West Africa

a Lonely Planet travel survival kit

Alex Newton
David

D1038973

West Africa

3rd edition

Published by
Lonely Planet Publications
Head Office: PO Box 617, Hawthorn, Vic 3122, Australia
Branches: 155 Filbert St, Suite 251, Oakland, CA 94607, USA
10 Barley Mow Passage, Chiswick, London W4 4PH, UK
71 bis rue du Cardinal Lemoine, 75005 Paris, France

Printed by
SNP Printing Pte Ltd, Singapore

Photographs by

Rosemary Balmford (RB)	K D Lee (KL)
Chris Barton (CB)	Alex Newton (AN)
Chris Beall (CBe)	Ann Porteus (Sidewalk Gallery) (AP)
Glenn Beanland (GB)	Peter Ptschelinzew (PP)
Manuela Colehi (MC)	Peter Robinson (PR)
Jason Edwards (JE)	April Smith (AS)
Eliot Elisofon (EE)	Mim Tsantis (MT)
David Else (DE)	David Wall (DW)
John Kurth (JK)	

Front cover: Tuareg man, northern Niger (David Wall)
Title page: Wodaabé man dressed for the Gerewol Festival during the Cure Salée, Niger (Margaret Jung)

First Published
1988

This Edition
October 1995
Reprinted with February 1997 Update supplement

National Library of Australia Cataloguing in Publication Data

Newton, Alex
West Africa – a travel survival kit.

3rd ed.
Includes index.
ISBN 0 86442 294 6.

1. Africa, West – Guidebooks. I. Else, David
II. Title. (Series: Lonely Planet travel survival kit).

916.604329

text © Alex Newton 1995
maps © Lonely Planet 1995
photos © photographers as indicated 1995
climate charts compiled from information supplied by Patrick J Tyson, © Patrick J Tyson, 1995

Alex Newton

Raised in a small southern town, Madison, Georgia, Alex Newton was one of the many Americans affected in the 1960s by John Kennedy's challenge to join the Peace Corps. Following almost three years' service in Guatemala as an agricultural advisor and four years on Wall St as a lawyer, he studied French and development economics and ended up in West Africa, where he spent seven years working on development assistance programmes before moving on to similar work in Ecuador and Bangladesh. Travelling by plane, river boat, new trains and cockroach-infested ones, buses and pick-up trucks stuffed like sardines, and on top of lorries, he has visited all 16 countries in West Africa and crossed the Sahara as well. Alex is also the author of Lonely Planet's *Central Africa – a travel survival kit* and is presently working with his wife Betsy Wagenhauser on the 3rd edition of *Bangladesh – a travel survival kit*. Now living in Bangladesh and always keen to meet interesting people, he and Betsy bid travellers passing through Dhaka to look them up.

David Else

After hitching around Europe for a couple of years, David Else finally crossed the Mediterranean and first reached Africa in 1983. Since then he has travelled all over the continent, from Algeria to Zimbabwe, and from Sudan to Senegal, via most of the bits in between. He has written several guidebooks for independent travellers, including Lonely Planet's *Trekking in East Africa*. He has also co-authored and contributed to three other Lonely Planet guides: *Africa on a Shoestring* and the travel survival kits to *Kenya* and *East Africa*. When not in Africa, David lives in the north of England, where he's permanently chained to a word processor, and travel means driving to London and back.

From the Authors

From Alex Thanks to David Else and John Kurth who have brought refreshingly new and different perspectives to the book. Special thanks go foremost to my wife, Betsy Wagenhauser, for tolerating my long hours at the computer and for suggesting John Kurth to assist me; also to my buddy Olivier Leduc of Abidjan who once again helped send me off on my extensive updating journey into the hinterlands; to Phil Jones for helping me with getting visas; to Fernando Molina of Quito, Ecuador, for his wonderful drawings of West African masks; and to Debra and Chuck Llewellyn for wining and dining me in Accra and allowing me to recover a bit in mid-stream in the comfortable environs of their home. Special thanks also go once again to the Lonely Planet team in Australia as I couldn't imagine working for a more professional, tolerant and interesting group of people.

John would like to thank and acknowledge the following for their help in updating the Nigeria chapter: Joanna Moffat (UK) for background information on Ife, Harriet Dodd (UK) for a tour of Lagos nightlife, Peter Coats (UK) for excellent background information on wildlife and parks in Nigeria, Ted Lazer (USA), a gracious host, Jacque Juilland (USA) for the use of his computer, and Felicity Keulthan (USA) for her patience and help in putting the Nigeria chapter together.

From David I'd like to thank the following people for their help or hospitality (or both) while I was writing and researching this book. Firstly to my wife Corinne, who was with me all the way: out on the road, and looking over my shoulder as I put the notes together back at home. Secondly to my long-time and long-suffering assistants Robin Saxby and Helen Long for their excellent work in The Gambia and Senegal. And thirdly, thanks to Chris Morris who dropped everything to and, armed only with a notebook and Tuareg head-dress, got the latest low-down on Niger.

I'd also like to thank in The Gambia: Sam, James, Emma, the Atlantic crew, and Nick from Box Bar Rd. In Senegal: Véronique and Philip Chiche, Elaine Wells, Boubacar Diaw (for help with all the sections on West African music), Robert Kohlhase. In Mali: Issa Guindo, Thomas Rehmet, Bernhard Sulzbach, Wolfgang Hahn. In Guinea: Jim Emerson. In Guinea-Bissau: Bridget and Alex, the intrepid mountain-bikers. In Sierra Leone: Paul Everett, Keith Budden, Peter Robertson, Lucy Bardner, Carla Short, Shannon Coughlin, Samantha Foody, Paul and Trish from the USA, George from Belgium, Cameron from Scotland, Jeff, Nigel and Cindy from Essex, Clark, Joan and Kathleen from the USA. In Niger: Suzanne Köler and Brigitte Wiess, Abdoulmohamine Khamed Ahayoub and Mahmoudoun Chihillou. All over Africa: the local people who live in all the places I passed through, the expats, the Peace Corps and VSO volunteers who all shared with me their knowledge, experiences and good company. In the UK, I'd also like to thank: Alan Morgan of the Africa Travel Centre in London (for flight details), Clare Mahdiyone of Kinkiliba Tours and Lisa Bellini of Robinson Crusoe Lodge (for the Casamance info), Steve McHardy (for additions on Mali), Philip Atkinson of the University of East Anglia (for the details on Mt Bintumani), and Peter Bennett (for political updates fresh from the Internet).

At the risk of appearing sycophantic, I'd also like to thank all the Lonely Planet staff in London and Melbourne for their help and support over the last few years: they really are jolly nice people to work for.

Dedication (from Alex)
This book is dedicated to Phil Jones of Arlington, VA, the godpappy of our new child Nicola, a saint and court jester and a truly great friend, the kind one could normally only dream of having. (Phil would respond: 'Yeah man, talk dirty to me.')

This Book
Alex Newton researched and wrote the first two editions of *West Africa – a travel survival kit*. For this, the third edition, he updated the introductory chapters, Benin, Burkina Faso, Côte d'Ivoire, Ghana, Liberia, Mauritania and Togo. David Else updated The Gambia, Guinea, Guinea-Bissau, Mali, Niger (with assistance from Chris Morris and Alex Newton), Senegal and Sierra Leone. Both authors updated Cape Verde, and John Kurth updated Nigeria.

From the Publisher
This edition of West Africa was edited by Samantha Carew with help from Diana Saad, Susan Noonan, Rachel Scully, Ian Ward, Kristin Odijk, Paul Smitz and Greg Alford, many of whom also helped proof the book. Adam McCrow coordinated the mapping with help from Andrew Smith, Louise Keppie, Maliza Kruh, Sally Jacka and Chris Love. Adam also produced the colour map with assistance from Paul Clifton. Margaret Jung did the illustrations and handled the layout, including the colour section. Thanks to Simon Bracken and Adam McCrow for the cover design. Special thanks to Sue Galley and Greg Herriman for invaluable design suggestions; to Charlotte Hindle in the UK office for design input; to Glenn Beanland for taking photographs for the colour section; and to Diana Saad for ongoing editorial assistance and optimism. Thanks also to Sharon Wertheim for indexing and to Helen Castle for help with research. A big thanks to Sue Drerup at Off the Beaten Track in South Yarra for letting us photograph exhibits in her wonderful gallery and use her reference books; to Ann Porteus of Sidewalk Gallery in Battery Point, Tasmania, for photos and slides; to Nick Schulz at Blue Moon Records, Fitzroy, and Graeme Counsel for help with the music sections, to Jenny Laidlaw at Rafiki in Fitzroy for letting us photograph her exhibits; to Peter Robinson for his fantastic bird photos; and finally, a very big thank you to David Else who responded enthusiastically, as always, to the mountain of extra work we asked him to do.

Thanks
Thanks to the many people who have written to us with advice, tips, and travellers' tales. Their names are listed at the back of this book.

Warning & Request
Things change – prices go up, schedules change, good places go bad and bad places go bankrupt – nothing stays the same. So if you find things better or worse, recently opened or long since closed, please write and tell us and help make the next edition better!

Your letters will be used to help update future editions and, where possible, important changes will also be included as an Update section in reprints.

We greatly appreciate all information that is sent to us by travellers. Back at Lonely Planet we have a hard-working readers' letters team to sort through the many letters we receive. The best ones will be rewarded with a free copy of the next edition or another Lonely Planet guide if you prefer. We give away lots of books, but, unfortunately, not every letter/postcard receives one.

Contents

Map Legend

BOUNDARIES

International Boundary
Regional Boundary
Marine Park Boundary

ROUTES

Freeway
Highway
Major Road
Unsealed Road or Track
City Road
City Street
Railway
Tram
Walking Track
Walking Tour
Ferry Route
Cable Car or Chairlift

AREA FEATURES

Park, Gardens
National Park
Forest
Pedestrian Mall
Market
Cemetery
Reef
Beach or Desert
Rocks

HYDROGRAPHIC FEATURES

Coastline
River, Creek
Intermittent River or Creek
Lake, Intermittent Lake
Canal
Swamp

SYMBOLS

✪ CAPITAL		National Capital
◉ Capital		Regional Capital
CITY		Major City
● City		City
● Town		Town
● Village		Village
■		Place to Stay
▼		Place to Eat
▼		Pub, Bar
✉	☎	Post Office, Telephone
❶	❸	Tourist Information, Bank
⊖	P	Transport, Parking
🏛	⌂	Museum, Youth Hostel
⌘	⚐	Caravan Park, Camping Ground
†	✝	Church, Cathedral
☪	✿	Mosque, Synagogue
⚚	⚛	Buddhist Temple, Hindu Temple

⊕	★	Hospital, Police Station
✈	✝	Airport, Airfield
◰	✿	Swimming Pool, Gardens
❖	🐘	Shopping Centre, Zoo
⌐	🅿	Golf Course, Petrol Station
←	A25	One Way Street, Route Number
	∴	Archaeological Site or Ruins
🏛	⚱	Stately Home, Monument
🏯	▣	Castle, Tomb
⌒	⌂	Cave, Hut or Chalet
▲	☀	Mountain or Hill, Lookout
☼	⚓	Lighthouse, Shipwreck
)(	⌒	Pass, Spring
		Ancient or City Wall
		Rapids, Waterfalls
		Cliff or Escarpment, Tunnel
		Train Station

Note: not all symbols displayed above appear in this book

Introduction

Call it mystique or adventure, whatever, West Africa has a power of attraction which, despite its sometimes primitive conditions, continues to entice Westerners to spend time and even careers here. They certainly don't come because it's 'comfortable'. In the rural Sahel, people live in hamlets scattered about the hot and dusty landscape studded with huge baobab trees. Others live in tropical cities such as Freetown and Monrovia where every time it rains the electricity goes off and the sewers overflow.

Which isn't to say that the environment isn't interesting. You can experience sandy deserts and rainforests and everything in between. But the physical environment and the wildlife are not West Africa's principal attractions as they are in East Africa. West

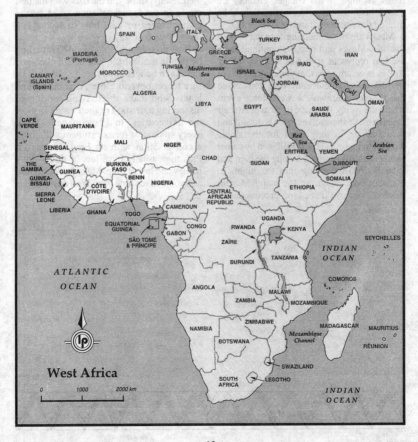

West Africa

0   1000   2000 km

Africa's draw card is its people. If you're interested in art, music or traditional African culture, head for West Africa.

In Timbuktu and elsewhere in the Sahel, you'll see nomadic Tuareg perched on their camels and covered with flowing embroidered material. Only their penetrating eyes appear from the white or indigo material wrapped around their heads. In the villages, you'll see men in traditional dress gathered around the chief discussing important village matters or shooting the breeze, while women dressed in brightly coloured material pound the millet, tend to the children or work in the fields. At night in the villages, chances are you'll hear drums and, in the Sahel, be offered the ritualistic three glasses of tea.

Masks are not something men carve only for sale. Masks and puppets continue to be used to represent spirits or help in telling stories in ceremonies that you may get to see first-hand. In September in Niger you can see the famous Gerewol, a week-long event where the young Wodaabé herders paint their faces to make themselves more beautiful and then line up in long rows for the single women to inspect. This is followed by camel races, ritualistic combat among the men and long hours of dancing into the night. In northern Nigeria during the major Muslim celebrations, you'll see long processions of the most elegantly dressed men galloping in mad fashion through town on their elaborately decorated horses.

What is just as interesting, however, is simply meeting people in the markets and villages. Africans are interested in people and one of the best ways to meet them is in the mud bars and local markets, talking with bread women, cigarette vendors, town crazies or millet-beer drinkers.

Africans have a different world view to Westerners, and the only way to penetrate this culture is to make a friend. A friend will take you to their village, introduce you to their family, show you the bars with the best music in town, and tell you when you're getting ripped off and how to accomplish tasks in the best way.

How do you meet this friend? Travelling by public transport in 2nd or 3rd class and staying in budget hotels is one way. Just be sure to get beyond those Africans around hotels who make their living serving or disserving tourists. Try the Peace Corps or the universities. In Francophone Africa, every student or former student will enjoy a conversation with an English speaker. Plus they usually have lots of time – little money and lots of time. Make just one friend and you will see how open West Africans can be.

Facts about the Region

GEOGRAPHY

West Africa is mostly flat. The principal hilly areas, rising to about 1000 metres, are good for hiking (see the boxed feature on Hiking in the Facts for the Visitor chapter).

The coastal areas are close to the equator, but all of West Africa is north of it. Abidjan is only 5° north of the equator, Dakar 14°.

West Africa has far fewer rainforests than Central Africa. Nonetheless, Liberia is almost completely covered in rainforests, as are large parts of Sierra Leone and south-western Côte d'Ivoire.

Heading inland from the coast the climate becomes drier and the Sahel begins in the southern areas of Mali, Burkina Faso and Niger. It extends northward to the edge of the desert. The landscape consists primarily of scrub trees and brush and large baobab trees (the ones that look like they are turned upside down with the roots in the air) and lots of natural laterite. Northern Mali and Niger and virtually all of Mauritania are pure desert.

CLIMATE

Heat

You probably think Africa is very hot. Look at the average highs (in centigrade) of the following cities:

	July	August
Rome	31°	31°
Singapore	31°	30°
Tokyo	28°	30°
Washington	30°	29°
Accra (Ghana)	28°	28°
Cairo (Egypt)	35°	35°
Dakar (Senegal)	31°	30°
Lagos (Nigeria)	28°	28°

In most of West Africa, high humidity is the problem, not heat. The only area that gets really hot is the Sahel near the desert (Senegal, The Gambia, Mauritania, Mali, Burkina Faso and Niger) but not year-round. Only from March to May does it get notice-ably hotter in most of West Africa. Put your face in front of a hair dryer and you'll know what it's like riding in a car with the windows down in the Sahel during this period. At least it's dry heat. While the Sahel can easily get 15°C hotter from March to May, many people prefer this to the humidity.

Rain

The rainy season in West Africa is from June to September. In the wetter countries (Guinea, Sierra Leone and Liberia), May and October are also rainy months. The wettest areas are (from west to east) Guinea, Sierra Leone, Liberia and south-eastern Nigeria. If possible, avoid visiting these areas during the heavy rainy period. The sun rarely shines and most dirt roads, except for the main arteries, become impassable.

In the rest of West Africa the skies are not cloudy all day during the rainy season. In the Sahel some people actually prefer this time of the year. The sun is not incessantly beating down and temperatures are a little lower.

The main problem during the rainy season is travelling upcountry off the major roads. Many of the dirt roads are passable only with 4WD vehicles, and the driving times are double. Without a 4WD you may have no hope of reaching some of those more remote spots. This is true even in the Sahel. In late July on the edge of the Sahara, you can find yourself surrounded by lake-size puddles of water that refuse to be absorbed by the life-less soils. People on tours shouldn't be concerned because 4WD vehicles are invari-ably used. Others who expect to do a lot of upcountry travel should have patience, a sense of humour and a good book – and be thankful that most major roads are either paved or all-weather.

The Harmattan

The November to February period may be a little cooler, but December to February is the time of the harmattan winds when the skies

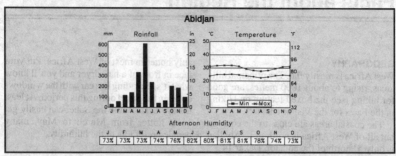

Abidjan

Rainfall — mm / in
Temperature — °C / °F — Min, Max

Afternoon Humidity

J	F	M	A	M	J	J	A	S	O	N	D
73%	73%	73%	74%	76%	82%	80%	81%	81%	78%	74%	73%

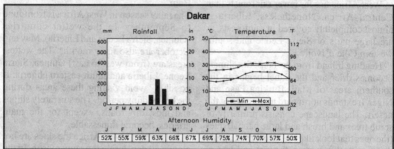

Dakar

Rainfall — mm / in
Temperature — °C / °F — Min, Max

Afternoon Humidity

J	F	M	A	M	J	J	A	S	O	N	D
52%	55%	59%	63%	66%	67%	69%	75%	74%	70%	57%	50%

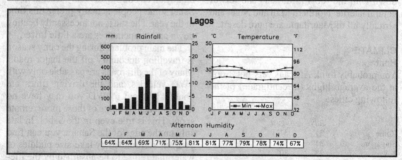

Lagos

Rainfall — mm / in
Temperature — °C / °F — Min, Max

Afternoon Humidity

J	F	M	A	M	J	J	A	S	O	N	D
64%	64%	69%	71%	75%	81%	81%	77%	79%	78%	74%	67%

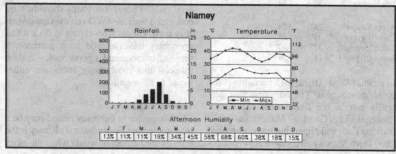

Niamey

Rainfall — mm / in
Temperature — °C / °F — Min, Max

Afternoon Humidity

J	F	M	A	M	J	J	A	S	O	N	D
13%	11%	11%	19%	34%	45%	58%	68%	60%	38%	18%	15%

A	B
C	D
E	

A: Mosque, Gao, Mali (PP)
B: Traditional architecture, Atar, Mauritania (AS)
C: Grand Mosque, Bobo-Dioulasso, Burkina Faso (AN)

D: Granaries, Mali (DE)
E: Dogon mosque, Mali (CB)

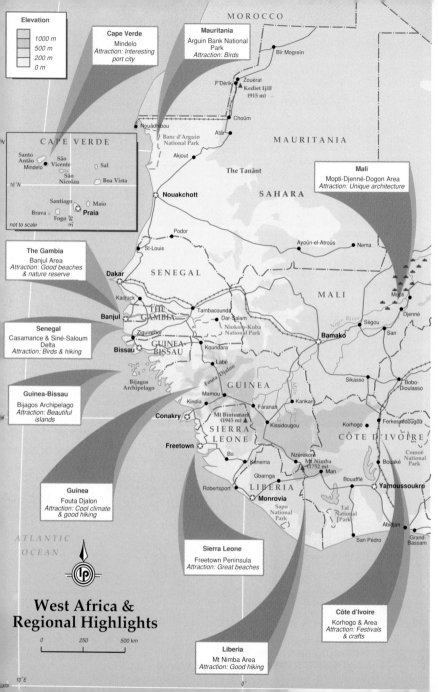

West Africa &
Regional Highlights

Elevation
1000 m
500 m
200 m
0 m

Cape Verde
Mindelo
Attraction: Interesting port city

Mauritania
Arguin Bank National Park
Attraction: Birds

Mali
Mopti-Djenné-Dogon Area
Attraction: Unique architecture

The Gambia
Banjul Area
Attraction: Good beaches & nature reserve

Senegal
Casamance & Siné-Saloum Delta
Attraction: Birds & hiking

Guinea-Bissau
Bijagos Archipelago
Attraction: Beautiful islands

Guinea
Fouta Djalon
Attraction: Cool climate & good hiking

Sierra Leone
Freetown Peninsula
Attraction: Great beaches

Côte d'Ivoire
Korhogo & Area
Attraction: Festivals & crafts

Liberia
Mt Nimba Area
Attraction: Good hiking

CAPE VERDE

Santo Antão
Mindelo
São Vicente
São Nicolau
Sal
Boa Vista
Santiago
Maio
Brava
Fogo
Praia
not to scale

16°N

MOROCCO

Bír Mogreïn

F'Dérik
Zouérat
Kediet Ijill
(915 m)

Choûm

Nouâdhibou

Banc d'Arguin
National Park

Atâr

MAURITANIA

Akjout

The Tanânt

SAHARA

Nouakchott

Podor

St-Louis

Ayoûn-el-Atroûs
Nema

SENEGAL

Dakar

Kaolack

Tambacounda

Dar-Salam

MALI

Mopti

Banjul
THE GAMBIA

Ziguinchor

Niokolo-Koba
National Park

Koundara

Bissau
GUINEA-BISSAU

Bijagos
Archipelago

Labé

Fouta Djalon

Niger River

Ségou

Djenné

San

Bamako

Sikasso

Bobo-
Dioulasso

GUINEA

Mamou

Kindia

Faranah

Kankan

Ferkessédougou

Kissidougou

Korhogo

CÔTE D'IVOIRE

Conakry

Mt Bintumani
(1945 m)

SIERRA
LEONE

Freetown

Bo

Kenema

Nzérékoré
Mt Nimba
(1752 m)

Man

Comoë
National
Park

Bouaké

Gbarnga

Bouaflé

Yamoussoukro

Robertsport

LIBERIA

Monrovia

Sapo
National
Park

Taï
National
Park

Abidjan

San Pédro

Grand-
Bassam

ATLANTIC
OCEAN

0   250   500 km

10°E

16°N

0°

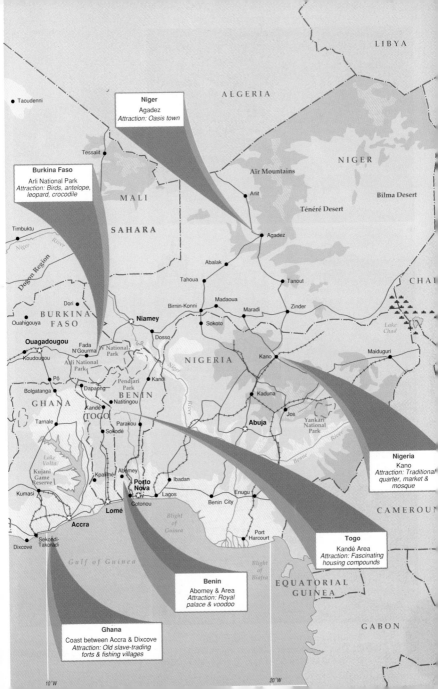

Niger
Agadez
Attraction: Oasis town

Burkina Faso
Arli National Park
Attraction: Birds, antelope, leopard, crocodile

Nigeria
Kano
Attraction: Traditional quarter, market & mosque

Togo
Kandé Area
Attraction: Fascinating housing compounds

Benin
Abomey & Area
Attraction: Royal palace & voodoo

Ghana
Coast between Accra & Dixcove
Attraction: Old slave-trading forts & fishing villages

LIBYA

ALGERIA

Taoudenni

Tessalit

NIGER

Aïr Mountains

Ténéré Desert

Bilma Desert

Arlit

MALI

SAHARA

Timbuktu

Niger River

Dogon Region

Agadez

Abalak

Tahoua

Tanout

CHAD

BURKINA FASO

Dori

Madaoua

Birnin-Konni

Maradi

Zinder

Lake Chad

Ouahigouya

Koudougou

Ouagadougou

Fada N'Gourma

W National Park

Niamey

Dosso

Sokoto

NIGERIA

Kano

Maiduguri

Po

Arli National Park

Bolgatanga

Dapango

Pendjari Park

Kandi

Kaduna

GHANA

Kandé

Natitingou

BENIN

Jos

Tarnale

TOGO

Parakou

Yankari National Park

Lake Volta

Sokodé

Kujani Game Reserve

Kpalimé

Abomey

Ibadan

Benin River

Kumasi

Porto Novo

Lagos

Benin City

Enugu

Accra

Lomé

Cotonou

Blight of Guinea

CAMEROUN

Sekondi-Takoradi

Dixcove

Gulf of Guinea

Port Harcourt

Blight of Biafra

EQUATORIAL GUINEA

Abuja

Benue River

GABON

10°W

20°W

A	B
C	D
E	F

A: Morning market, Ganvié, Benin (AS)

B & C: Dantopka market, Cotonou, Benin (AS)

D: Grand Marché & mosque, Djenné, Mali (DE)

E: Market, Abidjan, Côte d'Ivoire (AN)

F: Potato vendors, Vogan, Togo (AN)

of most West African countries are grey from the sands blown south from the Sahara. On bad days visibility can be reduced to one km, occasionally even less, resulting in plane delays or cancellations.

The harmattan begins in late November or early December. The worst part is usually over by around mid-February, although in the Sahel the skies remain hazy until the first May rains. Fortunately, some days are fairly clear, which is probably why most travellers aren't too troubled by the harmattan. People with contact lenses should be prepared for problems, regardless, while photographers can expect hazy results.

WHEN TO GO

For many, the best time is the cool, dry period from November to February but other important factors to consider are the harmattan, rain, heat, tourist-season congestion and, for some people, the game-park season.

- If you wilt in the heat, avoid visiting during the hot period (from March to May).
- If you're a photography nut, you'll get much better photographs in the rainy season from May to October. During the dry season, particularly December to the end of February, the skies get very dusty from the harmattan winds.
- If you're an animal lover, avoid visiting between 1 June to 30 November because this is when most of the game parks are closed.
- If you love the sun and beaches, avoid the rainy season (from May/June to mid/late October). Especially true for Guinea, Sierra Leone and Liberia.

Tourist Congestion

If you think this is a joke, you're not far off the mark. Still, hotels along the coast of Togo, Sierra Leone and The Gambia become literally packed with sunbathers on package tours from Europe from December to March (and to a lesser extent, in November and April). Also, the Casamance region of Senegal and the Dogon area of Mali are a small Mecca for Europeans during the extended Christmas season, but that's only six to eight weeks out of the year. So if you don't have hotel reservations in these areas or just want to avoid other travellers, pick another spot in West Africa during these periods. Otherwise you should have no problems finding bottom-end accommodation.

PLANNING AN ITINERARY

Having established when to visit West Africa (or when not to), your next decision is *where* to go. This may depend on the environment or landscape you want to travel through. Basically there are two main types: in the northern part of the region is the dry savannah area called the Sahel (this includes most of Senegal, The Gambia, Mali, Burkina Faso and Niger); south of here lies the moister, more vegetated tropical area (Guinea, Guinea-Bissau, Sierra Leone, Liberia, Côte d'Ivoire, Ghana, Togo and Benin). Nigeria spreads across both areas. Usually it is more interesting to see something of both. (A third West African environment is the desert, but most travellers don't see it because it's difficult to reach and travel around.)

Regional Highlights

At great risk of creating controversy, we have chosen a selection of 'regional highlights'. These are places most visitors find interesting, rewarding or enjoyable. Fortunately, very few of these places ever get overrun with visitors, and even then it's only at certain times of the year (see Tourist Congestion), so don't worry about having to combat the kind of crowds that haunt the Pyramids or the Taj Mahal.

And don't lose sight of the fact that in West Africa the 'feel' and the atmosphere of the places and the activities of their people are often more interesting than tangible tourist 'sights'. In Bamako, for example, you could tick off the city's official attractions (such as the main mosque and museum) in half a day, but if you spend more time here, strolling through the markets or along the river bank, sitting in pavement cafés to watch the world go by, or just talking to the locals, you'll get much more out of your visit.

With that in mind, you could have a memorable trip in West Africa without seeing any of the highlights on our list. In fact some travellers might avoid them, precisely *because* they are on this list! Still, some

REGIONAL HIGHLIGHTS

Country	Highlight	Features
Benin	Abomey & area	Royal palace, voodoo
	Natitingou area	Fascinating housing compounds
	Ganvié	Lagoon villages
Burkina Faso	Bobo-Dioulasso	Shady town with traditional feel
	Gorom-Gorom	Fascinating desert market
	Arli NP	Birds, antelope, leopard, crocodile
Cape Verde	Mindelo	Interesting port city
	Fogo Island	Volcano, good hiking
Côte d'Ivoire	Korhogo & area	Festivals, crafts
	Man area	Waterfalls, hills, good hiking
	Sassandra & Grand-Béréby	Fishing villages, good beaches
	Grand-Bassam	Colonial capital, good beaches
The Gambia	Banjul area	Good beaches, nature reserve, music
Ghana	Mole Game Reserve	Elephant, wart hog, lion
	Accra & area	Vibrant capital, university, gardens
	Kumasi & area	Festivals, crafts
	Coast between Accra & Dixcove	Slave-trading forts, fishing villages
Guinea	Fouta Djalon	Scenic hill country, cool climate, good hiking
Guinea-Bissau	Bijagos Archipelago	Beautiful islands, good beaches
Liberia	Mt Nimba area	Hill country, good hiking
	Sapo National Park	Virgin rainforest, pygmy hippos
Mali	Bamako	Lively capital with traditional feel
	Mopti	Interesting town, busy market & waterfront, good access to other nearby highlights
	Djenné	Fascinating architecture, especially the mosque
	Dogon Escarpment	Spectacular landscape & various hiking options (from a few days to a few weeks)
	Timbuktu	Historical city in desert setting, plus magical name
	Niger River by boat	Floating villages – an interesting way to travel & experience river life
Mauritania	Chinguetti & Ouadâne	Fascinating old oases towns
	Arguin Bank National Park	Great bird sanctuary, remote coast
Niger	Niamey	Capital city with desert feel
	W National Park	Elephant, lion, buffalo, hippo
	Agadez	Oasis town
Nigeria	Oshogbo & Ife	Artist centre, university
	Zaria	Interesting traditional quarter
	Yankari National Park	Excellent for birds & wild game
	Kano	Traditional quarter, market, mosque
Senegal	Dakar & Goreé Island	Modern capital, historical island/town
	St-Louis & Djoudj National Park	Colonial architecture, fishing activity, birds
	Siné-Saloum Delta	Quiet & scenic, birds & monkeys
	Casamance	Beautiful coastal region (good for cycling & hiking), great beaches
Sierra Leone	Freetown Peninsula	Remote beaches and others with good facilities
	Outamba-Kilimi National Park	Rainforest, chimp, monkey, hippo
	Tiwai Island Wildlife Sanctuary	Butterflies, birds, monkeys
Togo	Kpalimé	Mountainous cacao & coffee region, good hiking
	Kara area	Scenic hills, good hiking, markets
	Kandé area	Fascinating housing compounds

Days	Transport	Accommodation
2	Bush taxi, motorcycle-taxi, train	Variety of prices & quality
2	Taxi & bus (cheaper but often break down)	Hotels (medium-expensive)
2	Bush taxi (cheap) & then pirogue across lagoon	Hotel (expensive); rooms with locals
3	Taxi, mobylette, motorcycle	Variety of prices & quality
2	Bush taxi, minibus, bus	Mud huts & auberge
3	Bus, hitching (difficult), use of park vehicle (maybe)	Camping & attractive campement
3	Plane & ferry to islands (expensive); inter-island flights (medium); cheap to get around (bus/taxi/hitch)	Most major towns have at least one place to stay (cheap)
2	Bush taxi, train, bus	Cheap-medium; OK quality
3	Bush taxi, bus	As above
5	Bush taxi, bus	Cheap camping (Sassandra)
1	Bush taxi	Variety of prices
2-5	River boat, bush taxi, bus	Coast resorts, guesthouses & hotels
2	Bus; foot or vehicle within park	Hotel & camping
3	All types & prices	All types & prices
3	Taxi (no inner-city buses)	As above
7	Bus, tro-tro, bush taxi	Castle, hotels & guesthouses
3	Bus & bush taxi: cheap & straightforward	Cheap-medium, quality varies from bad to good
3	Boat (cheap & easy), plane (expensive & easy)	Cheap-medium, good quality
3	Bush taxis; travel impossible due to civil war	Yekepa (missions & one inn)
3	4WD necessary in the rainy season; civil war	Greenville (private rooms, no hotels)
1	Bus & train: cheap-medium & easy	All types & prices
2	Bus (cheap-medium, quick & easy), boat (slower & cheaper)	Cheap-expensive; bad-OK quality
1	Bush taxi: easy & cheap	Limited, cheap-medium, OK quality
2	Some parts easy to reach by bush taxi; remote parts reached with tour group, own vehicle or great patience	Local houses with basic facilities; cheap & very interesting
1	Boat: cheap, slow, unreliable Road: medium, slow, unreliable Air: expensive, quick, more reliable	Range of prices & quality from deluxe cabins to deck class
2-7	Large, unromantic passenger boats; pinasses (slower); pirogues (slowest)	As above
3	Bush taxis, trucks: cheap-medium	One or two places to stay (cheap)
2	4WD only	Camping
1	Bush & bush taxi: cheap, medium, easy	Wide choice of price & quality
2	Bush taxi, minibus (difficult to find) & charter	Camping or hotel (expensive)
3	Bus, bush taxi, truck: medium & easy	Cheap-medium; camping (cheap)
2	Bush taxi: cheap, easy & quick	Cheap-medium, OK-good quality
2	Bus, bush taxi & train: cheap, easy, quick	As above
2	Bush taxi: cheap, easy & quick	Hotel (expensive) & camping
2	Bus, bush taxi & train: cheap, easy, quick	All types & prices
3	Bus, bush taxi & train: cheap-medium, easy	All types & prices
2	Bush taxi & train: cheap & easy to St-Louis Taxi & tour to park: easy & medium	Cheap-medium; OK-good quality
2	Bush taxi: cheap, some parts easy	Cheap-medium, good quality
3	Bus & bush taxi (cheap); easy to reach & tour by foot, bike & bush taxi	Cheap, excellent quality, local-style rest houses
2	Bush taxi: easy & cheap to beaches near Freetown (remote beaches take more effort and patience)	Cheap-expensive, good to excellent quality (depends on location)
3	Difficult to reach; foot or canoe within park	Park tents (cheap)
2	Impossible to reach since1990 because of fighting	Not applicable
3	Train & minibus; charter taxi to get around	Variety of prices and quality
3	Bush taxi, minibus	Variety of prices and quality
3	Shared taxi or foot	Huts (cheap)

places (such as the Dogon Escarpment) are unique and particularly fascinating, and worth making an effort to reach. If you don't like it, you can always go somewhere else – that's what travel is all about. All the highlights listed are discussed in more detail in the individual country chapters.

GAME PARKS

You may hear that people go to East Africa to see the animals and to West Africa to see the people. You may also hear that there are no game parks in West Africa worth visiting. However, this is not the case. In fact, you'll find them quite interesting if you like the idea of stalking and observing the animals rather than sitting on your hotel porch and having them led by, and you may only be disappointed with the West African parks if you've been to East Africa.

The main problem with game parks in West Africa isn't the lack of animals – you can see elephant, lion, buffalo, wart hog, birds galore, various species of antelope, and hippo – it's the remoteness of the parks. All except W National Park near Niamey (Niger) are at least a day's drive from the nearest capital city. The parks are usually open from late November to the end of May.

Crowned crane (*Balearica pavonina*)
Found from Senegal to Nigeria in wet plains, grassy marshland and crops.

The major game parks in West Africa are:

Comoë National Park in north-eastern Côte d'Ivoire; a day's drive from Abidjan
Niokolo-Koba National Park in south-eastern Senegal; a long day's drive from Dakar
Arli National Park in eastern Burkina Faso; a day's drive from Ouagadougou
W National Park in south-western Niger and northern Benin; a three-hour drive from Niamey and part of the same park network as Arli
Pendjari Park in northern Benin
Yankari National Park in eastern Nigeria; several hour's drive east of Jos
Mole Game Reserve in northern Ghana
Kakum Nature Park in southern Ghana

If you're interested in seeing rainforests, the best parks are Taï National Park in far western Côte d'Ivoire and Bia National Park in far western Ghana. Sapo National Park in eastern Liberia is another, but seeing it is logistically very difficult.

ECONOMY
The Bad News

Overall, the economic situation in West Africa is bleak. Ten of the world's 36 poorest countries (in terms of per capita incomes) are there, but the situation may be much worse because of currency distortions. In 1994 the UN's human development index (based on life expectancy, adult literacy and GNP per person with purchasing power factored in) showed that seven of the 10 worst-off countries were in West Africa. The poorest countries are Burkina Faso, Mali, Niger, Guinea-Bissau (all with GNPs below US$250 per person), with Guinea and Sierra Leone at the absolute bottom. The latter has the world's lowest life expectancy (43 years) and until recently seems to have been doing everything possible to destroy its economy.

The Sahel tends to be poorer because the rainfall is so much more unreliable. A 50% drop in rainfall in Niger may mean a zero harvest – the same in rainy Liberia would not have nearly the same effect. It is so bad in the Sahel that many rural families cannot afford to have their only daily 'luxury' – a small glass of tea in the shade after a meal.

The overall picture is not improving –

many countries are now worse off than they were at independence 25 years ago. One contributing factor is the birth rates, which are the highest in the world. The yearly net population growth in Côte d'Ivoire, for example, is 3.6%, which means that the country's 13.5 million people will become 39 million by 2025. A more recent contributor to the continent's economic demise is AIDS, which is devastating Africa's working population. Also, exports are no more diversified in sub-Saharan Africa now than they were in the 1960s and per capita incomes are predicted to grow by only 0.3% during the rest of this century.

Most West African countries were self-sufficient in food production in 1960. Now they are net importers of even basic grains, except in years of adequate rainfall, which seems to have been about 50% of the time during the past 10 to 15 years. It's not just a question of rainfall; the population growth rate has not been matched by a concomitant growth in the agricultural sector even during years of good rainfall. The situation has not been reversed by assistance from the West.

Until the late 1980s, instead of letting food prices be determined by market forces, most governments in West Africa set official prices for the farmers. The intentions may have been noble, but invariably the set prices were too low, so farmers had little incentive to produce more than they could consume. In Mali, farmers used to go to jail for refusing to sell part of their harvests to the government at ridiculously low prices.

As a result, most agricultural projects failed and it mattered little who financed them. Many of the failures were well publicised. The USA financed the most projects, so its failures got the most publicity.

The United States...spent $4.6 million for a cereal-production project in Senegal that did not increase grain output by a single bag. It spent another $13 million on a livestock scheme in Mali and later admitted that nothing whatsoever had been achieved.
The Africans by David Lamb

It wasn't until the 1980s that most West African countries began buying the IMF (International Monetary Fund) and World Bank's argument that their economic policies were at the root of the problem. With droughts occurring almost every second year, the pressure was relentless to 'do something'. In Ghana, Guinea, Guinea-Bissau and other countries, the response was to begin handing segments of the economies back to the people, ordering some of the state-run, money-losing enterprises to make a profit or close down, thus reducing bloated bureaucracies and shifting their taxes away from farmers. One visible result in all three countries is that consumer products, once very scarce, are now plentiful.

The Gambia, Burkina Faso and Nigeria carried out major reforms along similar lines recommended by the IMF and the World Bank but with less visible success, calling into serious question the wisdom of the West's economic advice. Oxfam claims that the imposed structural adjustment programmes of these two institutions have been a 'fundamental failure' and that they are built on a fundamentally false premise: 'that sub-Saharan African economies can export their way to recovery'. As a result of those programmes, which have reduced food subsidies and effectively increased the public charges for health and education, real incomes have fallen rather than increased, and in some countries child malnutrition is on the rise. Also, the verdict still seems to be out as to whether the elimination of food subsidies has or will increase overall production of food for local consumption. During the 1980s, when the structural adjustment programmes began, about 60% of the countries in Africa experienced a drop in per capita cereal production. One of the worst cases was in Nigeria, where everybody seemed to be heading for the cities.

The Good News

There are some real success stories in West Africa. That of Côte d'Ivoire is well known, although since 1980 the economy has declined noticeably. Until 1984, Ghana had one of the worst economic post-independence records of any country in Africa. Since 1984, it has had the best and is now the

〜〜〜

The Poorest Countries on Earth
A classic example of a screwed up economy is that of Sierra Leone, which at independence was one of the five most prosperous countries in West Africa. Now it's last on the UN's list, making it the poorest country on earth, with Guinea running a close second. In the process, Sierra Leone has lost much of its natural resources. When it achieved independence in 1961, as much as 60% of the country was primary rainforest, with lots of very old trees; now only 6% is. Guinea too has one of the worst post-independence records in Africa, in large part because for almost 30 years after independence it refused French assistance. Senegal is a less dramatic example. It has received more outside assistance during the past 30 years than any other country in West Africa, yet its real growth rate per capita (slightly improved since 1985) has been near zero over this period. But most other West African countries are doing no better, so comparably it still stacks up near the top. ■

〜〜〜

showcase of West Africa and may soon surpass Côte d'Ivoire in per capita income. Nigeria continues to expand, but at a very slow rate, while the remaining West African countries show either no visible signs of improvement or, in the cases of Sierra Leone, Liberia and Togo, clear signs of deterioration.

On a per capita basis, the wealthiest countries (whether or not adjusting for purchasing power parities) are Cape Verde, Ghana, Côte d'Ivoire, Nigeria and Senegal. Similarly, in terms of the UN's overall human development index, those countries (in the same order) are also the best off. The remaining countries in West Africa are much lower on that index, considerably lower, for comparison purposes, than Bangladesh. While per capita incomes are a poor way to compare living conditions, they provide at least a basis for comparing the economic performance over the years of various countries.

Here's how the top countries in West Africa, based on per capita incomes, stack up now compared to several years after independence:

1963	1994
Liberia	Cape Verde
Ghana	Côte d'Ivoire
Côte d'Ivoire	Ghana
Senegal	Senegal
Sierra Leone	Nigeria
Mauritania	Mauritania

Clearly, Sierra Leone and Liberia have fallen the furthest. In terms of health conditions, education and per capita incomes, Cape

Verde is tops by far, but it's also more dependent on foreign aid than any other country in Africa as, due to the minimum rainfall there, it produces only about one-tenth of its food requirements. The 350,000 inhabitants also receive considerable amounts of money from relatives living abroad. So in terms of its economy, it's a model for no one; indeed, it's virtually a basket case.

As the model economy in West Africa during the l960s and '70s, Côte d'Ivoire has been for years the only net exporter of food in the area; Ghana may have now achieved this distinction as well. Côte d'Ivoire's success has come from cocoa (the world's largest producer), coffee (the world's third-largest producer), cotton (the highest in Francophone Africa), rubber (approaching the highest in Africa) and timber. Plus, until 1993 it had one of the region's most astute political leaders – Houphouët-Boigny. However, by the time of his death late that year, he had become a major liability, having virtually destroyed the economy with his famous St Peter's-like cathedral in Yamoussoukro.

Don't lose perspective – Nigeria is the economic Goliath of West Africa. Nigeria's GNP is greater than that of all the rest of West Africa. Why? Oil is one reason. Another is people – roughly 105 million. One out of every five Africans is a Nigerian and there are as many Nigerians as there are Africans in the rest of West and Central Africa, excluding Zaïre. And although the economy is not booming, it's still in far better shape than most.

Politics in West Africa

The end of the Cold War has had an amazing impact on African politics. Previously, African dictators could justify single-party politics on the theory that Africa was different and that what worked in the West wasn't necessarily the best system for Africa.

In reality that logic was a façade for tyranny, and throughout the '80s fewer and fewer African intellectuals were claiming with any conviction that single-party governments were democratic or that they were authentically African. But with the peoples of Eastern Europe throwing out their long-term dictators one by one, not just the intellectuals but also the masses in Africa have begun looking at their own leaders and wondering what right they have to stay in power for so long without periodic public approval. So, in large part as a result of the end of the Cold War, the seeds of democracy have sprung up like flowers after the first rains in the Sahara. Throughout much of West Africa, people are far more willing than in the past to openly criticise their governments. Travellers too can feel freer to talk politics with them.

The USA through the World Bank, and the French Government, not surprisingly, are playing a role in all of this. The Bank, never very forthright, seems to be demanding an end to one-party rule in exchange for more assistance. The French, hoping to prevent revolution, are also putting pressure for political reform on all of the French-speaking countries – hence the nickname 'Paristroika'.

One of the most autocratic governments for years has been that in Benin, so it is surprising to see that Benin has become one of the major laboratories for democracy in West Africa. At a major political gathering in 1990, the 400-odd delegates demanded and received Mathieu Kérékou's resignation (although he retained control of the army). A year later in neighbouring Togo, Gnassingbé Eyadéma, Togo's strongman for 24 years, was forced to hold a similar conference, with the identical result. He too retained control of the army and eventually regained full control after an election in early 1994 (which, according to many observers, was conducted in a grossly unfair manner).

In Mali, the masses rioted so forcefully against Moussa Traoré (in power since 1968) that in early 1991 he also was finally ousted. The new leadership is now supporting a multiparty system and open elections. In Côte d'Ivoire, everyone expected political chaos when their leader for some 35 years, Houphouët-Boigny, died, but his appointed successor has taken over in one of the smoothest transitions in recent history. In Niger, on the other hand, the new democracy movement with open elections has resulted in weak unstable governments, calling in to serious question whether most African governments are at a stage where they can handle democracy. And in The Gambia, a military coup in 1994 demonstrated that coups are still a real possibility everywhere.

Many African leaders don't like what's happening, but they're being forced to embrace the new democracy to remain in power. During the early 1990s, no leader was under greater pressure to do this than Ghana's Jerry Rawlings, who was undoubtedly shaking in his boots after the results in neighbouring Togo and Benin. After several years of forcibly resisting these pressures, Rawlings finally agreed in 1993 to call elections, which he won fairly and squarely, thereby giving his position complete legitimacy.

In short, multiparty politics has become the public cry of the '90s, and it will be interesting to see what develops. The countries which are leading the way are Senegal, Benin, Niger, Mali and Cape Verde, where the new democratic institutions are the strongest (Togo, Sierra Leone, Mauritania and Liberia are the laggards in this regard). Greater economic prosperity, unfortunately, does not seem to be a likely outcome, at least in the short term, nor does increased political stability. ■

EDUCATION

The only countries in which the adult literacy rate exceeds 50% are Cape Verde, Ghana, Côte d'Ivoire and Nigeria. Those with the lowest rates, all below 25%, are Burkina Faso, Sierra Leone, Guinea and Benin. In virtually all of the latter countries, the adult literacy rate for women is about one-third that of men. In Burkina Faso, for example, only 9% of adult women are literate – the lowest rate in the world for women – compared to 28% for the men in that country. Its overall adult literacy rate of 18% is the lowest in the world.

Low literacy rates are a result of the low

priority that governments tend to give education. In The Gambia and Niger, for example, education accounts for less than 10% of public expenditure. Education expenditure (as a percentage of GNP) has been slowly rising in every country in the region except Nigeria. In that country, it has remained the same for the last 25 years; just 1.5% of GNP, the fourth lowest in the world. The progress in other countries has had some effect. In Senegal, for example, education expenditure increased from 2.4% in 1970 to 4.6% in 1990. The adult literacy rate jumped twofold during the same period, to almost 40%.

However, the modest increase in public spending on education in other countries and the higher literacy rates are not nearly enough. These countries have a long way to go in improving their education systems. Niger, for example, has increased its adult literacy rates sevenfold during the past two decades, but it is still below 30%.

SOCIAL CUSTOMS

One of the highlights of visiting West Africa is meeting the people. Knowing the social customs will help you avoid embarrassing situations and enhance your chances of getting to know people.

Greetings

One of the basics is the great importance Africans place on greetings (*les salutations* in Francophone Africa). For example, when the Senegalese Wolof greet one another they observe a ritual that lasts up to half a minute, starting with 'Peace be unto you', 'Do you have peace?', 'How are you doing?' to 'Where are

the people of your compound?', 'Is your body in peace?', or 'Thanks be to God'. The typical African greetings go into all kinds of enquiries about the family, one's health, work, the weather, etc. Even if one is at death's door, the answer is always that things are fine.

In the cities, the traditional greetings may give way to shorter greetings in French or English. In either case, it's a social blunder to get down to business immediately or to walk past an adult in a house without greeting them. Those who do are likely to meet with a hostile or negative attitude.

If you can learn the ritual in the local language, you will be an incredible hit. Even if you can't, all it takes is a few words and you will find many friends. In the country chapters, greeting phrases are given in the most popular local language in the capital city. The unfortunate part is that many countries have four or five major languages and often another 20 or so minor ones. At least they'll know you're making the effort.

The emphasis on greetings makes the handshake important. It's a soft handshake, not the Western knuckle-cracker. In some coastal areas, particularly around Togo, you should try to learn the handshake between friends, which always ends up with a snap of the fingers. Even if you never succeed, Africans will find it amusing to teach you. Not to shake a man's hand when entering and leaving a social or business gathering is a real gaffe. In social settings you must go around the room, greet everyone and shake hands with the men. Do the same when you leave.

Shaking Hands

In most areas men and women don't shake hands unless the woman extends her hand. In the French-speaking countries the thrice-kissed cheek greeting (starting with the left) is the norm for friends and even casual acquaintances of the opposite sex.

Women have traditionally been considered inferior to men and for this reason they tend to show deference to men in their greetings. As noted, they usually don't shake hands, but African men usually shake the hands of Western women. In the Sahel, women travellers may encounter an elder who, in strict compliance with the Koran, refuses to shake hands. ■

Another consideration is eye contact, which is usually avoided, especially between men and women and particularly in the Sahel. A boy does not look his father in the eye. If he does, his father will be suspicious. Don't think that because a woman avoids eye contact she's being cold. Some eye contact is OK as long as it doesn't become a gaze.

Begging

In Africa, the only social security system for most people is the extended family. There is no government cheque to help the unemployed, sick or old. Most beggars are cripples, lepers, or those blinded by onchocerciasis (*oncho*). Nevertheless, because of the effectiveness of the extended family in providing support, and the general respect that Africans give to their elders, there are remarkably few beggars considering that West Africa is the poorest area on earth.

For travellers, the point to remember is that Africans do not look down on beggars. Alms giving is one of the pillars of Islam and giving to beggars is one of the means by which Muslims gain entrance into paradise. For those studying with a marabout (Muslim holy man), they are even expected to beg in order to feed themselves. For this reason, you will see even relatively poor Africans giving to beggars. You won't be violating traditional custom by giving to beggars and usually a coin equivalent to five or 10 US cents is adequate. If you don't have any, just say 'next time' (*'la prochaine fois'*).

Gifts

One great annoyance for most travellers is people everywhere approaching them and asking for hand-outs (*le cadeau*). They are not beggars because they only prey upon foreigners. Follow local custom and not your emotions. In general, Africans never offer gifts to strangers unless they appear to be truly destitute or they have rendered a significant service. Walking a block with you would not be a significant service but helping you for 10 minutes to find a room at night would probably warrant a tip. Africans would rebuff anybody else looking for a

hand-out. Your 'giving in' only encourages the recipient to prey upon the next traveller. Even if some children seem undernourished, in the long run your giving them pieces of candy or money can do a lot of harm.

On the other hand, Africans frequently are very open and friendly towards foreigners and even after a few minutes of talking they may consider you a friend. At that point they might offer you a meal or a bed for the night. In instances such as this a small gift would be customary. Giving is very important in African society. You are expected to give gifts to those above you in the social hierarchy, or to respected people. If your mother-in-law comes for the day, a gift to her is in order. It's not so much a case of reciprocity, rather, it's that if Allah (God) has been good to you, you should be willing to spread some of it around. Since non-African foreigners are thought to be rich, they're expected to be generous. Keep this in mind.

If you're travelling near the desert, take some tobacco with you for the men with whom you might strike up a brief friendship. Perfume makes an excellent gift for either sex, at least in the Sahel. Bring small Western items to show your appreciation. One of the best gifts is a photo; consider bringing a cheap Polaroid as a second camera.

Be aware, however, that most African men approaching you and saying that they just want to talk, be friends and help you out are not being friendly at all but merely looking for a cadeau. And for some men, this trade of preying off travellers is a living, particularly those who hang around hotels. Africans tend to scorn them. Avoid them unless you really need something and don't mind paying.

On a different note, Africans tend to expect tips in situations where in other countries tipping would not be customary. For instance, if you ask someone for directions to the bus station and they walk three blocks with you to the station, chances are they may ask for a cadeau. It's not just foreigners who have to pay such tips, though with Africans less is expected. If you're not prepared to offer a tip, don't ask for significant favours.

Bribery

Bribery, or 'dashing', is not just a way of life in West Africa, it's an annoyance that travellers are constantly faced with everywhere they go. From the minute you get off the plane or cross the border, you are likely to be confronted with a request for a bribe. A customs official may ask you to come into a small room for a body search and then ask: 'Don't you have something for me?' In countries that require you to declare your money (Nigeria, Sierra Leone, Ghana, Mauritania), the official may count your money and then ask: 'What is there for me?'.

State as unequivocally as possible that you are not going to give them anything, and to say the same each time they repeat the request. In virtually all cases, they will back down and let you through. Many travellers think if they don't offer something, the official will trump up some excuse not to let them through. This is a tremendous mistake because it only encourages them to do the same to the next traveller.

Occasionally the requests are accompanied by threats, such as denying entrance into the country. It is usually just a bluffing act, typically lasting several minutes. Refuse to pay and in those rare instances where officials proceed to carry out their threat, you can always back down. On my last trip to Africa, probably a good 50 officials, mostly those at the borders, asked for gifts, and never once did I give in.

If your documents are not all in order, you're more vulnerable. It helps to know the regulations, however, because sometimes officials trump up totally fictitious ones in order to create a bribe situation.

If officials are slow in processing a visa request, offering a small gift to speed up the process may be your only option. Also, if the borders have closed, offering a small gift for 'overtime' may open them up for you.

Dress

In general, Africans place great importance on clothing (les costumes in Francophone Africa), spending a huge portion of their non-food budget on clothes. Western informality is definitely not the norm, although it is making a few inroads with the young in the bigger cities. Visitors are in for a real treat because Africans can dress with a regal quality.

In the traditional areas of West Africa, men and women wear long dress or outfits. The most common name for the most elaborate outfits is the grand boubou. For men, this is an embroidered robe-like garment reaching the ground with pants and shirt underneath. A kaftan is a less elaborate variation. They are invariably worn at important occasions, and sometimes at work or on holidays.

The woman's boubou is similarly regal, long and embroidered. For more everyday wear, women wear a loose top and a length of cloth (pagne) around the waist for a skirt; this is made from the colourful cotton prints you see everywhere. The same wax or wax lookalike cloth is used in making men's casual clothes, which look like pyjamas. Because the designs are so distinctively African, it's initially surprising to learn that much of the better quality cloth actually comes from Holland. Yet the most unique are the handmade design fabrics, such as the tie-dyed, indigo wood-block prints and batiks, which are produced in individual cottage-type establishments.

With clothing such as this, it is not surprising that in the more traditional areas, especially the Sahel, shorts worn by either sex and tight pants worn by women are considered offensive. This may seem like a double standard because African women often go bare-breasted in the villages, yet they would be ridiculed for wearing tight pants. It's all a bit confusing, but women should keep in mind that clothes should not be revealing or suggestive. For men, standards are less strict.

Standards are different in the big cities such as Dakar. You'll see everything from the latest Parisian fashions to the most traditional outfits. Yet you will not see shorts being worn by either sex (unless jogging) or, in the Sahel, African women in pants. As for the villages, women travellers would do well to purchase some colourful wraparound pagnes or wear very loose-fitting long pants with socks.

Eating Traditional-Style

In villages and African-style homes in the cities, African food is eaten with the hands. Only the nomadic Tuareg of the Sahara traditionally used utensils. Visitors will usually be offered a spoon, if there is one. A bowl of rice and a bowl of sauce will be placed on the ground and those eating will sit around on a mat and dig in, but never before washing their hands. It is polite to take off your shoes.

The head of the household will distribute meat and vegetables to the visitors. Take a handful of rice or other staple and part of the sauce or meat, then form a ball – this is the hard part – and eat. Don't shy away, it's usually a lot of laughs for everyone. Getting your hands all gooey won't be pleasant the first time, but a washbasin is always passed around afterwards. You may even grow to like this way of eating because of the increased 'family' feeling that it fosters.

As with the Arabs, only the right hand is used in forming the ball of food because of the ancient practice of using the left hand for personal toiletries. A violation of this rule will cause a silent turmoil. Just because you're a tourist won't make much difference. ■

Social Events

Much of African life centres around special events, such as weddings, baptisms, funerals, holidays and village celebrations (*les fêtes*). If you get an invitation, by all means accept. Just be sure to bring your dancing shoes because, except at funerals, there will probably be dancing. At baptisms guests bring gifts for both the mother and father – a small amount of money is perfectly acceptable. There will be a ceremony followed by a meal, typically a slaughtered sheep or goat.

Weddings At weddings there is likely to be an official ceremony at the mayor's office followed by eating and dancing at someone's home. The wedding is the culmination of a week of activities involving visits to relatives, meals and the exchange of gifts; only relatives and the closest friends are invited.

The offering of kola nuts plays a special role in all of this (as well as at other occasions). They are the extremely bitter nuts sold everywhere on the streets and known for their mildly hallucinogenic effects. (Travellers looking for a 'high' are usually disappointed and find them too bitter.)

Marriage is such an expensive affair for the groom that many African men cannot afford to get married before their late 20s or 30s. Gifts to the bride's family can easily cost several hundred dollars in sheep, money and the like – not exactly peanuts in an area of the world where incomes of US$200 a year are typical. Still, in traditional society, men who could afford more than one wife usually would marry more (the Koran allows up to four). Despite what you may hear to the contrary from African men, the first wives definitely don't like the custom of multiple wives. On the other hand, there's not much they can do except go back to their families, where they're unlikely to be welcomed with open arms if the husband's only 'sin' was taking a second wife.

Fêtes Other celebrations of particular interest are the village fêtes. They may range from something fairly common, such as celebrating the end of the harvest, to something a little different, such as honouring the dead. There's usually traditional African dancing in a circle. Don't worry – you won't be asked to join in. If there's modern African music, however, you can expect to do some dancing.

Each fête is unique. In Niger, for example, they may include camel races or a wrestling match (*la lutte*). In other areas you may see African puppets used to tell stories, and elaborate dances with masks. If you get the chance to see one, by no means pass it up. The individual country chapters mention some of the more important celebrations.

Spectator Sports

Soccer is Africa's most popular sport, more

Woaley

If you like games of intellectual challenge, one of the first things you should do upon arriving in Africa is learn how to play woaley – a game similar to backgammon. The game goes by many different names, including *woaley* or *awalé* in Côte d'Ivoire, *ayo* in Yoruba (Nigeria), *aju* in Togo and Benin, *ouri* in Wolof (Senegal), *wori* in Malinké (Guinea) and *mankala* in Lingala (Zaïre).

For starters, buy a woaley board. Most are rectangular, about half a metre long with two rows of six cups each. Some boards also have a cup at one or both ends for storing captured peas (48 come with the game).

Even if games aren't your bag, you won't find a better way to meet Africans, especially if you're having trouble communicating. Woaley is a major pastime of Africans of all ages and has been since it originated in Egypt thousands of years ago. While it is designed for two people, teams are also possible. Finding an opponent is rarely difficult – opening the board amongst onlookers is usually all that's required.

The basics of play are not difficult, but mastering the game requires time. In Africa, one thing you will find is time, whether waiting for a bush taxi or simply cooling off in a bar or under a shade tree. There are several versions of the game played by different ethnic groups, and the game varies in complexity. So don't be surprised if your opponent's rules are slightly different from those explained here.

Starting Play All woaley boards have 12 cups and 48 peas. Four peas are placed in each cup. The first player starts by picking up all the peas from any cup on his/her side of the board and dropping them one at a time in each consecutive cup to the right, counterclockwise.

Capturing Peas A player scores by capturing peas; the winner is the one who captures the most. A player captures peas only when the last pea dropped falls in a cup on the opponent's side containing only one or two peas. When that happens, the player picks up all the peas in that cup and stores them for counting at the end of the game.

so than ever since the surprisingly strong showing in the 1990 World Cup matches of Cameroun's Cinderella team. There are games almost every Sunday in the major cities.

The biggest sports event in Africa is probably the Africa Cup football matches held every even year in the spring.

In Lagos, the two major running races are the Maltonic Marathon in the first week in April and the Milo Marathon in September. The West African International Marathon and 10-km race is held on 4 April in Dakar (Senegal) and attracts a few name runners.

RELIGION

Before the Muslims began making inroads into Africa about 1000 years ago, the traditional religions in Africa were almost all animistic and involved ancestor worship. Now, roughly half of all West Africans are Muslim, particularly those living in the Sahel. The exception is Burkina Faso, where the Mossi warriors successfully resisted the Islamic invaders. The country with the highest percentage of Muslims is Mauritania (95%), followed by The Gambia, Niger, Senegal, Mali, Guinea and Nigeria (primarily in the north) – all with more than 50%.

Christians, mainly Catholics, are concentrated along the coast with the highest numbers found in Ghana (40%), followed by Togo, Liberia, Benin and Côte d'Ivoire. The

In a well-executed move, a player may capture peas not only from the last cup but also from the next-to-last cup if it, like the last cup, contains only one or two peas (prior to the move). The player may also capture peas from the third-to-last cup if it too contains only one or two peas. The same is true of the fourth-to-last cup, etc. For instance, if the last pea falls into a cup with one or two peas and, say, the three cups immediately preceding it similarly contained only one or two peas prior to the move, the player would capture all the peas in all four cups.

End of Game The game ends when Player A has no peas left on his/her side and Player B must play at least twice consecutively in order to reach the opponent's side of the board. (In that instance, if Player B has various alternative moves but only one will allow him to get to A's side of the board, he has no option – he must make that move in order to keep the game going.) Ending up with no peas on the board does not mean you win the game, although it is beneficial in the scoring.

Scoring Each player counts the peas he/she has captured plus any peas remaining on the opponent's side of the board. Since there are 48 peas, any peas over 24 constitute a point. If, for example, your total is 30 peas (your opponent will have 18 peas), you will receive six points and your opponent zero. A match is whatever you decide – three games, 100 points, two hours, etc.

Rules & Clarifications The major rules of the game are as follows:

- Moves are always left to right, counterclockwise.
- A move is made by picking up all of the peas from any cup on your side of the board and dropping them one by one (and only one) in each consecutive cup to the right.
- A player is entitled to only one move at a time. (In some versions, the player continues until a cup is 'captured'.)
- A cup of peas may be 'captured' only when the last pea in a move falls in a cup (a) on your opponent's side of the board and (b) with only one or two peas in it prior to the move. (In some versions, it makes no difference on which side of the board the last pea falls. In other versions, the last pea must fall in a cup with three peas.)
- To capture multiple cups of peas, each preceding cup must similarly contain only one or two peas prior to the move. If, for example, the last two cups contain two peas and the third-to-last cup contains three peas and the fourth-to-last cup contains two peas, you would capture the peas only from the last cup and the next-to-last cup. (In some versions, multiple captures are not allowed.) ■

new US$300-million cathedral in Yamoussoukro (Côte d'Ivoire) is copied after St Peter's in Rome and is equally big.

Animism

Each ethnic group in Africa has its own religion, so there are literally hundreds of traditional religions in West Africa. However, there are some factors common to all of them.

Virtually all are animistic and accept the existence of a Supreme Being as well as reincarnation. The Creator is considered to be too exalted to be concerned with humans but there are numerous lesser deities with whom one can communicate, usually

through sacrifices, as well as deified ancestors. There are no great temples or written scriptures, and beliefs and traditions are handed down by word of mouth.

The lesser deities, who act as intermediaries between the Creator and mortals, are frequently terrifying and correspond to natural phenomena or diseases. The Ewé of Togo and Ghana, for example, have over 600 deities, including one representing smallpox. Africans pray to these deities in order to gain good health, bountiful harvests and numerous children. It would not be unusual to see an African offering a few ritualistic words to one of the deities before taking libations, Many of the village celebrations are in honour of one or more deities. The Dogon of Mali, for instance, have celebrations before planting and after harvests to ensure good crops.

The ancestors play a particularly strong role in African religions. Their principal function is to protect the tribe. They are also the real owners of the land, and while you can enjoy it during your lifetime, you cannot sell it without incurring their wrath.

Ethnic groups are usually broken down into clans, which include all individuals who can trace their origins to a particular ancestor. Each has its own taboos in relation to its protective genies. Certain ones cannot kill lions; others refrain from slaughtering pythons or caymans.

Magic is another element common to native African religions. Good magic keeps away evil spirits. The medicine men, or juju priests, are the ones who dispense charms, tell fortunes and give advice on how to avoid danger. They are frequently seen around the markets, usually with bags full of fetishes such as birds' skulls and shells.

The charms worn around the neck are called *grisgris* (gree-gree) and are found all over West Africa. In the Sahelian countries, it is not unusual to see a person with six or seven grisgris around their neck, each warding off a particular evil. If it hasn't been blessed by the medicine man, it's worthless.

The Five Pillars of Islam
Islam is the Arabic word for submission and underlies the duty of all Muslims to submit themselves to Allah. The five pillars of Islam are the basic tenets which guide Muslims in their daily lives:

1. The profession of faith (*shahada*). 'There is no God but Allah, and Mohammed is his prophet', is the fundamental tenet of Islam.

2. Prayer (*salat*). Muslims must face Mecca and pray at dawn, midday, mid-afternoon, sunset and nightfall.

3. Alms (*zakat*). Muslims must give a portion of their income to the poor and needy.

4. Fasting (*sawm*). Ramadan is the month of the Muslim calendar when all Muslims must fast from dawn to dusk. It commemorates when Mohammed had the Koran revealed to him.

5. Pilgrimage (*hadj*). It is the duty of every Muslim who is fit and can afford it to make the pilgrimage to Mecca at least once.

Islamic Customs It is worthwhile remembering a few basic points lest you commit some social error, or miss out on some of the goings on:

- Whenever you visit a mosque, take off your shoes. In some mosques, women are not allowed to enter; in others, there may be a separate entrance since men and women pray separately.
- If you have a taxi driver or guide for the day, he may need to do his prayer ritual. Look out for signs indicating he wants a few moments off, particularly around midday, late afternoon and sunset.
- Despite the Islamic proscription against alcohol, you may have heard that some Muslims drink like fish. Even so, it's impolite to drink alcohol in their presence unless they show approval.
- If a Muslim man refuses to shake hands with a woman, remember he's only following the Koran so don't take offence.
- There are some important Islamic holidays, during which time little gets done (see Cultural Events & Holidays in the Facts for the Visitor chapter). ■

Islam

In the early 7th century in Mecca, Mohammed received the word of Allah (God) and called on the people to turn away from pagan worship and submit to the one true God. His teachings appealed to the poorer levels of society and angered the wealthy merchant class. By 622 AD life had become sufficiently unpleasant for Mohammed and his followers that they were forced to flee to Medina. This migration, the Hejira, marks the beginning of the Islamic calendar, year 1 AH or 622 AD. By 630 AD they had gained a sufficient following to return and take Mecca. Mohammed died in 632 but within two decades most of Arabia was converted to Islam.

Muslims began infiltrating Africa about 1000 years ago. The Berberspeoples & languages; from Morocco, for example, began raiding the Sahelian areas, bringing about the demise of West Africa's first major kingdom, the Empire of Ghana. By the 14th century many African rulers, particularly in the Sahel, had adopted Islam, at least in part. The second great West African kingdom, the Empire of Mali, was almost always ruled by Muslims, and Timbuktu became a major centre of Islamic teaching.

Islamic penetration through the coastal forests was quite another matter. Even today there are not many adherents of Islam in the coastal areas except for the immigrants from the north.

LANGUAGE

Of the 16 countries in West Africa, French is the official language in eight, English in five, Portuguese in two, and Arabic in one. See the individual country chapters for details.

Some say it's an awful legacy of the colonial period that the official languages are non-African. Far from it. To choose one of the many local languages for the official language would be politically disastrous. Moreover, few would be able to speak it.

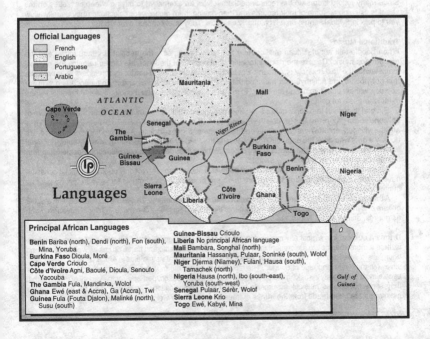

Official Languages
- French
- English
- Portuguese
- Arabic

ATLANTIC OCEAN

Cape Verde

Mauritania

Mali

Niger

Senegal

Niger River

The Gambia

Guinea-Bissau

Guinea

Burkina Faso

Benin

Nigeria

Sierra Leone

Côte d'Ivoire

Ghana

Liberia

Togo

Gulf of Guinea

Languages

Principal African Languages

Benin Bariba (north), Dendi (north), Fon (south), Mina, Yoruba
Burkina Faso Dioula, Moré
Cape Verde Crioulo
Côte d'Ivoire Agni, Baoulé, Dioula, Senoufo Yacouba
The Gambia Fula, Mandinka, Wolof
Ghana Ewé (east & Accra), Ga (Accra), Twi
Guinea Fula (Fouta Djalon), Malinké (north), Susu (south)
Guinea-Bissau Crioulo
Liberia No principal African language
Mali Bambara, Songhaï (north)
Mauritania Hassaniya, Pulaar, Soninké (south), Wolof
Niger Djerma (Niamey), Fulani, Hausa (south), Tamachek (north)
Nigeria Hausa (north), Ibo (south-east), Yoruba (south-west)
Senegal Pulaar, Sérèr, Wolof
Sierra Leone Krio
Togo Ewé, Kabyé, Mina

MUSIC

Perhaps nothing is more interesting about African culture than the music and dancing; you could do a tour of West Africa focusing solely on music. Amongst Africans, the pop music from West and Central Africa dwarfs in popularity that from the rest of Africa.

A good introduction to West African music can be found in *Africa Never Stands Still* (Ellipsis Arts, New York, 1994), a boxed set of three CDs with a 48-page book. You could also get on the mailing list of Original Music (☎ (914) 756-2767), Box 190, Lasher Rd, Tivoli, New York 12583, USA, or Music of the World, PO Box 3620, Chapel Hill, NC 27513-3620. Both have catalogues of African music (listing cassette and CD titles) and also books on African music which explains the significance of each style. In addition, Ronnie Graham's discography of leading musicians and bands entitled *The Da Capo Guide to Contemporary African Music* (*Stern's Guide to Contemporary African Music* in the UK) or, better, Chris Stapleton & Chris May's *African Rock* (*African All Stars: the Pop Music of a Continent* in the UK), both excellent introductions and available through Original Music. These and other recommended books on African music are listed under Books in the Facts for the Visitor chapter.

Record Stores

Outside Africa It's not easy to find record stores which have extensive collections of African music except in France where West African music has become extremely popular. Four of the best stores are:

Stern's African Record Centre 116 Whitfield St, Covent Garden, London W1P 5RW, UK (☎ (0171) 387-5550). They have a catalogue with over 1000 titles.
African Record Centre Ltd 2343 Seventh Ave, New York, New York, USA (☎ (212) 281-2717)
The Kilimanjaro Music Store Corner of Florida Ave and California St, NW, Washington, DC 20009 (☎ (202) 462-8200)
Afric Music rue des Plantes, 75014 Paris, France (☎ (01) 45-42-43-52)

Within Africa Once you're in West Africa, it's easy to find records and cassettes (but not CDs) of West and Central African music but most cassettes are of poor quality and records marked stereo are usually mono. Since many record stores do the recordings themselves, an alternative to buying cheap cassettes on the street is listening to some of their records and then having them record your selections (they usually allow you to pick individual songs) on a high quality cassette. They rarely charge over US$3.

Traditional Music

When people talk about African music, there are really two types – the traditional village music and the modern pop music. Despite the rising international popularity of the latter, the former remains the musical mainstay for the vast majority of Africans. But traditional music is much harder for foreigners to appreciate. It is polyphonic and polyrhythmic, meaning that there are many melodies and rhythms occurring simultaneously, without one dominating the other. To the uninitiated, it may sound monotonous and repetitive when in fact there is a lot going on.

Several things set traditional music apart from pop music. Historically, music has been the prerogative of only one social group, the *jalis* (*griot* is the French word often used in West Africa to denote this group). They are the villages' entertainers as well as oral historians and genealogists. At a wedding, for instance, it's usually a griot who does the entertaining. Yet despite their widely admired talents, they rarely enjoy personal esteem and are in one of the lowest social orders along with shoemakers and weavers. People often fear them because they know too many secrets.

A second feature of traditional music is that it serves a social purpose. Not only does each social occasion have its own type of music but, in addition, there are different kinds of music for women, young people, hunters, warriors, etc.

A third aspect of traditional music which sets it apart is the instruments. Unlike the pop groups with electric guitars and the like, the griots use only instruments that they themselves can make with local materials, such as gourds, animal skins, horns, etc.

Drums A quick visit to almost any museum in Africa will give you a good idea of the variety of drums. Nowhere is there a more imaginative assortment than in Africa – cylindrical, kettle and frame drums as well as goblet and hourglass-shaped drums. There is a certain mystical aspect of musical instruments in Africa, as though they were alive with their own language of sounds. The fact that goats are the most talkative animals and their skins are used almost exclusively in making drums is no coincidence. One reason, perhaps, for the variety of drums is that they serve not only as musical instruments but also for communication. The drums used for long-distance messages are often made from the trunks of trees and can easily weigh several hundred kg.

A
B
C D E

A: Drummers in Zala village, Man, Côte d'Ivoire (DW)
B: Balafon (xylophone), Ghana (GB)
C: Peg drum, Ghana (GB)

D: Drum, Accra, Ghana (AN)
E: Djembe drum, Ghana (GB)

A	B
C	D
E	F

A: Musical instruments, Cotonou, Benin (AS)
B: Talking drum, Ghana (GB)
C: Chekere, Ghana (GB)
D: Celebration near Cape Coast, Ghana (A)
E: AAMAL musicians, Kokrobite, Ghana (A)
F: Agung (cow bells), Ghana (GB)

Stringed Instruments These come in about as many varying forms as drums, ranging from a one-string lute to the multiple-string kora. The **kora** is the pre-eminent instrument of the jalis, and is arguably one of the most sophisticated instruments in sub-Saharan Africa. It is described as a harp-lute (due to its structural properties) and consists of 21 strings which are supported over a long neck made of rosewood. This neck pierces a large hemi-spherical gourd which is covered with cowhide. The rear of the gourd is often covered with interesting stud patterns. The instrument sits vertically in the lap of the player, who plucks the strings with the thumb and index finger of each hand. Kora players are often very highly skilled musicians and seeing a performance is a real treat.

Another stringed instrument that is played by the jalis is the **konting**. This is a lute-type instrument that is unfortunately becoming less common. It is said to be the originator of the banjo.

You're most likely to hear a kora in The Gambia, Senegal (particularly the Casamance region), Guinea and Mali. In Guinea, all you have to do is wander down the streets of Conakry any evening and you're likely to see a street dance; the kora is an indispensable part of the scene (as is the **balafon**, a xylophone-like instrument with small gourds hanging on the underside that give it a hollow sound). In Senegal, you can go out any Sunday to the Benedictine monastery outside Dakar and hear the kora and other traditional instruments being used to play Bach and the like – truly unique. For an impressive recording, look for *Soubindoor* by **Jali Musa Jawara**, younger brother of Guinean pop star Mory Kanté. For excellent kora music played in a traditional style, check out **Jali Nyama Suso** whose work, amongst other recordings, appears on a two-volume set called *A Search for the Roots of the Blues*. Two other master kora players are **Dembo Konté** of The Gambia and **Kausu Kuyateh** of Senegal; they have an exceptional duo album, *Simbomba*. Also look out for **Toumani Diabaté**, best known in Europe for being part of Songhaï, a 'world-combo' which includes a Malian griot on kora.

Kora

Wind Instruments The most notable wind instrument is the **flute**. Fulani shepherds are reputed to play the most beautiful flute music; their instrument is simply a length of reed. You'll also see flutes made from millet stalks, bamboo and gourds. Other wind instruments include animal tusk horns and trumpets made from gourds, metal, shells or wood. They are found all over West Africa and take a slightly different form in each area. If you're looking for something a little unusual to collect but light and inexpensive, flutes are a good buy.

Books Two of the best books on traditional African music are *The Music of Africa* by J H Kwabena Nketia and *African Music, A People's Art* by Francis Bebey. Unfortunately, hearing traditional African music in West Africa is quite difficult unless you stay in a village for a few days. One place that you're guaranteed to hear it every day of the week is at the Academy of African Music & Arts, 30 km west of Accra (Ghana); see that chapter for details.

Pop Music

If there's any one music that is king just about everywhere, it's unquestionably the modern Congo sound from Zaïre and the Congo. Hearing it for the first time, you might think it's Latin. That's because there's a lot of Latin influence in African popular music. Indeed, African pop music is an incredible mishmash of traditional, Latin and Afro-American music with elements of American jazz and rock.

It all started about 90 years ago with the coming of the colonial era. Africans for the first time were introduced to music with ballads. The influence came from three sources. First, there were the Africans who were forced to become members of regimental bands associated with the forts. The music they played was typically European – polkas, marches and the like. Second, there was the impact of the Christian religious groups with their songs. Finally, the increased trade with Europe brought sailors from all over the world and they brought not only their favourite ballads, but also instruments such as guitars, harmonicas and accordions.

Highlife Ghana was the richest country in the area and, not surprisingly, was where the influence of ballads was felt the most. What emerged was a Westernised music called 'highlife'. The Western influence was greater in the dance bands which played to the Black elite in the cities than in those which played in the hinterland. The latter combined acoustic guitars with rattles, drums and the like and developed a type of highlife that was substantially different from that of the dance bands. During WW II, the stationing of Allied troops in West Africa spread more new musical ideas, especially the then-popular 'swing' music. After the war, there were bands with sizeable repertoires, including calypso sounds. They began touring West Africa igniting the highlife fire everywhere, but at the same time continuing to assimilate foreign musical styles. Black music from across the Atlantic had a big impact, especially jazz, soul and, more recently, reggae.

Rumba Further to the south in Leopoldville and Brazzaville, there was another movement going on. During WW II, radio stations began popularising the early Cuban rumba stars, and new 'Congo-bars' were popping up offering not only refreshments but also dance music. The music was predominantly acoustic with solo guitars being accompanied by small brass ensembles. Bottles struck like cowbells provided the rhythmic accompaniment. However, the indigenous musical traditions of the Congo basin, called 'Le Folklore', remained the heart of the music, as it does today.

Orchestras With the arrival of the electric guitar and amplification, large orchestras emerged, many elaborating on traditional rumba patterns. In 1953, the popular band African Jazz featuring Dr Nico was established, followed three years later by the famous OK Jazz led by Franco, Africa's all-time, most influential musician (and still one of its most popular despite his recent death). In the late 1960s when President Mobutu of Zaïre began his well-known 'Authenticité' movement, new orchestras began trying to remain more faithful to traditional sounds while at the same time experimenting with some of the North American rhythms. The result was enormously successful, bringing a deluge of new orchestras that have dominated the African music scene ever since.

The Impact on Western Music African groups have incorporated African rhythms and developed their own unique sounds, with the result that African music is now having an impact on Western music.'The hottest music in France today is Afro-pop, a cultural melee in which African talking drums and Latin rhythms meet Western technology. For years Paris has been the Mecca for African stars who have quit Dakar or Kinshasa for the West; the problem is that their recordings, once recorded in Africa for Africans, are now recorded in Paris and directed more at international audiences, arguably losing some authenticity in the process. The major styles that have developed are listed below. Most of the stars are male. There are a few big stars who are left out simply because they either do not fall within any major style (Aicha Koné) or because the music is not uniquely African, such as Alpha Blondy – the reggae superstar who is huge throughout Europe – and Nayanka Bell (all from Côte d'Ivoire).

One of the more interesting things to do while in any major city centre is to go into a record shop and ask to hear some of the local recording stars – on the pretence that you might buy something, of course. There's no better way to learn the different styles, and maybe you *will* buy something. Each country chapter lists the most popular local recording stars. Chances are they'll be the leading stars five years hence.

The best cities in West Africa for hearing live performances are Lagos, Accra, Dakar and Bamako. On weekends in Accra and elsewhere in Ghana, you can find live bands at many of the nightclubs. Other cities where there are groups playing on a regular basis are Abidjan, Dakar, Praia, Niamey and Conakry.

Sahelian Pop Music Riding the crest of the 'World Music' wave is the music from the Sahel in West Africa, principally Mali, Senegal and Guinea. From these three countries come three of the most popular African singers – **Salif Keita**, **Youssou N'dour** and **Mory Kanté**.

In the 1960s and '70s Cuban music was a major influence on the musical styles of the region. Dance rhythms, such as the rumba, were very popular and orchestras from Cuba toured to sell-out concerts. At around the same time, the governments of Mali and Guinea were embarking on ambitious programmes aimed at revitalising their wealth of traditional customs and forms. Musicians, particularly, were encouraged to use the stories and melodies from the past in their compositions. The result proved enormously popular and was the origin of today's Sahelian pop style.

There were many superb recordings made during this period. Some original cassettes are still available in the region, though many

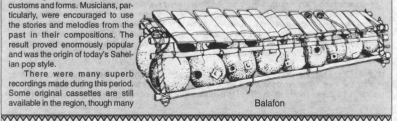

Balafon

releases are now on CD and can be purchased through good record stores worldwide. From Senegal, look out for the legendary **Orchestra Baobab**. Three of their albums are now on CD. Also, recordings by the **Star Band de Dakar** and **Super Etoile de Dakar** are worth hunting. The latter features a young Youssou N'dour.

From Mali, Salif Keita's original band – **The Super Rail Band** – are excellent, as are the follow up combination, **Ambassadeurs Internationaux**. In Guinea, over 80 records were made by the country's own label – Syliphone. They cover an enormous range of music; some of the big names are **Bembeya Jazz**, **Keletigui et ses Tambourinis** and **Camayenne Sofa**. Today's leading singers continue to incorporate elements from their musical tradition into their songs. **Youssou N'dour** is the leading exponent of *Mbalax* music – a Senegalese form that uses the sabar drum in a lead rhythmic role. **Salif Keita** blends traditional vocal styles with brass arrangements and synthesised instruments, whilst **Mory Kanté** fuses kora melodies with state-of-the-art technology.

These types of music are very popular today, and there are many cassettes available by these stars, and by lesser-known artists. For more details on the current scene, see the individual country chapters.

Blues lovers should check out recordings by Malian **Ali Farka Touré**, who has performed with John Lee Hooker. His blues guitar work and gravelly singing are probably the closest thing to blues to have originated in Africa.

Afro-Beat A fusion of African music, jazz and soul, Afro-beat (along with juju) is the most popular music today in Nigeria. The undisputed king of Afro-beat is **Fela Anakulapo Kuti**. Fela went to the USA in the late '60s and was greatly influenced by James Brown and Black American politics. He took Brown's jazz and mixed it with the many cultural intricacies of his own African music and developed a politicised Afro-beat. The instruments used by his orchestra are mainly non-African: guitars, trumpets, saxophones and electric pianos as well as drums. Yet the sounds are substantially African-inspired.

Because Fela Kuti's lyrics are always controversial and frequently political, he has never been popular with the politicians. In 1977 the military government burned his communal compound (called the Kalakuta Republic) on the outskirts of Lagos and in 1984 they detained him on spurious currency smuggling charges, sentencing him to five years in prison. The outcry was loud and, following a change of government in 1986, he was released. Another Nigerian musician whose music is kin to Afro-beat is **Sonny Okosun**, the granddaddy of Afro-reggae. His politicised 'jungle rock' music is a fusion of highlife, Santana rock and reggae, and his 1978 hit *Fire in Soweto* was a massive hit throughout West Africa.

Juju Music Juju music had its origins in Nigerian Yoruba music. As far back as the 1930s the highlife bands began playing it. The Nigerian civil war gave rise to the popularity of juju music. Many members of the highlife bands went east to Biafra, contributing greatly to highlife's nose dive in the west. So the Yoruba there turned to juju.

The music is characterised by tight vocal harmonies and sophisticated guitar work, backed by traditional drums and percussion. Today, it is one of the most popular music styles in Nigeria but its international appeal has totally evaporated.

The leading Yoruba musicians are Sonny Ade and Shina Peters, with **Ebenezer Obey** now a distant third. **Sonny Ade** was influenced by Afro-beat and has been the most famous since the late '60s, while **Shina Peters** is the new rising star and is particularly popular with the younger crowd.

Cape Verdean Music Although not very popular in West Africa, Cape Verdean music is nevertheless worth mentioning because of its distinctive, fast-paced Latin style. The dominant role of the guitar and electric piano without traditional African instruments are part of what sets it apart from other Latin-inspired music, such as that from Zaïre. The leading musicians can change quickly; those currently popular include **Tam Tam 2000, Bana** and **Paulino Vieira.**

Congo Music Senegalese pop music is the fad on the international scene, but the Congo music from Zaïre and neighbouring Congo continues to be at the top of all the pop charts throughout Black Africa. Indeed, it is the only music which is truly pan-African, its appeal stretching from Senegal to Zimbabwe. For one thing, it's some of the best dance music. The various musicians are always introducing new instrumentation and elements from other styles but they all retain the basic rumba framework. So if it sounds Latin, it's probably Zaïrean. If not, it's probably from neighbouring Congo or Gabon. The two biggest stars, both legends in their own time, are **Franco** of OK Jazz (who recently died), and **Tabu Ley** (or Rochereau as he is also called). Other leading musicians and groups include:

Male Artists Langa Langa Stars, Sam Mangwana, Bella Bella, Kanda Bongo Man, Papa Wemba, Dr Nico (deceased), Pierre Moutouari and Pamelo Mounka (both from the Congo) and Akédengué (Gabon).

Female Artists M'Bilia Bel, Tshala Muana, Abeti, M'Pongo Love (all from Zaïre) and Nayanka Bell (Côte d'Ivoire).

Makossa Music Cameroun's distinct makossa music has become so popular in recent years that it now trails only Congo music in popularity throughout much of West Africa. It's a fusion of Camerounian highlife and soul, and is strongly influenced by Congo music, with great use of the electric guitar. Like Congo music, the irresistible rhythms make you want to dance which, of course, is part of the reason for its popularity. Recognising it, however, requires a little structured listening.

The biggest star is still **Manu Dibango**, whose hit *Soul Makossa* in the mid-1970s put makossa music on the African musical map. His jazz-influenced music is more for listening, however, than for dancing. **Francis Bebey** and **Isadore Tamwo** are also extremely popular, while **Sam Fan Thomas** is Cameroun's king of makassi, a lighter sound than makossa but just as infectious. Other makossa stars include Sammy Njondji, Moni Bile, Toto Guillaume and Ekambi Brillant. ∎

Facts for the Visitor

VISAS & EMBASSIES
Visa Requirements
The cost of visas varies considerably. In the USA, for example, they cost from nothing for a visa to Nigeria or Guinea and only US$11 for one to Cape Verde to US$35 for a visa to Niger.

You'll need from one to four photos and in some cases proof of intention to leave the country (ie, a return ticket or one with a flight out of the country). Photocopies are OK.

If you buy a one-way airline ticket to Africa, chances are you won't have any significant problems. If you don't have a return ticket, an embassy may refuse to issue you a visa unless you submit a bank statement or guarantee (*caution bancaire* in French) showing proof of adequate funds to return, ie at least the price of a return airline ticket. The chances are good, however, that the same embassy in another African country may not require such. So move on and get the visa in another country.

West African embassies in Europe and North America often have stricter visa requirements than those in neighbouring countries in Africa. Some even demand to see a recent bank statement demonstrating sufficient funds or a letter from your travel agent. If you can't produce or afford what they request, consider getting the visa in Africa. Many people travelling on the cheap try to procure the majority of their visas in Africa for this reason. The main problem is that visas are often more expensive to buy in West Africa.

One quirk is that a few embassies still issue visas of only very short duration. Visas to Benin, for example, are usually good for a stay of only seven days. Don't worry. In those cases, getting extensions once you're there is usually fairly simple and routine. The other quirk, exit visas, are no longer required in any West African country.

Occasionally, an embassy may refuse to issue you a visa if you are not a resident of the country where you're trying to get the visa (eg the Nigerian embassy in Dakar) or if, theoretically, you could have obtained a visa in the country of your residence (eg the Ghanaian embassy in Ouagadougou). What's bizarre is that the same embassies in other African countries usually do not have the same requirement, so the easiest solution is often to obtain the visa elsewhere. On rare occasions, the embassies that impose this requirement will drop it if you present them with a *note verbale* from your embassy; the Ghanaian embassy in Ouagadougou is not one of those. A note verbale is a letter from an embassy or consulate stating that you are a citizen of that country. It includes your passport number and requests that you be issued a tourist visa so that you can visit the country for a certain period of time.

Some embassies in Africa routinely request a note verbale from your embassy even if you're a resident of the country – a definite problem if your country doesn't have an embassy or honorary consul. In that case, if you happen to be from a Commonwealth country, they will usually accept such a letter issued by the embassy or honorary consul of another Commonwealth country.

Multiple-Entry Visas
In addition to single-entry visas, some embassies issue multiple-entry visas, allowing you to enter many times during a given period. If you take the three-hour trip from Accra (Ghana) to Lomé (Togo) you'll need a multiple-entry visa to re-enter Ghana.

Embassies of Benin, Cape Verde, Côte d'Ivoire, Mali, Mauritania, Niger and Sierra Leone generally do not issue them. All embassies of Senegal issue them, and some embassies of Liberia, Ghana, Burkina Faso, The Gambia, Guinea and Guinea-Bissau do the same, especially those located outside Africa. In the case of Senegal, its embassies issue multiple-entry visas as a matter of course and they're usually good for stays of up to three months. For other countries, multiple-entry visas, if available, almost invariably cost more. Many embassies in Europe and elsewhere will not tell you about the availability of multiple-entry visas unless you ask. Once in Africa, many travellers regret not having asked because plans frequently change, sometimes requiring a second entrance into the same country.

West African Embassies

Many West African countries have diplomatic missions in various cities around the world (see the individual country chapters). For information about West African embassies in West African countries, see Obtaining Visas in West Africa (later), and the individual country chapters.

In Australia, travellers can get Nigerian visas from the Nigeria high commission in Canberra. The only place where a visa to other West African countries might be obtained is through a French diplomatic mission, whether it be the embassy in Canberra or one of the consulates in Sydney or Melbourne.

Visa Agencies

If you need visas to a number of African countries, it'll take a little time tripping around to all the embassies. In the USA, Canada and the UK there are businesses that will do this for you. In the telephone directory, they're usually listed under 'passport and visa services'.

Shop around because fees vary considerably. Also, agencies are sometimes misinformed and will tell you that an embassy imposes a requirement that no longer exists. So in some cases where a requirement is particularly onerous, you may

want to verify the requirements with the embassy directly. This is particularly true in the case of visas to Nigeria, the requirements for which are far more onerous at embassies outside Africa than at those within Africa.

One word of warning: start the process early. Count on two weeks for the agency to mail you the applications and receive them back, one week per visa requested, and one week to get the passport back to you.

In the USA, while some offices of DHL assist clients in obtaining visas, you'll probably be better off dealing with an agency which specialises in offering this service. In the USA and UK they include:

Visa Services Inc 1519 Connecticut Ave, NW, Suite 300, Washington, DC 20036 (☎ (800) 222-8472, (202) 387-0300); US$40 per visa plus the embassy's fee

International Visas LA World Trade Center, 350 S Figueroa St, Suite 185, Los Angeles, CA (☎ (213) 625-7175); US$50 per visa plus the embassy's fee

Travel Agenda 119 West 57th St, Suite 1008, New York, NY 10019 (☎ (212) 265-7887, fax 581-8144); US$25 per visa plus the embassy's fee (US$40 for business visas)

Hogg Robinson 7 Butler Place (near Victoria train station), London W1H 02V (☎ (0171) 222-8835) Sterling House, 19 Holborn, London EC1N 2JS (☎ (0171) 242-7541) 119-123 Kingsway, London WC2B 6PT (☎ (0171) 404-5454); UK£15 per visa plus the embassy's fee

Thames Consular Services 363 Chiswick High Rd, London W4 4HS (☎ (0181) 995-2492); UK£15 per visa plus the embassy's fee

The Visa Service 2 Northdown St, Kings Cross, London N1 9BG (☎ (0171) 833-2709, fax 833-1857); UK£15 for the first visa (less for each subsequent visa) plus the embassy's fee

Nigerian Visas

Obtaining visas to Nigeria poses unique problems. In recent years the Nigerian embassies in the USA, the UK and in many other countries outside Africa have become intent on making it extremely difficult to obtain a Nigerian visa. More specifically, the visa application must now be accompanied by a letter from a friend in Nigeria or company there inviting the applicant to come visit them and assume full financial responsibility for the person during their trip and/or a telegram from a hotel confirming the applicant's reservation. In Lagos, the only hotel which will do such is the Sheraton, which charges about US$180 a night for a room. One way around these intentionally onerous requirements is to obtain the visa in Africa as none of the Nigerian embassies there impose such requirements. However, many Nigerian embassies in Africa now issue visas only to residents, not to travellers! Moreover, that eliminates the option of flying directly to Nigeria. ■

The Visa Shop Trailfinders Travel, 194 Kensington High St, London W4 (☎ (0171) 938-3848, fax 938-3305); UK£18 per visa (UK£100 for Nigeria)

Obtaining Visas in West Africa

If you'll be travelling around West Africa for over three months, there's no way you can get all your visas beforehand. Most tourist visas to West African countries are valid for a maximum of three months from the date of issue, and sometimes less. Try to obtain as many as possible, however, because getting them in Africa is sometimes difficult and sometimes more expensive.

It's easy to get visas to Burkina Faso, Côte d'Ivoire and Togo in every country in West Africa except The Gambia. This is because wherever those countries have no embassies, the French consulate is responsible for issuing the visas (usually in 24 hours). Many French consulates also issue visas to Mauritania.

Obtaining Visas at the Border or Airport

The only countries that issue visas at the border are Benin, Guinea and The Gambia. In Benin, two border stations have this authority – Malanville and the one on the Lomé to Cotonou road. Similarly, in Guinea only the Guinea-Sierra Leone border town of Nongoa (across the river from the north-eastern tip of Sierra Leone) has this authority. The Gambia also issues visas at the major border crossings but they must be renewed in Banjul within 24 hours of arrival. Elsewhere, the chances are slim that border officials will let you in without a visa, although it occasionally happens.

The same is not true if you arrive at an airport without a visa. At the airport in Bissau, visas are issued as a matter of course (but double-check before leaving because rules can change). Elsewhere in West Africa, if you arrive at an airport without a visa, the chances are still better than ever that officials will either issue you a visa there (after some hassling) or send you to the foreign ministry for a visa. I met one traveller who had done this in five West and Central African countries and had never failed to get in. This will not work if you're flying from outside Africa

because the airlines won't let you on the plane without a visa. But in Africa, airlines virtually never ask to see travellers' visas to the country of destination. I certainly recommend against travelling without visas but if you decide to take the risk, make sure you look decent, have ample funds and have a good story as to why you couldn't get a visa.

Visas to Ex-Colonies

British high commissions used to issue visas to virtually all Commonwealth countries (Sierra Leone, The Gambia, Kenya, etc) wherever those countries didn't have embassies. In West Africa, they no longer do this for The Gambia, Nigeria or Ghana, but occasionally they still do in the case of Sierra Leone. The British high commission in Abidjan, for example, issues visas to Sierra Leone and Kenya, but the British high commissions in Accra and Freetown do not.

French embassies, on the other hand, do this without exception for Côte d'Ivoire, Burkina Faso and Togo (and with a few exceptions to Mauritania), which is why visas to those countries are very easy to obtain all over West and Central Africa. On the other hand, don't count on French embassies outside Africa having this authority.

If you're travelling to Guinea-Bissau or Cape Verde and there's no embassy where you live, call the Portuguese embassy. They will usually help you process visa applications to those countries.

MONEY
Currency

The principal currency of the region is the CFA (Communauté Financière Africaine) franc. The CFA franc is fixed against the French franc at a rate of 100:1. Benin, Burkina Faso, Côte d'Ivoire, Mali, Niger, Senegal and Togo (all the former French colonies except Mauritania and Guinea) use the CFA franc.

By tying the CFA to the franc and exchanging it freely with the French franc, France has given West Africa a hard currency, eliminating the possibility of a black market and allowing travellers to go from one CFA country to the next without exchanging money. Prior to 1994, however, this gross market distortion which made foreign commodities, particularly those from France, relatively cheap for those paid in CFA wages was a mixed blessing. While African consumers of foreign goods, mostly bureaucrats, appreciated their relatively low prices, the overvalued CFA made it virtually impossible for these countries to export anything other than highly valued natural resources, such as petroleum; it also made West and Central Africa the most expensive region in the developing world for foreign travellers.

Even though the CFA is hard currency, exchanging CFA in other countries isn't easy. In East Africa, the banks act like it's funny money. In the USA, even major banks won't accept it. In short, the CFA is hard currency only in West and Central Africa and France. One hitch is that there are actually two CFAs – the West African CFA and the Central African CFA. The latter is used in Cameroun, Central African Republic, Chad, Congo, Equatorial Guinea and Gabon. While there's usually not too much difficulty exchanging one for the other at offices of Air Afrique, Air Cameroon or Air Gabon (which all serve Central Africa and find either currency useful), the person on the street definitely won't do the same, and many banks won't either.

Black Market

No non-CFA country in West Africa currently has a substantially overvalued currency. A small parallel market (or black market) exists in Guinea; the black-market rate is about 10 to 15% more favourable than the bank rate. The exchange bureaus in Sierra Leone, Ghana, Guinea-Bissau and Nigeria, on the other hand, offer virtually the same rates as the moneychangers on the streets.

In Liberia, the US dollar has all but supplanted the Liberian dollar in Monrovia, especially for the few remaining foreigners there other than soldiers. Elsewhere in Liberia, the money situation is as much a mess as the political situation. In Mauritania, the ouguiya is overvalued but, strangely, there appear to be no moneychangers.

Changing money on the black market in non-CFA countries used to be risky, with the potential of stiff jail sentences. With the new floating exchange rates all over West Africa, most governments now don't seem to care. Where you still have to be careful is Mauritania and possibly Guinea. In Mauritania, border officials are very strict in searching travellers for undeclared currency and the penalties are potentially severe. Since there appears to be no black-market moneychangers anyway, declare all of your money upon entering Mauritania. In Sierra Leone, Nigeria and Guinea, exchanging money on the street is not nearly as open as it is in The Gambia and Guinea-Bissau.

Sometimes there's no alternative to exchanging money with moneychangers on the streets. If you're travelling overland by bush taxi, you won't find a bank at the border. How do you pay for the onward taxi? You purchase currency at the last town before crossing the border.

You'll almost always find moneychangers at the borders. In the cities, money dealers often hang around markets, banks and post offices. Taxi drivers invariably know where

Devaluation of the CFA
In early 1994, France devalued the CFA by a whopping 100%, sending shock waves throughout the CFA countries. Prices of most imported goods rose dramatically, not enough in most instances to completely offset the devaluation but enough to put many products outside the grasp of many buyers. Imported French cheese and yoghurt, for example, almost doubled in price, thus making locally produced substitutes much more attractive. Some companies couldn't adjust and eventually folded. French co-operators and other employees whose salaries were pegged to the French franc rejoiced as did local farmers. Almost everyone else tied to the local economy, however, suffered. The biggest winners of all are foreign travellers, who will find prices in West Africa to be far more reasonable. ∎

they are. One way to avoid having to change money with hordes of dealers around you is to hire a taxi to the site and invite one moneychanger inside, then close the windows or drive off. This way you can count your money in peace and significantly reduce the chances of getting ripped off.

Importing Currency

Hard Currency There is never a limit to the amount of foreign currency that you may import into a country unless, possibly, it's a huge amount. One of the biggest mistakes many travellers make is bringing too few French francs. In letter after letter, travellers warn of the problems of exchanging other currencies and travellers' cheques. You'll need cash for emergencies because cashing travellers' cheques and using credit cards in Africa is difficult, if not impossible, particularly in rural areas.

Even in English-speaking countries, French francs and CFA are sometimes preferred to dollars or pounds, especially near the borders of CFA countries. In rural areas you may find dollars and pounds impossible to cash, even at banks.

In CFA countries, the problem is even worse. In rural areas, banks won't touch dollars because they don't know the official exchange rate for that day. CFA and French francs, on the other hand, exchange at the official ratio of 100:1 everywhere, and most banks charge no commission for the exchange. Most stores will accept French francs as well.

Local Currency Except in CFA countries and Liberia, importing local currency is either prohibited or severely restricted – typically limited to the equivalent of about US$10. Enforcement of this regulation is fairly lax. In most West African countries customs officials rarely conduct body searches of travellers entering the country. The exception is Mauritania, where enforcement is strict and violating the rule could land you in the clink.

Exporting Currency

CFA Countries Taking CFA out of a West African country is virtually never a problem unless you are exporting large quantities; say, over US$1000 worth. The exact rules, however, are unclear. In many CFA countries, tourists are theoretically supposed to be able to take out more than local business people, and the limit is supposed to be higher if you're travelling to another CFA country. However, most border officials don't seem to know exactly what the rules are. If you run into problems, playing the ignorant tourist should help. Exporting other currencies from CFA countries is also not a problem.

Non-CFA Countries The rules in non-CFA countries are quite different. You are never allowed to take out more than the equivalent of about US$5 to US$10 in local currency; in some countries you can't take any. On leaving, it's not possible to reconvert local currency into foreign currency except in Guinea and The Gambia, and then only if you have bank slips showing you originally exchanged it at the official rate.

As for exporting other currencies, there appears to be no limit anywhere in West Africa; just be sure to declare your money

---

Currency Declaration Forms

At the time of writing, currency declaration forms were still being used in Nigeria, Ghana and Mauritania but no longer in Sierra Leone or Guinea. In Nigeria, Ghana and Mauritania, if you declare all your money and then exchange some of it on the street, there is a risk that customs officials at the airport or border from which you're leaving will hassle you because you won't be able to prove that all your money was exchanged at banks. They may make all kinds of threats so as to intimidate you into offering a bribe. The risk varies from very great in Mauritania to very small in Ghana. To avoid this possibility, when entering the country hide a small amount of hard currency (preferably French francs) where no one could ever find it. But in Mauritania, declare everything. ■

upon entry if the country uses currency declaration forms.

Credit Cards

The most widely accepted credit cards are American Express (AE) and Visa (V), followed by Carte Bleue (CB) and Diners Club (D). MasterCard (MC) and Eurocard (EC) are all but worthless except at major establishments such as 1st-class hotels. With American Express and Diners cards it's possible to obtain cash advances at their offices, and in over half of the capital cities in West Africa there is at least one bank that offers this service to Visa cardholders. For the French, obtaining cash is particularly easy with Visa and Carte Bleue cards issued by French banks. Nevertheless, except for the French, travellers' cheques are still much more preferable for obtaining cash.

Travellers' Cheques

It is difficult to cash travellers' cheques in West Africa. Commissions are high, sometimes 5%, and many banks won't accept them, particularly if they're US dollar, UK pound or German mark. Moreover, the banks are slow and occasionally make you wait until the afternoon when they know the day's exchange rate.

If you'll be spending most of your time in CFA countries, bring French franc travellers' cheques. Finding banks that sell them is not always easy, even in Europe (outside France); still, it's definitely worth the effort scouting around to find one that does. If you have no success, one easy solution which involves only a minimum amount of risk if you're flying to a CFA country is to bring all your money in cash and convert most of it into French franc travellers' cheques immediately upon arrival.

Otherwise, take American Express. They are accepted at banks in major West African cities (but only rarely at banks upcountry).

As for Thomas Cook, Citibank, Barclays and Bank America travellers' cheques, in the largest capital cities there are usually at least one or two banks that accept them (more in the non-CFA countries) but elsewhere,

you'll find that many do not accept them. In English-speaking countries, you shouldn't encounter many problems with Thomas Cook and Barclays cheques; elsewhere you will probably be no better off than those with Citibank and Bank America cheques.

Transferring Money

Transferring money can take weeks, and problems are often encountered. The bank may deny receiving money which has actually arrived. If money is wired, arrange for the forwarding bank to send separate confirmation with full details. You can then go into the African bank with the much needed proof that your money has been sent.

Foreign Banks

Citibank Abidjan, Dakar, Lagos (affiliate)
Barclays Abidjan, Accra, Freetown, Kumasi, Lagos
Chase Manhattan Abidjan, Lagos (affiliate)
Chemical Abidjan

Costs

The recent devaluation of the CFA means the cost of living is less. Still, travel is not as cheap as in many South American countries or in countries such as India and Nepal, so you'll still need to budget.

Budget Travelling A room in a very cheap hotel costs around US$6, or CFA 3000. Most beds have a single clean sheet, fans and sometimes bucket showers. Couples should budget about 25% more per room. In many cases a couple can take a single room as it will have a double bed.

A bare minimum budget for meals is US$4 a day; in most countries that will buy you breakfast, two simple African meals on the street, a large beer and a soft drink, and peanuts for snacking. Eating African street food does not mean eating poorly. The best African food is often that sold on the streets.

Finding cheap restaurants is not always easy. While the cheaper places may increase your risk of getting stomach problems, the actual risk will be minimal if you stick to things like rice and well-cooked meat and stay away from raw vegetables and fruits.

Even in relatively expensive cities such as Abidjan you can get excellent braised chicken, rice and a soft drink for about US$5.

If you insist on eating Western food you'll be hard-pressed to keep the average down to US$3 a meal, although in the largest cities it's fairly easy to live off Lebanese chawarma sandwiches (lamb and vegetables in pita bread with sauce), which cost CFA 400 to CFA 550, or about US$1. An alternative is surviving off simple street food, such as beef brochettes, bread and butter, peanuts and cassava chips. In the morning and evening, in many cities, particularly those in the CFA countries, you'll see men serving Nescafé, bread, butter and scrambled eggs at benches along the streets, for US$0.45.

As for transport, hitching rides on the major routes is sometimes fairly easy. Most drivers will expect you to pay, so establish this at the beginning. Most travellers take buses or bush taxis, of which there are various types and, therefore, prices. In descending order of cost, there are five-seater sedans, Peugeot 504s, buses and vans, and pick-up trucks. In Nigeria, Senegal and elsewhere, you can save from 20 to 30% by taking a van, for example, instead of a Peugeot, but the waiting and riding time can easily double. In most countries, you can expect to pay approximately US$1 for every 80 km in a van and US$1 for every 55 km in a Peugeot. In oil-rich Nigeria, transport costs are about half this.

Mid-Range Travelling Expect to pay US$80 to US$150 a night for a single room at a top hotel. A very decent two or three-star hotel with a good restaurant, a nice view and a pool will be about 60% less.

As for meals, many countries in West Africa are so poor that only a small percentage of the locals can afford to eat at restaurants. As a result, many restaurants cater to foreigners and serve only Continental cuisine. And these meals are usually expensive, particularly if some of the ingredients are flown in from Europe. Eating relatively modestly in a major city can easily cost US$30 for two at a restaurant and more at a fancy hotel.

Renting a car can easily cost US$100 a day or more. Going from one city to another, taking a share Peugeot 504 is much cheaper and you can make the trip more comfortable by renting two seats instead of one. For excursions out of town, consider hiring an all-day taxi instead of renting a car.

Tipping

Tipping is a problem in Africa because there are few clear rules applicable to all people. Africans are not in the habit of tipping but a small amount of tipping is expected from wealthier Africans. Tipping to most Africans is related to the concept of a gift (*cadeau*); rich people are expected to give cadeaux. Almost all foreigners appear rich, therefore a cadeau is expected unless the person obviously looks like a hitchhiker. Anyone going to a fancy hotel would be expected to tip, but there would not be the same expectation from a backpacker in a cheap hotel.

Everyone, even Africans, are expected to tip 10% at the better restaurants, but check the bill closely to see if service is included. It frequently is at restaurants and hotels in French-speaking Africa. At the other end of the scale are the African restaurants with almost all-African clientele – no tipping is expected from anyone. There's a grey area between these two classes of restaurants. Tipping at these restaurants is rarely expected from Africans and those who are obviously backpackers, but may be expected of wealthy-looking foreigners. Even the wealthier Africans will sometimes tip at all-African restaurants, not so much because it's expected but because it's a show of status.

In taxis, tipping is not the rule but well-heeled travellers are expected to tip about 10%, except for rides in shared cabs where tipping is almost unheard of. In bigger cities with numerous foreigners, such as Dakar, Abidjan and Lagos, the taxi drivers may still hope for a small tip, even from backpackers.

In general, follow local custom. Again, in Africa there is no uniform standard applicable to all Africans; rather, richer Africans are held to one standard and poorer Africans to another. Even if you view yourself as poor, Africans will probably view you differently.

In areas where the locals are unaccustomed to foreigners, travellers must be especially careful. You need to make a special effort to observe local customs and reflect on the possible consequences of your actions. Be as unobtrusive as possible and follow local customs to a tee. If you're unsure of what the customs are, ask. Gestures such as tipping or offering candy to children may seem innocuous but they can have the unwanted effect of encouraging the locals to view foreigners as a source of income.

WHAT TO BRING
Clothes
Travel light and keep your attire simple. Shorts are useful for the beaches and travelling upcountry, but women should not expect to wear them anywhere in public, even in modern cities such as Dakar (bring several wraparound skirts to put on over your shorts). Men can wear shorts anywhere, but doing so will only accentuate the differences with the locals, especially in the Sahel where Muslims predominate.

Pants are acceptable everywhere. But in the Muslim areas, Western women usually find it easier to develop a good rapport with African women if they wear similar clothes (long dresses), particularly in the villages.

A light sweater is advisable year-round, but especially from December to February in countries bordering the desert and Cape Verde. If you're crossing the desert in the winter, bring a heavy sweater.

Essentials
- Medical kit – see the later Health section
- Tampons, pads & contraceptives – often impossible to find outside major cities
- Suntan lotion – frequently available
- Foreign currency – hide at least US$100 worth of hard currency on you, preferably French francs
- Passport photos – bring lots; you'll need two or three for every visa and visa extension.
- Photocopy of critical documents

Recommended Items
- French franc travellers' cheques – see under Travellers' Cheques
- Washbasin plug & soap powder
- Mosquito repellent

- Water bottle
- Iodine tablets or crystals – handy whenever bottled water is not available (see the later Health section)
- Water Tech water purifier – much easier to use than iodine tablets or crystals. (Write to Water Technologies Corporation, Box 2495, Ann Arbor, MI 48106, USA.)
- Map – Michelin's map of West Africa (No 953) is far superior to others. Finding one in West Africa is difficult.
- Money pouch
- Day pack
- Hat
- Paperback books – one on African art will be a useful reference, plus books in English are frequently difficult to find
- Vitamin tablets (to help resist tempting salads)
- Film & photographic accessories – bring a variety of speeds of film; lighting conditions vary considerably
- Polaroid camera
- Alarm clock
- International Driving Permit (IDP) – some rental agencies will not accept licences from other countries
- Credit cards – required by most rental agencies
- French phrasebook – don't expect to find one easily in Africa
- Small calculator – for bargaining in markets
- Business cards – Africans like to make friends; giving someone your card is an indication you want to keep in contact. They can even be useful in dealing with police.
- Swiss Army knife

Especially for Budget Travellers
- Cassettes – Africans love music with a good beat from the West. Hard core blues and complicated jazz go over like a bad joke. You can be sure that bus and taxi drivers and many other Africans with cassette players will, for a change, want to hear your music. They also make good souvenirs for African friends you make along the way.
- Blank cassettes – if you wish to record African music during your trip, you'll have a very difficult time finding high-quality blank cassettes
- Plastic rain poncho – can double as a ground mat
- Sleeping bag liner – useful for camping and when the hotel's sheets are unbearably dirty
- Utensils
- Camping gear – useful only if you'll be crossing the Sahara, travelling in your own vehicle, or hiking considerably. In villages, you will not need such as the chief or someone else will usually find you a place to sleep.
- Student ID – occasionally useful for obtaining discounts, particularly in Nigeria and Ghana

CULTURAL EVENTS & HOLIDAYS

When planning your itinerary consider the special events throughout the year. The more important ones are listed below and are discussed more fully in the individual country chapters (* approximate date).

January

New Year's Day (1) – celebrated all over Africa

Paris-Dakar Car Rally (1-22) – Africa's biggest auto race; the route changes slightly every year. The drivers arrive in Niamey (Niger) around 15 January, Mali a few days later, and Dakar on the 22nd.

Togo Liberation Day (13) – a vast parade makes its way through the streets of Lomé

February

Festivals des Masques (10*) – in the Man region, western Côte d'Ivoire, the mask festivals of the Dan are the most spectacular festivals in Côte d'Ivoire, the acrobatic dancing events being the main attraction.

Argungu Fishing Festival (15-17*) – in Sokoto State, Nigeria, this spectacular festival offers displays of barehanded fishing, duck hunting, swimming and diving competitions, and canoe racing. Drinking, drumming and dancing continue into the night.

FESPACO – in Ouagadougou, Burkina Faso, this all-African film festival is held for 10 days every odd year during the last week of February (in even years it is held in Tunis).

March

Mardi Gras in Cape Verde & Guinea-Bissau – Cape Verde's major celebration, with street parades every day leading up to Lent

Tilsm Festival (14-16*) – near Kanté (Togo), the Bassar people spend over three days in this dry month trying to predict the crop. Men perform *sintou*, a magical dance that can last as long as the festival.

April

Senegalese National Day (4) – Senegal's biggest public celebration; coincides with the West African International Marathon in Dakar

Gomon Festival (8-9*) – in Oumé, central Côte d'Ivoire, you'll see memorable dancing, healing ceremonies and sacrifices

Niger's National Festival (15) – a major holiday in Niger involving one week of traditional dancing, wrestling and camel races

Festival des Masques (25*) – held around Bandiagara, Mali, the Masks Festival is the major festival of Mali's Dogon people and is celebrated in the Dogon villages in April or early May. Masked dancing is the major attraction.

May

Deer Hunt or *'Aboakyer' Festival* (6*) – this festival in Winneba, Ghana, is on the first Saturday in May and draws large crowds. The main event is the deer hunt, when several groups of men try to be the first to catch a deer, followed by royal processions through the streets, and dancing.

July

Fishing Festival (4*) – the first Tuesday of July, this colourful event in Elmina, Ghana, includes a parade of royally dressed chiefs

August

Grand Magal (5*) – a pilgrimage and celebration in Touba, Senegal, held 48 days after the Islamic New Year to celebrate the return from exile of the founder of the Mouride Islamic Brotherhood

Oshun Festival (28*) – this famous Yoruba festival in Osogbo, Nigeria (north-east of Ibadan), takes place on the last Friday in August and there's music, dancing and ritual sacrifice

September

Yams Festival (2*) – at the beginning of September, this festival in Bassar, Togo, has folk dancing, fire dances and traditional costumes

Aguaa Fetu Afabye Festival (4*) – this Cape Coast (Ghana) festival takes place the first Saturday in September. The pageantry is particularly colourful, and there's music and dancing all over town.

Niger's Cure Salée (7-8*) – there is no event on the continent more interesting than the annual celebration of Niger's Wodaabé (nomadic Fulani cattle herders who get together once a year to celebrate). The courtship rituals are particularly famous. The date is not fixed, but almost always occurs sometime in September. The celebration lasts a week, but the major events only about two days. The location is also not fixed; the principal Cure Salée (there are several) takes place west of Agadez, usually near In-Gall.

Guin Festival (8-11*) – this four-day festival in Glidjo-Aného, Togo, starts on a Thursday before the second Sunday in September. Processions the first two days are followed by dancing and celebrations during the last two days.

Biennial Festival (9-22) – in Bamako, Mali, this two-week festival takes place every two years, starting around the second week of September. It sponsors various sporting and cultural events.

October

New Yams Festival (1-15*) – Imo State, Nigeria

November

Abissa Festival (2*) – at Grand-Bassam, Côte d'Ivoire and, nearby at Gbregbo (near Binger-ville), it is the Festival of the Prophet Atcho

December

Igue Festival (7-15*) – in Benin City, Nigeria, this colourful seven-day festival is when the Oba people perform traditional dances in full regalia, and their chiefs hold a mock battle and dance in procession to the palace to reaffirm their loyalty

Cattle Crossing (10-12*) – the exact date is not fixed until November. This is a very interesting event in Diafarabé, Mali, when Fulani herders from the desert bring hundreds of thousands of cattle to an area about 200 km north-east of Ségou to cross the Niger River in search of greener pastures.

Christmas (25) – celebrated everywhere

Islamic Holidays

There are some very important Islamic holidays, when almost all of West Africa's commercial life comes to a stop. Since the Islamic calendar is based on 12 lunar months, with 354 or 355 days, these holidays are always about 11 days earlier than the previous year. The exact dates depend on the moon and are announced about one day in advance. For estimated dates, see the table.

Tabaski (Eid-al-Kabir) – also known as the Great Feast, Tabaski is the most important celebration throughout West Africa and is the major Muslim holiday. On this day Muslims kill a sheep to commemorate the moment when Abraham was about to sacrifice his son in obedience to God's command, only to have God intercede at the last moment and substitute a ram instead. It also coincides with the end of the pilgrimage (hadj) to Mecca. In most countries, it's a two-day public holiday, even in those not predominantly Muslim.

Feast of Ramadan (Eid-ul-Fitr) – the second major Islamic holiday, celebrated everywhere in West Africa, following the annual 30-day Muslim fast. The fast is sometimes referred to as *le carême* (kah-REM). Muslims who do the carême (many

---

The Hadj

Ask a wheat farmer from near Timbuktu what he's going to do with any profits from a development assistance project and he's likely to tell you that he'll use it to finance a pilgrimage to Mecca. Many other Muslims would say the same. All Muslims who are of good health and have the means are supposed to make the pilgrimage at least once in their life.

Those who do the pilgrimage receive the honorific title of Hadj for men, and Hadjia for women. For some, this can involve a lifetime of savings, typically several thousand dollars. It's not unusual for families to save up and send one member. Before the aeroplane, it used to involve a journey overland of a year or more, sometimes requiring stops on the way to earn money. So if you meet someone with the prefix Hadj or Hadjia, you may appreciate the honour this bestows on them in the community. ∎

---

do not, particularly those living in the cities) are usually weak during the afternoon because they are not allowed to eat or drink (exceptions include athletes and pregnant women) from sunrise to sunset. Work hours usually end around 1 or 2 pm. Especially interesting are the Sallah celebrations in Kano and Katsina (northern Nigeria).

Mohammed's Birthday – also widely celebrated, it occurs almost three months after Tabaski.

Estimated dates for major Muslim events:

event	1996	1997	1998
Ramadan begins	22 Jan	10 Jan	31 Dec
Eid-ul-Fitr	22 Feb	10 Feb	31 Jan
Tabaski	29 April	18 April	8 April
Mohammed's Birthday	28 July	18 July	7 July

Tabaski (Eid-al-Kabir)

Two weeks before Tabaski, sheep prices can jump 50% or more. One-third of the sacrificed animal is supposed to be given to the poor, one-third to friends, and one-third is left for the family. Those who cannot afford a sheep are really embarrassed – most will do anything to scrape up the money. If you can manage to get an invitation, you'll be participating in what is for most West Africans the most important and festive day of the year. It's mainly lots of eating and visiting friends following several hours at the mosque. ∎

POST & TELECOMMUNICATIONS
Post

The mail service is quite reliable in most of West Africa – it just takes a while getting there. From the USA the typical delivery time is two to four weeks depending on the town's size and remoteness. From Europe, the delivery time is about one-third less. However, delivery times considerably longer than this occur just frequently enough to make it impossible to rely on the mail for matters involving critical time constraints.

Contrary to what you may hear, it's rare that governments open the mail. But then there's the Peace Corps volunteer in Togo who was thrown out of the country for making unflattering remarks about the government on a postcard. Courier service is an alternative; DHL, for example, has offices in almost every capital city in West Africa and in some of the other major cities as well.

Telephone

Telephone connections between Africa and Europe/USA have improved greatly in recent years because international calls now go by satellite in virtually every country. Calls between African countries, however, are sometimes relayed through Europe, in which case the reception is usually bad – *if* you can get a call through.

The main problem is still the high cost; it's about four times more expensive than calling from abroad and there are no reduced rates at night. The other problem is the waiting time, which can be minutes or hours depending on the locality and time of day.

Calling from the USA or Europe to Africa is usually easier, and always less expensive. Direct dial is possible to some African cities. Between 5 pm and 6 am, the direct-dial rate from the USA and the UK to most of Africa is about US$0.85 a minute. This is also the easiest time to get a line. If you call during business hours in the USA or Europe, you may find it very difficult to get through – after 5 pm your chances increase.

TIME

Burkina Faso, Côte d'Ivoire, The Gambia, Ghana, Guinea, Guinea-Bissau, Liberia, Mali, Mauritania, Senegal, Sierra Leone and Togo are at GMT/UTC. Cape Verde is one hour behind; Benin, Niger and Nigeria are one hour ahead. None of the West African countries in this book observe daylight savings.

When it's noon in the following West African countries, the time elsewhere is:

	Benin, Nigeria & Niger	Cape Verde	Other West African Countries
London	11 am	1 pm	noon (same)
New York	6 am	8 am	7 am
Paris	noon (same)	2 pm	1 pm
Sydney	9 pm	11 pm	10 pm

ELECTRICITY

The electricity supply throughout West Africa is 220 volts, except for Liberia where it is 110 volts. Plugs are usually two round pins, like those in Europe.

LAUNDRY

Throughout West Africa, finding someone to wash your clothes is fairly simple. The top-end hotels often charge per item. At other hotels, a staff member or a local will do the job for a reasonable and often negotiable fee. Only the worst and dumpiest cheap hotels don't organise this service.

WEIGHTS & MEASURES

The metric system is used in West Africa.

BOOKS

Except for several commercial reference books, the following list of books is limited to those that are available in paperback and obtainable by mail – take several with you! An art book, in particular, will be handy for reference purposes.

For novels by African authors, contact Heinemann Educational Books at Michelin House, HE1 Fulham Rd, London SW3 6RB (☎ (0171) 581-9393) or at 70 Court St,

Portsmouth, NH 03801, USA (☎ (603) 778-0534). Heinemann carry over 270 titles in their African Writers Series.

For history books, contact Longman Publishers (Longman House, Harlow, Essex CM20 2JE, UK, and Addison-Wesley/Longman, Reading, MA 01867, USA) or Cambridge University Press (The Edinburgh Bldg, Shaftesbury Rd, Cambridge CB2 2RU, UK; and 510 North Ave, New Rochelle, NY 10801, USA); they publish the most titles. Ask Longman for their free history and African studies catalogues.

Background Reading

If you're interested in understanding the roots of Africa's problems, check out Haskell Ward's *African Development Reconsidered*. The themes that echoed most consistently through the conversations he had with Africans were that things work only when Africans feel they have done things for themselves and that Africa's lack of self-reliance lies at the heart of its problems. The systems imposed upon them following independence by well-meaning Western advisers have had very little to do with African needs; Africa's resulting dependence today on the West encompasses virtually every area of life.

For some truly fascinating and provocative reading touching on a number of topics, I highly recommend Blaine Harden's *Africa: Dispatches from a Fragile Continent* (Harper Collins, London, 1993, UK£7.99). In this 333-page work, he examines why African political leadership, which suffers from the 'Big Man' disease, has failed its people, but Harden believes there's hope, especially in the case of Nigeria. He also believes that African values still endure and are what make the continent a joy.

History

African Civilization Revisited: From Antiquity to Modern Times (Africa World, Trenton, New Jersey, 1990) by Basil Davidson is an engaging book which builds on Davidson's earlier eight-part documentary series on the history of Africa for British TV.

Africa in History (Phoenix, London & Colliers, USA, 1994, UK£8.99, 425 pages) is Davidson's latest book.

Modern Africa (Longman, 1994, UK£12.99) is a 300-page paperback focusing on African history since 1900, also by Basil Davidson.

The African Genius: An Introduction to African Social & Cultural History (Little Brown & Co, Boston, 1990) is another by Basil Davidson.

A History of Africa (Unwin Hyman, London, 1988, UK£14) by J D Fage is a well-written, 578-page paperback on African history.

A Short History of Africa (Penguin, London & New York, 1990, UK£6.99, 303 pages) by J D Fage & Roland Oliver is also very good.

Africa Since 1800 (Cambridge University Press, 1981) by Roland Oliver & Anthony Atmore is the last of a trilogy, the others being *Africa in the Iron Age* and *The African Middle Ages 1400-1800*. The book has three parts: the pre-colonial period up to 1875, followed by the partition and colonial rule (by theme rather than by region), and finally the roads to independence taken by different African territories, plus the post-independence decades.

Contemporary West African States (Cambridge University Press, 1989) by Donald Cruise O'Brien is recommended if you're looking for a thorough, if colourless, country-by-country account of conditions and events in contemporary West Africa. It covers Senegal, Côte d'Ivoire, Burkina Faso, Nigeria, Ghana, Liberia plus several countries in Central Africa.

West Africa: An Introduction to its History (Longman, 1977) by Michael Crowder covers West Africa and parts of Central Africa. *A History of West Africa 1000-1800* (Longman, 1992, UK£8.25) by Basil Davidson gives a detailed, 406-page account of early West African history. *West Africa Since 1800* (Longman, 1992, UK£8.25) by J B Webster & A A Boahen gives more of an in-depth treatment of later African history. Also worth reading is *Topics of West African History* (Longman, 1986) by Adu Boahen.

Art & Culture

African Art in Cultural Perspective (W W Norton & Co, London & New York, 1985, UK£7.95) by William Bascom is an excellent paperback focusing solely on sculpture, and covers West and Central Africa. Another good and compact but out-of-print paperback is *African Sculpture* by William Fagg & Margaret Plass.

African Art (W W Norton & Co, 1988) by Frank Willett is back in print for US$11.50, with 288 pages and 261 illustrations. It's a superb, introductory paperback on African art, providing a wider perspective than Bascom's book. The *Times Literary Supplement* called it 'the finest general introduction to African art'. Take this paperback or Bascom's; the art will make a lot more sense and you'll develop a more critical eye.

A Short History of African Art (Penguin, New York, 1987) by Gillon Werner is a 416-page paperback, good for the historical perspective.

African Arts is a superb quarterly published by the African Studies Center (UCLA, Los Angeles, CA 90024, US$20 yearly), with good photography and well-researched articles.

African Textiles (Icon Editions, Harper & Row, New York, 1989, US$19.95) by John Picton & John Mack is a bulky book with numerous photographs, and is the best on the subject.

African Hairstyles (Heinemann Educational Books, 1988, US$12.95) by Esi Sagay is a 208-page publication loaded with photographs of fascinating hairstyles from all parts of the continent.

Beads from the West African Trade (9310 Los Prados Lane, Carmel, CA 93923) by Picard African Imports is a six-volume paperback collection. Each pamphlet is fairly compact and focuses on a different category of beads, such as chevrons and millefiori.

African Traditional Architecture (Heinemann, 1982) by Susan Denyer has lots of photographs and is probably the best book available on traditional African architecture.

Music

African Rock (Obelishk Press, 1989) by Chris Stapleton & Chris May, an introductory 384-page book to non-traditional African music of all sorts, is highly recommended. In the USA, it is available through Original Music (418 Lasher Rd, Tivoli, New York 12583). In the UK, Paladin Press publishes it under the title *African All Stars: the Pop Music of a Continent*.

The Da Capo Guide to Contemporary African Music (Da Capo Press, New York, 1988), also available from Original Music, is another good introduction; it has some errors but is unbeatable if you're looking for a musician-by-musician guide with short country-by-country surveys. The section on Central African musicians and countries is good. In the UK, it is published by Pluto Press under the name *Stern's Guide to Contemporary African Music*.

The Music of Africa (Victor Gollancz Ltd, 14 Henrietta St, London WC2E 8QJ) by J H Kwabena Nketia is an excellent introduction to traditional African music.

African Music, A People's Art (Lawrence Hill & Co, Westport, CT, 1984) by Francis Bebey is a 184-page paperback and another excellent book on the traditional music of Francophone Africa. At the end of the book, the Camerounian author gives a selective discography with extensive recordings from six Central African countries and eight West African countries.

Politics & Economics

Squandering Eden (The Bodley Head, London, 1988) by Mort Rosenblum & Doug Williamson is a highly readable and still up-to-date book on Africa. Imbued with a non-patronising concern for the welfare of Africans and the African environment, it develops the theme that broad-based stable development in the interest of all Africans should be the goal, and that this is dependent on building a workable relationship between African landholders and managers, and their environment.

The Africans (Random House, New York, Seattle, 1984) by David Lamb, a best seller, is a portrait of modern-day Africa, rich in political and social detail. The analysis lacks depth but for entertainment it's unbeatable. Lamb, who has been twice nominated for the Pulitzer Prize, spent four years in the early '80s travelling to 46 countries, talking to both guerrilla leaders and presidents, and catching midnight flights to coups in little-known countries where desert people were supposedly doing unspeakable things to each other.

Africa: The People & Politics of an Emerging Continent (Simon & Schuster, New York, 1989) by Sanford Ungar is a guide to the present-day political, economic and social realities of Africa which tries to make sense out of a complex continent. It is highly readable and entertaining and pays particular attention to Liberia, Nigeria, Kenya and South Africa.

Political Economy of Africa (Longman, 1981), edited by David Cohen & John Daniel, is a selection of pieces, some with a leftist viewpoint.

West African States (Cambridge University Press, 1978), edited by John Dunn, is one of the best books focusing solely on West Africa.

The Economies of West Africa (St Martin's Press, New York, 1984) by Douglas Rimmer is an analytical and systematic economic survey of West Africa by a senior academic at the University of Birmingham.

Ecology

Africa in Crisis (New Society Publications, Philadelphia, 1986) by Lloyd Timberlake focuses on the political and environmental factors contributing to drought and famine in Africa, particularly the roles international aid organisations and African leaders have played in recent environmental disasters.

The Seeds of Famine: Ecological Destruction & the Development Dilemma in the West African Sahel (Rowman & Littlefield, Lanham, Maryland) has a narrower focus.

African Silences by Peter Matthiessen (Random House, New York, 1991) focuses on the author's journeys through parts of West Africa as well as through Zaïre, Gabon and the Central African Republic. The most compelling part of this deeply gripping, beautifully written book is his foray with other researchers to make estimates of the number of elephants in the Central African region; the numbers are smaller than feared.

Adventure

Impossible Journey: Two Against the Sahara (Penguin, New York, 1987) by Michael Asher is an enthralling account of the first successful west-to-east crossing of the Sahara. Written by an Englishman travelling with his new Ethiopian bride, it recounts their adventure on camel-back starting in Mauritania and passing through Mali and Niger before ending at the Nile. Problems

Novels

In 1986, Wole Soyinka of Nigeria won the Nobel Prize for literature, only the fifth person from a Third World country to win the prize. He has written three books, including *The Interpreter* and more recently *Ake*, a personal memoir of his childhood, but he is primarily a playwright. *A Dance of the Forests*, *The Man Died*, *Opera Wonyosi* and *A Play of Giants* are some of his more well-known plays. Heinemann publishes a number of his works. He is a man with a social vision who doesn't mind lambasting those in power, and uses a language which is far from simple.

The Palm-Wine Drinkard (Grove-Weidenfelf Press, New York, 1954) by Amos Tutuola of Nigeria was the first great African novel. For those seeking humour, there is no book more amusing than this 1952 Nigerian classic about an insatiable drunkard who seeks his palm-wine tapster in the world of the dead.

Things Fall Apart (Heinemann Educational Books, 1958) by Chinua Achebe of Nigeria is a classic of English literature and the most well-known African novel, having sold more copies than any other novel by an African writer. The story takes place in the mid-1890s at the time of the colonial takeover and portrays the collision between pre-colonial Ibo society and inrushing Western missionaries. Particularly interesting is Achebe's penetration beyond the great fact of colonialism to a probing moral examination of Africa and Africans. Achebe's historical imagination coupled with a mastery of the English language have led critics to compare him with Conrad and the like.

Anthills of the Savannah (Doubleday, New York and London, 1988), also by Chinua Achebe, is an anatomy of political disorder and corruption in a fictional African country resembling Nigeria. The book abounds with African humour and satire and is one of Achebe's most recent novels. It was a finalist for the 1987 Booker Prize in the UK.

The African Child (also called *The Dark Child*) (Farrar, Straus & Girous, New York, 1954) by Camara Laye of Guinea is the second most-widely printed novel by an African. Camara Laye was born in Guinea in 1924, studied in France and returned to write this largely autobiographical work of his childhood among the Malinké tribe, surrounded by ritual magic and superstition, and his emergence into manhood and independence. All the patience, curiosity, resolution and ferretings of the most accomplished anthropologist could not have elicited these facts.

The Beautiful Ones Are Not Yet Born by Ayi Kwei Armah of Ghana (1969) and *God's Bits of Wood* by Sembéné Ousmane of Senegal (1970), both published by Heinemann, are especially recommended. The former, about the political greed and corruption following Nkrumah's death, received rave reviews from the *New York Times*. Sembéné's novel, which is the most widely acclaimed to date by a Senegalese author, tells of the struggles of strikers on the Dakar-Niger train line in 1948.

Slave Girl (Fontana, 1979) and *Rape of Shavi* (Fontana, 1989), both by Buchi Emecheta of Nigeria, are two of a number of novels written by one of Africa's most successful women authors. Her books are invariably humorous and focus on the struggles of African women to overcome their second-class treatment by society.

A Bend in the River (Random House, New York, 1989) by V S Naipaul, a tale that takes place in Zaïre, is a good selection for those wanting a novel on rural African life by a Pulitzer Prize winner from Trinidad.

Reading the African Novel (1987) by Simon Gikandi and *Journeys Through the French African Novel* (1990) by Mildred Mortimer are two of the best works of criticism of the African novel; both are available through Heinemann. ■

plague them throughout the journey, including dodging bullets in the Sudan.

African Dances (Penguin, New York 1980) by Geoffrey Gorer is less a study of African dancing than it is the recounting of a White man's adventures from Senegal to Benin in 1935. Fascinating are Gorer's observations of African customs and lifestyles during colonial times, but they also reveal the very evident cultural prejudices of his era.

Travels in the Interior of Africa (Eland Books, 1983) by Mungo Park is the account by one of the famous early West African explorers (a Scot) of his expeditions to West Africa and Timbuktu in the late 18th century and early 19th century.

Travels in West Africa (1897, reprinted by Beacon Press, Boston, 1988, US$12.95), who was a Victorian free spirit, is a true classic and an engaging travelogue that details this flamboyant spinster's two trips through Gabon during the 1890s, sailing up the Ogooué River, crossing some 150 km of dense jungle, dealing with the Fang (reputedly a dreaded cannibalistic tribe at the time) and gathering fish specimens for a museum, all the time facing every calamity with fortitude and good humour.

Cookbooks

The Africa News Cookbook by Africa News Service Inc (Viking Penguin Inc, New York, US$12.95; and Middlesex, UK, 1985) is one of the few African cookbooks in print. This 175-page book is good and covers the entire continent. Each recipe has been carefully chosen to ensure that all ingredients are obtainable in the West.

A Safari of African Cooking by Bill Odarty (Broadside Press, Box 04257, Detroit, 1988, US$5) is also good. The 137-page paperback by the Ghanaian has 106 recipes, 43 from West African countries.

Magazines

West Africa (West Africa Publishing Co, London) is a weekly magazine with a reputation for the accuracy of its news.

Jeune Afrique (in French; Le Groupe Jeune Afrique, Paris) is a popular weekly magazine covering both Central and West African and world events, always with an African perspective.

New African (IC Publications, London & New York) has a reputation for accurate and balanced reporting, with a mix of politics, financial and economic analysis, features on social and cultural affairs, plus country and topic surveys.

Africa News (☎ (919) 286-0747), not found readily on the newsstands, focuses on crucial issues in Africa and is probably the most consistently reliable source of information about Africa in magazine format. This magazine also has a research centre with over 4000 books mostly on Africa,

over 150 periodicals, and 40 cabinets of newspaper clippings, press releases and reports, some quite old. The centre's address is Box 3851, Durham, NC 27702.

Africa Business (IC Publications, London & New York) is a monthly magazine providing a wide variety of news items, commentaries and feature articles.

Africa (Africa Journal Ltd, London), also a monthly magazine, covers African business, economics and politics.

Economic Digest (Middle East Economic Digest, London) is the best weekly providing business news, economic analyses and forecasts.

Africa Confidential (Miramoor Publications, London), an expensive bimonthly publication, is unquestionably the best in terms of giving the inside scoop.

Reference Books

Africa South of the Sahara (Europa Publications, London) is an expensive, respected reference book published annually with over 1100 pages of economic and commercial data, by country.

Africa Contemporary Record (Holmes & Meier, London), published annually, is even more detailed.

Africa Review (Walden Publishing Ltd, Essex, UK, and Box 830430 Birmingham, Alabama 35283, USA) is a more concise (235 pages) and affordable (US$89) annual digest of economic and commercial data on African countries, with general information on the African business environment.

Resource Guide to Travel in Sub-Saharan Africa (Hanz-Zell/Bowker-Saur, London) has less on economics and much more for tourists and visitors with an extensive, critically reviewed list of all guidebooks, maps, travelogues and specialist manuals to the region, plus detailed information on travel magazines, bookshops, publishers, libraries, tourist organisations, special interest societies and conservation projects. Volume 1 covers East and West Africa; volume 2 covers Central and southern Africa.

Overseas Bookshops

Bookshops in West Africa are listed in the individual country chapters. It's difficult to pick up any interesting reading material in English, even in Lagos and Accra. Books in French, however, are abundant, particularly in Dakar and Abidjan. For specialist books on Africa, it is better to buy them at home.

UK One of the country's truly outstanding travel bookshops is Blackwell's in Oxford.

In London, Foyle's (☎ (0171) 437-5660), 113 Charing Cross Rd WC2H OE5, one block from Cambridge Circus, claims to be the world's largest bookshop. Ask for their Africana section. Their travel section is good as well. Waterstone's (☎ (0171) 434-4291), next door to Foyle's, is also good for maps and travel guides.

Even better for maps, with a fairly good selection of travel guides as well, is Stanfords (☎ (0171) 836-1321), 12 Long Acre St, Covent Garden, London WC2P. It's the official outlet for the Department of Overseas Surveys (DOS) and has maps for individual countries in Africa. If you will be driving around West Africa, buy your maps here.

Africa Bookcentre at the Africa Centre (☎ (0171) 240-6649), 38 King St, Covent Garden, London WC2 8JT, has a small book department and is a good place to get practical first-hand information on Africa. The centre, which is a good place to meet people, also has a reading room with newspapers and magazines plus exhibitions and a cinema, etc. Other excellent London travel bookshops are The Travel Bookshop (☎ (0171) 229-5260) at 13 Blenheim Crescent W11; Daunt Books (☎ (0171) 224-2295) at 83 Marylebone High St W1M 4AL; and The Travellers Bookshop (☎ (0171) 836-9132) at 25 Cecil Court WC2N 4EZ.

USA In New York City, your best bets for maps and travel guides are Travelers Bookstore (☎ (212) 664-0995), 22 West 52nd St and Complete Traveler Bookstore (☎ (212) 685-9007) at 199 Madison Ave at 35th St. Two stores with good Africana sections are Barnes & Noble (☎ (212) 807-0099) at 105 5th Ave at 18th St, and Liberation Book Store (☎ (212) 281-4615), 421 Lenox Ave, on the corner of 131st St, Harlem.

In Washington, DC, the best store for travel books and maps is Travel Books & Language Center (☎ (301) 951-8533), 4931 Cordell Ave, Bethesda, MD, which is open seven days a week. The Map Store (☎ (202) 628-2608), 1636 Eye St, NW, carries Michelin maps of Africa.

In Chicago, The Savvy Traveller (☎ (312) 263-2100), 50 East Washington St, is the city's best-stocked source of guidebooks and has other travel literature and paraphernalia.

On the West Coast, two stores specialising in travel are Travellers Bookcase (☎ (213) 655-0575), 8375 West 3rd St, Los Angeles, CA 90048 – 2½ blocks east of the Beverly Center and Phileas Fogg's (☎ (415) 327-1754, (800) 533-3644), 87 Stanford Shopping Center, Palo Alto, CA 94304, open seven days a week. Travel Centres of the World (Box 1788, Hollywood, CA 90078) specialises in travel guides and hard-to-get, detailed maps. Contact the Adventurous Traveler Bookstore (☎ (800) 282-3963), PO Box 577, Dept E5, Hinesburg, VT 05461. Their catalogue covers 150 countries.

Canada In Montreal, one of the best travel bookshops is Librairie Ulysse (☎ (514) 843-9447), 1208 St-Denis, Montreal H2X 3JS. Another excellent one is Quillan Travel Store at 4B, 112-11 Ave, SE Calgary, Alberta T2G 0X5. It sells books, maps, videos and travel accessories by mail. Ask for their free travel catalogue, indicating your destination. Another bookshop is The Travel Bug (☎ (604) 737-1122), 2667 West Broadway, Vancouver, BC V6K 2G2. It carries many series and will sell by phone or mail. ITMB Publishing (☎ (604) 687-3320), 736A Gransville St, Vancouver, BC V6Z 1G3, has lots of scarce country road maps, but most are for other parts of Africa.

France One of the two largest travel bookshops in France is L'Astrolabe (☎ (01) 42-85-54-95), 46 rue de Provence, 75009 Paris (metro: Chaussée d'Antin). It has a huge selection of travel books and maps and lots of notices posted by people buying and selling gear and looking for travel partners. The other biggie is Ulysse (☎ (01) 43-29-52-10), 35 rue St-Louis en Ile, 75004 Paris (metro: Pont Marie), the oldest travel bookshop in Paris. It's open Tuesday to Sunday from 10 am to 8 pm. The selection of books is vast, particularly the section on the Sahara.

Gilbert Joseph (☎ (01) 43-25-57-16), 26

blvd St Michel, 75006 Paris (metro: St Michel) also has an excellent selection of maps and travel guides. Hachette Évasion (☎ (01) 46-34-89-52), 77 blvd St-Germain, 65006 Paris, has some books not found at Gilbert Joseph. For a late-night travel bookshop, try Librairie du Voyageur (☎ (01) 46-33-38-73) at 3 rue Blainville, 75005 Paris. It's open daily from 11 am to 11 pm.

If you can't find the maps you want at any of these stores, try the Institut Géographique National. It has an excellent retail shop at 107 rue la Boétie, 75008 Paris, and stocks recent maps of many former French colonies.

For African bookshops, try Présence Africaine (☎ (01) 43-54-15-88) several blocks from Gilbert Joseph at 25 rue des Écoles, 75005 Paris. It specialises in serious literature and other books on Africa, many by African authors, but has no travel guides. At 16 rue des Écoles you'll find L'Harmattan (☎ (01) 43-26-04-52), which, with Présence Africaine, are the two best bookshops in Paris focusing primarily on Africa.

Elsewhere in Europe In Holland, your best bet may be Geografische Boekhandel (☎ (020) 121-901), Overtoom 136, 1054 HN Amsterdam. In Germany, try Daerr Expeditionservice GmbH (☎ (089) 903-1519), Theresienstrasse 65, D-8011 Kirchheim/Munich, Ortsteil Heimstetten.

In Belgium, head for Peuples et Continents (☎ 511-2775) at 11 rue Ravenstein, 1000 Brussels. It's the oldest travel bookshop in Belgium and still the best. In Switzerland, there are excellent travel bookshops in the three largest cities: La Librairie du Voyageur (☎ 21-4544) at 8 rue de Rive, zone 1204 in Geneva; Travel Bookshop (☎ 34-3883) at 11 Seitergraben, zone 8801 in Zürich; and Atlas Librairie de Voyage (☎ 22-9044) at 31 Schauplatzgasse, zone 3011 in Berne. They all carry English-language travel books.

Australia In Melbourne, the International Bookshop (☎ (03) 9614-2859), 2nd floor, 17 Elizabeth St, probably has the largest selection of books on Africa. In Sydney try Gleebooks (☎ (02) 660-2333), 191 Glebe Point Rd, Glebe.

MAPS

For regional maps, Michelin (No 953 covers West Africa) is definitely the best.

FILM & PHOTOGRAPHY
Permits & Limitations

There are a few peculiarities about photography in Africa. One is photo permits. Virtually every West African country has dropped the requirement; the only hold-out may be Liberia. In years past, expatriates in countries with photo permits usually preferred to use discretion rather than going through the hassle of getting one. In Liberia, however, don't take a chance. If you take a photo in Monrovia city centre without a permit, the cops will pounce on you almost instantly, then haul you off to police headquarters if you don't bribe them well.

As for video cameras, most countries treat them like regular cameras but in some countries, such as Burkina Faso, a permit is required and the fee can be fairly high. The governments' concern is that you may be a commercial film maker and if that is the case, special permission is required virtually everywhere. If you wear a Hawaiian shirt and look like a tourist, you may be more convincing that you're an amateur. Alternatively, contact the country's embassy and ask them to cable for clearance but don't expect the embassies to know the rules.

In Liberia, even if you have a permit, what you can photograph will be greatly restricted – no dilapidated houses, for instance. Other countries prohibit photographing local religious services. The rules change from country to country. In Dakar, you can even take pictures of the presidential palace. In Togo, if you did the same, at a minimum your camera would almost certainly be confiscated and you would be put under intense interrogation for a day or two. At worse, you would be severely beaten by police as has happened to some travellers in Togo.

Freedom of Press
The press is much freer in the former British colonies of West Africa than in the former French colonies. None of the region's French-speaking countries, for example, have a free press, and until recently, only very limited criticism of the government was allowed. Democracy, however, is spreading. In Mali, private publications are now often quite critical of the government, although their circulations are small.

Senegal has only one daily national newspaper (government controlled). The six or so weeklies and other periodicals often criticise the government (to a certain degree).

Of the English-speaking countries, Nigeria (which has by far the greatest number of newspapers – some 30 national daily and weekly publications, and several dozen weekly news magazines) has the freest press. But even there, the government has frequently closed newspapers, particularly during 1994.

The Gambia, which has about eight newspapers, Ghana, which has seven dailies and weeklies and numerous periodicals, and Sierra Leone, which has even more, have considerable liberties of expression. However, Cape Verde has the freest press of all. It has about six weekly or monthly newspapers, several of which are opposition newspapers. ∎

Photographing People

Every respect must be shown for others' customs and beliefs. In some places the camera's lens may be seen as taking away something personal. As for objects, some are sacred and should be treated as such. The golden rule is to ask permission first – and take 'no' for an answer. In some instances, dress may be important. Wearing long pants and removing your shoes in mosques, for instance, may make it more likely that your guests won't object.

While many Africans are very sensitive to having their pictures taken, there are also many who enjoy being the subject of photos, especially if you are friendly. There are very few things more valuable to Africans than photographs of their family, relatives and friends. Your promise to send them one will be taken seriously; moreover, it is one of the most appreciated, and yet inexpensive, ways to express your friendship. The great pity is that maybe only one in 10 travellers actually send that promised photo. Reserve this, however, for true friends that you make along the way, otherwise you may simply be encouraging Africans to beg the same of future travellers.

Paying for pictures is highly controversial. Travellers need to be aware of the potential cultural ramifications of their decision on the locals and on future travellers. By paying for pictures you may be helping to create a situation where the locals come to expect – and beg for – a gift.

Special Concerns

Film in West Africa is expensive – US$6 to US$14 a roll – and only the most widely used film is sold. Also, even if the expiration date has not yet arrived, the film may have been damaged by the intense African heat. Light conditions vary widely, so bring all the film you'll need and a variety of ASA (ISO) films (100, 200, 400). In West Africa, you'll find lots of 100 ASA film and some 200 ASA, but rarely 400 ASA. That's because the sunlight in West Africa is frequently very intense. In the rainy season, you'll want more 200 ASA, even 400 ASA in the wetter coastal areas.

As for equipment, bring everything with you, especially extra batteries and cleaning equipment. Dust and dirt can get into your equipment, making it filthy in no time. A filter is also a good idea.

For two or three months starting in December, the harmattan winds cover the sky with fine dust particles from the desert. Visibility even along the coast can be reduced to a km or two; in the Sahel it's even worse. If photography is a primary reason for your visit, pick a time other than between December and mid-February.

All too often, pictures of Africans come out

Photographing Military Installations
In no country in this book may you photograph militarily sensitive installations. Depending on the country, this may include most or all government buildings (even post offices!), airports, harbours, the presidential palace, the ministry of defence buildings, dams, radio and TV stations, bridges, train stations and factories. In short, any photos that might aid a potential coup d'état – and more. Photographing police or military personnel is a major blunder. The problem for tourists is that prohibited areas are rarely put in writing or stated in specific terms. When in doubt, ask first. ■

with the faces too dark, with little or no detail. To avoid this, use a light meter. The general rule is to open up one or 1½ stops from what the metre reads. Alternatively, use a flash.

Finally, some airports have fairly old model x-ray machines for checking baggage which may not be safe for film. Although most airports now have the newer film-safe models, because of the uncertainty some travellers bring protective lead bags – they're fairly inexpensive. Those with high-speed film (1000 ASA and higher) may also want to bring protective bags because even the film-safe models are safe only for slow-speed film. Most importantly, since damage to film by x-rays is cumulative, even with newer machines you can damage film after repeated airport arrivals and departures. However, I wouldn't worry because I've yet to meet a custom official in Africa who wouldn't allow me to carry the film separately, thus avoiding the x-ray.

HEALTH

Travel health depends on your predeparture preparations, your day-to-day health care while travelling and how you handle any medical problem or emergency that does develop. While the list of potential dangers can seem quite frightening, with a little luck, some basic precautions and adequate information, few travellers to West Africa experience more than upset stomachs.

Travel Health Guides

Staying Healthy in Asia, Africa & Latin America, Dirk Schroeder, Moon Publications, 1994. Probably the best all-round guide to carry as it's compact but very detailed and well organised.

Travellers' Health, Dr Richard Dawood, Oxford University Press, 1992. Comprehensive, easy to read, authoritative and also highly recommended, although it's rather large to lug around.

Where There is No Doctor, David Werner, Macmillan, 1994. A very detailed guide intended for someone (eg, a Peace Corps worker) going to work in an undeveloped country, rather than for the average traveller.

Travel with Children, Maureen Wheeler, Lonely Planet Publications, 1995. Basic advice on travel health for younger children.

Predeparture Planning

Health Insurance A travel insurance policy to cover theft, loss and medical problems is a wise idea. There are a wide variety of policies and your travel agent will have recommendations. The international student travel policies handled by STA Travel or other student travel organisations are usually good value. Some policies offer lower and higher medical-expense options but the higher one is chiefly for countries like the USA which have extremely high medical costs. Check the small print:

- Some policies specifically exclude 'dangerous activities' which can include scuba diving, motorcycling, even trekking. If these activities are on your agenda you don't want that sort of policy.
- You may prefer a policy which pays doctors or hospitals directly rather than you having to pay now and claim later. If you have to claim later make sure you keep all documentation. Some policies ask you to call back (reverse charges) to a centre in your home country where an immediate assessment of your problem is made.
- Check if the policy covers ambulances or an emergency evacuation flight home. If you have to stretch out you will need two seats and somebody has to pay for it!

Medical Kit A small, straightforward medical kit is a wise thing to carry; it should include:

- Aspirin or panadol – for pain or fever
- Antihistamine (eg Benadryl) – useful as a decongestant for colds, allergies, to ease the itch from insect bites or stings or to help prevent motion sickness
- Antibiotics – useful if you're travelling well off the beaten track but it must be prescribed and you should carry the prescription with you
- Kaolin preparation (Pepto-Bismol), Imodium or Lomotil – for stomach upsets
- Rehydration mixture – for treatment of severe diarrhoea; particularly important if travelling with children, but is recommended for everyone.
- Antiseptic such as Betadine, which comes as impregnated swabs or ointment, and an antibiotic powder or similar 'dry' spray – for cuts and grazes
- Calamine lotion – to ease irritation from bites or stings
- Bandages and Band-Aids – for minor injuries
- Scissors, tweezers and a thermometer – mercury thermometers are prohibited by airlines
- Insect repellent, sun block, suntan lotion, Chap Stick (lip gel), water purification tablets and, if you'll be travelling in the Sahel, salt tablets and petroleum jelly
- A couple of syringes, in case you need injections in a country with medical hygiene problems. Ask your doctor for a note explaining why they have been prescribed.

Ideally, antibiotics should be administered only under medical supervision and should never be taken indiscriminately. Over-use of antibiotics can weaken your body's ability to deal with infections naturally and can reduce the drug's efficacy on a future occasion. Take only the recommended dose at the prescribed intervals and continue using the antibiotic for the prescribed period, even if the illness seems to be cured earlier. Antibiotics are quite specific to the infections they can treat, stop immediately if there are any serious reactions and don't use it at all if you are unsure if you have the correct one.

If you must buy drugs during your trip, buy them from a pharmacy that appears in good condition (many are listed in the country chapters) because the storage conditions in some are not the best. Also be sure to check the expiration date on any drugs you purchase. It's possible that drugs which are no longer recommended or have been banned in the West are still being dispensed in many Third World countries.

Health Preparations Make sure you're healthy before you start travelling. If you are embarking on a long trip, check your teeth are OK because in some areas of West Africa a visit to the dentist would be the last thing you'd want.

If you wear glasses bring a spare pair and your prescription. Losing glasses can be a real problem, although in many major cities you can get new spectacles made up quickly, cheaply and competently.

If you require a particular medication take an adequate supply as it may not be available locally or under a brand name no one recognises. Take the prescription, with the generic rather than the brand name, as it will make getting replacements easier. It's a wise idea to have the prescription with you to show you legally use the medication – some pharmacies may require it to sell certain drugs.

Immunisations Vaccinations provide protection against diseases you might meet along the way. With few exceptions, virtually all countries in West Africa require that you bring an International Health Certificate with a record of your vaccinations; it's available from your physician or health department.

Plan ahead for getting your vaccinations since some of them require an initial shot followed by a booster while some vaccinations should not be given together. Most travellers from Western countries will have been immunised against various diseases during childhood but your doctor may still recommend booster shots against measles or polio – diseases still prevalent in many developing countries. The period of protection offered by vaccinations differs widely and some are contraindicated in pregnancy.

In the USA, the Center for Disease Control (CDC) has established a special number (☎ (404) 332-4559) for international travellers information, giving details on its recommendations for all sorts of vaccinations, by region. It is easier and cheaper

Vaccinations

Yellow Fever Every country in West Africa requires you to have had a yellow fever vaccination, but about half of them waive the requirement if you're arriving directly from North America or Europe. Airport health officials, however, are sometimes unaware of this exemption, so get one anyway. In some countries you have to go to a special yellow fever vaccination centre. You will need to start the injections about three weeks prior to departure; protection lasts 10 years. Vaccination is contraindicated in pregnancy but if you must travel to a high-risk area it is probably advisable.

Cholera The list of countries requiring a cholera vaccination is constantly in flux as the list tends to expand whenever there's a cholera outbreak in the region. In some countries you must have one if you're coming from an infected area (ie the rest of Africa). The vaccination is not very effective, only lasts six months and is contraindicated for pregnancy.

Tetanus & Diptheria Boosters are necessary every 10 years and protection is highly recommended.

Typhoid Protection lasts for three years and is useful if you are travelling for long periods in rural, tropical areas.

Infectious Hepatitis (Hep A) Gamma globulin is not a vaccination but a ready-made antibody which has proven to be very successful in reducing both the chances of hepatitis infection and its severity, should you get it. Because it may interfere with the development of immunity, it should not be given until at least 10 days after administration of the last vaccine needed and as close as possible to departure because its effectiveness decreases rapidly. Even after three months it has lost over 50% of its effectiveness and by six months it's totally worthless. For this reason, getting a shot every four months is better than waiting for six months. ■

to reach this 24-hour number at a low-toll time, including weekends. In London, travellers can get all required vaccinations except, possibly, rabies at the Hospital for Tropical Diseases at 4 St Pancras Way NW1 OPE (easy bookings and friendly staff) as well as at Trailfinders Immunisation Centre (☎ (0171) 938-3999) at 194 Kensington High St. It also sells first-aid kits (UK£13).

Only two vaccinations are sometimes required to enter West African countries – yellow fever and, to a lesser extent, cholera. The average traveller will also need to take hepatitis and typhoid shots, and anti-malarial tablets. In addition, vaccinations for tuberculosis, tetanus, meningitis and polio are recommended for those planning to live in Africa for awhile and for those travelling on the cheap who may encounter fairly unsanitary conditions.

Basic Rules

Care in what you eat and drink is the most important health rule; stomach upsets are the most likely travel health problem but the majority of these upsets will be relatively minor. Don't become paranoid; trying the local food is part of the experience of travel.

Water The number one rule is *don't drink the water* and that includes ice. If you don't know for certain that water is safe always assume the worst and either boil or purify it. The latter is easier as water is sold on the streets everywhere in convenient, see-through plastic bags, which you can purify in a water bottle. An alternative is to buy mineral water, available in every capital city in West Africa and in many smaller cities and towns. The typical supermarket price is about US$0.80 per litre; hotels will sell it for up to three times that amount.

Take care with fruit juice, particularly if water may have been added to it. Milk should be treated with suspicion as it is often unpasteurised. Boiled milk is fine if it is kept hygienically, and yoghurt is always good. Tea or coffee should also be OK since the water should have been be boiled.

Water Purification The simplest way of purifying water is to thoroughly boil it.

Recent information and studies from CDC in the USA indicate that three minutes of vigorous boiling at sea level is all that is needed to kill all major waterborn bacterial diseases and viruses in water in the developing world (one minute for water in the USA) – not 10 minutes as previously recommended. Simple filtering will not remove all dangerous organisms so if you cannot boil water it should be treated chemically. Chlorine tablets (halazone, puritabs, steritabs or other brands) will kill many but not all pathogens (in particular, giardia and amoebic cysts).

Iodine is much more effective in purifying water and is available in tablet form (such as Potable Aqua) but follow the directions carefully and remember that too much iodine can be harmful. You can also use tincture of iodine (2%) or iodine crystals. Two drops of tincture of iodine per litre (quart) of clear water is the recommended dosage which should then be left to stand for 30 minutes.

Iodine loses its effectiveness if exposed to air or damp, so keep it in a tightly sealed container. Flavoured powder will disguise the taste of treated water and is a good idea if you are travelling with children. Iodine is contraindicated for pregnancy.

If for some reason you may have to drink untreated water, there are two things to remember. First, most water in African cities and towns comes from potable sources. Second, the risk is less in the dry season. The problem is that the water can become contaminated in the pipes. African water systems operate under low pressure so that seepage of sewerage and the like into the pipes is quite possible. This is a much bigger problem during the rainy season.

Food Salads and fruit should be washed with purified water or peeled where possible. It's an extremely rare restaurant that soaks its vegetables in an iodine solution. Hotels like the Meridien simply import their vegetables from Europe, but this doesn't avoid potential contamination through handling. Taking vitamin tablets helps resist the temptation to eat raw vegetables.

Ice cream is usually OK if it is a reputable brand, but beware of street vendors and of ice cream that has melted and been refrozen. Thoroughly cooked food is safest but not if it has been left to cool or if it has been reheated. Take great care with shellfish or fish and avoid undercooked meat. If a place looks clean and well-run and the vendor also looks clean and healthy then the food is probably safe. In general, places that are packed with travellers or locals will be fine, empty restaurants are questionable.

In some respects, eating at restaurants may be more risky than eating on the street with your hands. (The opposite is true when street food is eaten with plates and utensils.) Street food is usually safe because the ingredients are purchased daily.

Nutrition If you don't like African food, if you're travelling hard and fast and therefore missing meals, or if you simply lose your appetite, you can soon start to lose weight and place your health at risk.

Make sure your diet is well balanced. If you eat African food, you don't have to worry because it's very well balanced nutritionally, particularly if you supplement your meals, as the Africans do, with fruit. In addition, peanuts and boiled eggs are sold on the street and are a safe way to get protein. Fruit you can peel (bananas, oranges or mangoes for example) are always safe and a good source of vitamins. Try to eat plenty of grains (rice) and bread. If you're not eating enough, take vitamin and mineral supplements.

In the Sahel make sure you drink enough, don't rely on feeling thirsty to indicate when you should drink. Not needing to urinate or very dark yellow urine is a danger sign. Always carry a water bottle with you on long trips. There are people everywhere selling water in plastic bags; put this in your bottle and add the purification tablets. Excessive sweating can lead to loss of salt and therefore muscle cramping. Salt tablets can help but they're not a preventative. Adding salt to your food can help and it's fairly available virtually everywhere in West Africa.

General Health
A normal body temperature is 37°C, more than 2°C higher is a 'high' fever. A normal adult pulse rate is 60 to 80 beats per minute (children 80 to 100, babies 100 to 140). You should know how to take a temperature and a pulse rate. As a general rule the pulse increases about 20 beats per minute for each 1°C rise in fever.

Respiration rate (breathing) is also an indicator of illness. Count the number of breaths per minute, between 12 and 20 is normal for adults and older children (up to 30 for younger children, 40 for babies). People with a high fever or serious respiratory illness (like pneumonia) breathe more quickly than normal. More than 40 shallow breaths a minute usually means pneumonia.

Climatic & Geographical Considerations
Sunburn You can get sunburnt even through cloud. Use a sunscreen and take extra care to cover areas which don't normally see sun – your feet for example. A hat provides added protection, and use zinc cream or some other barrier cream for your nose and lips. Calamine lotion is good for mild sunburn.

Heat Exhaustion Dehydration or salt deficiency can cause heat exhaustion. Take time to acclimatise to the hotter temperatures and make sure you drink sufficient liquids. Salt deficiency is characterised by fatigue, lethargy, headaches, giddiness and muscle cramps and in this case salt tablets may help. Vomiting or diarrhoea can deplete your liquid and salt levels.

Heat Stroke This serious, sometimes fatal, condition can occur if the body's heat regulating mechanism breaks down and the body temperature rises to dangerous levels. Long, continuous periods of exposure to high temperatures can leave you vulnerable to heat stroke. Avoid excessive alcohol or strenuous activity when you first arrive in a hot climate.

Feeling unwell, not sweating very much or at all, and a high body temperature (39 to 41°C) are symptoms. Where sweating has ceased, the skin becomes flushed and red.

Severe, throbbing headaches and lack of co-ordination will also occur and the sufferer may become confused or aggressive. Eventually the victim will become delirious or convulse. Hospitalisation is essential but meanwhile get the victim out of the sun, remove their clothing and cover them with a wet sheet or towel and then fan continually.

Fungal Infections Fungal infections are more of a problem along the coast of West Africa than in the Sahel and even there only during the rainy season. They are most likely to occur on the scalp, between the toes or fingers (athlete's foot), in the groin (jock itch or crotch rot) and on the body (ringworm). You get ringworm (which is a fungus infection, not a worm) from infected animals or from damp areas, like shower floors.

To prevent fungal infections, wear loose clothes, avoid synthetic fibres, wash frequently and dry carefully. If you do get an infection, wash the infected area daily with a disinfectant or medicated soap and water and rinse and dry well. Apply an anti-fungal powder like the widely available Tinaderm. Try to expose the infected area to air or sunlight as much as possible and wash all towels and underwear in hot water and change them often.

Foot Problems If you'll be travelling in the desert and you wear sandals, the soles of your feet may get very dry and hard and, as a result, begin cracking. The French call this *le croco*. You'll need to change to shoes and socks or use petroleum jelly. If you wait until the cracks go very deep, they can be amazingly painful and become infected. Fortunately petroleum jelly is sold seemingly everywhere in Africa.

Infectious Diseases
Diarrhoea A change of water, food or climate can all cause 'the runs' but more serious is diarrhoea due to contaminated food or water. You may think that diarrhoea is inevitable, but there are in fact many short-term visitors to West Africa who never get it. It's water – not meat, noodles, rice, African

dishes such as *foutou* and the like – that has the greatest likelihood by far of giving you diarrhoea. But it's not just drinking water – your soft drink and fries may be safe but not the glass or utensils they are served with.

Despite all your precautions you may still have a bout of mild travellers' diarrhoea but a few rushed toilet trips with no other symptoms is not indicative of a serious problem. Moderate diarrhoea, involving half a dozen loose movements in a day, is more of a nuisance. Dehydration is the main danger with any diarrhoea, particularly for children, so fluid replenishment is the number one treatment. You'll also need to replace lost minerals in the body, particularly potassium.

Drink large quantities of unsweetened liquids such as tea, bouillon soup and bottled water. A good preparation is: the juice of one orange and a quarter of a teaspoon of salt together with 250 ml of water. The flow of fluids will also help relieve pains from muscle cramps as well as help to wash out whatever is down there. With severe diarrhoea a rehydrating solution is necessary to replace minerals and salts. Stick to a bland diet as you recover.

For normal cases of bacterial diarrhoea, drugs are not recommended except, perhaps, for Pepto-Bismol. It's also effective as a diarrhoea preventative. Four tablets a day will reduce your chance of illness significantly. However, it shouldn't be taken for more than three weeks. Lomotil or Imodium can be used in more severe cases; they bring relief from the symptoms although they do not actually cure the condition. Only use these drugs if absolutely necessary (eg, if you *must* travel). For children, Imodium is preferable but do not use these drugs if you have a high fever or are severely dehydrated. Antibiotics can be very useful in treating severe diarrhoea especially if it is accompanied by nausea, vomiting, stomach cramps or mild fever. In the USA, an excellent, wide-spectrum antibiotic is Ciprofloxin, or 'Cipro'.

Giardia This intestinal parasite is present in contaminated water and the symptoms are stomach cramps, nausea, bloated stomach, watery, foul-smelling diarrhoea and frequent gas. Giardia can appear several weeks after you have been exposed to the parasite, the symptoms may disappear for a few days and then return; this can go on for several weeks. Metronidazole (known as Flagyl) is the recommended drug but it should only be taken under medical supervision; the recommended dosage is three pills a day for a week. Nausea is a common side effect, and it often causes a rather severe reaction when alcohol is consumed during treatment.

Dysentery This serious illness is caused by contaminated food or water and is characterised by severe diarrhoea, often with blood or mucus in the stool. There are two kinds of dysentery. Bacillary dysentery is characterised by a high fever and rapid development; headache, vomiting and stomach pains are also symptoms. It generally does not last longer than a week, but it is highly contagious.

Amoebic dysentery develops more gradually. You won't experience fever or vomiting but it is a more serious illness. Although not a self-limiting disease, it will persist until treated and can recur and cause long-term damage. As with giardia, the prescribed treatment is Flagyl but in larger dosages (three pills three times daily for 10 days) or a new medicine Fasigyn (four pills per day over three days) followed by another medicine, like Diodoquin (for 20 days) or Humatin (for seven days) to prevent recurrence.

A stool test is necessary to determine which type of dysentery you have. If you don't know which kind you've got or whether you've even got dysentery, you'll do better with a wide-spectrum antibiotic. A good one is sulfamethoxazole (brand names Bactrin and Septra in the USA). In French West Africa, a very effective French drug available locally that some people swear by is Ercefuryl. If that's not available, try Centercine. Beware of needle-happy doctors. Africans tend to have an overly high regard for medicines taken by needles, and most doctors comply. Medicine taken through pills is usually just as effective.

Cholera The cholera vaccine is largely ineffective which is why the US State Department, for example, no longer gives the shot to any of its overseas employees – even where there's a cholera epidemic! Take it anyway (or at least get your vaccination certificate stamped) because you don't want to take the risk of being jabbed with a dirty needle at the airport or border station. It's a disease that is largely avoided by boiling water, so even in areas where there have been severe outbreaks several years ago (such as Peru and Ecuador), the number of foreigners getting the disease has been minuscule.

The disease is characterised by a sudden onset of acute diarrhoea with 'rice water' stools, vomiting, muscular cramps, and extreme weakness. It's possible to lose as much as 10% of your body weight within a day through diarrhoea and vomiting. You'll need medical help, but the initial treatment is always the same: dehydration salts. If there is an appreciable delay in getting to hospital then begin taking tetracycline. This drug should not be given to young children or pregnant women.

Viral Gastroenteritis This is not caused by bacteria but, as the name suggests, a virus, and is characterised by stomach cramps, diarrhoea, sometimes vomiting, and sometimes a slight fever. All you can do is rest and drink lots of fluids.

Hepatitis Hepatitis is a general term for inflammation of the liver. There are many causes of this condition: drugs, alcohol and infections are but a few.

The discovery of new strains has led to a virtual alphabet soup, with hepatitis A, B, C, D, E and a rumoured G. These letters identify specific agents that cause viral hepatitis. Viral hepatitis is an infection of the liver, which can lead to jaundice (yellow skin), fever, lethargy and digestive problems. It can have no symptoms at all, with the infected person not knowing that they have the disease. Travellers shouldn't be too paranoid about this apparent proliferation of hepatitis strains; hep C, D, E and G are fairly rare (so far) and following the same precautions as for A and B should be all that's necessary to avoid them.

Viral hepatitis can be divided on the basis of how it is spread. The strains spread by contaminated food and water are:

Hepatitis A This is a very common disease in most countries, especially those with poor standards of sanitation. Most people in developing countries are infected as children; they often don't develop symptoms, but do develop life-long immunity. The disease poses a real threat to the traveller, as people are unlikely to have been exposed to hepatitis A in developed countries.

The symptoms are fever, chills, headache, fatigue, feelings of weakness and aches and pains, followed by loss of appetite, nausea, vomiting, abdominal pain, dark urine, light coloured faeces, jaundiced skin and the whites of the eyes may turn yellow. In some cases you may feel unwell, tired, have no appetite, experience aches and pains and be jaundiced. You should seek medical advice, but in general there is not much you can do apart from resting, drinking lots of fluids, eating lightly and avoiding fatty foods. People who have had hepatitis must forego alcohol for six months after the illness, as hepatitis attacks the liver and it needs that amount of time to recover.

The routes of transmission are via contaminated water, shellfish contaminated by sewerage, or foodstuffs sold by food handlers with poor standards of hygiene.

Taking care with what you eat and drink can go a long way towards preventing this disease. But this is a very infectious virus, so if there is any risk of exposure, additional cover is highly recommended. This cover comes in two forms: Gammaglobulin and Havrix. Gammaglobulin is an injection where you are given the antibodies for hepatitis A, which provide immunity for a limited time. Havrix is a vaccine, where you develop your own antibodies, which gives lasting immunity.

Hepatitis E This is a very recently discovered

virus, of which little is yet known. It appears to be common in developing countries, generally causing mild hepatitis, although it can be very serious in pregnant women.

Care with water supplies is the only current prevention, as there are no specific vaccines. At present it doesn't appear to be too great a risk for travellers.

Strains spread by blood and bodily fluids:

Hepatitis B This is also a very common disease, with almost 300 million chronic carriers in the world. Hepatitis B, which used to be called serum hepatitis, is spread through contact with infected blood, blood products or bodily fluids, for example through sexual contact, unsterilised needles and blood transfusions. Other risk situations include having a shave or tattoo in a local shop, or having your ears pierced. The symptoms of type B are much the same as type A except that they are more severe and may lead to irreparable liver damage or even liver cancer. Although there is no treatment for hepatitis B, a cheap and effective vaccine is available; the only problem is that for long-lasting cover you need a six-month course. The immunisation schedule requires two injections at least a month apart followed by a third dose five months after the second. Persons who should receive a hepatitis B vaccination include anyone who anticipates contact with blood or other bodily secretions, either as a health-care worker or through sexual contact with the local population, particularly those who intend to stay in the country for a long period of time.

Hepatitis C This is another recently defined virus. It is a concern because it seems to lead to liver disease more rapidly than hep B.

The virus is spread by contact with blood – usually via contaminated transfusions or shared needles. Avoiding these is the only means of prevention, as there is no available vaccine.

Hepatitis D Often referred to as the 'Delta' virus, this infection only occurs in chronic carriers of hepatitis B. It is transmitted by blood and bodily fluids. Again there is no vaccine for

this virus, so avoidance is the best prevention. The risk to travellers is certainly limited.

Typhoid Typhoid fever is another gut infection that travels the faecal-oral route, ie contaminated water and food are responsible. Vaccination against typhoid is not totally effective and it is one of the most dangerous infections – medical help must be sought.

The early symptoms are like so many others: you may feel like you have a bad cold or flu on the way, headache, sore throat, a fever which rises a little each day until it is around 40°C or more. Pulse is often slow for the amount of fever present and gets slower as the fever rises, unlike a normal fever where the pulse increases. There may also be vomiting, diarrhoea or constipation.

In the second week the high fever and slow pulse continue and a few pink spots may appear on the body along with trembling, delirium, weakness, weight loss and dehydration. If there are no further complications, the fever and symptoms will slowly go during the third week. However, you must get medical help before this because common complications are pneumonia (acute infection of the lungs) or peritonitis (burst appendix), and typhoid is very infectious.

The fever should be treated by keeping the victim cool. Watch for signs of dehydration. Chloramphenicol is the recommended antibiotic but there are fewer side effects with ampicillin.

Worms These parasites are most common in rural, tropical areas and a stool test when you return home is not a bad idea. They can be present on unwashed vegetables or in undercooked meat and you can pick them up through your skin by walking in bare feet. Infestations may not show up for some time, and although they are generally not serious, if left untreated they can cause severe health problems. A stool test is necessary to pinpoint the problem and medication is often available over the counter.

Tetanus This potentially fatal disease is found in undeveloped tropical areas and is difficult to treat but is preventable with immunisation. Tetanus occurs when a wound becomes infected by a germ which lives in the faeces of animals or people, so clean all cuts, punctures or animal bites. Tetanus is known as lockjaw and the first symptom may be discomfort in swallowing, stiffening of the jaw and neck, then painful convulsions of the jaw and whole body.

Rabies Rabies is found in many countries and is caused by a bite or scratch by an infected animal. Dogs are a noted carrier. Any bite, scratch or even lick from a mammal should be cleaned immediately and thoroughly. Scrub with soap and running water then clean with an alcohol solution. If there is any possibility that the animal is infected, medical help should be sought immediately. Even if the animal is not rabid, all bites should be treated seriously as they can become infected or can result in tetanus. A rabies vaccination is now available and should be considered if you are in a high-risk category, eg if you work with animals.

Meningococcal Meningitis Sub-Saharan Africa is considered the 'meningitis belt' and the meningitis season falls at the time most people would be attempting the overland trip across the Sahara – the northern winter before the rains come. This very serious disease attacks the brain and can be fatal. A scattered blotchy rash, fever, severe headache, sensitivity to light, and neck stiffness which prevents forward bending of the head are the first symptoms. Death can occur within a few hours so immediate treatment is important.

Treatment is large doses of penicillin given intravenously, or, if that is not possible, intramuscularly, ie in the buttocks. Vaccination offers good protection for over one year but you should also check for reports of current epidemics.

Tuberculosis Although this disease is widespread in West Africa it is not a serious risk to travellers. Young children are more susceptible than adults and vaccination is a sensible precaution for children under 12 travelling in endemic areas. TB is commonly spread by coughing or by unpasteurised dairy products from infected cows. Milk that has been boiled is safe and the souring of milk to make *lait caillé* (soured milk available in the Sahel) or yoghurt kills the bacilli.

Diptheria Diptheria can be a skin infection or a more dangerous throat infection. It is spread by contaminated dust contacting the skin or by the inhalation of infected cough or sneeze droplets. Frequent washing and keeping the skin dry will help prevent skin infection. A vaccination is available to prevent the throat infection.

Sexually Transmitted Diseases Sexually transmitted diseases (STDs) are rampant in Africa, even in the lowly populated Sahel. Health officials estimate that 25% of the people in that region have venereal disease. Among prostitutes it can reach as high as 100% in some areas. Numerous studies confirm that in Africa it is men seeking commercial sex who carry infection from one prostitute to another and eventually to the real victims – their wives and girlfriends. The problem is so serious in Africa that STDs cause far more deaths in women than does AIDS (another STD) in men, women and children combined.

Sexual contact with an infected sexual partner spreads these diseases and while abstinence is the only 100% preventative, use of a condom is also effective. Gonorrhoea and syphilis are the most common of these diseases, and sores, blisters or rashes around the genitals, and discharges or pain when urinating are common symptoms. Symptoms may be less marked or not observed at all in women. The symptoms of syphilis eventually disappear completely but the disease continues and can cause severe problems in later years. Treatment of gonorrhoea and syphilis is by antibiotics.

HIV/AIDS HIV, which is the Human Immunodeficiency Virus, may develop into AIDS,

Acquired Immune Deficiency Syndrome. HIV is a major problem in many countries. Any exposure to blood, blood products or bodily fluids may put the individual at risk. In many developing countries transmission is predominantly through heterosexual sexual activity. This is quite different from industrialised countries where transmission is mostly through contact between homosexual or bisexual males, or via contaminated needles shared by IV drug users.

AIDS *(Sida* in French and Spanish) is devastating the working population of Black Africa. In 1994, the World Health Organisation (WHO) estimated that of the 15 million people worldwide infected with the disease, almost 10 million were Africans, with about 1.5 million new infections annually in Africa and about 500,000 new cases of the fully developed disease. It is already one of the leading causes of death in many areas of the continent. Over nine million African children will have been orphaned during the 1990s alone. A principal reason that AIDS is

so deadly in Africa is that STDs, which are rampant in Africa, greatly facilitate transmission of the AIDS virus. One recent study shows that if one partner has AIDS and either partner has a lesion caused by a STD, the chances of getting the virus in a single sexual act are about 40% if a condom isn't used!

As of early 1995, the following 12 countries in Africa were the worst hit: Uganda, Tanzania, Kenya, Zambia, Rwanda, Burundi, Angola, Zimbabwe, Malawi, Central African Republic, Zaïre and the Congo. While none of these countries are covered in this book, the disease has spread all over West Africa, the risk being greater in cities than in rural areas, although the difference is diminishing. In Nigeria, for example, prevalence rates have reached as high as 22% amongst men attending STD clinics.

In Africa, AIDS is transmitted primarily by heterosexual contact. Many prostitutes in the largest West African cities, such as Abidjan and Dakar, carry the virus. Avoiding sex with prostitutes is not enough, however,

Bilharzia (Schistosomiasis)

Bilharzia, or 'schisto', is a disease caused by tiny blood flukes. The worms live in snails found on the edge of lakes or slow moving rivers (there are few fast-flowing rivers in West Africa). Inside the snail, they multiply and emerge as free-swimming creatures and, like heat-seeking missiles, they hone in on humans and other mammals in the water. In as little as five minutes, they can bore painlessly through the skin. Once inside you, most of the blood flukes take up residence in the intestines, where they produce eggs for seven to 30 years. Because most eggs are eliminated (and start the cycle over again), the disease frequently doesn't cause problems other than malnourishment. However, if the eggs end up in the liver or spleen, they can disrupt blood flow and cause the organs to swell. In that case, the disease will be mildly painful and have a very debilitating effect over the years.

Anyone in the mud or shallow water along the edge of a lake or river is vulnerable, which is why you will hear warnings never to enter any freshwater bodies in Africa except those known to be safe. Even brief contact can lead to infection, so if you fall in accidentally, towel yourself off as quickly and as briskly as possible. However, don't let this scare you from missing out on every opportunity for a cooling dip. Since the disease requires a human host to complete the cycle, rivers in uninhabited areas, such as remote parks, are at low risk.

The first indication you're infected is a tingling and sometimes a light rash around the area where the worm entered. Weeks later, when the worm is busy producing eggs, a high fever may develop. A general feeling of being unwell may be the first indication but once the disease is established, abdominal pain and blood in the urine are other signs. For a mild case there may be no clear signs at all, which is why anyone living overseas for a few years must get checked for schisto upon return. There is no vaccine and until recently, the only cure was a dangerous treatment with strong dosages of arsenic which killed the worms but, hopefully, not you. Now a new drug, praziquantel (brand name Biltracide in the USA), clears it up with a single dose of pills. ■

Top: Mosque, Porto Novo, Benin (AS)
Middle: Market vendors, Cotonou, Benin (AS)
Bottom: Traditional houses, Boukoumbé, Benin (AS)

Top: Making millet beer, Ouahigouya, Burkina Faso (AN)
Bottom: Colonial religious relic, Grand-Bassam, Côte d'Ivoire (AN)

because Africans from all walks of life are known to carry the virus.

Compounding the problem is the presence of a different strain of AIDS virus – HIV-2. Strangely, the highest rates of people testing positive for this virus occur in isolated Guinea-Bissau, but it is spreading elsewhere. Equally perplexing, it has produced far fewer cases of AIDS than HIV-1, possibly because it doesn't usually cause AIDS. Beware, however, some experts speculate that it may just have a longer incubation period.

Other than sex, the major way of contracting AIDS in Africa is through blood transfusions and injections. Finding safe blood is difficult in Africa because most countries don't screen blood for transfusions, and embassies tend to be poor sources of information unless you can get to a medical person. As for injections, avoid them. At a minimum, make sure that a new syringe is used. Buy one from a pharmacy or bring one with you.

There is currently no cure for AIDS. Using condoms and avoiding certain sexual practices such as anal intercourse are the most effective preventatives.

Insect-Borne Diseases

Malaria Malaria, which in recent years has increased in severity throughout Africa, is probably the most serious disease in Africa, yearly affecting about one in five Africans and killing about one million of them. Most Africans can't afford the preventative treatment, which is why a typical African farmer may have malaria 25% of his lifetime.

It is spread by mosquito bites and is usually not fatal. However, without treatment malaria can have more serious, potentially fatal effects. Moreover, there is a rare type of malaria (falciparum) that is fatal and death can occur in a day or two if not treated immediately. It does not produce immediate symptoms, which is why some travellers have died from it after returning to their homes where doctors, unfamiliar with the disease, frequently incorrectly diagnose it as a mean flu.

Diagnosing malaria is not easy because it can mimic the symptoms of other diseases, particularly the flu – high fever, lassitude, headache, pains in the joints, and chills. As a rule, the onset is sudden, with a violent, shaking chill followed by a rapid rise in temperature. Headache is common. After several hours of fever, profuse sweating occurs. Even Peace Corps nurses who have seen it many times have difficulty diagnosing malaria, so you should be a little sceptical if some Joe Doe is 100% certain you've got it. The only sure way to diagnose malaria is by thorough examination of blood smears, and it's not everywhere that this can be done.

Anti-malarial drugs do not actually prevent the disease but suppress its symptoms. Chloroquine (brand name Aralen in the USA and Nivaquine in France and West Africa) is the usual malarial prophylactic and consists of a 500 mg tablet taken once a week for two weeks prior to travel and six weeks after you return. Chloroquine is quite safe for general use, side effects are minimal and it can be taken by pregnant women. It's also effective for treatment but in larger doses. Most travellers take anti-malarial drugs religiously at first but after arriving in Africa become progressively blasé about it; only an estimated 10% follow this régime to its conclusion – a mistake.

Unfortunately there is now a strain of malaria (plasmodium falciparum) which is resistant to chloroquine and within the last few years cases have been reported in virtually every West African country. So cholorquine is no longer completely effective. Fortunately, a relatively new malaria drug, mefloquine (brand name Larium in the USA), which is highly effective against chloroquine-resistant malaria has been approved in most of Europe and, since 1990, in the USA. Its side effects are claimed to be no worse than those of chloroquine but many travellers seem to disagree; they include, occasionally, hallucinations, dizziness, nausea, fainting, premature contractions of the heart, and vertigo. The primary disadvantage is that it cannot be taken by pregnant women, children weighing less than 15 kg, those taking heart/blood medications and those with a history of epilepsy or a significant psychiatric disorder. Mefloquine should be taken once a week. In the USA, physicians who are not able to find a supply can call ☎ (800) 526-6367 for information.

There are three other drugs which are effective to varying degrees against chloroquine-resistant malaria. The best is doxycycline (brand name Vibramycin in the USA), a tetracycline-based drug which must be taken daily. It cannot, however, be taken by pregnant women or children below eight years of age, plus it causes hypersensitivity to sunlight so sunburn must be avoided (use sun block). For those unable to take mefloquine or doxycycline, the recommendation is proguanil (brand name Paludrine in the USA), which is weaker than chloroquine and has almost no known side effects. It should be taken daily (200 mg) along with 500 mg of chloroquine weekly; together, they are about two-thirds as effective as mefloquine. Both of these drugs are considered safe during pregnancy and for small children. A final alternative is Fansidar. Because it has so many negative side effects, it is now recommended only for emergency treatment. Moreover, it cannot be taken by pregnant women or by people sensitive to sulphur.

All of these drugs only suppress malaria – they do not prevent it. The trick to avoiding malaria is to not only avoid mosquitos but make the mosquitos avoid you: don't use fragrances (mosquitos love perfume, aftershave lotion, etc), wear light clothing (they seem drawn to dark colours), cover bare skin and use a good repellent. Some travellers swear that eating garlic also works. Mosquitos don't like the flavour of garlic and if you eat enough daily, your skin will release the odour. The idea is to start eating garlic seven to 10 days before departure and continue such for the duration of your trip. It's worth a try! Fortunately, African mosquitos are active only at night, so they are less of a nuisance than you'd expect. Mosquito nets on beds offer protection, as does burning a mosquito coil. The risk of infection is higher in rural areas and during the wet season.

Sleeping Sickness In parts of tropical Africa tsetse flies can carry trypanosomiasis, or sleeping sickness, which causes physical and mental lethargy. It's caused by the tsetse fly, about twice the size of the common fly. The main problem is that it kills horses and cattle, leaving large areas of West Africa with few or no such animals. Swelling at the site of the bite, five or more days later, is the first sign of infection followed by fever within two to three weeks. Even in areas where tsetse flies are amply present, the risk of infection to short-term visitors is virtually nil, and it is easily treated.

Yellow Fever This disease is endemic in West Africa. The viral disease is transmitted to humans by mosquitos and the initial symptoms are fever, headache, abdominal pain and vomiting. There may appear to be a brief recovery period before it progresses to more severe complications, including liver failure. There is no medical treatment apart from keeping the fever down and avoiding dehydration but yellow fever vaccination gives good protection for 10 years and is an entry requirement to most West African countries.

Typhus Typhus is spread by ticks, mites or lice and begins as a bad cold, followed by a fever, chills, headache, muscle pains and a body rash. There is often a large painful sore at the site of the bite and nearby lymph nodes are swollen and painful. As the name suggests, tick typhus is spread by ticks and trekkers may be at risk from cattle or wild animal ticks. A strong insect repellent can help and serious walkers in tick areas should have their boots and trousers treated.

Bedbugs & Lice
Bedbugs live in various places, particularly dirty mattresses and bedding. Look for spots of blood on bedclothes or on the wall around the bed. Bedbugs leave itchy bites in neat rows. Calamine lotion may help.

Lice cause itching and discomfort and make themselves at home in your hair (head lice), your clothing (body lice) or in your

Other Weird African Maladies

You already know the source of the rumours why you should never go swimming in a lake or a river because you might go blind (from 'oncho', also called 'river blindness' but known more formally as onchocerciasis) or come down with some weird African disease that over a period of time ages you about 20 years (shisto).

But there are other maladies, one of them being the guinea worm. It grows up to a metre long inside the body, then emerges through a skin blister on the leg and is typically extracted by wrapping the worm around a matchstick and carefully pulling it out – over a month's period! Fortunately, foreign travellers are not at risk because it's contracted only from repeated use of very badly contaminated water.

You may have also heard that if your clothes aren't ironed or dried in a clothes drier, you'll get worms. It's true. A wet piece of clothing hanging outside to dry is the tumba fly's favourite place to deposit her eggs. If they are not ironed, the eggs will become larvae and bore into your skin. Often a small white spot can be seen at the site of the lesion. Fortunately, the larva always stays just below the surface of the skin. Even many old African hands don't know how simple the treatment is – put Vaseline over the wound to suffocate the worm. It will come out, although a little push may be necessary. Left untreated, these worms become twice the size of rice from eating your juicy flesh and are quite painful and more difficult to extract. ■

pubic hair (crabs). They get to you by direct contact with infected people or sharing combs, clothing and the like. Powder or shampoo treatment will kill the lice. Infected clothing should be washed in very hot water.

Women's Health

Gynaecological Problems Poor diet, lowered resistance due to the use of antibiotics for stomach upsets and even contraceptive pills can lead to vaginal infections when travelling in hot climates. Keeping the genital area clean, wearing cotton underwear and skirts or loose-fitting trousers will help to prevent infections.

Yeast infections, characterised by a rash, itch and discharge can be treated with a vinegar or even lemon-juice douche or with yoghurt. Nystatin suppositories are the usual medical prescription. Trichomonas is a more serious infection with a discharge and a burning sensation when urinating. Male sexual partners must also be treated and if a vinegar-water douche is not effective, medical attention should be sought. Flagyl is the prescribed drug.

Pregnancy Most miscarriages occur during the first three months of pregnancy, so this is the most risky time to travel as far as your own health is concerned. Miscarriage is not uncommon, and can occasionally lead to severe bleeding. The last three months should be spent within reasonable distance of good medical care. A baby born as early as 24 weeks stands a chance of survival, but only in a good modern hospital. Pregnant women should avoid all unnecessary medication, but vaccinations and malarial prophylactics should still be taken where possible. Additional care should be taken to prevent illness and particular attention should be paid to diet and nutrition. Alcohol and nicotine, for example, should be avoided.

Women travellers often find that their periods become irregular or even cease while they're on the road. Remember that a missed period in these circumstances doesn't necessarily indicate pregnancy. There are health posts or Family Planning clinics in many urban centres in developing countries, where you can seek advice and have a urine test to determine whether or not you are pregnant.

DANGERS & ANNOYANCES
Mugging

From what you may read in the newspapers you are probably prepared to hear that security is a major problem in West Africa, and that roasted tourist in peanut sauce is considered a delicacy. The good news is that the

Sahelian area of West Africa (Burkina Faso, Mali, Senegal, Mauritania, Cape Verde, southern Niger and also Guinea-Bissau) is one of the safer places in the Third World, and certainly safer than most large cities in the USA if not Europe as well. Which is not to say there aren't problems, only that they're less than in most other areas.

The Sahel certainly has thieves but homicides involving foreigners are still extremely rare. In terms of theft and muggings, all the capital cities in the Sahel are among the lowest 20% in the world. Still, travellers, particularly single women, can never let down their guard. In the late '80s an American woman travelling alone in her Land Rover in Burkina Faso was killed by her new Ghanaian boyfriend, apparently for her money.

In major cities along the coast, the picture is not the same. The worst cities by far are Lagos, Abidjan and Monrovia. For years, Lagos has had the reputation for being one of the most dangerous cities in all of Africa. Fortunately, the crime situation has stabilized. Many of the thefts and murders there involve taxi drivers, particularly those at the airport; taking a cab at night is still risky. Most visitors experience no problems, but even so, security is still a worry. In Abidjan, which since the late 1980s has gained a reputation almost as bad as Lagos, the crime rate has improved somewhat in recent years due to stricter law enforcement. Still, some of the thieves carry guns, and have entered restaurants there and robbed the patrons. Expatriates have been killed for their money. As for Monrovia, never one of West Africa's safer cities, five years after the successful 1990 rebellion the situation there and throughout the country is still potentially extremely dangerous for foreigners, as are certain interior regions of Sierra Leone.

As for other coastal cities, such as Accra, Dakar, Lomé, Cotonuou and Banjul, there are lots of petty thieves and many of them carry knives. Fortunately, the worst that usually happens is a loss of money and papers, but the scare can be horrific. In these cities, it's still fairly rare to hear of thieves carrying guns, but when they do, the news spreads like wildfire. Expatriates, it seems, frequently distort the picture.

Theft

By Western standards, theft in the Sahel is fairly tame while elsewhere in West Africa it is much worse. Particularly in cities along the coast, it is accompanied by muggings or the threat of armed violence just frequently enough that one must definitely be concerned about those possibilities as well. Women are more vulnerable and they have been robbed while jogging alone on seemingly safe beaches, and had their purses and jewellery snatched while leaving the grounds of hotels and restaurants.

Leave your purse or wallet behind. Either hide your money, take a small pouch bag which can be worn at all times, or wear clothing with lots of pockets, and leave most of your money, passports, credit cards, even watches, in the hotel safety boxes.

The police are less likely to hassle you if you carry a photocopy of your passport but if they do, the worst that usually happens is you have to fetch it or pay a bribe.

A final suggestion is to hire a local to accompany you when walking around a risky area. It's usually not too difficult to find a kid hanging around who wouldn't mind picking up a few shillings for warding off potential molesters.

Sexual Harassment

A frequent complaint of Western women living in Africa, particularly single women, is sexual harassment. You may have an 'admirer' who won't go away, or a border official may abuse you verbally. Rape, on the other hand, is statistically insignificant, perhaps in part because Black African societies are not repressive sexually.

One reason for such harassment is that Western women are frequently viewed as being 'loose'. Dress is sometimes a factor. Although you'll see African women in Western clothes in the larger, more modern cities of West Africa, most still dress conservatively, typically with skirts to the ground. When a visitor wears something significantly different from the norm, she will draw attention. In the mind of the potential sexual assailant, she is dressing peculiarly. He may think she's asking for 'peculiar' and aggressive treatment.

In general, look at what other women are wearing and follow suit. Long pants are not a problem but long dresses are much better. If you want to wear shorts, bring along a wraparound skirt to cover them when you're in public. Going bra-less is ill-advised.

If you're in an uneasy situation, act prudish – stick your nose in a book. Or invent an imaginary husband who will be arriving shortly either in the country or at that particular spot. Or, if you are travelling with a male companion, introduce him as your husband.

ACTIVITIES
Cycling
It's fairly rare to see foreigners travelling around West Africa on bicycles but in many ways it's the best way to travel. Cyclists tend to make contact with locals much more easily than other travellers. The appearance of a lone foreigner entering a village on a bicycle creates considerably more attention than the same individual hopping off a bus. And of course you see a lot more of the countryside.

Roads are not a problem; most countries in West Africa are connected by paved highways. The main problems are the long distances and the intense heat. The best time to bike is the dry 'winter' period from mid-October to the end of February. People in villages and small towns are occasionally willing to rent their bicycles for the day to travellers; ask at the markets.

Anyone in the UK considering doing some serious cycling in West Africa should contact and/or join The Cyclist's Touring Club, Cotterail House, 69 Meadow Godalming, Surrey GU7 3HS; they have lots of good information for members only, including information on crossing the Sahara by bicycle. Those in the USA should contact the International Bicycle Fund (☎/fax (206) 628-9314), 4887 Columbia Drive South, Seattle, Washington 98108-1919. A low-budget, socially conscious organisation, it

conducts four, two-week bicycle tours back-to-back a year in West Africa (eg Senegal/Gambia, Mali, Togo and Ghana last year) during October and November. The all-inclusive land cost ranges from US$990 to US$1290. For more information on biking in West Africa, see the introductory Getting Around chapter.

Soccer & Basketball
Bring along a deflated football (soccer) for a village family, a child or group, and you'll be the hit of the day. If you want to play, the universities and municipal stadiums are by far the best places to find a game.

Basketball is Africa's second most popular sport (after soccer) and for travellers it's one of the best ways to meet Africans because foreigners are usually warmly welcomed in friendly matches.

Hash House Harriers
This is a jogging group of predominantly expatriates which started back in 1939 when a bunch of Aussies in Malaysia began meeting to run through rice paddies (and anywhere else) to build up a thirst for drinking more beer. It's now an international organisation. In West Africa there are groups in Abidjan, Accra, Bamako, Banjul, Dakar, Kaduna, Lagos and Ouagadougou.

The runs, typically once a week on a Saturday or Monday, are open to everyone, and hashers from other clubs are particularly welcomed. The runs are not so tough as to prohibit non-joggers from participating. They run through African villages, through corn fields and in the hills, sometimes on city streets – anywhere. Since the starting point changes every week, the only way to find the Hash is to ask around the expatriate community or call the UK embassy or marine guards at the US embassy. But beware – the beer-drinking rituals afterwards are as important as the run.

Tennis, Squash & Swimming
You'll find tennis courts and swimming pools in almost every city with over 100,000 people, and in many smaller cities. Many major hotels have these facilities and even if

Hiking

West Africa has many interesting possibilities for hiking, but the setup in this region is very different from that in East or southern Africa. There are fewer large mountains, and less in the way of wilderness areas with good walking conditions, so much of the hiking tends to be in populated areas, where you pass through fields and villages on paths used by the locals. This is a great way to see something of the local people; and on foot you can meet on more equal terms rather than stare at each other through the windows of a bush taxi.

As well as people, if you're interested in wildlife, you can also go hiking in many of West Africa's national parks and reserves. However, most park walking trails (if they exist at all) are generally quite short, designed more as an introduction to the vegetation and its inhabitants than as a way of covering long distances.

If you want something more demanding, there are opportunities for longer treks or backpacking trips, but the region has little in the way of organised routes (such as you find on Kilimanjaro or the Drakensbergs) so you often need to use your imagination and be prepared to adapt your plans as you go.

In the table, we've outlined a selection of areas where hiking is possible. In some of these places (eg the wildlife reserves in The Gambia) the hikes are very short and routes easy to follow; in other areas (eg Mt Bintumani in Sierra Leone) the hikes are much longer, and routes difficult to find, so that guides and a certain degree of planning are required. But in most areas, you have a complete range of hiking options, from short strolls to major treks, which depend entirely on your own energy and inclination. For example, you can hike along the Dogon Escarpment in Mali for anything between a few hours and a few weeks, or explore the Cross River National Park in Nigeria on trails which take from one to five days to complete.

Travelling by bike (can be hired) is an ideal way to explore some of these areas (such as the Fouta Djalon in Guinea or the Casamance in Senegal). Parts of the Casamance and several of the region's national parks can also be toured by dugout canoe; a nice contrast to hiking on terra firma. In some places, because of the distances involved (or just to take a break from walking), it may also be necessary to use donkeys, hitching or public transport to get around. The range of transport, and the need for adaptability, is all part of the fun.

If you're a peak-bagger, the highest points in West Africa include the summits of Cape Verde's Mt Fogo (2839 metres), Nigeria's Chapal Waddi (2407 metres) and Sierra Leone's Mt Bintumani (1945 metres). There are also several other peaks in Nigeria (on the Jos Plateau and along the Cameroun border) above 1500 metres.

For more details on the places listed in the table, see the individual country chapters.

Mountaineering & Rock Climbing

West Africa has very little in the way of climbing, as opposed to hiking (ie walking), up mountains. The main peaks are not particularly high, and the rock is generally not suitable. While expatriates living in, say, Guinea or Ghana may find some outcrops suitable for short climbs or bouldering, as a visitor it's not worth lugging rock-climbing clothes and equipment around West Africa.

The main exception is the area of Hombori, a village between Mopti and Gao in Mali, where some spectacular rock formations jut out of the desert floor, reaching over 1000 metres in parts. One group of peaks, called La Main de Fatma (or Aiguilles de Garmi), attracts serious rock climbers from Europe and several routes and summits apparently still wait to be conquered.

Another area where some rock climbing has been done is the Bandiagara Escarpment, also in Mali. The famous French climber Christine Destiville established some routes (and made a film about the Dogon Country) here several years ago, and groups of climbers from various European countries occasionally come here on short exploratory trips. But the quality of the rock is not very good, and the climbing itself is generally unstructured. As far as we know, there is no climbing guidebook to the area.

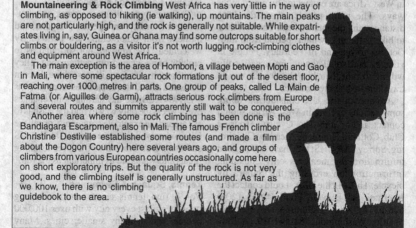

Country	Area	Features	Rating
Benin	Natintingou & Somba country	Interesting people & houses	E
Burkina Faso	Banfora area	Farmland, lakes, cliffs, waterfalls	V
Cape Verde	Brava Island	Scenic, hilly, rarely visited	V
	Mt Fogo (2839 m)	Major peak, no trees; major eruption in 1995	Stiff one-day hike, plus longer options
	Ribeira Grande Mountain	Scenic peak	As above
Côte d'Ivoire	Man area	Lush hills, waterfalls, villages, good views, traditional art	V
	Taï National Park	Dense rainforest, animals, birds; special permit required	E
The Gambia	Abuko Nature Reserve	Pristine, various habitats, birds	E
	Bijilo Forest Park	Coastal woodland, informative trails, birds	E
Ghana	Bia National Park	Dense rainforest, animals, birds	E
	Tongo (Bolgatanga area)	Scenic hills, villages	E
	Nakpanduri (Gambaga Escarpment)	Villages, good views	E
	Kakum Nature Park	Dense rainforest, birds, animals	E
	Mole Game Reserve	Wild game, trails, savanna	E
	Ho	Forested hill, villages	V
Guinea	Fouta Djalon	Large, scenic region of hills, forest, farmland	V
Guinea-Bissau	Bolama Island	Few visitors, good beaches, fields, villages	V
	Bubaque Island	Flat, more popular, good beaches, fields, villages	V
Liberia	Yekepa area (Mt Nimba 1752 m)	Lush hills, high mountain, forest	V
Mali	Dogon Escarpment	Spectacular landscape, traditional art	V
	Hombori area	Impressive sheer peaks	Mainly rock climbing
Nigeria	Bukuru (Jos Plateau area)	Large region of scenic hills	V
	Ganawuri Mountains (Jos Plateau area)	Scenic hills	V
	Gembu	Tea estates, cattle farms, friendly people	V
	Gwoza area	Rocky foothills of Mandara mountains	V
	Gashaka Game Reserve	High peak, various habitats & animals	V
	Cross River National Park	Lush rainforest, birds, gorillas	V
Senegal	Casamance	Scenic lowland region, excellent accommodation	V
	Siné-Saloum Delta	Coastal woodland, monkeys, birds; travel by canoe	E
Sierra Leone	Kabala area	Wooded hills, waterfalls	E
	Tiwai Island Wildlife Sanctuary	Pristine rainforest, animals	E
	Mt Bintumani (1948 m)	Remote region, mountain forest, high peak	H
	Sugar Loaf Mountain	Near Freetown, villages & views	E
	Outamba-Kilimi National Park	Rivers, forest, animals, birds	V
Togo	Fazao-Malfacassa National Park	Scenic forested hills	E
	Kpalimé area	Forested hills, butterflies	V
	Kandé area (Tamberma Valley)	Interesting people & houses	V
	La Fosse aux Lions (reserve)	Savannah woodland, cliffs	V

E – easy &/or short hikes (less than one day/10 km)
H – harder &/or longer hikes (more than 10 km, possibly over several days or in tougher conditions)
V – various lengths & standards ■

you're not a guest, you can use them – for a small price. There are squash courts in Dakar, Banjul, Conakry, Freetown, Monrovia, Abidjan, Yamoussoukro (Côte d'Ivoire), Grand-Bassam (Côte d'Ivoire), Ouaga, Accra, Lagos, Kaduna and Kano (Nigeria).

Other Water Sports
In (from west to east) Dakar, the Casamance beach area in Senegal, Banjul, Freetown, Abidjan, Sassandra (Côte d'Ivoire), Lomé and Lake Togo, **sailboards** are available for rent . The sport is practised everywhere, even on rivers in the Sahel. On the rivers, however, you risk taking home one of those weird African diseases – bilharzia.

There are also sailing clubs in most major cities along the coast, but renting a boat is virtually impossible except for Hobicats in Dakar and Banjul. Day sails on 10 to 18-metre crewed yachts are available in Dakar, Banjul, Freetown and occasionally Abidjan.

The underwater **diving** off N'Gor Island just outside Dakar is excellent for marine life, less so for coral. The diving is good down to about 30 metres. There is also a diving club in Abidjan though conditions are pretty murky and there's not a great deal to see. There are diving clubs/shops in both cities. Sierra Leone also offers fairly interesting diving south of Freetown.

About the only place in West Africa where you'll see **surfers** on a regular basis is at Assini beach in Côte d'Ivoire on Sundays; they're mostly young French men. They frequent the Ghana beaches on occasion as well. For a reef break, one of the best places is just outside Dakar near the airport, discovered by the *Endless Summer* surfers. Reefs along the coast of Mauritania undoubtedly make this one of the best places. Generally speaking, from Guinea eastward the waves are the one-big-crash type.

Golf
Abidjan and Yamoussoukro (both in Côte d'Ivoire) have the only two courses with grass greens and both are in very decent shape. The club house in Abidjan is so futuristic in design, it's suitable for a James Bond

movie. The next best courses are in Lagos, Kaduna and Kano.

The remaining cities, all with sand greens, are recommended only for addicts, or those wanting a few good photos showing golfing conditions that people back home won't believe. From west to east, the courses are in Dakar, Banjul, Freetown, Ouagadougou (semi-desert conditions), Abidjan, Yamoussoukro, Accra, Lomé (bad), and Oguta (Imo State, Nigeria).

Softball
There are laid-back games on weekends throughout West Africa. Americans are naturally the main participants but outsiders are always welcomed. The marine guards at the US embassies invariably know the details. You'll find teams in Praia, Dakar, Abidjan, Accra, Bamako, Ouaga, Niamey and Lagos.

Rugby
There are clubs in almost all the ex-British colonies. Visiting players are welcomed.

Fishing
For most travellers, deep-sea sports fishing is prohibitively expensive, costing well over US$100 a day per person. For those still interested, the countries where most deep-sea sports fishers head for are Senegal, Mauritania, Côte d'Ivoire and The Gambia, but there's fishing everywhere along the coast. From The Gambia to Liberia, fishing for barracuda is very popular, while in Cape Verde tuna is the main catch. Only the deep-sea fishing world is on to the fact that Dakar is one of the three or four best places in the world for sailfish; it's also excellent for blue marlin. Less well known is that other places along the coast, especially Abidjan, are right up there when it comes to blue marlin (also good for wahoo, barracuda and tuna). Mauritania is noted for surf casting and courbine is one of the main catches around Nouâdhibou. Air Afrique has a fishing centre there.

Charter boats are available only in (from west to east) Dakar, Banjul, Conakry, Freetown and Abidjan. The season for blue marlin and sailfish is from June to September. In Abidjan, there's a second season from November to mid-January. The major agencies offering special fishing trips are in Paris:

Jet Tours Departement Chasse et Pêche, 19 ave de Tourville, 75007 Paris (☎ (01) 46-02-70-22 or 47-05-01-95). They offer one-week fishing trips to Gabon. Prices range from 10,000 to 20,000FF depending on the number of people (one to four).
Au Coin de Pêche 50 ave de Wagram, 75017 Paris (☎ (01) 42-27-28-61/41-68). Their prices are lower.
Orchape 6 rue d'Armaille, 75007 Paris (☎ (01) 43-80-30-67 or 47-54-78-57, telex 640771).
Dominique H Dhouailly 37 rue La Fayette, 75009 Paris (☎ (01) 48-74-31-33). He concentrates on Côte d'Ivoire and Senegal.

FOOD

Food is one of the most interesting aspects of West African culture. African food is usually safer than Western food because it's cooked much longer (sometimes all day) and the ingredients, except for the staple (rice, etc), are invariably fresh that day. Restaurant food, on the other hand, may have been sitting in a refrigerator for some time.

Even people with sensitive stomachs can usually eat African food if they stick, at least initially, to less exotic dishes. I've yet to meet a traveller who didn't like, for instance, Senegalese *poulet yassa*, which might even be mistaken for Western cuisine, or one of Abidjan's renowned maquis serving braised chicken and fish. And African food is by no means always hot. Dishes with peanut sauce, for example, are usually quite mild.

The quality of food varies considerably from country to country. If you tried the food in Mauritania or Niger and thought it was unpalatable, you're not alone. This is mainly because so many of the inhabitants are nomads whose staples are dates and goat milk. The countries with the best African food tend to be those along the coast, where rainfall is plentiful and the crops are varied.

Where to Eat

The best place to find good African food is at somebody's home. The second-best place is frequently on the street corners, where many women earn their reputations as ter-

rific cooks, or at one of the many *gargottes* (basic eating houses and stalls).

African restaurants are a mixed bag. The expensive ones usually cater to foreigners and, with few exceptions, should be avoided. Many of the best places are no-name holes-in-the-wall, hardly deserving to be called restaurants. Ask the Africans; most of them know at least one great place.

On menus in all French-influenced countries you'll often find the *plat du jour*. It is the dish of the day and is usually at a special price. The *menu du jour* (often shortened to *le menu*) is the meal of the day – usually a starter, a main course and a desert – also at a special price.

Ingredients

The great variety of ingredients is what makes African food interesting. If you want to sample the best, make friends with an African woman and then give her some money (what you would have used for a restaurant) to make a meal. If you're curious about African ingredients and spices, accompany her to the market. Most African food is quite hot, but as you get closer to the desert, you'll find fewer hot dishes.

Okra A number of African dishes are made with okra, and the result is a slimy concoction. In the rural environment, you may be eating local-style (with your hands) in which case it's like dipping your hand into a bowl of raw eggs. There are any number of staples with which okra can be eaten. One is banana *foutou*; another is *fufu*. The former is basically a glob of mashed plantains and cassava. The latter is made with fermented cassava or, in Ghana, yams or plantain and manioc which is cooked and pureed, with no liquid added, and shaped into a ball. Picture mashed potatoes mixed with gelatine and very sticky. You grab a portion (with your right hand, please!) and dip it in the sauce while forming a ball.

If you're turned off by slimy okra, you won't be the only one. Okra dishes are plentiful on the streets, so it's easy to get the false impression that there's not much else.

vvvvvvvvvvvvvvvvvvvvvvvvvvvvvvv

Poulet Yassa (Senegal)
1 large chicken
450 grams (1 lb) shredded onions
180 grams (⅓ lb) butter
4 big peppers (mildly hot)
1 lemon
2 heads garlic, crushed
2 bay leaves
1 dessertspoon black pepper
salt to taste
chicken stock/water

Cut the chicken into four pieces, sprinkle with lemon juice and salt, and grill until brown. Melt the butter in a saucepan and sauté the chicken. Add the other ingredients and chicken stock/water (not too soupy), cover, and cook until tender. Garnish with tomato and lemon slices. Serve with rice. Serves four.

Jollof Rice (Nigerian Style)
450 grams (1 lb) meat (chicken, ham, beef, lamb)
225 grams (½ lb) rice
450 grams (1 lb) tomatoes
140 grams (15 oz) tomato purée
2 onions, sliced
1 large green pepper, sliced
3 dessertspoons butter
½ cup oil
1 teaspoon cayenne pepper or paprika
½ teaspoon thyme
½ teaspoon allspice
1 teaspoon black pepper
salt to taste

Cut the meat into small pieces and brown in a large saucepan with heated oil. Then put to one side. Fry the tomatoes, green pepper and onions in the same oil until soft, and then add the meat with the tomato purée and spices. Add the water and bring to the boil. Reduce the heat and simmer until tender. Add the rice to the pan and cook until all the water is absorbed and the grains are soft. Serves four. ■

vvvvvvvvvvvvvvvvvvvvvvvvvvvvvvv

Staples African food typically consists of a staple plus some kind of sauce. The preferred staple everywhere is rice; it is also more expensive because much of it has to be imported. In the Sahel, millet is the most common staple. It's a cousin of sorghum but

produces a smaller grain, and has foliage resembling a corn plant. The grain is placed in a wooden receptacle and pounded, sometimes for several hours. African villages are too small to support the mills seen in most towns and cities, and even in the cities many people cannot afford the extra cost of the service. (It's close to slavery. Ask a group of women in a small village to make a wish list, and a mill will be at the top.) Eaten with a tasty sauce, it can be surprisingly good.

Sauces
Sauces are the heart of African cuisine and each country has its own specialities. Because groundnuts (peanuts) are grown almost everywhere in West Africa, groundnut sauce is one of the most common. Peanut butter can be used as the main ingredient.

Jollof rice is a close cousin of Spanish paella and is one of the few African dishes that is well known throughout West Africa. Senegalese *poulet yassa* is a chicken dish which makes liberal use of onions and lemons. As for desserts, they are not a part of traditional African cuisine, although fresh fruits are sometimes eaten afterwards.

Many of the African sauces are difficult to duplicate outside Africa for lack of the proper spices.

DRINKS
Alcohol
While African cuisine is not everybody's cup of tea, everybody agrees that African beer is good by any standard. It is certainly better than the watery stuff found in the USA and is cheaper than that in Europe.

In all, there are about 45 beers (including about 10 European beers) brewed in West Africa, with Nigeria alone producing about 30. In Togo, German tourists say that Beer Benin, which now comes in both Pils and lager form, is as good or better than what they're accustomed to drinking at home. Part of the reason may be that the brewery in Togo was started by the Germans around the turn of the century and they still own an interest. While everyone has their own favourite beer, the following are some to look out for:

Beer Benin (Togo), Club (Ghana, Nigeria, Liberia), Flag (Côte d'Ivoire, Senegal), Star (Sierra Leone, Ghana, Nigeria), Harp and Gulder (Nigeria, Ghana).

Except in the coastal area between Sierra Leone and Nigeria, the majority of Africans don't drink beer. (Probably fewer than 1% of the women drink alcohol.) That's because they prefer soft drinks and so many are Muslims.

Home-made brew, on the other hand, is popular everywhere, even in Muslim areas. In West Africa palm wine ('vin de palme' in French) is a staple in villages along the coast. Yeast is added to the juice tapped from the palm-oil tree, and then this brew is allowed to ferment overnight. In Nigeria, it is even bottled in factories. Palm wine, which is white, goes by a different name in every language. In Sierra Leonean Krio, for example, it's called *poyo*; in Togo they have both palm wine and a clear whisky-strong version called *sodabe*, which will really knock your socks off. In the Sahel where it's too dry for palm-oil trees, it's the cheap 'millet beer' that gets the men wasted in the villages.

Nonalcoholic Drinks
Ginger Beer There's one nonalcoholic drink that is consumed so much throughout Africa that it could be called the drink of Africa – ginger beer. It's made with so much ginger that it burns the throat, and is too strong for many foreigners. In remote villages, they may have nothing else to offer you. The name changes from area to area and from ethnic group to ethnic group. Most Ghanaians, for example, call it *taka*.

Beware: the water is frequently contaminated because it's not distilled and rarely boiled.

ginger (12 pieces)
1 unpeeled pineapple
2 litres boiling water
sugar to taste

Beat ginger, add pineapple (with peel), pour boiling water over, stand overnight, strain, add sugar and chill.

Tea In the Sahel, if you have the opportunity to try the mint tea, don't pass it up. It's the principal drink of the nomads and is found mainly in Mauritania, northern Mali and Niger. Nothing like English tea, it's extremely sweet and served in small glasses. Don't let the sweetness turn you off; even those who normally drink tea without sugar learn to crave the sugar and caffeine high when they're in or near the desert.

Half the fun of drinking mint tea is the ritual. The unchangeable custom is for the tea to be served three times, progressively sweeter, taking at least an hour. For the men, this is always an occasion to relax and talk.

MARKETS
The markets in West Africa are the most vibrant and interesting in Black Africa. The best are those in Bamako, Lomé, Abidjan, Dakar, Kano, Niamey and Ouagadougou. But don't think you'll be wasting your time at some of the lesser markets.

Hassling
Most travellers love the markets, but a few find them extremely intimidating or annoying experiences – people grabbing you by the arm and not-so-gently pulling you over to the stall *pour voir seulement* (just to see). There's a huge difference between markets, however. Traders in the markets in the Sahel (Bamako, Ouagadougou, etc) are not very pushy, while those in Dakar and Abidjan definitely are. (The latter markets are also known to have thieves; see under Dangers & Annoyances.) If you're hesitant about the markets, don't start off with those two. Also, go early when the stalls are just opening and the vendors aren't in high gear; it's cooler then as well.

As for strategies in dealing with overly persistent traders, if you are really not looking for anything in that section, say no and move on. If they keep pulling you and you find it really offensive, let them know in no uncertain terms – if your actions are clear, they'll stop most of the time.

Bargaining
Bargaining, of course, is the name of the game. Most travellers expect the initial price to be three times the 'real' price. This is

usually true, but not always. With African cloth sold by the yard, for example, you can expect little or no lowering of the price. The same is true of gold and silver. If the trader tells you the price and you come back with an offer one-third that amount, don't be surprised if they become extremely ticked off, fold up the material and refuse to talk further. You'll feel like a real fool. So try to get a feel for prices beforehand. Ask knowledgeable locals or check out one of the hotel shops; prices in the market are typically half those in the stores.

Posting Your Purchases

No one likes to lug around souvenirs, so mail them home. Shipping is actually fairly reliable. Purchases not exceeding US$25 that are mailed to the USA enter duty-free. You may bring with you goods worth up to US$400 without paying duty. US$400 includes all purchases mailed as well.

Keep in mind that many developed countries do not charge duty on goods from underdeveloped countries to help them improve their export trade. In the USA, under the Generalised System of Preferences (GSP), goods from all countries of West Africa (except Nigeria) are exempt from duty. The major exceptions to this are textiles and shoes; gold, silver and jade have certain restrictions in terms of duty-free treatment.

Most countries, including Australia, Canada, the USA, Japan and virtually all countries in Europe, now prohibit the importation of ivory. To Australian customs officials, anything made from animal or plant matter is synonymous with the plague, and any such items will certainly be fumigated, if not confiscated. It is wise to check the customs regulations first.

Exporting Art

Art which is authentic and valuable cannot be exported under the laws of most African countries. Since very little art purchased by nonexperts fits this description, it's more a matter of being hassled by customs than doing something illegal. Moreover, in some countries such as Nigeria and Ghana, you'll have to get approval for export at the local museum, which is usually easily obtained but still a hassle. In those countries, if the piece looks at all old, it's best to let the museum see the piece before you purchase it. To protect yourself, either have the vendor accompany you to the museum before you purchase or get a written guarantee that they will refund your money if permission to export is denied.

Don't expect to travel upcountry and find something really valuable. Most of the museum-quality stuff has already been purchased. Also, knowing the difference between the real thing (ie old and used) and a forgery requires seeing and handling thousands of pieces. No book or sixth sense will enable you to bypass this process.

THE ART &
PEOPLE OF
WEST AFRICA

ART & TEXTILES

There's a great selection of good artwork in West Africa. Masks are as imaginative, and frequently amusing or terrifying, as anything you've dreamed. There are textiles rarely seen in Europe or the USA with a variety of pleasing colours and patterns. You can buy silver and gold jewellery as well as beads at prices far below what you'd pay elsewhere, and there is a fascinating assortment of spears, musical instruments, agricultural tools, etc.

To understand and appreciate African art, you need to know the context in which an object is used. Unlike Western art, almost all traditional African art is practical and has a day-to-day meaning. This art is involved in religion, health, village harmony and successful crops. So before you arrive, buy a book on African art and, after you arrive, go to an art museum (every capital city has one) or good art shop.

The following selections of African art and textiles are a few examples of the diversity in style and technique that you will find throughout West Africa.

Textiles

Probably the most well-known and expensive fabric in West Africa is the colourful kente cloth from Ghana. Other major textiles in West Africa include the elaborate Yoruba textiles from Nigeria, Tuareg wedding blankets found in Mali, Korhogo cloth from northern Côte d'Ivoire, country cloth from Liberia, and various textiles from the Sahel region (especially Mali, Burkina Faso and Niger).

Front Page: Colourful kente and adinkra cloth (centre) from Ghana (GB)

Top: Peasants shirt made from Mali mud cloth (GB)

Middle: Blanket seller in Mopti, Mali (KL)

Bottom: Colourful cloth, Mali (DE)

Also popular throughout West Africa is the blue indigo cloth of the Tuaregs, though some is not real indigo. The real stuff will rub off all over you. (Soaking the cloth in vinegar or very salty water will stop the dye running.) Some 'African' materials are actually made elsewhere, eg much of the colourful wax cloth comes from Holland.

Kente Cloth Clothing is one of the most obvious and important marks of distinction in Ashanti society. The basic garment of adult males is a long rectangular piece of cloth (*ntoma*) passed over the left shoulder and brought around the body and worn over shorts – like a toga. The most impressive of all materials used in such garments is kente cloth, which is woven in narrow, brightly coloured strips with dazzling complex patterns and a wealth of hues.

The Ewé also weave kente cloth, but the designs are somewhat different. The motifs used are all geometrical figures. Every design has a meaning, and some designs are reserved exclusively for royal families.

The earliest kente cloth was all cotton but, starting in the 18th century, Ashanti weavers began incorporating highlights using silk brought by the Dutch. Today, only the higher priced kente cloth contains silk (or imported rayon). The weaving is done exclusively by men, and almost always outdoors.

Kente cloth is worn only in the southern half of the country and unlike adinkra cloth, which is worn primarily on solemn occasions, is reserved mainly for joyous events. As a rule of thumb you should pay about US$3 per strip; a man's toga has about 22 strips. A slightly used piece would be somewhat cheaper and double-weave material is more expensive.

Top: Ashanti loom beaters for narrow loom, and heddle pulley (GB)

Middle Left: Ashanti cloth weaver, Ghana (EE)

Middle Right: Dye pits, Kano , Nigeria (DW)

Bottom: Artisan shop, Abomey, Benin (AS)

Adinkra Cloth Adinkra cloth is a colourful cotton material with black or dark brown geometric designs or stylised figures stamped on it. The word adinkra means farewell, hence Ghanaians consider adinkra cloth togas most appropriate for funerals (*ayie*), but they're also used at other special occasions. Unlike kente cloth which is worn exclusively by men, adinkra cloth is also worn by women. By legend, the art of adinkra originated in Côte d'Ivoire. King Adinkra of Gyaman was so enamoured with the Golden Stool that he had a replica made. The Ashanti king was so angered that he sent an army to capture it and melt it down. They succeeded, slaying the king and bringing back, as the spoils of victory, some of the cloth made there.

Originally the printing was done on cotton pieces lying on the ground. Today, the cotton fabric, which is of ordinary quality and cut in long pieces, is spread on a raised padded board and held in place by nails. The designs, which are all symbolic, are cut on calabash stamps, and the dye is made from the sap obtained from boiling the bark of a local tree called *badie* together with iron slags. The printer dips the calabash into the hot dye and presses it onto the fabric. Adinkra printers sometimes stamp over used pieces. Each colour has special significance; vermilion red, one of the more common colours, symbolises the earth and is used in funerals, while blue symbolises love and yellow is for success and wealth. Adinkra clothes are not meant to be washed.

Wood Carvings

Traditional African sculpture has some distinguishing characteristics. The sculptures are usually stylised, not naturalistic, and most are of a single form. If they are represented in pairs or groups, the figures rarely interact. Gender is very important, so the sizes of body parts are exaggerated, particularly the head, buttocks, breast and navel. The creators place more importance on spirituality than originality.

Woodcarver, Korhogo, Côte d'Ivoire (AN)

Masks In ceremonies, masks are used to disguise their wearers as they impersonate an ancestor or some other spirit. The dancers often work themselves into a frenzy as the spirit of the mask enters them. Certain masks possess great ritual significance, others are just for entertaining. In museums, you may see the large helmet masks of the Epa cult, the most spectacular of the Yoruba masks. The most common Dan mask is that of a human face, slightly abstract but with realistic features, a smooth surface, everted lips, slit or large circular eyeholes and calm expression. The slit-eye ones are used to keep women from seeing the uncircumcised boys during their initiation into adulthood. In the Senufo dances, such as *la dance des hommes-panthères* (dance of the leopard-men), masks play a critical role in reaching the gods and driving away bad spirits.

Figurines Yoruba women often carry twin dolls, or *ibeji*, because twins are believed to bring wealth and luck. If one of the twins dies, the corresponding doll is cared for in place of the dead child. The figure is regularly cleaned, and dressed and adorned with beads. This ritual ensures that the dead child is not forgotten and will be welcome if it returns.

Fertility Dolls Unlike in virtually every other West African country, the Ghanaians do not use masks. But this does not mean they do not believe in supernatural powers, and fetishes to invoke them. In Ghana, this is done through wooden and clay statuettes, often placed on altars in fetish houses.

The Ashanti fertility dolls (*akua-mma*) are a prime example. Carved in wood, they are flat and coloured black or dark brown. The dolls are, by

Top: Stilt dancer, Zala village, Man region, Côte d'Ivoire (DW)

Middle: Masks at the Central Marché in Man, Côte d'Ivoire (DW)

Bottom Left: Yoruba twins, Nigeria (GB)

Bottom Right: Akua-mma (fertility dolls), Ghana (GB)

tradition, used only by women; today they are still treated like magic. Women who are afraid of being infertile, and pregnant women who want to ensure beautiful children, carry them on their backs like children, with only the top of the head protruding from the cloth. Those who want children of both sexes carry two dolls. The woman's desire to have children is gradually transmitted to the doll, which, it is hoped, will bestow fertility on her.

The sculptor endeavours to make the dolls comely. The heads are invariably circular or oval, the necks appear to be a number of rings and the bodies are cylindrical with rudimentary arms.

Other Wooden Objects Woaley is a board game similar to backgammon that has been a major pastime of Africans of all ages since it originated in Egypt thousands of years ago. Woaley boards are nearly always rectangular, and about half a metre long with two rows of six cups each. Some boards also have a cup at one or both ends for storing captured peas (48 come with the game).

In West Africa, virtually all mud buildings have decorated doorways or thresholds. Mali's Dogon people, in particular, are well known for their elaborately carved house posts and doors from their dwellings.

When you buy a new wooden carving you may find it cracked by the time you get home. New wood must be dried slowly. Wrapping the carvings in plastic bags with a small water tray enclosed is one technique. If you see tiny bore marks with white powder everywhere, it means the powder-post beetle (frequently confused with termites) is having a fiesta. There are three remedies – zap the buggers with a microwave oven, stick the piece in the freezer for a week, or drench it with lighter fluid.

Top: Woaley board, Ghana (GB)

Left: Dogon door, Mali (DE)

Right: Dogon door latch (MC)

Jewellery

Jewellery is important to all Africans, both men and women, and in West Africa you'll find a large and fascinating variety. Most jewellery is also highly portable, making it one of the best things to collect during your travels.

For Africans, beads are often more than simple adornment. They are used to create objects representing spiritual values basic to the community and can play major roles in community rituals such as birth, circumcision, marriage and death. So like all African art objects, they can acquire more importance than may be initially appreciated.

In most of Black Africa the preferred metal is gold, but in and near the Sahara the nomads, particularly the Tuaregs and the Moors, prefer silver to gold, which is believed to bring bad luck. In West Africa, both metals are sold by the gram and the artwork is included in the price. Prices have been very stable over the past decade, gold selling for around CFA 4500 per gram and silver for around CFA 500 per gram (more if the quality is superior). While prices in CFA have shot up significantly from these levels since the devaluation, in foreign currency terms they are no more expensive than before.

Top: Silver maker, St-Louis, Senegal (AS)

Left: Jewellery vendor at Vogan market, Togo (AN)

Right: Brass dagger, bronze buckle and fertility doll (Ashanti), and Tuareg silver work (GB)

Beads Several hundred major bead styles are sold in Africa, including a variety of glass beads and shells. Prices vary considerably and some beads are quite expensive. Necklaces can be made to order; at markets, the vendors will usually string them for you on the spot.

The most common African bead is the glass bead, quite rare in Africa until the arrival of Europeans. Millefiori trading beads are highly decorative glass beads from Venice, featuring flowers, stripes and mosaic designs. Africans were intrigued by these Venetian beads, and some African artisans began making their own. Although they knew how to make glass before the arrival of Europeans, they found it easier to use discarded European bottles and medicine jars, which they pulverised into a fine powder.

Many glass beads are tiny and sold by the pound, hence their name 'pound beads'. Today, the Krobo in Ghana still melt powdered glass in small bead moulds, while the Nupe of Bida in central Nigeria wind molten glass on long iron rods to make beads and bracelets. However, many of the beads you'll see in African markets, particularly the chevron beads, still come from Europe. Referred to as *bakim-mutum* by bead traders throughout West Africa, they are commonly worn by village chiefs and elders as a sign of power and wealth.

In the Mopti-Djenné-Dogon area of Mali, you'll see fairly large amber beads worn by Fulani women. The Dogon and Berber also treasure amber and use it in their necklaces, bracelets and pendants. Berber women believe it can cure a variety of illnesses. The Dogon also use a large, thin, red bead as well as stone beads and black spindle whorls. Made of clay and stone and incised with geometrical patterns, the whorls,

Top: Yoruba beadwork banner, Nigeria (GB)

Middle: Mali amber beads in Nigerian baskets (GB)

Bottom Left: Trading beads from Nigeria, probably made in the Czech Republic (GB)

Bottom Right: Sand cast and millefiori trading beads, Ghana (GB)

used as beads for at least a thousand years, are recognisable by their enlarged central hole.

A variety of other elements are used in Africa in making beads, including coral, shells, copal, amazonite, silver, gold and brass. Poorer women sometimes have to make do with cheaper elements. Among the Bella (former slaves of the Tuaregs), for instance, plastic beads and imitation amber beads are sometimes used instead of coral, amber and stones, while coins may replace silver in jewellery.

Talismans & Other Jewellery Grisgris and necklaces are very popular with travellers. Grisgris are talismans that ward off a particular evil; Africans often wear many. In Agadez (Niger), you'll see Tuaregs, both men and women, wearing the famous Agadez silver crosses as pendants around their necks. Characterised by protective symbolism as with most jewellery from the Sahara, these come in various designs. Some incorporate circle and phallus designs, fertility symbols for both sexes; those representing a camel's eye or jackal tracks are symbolic of power and cunning. The best talisman of all in the Saharan area, however, is the Koran, often seen hanging in artisans' workshops.

Top: Handcraft stall at the Grand Marché in Bamako, Mali (DW)

Left: Tuareg amulets (GB)

Right: Tuareg crosses and amulets (GB)

All over West and Central Africa you'll find beautiful dark green malachite jewellery, which comes from the southern Shaba region of Zaïre. The price is as low as you'll find anywhere in the world and it makes an excellent substitute for ivory.

Rings in West Africa are sometimes stunning. In Burkina Faso, for example, you might see a Bobo bronze ring showing a tick bird, a warrior on horseback, or a frog poised on a water lily. Older Dogon men wear bronze rings as a sign of status; their rings can be quite large. Earrings, too, can be interesting. In the Dogon area, observe the womens' ears. Traditionally, they wear eight small rings on the rim of the ear, standing for the eight Dogon ancestors.

Bracelets are also very popular with travellers and are particularly interesting in West Africa, in part because of the incredible variety. Some brass bracelets are so huge as to be impractical to wear, but in Africa big often means better.

Cowrie shells are often used to decorate pieces of jewellery. Found mainly in the Indian Ocean, for a long time these shells were used as money in Africa.

Top: Woven and leather bangles, Mali (GB)

Bottom: Cowrie belt and bangles, Mali (GB)

PEOPLE

The number of ethnic groups in West Africa is mind boggling. Guinea-Bissau, a country of less than one million people, has 23 major ethnic groups. Almost all of the other countries have a similar ethnic diversity. The colonial powers ignored this diversity, so that today the area of the Malinké people, for example, constitutes part of three countries instead of one. The major difference between countries in this respect is that some countries have one or two ethnic groups which clearly predominate; other countries do not. In Mali, for example, the largest ethnic group, the Bambara, represent only 23% of the total population.

This pattern is repeated throughout Africa. The result is that Africans of the same nationality often have difficulty communicating with one another. In many cases the only way is by means of French or English, but a lot of Africans do not speak either language. Go to the market in Niamey (Niger) and you'll be hard-pressed to find a vendor who speaks the official language of the country – French.

This makes governing exceedingly difficult. For travellers, it can be frustrating but it is this ethnic diversity that makes travel in West Africa so interesting.

Each group has its own special characteristics. The Bozo of Mali and Niger, for example, are almost all fishers along the Niger River. The Dogon in Mali are mostly farmers who are famous for their cliff dwellings and their intensive agriculture. The Fulani, on the other hand, are professional herders.

Some ethnic groups are more well known than others. The Bambara and the Hausa have probably the most widely used languages in the western and eastern parts of West Africa, respectively. The Tuareg are famous for being the principal desert nomads, even though their numbers have declined. Thirteen of the more well-known ethnic groups in West Africa are described below. Most are found in one or two countries but a few, such as the Fulani, are spread throughout West Africa.

Women traders at a fish market in Nouakchott, Mauritania (AS)

Ashanti

Living in the heart of the 'Gold Coast' (Ghana) and once wealthy from gold, the Ashanti (ah-SHAN-tee) developed one of West Africa's richest cultures. The largest tribe in Ghana and one of the few matrilineal societies in West Africa, the Ashanti live in the cocoa and gold regions of central Ghana, with Kumasi as the capital. Their kings used to be weighed down with gold ornaments on special occasions but the kings' houses were never very elaborate, except for the exterior carvings.

The Ashanti's traditional wealth is reflected in their art and fabrics, especially the colourful and expensive *kente* cloth made with finely woven cotton and, sometimes, silk.

Bambara

The Bambara (BAM-bah-rah) are the major ethnic group of Mali. They are mostly farmers and they control the government. Their language, Bambara, is not only the dominant language of Mali but is almost identical to Dioula, the market language of Côte d'Ivoire, Guinea and Burkina Faso. The Bambara are famous for their art, especially the antelope-like masks, called *chiwaras*, which are perhaps the most well-known masks in African art.

Previous Page: Women fishing, Niger River, Guinea (CB)

Top: Ashanti women potters, Pankrono, Ghana (AN)

Bottom: Elders meeting, Mali (CB)

Dogon

Although numbering only about 300,000, the Dogon (DOH-ghon) are, nevertheless, quite famous for their cliff dwellings. As a result, their villages are a hot tourist attraction. Located in Mali in the area east of Mopti, their houses are perched on cliffs and resemble those of the cliff-dwelling Indians in the USA. Unlike many African villages where the houses show signs of the 20th century (metal roofs, etc), Dogon villages look the same as they did 400 years ago.

The Dogon are equally famous for their art – the doors and locks to their houses, for example, are some of the most artistically carved in Africa. Dogon masks are some of the most sought after in West Africa. When a Dogon dies, the spirit of the deceased takes up residence in a mask, so these are most important in funeral rites.

Below: Dogon woman and baby, Ende, Mali (AP)

Left: Dogon man, north of Bamba, Bandiagara Escarpment, Mali (DW)

Right: Dogon man, north of Bamba, Mali (DW)

Bottom: Mopti, Mali (MT)

Fulani

The origin of the Fulani (fou-LAN-ee), also known as Peul or Foulbé, is not certain, though it appears that they migrated centuries ago from Egypt and may even be of Jewish origin. Some are so fair that they look Caucasian.

Fulani are usually tall, elegant and thin, with aquiline noses, long dark hair, oval faces and a light complexion. The Fulani women are noted for their bright robes, elaborate hairdos and outrageously large gold earrings.

For centuries the Fulani have been cattle raisers throughout West Africa, and while some now combine farming with cattle, others are still nomadic herders who live in the pastoral zone and subsist entirely from raising livestock. A typical arrangement is for farmers to purchase cattle as a form of investment and turn them over to the Fulani, who tend them in return for occasional sacks of rice. Fulani herders can recognise every single animal in herds of 300 cattle and more.

Top: Peul (Fulani) man, Northern Bandiagara Escarpment, Mali (DW)

Bottom: Peul (Fulani) girl, Northern Bandiagara Escarpment, Mali (DW)

Hausa

The Hausa (HOW-sah) number over 20 million and are centred mainly in northern Nigeria and southern Niger. The largest Hausa city is Kano, for centuries the hub and distribution centre for the trans-Saharan trade. As one of the three major ethnic groups of Nigeria, the Hausa are predominantly Muslim and for the most part are farmers, traders and merchants (*commerçants*).

Because of their well-known commercial network which stretches across the continent, the Hausa, like the Bambara, have one of the most important languages in West Africa. The Hausa traders, who you will encounter hawking masks, statues and the like, form almost a subculture of their own.

Left: Boy with facial sacrification, Western Niger (DW)

Right: Djerma girl and pot by Niger River market, Niger (EE)

Ibo

The third-largest ethnic group in Nigeria, the Ibo (E-bow) are centred mainly in south-eastern Nigeria. Their numbers, like the Yoruba, are enormous compared to most other West African ethnic groups.

Resourceful and industrious by reputation, they have always been in conflict with the Yoruba and Hausa. This historic conflict was one of the catalysts for the Biafran War in the late 1960s.

Malinké

The Malinké (mah-LEEN-kay) are the major ethnic group in Guinea with a significant presence in southern Mali, north-western Côte d'Ivoire and eastern Senegal. They are closely related to the Bambara and are famous for having had one of the great empires of West Africa. It was during the Malinké Empire of Mali in the 14th century that Timbuktu, Djenné, Gao and Agadez began to blossom. These were not just the leading cities on the Sahara trade routes; they were centres of Islamic learning with major universities and palaces. The Malinké are also noted for having perhaps the best kora musicians in West Africa.

Moors

The Moors (or Maurs) are peppered throughout West Africa but are found primarily in Mauritania. Historically the Moors have been, like the Tuareg, nomads living from raising cattle and sheep. Living also in

Top: Young girl, Beyla, Guinea (MT)

Bottom: Moor man in traditional dress, Nouâdhibou, Mauritania (AS)

desert oases, they became involved in the date trade and other commerce, and are now well known as merchants.

The racial conflict between the Moors, Caucasian Muslims of Arab Berber origin, and the Negro Africans is fierce, and in the late 1980s it exploded in the form of race riots in Mauritania. As a result the government expelled large numbers of Black Senegalese from its territory. Senegal then did the same with its Moors. Until 1980, when slavery was finally abolished in Mauritania (in law if not entirely in fact), Moors had Black African slaves who were permanently attached to the households.

Mossi

The Mossi (MOH-see) occupy the central area of Burkina Faso and comprise about half the population of Burkina Faso as well as the bulk of Côte d'Ivoire's migrant labour force. They are noted for never having been conquered by the Muslims. As a result, in great contrast to neighbouring Mali and Niger, Burkina Faso is no more than 20% Muslim.

During their heyday, the Mossi had four kingdoms in Burkina Faso, each with its own courts and ministers maintaining a rigid social order. The Mossi have held on to their traditions very strongly, as can be witnessed today in Ouagadougou at the weekly Mora Naba ceremony.

Left: Women in typical dress, Grand-Bassam, Côte d'Ivoire (AN)

Right: Girl near La Guinguette, Bobo-Dioulasso, Burkina Faso (DW)

Songhaï

Located primarily in north-eastern Mali and western Niger along the Niger River, the Songhaï (SAUN-ghi) have traditionally been farmers and fishers as well as herders. They are a very proud people, famous for having had the last and most expansive of the Sudanic empires of West Africa in the 16th century. At its height, the Songhaï Empire extended from Senegal to Niger.

The great majority remain farmers who employ a unique method of planting rice along the banks of the Niger River as it rises with the rains, and sorghum as it lowers. They are now one of the poorest of African groups due to the droughts of the 1970s and '80s.

Tuareg

The nomadic descendants of the North African Berbers, the Tuareg are found all over the Sahara, especially in Mali, Niger and southern Algeria. They are a proud people and consider themselves Caucasian because of their Berber heritage. They are relatively easy to recognise by their fair skin and nomadic outfits, especially the ink-blue turbans covering all of their heads except their eyes. For most Africans, gold is the most highly prized metal, but for the Tuareg it's silver. Virtually all their jewellery is made out of silver, including the swords which no respectable Tuareg man would be seen without.

Tuareg unloading camel, near Timbuktu, Mali (CB)

Historically, they were warriors and raiders and were known for their possession of slaves, the Bella. Since the drought of the 1970s when their herds were devastated, many have had to abandon the nomadic existence.

Wolof

As the major ethnic group in Senegal (38%), the Wolof (WOH-loaf) are extremely proud and easy to distinguish – tall and thin with regular features and round heads, and frequently very black skin. They are also present in surrounding countries, particularly The Gambia. As with the Hausa, the Wolof are famous as traders, but because their trading technique sometimes appears overly persistent, they are not always appreciated by travellers or other Africans.

Primarily Muslims, the Wolof are related to several other major ethnic groups in Senegal. As a result, not only is the Wolof language virtually the national language of Senegal, but also tribal rivalries in Senegal have not been as strong as in other African countries.

Yoruba

The Yoruba (YOH-rou-bah) are one of the three major ethnic groups in Nigeria and are concentrated in the south of the country. They are predominantly Christian, and generally rather robust in appearance.

They are a significant ethnic tribe in West Africa if only because of their large numbers and the fact that their principal city, Lagos, is the largest in Black Africa. In addition the Yoruba, who were early exposed to Western education, are significant because of their well-known art, including phenomenal beadwork, appliqué cloth and woodcarvings.

Casamance, Senegal (PP)

BIRDS OF
WEST AFRICA

You don't have to be an intrepid bird-watcher to appreciate the beauty and diversity of West African bird life. With very little effort you'll be able to observe the rich bird life for which West African waters are famous. Hundreds of species are found south of the Sahara in some of the world's most important and impressive reserves. And unlike the region's game parks, most of the bird reserves are easy to reach and all are abundantly populated, particularly during the migratory season – November to April. Nigeria, Sierra Leone, Senegal and Mauritania are perhaps the best countries for bird-watching, while Benin, Burkina Faso, Côte d'Ivoire, The Gambia and Mali are also worthwhile.

Bird-watching is excellent in Nigeria. The famous **Yankari National Park** is something of an ornithologist's dream. Approximately 600 species of birds call Yankari home for a time; savannah, wetland, river and raptor species are all found here. The **Okomo Sanctuary** is less than an hour from Benin City and is host to cranes and hornbills. **Kamuku Wildlife Reserve** near the town of Birnin Gwari is another great place for bird-watching, as is the **Hadejia-Nguru Wetlands**, 200 km north-east of Kano, a project supported by the Nigerian Conservation Foundation (NCF), and an important resting point for migratory birds and indigenous water birds. **Gashaka Game Reserve**, near Yola and the Cameroun border, is the largest national park in Nigeria and has the most diverse ecology of any Nigerian park. It supports a staggering number of birds.

In Sierra Leone, **Tiwai Island Wildlife Sanctuary**, south of Kenema, has more than 120 bird species, including hornbill, kingfisher and the rare white-breasted guinea fowl. The smaller **Mamunta-Mayoso Wildlife Sanctuary** protects a wetland area about 30 km to the south of Makeni, and provides a vital refuge for many bird species. Around **Mt Bintumani**, the endangered rufus fishing owl has been sighted. The various habitats in **Outamba-Kilimi National Park** support many species of bird, including kingfisher, hornbill, heron, hawk, eagle, turaco, weaver, sunbird and the spectacular blue plantain eater.

In Senegal, the **Langue de Barbarie National Park**, 20 km south of St-Louis, is home to numerous water birds – pink flamingo, white pelican, cormorant, heron, egret and duck. North of St-Louis, **Parc National des Oisseaux du Djoudj** offers the opportunity to see a great spectacle of bird life: some three million birds migrating south from Europe pass through this area. Almost 300 species of bird have been recorded here, including up to 100,000 pink flamingo, and white pelican, spur-winged goose, night and purple heron, egret, spoonbill, black-tailed godwit, cormorant, great bustard, tree duck, kingfisher, stork and sunbird. **Niokolo-Koba** in the south-east is Senegal's major game park but the bird-watching is particularly good also. Amongst the 350 species recorded here are the red-throated bee-eater, saddlebill stork, spur-winged goose, white-faced tree duck, kingfisher, Senegalese coucal, crane, ibis, hammerhead, heron, Denham's bustard, the spectacular Abyssinian ground hornbill and violet turaco. Also good for bird-watching during the migratory season is the **Siné-Saloum Delta**, and during the dry season the **Casamance** is a temporary home to millions of migratory birds.

Mauritania's remote **Arguin Bank National Park**, not viewable during the mating season, is one of the top bird sanctuaries in Africa. Because of its secluded seashore, it's a crossroads for multitudes of aquatic birds migrating between Europe and northern Asia and most of Africa. Over two million broad-billed sandpipers have been recorded in the winter. Other migrants include black tern, flamingo, white pelican and spoonbill.

Over 400 species have been recorded in The Gambia. In **Abuko Nature Reserve** you'll find heron, hawk, grass warbler, dove, swallow and kingfisher. Birds are also plentiful in **West Kiang National Park**.

In Ghana **Kakum Nature Park**, **Owabi Wildlife Sanctuary**, **Bia National Park** and **Bui National Park** are all good for bird-watching. As

Prievious Page: Saddlebill Stork (JE)

is **Mole Game Reserve** where over 300 species of birds have been recorded.

The rainforest of Côte d'Ivoire's **Parc National d'Assagny** is home to a large variety of birds, and in **Parc National de la Marahoué** nearly 300 species have been recorded. **Comoë National Park** supports an abundance of bird life; one couple spotted 130 species in three days.

Mali also supports its share of birds. **Lake Faguibine**, 50 km north of Goundam, is one of the three best places in the Sahel for seeing migratory birds. Benin's **Pendjari Park** supports a variety of bird life and in Burkina Faso, the lake just outside Le Barrage and also **Ranch de Nazinga** and **Lake Tengrélalots** have lots of interesting birds.

The examples of West African bird life which follow are mostly widespread across the region and quite easy to recognise, even if you only have a passing interest in ornithology. Notes on distribution are specific to West Africa (ie, we have not provided a definitive range for the species) and the average length of the bird (from the tip of the bill to the tip of the tail) is given after the scientific name.

Black-Crowned Night Heron
Nycticorax nycticorax (56 cm)
Widespread in Senegal and The Gambia where there is adequate water sources for fishing and dense foliage for nesting, this bird is most active at dawn and dusk (more active in daylight hours in the breeding season). Coloured white, black and grey, it has a large head, short legs and large distinctive red eyes. Its harsh call can often be heard at night. When nesting they eat other heron chicks after drowning them.

Black-Head Weaver
Ploceus melanocephalus (15 cm)
Residing among grass and bushes of the waterways and savannah plains of Mauritania, Senegal, The Gambia, Guinea-Bissau and east to Mali and northern Nigeria, this twittering, colourful bird makes a tightly woven, ball-shaped nest in tree branches. The male of the species has a bright yellow neck and black head and throat; the female is more brown and smaller.

Left: Black-Crowned Night Heron (PR)

Right: Black-Head Weaver (JE)

Cape Cormorant
Phalacrocorax capensis (75 cm)
These highly gregarious birds which inhabit coastal waters are mostly blue-black and bottle-green. Some can be brown. The head becomes speckled with white during breeding which occurs in colonies of up to 120,000 individuals. Sexes are similar. They feed in large groups, and often with penguins and terns, on pilchards, anchovies, maasbanker, and occasionally lobsters, crabs and mussels.

Helmeted Guinea Fowl
Numida meleagris (56 cm)
This species is found in bush country and savanna woodlands. They are grey with white spots, and have a distinctive bony horn and a sparsely feathered blue (or red and blue) neck. They cackle loudly and congregate in large groups.

Top: Helmeted Guinea Fowl (RB)

Bottom: Cape Cormorants (left) and juvenile White Breasted Cormorant (right) (JE)

Crowned Crane
Balearica pavonina (100 cm)
Found on wet plains, grassy marshland and crops, the large, decorative crowned crane has a distinct 'fan' of feathers on its nape, and a red wattle. Similar, but not related, to the stork they have a long neck and long legs. They usually congregate in groups of about 15 (though at certain times will flock in their hundreds) and feed on vegetation, grain, large insects and small reptiles. At about one-metre long and with a loud, melodic cry they are impressive to watch in their ceremonial courtship dances: wings open, they bow to each other and leap nearly one metre before landing, circling each other and starting again.

Greater Flamingo
Phoenicopterus ruber (140 cm)
This tall bird is known to breed on Mauritania's Arguin Bank; they can also be found in their hundreds in Senegal during the non-breeding season on saline or alkaline lakes and lagoons. They cannot survive long on fresh water. Generally white with tinges of pink, they have crimson wings, black flight feathers and long legs. They are easily confused with the smaller lesser flamingo *(Phoenicopterus minor)* which has a dark red bill. Flamingos have a complicated and sophisticated system for filtering the foodstuffs out of the water. This is because the highly alkaline water would be toxic if consumed in large quantities. The greater flamingo supplements its algae diet with small molluscs, crustaceans and other organic particles from the mud. Their call is similar to a goose's honk.

Hammerkop
Scopus umbretta (55 cm)
This noisy bird is abundant in Senegal's waterways, particularly mangrove creeks, seasonal ponds and large rivers, though less common in forests. Numbers are increasing probably due to artificial structures such as dams and irrigation schemes. Though dull-brown in colour, their thick crest, large bill and short legs make them easy to recognise. They are most active from dawn to dusk. Both sexes help make huge nests, usually four-foot high, from mud and grass. They feed mainly on

Top: Crowned Crane (RB)

Left: Hammerkop (JE)

Right: Greater Flamingos (JE)

amphibia, and in Mali, on small fish, whilst wading in shallow water. In some parts of Africa, this bird is believed to have magical powers.

Hornbills
Bucerotidae (38 cm)
These large birds inhabit woodland savannah feeding mainly on fruit, and are distinguishable by their large, curved beaks and loud, raucous calls. The red-billed dwarf hornbill *(Tockus camurus)* is common in Liberia and easy to recognise by its red bill and distinctive call.

Left: Red-Billed Hornbill (PR)

Right: Trumpeter Hornbill (JE)

Little Egret
Egretta garzetta (61 cm)
Belonging to the same family as herons, the little egret has long legs and a slender beak. Found throughout West Africa, it wades and hunts in the shallow waters of mangrove creeks, marshy rivers and lakes, feeding on fish, frogs and insects. All white, it has yellow feet and a black bill, thus distinguishable from the great white egret *(Egretta alba)* which has a yellow bill (it changes from yellow to black in the breeding season, however). They commonly nest with the night heron *(Nycticorax nycticorax)* not far from water in trees and bushes.

Long-Tailed Shag
Phalacrocorax africanus (56 cm)
Abundant along West Africa's coast and on large bodies of water (particularly Mauritania's Arguin Bank), this medium-sized bird with a long tail is velvety black with an orange face. They dive for lengthy periods and feed on fish. They nest in trees, colonising with darters and other small herons, laying between three to five white eggs.

Nubian (Lappet-Faced) Vulture
Aegypius tracheliotus (100 cm)
This large, brown eagle-like member of the Accipitridae family, of which hawks and eagles are also members, is found in the semi-arid, semi-desert scrub of Senegal and The Gambia, and through to Mali, Niger and Nigeria. Like other vultures, they are fairly inefficient fliers and so rely to a large degree on finding rising hot-air thermals on which to glide and ascend. For this reason you won't see them in the air until well into the morning when the upcurrents have started. Usually solitary, they are silent birds – even when feeding with other vultures or having prey stolen from them by jackals. They feed mainly on small dead animals such as duikers and hares, and also on locusts and termites. Often mistaken for a hooded vulture *(Necrosyrtes monachus)*, this species has a larger head and heavier bill which it uses to break into a carcass with powerful blows. This species lays a single egg in a large stick nest in an acacia tree.

Left: Little Egret (JE)

Right: Long-Tailed Shag (PR)

Bottom: Nubian (Lappet-Faced) Vulture (JE)

Pied Kingfisher
Ceryle rudis (25 cm)
Spread throughout West Africa, these noisy birds are plentiful in mangrove creeks, large rivers and lakes (particularly Senegal, The Gambia and Nigeria where they breed). They dive for their meals of fish which they beat about before swallowing. A distinguishable feature is their huge black bill, and you can tell the sexes apart by the number of bands on the chest – the male has two, while the female has only one. They nest in a chamber at the end of a tunnel in a canal or river bank. These birds are quite tame, and gregarious in the non-breeding season.

Red-Throated Bee-Eater
Merops bulocki (25 cm)
This bird is easy to identify by its red throat, blue-green head, green body and square tail. They are found in small groups in the open woodland and grassy areas of Senegal, The Gambia and northern Nigeria and feed mainly on hymenoptera (bees, wasps, ants etc) and large insects. When they breed, they congregate in bigger groups, and nest in tunnels in river banks where they lay between two and five glossy white eggs.

Rollers
Coraciidae (35 cm)
These brightly coloured birds always have blue markings. They spend considerable time perched on bushes and telegraph wires looking for prey (insects and small reptiles). The blue-bellied roller *(Coracias cyanogaster)* is found in pairs or small groups in the savannah of The Gambia, Senegal, Sierra Leone, Côte d'Ivoire, Ghana and northern Nigeria. It has distinct blue underparts, a pinkish-fawn head and neck, and a green beak and feet. The sexes are similar.

Top: Pied Kingfishers (JE)

Left: Red-Throated Bee Eaters (PR)

Right: Blue-Bellied Roller (PR)

Saddlebill Stork
Ephippiorhynchus senegalensis (145 cm)
Found in Senegal and The Gambia in swamps and large rivers, these large black- and-white birds with huge red bills are solitary nesters.

Senegal Coucal
Centropus senegalensis (38 cm)
This species is one of seven coucals which occur in West Africa. It has an olive green head and upper back, red eyes, black bill and white or chestnut front. It is awkward in flight and spends most of its time on the ground where it preys on small vertebrates and grasshoppers. It's common throughout the region (particularly in Senegal and The Gambia) in reeds, thickets and dense undergrowth.

Senegal Thick Knee
Burhinus senegalensis (35 cm)
This sandy-coloured, black-streaked bird has large eyes and a round head. It frequents the open country of The Gambia and Senegal, nesting on bare ground near water.

Left: Saddlebill Stork (JE)

Right: Senegal Thick Knee (PR)

Bottom: Senegal Coucal (PR)

Spur-Winged Goose
Plectropterus gambensis (100 cm)
This nocturnal, long-necked bird is found in large inland waters of southern Mauritania, Senegal and The Gambia. It has a pink bill and pink feet, white underparts, green wings, and black upperparts, and feeds on grass seeds, fallen fruit, aquatic plant life, and sometimes small fish. They are difficult to approach and will shake their heads and lift their chins before flying off. When breeding they form smaller groups and seek smaller bodies of water, eg flood lands.

Spur-Winged Plover
Vanellus spinosus (28 cm)
These medium-sized wading birds are easy to identify by their white cheeks and neck, and black throat, breast and legs. Commonly found in the savannah and near rivers and lakes in Mauritania, Senegal and The Gambia they sometimes forgo a nest, and lay their eggs (between three and four) on bare rock or soil. They are noisy, aggressive and extremely gregarious.

Sunbirds
Nectariniidae (10 cm)
These small birds with hollow tongues feed on nectar and insects (species which feed on the latter have less curved and shorter beaks). The male's metallic colouring makes them easy to distinguish. In contrast, the females have dull plumage and are therefore difficult to identify. The yellow-bellied sunbird *(Nectarinia venusta)* can be found restlessly flying between orange or red flowers. While they suck nectar and have a similar appearance to the hummingbird, they cannot hover or fly backwards. Most males have a green throat and purple breast. Common in the savannah of Senegal and The Gambia, they are found in pairs, sometimes with different species.

Top: Spur-Winged Goose (JE)

Left: Spur-Winged Plover (PR)

Right: Yellow-Bellied Sunbird (JE)

Tawny Eagle
Aquila rapax (70 cm)
Commonly found in the open plains and semi-desert of most of West Africa, this eagle is generally brown and easily confused with other African eagles, especially in winter. Its varied diet includes termites, mammals (mice, gazelles etc) and lizards. It often poaches on the prey of other species and will even strike flying flamingos.

Western Reef Heron
Egretta gularis (61 cm)
Found in the coastal areas of Mauritania and south to the Gulf of Guinea islands, this slate-grey, medium-sized heron has a distinctive curved bill, white chin and throat, and brown bill. When feeding on fish, molluscs and grubs in shallow waterways, it first disturbs its prey by stirring the bottom with its feet. They are found in small groups and are generally silent.

Top: Western Reef Heron (PR)

Bottom: Tawny Eagle (RB)

White-Breasted Cormorant
Phalacrocorax carbo (85 cm)
This species is the largest of the African cormorants (see image on page 100). They have a white lower neck and upper breast. They feed mainly on fish, sometimes frogs and crustaceans, and breed in large groups, often with darters, other cormorants, herons and spoonbills. They have several predators, including the African fish eagle *(Haliaetus vocifer)* and black kite *(Milvus migrans)*.

White Pelican
Pelecanus onocrotalus (165 cm)
These large, gregarious birds can be found throughout West Africa on alkaline or freshwater lakes where there is an abundance of fish (fish make up 90% of their diet). Breeding colonies have been located in areas including south-west of Jos in Nigeria, on islets of the Mauritanian coast and north of the Senegal Delta. They are white all over with tinges of pink, have a blue bill and orange feet. The male and female are similar except that the female has a smaller crest. They feed in groups, either forming a half circle and driving the fish into shore, or plunging (singly) from a metre or so.

White Pelican (JE)

Getting There & Away

AIR
To/From the USA

Air Afrique (☎ (800) 456-9192) and Ghana Airways (☎ (212) 697-3270 or 371-2800) are the only airlines with direct flights from New York to West Africa, and they offer unbeatable deals. Air Afrique (which as of 1994 had never had a fatal accident), despite its recent financial difficulties, is probably a better airline, but Ghana Airways' flights from the USA and the UK are their best, giving Air Afrique strong competition. Air Afrique has twice-weekly flights from New York, stopping in Dakar (Senegal) and Abidjan (Côte d'Ivoire), and Ghana Airways has one flight a week to Accra (Ghana). Nigeria Airways' flights from New York to Lagos have been halted by the US Government because of the failure of Lagos' international airport to meet minimum safety standards. Service on Nigeria Airways' international flights from Europe to Lagos continue, however, and they are about on a par with those of Ghana Airways.

Iberia (☎ (800) 772-4642), Royal Air Maroc (☎ (718) 995-6991) and TAP Air Portugal (☎ (800) 221-7370) offer service to West Africa and charge the same or only slightly more. TAP Air Portugal is particularly good if you're travelling for two months or more as their fares (with a six-month restriction) are among the lowest available, but you may have to wait a day in Lisbon for a connecting flight. Also check Aeroflot (☎ (212) 397-1660) as its fares are generally rock bottom. It is much less reliable, however, which is why most agencies refuse to book flights on it. For all other flights via Europe, you'll have to pay considerably more and change planes to boot.

Fares Regular economy fares to and within Africa seem expensive but on a per-km basis are fairly standard for the industry. The problem is that there is not an array of special fares as in North America or Europe. If for whatever reason you fly to Africa on a full-fare economy ticket, buy only a one-way ticket because you can buy the return fare in local currency for about one-third less than the fare in dollars! However, if you're planning on getting visas in your home country, be warned that this could complicate things, as a few embassies in Europe and the USA (eg Nigeria, Ghana, Niger and Guinea) still require travellers to have an onward airline ticket. So check the visa requirements before you buy a one-way ticket.

Most travellers take advantage of one of the airlines' three special round-trip fares – APEX, excursion and youth fares. With Air Afrique, APEX is about a third less (US$1290 to Dakar and US$1536 to Abidjan) than the normal economy fare (US$2210 to Dakar and US$2525 to Abidjan). Excursion fares (US$1373 to Dakar and US$1641 to Abidjan) are only slightly higher on Air Afrique and offer far more flexibility.

APEX fares have far more restrictions than excursion fares. APEX fares must be purchased at least 30 days in advance, have a maximum stay limitation of, typically, 45 or 60 days, the return date cannot be changed without a 25% penalty, and no stopovers are allowed. In comparison, with excursion fares you are usually allowed at least one stopover (ie you could stop over in Dakar en route to Abidjan or, on Iberia, stop over in Spain en route to West Africa), you can stay much longer and there's no 30-day advance purchase requirement.

If you are flexible with your destination, definitely check Ghana Airways. Its flights to Accra are usually cheaper than Air Afrique's fares to Abidjan and Dakar. Most recently, Ghana Airways' round-trip fare from New York to Accra was US$1000, with a one-year return restriction. Also, if your trip will not exceed three weeks in duration, ask Air Afrique for its 'special APEX' fare which has a three-week return restriction; it

Air Travel Glossary

APEX APEX ('Advance Purchase Excursion') is a discounted ticket which must be paid for in advance. There are penalties if you wish to change it.

Baggage Allowance This will be written on your ticket: usually one 20-kg item to go in the hold, plus one item of hand luggage.

Bucket Shop An unbonded travel agency specialising in discounted airline tickets.

Bumped Just because you have a confirmed seat doesn't mean you're going to get on the plane – see Overbooking.

Cancellation Penalties If you have to cancel or change an APEX ticket there are often heavy penalties involved – insurance can sometimes be taken out against these penalties. Some airlines impose penalties on regular tickets as well, particularly against 'no show' passengers (see No Shows).

Check In Airlines ask you to check in a certain time ahead of the flight departure (usually two hours on international flights). If you fail to check in on time and the flight is overbooked, the airline can cancel your booking and give your seat to somebody else.

Confirmation Having a ticket written out with the flight and date you want doesn't mean you have a seat until the agent has checked with the airline that your status is 'OK' or confirmed. Meanwhile, you could just be 'on request'. Also, it is necessary to reconfirm onward or return bookings directly with the airline 72 hours before departure (see Reconfirmation).

Discounted Tickets There are two types of discounted fares: officially discounted (see Promotional Fares) and unofficially discounted. The lowest prices often impose drawbacks like flying with unpopular airlines, inconvenient schedules, or unpleasant routes and connections. A discounted ticket can save you things other than money – you may be able to pay APEX prices without the associated APEX advance booking and other requirements. Discounted tickets only exist where there is fierce competition.

Full Fares Airlines traditionally offer 1st-class (coded F), business-class (coded J) and economy-class (coded Y) tickets. These days there are so many promotional and discounted fares available from the regular economy class that few passengers pay full economy fare.

Lost Tickets If you lose your airline ticket, an airline will usually treat it like a travellers' cheque and, after enquiries, issue you with another one. Legally, however, an airline is entitled to treat it like cash and if you lose it then it's gone forever. Take good care of your tickets.

No Shows No shows are passengers who fail to show up for their flight, sometimes due to unexpected delays or disasters, sometimes due to simply forgetting, sometimes because they made more than one booking and didn't bother to cancel the one they didn't want. Full fare passengers who fail to turn up are sometimes entitled to travel on a later flight. The rest of us are penalised (see Cancellation Penalties).

On Request An unconfirmed booking for a flight (see Confirmation).

Open Jaws A return ticket where you fly out to one place but return from another. If available, this can save you backtracking to your arrival point.

is US$1005 to Dakar and US$1210 to Abidjan.

Travellers from 12 to 23 years of age can take advantage of Air Afrique's youth fare. The fare costs slightly less than APEX. The real advantage is that there are less restrictions – no advance purchase requirement (at least five days) and no 45-day return restriction. Ghana Airways does not offer a student fare from the USA, but along with Nigeria Airways they do offer student discounts within Africa, eg Nigeria Airways gives up to 40% off from Lagos to Nairobi, which is a huge saving but the flight is still not cheap.

A final factor to consider is the seasonal variation in prices. During the summer

Overbooking Airlines hate to fly empty seats, and since every flight has some passengers who fail to show up (see No Shows), airlines often book more passengers than they have seats. Usually the excess passengers balance those who fail to show up but occasionally somebody gets bumped. If this happens, guess who it is most likely to be? The passengers who check in late.

Promotional Fares Officially discounted fares like APEX fares which are available from travel agents or direct from the airline.

Reconfirmation At least 72 hours prior to departure time of an onward or return flight you must contact the airline and 'reconfirm' that you intend to be on the flight. If you don't do this the airline can delete your name from the passenger list and you could lose your seat. You don't have to reconfirm the first flight on your itinerary or if your stopover is less than 72 hours. It doesn't hurt to reconfirm more than once, especially if you reconfirm more than 72 hours in advance.

Restrictions Discounted tickets often have various restrictions on them – advance purchase is the most usual one (see APEX). Others are restrictions on the minimum and maximum period you must be away, such as a minimum of 14 days or a maximum of one year. See Cancellation Penalties.

Standby A discounted ticket where you only fly if there is a seat free at the last moment. Standby fares, which are not available in West Africa, are usually only available on domestic routes.

Tickets Out An entry requirement for many countries is that you have an onward or return ticket – in other words, a ticket out of the country. If you're not sure what you intend to do next, the easiest solution is to buy the cheapest onward ticket to a neighbouring country or a ticket from a reliable airline which can later be refunded if you do not use it.

Transferred Tickets Airline tickets cannot be transferred from one person to another. Travellers sometimes try to sell the return half of their ticket, but officials can ask you to prove that you are the person named on the ticket. This is unlikely to happen on domestic flights, but on international flights, tickets are almost always compared with passports. Also, if you're flying on a transferred ticket and something goes wrong with the flight (hijack, crash), there will be no record of your presence on board.

Travel Agencies Travel agencies vary widely and you should ensure you use one that suits your needs. Some simply handle tours while full-service agencies handle everything from tours and tickets to car rental and hotel bookings. A good one will do all these things and can save you a lot of money, but if all you want is a ticket at the lowest possible price, then you really need an agency specialising in discounted tickets. A discounted ticket agency, however, may not be useful for other things, such as hotel bookings.

Travel Periods Some officially discounted fares, APEX fares in particular, vary with the time of year. There is often a low (off-peak) season and a high (peak) season. Sometimes there's an intermediate or shoulder season as well. At peak times, when everyone wants to fly, not only will the officially discounted fares be higher but so will unofficially discounted fares, or there may simply be no discounted tickets available. Usually the fare depends on your outward flight – if you depart in the high season and return in the low season, you pay the high-season fare. ∎

months and around Christmas time, fares are typically US$200 to US$300 higher.

Discount Agencies Virtually all discount agencies place small adds in the Sunday travel section of local newspapers, especially the *New York Times* and the *Los Angeles Times*. There are only a few specialising in travel to Africa; some of the best are:

All Continents Travel
　5250 West Century Blvd, Suite 626, Los Angeles, CA 90045 (☎ (800) 368-6822 or (310) 337-1641)
Costa Azul Travel
　955 S Raymond Ave, Los Angeles, CA 90006 (☎ (800) 332-7202 or (213) 384-7200)

Falcon Wings Travel
    9841 Airport Blvd, Suite 818, Los Angeles, CA
    90045 (☎ (800) 230-4947 or (310) 417-3590)
Flytime Tours & Travel
    45 West 34th St, Suite 305, New York, NY 10001
    (☎ (212) 760-3737, fax 594-1082)
Hollywood Travel & Tours
    2025 I St, NW, Suite 709, Washington, DC 20006
    (☎ (202) 659-2522, fax 296-3636)
Magical Holidays
    601 Madison Ave, New York, NY 10022
    (☎ (800) 228-2208) or (212) 486-9600)
Maharaja Travels
    393 Fifth Ave at 37th St, New York, NY 10016
    (☎ (800) 228-2208 or (212) 486-9600)
Pan Express Travel
    25 West 39th St, Suite 705, New York, NY 10018
    (☎ (212) 719-9292/2937)
Spector Travel of Boston
    31 St James Ave, Boston, MA 02116 (☎ (800)
    727-1120 or (617) 338-0111)
STA Travel
    Phoenix, AZ (☎ (800) 777-0112)
Travel Trade & Tours
    (☎ (800) 935-8787, fax (212) 947-6786)

These discounters, called 'consolidators', are the equivalent of London's bucket shops. They have a quasi-legitimate status and are generally quite reliable. They undercut their competitors by buying large blocks of tickets at discount prices. It pays to call numerous agencies because their rates vary considerably. Most of them offer special round-trip fares on Air Afrique to Dakar and Abidjan, and on Ghana Airways to Accra, but prices vary considerably with the length of stay and when you go.

Three of the best and most reliable are Spector Travel of Boston, Falcon Wings Travel and STA Travel, which offers extra special fares for students under 26 years of age and normal, low-rate consolidator fares for everyone else. Spector Travel's round-trip fares to Abidjan from New York or Boston on Air Afrique are typical: US$1009/ 1252 with a maximum three-week/45-day return restriction.

Other examples include US$839/1040 to Dakar, US$919/1140 to Banjul, US$939/ 1165 to Nouakchott, and US$1009/1252 to all other West African capital cities. The above three-week return fares are, in effect, Air Afrique's special APEX fares but at a discount, and they carry the same restrictions.

If you want to stay longer than three weeks or pay less than 30 days in advance, call all the agencies. You will find that they're not all sticklers for the rules. Also, ask them for their fares with TAP Air Portugal. With Spector Travel, for example, you can get a round-trip, New York (or Boston) to Abidjan fare on TAP for US$1079 with a six-month return restriction.

One of the oldest and most popular agencies in New York is Maharaja Travels. Its fares are often the lowest of all, eg US$935 from New York to Accra, Abidjan or Bamako on Air Afrique with a maximum three-week return (US$1125 with a maximum 45-day return). In recent years, however, we have received several complaints about Maharaja. Costa Azul seems more reliable. While its discounts are not as substantial, it offers special fares to many West African destinations (eg US$1299 from LA to Lagos) and seems more flexible than most agencies. Likewise, Magical Holidays, which is also quite reliable and one of the largest operators specialising in Africa, offers great prices and maximum flexibility on one-year return air tickets as well as air-fare/hotel packages and full tours.

Another possibility is Friends of Togo, a model do-good organisation of mainly ex-Peace Corps volunteers to Togo. Twice a year, it negotiates hard-to-beat return fares with McDonald Travel to Lomé (Togo) for two weeks, available to nonmembers. There is one flight around the second week in June and another about a week before Christmas. The cost is typically around US$1200. For information, contact McDonald Travel (☎ (800) 334-8352), 1904 Front St, Durham, NC 27705.

If you wish to stay longer than 45 days, it may pay to fly to London or Amsterdam and buy a ticket from a bucket shop. This would also allow you to combine a trip to Africa with a trip to Europe. Unfortunately, some bucket shops are too understaffed to respond to mail, but you can always call. The only way to make a reservation is to pay for the ticket, which can be done by mail. Except during the Christmas holiday season, you'll be taking little risk by waiting until you arrive in London or Amsterdam to buy your ticket; the chances of getting a flight within a day or two are usually good. The wise will call first, however.

As for getting to Europe, the cheapest way is to act as a courier but you have to travel light. Return fares from New York to Europe as a courier are about US$400 in the summer season. If you're interested, subscribe to Travel Unlimited, Box 1058, Allston, MA 02134, a monthly publication which costs US$25 a year. It is filled with detailed information on courier agencies around the world, including fare listings by agency. Two among many in the USA are Now Voyager (☎ (212) 431-1616) and UTL Travel (☎ (415) 583-5074).

Those willing to travel to Europe on the spur of the moment should try stand-by brokers. Four brokers among many are Vacations to Go (☎ (800) 338-4962), Airhitch (☎ (212) 864-2000), Moments Notice (☎ (212) 980-9550) and Boston-based Last Minute Travel (☎ (617) 267-9800).

To/From Canada

There are no direct flights from Canada to West Africa, so most Canadians fly via Europe, frequently with Air Canada (☎ (800) 776-3000) to Europe, or connect with a flight out of New York to West Africa. APEX and excursion fares are also available on regularly scheduled flights to Europe from Canada. In addition, there are bucket shops in Montreal, Toronto and elsewhere that operate like those in the USA. In particular, there are some very cheap flights from Montreal to Paris. There are also some travel agencies which are not consolidators but nevertheless offer cheap flights; in Montreal you might try Tourbec (☎ (514) 288-4455 or 342-2961), 3419 rue Saint-Denis H2X 3L2. Also, NationAir (☎ (416) 922-0224), which is a small charter outfit with flights out of Hamilton (48 km from Toronto), has some good deals on one-year open return tickets

between Hamilton and London. The cost is about C$325 one way and C$600 return. NationAir also has flights to Brussels.

To/From the UK

Full-Fare Tickets Full-fare economy tickets to Africa seem terribly expensive but the cost per km is fairly standard on a worldwide basis. Excursion fares are cheaper but limit the passenger to a stay of, typically, 25 or 30 days. APEX fares are usually not available.

In general, fares are lower to Britain's ex-colonies, such as Nigeria, Ghana and The Gambia. Nigeria Airways offers the best deals. Their return London to Lagos fare, for example, is about UK£1000 economy (one-year maximum stay) and UK£900 excursion (25-day maximum stay).

Discount Tickets It's usually much cheaper to purchase tickets from a discount agency than from the airlines directly and the savings can be as much as 50%. In London (and Amsterdam), there are two distinct kinds of travel agencies. The first kind are the well-known ones like Thomas Cook which offer virtually no fare reductions unless you press them for their 'concession' tickets or go on one of their all-inclusive tours. The second group, known colloquially as bucket shops, offer rock-bottom prices on major airlines. These agencies are generally small operators (typically three to five people) and for the most part are quite reliable. They get their name from the fact that the airlines sell them a 'bucket' of tickets at a discount, and the savings are passed on to the passengers.

Round-trip fares offered by bucket shops from London to coastal West African cities range from as low as UK£350 to as high as UK£750, with most in the UK£495 to UK£595 range. Trailfinders' low-season return fares from London to Lagos and Accra, for example, start at UK£500 and UK£511, respectively. There's no advance purchase requirement and return dates can be changed.

Which airline you choose, how long you stay and when you fly (the Christmas season and approximately mid-May to mid-September are generally the high seasons, when prices generally rise about £100) all affect the ticket price. Nigeria Airways and Aeroflot are usually the cheapest but with the latter you'll have to spend at least a night in Moscow, at the airline's expense. If you prefer flying on a European airline, you'll probably find the fare costs no more on them than on most African airlines. As for the length of stay, round-trip tickets with a 30 or 45-day maximum return restriction are often about UK£75 to UK£150 cheaper than those with the return portion valid for up to one year. Airlines Travel PLC, for example, charges UK£350 year-round for a flight from London to Lagos on Nigeria Airlines with a one-month return restriction compared to UK£485 for the same flight with a one-year restriction. During the low season, Trailfinders can get you there on Alitalia for UK£500, maximum one-year return.

Some people think that because the tickets are so cheap, there must be something fishy going on. It's not true, as the great majority of bucket shops are quite reliable. The problem is that every now and then one goes bust, giving a black eye to the overall reputation of bucket shops. Shopping around for the better ones takes time but some of them are listed here. The better agencies are invariably members of the International Air Transport Association (IATA). Agencies must meet certain requirements to become members, so if the agency isn't a member of this association, you should probably look elsewhere.

It's important to go to at least three or four agencies because they don't all deal with the same airlines. Many agencies refuse to deal with Aeroflot, claiming it is too unreliable. Consequently, you'll find a wide variation in prices and availability of flights to a particular destination.

The lowest fares by far are to The Gambia. From October to April, major tour companies such as Kuoni offer package deals to The Gambia. These charter tickets are typically between UK£280 and UK£300. However, these agencies offer heavily dis-

counted 'flight only' tickets on their unfilled charters. In October, March and April, there are usually many unfilled seats. Fares on charter flights are available from Connections for as low as UK£129/199 one way/one-week return. (Connections' normal one-month return and three-month return fares to The Gambia were, in comparison, UK£369 and UK£499, respectively, at the time of writing.) Going Places offers a return fare with a three-week return restriction to Banjul on Monarch Airlines for UK£229. The cheapest way of all is simply to show up at the airport and look for a late availability flight; you can sometimes pick up a ticket for as low as UK£60 to UK£80.

To take advantage of some of the extra low charter-flight fares to The Gambia, you'll have to have all of your visas and vaccinations in order because they are likely to be available only on a space-available basis and can be purchased only a few days in advance. Go to the nearest bucket shop and ask the agent to check the price on a ticket-only basis through the major package-tour agencies such as Thompsons, Horizon or Kuoni. The maximum stay is usually from one to three weeks but, at this price, if you want to stay longer you can discard the return ticket or try to sell it in Banjul. Some travellers have managed to get the return portion for as low as UK£80. Many travel agents are unwilling to tell you about or help you with these flights, but one agency which will is Hogg Robinson (see list below). Also, you can deal directly with the charter companies themselves (for details see Package Tours, later).

As for youth fares, STA Travel, a student travel association, offers special fares for those under 26 years of age (eg UK£495 for a round-trip ticket to The Gambia on Swissair with a 90-day return restriction and UK£524 for a round-trip ticket to Accra on KLM with a 90-day return restriction), but many of its fares are no lower than those offered by more standard bucket shops.

The Air Travel Advisory Bureau (☎ (0171) 636-5000) is a free travel advisory service that can be very helpful. They refer enquirers to only reputable bucket shops but not always to the cheapest.

The following bucket shops, all of which are members of IATA, appear to be reliable and well established, and some of them will even respond by mail to enquiries:

Africa Travel Centre
    21 Leigh St, London WC1 9QX (☎ (0171) 387-1211, fax 383-7512). Part of a chain, with branches in Australia, New Zealand, USA and Kenya. Specialises in flights to all parts of Africa. Has a brochure-request service, video lounge and visa agency.
African Travel Specialists
    Victoria House, 98 Victoria St, London SW1E 5JL (☎ (0171) 630-5434, fax 630-5470). Concentrates on flights to West Africa; has good deals on Ghanaian and Nigerian airlines. Some staff are West African and have good local knowledge.
African World Travel Services
    Radnor House, 93 Regent St, London W1R 7TG (☎ (0171) 734 7181/2). Agency for almost all airlines serving West Africa from London; offers one-way fares.
Afro-Asian Travel Ltd
    Linen Hall, 162 Regent St, London W1R JTB (☎ (0171) 437-8255/6). Agency for most airlines serving West Africa.
Airlines Travel PLC
    44 Conduit St, London W1 (☎ (0171) 437-5555)
Connections
    93 Wimpole St, London W1 (☎ (0171) 495-5545). Government bonded.
Cruxton Travel
    (☎ (0181) 868-0942). Offers return fares to: Dakar UK£495, Lagos UK£495, Abidjan UK£530.
Euro Asean Travel Ltd
    35 Kensington Park Rd, London W11 2EU (☎ (0171) 221-0900). Responds immediately and informatively by letter to enquiries.
Going Places
    106 Bishopsgate, London EC2 4AX (☎ (0171) 628-3333)
Hogg Robinson Ltd
    Crazem House, Kingsway WC2 (☎ (0171) 405-1245). Consolidators for many airlines rather than a bucket shop.
The London Flight Centre
    131 Earls Court Rd, London (☎ (0171) 244-6411 or 727-4290). Deals with Aeroflot (among other airlines), eg UK£499 to Accra (one-year return restriction).

London Student Travel
    52 Grosvenor Gardens, London SW1 0AG (☎ (0171) 730-8111). Fares appear to be among the lowest.
STA Travel
    86 Old Brompton Rd, London SW7 (☎ (0171) 937-9962)
Trailfinders Ltd
    44-50 Earls Court Rd, London W8 6EJ (☎ (0171) 938-3366); 194 Kensington High St, London W8 7RJ (☎ (0171) 938-3939); and 58 Deansgate, Manchester M3 2FF (☎ (0161) 839-6969). This agency is one of the best and deals with most airlines except Aeroflot. Ask for a copy of their magazine *Trailfinders*.
The World Sports Supporters Club
    40 James St, London W1M 5HS (☎ (0171) 935-9107). Well-known, reliable agency unique in selling tickets on flights originating in Africa.

To/From France

Excursion fares from Paris usually come with a 30-day or 60-day maximum stay restriction. However, Air Afrique offers excursion fares originating in New York which allow young travellers to stay in West Africa for up to three months. Young people may find flying through Paris advantageous because Air France and Air Afrique offer a youth fare (ages 12 to 23) with a one-year return restriction for about 40% less than the regular economy round-trip fare. A normal return fare from Paris to Abidjan is 4800FF (4565FF to Ouagadougou) with a maximum stay of 60 days, and 7800FF for more than 60 days. One potential big advantage of flying with Air Afrique is that you can buy a return ticket from Paris with arrival in one African city and departure from another; the price is calculated as a return ticket from the furthest city.

The special fares offered by travel agencies in France are, in general, as good or better than those offered in London. However, most of them limit you to a maximum stay of 30 days. Some agencies offer special round-trip fares valid for a year; the typical price is about 25% higher than with the 30-day restriction.

French travel agencies offering special fares include:

Any Way
>46, rue des Lombards, 75001 Paris (metro: Châtelet) (☎ (01) 40-28-00-74, fax 42-36-11-41). One of the few agencies in France which acts like a bucket shop.

FUAJ
>Federation of Youth Hostels, 10 rue de Notre-Dame-de-Lorette, 75009 Paris (☎ (01) 42-66-18-18). Offers special fares to young people as well as organised tours.

GO Voyages
>2 rue du Pont-Neuf, 75008 Paris (metro: Madeleine) (☎ (01) 42-66-18-18 and, for information and reservations ☎ (01) 49-23-26-86). This agency offers 20 to 25% reductions on the normal seven to 30-day excursion rates, plus return tickets valid for up to a year for 25 to 50% more. Departures are from Paris and Brussels, some from London. Destinations include about half of the countries covered in this book.

Nouvelles Frontières
>87 blvd de Grenelle, 75015 Paris (metro: La Motte-Picquet) (☎ (01) 41-41-58-58); 31 allée de Tourny, 33000 Bordeaux (☎ 56-44-60-38); 34 rue Franklin, 69002 Lyons (☎ 78-37-16-47); and 11 rue d'Haxo, 13001 Marseilles (☎ 91-54-18-48). This agency offers return fares to Senegal, Mali, Côte d'Ivoire and Togo for about two-thirds the excursion fare. Paris-Abidjan return is about 4000FF, with a two-month return restriction. Many of its special fares, however, have a limited stay (one to four weeks), and limited cancellation rights. Ask about its reduced hotel rates and excursions.

Nouvelle Liberté
>26 rue Soufflot, 75005 Paris (metro: Luxembourg) (☎ (01) 43-25-43-99); 53 cours Clemenceau, 33000 Bordeaux (☎ (01) 56-81-50-50); Place des Jacobins, rue Jean-de-Tourne, 69002, Lyons (☎ 72-41-07-07); and 393 av du Prado, 13008 Marseilles (☎ 91-77-80-00). This agency has its own airline, Air Liberté, and can thus offer especially advantageous fares to various destinations.

Uniclam 2000
>11 rue du 4 Septembre, 75002 Paris (metro: Opéra) (☎ (01) 40-15-07-07); 16 rue du Dr-Mazet, 38000 Grenoble (☎ 76-46-00-08); and 19 quai Romain-Rolland, 69005 Lyons (☎ 78-42-75-85). This agency has some unbeatable fares. Tickets can be purchased to eight countries, from Senegal to the Congo, mostly good for one year. Round-trip Paris-Dakar is 3580FF. Prices are about 600FF less if the trip does not exceed four weeks. Flights during peak periods, such as at Christmas time, have a surcharge of about 700FF. The agency also offers package deals including hotels.

To/From Belgium

Sabena flies to Accra, Abidjan, Bamako, Conakry, Cotonou, Dakar, Kano, Lomé and Lagos. Travel agencies to try in Brussels include:

Acotra World
>Rue de la Madeleine, 51, Brussels 1000 (☎ (02) 512-86-07, fax 512-39-74). This agency offers special prices to teachers, students and recent students under 31 years of age. Destinations include Bamako and Lagos.

CJB L'Autre Voyage
>Chaussée d'Ixelles, 216, Brussels 1050 (☎ (02) 640-97-85, fax 646-35-95). Offers special fares for students and young people.

Nouvelles Frontières
>Blvd Lemonnier, 2, Brussels 1000 (☎ (02) 513-76-36). Offers the same fares as Nouvelles Frontières in Paris.

Services Voyages ULB
>Campus ULB, av Paul-Héger, 22, Brussels. Offers discount fares to students.

Taxistop-Airstop
>Promenade de l'Alma, 57, Brussels 1200 (☎ (02) 779-08-46). Offers discount fares.

To/From Germany

In Munich, ARD (☎ (089) 759-2609/45) at Königwieserstrasse 89, 8 Munich 71, specialises in cheap air fares to Africa. Its lowest fares usually have a 35-day return restriction; those with a one-year return restriction are about 50% higher. Lufthansa has flights to various West African coastal cities, including Abidjan, Accra and Lagos.

To/From Switzerland

From Zürich or Geneva, Swissair has flights to various West African coastal cities. For discount air fares, try Artou (☎ (022) 311-84-08), 8 rue de Rive, Geneva and Nouvelles Frontières (☎ (02) 732-04-03), 10 rue des Chantepoulet, 1201 Geneva.

To/From Australia

There are no direct flights from Australia to West Africa. The basic options are to fly via East Africa, North Africa or Europe. There are now some interesting Round-The-World (RTW) fares with Qantas and Continental, allowing you to stop in Nairobi and Harare.

The only direct flight to continental Africa is with Qantas to Harare but at A$2442 return

(90-day maximum stay) from Perth, this is one of the most expensive options. There are no cheap flights to West Africa from Zimbabwe.

A better option is to fly to Nairobi and then pick up a return ticket to West Africa from there. This usually involves flying to Singapore and connecting with another flight to Nairobi.

Ethiopian Airlines provides a weekly service from Bangkok (Thailand) to Addis Ababa, with onward flights to Niamey, Bamako and Dakar and to Lagos, Accra and Abidjan.

The high cost of flying to Africa makes flying via Europe a viable alternative. A low-season ticket to Europe costs around A$1700 return and you can then buy a bucket-shop ticket to West Africa in London or Paris.

A good place to start when you're shopping around is STA Travel or Flight Centres International; both have offices in all major cities.

LAND
Expeditions by Truck

There are numerous companies in the UK and some on the Continent which take travellers across the Sahara to West Africa or to East Africa via West Africa. The latter typically go through Algeria, Niger, Nigeria and Cameroun en route to Kenya; others pass through Mali, Burkina Faso, Togo and Benin instead of through Niger.

These trips take one to five months depending on the itinerary and are not for everybody. Truck breakdowns and border closings requiring drastic changes in itinerary are warnings that shouldn't be taken lightly. The overland vehicles are almost invariably remodelled trucks, with seats down the sides, carrying from 10 to 24 people. The price is very reasonable considering the distance covered and the time involved. Tracks, for example, offers a six-week, one-way trans-Saharan trip from London to Kano (and vice versa) for UK£875 plus the food kitty (UK£150) and return flight to London. Exodus Expeditions charges about the same for a six-week, one-way trip overland from Tunisia to Togo via the Reggane-Gao route, Timbuktu and Mopti. African Trails charges UK£800 (plus UK£130 for the kitty) for its eight-week trip from London to Ghana.

The base price of the classical London to Nairobi trip via West Africa varies anywhere from about UK£1000 to UK£2400, depending largely on the company, the number of passengers per vehicle (the more the cheaper), the length of the trip (which can vary from 15 to about 27 weeks), and the number of side excursions. Incidentals, including the food kitty (typically UK£20 a week), visa fees (typically around UK£220), optional trip insurance (typically UK£100 to UK£150), optional side trips, park entrance fees, return flights to London (typically UK£240 with Aeroflot) and spending money will, together, add at least another UK£1000 to UK£1500, thus doubling the base cost in many instances. Burkima Africa, for example, offers a 22-week trip from London to Nairobi for UK£1350 but emphasises that the UK£20 a week food kitty, return flight (UK£240), visas and other incidentals will probably add up to at least as much. Encounter Overland, which is one of the oldest and best outfits, offers a 16-week, one-way trip through 14 countries from London to Nairobi (and back) via West Africa for about the same amount, while Tracks offers a 15-week trip with a similar itinerary for UK£1900, including game park fees but not the kitty (UK£20 a week).

Tracks also offers a longer 18-week 'West African expedition' for UK£2350 plus kitty (UK£600) which is an extended London to Nairobi trip with more time spent in West African countries. The cheapest of all is probably Economic Expeditions, which has 24-passenger vehicles and charges just UK£1180 for a long 22-week trip, including the food kitty (an estimated UK£1950 including all visas, park entrance fees and return flight from Nairobi). In Germany, one of the most long-standing overland companies is Explorer, which offers a similar 15-week trip to Nairobi via West Africa.

These trips offer the opportunity (at a very reasonable price) to see just about every kind of environment that Africa has to offer. The disadvantage is that they involve a lot of time in a fairly slow truck. Most days are spent riding from sunrise to sunset; the rest of the time goes to eating, setting up tents, cooking and performing designated duties. Since the quality of the guides varies greatly, be sure that you meet your trip leader before signing up; a bad one can ruin the whole trip. For those with a little time to blow, these trips offer a safe way to see Africa and an unforgettable adventure at a cheap price.

Virtually all of the British companies offering such trips advertise in *TNT* or the Saturday edition of the *Guardian* in the overseas travel section, both published in London. There are about 20 or so small travel companies in the UK offering such trips; those in the USA are usually representatives of these companies. In Germany, they advertise in *Abenteuer & Reisen* and *Tours*. The most well-known companies include:

USA & Canada

The Adventure Center
1311 63rd St, Suite 200, Emeryville, CA 94608 (☎ (800) 227-8747 or (510) 654-1879) and 17 Hayden St, Toronto, Ontario M4Y 2P2 (☎ (416) 922-7584). This outfit acts as a clearing house for the top European companies, such as Guerba and Encounter Overland, and thus offers more trips than any other operator in the USA. Group sizes are usually kept to 20 people or less, nevertheless costs (eg US$4120 for a 16-week trip from London to Nairobi with Encounter Overland and US$3830 for a 15-week trip from Senegal to Tanzania with the same company) are lower than the norm in the USA because of its hook-up with European companies, which are generally cheaper than North American companies.

Himalayan Travel
Box 481, Greenwich, CT 06836 (☎ (800) 225-2380). Represents Tracks in London.

Safari-Center International
(☎ (800) 223-6046)

UK

Africa Explored
Rose Cottage, Summerleaze, Newport (☎ (0633) 880-224, fax 882-128)

African Trails
126B Chiswick High Rd, London W4 1PU (☎ (0181) 742-7724, fax 742-8621)

Bukima Africa
55 Huddlestone Rd, Willesden Green, London NW2 5DL (☎ (0181) 451-2446)

Economic Expeditions
29 Cunnington St, Chiswick, London W4 5ER (☎ (0181) 995-7707, fax 742-7707)

Encounter Overland
267 Old Brompton Rd, London SW5 (☎ (0171) 370-6845)

Exodus Expeditions
9 Weir Rd, Balham, London SW12 0LT (☎ (0181) 673-0859, fax 673-0779)

Explorer Expeditions
(☎ (0633) 257-561)

Guerba Expeditions
101 Eden Vale Rd, Westbury, Wiltshire BA13 3QX (☎ (0373) 826-611). One of the oldest, most highly regarded outfits.

Hobo Expeditions
Wissett Place, Halesworth, Suffolk IP19 8HY (☎ (0986) 600-873-124)

Kumuka Expeditions
40 Earls Court Rd, London W8 6EJ (☎ (0171) 937-8855)

Tracks
12 Abingdon Rd, London W8 6AF (☎ (0171) 937-3028/9, fax 937-3176)

Truck Africa
37 Ranelagh Gardens Mansions, Fulham, London SW6 3UQ (☎ (0171) 731-6142, fax 371-7445)

Germany

Explorer
Hüttenstrasse 17, 4000 Düsseldorf 1 (☎ (0211) 37-0011, fax 37-7079)

West African Travel
Wilhelm Leuscher Strasse 228, 6103 Griesheim (☎ (06155) 63-336)

Lama Expedition
Roderbergweg 106, 60311 Frankfurt/Main 60 (☎ (069) 447-897)

Travel Overland
Nordenstrasse 42, 8000 Munich 40 (☎ (089) 21-8353)

Ticket-Shop
Theresienstrasse 66, 8000 Munich 2 (☎ (089) 28-0850)

Other European Countries

Afriesj Expedities
Hemonystraat 33, 1074 BM Amsterdam (☎ (020) 662-3953, fax 675-5015). This outfit is the largest in the Netherlands specialising in adventure travel trips to Africa. Their programme includes several trips to West Africa in small groups using expedition trucks.

Caravanes de Jeunesse Belge
6 rue, Mercelis, Brussels 1050, Belgium (☎ (02) 511-6406)

Jerrycan Expedition
Rue Sautter 23, 1205 Geneva, Switzerland (☎ (022) 46-9282)

SEA
To/From the USA

From North America, the only shipping company that has fairly regular passenger-carrying freighters to West Africa appears to be Lykes Lines. Their freighters typically leave from New Orleans; itineraries vary but may include Dakar, Abidjan, Tema (Ghana) and Douala (Cameroun). Other than this, there appear to be only vessels chartered for a particular shipment. While they might accept a passenger or two, you'd have to go down to the docks to find out about them. For general information and enquiries, contact the Freighter Travel Club of America (see below) or Carolyn's Cruises (☎ (415) 897-4039), 32 Garner Drive, Novato, CA 94947.

There are several newsletters loaded with information on freighters:

Ford's Freighter Guide
    19448 Londelius St, Northbridge, CA 91324. It is published twice a year, costs about US$10 and lists more than 30 freighter companies and their itineraries.
Freighter Cruise Service Newsletter
    5925 Monkland Ave, Montreal, Quebec H4A 1G7. This is a free thrice-yearly newsletter (one of the best) with freighter schedules, including those to Africa.
Freighter Space Advisory
    This newsletter, which lists cabin types, rates and worldwide itineraries, is published twice monthly by Freighter World Cruises, 180 South Lake Ave, No 335-1, Pasadena, CA 91101 (☎ (818) 449-3106, fax 449-9573). Annual subscription costs US$33.
Freighter Travel News
    This is a monthly newsletter published by the Freighter Travel Club of America, Box 12693, Salem, OR 97309. The subscription fee, which is about US$25, includes membership and a question and answer service.
Traveltips
    This is published six times a year by Traveltips Cruise & Freighter Travel Association, PO Box 218-B2, Flushing, NY 11358 (☎ (800) 872-8584 or (718) 939-2400). The annual membership fee costs US$15 and includes a subscription to the magazine.

To/From Europe

From Europe, there are still a few romantics who occasionally hop on a freighter. It is only for those with a few extra shekels. A typical trip from Europe, say Antwerp, takes about eight days to Dakar, 13 days to Abidjan, and 17 days to Lagos.

Of the lines serving West Africa, you cannot do better than the Swiss Nautilus Line, c/o Keller Shipping AG (☎ (061) 237940), Holbeinstrasse 68, 4002 Basel; in Douala c/o Socopao, Quai de la Marine, 5; in Abidjan c/o Transcap. Its freighters, which are reportedly quite clean, leave from Genoa and Marseilles to the Congo, stopping at Dakar, Tema, Lagos and Douala. To Dakar, for example, Nautilus charges about 1000 Swiss francs one way; the price includes meals. If you're shipping a vehicle, count on paying about 50 to 75% extra for the vehicle, depending on its length and weight.

From the UK, your best bet is probably Grimaldi Lines (☎ (0171) 930-5683), Eagle House, 109 Jermyn St, London SW1Y 6ES. It has two large 42,500-ton, Italian flag vessels, the *Repubblica di Genova* and the *Repubblica di Amalfi*, periodically departing from Tilbury (London's port city) for Lagos. Each has a pool, gym, and TV lounge and can accommodate up to 65 passengers. Their rates are typical and vary according to the number of berths per cabin, the location of the cabins, and your destination. The one-way fare to Dakar, Conakry or Freetown ranges from US$1125 per person (including meals) for an inside four-birth cabin to US$2320 for a single outside cabin. The corresponding fares to Tema, Lomé, Cotonou or Lagos are 33% higher. Grimaldi's sales agencies include Strand Cruise & Travel Centre in London (listed below), Freighter World Cruises in Pasadena, CA (☎ (818) 449-3106, fax 449-9573), Transports & Voyages in Paris (☎ (01) 44-94-20-40), DER-Traffic in Frankfurt (☎ (069) 9588-1753) and A Verder in Amsterdam (☎ (020) 624-1677, fax 622-8093).

Another possibility is the UK West African Line; it has freighters from Tilbury to Lagos and even though it doesn't cater to passengers, there's often room for one or two on their freighters.

For information on these and other freighters from British ports with passenger service to West Africa, call Lloyds Shipping (☎ (0206) 772-277) and ask for its 'loading list'. Or consult the monthly *ABC Shipping Guide*, available from World Time Table Centre c/o Reed Travel Group (☎ (0582) 600-111), Church St, Dunstable, Beds LU5 4HB, UK. Better yet, call Strand Cruise & Travel Centre (☎ (0171) 836-6363, fax 497-0078), Charing Cross Shopping Concourse, The Strand, London WC2N 4HZ. A very helpful outfit, it has detailed brochures and sailing schedules and can make bookings on vessels of Grimaldi Lines, Polish Ocean Lines (POL) and others.

For sailings from Continental ports, contact POL, which offers some of the lowest fares. From Hamburg, it has five small, 7000-ton freighters serving the Hamburg to Douala route, with departures twice monthly and stops in Antwerp, Las Palmas and seven West African ports. The round trip from Hamburg to Douala and back takes from 60 to 80 days and costs UK£1240 per person in a twin cabin, including meals (UK£1360 in a single cabin). Most travellers are, of course, only interested in one-way fares, but these must be negotiated and depend on availability. POL's London agent is Gdynia America Shipping Lines Ltd (☎ (0171) 251-3389 or 253-9561, fax 250-3625), 238 City Rd, London EC1V 2QL. In Germany, try Hamburg-Süd Reiseagentur Gmbh (☎ (040) 370-5591), Ost-West-Strasse 59, 2000 Hamburg 11. In the Netherlands, contact Pakhold-Rotterdam BV (☎ (010) 302911), Box 544, Van Weerden Poelmanweg 25-31, Rotterdam.

From France, SITRAM (☎ (01) 49-00-02-01, Tour Atlantic, 92080 Paris Cedex 6; or ☎ (225) 36-92-00, 01 BP 1546, Abidjan 01, Côte d'Ivoire) has freighters twice a month from Bordeaux to Abidjan. The trip costs about 8500FF, ie about twice the one-way economy air fare. When there's not a full load, the ship stops in Dakar; otherwise, there are no intermediate stops.

From Antwerp, you can take Compagnie Maritime Zaïroise (CMZ) or Compagnie Maritime Belge (CMB), both of which offer fortnightly cargo services to Zaïre, stopping at Dakar and Abidjan. The trip is about 15 days to Zaïre and costs about 2000 Belgium francs (Bf) for a single-berth crew cabin per day. CMB has two cargo ships, the *Esprit* and the *Quellin*, with limited passenger accommodation; fares start at Bf2500 and Bf2000 per day, respectively. CMZ has a passenger boat, the *Kananga*, with single fares to Zaïre starting from Bf60,000, as well as cheaper cargo ships with fares from around Bf2000 per day. For more details, contact CMB (☎ (03) 223-2111, telex 72304), St Katelijnevest 61, B-2000, Antwerp.

PACKAGE TOURS

For older travellers and those who have significant fears of Africa even after reading this book (or perhaps because of it!), package tours are probably the best solution. Moreover, some of the more exotic offerings, especially with the French companies, allow you to do things that you could not possibly do otherwise. Nouvelles Frontières, for example, offers a one-week chartered sailing trip in the Casamance area of Senegal for about US$1000 plus air fare.

In the USA, one of the best tour agencies is African American Studies Program (see below). It offers study/travel programmes intended to increase your awareness of the many cultures in Africa. Prices range from about US$1100 to US$3000, including air fare.

Henderson Tours operating out of Atlanta has tours covering 11 countries from Senegal to Gabon. A 14-day tour of Senegal, The Gambia, and Côte d'Ivoire, for example, costs about US$1850 plus air fare. The agencies listed below are more affordable than many, with interesting itineraries.

Unfortunately, most agencies in the UK offer only beach vacations in The Gambia and Sierra Leone coupled with a few side trips into the interior. The attraction of these countries is obvious: miles of beautiful sand beaches, virtually guaranteed sun and, unlike most of West Africa, safe swimming. Particularly during the off-season (June to

October), it's sometimes possible to get a reduced stand-by rate for one of these package holidays if you're prepared to travel on the spur of the moment; such packages (air fare, hotel and half board) can be cheaper than the bucket-shop air fares. Some travellers just take the plane and chuck the hotel.

From the USA

African American Studies Program
120 South LaSalle St, Suite 1144, Chicago, Ill 60603 (☎ (312) 443-0929)

African Holidays
Box 36959, Tuscon, AZ 85740 (☎ (800) 528-0168)

Borton Overseas
5516 Lyndale Ave South, Minneapolis, MN 55410 (☎ (800) 843-0602). Trips to The Gambia and Senegal, which include canoe trips down river to the wildlife-filled Sine Saloum Delta, cost US$1090 and US$1050 (land cost), respectively, and are scheduled year-round.

Henderson Tours
931 Martin Luther King St, Atlanta, GA 30314 (☎ (800) 241-4644)

Magical Holidays
Previously listed.

Select World Tours
(☎ (800) 345-9690). Appeals to adventurous young professionals and has trips to Senegal, Togo and Côte d'Ivoire.

From the UK

Enterprise/Redwing Holidays
Ground Star House, London Rd, Crawley, West Sussex RH10 2TB (☎ (0293) 560-777)

Horizon Holidays Ltd
Broadway, Edgbaston Five Ways, Birmingham B15 1BB (☎ (021) 6432-7272)

Insight Travel
6 Norton Rd, Garstang, Preston, Lancashire PR3 1JY, UK (☎ (01995) 60-6095, fax 60-2124). This aptly named company runs excellent 'host-based' trips in Ghana. For more details, see Tours in that chapter.

Kuoni Travel Ltd
Kuoni House, Dorking, Surrey RH5 4AZ (☎ (0171) 499-8636 in London)

Twickers World
22 Church St, Twickenham, Middlesex (☎ (0181) 892-7600)

Thomson Holidays
Greater London House, Hampstead Rd, London NW1 7SD (☎ (0171) 439-2211)

From France

Africatour
9/11 av Franklin Roosevelt, 75008 Paris (☎ (01) 47-23-78-59)

Airtour Afrique
36 av de l'Opéra, 75083 Paris (metro: Opéra) (☎ (01) 42-66-90-89)

Bureau des Voyages de la Jeunesse (BVJ)
20 rue Jean Jacques-Rousseau, 75001 Paris (☎ (01) 42-36-88-18)

FRAM
120 rue de Rivoli, 75001 Paris (metro: Châtelet) (☎ (01) 40-26-30-31, fax 40-26-73-58)

Jet Tours
2 rue du Pont-Neuf, 75001 Paris (metro: Pont-Neuf) (☎ (01) 40-41-82-04); 5 rue Grolée, 69002 Lyons (☎ 78-37-47-87); and 276 av du Prado, 13008 Marseilles (☎ 91-22-19-19). Offers a wide assortment of moderately priced to expensive vacation opportunities in West Africa.

Nouvelles Frontières
Previously listed.

Rêve-Vacances
9 rue Kepler, 75016 Paris (☎ (01) 47-20-63-33)

Uniclam
Previously listed.

From Belgium & Germany

CJB
Brussels, previously listed.

Uniclam
Brussels, previously listed.

Afrika Tours Individuell
Schwanthalerstrasse 22, 800 Munich 2 (☎ (089) 59-6081)

Air Conti Flugreisen GmbH
Neurhauserstrasse 34, 8000 Munich 2

ARD
Konigswieserstrasse 89, 8 Munich 71 (☎ (089) 759-2609)

ADVENTURE TRIPS

Some organisations and travel agencies specialise in adventure travel, from canoe trips down the Niger River to camel trips across the desert. People on these trips experience Africa in ways that even most people living in Africa never have. Wilderness Travel, for example, offers a 23-day Mali adventure including a three-day boat trip on the Niger River to Timbuktu for US$4075, including air fare within Mali but not to/from Mali. It also offers a 17-day trip with a similar itinerary for US$3570 and, on occasion, a special 32-day expedition to Senegal,

The Gambia, Mali, Burkina Faso and Côte d'Ivoire for US$5895 plus air fare. Trips take place only during the November-February period.

Another up-market company is Turtle Tours, which sponsors five West African trips, including a 16-day overland expedition to Timbuktu via the desert and the Niger River, for about US$4500 plus air fare. Other trips include ones to tribal festivals in Ghana, Togo and Benin, to Mali's Dogon Country and, in September, to the famous Cure Salée in Niger. Forum Travel International specialises in eco-tourism and sponsors adventurous trips to Senegal, Mali, Mauritania and Niger. One trip, for instance, is billed as a study of the nature and cultures of Senegal, another involves exploring the Aïr Mountains in north-eastern Niger.

Spector Travel of Boston offers two-week, cross cultural exchange programmes in Senegal. On one trip, participants stay with Senegalese families in Dakar and study dance, music or weaving with local artists. The cost, including air fare from New York, meals and lodging, is typically around US$2200.

The International Bicycle Fund is a non-profit organisation dedicated to fostering increased use of bicycles for public transport. Its bicycle trips are a fantastic way to explore the countryside and meet the people. They normally last two weeks, consist of from six to 13 cyclists, are relatively inexpensive, cover about 550 km (mostly flat terrain), and focus on the cultural experience rather than on the biking; indeed, most of its participants are not serious bikers. The trips in West Africa invariably take place during October and November. In 1994, there were four trips – one in Mali, another in Senegal/The Gambia, another in Ghana and another in Togo. Tour prices, which include all meals and lodging (mostly in-village accommodation), range from US$990 to US$1290 plus air fare.

In the UK, companies to contact include Explore Worldwide, Afrikan Heritage and Kinkiliba Tours. Explore Worldwide, for example, offers a 16-day adventure to Djenne and Dogon Country in Mali; accommodation is basic and some travel is by canoe. The cheapest outfit is Afrikan Heritage, which offers a 14-day trip to The Gambia for just UK£435 including the flight, accommodation and travel insurance.

All trips are designed to provide the opportunity to participate in and observe cultural activities such as village festivals, workshops and bush and sea safaris. Kinkiliba Tours offers a tour of similar length to The Gambia and the Casamance region of Senegal for UK£392 plus air fare. Trips, which are limited to a maximum of seven people, include a nine-day adventure by Land Rover and dugout canoe to coastal communities and into the hinterlands and the opportunity to meet people. Participants spend their nights in village-run campements, socialising, dancing and drumming with the locals.

Terres d'Aventure, in Paris, offers a 16-day river and hiking adventure through Sierra Leone plus a 16-day adventure in Mali's Dogon area for about 17,500FF and 16,000FF, respectively. Another Paris-based outfit, Uniclam, is involved in a wide assortment of adventure tours, including trips in Mali's Dogon area for 14 days for about 10,000FF, the Agadez-Aïr Mountains (nine days for 8500FF) and Togo-Benin.

From the USA

Borton Overseas
   5516 Lyndale Ave South, Minneapolis, MN 55419 (☎ (800) 843-0602, fax (612) 827-1544). It has two-week adventure trips every January to West Africa, with changing itineraries; the cost is typically around US$3600 plus air fare.

Cross Cultural Adventurers
   Box 3285, Arlington, VA 22203 (☎ (703) 204-2717). It has two-week cultural trips to Timbuktu and Djenne which include travelling by canoe on the Niger River and some camping. The cost is US$3600 plus air fare.

Forum Travel International
   91 Gregory Lane, Suite 21, Pleasant Hill, CA 94523 (☎ (415) 671-2900)

International Bicycle Fund
   4887 Columbia Drive South, Seattle, WA 98108 (☎/fax (206) 628-9314)

Mountain Travel
   6420 Fairmont Ave, El Cerrito, CA 94530 (☎ (800) 227-2384)

Operation Crossroads Africa
(☎ (800) 422-3742)
Spector Travel of Boston
Previously listed
Turtle Tours
Box 1147, Carefree, AZ 85377 (☎ (800) 283-2334 or (602) 488-3688)
Wilderness Travel
801 Allston Way, Berkeley, CA 94710 (☎ (800) 368-2794, fax (510) 548-0347). The largest and most successful adventure travel agency in the USA, largely due to the outstanding quality of its guides.

From the UK
Afrikan Heritage
60B Rowley Way, Abbey Rd, London NW8 0SJ (☎ (0171) 328-4376)
Explore Worldwide
1 Frederick St, Aldershot GU11 1LQ (☎ (01252) 319448, fax 343170). Offers exploratory trips to Mali.
Kinkiliba Tours
(☎ (0181) 880-1090)

From France
Deserts
6-8 rue Quincampoix, 75004 Paris (metro: Châtelet-Les-Halles) (☎ (01) 48-04-88-40, fax 48-04-33-57). Specialises in trips to the desert, including to the Sahara, Mali and Niger.
Explorator
16 place de la Madeleine, 75008 Paris (metro: Madeleine) (☎ (01) 42-66-66-24, fax 42-66-53-89). Destinations include the Sahara region, Mali, Benin and Togo.
Moto Contact Évasion
26 route de Grasse, 06800 Cagnes-sur-Mer (☎ 93-22-50-31). Organises relatively expensive trips for motorcyclists and provides the air fare and all equipment, including motorcycles.
Nouvelles Frontières
Previously listed
Terres d'Aventure
16 rue Saint-Victor, 75005 Paris (metro: Maubert-Mutualité) (☎ (01) 43-29-94-50, fax 43-29-96-31) and 9 rue des Remparts-d'Ainay, 69002 Lyons (☎ 78-42-99-94). Offers various adventurous overland trips in West Africa, particularly in the Sahara region.
Uniclam
Previously listed

From Germany
Explorer
Hüttenstrasse 17, 4000 Düsseldorf 1 (☎ (0211) 37-0011, fax 37-7079)

Minitrek Expeditionen
Bergstrasse 153, 6900 Heidelberg 1 (☎ (06221) 40-1443)
Sliva Expeditionen
Postfach 548, 8000 Munich 33 (☎ (0211) 37-9064)
Travel Overland
Nordenstrasse 42, 8000 Munich 40 (☎ (089) 21-8353)

From Other European Countries
Explorado
61 Ave Legrand, Brussels 1050, Belgium (☎ (02) 648-22-69)
Jerrycan Expedition
Rue Sautter 23, 1205 Geneva, Switzerland (☎ (022) 469282)
Pampa Explor
Chaussée de Waterloo, 735, Brussels 1180, Belgium (☎ (02) 343-75-90). Specialises in trips in the Sahara.
Strichting Explorer
Manixstraat 403, 1017 PJ Amsterdam, Holland (☎ (020) 255424)

Crossing the Sahara

The first crossing by automobile was in 1922 when a group of French people in five Citroën trucks made the north-south crossing in 20 days. Now the adventure is done all the time. From November to early March, temperatures are fairly tolerable.

The desert offers lots of surprises. It's not all sand dunes like you saw in *Lawrence of Arabia*. On the contrary, huge sand dunes are seen only occasionally on the most popular routes. You'll see spectacular mountains in some areas, hard flat sand in other areas, and lots of rocks in still other areas, with an oasis now and then to clean your dirty body and perk up your spirits.

Each environment offers its own special memories. Don't be surprised if you see a camel caravan or two, with a princess perched on a fancy saddle with flowing white material draped over four posts to shield her from the sun. When you see this, you'll know you're really in the Sahara. If you meet a few Tuareg in the middle of nowhere, unless you're in northern Niger there's nothing to worry about even though they used to be famous fighters and to this day would no more be seen without their swords than cowboys used to be without their guns.

Despite what you may have heard and read, under normal conditions the trip is not particularly dangerous if the minimum precautions are observed. It's done all the time, even by motorcyclists who frequently go off the main routes and chart their own course. One warning, however, concerns crossing the Sahara during the hottest period, June to August. Only a few vehicles cross then and, if you're hitchhiking, be prepared for some long waiting periods. Those driving will have their equipment and provisions inspected by the Algerian police. If you don't seem prepared, they may not allow you to cross. A second even stronger warning is that in recent years the internal political situation in Algeria and northern Niger has become extremely dangerous. In both countries, foreigners have been attacked and killed; don't attempt a crossing without, at a minimum, consulting your embassy.

The best English-language book from a logistical standpoint is the *Sahara Handbook* (1990) by Simon & Jan Glen; it's a gold mine of information on equipment, routes and techniques. You can get a copy from Roger Lascelles Publishers (☎ (0181) 847-0935) at 47 York Rd, Brentford, Middlesex TW8 0QP, UK. Lascelles also publishes *Overland & Beyond* (1981) by Jonathan & Theresa Hewat; this anecdotal account of a transcontinental journey will give you a good idea of what you'll be up against in the Sahara and beyond.

ROUTE THROUGH NIGER

The Algiers-Tamanrasset-Agadez route, called the Route du Hoggar, is a far less popular route than in the past because of the violent political conditions in Algeria and northern Niger. This route was closed completely to tourist traffic in 1993 and 1994, although things may improve if peace returns to this part of Niger. (For more details, see the Niger chapter.)

The route is paved except for about 500 km. If your vehicle breaks down in the unpaved section, you are fairly assured of being able to hitch a ride. It's 1975 km between Algiers and Tamanrasset (Tam), another 835 km to Agadez, and 1020 km more to Niamey – a total of 3830 km.

The straight driving time is only 10 days (four days from Algiers to Tam, three days more to Arlit, and another three to Niamey). However, most people who rush the trip regret it afterwards. Allowing three to four weeks would be far more desirable. Nonetheless, people do it in two weeks all the time and thoroughly enjoy it. Agadez is one of the most interesting desert towns in West Africa, plus there are fabulous mountains along the way, making this one of the most interesting areas in all of West Africa. However, getting to and from the mountains requires a detour of at least a few days. The Hoggar Mountains are north-east of Tam; the Aïr Mountains are accessible from Agadez.

The road is paved between Algiers and Tam but north of Tam it is in terrible condition for long stretches, making travel very slow. The real 'crossing', however, is the sandy stretch between Tam and Arlit, just 598 km. Try to time your departure so that you spend the night in Gara Eckar, an area about 260 km south of where the pavement ends and 60 km north of In-Guezzam. You'll know you're there when you see the magnificent outcrops of wind-eroded sandstone rocks – ideal for photography in the late afternoon or early morning.

From the Niger border-control post at Assamakka to Agadez, you have the choice of going via Arlit or the old camel route via Tegguidam Tessoumi. The latter route is much less travelled but allows you to see the salt evaporation ponds at Tegguidam Tessoumi, where camels are loaded with salt for transport to northern Nigeria and elsewhere.

Don't worry too much about getting lost. The unpaved section has clearly visible stakes every few km, so it's fairly difficult to lose your way, although it sometimes happens. Count on three to four days from Tam to Agadez. In Tam, you must pass by the police and through customs. As for petrol, there are stations in Tam and in Arlit and you must have enough fuel to make the 598 km between the two, but bear in mind that you will use more petrol than normal. There is a petrol station (and water) at the border post, In-Guezzam, but you cannot rely on the petrol supply as it is often limited and the army gets priority.

Hitchhiking

Hitchhiking is not difficult except during the hottest part of the year, from June to August. If you can't pay, the only people likely to pick you up are other foreigners, as truckers always want payment. You must, however, be prepared to wait a few days. It's easier finding free rides in trucks between Algiers and In Salah than further south. If you get a ride in a truck, don't expect to get away cheaply – US$100 (dinars are usually not accepted) for the Tam-Agadez crossing is typical.

The waiting point for southbound travellers is Tam. For northbound travellers it is usually Agadez, sometimes Arlit. Anticipate waiting anywhere from a day or two in Tam in winter to a week in the summer. In Tam, the best places to catch a truck going south are the customs post and the petrol station; you can also try restaurants, such as the Restaurant de la Paix.

Women travelling alone will have fewer hassles if there are other travellers in the vehicle. There's safety in numbers against, for example, border officials who sometimes have nothing better to do than to get drunk and try to seduce women.

Travellers have varying experiences at Assamakka with the officials on both sides of the border. They treat most travellers politely or indifferently; the days when they acted like swine, demanding huge bribes, are largely but not completely over. As at all border crossings, the way you treat the customs and police officials can make a lot of difference to their reaction to you. Neat, clean 'border clothes' and tidy hair can work wonders. Friendliness and flattery can help too and you might bring along some cigarettes. Handing over money or expensive

items only makes it far more difficult for the people behind you.

Between Arlit and Niamey and between Tam and Algiers, you can hitch or take a bus. There are daily buses doing the Algiers-Ghardaia, Ghardaia-In Salah routes, and thrice-weekly In Salah-Tam services. There are also flights between Algiers and Tam, but finding space is frequently difficult.

ROUTE THROUGH MALI

The 1503-km Adrar-Gao route through Mali, known as the Route du Tanezrouft has always been far less travelled than the Route du Hoggar (through Niger). There are some misconceptions about this route, eg that it takes longer and is more rugged. Neither are true. For motorists and motorcyclists, there are even certain advantages. Because there are fewer sections of soft sand along the way, some travellers believe that the route is technically easier than the Tam-Agadez route even though the unpaved section is over 2½ times longer (1317 km as opposed to about 500 km).

The most important thing to consider before taking this route, however, is the security situation. Due to violent political conditions in the area around Gao this route was closed to tourist traffic in 1994 and early 1995, although things may change (see the Mali chapter for more details).

The paved section ends in Reggane, 185 km south of Adrar. From there it's a two to three-day drive to the Malian border (Bordj-Moktar). It is hard flat sand most of the way and a little monotonous. High markers are placed every 10 km and you can see them from a long distance. The only place the going gets a little rough is about halfway between the border and Gao. Count on another two to three days for that section. After Gao it's a day or two on difficult sandy road to Niamey, or two days on asphalted road to Bamako. So time-wise, the routes through Niger and Mali are about the same.

Many who take the Mali route find that the desert's vastness gives a heightened sense of adventure and exhilaration. A very isolated week in the desert simply leaves a greater impression than the more travelled Tam route involving only three or four days off asphalted road. Some may consider the near absence of other travellers an advantage. This consideration is more than outweighed by the significantly increased risk factor. Travelling alone is simply out of the question unless you really don't mind risking your life. Police in Adrar may insist that you travel with at least one other vehicle.

Petrol and water are available in Adrar, Reggane, Bordj-Moktar and Gao. The pump at the border is sometimes empty, in which case you may have to wait a few days. You can find out at Adrar or Gao whether there's petrol in Bordj-Moktar or when it should arrive. In any event, this is not a good route for petrol-guzzling vehicles. Bordj-Moktar may also be the only place for water between Reggane and Gao.

In Adrar, you must pass through customs (la douane), while in Reggane, you must pass by the police for an inspection of your equipment and documents. You'll also have to pass by the police in Bourem and Gao. If you're heading south, you'll have to pay CFA 1000 per vehicle at the border, so be sure to carry some CFA or French francs.

Finally, getting petrol is usually no problem in most of Algeria and Gao, but in Timbuktu it is sometimes rationed. There's almost always black-market fuel available; ask the filling station attendant.

Hitchhiking

If you are hitchhiking, this route can be difficult: you may have to wait for up to a week because there are only about five or six trucks a week that make this run. The best places to catch rides are Gao and Adrar, not Bourem or Reggane. There are regular buses between Adrar and Ghardaia as well as between Gao and Niamey. Between Gao and Mopti (now paved) there are daily bush taxis, but between Gao and Timbuktu you may have to wait a few days. The turn-off point for Timbuktu is three km north of Bourem but this section is worse than any part of the Reggane-Gao stretch.

ROUTE THROUGH WESTERN ALGERIA

The route through western Algeria is rarely attempted by travellers, especially since the violent struggle between the military government and Islamic groups seeking to install an Islamic government continues. These political disturbances, to which there is no end in sight, have claimed the lives of almost 70 foreigners. And the vast majority of Western residents, together with thousands of Francophile Algerians, have taken the hint and left.

Saharan crossings via this route in 4WD vehicles and on motorcycles do occur from time to time, however, so it's definitely possible. (Hitchhiking is not an option because few vehicles pass this way.) The road to Tindouf (in the far south-west corner of Algeria) is in reasonably good condition, however, from there south to Zouérat (974 km) involves some of the toughest driving in the Sahara, certainly far tougher than any of the other major crossings through Niger, Mali and Morocco. Moreover, you must carry enough petrol for the entire Tindouf-Zouérat stretch. Consequently, only the most intrepid travellers should attempt this.

ROUTE THROUGH MOROCCO

With the conflict in the Western Sahara now over, it's possible once again to travel overland south from Morocco through the Western Sahara to Mauritania. Indeed, because of all the political problems in Algeria and northern Niger, it is becoming the preferred route. The starting point for the serious crossing is Dakhla, which is on the coast in the Western Sahara, 1703 km by tarred highway due south of Casablanca via Marrakech. In Casablanca, Marrakech and Agadir, you can easily catch buses all the way to Dakhla. If you're travelling by vehicle, no special travel permit is required to make the trip to Dakhla, however, there are many police checks along the way. The police can contact each other, so make sure you keep telling them the same story.

Once in Dakhla, present yourself first to la Sûreté (the police), then to the 'province' to ask for permission to proceed towards

Mauritania, then to the army headquarters at the entrance to Dakhla to put your name on the list of people for the next convoy to Nouâdhibou. Convoys depart on Tuesdays and Fridays, and drivers must put their names on the list at least one day in advance. On the day of departure, cars come together in the morning at the army headquarters and leave around 9 am. Normally, it's easy to hitch if you have no transport as this is now the principal passage through the Sahara. Moreover, it's reported that you will probably find drivers glad to take you all the way to Nouakchott if you're willing to work hard when the vehicle gets stuck in the sand (which is virtually guaranteed between Nouâdhibou and Nouakchott). Nevertheless, if you wait until the day of departure to begin looking for a ride, you may not be lucky.

In Dakhla, there are two budget hotels next to the airfield and another on the main road into town (Dr 25 a person). There are plenty of restaurants where a meal costs around Dr 15. (In Laâyoune, a big city and a popular stopover en route south to Dakhla, there's plenty of *hôtels économiques*, especially in the lower city. They're not easy to find; one is near the Catholic church. Singles/doubles cost Dr 25/36.)

The coastal road from Dakhla to Nouâdhibou (464 km) is mostly tarred; the remainder is sandy road and marked by stakes. Only about 50 km or so is really rough driving. At night, those in the convoy camp in the desert along the road. The Moroccan army will guide the convoy to the last army post before the border. From there until the first Mauritanian military post (eight km), you're on your own as you pass over difficult sandy tracks amidst land mines.

Passing through the Mauritanian military post can be sheer hell. The process takes from two to 10 days for all the vehicles to clear! And there's no water or food, just sand, heat and wind. Also, there are quite a few mines scattered in this area, an unfortunate remnant of the conflict with the Polisario. The risk is minimal if you stick with the convoy and follow their instructions for the eight km between the two border posts.

Once the vehicles are cleared through the Mauritanian military post, a guide will lead the cars through another minefield to Nouâdhibou. Everyone must then pass through customs at the entrance to town. The officials here live off bribes, so be very respectful and avoid aggravating them. As at all border posts, you must declare your currency. If you miscount or add improperly and they find out, you're in for real trouble. Only a major bribe may keep you out of jail. So don't make mistakes here! After you have cleared this hurdle, you must register with the commissariat and get a permit there to leave town.

After all this, you may think you can celebrate – wrong! Departing Nouâdhibou, you'll soon find that your journey has just begun in terms of driving because the worst section by far is between here and Nouakchott. This sandy diabolical route has metal markers every five km but it is not well marked in sections. To avoid getting lost, you absolutely must follow a truck or other vehicle or take a guide. To do otherwise is suicidal. There is hardly any sign of life along the way, just lots of loose sand to get stuck in. Trucks make this trip in 24 hours straight driving time. With luck, you may get to Nouakchott in two days, but count on taking three.

WHAT TO TAKE

A complete medical kit is indispensable for motorcyclists and highly recommended for everybody else. Make sure it includes salt tablets to avoid dehydration, ointment for the eyes (for sand irritation), plus skin cream, sun block and Chap Stick. Because you won't be able to get quickly to a doctor in an emergency, bring an antibiotic as well. Fasigyn and Flagyl (metronidazole) are effective prescription medicines for amoebic dysentery and giardia, but difficult to obtain in Africa.

From December to February, you'll need warm clothing at night because near freezing temperatures are not unusual. During the rest of the year, except from May to August, it can still get chilly at night, so bring a sweater. You'll need a sleeping bag/pad for the same reason, also sunglasses and a hat. Pick up a *chèche*, the cotton cloth that Tuareg wrap around their heads. It can be useful to help prevent dehydration and it keeps the sand out of your eyes. Plastic bags come in very handy since sand gets into everything. If you'll be crossing by motorcycle, consider bringing some facial mist spray.

If you're driving, don't wait until arriving in Algeria to get 20-litre jerry cans. They cost about 10 times as much in Algeria as they do in the UK. Count on using at least twice as much petrol per km than usual because the sand retards movement.

Metal sand ladders (*plaques de désensablement*) are indispensable. You can buy them along the way, but they become much more expensive south of Ghardaia. You'll also need a compass and a mirror, two good spare tyres, a three-tonne hydraulic jack with wide supporting board, and a fire extinguisher – overheated engines have been known to catch fire.

As for water, count on using at least seven litres per person per day, more if you're riding a bike. Obviously, it's best to have an extra supply. For cooking, bring a kerosene stove. In French West Africa, kerosene is *petrole* and usually not difficult to find because most petrol stations in French West Africa have a single pump labelled 'petrole'.

You are permitted to bring in (duty-free) one bottle of scotch or two bottles of wine per person, plus a carton of cigarettes. Hold firm if custom officials say you cannot bring in liquor. They want it desperately. Alcohol, even Algerian wine, is not sold anywhere in Algeria except at major hotels, and then only to tourists at exorbitant prices. Naturally, the Algerians want this forbidden fruit. So don't be surprised if a border official asks if you have any to sell. The selling price of whiskey is the equivalent of a night at the best hotel in town. Wine, on the other hand, is much less valuable. Cigarettes make such good presents that you should consider bringing some even if you don't smoke.

In London you can get everything you need (sand ladders, jerry cans, shovels with a large blade, tow rope, tyre pumps, puncture repair kits, etc) at Brownchurch Landrovers Ltd (☎ (0171) 729-3606), 308 Hare Row

(off Cambridge Heath Rd), London E2 9BX. In Nice, try *Nice Off-Road Centre* (☎ (93) 82-1977) at 107 ave Cyrille Besset.

If you're heading south-north instead of north-south, you'll find just about everything you need in Arlit. Traders there sell everything imaginable. Finally, a few non-essentials that experienced overland travellers highly recommend are a short-wave radio, binoculars for viewing the wildlife, welding rods (local workshops don't always have them), a logbook and French franc bills (easily exchanged).

TYPE OF VEHICLE

What one usually reads and hears is that a 4WD vehicle is required for crossing the Sahara. This is crap. The Sahara has been crossed in all kinds of vehicles, including bicycles. I crossed it in a 10-year-old Volkswagen van without experiencing problems; others have crossed in even less appropriate vehicles. You are likely to see as many Peugeot 504s as Toyota Landcruisers and you'll undoubtedly see a few Deux Cheveaux as well.

This is not to say that a Toyota Landcruiser or the equivalent isn't preferable, but it's speed, not traction that will keep you from getting stuck. Once you're stuck, it is the sand ladders that will get you out. The main advantage of a 4WD is its high clearance.

Bicycle

Biking across the desert obviously shouldn't be taken lightly. The 598-km distance between Tamanrasset and Arlit can be biked in about 16 days. You should expect to consume from 10 to 12 litres of water a day. Carrying enough food for 16 days is possible but carrying sufficient water is not. So you'll either have to make arrangements for someone to supply you with water en route or plan on borrowing water from passers-by. Those who have attempted this have relied successfully on the generosity of passing vehicles for water. It may sound dangerous but the only real danger, according to one person who has successfully done this, is losing the route. For other problems, such as a mechanical failure, you could simply catch a ride to Arlit or Tamanrasset.

VEHICLE DOCUMENTS
International Driving Permit (IDP)

Most countries in West Africa will recognise your regular driving licence but get an IDP anyway. First, in some countries such as Nigeria, your regular licence is not legally sufficient. Second, even in those countries where it is, don't expect the local African police to know this. They probably will have never seen a licence the likes of yours and may doubt its validity. Finally, for those who get into trouble with the law, having two licences will allow you a certain amount of liberty, shall we say, if the police take your IDP and tell you to report somewhere.

Car Insurance

Almost no country in Africa will allow you to drive without third-party automobile insurance – a Green Card (*la Carte Verte*). Getting insurance in Europe is next to worthless because coverage does not extend below about 20° latitude north (ie only Algeria, Morocco, Tunisia, Libya and Egypt).

Whether or not you have a Carte Verte, many countries in West Africa (Niger, Mali, Benin and Algeria among others) require you to buy insurance locally. You can usually buy it at the border or in the closest major town. In Algeria, it's very cheap – about 65 dinar for 10 days. In Niger, you can buy it at or near the border. The cost comes to about US$1 per day, and it's valid for most countries in West Africa, including Mali, Burkina Faso, Togo and Benin. (If you buy it in Mali, the minimum 15-days insurance costs CFA 18,000; around US$36.) Insurance purchased in Africa is often not worth the paper it's written on, but it's a requirement none-theless. Prices of third-party liability insurance in West Africa vary widely, from about UK£50 to UK£150 for insurance covering all West African countries for a period of three months. Prices in The Gambia seem to be among the lowest. Many Europeans travelling on the cheap simply take their regular insurance card along and count on the fact that the border guards won't look in the back to see in which countries the insurance is valid. In Nigeria and some other countries, this assumption often proves correct.

Companies/organisations which issue insurance include: Campbell Irvine Ltd (☎ (0181) 937-9903/6981), 46 Earls Court Rd, London W8 6EJ; Automobile Club de l'Ile de France, 14 av de la Grande Armée, 75017 Paris; and ADAC, Am Westpark 8, 8000 Munich 70 (also Bundersalle 9-30, Berlin 31).

Carnet de Passage

A *carnet de passage en douane*, or triptyque, is a temporary import/export document for the vehicle and allows you to bring a car into a country without paying the normal customs duty or lodging a deposit with customs. It is intended to ensure that you don't sell your vehicle en route without paying duty. If the vehicle is not exported when you leave, the country can obtain payment of the duty from the issuing organisation and eventually you.

Carnets are issued by automobile associations in many countries but not in the USA, so Americans must get theirs in Europe. In Britain, RAC and AA both issue them. In Germany, they're issued by ADAC and AVD (Lyonerstrabe 16, 60311 Frankfurt 71). In France, they're issued by the Automobile Club de l'Ile de France (see Car Insurance, above). In all of these countries, including France, getting a carnet is no problem; AA members usually get a discount. However, if you're a foreigner or have a vehicle with foreign licence plates, they may demand that you be a member of the automobile association in your country before they'll issue you a carnet. All of them demand a guarantee. There are two types – bank guarantees and insurance company guarantees. For a bank guarantee, you must put up collateral equal to the estimated amount of the duty. The cost is frequently prohibitive. In Australia, for example, the AA requires a bank guarantee equal to 300% of the value of the vehicle! Insurance companies, on the other hand, demand much less up-front money. They will issue a bond upon payment of a refundable premium equal to a small percentage of the estimated amount of the duty. If the company must pay on a claim, it has the right to collect the same from you. (If you purchase a double indemnity bond, which costs twice as much, the insurance company will waive the right to recover against you.) In the UK, the AA uses Alexander Howden Ltd (☎ (0171) 623-5500, 8 Devonshire Square, London EC2M 4PL); their premium is only 3% and is good for one year (you can't get a price reduction by asking for a lesser period of coverage). A bond takes about a week to get.

While Nigeria and many other countries in Africa require a carnet, Algeria, Morocco, Tunisia, Niger, Mali and Côte d'Ivoire do not. In Benin and Togo, they can be purchased at the border. In Senegal, they are no longer required for stays of up to 30 days. (The customs office will issue you a free *passavant de douane* valid for 30 days.) Carnets issued in the UK (and possibly elsewhere in Europe) do not cover Guinea, but for CFA 10,000 you can get a carnet covering that country at the Guinean embassy in Dakar. This means that you can drive from Europe to the coast of West Africa (but not Nigeria) without getting one beforehand, regardless of which route across the Sahara you choose. Many motorcyclists don't bother with carnets and seem to experience no significant problems. Vehicle owners, however, should definitely get them so as to avoid the problems of having to buy one each time you cross a new border.

Even with a carnet, in Algeria (which doesn't require a carnet) you will have to pay double the new value of your vehicle if your car dies in the desert and you leave it there – Algerian authorities will assume you sold it! So if your car is a heap or you come without tools to repair it, you'll be taking a big risk in that country.

SELLING VEHICLES
Most new or used automobiles can be sold in Africa for about the same price or a little more than in Europe.

To sell your vehicle, you will have to turn it over to customs who will not release it until the prospective purchaser pays the duty; even then, the buyer may have to bribe someone. The paperwork is less in Togo and Benin, making them two of the most attractive places to sell automobiles, followed by Côte d'Ivoire and Senegal. In Mali, finding a buyer is reportedly very easy if it's a French vehicle. In Niger, temporarily imported vehicles cannot be sold unless the owner has resided there at least two months. Left-hand drive Peugeot 504s and non-diesel Mercedes 280s are the easiest to sell. As for large motorcycles, Abidjan and Dakar are the best markets. If you do sell your vehicle, make sure you discharge the carnet correctly in the country where you sell it; otherwise on arrival home you risk receiving a bill for unpaid import duty from your automobile association.

For those unable to find a buyer, one alternative is to ship it back. If you don't want it stripped, put it in a container. This can be quite expensive but you can save a lot of money by being flexible on where you pick it up because prices to various ports in Europe vary enormously. Dakar, Accra and Abidjan are the best ports for shipping. Those using the Swiss Nautilus Line have reported satisfaction with the service. The cheapest, however, may be the Black Star Line in Ghana; travellers have shipped their motorcycles from Tema back to northern Europe for US$400.

SHIPPING YOUR VEHICLE
By Freighter from Europe
Shipping a vehicle or motorcycle from Europe to West Africa is complicated and a bit risky but it's done all the time, more so in recent years because of the great danger and near impossibility of crossing the Sahara by vehicle via Algeria due to the serious political disturbances there. The most commonly used ports for shipping are Tilbury, Marseilles, Antwerp, Rotterdam and Hamburg (the most commonly used shipping lines are those previously listed in this chapter under Sea).

Insuring the contents of the vehicle for shipment is extremely difficult and costly. The recommended solution is to bring the essential equipment with you and chain or lock all of the other equipment into fixed boxes inside the vehicle. Regardless of what you may be told by your shipping agent, the chances are good that your vehicle will be left unlocked both for the crossing and when it goes into storage at the destination port (typically Dakar, Abidjan or Tema). Thieves seem to particularly like tools, high-lift jacks and tarpaulins, so if possible take special precautions with these items.

Getting a vehicle out of port is frequently a nightmare. In Dakar, for example, the procedure is as follows: the bill of ladding (shipper's receipt) must be stamped by your shipping agent in Dakar to prove that you have paid your disembarkation fee. Despite the fact that your agent in Europe may tell you that this will cost only UK£30, officials in Dakar will probably demand in excess of UK£100. The Touring Club of Senegal (ie RAC), which is located near the port, must stamp the cover of your carnet. Thereafter, the Chef de Visite at the port must stamp and remove the entrance part of the carnet. Next, the port commandant must stamp the carnet which he will probably only do when you have paid the disembarkation fee for a second time. At that point the vehicle can be brought through customs. If you're lucky and you're willing to offer a few bribes along the way, the vehicle may be yours in as little as 48 hours.

By Ferry

From France From Marseilles, Société Nationale Maritime Corse-Méditerranée (SNCM) and Compagnie Tunisienne de Navigation (CTN) offer ferry connections to Tunis, Algiers and Oran. From Sété, SNCM and Compagnie Nationale Algérienne de Navigation (CNAN) have ferries to Algiers, Oran and Tangiers.

Since Marseilles and Sété are the two most popular points of departure, getting a reservation for an automobile during the summer is difficult. You can reserve by calling SNCM in Paris (☎ (01) 49-27-91-20, telex 214386) at 25 rue St-Augustin; in Marseilles (☎ 91-90-64-70, telex 401089) at 29 blvd des Dames; in Sété (☎ 67-74-70-55, telex

490545) at 4 Quai d'Alger; and in Algiers (☎ (02) 74-0585, telex 67100) at 6 rue de Beziers. Its agent in the UK is P&O Ferries (Arundel Towers, Portland Terrace, Southampton SO9 4AE). If you use an agent, book at least several weeks in advance. Otherwise on arrival you may find that they have no knowledge of your reservation.

The journey from Marseilles to Algiers takes from 20 to 25 hours depending on the ferry. During much of the year, SNCM has about 20 crossings a month from Marseilles to Algiers, all between 11.30 am and 6 pm, with only an occasional crossing on Sundays. The cost for a vehicle one way is expensive (there are reductions for round-trip fares), averaging about 2000FF regardless of which route you take. The exact cost depends on the length of the vehicle and the season (about 20% more expensive during the summer). These boats are not like the average ferry but are one-class tourist ships with comfortable accommodation, superb meals and nightly entertainment. For travellers, the price is about 900 to 1500FF. There are reduced rates for students and young people.

From Italy CTN offers service from Genoa to Tunis for about half the price of Marseilles to Tunis. It is represented in Europe by SNCM. The Italian company Tirrenia offers service to Tunis from Genoa, Naples, and Sicily (Palermo and Trapani). You can take a slow train from Naples to Sicily. There are no reductions for round-trip fares, but they do offer reduced rates for students in the off season. Tirrenia is represented by CIT in Paris (☎ (01) 45-00-99-50), Brussels (☎ (02) 513-8599), Geneva (☎ 31-5750) and Amsterdam (☎ (020) 24-1677). Their tourist ships are similar in quality to those of SNCM.

From Spain In Spain, you can cross the Mediterranean from one of three ports: Algeciras (southern tip of Spain), Alicante and Malaga. Ferries from Algeciras go to Morocco (Tangiers and Ceuta), while those from Alicante and Malaga go to Melilla (northern Morocco). Algeciras-Ceuta is the cheapest route (roughly 100/350FF per person/vehicle) and serviced six days a week, several times daily. The trip takes only 90 minutes, but during the summer you have to queue for many hours. Algeciras-Tangiers costs about 50% more, and there are half as many crossings a week. Alicante-Melilla (or Malaga-Melilla) is over twice as expensive as Algeciras-Ceuta and takes eight hours. But you can cross every day except Sunday, and you'll save petrol and about 1000 km of driving to Algeria.

There are also connections between Alicante and Oran/Algiers, but they are less frequent (several times a week to Algiers; once a week to Oran in the summer). For more information, call Melia in Paris (☎ (01) 47-42-70-59). Both Melilla and Ceuta are free ports. If you will make significant purchases (petrol, alcohol, cigarettes, etc), it may be worth your while to go via one or the other.

ALGERIAN FORMALITIES
Algerian visas are not required for citizens of Denmark, Finland, Ireland, Italy, Norway, Spain, Sweden and Switzerland. Britons, previously exempted, must now get visas. In London, the Algerian embassy issues visas in 48 hours; the cost varies according to nationalities, eg UK£16 for Australians and free for Britons. If you travel from south to north through Algeria, you can get a visa easily at the Algerian embassies in Bamako, Niamey, Lagos, Cotonou, Accra or Abidjan. All issue visas either the same day or within 24 hours.

Going north-south, you are well advised to get your Algerian visa before leaving Europe. They are not available on arrival at the border, port or airport; the embassy in Tunis is currently issuing visas only to Tunisian residents, and the situation in Morocco can be equally tenuous. In Algiers, you can get visas to Niger and Mali within 24 hours, although they may direct you to their consulates in Tam. When going south to Niger, you no longer need

to get an exit visa from the police in Tam; they'll give it to you at the border.

You must change the equivalent of about US$100 at the Algerian border regardless of how long you stay. This can make a short trip through Algeria expensive. Don't expect to be able to re-convert the local currency (dinar) into hard currency at the border. There is a substantial black market that brings as much as three times the official rate. Be sure to keep every bank receipt, otherwise you'll have serious problems at the border when leaving.

LEAVING WEST AFRICA
In about half the countries in West Africa, the airport tax is included in the ticket price. In the others, the tax is levied at the airport when you're leaving. If you're not prepared, you may have to cash a US$50 bill to pay a US$10 tax. See the individual country chapters for more information.

WARNING
This chapter is particularly vulnerable to change – prices for international travel are volatile, routes are introduced and cancelled, schedules change, special deals come and go, and rules and visa requirements are amended. Airlines and governments seem to take a perverse pleasure in making price structures and regulations as complicated as possible. You should check directly with the airline or travel agency to make sure that you understand how a fare (and ticket you may buy) works. In addition, the travel industry is highly competitive and there are many schemes and bonuses. The upshot of this is that you should get opinions, quotes and advice from as many airlines and travel agencies as possible before you part with your hard-earned cash. The details given in this chapter should be regarded as pointers and are not a substitute for careful up-to-date research.

Getting Around

AIR
African Airlines

African airlines have been described by readers of the *African Economic Digest* as frightening, unreliable, dangerous, unpleasant, unpredictable, uncaring, over booked, impertinent and dirty. Few travellers realise, however, that as of 1994 Air Afrique was in the select company of less than 30 airlines in the world that had never had an accident fatality.

Service varies greatly even with the same airline. Sometimes it is excellent. Take Nigeria Airways from Abidjan westward and it'll be half full and with very good service; take the same airline from Abidjan to Accra and you may think you're on a cattle car. There's some correlation between service and safety, but not always. The real concern is the quality of the maintenance operations. Foreign pilots operating in Africa say it varies greatly. Most of the airlines are serviced routinely in Europe and many have contracts with well-established foreign airlines which provide the pilots and maintenance personnel. There is, then, an element of control. In general, airlines worldwide are about eight times safer now than in 1960, and the same holds for airlines flying in Africa.

So despite the horror stories you may hear, in general you need not worry about flying on African airlines. There's no reason, however, not to try taking one of the better airlines, but in many instances there is no choice. If a foreign ambassador wants to get from Bissau to Dakar, he or she will take the local airline – and so will you. Don't be terribly surprised if, on occasion, you have to wait at the airport for a half day or so (never go to the airport without a good book and several magazines), or during the flight they're doing things to keep the door from coming off, or the luggage is stuffed in the back preventing an emergency exit. These things happen every now and then. If it's any comfort, most of the pilots are well trained and many have gained experience in areas of the world where safety standards are more rigorous. When you do have a choice, the list of airlines below in descending order of quality (safety and service) is intended to give you some basis for choosing:

1 Ethiopian Airlines, Air Afrique, Air Gabon and Cameroun Airlines – the order in which the readers of *Africa Economic Digest* have rated the African airlines serving West Africa
2 Air Mauritanie, TACV (Cape Verde), Air Ivoire and Air Burkina seem to have the best reputation of the airlines which offer service primarily within the country.
3 Ghana Airways and Nigeria Airways – in terms of service, Ghana Airways wins hands down on the inter-Africa routes and provides service comparable to that of Nigeria Airways on routes to Europe. Nigeria Airways' service to/from London is excellent and punctual, but on its inter-Africa routes, Nigeria Airways has one of the worst reputations of any airline in West Africa. It's the type of airline you board without knowing whether there's really a seat for you. In terms of safety, however, Ghana Airways and Nigeria Airways seem to be on an equal footing and superior to those in category four.
4 All other African airlines operating in West Africa are included here except for those in the category below. Foreigners take these airlines all the time, especially when there's no alternative.
5 You'll be glad to know that the worst airlines (Air Mali, Air Liberia, Air Niger and Sierra Leone Airlines) all went bust during the late 1980s and are no longer flying. The worst today are probably Linhas Aéreas du Guinea-Bissau and Air Guinea.

Changing Tickets

You may find that tickets written by Nigeria Airways and Ghana Airways are not accepted by other airlines unless written outside Africa, ie paid for in hard currency. If you buy a ticket on Nigeria Airways in Dakar, for example, and want it endorsed to another airline, keep dreaming.

Confirming Reservations

Flight schedules change frequently so you must reconfirm your reservation in person before the flight, even if the ticket says 'OK'. Telephone reconfirmations are never accepted because your ticket must be stamped. The regulations say to reconfirm within 72 hours of the flight – that means not later than 72 hours. However, you can usually reconfirm up to a week in advance. If you reconfirm within 72 hours, you will more than likely find that your reservation is still valid. You can reconfirm on the day of the flight, but if the flight is full your reservation may be cancelled.

If you're put on the waiting list, don't panic. African airlines usually don't over book, so your chances of getting on are frequently good. It's usually not how far up the waiting list you are that counts, but who gets to the check-in counter first. The standard check-in time is two hours before flight departure; get there even earlier if you're on the waiting list. The check-in line will probably resemble a rugby scrum, so look immediately for a young local (a 'friend') who'll assist you – it's worth every cent.

Hassles at the Airport

For all too many travellers, the most harrowing experiences are at the airport. Lagos airport has the worst reputation by far. Checking-in can be a nightmare. It's rare that the good guy who respects the queue doesn't get on the plane, but it's just frequent enough to cause many people, Africans and foreigners alike, to lose their civility.

There is a way out of this, however. Find one of the enterprising locals who make a living by getting people checked in. It will only cost you a dollar or two, more when you don't have a confirmed seat, and don't be surprised if the person behind the counter insists you show your appreciation to them as well.

Costs of Flying

Flying in Africa is not cheap because distances are fairly long (Dakar to Abidjan, for example, is equivalent to flying halfway across the USA), and you can't get anything cheaper than the round-trip excursion fare (two-thirds the standard economy fare). To get this special round-trip fare, you must stay at least seven days. But take a four-day trip from, say, Lomé to Niamey or Abidjan to Bamako (about 1000 km) and you'll pay the full economy fare both ways (about US$300

return). Occasionally, you can get a cheaper fare by taking smaller airlines, such as Air Ivoire and Air Burkina, which charge 20% less. Air Burkina also offers 35% student discounts on top of this, eg about US$60 from Bamako to Ouagadougou.

BUS

The big change on the West African transport scene during the last 13 years is that big buses are becoming more popular than bush taxis on many long-distance runs. The main reason is that they're cheaper (typically 15 to 25%) than Peugeot 504s and more comfortable. Sometimes they are slower with frequent stops, and in such instances those with money usually still prefer the Peugeot 504s. Many buses don't have fixed schedules, so the waiting time can be longer.

The best bus systems are in Ghana, Côte d'Ivoire, Senegal, Mali, Burkina Faso and Niger. In Ghana, the state transport system is topnotch, has a set schedule, connects all the major towns and is dirt cheap. The problem is that it is so popular that getting a seat is frequently difficult. Niger has a public and a private bus system. The government buses have fixed schedules and are as fast as bush taxis and more comfortable. Consequently, to get a seat you must invariably reserve a day or two in advance.

In Nigeria, where everyone seems to be in a rush, buses are slower than bush taxis but much faster than the trains and, hence, are an excellent way of travelling long distances at night. Côte d'Ivoire has a huge, privately owned fleet of modern, comfortable buses with fixed schedules but, unlike Ghana, these serve only the major cities. In Burkina Faso and Mali, buses were once rare but are now more popular than bush taxis on many of the longer distance runs.

Other countries where you'll find buses are Guinea, Sierra Leone (where they are in bad shape but frequently the only option) and Cape Verde (where bush taxis don't exist). Otherwise, count on using one type or another of bush taxi.

TRAIN

As West Africa's bus system improves, the

train system deteriorates. The three longest lines (Dakar-Bamako, Abidjan-Ouagadougou and Lagos-Kano-Maiduguri) are all worse than they were 13 years ago, while the train in Guinea has ceased altogether.

Most budget travellers, however, are reasonably pleased with the trains and a ride on one may well be one of your more memorable experiences.

Over half the countries in West Africa have trains and many are still fairly decent. The best are now those in Ghana and in Burkina Faso. In Ghana, the train which most foreign travellers take is the Kumasi-Takoradi line, especially the overnight train which allows you to save on the cost of a hotel. It has sleepers as well as both 1st-class and 2nd-class compartments. The other lines in Ghana (Accra-Kumasi and Accra-Takoradi) provide only 2nd-class coaches and are much better served by buses and bush taxis. Other train lines well used by foreigners are Dakar-Bamako and Abidjan-Ouagadougou. The cars on these latter two lines are now ageing considerably. Taking the Abidjan-Ouagadougou train, you'd never guess that 13 years ago it had air-con and was virtually in the same league as the delightful Nairobi-Mombasa train. Côte d'Ivoire is experiencing hard times and the train reflects it. The toilets are atrocious and the only food is soft drinks and sandwiches. However, if you take the train which runs only within Burkina Faso and does not continue to Côte d'Ivoire, you'll be pleasantly surprised – the train is not only punctual but the cabins are very comfortable and, in 1st class, air-conditioned.

On some of the trains on the Dakar-Bamako and Abidjan-Ouagadougou runs, you may find sleeping cars with compartments limited to two people, giving you a bit of privacy. On most trains however, the sleeping cars all have four bunks per compartment; nevertheless, the 1st-class sleeping cars sometimes aren't all filled, so you may have a bit of privacy anyway, at least for part of the journey. In Nigeria the trains are older but still offer meals and sleepers; however, they are pitifully slow and you're sure to arrive later than scheduled. In Togo, take

along some wine, cheese and friends on the six-hour train ride from Lomé to Kpalimé – arriving on time only spoils the party.

Below is a summary of possible train routes; the country chapters give the specifics. The best trains in West Africa are:

Ghana (Kumasi to Takoradi); eight hours
Burkina Faso (Ouagadougou to Bobo Dioulasso); five hours
Senegal-Mali (Dakar to Bamako); 30 to 35 hours
Senegal (Dakar to St-Louis); five hours
Côte d'Ivoire-Burkina Faso (Abidjan to Ouagadougou); 26 hours

The other routes are:

Ghana (Accra to Kumasi and Accra to Takoradi; 2nd class only)
Nigeria (Lagos to Kano and Port Harcourt to Maiduguri); both 40 hours or more
Benin (Cotonou to Parakou); 12 hours
Togo (Lomé to Kpalimé and Lomé to Notsé); six and five hours respectively

BUSH TAXI

There are three classes of overland transport that could come under the title 'bush taxi' (*taxi brousse*): the Peugeot 504s, the minibuses and the pick-up trucks. You may think that they are those beat-up old vehicles that take three hours to fill up and are packed like sardines, with an accident rate you'd just as soon not know about. The answer is yes, but not for all bush taxis.

There's usually some correlation between the quality of the vehicles and the wealth of the country. Comparing bush taxis in Nigeria and Mali, for example, is like equating diamonds and glass. The latter are generally in terrible condition; the former may be relatively new. So just because it's a bush taxi doesn't mean the trip will be unbearable.

It's also not true that the waiting time is always long. For well-travelled routes such as Dakar-Banjul, Abidjan-Bouaké, Lomé-Accra and Lomé-Cotonou, the waiting time is typically no more than 15 to 45 minutes. In Nigeria, the average waiting time is more like 15 minutes. However, going from Bamako to Ouagadougou could involve a half day's wait or more, especially if you arrive at the wrong time. From 6.30 to 8.30 am is usually the best time to catch bush taxis.

Bush taxis are almost always located at a bush taxi station (*gare routière*). Just remember that most major cities have several, one for each major road leading out of town.

Peugeot 504

These cars, assembled in Nigeria, are referred to by various names, including cinq-cent-quatre, peugeot, sept-place and brake. They are quite comfortable when relatively new and are usually not packed like sardines (more than eight including driver). If one is overstuffed, all it takes to change a nightmare to a pleasant ride is to buy an extra seat. Throughout the CFA zone the cost of a bush taxi is roughly CFA 750 (US$1.50) per 100 km but on three international routes (Bamako-Abidjan, Ouagadougou-Abidjan, Ouagadougou-Lomé) the cost is about double this. It is for this reason that some travellers on the Ouagadougou-Lomé route, for instance, take a bush taxi or bus to the border and then catch another on the other side; the savings can be as much as 30%. The down side of switching vehicles at the border is that it can prolong the trip considerably, sometimes up to an entire day.

If you want to charter a Peugeot all to yourself, the price is easy to calculate if all you're doing is going from A to B and back. Take the price of one seat and multiply it by the number of available seats and then do the same for the return portion. Don't expect to pay less just because you're saving the driver the time and hassle of looking for other passengers – time is not money in Africa.

Minibus

At many gare routières, you may find no Peugeot 504s, but only minibuses. Typically about 25% cheaper than the Peugeots, they are not necessarily less comfortable, particularly if the Peugeots are stuffed with four people on the back seat. The big disadvantage is that they are always a little slower and have longer waits at the numerous police checks because there are more passengers to search. One of the best van systems is in Togo, where bush taxis are becoming rarer and large buses don't exist.

Pick-Up Truck

With wooden seats down the sides, covered pick-ups (*bâches*) are definitely 2nd class, but sometimes the only kind of bush taxi available. These trucks are invariably stuffed with not only people, but probably a few chickens as well, and your feet may be higher than your waist from resting on a sack of millet. The ride is guaranteed to be unpleasant unless you and your companions adopt the African attitude, in which case each time your head hits the roof as the truck descends

---

Luggage Fee

Everywhere in West Africa, when you travel by bush taxi, there is always an extra fee for luggage. While such fees may at first seem arbitrary and unfair, the practice is standard and applies to all passengers. The only thing that is a bit arbitrary is the amount, which varies according to the size of the baggage and is in the sole discretion of the driver or his assistant. The baggage charge is partly based on the fact that in many countries bush taxi fares are fixed by the government or by a driver's syndicate and, therefore, may not reflect true costs. For instance, drivers must often pay bribes to the police for a whole host of reasons, sometimes to prevent them from making excessively long searches, especially at border crossings. Thus, the baggage fee for transport crossing a border is often relatively high. The only way the driver or his assistant can earn a bit extra is to charge for luggage. Local people accept this, so travellers should too, unless of course the amount is beyond reason.

The fee for a medium-sized sack is usually around 10% of the fare and more for large sacks, so this is just another reason for travelling light. Some travellers carry bags the size of a fridge and they're often the ones complaining the loudest. If you think you're being overcharged, ask other passengers – but out of earshot of the driver as they will otherwise be reluctant to speak. ∎

into yet another big pothole, a roar of laughter rings forth instead of a cry of anguish. There's nothing like African humour to change an otherwise miserable trip into a tolerable, even enjoyable experience.

Truck

While not falling under the general title of bush taxi, in a few instances the only thing available is a truck stuffed with what at first glance you may think is cattle. Even unflappable old African hands are taken aback by the fact that until 1986, this was the only mode of overland transport offered on a regular basis between two neighbouring Sahelian capitals, Niamey and Ouagadougou. Fortunately, a World Bank project has improved not only the condition of the road but, as a side effect, the subhuman transport system as well. See the individual country chapters for details.

CAR

If you'll be travelling by road, the location of the principal routes is a major consideration. Some dirt roads are all-weather while others are not and you can't necessarily tell this from the Michelin road map.

Travelling times for the major routes are given below. A 'day' means from seven to 10 hours driving time in a private vehicle, eight to 14 hours in a bush taxi.

Dakar to: Nouakchott (one full day), Banjul (six hours), Casamance (eight hours), Bamako (four to five days, or 35 hours on the train – you can take a vehicle), Conakry (three to four days, four to five by bush taxi), Bissau (1½ days)

Abidjan to: Bamako (two full days), Ouagadougou (two full days, 25 hours by train), Accra (one long day), Cotonou (two days), Monrovia (two full days), Freetown (four full days)

Ouagadougou to: Bamako 1½ days, two by bush taxi, Mopti (two days), Lomé (two days), Niamey (one day), Accra (two days)

Niamey to: Agadez (one to 1½ days), Gao (1½ days, 2 days by bus), Ndjamena (four days), Kano 1½ days

Lagos to: Kano (one very long day), Enugu (one day)

Rental

Renting a car in West Africa is invariably ridiculously expensive. You can easily spend in one day what you'd pay in the USA for a one-week rental of the same model. For those still interested, there are car rental agencies in almost every capital city. Just go to the city's major hotel to find one. There is little difference in price between car rental agencies except in large cities where there may be a number of small operators.

If the small operators charge less, it's usually because the vehicles are older and sometimes not well maintained. While you can sometimes get a good deal, the problem is that you can never be sure about the car's condition. If you can't afford to be stuck in the middle of nowhere with a broken-down vehicle, stick with Hertz, Avis and Europcar. As in the USA and Europe, you will usually need to have a credit card to guarantee payment, or put down a large deposit. Nowhere in West Africa may you take a rental car across a border or leave it in another city.

Hertz, Europcar and Avis are all well represented in West Africa, but they are not the only ones. Their brochures sometimes fail to include some of their more obscure representatives. Their locations are listed in the individual country chapters.

Before you rent a car consider whether you might not be better off hiring a taxi by the day. If your rental car breaks down, it's your problem instead of the taxi driver's and if you don't speak French and you're in a French-speaking country, the headache will be greater.

The following table compares typical prices of rental cars (fairly uniform throughout West Africa) to those of all-day taxis (highly negotiable, anywhere from about CFA 12,000 to CFA 22,000 plus fuel if you bargain well). All the fares are in CFA:

distance	subcompact	taxi
100 km	40,000	20,000
200 km	58,000	25,000
300 km	76,500	31,000

These prices in Burkina Faso include all costs except petrol – insurance, tax, and chauffeur (required in many countries). Note that for a day's drive of just 300 km, you'll pay about US$150 plus fuel. So if you rented a car to, say, travel around Senegal for a week, you'd probably end up paying over US$1000, but still a lot less than before the devaluation of the CFA. You have to shop around.

The major problem with hiring taxis by the day is that many taxi drivers have never done it before. If you'll be staying within the city limits, the price should include petrol and coming to an agreement shouldn't be too difficult. The problem comes when you want to travel outside the city. In that case, if you try to negotiate a price including petrol, you'll be asking for trouble. They'll reduce the speed to a slow trot and complain incessantly every time you take even the most minor detour. Their attitude will ruin your trip – no joke. Getting the driver to agree to a fixed rate plus petrol is conceptually easy to understand and requires no estimate of petrol consumption. If you change your itinerary, it won't matter to them because you're the one paying for the petrol. Still, it's not always easy to negotiate because they may never have done such before and may not speak English or French very well. Go to the nearest major hotel and explain to the door attendant what you want and then have them explain it to the driver. Once this is settled, your only other problem is calculating the petrol usage. If the petrol meter is not working, you're asking for an argument at the end of the day. Get another driver!

The second major problem with hiring a taxi is that it is more likely to break down than a rental car. Inspect the car beforehand; if you hear a lot of rattling, choose another.

MOPED
In French West Africa, you'll find French-made, motorised 'Mobylettes' everywhere you travel. Elsewhere in the region, Asian-made mopeds are more popular. With few exceptions, in most towns there is no one in the business of renting them. So to rent one, in most places you'll have to find a local willing to rent you theirs. The best place to ask is usually around the market, particularly

at the spots where new ones are sold. There are rarely standard prices, so hard bargaining is usually required; 2500 CFA per day is a typical price. Many travellers who do rent them end up getting flat tyres and having mechanical problems. Since getting flats is almost certain, rent or purchase a tyre pump (about CFA 5000) and patches and tools for fixing flats. Second, rent or buy a basic tool kit, the minimum being an adjustable wrench and two screwdrivers. Third, wear a helmet as conditions can be quite dangerous. Finally, check the tyres and brake cables; the latter are often loose, so you may need to tighten them.

BICYCLE
There seems to be almost unanimous consensus among those who have travelled around West Africa by bicycle that cycling is the very best way of discovering Africa. It's not the most comfortable way to tour Africa, but you'll get into the country a lot more and you'll stay more frequently in small towns and villages, interact more with the people, and eat African food more frequently. In general, the more remote areas you visit, the better the experience. You may have to travel on dirt tracks and ask your way from village to village; you may even see no cars for weeks on end but virtually everywhere you go you can count on sharing the road with lots of other cyclists. In little villages in those areas you will have to ask each night where you can pitch a tent. The *chef de village* is invariably the one to ask. Even if you don't have a tent, he'll find you a place to stay.

What to Bring
If you'll be bringing a bicycle, also bring spokes, tubes, brake pads, cables, a spare tyre, a chain, a puncture kit and a decent set of tools as Western cycle parts are not available anywhere in West Africa. Buy tyres as thick as possible, at least a 32 inch. Also, you need to work out a way to carry at least four or so litres of water comfortably as the heat can get intense and distances between villages can be great. Because long distances tend to be a major drawback to biking in West

Africa, consider starting off along the coast of Ghana or in The Gambia and southern Senegal: the distances between major points of interest in these areas are not so great.

For more information on cycling, see Activities in the Facts for the Visitor chapter. Adventure Trips in the Getting There & Away chapter has information on the various cycling trips in West Africa sponsored by the International Bicycle Fund. Even if you decide not to bike with them, they're an excellent source of information on cycling in West Africa.

HITCHING

Hitching is never entirely safe in any country in the world, and we don't recommend it for single women. Travellers who decide to hitch should understand that they are taking a small but potentially serious risk. People who do choose to hitch will be safer if they travel in pairs and let someone know where they are planning to go. See the individual country chapters for details.

LOCAL TRANSPORT
Bus

There are well-developed systems in Abidjan, Dakar and Conakry. Also, in Banjul and Freetown, there is a fairly extensive network of buses connecting the city centre and suburbs. In most other cities, the shared taxi system takes the place of buses.

Taxi

Only in Dakar, Abidjan and Ouagadougou do taxis have meters (*compteurs*). For all others, either bargaining is required (especially the bigger cities), or you'll be given the legally fixed rate which is not negotiable. Typical fares are given in the country chapters. Fares have been very stable over the last few years, so be wary if the quoted price is much higher. If you can't speak French, be content if you pay no more than a 25% premium. The price always includes the luggage unless you have a particularly bulky item. Also, fares invariably go up between 9 pm and midnight; the country chapters specify the time. Don't be surprised if the driver tells you an earlier hour.

Don't expect that bargaining is always required with taxis. The fare at most airports into town is fixed by law. Taxi drivers at Dakar Airport, however, totally disregard the fixed rates and generally act as though they received their training in New York. Still, many drivers in other cities are honest and will quote the correct fare. The problem is how to tell if the quoted fare is the correct one. Check first with an airport official.

There are two bases for calculating taxi fares – one when you hop in a cab with other people going in the same direction, and another when you 'charter' (as they frequently say in English-speaking Africa) one to yourself. (In French-speaking countries, the word *déplacement* is sometimes used.)

From the hotels, the rate is always the charter rate, plus there's usually a 50 to 100% premium on top of that to cover their waiting time. When you hail a cab on the streets in the city centre, it's not always easy to know which rate you're being offered, so be sure to clarify it.

In virtually every capital city, taxis are thicker than flies during the day, but at night they seem to turn into pumpkins except in Abidjan, Dakar and Accra. If you're having problems at night finding a taxi, the major hotel in town is invariably a place to pick up one. If it's a long walk to get there, consider looking for a local to help you find one.

Warning Drivers tend to be sleepy from 18-hour work days and may race along at hair-raising speeds, particularly in the big cities. Rather than saying nothing, raise your voice and encourage other travellers to do the same.

TOURS

Compared to most areas of the world, West Africa has very few tour operators. Tour companies are usually located in the capital cities, and typically offer anywhere from one-day to one-week trips. On most tours, the larger the group, the lower the cost per person. Despite the fledgling tourist industry in some parts of West Africa, the companies seem to be quite reliable. For more information, see the individual country chapters.

Benin

Benin has one of the hottest attractions in all of West Africa – fishing villages built on stilts in the middle of a lagoon that stretches past Porto Novo. It's only a 25-minute drive from the heart of Cotonou to the launching point where you'll find canoeists ready to take you around the lagoon. Most tourists head for Ganvié, which has become something of a tourist trap, but you can pass it up for smaller, more pristine villages that are equally interesting.

In comparison, Cotonou may not seem so remarkable but, like the rest of Benin, it is shedding its traditional lethargy as the country emerges from its Marxist past. And if you're into African cooking, you may love the city; the selection and quality of African restaurants is unbeatable in West Africa.

In the rural areas, life in some respects goes on as it has for centuries. Voodoo, which has its origins in Benin and eastern Togo, still plays a prominent role, as it does in Haiti. Even today, fetishism is prevalent. You'll get a sense of this in Ouidah, the old slave-trading centre on the coast, and Abomey, the centre of the kingdom of Dahomey, one of the greatest empires in West Africa. The history of the king's palace, once the largest in West Africa and now a museum, is unique in that only women were used to protect the king.

Up north, you can visit Pendjari Park, one of the better game reserves in West Africa and, nearby, the fascinating castle-like settlements of the Somba.

Benin is a small, obscure country, but when it does something, it does it in a big way. The people in this area established one of the largest slave-trading operations in West Africa and also one of the most powerful kingdoms. Since independence, Benin has had the third-highest number of coups in Africa (Burkina Faso and Nigeria have had more) and adopted Marxism – it's the only country in West Africa to do so wholeheartedly. Now, however, democracy has taken a firm hold.

PEOPLE'S REPUBLIC OF BENIN

Area: 112,620 sq km
Population: 5.2 million
Population Growth Rate: 3.2%
Capital: Porto Novo
Head of State: President Nicéphore Soglo
Official Language: French
Currency: West African CFA franc
Exchange Rate: CFA 500 = US$1
Per Capita GNP: US$450
Inflation: 1%
Time: GMT/UTC + 1

Facts about the Country

HISTORY

Over 350 years ago, there were numerous small principalities. One of the chiefs had a quarrel with his brother and, around 1625, settled in Abomey. He then conquered the neighbouring kingdom of Dan, which became known as Dahomey, meaning 'in Dan's belly' in Fon. Each successive king pledged to leave more land than he inherited, a pledge they all kept by waging war with their neighbours, particularly the powerful Yoruba of Nigeria. At the same time, the

BURKINA FASO
NIGER
Parc National du W
Gaya
Malanville
Pendjari River
Parc de la Pendjari
Niger River
Kandi
Tanguieta
Natitingou
Boukoumbé
Kara
Djougou
Parakou
Ouémé River
TOGO
Benin
0   50   100 km
Savalou
Savé
Dassa Zoumé
Ibadan
Abomey
Bohicon
Pobè
NIGERIA
Bopa & Possotomé
Lokossa
Lake Ahémé
PORTO NOVO
LAGOS
LOMÉ
Ganvié
Cotonou
Grand Popo
Ouidah
Gulf of Guinea

Suggested Itineraries

With the recent political turmoil in Togo, **Cotonou** has become at least as popular as Lomé as a place to relax for a few days, enjoying the beach environment, wonderful African food and nightlife, and artisan shops. Add several more days to explore nearby **Porto Novo** and **Ganvié** but return to Cotonou in the evening. Porto Novo is a small tranquil town, and you can explore the lagoon from this eastern end of the country as easily as from the Cotonou side.

Those interested in voodoo will want to spend at least a day in **Ouidah**, which also has two good museums, while beach lovers will want to spend a few days at **Grand Popo** further west. However, if what you're looking for is a tranquil water environment, but not necessarily the sea, head for the **Lake Ahéné** area north of Grand Popo as it's surrounded by fishing villages and there's a decent hotel. Most travellers overlook this relatively unknown area and head directly to **Abomey** to see the royal palace. You can rent bikes there to explore the surrounding area, which is full of voodoo relics. **Parakou**, further north, is a good stopping point for a day, then head to **Natitingou** and **Pendjari Park**. You could easily spend almost a week here, climbing and cycling, exploring the castle-like houses, cooling off in various waterfalls and looking for wildlife. ∎

Portuguese and then other European powers established trading posts along the coast, notably at Porto Novo and Ouidah.

The Dahomey kingdom soon became rich by selling slaves – usually prisoners of war – to these traders and received luxury items and guns in return, thus increasing the internal strife. For well over a century, an average of 10,000 slaves a year were shipped to the Americas, primarily Brazil and the Caribbean and particularly Haiti, taking their knowledge and practice of voodoo with them. As a result, southern Benin became known as the Slave Coast.

In the late 1800s, the French gained control of the coast and defeated the kingdom of Dahomey, making it a colony and part of French West Africa. During the 70-year colonial period, great progress was made in education. Dubbed the 'Latin Quarter of West Africa' by the French, Dahomey became famous for its educated elite. These citizens were employed by the French and the Senegalese as principal advisors to government officials throughout West Africa. This eventually backfired – the educated elite became extremely vocal and began agitating for assimilation and equality, even producing a newspaper that attacked the French.

No progress was made, however, in developing the palm industry. Incredibly,

Dahomey was exporting the same amount of palm products on the eve of independence in 1960 as it was in the mid-1800s.

Independence

After WW II, the people of Dahomey formed trade unions and political parties. Hubert Maga became a famous politician during this period. When Benin became independent in 1960, he became the country's first president.

Almost immediately, the former French colonies started deporting the Dahomeyans who had been running the administration. Back in Dahomey without work, they were the root of a highly unstable political situation. Three years after independence, after seeing how easily some disgruntled army soldiers in Togo staged a coup, the military did the same in Benin.

During the next nine years, Benin became the Bolivia of Africa, with four more successful military coups, nine more changes of government and five changes of constitution – what the Dahomeyans called in jest *le folklore*. However, reflecting the civil manner of the Fon, not a single president was ever killed! When the army deposed General Soglo in 1967, they politely knocked on his door and told him: 'You're through'.

The Revolution

In 1972, Lt Col Mathieu Kérékou, a Catholic from the north representing a group of middle and junior-grade officers, seized control and formed a revolutionary government, renaming the radio station 'the voice of the revolution'. Anti-White sentiment erupted a few months later, with crowds attacking foreign-owned stores and the French Cultural Centre. Initially portraying themselves as a group of officers outraged by tribalism and political chaos, Kérékou's government soon attracted more radical elements.

Two years after his coup, Kérékou announced that Marxism would be the country's official ideology. To emphasise the change, he renamed the country Benin. The transition was rough: a presidential guard assassinated the Minister of Interior over a moral scandal implicating Kérékou's wife, the USA withdrew its ambassador, and workers held strikes in Cotonou for higher salaries. In 1977, in a coup attempt presumably instigated by Beninese exile groups, a force of Europeans and Africans headed by a French mercenary landed at Cotonou Airport, only to fly away after several hours of unsuccessful fighting. A commission of enquiry later revealed that Gabon and Morocco had helped organise the operation and implicated the French as well. Outraged by the accusations, Gabon broke off diplomatic relations and expelled all 9000 Beninese living there, and the French reduced their aid by a third.

As part of the revolution, the government required schools to teach Marxism, set up collective farms and ordered students to work part time on them. It assigned areas of cultivation and production goals to every district and village, formed state enterprises, created a single central trade union, inculcated a more militant spirit in the army and warned churches to support them or get out – à la the Soviets.

However, the revolution was always more rhetorical than real. Most farming remained in private hands; state and collective farms represented no more than 10% of the cultivated land. In the commercial sector, private businesses continued to handle about two-thirds of the trading. The economy fell into a shambles: inflation and unemployment rose and salaries remained unpaid for months. People soon lost interest in the Marxist-Leninist ideology foisted on them by the régime. In one year alone, there were six attempted coups. In the late 1980s, workers went on strike and were soon joined by students who protested in the streets. In Porto Novo, portraits of Kérékou and Beninese flags were burned in the streets and shops were looted. The government responded by giving 'shoot on sight' orders to the military but the strikers and demonstrators were not discouraged. Then the BCB bank collapsed due to fraud.

In December 1989, the French ambassador sent a memo to Kérékou recommending that the government hold a national conference and adopt specific constitutional changes. Kérékou followed the advice and in early 1990 renounced Marxism-Leninism and called for a conference to draft a new constitution. Dissidents used the occasion to blame Kérékou's government for leading the country into total bankruptcy, and for corruption and human rights abuses. To Kérékou's total surprise, the 488 delegates then engineered a coup, leaving him head of the army. A new cabinet was formed with Nicéphore Soglo (a former dissident) as prime minister. There were calls for a new constitution and free multiparty elections in 1991. Soglo defeated Kérékou in a free and open election. In exchange, France stepped up aid significantly.

Thus, in one of the quickest reversals in modern African history, Benin has gone from one of the most autocratic governments in Africa to one of the most democratic. Today, Africans across the continent who are discontent with their non-elected political leaders are pointing to Benin as a model on the African political front, leading the way to new political possibilities.

Benin Today
The dust is beginning to settle and talk is dying down after the major devaluation of the CFA French franc. Despite this setback, the future of the Republic of Benin looks considerably optimistic. With the implementation of a multiparty democracy, President Soglo has been working to foster trade and diplomatic relations with external creditors. His seat as chairman of the Conference of Heads of State and Government of the Economic Currency of West Africa (ECOWAS) and his former position as an administrator for the World Bank have enhanced Benin's profile, as will the summit of Francophone states to be held here in late 1995. All of this may help to attract foreign investment.

Since the instabilities and disruptions of the 1991-92 period, the country has made strides towards some significant economic gains and more importantly has experienced little civil unrest. Benin has received a good portion of the some 300,000 refugees from Togo who have fled the violence caused by supporters of President Eyadéma. As a result, diplomatic negotiations between the two countries have ceased and future relations look bleak until the political turmoil in Togo is settled.

GEOGRAPHY
Located between Nigeria and Togo, Benin measures roughly 700 km long and 120 km across in the south, widening to over 200 km in the north. It is a small country, about two-thirds the size of Portugal. Most of the coastal plain is a sandbar that obstructs the seaward flow of several rivers. As a result, there are lagoons a few km inland all along the coast. The biggest lagoon is Lake Nokoué, which forms the northern city limits of Cotonou and the southern limits of Porto Novo, the country's nominal capital. Lake Nokoué's outlet to the sea passes through Cotonou, dividing the city almost in half. The famous fishing town of Ganvié is constructed on stilts in this lagoon. The country's major river, the Ouémé, flows southward into Lake Nokoué and has a wide marshy delta with considerable agricultural potential.

As you travel inland, the land remains flat but the coastal plains are replaced by a forested plateau with dense vegetation. The country's third and fourth-largest towns, Parakou and Abomey, are in this area. In the far north-west, where Benin's two major game parks (Pendjari and W) are, the Atakora mountains reach a height of 457 metres.

CLIMATE
In the south, there are two rainy seasons – April to mid-July and mid-September to the end of October – while the north has one rainy season from June to early October. Areas in the Atakora region occasionally receive heavy rainfall. The climate in the north is tropical with temperatures reaching 46°C, and in the south ranging from 18° to 35°C. Harmattan winds blow from the north

from December to March. The hottest time of the year is from March to June.

GOVERNMENT

The Marxist-inspired *Loi Fondamentale* of 1977 was rescinded in 1988 and a new constitution was ratified two years later. The latter vested legislative authority in the hands of a 64-member national assembly and executive power in the president, who is elected by universal suffrage for five-year terms with a maximum of two terms, and in his Council of Ministers, including a prime minister which he appoints. Since 1993, there has been a seven-member constitutional court, which assumed the functions of the Haut Conseil de la République (HCR), a body that was set up during the transition. The setting up of this court formally completed the transition to democracy.

The constitution also created a true multiparty system. The main political parties today are the Rassemblement Africain pour le Progrès (RAP), which is the ruling party, the Union National pour la Démocratie et le Progrès (UNDP) and the Rassemblement Démocratique Dahoméen (ROD). The latter two are the main opposition parties and are reportedly considering merging.

ECONOMY

Benin is primarily a country of subsistence farming, with agriculture accounting for approximately 36% of GNP. Yams, cassava and corn are the principal food crops, followed by sorghum, beans, millet and rice, while cotton and palm oil are the main export crops. Cotton, the production of which has grown spectacularly during recent years, now accounts for over three-quarters of export earnings. Industry contributes only about 12% to GDP and manufacturing contributes less than 10%.

The GNP per capita is rising and is now US$450, which is above the West African average, but the annual population increase is 3.2%, which is on the high side. With the assistance of the Enhanced Structural Adjustment Facility (ESAF), the Soglo administration is trying to increase economic growth so as to finance improvements to the social infrastructure and reduce its budget deficit, which is now under 7%. The privatisation programme, on the other hand, is continuing to move at a snail's pace.

POPULATION & PEOPLE

Within the narrow borders of Benin is an array of different ethnic groups, which adds to the diversity and charm of the country. Despite the underlying tensions between the southern and northern regions, the various groups live in relative harmony and have intermarried. Most of the ethnic groups are patrilineal and many still practise polygamy. It appears, however, that this practice is becoming increasingly rare among urban and educated Beninese. Marriages were and are still arranged by the families and divorce is rare. Most families support themselves through agricultural production, their daily activity during the planting and harvesting seasons. Women control the local food distribution system, including the transport of produce to the market and the subsequent barter and sale.

Among the country's 5.2 million inhabitants are only about 240 doctors but there are over 11,000 nurses, and health care centres, although scarce in the north, can be found all over the country. As a result, infant mortality (8.8%) is the third lowest in West Africa. Nevertheless, life expectancy is still only 47 years, which is well below the average for West Africa.

Over half of Benin's people are members of one of five ethnic groups – the Fon, the Yoruba, the Bariba, the Betamaribé and the Fulani.

The Fon (and the related Adja) comprise nearly 40% of the population in Benin. Migrating from south-western Nigeria in the 13th century to southern parts of Benin, they established a kingdom in what is known today as the village of Allada.

The Yoruba (locally called Nagot), who also migrated from Nigeria, occupy the southern and mid-eastern zones of Benin and are the second-largest ethnic group in the country, comprising 12% of the population.

Many of them are noted for being active commercial travellers and traders.

The Bariba, who live primarily in the north and comprise about 8.5% of the population, are found mostly in the Borgou region. According to legend, they migrated from the Bussa and Ife areas of Nigeria. Their most famous kingdom in Benin was centred at Nikki, and they have remained relatively aloof towards southern Beninese because of their distant location and the slave raids which occurred in the north prior to the arrival of the colonial powers. This has resulted in a political and socioeconomic rift between the two areas.

The term Somba is a misnomer for the Betamaribé who live in the north-west, in the area of the Atakora mountains. They received this name as a result of the international attention given to their unique two-storey castle-like domiciles called *tata sombas*. One of the most fascinating groups in Benin, they were one of the first groups to arrive in the country. They have lived for hundreds of years in seclusion from industrial and Western influence and have managed to keep much of their traditional culture intact.

The Fulani, commonly referred to as the Peul, live primarily in the north and comprise 5.6% of the population. They are scattered throughout West Africa and many continue living as nomadic cattle herders. It is said that they have a mixed ancestry of Berbers and Toucouleurs; regardless, they continue migrating southward from the Sahara into the western region. Today, the Fulani,

despite their symbiotic relationship with the Bariba, are the least respected ethnic group in Benin because of their traditional nomadic lifestyle and lack of formal training.

ARTS & CULTURE
Artwork
The cultural history of Benin is rich, and for over a century the people's art has brought international attention to the legendary kingdom of Dahomey. Artistic expression was able to flourish with the help of the

16th-century bronze queen mother head – the queen mother held a powerful position in the royal family and had a right to her own altar.

Illiteracy
Historically noted for having a large number of intellectuals, Benin nevertheless has, according to UN publications, the third-highest rate of illiteracy (77%) in the world, exceeded only by Sierra Leone and Burkina Faso. For women, the situation is particularly bad as the literacy rate for them (16%) is half that for men. Education is primarily public and secular with minimal cost to the student. Primary school is a six-year compulsory programme with secondary school being a seven-year programme. Efforts are definitely being made to increase literacy as some 52% of school-age children are now enrolled in primary school, a rate higher than most countries in West Africa including Senegal. Enrolments in private schools in Cotonou are also growing while the University of Benin now has nearly 11,000 students. ■

Openwork cylinder

kingdom of Abomey. Traditionally, art served a functional and spiritual purpose, but in the case of the vainglorious kings, crafts people and sculptors were called upon to create works that evoked heroism and enhanced the image and prestige of the rulers. Until the 19th century, these Fon kings forbade artists and brass/silver casters to work outside of the palace walls. They became the historians of the era, particularly with the richly coloured appliqué tapestries that depicted the events of past and reigning kings. Originally hung on walls and paraded during ceremonies, they are still being made and are described as 'one of the gayest, liveliest of contemporary art forms'. You won't have any problem finding modern day examples – black material with figures cut out of imported coloured cloth and sewn on which illustrate, for example, animals, hunting scenes and the panther god Agassou.

The bronzework of Benin and Nigeria continues to be revered and collected by curators internationally. Bronze sculpture functioned as a celebration of royalty and served only aesthetic purposes. The sculptors of Ife (the progenitors of bronze casting) have produced almost no bronze or brass in several hundred years. Bronze casting is said to have been halted after a death decree was sent out by an enraged successor to a powerful Ife leader who had been immortalised with a life-size bronze statue.

Don't miss the bas-reliefs at the palace of Abomey. These were polychrome bas-reliefs in clay that were used to decorate the palace, temples and chiefs' houses. The palace has been restored by the Getty Conservation Institute and has been designated by UNESCO as one of the nearly 500 worldwide historic sites of common heritage in humanity.

The art of woodcarving still exists in Benin. In the areas of Allada and Abomey are some very skilled crafts people who carve ritual masks, tables and beautiful armchairs.

Dance & Ceremonies

There's a great variety of traditional dances and songs which you may encounter while travelling through the interior of Benin. Depending on the circumstances and events, these dances and ceremonies may be of a religious or cultural nature, or concern the vital forces of the universe. They may also give praise or a simple manifestation of joy, sorrow, or communion with the spirits of the dead. Some dance is choreographed in groups but more often it is individual and involves intricate body expression. There are traditional festivals such as La Gani in Nikki, a celebration of culture, identity and the memory of their great kingdom. There are other planned and spontaneous festivities that you may stumble upon such as the Zangbeto, a dance of ghosts, or the Egoun, a dance of masquerades. If you see a growing crowd of people running down the road following what appears to be a dancing haystack, catch up. Of all the things you can see while in Benin, these life-affirming traditional dances and ceremonies are likely to be the most enrapturing.

Voodoo
The ancient practice of worshipping spirits and fetishes has made Benin the 'cradle of voodoo'. It is comprised of a supreme God and a lesser pantheon of deities (the voodun). The voodun have the power to control the fate of humans by interceding on behalf of the worshippers and convening with the supreme deity. Those who possess or have mastered this divining ability to communicate with the spiritual world of voodun are called fetishers, juju priests or traditional medicine men. There is always a sacrificial offering made as a show of loyalty and respect to the spirits, but also on occasion to gain special favours, such as the birth of twins. In addition, if before approaching the other gods, an offering isn't made to Legba, who is the messenger between the gods and represented by a phallus, bad things might happen. Such sacrifices are usually palm wine or gin, but it is not uncommon to use the blood of rare birds, valuable animals and skulls of men.

Charms, called gris-gris, and fetishes prepared by the priests serve to protect the believer who may wear these charms or figurines on the arm, leg or around the neck, and may suspend them from the doorway of the house or in the central living area. Fetish temples can be found everywhere in Benin and ceremonies of sacrifice and adoration are today still quite common, particularly in northern areas such as the Borgou and Atakora regions. Despite the increasing 'Christianisation' of the country and the profane interest of voodoo adepts (usually greed or jealousy), this divine art and belief continues to live in the minds and souls of the people. The voodoo culture is also a part of the religion in Cuba, Haiti, Brazil and the USA, having been carried to these countries by slaves who were taken from the coast of Benin.

If you buy a fetish, make sure you learn which voodoo spirit it represents. ■

RELIGION
The history of religion in Benin has a most remarkable character that has been the subject of much scholarly research and public curiosity. While 20% of the population practise Christianity (Roman Catholics and fewer Protestants) and 15% are Muslims, most retain beliefs in a polytheistic spiritual world that influences all realms of life. There is no separation between humans and spirit; all is interconnected. Animism is simply the worship of the spirit in all things. This concept is called voodoo.

LANGUAGE
French is the official language in Benin. The majority of the people speak Fon in the southern parts while Bariba and Dendi are the principal languages in the north. Villages bordering Nigeria and Benin speak Yoruba, which is commonly referred to as Nagot (nah-GOH). The word for foreigner is *yovo*. While travelling into the interior of Benin you may hear the chant most young children have been taught: *Yovo, yovo, bon soir* (or *cadeau*), *ça va bien?, merci*.

Expressions in Fon
Good morning.	*AH-fon GHAN-gee-ah*
Good evening.	*kou-DOH BAH-dah*
How are you?	*ah-DOH GHAN-gjee-ah?*
I'm fine.	*un-DOH GHAN-gee-ah NOH-dang-gee*
Thank you.	*AH-wah-nou*
Goodbye.	*OH-dah-boh*

Expressions in Yoruba
Good morning.	*eh-KAH-roh*
Good evening.	*EE-kou-roh-lay*
How are you?	*BAH-un?*
I'm fine.	*AH-dou-pay*
Thank you.	*oh-SHAY*
Goodbye.	*OH-dah-boh*

Facts for the Visitor

VISAS & EMBASSIES
Benin Visas
Visas are not required of nationals of Denmark, France, Germany, Italy and Sweden. The Benin embassy in Washington requires US$20 and two photos for single-entry visas valid for

stays of up to 90 days. Multiple-entry visas are not available. The embassy normally takes nine days to process applications, but if you're in a hurry they'll usually speed up the process. There is no embassy in London, so travellers from the UK must get one in Paris or elsewhere. If you're in a real hurry and don't have time to get a visa, you could fly to Lomé, Togo, (Americans and most Europeans don't need visas to Togo) and take a taxi from there to Cotonou (three hours). As noted below, Benin visas are readily obtainable at the border en route.

There are Beninese embassies in both neighbouring Nigeria and Niger as well as in Ghana but not in Togo or Burkina Faso. If you will be travelling to Nigeria before coming to Benin, get a Benin visa in Lagos. This embassy gives reliable same-day service, the cost is minimal (roughly US$4), and it's valid for a seven-day trip. If you're travelling from Togo, you can get a visa at the border on the coastal road. The border is open 24 hours, but you might have to grease someone's hand to get a visa at night. It costs CFA 2000 but is good for only 48 hours; however, extensions are easy to obtain. It is reported that you can also get 48-hour visas at the northern border at Malanville, but get one in Niamey if at all possible as you risk being sent back to Niamey anyway, given only two days to arrive in Cotonou, or paying a huge bribe. No other Benin border station issues visas.

Visa Extensions

Visa extensions for up to 30 days are issued without problems in 24 to 48 hours by the immigration office of the Ministry of Interior (☎ 31 42 13) in Cotonou. A 30-day extension costs CFA 7000 and you'll need three photos. Applications are accepted only at 11 am.

Exit Visas

Exit visas are not required if you're leaving by road. However, except for French nationals, they are still required if your visit exceeds 48 hours and you're flying out. The process usually takes 24 hours, although you can usually get it the same day if necessary. Immigration is in charge of this service and

is open weekdays until 8 pm and on Saturday morning. If you arrive at the airport without your exit visa, be prepared to negotiate a small fee with the police. Check the exit visa requirement upon entering – the rules can change.

Benin Embassies

Belgium 5 Ave de l'Observatoire, Brussels 1180 (☎ (02) 354-94-71)
France (consulate) 89 rue du Cherche-Midi, 75006 Paris (☎ (1) 42-22-31-91)
Germany Rüdigerstrasse 10 Postsech, 5300 Bonn Mehlem (☎ (0228) 34-40-31/2)
USA 2737 Cathedral Ave, NW, Washington, DC 20008 (☎ (202) 232-6656)

Benin also has embassies in Abidjan, Accra, Algiers, Kinshasa, Lagos, Niamey and Ottawa. There's a consulate in Basel.

Other African Visas

Ghana The embassy takes two days to issue visas, requires four photos and charges CFA 12,000 (CFA 30,000 for multiple entries), which is considerably more than the Ghanaian embassy in Togo charges.
Niger The Niger embassy issues visas within 24 hours but almost never the same day, even if you beg. It's open Monday to Friday from 8 am to noon and 3 to 6.30 pm (CFA 15,000; two photos).
Nigeria The embassy is open weekdays from 10 am to 2 pm and issues visas in 24 hours. It requires two photos. The price depends upon your nationality; for Americans, visas are free. Germans, Australians, Japanese and the French must pay anywhere from CFA 500 to CFA 4000, while Britons must pay over CFA 10,000. However, since the embassy gives visas only to residents of Benin, travellers should not count on getting a Nigerian visa here.
Other Countries The French consulate issues visas in 24 to 48 hours to Togo, Burkina Faso, Cameroun, Côte d'Ivoire, Central African Republic, Gabon, Mauritania and Senegal.

Foreign Embassies

See the Cotonou Information section for a list of embassies in the capital.

DOCUMENTS

A passport and an International Vaccination Certificate are required. In small villages it may be advisable to pay a courtesy call on the police if you'll be staying overnight. They can be very helpful.

Car owners cannot enter the country

without insurance from a company in Africa. If you have insurance from elsewhere, chances are you'll be admitted anyway as this rule is not always strictly enforced. Regardless, you cannot get insurance at any Benin border stations, so you must get insurance in the capital city of the neighbouring country from which you're coming. This rule could change, so enquire.

CUSTOMS
There is no restriction on the amount of CFA or other currencies that you may import or export, but if you import a large amount you should declare it because you will be allowed to export only what you declare.

MONEY
1FF	=	CFA 100
UK£1	=	CFA 775
US$1	=	CFA 500

The unit of currency in Benin is the West African CFA. There's a thriving black market for the Nigerian naira and CFA around the Jonquet (jon-KAY) district in Cotonou. The rate for the CFA is essentially the same as the bank rate; the difference is you can get money any day and virtually at any hour. If you're at the airport and the bank is closed, you could walk or ride to the Sheraton only one km away and change money there. They don't require that you be a guest at the hotel and they don't charge a commission on travellers' cheques. The best bank for changing currency is the Bank of Africa, which offers the lowest exchange rates and charges no commission for travellers' cheques. Also try Ecobank-Bénin, open on Saturday from 9 to 11.30 am, and the Financial bank. At the latter, you can draw money with your Visa credit cards. However, if your card is not tied to a bank in France, you may encounter difficulties.

BUSINESS HOURS & HOLIDAYS
Businesses are open weekdays from 8 am to 12.30 pm and 3.30 to 6.30 pm, and Saturdays from 8 am to 12.30 pm. Government offices are open weekdays from 8 am to 12.30 pm

and 3 to 6.30 pm. Banking hours are 8 to 11.30 am and 3 to 5.30 pm weekdays. Ecobank-Bénin (Saturdays from 9 to 11.30 am) and the bank at the Sheraton are open in Cotonou on weekends.

Public Holidays
1 January, 16 January (Martyr's Day anniversary of mercenary attack on Cotonou), End of Ramadan, Good Friday, Easter Monday, Tabaski, 1 May (Worker's Day), Ascension Day, Whit Monday, 31 May, 1 August (Independence), 15 August (Assumption), Mohammed's Birthday, 26 October, 1 November (All Saint's Day), 30 November (National Day), 25 December, 31 December (Harvest Day).

POST & TELECOMMUNICATIONS
The post office and poste restante are excellent in Cotonou. To mail packages overseas, head for the Centre de Tori (☎ 30 10 48), opposite the airport in Cotonou. Packages up to five kg cost about CFA 11,600 or less.

For overseas telephone calls and faxes, go to the telecommunications office, in the heart of Cotonou on Ave Clozel, two doors west of the well-known Soneac bookshop, and open Monday to Saturday from 8 am to 8 pm. You can also make overseas calls from the main post office, which is open until midnight for that purpose only. The cost to the USA is about CFA 2500 for the first minute and half that for the remaining minutes; calls to Europe are slightly less. At the telecommunications office you can also make an international call and have the person ring you back. The cost of faxes and telefaxes is CFA 2400/3000 a minute to the USA/Canada, which is about half the Sheraton's rate. The fax service at both the telecommunications office and the Sheraton is good, however, faxes sent from the former may or may not get through, so double-check. Finally, if you need telephone numbers or business locations dial ☎ 12.

PHOTOGRAPHY
A photo permit is not required, but be careful when taking shots of museums, fetish

temples and cultural and religious ceremonies. You could upset a lot of people and end up being cursed. These rules are not so clear cut, so it's best to ask first. Fortunately, unlike other African countries, the police in Benin don't seem very concerned these days about travellers taking photographs.

HEALTH

Yellow fever and cholera vaccinations are both required. Anti-malarial treatment is recommended and it is best to only drink water that has been treated.

In Cotonou, the Polyclinique Les Cocotiers (☎ 30 14 31) is a private and efficient clinic at the Carrefour de Cadjehoun, across from the PTT Cajehoun. It is better than the government's nearby Hôpital CNHU (☎ 30 01 55).

DANGERS & ANNOYANCES

Benin is a relatively secure country with only limited incidents of crime that the typical tourist can avoid by simply being cautious.

Never walk on the beach alone, and even when walking with someone don't carry or wear any valuables. Even a cheap watch can attract thieves and there have been numerous muggings on the beach. Beaches are closed at night, so avoid being there after sundown. The beachfront between the Sheraton and Hôtel de la Plage is the area that has seen the largest increase in muggings. Also take care in the Jonquet and Ganhie business districts from the late afternoon onward.

Beggars are quite common in the shopping districts and can be quite persistent but they generally do not pose a security problem unless you attract hordes of them around you by giving gifts.

ACCOMMODATION & FOOD

Even after the devaluation, it is still fairly easy to find rooms (with fans) for under CFA 3000 all over the country, even in Cotonou. Several of these have restaurants attached. Most towns have very decent mid-range hotels.

Beninese food is unquestionably among the best in West Africa. It's also very similar to Togolese cuisine. (See Food in the Togo chapter for details.)

Getting There & Away

AIR
To/From Europe & the USA
There are direct flights from Paris on Air France and Air Afrique and from Brussels on Sabena. From London, the cheapest fares are those from bucket shops. Many of them do not deal with Aeroflot, but its fares are often the cheapest if they're obtained through one of those agencies. If the flight schedules to Cotonou are not convenient or if you're having problems getting a visa to Benin, consider flying to Lomé (Togo) and taking a taxi from there to Cotonou (three hours). Benin visas are readily obtainable at the Togo-Benin coastal border crossing.

From the USA, you can take Air Afrique twice weekly from New York to Abidjan, transferring there to Cotonou on the same airline. Or check the discount travel agencies found in many major US cities; some of the more well-established ones are listed in the introductory Getting There & Away chapter. Most offer amazingly low fares. Henderson Travels in Washington, DC, for example, has very competitive round-trip fares to Benin via Paris starting at around US$1300.

To return to Europe, check Aeroflot in Cotonou; it appears to have the lowest fares but you may have to go through one of the numerous travel agencies in Cotonou to obtain these. Standard economy fares to Europe on most major airlines (Air Afrique, Sabena and Air France) are all similar.

To/From West Africa
Since the devaluation, airfares in CFA have almost doubled. One-way fares to Niamey and Ouagadougou, for example, are now CFA 97,500 and CFA 105,000, respectively, on Air Afrique. However, Air Burkina's fares are about 20% less and it has several flights a week on this route. If you're headed to East Africa via Lagos, you may find it cheaper to fly from Cotonou to Lagos (CFA 15,000) and transfer airlines there rather than going overland to Lagos. This way you'll avoid having

to get a Nigerian visa and the hassles of Lagos and the airport because you'll spend your time in the transit lounge.

LAND
Bush Taxi & Minibus
To/From Niger Getting a taxi from Cotonou to Parakou is easy and takes from six to eight hours; to the Niger border it's another six hours. The entire trip costs CFA 8000.

To/From Nigeria The trip by bush taxi from Lagos to Cotonou costs CFA 2500 and takes about three hours. Minibuses are cheaper (CFA 2000) but the trip takes much longer.

Bush taxis leave for Lagos frequently throughout the day in Cotonou from the Gare du Dantokpa. If you want to stop at Porto Novo en route, you could take one headed for the border and get off at the turn-off north for Porto Novo. To continue your journey simply hail a cab from that intersection as most taxis will be headed for the border. Going to/from Lagos, you could save money by taking a taxi just to the border and changing there because taxi fares on the Nigerian side are much lower than in Benin. If you do this, you will need to change money at the border or carry naira with you.

To/From Togo Peugeot 504 bush taxis from Lomé make the trip to Cotonou in only three hours. The fare is CFA 2000 by minibus and CFA 2500 by bush taxi. In Cotonou, bush taxis leave for Lomé at all hours of the day and into the early evening from the Gare de Jonquet not far from the centre of town.

Car
The driving time from both Lagos (Nigeria) and Lomé (Togo) to Cotonou is only three hours. Avoid arriving or leaving Lagos at rush hour – it's a mess. The coastal route to Lomé and to Lagos is open 24 hours.

The Cotonou to Parakou road is paved, so you can travel the entire 1062 km from Niamey (Niger) on tarred road – an easy 15-hour drive. The northern border of Benin is open from 7 am to 7.30 pm, so keep that

in mind when leaving Cotonou if you don't want to end up sleeping at the border.

The 200-km road from Parakou to Kara (Togo) is in good condition and tarred on the Togo side. If you're headed from Parakou to Lomé via Kara you can make it in one long day, but you could also stop at Kara, which is a good overnight spot.

Getting Around

BUSH TAXI
Benin has no large buses, so minibuses and Peugeot 504 bush taxis are the principal means of public transport between towns. In Cotonou, there are four principal *gare routières* (taxi parks), each serving different areas and routes; see the Cotonou Getting There & Away and Getting Around sections. A Peugeot 504 costs CFA 2000 to Abomey, CFA 2500 to Lagos or Lomé, and CFA 5000 to Parakou, while minibuses generally cost about a quarter less and take much longer.

Some travellers recommend avoiding the gare routières and catching taxis as they leave town. Most taxi drivers at the gares will say almost anything to get you into their taxis, the most popular being that the car is leaving 'tout de suite' (right away). Wrong! In this context, 'right away' and 'in a little while' are conditioned responses to entice you into the car. They never leave town, however, until full or nearly so, and that's often difficult to predict. If you get into the car, don't pay until it's ready to depart as this will allow you the option of leaving. The drivers will press you to pay but don't give in as the last thing they want is to lose a potential customer.

To avoid the gare, stand along Blvd St Michel or near the university hospital where most taxis (for whatever destination in Benin) pass before departing Cotonou. Just yell out your destination to passing taxis which are honking and sooner or later one will pull over. However, for taxis to Lomé and Lagos, you will need to go to the gare routière because they don't leave there until full.

TRAIN

The train between Cotonou and Parakou via Bohicon (the stop for Abomey, nine km to the west) takes from eight to 10 hours. There's a daily train every morning in either direction and every other day there's also an evening train with a sleeper coach. There is no dining car on the sleeper train, so bring a snack. Bedding (ie a sheet) is provided, but bring warm clothing.

You can buy fruit, bread, acasa, ablo, agouti and small fish at all the frequent stops en route. The Pahou stop is my favourite; you can pick up some delicious ablah, a firm dough that the women serve with a hot pimente sauce, as well as petit poisson (small grilled fish). The only things served on the train are lukewarm soft drinks and beer. If you want mineral water, bring your own.

Second-class seats on the train are slightly cheaper than seats in a van and are significantly cheaper than those in a bush taxi. A minibus from Cotonou to Abomey, for example, costs CFA 1000; a 2nd-class train to nearby Bohicon costs CFA 750. Seats in 2nd class are a little hard but the cost (CFA 2500 to Parakou) is half the price of a Peugeot 504 bush taxi, and finding a seat is seldom a problem.

First class, which costs CFA 1500 to Bohicon and CFA 5100 to Parakou, is about as comfortable as that on any train in West Africa. The train also has a *couchette* (sleeping car) on the night run; a bunk is CFA 3000 to Bohicon and CFA 6300 to Parakou.

CAR

Petrol costs about CFA 150 a litre, the lowest in the CFA zone, but in recent years the price has fluctuated a bit because of the political turmoil in Nigeria and Benin's critical dependency on Nigeria for its petrol. In Nigeria, petrol is much cheaper, so much of it is carried illegally across the border into Benin and sold on the black market here at prices slightly below the official rate. Just look for the guys along the roads with one to five-litre bottles.

Rental cars are readily available in Benin. See the Cotonou Getting Around section for details on rates.

MOTORCYCLE-TAXIS

In all cities and towns, you'll find motor-cycle-taxis, commonly referred to as 'zemi-johns'. While they are by far the fastest and most convenient way of getting around the cities, they are not as safe as regular taxis. They are virtually everywhere in Cotonou and also in the larger towns. You'll recognise them by the driver's yellow and green shirt (purple and green in Parakou). Hail them just as you would a taxi, but they'll usually track you down first. Be sure to discuss the price before getting on or upon arrival at your destination the driver may demand an obscene fare. The typical fare is CFA 100 to CFA 200, depending on the length of the trip.

Cotonou

Founded in 1830, Cotonou (ku-TONU) meaning 'mouth of the river of death' in Fon, owes its birth to the abolition of the slave trade. With the arrival of a democratic government, the influx of both Togolese and Nigerian expatriates and the expansion of the private sector, Cotonou is no longer the lethargic town it once was.

In addition to some fairly good beaches only a few km from the centre of town, Cotonou offers several good nightclubs, two international-level hotels, and good crafts centres. It is also one of the best places in West Africa for trying African food. Only a short drive from its centre brings you to Ganvié – an unusual, picturesque, major tourist attraction.

Most importantly, the Beninese are still quite friendly despite the growing number of foreigners invading the place. So even if Cotonou seems a little boring at first glance, stay a while. The more you get to know the city, the better it gets.

Orientation

The heart of town is the intersection of Ave Clozel and Ave Steinmetz. Going eastward on Ave Clozel, one of the city's two main drags, you'll pass over the old bridge (the one closest to the ocean) into the Akpakpa section; the road eventually turns into the highway to Porto Novo and Lagos. The new bridge is the one further inland; the wide Blvd St Michel (or Ave du Nouveau Pont), the other main drag, passes over it into Akpakpa, eventually connecting with Ave Clozel. The nicest residences are in the opposite direction, out near the Sheraton, in the Patte d'Oie, Haie Vive and Cocotiers sections.

Information

Tourist Office The Direction du Tourisme et de l'Hôtellerie (☎ 31 49 05), at the Carrefour des Trois Banques, has an 80-page booklet, *Passeport pour le Bénin*, in French or English for CFA 500. The staff can sometimes be a useful source of information.

Money The best bank for changing money is the Bank of Africa (BOA), which is near the centre on Ave Jean Paul II, a block west of Air Afrique. It offers the lowest exchange rates and like most banks here, including the one at the Sheraton, charges no commission on travellers' cheques. On Saturday until 11.30 am, you can change money at Ecobank-Bénin, near Marché Ganhi; all other banks are closed on the weekend except the one at the Sheraton.

Foreign Embassies The addresses or telephone numbers of some embassies are:

Chad Akpakpa district, 2½ blocks north of Cinéma Concord (☎ 30 08 24)
Egypt (☎ 30 08 42)
France Route de l'Aéroport near the Presidential Palace (☎ 30 08 24, telex 5209). The French consulate is in the centre, one block behind the post office. It, not the embassy, issues visas.
Germany In Patte d'Oie, one block from the US embassy (☎ 31 29 67, telex 5224)
Ghana Route de l'Aéroport (☎ 30 07 46)
Niger One block behind the post office (☎ 31 40 30)
Nigeria Blvd de la Marina, several hundred metres east of the Sheraton (☎ 30 04 70, telex 5247)
USA Rue Caporal Anani Bernard, Patte d'Oie, near the French embassy (☎ 30 06 50, fax 30 19 74)
Zaïre Cocotiers (☎ 30 19 83)

Honorary consulates include Belgium (☎ 30 18 75) in Cocotiers, Italy (☎ 31 25 74), the Netherlands (☎ 31 30 05), Switzerland (☎ 30 14 68) in Cocotiers and the UK (☎ 30 16 01).

Travel Agencies Two of the best agencies are Bénin-Tours (☎ 30 01 00, fax 30 11 55, telex 5111) at the Sheraton and Sacodi Voyages (☎ 31 25 60, fax 31 38 09) at the Hôtel de la Plage. They offer a wide assortment of information and tours, including *pirogue* (dugout canoe) fishing and trips by boat from Cotonou to Ganvié. Two others include Sitrexci Voyages (☎ 31 47 80), on Rue Goa and good for discounted fares, and C&C Bénin Voyages (☎ 31 47 46), on Ave Clozel, several blocks east of the old bridge.

Bookshops Papeterie Soneac on Ave Clozel across from the main post office is the largest and most popular bookshop in town. It sells the *International Herald Tribune*, *Newsweek*, *Time* etc and has a large selection of books and postcards. The next best bookshop is the Librairie Nôtre-Dame, which is adjacent to the cathedral and has an excellent selection of cultural and historical books on Benin. If you still cannot find what you're looking for, try Librairie Buffalo two blocks to the north.

Supermarkets In the heart of the city around Marché Ganhi are a number of good supermarkets. The newest and largest is Prisunic. American 24 is just across the street and has many expensive US products while La Pointe has an impressive selection of wines and imported fruit. For speciality items, try the reliable Mayfair on Ave Missé Beau; you'll find pita bread, popcorn and a wonderful selection of chocolates. Be sure to check the expiration dates of everything you buy. Locally bottled mineral water is sold at all of the supermarkets; you'll find chilled bottles at La Gerbe d'Or and La Caravelle.

Pharmacies The most well-stocked pharmacy is Pharmacie Camp Ghezo (☎ 31 55 52), one block north of Olymp Coiffure, just around the corner from the US embassy. For an all-night pharmacy (*pharmacie de garde*), try Pharmacie Jonquet (☎ 31 20 80) on Rue des Cheminots in the Jonquet district, or look

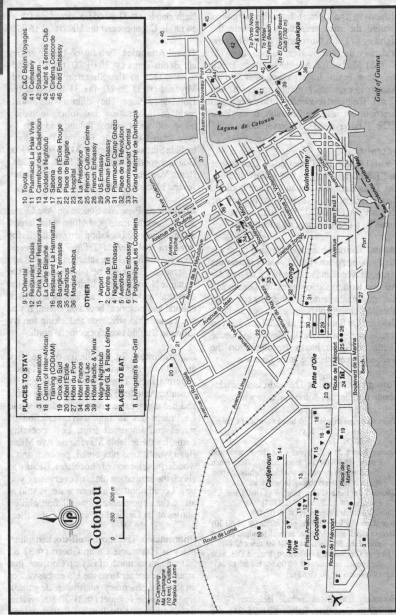

Cotonou

PLACES TO STAY

- 3 Bénin Sheraton
- 18 Centre of Inter-African Training (CODIAM)
- 19 Croix du Sud
- 20 Hôtel l'Étoile
- 27 Hôtel du Port
- 34 Hôtel France
- 38 Hôtel du Lac
- 39 Hôtel Pacific & Vieux Nègre Nightclub
- 44 Hôtel GL & Place Lénine

PLACES TO EAT

- 8 Livingston's Bar-Grill
- 9 L'Oriental
- 12 Restaurant l'Oasis
- 15 China House Restaurant & La Carte Blanche
- 16 Restaurant La Harmattan
- 28 Bangkok Terrasse
- 35 Atlanticus
- 36 Maquis Akwaba

OTHER

- 1 Airport
- 2 Centre de Tri
- 4 Nigerian Embassy
- 5 Aeroflot
- 6 Ghanian Embassy
- 7 Polyclinique Les Cocotiers
- 10 Toyota
- 11 Pharmacie La Haie Vive
- 13 Carrefour des Cadéhoun
- 14 Golden's Nightclub
- 17 Sabena
- 21 Place de l'Étoile Rouge
- 22 Place de Bulgarie
- 23 Hospital
- 24 La Présidence
- 25 French Cultural Centre
- 26 French Embassy
- 29 US Embassy
- 30 German Embassy
- 31 Pharmacie Camp Ghezo
- 32 Place de la Révolution
- 33 Commissariat Central
- 37 Grand Marché de Daniokpa
- 40 C&C Bénin Voyages
- 41 Cemetery
- 42 Stadium
- 43 Yacht & Tennis Club
- 45 Cinéma Concorde
- 46 Chad Embassy

on the windows of other pharmacies for postings of other all-night places.

Grand Marché de Dantokpa

If there were a 'must see' in Cotonou, it would be the huge, picturesque Grand Marché de Dantokpa which borders the lagoon and Blvd St Michel. This lively market has everything from food items (which occupy the entire 1st floor) dungarees, blank cassettes, radios, wax cloth, baskets, religious paraphernalia and pottery, to bats' wings and monkeys' testicles. The wax cloth selection is the best in Cotonou and, like all items, it's all sold in one given area. This market is truly fascinating with all the activity, variety of items for sale and the people who give it vibrancy.

One of the more amusing things you may find here is a love fetish, *le fetishe d'amour*. Rub it into your hands, whisper a girl's or boy's name to it seven times, touch the person and he or she is yours. The price is determined in a ceremony where a fetisher hurls into the air a piece of rope with bits of animals hanging off it, to the sound of chanting and gongs. If you're on a tight budget, say so because the fetishers, taking compassion on the poor, have been known to throw the rope again – and lower the price.

Beaches

The best beach is the one behind Hôtel PLM-Aledjo, extending east to Hôtel El Dorado (four km east of the centre). It is the safest and cleanest beach but gets crowded on weekends. The best beaches of all, however, are well west of Cotonou – at Ouidah (41 km) and, best of all, Grand Popo (80 km).

Places to Stay – bottom end

The Centre of Inter-African Training (COD-IAM), near the Ministry of Interior, often has rooms for CFA 3500. They have screens, shared showers and exterior toilets.

The long-standing *Hôtel Babo* (☎ 31 46 07) has for many years been the most popular cheap hotel. Unattractive rooms with cockroaches cost from CFA 2500 to CFA 4000 (with fan and personal toilet). Request one

on the top level as they are more spacious and airy. It's on Rue Agbeto Amadoré, five blocks south of St Michel church.

Two blocks to the east is *Hôtel Camer*. It has spartan but large, clean and airy rooms for CFA 3000 (CFA 3500 with private bath and flush toilet) – check the sturdiness of your bed. There's a lively open-air bar next door.

At *Hôtel Pacific* (☎ 33 01 45) you simply cannot beat the price for the quality of the rooms, attached baths and the relatively central location. Ventilated singles/doubles cost CFA 4000/8000, including breakfast. Ask for a room in the back as those on the street side are a bit noisy. It is just east of the old bridge, on the road to Porto Novo. If you walk across the bridge at night, be alert as robberies have occurred there.

Hôtel Crillon, in the centre just behind the ex-Ciné Vog (eastern side), is not a bad choice either. It has rooms with fans starting at CFA 4700, including breakfast, amazingly clean bathrooms and friendly service. Check the mattress before taking your room, however, because some of them are in terrible condition. Just around the corner on Ave Steinmetz is *Hôtel Concord*, with rooms starting at CFA 5000. A Peace Corps favourite, it has good management, very clean rooms and private baths. It is often completely booked, however, so you may have to go early in the morning to get a room.

If you're desperate or want a room by the hour, try *Pension Le Muguet*, directly behind Le Must nightclub. It's a brothel and rents rooms with fans mostly by the hour. While hourly rates are fixed, the nightly rate seems to range from CFA 2500 to CFA 3000. The rooms are cheap but you'll get what you pay for because at night the area is one of the noisiest and most dangerous in Cotonou.

Camping The only camp site near Cotonou is *Camping Ma Campagne* (☎ 36 01 63), 13 km from the heart of Cotonou on the coastal road to Lomé. It's clearly marked and only five km from the launching point for boats to Ganvié. The facilities are not the best, but camping costs only CFA 1000 per person and the bar's frosty beers are reasonably priced.

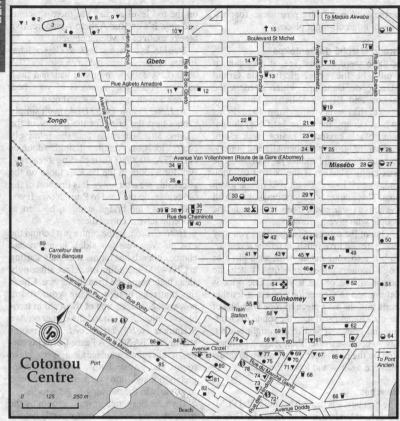

Cotonou
Centre

Meals here cost around CFA 1500. The owner, Felix, is a repository of wisdom on tribal life in Benin, Niger and Togo. He can also show you the five-km dirt path that leads to the nearest beach. Motorcycles can travel on that path but not cars. To get here from central Cotonou, stand by the main mosque on Blvd St Michel and look for a minibus headed this way; the fare is CFA 200.

Don't try camping at an unofficial camp site, even in a car; it's illegal and if the police find you, you could spend a night in jail. The worst possible place is the beach. The thieves are notorious, and the risk of getting arrested there is higher.

Places to stay – middle

Hôtel Bodega (☎ 31 44 97) has poor-quality rooms starting at CFA 7000 (overpriced), with a fan and shared bath that is not separated by a complete wall. The restaurant below has an upbeat ambience with great pizza and cold beer on tap. About five blocks north of Blvd St Michel on St Jean is the 25-room *Hôtel de France* (☎ 32 19 45), which is a bit off the beaten path but all the taxi drivers know it. It's well maintained and has spacious, clean rooms with fans and carpets for CFA 6500 (CFA 8500 with air-con). The hotel has a secure place

PLACES TO STAY

5	Hôtel de l'Union
12	Hôtel Babo
22	Hôtel Camer, Hôtel des Familles & Buvette au Petit Coin
36	Pension Le Muguet
48	Hôtel Concord
49	Hôtel Crillion
52	Hôtel Vickinfel
55	Hôtel Bodega & The Marilyn (Bar)
82	Hôtel de la Plage
90	Maquis La Résidence

PLACES TO EAT

1	Restaurant Sorrento
6	Maquis Pili-Pili
8	Chez Ogot
9	Mama Bénin
10	Restaurant La Serre
11	Restaurant L'Amitié
14	La Cabane
16	Le Source Grill
25	Street Food
26	Street Food
29	Le Méditerranean
38	China Town
41	Au Feu de Bois Restaurant
43	La Terrasse
44	Le Lagon Grill
45	Chez Fatou
47	Calao & Ex-Vog Ciné
53	Royal Toffa
56	Costa Rica
57	Le Buchon
58	La Gerbe d'Or
60	Sandwich Vendors
61	Pâtisserie La Caravelle

67	Mik-Mac (Restaurant-Bar)
71	Restaurant La Verdure
73	Street Food
74	Edelweiss
77	Africa Queen

OTHER

2	Artisans du Soleil (Boutique)
3	Stadium
4	Halle des Arts, New York, New York Nightclub & Centre de Promotion de l'Artisanal
7	Ex-Ciné Bénin
13	Banana Nightclub
15	St Michel Church
17	Lively Bar
18	Gare du Dantokpa
19	Dani's Bar
20	Air Gabon
21	Nigeria Airways
23	Coronné d'Or
24	Cheap Bar & Street Food Area
27	Gare Abomey & the Fripe Area
28	Autogare Missébo
30	Cameroun Airlines
31	Buses for Ouidah
32	Mosque
33	Autogare Jonquet
34	Cheap Bar & Street Food Area
35	Peace Corps
37	Le Must & Playboy (Le Rêve) Nightclubs
39	2001 Nightclub
40	Afrikan Nights (Nightclub)

42	Gare Itajara (for Parakou)
46	Flash Video
50	Pharmacy
51	Institut Cartographique
54	Espace Goa Department Store
59	Florida Nightclub, Air France & Sitrexci Voyages
62	Librairie Buffalo & So What Nightclub
63	Photo Nina
64	Gare de l'Ancien Pont (for Porto Novo)
65	Librairie Notre-Dame & Cathedral
66	New Gate Nightclub
68	Three Musketeers Bar-Restaurant
69	Prisunic Supermarket
70	La Pointe Supermarket
72	Ecobank-Bénin
75	Marché Ganhi & Music Vendors
76	American 24 Supermarket
78	Financial Bank
79	Papeterie Soneac (Bookshop) & Télécommunications
80	Niger Embassy
81	Post Office
83	Sonacop Station
84	Sonacop Station
85	French Consulate
86	Air Afrique
87	BOA Bank
88	Direction du Tourisme et de l'Hôtellerie
89	Ministry of Interior

to park cars and asks that guests pay for all their expenses on a daily basis.

Several km to the west is the three-storey *Hôtel l'Étoile* (☎ 30 26 41), which is on the north-west side of Étoile Circle. Despite the remote location, it gets its fair share of business and has rooms with fans starting at CFA 6000 (CFA 12,000 with air-con). There is a restaurant and small bar and the menu of the day is CFA 3500. For a more central location, check *Hôtel de l'Union* (☎ 31 27 66) on Blvd St Michel facing the Halle des Sports. Rooms cost CFA 7500 (CFA 12,500 with air-con) but the service is awful and the rooms are tiny and dark. The only attractions

are the bar, which is fairly lively, and a dried-up dead alligator on the 2nd level, which you can see without staying here.

Hôtel El Dorado (☎ 33 09 23) has a nice breezy ambience and is good value among the mid-range hotels. The standard rooms with fans cost CFA 11,000 and have large bathrooms, comfortable beds and tile floors. You can also get larger bungalows for CFA 20,000. The facilities include tennis courts, an excellent long pool and a small one for children, a workout room, massage parlour, ping-pong tables and a clean private beach. The main drawback is the location, four km east of the centre. Finding taxis to go there is no problem

(CFA 150 for a moto-taxi), but finding one at night to take you into town is nearly impossible. Also, on weekends the pool and beach here are often very crowded.

Much further east along the coastal highway, 17 km from central Cotonou, is the new *Hôtel Palm Beach*, which is a nice hideaway right on the beach with one of the best restaurants for grilled and fresh seafood. Rooms are spacious and start at CFA 15,000 with air-con and TV. It's possible to wade in the water but swimming can be dangerous because of the strong undercurrents. If you don't have wheels, you'll need to arrange transport for your return to Cotonou.

Hôtel GL (☎ 33 16 17, fax 33 26 27), east of the new bridge, has carpeted, spacious and air-con rooms for CFA 14,000, including breakfast, telephones and TV. There is also a restaurant and a small bar.

Hôtel du Port (☎ 31 44 43) is the best mid-range hotel because of its professional service and high-quality rooms. Prices range from CFA 16,000 for a carpeted air-con room with private bath to CFA 28,000 for a spacious pool-front bungalow. The restaurant is quite expensive but they have Sunday barbecue specials that are delicious.

If you're desperate, consider the smelly, run-down *Hôtel de la Plage* (☎ 31 25 60) nearby. Unventilated rooms with sagging, smelly mattresses and mosquitoes start at CFA 12,000. The CFA 15,000 units with air-con and private baths are slightly better but still very poor value. It has a small pool out the back, and accepts American Express.

Places to Stay – top end
For luxury accommodation, head for the huge *Bénin Sheraton* (☎ 30 01 00, fax 30 11 55, telex 5111), on the beach on the outskirts of town near the airport. Rooms cost CFA 78,000 (CFA 10,000 more for an ocean-view room). The long-standing *Croix du Sud* (☎ 30 09 54, fax 30 02 18, telex 5032) is nearby and much better value. It has a lively feel and good amenities, including the United Nations Club which has a pool, tennis courts, volleyball and horses. Singles/

doubles cost CFA 22,000-25,000/25,000-28,000, including breakfast.

If you're looking for a beach hotel and won't be going to the centre very often, you may prefer the four-star *Hôtel PLM-Aledjo* (☎ 33 05 61 or 33 11 58, fax 33 15 74, telex 5180). Large singles/doubles cost from about CFA 35,000/40,000, including 15% tax. The Aledjo restaurant serves good but expensive food. Except in the peak of the winter season, the place is like a mortuary, and finding a cab can be a pain.

The only top-end hotel near the centre is *Hôtel du Lac* (☎ 33 19 19, telex 5311). It has been completely renovated and is under new management. The rooms are sunny, spacious and exceptionally clean with TVs and telephones. Singles/doubles cost CFA 20,000/36,000 including 15% tax and breakfast. There is an excellent restaurant, with a sedate ambience and great lagoon and port views.

Places to Eat
Superb brochettes (beef kebabs) can be found all over Cotonou in the late afternoon and at night. Just look for the smoking grill piled with meat on sticks for CFA 100 to CFA 200. There are also omelette men who set up shop around sundown and work until 10 am the following morning. They are everywhere and you can usually spot their long tables with hot chocolate, coffee and tea containers spread across the top. You can get an entire breakfast for CFA 300. Be sure not to miss the seasonal plantains, yam fries and deep-fried sweet potatoes usually found in front of *buvettes* (small bars) in the late afternoon and evening. The sandwich ladies, right off Ave Clozel, 100 metres north of La Gerbe d'Or pastry shop, allow you to create your own sandwich with avocado, spaghetti, beef, eggs, pasta and loads of other stuff.

Coffee Shops & Bakeries The most popular place for fresh bread, croissants and other pastries is *La Gerbe d'Or*, which opens at 7 am. On the lower level they sell bread, pastries, yoghurt, milk and ice cream. On the 2nd level is the restaurant/ice-cream parlour (closed Monday) which has a full menu plus quick sandwiches, hamburgers and fries. This is the only place in Benin to get real ice cream, and the banana splits are absolutely delicious. Down the street, on Ave Clozel at the intersection with Ave Steinmetz, is *Pâtisserie La Caravelle*, which has a quaint coffee shop and a terrace restaurant overlooking the city centre. They have excellent fish and shrimp. It's open daily.

African *Restaurant L'Amitié* (Senegalese), on the same street as Hôtel Babo, has excellent peanut sauce and spicy rice dishes for less than CFA 700. It's a great lunchtime place and it ranks among the best. They serve from noon to 4 pm and from 8 pm until late.

Le Source Grill, on Ave Steinmetz three blocks north of Air Gabon, opens at sundown. It has delicious chicken and fries for less than CFA 1000, good salads (untreated) and some of the coldest beer in town.

Le Lagon Grill on Ave Steinmetz, 100 metres from Hôtel Concord, has grilled chicken and fries, and is open late. The longstanding *Mama Bénin* has an overwhelming selection of West African dishes (CFA 300 to CFA 1000). It's behind the ex-Ciné Bénin, and open for lunch and dinner.

Chez Ogot, just down the street from Mama Bénin, opens around 7.30 pm, and you can choose from a selection of rice, pounded yams and maize to accompany your piping-hot sauces. It's always crowed but squeezing in is no problem. *Chez Fatou* has for years been a popular hang-out and pick-up joint with very good Nigerian food. The prices are reasonable and it's open at all hours of the night. It's 100 metres from the ex-Ciné Vog and across Ave Steinmetz.

Maquis Pili-Pili (☎ 31 50 48) is one of Cotonou's best. Two blocks behind Hôtel de l'Union, it's a slightly up-market restaurant with a great ambience and excellent food. Prices range from CFA 2000 to CFA 3500.

Maquis Akwaba is another great restaurant right off Blvd St Michel near St Michel market. It is most impressive, with dishes from Senegal, Nigeria, Cameroun and Côte d'Ivoire. Call about their Sunday specialities; you can also make special requests.

Royal Toffa (☎ 31 23 33) is where the Beninese ministers and diplomats go. Prices are high but the food is said to be only average. The menu is African and European. *Maquis La Résidence* has a secluded location, excellent service and delicious grilled fish. Be prepared to pay at least CFA 5000 per person, however.

Lebanese *Le Méditerranean* (☎ 31 02 41) is the new rave of many Peace Corps volunteers. It has good hamburgers and Lebanese chawarmas and falafel sandwiches with fries from CFA 500 to CFA 2500. *Mik-Mac* (☎ 31 39 79), which is directly across from La Caravelle, has similar fare but quicker service and takeaway service. One of the best restaurants in town is *L'Oriental* (☎ 30 18 27). With the exception of the Sheraton, it has the best and largest buffet in Cotonou; it's on Wednesday and Sunday nights and costs CFA 4000. It's open every evening and is in Quartier Haie Vive; take the first road after Pharmacie La Haie Vive.

French For relatively moderate prices, it's hard to beat the very popular *Calao* (☎ 31 24 26), with its adjoining sidewalk bar. It's an attractive small restaurant in the heart of town next to the ex-Ciné Vog on Ave Steinmetz. *Costa Rica*, near Hôtel Bodega, is a great place for pizza, grilled steak and shrimp. It has great draught beer on tap too. Directly across from it is the new *Le Buchon*, with an impressive menu.

Le Bodega reportedly has great pizza; a plate costs around CFA 3000. *Edelweiss* (☎ 31 27 40), just behind Marché Ganhi, is pretty dead these days, but the menu is huge with appetising main dishes from CFA 2900 to CFA 5000. *Restaurant La Serre* is the talk of the town and has more than just French food to offer for reasonable prices. It's around the corner from the intersection of Blvd St Michel and Rue de Soc Gbeto. Prices are in the CFA 2500 to CFA 5000 range.

Restaurant La Harmattan (☎ 08 08 91) has been around for years and has a longstanding reputation among expatriates, though you'll rarely hear them raving over the food. It's just across from the statue at the Place des Martyrs and under a large straw hut. *La Terrasse* (☎ 31 52 08), on Rue Guinkomey a block north-west of Flash Video, is an up-market restaurant with specialities such as Spanish rice dishes, couscous, raclette and fondu; most main courses are around CFA 4000. It has irregular hours, so check before coming here.

Italian *Sorrento* (☎ 31 57 79) is the only authentic Italian restaurant in Cotonou. It has decent pizza and other Italian and French dishes. It's within the Halle des Arts complex (in the back) on Blvd St Michel, two km from the centre, and is open for lunch and dinner. For a pizza place closer to the centre, try *L'Estaminet* a block west of ex-Ciné Vog.

Asian *China Town* is in the heart of Jonquet across from Le Must nightclub. It's a simple but nice place with low prices, good food and cordial service. Also try the new and attractive *Bangkok Terrasse*. The interior is simply charming but the portions are small.

Entertainment

Bars There are buvettes all over Cotonou, and both beer and mixed drinks are unquestionably cheaper at them than elsewhere. The liveliest bars in town are along the Jonquet strip after sundown. The bar facing the Peace Corps is a good place to meet volunteers if you're looking for information on places to see and things to do in Benin. *Le Calao* has a nice sidewalk bar with good beer on tap. It's very animated in the evenings. *Three Musketeers* has a quiet, more up-market bar on the ground level with satellite TV, a pool table, darts, snack foods and draught beer on tap. *Livingston's*, which attracts mainly expatriates, is in a nice neighbourhood and features an open-air patio and good music.

Live Music As Cotonou continues to grow, the choice of evening activities looks very promising. There are a number of places where you can go to hear live music from both the Orient and the Occident. *The Marilyn* jazz bar next to Hôtel Bodega is a classy place featuring local musicians. *So What* is the most popular jazz club and has a variety of traditional Benin musical performers and contemporary jazz artists. It's a nice and casual open bar, above Librairie Buffalo. *La Cabane* is a restaurant-jazz bar that has an outstanding jazz band with special guest singers Wednesday to Saturday. The new *Case de la Musique* needs more publicity but it's definitely a place to check out if you want to see young Beninese music artists showcased. Be sure to enquire also about upcoming events at the French Cultural Centre (☎ 30 52 14), which attracts many excellent musical groups from abroad.

Nightclubs There are a number of good nightclubs in Cotonou, regardless of the type of crowd and music you're in search of. The Jonquet strip is full of them – wild and wicked. *Afrikan Nights* is the newest and has a mix of current US and African music. Just down the street is the live, uncensored *2001*; crowded and good for dancing. It's small and smoky. Other more decadent places in the area are *Le Must* and *Playboy*. They are equally animated with good, upbeat music. In the Halle des Arts is the plush *New York, New York* which is a haven for prostitutes with fetishes for mirrors. The *New Gate* is an elite dance club with upper-class Beninese clientele. The music is contemporary West and Central African and the dress is semiformal. It's behind the Co-op supermarket just before the old bridge.

Florida, in the heart of town on Rue Goa, is a great couple's place for dancing. *Le Téké* at the Sheraton is a lot of fun on holidays and special occasions when there's a crowd, otherwise it's usually pretty dead. A better choice would be *Golden's* on the western side of town behind the mosque in Cadjehoun. It's one of the biggest clubs in Cotonou and the music and drinks are tops. *Le Vieux Nègre* is a fabulous Camerounian nightclub that often spotlights dancers from Cameroun to perform traditional dances. It's across the old bridge, next door to Hôtel Pacific.

Cinemas In 1993, all movie houses in

Cotonou closed because of the increasing popularity of video tapes. You can still see good films at the American and French cultural centres, however. They both offer monthly pamphlets on upcoming programmes and films. If you have access to a video player, you can get movies for CFA 1000 at Flash Video on Ave Steinmetz facing the ex-Ciné Vog.

Things to Buy

Artisan Goods There is a wide variety of wonderful souvenirs to buy in Cotonou. If you're not looking for anything in particular and just want to browse, the *Centre de Promotion de l'Artisanal*, just west of the Halle des Arts on Blvd St Michel, is a good place to do this. The shops there offer a wide variety of wood carvings, bronze sculptures, batiks, leather goods, jewellery and the famous Benin appliqué cloth.

Artisans du Soleil is a unique artisan shop selling a variety of handmade goods such as tablecloths, boxer shorts, accessory bags, and oak and ebony wood crafts. It's open on Monday after 3 pm and Tuesday to Saturday from 9 am to noon and 3 to 7 pm.

The *Coronné d'Or* (☎ 31 58 64) on Ave Steinmetz, a block south of Nigeria Airways, has an impressive selection of bronze, wall hangings, wood sculptures and original jewellery with African stones. The people here also design jewellery, and clean and restore jewellery and art. It is open Monday to Saturday from 9 am to 1 pm and 3 to 8 pm.

Leather & cotton cushion

Hôtel du Port has a nice boutique where many people go to buy stones for making jewellery; outside Africa, these stones can be very expensive. Open every day from 10 am to noon and 3 to 7 pm, it also sells beautiful bathrobes, handbags, jewellery and other artwork from Togo, Côte d'Ivoire and Zaïre.

Clothes There's a good used-clothes market behind Gare Abomey called the 'dead yovo' market, named so because it was thought that these US and European donations were clothes of people who had died. It is a good place to find running shoes that somehow make their way over from Lagos.

Music For records or cassettes of Beninese music, the best place is along the road just to the rear of Marché Ganhi. You'll find an entire block of young men standing in front of their huge portable cassette players outblasting each other. Once you can get them to turn the music down so that you're not screaming at each other, they can be really helpful. Angelique Kidjo is very popular these days. Other well-known Beninese recording artists include Yonass Pedro, Nel Olivier and Yelouassi Adolphe. Koffi Olomidé and Aureleus Marbele are also popular to varying degrees. The cassette vendors also have a large selection of Beninese artists playing traditional music. Cassettes cost from CFA 700 to CFA 900.

Getting There & Away

Air Aeroflot (☎ 30 15 74) and Air France (☎ 30 10 10) are out on Route de l'Aéroport; Air Afrique (☎ 30 15 15) is on Ave Clozel; Ghana Airways (☎ 31 42 83); Nigeria Airways (☎ 31 52 31/2), Air Gabon (☎ 31 20 67) and Cameroun Airlines (☎ 31 52 17) are all on Ave Steinmetz, halfway between Ave Clozel and Blvd St Michel.

Bush Taxi & Bus Bush taxis for Lomé and Ouidah leave from Autogare Jonquet on Rue des Cheminots, 2½ blocks west of Ave Steinmetz. Those for Parakou leave from Gare Itajara a block away. Gare Abomey, which serves Abomey and is often called

Misséba (mee-SAY-boh), is at the eastern end of Ave Van Vollenhoven, one block east of Ave Steinmetz. Bush taxis for Lagos leave from Gare du Dantokpa at the new bridge, while those for Porto Novo leave from there and from Gare de l'Ancien Pont, on the corner of Ave Clozel and Rue des Libanais. A minibus costs about CFA 250 to Porto Novo.

Abomey-Calavi, 18 km north-west of Cotonou, is the embarkation point for trips to Ganvié. The main motor park for Abomey-Calavi is Gare du Dantokpa near the new bridge, but standing along Blvd St Michel will give you a head start.

Train The train station is in the heart of town one block north of Ave Clozel and several blocks west of Ave Steinmetz. The Cotonou to Parakou train leaves every day from both places at 8.34 am, arriving from eight to 10 hours later. There is also a night train, which departs Cotonou at 7.15 pm on Tuesday, Thursday and Saturday, arriving about 7 am the next morning; it departs Parakou at 6 am Wednesday, Friday and Sunday. There's usually space, even at the last minute.

Getting Around

To/From the Airport The official fare for a taxi from the centre to the airport is CFA 2000 (CFA 700 to/from the Sheraton). From the centre you can get this price but at the airport most drivers will probably demand a higher price. You can cut costs, if you don't have much to carry, by walking from the airport down Route de l'Aéroport to the Place des Martyrs (20 minutes) and catching a shared cab from there to the centre, which is only CFA 100 to CFA 200. There's a departure tax of CFA 2500.

Taxi Most motorcycle-taxi fares vary according to the distance, but CFA 100 is typical. Fares of regular taxis are CFA 100 for a shared taxi (double that for fairly long trips) and CFA 500 for a taxi to yourself. By the hour, taxis cost about CFA 1500, CFA 500 more if you include the Sheraton in the trip. Rates double at 9 pm. You'll find it difficult to negotiate a fare for the entire day

but it's usually worth the effort because settling for an hourly rate, while less confusing, will cost you more. CFA 12,000 plus petrol for the day would be a fair price.

Car Hertz (☎ 30 19 15; cards AE, D) and LAB Car Rental (☎ 33 15 84) both have booths at the airport; Bénin Tours is at the Sheraton (☎ 30 01 00, fax 30 11 55, telex 5111). Typical rates for a Citroën or the equivalent are about CFA 15,500 by the day plus CFA 165 per km, plus CFA 5000 a day for insurance and 12% tax (ie about CFA 60,000 plus petrol per day if you average 200 km per day). A chauffeur costs CFA 3000 to CFA 7000 a day but is not compulsory. A Peugeot 504 costs roughly 10% more.

AROUND COTONOU
Ganvié

The number one attraction near Cotonou is Ganvié (ghan-vee-AY), where the 12,000 inhabitants live in bamboo huts on stilts several km out on Lake Nokoué. It's a place that has been overrun by so many tourists that many children find it profitable to beg and will allow you to photograph them if you pay. While their opportunistic rationale is clearly understandable, you'll only be contributing to the problem if you agree.

However, for those travellers with a human eye Ganvié provokes a mixture of fascination, pathos and most certainly respect. While it is possible to explore other less-visited villages on the lagoon, visiting Ganvié is still worthwhile, especially if you have a knowledgeable guide.

In the 18th century, the Tofinu fled here from the warring Fon in the north, where the land was no longer sufficient to feed everyone. The swampy area around Lake Nokoué was excellent protection against the Fon and Dahomey kingdoms because a religious custom banned their warriors from venturing into the water.

All the houses, restaurants, boutiques and the one hotel and post office in Ganvié are on pilings (wooden sticks) about two metres above water level. The people live almost exclusively from fishing. As much breeders of fish as fishing people, the men plant branches on the muddy lagoon bottom.

When the leaves begin to decompose, the fish congregate there to feed. After many days, the men return to catch them in a net. Most of the pirogues are operated by women, who do the selling. Loaded with spices, fruits and fish, these pirogues are a colourful sight.

The best time to see Ganvié or other villages on the lagoon is in the early morning when the women are en route to the market and it is still fairly cool. Unfortunately, the pirogue rental place doesn't open until 8 am. Alternatively, try the late afternoon when the sun has lost its force.

Taking close-up photographs is nearly impossible because the people, especially the women, object to having their pictures taken. They don't like being exploited by professional photographers who want their photos for postcards; they are likely to have other reasons as well. In short, respect their sensitivity to photography.

Places to Stay & Eat It's possible to sleep in Ganvié; some of the locals don't mind renting rooms although there is the *Aptam Inn* – a quaint little bungalow-hotel which has very nice huts and decent bathrooms with flush toilets. The quoted price is CFA 10,500 which includes a three-course dinner with dessert and breakfast. However, the price is negotiable; you should be able to get a double without meals for around CFA 2500. Bring your own food because the set menu at the restaurant costs at least CFA 2500 and there are virtually no alternatives to eating there. Regardless of where you stay in Ganvié, sleeping here can be expensive because you must pay twice for the pirogue (the second time to pick you up), about CFA 2500 extra per person. However, you may be able to negotiate or hitch a pirogue ride with someone who is going to the morning market at the launching point in Abomey-Calavi.

Alternatively, there's the *Ganvié Bungalow Hôtel* (☎ 36 00 39) in Abomey-Calavi at the launching point. It has four very decent air-con rooms for about CFA 7000. Next door is *La Pirogue*, a pleasant restaurant that offers a four-course meal for CFA 3000 plus à la carte selections.

Getting There & Away To get to Ganvié you must go 18 km to the western side of the lagoon at Abomey-Calavi, a 25-minute ride. A shared Peugeot 504 bush taxi from Cotonou costs CFA 500. Most of them leave from the Gare du Dantokpa in Cotonou, or just stand along Blvd St Michel. Most drivers will let you off right at the embarkation point but if not, just walk down the hill (one km). You'll need to return to the top of that hill to find a taxi leaving Ganvié. A taxi (not shared) from Cotonou costs CFA 3000 but the driver is likely to demand twice that much if he thinks you're a tourist.

You can catch a motorised boat or pirogue to Ganvié across the lagoon. By motorised boat, the trip over and back takes about 1½ hours and the cost for one person is CFA 5500 (CFA 4000 for two to four people and CFA 3000 for five to nine people). By pirogue, the cost is CFA 4500 (CFA 3000 for two to four people) and the round trip takes 2½ hours. The trip by pirogue is more serene plus you'll be able to talk to people passing by and hear the fishers singing. For about CFA 1000 a person more, you can negotiate a long trip around the lagoon. This is worth the extra cost because on the small trip you get to see only a small part of Ganvié.

It's possible to get a cheaper pirogue ride to Ganvié or some of the less-visited lagoon villages with some of the independent pirogue men from other points around the lagoon, but finding them is no easy task. One such place is Akossato, a village five km north of Abomey-Calavi. However, some of these unregulated pirogues are less seaworthy and in recent years there have been cases of pirogues capsizing. This can be risky because there are fairly deep channels which you must cross to arrive at Ganvié. In addition, you may run into problems with officials. In Akossato, for example, if you're told to meet your pirogue at Sova, this may be just a scam. One traveller reported that when he arrived at Sova, which is several km off the main road, a man claiming to be a representative of the tourist agency demanded the full regulated price, which resulted in lots of yelling and screaming. The traveller stuck to his originally agreed-upon price, however, and eventually won.

The South

PORTO NOVO

Porto Novo is one of the more interesting towns in Benin. Even though the president lives in Cotonou and everything transpires there, Porto Novo, 32 km to the east, remains the nominal capital.

Dating back to the 16th century, Porto Novo was named by the Portuguese after a town in Portugal to which it bore a certain resemblance. The town has numerous buildings dating from early colonial times and has apparently seen better days. The Portuguese and wealthy Yoruba families once lived here and you can see a few of their homes, now dilapidated, in the old quarter to the east of the market.

Today, Porto Novo is a town of 160,000 people and is fairly active because of its proximity to Nigeria. It's possible to cover the town on foot but there are motorcycle-taxis everywhere willing to take you anywhere for a song.

Three km north of the city centre is Ouando, which has a fairly active market and some lively night spots. Porto Novo is also a good place to look for pirogues to take you to some of the less-visited villages on the lagoon. You can also change money at the Financial bank and make telephone calls from the post office two blocks away.

Musée Éthnographique de Porto Novo

Opened in 1966, but revamped with funding from President Mitterrand after his visit in 1983, what was once a colonial-style structure housing orphans is now an interesting museum. Retracing the history of the kings of Porto Novo, it has a wonderful collection of old Yoruba masks, some dating back to the 17th century. Other items on display are Fa (spiritual and calendar-like) fetishes, carved drums, arms, implements and costumes. Located 1½ blocks north-west of Place Jean Bayal, it's open every day from 9 am to noon and 3 to 6 pm. The entrance fee is CFA 1500.

Palais Royal du Roi Toffa

Now officially called the Musée Honmé (☎ 21 35 66, fax 21 25 25) but better known as the Palais Royal, this walled compound was the residence of King Toffa who signed the first treaty with the French in 1883, conferring much territory to them. The kingdom of Porto Novo was one of the longest lasting in Black Africa. It ended with the 25th king in 1976 when the five dynasties in Porto Novo had a disagreement and let the kingdom die.

Far from luxurious by Western standards, but nevertheless fascinating, the Royal Palace gives you a good idea of how African royalty lived. Constructed in the late 17th century and remodelled numerous times, it has finely carved doors, interesting old photos and King Toffa's royal carriage. It is on Rue Toffa two blocks south of the central market, has a CFA 1000 entrance fee and is open every day from 9 am to noon and 3.30 to 6 pm. Enquire about Paulin Sourou Zoffoun, a very knowledgeable tour guide. His tour lasts about an hour.

The palace is also a good place to organise inexpensive tours of Porto Novo's historical sites, the surrounding villages and the lagoon. If you can contact the museum's director, he will make all arrangements provided you give him 48 hour's notice.

Grand Marché d'Adjara

This market is held every fourth day, and is one of the most interesting in Benin. It's 10 km east of Porto Novo on a back road to Nigeria. You'll find drums and other musical instruments, unique blue and white tie-dyed cloth, some of the best pottery in Benin, locally made baskets, bicycles and the usual fare. Pirogues are used to transport goods from nearby Nigeria. Be sure not to miss the pork brochettes, which are reputed to be the best in all Benin; they're delicious.

Other Things to See & Do

When you're in the market area, don't miss the unique old Brazilian-style church just one block to the north. Built originally as a church in the late 1800s, it has been converted into a **mosque** and painted in seemingly 20 different hues, making it perhaps the most colourful building in West Africa.

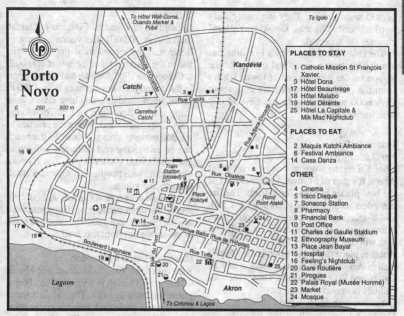

Porto Novo

To Hôtel Well-Come,
Ouando Market &
Pobé

To Igolo

Kandévié

Catchi

Route d'Ouando

Rue Catchi

Carrefour
Catchi

Rue Adgara-Dégadji

Train
Station
(closed)

Rue Obalédé

Place
Kokoyé

Rond
Point Ataké

Avenue Ballot (Rue de l'Hôpital)

Rue du Pont

Boulevard Lagunaire

Rue Toffa

Lagoon

Akron

To Cotonou & Lagos

PLACES TO STAY

1 Catholic Mission St François Xavier
3 Hôtel Dona
17 Hôtel Beaurivage
18 Hôtel Malabo
19 Hôtel Détente
25 Hôtel La Capitale & Mik Mac Nightclub

PLACES TO EAT

2 Maquis Katchi Ambiance
6 Festival Ambiance
14 Casa Danza

OTHER

4 Cinema
5 Iraco Disque
7 Sonacop Station
8 Pharmacy
9 Financial Bank
10 Post Office
11 Charles de Gaulle Stadium
12 Ethnography Museum
13 Place Jean Bayal
15 Hospital
16 Feeling's Nightclub
20 Gare Routière
21 Pirogues
22 Palais Royal (Musée Honmé)
23 Market
24 Mosque

For a pirogue ride to some **lagoon villages** rarely visited by foreigners, the best place to enquire is next to the lagoon, about 200 metres east of the bridge. There's no fixed price because the pirogue men are rarely approached by foreigners for rides. A trip in a non-motorised pirogue to the nearest three villages takes about four hours. For this they may ask around CFA 8500, but you should be able to bargain down the price.

Places to Stay – bottom end

Ask around for inexpensive places to sleep in Porto Novo as new places are always popping up . Porto Novo has three cheap hotels. The best and the most central is *Hôtel Détente*, which has a large paillote in the back – perfect for drinks, reading and viewing the lagoon. Inside is a bar and restaurant. Clean rooms with fans, armchairs and shared bathrooms cost CFA 2500. Coming across the bridge, the hotel is about 300 metres to your left (west).

If Hôtel Détente is full, try *Hôtel Well-Come* (☎ 21 33 08), three km from the centre in Ouando, about 150 metres west of Marché Ouando. It is now almost defunct because of the CFA devaluation, however, a room with a large bed, fan and shared bath costs CFA 2500 (negotiable) at night; much less by the hour. You can eat here (order in advance).

Hôtel La Capitale (☎ 21 34 64) is a four-storey hotel on Rue Toffa, half a km east of the Royal Palace and not far from the market. It has a fancy nightclub (Mik Mac) but no restaurant and overpriced rooms with fans for about CFA 6000. Also check out one of the three *Catholic missions*; one is on the road to Ouando, 1.5 km from the centre.

Places to Stay – top end

The most expensive hotel in town is the *Hôtel Dona* (☎ 21 30 52, telex 5032) on Rue Catchi, one km north of the centre. The comfortable rooms cost CFA 6000/8500 for singles/doubles with fans and CFA 9500/

11,500 with air-con. They are rarely fully booked and Thomas Cook travellers' cheques are accepted.

The *Hôtel Beaurivage*, with 13 rooms, has a more lively ambience and overlooks the lagoon on the western end of town, 1.5 km from the centre. Air-con rooms cost about CFA 8000 with two beds and CFA 11,000 with one big bed.

Places to Eat

For African food, it's hard to beat *Comme Chez Soi* on the western side of Rond Point Ataké. It's part of *Festival Ambiance*, one of the best places in town for a drink. The bar has good music, small beers for CFA 150, and a relaxing atmosphere. The restaurant offers a number of selections and a filling dish will cost you from CFA 250 to CFA 400. Another place that looks good is the *Maquis Katchi Ambiance* at the intersection of Rue Catchi and Route d'Ouando. One of the specialities is agouti (African rat).

For Western food, a good choice is *Casa Danza*, a block south of the ethnographic museum on the same street. It's attractive and you can get a decent meal (but painfully slow service) for around CFA 1000 to CFA 2500. There's also the *Restaurant La Royale* near the Royal Palace. Very reasonably priced, it has a full menu plus lighter fare including sandwiches and ice cream. Your other alternatives may be the hotels *Dona* and *Beaurivage*, which are much more expensive. At the Dona, for example, the three-course menu of the day costs CFA 2500. The new *Feeling's* nightclub, centrally located on Blvd Lagunaire about three km from Hotel Beaurivage, has a restaurant that is open from around 6 pm until very late. It has European and African dishes costing from CFA 800 to CFA 2500.

Getting There & Away

Taxis to and from Porto Novo are available all day. They cost CFA 250 and leave from the intersection in front of the bridge in Porto Novo. In Cotonou, they leave from Gare du Dantokpa and Gare de l'Ancien Pont.

OUIDAH

Located 42 km west of Cotonou is Ouidah (population 30,000), the voodoo centre of Benin and the second most popular tourist site in the country. Until the wharf was built at Cotonou in 1908, Ouidah had the only port in the country. Its heyday was from 1800 to 1900, when Ouidah was where slaves were shipped from Benin and eastern Togo to the USA, Brazil and Haiti, where the practice of voodoo remains strong. A walk to the beach can be interesting and culturally enlightening; it's four km south of town. You'll pass a big lagoon with people fishing and a small Ganvié-like village.

Many travellers pass Ouidah without ever seeing the town because of the bypass road around the northern side. The centre of town is about two km from this road.

Musée d'Histoire d'Ouidah

Also called the Voodoo Museum, the Musée d'Histoire d'Ouidah is part of an old Portuguese fort built in 1721. The exhibits focus on the slave trade and Benin's consequent links with Brazil and the Caribbean. There are also all sorts of mystical artefacts of the voodoo culture and rooms presenting Benin's influences on its descendants in Haiti, Brazil and Cuba. You'll be shown skulls, ghost clothes, Portuguese gifts to the kings of Dahomey, old maps, engravings, photos showing the influence of Dahomeyan slaves on Brazilian culture, and traces of Brazilian architecture that the repatriated slaves brought back with them to Africa. There's also a souvenir shop with books on the history of Benin and its participation in the trade. The museum is open every day from 9 am to 6 pm; the entrance fee is CFA 1500 which includes a guide. It's two blocks east of the market.

Route des Esclave

Ask about the Route of the Slaves before leaving the fort as someone there may offer to accompany you as a guide. The four-km path, which is the major road to the beach, starts next to the Sonacop petrol station. If you don't want to walk, you can always find

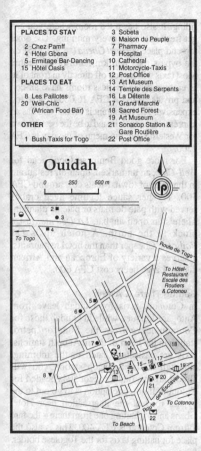

PLACES TO STAY	3	Sobeta
	6	Maison du Peuple
2	Chez Pamff	7	Pharmacy
4	Hôtel Gbena	9	Hospital
5	Ermitage Bar-Dancing	10	Cathedral
15	Hôtel Oasis	11	Motorcycle-Taxis
		12	Post Office
PLACES TO EAT	13	Art Museum
		14	Temple des Serpents
8	Les Paillotes	16	La Détente
20	Well-Chic	17	Grand Marché
	(African Food Bar)	18	Sacred Forest
		19	Art Museum
OTHER	21	Sonacop Station &
			Gare Routière
1	Bush Taxis for Togo	22	Post Office

Ouidah

a motorcycle-taxi . There are lots of fetishes along the way as well as monumental statues of old African symbols. This is the route that the slaves took to the coast to board the ships. Numerous historical and supernatural legends are associated with this road, giving it significance even to the residents of Ouidah today.

You'll pass through three villages en route to the beach. At the first village, enquire about the Voodoo chief, Daagbo Hounon, a wise fetisher who loves foreigners and can prepare magical potions for you. If you ask for his services, he'll expect a gift; gin is

what he likes most. This village is also noted for holding a periodic celebration for twins. The third village was the actual holding point for slaves as the fort was only for taking head counts. There is a beautiful memorial here in honour of those departed slaves. Overlooking the ocean is a hotel that's been in construction for nearly five years and the remains of a church, but little else. The beach here is special and symbolic in regard to the final departure of slaves.

Art Museums
There is a new unnamed art museum in the centre behind the post office; it features contemporary art relating to voodoo and its traditions. Also, in 1992 the Casa do Brazil (better known as La Maison de Brazil) was turned into a museum. It displays works depicting voodoo culture and the Black diaspora, and has a good collection of B&W pictures of voodoo rituals – don't miss it. The house itself is the former residence of the Brazilian governor and was later occupied by a Portuguese family until they were ousted in the early 1960s. During those later years, the old 'governor' used to raise a Portuguese flag every morning, claiming the property was Portugal's! The entrance fee is CFA 1500 (includes the cost of a guide). La Maison de Brazil is a 15-minute walk from the centre, near the civil prison.

Temple des Serpents
Snakes are especially important in Ouidah because, traditionally, they were fetishes and the principal object of worship. This explains why there's a Sacred Python Temple here. It's in the centre of town, half a block from the cathedral, but has become more or less a tourist trap and less sacred because of this. A small tour costs a rip-off CFA 1000 (CFA 500 extra for photos) for which you'll get an explanation of the temple and some of the voodoo traditions. Don't expect too much, however. Inside the temple they'll lead you into a very small room, lift up some boards, and voilà – four harmless, sleeping snakes.

Sacred Forest
Erected primarily for the 1992 Oudiah

Culture Festival, this park consists of a small array of African deities representing fascinating legends and myths. Unfortunately, much of the significance of this place is lost on viewers because there is no guide to elaborate on it. The deities are placed on the spiritual grounds of King Kpassé, the founder of Ouidah, who foretold of his sudden departure. Upon his disappearance, in the very spot where he made the announcement, a rare and huge tree grew up, and it is alive even today. There is also a crumbling, once elaborate house built by Kpassé's son in honour of his father. Be sure to bow before King Legba – 'guardian of the house' – when you enter the park.

Places to Stay & Eat

One of the best places in town for the low price is the *Ermitage Bar-Dancing* (☎ 34 13 89), a block east of the huge Maison du Peuple. It has a very African feel and a pleasant terrace bar, and is definitely the place to go for a drink at night. The military like to stop by and chat with travellers. The three rooms here cost CFA 4000 each, but the friendly family who run this place will probably let you have one for CFA 3000.

Another possibility is the *Hôtel Escale des Routiers* at the eastern entrance to town. Rooms cost around CFA 3500 (negotiable). Units are clean and have fans. The atmosphere is sterile, except for in the restaurant.

Others prefer *Chez Pamff*, on the northern edge of town, behind Sobeta. From Hôtel Gbena on the bypass road, take the road north for one long block, then your first right for several hundred metres. It has a great ambience and a large selection of alcoholic drinks. Its rooms have fans and are excellent for CFA 3500. Chez Pamff also has excellent African dishes starting at CFA 800.

There are two up-market hotels in Ouidah. The best for the money is the new *Hôtel Oasis* (☎ 34 10 91), which is in the heart of town just blocks from the fort and opposite the Sonacop petrol station. It has spacious, clean and airy rooms with air-con and private baths for CFA 10,500. The restaurant, which has friendly staff, serves special African dishes upon request that are both excellent and

filling. It also has a tea room where you can get fresh hot bread every morning. The other top-end place is *Hôtel Gbena* (☎ 34 12 15), on the bypass road two km north of the centre. Most taxis will let you off directly in front of it. Even though the spotless rooms have air-con and private baths, at CFA 16,000 they're too expensive. The restaurant is French and has an impressive menu. It is said to be the best in town for Western food; the menu of the day is CFA 2500.

For more good Beninese food, head for *Well-Chic*, an unmarked, open-air restaurant in the heart of town. Meals cost around CFA 300. Try her sauce légume avec crabes served with pâte de maïs or pâte de plantain. There's an open-air bar, *La Détente*, just a block to the north. A notch up is *Les Paillotes*. Cheaper than the hotel restaurants, it serves a variety of European and African dishes. Large beers cost CFA 600.

Getting There & Away

In Cotonou, taxis for Ouidah leave from Autogare Jonquet, while in Ouidah those for Cotonou leave from the Sonacop petrol station in the heart of town. At both stations, taxis are easiest to catch in the morning, although at the Sonacop station you will almost always find Peugeot 504s headed for Cotonou. If not, one option is to go out to the bypass road at the intersection near Hôtel Gbena and try hailing one from there – the fare to/from Cotonou is CFA 400. This is also the place for hailing taxis for the Togolese border.

GRAND POPO

Some 80 km west of Cotonou and 15 km east of the Togo border, Grand Popo is renowned for its **beaches** and is the best get-away spot in Benin for travellers to spend a few idle days on the sand. Travelling here via the coastal highway from either Cotonou or Lomé, you may see white flags flying from poles in small villages along the way; they identify voodoo practitioners.

The only hotel is the popular and highly recommended *L'Auberge de Grand Popo*, which has a very casual atmosphere and is right on the beach. Recently expanded, it has

16 new rooms in a restored colonial building plus additional space for camping. Many visitors go just to camp on the beach. The auberge is run by a Briton, John, who charges CFA 3000/5000 for singles/doubles with fans and from CFA 7000/8000 to CFA 11,000/12,000 for the newer, more spacious air-con rooms. Camping costs CFA 500 per person, which includes access to clean wash-rooms – tents, mattresses and mosquito nets are provided. If it rains, campers can move their gear and mattresses into the restaurant. The menu is quite impressive and the seafood is said to be some of Benin's very best. However, meals are not cheap. Most main courses cost between CFA 1500 and CFA 2000, while Cokes and beers cost around CFA 300 and CFA 450, respectively. The only alternative is to search for food in the village; there's plenty available. Ask John about excursions in Benin as he is a good source of information.

Getting There & Away

From Cotonou, take a taxi from Autogare Jonquet and have it drop you off at the Grand Popo junction on the main coastal highway, 20 km east of the border. The fare is CFA 800. You'll probably have to walk 3.5 km from there to the hotel as very little traffic passes by, but if you're nice, the driver may drop you off right in front. Leaving shouldn't be difficult as there will almost surely be someone there with a vehicle who will be willing to drop you off at the main road.

LOKOSSA

Lokossa is halfway between Grand Popo and Abomey, and is a convenient spot to find taxis east to Possotomé and Bopa and north to Abomey. Hôtel Étoile Rouge has a bar-res-taurant and 20 rooms, four with air-con. If you stop here, check the lively **market** (it operates every five days).

BOPA & POSSOTOMÉ

If you're looking for a place that's off the beaten path, head for **Lake Ahémé**, which is 40 km south-east of Lokossa. There are fishing villages all around the lake, the main ones being Bopa and Possotomé, and the

setting is very tropical, with coconut trees everywhere. Few travellers come this way, so you may be the only foreigner around. The people in the villages are very friendly and will treat you as though you were an old friend, taking you to their homes, introduc-ing you to local customs and foods, and helping you to make arrangements for pirogue trips around the lagoon.

Bopa, which is on the western side of the lake and connected by road to Lokossa, is a fascinating village as the practice of voodoo here may be the most avid of that practised anywhere in Benin. If you're interested in seeing a **fetish temple** and getting an insider's view on the practice of voodoo, charms and spells, ask to see Mr Agbogbo, a renowned and powerful fetisher who may let you see more than you expect.

Possotomé, which is near Bopa, is quite interesting and famous for its hot **thermal springs**, the country's primary source for mineral water. You can visit the factory here which has been set up near the source for bottling the water. From the village you can rent a pirogue for a trip to the nearby fishing villages, including Bopa and Oussa Tokpa, or simply to ride around the lagoon.

Places to Stay & Eat

Near the thermal springs at Possotomé is a new 20-room hotel, Le Village Ahémé (☎ 45 02 20 or 32 30 15). It's on the water's edge and has ventilated bungalows for CFA 5000 (CFA 11,500 for a double with air-con) and a surprisingly good restaurant with excellent service. Breakfast costs CFA 1500 and full meals cost around CFA 3000. The relaxing tropical ambience here is simply delightful. In addition, the friendly owner will do everything possible to introduce you to the area, including making arrangements for pirogue rides around the lake and seeing traditional festivals.

Getting There & Away

As you're heading north from the coastal highway turn-off towards Lokossa, some 20 km south of Lokossa you'll come to the Marché de Comé intersection. Take the dirt road heading east just after the Co-op store and go for 17 km to the lake at Possotomé. The fork to the left heads towards the hotel and Bopa. The former is about 500 km down that road, on your right. For a bush taxi to either village, look around the intersection. The best time to find vehicles there or to hitchhike is in the morning.

ABOMEY & BOHICON

If you have time to visit only one town outside Cotonou, Abomey would be a good choice. It's 144 km north of Cotonou on an asphalt road. Abomey is Fon country and was the capital of the great Dahomey kingdom. The main attraction is the restored Royal Palace of the Fon and the museum inside, which covers the history of the kingdom.

Royal Palace Museum

Before the arrival of the French, the palace compound must have been the most incredible structure in West Africa. The first palace was constructed in 1645 by the third king of Dahomey; each successive Fon king built his own palace so that by the 19th century the palace compound was huge, with a four-km-long perimeter and a 10-metre-high wall enclosing an area of 40 hectares and a court of 10,000 people.

Today's palace-museum dates from 1818 and consists only of the palaces of the last two great kings to build there, Ghézo and Glélé. Fleeing from the French in 1892, Glélé's son, Béhanzin, the 10th king, ordered the palaces to be burned. So only a small part of the palace compound is standing – the courtyards and ceremonial rooms, and the houses where the kings' wives lived.

A large part of the palace compound was devoted to altars for dead kings, who were buried there. The people thought it fitting that their deceased kings have entourages in the afterlife, so they held an annual human sacrifice, mainly of convicts and prisoners of war. This was one of the aspects of Dahomey culture that most struck the early European explorers, and rumours abounded.

On the exterior of the palace are bas-reliefs which depict the history of the Abomey kingdom. Although some of the reliefs were destroyed in the fire, some have been saved and restored. These reliefs are a major factor in the palace's classification by UNESCO as one of the 485 historic sites of common humanity in the world.

Inside the museum a guide will show you rooms containing the relics of the kings. In one room, the Room of Arms, are the thrones of 11 of the 12 Dahomey kings – the last king was a puppet of the French and his subjects threw away his throne. These 11 thrones are all of elaborately carved wood and a few are decorated with silver and copper. Ghézo's throne is particularly large and is mounted on four skulls (not real) of vanquished enemies. Behind the 11 thrones are the magnificent appliqué tapestries of the royal family. These tapestries, which have been restored, depict some of the country's bloody history, particularly battles. One of them shows a scene of Glélé using a dismembered leg to pound his enemy's head. In the same

---

King Roi Glélé

The greatest of the Dahomey kings was Roi Glélé, the ninth king who ruled during the late 19th century, just before the arrival of the French. Like all the kings, he had a colony of artists who worked exclusively for him, which is why the royal palace was so magnificent. Most interesting, King Glélé was said to have had about 800 wives, 1000 women slaves to attend to them, an army of 10,000 soldiers and, most unusual, 6000 women bodyguards – Amazons as they were called. In Dahomey the kings owned everything. Women and children were the only property that could be inherited, so they were men's greatest source of wealth. Whenever a male subject died, all of the man's property was brought to the king for distribution, and he usually kept a few of the wives for himself. From the time of the fourth king on, kings had so many wives that they began using them as bodyguards, in part because they considered women less treacherous than men. ■

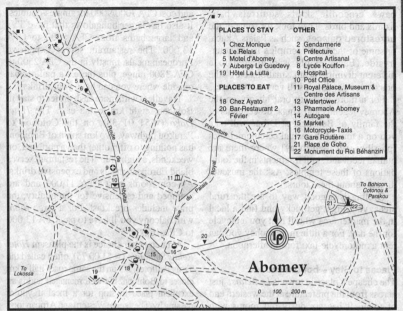

PLACES TO STAY
1 Chez Monique
3 Le Relais
5 Motel d'Abomey
7 Auberge Le Guedevy
19 Hôtel La Lutta

PLACES TO EAT
18 Chez Ayato
20 Bar-Restaurant 2 Février

OTHER
2 Gendarmerie
4 Préfecture
6 Centre Artisanal
8 Lycée Kouffon
9 Hospital
10 Post Office
11 Royal Palace, Museum & Centre des Artisans
12 Watertower
13 Pharmacie Abomey
14 Autogare
15 Market
16 Motorcycle-Taxis
17 Gare Routière
21 Place de Goho
22 Monument du Roi Béhanzin

Abomey

0   100   200 m

rooms are carvings of the panther Agassou. Agassou was a fetish animal of the royal family and, so the tale goes, was born from the union of a woman and a speaking beast. Unfortunately, a fire in late 1993 destroyed a large part of this room, so it's likely to be disordered until the reconstruction is completed.

In other museum buildings, you'll see lots of voodoo, skulls, Portuguese artefacts, ranging from pistols to sets of china, and the traditional housing of King Glélé's 800 wives. You may not take photos of any of this! The palace-museum is open every day from 9 am to 3.30 pm. The entrance fee is CFA 1500, which includes a guide.

Centre des Artisans

The museum tour takes about an hour, at the end of which your guide takes you to the Centre des Artisans next door where you'll see artisans making appliqué cloths. The quality is better than that of most appliqué cloth found in Cotonou but asking prices are

high, so you'll have to bargain hard. (If you're really interested in appliqué cloth, ask at the museum for the Yemandje family; their workshop is not far away and prices are generally lower). At this centre you'll also see artisans working on all kinds of other modern-day crafts, particularly wooden carvings, bronze statues and tablecloths, mostly of souvenir quality. If you're looking for bronze pieces, get them here because the work tends to be much more original than that found in Cotonou. Even if you can find pieces of comparable quality in Cotonou, they'll cost you twice as much.

Other Things to See

Besides the palace, you could check the **market**, which is quite good and not the least bit touristy. Market day occurs every fourth day, but the main market continues throughout the week. Stalls in the voodoo section are filled with all sorts of dead insects and animals; the selection includes monkey paws, crocodile skulls, squirrels, bats, lizards and birds. Then look for some of the **unrestored palaces**, such as Palais Akaba, or some of the **fetish temples** in the countryside. Each temple is dedicated to a different divinity (death, smallpox etc) – the practice of voodoo is still very active here.

For a more in-depth oral history on the Abomey legends and kings, descendants of the family of Béhanzin at Djimé will take you on a tour of the actual ceremonial sites (possibly still used today) where there are human teeth and skull fragments in the foundations of these temples. Ask the museum director about these tours.

Cycling is a good way to see the rural areas; you might get lucky and find a local in the market area who'll rent you a bicycle for the day. For a little more money you can rent a motorcycle-taxi for the afternoon.

Places to Stay – bottom end

The cheapest place in town is *Le Relais*, just across from the préfecture at the western end of town. It has six dusty old rooms with shared bath for CFA 2000.

The most popular cheap establishment in Abomey is the pleasant *Chez Monique* (☎ 50 01 68), or 'A La Lune', at the far western end of town down a dirt road. The garden has a delightful tropical ambience with animals, exotic birds and straw huts. There are nice rooms available (from CFA 5000) that are screened and have fans and exceptionally clean shared baths. The meals are very good but not cheap, mostly CFA 1500 a plate. Make reservations as rooms are often fully booked.

Auberge Le Guedevy, about two km from the centre, is a modern two-storey hotel that has a good restaurant with a European and African menu and a wide selection of cold drinks. Rooms are more reasonably priced here and cost CFA 4500 for a double with fan, shower and toilet (CFA 6500 with air-con).

Places to Stay – top end

Motel d'Abomey (☎ 50 00 75) on the western side of town, one km from the centre, is the largest and best hotel in Abomey. The rooms are pretty basic with carpeting and air-con

and cost CFA 7000/9000 for singles/doubles. It also has larger bungalows that have TVs and large baths from CFA 8000 to CFA 13,000. The restaurant serves expensive European meals, mostly in the CFA 2500 to CFA 3800 range, plus there's a paillote bar outside where you can have your drinks.

Travellers with more cash prefer to stay in Bohicon, eight km to the east. The *Hôtel Dako* (☎ 51 01 38), on the Cotonou to Parakou highway, two km south of Bohicon, has nothing to offer other than a pool and, on weekends, a nightclub. The restaurant serves bland European meals and expensive drinks. Air-con rooms cost CFA 11,000 and are cramped and expensive for the quality; the price includes breakfast. For a large room with balcony you'll have to pay CFA 13,000 to CFA 16,000.

A much better choice is the pleasant *Hôtel Relais Sinnoutin* (☎ 51 00 75), often called the Trois Paillotes. It's on the same road, half a km closer to Bohicon. It's well managed and is an excellent place to stop for a meal if you're passing by. They serve Western and African food costing anywhere from CFA 1000 to CFA 1500. A spotlessly clean room with fan and shared bath costs CFA 5000 (CFA 6000 with private bath), while air-con rooms cost CFA 10,000.

Places to Eat

Just across the street from Hôtel Dako in Bohicon is the maquis *La Bonne Marmite* that has wonderful African sauces with couscous, rice and pounded yam at lunch (before 2.30 pm) and in the evening. You can expect to pay from CFA 200 to CFA 600 for a filling meal. Alternatively, there is the ever-popular *Mochas*, right at the crossroads in Bohicon. It has the loudest music in town and delicious beef brochettes. There is also a woman here with a wide range of sauces as well as salad. The tasty food makes the music more bearable. For tasty chicken, try *Chez Chantal*, in the same area, near the petrol station. In Abomey, look around the market for cheap street food. At the stall called *Chez Ayato Adjara* you can get a delicious meal for CFA 250. A speciality here is pâte de maïs with meat and cheese sauce or with gumbo sauce; both are excellent.

Entertainment

During the day, you could try the pool at Hôtel Dako; it's open every day from 10 am to 6 pm and costs CFA 1000. For dancing, try *The Prestige* at Motel d'Abomey; it's the newest and fanciest place in town and completely overshadows *Le Refuge*, which appears to be on its last leg. For a nightclub in Bohicon, try *Le Moulin Rouge*; it's reputed to be the best.

Getting There & Away

Bush Taxi In Cotonou, taxis for Abomey leave throughout the day and early evening from Gare Abomey, or more conveniently from anywhere on St Michel (CFA 1000, 2½ hours). Shared taxis and motorcycle-taxis ply between Abomey and Bohicon during the day and early evening; the fare is CFA 100. Vehicles continuing on to Parakou leave frequently from the gares routières in Abomey and stop off in Bohicon. In Bohicon, to hail a taxi headed north towards Parakou, just stand along the main road and wave your hand.

It's possible to rent bicycles for about CFA 800 a day – just ask around town. A ride into the countryside will take you to all sorts of villages; keep an eye out for fetish temples and brightly painted statues of the Dahomey kings.

Train The Cotonou to Parakou train leaves in either direction at 8.34 am. The evening train from Cotonou leaves at 7.15 pm on Tuesday, Thursday and Saturday and at 6 pm on Wednesday, Friday and Sunday from Parakou. From Cotonou, the train takes 2½ hours to get to Bohicon, where you must catch a taxi to Abomey (nine km to the west). The Cotonou to Bohicon fare is CFA 1500 for 1st class, CFA 750 for 2nd class and, on the night train only, CFA 3000 for a sleeper. The evening train arrives and departs Bohicon quite late at night and finding a room at that hour can be a problem, so consider taking the day train instead.

DASSA ZOUMÉ

Dassa Zoumé, which is 200 km north of Cotonou on the main north-south highway, lies roughly halfway between Cotonou and Parakou. It's one of the most picturesque places in Benin.

Dassa, the 'city of 41 hills', has a buzzing population of 30,000 and is the next major town you'll come to after Bohicon. It has some awesome **rock formations** that have houses built around them. Dassa is also renowned for the annual '**pilgrimage**' (la grotte) for Catholics throughout West Africa who come and walk to the top of the hill to pay tribute to the Virgin Mary who it is said once appeared here. It's a major gathering that has become more social than religious, and is held the third Sunday in August.

For details of how to get to Dassa Zoumé, see the Savé Getting There & Away section.

Places to Stay & Eat

For cheap lodging, ask around the gare routière. The most expensive place in town is the *Auberge de Dassa* (☎ 53 00 98), which faces the rond point on the major highway. It has 11 rooms with fans for CFA 7950 (CFA 12,950 with air-con) and an excellent restaurant with great pepper steaks as well as desserts. It also has draught beer, a satellite TV and mountain bikes for hire. For things to do and see in Dassa, ask for Allen, the manager; he can tell you about fishing excursions and finding the nearby hippo hang-out.

SAVÉ

Savé, 160 km south of Parakou, is the home of many Yoruba people who migrated from Nigeria, and a convenient place to cross over to Nigeria by land. If you enjoy rock climbing, stop here as there are accessible **rock formations**. Many of these rocks have a great deal of history behind them and are considered sacred, hence the name 'la montagne sacrée'. Centuries ago, to counter attacks from their enemies from the south, the inhabitants would flee to the rocks and strategically place boulders, then roll them down the hills as the enemy approached. There are also areas in these hills where village elders would go to pray to the deities.

Places to Stay & Eat

One of the cheapest places to stay is the

increasingly decrepit *Roc Motel*, which has rooms with shared baths for CFA 4000. The restaurant functions only if they can find a cook, which is not always the case, or if the owner from Cotonou appears. The extremely rustic *campement* at the northern exit to town is even cheaper. If these places are full, enquire about the *Savé Idadu Hôtel*.

The town's nicest hotel is the new *Les Trois Mammelles*, which is an overly ambitious three-storey hotel that has large spacious rooms with comfortable beds, and balconies overlooking the hills and much of Savé. The place is somewhat moribund as it's never fully booked, but because business is so slow, the CFA 6000 price is entirely negotiable. The restaurant is decent but many of the items on the menu are not available. There's a chic nightclub next door which attracts a few people on weekends. Just above the nightclub is the more popular open-air bar where you can enjoy the view of Savé over a cold beer. Many travellers with vehicles headed north stop here.

If you have wheels and you want to get away from town, head out to the animal breeding campement, a French-financed project; it's about 14 km from town and is an amazingly peaceful and lovely place. They have nice paillote rooms for only CFA 1000. Ask for Paul, the genial director; he has been known to give travellers tours by motorcycle of the surrounding hills.

Getting There & Away

Getting to Dassa and Savé is relatively painless by taxi. For direct taxis from Cotonou, you can catch them under the new bridge by the Dantokpa marketplace. Taxis leave in the early afternoon once they fill up. The fare is CFA 2000 to Dassa and CFA 2500 to Savé. It's quicker to stand along Blvd St Michel and catch a taxi just to Bohicon. In Bohicon, it's fairly easy to hail taxis as they pass through the centre of town; the fare is CFA 800 to Dassa and CFA 1000 to Savé.

You can also get to Dassa and Savé by train. The day train from Cotonou arrives at Bohicon usually between 11 am and noon and at Dassa and Savé roughly one and two hours later respectively.

The North

PARAKOU

Parakou (population 80,000) is a bustling metropolis at the end of the railroad. It was once a major slave-market town in the 19th century. Today it is the administrative capital of the Borgou. Virtually everything you can find in Cotonou can be found in Parakou. While there's not much to see, it is a convenient place to stop for the night if you're heading further north or to the game parks.

The centre of town is the area around the cinema at the intersection of Rue de la Gare and Route de Transa. There are four banks including the Financial bank, BCB, Ecobank-Bénin and the Bank of Africa. The market is three blocks away, to the southeast. There are hotels all over town. Using motorcycle-taxis is the cheapest and easiest way to get around.

Places to Stay – bottom end

One of the cheapest place to stay in Parakou is *Les Cocotiers*, which is near the train station and quite dumpy. It has dingy little rooms virtually in decay with fans and shared baths including showers for CFA 2000/3000 for singles/doubles. A much better place for roughly the same price is the long-standing *Hôtel Les Canaries* (☎ 61 11 69), which is roughly 400 metres east of the train station. It has two courtyards with rooms facing them. Singles/doubles with fans, shared baths and mediocre showers cost CFA 1800/3000 (CFA 4200/5900 with private bath and CFA 4800/7100 with air-con). The restaurant closes fairly early. In addition, about 200 metres north-east along the road running in front of the hotel you'll come to an intersection where there's excellent street food.

A notch up is the new *Auberge Mon Petit Père* (☎ 61 10 57), on the northern side of town on the Route de Malanville. It's a delightful six-room auberge with spotless singles/doubles with fans for CFA 3500/4500, and excellent meals include couscous, pounded yam and other African specialities.

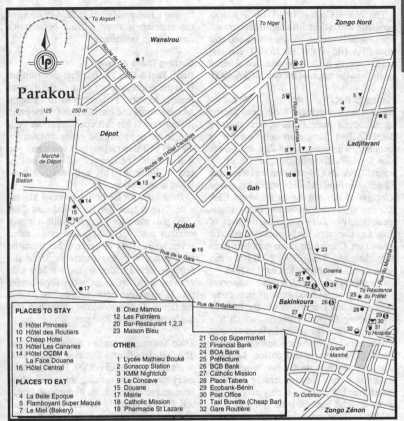

Parakou

0   125   250 m

PLACES TO STAY
6   Hôtel Princess
10 Hôtel des Routiers
11 Cheap Hotel
13 Hôtel Les Canaries
14 Hôtel OCBM &
     La Face Douane
16 Hôtel Central

PLACES TO EAT
4   La Belle Epoque
5   Flamboyant Super Maquis
7   Le Miel (Bakery)

8   Chez Mamou
12 Les Palmiers
20 Bar-Restaurant 1,2,3
23 Maison Bleu

OTHER
1   Lycée Mathieu Bouké
2   Sonacop Station
3   KMM Nightclub
9   Le Concave
15 Douane
17 Mairie
18 Catholic Mission
19 Pharmacie St Lazare

21 Co-op Supermarket
22 Financial Bank
24 BOA Bank
25 Préfecture
26 BCB Bank
27 Catholic Mission
28 Place Tabera
29 Ecobank-Bénin
30 Post Office
31 Taxi Buvette (Cheap Bar)
32 Gare Routière

Another great place is the *Flamboyant Super Maquis*. It's an authentic African maquis with two guest rooms in super condition. Singles/doubles cost CFA 4000/6000 (negotiable if you eat there). The long-standing but declining *Hôtel OCBN* (☎ 61 10 57), in a quiet area just east of the train station and surrounded by trees and shrubs, has large, clinically clean singles/doubles for CFA 3500/4500; breakfast is CFA 700.

Places to Stay – top end
For years, the most popular top-end hotel has been the *Hôtel des Routiers* (☎ 64 04 01). It's a French-run establishment on Route de Transa, half a km north of the heart of town. You can't help but relax in the garden setting with its clean pool. There's also an excellent tennis court and a good French restaurant. The air-con rooms range in price from CFA 10,500 (shared bath) to CFA 15,500.

The new *Hôtel Princess* (☎ 61 01 32), however, is now the liveliest hotel in town and has a wide range of rooms. For CFA 6800 to CFA 9800, you can get a small room with a fan and private bath. The deluxe rooms (CFA 11,900 to CFA 16,300) are spacious, carpeted bungalows with telephones and satellite TVs.

BENIN

The *Hôtel Central* (☎ 61 01 24) lacks ambience and is thus difficult to recommend. The rooms, however, are quite cosy and cost from CFA 10,500 to CFA 15,000. The restaurant serves both European and African meals, and the menu of the day is CFA 4000.

Places to Eat

For inexpensive African food, head for the unmarked *La Face Douane*, next door to Hôtel OCBM. It is extremely popular at seemingly all hours of the day and serves pâte for CFA 100 plus several sauces for around CFA 250. My favourite place is the *Flamboyant Super Maquis*, which has a large selection of African dishes for about CFA 300 and a pleasant ambience. Many locals speak highly of *Les Palmiers* at the back of Hôtel Les Canaries, but business seems to be off and on. One of the more popular dishes is chicken and fries (CFA 1500) but when business is slow the cook is hard to find.

Chez Mamou is a small buvette that serves good cheap street food such as rice, couscous, salad and chicken. It's in the heart of town facing *Le Miel* (bakery), which is a good place for vegetarian sandwiches, ham and cheese sandwiches, ice cream and, in the mornings, croissants and coffee. *La Belle E'poque*, which is on the northern side of town, has a reputation for serving excellent French fare but the pizza is only average and prices are a bit high for what you get.

All of the larger hotels in Parakou have good restaurants, particularly those at *Auberge Mon Petit Père* and *Hôtel Princess*. The one at *Hôtel des Routiers* is also excellent but expensive. The most outstanding restaurant in town, however, is *Maison Bleu*, which is also one of the best French restaurants in Benin outside of Cotonou. The chef is talented and the wide choice on the menu is refreshing. Main dishes range from CFA 1800 to CFA 4000.

Entertainment

For a nightclub, try *KMM* on Route de Transa, two blocks north of Hôtel des Routiers. It has been renovated and is now the fanciest club in Parakou. *Le Concave* is a lot of fun. It's more casual and much less expensive than KMM but finding a motorcycle-taxi in the wee hours of the morning is more difficult because it's further from the centre.

Getting There & Away

Bush Taxi & Bus The bustling gare routière is in the centre, a block from the market on Rue du Marché. Peugeot 504s to Cotonou take six hours and cost CFA 5000. Beware: if your taxi is not full upon departure or if people are not going the entire destination, the taxi will stop endlessly in route and you will probably be dumped off into another taxi in Bohicon. This will lengthen your travel time considerably.

Bush taxis for the border town of Malanville (Niger) take five hours and cost CFA 3000 plus extra for luggage, while a bus or minibus costs CFA 2000 and takes about seven hours. They all leave either from the gare routière in the centre or from the Sonacop petrol station on the northern side of town. Bush taxis east to the Togo border take at least three hours because the road is not tarred. The Togo border closes at 6 pm; the Niger border at 7.30 pm.

Train You can save money by taking the train. The 2nd-class fare to Cotonou is CFA 3300 while 1st class costs CFA 5500. The train leaves every day at 6 am, arriving about nine hours later, and also at 6 pm on Wednesday, Friday and Sunday, typically arriving around 8 am. The latter train has a couchette; the cost is CFA 6600, but neither train has a dining car. Getting a seat at the last moment is seldom a problem.

DJOUGOU

Djougou (population 30,000) is a lively crossroads town 134 km north-west of Parakou. Most people passing through are on their way to Togo or Natitingou. If you're travelling to Kara, there are good connections to the border. It's also fairly easy to find vehicles headed north to Natitingou. The gare routière is next to the market.

If you're looking for **hiking** opportunities, don't overlook the area around Djougou. The famous Somba people live mostly to the north but the **Taneka villages** near Djougou are also very picturesque. Their round houses have *banco* (mud) walls and grass roofs topped with jars.

The cheapest lodge in town is a tiny *hotel* near the stadium which charges about CFA 1500 for a double with fan, shower and toilet. The only other place to stay in Djougou is the *Motel de Djougou* (☎ 80 00 69), which is not very good for the price. It has eight rooms, five with fans, plus a bar-restaurant. Singles/doubles with fans and attached showers cost CFA 5000/6000. For cheap African food, try the area around the gare routière and adjoining market.

NATITINGOU
Over 200 km north-west of Parakou and pleasantly located at an altitude of 440 metres in the Atakora mountains, Natitingou is the starting point for excursions to Somba country to the east and south, as well as to Pendjari Park to the north.

Things to See & Do
Officially called the Musée d'Arts et de Traditions Populaires de Natitingou, **Le Musée de Natitingou** is behind the tourist agency, Atacora. It has an interesting history and some interesting artefacts from the Somba region. What began as a house for the colonial administrator took nearly half a century to complete due to a fatal accident which occurred during construction and hostilities

leading up to independence in 1960. In 1991 the house was converted into a museum, with two galleries and three rooms. The exhibit includes various musical instruments (bells, violin and bow, drums and flutes), jewellery, crowns, skirts and other ceremonial artefacts. Most interesting is the Habitat room which has the different types of tata somba models with an explanation of why certain models are used. It is open Tuesday to Saturday from 8.30 am to 1 pm and 3 to 7 pm.

Be sure to stop off and have a look at the **Carrefour des Artisans** which is a locally organised artist association that displays and sells authentic work of many northern artists. It's just before Hôtel Tata-Somba in a very quaint tata somba. Prices are fixed but the profits support the organisation.

You could also check **Les Chutes de Kota**, a waterfall 15 km south-east of Natitingou off the main highway, on a well-maintained dirt road. It's a nice place to have a picnic and for at least half the year, during the rainy season, you can swim in the pool of water at the bottom of the falls. There is also a tiny bar where you can get soft drinks and beer. A motorcycle-taxi will take you there for about CFA 400 but you'll have to ask the driver to stay or come back for you.

Places to Stay & Eat
The *Auberge Tanekas* (☎ 82 15 52), or Chez

The Somba
Commonly referred to as the Somba, the Betamaribé are concentrated to the south-west of Natitingou in the plains of Boukoumbé on the Togo border, and to the south-east around Perma. Unlike most Africans who live in close-knit villages, the Betamaribé live in the middle of their cultivated fields so that their compounds are scattered over the countryside. This custom is a reflection of their individualism and helps them maintain a good distance from their neighbours.

The Betamaribé, like their close relatives in Togo, the Tamberma, have avoided Islamic and Christian influences. Most are devout animists and sacrifice animals in ceremonies. Once famous for their nudity they now wear clothes, but they still hunt with bows and arrows, which make great souvenirs. They don't like people taking photos of them, and you're strongly advised not to get out of your car and approach the houses, especially if you have a camera. Of course, if someone invites you to their home, that's an entirely different matter. Don't hesitate to accept.

What's most fascinating about the Betamaribé is their houses. Called *tata somba*, they consist of small, round, tiered huts that look like miniature fortified castles. The ground floor is reserved for the animals. The kitchen is on the intermediate level. From there, you ascend to the roof where there are rooms for sleeping and a terrace for daytime living. ∎

To Boukombé &
Pendjari Park

Moto-taxi Stand

PLM Hôtel
Tata-Somba

Co-op Supermarket ●

■ Hôtel Bourgogne

Chez Victoire &
Good Street Food ▼
● Carrefour
des Artisans

Market

● Carrefour
Principal

Pharmacy

▲ Musée de
Natitingou

Rue du Marché (Le Goudron)

● City Government
Offices

Sonacop Station 🅿
Gare Routière 🚌

CEG Secondary School
■ Hôtel Kanta Borifa

Nightclub ▼

Auberge Tanekas ■

To Chutes de Kota
(Waterfall)

Natitingou

LP

0   0.5   1 km

To Djougou
& Parakou

Sam, is nice and quiet and one of the cheapest places to stay in Natitingou. It's on the southern outskirts of town on the road to Djougou, on your left as you enter Natitingou and about two km from the centre. Spacious singles/doubles with fans and interior showers cost CFA 4500/5500. The owner has been known to act as a guide. The hotel's restaurant is also quite popular and offers chicken, steak and ome-lettes, also African specialities; the menu du jour costs around CFA 2200 and most main dishes are in the CFA 1200 to CFA 2500 range. On the road to the secondary school, CEG, is the eight-room *Hôtel Kanta Borifa* (☎ 82 17 66). It has quiet, clean singles/doubles for CFA 4500/5500 (CFA 7500/8500 with air-con) plus a restaurant. The owner can arrange for you to see a tata somba.

Hôtel de Bourgogne (☎ 82 12 40) is an eight-room, two-storey hotel with a restau-rant and overpriced singles/doubles for CFA 7000/9000 with air-con. The three rooms with fans cost less. The new *Hôtel Bellevue*

(☎ 82 15 27) has eight guest rooms, four with fans and four with air-con. Prices are similar to the Bourgogne's, plus it has a restaurant.

The best hotel by far is the *PLM Hôtel Tata-Somba* (☎ 82 11 24, fax 82 15 84, telex 5354, Paris ☎ 05-28-88-00), which has the liveliest ambience during the park's open season. It has 24 air-con singles/doubles with private baths for CFA 20,000/24,000 (CFA 15,000/18,000 from 1 June to 30 Septem-ber). The facilities include a restaurant (CFA 1500 for breakfast and CFA 4500 for meals), a pool and a reproduction of a tata somba. You can also book rooms for the two lodges at Pendjair Park here.

For cheap beer and street food, or just hanging out, head for *Chez Victoire* in the centre of town. *Le Refuge*, behind the small market, is another place for cheap food.

Getting There & Away

There's usually at least one vehicle every morning from Parakou to Natitingou. It starts filling up early in the morning. If you miss it, don't worry; there are many more vehicles to Djougou (134 km) and from there it's usually not difficult to find a ride on to Natitingou. For a vehicle from Natitingou to Parakou or Cotonou, go early in the morning to the taxi stand. A taxi direct to Cotonou costs around CFA 7000. Buses are cheaper but they are much slower and break down frequently. There are other taxis for Parakou and Cotonou that leave during the course of the day when they fill up.

Those driving will find petrol in Natitingou. If you encounter mechanical problems, try Garage St Joseph – the mechanics are report-edly competent and their charges are fair.

BOUKOUMBÉ

Located some 43 km south-west of Natitin-gou via a very scenic road, Boukoumbé, which is on the Benin/Togo border, is defi-nitely a place worth visiting if you're in the Natitingou area. Some 15 km before town you'll pass near **Mt Kousso-Kouangou**, the tallest mountain in Benin. Three km further along this road you'll pass the **Belvédère de Koussou-Kouangou**, an observation point which offers fantastic views of the area.

The Boukoumbé **market**, which Peace Corps volunteers rave about, is the town's major attraction and a 'must see'. The market here is as much a social event for people from near and far in the region to get together and drink 'chouk' (sorghum beer) and party as it is for marketing produce. Boukoumbé is one of the few areas in Benin where you can buy traditional smoking pipes, which are truly rare souvenirs. If you ask around, you'll also find a workshop run by local artists; they have a number of items for sale including woven grass bracelets and carved wooden imprints. Be sure to search out the town's Peace Corps volunteers as well. If you make friends with them, perhaps offering a beer or two, they may offer to introduce you to a local who owns a tata somba or make arrangements for you to see one of these compounds, which are as numerous in this area as they are around Natitingou.

Every four years or so, for an entire season, there is the infamous '**whipping ceremony**' where young men run around naked with whips, literally beating the crap out of other young men in surrounding villages. It is said to be a rite of passage into manhood displaying who is the most powerful and highly esteemed.

Places to Stay & Eat
Several hundred metres off the road which runs by the Catholic mission is a nice new hotel with three decent rooms, the *Auberge Villageoise de Tourisme*. It has a restaurant. While the *Catholic mission* doesn't usually open up its rooms for travellers, if the hotel is full and your story is pathetic enough, the priests there may find space for you.

Chez Pascaline in the Zongo area is the best place to eat in Boukoumbé. It is reportedly 'wickedly nice', with fantastic and inexpensive wild-game meat, salads, rice and beans. This is also a good place to enquire about lodging with locals and the possibility of visiting nearby tatas. Street food can be found in the market area.

Getting There & Away
There is at least one taxi every day from Natitingou to Boukoumbé; the fare is CFA 800. The trip only takes two hours but the waiting time can be longer as the taxi starts filling up around 9 am and may not leave before 3 pm. To avoid such a long wait, you might try hitching a ride with a project vehicle or with tourists. The road is usually in decent condition, except during the heavy rainy season. From Boukoumbé, if you're adventurous you might try crossing over into Togo via Nadogo, then heading south-west to Kandé. This is much easier on Wednesday, which is market day in Nadogo.

PENDJARI PARK & W NATIONAL PARK
Benin has two national parks in the far north: Parc de la Pendjari and, about twice as large, Parc National du W. Pendjari is adjacent to Parc National d'Arli in Burkina Faso (see that chapter for details), while W Park is adjacent to the park of the same name in Niger. The three form, in effect, one big park and are surrounded by buffer zones managed for hunting (*zones cynégétiques*).

Parc de la Pendjari, 45 km north of Natitingou, is bordered on its western side by the Pendjari River. It's much more developed for tourism than the Benin side of W Park, so it receives most of the visitors. It's open only from 15 December to 15 May, the best viewing time being near the end of the dry season when the animals hover around the water holes. The park usually isn't particularly attractive then because much of the vegetation is burnt off by fires.

Half the fun is looking for the animals. A recent census indicates that there are approximately 850 elephants, 2000 buffalo, 1250 hippos and 350 lions in Pendjari Park. However, don't be surprised if all you see are some forlorn-looking antelope and a few wart hogs, monkeys and hippos because even during the dry season the place often seems almost barren of wildlife.

The park entrance fee, which is good for 30 days, is CFA 3000, plus you must pay a camera fee of CFA 500 and also CFA 1000 for each night you stay in the park. They may request your ID.

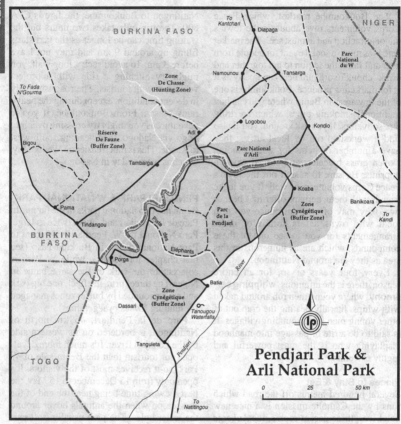

BURKINA FASO

To
Kantchari

Diapaga

NIGER

Parc
National
du W

Zone
De Chasse
(Hunting Zone)

Namounou

Tansarga

To Fada
N'Gourma

Logobou

Kondio

Réserve
De Faune
(Buffer Zone)

Arli

Parc National
d'Arli

Bigou

Tambarga

Koaba

Zone
Cynégétique
(Buffer Zone)

Banikoara

Pama

Parc
de la
Pendjari

To
Kandi

BURKINA
FASO

Tindangou

Piste des Éléphants

Porga

River

Batia

Zone
Cynégétique
(Buffer Zone)

Dassari

Tanougou
Waterfalls

TOGO

Tanguieta

Pendjari

**Pendjari Park &
Arli National Park**

0   25   50 km

To
Natitingou

Places to Stay & Eat

Many visitors stay in Natitingou and make excursions from there, but you'll have a better chance of seeing animals if you stay at the park itself. In Tanguieta, which borders the park, there are two very rustic *campements* – one of these is beside the river and has low prices. There's also *Chez Basile*, which is a small hotel-restaurant in town. You'll also find the best hospital in northern Benin plus a thriving market on Mondays.

Most people keep going to Porga. There, at the entrance to the park, is the *Campement de Porga* (Natitingou ☎ 82 11 24, fax 82 15

84 c/o Hôtel Tata-Somba). It's a larger place with a restaurant (breakfast CFA 1750, meals CFA 5000) and 15 basic singles/doubles with fans which are overpriced at CFA 12,000/13,500 (CFA 18,000/20,000 with air-con). Despite the fans and air-con, the rooms can become suffocating because the generator cuts down before midnight. Nile perch from the Pendjari River and game in season are the specialities of the restaurant.

Very early morning is the best time for spotting animals because that's when they tend to congregate at the water holes. For this reason, you'll have a better chance of seeing

The Waterfalls
If you stay in Tanguieta, consider a trek north-east on the Batia road to La Chute de Tanguieta or La Cascade de Tanougou, two waterfalls. The road to the former is quite bad but the site is beautiful. The latter, which is much more accessible, is about 15 km before Batia and off to your right (east). During the rainy season, the pools at the bottom are great for swimming, but during the dry season they contract considerably. Even then, however, the atmosphere is relaxing. ■

animals if you stay inside the park. Because of the presence of lions, there are only certain areas, including the Mare Yangouali and Pont d'Arli, where camping is permitted. The park wardens can show you where.

The larger *Campement de Pendjari* (Natitingou ☎ 82 11 24, fax 82 15 84 c/o Hôtel Tata-Somba), inside the park via the Porga entrance, has various bungalows with 29 rooms altogether. Units have fans, washbasins and shared baths. It charges CFA 15,000/17,000 for singles/doubles (CFA 20,000/22,000 with air-con) and CFA 1750/5000 for breakfast/dinner. Both campements close from 15 May to 15 December.

Getting There & Away
The major entrance points to Pendjari Park are roughly 100 km north of Natitingou. To get to the park from Natitingou, take the dirt road heading north for 45 km to the fork in the road at Tanguieta. It's a village on the southern tip of the park. From there most people head north-west for 59 km to Porga at the Burkina Faso border. This village is the main entrance to the park and there's a campement near the gate. Alternatively, you could head north-east from Tanguieta to the village of Batia (41 km), the other park entrance. Many people prefer this latter entrance because the route is almost one-third shorter and in equally good condition.

To get to W Park, go north-east from Batia for some 100 km to the intersection with the dirt road connecting Kondio (Burkina Faso) and Kérémou. The latter, to the south-east, is the major entry point on the Benin side.

You can't hike in the park, so go to the hotel in Natitingou and make friends with travellers who have vehicles. Or hitch a ride

to Porga and try the same with the guests at the campement there. Or arrange to rent Hôtel Tata-Somba's Land Rover. You'll have to share it to make it affordable.

KANDI
Kandi, 213 km north of Parakou on the highway to Niger, is worth a stop to check the lovely **market**. The Bariba and the Peul give it a distinctive northern character, as do the voluptuous mango trees all over town.

There are two roughly comparable places to stay. At the southern entrance to town you'll find the *Auberge du Carrefour*, while at the opposite end of town is the *Baobab 2000*, sometimes referred to as the campement. At either place you'll be brought a bucket of water for bathing. For food, try the *Gargoterie de Kandi* behind the market.

MALANVILLE
Malanville is in the far north at the Niger border, on the main Cotonou to Niamey highway. The ride from Parakou passes through some interesting terrain. Look for the women selling good red-skinned cheese on the way. **Market** day (Sunday) can be quite interesting because so many different races of people converge in this area.

Places to Stay & Eat
The only hotel appears to be the dirty *campement* at the entrance to town. You can get street food all around the lively gare routière.

Getting There & Away
A bush taxi from Malanville to Parakou typically takes five hours and costs CFA 3000, while a bus or minibus (if you can find one) costs CFA 2000 and takes up to seven hours.

Burkina Faso

If you ask someone what there is to see in Burkina Faso, 'nothing' may be the response. Yet its popularity among travellers is tops in the Sahel – proof again that in West Africa, people count more than places.

Ouagadougou (wah-gah-DOU-gou) is smaller than most Sahelian capitals – you can walk to most places in the core central area – and you might think life in one of the five poorest countries on earth would be fairly tranquil. Far from it: you'll find bustling streets crammed with *mobylettes* (mopeds), while the Grand Marché is one of West Africa's most active.

One reason travellers like Ouagadougou, or Ouaga, is that it is so easy to meet the locals in the morning at one of the many street-side tables where you can get coffee and bread, or in the evening at one of the many bars for which the city is famous.

In the rest of Burkina, village life is fascinating. In Gorom-Gorom, a dry north-eastern area near the desert, the people are accustomed to having foreigners living in their African-style huts and participating in village life, even weeding and pounding millet, but elsewhere villagers are less accustomed to visitors and may be a little reluctant to accept them so readily.

BURKINA FASO

Area: 274,122 sq km
Population: 9.5 million
Population Growth Rate: 3.1%
Capital: Ouagadougou
Head of State: President Captain Blaise Compaoré
Official Language: French
Currency: West African CFA franc
Exchange Rate: CFA 500 = US$1
Per Capita GNP: US$320
Inflation: 0%
Time: GMT/UTC

Suggested Itineraries

The city of **Ouagadougou** is interesting and friendly and can easily be covered on foot. Travellers like hanging out here for a few days, absorbing the good vibes. Thereafter, most of them hop on the train for the small city of **Bobo-Dioulasso**. If you're in no hurry, you could stop off en route at the sleepy town of **Koudougou**.

From Bobo you could head south to **Banfora**, an area in the country's 'green' belt with large expanses of sugar-cane fields, lakes, waterfalls, rocky cliffs and, consequently, exceptionally good hiking (allow at least three days here). Or you could head east to **Gaoua**, a more remote area noted for its architecture. Alternatively, go north to **Ouahigouya**, the country's third-largest city and a potential gateway into Mali. East of Ouahigouya is **Gorom-Gorom** – home to the most fascinating market in Burkina. The nearby town of **Dori** is also a good place to absorb the dry desert atmosphere. A good place to end your trip might be Burkina's major game park, **Arli**, in the far south-east. Plan on staying here at least two or three nights. ∎

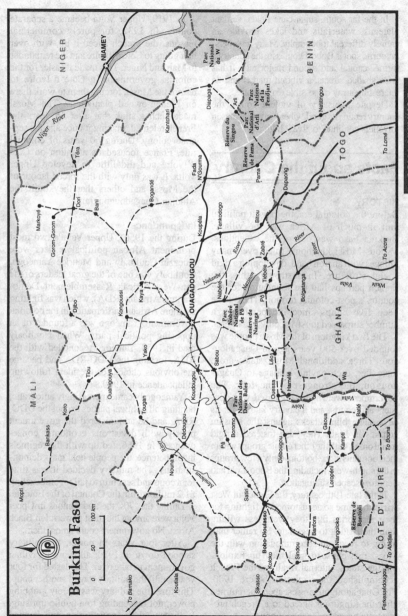

In the far south, sugar-cane fields, verdant plateaus, waterfalls and lakes provide an entirely different topography. Many travellers' favourite spot is Bobo-Dioulasso, the country's former capital and second major city. It has wide shaded streets, a vibrant market and an interesting array of possible excursions.

Despite a history of violent coups, the country retains its good 'vibes' – a major reason travellers continue to give it high marks.

Facts about the Country

HISTORY

Before the colonial era, the largest political unit in much of Africa was the village. Burkina Faso was one of the exceptions. Various Mossi kingdoms ruled over many villages with an iron hand, developing a rigid social structure. In destroying this, the French perhaps laid the foundation for the country's post-colonial turmoil. There have been five coups since independence, a number surpassed in Africa only by Nigeria.

The first kingdom of the Mossi people was founded over 500 years ago in Ouagadougou. Three additional Mossi states arose thereafter, each paying homage to Ouagadougou, the strongest of the four. The governments were highly organised, with ministers and courts, and a cavalry known for its devastating blitz attacks against the Muslim empires in Mali. They also fostered a rigid social order, with the other ethnic groups within their domains at the bottom. Only a few groups in the south-west, including the Bobo, Lobi and Senufo, escaped subjugation.

In the late 19th century, the French in West Africa became so accustomed to fighting for their territories that they were less willing than the British to negotiate. So rather than trying to reach an accommodation with the Mossi, they chose to break them up. Exploiting the states' internal rivalries, the French accomplished their mission before 1900. The Ouagadougou king escaped but returned after the kingdoms agreed to a French protectorate based in Ouagadougou.

In 1919, Upper Volta became a separate colony. In 1932, for purely commercial reasons, the French sliced it up, with over half going to Côte d'Ivoire and the remainder to Mali and Niger. This made it easier for the colonial government in Côte d'Ivoire to recruit the Mossi, forcing them to work there on French-owned plantations. The Mossi made such a stink that after 15 years the French relented, making it once again a separate colony. During 60 years of colonial rule, France focused its attention on Côte d'Ivoire and did little to develop Upper Volta. It was only with the forced labour of the Mossi and others that they built the Abidjan-Ouagadougou train.

Independence

During the 1950s, Upper Volta's two most prominent African political leaders were Ouezzin Coulibaly and Maurice Yaméogo. Coulibaly was one of the great leaders of the pan-West African Rassemblement Démocratique Africain (RDA), which was fighting for more African participation in the colonial government. Yaméogo was a founder of an opposing political party. When Coulibaly died in 1958, Yaméogo reconciled with the RDA, forming the UDC-RDA and became the obvious choice for president following independence in 1960.

Yaméogo became increasingly autocratic, banning all political parties except the UDC-RDA, and he administered the government poorly with disastrous economic consequences. In 1966, fed up with the régime's incompetence, the people held mass demonstrations. The military decided it was time for a coup and sent him to jail for embezzling £1.2 million from the Council of the Entente.

During the '70s, the trade unions in Upper Volta were among the most powerful in Black Africa. No government could ignore them.

After four years in power, the military stepped down in 1970, allowing a civilian government to take over. This lasted for four years, until the military staged another coup. This time, the military was merely grabbing power, not responding to a public uprising. It suspended the constitution and banned political activity. Getting rid of the powerful trade unions was not so easy. Following a nationwide strike in 1975, the unions forced the government to raise wages but labour leaders were still not satisfied. In 1978, after several years of pressuring the government, the unions got the new constitution and general elections that they wanted. However, their man lost to the incumbent president.

In the next five years, there were three more coups. The most notable was in 1983 when Captain Thomas Sankara, an ambitious young military star with left-wing ideas, staged a bloody coup and seized power.

The Sankara Era

Burkina Faso, Sankara's new name for the country, became the most revolutionary on the continent. Sankara wondered why it was that after almost a quarter of a century of receiving more foreign aid per capita than just about any country in Africa, Burkina remained one of the world's five poorest nations. He concluded that it was because the people were not being consulted and were not involved in the development process. The new government's central theme, therefore, was that development rests ultimately with the people, not foreign aid-donors. The flip side of this Maoist coin was that only group action counts; individual motivation was virtually frowned upon.

Sankara's approach was unconventional. Modest Renault-5s, for example, were the official car of the president and his ministers. Blitz campaigns were his style. In one 15-day marathon, the government vaccinated about 60% of the children against measles, meningitis and yellow fever. UNICEF called it 'one of the major successes of the year in Africa'. Adopting the Chinese barefoot doctor model, Sankara called on every village to build a medical dispensary. The government then sent several people from each village for training, making them front-line medical advisors. Between 1983 and 1986, over 350 communities built schools with their own labour and the education of school-age children increased by one-third to 22%.

Ouagadougou looked a bit shabby, so Sankara ordered all houses on the principal streets to be painted white, then levelled the decrepit central market, thinking that some foreign government would help finance a new one. The French eventually came through. In 1985, he dismissed all but three of the cabinet members, sending them to work on agricultural co-operatives. It was mainly show; a month later, they were back at their old jobs. Then Sankara ordered an across-the-board 25% cut in government salaries and ordered all rents for 1985 to be handed to the government instead of the landlords. His pet project was the Sahel railway, a 375-km railroad project connecting Ouagadougou and Tambao at the Niger border, the site of rich manganese and limestone deposits. Although economists said it wouldn't be profitable, Sankara moved ahead. In early 1987, he inaugurated the first leg, the 33-km stretch to Dousin, all done with 'voluntary' village labour. Today, it reaches Kaya.

Sankara was amazingly charismatic. The masses loved him for his blunt honesty and could listen to him for hours. In early 1986, he brought the country to war with Mali over an ancient border dispute involving Agacher, an area supposedly rich in manganese (but too costly to mine). His popularity soared still further. The war ended five days later, but not before both sides had dropped a few bombs, causing an estimated 60 deaths.

While Sankara had widespread support, he antagonised trade unions, landlords and many Western countries. By his constant attacks on Western imperialism, his back-slapping antics with Libya's Gaddafi, and actions like throwing out the Peace Corps, Sankara particularly alienated the Americans and the French. Sankara was one of the most interesting political figures in West Africa and his motives seemed irreproachable, but he did not live to see if his socialist policies would work. In late 1987, a group of junior officers seized power. Sankara was taken outside Ouagadougou and shot.

Burkina Faso Today

While many Western countries were relieved to see Sankara gone, many people on the street were understandably furious. The economy improved under Sankara and there was little corruption in the government. Its financial books were kept in good order, debt financing was kept to a minimum, and budgetary commitments were adhered to. Most importantly, the people developed a genuine pride in their country, as Sankara, with favourable press, put Burkina on the map.

The new junta, headed by Captain Blaise Compaoré, Houphouët-Boigny's son-in-law and Sankara's former friend and co-revolutionary, attempted unsuccessfully to discredit Sankara with its 'rectification' campaign, which was to correct the 'deviations' of the previous government while embracing the revolution. Their first act – dismantling the local cells of the revolutionary defence committees that had threatened and often replaced traditional power structures in rural areas – couldn't have been more counter-revolutionary. The government then undermined the revolution by raising government salaries and removing some food subsidies.

Today, Burkinabé society is suffering from a serious malaise and even top government officials privately acknowledge as

much. Many people still mourn Sankara. Relations with the USA, which has withdrawn all foreign assistance, are bad because of the government's assistance to the rebel leader Charles Taylor in Liberia. More importantly, no one is sure exactly where Compaoré's government is headed. The 'rectification' seems determined not so much by conscious policy decisions as by a tendency to bend before varying pressures. Political splinter groups have sprouted everywhere. Also, street crime is on the rise. Most important, Burkina is no longer in the limelight and that is having an adverse effect on an invaluable asset – national pride.

GEOGRAPHY

Landlocked in the Sahel, Burkina Faso is a flat, arid country of bush, scrub and reddish laterite soil. To the north, the vegetation thins out and the land becomes sandy and desert-like. In the far south around Banfora the rainfall is heavier and there are forests and irrigated sugar-cane fields. The area from Banfora eastward to Ghana has beautiful rolling plateaus and green woodlands.

The French named the country Upper

The Environment

Environmentally, Burkina is facing severe problems due in large part to the population growth rate, which is high even by African standards. The problem is extremely complex, however, and government and donor agencies are slowly coming to realise that their attempts during the '70s and '80s to find relatively simple technical solutions haven't worked. Environmental problems here are symptomatic of the country's multiple socioeconomic problems, not just population growth. One thing for sure is that traditional land-use systems, while once well adapted to this Sahel region, are proving inadequate to the challenge. One of the most visible consequences of this is deforestation. Ouagadougou is now surrounded by a 70-km swath of land virtually devoid of trees. That's because wood accounts for 94% of the country's energy consumption. Arriving at Ouagadougou overland, you'll see cart after cart bringing wood from afar to the city. This, along with slash-burn agriculture and wild grazing of animals, is resulting in increased desertification, particularly in the north. So as the population rises, the land's carrying capacity is decreasing – an ominous trend throughout the Sahel.

Environmental damage is so bad that the country is estimated to be losing 9% of GNP annually because of it. To combat this, the country has been experimenting since 1981, with the assistance of Oxfam, in encouraging farmers to return to traditional methods, particularly the building of *diguettes* – stone lines laid along the contours of fields. By slowing water runoff, the stones maximise water penetration and reduce erosion, thus conserving soil. These diguettes have had an amazingly beneficial impact, in some instances increasing soil levels by 15 cm in a single year. As a result, more and more villages are building them and as you travel around the country you might see some. ■

Volta after its three major rivers – the Black Volta, the White Volta and the Red Volta. All of them flow into the world's largest artificial lake – Lake Volta in Ghana. You might think these rivers are the saviour of this arid country, but the waters attract black flies which transmit river blindness disease (onchocerciasis). As a result, until recently Burkina had the world's highest incidence of this dreaded disease. Entire villages along the rivers were evacuated because of it and the victims are the beggars in Ouaga and elsewhere. The World Health Organisation's (WHO) 18-year-old black fly spraying programme has succeeded beyond expectations, as new incidences of the disease have virtually disappeared, permitting deserted villages to be resettled. There has also been a major breakthrough in the treatment of the disease with the introduction of a new drug called mectizan. It doesn't completely cure the disease but offers considerable relief and, after long usage, may become a cure.

CLIMATE

The weather pattern is similar to that in the rest of the Sahel. The rain falls from June to September. From December to February the weather is cooler and the harmattan winds produce hazy skies. The hot season is from March to early June.

GOVERNMENT

The head of government is the president; the country also has a National Assembly. Presidential elections were held in 1992 but Compaoré was the only candidate and of course won. However, 72% of the people abstained from voting, which suggests that his support is actually very weak. Elections were also held in 1992 for the National Assembly. Over 45 political parties participated but Compaoré's party, the Popular Democracy-Labour Movement (ODP-MT), won; still, the results were disputed.

ECONOMY

During Sankara's reign, GNP rose from an average of 3.1 to 4.6% per annum, making Burkina one of the very few countries in Africa to enjoy per capita GNP growth during the 1980s. On the negative side, he caused foreign investment to nose-dive and turned a blind eye to the country's population growth rate, which soared from 2.7% in the 1970s to 3.5% in the 1980s.

Today, the economy is continuing to improve, but barely enough to keep up with the country's population growth. Agriculture employs 90% of the work force and in 1994 Burkina was one of only five African countries in a position to export food. But this depends on there being sufficient annual rainfall. While cotton exports, which generate 48% of foreign earnings, are doing well, the country's cattle trade is being destroyed by the European Union (EU) which is dumping European beef on the West African market, depressing prices considerably. Most important, the distribution of incomes may be becoming more skewed, perhaps because the government is following International Monetary Fund (IMF) policy so well. Ostentatious displays of status are now back in vogue among the rich, and street crime is on the rise, which suggests that some segments of the economy may be worse off. In sum, while Burkina has followed very closely the West's recommendations for freeing the economy from government control, the results to date suggest that this approach is hardly a panacea for struggling economies with little export potential.

POPULATION & PEOPLE

With some 9.5 million people, Burkina Faso is one of the more densely populated countries in the Sahel. It's overpopulated, which is why the country's major export is people – over 500,000 Burkinabé work in neighbouring countries, primarily Côte d'Ivoire. While the remittances they send home assist the economy, the emigration of so many young people is a catastrophe for agriculture. It all helps intensify the famines that occur during the periodic droughts.

Concentrated in the central plateau area, including Ouagadougou, the Mossi are only one of about 60 ethnic groups in Burkina, each with its own language. You'll encounter

BURKINA FASO

the Bobo in the west around Bobo-Dioulasso, the Fulani or Peul (Sankara was Fulani-Peul) primarily in the north, the Gourmantché in the east, and the Lobi in the far south-west around Gaoua.

The Mossi are famous for having the longest continuous royal dynasty in West Africa, dating back about 500 years, when the war-mongering Mossi founded an empire in Ouagadougou. There were four Mossi kingdoms each with its own king, or *naba*. Strongly individualistic, they were one of the few peoples in the Sahel to successfully resist the Muslims. They even sacked Timbuktu, a Muslim stronghold, at the height of its power in 1333. The dynasty continues because the chief of the Ouagadougou kingdom escaped the French. You can see the naba of Ouagadougou, who is in effect the Mossi emperor, on Friday mornings at the weekly Moro-Naba ceremony (Moro is singular for Mossi).

Art of Burkina Faso

Each ethnic group in Burkina has its own artistic style, but the art of the Mossi, the Bobo and the Lobi is the most famous. In the museums in Ouaga and Bobo you'll see examples of all three. The Mossi are best known for their tall wooden antelope masks, which are usually over two metres high and painted red and white. The female and male antelope masks are distinguishable by the top piece; the former has a human female figure on top while the latter is surmounted by a nonhuman plank-like structure. At the bottom of the mask is a small oval face bisected by a serrated vertical strip, with triangular eyeholes on either side. They were originally worn at funerals and when guarding certain fruits.

The Bobo are famous for their large, horizontal butterfly masks, which are typically 1.5 metres wide and painted red, black and white. They are worn during funeral rites and when invoking the deity *Do* in ceremonies asking for rain and for fertility of the fields at planting time and after the harvest. The form of a butterfly is used because butterflies appear in great swarms immediately after the first rains and are thus associated with the planting season. The dancer twists his head about so that the mask almost appears to be spinning. Other animals used for these zoomorphic masks include the owl, buffalo, antelope, crocodile and scorpion but rather than being horizontal, these masks are usually tall like the Mossi antelope masks, only wider with bold coloured patterns similar to those of the butterfly masks. The use of all these masks, however, is identical. The Bobo are also noted for their helmet masks which are frequently used in the famous 'fêtes des masques' of that region.

Do mask

The Lobi, in southern Burkina, don't use masks. Most of their woodcarvings are of human figures, typically 35 to 65 cm high, representing deities and ancestors. They are used for ancestral shrines and years ago were found in all homes. Other wooden carvings of the Lobi which you might see are staffs and three-legged stools with human or animal heads and combs with human figures or geometric decorations. The most distinguishing features of their carvings (which were not done by specialists and are not so well known except by African art specialists) are their rigid appearance, with arms straight down by the sides of the body, and their realistic and detailed rendering of certain body parts, particularly the navel, eyes and hair. ■

Blade mask

RELIGION

Because the Mossi were so successful in resisting the Muslim invaders during the centuries before the colonial period, today not more than 25% of the people of Burkina are Muslim. Most of them reside in the north. The remainder are animists.

LANGUAGE

The official language is French. There are a number of African languages. Over half the people speak Moré (MOR-ay), the language of the Mossi. Dioula (JOU-lah) is the major language spoken in the market.

Expressions in Moré

Good morning.	*YEE-bay-roh*
Good evening.	*nay-ZAH-bree*
How are you?	*lah-FEE-bay-may?*
I'm fine.	*lah-FEE-bay-lah*
Thank you.	*when-ah-TAH-say*
Goodbye.	*un-PUS-dah BAR-kah*

Expressions in Dioula

Good morning.	*e-nee-SOH-goh-mah*
Good evening.	*e-nee-WOU-lah*
How are you?	*e-kah-kay-nay-WAH?*
I'm fine.	*ah-HON kah-kay-nay*
Thank you.	*e-nee-chay*
Goodbye.	*AM-bay SOH-goh-mah*

Facts for the Visitor

VISAS & EMBASSIES
Burkina Faso Visas

Visas are required by all. In London, the Burkina Faso consulate charges UK£17.50 for multiple-entry visas valid for three months from the date of issue. Bring two photos. In Washington, the embassy processes visas in 48 hours, requires two photos and proof of a yellow fever vaccination, and charges US$20 for a visa valid for three months for a visit of equal duration.

Visas are easy to get in virtually every country in Africa because French embassies issue them in countries where Burkina is not represented, and the process takes from 24 to

48 hours. However, the cost of a three-month visa is often higher than outside Africa, eg CFA 20,000 in most of West Africa but CFA 40,000 in Abidjan. In Algiers, the Burkina Faso embassy requires two photos and takes 24 hours to issue visas valid for 30 days. Exit permits are not required.

Burkina Faso Embassies

Belgium 16 Place Guy-d'Aarezzo, Brussels 1060 (☎ (02) 345-99-12)

France 159 blvd Haussmann, 75008 Paris (☎ (1) 43-59-21-85)

Germany 18 Wendelstadtallee, 5300 Bonn-Bad Godesberg (☎ (0228) 33-20-63)

UK 5 Cinnamon Row, Plantation Wharf, London SW11 3TW (☎ (0171) 738-1800, fax 738 2820)

USA 2340 Massachusetts Ave, NW, Washington, DC 20008 (☎ (202) 332-5577)

Burkina Faso also has embassies in Algiers, Abidjan, Accra, Bamako, Cairo, Copenhagen, Lagos, Ottawa and Rome.

Other African Visas

Algeria & Senegal The Algerian embassy issues visas within 24 to 48 hours. The Senegalese consulate is open weekdays from 8 am to noon and issues visas within 24 hours. Both are in Ouaga.

Ghana Getting a Ghanaian visa can be problematic as the embassy may tell you that you must be a resident of Burkina. However, if you indicate in your application form that you reside in a country without a Ghanaian embassy and are persistent with the staff, your chances of being issued a visa are good. You will need to provide information on your hotels in Ghana, eg names and telephone numbers. The embassy, open weekdays from 8 am to 2 pm, charges CFA 6000 for visas (CFA 3000 for three-day transit visas) and issues them within 24 to 48 hours. Bring four photos.

Nigeria The embassy in Ouaga issues visas in 48 hours; it's open weekdays from 8 am to 3 pm. The price varies according to nationality, from about CFA 350 for Americans to over CFA 10,000 for Britons. You'll need one photo.

Other Countries You can get visas in Ouaga for Togo, Côte d'Ivoire, Central African Republic, Mauritania and Gabon at the French consulate, which gives same-day service if you come in the morning. Single-entry visas cost CFA 6000 for stays of one to five days and CFA 20,000 for stays of up to three months. Bring two photos. You cannot get visas in Ouaga to Mali, Niger, Chad or Benin. If you can convince the Malian border officials that you reside in Burkina and couldn't get a visa, occasionally they will allow you through provided you apply for a visa upon arriving in Bamako. Don't try this if arriving by air.

Foreign Embassies
See the Ouaga Information section for a list of foreign embassies found in the capital.

DOCUMENTS
To enter the country, all you need is a passport and an International Vaccination Certificate. Those driving need a *carnet de passage en douane*.

CUSTOMS
There's no restriction on the import or export of CFA or foreign currencies. If you purchase artwork in Burkina that appears to be old, you will not be permitted to take it out of the country without the prior approval of the Director of the National Cultural Patrimony in Ouaga. To obtain this, you must submit a written declaration including a receipt to the Director. If approval is obtained, you will be issued with a certificate of exportation provided you pay the required fee per piece.

MONEY
1FF	=	CFA 100
UK£1	=	CFA 775
US$1	=	CFA 500

The unit of currency is the West African CFA franc. The best banks for changing money are the Banque Internationale du Burkina (BIB) and the Banque Internationale pour le Commerce l'Industrie et l'Agriculture (BICIA). Both change US dollar and UK pound travellers' cheques and, most unusually for Africa, charge no commission. So if you'll be leaving here for another CFA country, change your money here before leaving. Other banks include the BICAO and the Banque Nationale de Paris. It is now possible to withdraw cash with a credit card at most of these banks.

BUSINESS HOURS & HOLIDAYS
Business hours are weekdays from 7.30 am to 12.30 pm and 3 to 5.30 pm, and Saturday from 9 am to 1 pm. Government offices are open weekdays from 7 am to 12.30 pm and 3 to 5.30 pm; closed Saturday and Sunday.

Banking hours are weekdays from 7 to 11.30 am and 3.30 to 5 pm; closed Saturday and Sunday.

Public Holidays
1 January, 3 January, End of Ramadan, Easter Monday, 1 May, Tabaski, Ascension Thursday, Whit Monday, 4 August (Revolution Day), 15 August, Mohammed's Birthday, 1 November, 25 December.

POST & TELECOMMUNICATIONS
The poste restante in Ouagadougou is reliable and costs CFA 200 per letter.

The city dialling codes are 30 or 33 for Ouaga, 9 for Bobo, 88 for Banfora, 55 for Ouahigouya and 4 for Koudougou. Calling Europe, the USA or Australia is fairly easy. You can call from the main post office in Ouagadougou every day until 10 pm; the cost per minute is CFA 902 to Europe and CFA 1458 to North America and Australia. You can also use the hotel phones but they are more expensive. As for telexes, in Ouagadougou you can use the post office or the Silmandé and l'Indépendance hotels.

PHOTOGRAPHY
A photo permit is not required so long as you do not photograph any sensitive places; the official list is as follows: airports, reservoirs, bridges, banks, any military installations or police stations or government buildings including the Presidential Palace and post offices, train stations and *gare routières* (bush taxi parks), TV/radio stations, petrol stations, grain warehouses, water towers, industrial installations and indigent people.

A permit is required for a video cassette recorder. The Ministère de l'Environnement et du Tourisme has simplified procedures considerably but the permit is still costly, around CFA 50,000 (CFA 3000 for a photo permit).

HEALTH
Malaria is a serious problem in Burkina. A yellow fever vaccination is required. Vaccination against cholera is required only if

you've been in a country with a recent outbreak. Oncho, once a major problem here, has been essentially eradicated.

The Hôpital Yalgado Ouédraogo (☎ 33 46 41) in Ouagadougou should be used only in emergencies. One of the better pharmacies in Ouagadougou is Pharmacie Nouvelle in the central area near Ciné Burkina. For the name of an all-night pharmacie (*pharmacie de garde*) in Ouaga, consult the second page of the *Sidwaya* newspaper.

DANGERS & ANNOYANCES

Burkina is one of the safer countries in West Africa but crime is rising here as elsewhere, so travellers, particularly women travelling alone, need to be on their guard. Travellers have been attacked and robbed within minutes of arriving at the markets in Ouagadougou and Bobo-Dioulasso. Most crimes occur in those two cities and, fortunately, most are limited to petty theft. Occasionally, thieves are armed with knives. In Ouaga, the worst areas are around the market and the post office and along Ave Yennenga, particularly at night. During the day, travellers have been robbed by two fellows on a mobylette, one grabbing the traveller's bag while they pass by. In addition, the zones around the Presidential Palace and the Conseil de l'Entente in Ouaga are guarded and are strictly off limits. Serious incidents do sometimes happen. In the late 1980s, an American woman travelling on her own was killed by her new Ghanaian boyfriend, apparently for her money and her 4WD. So don't take security lightly, particularly at night in the cities. If you have problems in Ouaga, contact the commissariat central (☎ 30 62 71).

ACCOMMODATION

Accommodation in Burkina Faso is basically the same as you'll find all over West Africa, ranging from filthy dumps to fairly deluxe hotels in the country's largest two cities. It's fairly easy to find rooms for between CFA 3000 and CFA 4000, not so for less than this. The government imposes a lodging head tax of CFA 300 per person per night (sometimes included in the quoted rate) and, except for the cheapest hotels, there is also a 15% tax.

FOOD & DRINK

Food in Burkina Faso lacks the variety of that found in most countries along the West African coast. Sauces are the mainstays, eg *riz sauce* (rice with sauce), *riz gras* (rice with vegetable sauce), *sauce du poisson* (a fish-based sauce), *boeuf sauce aubergine* (sauce with beef and eggplant), *mouton sauce tomate* (sauce with mutton and tomatoes), *ragoût d'igname* (a yam-based stew), *riz sauce arachide* (rice with peanut sauce) and *sauce gombo* (a sticky okra-based stew). Sauces are always served with a starch, usually rice or some kind of *paté* (a pounded dough-like substance made with millet, corn, yams etc) and eaten with the bare right hand. In rural areas, bush rat is a tasty local delicacy. Lunch is the main meal; at night, grilled dishes such as poulet and poisson grillé and beef brochettes are popular, particularly in the cities. Water is the most common drink, but try the nonalcoholic ginger beer or Senegalese *bissap*, a reddish drink made with bissap flowers.

Getting There & Away

AIR

From Europe, there are direct flights from Paris and Brussels. From the USA, you'll have to transfer in Paris, Dakar or Abidjan. From London, the cheapest is Aeroflot via Moscow.

Within Africa there are direct flights to Ouagadougou from Bamako (CFA 48,000), Dakar and Niamey. Air Burkina and Air Ivoire have flights to Abidjan and Bouaké (Côte d'Ivoire) and their fares are 20% less than those of Air Afrique.

LAND

Bus

In Burkina, buses and vans are called *cars*. In Ouaga, they all leave from the gare routière. None ply the Ouaga-Lomé route – only bush taxis (Peugeot 504s) and minibuses.

To/From Ghana If you're headed for Ghana, the fastest way is with a large Ghanaian STC bus. Somewhat dilapidated but still reasonably comfortable, they leave from Ouaga for Accra on Mondays and Fridays. (The return trips to Ouaga are on Wednesdays from Kumasi and Saturdays from Accra; the departure time is 8 am.) The departure from Ouaga is at 9 am according to the schedule but closer to 10.30 in practice. Buses leave from the gare routière in Ouaga, but you must buy your ticket in advance from the STC office (☎ 30 87 50) in town. The cost from Ouaga is CFA 6700 to Kumasi and CFA 7200 to Accra. It's a long, gruelling, 24-hour trip all the way to Accra, which is why some travellers recommend breaking the trip at Tamale. If the schedule isn't convenient, take a government RNTC/X9 (more commonly known as X9) bus from Ouagadougou to the border town of Pô and hitch from there; they leave every day except Tuesday and Sunday at 9 am from the X9 station.

To/From Côte d'Ivoire There are large buses every day from Ouaga to Yamoussoukro and Abidjan. Sans Frontières, Les Comètes Binkady and Linko Lemgo do the trip which takes at least 24 hours and sometimes much more due to overnight stays at the border and occasional long waits in Bouaké. At about CFA 14,000 they cost less than a 1st-class seat on the train (CFA 16,400) but more than a 2nd-class seat (CFA 11,000). Sans Frontières' *cars* for Yamoussoukro depart Ouaga daily at 10 am and at 3 pm; the cost is CFA 13,500.

To/From Niger Faso Tours, SNTN and X9 are the principal companies with bus connections to Niamey. The large Faso Tours *car* leaves for Niamey on Mondays while that of SNTN leaves on Thursdays. (They depart Niamey for Ouaga on Tuesdays and Wednesdays.) They both depart at 7 am from the Faso Tours office in town, 1½ blocks west of the market, and tickets must be purchased a day or more in advance. Regardless of what you may be told, the trip takes at least 12 hours, with over two hours at the border, which involves several laborious luggage checks. The cost is CFA 7000 from Ouaga and CFA 9000 from Niamey. X9 also has buses for Niamey (CFA 7000), departing Ouaga on Tuesdays and returning on

Thursdays. You can also catch a daily Sans Frontières *car* to the Niger border (CFA 4000) and a bush taxi from there to Niamey; the *car* leaves at 9 am from the Sans Frontières office in Ouaga on Ave Coulibaly; advance reservations are required. All other buses on this route have discontinued service.

To/From Togo There are no *cars* to Lomé but STCB (on Ave de la Liberté near Ave Dimdolobsom) connects Ouaga with Dapaong in northern Togo. The trip takes about eight hours and costs CFA 4000. Most travellers end up taking Peugeot 504s or minibuses, both inferior. An X9 used to leave Ouaga on Saturdays and Lomé on Wednesdays; check if this service has resumed.

To/From Mali Sans Frontières offers the best service to Bamako. Its *cars* depart Bobo every day at 3 pm except Sundays (CFA 8000). Faso Tours, which is not as good, has a *car* (CFA 6000) departing every Monday and Thursday morning from Bobo.

Bush Taxi & Minibus
From Ouagadougou there are bush taxis for Côte d'Ivoire, Niger, Togo and Ghana. Minibuses often cost about 25% less than Peugeot 504 bush taxis.

To/From Côte d'Ivoire A Peugeot 504 direct from Ouaga to Abidjan is CFA 14,000, and to Bouaké/Yamoussoukro it's CFA 13,000. It works out cheaper to split this trip up. Take a bush taxi from Ouaga to Bobo (CFA 3000), then to Ferkessédougou (CFA 6000), and on to Abidjan (CFA 3500 by bus); total cost is CFA 2250 less than a direct trip by bus.

From Bobo bush taxis cost CFA 7500 to Bouaké and CFA 11,000 to Abidjan.

To/From Ghana Taking a series of minibuses from Accra to Ouaga costs about CFA 7500, which is about the same price as the STC bus. From Ouaga to Pô at the border costs CFA 2500 by bush taxi and another CFA 1000 from there to Bolgatanga.

To/From Mali A Peugeot 504 from Ouaga to

Mopti costs CFA 8000. From Bobo there is at least one vehicle a day, often more. For a *car* to Mopti (10 to 12 hours; CFA 7500), reserve a seat the day before but don't pay, otherwise you'll be stuck with that *car*. Remember, it may take eight hours for the vehicle to fill up.

From Bobo there are also bush taxis to San (CFA 5500), Ségou (CFA 6500) and Bamako (CFA 8000). If you're travelling between Sikasso (Mali) and Bobo, be prepared for a bumpy ride on corrugated road. It's an all-day trip including waiting time.

To/From Niger There are no Peugeot 504s or minibuses connecting Ouaga and Niamey. You must take one to the border and change there. If you leave early, the trip can be done in one day.

To/From Togo On the Ouaga-Lomé route it's also cheaper to do the trip in stages. A direct Peugeot 504 costs CFA 12,500. If you pay this rate, you'll be taking a risk as for years the drivers have operated a major scam on this route, dropping passengers off at the border and giving them CFA 3000 or so to continue their journey to Lomé. If you're headed south from Ouaga, take a taxi or minibus from the gare routière in Ouaga to the border town of Bitou, not Dapaong some 35 km into Togo. The fare is CFA 4000 to Bitou and, inexplicably, CFA 7500 to Dapaong, which is part of the scam operated by the Burkina taxi syndicate. From Bitou, you can catch a taxi to Dapaong and minibuses to Lomé for a total of CFA 3500 to CFA 4000. The Togo border closes at 6 pm, but passage after hours is usually possible. Alternatively, it's just as cheap to take a bus south from Ouaga to Accra (CFA 7500) and a bush taxi from there east to Lomé.

Train
To/From Côte d'Ivoire The Abidjan-Ouaga train, which has declined considerably in recent years, is still a popular way to travel and fares are competitive with the buses. The big advantage is that meeting people is easier. The Express leaves on Tuesday, Thursday and Saturday. It departs Ouaga at 7 am and typically takes 27 hours. The fare to Abidjan is CFA 16,400 in 1st class (CFA

19,900 for a *couchette* – sleeping berth) and CFA 11,000 in 2nd class. From Ouaga, 1st/2nd-class fares are CFA 3600/2400 to Bobo and CFA 7600/5400 to Ferké.

The 7 am Express from Ouaga arrives in Koudougou at 8.35 am, Bobo-Dioulasso at 2.15 pm (20-minute stopover), Banfora at 4.39 pm, Ferkessédougou at 8.31 pm, Bouaké at 2.10 am, and Abidjan at 9.10 am. From Abidjan it leaves daily at 8.30 am, arriving in Banfora the next day at 1.05 am, Bobo at 3.10 am, and Ouaga at 10.30 am. Schedules change frequently, however, so double-check at the Ouaga train station (☎ 30 60 47). Departures from Ouaga and Abidjan are usually quite punctual, but arrivals are usually several hours behind.

Sleeping berths cost CFA 3500 more than 1st class. They are usually for four people and have clean sheets, but the shared toilets are filthy. The restaurant provides only sandwiches and drinks these days, so most travellers now resort to buying food and drink from the vendors at stops along the way. For a berth, you must reserve at least a day in advance if not more at the train station.

Second-class cars tend to be much more crowded, thus considerably worse. Whether or not the ride in 2nd class is tolerable often depends on whether you can get a seat. You are much more likely to find one if you get on the train when it leaves at either end than if you pick it up en route. Even if you get a seat, long hours of sniffing rotting mangoes in the heat can make the trip miserable. They do sell drinks, which helps. Try breaking the trip in Ferkessédougou.

There is also a new train called the Étalon which connects only Ouaga and Bobo-Dioulasso and is far better than the Express (see Getting Around).

Finally, during certain parts of the year students with ID cards can get 30% discounts on 2nd-class fares, even to as far as Abidjan.

Car
At CFA 360 a litre (CFA 445 for premium and CFA 310 for diesel), petrol is significantly more expensive than in Niger and Togo but also cheaper than in Mali and Côte d'Ivoire (CFA 395).

The nonstop driving time from Ouagadougou to Lomé (Togo), Accra (Ghana) or Abidjan (Côte d'Ivoire) is about 20 hours; all the roads are paved and in good condition except for certain stretches in Togo which have lots of potholes. The straight driving times from Ouagadougou to Niamey (Niger) and Bamako (Mali) are about 10 and 16 hours, respectively; both routes are paved all the way. Borders with Ghana and Mali close at 6 pm sharp; the border with Togo closes at the same time but if you arrive later, a 'gift' for supplementary hours will usually get you across. The borders with Niger and Côte d'Ivoire close at 6.30 pm; getting across them after that hour is extremely difficult but has been done on occasion. Foreign cars entering Côte d'Ivoire, however, need a *laissez passer*, which is issued only during official hours.

If you're driving from Niamey to Ouaga, a more adventurous route is north from Niamey along the Niger River for 62 km to Farié, where for CFA 700 you can take a ferry across and proceed south-west to Ouaga via Gothèye, Dori and Kaya. This route is scenic, off the beaten path and in fairly good condition except from mid-July to September.

Getting Around

AIR
From Ouagadougou, Air Burkina has flights about four times a week to Bobo-Dioulasso, the Wednesday flight of which continues on to Bamako (Mali).

BUS
Burkina has a large number of private bus companies, so getting around the country is fairly easy and inexpensive. Many companies, such as those of Sogebaf and Sans Frontières, have large *cars* with guaranteed seating and schedules with fixed departure times, so in most instances you don't have to wait until they fill up. Most of them leave from their own offices rather than the gare routières, so knowing the names of the companies helps. They are also no more expensive than minibuses, which are often over crowded and less comfortable.

The government-owned RNTC (Régie Nationale des Transports en Commun), better known simply as X9, has large buses plying over 15 different routes throughout the country, all starting from either Ouaga or Bobo-Dioulasso. No other company comes close in terms of coverage. However, for a given destination there are other companies which offer more frequent services and, for this reason, are often preferable. It's best to arrive at the X9 station several hours early because the X9 buses fill up fast.

BUSH TAXI & MINIBUS
These connect Ouagadougou with the major towns. Most leave from the gare routières, and the morning is the best time (frequently the only time) to find them. There are also lots of bush taxis and minibuses in Bobo-Dioulasso, connecting Bobo with towns in the south-eastern section of the country.

Minibuses are usually one-third cheaper than Peugeot 504s. The large *cars* are much more comfortable, cheaper than minibuses and bush taxis, leave more frequently and cover towns that the *cars* do not reach.

TRAIN
The Étalon plies between Ouaga and Bobo-Dioulasso three times a day. It's one of the best trains in West Africa and is far superior to the Express which runs between Ouaga and Abidjan. The 1st/2nd-class fare is CFA 4000/2500 (CFA 6000/4000 round trip). The 1st-class compartments have comfortable seating, air-con, bar service, guaranteed seating and, unfortunately, videos which are loud with terrible B-grade flicks. The 2nd-class ones are virtually the same but without air-con. The seating is not guaranteed, so board early. There is also a 2nd-class train which connects Ouaga and Kaya on Tuesdays and Saturdays.

HITCHING
Hitching is not common in Burkina Faso. Virtually all drivers will expect payment – the equivalent (or more) of a seat in a bush taxi.

TOURS

The tour industry in Burkina Faso is in its infancy. See Travel Agencies in the Ouagadougou section for details.

Ouagadougou

Ouaga has a relaxed atmosphere and continues to be a favourite among travellers. Its bicycle lanes make it a progressive city amongst its African counterparts. You can cover most of the central area on foot. Meeting Africans and other travellers is relatively easy, especially in the bars and pastry shops in the centre.

One of the first things you'll see is the city's pride and joy – the attractive user-friendly central market. It's even landscaped, a first in West Africa. In addition to food stuffs, you'll find all kinds of materials and crafts for sale.

Unlike most other major Sahelian cities, Ouaga is not dominated by Muslims, hence the nightlife is better than just about anywhere else in the Sahel except Dakar. Several places have live music almost every night of the week; some of it is under the stars.

Ouagadougou is the capital of African film and the best time to be here is during FESPACO, which is the premier African film festival. The city's atmosphere is festive, plus the films, almost all produced by Africans, are fascinating and an excellent way to learn about Africa.

Orientation

The main street running east-west through town is Ave Nelson Mandela along which are the post office, the intriguing Maison du Peuple assembly hall and the Ran Hôtel, behind which is the train station. On the eastern end is the circular landmark Place des Nations Unies where the street splits into Blvd de la Révolution du 4 Août (or just Blvd de la Révolution), which heads toward the Palais Présidentiel, and Ave d'Oubritenga, which heads toward the National Museum, Hôtel Silmandé, the Zone du Bois and out of town toward Niamey.

The western end of Ave Mandela ends in the Place de la Révolution where the street splits into Ave Kadiogo heading south-west toward Bobo-Dioulasso and Ave Yatenga heading north-west toward Ouahigouya.

The heart of town is the handsome Grand Marché completed in 1989. The Hôtel Central and the famous Restaurant L'Eau Vive both face it. The main mosque and most banks, bookshops, cinemas and pastry shops are nearby.

A block to the east of the market is Ave

BURKINA FASO

FESPACO

The nine-day Pan-African Film Festival, FESPACO, is held every odd year starting the last or next-to-last Saturday in February (in even years it is held in October in Tunis). In recent years it has become such a major cultural event that it attracts celebrities from around the world. This home-grown event started in 1969 when it was little more than a few African film-makers getting together to show their 'shorts' to interested audiences. Since then it has helped stimulate film production throughout Africa. In 1993, more than 150 films, many full-length, were viewed by some 650,000 spectators. Three of the star Burkinabé film-makers who have won prizes here and developed international reputations are Idrissa Ouedraogo, who won the 1990 Grand Prix at Cannes for *Tilaï*, Souleymane Cissé, who won the Prix du Jury at the 1987 Cannes Festival for *Yeelen*, and Gaston Kaboré. Among the film-makers from other West African countries, those from Mali and Senegal have stood out, garnering quite a few prizes here.

Ouaga is always at its best during FESPACO as the city is invariably spruced up a bit then and everyone seems to be in a festive mood. All the city's cinemas are used, each screening different films starting in the late afternoon. Hotel rooms are hard to find, so advance booking is definitely advisable. For videos of award-winning African films, contact California Newsreel (☎ (415) 621-6196), 149 9th St, Suite 420, San Francisco, CA 94103, USA. ■

BURKINA FASO

PLACES TO STAY
1 Hôtel Silmandé
3 Hôtel Ricardo
10 Hôtel Le Pavillon Vert
11 Hôtel L'Entente
13 Hôtel Ouidi
18 Hôtel Le Dapoore
26 Hôtel de l'Indépendance
30 Hôtel Don Camillo Annex
39 Pension Guigsème
41 Hôtel Avenir
48 Hôtel Kilimanjaro
51 Hôtel Oubri
55 Ouaga Camping
56 Hôtel OK Inn

PLACES TO EAT
15 La Paillote
20 Restaurant La Jardin Bambous
33 Le Belvédère
34 Les Cascades
35 Restaurant Côté Jardin
37 Black & White Maquis
38 Hamburger House
44 Restaurant Tam-Tam & Sogebaf Bus Station
47 La Chaumière
54 Cité l'An II

OTHER
2 Crocodile Club
4 National Museum
5 Yalgado Hospital
6 Avenir Auto Location
7 Bar Matata
8 STCB Bus Station
9 Harlem Bar-Dancing
12 Palais du Ouidi Naba
14 STBF Bus Station
16 Shell Station
17 Marché Sankariaré
19 Gendarmerie
21 UNESCO
22 Nigerian Embassy
23 Italian Embassy
24 Palais Présidentiel & Ministries
25 French Embassy
27 X9 Bus Station
28 Race Track
29 Stade du 4 Août
31 Lycée Marien Ngouabi
32 Grand Marché
36 US Embassy
40 Cathedral
42 Gare Station BP
43 Trans-Mif Bus Station
46 Sans Frontières Bus Station
49 Le Soir au Village (Nightclub)
50 Moro-Naba Palace
52 Senegalese Consulate
53 Airport
57 Gare Routière

To Kaya
To Ouahigouya

Reservoir
Reservoir

Route de Fada N'Gourma

Blvd Charles de Gaulle

Avenue Yatenga
Avenue de la Liberté
Train Station
Rue des Écoles
Avenue d'Oubritenga

Boulevard de la République

Avenue N Mandela

Avenue du Conseil de l'Entente

Canal

Avenue Ché Guevara

Ave Kouanda

Avenue Nkrumah

Ave Boumedienne

Avenue Kadiogo (Route de Bobo)

Coulibaly

Ave

See Ouagadougou Centre Map

To Bobo-Dioulasso & Le Camping Poko-Club

Avenue de la Résistance du 17 Mai

Avenue Bassawarga

Rond-Point de l'Avenue Bassawarga

To Fada N'Gourma, Niger & Togo

Ouagadougou

0   0.5   1 km

Boulevard Circulaire

To Léo   To Pô

Boulevard Circulaire

Yennenga. (It runs north-south and parallel to Ave de la Résistance du 17 Mai.) Along this wonderfully vibrant street are numerous cheap hotels and cheap places to eat. On Ave de la Résistance, there's the Hôtel de l'Indépendance and the Ministère de l'Environnement et du Tourisme, both at the northern end, while the airport is 1.5 km to the south. If you continue south on either road for several km you'll come to Ave Bassawarga and the city outskirts where there is a major intersection, Rond-Point de l'Avenue Bassawarga, several hundred metres east of which is the gare routière.

Another major area of town centres around Marché Sankariaré, half a km north of the train station. It borders Ave de la Liberté (which runs parallel with Ave Mandela). Some inexpensive hotels and cheap drinking places are on or near this avenue.

Information
Tourist Office The tourist office is on the ground floor of the Ministère de l'Environnement et du Tourisme (☎ 33 38 10 or 30 63 99) on Ave de la Résistance du 17 Mai, just south of the Hôtel de l'Indépendance. They have some information on Arli Game Park and Nazinga Park. Enquire here if you want lodging at either. They may suggest that you call Mrs Bada or Mr Ouedraogo (☎ 31 19 59) for further information and to book a room.

Money The BIB facing the central market gives good rates and efficient service and charges no commission for changing travellers' cheques. The BICIA on Ave Nkrumah, three blocks south of the Place des Nations Unies, does the same. Both are open Monday to Friday from 7 to 11.30 am and 3.30 to 5 pm.

Post Office The post office and telecommunications are a block west of the Place des Nations Unies; the latter has public phones, which are easily accessible.

Foreign Embassies The following countries have embassies or consulates in Ouaga:

Algeria Ave Oubritanga at the Place des Nations Unies (☎ 30 64 01)
Belgium two blocks north-west of the US embassy (☎ 30 67 33)
Canada Ave de la Résistance du 17 Mai, one block south of Hôtel de l'Indépendance (☎ 30 00 39/01 61, telex 5264)
France Blvd de la Révolution, 100 metres west of the Palais Présidentiel (☎ 33 22 70, telex 5211)
Germany (& GTZ) Rue Joseph Badoua, next to Air Ivoire, open weekdays 9 to 12 am (☎ 30 67 31, telex 5217)
Ghana one block north of the cathedral and just to the west of Ave Bassawarga (☎ 30 76 35)
Italy 50 metres off Ave d'Oubritenga, facing the Nigerian embassy (☎ 33 22 57)
The Netherlands two blocks south of the Place des Nations Unies (☎ 30 61 34)
Nigeria Ave d'Oubritenga, one km north-east of the Place des Nations Unies (☎ 30 66 67)
Senegal (consul) north of Hôtel Oubri (1½ blocks) and two blocks west of Librairie-Papeterie de la Paix, which is at the southern end of Ave Yennenga (☎ 31 28 11)
USA Ave Raoul Follereau, south of the French embassy (☎ 30-6723, fax 30 89 03, telex 5290)

Honorary consulates include those of Denmark (☎ 33 43 10), Spain (☎ 30 61 60), Sweden (☎ 33 33 75), Switzerland (☎ 30 67 29) and the UK (☎ 30 67 24).

Travel Agencies Some of the best travel agencies are Savannah Tours (☎ 30 60 60, fax 30 67 67) at the Hôtel de l'Indépendance; Faso Tours (☎ 30 66 71, telex 5377) at 3 Rue Amirou Thiombiano (ex-Lumumba), one block west of the market; Flash Voyages (☎ 31 39 33) on Ave Loudun; Sahel Excursions Voyages at the main office of the BIB bank; and Promo Voyages. Most will organise trips to Arli Game Park and elsewhere.

Bookshops The city has no good bookshops. The best for English newspapers and magazines are at Hôtel Silmandé and Hôtel de l'Indépendance. Two other bookshops, both facing the market, are Librairie Socifa, which carries the *International Herald Tribune*, and Librairie Générale. All of these places sell an excellent map of Ouaga (CFA 2000. For other maps, check the Institut de Géographie on Blvd de la Révolution near

BURKINA FASO

the Palais Présidentiel; open weekdays to 5 pm.

Supermarkets One of the best supermarkets is the new Marina Market facing the Grand Mosque in the city centre. Prices are reasonable, eg bottled water for CFA 350 and locally made yoghurt for CFA 125. It's open every day until 10 pm except on Sundays when it closes a few hours earlier. Self-Service, which is just west of the market near Peyrissac, is equally good but closes earlier, around 7.15 pm, and is closed on Sundays.

National Museum

The Musée National is at Lycée Bogodogo (the school) on Ave d'Oubritenga, one km north-east of the Place des Nations Unies and before the hospital. The modest 100-piece collection is in one large poorly lit and unventilated room. There are Lobi wooden statutes, masks (from Bobo, Gurunsi and Mossi, including some strikingly tall ones of the Bwaba and Karanga people) and tradi-

tional outfits of the Nankana, Dagara, Moaga Senufo and Peul. There are also good collections of door latches, musical instruments and metal necklaces and bracelets plus lots of clay pots and jars, wooden stools and baskets. It's open from 8 am to 12.30 pm and 3.30 to 6.30 pm except Sunday and Monday. Entrance costs CFA 500.

Other Sights

Besides the attractive new **Grand Marché**, check the **cathedral** on Ave Bassawarga near the Moro-Naba Palace. It's the largest church in the interior of West Africa. There's also the **Maison du Peuple**, a striking public auditorium on Ave Mandela inspired by Burkina's traditional housing architecture.

Activities

Nonguests can use the long **swimming** pool at the Ran Hôtel for CFA 700/1000 weekdays/weekends. The pool at Restaurant La Colombe costs CFA 700 as well and is far more tranquil but not so clean. Pools at the

---

Moro-Naba Ceremony

The Moro-Naba of Ouagadougou – the emperor of the Mossi and the most powerful traditional chief in Burkina Faso – is a Muslim even though the Mossi people themselves are not Muslim. No order of his is ever disobeyed. He's also very well in with the government, which alway consults him before adopting any major new policy or programme. Most Moro-Nabas have been imposing-looking persons, in part due to their ritual drinking of millet beer, and the present one, the 37th, is no exception.

One of the few 'must sees' of Ouaga is the Moro-Naba ceremony, *la cérémonie du Nabayius Gou*. It takes place every Friday around 7.15 am outside his palace. From Ave Mandela, take Ave Bassawarga south a block or two beyond the cathedral, then about two blocks to your right until you reach the western side of his very plain palace. The ceremony is a very formal ritual that lasts only about 15 minutes and is accompanied by drums. With the Moro-Naba seated on his throne, one by one his ministers and advisors, mostly lesser village chiefs all dressed in traditional costumes, arrive, greet one another, and then sit in their appointed places in front. When they're all there, the important ones then greet the Moro-Naba himself, who is seated on his low throne, with his saddled and elaborately decorated horse nearby. Actually, with the same words and gestures every time, they are advising him not to go to war. The ceremony, which then ends, is hardly breathtaking but it is interesting for the small details, particularly the attire and gestures of the elders and the horse's decoration. Spectators must stand a fairly good distance away and photographs are not allowed.

The story behind this pantomime is as follows. Long ago, the king's eldest son, who was to succeed his father to the throne, decided that his time to reign had come and sent a slave to his father advising him of such and 'giving' him three days to live. The old emperor, not giving in so easily, mounted his horse and prepared to go to war against his hereditary enemy. As he was about to depart, his ministers and advisors begged him not to go fight. Showing concern for his people, he agreed, dismounted and returned to the palace. ■

Indépendance, the Ricardo and the Silmandé are more expensive.

There are also **tennis** courts at the Silmandé which nonguests can use and a **billiards** table at the Indépendance.

Places to Stay – bottom end

Price quotes in this category include taxes. The best place for the price and ambience is the well-marked *Fondation Charles Dufour* on Rue de la Chance, five blocks south of the market. Madama Yameogo, the friendly owner-manager, is the adopted son of Frenchman Charles Dufour, who started this truly unusual place in 1985 and is now deceased. Profits from the hotel and membership in the foundation (CFA 8000), which you can join, go to support 22 orphans whom Madama has adopted and whom you can visit. It has two double rooms and one, four-bed dormitory. The price of a bunk bed with a clean sheet and a mosquito net is CFA 1500 a person. If all the beds are taken, Madama will let you sleep on a mattress on the floor for CFA 1000 or camp outside in the courtyard (CFA 750). There's a clean shared bathroom, laundry service and limited food (eg CFA 300 for breakfast, CFA 250 for omelettes, CFA 75 for coffee and CFA 700 for dinner); you can use the kitchen.

La Rose des Sables (☎ 31 30 14), a pleasant homey lodge, three blocks directly south of the Catholic compound, has five small, clean rooms with fans and a central patio with a lovely garden, and the friendly owner serves beer and food. Some women may prefer the nearby *Centre d'Accueil des Soeurs Lauriers* (☎ 33 49 09), several blocks to the west of Fondation Charles Dufour and 100 metres before the cathedral. Travellers are welcomed and charged CFA 4000 per person for a spotless room with mosquito net and Continental breakfast. Lunch or dinner here costs CFA 800. The men's equivalent (same price) is the unmarked austere *Centre Missionaire Fraternité des Pères*, which has four-bed dormitories and is just a block away.

Of the cheap hotels along Ave Yennenga, south of the central market, the once highly recommended *Pension Guigsème* has become grubbier but it's still not bad for the price. Rooms with wide beds, fans and washbasins cost CFA 3000; the shared baths are passable but don't be surprised if you're attacked by a squadron of mosquitoes. The restaurant next door is decent but not so cheap.

Almost directly opposite is *Hôtel de la Paix* (☎ 33 30 23), which is slightly more expensive and no better. Reasonably clean singles/doubles with fans (some work) and interior showers cost CFA 3600/3900 (CFA 4150/4450 with full private bath; CFA 5800/6100 with air-con) but there's no restaurant.

There are two more hotels further north on Ave Yennenga towards the market. *Hôtel Idéal* has larger rooms (CFA 4300) than the Guigsème. However, the music is sometimes loud and men may encounter drunken prostitutes banging on the door in the middle of the night. Nearby is *Hôtel Yennenga* (☎ 33 58 24), which is the best hotel on Ave Yennenga and the closest to the centre. Rooms (CFA 3600/4150) are quite decent and reasonably spacious, with fans, interior showers and clean sheets. There's no restaurant but you can have a drink in the courtyard.

If you'd prefer to be in the very heart near the Grand Marché, you'll have to pay more. *Hôtel Delwendé* (☎ 30 87 57), on Rue Amirou Thiombiano, has very decent singles/doubles with fans and private baths but they're overpriced at CFA 7200/9800 (CFA 8350/10,950 with air-con). The hotel's nicest feature is its 2nd-floor balcony, which is a good place for drinks and hanging out.

On the northern side of the city behind the train station and near Marché Sankariaré *Hôtel L'Entente* (☎ 31 14 97) has clean cell-like rooms for CFA 3550 with overhead fans and shared baths. The hotel's best feature is its active street-front terrace bar; you can also get cheap food here, eg riz gras and riz sauce. If it's full, try *Hôtel Ouidi*, which is one km to the west. Rooms with fans and interior showers cost CFA 4000. There's a bar but no restaurant.

The French-run *Hôtel Le Pavillon Vert* (☎ 31 06 11), on Ave de la Liberté facing the

BURKINA FASO

BURKINA FASO

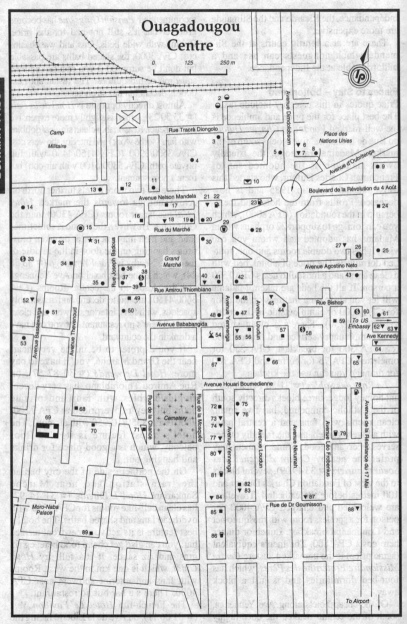

Ouagadougou Centre

0   125   250 m

Camp Militaire

Rue Traorè Diongolo

Place des Nations Unies

Avenue Dimdolobsom

Avenue d'Oubritenga

Boulevard de la Révolution du 4 Août

Rue Traorè Diongolo

Rue Nelson Mandela

Rue du Marché

Rue Joseph Badoua

Grand Marché

Rue Amirou Thiombiano

Avenue Agostino Neto

Rue Bishop

To US Embassy

Ave Kennedy

Avenue Bassawarga

Avenue Thevenoud

Avenue Yennenga

Avenue Loudun

Avenue Bababangida

Avenue Houari Boumedienne

Cemetery

Rue de la Mosquée

Rue de la Chance

Moro-Naba Palace

Avenue Yennenga

Avenue Loudun

Avenue Nkrumah

Avenue Léo Frobenius

Rue de Dr Goumisson

Avenue de la Résistance du 17 Mai

To Airport

PLACES TO STAY

12	Ran Hôtel
16	Hôtel Central
17	Hôtel Relax
24	Hôtel de l'Indépendance
34	Maison des Jeunes
49	Hôtel Delwendé & Le Pub
56	Hôtel Continental, Café de la Paix & La Sorbetière
57	Hôtel Belle Vue
59	Hôtel Nazemsé
67	Hôtel Yennenga
68	Centre Missionaire Fraternité des Pères
70	Centre d'Accueil des Soeurs Lauriers
71	Fondacion Charles Dufour
72	Hôtel Idéal
82	Pension Guigsème
85	Hôtel de la Paix
89	La Rose des Sables

PLACES TO EAT

6	La Fontaine Bleue
7	Le Verdoyant
18	Restaurant L'Eau Vive
21	Pâtisserie La Bonbonnière
27	Restaurant La Colombe
40	La Gourmandise
45	Le Vert Galant
52	La Forêt
55	Marina Market & Café ONU
62	Restaurant Le Belvédère
63	Les Cascades
64	Le Tambarze
65	Pâtisserie de Koulouba
73	Chez Awa
74	Restaurant Riale
76	Chez Tanti Bintou
77	Café Salif
80	Faso Café
83	Café Étalon
84	Orient Bar & African Food
87	Maquis Pili-Pili
88	Restaurant Allah Barka

OTHER

1	Train Station
2	Bus Companies for Kaya
3	Mission Protestante
4	Maison du Peuple
5	Centre Artisanal
8	Algerian Embassy
9	UN
10	Post Office
11	Air France & Sortilèges Artisan Shop
13	French Cultural Centre
14	Place de la Révolution
15	Place du Cinéaste Africain
19	Librairie Socifa
20	Pharmacie Keneya
22	Shell Station
23	Total Station
25	Tennis Club
26	Tourist Office
28	Palais de Justice
29	Wassa Club
30	Librairie Africatex
31	Haut Commissariat
32	Air Afrique
33	BCEAO Bank
35	Faso Tours & Open-Air Bar
36	Toyota
37	Peyrissac & SICA (Peugeot Dealer)
38	BIB Bank
39	Self-Service Supermarket
41	Top Music
42	Librairie Socifa
43	Canadian Embassy
44	Air Algérie, Ethiopian Airlines & Aeroflot
46	Photo Shop
47	Ciné Burkina
48	Librairie Attié
50	Air Ivoire & German Embassy
51	Air Burkina
53	Ghanaian Embassy
54	Grande Mosquée
58	BICIA Bank
60	BIB Bank & Sahel Excursions Voyages
61	Mini-Alimentation
66	Flash Voyages
69	Cathedral
75	Super Sound Music Shop
78	Tagui Station
79	Jimmy's Discotheque
81	African Queen (Nightclub)
86	Ludo Bar

market, is much better, highly recommended and quite popular with travellers. With grass-covered *paillotes* (sun shelters) in a central shady courtyard, it has possibly the nicest ambience of all the cheaper hotels. Ventilated singles/doubles with shared baths cost CFA 3000/3500 (CFA 6000/6500 with private bath and CFA 7500/8000 to 9000 with air-con). There's also an excellent restaurant with a good menu; most dishes are in the CFA 1200 to CFA 1600 range including spaghetti, rabbit, poulet sauce arachide (chicken with peanut sauce) and various other chicken dishes. If it's full, try the new, nearby *Hôtel Le Dapoore* (☎ 31 33 31), just north of Rue du Capitaine Ouedraogo and

well marked on both it and Ave Liberté. Rooms are excellent value at CFA 5000/6000 plus taxes for singles/doubles with fans and CFA 6500/7500 with air-con. The restaurant serves mainly fancy French fare, eg CFA 2500 for steak au poivre and CFA 4000 for the four-course menu.

At *Hôtel Oubri* (☎ 30 64 83), five blocks west of the airport on Rue de la Mosquée, some travellers have had items stolen from their rooms (CFA 6950/8250 singles/doubles with air-con and private bath). There are also some tiny, somewhat grubby singles with fans and interior showers for CFA 4400 to CFA 5425 but they're usually all taken, and dormitory beds cost CFA 3000. This place has a nice little terrace, good food and African music.

Camping There are two camp sites outside Ouaga. Travellers without vehicles usually prefer *Ouaga Camping*, or Chez Bouda Abel (☎ 30 48 51), because of the location one km behind the gare routière on the south-eastern outskirts of town. Follow the signs behind the gare routière; it's down a dirt road. The bare, treeless ambience is dreadful and the pool is dirty and dry. Bouda charges CFA 1500 a person for camping and CFA 3000 for a stuffy bungalow for two people (CFA 3500 with fan). The bungalows have poor-quality beds and marginally clean shared baths. You can order food but you'll do better eating elsewhere. Catch the No 3 bus to town from the main road or take a shared bush taxi (CFA 300).

Those with vehicles will do much better to head for *Le Camping Poko-Club* (☎ 30 24 06). It's clearly marked 12 km out on the road to Bobo, near the 13-km post and one km beyond the police checkpoint. Its prices are similar and even though there isn't much shade, the ambience is much better and the restaurant is quite good.

Places to Stay – middle

The pleasant colonial-era *Ran Hôtel* (☎ 30 61 06, telex 5273; cards AE, D), on Ave Mandela near the train station, gets high marks for its long pool and central location, although the restaurant is mediocre. The air-con singles/ doubles cost CFA 16,500/ 18,000 plus taxes (CFA 19,500/22,500 for a bungalow).

During the high season (November to February) a number of tour groups specialising in inexpensive overland adventures stay at my favourite in this category, the *Hôtel Ricardo* (☎ 30 70 72, fax 33 60 48). It offers good views of the reservoir, has a long clean pool and a relaxed atmosphere, and is well managed. Singles/doubles with air-con cost CFA 17,800/19,800 including all taxes. It also has one of the best hotel restaurants, with good pizza, paella and grillades. The main drawback for those without vehicles is the remote location on the outskirts of town

behind Reservoir No 2; finding a taxi is not easy.

Hôtel Nazemsé (☎ 33 53 28, telex 5375; cards AE, D) has a sterile feel but it's fairly close to the centre, a block east of the BICIA bank. It has an air-con lobby and car rental agency. Singles/doubles with air-con and TV cost CFA 16,000 to 19,500/18,000 to 21,500 including tax. *Hôtel Belle Vue* (☎ 30 84 98), nearby facing the BICIA, is much better. The rooms (CFA 8280/9280 singles/doubles) are a bit small and those out the back have no windows, but they all have TVs, air-con and decent attached baths, plus you can get breakfast in the restaurant. The terrace is great for drinks after 5 pm.

If you want to be in the very heart of town, *Hôtel Central* (☎ 33 34 17), which faces the market, has a lively bar and good pizzas in the CFA 1600 to CFA 3200 range. The Central's old air-con singles/doubles cost only CFA 6500/7500 plus 15% tax but they're being destroyed and replaced by 48 much more expensive units. Another central place good for the price is the popular new *Hôtel Continental* (☎ 30 86 36), next to the Café de la Paix. Spacious carpeted singles/ doubles with TVs cost CFA 10,000/11,000 plus 15% tax. If you're desperate, try *Hôtel Avenir* (☎ 34 06 21/2), which is remotely located on the western side of town and has overpriced rooms at CFA 12,500/14,000 plus tax.

Places to Stay – top end

The top hotel is Pullman's *Hôtel Silmandé* (☎ 30 01 76, fax 30 09 71, telex 5345; cards V), which has a nice long swimming pool and a nightclub, but the expensive restaurant is nothing to rave about (entrée CFA 4000). The rooms (for CFA 66,000 including 15% tax) are fairly small, and it's inconveniently located on the outskirts of town next to the reservoir. It also has tennis courts, shops and a casino. One alternative is the *Hôtel de l'Indépendance*, one km east of the Grand Marché (☎ 30 60 60, fax 30 67 67, telex 5201; cards AE, D, MC). Despite many complaints, it is still doing good business because of the lower prices (CFA 31,395/35,710 including 15% tax), long pool, numerous stores and more central location. The CFA 3250 breakfast here is a rip-off. You'll do better having coffee and croissants at La Boulangerie down the street. Next to the hotel is the city's major tennis club, to which guests have limited access. The hotel also features TV/video, a bar with billiards table, casino and shops.

The best deal (CFA 20,000/23,000 including 15% tax, and five bungalows for CFA 27,500) is at the *Hôtel OK Inn* (☎ 30 40 61, fax 30 48 11, telex 5418; cards AE, D). It has a clean short pool, a decent restaurant and artisan vendors. Prices are lower because of the poor location – five km from the centre on the southern outskirts of town on the Route de Pô, 100 metres beyond the gare routière. It does offer, however, free minibus service into town about five times a day starting at 8 am.

Places to Eat
Cheap Eats For very cheap fare in the centre, eg braised fish (CFA 100) and Ivoirian attiéké (shredded manioc) (CFA 100), you can't beat the *Café ONU* facing the mosque. Some of the hole-in-the-wall places along Ave Yennenga, like *Faso Café* (one block south of the Hôtel Idéal), also serve spaghetti, steak, etc for CFA 400 to CFA 600. One place that has been very popular with travellers for years is the *Café de la Paix* on Ave Loudun, one block east of the mosque and facing the Ciné Burkina. It's a good notch above most of those along Ave Yennenga but slightly more expensive.

For sandwiches and beer, popular places around the market include *La Gourmandise* facing the market on Rue Amirou Thiombiano (one flight up) and *Le Pub* next to the Hôtel Delwendé. Neither are particularly cheap. In the US embassy area on Blvd de la République, the popular *Hamburger House* has hamburgers from CFA 850, hot dogs for CFA 900 and milkshakes for CFA 650. Open to midnight; closed Wednesdays.

African One of the best areas for cheap African food is along Ave Yennenga. My favourite, just south of Hôtel Idéal, is *Chez Awa*. The da and the tiga diga na here are as

good as home-made; for CFA 300 you can also get riz sauce aubergine (rice with aubergine sauce), frites (fries), a huge bowl of yoghurt, steak or poisson braisé. Tasty cool bissap, a local drink made of local reddish fruit, is also available for CFA 50 but the water is not boiled. Nearby is *Restaurant Riale*, where you can get tasty potato ragoût for CFA 300 and a big bowl of yoghurt for CFA 250 (CFA 125 for a half bowl). Across the street is *Chez Tanti Bintou*; Tanti specialises in fresh yoghurt, which is available only from about noon to 6 pm. Further on the same block is *Café Salif*, which is very ordinary but even cheaper, eg CFA 100 for a half bowl of yoghurt. The cheapest place of all is a bit further south near Hôtel de la Paix. From the hotel, go about 50 metres west on a dirt side street. For CFA 50 you can get rice with three kinds of sauce.

Le Tambarze is on Ave de la Résistance, four blocks south of the Indépendance. It's a small rustic place with a pleasant terrace and specialities such as couscous, ragoût and riz gras. *Hôtel Le Pavillon Vert* on Ave de la Liberté has good African food (see under Places to Stay – bottom end).

For a more up-market restaurant in an outdoor setting, try *La Forêt* (☎ 30 72 96) near the centre on Ave Bassawarga, a block south of the modern BCEAO bank. Set in a pleasant garden with shady trees, this tranquil restaurant offers only a few selections each day, all well prepared.

Another good place in a relaxing outdoor setting with lots of trees is *La Colombe* (☎ 31 04 45) on Ave Agostino Neto, just south and around the corner from the Hôtel de l'Indépendance. It has a different African speciality every day, eg poulet yassa on Fridays for CFA 1700. Most dishes cost from CFA 1500 to CFA 2000; excellent steaks CFA 2500. You can use the swimming pool here for CFA 700.

African Maquis Ouaga now has a number of Ivoirian-style *maquis* specialising in braised dishes; they are best at night. One is *La Fontaine Bleue* (☎ 30 70 83) on Ave Dimdolobsom across from the Centre Artisanal. The menu includes poulet braisé for CFA

1200, poisson braisé for CFA 2500 and Côte d'Ivoire-style attiéké for CFA 500 as well as pizzas from CFA 1500 and large beers for an outrageous CFA 800. Another is the popular *Cité l'An II*, a spacious open-air place on the main highway between the airport and the gare routière and very dimly lit at night. You can get poulet braisé for CFA 1400, capitaine braisé for CFA 1800, brochettes for CFA 1000 and large beers for a reasonable CFA 285.

Another place specialising in grilled chicken is the attractive and breezy *La Paillote* on Ave Kouanda, 700 metres north of the Place de la Révolution. You can get cheaper fare at *Restaurant Allah Barka* (on Ave de la Résistance), eg CFA 500 for poisson braisé and CFA 600 for poulet braisé, but the atmosphere here is not nearly as nice. However, the food, particularly the Senegalese poulet yassa and the poulet major, is quite good. The *Black & White Maquis*, just beyond Hamburger House, is laid-back. Brochettes cost CFA 1600, poulet yassa CFA 1500 and large beers CFA 550. There are also hamburgers for CFA 2000.

French *Restaurant L'Eau Vive* is an Ouaga institution known throughout West Africa. It is run by an order of nuns and is closed on Sundays. The food (French and a few African selections) is very good and service comes with a smile. Well marked, it faces the market, just 50 metres east of the Hôtel Central. A typical meal costs CFA 4000.

The long-standing *La Chaumière* (☎ 31 18 25), 1.5 km from the centre on Ave Coulibaly, just beyond the Moro-Naba Palace, has Alsatian and Belgian specialities (closed Thursday). The new French-run *Côté Jardin* (☎ 30 84 15) has a more personable owner. Most dishes are in the CFA 3000 to CFA 4000 range and everything is home-made including the ice cream. The popular *Les Cascades* (☎ 30 87 36), which is closed Mondays, is a block to the west on the same street and very similar, with a fancy menu. Most dishes are in the CFA 2200 to CFA 3800 range, eg capitaine fumé for CFA 2400.

Finding moderately priced French restaurants is no easy trick. One of the best is the popular and breezy *Restaurant Tam-Tam* (☎ 30 28 04) on Ave Kadiogo. Open daily to midnight (closed Tuesdays), it specialises in grilled dishes for CFA 1200 to CFA 2000, and has steak provençal for CFA 1700, steak au poivre for CFA 2300, and large beers for CFA 450. Cheaper still and much more rustic is the *Café Étalon* next to Pension Guigsème on Ave Yennenga. At night they bring the tables outside on the dirt pavement. You can get an excellent steak and superb frites here for CFA 1400 as well as cheaper African dishes such as soupe de poisson for CFA 1000, couscous for CFA 600, riz sauce for CFA 600 and large beers for CFA 400.

Italian The pizzeria at the *Hôtel Central* is quite good but *Le Verdoyant*, also in the centre across from the Artisanal, is much more popular, with excellent lasagne as well. Another good choice but much less convenient is the *Hôtel Ricardo* behind reservoir No 2, about three km from the heart of town. It's open every day and has excellent pizza cooked in a wood-burning oven as well as numerous Franco-Italian dishes. Until 8 pm, you can take a No 5 city bus from Place des Nations Unies to get there.

Le Belvédère (☎ 33 64 21) on Ave Raoul Follereau (closed Tuesdays), has the best ambience, with an outdoor garden setting. It serves Italian and Lebanese food and has some of the best pizza in town. Most selections are in the CFA 2200 to CFA 3800 range, eg CFA 3200 for cannelloni and CFA 2400 for tagliatelle à la bolognaise.

Another relatively expensive place in the centre is the air-con *Le Vert Galant* (closed Sundays) on Rue Amirou Thiombiano, 2½ blocks east of the market. It has French fare, spaghetti carbonara for CFA 3000, osso bucco for CFA 3600 and expensive ice-cream desserts for CFA 2200.

Oriental Of the top Chinese-Vietnamese restaurants, try *Le Jardin Bambous* (☎ 31 35 14), on Ave d'Oubritenga just beyond the gendarmerie (open every day), and *Le Lotus d'Or*, at 35 Ave Kadiogo (Route de Bobo), 1.5 km west of the central area.

Pastry Shops Ouaga is noted for its pastry shops, most of which serve as social meeting places; the hours are usually 6 am to noon and 3 to 7 pm. The longest running is *Pâtisserie La Bonbonnière* on Ave Nelson Mandela, a block north of the market and facing the Maison du Peuple. One of the most popular these days, however, is *La Gourmandise* facing the market's south-eastern corner; it's on the 2nd floor and is great for watching the crowds plus it's open until midnight. It's not cheap; most pastries are around CFA 350. *La Sorbetière*, facing Ciné Burkina, is similar and a popular breakfast spot for wealthier Burkinabé.

Business is booming at the *Pâtisserie de Koulouba*. It has the widest selection by far, but is one km from the centre on Ave de la Résistance. Still another is the *Salon de Thé Super Printemps*, which is east of the market and has reasonable prices, eg CFA 165 for Cokes, CFA 200 for coffee, CFA 160 for croissants and CFA 270 for sandwiches made with French bread and pâté.

Entertainment
Bars A pleasant watering hole in the heart of town is the *Wassa Club* (☎ 31 02 33), a block east of the market on the diagonal road leading towards the Place des Nations Unies. In the thick of everything, it's blocked off from the crowds by bushes and completely shaded by trees. This hip open-air place has Cokes for CFA 300, large beers for CFA 400, African meals for around CFA 2000 and live music every night starting around 9.30 pm. There are also occasionally theatrical performances. For cheaper brew during the day, try the shady terrace next to Faso Tours on Rue Amirou Thiombiano; it's popular with working people.

For late-night drinking with Africans, the liveliest area is along Ave Yennenga. The *Ludo Bar*, 60 metres south of the Hôtel de la Paix, is cheap and has a large drinking area at the back. *African Queen* nearby is also good.

Fancier is *Hôtel de l'Indépendance* which offers a choice of a drink around the pool or inside with air-con and a billiard table.

Nightclubs One of the best dancing places in Ouaga is *Harlem Bar-Dancing*, three blocks or so east of Sankariaré market off Ave de la Liberté. Very popular with Africans, it has a spacious open-air area at the back with a full band setup and a large dance floor. Large beers are reasonably priced at CFA 350 and you can get food here as well. The music begins around 9.30 pm every night. The similar *Bar Matata* is four blocks further east on Ave de la Liberté. Dancing to an excellent band starts around 9 pm. Two more laid-back 'in' dancing spots are *Number One* (☎ 30 28 58) on Ave Ché Guevara, which also serves good capitaine, and *Maquis Pili-Pili* on Ave Nkrumah, which often has live blues music on weekends and also serves food.

For the city's hottest disco, head for *Jimmy's Discotheque*. Like most of the more flashy places, Jimmy's has air-con and a cover charge (CFA 2500). Not well marked, it's one block north and several blocks east of Hôtel de la Paix. Other similar places include the *2000 Nightclub*, *Le Soir au Village*, on Ave Coulibaly two km southwest of the centre, and the *Crocodile Club*, a swanky disco just west of Hôtel Silmandé.

Cinema Ciné Burkina was built for FESPACO in the late '60s. With a wide screen and good seats, it's still one of the better movie theatres in West Africa and one of the few where African-produced films are regularly shown, in addition to the latest international productions (6.30, 8.30 and 10.30 pm shows; CFA 650). It's two blocks south-east of the market on Ave Yennenga. For an open-air cinema, try the Oubri several blocks east on Rue Amirou Thiombiano.

Things to Buy
Artisan Goods The Grand Marché is one of the best in West Africa. Fabrics are a particularly good buy as are baskets, leatherwork, bronze, pottery and blankets from Dori and Mali. Most are found on the 2nd floor. Local Faso Fani cloth sells for about CFA 1250 a metre while imported wax prints are a bit more expensive. The 2nd floor in the back is

also the best place in Ouaga for beads. You can find entire strands or individual beads for sale. Masks and statues are also sold here and in front of the Ran and Indépendance hotels, but examine them closely as they are often falsely aged to appear antique.

One of the best places for African art, particularly wooden carvings, is Sortilèges (☎ 31 60 80) in the centre on Ave Mandela, next to Air France. The selection is not extensive but the quality is high and prices are marked and reasonable (weekdays until around 5.30 pm; Saturdays until 1 pm). Another place to check is the tiny Boutique d'Artisanat at the nearby Wassa Club.

The Centre National d'Artisanat d'Art (☎ 30 68 35) has a large showroom of bronze objects, and also pottery, batiks and other materials. The quality is disappointing but the centre is worth checking to see what crafts are being produced in Burkina. It's on Ave Dimdolobsom, 100 metres north of the Place des Nations Unies, and is open weekdays from 8 am to noon and 3 to 6 pm, and Saturdays from 8 am to noon.

In late October, don't miss the annual International Art Exhibition of Ouaga in front of the Maison du Peuple. Artisans and art dealers from virtually everywhere on the continent come here to sell their sculptures, masks, leather, pottery and textiles.

Embroidered tablecloths and napkins are the speciality of Le Centre de Formation Feminine Artisanale, a women's co-operative sponsored by the Austrian Catholic mission. It is in Gounghin, off the road to Bobo-Dioulasso and several km west from the city centre on the western outskirts of town. The hours are weekdays from 7.30 am to noon and 3.30 to 5.30 pm and Saturdays until noon. The tannery, Le Centre de Tannage, is on the eastern outskirts of town on the road to Niamey, facing the prison and three km from the centre. Take bus No 1 along Ave Mandela to get there or to the women's co-operative. The tanners there make purses, small boxes and wall hangings of brushed leather with burnt-in designs. Or pass by one of the tannery's outlets in the centre – at the Hôtel de l'Indépendance and

on Ave Loudun south of Ciné Burkina. The quality is not exceptional, but you may find a good souvenir.

Music For cassettes of African music, try Top Music on Ave Yennenga, a block north of Ciné Burkina, or Musique Sans Frontières, on the same street, just north of Pension Guigseme. The latter stocks a huge range of cassettes from many African countries, plus has recordings of local musicians. Top Music is open to 10 pm and sells cassettes for CFA 1100. A group from Bobo that's making waves, however, is Farafina, led by the master drummer, Mahama Konaté. Other local stars include Nick Domby, Youssou Camporé, Georges Ouedraogo, Nakelse Emmanuel and Namenédé, a female vocalist.

Getting There & Away

Air Within Africa, the most heavily travelled route from Ouagadougou is to Abidjan (CFA 101,000); there are flights virtually every day, primarily on Air Afrique and Air France but also on Air Ivoire and Air Burkina. The latter two offer fares which are 20% less than the others (eg CFA 48,000 from Ouaga to Bamako and about CFA 95,000 to Cotonou on Air Burkina) but they are still no bargain compared to travel overland unless you can get a student discount (CFA 28,000 from Ouaga to Bamako, for example). There are also fairly frequent connections to Lomé (CFA 111,300 one way on Air Afrique and about CFA 85,000 on Air Burkina) but only two flights a week to and from Bamako, Dakar, Niamey and Cotonou. Air Afrique, Air Burkina and Ethiopian Airlines serve these three routes; flights on Ethiopian Airlines continue to Addis Ababa, with connections to Nairobi. Air Algérie has flights on Thursday nights to/from Algiers.

Most of the airlines' offices are within several blocks of the market, and open weekdays to 5.30 pm and Saturday mornings.

Air Afrique Ave Nasser at Place de la Révolution (☎ 30 60 20/1)
Air France Ave Mandela (☎ 30 63 65/6/7)
Air Ivoire Rue Joseph Badoua, west of the market (☎ 30 62 07)

Air Burkina Ave Bassawarga (☎ 30 61 44 or 31 53 25)
Air Algérie Ave Nkrumah at Rue Bishop (☎ 31 23 01/2)
Aeroflot Ave Nkrumah at Rue Bishop (☎ 30 71 29)
Ethiopian Airlines Ave Nkrumah at Rue Bishop (☎ 31 00 82)
Sabena (☎ 30 15 95)

It is also possible to charter a plane to some exotic place such as Timbuktu. Allain Long (☎ 30 09 38) has a five-seater plane for CFA 102,000 an hour; the round trip to Timbuktu takes less than four hours. Dominique Vignon (☎ 33 28 15) can also make arrangements for chartering either a two-seater or three-seater plane from the Aero Club.

Bus All large buses (*cars*) for international destinations leave either from their offices or, less frequently, from the gare routière. (See Getting There & Away, earlier.)

Most major bus companies serving strictly in-country destinations leave from their own offices, so knowing their names can be critical. Those for Bobo, Ouahigouya and Koudougou leave at all hours of the day; buses for most other destinations in Burkina leave only in the morning, between 7 and 9 am. The major companies operating on the Ouaga-Bobo route are Sans Frontières (departures at 7 and 10 am, and 2 pm); Sogebaf (☎ 30 36 27, nine departures a day between 6 am and 7 pm from its station on Ave Kadiogo); STBF (☎ 31 27 95, departures from its office on Ave Yatenga at 8 am, 2 and 6 pm); X9 (☎ 30 42 96, departures from its main station on Ave Yatenga at 7 am and 2 pm); Trans-Mif (☎ 30 22 69, Ave Kadiogo); Guimbi Voyages (Ave Coulibaly) and, worst of all, with buses in bad condition, Faso Tours (departures on Sundays from its office on Rue Amirou Thiombiano).

Many also serve other cities in Burkina. For buses to Ouahigouya via Yako, for example, you can take Trans-Mif (1 pm, return at 6.30 am), Sogebaf (noon, 4 pm and midnight, return at 6 and 9 am, and 2 pm), STBF (8 am and 2 pm, return at 6.45 am and 2 pm) and X9 (8 am except Sunday, return at 3 pm). The cost is CFA 2000 and the trip takes about three hours. For service just to Yako, try Air Yako (just west of

the market), which has the most frequent service but not the best buses. Buses for all of these companies leave from their individual offices, not the gare routière.

For service south-west to Gaoua (CFA 3500), try Trans-Mif. Its buses depart every day at 7 am for Gaoua (7 am from Gaoua), arriving Gaoua around 3 pm, passing through Sabou (CAF 1250), Pâ (CFA 2000) and Diébougou (CFA 3000), with service onward to Kampti (CFA 4500) on Tuesdays and Saturdays. You can also take an X9 bus to Gaoua; see the schedule below.

Most companies serving Kaya are stationed together near the centre, 300 metres east of the train station. Air Sannatenga Kaya has about 10 departures a day, from 7 am to 6 pm. Ouedraogo Adama, has buses departing at 8 am, noon and 2 pm (CFA 1500).

X9 provides the most extensive service, with over 15 routes in all. Below is the schedule of departures from Ouaga; returns are the same day unless shown otherwise.

destination	departure time	frequency
Bobo	7 am & 2 pm	daily
Ouahigouya	8 am	daily except Sun
Pô	9 am	Mon, Wed, Thur, Sat, Sun
Fada N'Gourma/ Diapaga	8 am	Mon, Sat (returns next day)
Dori-Gorom	8 am	Mon, Wed, Sat (returns next day)
Gaoua	8 am	Mon, Wed, Sat (returns next day)
Dédougou/Nouna	8 am	Mon, Wed, Sat (returns next day)
Tenkodogo	2 pm	Wed
	9 am	Thur
	9 am & 2 pm	Sat
Kaya	8 am	Tues, Sat
Bogandé	8 am	Mon, Wed
Kongoussi/Djibo	8 am	Wed, Sat
Tougan	8 am	Mon, Sat (returns next day)
Zabre	8 am	Wed, Sun
Léo	9 am	Sat
Hamélé	8 am	Mon

Bush Taxi & Minibus Bush taxis for all neighbouring countries leave from the gare routière on the road to Pô on the southern outskirts of town, four km from the centre. Take bus No 3 to get there; it passes along Ave d'Oubritenga, Ave Mandela and Ave Bassawarga. See the Burkina Faso Getting There & Away section for details of international routes and prices.

Most bush taxis and private minibuses for towns throughout Burkina Faso leave from the gare routière, usually between 7 and 9 am (also at 2 pm for those to Bobo). You can also find bush taxis stationed at the BP station on the road to Bobo, about two km west of the central area; they're usually headed for places to the west such as Bobo-Dioulasso. Take bus No 1 to get there. Typical fares in CFA are:

destination	bush taxi	minibus
Bobo	3500	2750
Dori	4500	3000
Fada N'Gourma	3000	2500
Gorom-Gorom	6000	4000
Kantchari	5100	4000
Koudougou	1000	1000
Léo	3000	2500
Ouahigouya	3000	2000
Pô	2500	2500

Peugeot 504s to Bobo take from five to six hours, barely less than the train. It's sometimes possible to find Peugeot 404 pick-up trucks; they charge about CFA 2500 to Bobo.

Train The new Étalon, which connects Ouaga and Bobo, departs every day in either direction promptly at 6 am, 12.30 and 7 pm. The trip takes five hours and costs CFA 4000/2500 1st/2nd class (CFA 6000/4000 round trip). The Express for Abidjan leaves on Tuesdays, Thursdays and Saturdays at 7 am and typically takes about 27 hours. There is also a 2nd-class train departing for Kaya at 7.45 am on Tuesdays and Saturdays, returning the same day. For more information, see the earlier Getting There & Away section.

Getting Around
To/From the Airport The cost of taxis to the centre (two km) is about CFA 1000 (50 to 100% more to the Hôtel Silmandé). It's also possible to walk; Ave Yennenga, with its

hotels, is only one km away. You could also catch the No 5 bus heading north on Ave Nkrumah (two blocks west of the airport) toward the Place des Nations Unies.

Bus X9 has buses which cover the city but few travellers use them because shared taxis are almost as cheap. Buses start running at 6 am and stop at 8 pm. The names of the city neighbourhoods are posted on the front of the buses, and bus stops are clearly marked as well. The buses are small and are typically packed at rush hour. Fares are CFA 100 for a single trip and CFA 150 for a connecting trip.

Most of the six bus lines pass along Ave Nelson Mandela at one point or another; the post office and the Place des Nations Unies are major bus stops:

No 1 goes east-west from the Zone du Bois along Ave d'Oubritenga, Ave Mandela, and Ave Kadiogo (the road to Bobo).

No 2 also goes east-west but starts out on the Hôtel Silmandé Rd, passes along Ave d'Oubritenga and Ave Mandela, and then heads north-west on Ave Yatenga (the road to Ouahigouya).

No 3 starts beyond the gare routière and passes the gare, then heads north on Ave Bassawarga to the centre of town, then east on Ave Mandela and Ave d'Oubritenga out to the Zone du Bois.

No 4 takes a more circuitous route, passing north along Ave Yennenga to Ave Mandela, then east along Ave Mandela and Blvd de la Révolution, then north again to Ave de la Liberté, then west along Ave de la Liberté past Marché Sankariaré toward the stadium.

No 5 goes north-south, starting on the southern end several hundred metres west of the gare routière and passes north along Ave Nkrumah (near the airport) toward the Place des Nations Unies, continuing northward on Ave Dimdolobson and across the reservoir and past Hôtel Ricardo.

No 6 goes east-west, starting on the eastern end out beyond the university and heading west on Ave de Gaulle and Ave Boumedienne toward Place de la Révolution, then north on Ave Kouanda through Ciné An III and eventually westward.

Taxi Taxis are green coloured and most are shared. There are also a few metered ones but they are more expensive and should be avoided. Fares in shared taxis are typically CFA 200, and about CFA 500 for a taxi to yourself (more for long journeys), CFA 2000 by the hour, and about CFA 15,000 plus petrol by the day. Serious bargaining is required to get these hourly and daily rates. Rates double at 10 pm.

Taxis are not too difficult to find during the day. About the only places you'll find them at night are at the petrol station near the Wassa Club and outside the Ran and Indépendance hotels.

Car One of the cheapest car rental agencies is Express Auto Location at the Ran Hôtel (☎ 30 61 06, telex 5273). Its daily charges for a Peugeot 303 with air-con or a Peugeot 505 without air-con are CFA 10,000 plus CFA 2000 for insurance, CFA 2500 for a driver (CFA 5000 for driving outside the city), CFA 60 per km (CFA 80 outside Ouaga) and 22% tax. At the Hôtel de l'Indépendance you'll find Savannah Tours (☎ 30 60 60, fax 30 67 67) and, more expensive, Burkina Auto Location (☎ 30 68 11/60 60, telex 5201; cards AE, D, MC). The

former rents subcompacts for CFA 15,000 and CFA 20,000 a day including unlimited mileage, insurance and tax, while the latter charges CFA 14,875 per day plus CFA 3850 for insurance and CFA 5000 for a chauffeur (required for out-of-town driving) plus CFA 130 per km (CFA 160 per km out of town) and 22% tax. There's also Rent-a-Car/Avis on Rue de la Chance and at Hôtel Silmandé (☎ 30 01 76, fax 30 09 71). You could also try Faso Auto Location (☎ 33 53 81) at Hôtel Nazemsé. If price is your main concern, try Avenir Auto Location (☎ 31 33 59), which faces the Hôtel de la France (closed). It may still have the lowest prices of all, but how reliable the vehicles are is anyone's guess.

AROUND OUAGADOUGOU
Koudougou

For a short day trip out of Ouagadougou, try Koudougou, 97 km to the west. It's Burkina's third-largest city and is fairly spread out,

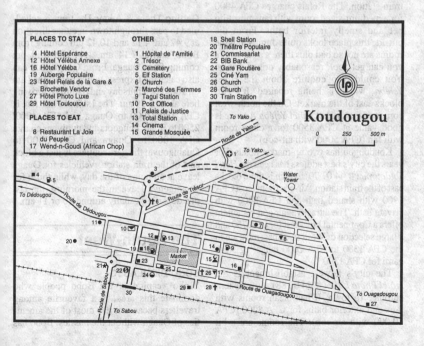

PLACES TO STAY
4 Hôtel Espérance
12 Hôtel Yéléba Annexe
16 Hôtel Yéléba
19 Auberge Populaire
23 Hôtel Relais de la Gare & Brochette Vendor
27 Hôtel Photo Luxe
29 Hôtel Toulourou

PLACES TO EAT
8 Restaurant La Joie du Peuple
17 Wend-n-Goudi (African Chop)

OTHER
1 Hôpital de l'Amitié
2 Trésor
3 Cemetery
5 Elf Station
6 Church
7 Marché des Femmes
9 Tagui Station
10 Post Office
11 Palais de Justice
13 Total Station
14 Cinema
15 Grande Mosquée
18 Shell Station
20 Théâtre Populaire
21 Commissariat
22 BIB Bank
24 Gare Routière
25 Ciné Yam
26 Church
28 Church
30 Train Station

Koudougou

To Yako

To Yako

Water Tower

0   250   500 m

To Dédougou

Route de Dédougou

Route de Trésor

Route de Yako

Market

Route de Ouagadougou

To Ouagadougou

To Sabou

Route de Sabou

with wide shaded avenues. It is usually quite tranquil during the day. The bars, market and hotels are good places for meeting the locals. You can take the train or bush taxis to get there. The heart is the market, which seems unusually large for such a small town, and the train station two blocks away. There's a BIB bank in the centre.

Places to Stay One of the cheapest and most convenient places is the *Auberge Populaire*, two blocks north of the train station and near the market (CFA 1800). The place is a dump, with no electricity or running water (a bucket of water can be supplied).

Hôtel Espérance is highly recommended: CFA 2500 for a clean room with fan, beds with two sheets, interior showers and basin. The main problem is that it's about one km west of the centre. It's a much better buy, however, than the more expensive *Hôtel Relais de la Gare*, only a block north of the train station. The Relais charges CFA 4000 for a medium-sized room with fan, mosquito net and smelly interior baths. From the outside this place looks quite dumpy, but the rooms are not so bad plus there's a bar where you can get cool, reasonably priced drinks. You could also enquire about the *Hôtel Yéléba*, which is being repaired. It's two blocks east of the market. On the north-west corner of the market *Hôtel Yéléba Annexe* is good value at CFA 3500 for a clean room with fan (CFA 5000 with air-con).

Koudougou has two up-market hotels. For years the city's best address has been the *Hôtel Toulourou* (☎ 44 01 70), which is three blocks east of the train station. Air-con rooms cost CFA 6900 with shared bath and CFA 8400 with private bath. The attractive, air-con restaurant offers a Continental breakfast for CFA 750 and a large selection of Western dishes; most are in the CFA 1300 to CFA 2000 range, eg steak garni for CFA 1300.

The city's newest establishment is the *Hôtel Photo Luxe* (☎ 44 00 88) at the eastern entrance to town. It has clean rooms with fans and exterior baths for CFA 8000 (CFA 10,000 with air-con). The rooms are a bit small but they are quite neat, plus there's a restaurant and a nightclub.

Places to Eat In addition to the Toulourou and Photo Luxe hotels, there are a few small places serving food and drink. The best place for African food, day or night, is the *Restaurant La Joie du Peuple*, just down the street from the Marché des Femmes, about one km north-east of the central market. Spacious and well maintained, it's an open-air place with lots of chairs, large funky paintings on the walls, recorded music playing and three or four African sauces to choose from. At night, it's also the best place to come for drinks and dancing. For dancing, you could also try the *Night Club Le Kon-Kiss* nearby.

For African food near the centre try *Wend-n-Goudi*, a hole-in-the-wall one block south of the main mosque. The food is cheap and ordinary. You can also get brochettes on the street next to the Hôtel Relais de la Gare and cold drinks on the hotel's front terrace.

Getting There & Away The train is scheduled to pass through town in either direction at 9.42 am, 4.12 and 10.42 pm coming from Bobo, and at 7.14 am, 1.44 and 8.14 pm coming from Ouaga. From Ouaga, you can also catch the Express, which departs at 7 am on Tuesday, Thursday and Saturday, arriving here about 8.30 am. The 1st/2nd-class fare is CFA 1800/1000 to Ouaga and CFA 4000/2500 to Bobo. Peugeots and minivans charge CFA 1000 to Ouaga and CFA 3500 to Ouahigouya; the gare routière is just a block east of the train station. Vehicles for Ouaga leave at all hours of the day, while those for Ouahigouya leave in the morning, the last one departing usually around 10 or 11 am.

The South-West

BOBO-DIOULASSO

'Bobo', capital of the Bobo people who dominate this area, is a favourite among travellers because it has most of the amenities of Ouaga without the hassles. Bobo has wide tree-lined streets, mango trees everywhere, a thriving market providing good souvenirs, cafés, a relaxed pace and good nightlife.

With some 200,000 inhabitants, Bobo is small enough for you to go almost everywhere on foot. Just don't go down dark alleys at night because thieves have recently become a serious problem. The surrounding areas are also interesting and for visiting them, a bicycle can come in handy; people in the market will rent you theirs for the day.

The best time to be here is during La Semaine Nationale de la Culture, held in Bobo every even year during the last week of April, thus alternating with the biannual film festival in Ouaga. During that week, there are performances of all kinds including music, dance and theatre.

Orientation

The heart of town is the central market, half a km directly east of the train station. Ave de la Nation leads south-east from the station for one km to a large roundabout called Place de la Nation, passing the post office along the way. Ave de la Liberté leads north-east from the train station for one km to another roundabout. The town's commercial core is the triangular area defined by these roundabouts and the train station, with the market in the centre. The area south and east of the market is where you'll find many of the hotels, restaurants and banks.

From the Place de la Nation, Ave du Général de Gaulle heads east toward the new gare routière on the outskirts of town and the road to Ouaga, while Ave de l'Indépendance heads west toward Sikasso. The road south to Banfora heads off from the latter.

Another of the seven roads intersecting with Place de la Nation is Ave Binger, which runs north for 15 blocks where it intersects with Blvd de la Révolution, a wide east-west thoroughfare. This is not to be confused with Ave de la Révolution, which starts at the same roundabout, runs northward almost parallel with Ave Binger, and also intersects with Blvd de la Révolution.

Information

Money BICIA, a block south of the market and BIB near the Auberge are the best for changing money. They change money at once, accept US dollar travellers' cheques (Visa, Barclays, American Express), and charge no commission. They are open from 8 to 11 am and 3.30 to 5.30 pm Monday to Friday. Banks in Mali and Côte d'Ivoire couldn't be more different, so if you're headed to either country, change your money here!

Bookshops The best bookshop (Librairie Socifa) faces the central market as do Librairie Nova and Librairie La Savane. They sell excellent maps of Bobo and Ouaga for CFA 1000, as does the Institut Géographique just beyond the commissariat, a block east of the Place de la Nation roundabout.

Museum

The Musée Provincial du Houët is in a small Sudanese-style building facing the Place de la Nation roundabout. The main building has two rooms, one exhibiting modern African paintings, batiks, sculpture, etc, and the other exhibiting traditional art of the region, including a Senufo carved wood doorway, Peul hats, funeral and dance masks, Bobo masks, a Mossi funeral statue, Senufo and Gurunsi clothing, beads, necklaces of cowrie shells, other jewellery and Mossi door locks. Outside are three full-sized models of traditional houses. One is Bobo, decorated and furnished and similar to those in Koumi. The others are Peul and Senufo. It's open from 8 am to noon and 3.30 to 6 pm; Sunday from 9 am to 1 pm; closed Monday (CFA 300).

French Cultural Centre

The Centre Culturel Français Henri Matisse is a block away and very popular with the locals. In front you'll find a shady area with lots of magazines and other material and plenty of chairs for reading as well as soft drinks on sale. This area, which is a good place to hang out, is open every day except Sunday until around 6 pm. The centre also has a library, theatre, cinema and video room; notices of events are posted all around.

Fêtes des Masques

Every so often there is a great funeral in the Bobo region, typically that of a village chief, which takes place six months or so after the death and is accompanied by a late-night 'fête des masques' in which the Bobo helmet masks and other masks are used. If you're in the area when one takes place and you're invited to observe, don't miss it.

A typical dance features masked men and an orchestra of narrow drums beaten with curved canes, and flute-like instruments. The masked dancers are sometimes dressed in loose raffia pyjama-like outfits which are bulky and coloured brown and black. Attached to the mask is a mop of brown raffia, falling over the head and shoulders to the waist. The masked men often carry long pointed sticks with metal jangles round the middle, making enormous jumps with them. Each masked dancer, representing a different spirit, performs in turn, jumping about and waving his stick, looking for evil spirits which might prevent the deceased from going to paradise. The onlookers, especially the children, are terrified and run away from him. No one dares to approach as the dancer becomes increasingly wilder, doing strange acrobatic feats and waving his head backwards and forwards, eventually catching someone and hitting them. That person, however, may not complain.

After a while, that chase ends and another begins. The entire affair can last for hours. ■

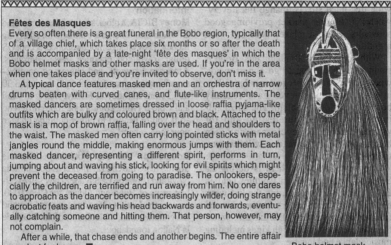

Bobo helmet mask

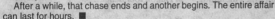

Market

The Grand Marché is one of the best in West Africa for a city of its size, and the Sudanese architecture gives it a nice feeling. It has an excellent selection of African cotton prints and cheap tailors who can make shirts (CFA 800) and dresses out of the material in very short order (CFA 400 for drawstring pants). There's also a good selection of masks, drums and objects in bronze and gold.

After scouring the marché, ask the kids there to lead you to the 'bronzier' who lives nearby; many of them know him. He makes wonderful bronze statues using the wax technique and, being very friendly, will let you photograph him at work. In addition, between the market and the Auberge, you'll find about six small shops which are the best places for buying souvenirs.

Mosque & Kibidwé District

Three blocks east of the market on Ave de la Révolution is the Grande Mosquée. Built in 1880 it is an excellent example of Sudanese mud architecture. For a tour including a view from the top, the caretaker will demand an exorbitant CFA 1000. If you say you don't want

to go on the roof, which is far less interesting than the interior, you may be able to bargain the price down considerably. The intriguing maze-like interior has a low ceiling and is very plain with mud walls, numerous pillars and no adornments whatsoever. The women sit at the back and the men in front, with the nobles and *grand marabouts* (Muslim holy men) on the first row and the emir facing them.

Just across the street to the east is the beginning of the old Kibidwé district. This 'vieux quartier' is the oldest section of town and is well worth exploring. The area is full of artisans (primarily blacksmiths, potters and weavers) and observing them at work can be fascinating. However, seeing them in a tranquil environment can be very difficult as children wait outside the mosque, ready to pester foreigners. To avoid them, see the old district first, entering from the far eastern side and making your way westward, ending at the mosque which you can then visit. You may also receive less attention if you go very early in the morning.

Places to Stay – bottom end

There are two places on the south-western side of town near the gare routière which are highly recommended. The best for the money is *Casafrica* (☎ 98 01 57) in Quartier Le Petit Paris. To get there, take the road to Sikasso; two blocks beyond Brasserie Brakina and a block before the turn-off for Banfora you'll see a sign for the hotel. From the train station or city centre, you'll probably want a taxi. They charge CFA 3000 including tax for a good size room with mosquito net, fan and shared bath (CFA 3500/4000 for a single/double with private bath). Travellers can also pitch tents for CFA 1000 a person. The atmosphere is quiet and relaxing, and someone always seems to be playing the banfora or drums. There's also space for parking. Good meals include omelettes (CFA 300), riz sauce (CFA 500), pizza (CFA 600), grilled half chicken (CFA 700), steak au poivre (CFA 900), soft drinks (CFA 175) and large beers (CFA 300).

Campers may prefer the new six-room *Campement Le Pacha*, half a block east of the gare routière. Camping costs CFA 1000 a person (no charge for vehicles). The rooms, however, are far inferior to those at Casafrica. They cost CFA 2800 and CFA 4000 plus tax but with no fans (CFA 500 extra). The cheaper rooms are barely big enough for a bed with mosquito net. Toilets are African style and shared. There are hammocks in the shady yard, books, parking, drinks (CFA 450 for a large beer) and a grill.

Hôtel Okinawa (☎ 99 02 55), one km north of the train station, is more like a traditional African compound than a hotel. Singles/doubles with a bed and shower cost CFA 2000/2500 (CFA 3000 with fan and interior toilet). The people are friendly, and there's a shaded patio in the middle, but the loud music and prostitutes make relaxing difficult. The menu includes horse for CFA 200, braised fish for CFA 600 to CFA 1200, and braised chicken for CFA 1000.

Hôtel-Bar Liberté on the same street as the Okinawa, but five blocks closer to the train station, is similar. There's a loud stinking factory next door, a cement patio, and it's difficult to get food. Small dark rooms with interior showers cost CFA 2000 (CFA 2500 with fan). If you're desperate and want a place nearby, try *Hôtel de l'Unité* on Ave de l'Unité, six blocks north of the train station. This sterile place, which is definitely not recommended, has rooms with fans and shared baths for CFA 2500 (CFA 3000 to CFA 3500 with private bath).

A good choice away from the centre is the tranquil *Hôtel de l'Amitié* (☎ 97 22 12), on the north-western outskirts of town in Quartier Accart-Ville Nord. Very clean rooms with tiled floors, double sheets and baths cost CFA 3000 (CFA 3500 with fan) and are excellent value. You can also eat cheaply here, eg CFA 350 for an omelette and CFA 400 for steak.

In the centre, excellent value is *Hôtel Hamdalaye* (☎ 97 07 18), three blocks north of the market. The new owner has spruced this place up a bit and added a decent cheap restaurant; rooms cost CFA 3200 plus tax and have tiled floors, beds with two fresh sheets and good tiled showers. It's now much better for the price than the nearby *Hôtel Central* (☎ 97 01 47), formerly the Hôtel de la Paix, facing Ciné Bobo 90. It charges CFA 4025/5750 including 15% tax for a tiny single/double with fan and shower (CFA 5175/6900 with interior bath). It also serves food and drinks.

For just slightly more money you could stay at the much nicer *Hôtel L'Entente* (97 12 05), which has large, clean singles/doubles with fans, mosquito nets, washbasins and clean showers for CFA 4325/5200 including 15% tax (CFA 9500/9800 with air-con). You can have drinks under their attractive paillotes. It's on Rue du Commerce (which runs alongside the market), 1½ blocks east of the market. It's better value than the *Hôtel Teria* (☎ 97 19 72), formerly the Commerce. It's around the corner to the south on Ave Alwata Diawara and charges CFA 4565/5200 for small singles/doubles with mosquito nets, fans and private showers (CFA 6385/8185 with air-con). At the restaurant there are dishes for as little as CFA 300.

Places to Stay – middle

Some travellers still rave about the friendly *Hôtel Soba* (☎ 98 09 17), in the centre next to Cinéma Houët on Ave Ouédraogo. A

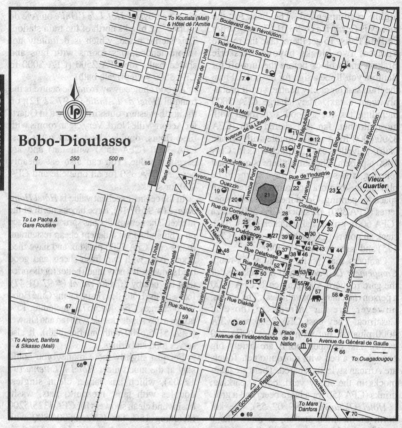

Bobo-Dioulasso

0   250   500 m

double room with fan but no mosquito net is CFA 5590 including 15% tax (CFA 8235 with air-con). For more than one night, you should be able to bargain down the price about 20%. The showers have warm water and the toilets even have toilet paper, but it's not particularly good value.

There's also the attractive *Hôtel La Renaissance* (☎ 98 23 31) on Rue Malherbe, three blocks south of the market. Not to be confused with the Bar Renaissance nearby, it has very neat singles/doubles with fans, mosquito nets and private showers for CFA 4000/4500. There's only one shared toilet,

however, for the eight rooms. It's a pleasant place for drinks and meals too.

Places to Stay – top end

For years, *L'Auberge* (☎ 97 14 26, fax 97 21 37), with its clean pool, central location, sidewalk terrace for sipping drinks and watching the crowds, and good restaurant has been the best place to stay. Nonguests can use the billiards table (CFA 500 a game) and, if it's not crowded, the pool (CFA 1000). Singles/doubles with air-con are CFA 16,445/17,940 including tax. It's on Ave Ouédraogo, a block south of the market.

PLACES TO STAY		52	L'Eau Vive	34	BICIA Bank & Cinéma Houët
1	Hôtel Okinawa	70	Le Concorde	37	BIB Bank
2	Hôtel de L'Unité			39	La Kazar Nightclub
6	Hôtel-Bar Liberté	**OTHER**		43	Rakieta Bus Station
11	Hôtel Hamdalaye			44	Hilton Nightclub
14	Hôtel Central	3	Sogebaf Bus Station	45	Cinema
17	Ran Hôtel	4	Gare de Dédougou	46	Le Must (Nightclub) &
27	L'Auberge	5	Marché du Soir		Street Food
30	Hôtel L'Entente	7	Traditional Weavers	49	Sûreté
35	Hôtel Soba	8	Gare de Mopti	50	ONATEL Telephone
38	Relax Hôtel	9	Total Station		Office
40	Hôtel Teria	10	Stadium	51	Post Office
48	Hôtel Le 421	12	Ciné Bobo 90	54	Mazawan (Nightclub)
53	Hôtel Watinoma	13	Sans Frontières Bus	56	Commissariat
55	Hôtel Diyanan, DHL &		Station	57	Jardin Zoologique
	Air Burkina	15	Librairie Socifa	58	Faso Tours
59	Hôtel Soma	16	Train Station	60	Hospital
67	Casafrica	18	Cathedral	61	Le Colsa Bar
		19	Sotraco Bus	62	Tennis Club
PLACES TO EAT		20	Air Afrique & Mobylette	63	Gendarmerie
			Rentals	64	Musée Provincial du
25	Street Food	21	Grand Marché		Houët
31	Café des Amis & La	22	Mission Protestante	65	Centre Culturel
	Sorbetière		Américaine		Français Henri
36	La Boule Verte	23	Grande Mosquée		Matisse (French
41	Restaurant Togolais	24	BND Bank		Cultural Centre)
42	Boulangerie La Bonne	26	Artisan Shops	66	Haut Commissariat
	Miche & Salon de Thé	28	Sogobim Supermarket	68	Brakina Brewery
47	Restaurant	29	Air Ivoire	69	Catholic Mission
	Delwinde	32	Mairie		
	(Chez Tanti Abi)	33	Place de la Révolution		

The *Ran Hôtel* (☎ 98 18 45/6, fax 97 09 00) opposite the train station, half a km west of the centre, has singles/doubles for CFA 19,320/23,115 including tax; breakfast is extra. Non-guests can use the pool for CFA 1500. On weekends the nightclub next door can be noisy. You can make reservations at the train station in Ouaga, Abidjan or Bouaké.

Excellent and less expensive is the popular *Hôtel Watinoma* (☎ 98 21 62). Air-con singles/doubles cost CFA 11,570/12,675 including tax. It's on the corner of Rue Malherbe and Ave Binger, and has a French restaurant. The new *Hôtel Diyanan* (☎ 97 01 69, fax 97 18 63), six blocks south of the market, looks nice outside, but inside it's cheap, and business is slow. Singles/doubles cost CFA 13,500/16,500 including tax.

Places to Eat
Cheap Eats Two blocks south-east of the market is the well-known *Boulangerie La Bonne Miche*, which is good for bread and pastries. A block north and across from Hôtel L'Entente is the relaxing *Café des Amis* (good for light snacks), and *La Sorbetière*, one of the best ice-cream places in town, with four or five flavours (CFA 150 per scoop).

A good area for street food, day and night, is around Cinéma Houët on Ave Ouédraogo; the men here sell whole grilled chickens for CFA 1000 while the women sell much cheaper African sauces. For really cheap food, try the fried yams sold outside Hôtel Okinawa; the cost for a big serving and sauce is CFA 100. You can also get good riz sauce around the market for CFA 100.

African An excellent place for African food is the *Restaurant Togolais*, on Rue du Commerce, across from Hôtel L'Entente. Every day the Togolese woman here makes five or six dishes, such as sauce de poisson and sauce de feuille, all served with rice or paté (noodles). Most dishes are CFA 200. The salads are also very good.

Her food is generally better than the large, well-known *Restaurant Delwinde* (Chez Tanti Abi) on Ave Alwata Diawara, just south of Ave Ouédraogo. Its best feature is its unusually extensive menu: riz gras and riz sauce for CFA 300, sauce arachide, foutou for CFA 350, spaghetti for CFA 200, ragoût d'igname, etc. The quality is ordinary but unlike many African restaurants they serve food well into the evening. A block north on the same street is *Hôtel Teria*, which has a restaurant where you can also get inexpensive African food, eg riz sauce for CFA 300, couscous for CFA 500 and chicken for CFA 700. The *Hôtel L'Entente* around the corner on Rue du Commerce has similar fare.

For a laid-back African setting and clientele, take a taxi to *Le Concorde*, on Ave Louveau, 300 metres south-east of the Place de la Nation. The informal, outdoor setting and dance floor are special. The food is limited to brochettes, kidneys and grilled chicken or steak. Late at night, the dancing starts.

French *L'Eau Vive* (meaning 'living water') is the sister restaurant of the one in Ouaga and serves equally terrific French food, plus you can eat under the stars. The special three-course menu costs CFA 2300. Main dishes include steak frites (CFA 1500) and rabbit in wine sauce (CFA 2900). You could also go there just for one of their fabulous ice-cream desserts (CFA 900 for simple ice cream; CFA 1800 for a sundae). The restaurant (closed Sundays) is on Rue Delafosse at the intersection with Ave Alwata Diawara.

The city's other top French restaurant has similar prices. It's at *L'Auberge* at the intersection of Ave Ouédraogo and Ave de la République. *La Boule Verte* across the street offers a variety of dishes, most in the CFA 1900 to CFA 2300 range. Their cheese crêpes are said to be quite good.

Entertainment
Bars *Le Rêve* has closed but *Le Colsa* nearby, two blocks north-west of the Place de la Nation, is a tranquil open-air bar that has become popular in place of Le Rêve. It's best at night; you can have a large beer for only CFA 285 and listen to the soft background music.

For years, the street-side terrace of the *Auberge*, a block south of the market on Ave Ouédraogo, has been *the* place for a drink and watching the crowds. The drinks aren't cheap but the location is ideal.

Nightclubs *Mazawan* on Ave de la Révolution, five blocks south-east of the market and *La Kazar*, nearby, are popular. Other top places for dancing include *Le Must*, which has air-con and is on Ave Ouédraogo, and *Black & White*, around the corner on Ave Binger at the intersection with Rue du Commerce. Its terrace is packed with people drinking until late. Most of these places have cover charges, typically CFA 500. *Hilton Nightclub* nearby on Ave de la Révolution is a bit grubby and often crowded and is more for drinking than dancing. Try also *Le 421*, an air-con disco south of the market on Rue Malherbe at the intersection with Ave de la Nation, and the long-standing *Le Concorde* which is a restaurant with an open-air dance floor in the centre.

Cinemas The modern Ciné Bobo 90 on Ave de la République, three blocks north of the market, is an excellent movie theatre and shows good films nightly at 8.30 and 10.30 pm (CFA 500). The older and inferior Cinéma Houët is a block south of the market on Ave Ouédraogo.

Getting There & Away
Air Air Burkina (☎ 97 13 48) has flights to Ouaga on Tuesday, Wednesday, Friday and Sunday, to Abidjan (CFA 32,100) on Tuesday, Friday and Sunday, and to Bamako (CFA 40,000) on Wednesday. Air Burkina is on Rue Malherbe, six blocks south of the central market and two blocks east of the post office. Air Afrique (☎ 98 19 21) faces the market.

Bus There are a number of companies with large, comfortable *cars* offering service to Ouaga, Abidjan and elsewhere. The best bus companies have their own offices, usually near the centre of town. Most other companies can be found at the gare routière ('Gare de Gare Bas' or 'la grande gare'), which is on the western side of town, about three km from the city centre. Rue Malherbe leads to it from the centre.

Sans Frontières, 1½ blocks north of the central market, has buses every day to Ouaga (7 am, 2 and 6 pm) and Abidjan (4 and 6 pm) and every day except Saturday to Bamako (3 pm). The cost is CFA 3000, CFA 11,500 and CFA 8000, respectively. Another good one is Sogebaf, on Blvd de la Révolution, seven blocks north of the market. It offers daily service to Abidjan and has nine coaches a day to Ouaga (6, 7, 8, 10, 12 am and 2, 4, 5.30 and 7 pm) and one a day to Ouahigouya (10 am). Those departing for Ouaga at 6 am and 7 pm also continue on to Ouahigouya. The trip takes about five hours to Ouaga, nine hours to Ouahigouya and about twice that to Abidjan.

Faso Tours (☎ 98 11 40), on the corner of Rue Malherbe and Ave de la Concorde, has *cars* which have become very run-down (avoid if possible). It provides services to Bamako (CFA 8000) on Mondays and Thursdays, Sinkasé on Saturdays, and Ouaga (CFA 2500) on Sundays, continuing to Niamey (CFA 10,000) on Monday. All departures are at 7 am. (They depart Bamako on Wednesday and Saturday, Accra on Friday and Niamey on Wednesday.) It also provides a service to Gaoua, departing Bobo on Tuesday, Thursday, Friday and Sunday and returning the following day. The fare is CFA 2500.

If you're headed to Banfora only, your best bet is Sotraco, which charges only CFA 400, departing at 7 am every day. Another is Rakieta (☎ 97 18 91), which has buses departing punctually nine times a day between 7 am and 7 pm; the cost is CFA 800 and seats are guaranteed.

Other companies to enquire about include STBF (departures in either direction at 8 am, 2 and 6 pm) and Guimbi Voyages. If you're headed to Mali and you come here around 7 am, you'll find several buses and Peugeots headed for Bamako (CFA 8000), also

Koutiala (CFA 5000), Ségou (CFA 6500) and Mopti (CFA 7000). The best company for Mopti, however, is SOBA, which provides a daily service. Buses leave between 3 and 5 pm; the trip takes about 12 hours and costs CFA 7000. You'll also find Peugeot bush taxis (same price) headed for Mopti outside the SOBA office, which is more commonly referred to as the Gare de Mopti. It's near the centre on Ave Ponty, five blocks north of the market.

If you're headed to Dédougou, head for the Gare de Dédougou at the Marché du Soir. The company there has buses departing daily at 3 pm; the trip takes six hours and costs CFA 2500 plus baggage.

X9 buses also leave from the centre; the station (☎ 98 07 86) is on Ave Binger near the mairie (town hall). Departures are:

destination	departure time	frequency
Ouaga	7 am & 2 pm	daily
Banfora/ Niangoloko	8 am	daily except Fri
Gaoua	8 am	Mon, Thur, Sat
Hamélé	8 am	Mon, Wed, Sat
Dédougou	8 am	Mon, Thur
Koloko	8 am	Sat
Tougan	8 am	Fri, Sun
Batié	8 am	Tues

Bush Taxi & Minibus Virtually all minibuses and Peugeot 504 bush taxis leave from the gare routière on the far western side of town, three km from the centre. To get there, head west out on Rue Malherbe. Fares are CFA 3500 to Ouaga and CFA 1000 to Banfora; slightly higher than the bus fare.

Train According to the schedule, the Express leaves Ouaga and Abidjan on Tuesdays, Thursdays and Saturdays, arriving Bobo at 2.15 pm headed for Abidjan (3.10 am the next day headed for Ouaga); late arrivals from Abidjan are virtually guaranteed. Fares are CFA 4000/3000 (1st/2nd class) to Ferkéssédougou, CFA 8000/5200 to Bouaké and CFA 12,800/8600 to Abidjan. For a berth on the train, you must book a day or more in advance, either at the train station or at the Ran Hôtel. For information on schedules, berths or student discounts (30 to 50%), enquire at the train station (☎ 98 23 91).

There are also three local trains every day between Ouaga and Bobo, leaving in either direction at 6 am, 12.30 and 7 pm. Unlike the Express, these trains are amazingly punctual. The five-hour trip costs CFA 4000/2500 1st/2nd class (CFA 3800/6000 round trip). See Getting There & Away in this chapter.

Getting Around

Taxi Taxis are plentiful. Most trips in town, including those to the gare routière, are CFA 100; luggage is extra.

Bicycle & Mobylette To rent a bicycle for the day, ask around the market. CFA 1500 a day is a reasonable price, but you'll have to bargain hard. For a mobylette, expect to pay about CFA 2500 a day until 5 pm (CFA 3000 is the typical asking price). A good place to find them is outside the Air Afrique office facing the market. You can also rent motorcycles there for CFA 5000 a day. During the rainy season, seeing the surrounding villages by bicycle or mobylette can be quite difficult because of the mud.

AROUND BOBO-DIOULASSO

In the countryside, notice the Bobos' traditional houses, distinguished by their tall conical roofs. They mingle with narrow storehouses, joined together with earth walls that give the compounds the look of squat medieval castles.

The following places of interest can easily be reached on bicycles from Bobo.

La Mare aux Poissons Sacrés de Dafra

This sacred fish pond, eight km south-east of Bobo near Dafra (or Dafora), is a little hard to find but is not to be missed. The hills and the pond's setting in a crevice below a cliff are memorable, the fish less so. You'll find people there virtually every day of the week. They come with chickens, which they kill and feed to the huge fish. A taxi there and back will cost you about CFA 5000 if you bargain well; the excursion shouldn't take more than two hours. It's a 10-minute walk

from where the taxi stops. Around the pond you'll see chicken feathers everywhere. The people say the fish are more active Monday to Friday, and that photographs make them hide. Also, wearing red is prohibited.

Getting There & Away From the Place de la Nation in Bobo, take Ave Louveau towards the south-eastern end of town and then ask around for the turn-off to your right for Dafra (not shown on the Michelin map); the village is about eight km away. Once you get near the village, ask again for directions because the pond is a little hard to find, but everybody knows it.

La Guinguette

La Guinguette is a bilharzia-free, crystal-clear bathing area 18 km from Bobo in a verdant forest, La Forêt de Kou. In colonial times, it was reserved exclusively for the colonialists. Now, it's a popular place with Africans on weekends; during the week you'll have the place to yourself. Thieves are a serious problem, day and night. Camping is possible but unless you're with a group, it's safer to ask the villagers for permission to sleep in the village.

Getting There & Away From Bobo, take the Sikasso Rd and, just after passing through Koumi (15 km), turn right then take the left fork along a narrow rough dirt track. After passing two villages, take a sharp right alongside the forest and follow the track to the river. On the way, stop in Koumi to see some interesting Bobo architecture. The two-storey houses are reminiscent of those of Indian tribes in south-western USA. Consult the chief before taking photos.

Mare aux Hippopotames

Some 66 km north-east of Bobo there's a lake filled with hippos. For CFA 500, you can hire a local fisher on the lake to take you in a pirogue to see the hippos. If you've never been on the water with hippos you'll find them a little more aggressive and dangerous than you thought. Indeed, there are more people killed in Africa every year by hippos than by any other animal. The lake has bilharzia, so forget about swimming.

Getting There & Away Getting here is complicated without a vehicle. The turn-off for the lake is Satiri, 44 km north-east of Bobo on the dirt road to Dédougou (176 km). You could take a Dédougou bus from the Gare Routière and get off in Satiri but you'll probably have to pay the full Dédougou fare (roughly CFA 2000). From Satiri there's a rough dirt road west which, after about 15 km, forks off to the left (south) towards the lake. Unless you walk the 22 km, you'll either have to hitch a ride which would be extremely difficult except possibly on weekends during the dry season or get a group together and hire a taxi for the round trip, probably the only feasible way of getting here for most travellers. From July to September this road is probably impassable.

BANFORA

Banfora is a small pleasant town on the Ouagadougou-Abidjan train line that offers interesting hiking/biking possibilities. The

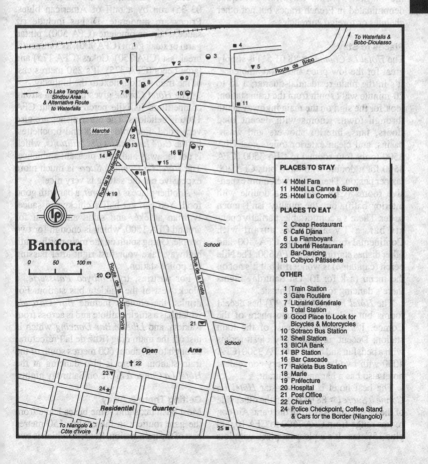

Banfora

0   50   100 m

To Waterfalls &
Bobo-Dioulasso

Route de Bobo

To Lake Tengréla,
Sindou Area
& Alternative Route
to Waterfalls

Marché

Rue de la Préfecture

Rue de la Poste

Route de la Côte d'Ivoire

School

School

Open   Area

Residential   Quarter

To Niangolo &
Côte d'Ivoire

PLACES TO STAY
4   Hôtel Fara
11 Hôtel La Canne à Sucre
25 Hôtel Le Comoé

PLACES TO EAT
2   Cheap Restaurant
5   Café Djana
6   Le Flamboyant
23 Liberté Restaurant
    Bar-Dancing
15 Colbyco Pâtisserie

OTHER
1   Train Station
3   Gare Routière
7   Librairie Générale
8   Total Station
9   Good Place to Look for
    Bicycles & Motorcycles
10 Sotraco Bus Station
12 Shell Station
13 BICIA Bank
14 BP Station
16 Bar Cascade
17 Rakieta Bus Station
18 Marie
19 Préfecture
20 Hospital
21 Post Office
22 Church
24 Police Checkpoint, Coffee Stand
    & Cars for the Border (Niangolo)

heart of town is the market, which is opposite the BICIA bank and Shell petrol station and two blocks south of the train station. The town is fairly spread out with little to see.

What is interesting is the surrounding area, certainly one of the more beautiful areas in Burkina, which is perfect for a tour on two wheels. The major attractions are Lake Tengréla (10 km to the west) and the nearby Karfiguéla waterfalls plus, much further to the west, the incredibly stunning rock formations around Sindou.

For changing money, the BNDB facing the market accepts travellers' cheques denominated in French francs but not other cheques or foreign currencies.

Places to Stay

The *Hôtel Le Comoé* (☎ 88 01 51) is simply great for the low price and good ambience. It's in the main residential quarter, a 15 to 20-minute walk south from the train station; look for the sign on the main highway south through town. Rooms with decent tiled floors, fans, interior showers and wash-basins, and clean exterior toilets cost CFA 3500 (only four rooms) to CFA 3500 (CFA 4500 for a double with bath) plus CFA 300 tax per person. There are newer, more expensive rooms (CFA 6440 for a double with interior bath), but the quality isn't much better. There's a comfortable, partially open-air bar, a TV and a restaurant with Continental breakfasts for CFA 400 and other dishes starting from CFA 600. The Nile perch (capitaine) is wonderful but it's not on the menu (ask for it). On Saturday nights there's dancing to recorded music.

The *Hôtel Fara* (☎ 88 01 17) has decent rooms but it lacks the atmosphere of the Comoé. It's 300 metres east of the train station. Decent, immaculately clean rooms with a bed, fan and bath cost CFA 3500 (CFA 4000 with two beds). This very convenient hotel also has a bar and restaurant.

The best hotel is the two-star *Hôtel La Canne à Sucre* (☎ 88 01 07) on the other side of the paved highway from the Fara. Air-con rooms range from CFA 7500 to CFA 10,000 plus 15% tax. It's a pleasant place with lots

of shade trees and has a decent restaurant where you can dine inside or outside. The menu includes capitaine for CFA 1700, steak for CFA 800 and large beers for CFA 400.

Places to Eat

Le Flamboyant, a shady sidewalk café, is in the heart of town between the train station and the market facing the Total petrol station. It's the cheapest place in town. Nearby and behind the market there's *Restaurant de l'Harmattan*; it has good grilled chicken and brochettes plus a nice ambience and music.

The best restaurant is *Café Djana* (☎ 88 03 35) run by a buff of American blues. Prices are moderate. Dishes include riz sauce, soup or omelette (CFA 500), pintad garni or steak garni (CFA 900), a Continental breakfast (CFA 750), Cokes (CFA 175) and large beers (CFA 375). It's 250 metres east of the train station, next to the highway.

The *Hôtel Comoé* gives the Djana strong competition. Its Nile perch for about CFA 1200 is delicious. The other dishes are also very good. For cold drinks and brochettes, try the *Café Le Creuset des Militants*, which is not far away and has a pleasant ambience. The *Hôtel La Canne à Sucre* is much more expensive but the setting is very nice.

Another place is *La Forêt*, a bar with good food. You can get half a chicken in sauce, Ivoirian attiéké, and salad and bread for around CFA 1500, which is enough for two people. Going south on the main north-south highway, take your first right after passing the police station.

For pastries, try *Colbyco Pâtisserie*, a block west of the Rakieta bus station. For drinks, the choices include *Bar Cascade* which has a single paillote and is across from Rakieta, and *Liberté Bar-Dancing* which is just off the main drag (Rue de la Préfecture) through town, about 600 metres south of the train station. There is also dancing at the *Hôtel La Canne à Sucre* on Saturday nights.

Getting There & Away

Most bush taxis and some buses leave from the gare routière in the centre, 150 metres east of the train station. Rakieta, which is two blocks east of the market, offers the best service to Bobo; its buses, which are comfortable and offer guaranteed seating, leave on schedule, departing at 7, 8, 9, 10 and 12 am, and 2, 4 and 6 pm (CFA 800; 1½ hours). Bush taxis charge CFA 1000. Sotraco, which is nearby, also offers services to Bobo but not as frequently (CFA 400).

Getting a ride on one of the large buses headed south to Ferkessédougou and Abidjan is generally impossible because they are usually full, so you'll have to hitch or take a Peugeot bush taxi to the border (the road is sealed) or wait for the daily afternoon train. You'll find bush taxis at the gare routière and on the main drag about 600 metres south of the train station. Most departures for the border are in the morning. The border closes punctually at 6.30 pm, so if you can't make it to the crossing by then, you could always take the south-bound train, which passes through around 4.24 pm on Tuesdays, Thursdays and Saturdays. The train normally takes four or five hours to Ferké, which is a bit longer than by bush taxi, but the train is usually fairly punctual and taking it avoids your having to sleep at the border and wait in line for customs.

AROUND BANFORA
Karfiguéla Waterfalls
Some 12 km north-west of Banfora, the rocky Les Cascades de Karfiguéla are interesting year-round, but more so in the rainy season. Camping is possible but you'll have to bring you own water in the dry season as the water is too dirty to use then. In addition, the pools below the falls may be infested with bilharzia. Those without vehicles can hike or rent a bicycle, mobylette or motorcycle, although in the rainy season a bicycle won't make it. On the way, you'll pass through irrigated sugar-cane fields: quite a contrast to the dry land in most of Burkina.

Travelling from Bobo to Banfora, you could also stop off at the **Chutes de la Comoé**. Less impressive than Karfiguéla Falls but easier to get to, they are near Toussiana, about 25 km north of Banfora and just west of the highway to Ouagadougou.

Getting There & Away There are two equal-distance routes to Karfiguéla Falls: one north-east then west, and one west then north-west. My guide and I, both on a rented mobylette, took the former. From the train station, we took the Bobo road for about one km and just beyond the petrol station turned left over the tracks, continuing on a dirt road for 10 km or so. There are no signs.

Those headed for Lake Tengréla usually take the other route. From the train station, head west, then take a right (west) past the lycée and over the train tracks toward Tengréla (10 km). Before the village you should see a sign pointing right (north) toward the falls. If not, ask passers-by to point out the road. The falls are roughly eight km down that track.

If you want a guide, the standard all-day price is CFA 2500 which includes the price of a mobylette (you ride on the back). A guide costs about CFA 1500 extra if the owner does not come with the bike. If you're staying at the Hôtel Le Comoé, the chances are good that a young man will come around offering this service. He's friendly and the hotel staff know him well.

Lake Tengréla
Lake Tengréla is about 10 km west of Banfora on a good dirt road. To get there, simply take the second mentioned route to the waterfalls but continue west to Tengréla instead. The lake is one km or so beyond the village. You'll see fishers in their boats bringing in the nets, lots of interesting birds and maybe one of the lake's four hippos bobbing its head up and down. The fishers will be more than willing to take you on a short trip around the lake in their pirogues; expect to pay about CFA 1000 with hard bargaining. Camping is also possible along the lake. Allow a day to see both the lake and the waterfalls.

Sindou Rock Formations
To see some exceptionally weird and intriguing rock formations, head for the area around Sindou. It's 50 km to the west of Banfora via Tengréla and Douna. The road

is miserable, so you'll need a motorcycle or car. After passing Douna, you'll see the cliffs in the distance, just beyond Sindou.

If you're a serious hiker, the Sindou area is definitely the place to go. To get an excellent idea of what awaits you, see the photographs in the lobby of the Hôtel La Canne à Sucre in Banfora. The hotel can help arrange a tour (expensive). While you're in Sindou, walk around the picturesque village. There are also some waterfalls (Les Chutes de Léraba) to the north-east, a few km beyond Tourny (34 km north of Sindou), but they're not easy to get to.

GAOUA
Some 210 km south-east of Bobo via Diébougou, Gaoua is the centre of Lobi country.

Loropéni
Loropéni, 39 km west of Gaoua, is the site of some ancient ruins, the exact origins of which are not known. The Lobi call them the *maison de refus*. They're several km out of town and not easy to find, so pick up a guide.

Places to Stay & Eat
For cheap accommodation try *L'Hôtel de Poni*, which faces the main square and charges CFA 3500 for a room, or the *Hôtel 125*. The *Hôtel Hala* just outside town offers

the best accommodation by far and serves excellent Lebanese fare. For cheap food, your best bet is *La Porte Ouverte* which serves good riz sauce and other basic fare, mostly for CFA 100 a plate.

Getting There & Away
Trans-Mif (☎ 30 22 69 in Ouaga) provides a daily service between Ouaga and Gaoua. Departures are at 7 am from either direction (CFA 3500 from Ouaga, CFA 2000 from Dano and CFA 1000 from Diébougou). On Tuesdays and Saturdays the bus continues on to Kampti for CFA 1000 more. X9 also provides service on this route. Buses depart Ouaga on Mondays, Wednesdays and Saturdays at 8 am and return the following days.

From Bobo, your best bet may be Faso Tours. It has buses on Tuesdays, Thursdays, Fridays and Sundays; they depart Gaoua for Bobo on the following days. The fare is CFA 2500. There are also X9 buses from Bobo to Gaoua every Monday, Thursday and Saturday at 8 am from Bobo and every Monday, Wednesday and Saturday at 8 am from Ouaga. They return the following days. It's also possible to find bush taxis and minibuses at the gare routière in Bobo headed for Diébougou and Gaoua. Market day is Friday in Loropéni and Sunday in Gaoua, so in Banfora, Thursday and Saturday are the best days to find taxis for

---

Lobi Traditions
Lobi traditions are some of the best preserved in Africa. The *dyoro* initiation rites, which take place every seven years, are a reminder of this. For three to six months the young boys undergo severe physical tests of their manhood and learn the oral history of the Lobi and the do's and don'ts of their culture. Lobi art, in particular the wooden carvings (which play an essential role in protecting the family), is highly regarded by serious collectors.

What's most fascinating for travellers, however, is the architecture of the Lobi homes in the countryside. The mud-constructed compounds are rectangular and sometimes multistorey. Each is like a miniature fortress, with high mud-brick walls. Unlike most Africans who live in villages, the Lobi (like the Somba-Tamberma in northern Togo and Benin) live in their fields, with housing compounds scattered all over the countryside, often separated several hundred metres from one another.

With such strong traditions, it's not surprising that in the rural areas the Lobi don't warm easily to foreigners. It is in areas such as these that foreigners must be particularly cautious about what they do. Taking photos without express permission or even offering sweets to children, for instance, should be avoided. In towns such as Gaoua, however, the Lobi can be very friendly, and if they plead with you to have some of the local millet beer (chapalo), by all means accept. ∎

Loropéni and Gaoua (197 km), respectively. Parts of the road are in awful condition, so the trip to either town takes a full day.

The dirt road east from Bobo to Gaoua (210 km) via Diébougou is in good condition, as is the road from Ouaga to Gaoua (385 km) via Pâ and Diébougou. From Ouaga, you can drive there in five or six hours.

BOROMO

Boromo is halfway between Ouaga and Bobo-Dioulasso. If you stop here for the night and want a cheap room, try *Le Campement* (CFA 2000 with shower).

The South & South-East

FADA N'GOURMA

Some 219 km east of Ouaga on the Ouaga-Niamey highway, 'Fada' is the major town on this route. It's also the turn-off point for Natitingou and Pendjari Park, both in Benin. Normally very tranquil, Fada is spread out, with wide, shaded avenues. The heart of town is the market and the tiny autogare nearby, both on the main drag. If you're stuck here at night with nothing to do, try the cinema at the back of the autogare. There's also a BIB bank, but you're unlikely to be able to cash travellers' cheques here.

Places to Stay & Eat

The cheapest place is *Le Campement* just across the main highway from the autogare. If you arrive late at night, go around to the back of the building where the friendly caretaker sleeps, otherwise he'll never hear you. The rooms are clean with one or two comfortable single beds with clean sheets, bucket showers and moderately clean exterior toilets (singles/doubles CFA 1500/2500).

The best hotel is the *Auberge*. It charges CFA 4000/5000 plus tax for singles/doubles with fans and private baths with running water (CFA 5500/7500 with aircon). There are several paillotes with comfortable chairs, a rustic bar where steak and chips are CFA 1200 and big beers are CFA 350. If you arrive late at night, however, the guard may refuse to respond, even if there's room.

There's also the *Hôtel Nungu*, about two km west of town on the main highway. A room with two beds costs CFA 3000, but this

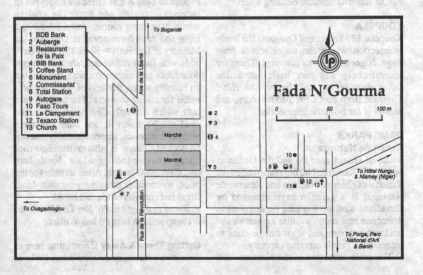

```
1   BDB Bank
2   Auberge
3   Restaurant
    de la Paix
4   BIB Bank
5   Coffee Stand
6   Monument
7   Commissariat
8   Total Station
9   Autogare
10  Faso Tours
11  Le Campement
12  Texaco Station
13  Church
```

Fada N'Gourma

To Bogandé
To Bandé
Ave de la Liberté
Rue de la Révolution

Marché
Marché

To Ouagadougou

To Hôtel Nungu & Niamey (Niger)

To Porga, Parc National d'Arli & Benin

0   50   100 m

place has little to recommend it other than the friendly staff.

For cheap African food, try the autogare; there are usually several people selling food. Between it and the market is a small stand where you can get coffee and bread. For European food, the best places are the *Auberge* and the *Restaurant de la Paix* next door. The latter has an attractive eating area outside under some trees.

Getting There & Away

Bush taxis and minibuses from Ouaga leave from the autogare; the cost is CFA 3000. The X9 buses to Fada leave Ouaga every Monday and Saturday at 8 am, returning the same day. They cost CFA 2000. Leaving Fada, you might be able to hop on one of the Sans Frontières buses that ply daily in either direction between Ouaga and the Niger border. They are usually full, however.

Whether you're headed to Ouaga or Niamey, you'll probably spend hours waiting for the vehicle to fill up. If you're headed to Benin or the western entrance of the Parc National d'Arli, you'll have a difficult time hitching a ride as few vehicles ply this route. For Arli, most people continue east to Kantchari before heading south.

KOUPÉLA

Koupéla, 137 km east of Ouaga, is the lively intersection where the major routes from Togo, Niger and Ouaga converge. There are several cheap and very basic hotels: the *Hôtel Bon Séjour* and, better, the *Hôtel Calypso*. Both cost CFA 2000 a room, and neither is far from the intersection.

GAME PARKS
Ranch de Nazinga

South of Ouaga near Pô and the Ghanaian border, the Ranch de Nazinga (also called the Ranch de Gibier de Nazinga and Réserve de Nazinga) is a game reserve managed by Canadians who are working on a project to determine how much wildlife a given area of land can support, and what can be done to increase the land's carrying capacity.

The main attraction is the elephant, and

you are more likely to see them here than at the main game park, Arli. There are also plenty of roan antelope, monkeys, baboons, wart hogs, crocodiles and birds. A guide is compulsory on each game drive and, unlike most game parks, here you can get out and walk wherever you like. This can be dangerous, however, as visitors have been charged by elephants. Viewing is best during the dry season because once the rains start, food is easier to find and the herds of animals disperse. Start your viewing no later than 5.30 am. Entrance is CFA 5000 for foreigners and CFA 1000 per vehicle.

If you have some extra time, consider a side trip to **Tiébélé**, which is 40 km due east of Pô via a dirt track. It's in the centre of Gourounsi country and famous for its fortress-like traditional houses, which are window-less and uniquely decorated in various geometrical patterns in red, black and white by the local women. They will gladly show you their handiwork, which is executed with guinea fowl feathers. From there, you could go another 10 km to **Boungou**, which is on the border and famous for its potters.

Places to Stay & Eat There are two types of lodgings – chalets and huts. The chalets, which have three rooms, cost CFA 5000 a night and must be reserved in Ouaga at the Ministry of Tourism (☎ 30 62 25). They have beds with foam mattresses, sheets, screens, door locks and bathrooms with fixtures but no running water. Buckets of water are provided for taking showers. The paillote-roof huts, which cost only CFA 500 a person and need not be reserved, are bare structures without mattresses, screens or doors that can be locked. There is also a thatched-roof dining area overlooking a lake. Meals here cost CFA 3900 and are often terrible for the price, so consider bringing your own food. Breakfast consists of tea and bread.

If you're caught in Pô, *Bar La Montagne*, is cheap and the best Pô has to offer.

Getting There & Away If you come here in your own vehicle, make sure it has 4WD as the road leading to the park is very rough. From Ouaga, the total driving time is three hours. Take the tarred 142-km road south to Pô, then a dirt road west toward Léo. After 15 km you'll come to a sign pointing south to Nazinga some 40 km further. Hitchhiking from that point is virtually impossible, although you may have more chance on weekends when expatriates and tourists from Ouaga are likely to visit. Alternatively, hire a taxi in Pô. Few travellers without vehicles ever make it here. If you don't have wheels, check with the people at the Ministry of Tourism in Ouaga. They oversee the project and sometimes know people heading that way. You can also rent a 4WD vehicle inside the park to take excursions. The cost is CFA 15,000 per day or CFA 7500 per half-day.

The easiest way to get here is with Faso Tours (☎ 30 66 71). It has one-day tours to Nazinga every Saturday, departing Ouaga at 6 am and returning around 6 pm. The price, CFA 25,000 per person (minimum four people), includes transport, food and non-alcoholic drinks.

Parc National d'Arli

In the south-east corner of the country on the border with Benin, Arli is Burkina's major game park. It's a small park of only 76,000 hectares, but it's contiguous with three reserves to the west: Arli, Singou and Pama. The park itself lies on a flat, flood-prone lowland area bordered to the south-east by the Pendjari River, and it's part of the same ecosystem as Pendjari Park just across the river/border (see the map in the Benin chapter). You'll find all the animals here that you do there – elephant, wart hog, baboon, monkey, lion, hippo, leopard, crocodile and various species of antelope and birds.

The park's main entrance is by the park lodge at Arli on the eastern edge near Benin. Travellers on the cheap with their own vehicles may prefer entering through the western entrance at Tindangou because of the cheaper lodging in Pama.

There are lions in the park so walking around is prohibited. If you come by bus, try your luck at the park lodge; for a price, you may be able to join the hotel's vehicle on a morning or afternoon tour. Otherwise, the weekend tourists might let you join them.

With your own vehicle, you can also see the Burkina side of **Parc W**, or W National Park, to the east of Arli on the Niger border; the entrance is via Diapaga. Both it and Arli are open from 15 December to 15 May. Entrance is CFA 2000 per person, plus CFA 1000 for the obligatory guide.

Places to Stay & Eat The park's main lodge is the *Campement d'Arli* (☎ 79 00 79). It's a very attractive lodge with steep thatched-roof bungalows and an air-con bar-restaurant overlooking a clean pool. Singles/doubles with air-con and private bath cost about CFA 20,000/22,000 plus taxes, and the fixed menu is about CFA 5000. There is also a vehicle for taking visitors around. If the phone is out of order, you can make reservations at the Ministry of Tourism in Ouaga.

Camping by the hotel is permitted. Also inexpensive is the *campement* in Diapaga or, better, *Chez Madame Bonazza* in Pama. Ms Bonazza, an Italian, has some inexpensive bungalows and serves good food. Apparently, her husband was eaten by the lions.

Getting There & Away For the eastern entrance at Arli, take the Ouaga-Niamey highway to Kantchari (389 km) near the border, then head south on a dirt road to Diapaga (56 km), Namounou (25 km) and Arli (48 km). The nonstop driving time is about seven hours. X9 buses leave Ouaga for Diapaga on Mondays and Saturdays and return the same day. From Diapaga or Namounou you can hitch to Arli.

Those with high-clearance vehicles may prefer the alternate route via the western entrance, which is somewhat more scenic and offers the chance of seeing some animals along the way. At Fada N'Gourma head south to Pama (109 km), then Tindangou 15 km further; the road is fair. From there it's a straight 85-km trip north-east to Arli lodge. Coming this way will save you about 90 km, but it takes about 1½ hours longer.

The North

OUAHIGOUYA

If you're headed to Dogon country in Mali, the most direct route from Ouaga is through Ouahigouya (wah-ee-GOU-yah), which is 182 km north-west of Ouaga by sealed road and is the country's fourth-largest city. Like many towns in Burkina, Ouahigouya is spread out. It's also a fairly lively town, particularly on Saturday nights. Much of the activity during the day is around the new market, in the centre, and on the long main drag. At night, much of the activity is around the cinema facing the autogare. Finding a taxi is virtually impossible, so if you're without a vehicle, you should expect to walk just about everywhere unless you can find someone with a mobylette.

If you're here at the end of Ramadan, head for Ramatoulaye, which is 25 km east of town, between Baghélogo and Rambo. Following Ramadan, there's a famous pilgrimage to the mosque in that village which shouldn't be missed.

Le Barrage

If you have wheels, visit the lake just outside town, to the north; the dam here was constructed in 1987 for water and irrigating crops. The best time to come is around 7 am. You can see the fishers working their nets, farmers everywhere tending their fields, and lots of birds.

Places to Stay – bottom end

The once lively *Hôtel du Nord* near the autogare is closed, but in its place is the lively *Auberge Populaire*, a two-storey structure on the main drag across from the autogare and not well marked. The rooms, which cost CFA 2500, are a bit noisy because of the loud radio in the bar but they are reasonably spacious and clean with noisy fans, mosquito nets, interior showers and basins, and shared toilets. As at most hotels in town, water is available usually only in the morning. This hotel is very active, with lots of people at night in the spacious bar area. Food is cheap, eg CFA 200 a plate with about five choices of various African dishes, soft drinks for CFA 185 and large Sobbras for CFA 385.

The 10-room *Hôtel Tahiti* (☎ 55 03 09), which is about 300 metres north of the autogare and a block behind the Tagui petrol station on the main drag, is not so bad if all you want is a clean bed (CFA 2000 for an unventilated room with a decent bed and shared bath). There's no restaurant, and it's exceedingly quiet, almost morgue-like.

Four blocks further north and two blocks

Maison du Naba Kango

A short walk eastward past the market, the Maison du Naba Kango dates back to the days of the Yatenga kingdom, which was one of the ancient rivals before the colonial period of the Mossi kingdom centred in Ouaga. The compound, a traditional mud construction, consists of a number of small buildings, including various houses for the naba's 30 or so wives, several granaries, a small plain reception room for guests, and a fetish house inside which even the naba's children are forbidden to see.

It's the naba's power, not his wealth, that's important, so don't let the modesty of the compound fool you. The naba, who is king of the Yatengo province (which is mainly Mossi people), with over 30 wives and over 60 children, is a very powerful man and no ordinary village chief, second only to the naba of Ouaga. When the government makes important decisions which need public support, the chief ministers, sometimes as many as 10 in a single visit, are usually sent here first to consult him. For travellers, what's most interesting is the opportunity to meet him. To see the naba, you must bring a present; money is most appreciated. If he's unavailable, one of his young sons (*les princes*) who hang out around the compound will probably greet you. They're very friendly and will probably be delighted to show you around, including to where some of the local women make chapalo, the local millet brew. For their time, they'll expect a tip, of course. ∎

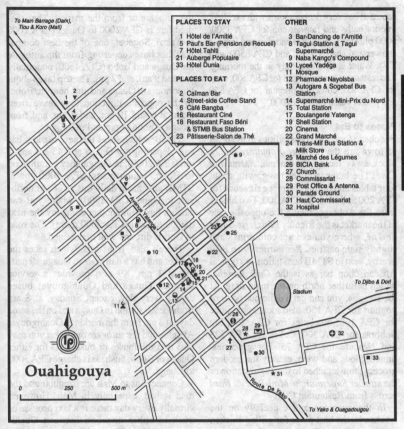

PLACES TO STAY

1 Hôtel de l'Amitié
5 Paul's Bar (Pension de Recueil)
7 Hôtel Tahiti
21 Auberge Populaire
33 Hôtel Dunia

PLACES TO EAT

2 Caïman Bar
4 Street-side Coffee Stand
6 Café Bangba
16 Restaurant Ciné
18 Restaurant Faso Béni & STMB Bus Station
23 Pâtisserie-Salon de Thé

OTHER

3 Bar-Dancing de l'Amitié
8 Tagui Station & Tagui Supermarché
9 Naba Kango's Compound
10 Lycée Yadéga
11 Mosque
12 Pharmacie Nayolsba
13 Autogare & Sogebaf Bus Station
14 Supermarché Mini-Prix du Nord
15 Total Station
17 Boulangerie Yatenga
19 Shell Station
20 Cinema
22 Grand Marché
24 Trans-Mif Bus Station & Milk Store
25 Marché des Légumes
26 BICIA Bank
27 Church
28 Commissariat
29 Post Office & Antenna
30 Parade Ground
31 Haut Commissariat
32 Hospital

Ouahigouya

0   250   500 m

west of the main drag you'll find *Pension de Recueil*, better known as Paul's Bar. Not well marked, this place is obvious at night because of the red light over the doorway. For the price, Paul's is unbeatable – CFA 1800 for a small room out the back with a double bed and firm mattress, clean sheets and shared basic showers (CFA 2300 with fan). You can have a drink in the shady courtyard (food is not served).

Places to Stay – top end

The city's top address is *Hôtel Dunia* (☎ 55 05 95), which charges CFA 5000/8000 plus

tax for rooms with fans/air-con and modern private baths (CFA 12,500 with TV) and attracts lots of foreigners. Run by a friendly Lebanese couple since the early 1970s, this homy, two-storey place has a sitting room with a satellite TV, a small pool which is often empty, and a shady area in front which is pleasant for a meal or drink. The food here is the best in town. The Dunia is on the south-eastern side of town on the Route de Señanega, a 20-minute walk from the centre.

A notch down is the government-owned *Hôtel de l'Amitié* (☎ 55 05 21/2), a large, three-storey place, one km north-west of the centre. It has very decent rooms with excellent interior baths and fans/air-con for CFA 3500/6000 plus tax (CFA 2500 with fan and interior shower and shared toilet, and CFA 8500 with TV). Water is available only in the morning. The restaurant has riz pilipili for CFA 300, soup for CFA 400, couscous oriental for CFA 850 and poulet yassa for CFA 1000.

Places to Eat

For cheap food, two possibilities in the heart of town are the *Auberge Populaire* and, a block away facing the cinema, *Restaurant Ciné*. The latter is rather basic, with about four tables and ordinary fare, eg riz sauce for CFA 200 and steak for CFA 300. Two blocks from the Auberge, facing the opposite side of the market is the friendly *Pâtisserie-Salon de Thé*, where you can get cold drinks and slightly stale pastries. *Restaurant Faso Béni* nearby, next to STMB bus station, is a typical African chop bar as is the *Café Bangba*, which is further north on the main drag. At the Bangba, you can get a delicious bowl of yoghurt for CFA 150, also local apple juice for CFA 160, omelettes for CFA 200, big Sobbras for CFA 300, Cokes for CFA 225 and Nescafé for CFA 75. For groceries, tinned goods and wine, etc, try the modern grocery store attached to the Tagui station or the smaller *Supermarché Mini-Prix du Nord* across from Restaurant Ciné.

In the evenings and especially on the weekends, the best place for grilled chicken and brochettes is the *Caïman Bar* which is on the northern edge of town, just behind Hôtel de l'Amitié. This spacious, largely open-air place is mainly for drinks, however, and on weekend nights most of the 70-odd chairs are taken, even at midnight. The ambience is dark and relaxing and a bit up-market. On Saturdays, it's a good place to hang out until the nearby *Bar-Dancing de l'Amitié*, which is open only on Saturday nights, livens up, typically around midnight. It has a large open-air dance floor, lots of chairs, loud recorded music (entrance CFA 300).

Getting There & Away

Virtually all *cars* and other buses leave from the autogare or from the market. The standard fare is CFA 2000 to Ouaga (CFA 1000 to Yako). Sogebaf, one of the best companies, has buses departing from the autogare for Ouaga and Bobo (CFA 4500) punctually at 6 and 9 am, and 2 pm. The trip takes about three hours to Ouaga and nine hours to Bobo. In the opposite direction they leave from Bobo at 6 and 10 am, and 7 pm, and from Ouaga at noon, 4 pm and midnight.

STMB, which faces the new market, has *cars* departing for Ouaga at 6.45 am and 2 pm (CFA 2000); in Ouaga, they continue on to Bobo, which costs CFA 3000 more. STMB also has a daily bus at 11 am northeast to Djibo (CFA 1500), where you can catch a bus with another company the next day on to Dori (CFA 3000 more). The road to Dori is dirt and well maintained.

There's also Trans-Mif, which faces the market and has a daily *car* to Ouaga, departing at 1 pm. X9 also provides a service between Ouaga and Ouahigouya; buses depart every day, except Sunday, at 8 am from the X9 station in Ouaga and on the same days at 3 pm from the market in Ouahigouya. At or around the autogare or market you may also find minibuses or bush taxis for either Ouaga or Bobo; bush taxis charge CFA 3000 to Ouaga.

Connections to Mali are irregular and the road is bad, especially in Mali. However, virtually every day there is a taxi brousse or truck in either direction between Ouahigouya and Koro. The road is pretty rough and there's very little traffic on it and you may have to wait all day for the vehicle to fill up and then sleep at the border, which can make the trip slow and miserable. If you can't find a vehicle at the autogare to Koro, you might find one headed for Tiou and the border. The chances of finding a vehicle are less during the peak of the rainy season (especially August) when the sandy road occasionally becomes impassable. The road is rough to Tiou (36 km), then good to the border (25 km), then bad again to Koro (30 km). A truck or minibus to Koro is CFA 2000 plus CFA 250 for a rucksack. If you leave on a Friday you can enjoy the market in Koro (Saturday).

KAYA

Kaya is 98 km north-east of Ouaga and is a potential stopover on the way to Dori and Gorom-Gorom. **Market** day is every three days and it's a rather low-key affair, with a wide selection of fabrics and leather items in addition to meats, vegetables, etc. Places to visit include the Swiss-funded **Morija reha-bilitation centre** in town, the **Marché du Bétail** on the road to Dori (three km from the centre), the tanners and weavers, including Sambarij, perhaps the most well-known artisan du cuir (ask around the market for someone to guide you where they work) and **Lac Dem**, 16 km north-west of town via a rough dirt road (look for a sign near the market). Those without vehicles can try renting a mobylette at the market.

Places to Stay & Eat

The cheapest place is the friendly *Mission Catholique* on the north-western outskirts of town toward Kougoussi. It has two unventilated rooms and showers for CFA 2000. For about the same price you can also stay at the *Relais Touristique* (or Petit Auberge Populaire), which is a group of well-marked small buildings on the eastern side of town on the road to Dori. The rooms are nothing special, with no fans or mosquito nets, but there's a good breeze from the nearby lake. Even if you don't stay here, the Relais is the best place in town for a cold drink or meal as the hotel's terrace offers a scenic view of the nearby dam. Decent cheap food includes brochettes (CFA 100) and fries (CFA 400).

The best hotels are the new 20-room *Hôtel Salmatenga*, on the city's southern edge near the police post, and, more expensive, the new *Hôtel Zinoogo*, which has the best rooms and public bathrooms in town. It also has one of the city's top restaurants; another is the *Mon Chou* on the road east to Dori. Other places to eat include *La Paillote* on the road south to Ouaga and *Resto Les Amis* in town. For cheaper African food try the market area.

Getting There & Away

The most interesting way to get here from Ouaga is on the train. It has only 2nd-class compartments and leaves Ouaga on Tuesdays and Saturdays at 7.45 am, returning the same day. Otherwise, take a minibus. They leave throughout the day from sun up to sun down and cost CFA 1500. Air Sannatenga Kaya has nine departures daily until 7 pm; Ouedraogo Adama is another company. In Ouaga, they leave from several blocks east of the train station. X9 has a bus service on Tuesdays and Saturdays, departing Ouaga at 8 am and returning the same day. On Mondays, Wednesdays and Saturdays, you can catch the X9 bus to Dori; it passes through Kaya. Otherwise, take a bush taxi; they leave from the gare routière in Ouaga.

If you're headed to Ouahigouya, you can take a minibus every day from the gare routière headed in that direction, passing through Kongoussi, which is a small tranquil town with no electricity or tourists and only one place to stay, *Hôtel Major*.

DORI

Some 261 km north-east of Ouaga via Kaya, Dori has a small **market** every day. It doesn't rank with the one in Gorom-Gorom but it's still interesting and all the various ethnic groups of the region (Peul, Songhaï, Tuareg etc) can be seen here. Also check the two women's co-operatives for hand-woven fabrics, eg tablecloths, napkins, aprons and children's items. Dori blankets are available at the Liptako co-operative for between CFA 3000 and CFA 10,000, depending on the size and colours, as well as at the market. At the latter you can get a nine-panel blanket for about CFA 4500.

About 35 km south of Dori on the road to Kaya you'll pass through **Bani**, a predominantly Muslim settlement which is famous for its exquisite mosques built by highly skilled artisans from Mali. It's definitely worth stopping to check out these cathedral-like banco (mud) structures (nine in all).

Places to Stay & Eat – bottom end

One of the cheapest places to stay is the *Centre d'Hébergement Populaire* (or Auberge Populaire), which is on the northern

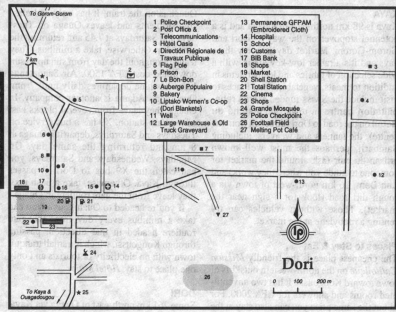

To Gorom-Gorom

7 km

1	Police Checkpoint
2	Post Office & Telecommunications
3	Hôtel Oasis
4	Diréction Régionale de Travaux Publique
5	Flag Pole
6	Prison
7	Le Bon-Bon
8	Auberge Populaire
9	Bakery
10	Liptako Women's Co-op (Dori Blankets)
11	Well
12	Large Warehouse & Old Truck Graveyard
13	Permanence GFPAM (Embroidered Cloth)
14	Hospital
15	School
16	Customs
17	BIB Bank
18	Shops
19	Market
20	Shell Station
21	Total Station
22	Cinema
23	Shops
24	Grande Mosquée
25	Police Checkpoint
26	Football Field
27	Melting Pot Café

To Kaya & Ouagadougou

Dori

0   100   200 m

BURKINA FASO

side of town on the road to Gorom-Gorom, about 200 metres from the market. It has electricity, reasonably clean rooms for CFA 1000, shared showers and a bar. Another very basic place is the *Save the Children Guesthouse*. For cheap food, you can't do better than the *Melting Pot Café*. It has riz sauce for CFA 150, spaghetti for CFA 150, yoghurt for CFA 125 and large beers for CFA 250. For inexpensive grilled meats, the best place is a stand in the centre next to the customs office. *Café des Amis* is good for coffee, tea and other drinks.

Places to Stay & Eat – top end
Many travellers like *Le Bon-Bon* (☎ 66 00 44), a friendly homy place closer to the market. Sometimes called Chez Jean, it is a small guesthouse with a sitting room, dining area and three comfortable guest rooms with twin beds and ceiling fans. Singles/doubles including breakfast cost CFA 5000/7500 plus tax. You can sleep on the terrace for CFA

2000 or pitch one of the hotel's tents. A tasty spaghetti dinner costs about CFA 600. If you call in advance to make a reservation, they will have a delicious dinner waiting for you.

The top address is the *Hôtel Oasis*, which was built by the Italians to house its road construction workers and has been converted into a hotel. The cabins, which cost CFA 14,000 plus taxes, have sitting areas, air-con, fans and refrigerators. The electricity is cut off after midnight, so they can still get hot. It also has a pinball machine and a good restaurant with cold drinks and moderately priced meals, eg CFA 350 for riz sauce and CFA 1000 for steak and chips.

Getting There & Away
Bush taxis/minibuses cost CFA 4500/3000 from Ouaga. They leave every morning from the gare routière in Ouaga. X9 buses leave Ouaga on Mondays, Wednesdays and Saturdays at 8 pm, returning the following day.

GOROM-GOROM

Of all the towns in the north-east, Gorom-Gorom is probably the most interesting. The biggest attraction is the Thursday **market** which gets into full swing around 11 am.

Places to Stay & Eat

Le Campement Hôtelier, run by the villagers, consists of a series of well-constructed African-style mud huts that fit perfectly into the environment. They are reasonably comfortable and have toilets, plus there's a bar and restaurant. A double costs CFA 3000. You can also get food here, eg CFA 1000 for spaghetti, but it's also possible to get food in town. If you want to take excursions, ask the campement staff; they can usually make arrangements. The grubby *L'Auberge Populaire* in the centre may still be in operation.

Getting There & Away

The road from Dori is in good condition. X9 buses run the Ouaga-Gorom route, leaving Ouaga at the X9 bus station on Mondays, Wednesdays and Saturdays at 8 am, and Gorom-Gorom the next days at the same hour. The cost is CFA 3000. You can also take a bush taxi/minibus from Ouaga; they cost CFA 6000/4000 and leave virtually every day from the gare routière in Ouaga.

MARKOYÉ

Markoyé is 45 km north-east of Gorom-Gorom on a sandy track towards the Niger border and can be visited as a day trip from Gorom-Gorom. The attraction here is the Monday camel and cattle **market**. If you're hitchhiking, that's about the only day you can count on catching a ride.

Gorom-Gorom Market

The Gorom-Gorom market is unquestionably the most colourful market in Burkina if not the entire Sahel and may be the country's largest as well. There are all kinds of interesting things for sale – African cotton prints, an amazing variety of beads, and leather products including sandals, knife covers and bags. You'll also find food products used in the desert, including dates, *lait caillé* which is curdled milk, sweet-tasting *tamaré*, which is a red bean-like fruit that grows in the wild and is sold in the form of a ball and used by the nomads as a thirst quencher, and *gib-gib*, which is a large rock-like sweet made from crushed seeds. Don't forget to check the animal market on the edge of town next to a pond; camels, goats, sheep, donkeys and cattle are all on sale here.

It's the interaction of the numerous Sahelian and Saharan ethnic groups, however, that most makes this market fascinating – the Tuareg proudly on their camels plus their ancient slaves the Bella, the Peul herders and the Songhaï farmers, each in their own groups, wearing their traditional garb and gossiping, trading their wares and meeting old friends. The combination of indigo, neon yellow and red turbans, colourful boubous and beads and silver coins in the women's elaborate hairdos combine to make this a colourful spectacle.

Trying to distinguish the various ethnic groups can be quite intriguing. The Tuareg men are easily identified by their proud attitude and long flowing robes *(boubous)*, the indigo cloth wrapped around their heads and the elaborate silver swords by their sides. The Bella, both men and women, usually wear black or grey gowns with wide belts of richly decorated leather. Most elaborately dressed of all are the Peul women. Their hairdos, for example, are far more complex than those of the Bella and are usually braided and decorated at the ends with tiny chains and colourful beads. Most amazing of all are their huge earrings, which come in many different forms but usually consist of beads or, in rare cases, pure gold. An incredibly colourful dress of potentially any combination of hues completes the outfit. ■

Cape Verde

The Galapagos Islands were not the only place that provided Charles Darwin with the inspiration for his theory of evolution. Cape Verde (Cabo Verde) played a role too. Only the fit survive here. By some measures it's the driest country in Africa; most of these islands receive rainfall only once or twice a year. When Darwin visited the islands over one hundred years ago, he wrote:

The island would generally be considered as very uninteresting; but to anyone accustomed only to an English landscape, the novel aspect of an utterly sterile land possesses a grandeur which more vegetation might spoil.

But there's more to Cape Verde than the environment. The people, for instance, are like none on the continent because they look and act more Portuguese than African. Don't be surprised by the absence of African tribal life or umpteen local languages. There are Mediterranean-style houses with verandas upstairs, plazas around orchestra stands, cobbled streets, *vino verde* with your Portuguese meals, distinctive fast-paced music with Latin rhythm as well as African inspiration, and a relatively well-educated *mestizo* (mixed race) people – almost all with relatives in the USA.

Cape Verde may not be action-packed, but if the idea of islands with a Portuguese ambience and a lunar setting seems intriguing, you'll be delighted with a visit here.

Facts about the Country

HISTORY

The history of Cape Verde is dominated by three overriding facts: there were no people of any sort on the islands when the Portuguese first arrived; the environment has become increasingly fragile over the centuries, largely due to the impact of people and overgrazing; and it's further from the African mainland and

closer to the Americas than any other African country. It's hardly surprising, therefore, that Cape Verde developed along lines somewhat different from the rest of Africa.

Early History

When Portuguese mariners first landed on the Cape Verde islands in 1456, the islands were barren of people but not of vegetation. Seeing the islands today, you may find it hard to imagine that they were sufficiently *verde* (green) in those years to entice the Portuguese to return six years later to the island of Santiago (São Tiago) to found Ribeira Grande (now Cidade Velha), the first European city in the tropics, and plant vineyards.

Cape Verde

0   50   100 km

century was another blow. Cape Verde's heyday was over.

It was then, in 1832, that Charles Darwin passed by. The landscape had become the antithesis of the Galapagos. His description in *The Voyage of the Beagle* still holds true:

A single green leaf can scarcely be discovered over wide tracts of the lava plains; yet flocks of goats, together with a few cows, contrive to exist. It rains very seldom, but during a short portion of the year heavy torrents fall, and immediately afterwards a light vegetation springs out of every crevice. This soon withers; and upon such naturally formed hay the animals live. It had not now rained for an entire year. When the island was discovered, the immediate neighbourhood of Porto Praya was clothed with trees, the reckless destruction of which has caused here, as at St Helena, and at some of the Canary islands, almost entire sterility. The broad, flat-bottomed valleys, many of which serve during a few days only in the season as water-courses, are clothed with thickets of leafless bushes. Few living creatures inhabit these valleys.

Around this time, Cape Verdeans started emigrating to New England. This was a popular destination because whales abounded in the waters near Cape Verde, and as early as 1810 whaling ships from Massachusetts and Rhode Island recruited crews from the islands of Brava and Fogo.

At the end of the 19th century, with the advent of the ocean liner, the island's position astride Atlantic shipping lanes made Cape Verde an ideal location for resupplying ships with fuel (imported coal), water and livestock. The deep, protected harbour at Mindelo on São Vicente became an important commercial centre.

However, the droughts continued. During the first half of the 20th century, the following percentages of the population were wiped out: 15% in 1900-03, 16% in 1920-22, 15% in 1940-43 and 15% in 1946-48. Starvation was becoming a way of life. The Portuguese still did nothing, neither helping to build water retention dams nor taking other measures to cope with the droughts.

Working on the plantations was no easy task, so almost immediately the Portuguese brought slaves from the West African coast to do the hard labour. The islands also became a convenient base for ships transporting slaves to Europe and the Americas.

The wine exported to Portugal was of excellent quality and added to the islands' prosperity. However, it was this very prosperity that attracted pirates who occasionally attacked the towns. England's Sir Francis Drake sacked Ribeira Grande in 1585.

Droughts

Cape Verde continued to prosper, but in 1747 the islands were hit with the first of many droughts that have plagued them ever since. The situation was made worse by people chopping down trees and goats destroying the ground vegetation which provided moisture. Three major droughts in the late 18th and 19th centuries resulted in well over 100,000 people starving to death. The proportion of the population that died in each was incredible: 44% in 1773-76, 42% in 1830-33 and 40% in 1863-66. The Portuguese government sent almost no relief during any of the droughts. The decline of the lucrative slave trade in the mid-19th

Independence

Although the Cape Verdeans were treated badly by their colonial masters, they fared slightly better than Africans in the other Portuguese colonies because of their lighter skin. A small minority received an education; Cape Verde was the first Portuguese colony to have a school for higher education. By the time of independence, a quarter of the population could read, compared to 5% in Portuguese Guinea (now Guinea-Bissau).

This ultimately backfired when the literate Cape Verdeans became aware of the pressures building up on the mainland for independence and started their own joint movement for independence with the natives of Guinea-Bissau. A Cape Verdean intellectual, Amilcar Cabral, founded the African Party for Independence in Guinea and Cape Verde (PAIGC) in 1956, later renamed the Partido Africano da Independencia de Cabo Verde (PAICV). Because the Cape Verdeans were better educated than the Guineans, they naturally took over the leadership.

But the Portuguese dictator Salazar wasn't about to give up his colonies as easily as the British and French had given up theirs. Consequently, from the early 1960s, the people of Cape Verde and Guinea-Bissau fought one of the longest African liberation wars. (For more details see the Guinea-Bissau chapter.) In fact, most of the fighting took place in the jungles of Guinea-Bissau because the liberation movement simply wasn't as strong in Cape Verde. Also, middle-class Cape Verdeans were not keen to dissociate themselves from Portugal, and the islands were more isolated. Finally, in 1975, Cape Verde gained independence from Portugal. For five years afterwards, Cape Verde and Guinea-Bissau (which had gained its own independence in 1974) talked about a union of the two countries, but a 1980 coup in Guinea-Bissau that deposed the president (of Cape Verdean origin) put an end to that.

In 1985, Cape Verde witnessed its seventeenth consecutive drought year and its thirty-first in the 20th century. There was only a third as many cattle as there had been in 1969. Only Santo Antão island remained green enough to warrant the islands' original name. The following year Cape Verde had heavy rains, ending its longest and harshest drought ever. This time, however, people had not died. The USA and Portugal made up most of the 85% food deficit and are continuing to do so.

Cape Verde Today
Since 1986, the weather has continued to be kinder and crop yields have doubled. Whether the increased rains are merely a freak accident, nobody knows. During the last century, the norm has been 100 to 200 mm of rain between late August and early October, followed by a 10-month drought. Survival is still the name of the game, and coping with the elements the only strategy. There's a gamble in everything Cape Verdeans do. If farmers plant before the rains and the rains are minimal, they can lose everything.

One of the things you'll remember most about your trip to Cape Verde is the strength of the people's attachment to their homeland. Even if the droughts return, Cape Verdeans aren't about to desert these islands. True, there's still a trickle of people leaving the islands every year, but if you talk to some of the older people you'll find some who have spent most of their lives abroad, yet returned here to retire. Since 1991, this peaceful island has become a flourishing democracy and started opening its economy, resulting in increased private investments from abroad and a higher growth rate.

GEOGRAPHY
The Cape Verde islands are in the Atlantic Ocean, 620 km west of Mauritania. There are 10 major islands (nine of them inhabited) and five islets, all of volcanic origin. The capital city is Praia on Santiago, and almost half of the population live on this island. The island's interior is mountainous and is far more interesting than that of São Vicente, which has the country's major harbour and second-largest city, Mindelo.

Two other important islands are Santo Antão, which is easily accessible from Mindelo and has the highest rainfall, the greenest environment and the second-highest population, and Fogo, with the islands' highest peak, Mt Fogo (2839 metres).

Sal Island (population 6000), as the name suggests, produces salt – enough for export. Flat, sandy and visually uninteresting, Sal Island has the major international airport, the country's top hotel and many km of sunny white beaches. Brava, famous as an important whaling centre in the 19th century, is the smallest of the inhabited islands. Few people live there, but it is one of the most picturesque of the islands. Another scenic island is São Nicolau, which is also worth visiting, but the two remaining islands, Boa Vista and Maio, are flat and boring.

Soil erosion is a major environmental problem. The islands' steep slopes, torrential rains, rapid water run-off and strong winds cause extensive erosion. The flash flood in 1984 on Santiago Island, for example, swept away two major bridges near Tarrafal and Porto Formosa and carried precious topsoil right into the sea. The inhabitants add to the problem by cultivating in steep and arid areas and pulling up vegetation by the roots for fuel.

Since 1976, the country has been making heroic efforts to combat these problems. Take a trip into the countryside and you'll see the evidence – some 15,000 contour ditches to slow water run-off and 2500 km of check-dams for controlling streams. It's working, and the people are building more. You may think these small dams are for irrigation too, but they're not. Pumping water would require resources way beyond Cape Verde's means.

Cape Verde also has the best reafforestation programme in Africa, so in rural areas you'll probably see new trees, particularly if you go to Mindelo by plane. Local experts and research by international organisations have produced a type of acacia which is well adapted to the conditions of the islands. Over 50,000 hectares have been planted since independence, and the country is well on target for planting 115,000 hectares by the year 2000. As a result, the country is nearing self-sufficiency in wood fuel for the first time in its history.

CLIMATE
Rainfall is not evenly distributed. On the western slopes of Fogo, for example, there is sufficient rainfall to grow coffee. In most areas, however, rainfall is typically limited to several downpours between late August and early October. The rest of the year is marked by gusty winds and, particularly during the harmattan season between December and February, by low visibility caused by dust from the Sahara.

Cape Verde has the lowest temperatures of any country in West Africa. The hottest period is from July to October, with temperatures reaching 27°C in September. Due to ocean currents, the sea is also considerably chillier than along the West African coast. From December to March, you'll need a heavy sweater; during the rest of the year, a windcheater is advisable.

GOVERNMENT
Politically, the country is a stable democracy and has an outstanding human rights record and no political prisoners. The quarrel with Guinea-Bissau after the 1980 coup has almost been forgotten. In early 1991, Cape Verde held its first-ever direct presidential and multiparty parliamentary elections and the country's astute president, Aristides Pereira, was defeated by Antonio Mascarenhas Monteiro, a former Supreme Court judge. Real day-to-day power, however, resides in the new prime minister, Carlos Veiga, a Portuguese-trained lawyer who was previously president of the country's Bar Association and now heads the 69-member People's National Assembly, which is elected every five years. The next elections will be in January 1996.

Veiga's party, the Movimento Para a Democracia (MPD), which was created less than a year before the elections, was swept into power with more than 70% of the vote on a platform of a more market-orientated economy. In effect, this wasn't so different from what the defeated PAICV was advocating and had already begun implementing. This smooth transition of governments is regarded as a model for peaceful and democratic change in Africa. Today, Veiga's government is encouraging foreign and joint ventures in fishing, light industry and tourism, and it's having some success as there is now considerable private sector involvement in construction.

ECONOMY
Even though only 10% of the land is arable and over two-thirds of its food has to be imported, the country and the people are doing relatively well. Indeed, based on the UN's quality of life index, Cape Verde comes

out on top in West Africa. Health standards and the level of literacy are the highest in West Africa; almost 60% of the state budget is spent on health and education. From 1975 to 1990, life expectancy leapt from 46 years to 67 years, third only to Mauritius and the Seychelles in Africa and 50% higher than the sub-Sahara African average of 51.8 years.

Cape Verde has the most successful food-for-work programme in Africa, maybe the world. Roughly a third of the economically active rural population, mainly farmers, are employed this way. Many others are employed in the transport services sector, which accounts for over two-thirds of the country's foreign earnings. This stems from Cape Verde's strategic position as a refuelling and servicing point for international air and maritime traffic, including South African Airways flights to the USA and Europe.

Cape Verde is relatively well off, even though GDP per capita is only about US$300. This is because for every US$1 earned at home, Cape Verdeans get another US$1 from relatives abroad, and another US$1 from foreign aid, resulting in a GNP per capita of US$890. In the last 100 years, over half a million Cape Verdeans have emigrated. There are as many Cape Verdeans living in the USA as there are in Cape Verde and as many again have gone to Portugal and other European countries. The remittances they send back are higher than the GDP itself and cover over 95% of the commercial deficit, which in 1990 was over US$100 million.

Cape Verde also receives more per capita foreign aid (primarily from the USA, Portugal and the International Development Association) than any country in the world except Israel; it is the highest per capita recipient of US grain in Africa. With real growth now averaging 5.5% a year, the country is on a roll and is even attempting to attract tourists by building hotels and tourist facilities on Sal, an island with an international airport and limitless sunshine.

POPULATION & PEOPLE

Cape Verde has a population of 407,000 and one of the lowest growth rates in Africa. It is also the only country in West Africa with a primarily *mestizo* (mixed European and African descent) population. The arrival of White people in significant numbers dates back five centuries, long before colonial settlement on the African mainland. The intermixing of the Portuguese settlers and their African slaves began early and forged a distinct Cape Verdean nationality with its own highly individual culture.

CULTURE

The vestiges of Portuguese culture are much more evident than those of African culture (although this is less true on Santiago Island, which has a significant number of people of African ancestry). The food is basically Portuguese, but their *moradeira* music is distinctive – Latin in rhythm but with a different pace, usually much faster and good for dancing.

RELIGION

About 80% of the people are Roman Catholics. At the time of independence in 1975, the church was the single largest landowner in the country. Subsequent land reform has reduced these holdings but the church remains a powerful entity in the country.

LANGUAGE

Portuguese is the official language. People also speak Crioulo, an Africanised Creole Portuguese. It is slightly different from the Creole spoken in Guinea-Bissau, and is not spoken nearly as much. See that chapter for expressions in Crioulo.

Facts for the Visitor

VISAS & EMBASSIES
Cape Verde Visas

Visas are required by everyone. Getting one is easy in the USA. Simply mail your passport, one photo and US$13 to the Cape Verde embassy in Washington. Visas are issued routinely for stays of 30 days and more if you ask. In Lisbon, the Cape Verde embassy processes visa applications in 24 hours and requires only one photo and US$6. If you are flying into Cape Verde direct from Europe, you can get a visa at the airport on arrival. You need a photo and from US$15 to US$20. In West Africa, Cape Verde has an embassy in Dakar (see the Senegal chapter for details). If there's no Cape Verdean embassy where you are, try the nearest Portuguese embassy – it may have authority to process applications.

Visa Extensions
For visa extensions, see the Ministry of Foreign Affairs at Praça 10 de Maio in Praia.

Cape Verde Embassies
France (consulate) 92 blvd Malesherbes, 75008 Paris (☎ (1) 42-25-63-31)
Germany Fritz-Schaeffer-Strasse 5, 53113 Bonn (☎ (0228) 26 50 02)
USA 3415 Massachusetts Ave, NW, Washington, DC 20007 (☎ (202) 965-6820)

Cape Verde also has embassies in The Hague, Lisbon, Moscow and Rome, and consulates in Basel, Boston, Geneva, Hamburg, Las Palmas, Luxembourg, Rotterdam, Stuttgart and Vienna.

Other African Visas
Senegal The embassy, open weekdays from 8 am to 4 pm, requires 440 CVE and two photos for one-month visas – issued in 24 to 48 hours.
Other Countries The French embassy in Praia issues visas in 24 hours to Burkina Faso, Côte d'Ivoire and Togo.

Foreign Embassies
See the Praia and Mindelo Information sections for details of diplomatic missions in those places.

DOCUMENTS
The only document you'll need is your passport. Proof of yellow fever vaccination is not officially required if you are arriving direct from the USA or Europe, but may be required if you are coming from the African mainland. Renting cars is less expensive on Cape Verde than in any other West African country so consider bringing your driving licence and credit cards. An International Driving Permit (IDP) is not required.

CUSTOMS
There is no restriction on the import of local or foreign currencies, but you may not export more than what you declare on arrival, or the equivalent of about US$100 if you don't declare. Customs formalities, however, are very relaxed, so you'll rarely have problems.

MONEY
UK£1 = 140 CVE
US$1 = 80 CVE

The unit of currency in the country is the Cape Verde escudo (CVE). It's not a hard currency, but there's virtually no black market. It is also one of the most stable currencies in Africa. Over the last 10 years, the exchange rate with the US dollar, for example, has changed very little. Banks accept travellers' cheques denominated in most major currencies, although US dollars are most easily dealt with.

If you arrive on a weekend, the Hotel Praia Mar in Praia will change US dollars or CFA for escudos even if you are not staying there. The hotel will also accept American Express travellers' cheques. Banks for changing money are the Banco de Cabo Verde and Banco Nacional Ultramarino.

BUSINESS HOURS & HOLIDAYS
Business hours are weekdays from 8 am to noon and 2.30 to 6 pm, and Saturday from 8 am to noon. Government offices are open on weekdays from 8 am to noon.

Banking hours are weekdays from 8.30 am to 2 pm; closed weekends.

Public Holidays
1 January, 20 January (National Heroes' Day), Good Friday, 1 May, 19 May, 1 June (Youth Day), 5 July (Independence), 15 August (Assumption Day), 1 November (All Saints' Day), 25 December.

POST & TELECOMMUNICATIONS
The postal service is very reliable, including the poste restante.

The country has no telephone area codes. There are telephones for international calls at the post offices. Calling Europe and the USA is no problem. The cost is about 400 CVE and 520 CVE per minute, respectively.

CAPE VERDE

There are telex and fax machines at many of the post offices and major hotels.

PHOTOGRAPHY

No permit is required and you should not encounter any problems. Nevertheless, avoid photographing military installations.

HEALTH

A yellow fever vaccination is required if you have been in an infected area within the previous six days. Malaria is not a major problem on the islands.

The hospital in Praia on Rua Martines Pidjiguita has Cuban doctors and is not too bad, but the one in Mindelo on Avenida 5 de Julho is definitely better.

Two of the better pharmacies are Farmacia Higiene at Praça 12 de Setembro in Praia and Farmacia Higiene on Rua Libertadores d'Africa in Mindelo.

DANGERS & ANNOYANCES

Praia is the safest capital city in West Africa. Mindelo and the other major towns are

---

CAPE VERDE

Cape Verdean Literature

While Cape Verde has the smallest population of any country in West Africa, its literary tradition is one of the richest, diverse and most developed in the region. The rough seas that separate the islands have resulted in marked linguistic, literary and cultural differences between them. In São Vicente, for example, the local Creole language includes some English and French words, while in Santiago the language has a stronger African influence. Some writers, such as Kaoberdiano Dambara, write mainly in Crioulo while others, like Onésima Silveira, write in Portuguese, the dominant literary tongue in Cape Verde today.

Prior to independence, a major theme in Cape Verdean writing was the longing for liberation. As far back as 1936, a small clique of mixed-race intellectuals founded a literary journal, *Claridade*, which lasted until 1960. Their aim was to express a growing Cape Verdean identity including an attempt, by using Crioulo in some of their writings, to elevate this so-called 'pigeon' (pidgin) language to one of literary merit. Since independence, the journal has been replaced by *Raizes*, which has also helped revive both Portuguese and Crioulo writing.

The dominant themes of the local literature have been the sea and the oppression of the slave trade. The poet, Jorge Barbosa, became well known with his publication of *Arquipélago*, which is laden with melancholic reflections on the sea and longings for liberation. Expressing the contradictory desires of many Cape Verdeans to leave a country with a declining economy and to establish a national identity, he wrote in 'Poema do Mar': 'The demand at every hour, to go is brought to us by the sea, the despairing hope for the long journey, and yet always be forced to stay'. *Two Languages, Two Friends – A Memory* by Jorge Barbosa (ICDL, Praia, 1986).

Racial discrimination is a principal theme of more recent writings. In *Judgment of the Black Man* (from *Poems of Black Africa* edited by Wole Soyinka; Heinemann, Oxford, 1987) Dambara writes:

> The white man looked him in the face
> my black brother did not stir
> The white man shouted, roared, beat and kicked him
> my black brother did not tremble
> In his eyes there kindled flames
> of rage, of dried tears, of force
> My black brother did not stir
> did not answer, did not tremble
> In his steady eyes there kindled the flame
> of a force which only the black man knows

If you're interested in Cape Verdean literature, check the Instituto Caboverdiano do Livro (ICDL) and the French Cultural Centre in Praia. Publications in English on Cape Verde in addition to those above include *Cape Verde; Politics, Economics and Society* by Colm Foy (Pinter, London, 1988); *Atlantic Islands* by T Duncan (University of Chicago Press, London, 1972); and *The Fortunate Isles* by Basil Davidson (Century Hutchinson, London, 1989). ■

equally safe. Wallet snatchings (rare) are about as serious as crimes get.

ACCOMMODATION

Cape Verde's selection of hotels is limited both in number and range of quality, but finding a room is generally not a problem because so few visitors come here and room prices are low. All of the major towns on the islands have at least one place to stay, but minor towns generally do not. If you're caught for a night in a place without accommodation, unlike other parts of West Africa where the village chief will find you a place to stay, in Cape Verde you'll have to work through ordinary citizens.

FOOD

Cape Verdean food is basically Portuguese, but some dishes are unique to the islands. One of the most unusual and delicious is *pastel com diablo dentro* (pastry with the devil inside) – a mix of fresh tuna, onions and tomatoes, wrapped in a pastry blended from boiled potatoes and corn flour, deep fried and served hot. If you come across these, don't miss trying them!

Soups too are popular in Cape Verde. One of the most common is *coldo de peixe* (fish soup) which has a bit of everything – fresh fish, green bananas, tomatoes, cabbage, potatoes, sweet potatoes and onions, seasoned with numerous spices and thickened with manioc flour. Or try *caldo de camarâo* (shrimp soup).

Other local specialities include *bananas enroladas* (ripe bananas wrapped in pastry and deep fried) and *manga de conserva* (an unsweetened chutney-like concoction served on occasion as a condiment).

ENTERTAINMENT

Entertainment on the islands is extremely limited, and available only in Praia and Mindelo. It consists of a few bars and nightclubs, several cinemas, and in joining the young in promenading around the plazas on an evening and weekend.

Getting There & Away

AIR

From Europe, there are daily flights from Lisbon (US$1376 excursion fare), as well as direct flights three times a week from Amsterdam, twice a week from Frankfurt, and once a week from Paris and Moscow. You can also fly direct from New York and Johannesburg three times a week on South African Airways, and from Buenos Aires and Rio de Janeiro.

From West Africa there are four flights a week from Dakar (CFA 85,900/US$120), two a week from Banjul and one flight (on Wednesdays) from Bissau.

All international flights except those from Dakar and Bissau arrive at Sal Island; TACV offers frequent onward flights to Praia and Mindelo.

Making reservations for flights between Praia and Dakar is hard (or impossible) unless it's done in person. This is only a problem if you are flying direct from the USA or Europe to Cape Verde. If you plan on spending a few days in Dakar everything can be arranged there.

Returning from Praia to Dakar, you'll have the same problem. When you arrive in Praia go (immediately) to the TACV or Air

CAPE VERDE

Cape Verdian Shrimp Soup

Slice two green (unripe) bananas in rounds, and soak them in just enough water to cover them with one teaspoon of salt. Drain the bananas after 15 minutes. Meanwhile, wash 1½ kg of fresh unshelled shrimp (with heads, if possible), and cook them for six to eight minutes in two cups of boiling water with one teaspoon of salt. Once cooked, peel off the shells and remove the heads. Keep the heads and cooking water (stock) to one side. Sautè one large sliced onion until golden brown, then stir in two large cloves of crushed garlic, three medium chopped tomatoes, three chopped chilli peppers, and add the shrimp. Blend or sieve the shrimp heads and add them to the mixture with the stock. Finally add four potatoes chopped into chunks, and the drained bananas, and cook for 20 minutes, or until everything is tender. Accompanied with rice on the side, this will feed from six to eight people. ■

Senegal office to make a reservation. They may tell you that there are no seats for the next two weeks. This is not unusual because the flights are almost always full. So your one-week trip could easily turn into a two-week trip or more. During Mardi Gras, count on staying a month unless someone has previously reserved and paid for you.

Still, if TACV tells you the plane is full, it's a half-truth because five of the 45 or so seats on most flights are reserved for the government. TACV can't sell any of the five until it knows how many will be used, usually a day or two before the flight leaves. So it's not unusual for several spaces to become available in that time.

SEA

There is a boat that connects Dakar and Praia once a month but don't expect to save much money by taking it. The round-trip fare for deck class is about the same as the round-trip excursion ticket on the plane. In Praia, enquire at the Agencia Nacional de Viagems in the centre on Avenida 5 de Julho near the US embassy. In Dakar, enquire at the port.

There are regular freighter connections between Mindelo and the Canary Islands, Portugal and Holland (Rotterdam). From the USA, Delta Lines carries the food shipments from New Orleans, but there's nothing on a fixed schedule and it'll probably cost you as much as the plane. If you are very lucky, you might even find a yacht headed towards the USA or the Caribbean. Most of those leaving from the West African coast stop here.

Getting Around

AIR

For flying around Cape Verde, TACV serves all the inhabited islands. Between Praia and Mindelo there are at least two flights a day, and there are three to five flights a day between Sal and either Praia or Mindelo. There are also two flights a day between Praia and Fogo Island. Between Praia or Mindelo and the other islands, the connections are much less frequent, typically two to four times a week. Examples

of one-way fares include 6110 CVE for Sal-Mindelo, Mindelo-Praia or Praia-Sal; 3800 CVE from Mindelo to Santo Antão; and 3230 CVE from Praia to Fogo. Fares purchased abroad in dollars are over one-third higher (eg US$105 from Sal to Praia or Mindelo), so wait until arriving in Cape Verde to purchase your inter-island tickets.

Reserving seats on the round-trip portion of inter-island flights is a problem. Agents at TACV in Praia or Mindelo may tell you that you must wait until you arrive on an island to reserve your flight back. Don't believe them. It's a matter of radioing the TACV office on the island and making a reservation. If they say there are problems with the radio, be sceptical. The problem is that the TACV office is usually deluged with people, especially in Praia, and their agents don't want to take the time to do this. The solution is to try to catch them when the office isn't so swamped, usually first thing in the morning or late in the afternoon. Let them know very clearly that you simply can't risk taking the flight without some certainty of getting back by a given day. Be very polite.

Another problem is the harmattan, the dusty wind from the Sahara that can reduce visibility to less than one km. This happens from December to March. The skies may be relatively clear one day, very hazy the next. Sometimes the winds won't let up for a week or more. Your return flight may be postponed, even cancelled, or you can be left stranded on an island for days.

BUS & TAXI

For getting around the islands, TRANSCOR, the government bus company, provides an extensive service on Santiago Island, with regular connections to most of the major towns. On the other islands you may have to rely on taxis or hitchhiking. Hitching rides is easier in Cape Verde than in any other West African country because Cape Verdeans are very willing to pick up travellers if they have room. However, vehicles are quite scarce and payment might be expected – ask to avoid any misunderstandings.

CAR

The Alucar rental company has offices in Praia, Mindelo and on Sal Island. Cape Verdeans back from the USA for a short holiday are the major customers. An ordinary driving licence is all that's required. The cost of renting a car is lower in Cape Verde than in any other West African country, typically about US$85 to US$105 a day plus petrol.

BOAT

There are ferry connections to all nine inhabited islands. Two boats, the *Sotavento* and the *Barlavento*, follow a regular schedule, but only stop at each port for a few hours, making island-hopping impossible. One or the other connects Praia with Fogo and Brava, leaving Praia on Tuesdays and Thursdays. For more information, see the Getting There & Away sections under Praia and Mindelo.

The major problem with these ferries is that some of them have no cabins. There are only a few benches, and they aren't comfortable. So you must resort to looking for a corner, and it'll probably have to be outside where it gets very cold and windy.

TOURS

The only travel agency in Cape Verde is Cabetur (CAB-tour), which has offices in Praia, Mindelo and on Sal Island (☎ 411545, fax 411098). If you send them a fax of your itinerary, they can make hotel and flight arrangements for all inter-island travel and for car rental as well. The easiest branch to contact is the one on Sal Island. Ask for Clara; she speaks French and Portuguese but very little English.

Santiago Island

This was the first island to be settled and is the major island of the Cape Verde Archipelago. Attractions include the relaxed capital city, Praia, the first settlement, Cidade Velha, the deserted beaches around Tarrafal on the opposite end of the island, and the mountainous interior.

PRAIA

Tranquillity rules in this small city of 65,000 inhabitants. The central market is small (by West African standards), but interesting.

If there are areas of town where the electricity hasn't been cut off, you will find a lively place to get a drink and listen to some local music, one of the best treats that Cape Verde has to offer. The beaches are another. There are two near the Hotel Praia Mar on the southern edge of town.

Orientation

The centre of Praia is on a fortress-like plateau (*Platô*) overlooking the ocean. The principal residential sections are on surrounding plateaus and in the valleys between.

A few blocks south of the market, in the heart of town, you'll find the central plaza (*praça*) with a covered bandstand. In the evenings, people congregate here, waiting for the next show at the cinema.

Information

Money The only bank for changing money is the Banco de Cabo Verde on Avenida Amilcar Cabral (open weekdays 8.30 am to 2 pm).

Foreign Embassies The following countries have embassies or consulates on Santiago:

Brazil Near Hotel Marisol (☎ 615607)
France 500 metres south of Hotel Marisol on the same street (☎ 615589/91)
Portugal In the Achada de São Antonio quarter near the National Assembly (☎ 615602/3)
Senegal Rua Abilio Macedo, facing the US embassy (☎ 615621)
USA In the centre on the Platô at Rua Abilio Macedo 81 and near the northern end of Rua Guerra Mendes (☎ 615616, fax 611353)

Honorary consulates include those of Belgium, Germany, the Netherlands, Norway and Spain.

Travel Agency The only travel agency is Cabetur (☎ 615551 or 611737, fax 615553, telex 6032). It's in the centre on the Platô at Rua Sorpa Pinto 4. It can make all arrangements for

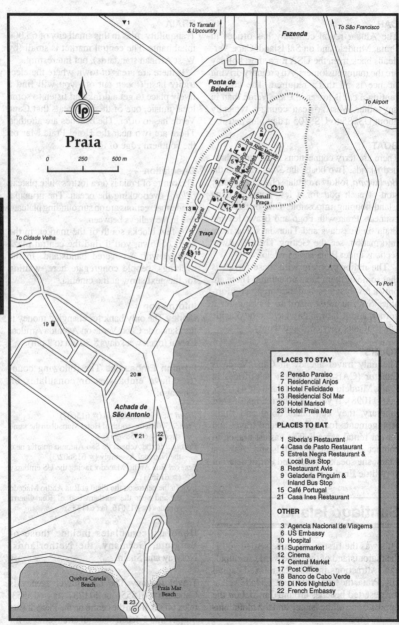

Praia

0   250   500 m

To Tarrafal
& Upcountry

Fazenda

To São Francisco

Ponta de
Beleém

To Airport

To Cidade Velha

Rua Abílio Macedo

Rua Guerra Mendes

Avenida Amílcar Cabral

Avg. de Julho

Small Praça

Praça

To Port

Achada de
São Antonio

Quebra-Canela
Beach

Praia Mar
Beach

To Port

CAPE VERDE

PLACES TO STAY

2   Pensão Paraiso
7   Residencial Anjos
16 Hotel Felicidade
13 Residencial Sol Mar
20 Hotel Marisol
23 Hotel Praia Mar

PLACES TO EAT

1   Siberia's Restaurant
4   Casa de Pasto Restaurant
5   Estrela Negra Restaurant &
    Local Bus Stop
8   Restaurant Avis
9   Geladeria Pinguim &
    Inland Bus Stop
15 Café Portugal
21 Casa Ines Restaurant

OTHER

3   Agencia Nacional de Viagems
6   US Embassy
10 Hospital
11 Supermarket
12 Cinema
14 Central Market
17 Post Office
18 Banco de Cabo Verde
19 Di Nos Nightclub
22 French Embassy

travel to other islands, including lodging, as well as help you locate car rental in Praia.

Bookshops For books on Cape Verde try the Hotel Praia Mar; it also has postcards. The Instituto Caboverdiano do Livro off Avenida Amilcar Cabral sells books and maps.

Beaches

There aren't many beaches because the coast is rocky. The most popular is a tiny beach just east of the Hotel Praia Mar, and it's packed on weekends. The beach west of the Praia Mar, Quebra-Canela, a 10-minute walk from the hotel, is better because it's not so packed and the body-surfing is good. As elsewhere in Cape Verde, the water is never very warm. From December to March it's downright cold.

The best beaches by far on the southern side of Santiago Island are 10 to 12 km north-east of Praia at São Francisco, an isolated area with many deserted coves and several good beaches. There's no bus, so you'll have to take a taxi or walk. Take the airport road and head north just after crossing the bridge.

Places to Stay

There are frequent blackouts and only the top two hotels have stand-by generators, so you should bring candles. In addition to room rates, all hotels charge a 10% tax.

For the cheapest rooms in town, try the *Pensão Paraiso* (☎ 613539) on Rua Guerra Mendes, 1½ blocks north of the US embassy; or *Residencial Sol Atlántico* (☎ 612872) on Avenida Amilcar Cabral facing the praça. Both charge 1100/1350 CVE for singles/doubles.

The most popular of the cheaper hotels is the *Hotel Felicidade* (☎ 615585) in the centre of town on Rua Guerra Mendes, 1½ blocks north of the praça. Clean singles/doubles cost 1500/3200 CVE. The rooms with double beds have private baths; there's also a restaurant. If it's full, which is often the case, try *Residencial Serjinho*, a block to the west facing the Café Portugal.

The modern *Residencial Anjos* (☎ 614178 or 614295) costs 2000/2700 CVE for singles/doubles, including breakfast. It's excellent value, with rooms almost as nice as

the Praia Mar. It's in the centre of town but has no restaurant (there are several nearby).

At *Residencial Sol Mar* singles/doubles cost 2600/3750 CVE. It's half a block south of the central market towards the park.

The best hotel by reputation is the *Pousada Praia Mar* (☎ 613777), usually just called the Praia Mar, with singles/doubles for 5000-6000/7000 CVE (including breakfast); 500 CVE less without hot water. It has a stand-by generator, tennis court, saltwater pool, ocean-view bar and a nightclub. The air-con usually doesn't work, but it's rarely needed. The city's two best beaches are nearby, but the hotel is three km from the town centre. Travellers' cheques are accepted but not credit cards.

Some people prefer the *Hotel Marisol* (☎ 613460), which also overlooks the sea but is much closer to town. It has singles/doubles for 3900/4650 CVE, including breakfast. It has a stand-by generator, decent rooms, a good restaurant and fans.

Places to Eat

City Centre All of the restaurants in the centre of town are inexpensive but for value you can't beat *Casa de Pasto* (or *Amelia's*) on Avenida Amilcar Cabral, four blocks north of the praça. It attracts a mixed clientele and is always packed at lunchtime. A big three-course Cape Verdean meal costs about 500 CVE. It's open daily, except Sunday, until 9 pm.

Estrela Negra, on Avenida 5 de Julho, is more rustic and not nearly as good. The daily special costs about 375 CVE. The Felicidade's top-floor *Restaurante Panorama* has a good lunch buffet on Sundays.

The *Cachito Snackbar*, across from the main plaza, offers the widest selection of lighter meals, including various sandwiches. It's open daily except Sunday until midnight. The *Café Portugal*, just east of the market, is similar but the selection is usually limited to the meal of the day. The *Restaurant Avis*, on the same street one block to the north, is open every day from morning to 11 pm.

The *Geladeria Pinguim* on Avenida Amilcar Cabral is the town's most modern ice-cream parlour, with a good selection of ice creams, sundaes and other fancy concoctions as well as sandwiches. However, you can order these only between 4 and 10.30 pm; only drinks are served during the rest of the day.

Suburbs Even the most expensive restaurants in town are all very moderately priced. The restaurant at the *Hotel Marisol* is many people's favourite. It's open daily, and the evening trading hours, 7.30 to 10 pm, are typical for most restaurants. A typical Portuguese meal with wine costs 950 CVE, and there's a very good ice-cream parlour. The *Pousada Praia Mar* is a close runner-up but the atmosphere is terribly boring.

One of my favourites is the *Casa Ines Restaurant*, between the two hotels south of town. It's more like a family restaurant and is basic but extremely popular, partly because it has a generator. The grilled meats are particularly good. Most dishes cost from 250 to 500 CVE. To get there take the road leading up to the bluff between the Marisol and the Praia Mar. At the first main intersection at the top, veer to your right, and stop at the first houses on your right for directions. It's to your right about 150 metres down an alley at the edge of the bluff.

Ponte has an entirely different ambience – like a nightclub, with low lights, a bar and few tables. The menu is very limited but the Portuguese fare is good, and most dishes cost 450 to 900 CVE. It's two km north of the plateau on the main road inland.

Casa de Pasto Churraqueria (open daily), which has an outside terrace, is on the same road but 200 metres nearer town. The speciality is grilled meat; most plates cost around 700 CVE. *Churraqueria Siberia* is better known and noted for its grilled chicken (850 CVE). It's two km north-west of the plateau.

Entertainment

Bars In the centre, the best places for a drink are the *Café Portugal*, the *Restaurant Avis* and the praça, where throngs of people mingle from the late afternoon onwards.

For local colour and a sip of the local brew (grogo), try *Casa de Poto's* bar in the heart of the plateau. Local expatriates tend to head more toward the terrace bars at the *Marisol*, the rooftop terrace of *Hotel Felicidade* and, for the best ocean view, the *Hotel Praia Mar*.

Nightclubs For open-air dancing and lively Cape Verdean music, head for the inexpensive *Di Nos*, one km to the south-west of the plateau. It's the best nightclub in town. People of all ages come here, but the younger crowd predominates. It's usually open Friday to Sunday, starting around 10.30 pm, unless there's a blackout in that area of town. It's a 20-minute walk up the bluff from the Hotel Marisol.

The *A Teia* (The Spider's Web) also has live Cape Verdean music on weekends, but it's fancier and has a cover charge. It's on the northern side of town in the Fazenda section, half a km north of the plateau.

For disco dancing, try *Pilão* at the Hotel Praia Mar. It has taped music – mostly American but some Cape Verdean. It's popular on weekends. There's a cover charge unless you're staying at the hotel.

Cinema The *Cine-Teatro*, just north of Hotel Felicidade on the same block, shows foreign films, either in Portuguese or dubbed in Portuguese. Shows are at 6.30 and 9.30 pm.

Music In Praia, nightclubs are the best place for hearing Cape Verdean musicians. Occasionally bands also perform on weekends at 5 de Julho park in the new part of town and Galarias Praia is probably the best place for finding cassettes of their music. The group Tam Tam 2000 is popular as is the female vocalist Cesaria Evora. Popular male musicians include Bana, Paulino Vieira (guitar), Masa Abrantes, Chico Serra (piano) and Luis Morais.

Getting There & Away

Air TACV has typically three to five flights a day to Sal (6110 CVE), at least two flights a day to Mindelo (6110 CVE) and to Mosteiros on Fogo Island (3230 CVE), five flights a week to Maio, four flights a week to São Nicolau, three flights a week to Santo Antão and two flights a week to Boa Vista. In Praia, TACV (☎ 615813, telex 6065) is on the plateau at 11/13 Rua Guerra Mendes, a block north of the praça. Air Senegal is 2½ blocks further north on Avenida 5 de Julho.

If you have a return ticket, be sure to reconfirm your return flight as soon as possible after arrival.

Bus TRANSCOR has buses to virtually every town in the interior: Cidade Velha, Tarrafal, Assomada (also known as Santa Catarina), São Domingos and Pedra Badejo. There are several buses a day to/from these towns. In Praia there is no bus station, but a major departure point is in the centre along Avenida Amilcar Cabral very near Geladeria Pinguim.

Ferry The ferry between Praia and Mindelo takes 16 hours and costs about 1000 CVE. Itineraries are flexible so you need to check sailing days and times a few days in advance.

In Praia, tickets can be purchased at the Agencia Nacional de Viagens on Avenida 5 de Julho, near the US embassy. You cannot buy a ticket on the boat. The port is about 2.5 km from the plateau. To get there, take the road to the airport and take a right just after crossing the bridge and follow that road for 1.5 km.

Getting Around

To/From the Airport A taxi into Praia (four km) costs 350 CVE including baggage. There are no buses to the centre.

Bus Buses on the plateau go to every section of Praia, but the service is infrequent.

Taxi Taxis are black and not too difficult to find on the plateau. Fares are about 150 CVE for a short trip in town. If you want to hire by the hour, bargaining is required as the drivers are not accustomed to hourly rates. Expect to pay not less than 1300 CVE per hour. There are no taxis at the hotels, but the hotel receptionist will call the taxi company for you. The pick-up charge is about 150 CVE. After 8 pm, taxis disappear, but you can call and arrange to be picked up.

Car Alucar rents cars for 4300 to 5300 CVE a day including 100 free km, plus 50 to 70 CVE per km for the excess, depending on the model.

CIDADE VELHA

For a half-day trip out of Praia, go to the old town of Ribeira Grande, now called Cidade Velha, or the Old City. It's 10 km west of Praia and was the first town built by the Portuguese on the islands. The ruins of the first cathedral and of **Fort Real de São Felipe** that dominate the village are of particular interest. Walk up to the old fort; it's remarkably well preserved and commands a spectacular and unforgettable view of the present-day village, which nestles in a fertile valley of gardens hemmed in by lunar canyon walls, providing quite a contrast. The harbour below is littered with cannons, shot and wine jars.

Sir Francis Drake stopped here in 1585 on one of his many voyages and his men plundered the town and the four forts before setting them aflame. Before he burned the town, it was the most important Portuguese settlement outside Portugal. Don't miss Cidade Velha as the country's impoverishment has left it suspended in the 16th century.

Getting There & Away

There are only a few buses a day connecting Praia and Cidade Velha, so you might consider walking (2½ to three hours), hitchhiking, or taking a cab.

SÃO DOMINGOS & TARRAFAL

For a short trip out of Praia, head for São Domingos, which is only about 25 km north of the capital on the road to Tarrafal. The town itself is nothing special but the gardens in the valley are lovely and the surrounding area will give you an idea of what the stark mountainous interior is like.

Better still, head all the way to Tarrafal, a small fishing village at the northern end of the island. The beaches just south of Tarrafal are some of the best on the island, while about one km north of Tarrafal bay there's a rocky cove with caves and protected pools for snorkelling.

Places to Stay & Eat

For food and lodging in Tarrafal, try *Aldeia Turística*, an inexpensive pension which has very decent food, and is next to the beach. A bungalow room costs about 1500 CVE. Alternatively, try the *Pensão Tata* in the centre. It charges around 1750 CVE for a room, including breakfast.

You'll find neither food nor lodging in São Domingos, but further north in Assomada, in the centre of the island along the same road, you'll find both. If you go via the eastern coastal route and stop off in Pedra Badejo (roughly halfway), you will probably have a tough time finding a place to sleep, but there's a restaurant with great views overlooking the ocean.

Getting There & Away

Tarrafal is a 3½-hour bus trip from Praia, and there are two buses a day. The more interesting one passes through the mountainous interior via São Domingos and Assomada; the other goes along the eastern coastline via Pedra Badejo, leaving Praia daily at 3 pm and Tarrafal at 6 am. In Praia, they leave from Avenida Amilcar Cabral. Each of these towns en route has additional daily buses connecting them with Praia.

Alternatively, you could rent a taxi by the hour, or hitchhike. Cape Verdeans are great about picking people up. Just don't expect many vehicles with extra seats to pass by.

São Vicente Island

São Vicente is Cape Verde's second most-important island. Mindelo, the island's capital and port, is the liveliest city in Cape Verde and well worth a visit. The interior of São Vicente, however, is less interesting than that of Santiago, Santo Antão or Fogo. If you travel inland, two places you might head for are Mt Verde, the island's highest peak, and

the beaches at Baia das Gatas, 15 km to the east of Mindelo.

MINDELO

With 35,000 inhabitants and the country's deepest port, Mindelo hardly plays second fiddle to Praia. It's a livelier town, perhaps because of the ships passing through. Certainly the bars and nightclubs are more numerous and the restaurants a cut above. The Praça Amilcar Cabral is the liveliest place in town from 6 to 11 pm; don't miss it. Half of what there is to see and do is on just two intersecting streets: Avenida 5 de Julho, which runs north-south alongside Praça Amilcar Cabral, and Rua Libertadores d'Africa, which is marked at the eastern end by the pink Palácio de Presidente and at the western end by the main bay.

The colonial houses are colourfully painted and very picturesque. Most are two-storey houses with balconies and shuttered windows, and the architecture is very Portuguese. Filling out the picture are streets in stone, palms and other trees, small bars on every other corner, each with their own special character, all surrounded by the sea on one side and tall barren hills on the other. In the USA, this town probably would have been restored and become a tourist trap. Left as is, it still has a lot of charm.

Information

The Banco de Cabo Verde is at the intersection of Rua Libertadores d'Africa and Avenida 5 de Julho.

Belgium, Denmark, Germany, the Netherlands, Norway, Portugal, Spain and Switzerland all have honorary consulates in Mindelo.

For a supermarket, try Casa Miranda. For books, try the bookshop facing the park behind the Palácio de Presidente. For records of Cape Verdean music, the best place is Discoteco do Bana behind Café Portugal.

The only travel agency is Cabetur (☎ 313847/59, fax 313842) at Rua Senador Vera Cruz 57. It can make all arrangements for travel to other islands, and assist you with car rental on Mindelo.

Mindelo's Mardi Gras
Mardi Gras (in February) is by far the best time to be in Cape Verde but it's also when the islands are most crowded. While celebrations and parades are held all over the islands, those at Mindelo are the best. Preparations begin several months in advance and on Sundays you can see the various groups practising, marching up and down the streets. ■

Activities
The main **beach** is on the north-western outskirts of town just beyond the port area, about 1.5 km from the centre. The best **jogging** area is along Avenida República, which runs along the bay and out to the port and beach beyond. If you walk up **Monte Verde** just outside Mindelo, you'll get a fine view of the city and harbour.

Places to Stay – bottom end
Pensão Chave d'Ouro (☎ 311050) costs 800/1000 CVE for singles/doubles plus 10% tax. It's on the corner of Rua Libertadores

d'Africa and Avenida 5 de Julho, across from the main bank and one floor up.

You can get a cheaper room at the *Pensão Casa Rialto*, which has singles/doubles for 700/900 CVE plus 10% tax. There are only three or four rooms with a common bathroom, but they are clean and the beds are comfortable. It's a block north of the Café Portugal.

Places to Stay – top end
At the *Aparthotel Avenida* (☎ 313435) rooms cost 2970/3470 CVE for singles/ doubles, plus 10% tax. The rooms are wood-panelled and the price includes breakfast. It's a small hotel in the centre on Avenida 5 de Julho between Rua

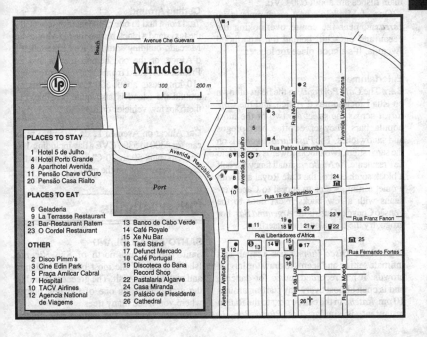

Mindelo

0   100   200 m

PLACES TO STAY
1 Hotel 5 de Julho
4 Hotel Porto Grande
8 Aparthotel Avenida
11 Pensão Chave d'Ouro
20 Pensão Casa Rialto

PLACES TO EAT
6 Geladeria
9 La Terrasse Restaurant
21 Bar-Restaurant Ratem
23 O Cordel Restaurant

OTHER
2 Disco Pimm's
3 Cine Edin Park
5 Praça Amilcar Cabral
7 Hospital
10 TACV Airlines
12 Agencia National de Viagems
13 Banco de Cabo Verde
14 Café Royale
15 Xe Nu Bar
16 Taxi Stand
17 Defunct Mercado
18 Café Portugal
19 Discoteca do Bana Record Shop
22 Pastalaria Algarve
24 Casa Miranda
25 Palácio de Presidente
26 Cathedral

Avenue Che Guevara
Beach
Port
Avenida República
Avenida 5 de Julho
Rua Nkrumah
Avenida Unidade Africana
Rua Patrice Lumumba
Rua 19 de Setembro
Rua Libertadores d'Africa
Rua Franz Fanon
Rua Fernando Fortes
Avenida Amilcar Cabral
Rua da Luz
Rua da Moeda

Libertadores d'Africa and Praça Amilcar Cabral. *Porto Grande* (☎ 313838), nearby, charges 2200/2700 CVE for singles/doubles, plus 10% tax. The price includes breakfast. Each room has a balcony overlooking the city's beautiful but noisy park.

The new *Residencial Sodade* (☎ 313556) has singles/doubles for 1900/2100 CVE.

Places to Eat

The *Pensão Chave d'Ouro* in the heart of town is one of the best places for traditional Cape Verdean food. A full meal costs about 400 CVE. For snacks, try the *Geladeria* on Avenida 5 de Julho next to the Aparthotel Avenida.

O Cordel Restaurant is small and quiet with air-con and impeccable service. Most main dishes are 400 to 600 CVE but their speciality, lobster, costs 1100 CVE. It's in the centre across the street from the pink Palácio de Presidente. *Ratem*, with soft music, air-con and some interesting selections, is two blocks away and seems about as good. Most main dishes are about 600 CVE.

One of Mindelo's best restaurants is *La Terrasse*, near the centre overlooking the ocean and on a hill behind the Aparthotel Avenida. It's a good place for lobster.

Entertainment

Bars The *Café Portugal*, in the heart of town on Rua Libertadores d'Africa, and the *Café Royal* across the street are two of the most popular bars. They serve coffee, beer, pregos and sandwiches. The *Pastalaria Algarve* is on the same street, two blocks towards the Palácio de Presidente. *Xe Nu Bar*, a small fancy bar half a block south-east of the Café Royal and with a quiet setting, seems to appeal to Cape Verdeans with a few bucks. Next door to the Pensão Chave d'Ouro is the *Argentina Bar*. For grogo, try the bars along the waterfront.

Nightclubs *Disco Pimm's* has a small and intimate setting and seems to draw the largest crowds. It has recorded music for dancing and is open almost every day starting around 10 pm. *Ratem*, in the centre next to the Ratem restaurant, is similar. The *Piano Bar*, *Je*

T'Aime and *Bar Calipso* are further from the centre and are also worth trying.

Cinemas The *Cine Edin Park* next to the Porto Grande has foreign films, all dubbed in Portuguese. Shows are at 6 and 9 pm.

Getting There & Away

Air TACV (☎ 311524) usually has about three flights a day to Sal (6110 CVE), at least two flights a day to Praia (6110 CVE), three flights a week to nearby Santo Antão (3800 CVE) and less frequent flights to neighbouring islands. Their office is in the centre on Avenida 5 de Julho near Aparthotel Avenida. If you will be returning by air, be sure to confirm your flight soon after arrival.

Ferry Ferry timetables change regularly, so for schedules and prices, see the Agencia Nacional de Viagems. It's on a side street, one block south of the intersection of Rua Libertadores d'Africa and Avenida 5 de Julho.

Getting Around

Taxi For a taxi to one of the interior towns, try the taxi stand a block behind the old Municipio Mercado building south of Rua Libertadores d'Africa, or the one behind the Palácio de Presidente. A taxi from the airport into town (10 km) costs about 500 CVE. Hitchhiking around the island is also quite possible, but there are few vehicles on the roads.

Car Alucar on Avenida 12 de Setembro rents cars for 4300 to 5300 CVE a day including 100 free km, plus 50 to 70 CVE per km for the excess, depending on the model.

Other Islands

SANTO ANTÃO ISLAND

Santo Antão, just north of São Vicente Island, is one of the most beautiful islands and well worth a visit. The greenest island in the archipelago, its one of the few places where you'll see many trees.

Ribeira Grande, the capital city on the

northern tip of the island, and Porto Novo, the major port some 20 km away on the eastern coast, are nothing special. What is special, however, is the hilly and relatively lush interior; hikers will love it. The major hike is **Ribeira Grande mountain**, some 10 km south of Ribeira Grande town; getting to the top and back takes most of a day. Other hikes that travellers recommend for the scenery are the coastal road from Ribeira Grande east to **Janela** (12 km), the valley that starts inland from **Paúl** (which is between these two coastal towns and where much of Cape Verde's grogo is distilled), and the narrow Ribeira Grande to Porto Novo road which winds up to **La Cova** in the centre at 1170 metres, with pine trees all around.

Places to Stay & Eat
In Ribeira Grande the *Residencial Aliança* (☎ 211246) has clean singles/doubles for 2000/2200 CVE. Cheaper is *Casa Melo*. Both places offer good meals, reasonably priced at around 500 CVE. The friendly owners will even find you a taxi if necessary.

Getting There & Away
Air TACV has flights on Tuesday, Friday and Saturday to/from Mindelo, connecting with flights to/from Praia; the one-way fare is 3800 CVE from Mindelo and 6110 CVE from Praia. The airport is at Ponta do Sol, five km north-west of Ribeira Grande.

Ferry Most travellers take the ferry because it's much cheaper and more convenient, with one crossing every day both ways between Mindelo (440 CVE one way) and Porto Novo. The trip takes an hour, but even on this short stretch the seas are often quite rough. Tickets are available from the Agencia Nacional de Viagens in Porto Novo at the harbour; buy them in advance.

FOGO ISLAND
The major attraction of Fogo Island is **Mt Fogo** volcano (2839 metres), which dominates the centre of the island. It erupted in April 1995. For details, see the boxed story on Mt Fogo. Ferries dock at São Felipe, on the south-

western corner of the island overlooking Brava Island to the west. Planes, however, still land at Mosteiros on the northern tip of the island. There's a road encircling the island, mostly cobbled and bumpy, but the major route goes along the scenic eastern coast and is punctuated by hamlets.

São Felipe
Perched on a cliff above a harbour, São Felipe is reminiscent of a sleepy town in Portugal, with small plazas and brightly painted houses with balconies. Finding a place to eat, drink or sleep is usually not a problem. Below town there's a black sandy beach that's clean, safe and usually deserted.

Places to Stay & Eat The only cheap place may be the unnamed two-storey *pensão* half a block from the market. It has several big rooms and beds with decent but sagging mattresses, shared bath and no restaurant. Rooms cost 200 CVE. The *Vulcão* near the market has one or two rooms and serves one meal only.

Hotel Xaguate, or *Hotel São Felipe*, (☎ 811222) has singles/doubles for 2500/2700 CVE, plus 10% tax. Prices include breakfast. The more expensive rooms have balconies. If you arrive by ferry, you'll pass it on the way into town. Reservations can be made in Praia at the Praia Mar Hotel.

For a cheap meal, try one of the several bars in town or the central market.

Getting There & Away
Air TACV has twice-daily connections between Praia and Fogo (about 3200 CVE) but flights are often cancelled during the hazy harmattan season. The airport presently being used is in Mosteiros on the opposite end of the island from São Felipe. There's a bus service to São Felipe (about 600 CVE).

Ferry The ferry between Praia and Fogo costs about 1000 CVE (one way). Schedules change, so check with Arca Verde in Praia.

BRAVA ISLAND
Brava Island, the smallest of all the inhabited islands and only three hours west of Fogo by

ferry, is mountainous and one of the most scenic islands, offering some of the best hiking opportunities in Cape Verde. The starting point is **Nova Sintra**, the tiny capital village. It has no amenities for travellers. There are ferries direct from Fogo, and TACV now also has flights here.

SAL ISLAND

All international flights land on Sal except those from the African mainland, which go to Praia. There's lots of sunshine and long beaches. The government is trying to attract foreign sunbathers by building modern hotels.

Espargos, a tiny village within walking distance of the airport, offers cheap food and lodging. The higher priced hotels such as the Novotel are in Santa Maria, 18 km away.

The Cabetur travel agency (☎ 411545 or 411087, fax 411098) is at the airport.

Places to Stay & Eat

In Espargos, *Pensão Angela* (☎ 411327) has singles/doubles for about 1500/1900 CVE, and good food. The *Residencial Central* (☎ 411210) on the main square has pleasant singles/doubles for 1900/2200 CVE. You can get meals here. Also good is *Hotel Atlántico* (☎ 411210), a B&B with singles/doubles for 2500/3300 CVE. If you tire of the food at these places, try the friendly *Caravellas*; meal costs around 450 CVE.

Sal has three tourist hotels, all on the beach in Santa Maria. The most reasonably priced is the new *Hotel Albatraz* (☎ 421300) where singles/doubles cost 3300/4600 CVE. The longer-standing *Hotel Morabeza* (☎ 421020) has singles/doubles for 5000/6000 CVE; breakfast is 600 CVE extra. The top hotel is the *Novotel Belorizonte* (☎ 421080, fax 421210, telex 4080). It's also the most expensive with single/double bungalow rooms for 5300/7000 CVE. Take the hotel's free shuttle bus to get here.

Other towns with lodging and restaurants are Porto Novo and Paûl, which is very picturesque. In both places there's a pensão with rooms for around 1000 CVE, and cheap restaurants.

Getting There & Away

TACV has three to five flights a day to Praia (6110 CVE) starting before dawn; three flights a day to Mindelo (6110 CVE); and less frequent flights to the other islands.

Mt Fogo

Hiking on Mt Fogo near the centre of the island can be great fun. It's not so difficult to reach the top, although it can be difficult getting to the base. The volcano has a very high rim all along the western half. On the other side, the rim dips down somewhat, permitting a road to pass across it from south to north starting at Achada Furna, which is well south of the crater.

The volcano erupted in April 1995, apparently wiping out most of the farming area called Cha das Caldeiras in the centre of the crater, destroying some 5000 structures and leaving thousands homeless.

Previously, you could take a taxi from São Felipe to Cha das Caldeiras, find a guide there and hike to the summit of the major cone (four to five hours). From the top there was a magnificent view of the volcano's eight-km-diameter crater and you could get a good idea of how this entire archipelago was born. This cone probably still exists, but it is not clear whether a taxi can reach Cha das Caldeiras, or if you can hike the cone. Regardless, if it's still possible to enter the centre of the crater, you may still be able to leave through the northern rim and then hike clockwise or counterclockwise around the volcano's outer rim back to São Felipe.

Even if hiking inside the crater is no longer possible, you may be able to hitch a ride to Achada Furna and then hike up to the outer rim from there, then down into the crater itself. However, such a trip normally takes more than a day. (You can also reach the rim from other points along the road below the southern rim, but you won't be able to climb down into the crater because the walls of the crater on the western half are almost vertical.)

If taxis aren't running from São Felipe to Cha das Caldeiras you could try hitchhiking, although you'll need lots of luck and patience because very few vehicles go this far. Alternatively, hitch to Achada Furna or the junction where the road splits in opposite directions around the volcano (about 12km from São Felipe). It's normally much easier hitching to both of these points. ∎

Côte d'Ivoire

Once the favourite showcase in Africa of liberal economists, the 'Ivory Coast' has fallen on hard times. It is, on a per capita basis, now far and away the world's most indebted nation and seems destined to be overtaken soon by Ghana as West Africa's wealthiest country. Abidjan now rivals Lagos as the region's most dangerous city, while serious labour unrest has become the biggest headache for the country's new president, Henri Konan-Bédié.

Surprisingly however, Abidjan retains its glitter despite these problems. You'll find skyscrapers, a beautiful lagoon setting without rival in West Africa, the Ivoire (West Africa's most famous hotel) and even an ice-skating rink. Most striking of all is the splendid modern cathedral which dominates the skyline like the opera house in Sydney.

Known as the 'Paris of West Africa', Abidjan has about 25,000 French people but, more significantly, it attracts Africans from all over West Africa, making it West Africa's most cosmopolitan city. Partially as a result of this migration, Abidjan has lots of vibrant African quarters, but the nightlife, as with almost everything else in Abidjan, has lost some of its vitality because of the city's high crime rate.

Travellers turned off by modern cities and sky-high prices used to give Côte d'Ivoire only a cursory look before passing on. With the CFA's devaluation, the high-price days are gone. Moreover, there's lots to see upcountry, including the picturesque former capital of Grand-Bassam and Assini beach nearby, the mountainous region around Man, the fascinating Senoufo area around Korhogo, Comoë National Park (West Africa's largest), Grand-Béréby beach and the remote fishing village of Sassandra. And don't miss the capital Yamoussoukro; that's where you'll find Houphouët's folly. Built under orders from former President Houphouët-Boigny, it's a near replica of St Peter's in Rome. It's truly magnificent, particularly the stained-glass windows, but with a price tag of US$400

REPUBLIC OF CÔTE D'IVOIRE

Area: 322,465 sq km
Population: 13.8 million
Population Growth Rate: 3.9%
Capital: Yamoussoukro
Head of State: President Henri Konan Bédié
Official Language: French
Currency: West African CFA franc
Exchange Rate: CFA 500 = US$1
Per Capita GNP: US$720
Inflation: 1%
Time: GMT/UTC

million, the cathedral is an embarrassment to many Ivoirians – particularly when the government is many months in arrears in paying the bureaucrats their salaries. It and the rest of the country's hinterland are easily reached by one of the best road systems in Africa. In short, even if Abidjan doesn't interest you, the rest of the country almost certainly will.

Facts about the Country

HISTORY
Not much is known about Côte d'Ivoire prior to the arrival of European ships in the 1460s.

251

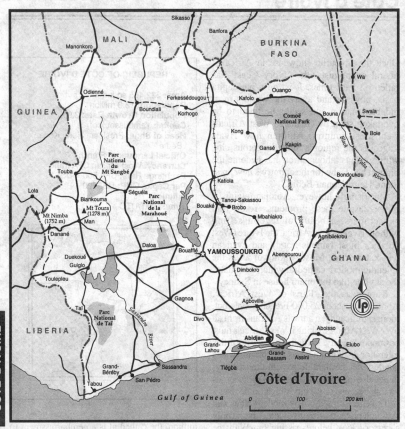

Côte d'Ivoire

The major ethnic groups all came rather recently from neighbouring areas. The Krou people migrated eastward from Liberia around 400 years ago; the Senoufo and Lubi moved southward from Burkina and Mali. It wasn't until the 18th and 19th centuries that the Akan people, including the Baoulé (BAH-ou-lay), migrated from Ghana into the eastern area and the Malinké from Guinea into the north-west.

The Portuguese were the first Europeans to arrive. Compared to neighbouring Ghana, Côte d'Ivoire suffered little from the slave trade. European slaving and merchant ships preferred other areas along the coast with better harbours. France didn't take any interest until the 1840s when the French, under Louis-Phillipe, enticed local chiefs to grant French commercial traders a monopoly along the coast. Thereafter, the French built naval bases to keep out non-French traders and began a systematic conquest of the interior. They accomplished this only after a long war in the 1890s against Mandinka forces headed by the illustrious Samory Touré. Even then, guerrilla warfare by the Baoulé and other eastern groups continued until 1917.

Suggested Itineraries

While **Abidjan's** reputation for crime deters some people from staying for long, because of the devaluation it is now not nearly so expensive. Consequently, travellers who would normally exit after a day or two should consider staying a bit longer. Abidjan can be used as a base for trips to nearby **Grand-Bassam**, **Assini**, **Jacqueville** and **Tiégba**, all on the coast.

Travellers looking for a good beach should head further west to **Grand-Lahou**, which has a rarely visited rainforest nearby; **Sassandra**, which has some amazingly cheap beach bungalows; or **Grand-Béréby**, which is an expensive resort. If you have obtained an entry permit in Abidjan to **Taï National Park**, you could then head on further west to see it. However, a trip to this enormous virgin rainforest, the largest in West Africa, is truly only for the adventurous because the park is generally not open to visitors and accommodation outside the park is extremely basic.

You could then head north to the titular capital **Yamoussoukro** for the required viewing of the amazing basilica. A day here is enough, so plan on heading from there either west towards **Man** or north towards **Korhogo** and **Comoë National Park**. Man and Korhogo themselves are nothing special but the regions surrounding them offer the best opportunities for experiencing the traditional culture and, in the case of Man, hiking in the mountains. ■

Colonial Period

Once the French had complete control and established their capital, initially at Grand-Bassam, then Bingerville, they had one overriding goal – to stimulate the production of exports. Coffee, cocoa and palm oil were soon introduced along the coast, but the opening of the interior had to await the building of the railway. Because of its rocky plateau, Abidjan, not the capital Bingerville, was chosen as the railway hub. To build the railroad north to Ouagadougou (Burkina Faso) and work the cocoa plantations, the French conscripted African workers from as far away as Upper Volta (now Burkina Faso). In 1932, to facilitate this, they even made Upper Volta part of Côte d'Ivoire. By then, cocoa was the country's major export. It wasn't until the late 1930s that coffee began to challenge cocoa as the main export earner.

Côte d'Ivoire stood out in West Africa as the only country with a sizeable population of 'settlers'. Elsewhere in West and Central Africa, the French and English were largely bureaucrats. As a result, a good third of the cocoa, coffee and banana plantations were in the hands of French citizens. The hated forced-labour system was the backbone of the economy.

Houphouët-Boigny

Around 1905, a wealthy Baoulé chief had a son, Houphouët-Boigny (WHO-fuet BUIN-

yee), who was to become Côte d'Ivoire's father of independence. Houphouët-Boigny studied medicine in Dakar and thereafter became a medical assistant, prosperous cocoa farmer and local chief.

In 1944, he turned to politics and formed the country's first agricultural trade union – not of labourers but of African planters. Annoyed that colonial policy favoured French plantation owners, they united to recruit migrant workers for their own farms. He soon rose to prominence and within a year, after converting the trade union into the Parti Démocratique de Côte d'Ivoire (PDCI), he was elected a deputy to the French parliament in Paris. A year later, he had allied the PDCI with the West African Rassemblement Démocratique Africain (RDA), becoming the RDA's first president. That year the French abolished forced labour.

In those early years, Houphouët-Boigny was a radical. The RDA was closely aligned with international Marxist organisations and staged numerous demonstrations in Abidjan that resulted in many deaths and arrests. It wasn't long, however, before Houphouët-Boigny adopted a more conciliatory position. France reciprocated, making him the first African to become a minister in a European government.

Even before independence, Côte d'Ivoire was easily French West Africa's most prosperous area, contributing over 40% of the region's total exports. Houphouët-Boigny feared that when independence came, Côte d'Ivoire and Senegal would end up subsidising the poorer colonies if they were all united in a single republic. His preference for independence for each of the colonies coincided with French interests. At independence in 1960, most of the former French colonies were lightly populated, weak and dependent on their former ruler.

Independence

Houphouët-Boigny naturally became the country's first president. He was the last of the old-guard presidents who ushered in independence in the early '60s. Leaders throughout Africa offered varying strategies for development. Houphouët-Boigny was at one extreme, favouring continued reliance on the former colonial power.

He was also one of the few who promoted agriculture and gave industrial development a low priority – at least initially. While almost every other country in Africa was cheating the farmer with low produce prices to subsidise industrial development, Houphouët's government gave farmers good prices and stimulated production. Coffee production increased significantly, catapulting Côte d'Ivoire into third place behind Brazil and Colombia in total production. Cocoa did the same; by 1979, Côte d'Ivoire had become the world's leading producer. It also became Africa's leading exporter of pineapples and palm oil. The Ivoirian 'miracle' was, foremost, an agricultural miracle. Almost everywhere else in Africa, agriculture failed to deliver the goods.

French technicians masterminded the programme. In the rest of Africa, Europeans were largely driven out following independence. In Côte d'Ivoire, they poured in. The French community grew from 10,000 to 50,000, most of them teachers and advisors. Critics complained that Houphouët-Boigny had sold out to foreign interests. In 1975, two out of three top managerial personnel were foreigners, mostly French. However, Houphouët-Boigny was clearly calling all

the major shots and, with a strong economy, few Ivoirians complained. For 20 years, the economy maintained an annual growth rate of nearly 10% – the highest of Africa's non-oil exporting countries. Abidjan has grown from 60,000 people in 1945 to over two million today.

The fruits of growth were widespread. One reason was that the focus of development was on farming, the livelihood of most of the people. Another reason was the absence of huge estates. Most of the cacao and coffee production, for instance, was in the hands of hundreds of thousands of small producers. Literacy rose from 28 to 60% – twice the African average. Electricity reached virtually every town and the road system became the best in Africa, outside South Africa and Nigeria. Still, the numerous Mercedes and the posh African residences in Abidjan's Cocody section were testimony to the growing inequality of incomes and the beginnings of a class society.

Politically, Houphouët-Boigny ruled with an iron hand. The press was far from free. Tolerating only one political party, he eliminated opposition by largess – giving his opponents jobs instead of jail sentences. Several half-hearted coup attempts in the early '60s were easily suppressed. All those arrested were eventually released. Later, he even made one of them a minister.

Not all the investments were wise: Houphouët-Boigny was Africa's number one producer of 'show' projects. So many millions of dollars were poured into his village, Yamoussoukro, that it became the butt of jokes. The four-star hotel there still has an occupancy rate of less than 5%; the losses are staggering. Many of the state enterprises were terribly managed; graft was rampant. But the economy did so well that the government could afford to err.

The Big Slump

The world recession of the early '80s sent shock waves into the Ivoirian economy. The drought of 1983-84 was a second wallop. For four years (1981-84) real GNP stagnated or declined. In 1984, the rest of Africa was gleeful as the glittering giant, Abidjan, was brought to its knees for the first time with constant blackouts. Overcutting of timber finally had an impact and revenue slumped. Sugar had been the hope of the north, but world prices collapsed, making a fiasco out of the huge new sugar complexes there. The country's external debt increased threefold and Côte d'Ivoire had to ask the IMF for debt rescheduling. Rising crime in Abidjan made the news in Europe. The miracle was over.

Houphouët-Boigny slashed government spending and the bureaucracy, revamped some of the poorly managed state enterprises, sent home a third of the expensive French advisors and teachers (the French population is now down to 28,000 from a high of 50,000) and, most difficult of all, finally slashed cocoa prices to farmers in 1989 by 50%. Hard times had finally forced the government to keep its promise of increasing the number of Ivoirians in management positions.

Early 1990s
In 1990, hundreds of civil servants went on strike, joined by students who took to the streets protesting violently, blaming the economic crisis on corruption and the lavish lifestyles of government officials. The unrest was unprecedented in its scale and intensity, shattering Houphouët's carefully cultivated personality cult and forcing the government to come out several months later in favour of multiparty democracy. The 1990 presidential elections were opened to other parties for the first time causing Houphouët-Boigny to receive only 85% of the vote instead of the typical 99.9%.

Houphouët, however, was becoming increasingly feeble, intensifying the guessing game of whom he would appoint as his successor. A master politician, he kept everyone speculating. Making a special effort to show no ethnic favourites, he wore three-piece suits rather than a Baoulé costume. He also held no political prisoners or grudges against politicians who caused major scandals.

Finally, in late 1993, at the estimated age of 88, 'Le Vieux' (the old man) died. His funeral, which took place at the Basilica in Yamoussoukro, was large and impressive, with many African heads-of-state in attendance, but only one non-African head of state, France's President Mitterand. He was accompanied by a delegation numbering 80 including virtually the entire cabinet! In great contrast, Washington could muster up only one obscure cabinet member. Naturally the Ivoirians were peeved, particularly since Houphouët had been such a strong ally of the West throughout the Cold War and an ardent supporter of free-market economies.

Houphouët's silently hand-picked successor was Henri Konan-Bédié, a Baoulé and speaker of the National Assembly. (The recently amended constitution designated the speaker as first in succession.) Although he was far from universally popular among PDCI party barons, after some brief political infighting in the days following the funeral with Prime Minister Alassane Ouattara, his main rival, Bédié emerged in complete control and Ouattara resigned.

Côte d'Ivoire Today
While the country has experienced well over a decade of continuous decline, with its gross national income per capita falling from US$1290 in 1978 to US$700 in 1992, the end of the bad times may be in sight. The recent devaluation of the CFA is having, as expected, a favourable impact on exporters and since Côte d'Ivoire is the leading exporting country in the CFA zone, it stands to benefit the most.

On the political front, even with the CFA devaluation, which occurred less than a month after the old man's death, and the country's continuing economic problems, no major crises occurred during Bédié's first year in office, and life continues pretty much as usual.

In short, Côte d'Ivoire has made the transition amazingly well, dumbfounding the many political pundits who had predicted chaos. With crime now on a downward trend in Abidjan because of more vigorous law enforcement, new open elections in late 1995 and the CFA devaluation apparently

CÔTE D'IVOIRE

CÔTE D'IVOIRE

The Environment
The major threat to the country's diverse flora and fauna is the expansion of agricultural lands, from 3.1 million hectares in 1965 to close to eight million in 1995. The rainforests are being cut down at a tragic rate; between 1977 and 1987 Côte d'Ivoire lost 42% of its forest and woodland – the highest loss in the world. The same figures for neighbouring Ghana and Liberia, for example, were 8% and 0%, respectively; for Brazil it was 4%. Since then, the volume of timber exports has declined by about one-third, but hardwood exports are still on a level with those of Brazil, a country over 20 times larger. The timber industry is one of the culprits; every day you can see hundreds of logs floating in the lagoon around Abidjan and ships being loaded with mahogany, samba, sipo, bété and iroko. As a result, the only remaining virgin forest is the 3600-sq-km Taï National Park in the far south-eastern corner of the country. ■

---

having positive effects after the initial shock, things are beginning to look up.

GEOGRAPHY
Côte d'Ivoire (322,465 sq km) is about the size of Italy but has less than 20% of Italy's population density. Except for the western area around Man, which is rolling hill country with several peaks over 1200 metres, Côte d'Ivoire is fairly flat. In the south is Yamoussoukro, the country's new capital à la Brasilia, and all the cacao and coffee farms. You'll see remnants of the rainforests that once covered the entire area. As you move north, the land becomes savannah. This is where you'll find Bouaké, the country's number two city, and, further north, Korhogo and Comoë National Park.

The coastal area is unusual in that a lagoon, several km inland, starts at the Ghanaian border and stretches for 300 km along the entire eastern half of the coast. From Abidjan you can sail westward on this lagoon for a week and never see the sea. To get to the sea you must go through the Vridi Canal, built in the early 1950s to give Abidjan a harbour.

CLIMATE
In the south, the rains fall heaviest from May to October, usually letting up in August. In the drier northern half, the rainy season is late May to early October, with no August dry spell. The south is humid, but temperatures rarely rise above 32°C. From early December to February the harmattan blows down from the Sahara and greatly reduces visibility in the northern mountain regions.

POPULATION & PEOPLE
There are over 60 ethnic groups amongst the country's 13.8 million people. The four principal ones are the Akan (Baoulé and Agni primarily) in the east and central areas, the Kru (Bété and Yacouba primarily) in the west near Liberia, and the Senoufo and Mandé in the north.

The Akan constitute about 35% of the population, the largest single group being the Baoulé (15% of the population), who separated from the Ashanti in Ghana around 1750 under the leadership of Queen Aura Poku and migrated west into the central area. The Akan are far from politically united, however, greatly reducing their importance as a coalition and forcing the powerful Baoulé lobby in the government to carefully court the country's other ethnic groups.

The Senoufo are renowned for their artisans who are separated into specific castes (carvers, bronze workers and welders). Primarily animists, they are concentrated around Korhogo, while the Yacouba (or Dan), who are known for their impressive masks and dancers on stilts, live in the mountainous region around Man.

GOVERNMENT
The head of state and commander in chief of the military is the president, who is elected by universal suffrage every five years. The president in turn appoints a council of ministers including the prime minister. The legislature consists of a National Assembly whose 175 members are also popularly elected to five-year terms. The speaker of the

Assembly is authorised to assume the presidency in case of the president's death. The ruling party, the PDCI, has operated for many decades, but multipartyism has existed only since 1990. There are now some 40 officially recognised opposition parties, the main one being the Front Populaire d'Ivoire (FPI) led by Laurent Gbagbo.

ECONOMY

In the agriculture sector, Côte d'Ivoire rates many superlatives – largest producer of cocoa in the world, largest producer of coffee in Africa (and third-largest in the world), and largest producer of cotton in Francophone Africa. However, despite serious efforts at diversification (palm oil, rubber, bananas and pineapples in the south, and sugar cane and cotton in the north), coffee and cocoa still represent over half of export earnings – about the same as in 1960. As a result of the collapse of these commodities on world markets starting in the early 1980s, Côte d'Ivoire has become the world's largest debtor on a per capita basis.

The rude shock of the CFA devaluation has done little for the debt problem, but it is giving a spurt to the economy as economists predicted, resulting in a positive growth rate in 1994, the first in years. Future growth is likely but as long as world prices for coffee and cocoa are depressed, a return to fast economic growth will be difficult. Increased privatisation of the country's many public enterprises might help, but so far the country is moving only very slowly in this direction, with only six companies privatised to date.

One bright prospect is that of oil and gas. Two new offshore oil and gas fields are expected to make the country self-sufficient in both. In sum, the country's long years of decline may be over.

ARTS & CULTURE
Wooden Carvings

The art of Côte d'Ivoire is among the most outstanding in West Africa. Three groups stand out – the Baoulé, the Dan (or Yacouba) and the Senoufo. They are known best for their wooden carvings, so if you're looking for

Wooden pith helmet carved by the Baoulé people during the colonial period

masks, Côte d'Ivoire is a good place to come. While most of this talent has been lost, a few artisans are still doing good work, and high quality older pieces, all expensive, can still be found.

Dan masks, which demonstrate a high regard for symmetry and balance, are a good example of expressiveness achieved primarily through form. Traditionally, they were often carved spontaneously, inspired perhaps by a beautiful face. The most common mask is that of a human face, slightly abstract but with realistic features, a smooth surface, everted lips, slit or large circular eyeholes and calm expression. These masks often have specific uses; that representing a woman, for example, might be used to keep women from seeing the uncircumcised boys during their seclusion during initiation. Another common Dan carving is that of a large spoon for serving rice; such spoons typically have two legs of human form and rest standing up on the legs.

Baoulé masks typically represent an animal or a human face. The facial masks, traditionally used in commemorative ceremonies, are very realistic and somewhat unique as they are often intended to portray particular individuals who can be recognised by their facial marks and hairdos. Other Baoulé masks, however, are not at all realistic. The humorous *kplekple* horned mask representing a disobedient child, for example, is very stylised with a powerful expression and not at all naturalistic or carefully finished. The same is true of the painted antelope and buffalo masks, which have large open mouths and are intended to represent evil

---

Literature of Côte d'Ivoire

Côte d'Ivoire's most famous writer is Bernard Dadié; he is also the country's most prolific and widely translated novelist. Born in 1916, he has a style that is both warm and simple, which he maintains even when expressing his dissatisfactions. One of his first novels, *Climbié* (Heinemann Books, London, 1971), is an autobiographical account of his childhood. Writing about his journey to France, he explains, 'Paris has not digested me because I resisted. The Gods from home, obstinate and patient, pulled me in another direction'. Other works translated into English include *The Black Cloth* (University of Massachusetts Press, Amherst, 1987) and *The City Where No One Dies* (Three Continents Press, Washington, DC, 1986).

Other well-known Ivoirian novelists include Aké Loba and Ahmadou Kourouma. The former is best known for *Kocoumbo* (abstracted in *African Writing Today* by editor Ezekiel Mphahlele, Penguin, London, 1967), an autobiographical novel of an African suffering the effects of being uprooted and poverty-stricken in Paris and being drawn towards militant communism. The latter's hit novel is *The Suns of Independence* (Heinemann Books, Oxford, UK, 1981), which recounts with wry humour the story of a disgruntled village chief who was deposed following independence, losing his subjects and his power in the process, and had to adjust to an altogether different life. ∎

---

spirits; women who see one during a night-long dance will die.

Senoufo masks are highly stylised like the animal masks of the Baoulé. The most famous perhaps is that of the 'fire-spitter' helmet mask, which is a combination of antelope, wart hog and hyena. Powerful and scary, it is said to represent the chaotic state of things in primeval times. The human facial masks, on the other hand, can often have a very insipid expression. One that you'll see everywhere in the tourist markets, and typically of very low quality as a result thereof, is the Sakrobundu mask of the mother of the clan. It features a highly stylised hairdo, thin eyes, small round mouth, various facial markings and two horns.

Pop Music

The country's most well known singer is Alpha Blondy, who is the top reggae singer in Africa and world famous. Three other Ivoirian *vedettes* known Africa-wide and in Europe are the reggae superstar Serge Kassy and female vocalists Aicha Koné and Nayanka Bell. Additional Ivoirian stars include Soro Nghana, Antoinette Kouna, Monique Ceka, Jimmy Hyacinte and Mariatou.

RELIGION

Even though the country has two of the largest Catholic cathedrals in the world, only about 12% of the people are Christian and many of those are Protestant. Some 23% – and especially the Malinké – are Muslims, primarily in the north. The remaining 65% of the people practise traditional religions involving ancestral worship. The dead are transformed into spirits and are in constant contact with the living. Through various rituals, the living seek their blessings and any protection they can afford. One group that has held particularly strongly to traditional beliefs are the Senoufo. The strong influence of such beliefs on the social system is reflected in their Poro cult, which is a system whereby children are instructed over many years in the oral history and social mores of the Senoufo and eventually initiated into it.

LANGUAGE

French is the official language. The principal African languages are Yacouba (in the area of Man), Senoufo (Korhogo), Baoulé (Yamoussoukro), Agni (Abengourou) and Dioula (JOU-lah), the market language everywhere.

Expressions in Dioula

Good morning.	*e-nee-SOH-goh-mah*
Good evening.	*e-nee-WOU-lah*
How are you?	*e-kah-KAY-nay-wah?*
I'm fine.	*ah-HON kah-kay-nay*
Thank you.	*e-nee-chay*
Goodbye.	*AM-bay SOH-goh-mah*

Expressions in Senoufo

Good morning.	*foy-YEH-nah*
Good evening.	*chang-WAH-nah*
How are you?	*kad-JOH-nah?*
I'm fine.	*meen-CHOK-low-goh*
Thank you.	*meen-mon-CHAR*
Goodbye.	*meen-KAR-ee*

Expressions in Yacouba

Good morning.	*un-ZHOO-bah-boh* (man)
Good morning.	*NAH-bah-boh* (woman)
Good evening.	*un-ZHOO-attoir* (man)
Good evening.	*NAH-attoir* (woman)
How are you?	*bwee-AR-way*
Thank you.	*BAH-lee-kah*
Goodbye.	*KHOD-an-kway*

Facts for the Visitor

VISAS & EMBASSIES
Côte d'Ivoire Visas

Nationals of Denmark, Finland, France, Ireland, Italy, Norway, Sweden, the USA and the UK don't need visas for stays of up to 90 days. Visas are usually valid for three months and good for visits of up to one month. Many Ivoirian embassies outside of Africa demand to see a return airline ticket, but those in Africa rarely do.

French embassies in Africa (and maybe elsewhere) issue visas to Côte d'Ivoire in those countries without Ivoirian embassies, usually within 24 hours. The cost is typically CFA 20,000. So you can get them very easily in every West or Central African country except The Gambia.

Côte d'Ivoire Embassies

Belgium 234 Ave Franklin-Roosevelt, Brussels 1050 (☎ (02) 672-23-57)
France 102 ave R-Poincaré, 75116 Paris (consulate) (☎ (1) 45-01-53-10)
Germany Königstrasse 93, 53115 Bonn (☎ (0228) 21-20-98/9)
UK 2 Upper Belgrave St, London SW1X 8BJ (☎ (0171) 235-6991)
USA 2424 Massachusetts Ave, NW, Washington, DC 20008 (☎ (202) 797-0330)

Côte d'Ivoire also has diplomatic representation in Accra, Addis Ababa, Algiers, Amsterdam, Bangui, Berne, Brasilia, Cairo, Copenhagen, Dakar, Freetown, Geneva, Kinshasa, Lagos, Libreville, Madrid, Monrovia, New York, Ottawa, Rabat, Rome, Tokyo, Tunis, Vienna and Yaoundé.

Other African Visas

In Abidjan, you can get visas to all West and Central African countries except Cape Verde, Equatorial Guinea and Guinea-Bissau.

Algeria The embassy requires four photos but issues visas only to citizens and legal residents of Côte d'Ivoire.
Benin There's no need to get a visa to Benin if you'll be travelling overland from Togo because you can get one valid for a two-day stay (and renewable in Cotonou) at the border on the Lomé-Cotonou route. Getting one in Abidjan is expensive. The Benin embassy, which is open weekdays from 8 am to noon and 3 to 6 pm and gives same-day service, requires one photo and CFA 20,000 for visas good for stays of three months. The embassy is in Deux Plateaux. Take SOTRA bus No 21 to the end, then Bus 35 until two stops before the end.
Burkina Faso Visas to Burkina Faso cost a whopping CFA 40,000 and are good for stays of three months. The embassy requires two photos and issues visas in 48 hours. It is open weekdays from 8 am to 12.30 pm and 1.30 to 4.30 pm.
Cameroun Cameroun visas good for stays up to three/six months cost CFA 15,000/30,000. The embassy, open weekdays from 8 am to 1 pm, requires two photos and 48 hours to process applications.
Chad The embassy, which takes 24 hours to issue visas, sometimes less, requires two photos and CFA 10,000 for single-entry visas valid for one-month stays.
Ghana The embassy receives visa applications only on Monday, Wednesday and Friday from 8.30 am to 1 pm. It requires four photos, CFA 6000 and 48 hours to issue visas.
Guinea The embassy is open weekdays from 9 am to 3 pm, charges CFA 20,000, requires three photos, and issues visas usually within 48 hours. A letter of recommendation from your embassy is not required.
Kenya & Sierra Leone The British high commission, open weekdays from 8.30 am to noon, issues visas to Kenya and Sierra Leone but not to The Gambia. Bring CFA 30,000 and one photo; the process takes 48 hours.

CÔTE D'IVOIRE

Liberia One-month Liberian visas cost CFA 8000, require two photos, and are issued the same day.

Mali Visas cost CFA 5000, require two photos and are issued the same day if you come in the morning. The embassy is open Monday to Thursday from 8 am to 2.30 pm, Friday from 8 am to 12.30 pm.

Mauritania The embassy is open weekdays from 8 am to 1 pm, charges CFA 6000 for visas and often gives same-day service.

Niger The embassy requires three photos and about CFA 9000; the process takes two to three days.

Nigeria The embassy's charges are far higher than those at other Nigerian embassies and they vary considerably: eg CFA 11,900 for Americans, CFA 24,000 for Canadians, CFA 33,220 for Australians and CFA 66,270 for Britons. The embassy, open weekdays from 9 am to 3.30 pm, also requires two photos and 48 hours to issue visas.

Senegal The Senegalese consulate, open Monday to Thursday from 8 am to 3 pm and on Friday and Saturday from 8 am to 12.30 pm, no longer issues visas to The Gambia (which has an honorary consulate in Treichville). For three-month multiple-entry visas to Senegal, it requires CFA 7000 and two photos and issues visas in 48 hours.

Zaïre The embassy, open weekdays from 8 am to 3 pm, requires five photos; same-day service. Its charges for single/multiple-entry visas are the same as in all CFA countries: CFA 22,000/34,000 (one-month stay), CFA 38,000/50,000 (two-month stay) and CFA 54,000/62,000 (three-month stay). A transit visa, however, costs just CFA 14,000 (CFA 26,000 for two entries).

Foreign Embassies

See the Abidjan Information section for a list of embassies in that city.

DOCUMENTS

Except for Africans of certain nationalities, everyone needs a passport and an International Health Certificate. If you have a car, you'll need a *carnet de passage*. If you don't have one, you can purchase a *laissez passer* at the border. It's good for two weeks and is not renewable.

CUSTOMS

Importing foreign currency is not a problem but if you'll be exporting large amounts of cash, declare it on arrival, otherwise customs officials may give you problems on departure. Theoretically, there is a limit on the amount of CFA that you may export (roughly CFA 75,000) but in practice customs officials don't seem to care and many times they don't even ask how much you're carrying.

MONEY

UK£1 = CFA 775
US$1 = CFA 500

The unit of currency is the West African CFA franc. The airport bank gives decent rates, so change money there if you arrive by plane; it's open every day from the first arrival to the last. Before changing money, it definitely pays to shop around for the best rates as some banks, such as Citibank, offer excellent rates but also high commissions while others, such as BICICI (Banque Internationale pour le Commerce et l'Industrie en Côte d'Ivoire), charge no commissions but offer significantly lower rates. Barclays offers good rates but it changes only Barclays travellers' cheques. Citibank's service is good and its rates are even better, but for travellers' cheques it's usually best only when fairly large amounts are being exchanged.

The French usually have no trouble obtaining cash with their credit cards as the cards are usually issued by French banks affiliated with ones here. Travellers from other countries may find doing this more difficult. Citibank is one place you can get cash with your Visa card; others are SIB (Société Ivoirienne de Banque), which has a weekly limit of CFA 100,000, and BICICI. If you have an American Express credit card and want money, you won't be able to obtain it without a personal cheque, so consider bringing one along just in case.

Banks that change money include Barclays, Citibank, BICICI, BIAO (Banque Internationale pour l'Afrique Occidentale), SGBCI (Société Générale de Banques en Côte d'Ivoire), SIB, Ecobank and Banque Atlantique.

BUSINESS HOURS & HOLIDAYS

Business hours are weekdays from 8 am to noon and 2.30 to 6 pm, and Saturday from 8 am to noon. Government offices are open weekdays from 7.30 am to noon and 2.30 to

Fête du Dipri

The festival commences around midnight. The entire village lies awake within the security of their huts. Evil lurks about. The Angrekponé secret society chants in the distance calling for the Diori to be a failure. Slowly and quietly only the women and children sneak out of their huts and, naked, they carry out nocturnal rites to exorcise the village to be rid of the spells of the Angrekponé. Before sunrise, the chief appears and calls out to his people: 'O Loh Loh Ao! Chase out the evil'. Then the entire village emerges screaming out these words. The drums begin to pound, mass hysteria permeates the air, and the villagers covered in kaolin enter into trances. Bodies squirm in the dust, eyes roll up into their sockets, an adolescent beats himself, women cook eggs and bananas in their hands, and in the main street children beat the red dust with sticks. Pandemonium reigns. This frenzied behaviour continues till noon, then the magic exercises begin. The Sékékponé society plunge knives deep into their bellies. Onlookers gaze as the healing process begins immediately. Finally by late afternoon, the Sékékponé and Angrekponé confront each other. In a silent battle, the loser hands an egg to the victor and departs. The Abidji, as the sun sets, perform their final purifying ablutions and the festival comes to an end.

Christine Robinson ■

5.30 pm, and on Saturday from 7.30 am to noon.

Banking hours are weekdays from 8 to 11.30 am and 2.30 to 4.30 pm, and Saturdays from 8 to 11.30 am.

Public Holidays

1 January, Easter Monday, 1 May, End of Ramadan, Ascension Thursday, Whit Monday, 15 August, 1 November, 7 December (National Day), 25 December.

CULTURAL EVENTS

One of the more famous festivals is the Fêtes des Masques in the Man region, which you are most likely to see in villages during the month of February. Some of the other important ones are the Fête de l'Abissa in Grand-Bassam (late October or early November, lasting a week), the Fête des Haristes in Bregbo near Bingerville (1 November), the carnival in Bouaké (March), and the Fête de Papa Nouveau at Toukouzou near Jacqueville (12 September).

If you're here in late April, don't miss the **Fête du Dipri** (yam festival) in Gomon (also at Yaobou), 100 km north-west of Abidjan. (For dates, consult the Ministry of Tourism or the community liaison officer of the US embassy.)

POST & TELECOMMUNICATIONS

The post restante service in Abidjan's main post office (Plateau) is pathetic; they won't let you sort the letters, nor are they particu-

larly friendly. Letters, if they arrive, cost US$1 each to collect.

International telephone calls and faxes can be made easily between 7 am and 7 pm at the nearby EECI building on Ave Houdaille. A three-minute (minimum) call to Australia or the UK costs US$18/8. To the USA a daytime call costs US$15 and a night call (between 7 pm and 7 am) costs US$10. You can also make international calls using phonecards, which range in price from US$3 to US$25.

PHOTOGRAPHY

A photo permit is not required. Côte d'Ivoire is not uptight about people taking snapshots but, as in virtually all African countries, taking photos of military installations and airports is prohibited.

HEALTH

A vaccination is required for yellow fever but not for cholera unless there's an outbreak.

The two best hospitals are the Polyclinique Internationale Sainte Anne-Marie (☎ 44 32 29) in Deux Plateaux and the hospital in the north in Ferké run by Baptist missionaries. The second page of the newspaper, *Fraternité Matin*, specifies which pharmacies in Abidjan are open at night.

DANGERS & ANNOYANCES

Since the late 1980s, Abidjan has had perhaps the worst reputation for crime in West Africa, sometimes exceeding that of Lagos. Armed people have entered restaurants and robbed

CÔTE D'IVOIRE

everybody. Treichville, the market and *gare routière* (bush taxi/bus park) in Adjamé, and around Vridi Canal are the most dangerous areas, but no part of town is safe for walking alone after dark. Also, walking over the two bridges to Treichville is very dangerous even during the day with lots of people around. Anybody who looks wealthy is at greatest risk but not even backpackers are safe.

Most theft is not planned. The trick is not to provide the temptation. At night, avoid walking around alone. Leave all jewellery, watches, purses and wallets at the hotel; most have safe boxes. The real value of what you're wearing makes no difference. If you've bought gold, don't wear it. Fortunately, most major nightclubs now have door attendants who escort people to and from their cars. Fortunately, too, the government's recent crackdown on crime (shoot first and ask questions later), while perhaps morally questionable, is making the city noticeably safer.

If you are attacked or lose anything, especially if you intend to claim insurance reimbursement, call or see the Commissariat du Premier Arrondissement in Abidjan (☎ 32 00 22). Each certificate regarding theft costs around CFA 7000.

ACCOMMODATION

Since the devaluation, accommodation has become much more affordable. In Abidjan there are lots of choices for CFA 4000. There are also decent mid-range hotels in the centre for CFA 7000 to CFA 15,000.

Outside of Abidjan, rates are slightly lower and you can even find places under CFA 3000 without too much difficulty. Some are complete dumps and others are decent, particularly some of the Catholic missions, many of which accept travellers.

FOOD

Attiéké (AT-chay-kay) is a side dish and one of Côte d'Ivoire's best known and liked specialities. You may think it's couscous but in fact it is grated manioc. You'll find attiéké at all the *maquis* (mah-KEY) – Côte d'Ivoire's claim to fame in the African culinary world.

A typical maquis is a cheap open-air res-

taurant with chairs and tables in the sand and some amusing African paintings on the wall, perhaps of a woman with her spider-like hairdo and a bottle of Flag, the country's most popular beer. All they normally serve is braised chicken and braised fish smothered in onions and tomatoes, served with attiéké. Some also serve beef brochettes and chicken *kedjenou* (KED-jeh-nou), a chicken dish made with vegetables and a mild sauce. I've never seen anyone get sick from eating at a maquis. If you're worried about the raw tomatoes or hot peppers, push them aside.

Another popular side dish is *foutou*, a dough made of boiled yams, cassava or plantains pounded into a sticky paste, similar to mashed potato. Foutou, rice and other staples are invariably served with a sauce, two of the more common ones being *sauce arachide* made with groundnuts, or a hot *sauce graine* made with palm oil nuts.

One of the more popular street foods is *aloco* (ah-LOH-coh), which are ripe bananas fried in palm oil, spiced with steamed onions and chilli and eaten alone or with grilled fish.

Getting There & Away

AIR

From Europe, there are direct flights daily from Paris, four times a week from Geneva and Zürich, three times a week from Brussels, twice a week from Rome and once a week from Lisbon.

From the USA, there are direct flights twice a week from New York to Abidjan with Air Afrique, with a stop in Dakar. Ethiopian Airlines offers four direct flights a week from Addis Ababa, with connecting flights to Nairobi and Bombay, while Air Afrique offers twice weekly service to/from Johannesburg via Brazzaville. You can also fly directly to Abidjan from Morocco and Egypt (once a week) and from every Central African country except Chad and the Central African Republic. To get to/from South America, the most direct route is through

Lagos or Dakar; Varig has flights from Brazil to both cities.

Within West Africa, there are daily flights to Abidjan from Lagos, Lomé, Accra, Bamako, Conakry and Dakar. The major carriers are Air Afrique (the best one), Nigeria Airways and Ghana Airways. There are also at least four flights a week between Abidjan and Ouagadougou, Niamey, Freetown, Cotonou and Banjul. There are two flights a week to/from Nouakchott and, because of the continuing political mess in Liberia, still only three flights a week to/from Monrovia. However, a small company, Weasua Air Transport (☎ 27 69 09), has daily flights every day to Freetown, stopping en route in Monrovia.

Since the devaluation, fares have almost doubled, eg: CFA 51,000 one way to Accra, CFA 109,000 one way to Bamako and over CFA 200,000 to Dakar. However, some smaller airlines are cheaper and just as good, in particular Air Burkina and Air Ivoire. The latter, for example, has flights two or three times weekly from Abidjan to Ouagadougou, Bamako, Accra, Monrovia and Conakry and charges about 20% less than Air Afrique and other major airlines. Air Burkina, which also serves the Abidjan-Ouaga route, matches Air Ivoire's fares.

LAND
Bus
You can get to Abidjan by bus direct from Accra, Ouagadougou and Bamako. However, travellers rarely take these long-haul buses the entire distance except on the Abidjan-Accra route because the trip is too gruelling and too much of interest is missed along the way.

To/From Burkina Faso There are large, comfortable *cars* departing every day from Abidjan, Yamoussoukro and Bouaké to Bobo-Dioulasso and Ouagadougou. Two of the best companies are Sans Frontières (two departures a day in either direction) and Sogebaf (one departure a day). Others include Les Comètes Binkady, Linko Lemgo, TST, Sotraco, Sotrabi and Sonabi.

In Abidjan, Yamoussoukro and Bouaké, they all leave from the gares routières. The trip to Ouaga takes at least 24 hours and sometimes much more due to overnight stays at the Burkina Faso border, which closes at 6.30 pm (lodging is available), and occasional long waits in Bouaké (up to seven hours!), so many travellers regret that they didn't break the trip up.

The cost from Abidjan to Ouaga, at CFA 14,000 (CFA 11,500 to Bobo), is less than a 1st-class seat on the train (CFA 16,400) but more than a 2nd-class seat (CFA 11,000). If you depart from Bouaké, it's better to go only to Bobo (CFA 7500) and catch another bus to Ouaga (CFA 3000) than to take a direct bus to Ouaga (CFA 12,500).

To/From Ghana The only direct bus service between Abidjan and Accra is provided by the Ghanaian STC company; the buses are large and comfortable but not very punctual. They leave daily in both directions at 8 am and arrive 12 to 14 hours later depending on the delay at the border, which lasts between two and four hours. Late departures are common. The fare is CFA 5000 (CFA 3500 for Abidjan-Takoradi) plus CFA 500 for luggage. There's also a CFA 1000 charge at the border. Tickets must be purchased the day before departure.

To/From Mali *Cars* for Bamako all leave from Gare d'Adjamé in Abidjan; there are departures every day. There are several companies that do the trip. TOKF, next to Sabé Transport at Gare d'Adjamé, has large buses leaving every day at 2 pm; the fare is CFA 8000 to Sikasso, CFA 10,000 to Bougouni and CFA 12,000 to Bamako. The trip to Bamako takes about 1½ days and is very gruelling; breaking the trip up would be better. Other companies with similar buses and fares are Sotranso and Centraci. Sotranso's buses leave Abidjan around 4 pm and arrive Bamako two days later around 5 am.

Bush Taxi
Bush taxi Peugeot 504s offer more frequent service than the buses, but they can be more

expensive and take just as long, sometimes longer. From Yamoussoukro to Man, for example, they cost CFA 4500 compared to CFA 3500 for a big bus, and they both do the trip in the same time.

To/From Burkina Faso A Peugeot 504 direct to Ouagadougou is CFA 14,000 from Abidjan and CFA 13,000 from Bouaké or Yamoussoukro. The trip takes 20 to 24 hours from Abidjan, and you can usually save money by splitting this trip up. Take a bus from Abidjan to Ferkessédougou (CFA 3500), then a bush taxi from there to Bobo-Dioulasso (CFA 6000) and another on to Ouaga (CFA 3000); the total cost is CFA 2250 less than a direct trip by bus. If you're headed just to Bobo, the trip by bush taxi costs CFA 11,000 from Abidjan and CFA 7500 from Bouaké. While the Burkina border closes at 6.30 pm, a 'competent' driver can reportedly get across as late as 8 pm. The same does not hold for buses.

To/From Ghana From Abidjan, you may have to go first to Aboisso and find another taxi from there to the border. From the Ghanaian border there are taxis that will take you all the way to Accra. The total cost is about the same as the STC bus, and the trip takes just about as long as the bus and is not nearly as comfortable.

To/From Liberia & Guinea Travellers headed west to Liberia or Guinea can make it from Abidjan to Man in eight hours by bus or bush taxi and from there to Danané (CFA 1200) and on to Monrovia in another long day provided overland travel in Liberia again becomes possible. You'll find taxis all along the way; no walking is required. Make sure you get your passport stamped in Danané, where you must catch a van to the border (CFA 800, two hours). Liberian border officials are looking for bribes, so have your documents in order. You'll find taxis just on the other side to take you to Kahnplé, then Sanniquellie. The turn-off for Guinea is in Danané; from there you take a series of bush

taxis to Lola and Nzérékoré, a distance of 210 km from Danané.

To/From Mali It is a long and gruelling trip between Abidjan and Bamako; most travellers who have travelled this route recommend breaking it up. You could, for example, take a bush taxi for the Bamako-Ferké section and a bus or train for the remainder. If you go via Odienné, expect very light traffic between there and Bougouni (Mali).

Train

To/From Burkina Faso The Ouagadougou choo-choo, which has declined considerably in recent years, is still a popular way to travel and fares are competitive with the buses. The big advantage is that meeting people is easier. There is only one train, the *Express*, and it leaves only three times a week, Tuesday, Thursday and Saturday, in either direction. It departs Abidjan at 8.30 am and Ouaga at 7 am and typically takes about 27 hours, several hours longer than scheduled. The fare to Ouaga is CFA 16,400 in 1st class and CFA 11,000 in 2nd class (CFA 12,800 and CFA 8600, respectively, to Bobo-Dioulasso). A sleeping berth (*couchette*) in 1st class costs an additional CFA 3500 regardless of where you get on or off.

Finding a seat on the train is usually easy in Abidjan, but more difficult as the trip progresses. To be sure of getting one you should book at least a day ahead, preferably several days in advance. During certain parts of the year students with ID cards can get discounts of 30% or more on 2nd-class fares, so if you have a card, ask about this.

According to the schedule, the *Express* from Abidjan arrives in Bouaké at 3.05 pm, Banfora at 1.05 am, Bobo at 3.10 am and Ouaga at 10.30 am. Schedules change frequently, however, so double-check at the RAN station.

Some travellers find 2nd class unbearable because of the incredible overcrowding and heat. For this reason, consider taking 1st class or breaking up the trip. For a description of the train, see the introductory Getting There & Away Section in the Burkina chapter.

Car & Motorbike

Petrol and diesel fuel *(gasoil)* cost CFA 445 (CFA 405 for regular) and CFA 270 a litre, respectively, which is about as high as you'll find in West Africa. The road system is excellent.

To/From Burkina Faso & Mali From Abidjan, the driving time north to Ouagadougou or Bamako is about 24 hours nonstop, or two long days. Both routes are paved all the way. Both the Malian and Burkina borders close around 6.30 pm and reopen at 8 am. While some people have managed to cross after closing time, most don't succeed. Moreover, foreign cars entering Côte d'Ivoire need a *laissez passer*, which is issued only during official hours.

To/From Ghana The coastal road connecting Abidjan and Accra is paved all the way and is in excellent condition. The nonstop driving time is 10 to 12 hours.

To/From Liberia The unpaved section between Man and Ganta (Liberia) is in good condition, so you can pass year-round once overland travel again becomes possible. You can also go along the Ivoirian coast via Tabou, Zwedru (Liberia) and Gbarnga; this route takes three to four days and is paved only about half the distance. Only expert drivers with 4WD vehicles should attempt it from May to November, when the Liberian section becomes very muddy.

Note If you have a big motorcycle, Abidjan is a good place to sell it, but you may need three weeks or so to find a buyer. Some travellers recently have received what they paid in Europe.

Getting Around

AIR

From Abidjan, Air Ivoire flies to five cities, including Bouaké every day, San Pédro and Odienné four times a week, Korhogo three times a week and Man twice weekly. Prices are quite reasonable, eg: CFA 16,250 to Bouaké and CFA 18,125 to Man or Korhogo.

There's an airport tax of CFA 800 on domestic flights and CFA 3000 on international flights. When you reconfirm, check whether the tax is included in your ticket.

BUS

The country's large modern buses are cheaper, more comfortable and more popular than most bush taxis. They're also cheaper than the train. Most of the buses are in excellent condition, have assigned seats and leave on set schedules; there are many companies and picking one is easy because those for, say, Man are usually grouped in the same general area.

A great advantage of the buses is that they ply the long routes at night and you can, therefore, save on accommodation. With most companies, if you arrive at, say, 3 am, you can sleep on the bus until dawn. While this seems safe in towns such as Korhogo or Man, doing the same in Abidjan would not be wise.

In Abidjan, buses all leave from the gare routière in Adjamé; the fare is CFA 3500 to San Pédro, CFA 4000 to Bouaké and CFA 4500 to Man and Korhogo.

BUSH TAXI

Côte d'Ivoire has a good system of bush taxis running throughout the country. Their main advantage is that they leave at all hours of the day and not at fixed schedules. Some are Peugeot 504s; others are minibuses. If the Peugeots are too crowded for your liking, buy an extra seat. In general, fares are only slightly higher than those of buses.

TRAIN

In addition to the daily Abidjan-Ouagadougou *Express* which leaves Abidjan at 8.30 am, there's a *Rapide* that costs about one-third less and plies the Abidjan-Bouaké route once a day, stopping at Anyama, Yapo, Agboville, and Dimbokro (among others), but not at Yamoussoukro.

CAR

Since the devaluation, rental cars are a bit more affordable. All the major operators are represented. See the Abidjan Getting There & Away section for details.

TAXI

With the devaluation, taxis in Abidjan are no longer so terribly expensive. Taxi drivers there are still notorious for rigging their meters, however. Also, rates double from midnight (not before!) to 6 am; during those times the red No 2 meter is used. Africans and the local French don't tip, but taxi drivers often expect tips from foreigners and those going to hotels.

Abidjan

Abidjan was an unimportant town until 1951 when the French finished the Vridi Canal connecting the lagoon with the ocean, giving the city an excellent harbour. Since then, the city's population has skyrocketed, from less than 100,000 people to 2.5 million today, spread over four peninsulas around the lagoon.

Abidjan has two faces. Visitors travelling first class tend to see only the wealthy side, especially Le Plateau, the central area with the skyscrapers, and Cocody, the posh residential section where you'll find the Hôtel Ivoire. Les Deux Plateaux, another posh residential section, is nearby.

The sections where ordinary people live such as Treichville, Marcory and Adjamé are far more interesting. Linked to Le Plateau by two major bridges, Treichville is where you'll find the largest of the city's four markets and the most nightclubs. A thorough tour of the Treichville market can easily take half a day. The one in Adjamé is also good. A few words of Dioula, the major market language, will help make the traders think you're an old hand at African bargaining.

Orientation

The modern commercial centre is Le Plateau. Two of its landmarks are the modern Pyramid building and, several blocks away, the Marché du Plateau. One of the major commercial streets is Ave de Gaulle, more commonly known as Rue du Commerce and not to be confused with the six-lane Blvd de Gaulle, which runs along the edge of Le Plateau, acting as a bypass route. At the western end of Rue du Commerce is the Gare Sud bus station (SOTRA terminal) and, nearby, the Novotel.

To the north of Le Plateau is Adjamé with its huge gare routière and market, while to its south and across the lagoon is Treichville and the port area, with Marcory just beyond and the airport and the ocean further south still.

Information

Tourist Office There is no longer a tourist office, and the Ministry of Tourism (☎ 21 82 28, fax 21 73 06), in the CCIA building at the Cité Administrative, a modern government complex just west of the catherdral, is not set up to receive travellers. Brititsh citizens should pass by their embassy because the staff there are friendly and full of helpful suggestions.

Money All of the banks are in Le Plateau, including Citibank (☎ 32 46 10, fax (225) 32 78 85) at 28 Ave Delafosse opposite the Pyramid building; BICICI (☎ 32 03 79) nearby on Ave Franchet d'Espérey; BIAO (☎ 32 07 22) on Ave Joseph Anoma (ex-Barthe); SGBCI (☎ 32 03 33) on the same street; SIB (☎ 21 00 00) at 34 Blvd de la République; Barclays (☎ 32 28 04) in Immeuble Alpha 2000 on Rue Gourgas; and the Chemical Bank representative in the same building as Barclays.

To get the best rate, you must shop around. Citibank, which is open weekdays from 8 am to 1 pm, usually offers the highest rates but charges a commission of CFA 6000 for cashing travellers' cheques regardless of the size of the transaction. Service here is now very quick and they'll give you cash with your Visa card to boot. BICICI, which is only about a block away and open weekdays from

8 to 11.15 am and 2.45 to 4.45 pm, offers much lower rates but charges no commission. It also offers quick service and will accept many kinds of travellers' cheques. Neither bank accepts Central African CFA. To exchange them, the best place is Air Gabon, which is on the same street as Citibank and a block away.

Foreign Embassies

All of the following embassies are in Le Plateau:

Algeria 53 Blvd Clozel (☎ 21 23 40)

Austria Immeuble N'Zarama, Blvd du Général de Gaulle near Ave Chardy (☎ 33 23 16)

Belgium Immeuble Alliance, Rue Lecoeur (☎ 21 00 88)

Brazil Immeuble Alpha 2000, Rue Gourgas (☎ 22 23 41)

Burkina Faso 2 Ave Terrasson de Fougères (☎ 32 13 13)

Cameroun Immeuble Le Général, Rue Botreau-Roussel (☎ 32 20 86/7)

Canada Immeuble Trade Center, 23 Ave Noguès corner Rue 5 (☎ 32 20 09, telex 23593)

Central African Republic Résidencial Atta, Ave des Anciens Combattants (☎ 21 36 46)

Chile Immeuble Jeceda (☎ 21 92 37)

Denmark Immeuble Le Mans, Rue Botreau-Roussel (☎ 33 17 65)

Egypt Immeuble El Nasr, Ave Général de Gaulle (☎ 32 79 25)

Ethiopia Nour al Hayat, 4th Floor, Ave Chardy (☎ 21 33 65)

France Corner of Rue Lecoeur & Rue Jesse Owens (☎ 20 20 04). Also issues visas to Togo.

Germany Immeuble Le Mans, Rue Botreau-Roussel (☎ 32 47 27 or 21 47 27, telex 23642)

Ghana Résidence La Corniche, Blvd de Gaulle (☎ 33 11 24)

Guinea Immeuble Crosson Duplessis, corner of Ave Crosson Duplessis & Rue 2 (☎ 32 94 94 or 32 86 00)

Japan Immeuble Alpha 2000, Rue Gourgas (☎ 21 28 63, telex 23400)

Liberia Immeuble Taleb, Ave Delafosse (☎ 22 23 59 or 32 85 17)

Mali Immeuble Maison du Mali, Rue du Commerce (☎ 32 31 47)

The Netherlands Immeuble Les Harmonies, corner of Blvd Carde and Ave Jamot (☎ 21 31 10 or 21 77 12)

Nigeria Corner of Blvd de la République & Ave Jamot (☎ 21 19 82 or 22 30 82)

Norway Immeuble N'Zarama, Blvd du Général de Gaulle near Ave Chardy (☎ 22 25 34)

Senegal (consulate) Immeuble Crosson Duplessis, corner of Ave Crosson Duplessis & Rue 2 (no phone)

Sweden Immeuble Alpha 2000, Rue Gourgas (☎ 21 24 10)

Switzerland Immeuble Alpha 2000, Rue Gourgas (☎ 21 30 02 or 21 17 21)

Tunisia Immeuble Shell, Ave Lamblin, 4th floor (☎ 32 23 04)

UK Immeuble Les Harmonies, corner of Blvd Carde and Ave Jamot (☎ 22 68 50/1, fax 22 32 21). It also issues visas to Sierra Leone and Kenya.

USA 5 Rue Jesse Owens, at northern end of Rue Gourgas (☎ 21 09 79, fax 22 32 59, telex 23660)

Zaïre 29 Blvd Clozel, 3rd floor (no phone)

Other embassies include: Benin (☎ 41 38 79, Rue des Jasmins, Deux Plateaux), Chad (☎ 32 35 35, 5 Rue des Selliers), Finland (☎ 41 50 01, Le Vallon Lot No 1385), Gabon (☎ 44 51 54, Direction de Géologie à Cocody), India (☎ 44 52 31, Impasse Pokou Lot No 36), Italy (☎ 44 61 70, 16 Rue de la Cannebière, Cocody), Mauritania (☎ 41 16 43, Rue Pierre et Marie Curie, Deux Plateaux, east of Blvd Latrille), Morocco (☎ 44 52 31, 24 Rue de la Cannebière, Cocody), Niger (☎ 26 50 98, 6 Blvd Achalme, Marcory) and Spain (☎ 44 48 50, Impasse Pokou Lot No 33).

Travel Agencies

American Express is represented by SDV Voyages (☎ 20 21 98, fax 20 21 99, telex 42438) in Treichville, on Ave Cristiani just west of Gare Lagunaire. It's open weekdays from 7.30 am to 12.30 pm and from 2 to 6 pm and on Saturday until 12.30 pm and is good primarily for airline reservations. If you have an American Express card, you can purchase travellers' cheques but you need a personal cheque to do this.

In the centre on Ave Chardy is the large Afric Voyages (☎ 21 21 11, fax 21 28 88), whose main business is also making airline reservations; it accepts credit cards but not travellers' cheques. Three other agencies which are good for airline reservations are Espace Voyages (☎ 21 26 46, fax 21 29 44) on Ave Houdaille facing Immeuble EECI, the World Travel Agency (☎ 35 14 85, fax 35 17 63), also in Le Plateau, and Socopao Voyages (☎ 32 85 30) on Blvd de Marseilles in the port area,

CÔTE D'IVOIRE

CÔTE D'IVOIRE

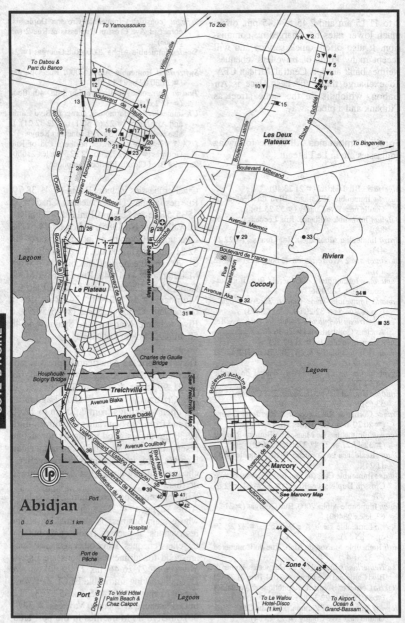

To Yamoussoukro

To Zoo

To Dabou &
Parc du Banco

To Bingerville

Boulevard de Gaulle

Rue de Williamsville

Boulevard Latrille

Route de Gobélé

Les Deux
Plateaux

Adjamé

Boulevard Attognoua

Avenue Reboul

Boulevard de la Paix

Boulevard Mitterand

Avenue Mermoz

Boulevard de France

Rue Washington

Avenue Aka

Riviera

Cocody

See Le Plateau Map

La Corniche

Lagoon

Le Plateau

Boulevard de Gaulle

Charles de Gaulle
Bridge

Houphouët-
Boigny Bridge

See Treichville Map

Lagoon

Treichville

Avenue Blaka

Avenue Dadié

Avenue Coulibaly

Boulevard Vallery Giscard d'estaing (Autoroute)

Blvd Naman Yamoussou (Autoroute)

Rue 12

Boulevard Acha Ime

Avenue de la TSF

Marcory

See Marcory Map

Autoroute

Abidjan

0   0.5   1 km

Port

Boulevard du Port

Boulevard de Marseille

Hospital

Port de
Pêche

Port

Digue de Vridi

To Vridi Hôtel
Palm Beach &
Chez Cakpot

Lagoon

Zone 4

To Le Wafou
Hotel-Disco
(1 km)

To Airport,
Ocean &
Grand-Bassam

200 metres before the train station. If an agency doesn't have its own computer terminals, you'll be better off dealing directly with the airlines because agencies without terminals often make mistakes.

For package tours of the interior, try Start Voyages (☎ 22 39 86, fax 22 39 82) at 17 Rue Delafosse in Le Plateau. It offers package tours to Man, Korhogo, Comoë National Park, Yamoussoukro, etc. Another one is L'Oiseau (☎ 32 74 78, fax 32 75 25) at Résidence Nabil on Ave Nogués in Le Plateau.

Bookshops The best bookshop is the Librairie de France on Ave Chardy near Blvd de la République. The next best are the bookshops at the Hôtel Ivoire (open to 8 pm) and Librairie Le Calumej at the Centre Commercial du Vallon in Deux Plateaux, followed by the small bookshop at the Novotel. All over town you'll find local newspapers for sale including the two opposition papers, *Le Changement* and *Notre Temps*.

Supermarkets The two best supermarkets are Nour-al-Hayat, which is in Le Plateau on the corner of Rue Lecoeur and Ave Chardy and open every day including Sunday mornings, and the Hayat supermarket at the Hôtel Ivoire in Cocody.

Hôtel Ivoire
The city's number one attraction is the Hôtel Ivoire, which has everything from an ice-skating rink, bowling alley, seven tennis courts, cinema and casino to a grocery store and a major art shop in the basement. Take bus No 86 from the Gare Sud, bus No 84 from the Gare Nord and bus No 74 from the Gare de Marcory.

St Paul's Cathedral
The city's eye-catching modern cathedral, outdone only by the one in Yamoussoukro, is definitely worth checking out, particularly for a trip up the tower. Designed by an Italian and consecrated by the Pope in 1985, it is open every day from 8 am to 7 pm; entry to the tower costs CFA 300. Mass is on Saturday at 7 pm and on Sunday at 8, 9.30 and 11 am. It is best seen on Sundays at 9.30 am, when there's a chorus.

The Outdoor Laundrette

Every day, some 375 *fanicos* (washermen), mostly Burkinabé and none Ivoirian, jam together in the middle of a small stream near the Parc du Banco frantically rubbing clothes on huge stones held in place by old car tyres. Afterwards, they spread the clothes over rocks and grass for at least half a km (never getting them mixed up) then iron them. Any washer not respecting the strict rules imposed by the washers' trade union which allocates positions is immediately excluded.

The soap is black and sold by 15 women who make it from palm oil in small wooden sheds on the hills surrounding the stream. It all starts at dawn when the fanicos head off on their rounds to collect the laundry in various parts of Abidjan; they begin arriving in single file at the stream around 6.30 am. The best time to be here is between 10.30 am and noon when the action is at its peak; you'll get some superb photos. In the afternoon, all you'll see is drying clothes. Every one will try to be your guide, but you don't need one. ∎

Musée National

At the V-shaped intersection of Blvd Carde and Blvd Nangui-Abrogoua is the Musée National d'Abidjan (☎ 22 20 56), which is open from 9 am to noon and 3 to 6 pm every day, except Sunday and on Monday morning. The collection of over 20,000 art objects is good by African museum standards and includes wooden statues and masks, pottery, ivory and bronze. The display is disorganised and the lighting is poor, but this may change when the ongoing repair work is completed. It's a 1.25-km walk from Le Plateau market, and lots of SOTRA buses pass nearby.

Parc du Banco

On the north-western edge of town near the beginning of the road to Dabou is the Parc du Banco, a rainforest reserve and a pleasant, cool place for a walk. The entrance fee is CFA 300. Several hundred metres beyond the dirt road entrance to the park you'll see an unforgettable spectacle, Africa's largest **outdoor laundrette**, where hundreds of men wash clothes in a stream. From the Gare Nord, take bus No 20, 34 or 36; from Gare Sud, take bus No 20.

Zoo

The zoo, on the north-east edge of town, is one of the best in West Africa, but nothing special by Western standards. It's open every day from 8 am to 6 pm. Bus Nos 75 and 76 departing from the Cité Administrative/museum go there, as does No 49 from the Cocody market and Deux Plateaux.

Activities

The Hôtel Ivoire is a good place to go swimming; the pool fee for nonresidents is CFA 3000. It also has seven tennis courts while the Hôtel Forum Golf has two. At the latter you can also rent sailboards. The Ivoire Golf Club has the best 18-hole golf course in West and Central Africa. The Forum Golf's pool costs CFA 3500.

Places to Stay – bottom end

Camping There are two camping spots. One is *Coppa-Cabana* along the ocean road to Grand-Bassam, 17 km east of Abidjan. It's run by two French brothers, Jeannot and Jean, who charge about CFA 1000 per person for camping and nothing for vehicles. There are good showers, washing facilities and a bar-restaurant with slow service. Take bus No 17 to get there.

The second camp site, *Les Vagues de Vridi*, is in the Vridi Canal area facing the ocean, on Rue de l'Océan between the Hôtel Palm Beach and Coco beach. Jean-Claude, the friendly owner, charges CFA 1000 per person for camping and CFA 1500 per person for a bare room, with no charge for vehicles. In addition to electricity and clean showers, there's a bar with large beers for CFA 300 plus a restaurant with food *sur commande* and food stalls nearby. Bus Nos 7, 17, 18 and 24 all pass nearby.

Some travellers who prefer sleeping in their cars recommend the parking lot of the *Hôtel Akwaba* (☎ 36 91 66); it's also in the

Vridi Canal area near the ocean. The guard will expect a tip.

Treichville In the past, many travellers have liked staying in Treichville because of its lively ambience. These days, there's far less going on and it's as dangerous as ever. If price is your only concern, if you don't mind being in the heart of Treichville's sleazy nightclub district, and you aren't bothered by the high crime rate, try *Hôtel aux Toulouroux* (☎ 32 64 48), which is on Ave 13 near Rue 8 and pretty good for the low price. The beds have sheets and the rooms, which cost CFA 1500 (CFA 2000 with fan), have working attached showers.

It's superior to the better known *Hôtel du Janick Bar*, which is 1½ blocks away on the corner of Ave 12 and Rue 9. The once-famous Janick Bar itself is closed, so the noise level here is more tolerable than in years past. The hotel upstairs charges CFA 2600 for a fairly grubby room with shower and clean sheets.

If you'd prefer to be away from the heart, inspect the grubby *Hôtel Fraternité* on Ave 25 between Rue 43 and Rue 44 (Blvd Mamadou Konaté), over one km south-east of the market. Ask for Cinéma l'Entente; the hotel is one block north. It charges CFA 2400 for a small dirty room with shared shower (CFA 3400 with fan).

Another possibility is *Hôtel Madani* further north on the corner of Ave 7 and Rue 25. A reasonably clean double with a basin and shower costs CFA 2000 (CFA 2500 with fan). *Hôtel de l'Amitié*, on Rue 21 between Ave 23 and Ave 24, is more expensive and best forgotten. It charges CFA 3500 for a grubby room with basin, dirty private shower and fan (CFA 4500 with air-con).

If none of the preceding places sound appealing, don't worry as there's one place that is three times better and no more expensive – the pink five-storey *Hôtel Le Succès* (☎ 32 18 39) on Ave 14 between Rue 24 and Rue 25. It has been completely renovated and painted and is now highly recommended. The sheets are fresh and there are decent attached showers and shared toilets. Rooms here are a

bargain at CFA 2500 (CFA 3000 with fan and CFA 4000 with air-con).

If it's full, you'll have to pay a bit more for similar quality. *Hôtel Le Prince* (☎ 32 71 27) on Ave 20 between Rue 19 and Rue 21 is very popular with travellers and charges CFA 4500 for a room with fan and private bath (CFA 6500 for a larger room with air-con). Bus Nos 3 and 21 pass nearby and will drop you in the middle of Le Plateau, at the Pyramid building.

Another good place is *Hôtel Atlanta* (☎ 33 24 69) on Ave 15, between Rue 13 and Rue 15. Rooms cost CFA 5000 and have telephones, clean sheets, private baths, and air-con which is reasonably quiet.

Marcory Marcory is a bit safer than Treichville and Adjamé. The best known place is the multi-storey *Hôtel Konankro* (☎ 26 16 28) on the main drag, Ave de la TSF. It has a pleasant street-side bar (large beers for CFA 375), a decent restaurant and rooms with fans and private baths for CFA 2500 (CFA 5000 with air-con). The *Pousada*, two blocks south, is the same or cheaper.

Adjamé Many budget travellers prefer the Adjamé area three km north of Le Plateau because the city's major gare routière is there and there are plenty of lively bars and cheap restaurants. It is no safer, however, than Treichville.

An excellent place for the money is *Hôtel de la Gare* (☎ 37 18 56), half a block east of the gare routière and often full by mid-morning. The rooms are reasonably spacious and clean with fresh sheets, interior hot-water showers and basins and shared toilets. They cost CFA 3000 (CFA 3500 with fan and CFA 4000 with quiet air-con). Units out the back are noisier. There's also a good cheap restaurant.

Cocody One traveller reports having stayed at a *Mission Biblique* in Cocody, which apparently costs CFA 3000 and is real luxury. It sounds like a winner, so let us know more if you find this place.

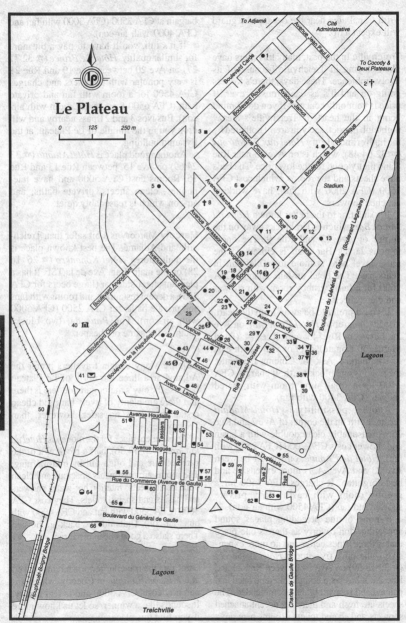

Le Plateau

PLACES TO STAY

3 Ibis Plateau Hôtel
9 Hôtel Tiama & Dimbo Pub
39 Sofitel Abidjan
56 Hôtel-Bar des Sports
58 Résidence Nabil
60 Novotel
62 Grand Hôtel

PLACES TO EAT

7 Maquis du Stade
11 Pizzeria Bruno
12 La Maison des Combattants
23 La Maquis Pâtisserie
24 Hamburger House
29 Restaurant du Dragon
31 Restaurant Phong & Restaurant Le Paris Village
32 Restaurant Chez Tong & Village Kim-Hoa
34 Restaurant Maharaja & Restaurant Lady Creole
37 Chalet Suisse Restaurant
38 Restaurant l'Escale Kreyole, La Taverne Don Antonio, Le Bagheera Disco & Restaurant Tuan
46 Southern Fried Chicken Restaurant
52 Cheap African Lunch Restaurants
53 Restaurant Le Ficus
57 Chawarma Restaurants

OTHER

1 Immeuble Les Harmonies (UK & Dutch Embassies)
2 St Paul's Cathedral
4 Nigerian Embassy
5 Burkina Faso Embassy
6 Zaïrian Embassy
8 Church
10 US Embassy
13 French Embassy & Consulate
14 SIB Bank
15 Church
16 Ecobank
17 Sabena
18 Immeuble Alpha 2000 (Swiss, Japanese & Brazilian Embassies, Barclays & Chemical Banks)
19 Librairie de France
20 Cinéma Les Studios
21 Nour-al-Hayat (Belgian Embassy & Shopping Complex)
22 Tiger Photo
25 Marché du Plateau
26 BICICI Bank
27 Le Paris Cinéma, Ethiopian Airlines, Afric Voyages & Maquis Le Paris
28 American Airlines
30 Pyramid Building & French Cultural Centre
33 Acapulco
35 Chardy Tennis Club
36 L'Oxygen Nightclub, Portuguese & Austrian Embassies
40 Presidential Palace
41 Post Office
42 Score Supermarket
43 Air Afrique
44 Air Gabon
45 BIAO Bank
47 Citibank & TAP Air Portugal
48 Alitalia
49 Air Ivoire
50 La Plateau Train Station
51 Air Burkina
54 Immeuble Trade Centre (Canadian Embassy)
55 Guinean & Senegalese Embassies
59 Immeuble Le Général (Cameroun Embassy & Air Guinée)
61 Nigeria Airways
63 Malian Embassy
64 Gare Sud Bus Station (SOTRA Terminal)
65 Ghanaian Embassy
66 Ferry Terminal (Gare Lagunaire)

CÔTE D'IVOIRE

Places to Stay – middle

Le Plateau One of the best value places in Abidjan is the *Grand Hôtel* (☎ 32 12 00, telex 23807), in Le Plateau at the eastern end of busy Ave de Gaulle (Rue du Commerce). It's a very respectable hotel and centrally located, with singles/doubles for CFA 12,000/15,000 (CFA 14,800/19,700 if you stay just one night). American Express and Diners cards are accepted.

The *Hôtel des Sports* (☎ 32 93 70), at the western end just beyond the Novotel, is cheaper but not as good. Its sparsely furnished air-con rooms with clean baths cost from CFA 6000 to CFA 8000, but if you'll be staying more than one night, you can usually negotiate the CFA 8000 rooms downward by CFA 1000 or more. There is an active bar-restaurant downstairs but drinks are not cheap. Travellers have had money bags stolen from their locked rooms, so don't leave valuables behind.

Adjamé In Adjamé, try *Hôtel Patient* (☎ 37 22 41), on the northern side of the huge intersection bordering the Adjamé train depot and conveniently close to the Adjamé SOTRA bus terminus. Spotless singles/doubles cost CFA 6500/7500 (CFA 8500 with air-con). The atmosphere is slightly sterile but the management is helpful and bargaining is possible.

If you'd prefer to be closer to the Gare Routière d'Adjamé, try *Hôtel Banfora* (☎ 37 02 52), on Ave 13, 80 metres east of the south-eastern corner of the gare. It has air-con rooms with private bath for CFA 7500, and a restaurant. It seems a bit better than the long-standing *Hôtel du Nord* (☎ 37 04 63) which has a tiny lobby with TV and two small ground-floor rooms with air-con for CFA 6000 and air-con singles/doubles upstairs for CFA 7500/8500. It's half a km east of the gare routière and two blocks south of the large 220 Logements roundabout.

Treichville In the somewhat dangerous Treichville area, there are very few mid-range hotels. The best is the long-established *Treichôtel* (☎ 32 89 65) on Ave 16 (Ave de la Reine Pokou). It's fairly modern and well maintained, and is on a major traffic artery. An air-con room with private bath costs CFA 8000.

Marcory You'll do much better for the money in the lively Marcory area just east of Treichville. *Hôtel Le Repos* (☎ 35 32 57) has air-con rooms for CFA 5000. Just a block away is the equally good and identically priced *Hôtel Le Souvenir* (☎ 35 12 56). It has a fairly decent-looking restaurant. Both places are one or two blocks east of the landmark Hôtel Konankro on Ave TSF and one block to the south on a dirt road.

The top hotel in Marcory is *Hôtel Hamanieh* (☎ 26 91 55), a modern five-storey establishment with air-con singles/doubles for CFA 10,000/13,000. All major credit cards are accepted.

Places to Stay – top end

The most famous hotel in all of West and Central Africa is the 750-room *Hôtel Ivoire* and it's still the city's finest, with an incredible array of facilities. The modern and ever-active *Novotel*, in the centre on Rue du Commerce, is quite decent. The refurbished *Tiama* is also in the centre and a bit nicer, but it's much more expensive than the Novotel

and seemingly not worth the big difference in price.

In the Riviera area bordering the lagoon, the *Forum Golf Hôtel* is almost as nice as the Ivoire and is much better value. The ambience here is tropical and much more relaxed than the hyperactive Ivoire. The only problem is the location – about five km beyond the Ivoire, a 15-minute taxi ride to the centre. The *Palm Beach*, a 20-minute drive south of the centre, is the furthest hotel from the centre but it gives the best value of all the top-end hotels plus it's the only hotel near the beach. The saltwater pool is emptied every other day and is quite popular.

If you don't want to stay so far out, then try the very decent *Ibis Plateau* or the nearly identical *Ibis Marcory*, both of which have small pools. The former is in Le Plateau near the centre, while the latter is better if all you want is a decent overnight hotel not far from the airport.

Hôtel Ivoire Inter-Continental (☎ 44 10 45, fax 44 00 50, telex 23555), CFA 35,000 per person (CFA 40,000 for the tower), pool, tennis, bowling, ice skating, sauna, movie theatre, casino, nightclub, supermarket, bookshop, Europcar; cards AE, D, V, CB, MC.

Forum Golf (☎ 43 10 44, fax 43 05 44, telex 26112), CFA 50,000/56,000 for singles/doubles, pool, tennis, sailboards; cards AE, D, V, CB, MC.

Hôtel Tiama (☎ 21 08 22, fax 21 64 60, telex 23494), CFA 50,000 per room, Budget; cards AE, D, V, CB, MC.

Novotel (☎ 21 23 23, fax 33 26 36, telex 23264), CFA 27,500/31,500 for singles/doubles, pool, Europcar; cards AE, D, V, CB.

Ibis (Plateau ☎ 21 01 57, fax 21 78 75; Marcory ☎ 24 92 55, fax 35 89 10), CFA 33,000/36,000 (Plateau), CFA 19,500/21,500 (Marcory) for singles/doubles, small pool, car rental; cards AE, D, V, CB.

Palm Beach (☎ 27 42 76, telex 42236), CFA 16,000-18,500/19,000-21,500 for singles/doubles, saltwater pool, satellite TV; cards AE, D, V, CB.

Places to Eat

Cheap Eats In the Adjamé area, it's hard to beat *L'Escale* at the Hôtel de la Gare, just east of the gare routière. There are lots of choices, from omelettes (CFA 175) and riz sauce (CFA 250) to roasted chicken (CFA 600). In the Cocody area, head for the *Allocodrome*

Treichville

0   125   250 m

CÔTE D'IVOIRE

PLACES TO STAY

15 Hôtel aux Toulouroux
16 Hôtel du Janick Bar
18 Hôtel Atlanta
19 Treichôtel
20 Hôtel Le Succès
24 Hôtel Le Prince
25 Hôtel de l'Amitié
27 Hôtel California
28 Hôtel Fraternité

PLACES TO EAT

4   Maquis Food Alley
7   Chez Babouya Restaurant
8   La Caravelle Chawarmas
10 Restaurant La Grand Rose
12 Restaurant Tout Est Bien
17 Samiranis Chawarma Stand
21 Restaurant Chez Valentin
23 Restaurant Chez Filine
29 Maquis Chez Filine
32 Cotton Club Super Maquis
33 Maquis 100 Boules Arras

OTHER

1   Gare Lagunaire Treichville
    (Ferry Terminal)
2   SDV Voyages
    (American Express)
3   Agip Station & 3A Express
    (for Jacqueville)
5   Méridien BIAO Bank
6   La Canne à Sucre
    Nightclub
9   Mosque
11 Bus Stop
13 Chez Tanti (Koutoukou)
14 Caravanes Nightclub
22 Train Station
26 Le Privilège Nightclub
30 Cinéma L'Entente
31 La Cabane Bambou Nightclub
34 Whiskey à Gogo &
    Nightime Street Food

Boulevard Mamadou Konaté (Rue 44)

Boulevard Nanan Yamoussou (Rue 38)

Autoroute

Lagoon

Houphouët-Boigny Bridge

Charles de Gaulle Bridge

Avenue Christiani

Avenue Victor Blaka

Marché de Treichville

Boulevard Delafosse

Rue 7

Rue 8

Rue 9

Rue 11

Rue 13

Rue 15

Rue 18

Rue 21

Rue 23

Rue 24

Rue 25

Boulevard du 6 Février (Rue 12)

Boulevard Gbon Coulibaly

Boulevard Valéry Giscard d'Estaing (Autoroute)

Boulevard de Marseille

Boulevard de Port

Rue des Galions

Park

Avenue 3

Avenue 4

Avenue 5

Avenue 6

Avenue 7

Avenue 9

Avenue 10

Avenue 11

Avenue 12

Avenue 13

Avenue 14

Avenue 15

Avenue 16

Avenue 17

Avenue 18

Avenue 19

Avenue 20

Avenue 22

Avenue 23

Avenue 24

Avenue 25

Avenue 26

Avenue 27

Avenue Gabial Dadié (Avenue 8)

Avenue de la Reine Pokou (Avenue 16)

Avenue Ouezzin Coulibaly (Avenue 21)

Avenue Laurent Clouzet

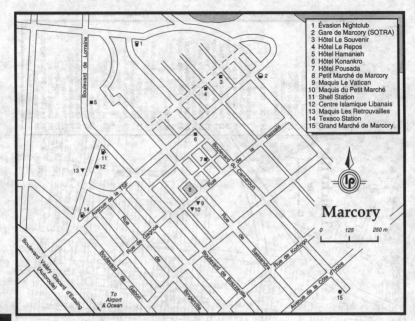

1 Évasion Nightclub
2 Gare de Marcory (SOTRA)
3 Hôtel Le Souvenir
4 Hôtel Le Repos
5 Hôtel Hamanieh
6 Hôtel Konankro
7 Hôtel Pousada
8 Petit Marché de Marcory
9 Maquis Le Vatican
10 Maquis du Petit Marché
11 Shell Station
12 Centre Islamique Libanais
13 Maquis Les Retrouvailles
14 Texaco Station
15 Grand Marché de Marcory

Marcory

0   125   250 m

CÔTE D'IVOIRE

on Rue Washington, about 200 metres north of Blvd de France and not far from Cocody market. Amazingly popular, particularly at night, it's a large outdoor area open for business from mid-morning to very late at night. Some 30 or so vendors grill fish, chicken and beef while patrons eat on the benches. Portions cost from CFA 200 to CFA 600. To satisfy your sweet tooth, check the pastries at the fancy *Opera Glacier* next door.

In Le Plateau, head for Rue 6, just north of Rue du Commerce. At lunchtime, on either side of Rue 6, women set up stands outside with various sauces such, as sauce de feuille (vegetable sauce) served with rice or foutou; patrons can pick their favourite and eat inside. A plate costs CFA 250.

For non-African fare, it's hard to be beat the Lebanese chawarma and falafel sandwiches sold all over town. At most places they cost CFA 400. In Le Plateau, there's *Charlie*, a chawarma place at the Pyramid building on the corner of Rue Botreau-Roussel and Ave Franchet d'Espérey. In Deux Plateaux, the best chawarma place is *Restaurant Georges V* facing Score supermarket on Rue des Jardins; you can also get full meals for CFA 1800 and Vietnamese nems next door for CFA 100 each. In the Adjamé area, there's *Le Printemps* and, next door, *Chez Hassan* at the 220 Logements roundabout, next to Score supermarket. In Treichville, you'll find *Samiranis* on the lively Rue 12 (Blvd du 6 Février) between Ave 12 and Ave 13 and, nearby, *La Caravelle* on Ave Dadié just west of the park.

For superb hamburgers, head for *Snackarama* at the Hôtel Ivoire's bowling alley; they cost CFA 2500. *Hamburger House* is also very popular; a hamburger costs CFA 1300 (CFA 2200 with a Coke and chips). One outlet is in Le Plateau on Ave Chardy near Rue Botreau-Roussel and open from 11 am to 1 am; another is in Deux Plateaux at Centre Commercial du Vallon. The *Restaurant Tiama*, near the Hôtel Tiama, serves both French and African food. It's a good place and is not expensive by Abidjan standards.

As for ice cream, the best places are not cheap – about CFA 300 a scoop – but the quality is outstanding. They are the *Dimbo Pub* at the Hôtel Tiama in Le Plateau, and the ever-popular *Festival des Glaces* in Du Vallon shopping centre next to Score supermarket in Deux Plateau.

African In Le Plateau, an upmarket place for African food is *Le Corcorde*, which is an attractive thatched-roof addition to the long-standing *Restaurant des Combattants* in the same compound. Both are half a block east of the US embassy and open day and evenings until around 8.30 pm. Le Corcorde also serves French food. Dishes at both places are mostly in the CFA 2000 to CFA 2500 range. Also good is *Restaurant Le Ficus* on Ave Crosson Duplessis. It has three different African specialities every day, always with sauce. A big plate costs from CFA 700 to CFA 800. For really cheap food, try the vendors just outside the *Maquis du Stade*.

A great place in Treichville is an alley just north of Ave Victor Blaka and 1½ blocks east of Treichville market. During the day the women there sell various sauces such as sauce capitaine (fish sauce) and sauce gombolais (gombo sauce). A very filling plate costs CFA 350. At night, they sell maquis food such as braised chicken with attiéké. Clients sit on benches.

If you're on the eastern side of Treichville, try *Chez Fifine*. She serves foutou banane for CFA 400 and several other African dishes at similar prices during the day and, at night, maquis food including braised fish and attiéké for CFA 1800. From the Cinéma l'Entente on Rue 44 (Blvd Mamadou Konaté), it's half a block east.

Also in this area is *Tout Est Bien*, which has excellent Ivoirian food such as foutou avec sauce; a big plate costs CFA 600. Senegalese food is the speciality at *La Grande Rose*; it's on Ave Dadié just east of the park in Treichville; a three-course meal costs CFA 1500.

In Marcory, a fantastic place for cheap chop is the *Maquis du Petit Marché*, next door to the famous Maquis Le Vatican and 20 metres west of the Petit Marché de Marcory. During the day there are about eight different delicious sauces to choose from; a plate of foutou and sauce costs CFA 350. At night it becomes a maquis with poulet braisé and attiéké for CFA 1500, which is about as cheap as you'll find in Abidjan. If you're in Zone 4 further south, try the well-known *Maquis Chez Mado* on Rue Calmette; it's inexpensive and specialises in Camerounian fare.

For Senegalese and Moroccan food in a fabulous environment, head for *Chez Babouya* in Treichville, Abidjan's most unusual restaurant. It resembles a Mauritanian tent with cushions on the floor, low tables and an amazing collection of photographs of old Hollywood movie stars. Since 1965, the affable Mauritanian owner has been serving only four well-prepared dishes (two Senegalese and two Moroccan). The cost, including wine, comes to about CFA 4000 a person. It's on the corner of Rue 7 and Ave 6, and is open every evening (usually closed during August and September).

Maquis A visit to Abidjan is not complete without dinner at a maquis – a special type of Ivoirian restaurant open only in the evenings (a few now also serve lunch) with wonderful food. The rustic ones are typically open-air with wooden benches and maybe sand for a floor. Even if you don't like typical African sauces, you almost certainly will like maquis food. Unfortunately, maquis have become so popular that some normal restaurants have taken the name. If the restaurant doesn't serve braised food, it's not a real maquis.

Eating at a maquis is much more expensive than eating traditional food such as rice and sauce. A plate of chicken typically costs CFA 2000 to CFA 2500. You'll spend less if you order fish (CFA 800 to CFA 1500).

Everyone swears they know the best maquis in town. Marcory has the most maquis. You could ask a taxi driver if he knows *un vrais maquis* or just head for

Marcory and ask there. You'll find several near the main drag, Ave de la TSF.

Marcory & Treichville The most famous maquis is the long-running *Maquis Le Vatican* in Marcory. Known by all the taxi drivers, it faces Marcory's Petit Marché (also called the ancien marché) two blocks south of Ave de la TSF. Poulet braisé costs CFA 2800 a plate. A slightly cheaper maquis is the *Maquis Les Retrouvailles* on Blvd de Lorraine, facing the Centre Islamique Libanais in Marcory. This place, which is open for lunch and dinner, is laid-back, rustic and partially open-air.

In Treichville, one of the best areas for maquis food, particularly late at night, is around the landmark Cabane Bamboo nightclub. This area includes the open-air grills facing the club, the *Maquis 100 Boules Arras* just down the street and the air-con *Cotton Club Super Maquis*, next door to the nightclub and a bit more expensive.

Le Plateau The well-known and long-established *Maquis du Stade* on the corner of Blvd de la République and Ave Crozet is open for lunch and dinner, and has a much more extensive menu than most maquis. There are several dishes with African sauces, eg poisson avec du sauce for CFA 700. It also has half grilled chicken for CFA 1200 and large Mamba beers for CFA 700.

Also open for lunch and dinner is *Maquis 'Guichet 23'* between Le Plateau train station and the post office across the street. One of its specialities is poulet braisé. It's friendly and if you arrive in Abidjan by train, you can safely leave your luggage there while you look for a hotel.

Deux Plateaux The most popular maquis area by far in Deux Plateaux is the *Maquis St Cecille*, next to the commissariat and about two km north of Score. It's an area with 10 or so small open-air maquis, including *Maquis Chez Willy* where grilled chicken and fish are at rock-bottom prices.

Italian One of Abidjan's most popular restaurants is the moderately priced *Pizzeria St Remi* (☎ 41 51 40). It has the best pizzas in town and numerous pasta and French dishes. Most dishes are in the CFA 2500 to CFA 3000 range. It is on the wide Blvd Latrille in Deux Plateaux. For lunch, call ahead because they're not always open then. Another place in the Deux Plateaux area, on Rue des Jardins, is *Au Pastel Pizzeria* (☎ 41 35 80); it's fancier with higher prices.

In Le Plateau, *Pizzeria Bruno* on Blvd de la République, near Hôtel Tiama, is a very popular and inviting lunch spot. It offers good pizza in the CFA 3000 to CFA 3800 range, and a special of the day for CFA 3500. It's closed on Sunday. Another thriving place in Le Plateau for pizza and Italian food is the *La Taverne Don Antonio* (☎ 21 89 51), which is near the Sofitel and a bit fancier. Most dishes cost between CFA 3000 and CFA 4500.

Seafood The long-standing *Chez Cakpot* (CACK-poh) (☎ 27 40 86) gets rave reviews and is highly recommended. The selection is limited – primarily grilled gambas (prawns) and langostines (crayfish) – but the location is special; you're seated only 30 metres from the ocean. Open every day from noon to 10 pm, it's at the beginning of Rue du Vridi Canal, which most taxi drivers know, a 20-minute ride south from Le Plateau. The cost of gambas and fries is CFA 6500 (CFA 7500 with langostines).

The new *Petit Bateau* (☎ 25 29 67) next door is very similar, with marginally lower prices and a much more extensive menu including a special three-course menu for CFA 7000.

The best seafood restaurant by reputation is the expensive *Restaurant des Pêcheurs* (☎ 25 42 35) at the Port de Pêche in the port area. It's open for dinner every day and for lunch, except Sunday; it also has rooms for CFA 11,000.

Asian For the money, you can't beat the city's Asian restaurants. The most popular by far is the *Nuit de Saigon* (☎ 41 40 44) on Rue des Jardins in Deux Plateaux, one km north of Score. It's a very attractive place with a

CÔTE D'IVOIRE

large menu and open every day for lunch and dinner. Most dishes are in the CFA 2000 to CFA 3000 range.

Two other Asian restaurants on the same street but closer to Score are *Restaurant Le Phenix* (☎ 41 33 13) and *Restaurant de Jade*. The Phenix is a bit cheaper, with most dishes in the CFA 1800 to CFA 2400 range (eg gambas au vert noir for CFA 2200), while the Jade serves primarily Chinese food, mostly in the CFA 2200 to CFA 3500 range, except for the vegetarian dishes which start around CFA 1600. Both are open every day for lunch and dinner.

In Le Plateau, there are four Vietnamese restaurants which are all excellent and close together: *Restaurant Tuan* (☎ 21 63 80) on Blvd de Gaulle just north of the Sofitel, *Restaurant Phong* around the corner on Ave Chardy, *Restaurant Chez Tong* (☎ 21 41 92) on the corner of Rue Botreau-Roussel and Rue Paris-Village, and *Village Kim-Hoa* (☎ 21 54 18) next door. They're all very similar, with prices almost identical to those of the Nuit de Saigon.

French The *Café de Paris*, on Ave Marchand near Blvd de la République in Le Plateau, serves standard French fare at relatively moderate prices. If you're looking for an outstanding French restaurant, you'll pay a lot more. Two of the city's best, both long-standing 'institutions' in Abidjan, are *Chez Valentin* (☎ 32 47 31) on Rue 16 in Treichville, which is quite expensive, and *Le Chalet Suisse* (☎ 21 54 80), more moderately priced and frequently full. The popular Suisse is on the corner of Ave Chardy and Blvd de Gaulle, facing the lagoon.

Le Paris-Village (☎ 22 26 17) on Ave Chardy, several doors up from the Suisse, is a newer place with a fixed menu for CFA 5500.

Miscellaneous The best Lebanese restaurant by reputation is the long-standing *Istambul* (☎ 24 25 73) in Marcory on Blvd de la Paix facing the Agip station. Prices are relatively moderate by Abidjan standards and the food is excellent.

For something out of the ordinary, try

Restaurant Maharaja (☎ 22 73 73 in Le Plateau) at 30 Ave Chardy near Blvd de Gaulle; it's the city's only Indian restaurant and is open every day. For Antillian food, you have a choice between *Lady Créole* (☎ 21 66 67), a fancy restaurant several doors down, and *L'Escale Kreyole* (☎ 22 40 46) around the block next to the Sofitel. They're all a bit expensive but no more so than many other top restaurants.

Entertainment

Bars During the day, two laid-back, moderately priced places are *La Maison des Combattants* and *Café des Sports*; the latter, at the far western end of Rue du Commerce just beyond the Novotel, is always packed. At night, French co-operants (technical advisors) can be found at *Acapulco*, an expensive cosy bar on Ave Chardy near the lagoon.

From around 5 to 10 pm, the lobby of *Hôtel Ivoire* resonates with the sounds of a lively African band, and the *Sofitel Abidjan* features a great pianist/vocalist.

Nightclubs Abidjan's two best known nightclubs are quite reputable and are in Treichville: the long-running *La Canne à Sucre*, on Blvd Delafosse, and *La Cabane Bambou*, several km east on Ave Laurent Clouzet (Ave 27). The newer *Whiskey à Gogo* across from Cabane Bamboo is now very popular as well. These may be the only places in town where you can dance to an African band. All three are open every day except Sunday. Finding a dancing partner, or a cab when you leave, is never a problem. All have door attendants/bouncers. As at most major nightclubs, the cover charge, CFA 4000, includes a drink. People don't begin showing up until 11 pm.

All the other 'name' nightclubs are fancy, undistinguished discos with recorded music. In Le Plateau, the two liveliest discos are on Blvd de Gaulle just north of the Sofitel and facing the lagoon: *L'Oxygen* and *Le Bagheera*. In the port area, try the disco at *Le Wafou*; it's very spacious and often mobbed on weekends.

Treichville has the reputation for being

where the action is; it's also where sailors have traditionally headed for. However, rogues have caused so many problems that the area is not nearly so lively as in former years. Many places have closed. However, there are still two clubs open on the dark side street, Ave 12, and neither is expensive. Also, unlike the fancy discos, they get going early, around 9 pm. If you'd like to try the local firewater, *koutoukou*, before visiting the bars, ask around; you may find some places nearby.

Cinemas All movies from English-speaking countries are dubbed in French. The standard admission price is CFA 1500 and there are usually three or four showings a day. The three best theatres, all excellent, are: Cinéma Ivoire at Hôtel Ivoire (showings at 3, 6 and 9 pm); and, in Le Plateau, Le Paris Cinéma on Ave Chardy and Cinéma Les Studios on Blvd de la République, near Le Plateau market. Les Studios has five separate studios/showings while Le Paris has two.

Older classic films are shown periodically at the French Cultural Centre (☎ 21 15 99) in the centre next to the Pyramid building, the Goethe Institut (☎ 44 14 22) on Ave Jean Mermoz in Cocody, and the American Cultural Centre (☎ 44 05 97). These centres also have various cultural events, usually announced in the daily Fraternité Matin and the weekly Abijdan 7 Jours.

Things to Buy

Artisan Goods For fabrics, beads, bronze, cheap woodcarvings and malachite, head for the markets. Marché d'Adjamé is the cheapest but Marché de Treichville (top floor), which closes around 2.30 pm, has the widest selection, especially for beads and cotton materials. Watch out for pickpockets. Prices for the wax cotton prints vary widely, from about CFA 1300 to CFA 5500 a metre, depending on where they're made (those from Holland are the most expensive), the number of colours and the popularity of a given print. The top floor of the Marché de Cocody (which is about one km north of the Hôtel Ivoire) is more compact and less con-

fusing but slightly more expensive. In Le Plateau, try the Marché Sénégalais along the wide Blvd de la République, and the Marché du Plateau one block away.

The best place by far to find excellent, high-quality masks and other woodcarvings is La Rose d'Ivoire at Hôtel Ivoire. It's like a museum and surely the best shop of its kind in West Africa. Don't expect any bargains however. It's open every day from 9 am to noon and 3 to 8 pm. Even if you don't care to buy anything or can't afford the high prices, it's a great place to develop an eye for good quality in African art. The French-run Galeria Akagni next to the Novotel has fantastic pieces but prices are sky high and the selection is much more limited.

Gold & Silver The best selection of silver and 18-carat gold is at the Hôtel Ivoire, however, the small jewellery shops in Treichville are cheaper. There are several along Blvd Delafosse facing the Bracodi brewery – about 700 metres to your right after crossing the Houphouët-Boigny bridge. Everything is sold by the gram – about CFA 10,000 for gold and CFA 1200 for silver.

Music Abidjan is one of the better places in West Africa to buy recordings of African music. The record shop at the Hôtel Ivoire is the best. In Le Plateau, try Studio 33 on Ave Chardy next to the Librairie de France, and Disc Discount on the top floor of Nour-al-Hayat nearby. Cassettes sold on the street are a third of the price but of poor quality. If you don't want records or can't afford those at the Ivoire, look on Ave 16 in Treichville for African-run record shops; they can record your selections of their music on your blank cassettes (good one are available from the Hôtel Ivoire).

Getting There & Away

Air Abidjan Airport is the worst in terms of hassling. The minute you arrive you'll be seized upon by young men offering to change money, be your guide, find you a cheap hotel, etc. Hold your belongings and jump into the first taxi.

Ghana Airways, Nigeria Airways and Air Afrique provide the most flights connecting Abidjan with other West African capital cities. Air Ivoire flies to Bouaké every day and to San Pédro (Tuesday, Thursday, Friday, Sunday), Korhogo (Friday, Saturday, Sunday), Odienné (Wednesday, Saturday, Sunday) and Man (Wednesday, Saturday). It also has two or three flights a week to Bamako, Ouagadougou, Accra, Monrovia and Conakry.

All the major airlines are in Le Plateau:

Air Afrique On Ave Anoma opposite Score supermarket (☎ 20 30 00 or 20 33 89)
Air France As above (☎ 21 12 78/9 or 21 76 78)
Air Burkina Ave Houdaille near Blvd de la République (☎ 21 89 19)
Air Gabon Ave Delafosse at Rue Daudet (☎ 21 55 06 or 21 74 29)
Air Guinée Immeuble Le Général, Rue Botreau-Roussel, north of Rue du Commerce (☎ 32 60 64)
Air Ivoire Ave Houdaille, two blocks north of Rue du Commerce (☎ 21 34 29 or 21 26 73)
Air Zaïre Immeuble BNDA, Ave Anoma at Rue Lagarosse (☎ 22 42 47)
Cameroon Airlines Immeuble Pyramid, Ave Franchet d'Ésperey (☎ 21 19 19)
EgyptAir Rue Alphonse Daudet at Delafosse (☎ 32 57 19)
Ethiopian Airlines Ave Chardy near Rue Lecouer (☎ 21 93 32)
Nigeria Airways On Rue du Commerce one block east of Rue Botreau-Roussel (☎ 32 26 01/14)
Sabena Immeuble Alliance on Rue Lecoeur (☎ 21 29 36)
Swissair Immeuble Le Mans, Rue Botreau-Roussel (☎ 21 55 72)
TAP Air Portugal Rue Botreau-Roussel, corner of Ave Delafosse (☎ 21 17 55)

Bus The main bus station is the Gare Routière d'Adjamé, some four km north of Le Plateau. All of the country's large buses on domestic routes leave from there as well as those headed for Mali and Burkina Faso. See Getting There & Away, earlier in this chapter, for details of international services.

For service to Bouaké, UTB is best. It's also easy to locate because the UTB office is the only two-storey building inside the gare. It has buses every 30 minutes in both directions between Abidjan and Bouaké starting at 6 am with the last departing at 11 pm. The

cost is CFA 4000 and the trip takes five hours. Sotranso offers less frequent service on the Abidjan-Yamoussoukro route for CFA 2500.

For San Pédro, one of the best companies is Sabé Transport (☎ 25 64 17), which is just south of UTB; it has departures at 9.30 am and 10 pm. La Gazelle du Sud-Ouest has departures between 10 am and 10 pm; the trip via Gagnoa takes about eight hours and costs CFA 3500. The fare via the coastal road may be less. Two other companies serving this route are Gibokle (departure at 10 am) and Tramoci (departures at 10.30 am and 8 pm). Gibokle also has direct buses to Sassandra in the morning and evening; the trip takes five hours and costs CFA 2500.

For Korhogo, SWTK leaves in both directions at 6 pm only, STVF has buses in both directions at noon and 8 pm, while CTK has buses at 6 am, noon and 6 pm (the return schedule is 7 am, noon and 8 pm). They all cost CFA 4500 and take from eight to 10 hours.

UTB, CTM, Tramoci and Les Montagnes buses cover the Abidjan-Man route. Les Montagnes buses leave Abidjan at 6.30 pm and Man at 8.30 pm; Tramoci's leave in both directions at 6 pm; CTM's leave in both directions at 9 am, and 1, 5.30 and 8 pm; UTB's two buses leave in the morning. The trip takes eight hours and costs CFA 4500.

There are two other small stations in Treichville. The STC station (for buses to Ghana) is two blocks off the autoroute. Heading south thereon, take a right at the major intersection after the Palais des Sports (boxing stadium), then a left after about 100 metres, then your next left. Departures are daily at 8.30 am and tickets should be purchased a day in advance. The fare is CFA 5000 plus another CFA 1000 at the border. Anticipate a late evening arrival in Accra.

Buses for Jacqueville leave from the tiny unmarked Gare de Jacqueville on Ave Cristiani in Treichville, 200 metres east of Houphouët-Boigny bridge. The only company serving this route is 3A Express; it has frequent departures between 6 am and 7 pm (CFA 800).

Bush Taxi & Minibus Most bush taxis leave from the gare routière in Adjamé. Peugeot 504 bush taxis cost about 30% more than the large *cars*, eg CFA 6000 to Man compared to CFA 4500 for the latter.

Bush taxis and minibuses for destinations east along the coast (eg Grand-Bassam, Aboisso and Noé at the Ghanaian border) leave primarily from the Gare de Bassam on the wide autoroute in Treichville at the large intersection with Rue 38, just beyond the round Palais des Sports. A bush taxi costs CFA 300 to Grand-Bassam (35 minutes) and CFA 1200 to Aboisso (1½ hours).

Bush taxis and minibuses for Bassam and Aboisso also depart from Gare Routière d'Adjamé and cost CFA 100 more. Finding one direct to Noé is next to impossible, so expect to change taxis in Aboisso; it's another CFA 1000 plus baggage in a minibus from there. At Elubo across the border you'll have no problem finding taxis or buses to Takoradi and Accra.

Train There are three stations in Abidjan: Treichville, Le Plateau and Adjamé. The *Express* for Ouagadougou leaves Treichville Tuesday, Thursday and Saturday at 8.30 am and Ouagadougou at 7 am. There's also a daily *Rapide* between Abidjan and Bouaké; it costs about one-third less, stopping at numerous stations en route. The 1st/2nd-class fare is CFA 8800/5600 to Ferkessédougou, 12,400/8600 to Bobo and CFA 16,400/11,000 to Ouaga. A sleeper car in 1st class costs CFA 3500 extra.

A typical trip takes about 27 hours even though it's scheduled to take about 25½ hours. The timetable below could easily

from	to	departs	arrives
Treichville	Ouaga	8.30 am	7 am
Bouaké	Bobo	3.05 pm	2.15 pm
Ferké	Banfora	8.35 pm	4.39 pm
Banfora	Ferké	1.05 am	8.31 pm
Bobo	Bouaké	3.10 am	2.10 am

change, so call the SICF train station in Treichville (☎ 21 02 45) to be sure. Departures are usually punctual, so don't be late, and if you're a student, don't forget to bring your ID and come well in advance to get a discount.

Car Rental cars are a bit more affordable since the devaluation but still expensive. Avis, for example, charges CFA 18,670 per day, CFA 195 per km, CFA 6750 per day for insurance, plus 20% tax for its cheapest model, a subcompact air-con Mazda 121 – about CFA 77,300 (US$150) for a day's drive of 200 km! The better alternative is to hire a taxi by the hour or day.

Agencies include: Europcar (☎ 25 12 27, fax 25 11 43), Hertz (☎ 25 77 47, fax 25 82 52), Avis (☎ 32 80 27, fax 32 66 75), Budget (☎ 25 60 11, fax 25 45 09), Abidjanaise de Location Auto-Mobile (☎ 35 60 11), Locauto (☎ 35 54 95), Civcars (☎ 35 89 51) and Mattei (☎ 32 30 34).

Boat If you're looking for a ship back to Europe, contact Sitram at the port in Zone 4. It has ships plying the Abidjan-Marseille route. A berth, however, can easily be several times the price of an airline ticket.

Getting Around

To/From the Airport Abidjan Airport can be called on ☎ 27 78 93. The bank at the airport is open daily from 8.30 am to noon and 3 to 8 pm, sometimes later to fit airline schedules. You'll also find a restaurant and free shuttle service to the major hotels. If you reserve ahead, Hertz, Avis and Europcar will meet you there with a car.

A taxi costs about CFA 1100 to Marcory, CFA 1500 to Treichville, CFA 2000 to Le Plateau (16 km) and CFA 3000 to Cocody (Hôtel Ivoire area). If you're travelling between midnight and 6 am, rates double. Bus No 6 connects the airport with the central area; the cost is CFA 140.

Bus The city's green SOTRA buses are extremely crowded and thus uncomfortable. However, they are cheap and in good condition – CFA 115 for most destinations and CFA 140 for outlying areas. The system is confusing because of the many routes.

The major bus station in Le Plateau just north of Houphouët-Boigny bridge is the Gare Sud. Other frequent stops are at the landmark Pyramid building and along Blvd de la République at Score supermarket and the intersection with Ave Chardy.

Other principal stations are the Gare Nord in Adjamé just north of the train station, Gare de Marcory at the northern end of Ave de la TSF in Marcory, Gare de Vridi Canal, Dépôt Cocody just beyond the University of Abidjan, Terminus Gobélé in Deux Plateaux, and Gare Koumasi in Koumasi. The buses on most lines operate from about 5.45 am to between 9 and 10 pm. Some useful routes include:

No 0/9 Gare Nord, Plateau (Cité Administrative, Blvd Clozel, Ave Delafosse, Pyramid building, Rue Roussel), Gare de Marcory

No 2 Gare Nord, Adjamé market, Plateau (National Museum, Blvd Clozel, Blvd République, post office), Blvd de Marseille, Gare de Marcory

No 3 Adjamé train station, Plateau (National Museum, Blvd Clozel, Ave Delafosse, Pyramid building, Rue Roussel, Ave de Gaulle), Treichville market, Gare de Bassam, Gare de Marcory

No 6 Airport, Blvd Marseille, Treichville hospital, Treichville market, Gare Sud

No 12 Gare Nord, 220 Logements roundabout, Plateau (Cité Administrative, Blvd Clozel, Blvd République, Gare Sud), Treichville market, Gare de Bassam

No 18 Gare Sud, Treichville market, Gare de Bassam, autoroute, airport turn-off, Hôtel Palm Beach, Vridi Canal

No 22 Gare Nord, Plateau (Cité Administrative, Blvd Clozel, Blvd République, post office), Treichville market

No 24 Treichville market, port area, Vridi Canal, Hôtel Palm Beach, autoroute, Koumasi

No 25 Gare Sud, Ave Cristiani, Treichville market, Gare Koumasi

No 26 Gare Koumasi, Plateau (Rue Roussel, Pyramid building, Ave Delafosse, Blvd Clozel, Cité Administrative), Gare Nord

No 28 Plateau (Gare Sud, Blvd République, Blvd Clozel, Cité Administrative), Cocody market, University of Abidjan, Riviera, Hôtel du Golf

No 31 Treichville market, Gare de Marcory

No 35 Gare Nord, Ave Reboul, Terminus Gobélé Deux Plateaux

No 74 Gare de Marcory, Plateau (Rue Roussel, Pyramid building, Score, Plateau, Blvd Clozel, Cathedral), Cocody market, Hôtel Ivoire

No 81 Gare Nord, Ave Reboul, University of Abidjan, Route de Bingerville

No 82 Plateau (Gare Sud, Blvd République, Blvd Carde, Cité Administrative, National Museum), Ave Reboul, Deux Plateaux

No 84 Gare Nord, Ave Reboul, Marché Cocody, Hôtel Ivoire

No 86 Plateau (Gare Sud, Rue Roussel, Pyramid building, Blvd Clozel, Cité Administrative), Adjamé market, Gare Routière d'Adjamé, 220 Logements roundabout, Cocody market

If you're going from one side of town to another, minibuses and shared taxis are much better because they don't stop en route and are thus much faster. One route, for example, is between the Gare de Bassam in Treichville and Blvd de Gaulle at the intersection just north of the gare routière in Adjamé. The fare is CFA 150 in a shared taxi and CFA 100 in a minibus.

Taxi Taxis have meters and are reasonably priced. The fare from the gare routière in Adjamé to Le Plateau, for example, is about CFA 550. Taxis by the hour cost about CFA 3000 if you bargain. Make sure the meter is on as drivers often 'forget', knowing they can extract more from you this way. Also, make sure the meter is set on tariff 1. The drivers can use the tariff 2 rate only between midnight and 6 am. Racing at death-defying speeds is quite normal. Ask your driver not to; the number of fatal accidents is surely Africa's highest. Sea belts are compulsory.

Boat Abidjan has an excellent ferry system on the lagoon and taking a *bateau-bus* is a great way to the see the city and the environs. The terminal in Le Plateau (La Gare Lagunaire du Plateau) is just east of Houphouët-Boigny bridge. The other major terminals are just across the lagoon in Treichville (there are no connections between the two) and in Abobo-Doumé. A trip over to Abobo-Doumé takes only eight minutes and costs CFA 175. There are several departures every hour. The ferries operate from about 6

CÔTE D'IVOIRE

am to 8.30 pm. If you get off in Yopougon, you'll find one of the famous Harris churches (a Christian-animist mixture), recognisable by the Christ figure on a cross outside – unusual for Africa.

You can also take a special sightseeing tour (CFA 1500) – a 1½-hour ferry ride takes you around the lagoon with a stop at Île du Boulay for a cold drink. Departures from the Le Plateau terminal are on Wednesday at 3 pm, Thursday at 9 am and 3 pm, and Saturday and Sunday at 9.30 am and 3 pm (minimum 10 people).

AROUND ABIDJAN

There are two nearby excursions that can be done as day trips or weekend excursions. Both are easily reached by public transport.

Île du Boulay

For a lazy day on the beach, take a ferry to this island several km from Le Plateau. It has inexpensive cabins (CFA 7000) for an overnight stay, and a seafood restaurant with authentic Ivoirian recipes. On Sundays at 10 am, you can catch the bateau-bus at Gare Lagunaire in Le Plateau. It returns around 5 pm. The price (about CFA 9500) includes a sumptuous meal.

Bingerville

Another possibility, 15 km to the east via Blvd Mitterand, is Bingerville (BAN-gervil). It is a charming town on a plateau overlooking the lagoon, and was the capital until the 1930s. A walk through the old botanical gardens near the centre of town is a must. The Governor's Palace, now an orphanage, is a particularly good example of colonial architecture. The Atelier d'Art, a school of art for young Africans, has a number of rooms displaying their work, and it is open from 8 am to 6 pm.

From Bingerville, you could continue 25 km by a good dirt road to Grand-Bassam; there's a ferry crossing en route and the wait usually isn't very long.

East Coast

GRAND-BASSAM

The best one-day excursion from Abidjan is to Grand-Bassam (bah-SAHM), 43 km to the east. What you'll find are the remnants of a bygone era. The narrow strip of land between the ocean and the lagoon, now called the old town, is where the first French colonists set up their capital, separating themselves from the locals whose own town across the lagoon grew up as servants' quarters. It's divided into three sections, with the old administrative quarter in the middle, the commercial centre to the east and the residential quarter to the west.

Grand-Bassam was declared the capital of the French colony in 1893, but only six years later a major yellow fever epidemic broke out, lasting four years and provoking the French into changing the capital to Bingerville. Bassam, it seemed, was headed for oblivion. Construction of a jetty two years later, however, brought new life. Buildings went up everywhere; spacious balconies, shuttered windows and pretentious archways were 'in'. In 1931, this 30-year golden age came to an end when the French built another jetty in Abidjan. Customs houses, the Governor's Palace, a tax office, an elegant post office, huge ornate storehouses and numerous two-storey homes with elegant verandas were all left to decay. The *coup de grâce* was the opening of the Vridi Canal in Abidjan in 1951.

Today, people from Abidjan head here on Sundays during the dry season to soak up the sun and have lunch at one of several hotels along the beach. Beware of the surf here, however; it's very dangerous, and almost every year someone drowns here. At the western entrance to town, there's a long series of stalls filled with local crafts – a good place to pick up souvenirs. From there you'll pass through the vibrant Nouveau Bassam (the new section where most people now live), around the Place Imperial roundabout where the market and gare routière are

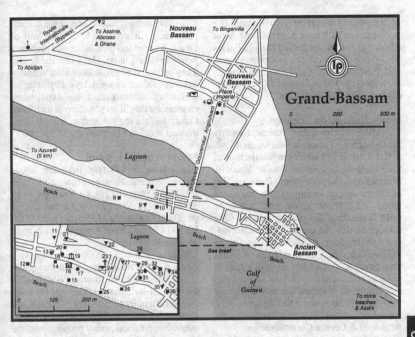

Grand-Bassam

PLACES TO STAY

8   Hôtel Assoyam Beach
10 Hôtel Le Madrague
12 Taverne La Bassamoise
14 Hôtel Koral Beach
15 Auberge de la Plage
      du Parrain
25 Hôtel Le Wharf
26 Hôtel La Paillote
33 Auberge Le
      Treich-Lapléné
36 Chez Antoinette

PLACES TO EAT

2   Good Maquis
9   Restaurant Le Village
11 Jardin Orchiders

13 Maquis du Stop Loulou
21 Restaurant Vietnamien
      & Artisan Shop
22 Restaurant La Pirogue
      Aumilo
27 Maquis Chez Gaston
28 Le Quai Restaurant
29 Maquis Toumodi &
      Galerie Arwechall
34 Foutou Restaurant
35 Maquis

OTHER

1   Artisan Stalls
3   Post Office &
      Commissariat
4   Gare Routière
5   Score Supermarket

6   Market
7   Old Prison
16 Old Palais de Justice
17 Nick Amon's Atelier
      d'Art
18 Mairie
19 Musée du Costume
      (Old Governor's
      Palace)
20 Gendarmerie
23 Church
24 Old Post Office
30 Artisanat
31 Centre Ceramique
32 Artisan Shops &
      Fondation
      Borremans
37 Old Speakers' Pulpit

CÔTE D'IVOIRE

located, and over the lagoon bridge to the sleepy old town and the beach.

The best time to visit is in November during the colourful week-long Abissa Festival, when the N'Zima people honour their dead.

Old Buildings

The colonial-era buildings, built mostly between 1894 and 1920, are virtually all in the old section near the water. The Governor's Palace (now the costume museum), with its imposing outer staircase, and the mairie (town hall) have been restored. Most of the remainder, including the old Palais de Justice, post office, customs houses and hospital, are mostly vacant and in various stages of decay but all very interesting.

Musée National du Costume

The Musée National du Costume, formerly the Governor's Palace, is well worth a visit. It has a small but interesting collection of traditional clothing of the Baoulé, Senoufo, Malinké and Yacouba tribes. There are also examples of old Korhogo cloth, miniature models of Ivoirian architecture, and some truly fascinating old photographs of Côte d'Ivoire during the colonial period, including construction of the Abidjan-Ouaga railway. They also have an artisans' workshop and a pamphlet on sale with a map of old Bassam and descriptions of all the colonial buildings. It's open Tuesday to Sunday from 9 am to noon and 3 to 5.45 pm.

Artisanat & Centre Ceramique

The Artisanat is a co-operative located in a large building just south of the main drag through the old section, some 300 metres east of the bridge. It has a fairly wide selection of artisan goods including fabrics and new woodcarvings. Items are souvenir quality and prices are reasonable. It's open every day from 8 am to 5 pm (6 pm on weekends) as is the ceramic centre next door. Whether or not you're interested in buying pottery, a visit to the latter can be interesting just to observe the artisans at work.

Places to Stay – bottom end

Chez Antoinette is a homey pension a good block off the beach. Rooms with fan cost CFA 4000, and there's also a bar. This place is often full, so come early. If you'd prefer to be on the beach, check *Auberge de la Plage du Parrain*, just behind the old Palais de Justice. It has fairly dark singles/doubles with mosquito nets and tiny showers but no fans for CFA 3500/4000. It's also very clean and friendly and you can eat next door.

To save money, stop at one of the numerous beach villages five to 20 km west of Grand-Bassam and pick out one of the many *paillotes* (straw huts) which line the beach. They're rented to expatriates on a seasonal basis but vacant on weekdays. If you go on a Sunday and talk to some expatriates, chances are they'll let you sleep in their huts. Otherwise, ask the villagers to rent you one; the cost shouldn't be more than CFA 1000.

Places to Stay – top end

Grand-Bassam has five first-rate hotels facing the ocean. From east to west they are: *La Paillote* (☎ 30 10 76), *Le Wharf* (☎ 30 15 33, fax 30 10 68), *Taverne La Bassamoise* (☎ 30 10 16), *Hôtel Le Madrague* (☎ 30 15 64, fax 30 14 59) and *Hôtel Assoyam Beach* (☎ 30 15 57 or 30 1474).

With a pool (CFA 2000 for nonguests), tennis court, a terrace restaurant facing the ocean and 15 air-con rooms (CFA 16,000), the colonial-style Bassamoise is the top hotel by reputation. The restaurant is French and most dishes are in the CFA 4000 to CFA 5000 range. Nevertheless, many people prefer the six-room Paillote. It has a friendly, more informal atmosphere, excellent food and a saltwater pool. With food factored in, it is also less expensive – CFA 13,000/22,000 including half board for rather plain singles/doubles with air-con and hot-water baths.

If it's full, try the attractive Assoyam. It is doing good business and has a lively ambience, a small salt-water pool and 20 air-con rooms for CFA 15,900. The Madrague also has a pool but at CFA 15,000 for a room, it's overpriced.

To save money, check the Wharf. It's a nice tranquil place right on the beach with lots of shade, friendly French owners and eight air-con rooms for CFA 9000.

Don't overlook the new *Auberge Le Treich-Lapléné*. It's on the main drag through the old section and has a private beach just three short blocks away. This three-storey place has been so thoroughly modernised that you'd never know it was formerly a colonial mansion. It has a TV room and restaurant, plus cheap eats (foutou etc) next door. Room prices range from CFA 7500 to CFA 15,000; the cheapest units are standard size, have air-con and are good value.

Places to Eat

In the old town, a good place for Ivoirian chop is on the street just east of the Auberge Le Treich-Lapléné. A bowl of fish sauce and foutou costs CFA 200. A few doors to the west you'll come to *Maquis Toumodi*; it offers various sauces for CFA 500 to CFA 600, including some Senegalese specialities. Another possibility is the cheap open-air restaurant adjoining the *Auberge de la Plage du Parrain*, directly on the beach. Otherwise, for cheap food, grilled brochettes and African sauces, you may have to head for Nouveau Bassam, particularly around the market and the gare routière at the Place Imperial roundabout.

After crossing the bridge going to the old town, the first place you'll pass, on your right, is *Jardin Orchiders*. Just across the street on the main drag is the ever-popular *Restaurant Vietnamien*, a long-time favourite and cheaper than the average. Vietnamese dishes, all about CFA 1000, include crevettes aux légumes (shrimp with vegetables) and ginger chicken. Large Flag beers cost CFA 450 and Cokes CFA 250.

Going eastward along the main drag in the old town you'll come to *Restaurant La Pirogue Aumilo*, a thatched-roof restaurant overlooking the lagoon, then *Chez Gaston*, a comfortable maquis with typical maquis food and prices, and then the attractive *Restaurant Le Quai*, also known as Chez Pierrot. The latter's delightful atmosphere overlooking the lagoon is as much an attraction as the food, which is both African and French. Most dishes are in the CFA 2000 to CFA 2500 range including grilled fish (CFA 2000) and spaghetti (CFA 2200).

Things to Buy

Old Bassam There are lots of artisan shops in the old section. Just after crossing the bridge and next door to Restaurant Vietnamien is an excellent unmarked shop

run by Karim Coumara, who used to work at the costume museum. He will tell you what's old and what isn't old and show you fine books on African art to help you better appreciate some of the sculptures on sale. His asking prices are often quite reasonable, so you may not have to bargain much.

Several blocks eastward on the main drag you'll come to the old Place Commerciale, where you'll find some more shops. Facing Restaurant Le Quai, for example, is the Galerie Arwechall, which is friendly and not at all pushy and has good quality work. And whether or not you're interested in purchasing modern African oil paintings, don't miss Nick Amon's Atelier d'Art (☎ 30 17 09), a studio just east of the old Palais de Justice. Nick's brilliantly coloured paintings are among the best of their kind in the country.

New Bassam On the far western outskirts of Nouveau Bassam is a series of artisan stalls with all kinds of locally made crafts, especially materials and wooden carvings. Most of the wooden objects with a dark natural tone are stained with shoe polish which can rub off – something to be aware of if you're buying a stool for instance. Also, what's sold as Ghanaian *kente* cloth may not be the real thing. Bargaining is definitely required.

Getting There & Away

Minibuses (CFA 300) and bush taxis (CFA 400) leave Abidjan from the Gare de Bassam on the autoroute in Treichville; the ride takes about 35 minutes. In Grand-Bassam, the gare routière is in the heart at the Place Imperial roundabout, 300 metres north of the bridge. You can also catch minibuses and bush taxis from there to Aboisso; they leave quite frequently and cost CFA 1000. If you're caught there for the night, try *Hôtel Bemesso*; it has rooms with showers and fans for around CFA 3000.

Getting Around

In Grand-Bassam, shared taxis cost CFA 100 for rides anywhere in town; however, they're not always easy to find.

CÔTE D'IVOIRE

ASSINI

Some 43 km east of Grand-Bassam, Assini (ah-SEE-nee) has by far the best beaches near Abidjan. Many foreigners own bungalows here (where you may be able to sleep), but usually stay only on Sundays. The rest of the week, there are few people except the Africans guarding the huts.

Other than the bungalows, the only accommodation is at one of the three resort hotels: the 380-room *Club Med* (☎ 30 07 17 or 32 35 80); the similar 338-room *Club de la Valture*; and *Les Palétuviers* (☎ 30 08 48). The charge for a couple including meals is about CFA 75,000 (about half that for the day including lunch).

In Assouindé (ah-SWIN-day) nearby, there's a more reasonably priced place several hundred metres from the ocean. The *Assouindé-Village* (☎ 35 36 85) has 45 bungalows for about CFA 22,000/40,000 a single/double with half board. Reservations are required.

Getting There & Away

Getting here from Abidjan (86 km) may be a little difficult. Also, most people with cars leave them on the northern side of the lagoon and hire a *pirogue* (dugout canoe) to take them across. Consider driving to Assini village and then following a track to Assouindé on the peninsula of the lagoon and leaving the car there. Buses and bush taxis from Abidjan leave from the Gare de Bassam; take one headed for Aboisso and get off 25 km beyond Grand-Bassam at the paved turn-off south for Assini; it's 18 km further so you'll have to hitch.

West Coast

JACQUEVILLE

Some 50 km west of Abidjan, Jacqueville (JHOCK-vil) is a two-hour ride from Abidjan. It was once a centre for the slave trade, but today there's little vestige of that or the town's colonial heritage except for several dilapidated colonial houses along the coast. The palm-lined beach here is actually a little nicer than at Bassam, but very few travellers come this way.

Places to Stay & Eat

If price is your only concern, head for *Hôtel Relax*, 600 metres from the bus terminal. However, if you have a few CFA to spare, try *Le Campement de Jacqueville* (☎ 31 51 21), only a short walk from the bush taxi stand and on a nice stretch of beach. Attractive thatched-roof bungalows cost around CFA 8000; camping is about CFA 3000. There's also a pleasant open-air restaurant.

The top establishment is the modern *Hôtel Le M'Koa* (☎ 32 79 80), which faces the lagoon and features a pool and a private beach not far away. It's a very nice place, with 22 air-con units, but the rooms and the restaurant are a bit overpriced.

Getting There & Away

On the Abidjan-Jacqueville route, 3A Express has buses departing in either direction between 6 am and 7 pm. In Abidjan they leave from the tiny Gare de Jacqueville on Ave Cristiani in Treichville, just east of Houphouët-Boigny bridge; the fare is CFA 800. You may also occasionally find vehicles headed for Jacqueville at the Gare Routière d'Adjamé. If you're hitching, the best time to go is Sunday when a few expatriates escaping the Grand-Bassam crowds head this way. If you're driving, be prepare for a 20-minute ferry crossing en route.

DABOU

Dabou is 49 km west of Abidjan and a potential rest stop for those en route to Tiégba or Grand-Lahou. If you get stuck here, the principal hotel is *Le Fromager*, which has rooms for CFA 4500 (CFA 8500 with air-con) and meals for about CFA 2500.

TIÉGBA

About 60 km west of Dabou, Tiégba is a fascinating lagoon village with houses built on stilts – Côte d'Ivoire's equivalent of Ganvié, a famous lagoon village in Benin. You can hire a pirogue for a trip around **Ébrié Lagoon**.

The only place to stay is *Aux Pilotis de l'Ébieyé* (☎ 37 09 99) near the boat dock on the mainland, where there's electricity and piped water and where most people now live. It has four clean guest rooms and is also a good place to come just for a drink; the terrace bar faces the lagoon. The people here may also be able to arrange pirogue excursions.

Getting There & Away

From Abidjan, take a Peugeot 504 bush taxi or bus from the gare routière in Adjamé to Dabou and a minibus *(mille-kilos)* from there to Tiégba. The turn-off for Tiégba is about 30 km west of Dabou on the Dabou to Grand-Lahou road; from there you take a 30-km dirt road in poor condition through rubber plantations.

GRAND-LAHOU

Some 142 km west of Abidjan, at the mouth of the Bandama River, Grand-Lahou was founded by the English and the Dutch, and in 1890 was turned into an important trading post by the French. Thereafter, it witnessed a brief period of prosperity and then virtually died. Today it's a tranquil village on the sea, and is similar to Grand-Bassam except that the old colonial buildings are all seriously decaying and abandoned and there are fewer palm trees. The modern section, called Grand-Lahou II, is on the mainland while the old section is on a thin sand bar facing the ocean.

Surfers like Grand-Lahou as it is one of the best spots in the country for **surfing**. Because of the larger waves and undertow, swimming here is also more dangerous, so be careful. Lahou is also a great place for nature lovers as a few km up river is the **Parc National d'Assagny**, which is a wonderful rainforest and home to a large variety of birds and some of the country's few remaining forest elephants. There are some elevated observation decks for viewing, and guards are available to accompany you on a walk through the park. Trips here by pirogue can be arranged at the Campement.

Places to Stay & Eat

At the far eastern end of the sand bar at the mouth of the Bandama River is the popular *Campement*, which is in a nice shaded area between the beach and the lagoon. It has a bar-restaurant and 40 bungalows with mosquito nets and showers for about CFA 8000. For cheaper accommodation, try *Chez Tantie Agathe* in the middle of the old section of town. Cheap paillotes with no electricity or water cost about CFA 1500.

Getting There & Away

The new road is finished and there are now direct buses to Grand-Lahou (174 km) from the Gare Routière d'Adjamé in Abidjan. If the buses have all left, you could still take one to Dabou (76 km) and try finding one there headed for Grand-Lahou.

Upon arriving in the new section of town, you'll have to take a ferry across Tagba Lagoon to the old quarter facing the ocean; it operates daily from 7 am to 6.30 pm. If you're the adventurous type and are headed back to Abidjan, ask around for a *pinasse* headed that way. These are large motorised canoes and travel usually at night; the trip takes about 10 hours.

SASSANDRA

Sassandra, 71 km east of San Pédro, is best known for its wonderful beaches. But what makes it special is that it's also an interesting Fanti fishing village, with an active port and a scenic river to explore by pirogue. And if you're up to trying some palm wine (*bangui* – highly recommended), there's plenty of it here. The town was once an important trading post, but when the port at San Pédro was built, it went into decline. Today, you can still see several old colonial buildings, such as the Governor's House, and the town is small enough to cover easily on foot.

Beaches

The beaches are all west of Sassandra along a well-maintained dirt road that intersects with the main highway into town, about one km before the roundabout. The first one, Batélébré, better known as Plage Le Bivouac, is only a km or two west of town but it's a good

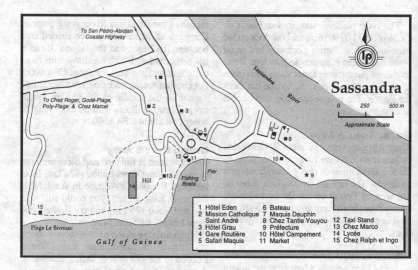

Sassandra

0   250   500 m

Approximate Scale

Sassandra River

Gulf of Guinea

Hill

Pier

Fishing Boats

To San Pédro-Abidjan Coastal Highway

To Chez Roger, Godé-Plage, Poly-Plage & Chez Marcel

Plage Le Bivouac

1 Hôtel Eden
2 Mission Catholique Saint André
3 Hôtel Grau
4 Gare Routière
5 Safari Maquis
6 Bateau
7 Maquis Dauphin
8 Chez Tantie Youyou
9 Préfecture
10 Hôtel Campement
11 Market
12 Taxi Stand
13 Chez Marco
14 Lycée
15 Chez Ralph et Ingo

walk as you must go over a hill to get there. You can also get there by taxi.

For the remainder, you'll have to hitch a ride or take a taxi from Sassandra along that dirt road. They include Grand Drewin-Plage (10 km), Latéko-Plage (12 km), Godé-Plage (14 km) and, best of all and the most peaceful, Poly-Plage (16 km), with a tiny Fanti fishing village just beyond. The beach at Poly-Plage is great, but the waves here are not so big as at Le Bivouac. A taxi from Sassandra to Poly-Plage costs about CFA 4000 and unless you arrange to be picked up, you'll probably have to walk back as there's virtually no traffic on this road.

Places to Stay

On the Beaches If you come to Sassandra primarily for the beach, you'll have several options, all west of town. Prices at all of them are similar.

The only one within walking distance of town is *Chez Ralph et Ingo* at Plage Le Bivouac. It's a new place right on the sandy beach, beneath the palm trees. Tents cost CFA 2000 (CFA 1000 per person if there are more than two of you). The cost of pitching your own tent is CFA 1000 (per tent). There's no electricity but you can get cold Cokes (CFA 350), small Flag beers (CFA 500) and food including spaghetti, bouille d'igname, fries and, most

Sassandra River

Be sure to take a pirogue trip up the tranquil and scenic Sassandra River; if you're lucky you may see some monkeys and other wildlife. The guide services offered by the hotels are expensive, so find your own. The place to enquire is along the river, 50 metres before the Campement. A reasonable asking price is about CFA 1500 an hour, but you may be able to bargain this down to around CFA 1000 if you rent one for several hours.

A trip to the mangroves takes about two hours (round trip); you'll see lots of trees, monkeys, crabs, herons, and perhaps a bush rat *(agouti)*. The hippo area is further up river, about a six-hour round trip. The young men who offer this service might also take you to the bars in town (where you'll hear reggae music), buy a lobster on the beach and cook it for you, and get you anything, including all the bangui you can drink. ■

CÔTE D'IVOIRE

expensive, a big plate of chicken with trimmings (around CFA 4000). Walking here from town takes about an hour by way of a path via the lycée (school); if you walk up to Chez Marco near the lycée, they'll point you to the path. At night you'll need a torch. Otherwise you'll have to take a taxi (CFA 1000). Or better, take a taxi up to the lycée (about CFA 300) and walk down from there.

Further west, about eight km from town, is *Chez Roger*. It has thatched-roof shelters and food. At Godé-Plage (a further 12 km) there's an African-run place with shelters for CFA 1000 a person plus food and drink.

Four km further is *Chez Richard & Ousman* at Poly-Plage. The sign, which the villagers nearby are constantly tearing down, says 'Camping Farafina Beach' but everyone calls the beach Poly-Plage. It's very similar to Ralph & Ingo and the Ivoirian guys who run it are just as friendly. Their meals are delicious, especially the fish dishes, but prices are no lower than at Ralph & Ingo, so consider bringing some food with you. They have bamboo huts on the beach for CFA 2500 with mosquito nets, basic but clean toilets and, most important, comfortable hammocks.

A short distance beyond is *Chez Marcel*. Finally, about 18 km from Sassandra is *L'Arbre du Voyageur* (☎ 72 06 63), apparently a bit more expensive.

In Town If you'd rather stay in town, head for *Chez Tantie Youyou*. This place under the coconut palms along the banks of the Sassandra River has a wonderful relaxing ambience. Tantie has 15 rooms with fans, mosquito nets and shared outdoor showers for CFA 3000 (CFA 4000 with attached shower) and serves some of the best African food in town, especially the seafood. It's on the eastern side of town just before the Campement. If you're really short on cash, inquire about *Le Sphynx*, which may still be in operation. It's across from the gare routière and near the wharf and reportedly has good cheap food and rooms for CFA 1500.

At *Chez Marco*, a round thatched-roof building up the hill overlooking the harbour, some mud cabins are being built.

Otherwise, check the small French-run *Hôtel Grau* (☎ 72 05 20) on the road into town, 200 metres before the roundabout, or the two-storey *Hôtel Eden* (☎ 72 04 64), which is on the same road at the northern entrance to town, one km before the roundabout. The former has spacious rooms with overhead fans and clean attached baths for CFA 5000 (CFA 8000 with air-con) plus a bar and a restaurant with good service. The latter, which is a bit nicer, has rooms with fans, balconies and attached showers for CFA 6000 (CFA 8000 with air-con). There's also a bar-restaurant.

The only upmarket hotel is the *Campement* (☎ 72 0515, Abidjan ☎ 24 74 64), a tranquil tourist hotel on the town's eastern edge, with a restaurant overlooking the ocean. Unfortunately, the beach here is too cluttered to use. Its 25 rooms, which have fans and attached hot-water showers, are spacious and OK but nothing special. Singles/doubles cost CFA 14,000/19,000 (half board). They also have a cheaper *Annexe*, about one km away on the banks of the Sassandra River. Singles/doubles cost CFA 8000/10,000. Either place will arrange half-day tours up the river but they are expensive – CFA 5000 per person, minimum five people.

Places to Eat
For street food, look around the market, the roundabout and the gare routière. The best place in this area, however, is *Safari Maquis*, a very rustic place just east of the gare and over the short bridge. The menu includes fish brochettes for CFA 800, breaded sole for CFA 1500 and a whole grilled chicken for CFA 3500, also large beers for CFA 500.

At night, try the open-air maquis at the back of the *Bateau*, the city's main brothel. One of several hole-in-the-walls is *Maquis Dauphin*; they're more for drinking than eating but you should be able to get some brochettes.

An excellent place for the price is *Chez Tantie Youyou*. The speciality is grilled carp (CFA 1500) with fries (CFA 500); other dishes include spaghetti (CFA 600), fish brochettes

(CFA 1500) and langouste (CFA 5000). A petit déjeuner costs CFA 500, and you can eat inside or on the sand under the palm trees. Or head up the hill to *Chez Marco*; the food here is similarly priced plus you get a great ocean breeze and a view of the harbour.

Getting There & Away

Buses ply daily between Abidjan and Sassandra, leaving around 8 or 9 am from either end and again around 10 or 11 pm. The trip via the coast takes about five hours and the fare is CFA 2500. One of the bus companies serving Sassandra is Giboklé, which leaves from the Gare Routière d'Adjamé in Abidjan and from the gare just east of the main roundabout in Sassandra. From here to San Pédro costs CFA 1500 in a Peugeot 504 bush taxi and the trip takes 1½ hours. In San Pédro, they leave from the main gare routière at the northern entrance to town but you may have to wait a while for the vehicle to fill up.

Taxis around town are not expensive, but you'll have to bargain hard to get a fair price. Getting a taxi to Le Bivouac and Poly-Plage for less than CFA 1000 and CFA 4000, respectively, is extremely difficult.

SAN PÉDRO

Roughly 280 km west of Abidjan as the crow flies, San Pédro is the country's second major port and is fairly bustling. Much of the country's timber and palm oil is exported from here. Built from nothing starting around 1968, it has not grown as much as the designers had expected nor is it a particularly interesting city, so most travellers head directly on to Sassandra, 71 km to the east, or Grand-Béréby, 59 km to the west.

The city is spread out, with lots of empty areas, so walking around is difficult except in the Cité, which is the commercial centre and where you'll find most hotels and cheap restaurants. The main drag is Blvd de la République, better known as the Rue du Commerce, which runs through it, starting at the port and heading northward for four km to Séwéké, or Quartier Le Village, where the gare routière and the main

market, the Marché du Village (or Marché San Pédro) is located. The top residential section is the Quartier Litiro, which is just west of the Cité and south of a lake and Quartier du Lac, while the main public beach is one km west of the port, just beyond the Maquis l'Horizon.

Places to Stay – bottom end

The better cheap hotels are in the Cité. A good choice would be the three-storey *EnHôtel* (☎ 71 20 98, fax 71 20 93), which has clean rooms with fan for CFA 3000 to CFA 4500 (CFA 8000 with air-con) plus a thatched-roof restaurant next door. The cheapest rooms have thin carpet, single beds, balconies and decent attached baths.

There are three almost equally good alternatives in the same area. None of them have restaurants but there are lots in the area. One is the popular *Hôtel Bahia* (☎ 71 27 33), which has a friendly Ghanaian owner and 15 clean rooms with air-con for CFA 5000 (three with fans CFA 5000). The *Hôtel Poro* (☎ 71 22 60) charges CFA 3000 for a clean room with fan (CFA 5000 with air-con), and the eight-room *Hôtel Le Relais* has clean small rooms with private baths for CFA 4000 and CFA 5000.

If you rather be on the water, try the isolated *Auberge Ponty*, which is well out of town, one km beyond the top-end Hôtel Balmer. There are cold drinks but no food and the ambience is morbid, but rooms, which cost CFA 3000, have mosquito nets and showers and the beach is a stone's throw away. Also, if you want to camp, this would be a good place to ask.

Places to Stay – top end

The city's top establishment is *Hôtel Balmer* (☎ 71 22 75 or 71 25 03, fax 71 27 83, Abidjan ☎ 22 49 37), which is four km west of the port out on Route de l'Hôtel Balmer – a CFA 1000 taxi ride and fairly isolated. Ideally located at a rocky site overlooking the sea, it's a great place, with wonderful breezes and pounding waves just beyond, with a nice sandy beach to one side. In addition, the grounds are large and lovely. They'll also meet you at the airport if

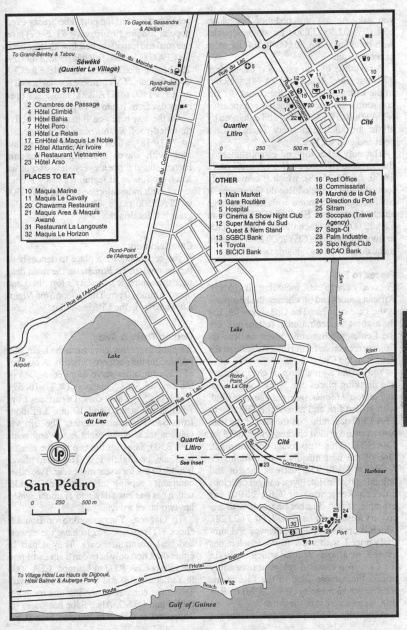

To Gagnoa, Sassandra & Abidjan

1

Rue du Marché

To Grand-Béréby & Tabou

Séwéké (Quartier Le Village)

2
3

Rond-Point d'Abidjan

4

Rue du Commerce

6

7

8

9

Rue du Lac

5

10

11

12

16

17

18

19

20

21

22

13

15

14

Quartier Litiro

0   250   500 m

Cité

PLACES TO STAY

2   Chambres de Passage
4   Hôtel Climbié
6   Hôtel Bahia
7   Hôtel Poro
8   Hôtel Le Relais
17 EnHôtel & Maquis Le Noble
22 Hôtel Atlantic; Air Ivoire
    & Restaurant Vietnamien
23 Hôtel Arso

PLACES TO EAT

10 Maquis Marine
11 Maquis Le Cavally
20 Chawarma Restaurant
21 Maquis Area & Maquis
    Awané
31 Restaurant La Langouste
32 Maquis Le Horizon

OTHER

1   Main Market
3   Gare Routière
5   Hospital
9   Cinema & Show Night Club
12 Super Marché du Sud
    Ouest & Nem Stand
13 SGBCI Bank
14 Toyota
15 BICICI Bank

16 Post Office
18 Commissariat
19 Marché de la Cité
24 Direction du Port
25 Sitram
26 Socopao (Travel
    Agency)
27 Saga-CI
28 Palm Industrie
29 Sipo Night-Club
30 BCAO Bank

Rond-Point de l'Aéroport

Rue de l'Aéroport

Lake

San Pédro River

To Airport

Lake

Lake

Rond-Point de La Cité

Quartier du Lac

Rue du Lac

Quartier Litiro

Cité

See Inset

23

Commerce

Harbour

San Pédro

0   250   500 m

30

25
24
27
26
29   28   Port

31

Balmer

To Village Hôtel Les Hauts de Digboué,
Hôtel Balmer & Auberge Ponty

Route   de   l'Hôtel   Beach

32

Gulf of Guinea

CÔTE D'IVOIRE

you ask. Air-con thatched-roof bungalows cost CFA 22,500/33,500 for singles/doubles with breakfast (CFA 30,000/46,500 for more expensive units).

A favourite of tour groups is the modern 27-room *Hôtel Arso* (☎ 71 24 74), which is in the Litiro district near the centre. Its air-con rooms are fine and much less expensive (CFA 8000 to CFA 10,000) and enhanced by all the surrounding greenery. There is also a pool and cars for hire.

The only other top-end establishment is the 80-room five-storey *Hôtel Atlantic* (☎ 71 18 50, fax 71 15 48), which is conveniently located in the centre on Rue du Commerce. It has average-sized rooms with fans and large attached baths for CFA 5000 (CFA 10,000 to CFA 12,000 with air-con), also a breezy porch in front for eating at (CFA 2500 for the French menu du jour) plus a billiards table.

Places to Eat

For really cheap eats, including all kinds of African sauces and brochettes, the best place is the gare routière. The Cité, however, has the highest concentration of restaurants. Try the Lebanese chawarma place on Rue du Commerce across from Hôtel Atlantic or the market in the Cité.

You'll find a great strip of cheap maquis and drinking places one block south of the market too. *Maquis Awané* is one of several, with grilled fish and attiéké for CFA 800 to CFA 1500 depending on the size of the fish, also an entire grilled chicken with attiéké for CFA 3000. This strip really hops at night. One of the best maquis is the *Maquis Le Noble* (☎ 71 20 93), just east thereof and adjoining the EnHôtel; you can get delicious chicken kedjenou for CFA 3300, for example. If you'd rather be inside with air-con, try *Restaurant Le Cavally* (☎ 71 23 28), which is only several blocks away and similarly priced, with a few Togolese selections as well, or *Maquis Marine* which is also in the Cité. You can also get good reasonably priced Vietnamese food in the Cité at the *Restaurant Vietnamien* (☎ 71 24 08) on Rue du Commerce next to the Atlantic.

Another good place for eating is along the beach just west of the port. The breezy ever-popular *Maquis l'Horizon* (☎ 71 29 67) is on this road and just off the beach, with large beers for CFA 600, braised fish with attiéké for CFA 2500, half grilled chicken with attiéké for CFA 2000, and lots of Vietnamese specialities all in the CFA 1500 to CFA 2500 range. It's open every day from 10 am to 10 pm.

On the way here you'll pass the attractive thatched-roof *Restaurant La Langouste* (☎ 77 19 18), which is the city's top restaurant, with waves breaking just beyond. French-run and open every day, except for lunch on Sunday, it features a fancy French menu, with most selections in the CFA 3500 to CFA 5500 range. The Langouste is also great just for drinks.

Entertainment

If you're looking for a place to dance, head for the modern *La Baraka* on the main drag near the centre; it's the city's top disco and opens around 10 pm. The air-con *Sipo Night-Club* nearby in the Cité is similar.

Getting There & Away

All public vehicles leave from the main gare routière on the northern outskirts. A number of bus companies serve San Pédro. One of the best is Sabé Transport (☎ 71 16 57), which has large new *cars*. Departures from Abidjan are at 9.30 and 10 pm, and those from San Pédro are similar. The trip via Gagnoa takes about eight hours and costs CFA 3500; fares for the trip via the coastal road may be slightly less. The video player is loud, so ask for a seat in the rear. Two other companies serving this route are Giboklé, which has one bus a day, and Tramoci, which has two buses a day.

To Gagnoa, Yamoussoukro or Bouaké, check UTB as it seems to have the newest and best maintained *cars*. They depart in either direction only between 8 am and 1 pm; the fare is CFA 3000 to Gagnoa, CFA 5000 to Yamoussoukro and CFA 6000 to Bouaké. Two other companies serving this route are CTKS and UTSO. Also, Sabé has buses on Thursdays to Gaoua in Burkina Faso (CFA

15,000), passing through Yamoussoukro and Bouaké.

Between San Pédro and Man there are typically only two or three departures a day, mostly minibuses but also Tramoci. The minibuses leave only when full, usually not before noon, and charge CFA 4000. If you're headed west to Tabou (or Grand-Béréby en route) or east to Sassandra, you'll have to take a bush taxi; they charge CFA 1500 to either town and the trip takes about 1½ hours.

Finally, you can also fly to San Pédro from Abidjan. Air Ivoire (☎ 71 25 52), which has an office on Rue du Commerce in the Cité, provides service on Tuesday, Thursday, Friday and Sunday; the fare is CFA 18,150.

GRAND-BÉRÉBY

The best beaches in Côte d'Ivoire are in Grand-Béréby, a fishing village eight hours by car from Abidjan and 59 km west of San Pédro. On one side is a protected bay, with calm waters, perfect for children, while on the other the surf is pretty good. It's also the only halfway decent place in the country for skin diving.

Places to Stay

The popular *Hôtel La Baie des Sirènes* (☎ 71 15 20 or 71 29 94; Abidjan ☎ 32 60 12, ask for Madame Daguero) has 75 attractive bungalows right on the ocean, langouste is on the menu every night and there are occasional folkloric shows. The cost is about CFA 50,000 for a double. Getting a room is next to impossible around Christmas time and on any three-day weekend. If you call in advance, they may be able to arrange for a guided tour of Taï National Park, 230 km to the north. If you arrive by plane, someone from the hotel will meet you at the airport.

The only alternative is *Hôtel Mani* in the village. It has an affable Ivoirian owner, a restaurant and 10 bungalows which cost about CFA 3000.

TAÏ NATIONAL PARK

From Grand-Béréby or San Pédro, consider a side trip to Taï National Park, one of the last remaining areas of virgin rainforest in West Africa. You'll see trees up to 46 metres high, with massive trunks and huge supporting roots. They block out the sun, preventing dense undergrowth from developing, and this makes walking through the forest quite easy. Walking in a primary forest is a unique experience. The towering trees, hanging lianas, swift streams and interesting wildlife combine to create a peaceful and enchanting environment. (Even though there's plenty of wildlife, you're only likely to see monkeys.)

The park is in a very rainy humid area, so the best time to visit is December to February, when there's a marked dry season. You need a permit from the Ministère des Eaux et Forêts in Abidjan and this rule is now

CÔTE D'IVOIRE

Chimpanzees of the Taï

Two Swiss researchers, Hedwige Boesch and her husband Christophe Boesch, who helped Dian Fossey in Rwanda with her famous research with the mountain gorillas, have been doing some fascinating research in Taï with chimpanzees since the late 1970s. The chimps live in large communities of 60 to 80 individuals but forage in small groups. Particularly interesting is how they have learned to select and use stones for cracking nuts. If you're in the park during kola nut season (November to February), listen for the cracking sounds; they can be heard up to one km away.

Equally fascinating is how the chimps hunt for monkeys. It's a group activity which includes a high degree of teamwork to catch the more agile monkeys. If they discover a monkey high up in a tree, the group of chimps will silently encircle it while some, including a 'blocker', climb up and force the monkey to jump to an adjacent tree. When he jumps, another chimp already in place may pull the branch aside, causing the monkey to fall into the hands of the chimps below. These tactics are quite different, for instance, from what Jane Goodall has observed of the Gombé chimps in Tanzania. The tragedy is that if poaching and illegal logging continue (already one-quarter of the park has been destroyed), fascinating research such as this may be short-lived. ■

strictly enforced. If you come without one, you'll be denied entrance. The ministry may also have information on a German guy who has been involved in chimp research at Taï and is reportedly in the process of organising trips there for travellers.

The park is definitely not user-friendly and it's extremely easy to get lost. One Dutch couple, after being lost for two days, had to be rescued by the army. So don't deviate from the path and carry a compass and, if possible, a map. Be especially careful in the swamp areas as it's easy to become disoriented, and don't be overconfident about bushwhacking through the forest as things look deceptively similar.

Places to Stay

There are two research stations in the park but visitors are no longer allowed to stay at them. In the town of Taï you can stay at the *Hôtel Nzè*, which has a bar with good music and beds for about CFA 1000 a person. It's very rustic and you'll have to draw water from a well to take a bucket shower.

Getting There & Away

Getting to the park is not easy. It's only a few km from the Liberian border, 202 km directly north of Tabou via Grabo and 118 km south of Duekoué. There are bush taxis from Tabou to Grabo but getting one from there to the town of Taï (134 km) could be a problem.

From either Man or San Pédro, take the large Man-San Pédro bus and get off in Duekoué (316 km from San Pédro), then a bush taxi further south to Guiglo (32 km) where there's a daily minibus further south to Taï (86 km). The total cost comes to about CFA 5000 from Man and more from San Pédro. You should check in with the park guards at the southern entrance to Taï town. From there it's about a 30-km walk to the research station. If you're in Taï on a Friday (market day), you can get rides south to the research station turn-off. If the driver doesn't know the turn-off, ask the park guards in Taï to explain it to him. From the turn-off you walk east on a dirt track for 10 to 15 km to the station. En route you'll come to a fork; take the right track. The caretaker of the station,

Teo, periodically drives back and forth to Taï, so you might be able to return to Taï with him.

If this sounds too complicated and you're in Grand-Béréby and have money to spare, see the owner of the Hôtel La Baie des Sirènes; he arranges trips, but only if you call ahead and you have a permit.

BOUBÉLÉ & TABOU

Some 80 km west of Grand-Béréby, the Fanti fishing village of Boubélé is recommended if you're looking for an out-of-the-way place on the beach. About 19 km east of Tabou (near the Liberian border), you'll see an arrow pointing south towards Boubélé and the beach four km away. You'll pass through a superb palm tree forest on the way. There is a surprisingly nice first-class hotel here, which has put this place on the map. Tabou is 19 km further west from the Boubélé turn-off. If you're headed for Liberia, get your passport stamped here. The border is a river about 15 km further west and reachable by bush taxi.

Places to Stay

In Boubélé, the *Village Hôtel de Boubélé* (reservations Abidjan ☎ 43 01 74) is in a superb location along the Houo River and next to the ocean. It costs about CFA 20,000 for an air-con bungalow with mosquito nets and full board. Meals are served in a thatched-roof restaurant. The owner meets clients at the airport and will make arrangements for trips with the local Fanti fishers. A good hour's walk down the beach will bring you to Tolou where, for CFA 1000 a person, you can rent one of the six, palm-leaf huts on the beach. Fresh water is available and the people are very friendly. This place is fantastic.

In Tabou, the *Hôtel Campement* at the beach on the far eastern side of town has doubles from CFA 2500 to CFA 6000. With a garden and large veranda, this place has a homely atmosphere and the staff are very friendly. If it's full, try the two-storey 12-room *Hôtel Kleh* (☎ 72 40 98), just behind the Palais de Justice. It has air-con rooms and a restaurant.

The West

MAN

Although Man is not an attractive place, it is nestled in lush green hills, giving it the most beautiful location of any inland city. However, don't overlook the market in town – it's first-rate. You'll find a wide assortment of fabrics and wooden carvings (some of high quality) on the top floor.

Two other places to pick up carvings are the artisan shop facing Hôtel CAA and the one outside the Hôtel Les Cascades. The blackened masks with big lips and slit or hollow eye holes are Dan (Yacouba); they're used to keep women from seeing the uncircumcised boys during their initiation into adulthood. The dark spoons which stand on two feet are also Dan. If you see some less naturalistic, fairly grotesque masks, they may be Guère.

Dan (Yacouba) mask

Information

The tourist office at the northern end of town next to the Catholic church has a good detailed map of the area with a list of festivals and places of interest.

There are four banks but, as in much of the country outside Abidjan, you will probably find that none of them change travellers' cheques except those denominated in French francs.

Places to Stay – bottom end

For the price, you can't beat the attractive *Centre Bethanie*, also called, incorrectly, the Mission Catholique. Headed by Sister Therese, a Swiss, this tranquil friendly place is on the western side of town on Route du Lycée Professionel, about 2.5 km from the centre on your right, 150 metres off the road on a hill. Rooms have mosquito nets, porches and private baths, and the cost is CFA 2500

CÔTE D'IVOIRE

Les Fêtes des Masques

The best time to be in the Man region is when there are festivals with masked dancing (February is particularly good). In some villages you can see impressionistic masked dancers on stilts up to three metres high. The masks vary in importance; each village has several great masks which represent the memory of that village. Masks in this area play a particularly important role. They are not made simply to disguise the face during celebrations or as works of art – the mask is for ritual. It's a divinity, a depository of knowledge. It dictates the community values that protect society and guard its customs. No man ever undertakes any important action without first addressing the mask to ask for its assistance. Whether the crops will be good or bad depends upon the mask; whether you will have a son or daughter depends on the mask. So the Africans here glorify it during times of happiness and abundance.

To find out where and when a festival is on, go to the tourist office in Man or call one of the major hotels there. In addition, it's possible to commission a dance through a guide, some of whom hang out at the better hotels. One place where you can pay for a performance is Booni, a very traditional friendly village in the beautiful mountainous area near Zala. (See the section on Touba.) ∎

for a single plus CFA 500 for breakfast. Although it is over two km from the centre (about CFA 200 by taxi), it is convenient for the waterfalls which are about two km further west. If it's full, try the *Collège Catholique pour les Garçons*, which is on the same road, half a km closer to town; its rooms cost about the same and are not so clean.

In the centre, if you can tolerate noise, try *Hôtel Mont Dent*; its rooms with clean beds and interior showers are good value at about CFA 2500 (CFA 1000 more with fan and bath). It's on the road leading to the Hôtel Les Cascades, two blocks south-east of the market. A much better place is *Hôtel CAA*, which is relatively new and nearby, behind the hospital and below Hôtel Les Cascades. Immaculately clean doubles cost CFA 4000.

Another fairly decent place near the centre is *Hôtel Fraternité* (☎ 79 06 89). A room with private bath costs CFA 3000 (CFA 500 more with fan). The place is a little grubby but the baths are clean enough, plus there's a small bar with a pleasant relaxing ambience. It's about 100 metres from the main gare routière.

Directly behind the Fraternité on the same block is the *Hôtel Tanty Akissi* (☎ 79 04 78).

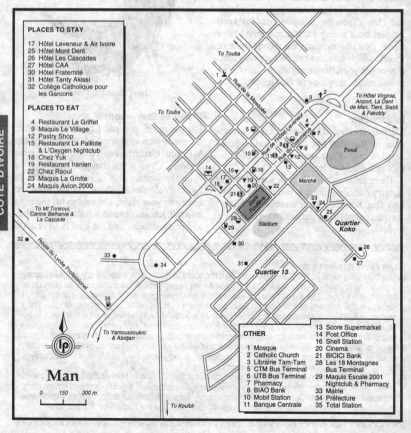

PLACES TO STAY
17 Hôtel Leveneur & Air Ivoire
25 Hôtel Mont Dent
26 Hôtel Les Cascades
27 Hôtel CAA
30 Hôtel Fraternité
31 Hôtel Tanty Akissi
32 Collége Catholique pour les Garcons

PLACES TO EAT
4 Restaurant Le Griffet
9 Maquis Le Village
12 Pastry Shop
15 Restaurant La Paillote & L'Oxygen Nightclub
18 Chez Yuk
19 Restaurant Iranien
22 Chez Raoul
23 Maquis La Grotte
24 Maquis Avion 2000

OTHER
1 Mosque
2 Catholic Church
3 Librairie Tam-Tam
5 CTM Bus Terminal
6 UTB Bus Terminal
7 Pharmacy
8 BIAO Bank
10 Mobil Station
11 Banque Centrale
13 Score Supermarket
14 Post Office
16 Shell Station
20 Cinema
21 BICICI Bank
28 Les 18 Montagnes Bus Terminal
29 Maquis Escale 2001 Nightclub & Pharmacy
33 Mairie
34 Préfecture
35 Total Station

To Touba
To Touba
Rue de la Mosquée
To Hôtel Virginia, Airport, La Dent de Man, Tieni, Siabli & Fakobly
Rue de l'Hôtel Leveneur
Rue du Commerce
Pond
Marché
Gare Routière
Quartier Koko
Stadium
To Mt Tonkoui, Centre Bethanie & La Cascade
Route du Lycée Professionel
Quartier 13
To Yamoussoukro & Abidjan

Man
0   150   300 m

To Kouibli

CÔTE D'IVOIRE

Rooms (CFA 3000) have fans and interior showers (CFA 500 more with full interior bath). The place is a little grubby but the beds are fairly clean and it's only 300 metres south of the market on a quiet back street. Tanty also prepares good African food.

The friendly *Hôtel Virginia* (☎ 79 06 91) on the eastern outskirts of town, about one km from the centre just off the road to the airport and Fakobly, has quite clean rooms with fans and full baths for about CFA 4000. However, there's no atmosphere, no restaurant, and it's a 20-minute walk to the centre.

Hôtel Mendeba (☎ 79 03 41), three km from the centre on the southern outskirts of town is great value but the remote location is a major drawback. Its rooms are very clean, have fans and private baths, and cost about CFA 3000. The *Hôtel Le Petit Coin* close by has similar prices.

Places to Stay – middle

For a good medium-priced place in the centre, head for the *Hôtel Leveneur* (☎ 79 09 41 or 79 00 39), a block north-west of the main gare routière. It's highly recommended for the atmosphere and the price – it has 12 clean rooms with air-con and private bathrooms for CFA 7000 to CFA 9000 (CFA 6000 with shared bath) and a pleasant restaurant with a menu (five choices) for CFA 1500. The street-side terrace is a good place to have a drink and meet people, and you're within easy walking distance of everything in town.

Many prefer the *Hôtel Beau-Séjour Les Masques* (☎ 79 09 91). For travellers with vehicles it's a good choice. The thatched-roof bungalows, which are decorated with local paintings and cost about CFA 9000, are a good deal and have air-con, TV and refrigerator. The Beau-Séjour also has ordinary air-con rooms with baths for CFA 5000. The French menu costs about CFA 2200. It's on the south-western edge of town, three km from the centre, off the road to Abidjan.

Places to Stay – top end

The best hotel is the *Hôtel Les Cascades* (☎ 79 02 51, fax 79 07 73; cards AE, V, CB)

on a hill overlooking the city, 300 metres east of the market. The principal attractions are the clean pool and the attractive location near the centre. Modern air-con singles/doubles around the pool cost CFA 11,500/14,000 (CFA 1500 more with TV and refrigerator). If you don't stay here, you can still use the pool for CFA 700 (CFA 1000 on weekends).

Places to Eat

African The best place for cheap street food, primarily African sauces, is around the main gare routière. During the day, try *Chez Raoul*, a popular shed facing the north-eastern side of the gare. At night, the best place is beside the petrol station just south of the BICICI bank, facing the gare. The selection is extensive and the food is excellent. Another possibility is *Restaurant Le Griffet* on Rue du Commerce; it has similar fare.

Man also has several typically rustic open-air maquis with braised dishes at very reasonable prices. One is the *Maquis Avion 2000*, a block east of the market. Closed Sunday, it has lots of relaxing armchairs and at night becomes a maquis with poisson grillé for about CFA 500 to CFA 700. Another is *L'Univers*, which is half a block west of the north-western corner of the market. *Le Tirbo*, which is similar, has also been recommended.

For an upmarket maquis, try *Maquis Le Village*, which is near L'Univers and open only in the evenings. It's a pleasant restaurant with a huge attractive paillote and good braised chicken for about CFA 2500 a plate.

Continental *Hôtel Leveneur* in the centre of town is a reasonably priced place for good French food. The plat du jour costs about CFA 1800 and there are five choices. You can also get good sandwiches here for about CFA 900. Nearby is *Chez Yuk* (closed Sundays). This sidewalk café is a better place for drinks and snacks than for full meals.

Half a block north of the Leveneur is the French-run *La Paillote* (or Chez Simon). It has the best reputation in town. Simon's place has a huge thatched-roof paillote in an inner garden; the menu is mostly French, with a few African selections including chicken kedjenou. Most dishes are around CFA 2500.

For lighter food, there's great Lebanese chawarma sandwiches (CFA 400) and hamburgers across the street at the popular *Restaurant Iranien*, and pastry at an expensive pastry shop on the main drag across from the Score supermarket.

Entertainment

L'Oxygen is a popular disco in the centre, half a block north of the Hôtel Leveneur. There's also *Maquis Escale 2001* on the main drag just south of the Texaco station. It's lively until the wee hours of the morning.

Getting There & Away

Air Air Ivoire has flights from Abidjan on Wednesday and Saturday; the one-way fare is CFA 18,150.

Bus There are at least three bus companies with service to Abidjan (CFA 4500, eight hours). Les 18 Montagnes, facing the southern side of the gare routière, has one bus a day at 8.30 pm in either direction. UTB, on the corner of Rue du Commerce and Rue de la Mosquée, has buses for Abidjan at 9 and 11.30 am, while CTM three blocks westward has buses at 9 am and 1, 5.30 and 8 pm, stopping briefly at Bouafflé en route. These companies also offer service to Yamoussoukro.

Getting from Man to either San Pédro or Odienné is much more difficult because only Tramoci and maybe one other company serve these routes. There are, however, minibuses serving these routes, with two or three departures a day to/from San Pédro. Tramoci also has one bus a day at 6 pm to/from Abidjan. Prices of buses are as follows: CFA 4000 to San Pédro, CFA 3500 to Bouaké and CFA 3000 to Yamoussoukro.

Bush Taxi The main gare routière for minibuses and bush taxis is on Rue du Commerce. Peugeot 504 taxis cost about CFA 7000 to Abidjan, CFA 6000 to Man, CFA 5500 to Bouaké and CFA 5000 to Yamoussoukro. Minibuses are cheaper and much

slower. Those headed north to Biankouma (CFA 500), Touba and Odienné leave from the gare routière on the Touba road, two km from the centre, while those headed for Danané leave from the central market.

Waiting for a van to Odienné to fill up can take hours, so you might try catching the courrier postal; this vehicle leaves every day from the post office between 7 and 9 am, arriving Odienné in the early afternoon.

AROUND MAN
La Cascade & Mt Tonkoui

The number one attraction in Man is La Cascade, a waterfall in a superb bamboo forest five km west of town on the road to Mt Tonkoui. Take a cab or walk; you are likely to be pestered by kids offering to be your guide. The hike can be done in an hour but plan on taking longer as you'll want to stop along the way to admire the scenery.

The waterfall is a touristy sight that even the locals frequent, and you can swim at the bottom. As the dry season progresses however, the water slows to a trickle, making a visit here hardly worth the CFA 200 entrance fee. There's a swinging bridge made of vines *(pont de lianes)* and an attractive restaurant in the gorge. The food is expensive but the wooden deck is a wonderful place for a drink while viewing the falls.

The base of Mt Tonkoui (1223 metres), the second-highest peak in Côte d'Ivoire, is 15 km further (45 minutes by car) on the same road. The road winds towards the top where there's a telecommunications tower. You may be blocked midway from going to the summit. If not, people working there sometimes allow travellers to climb to the top of the tower. The views are fantastic, particularly from the tower (Liberia and Guinea are clearly visible), except during the hazy harmattan season.

La Dent de Man

For hikers, a major attraction is the Tooth of Man – the guardian angel of Man – a steep tooth-shaped mountain north-east of town. You'll find the hike up more interesting and challenging than the road up Mt Tonkoui.

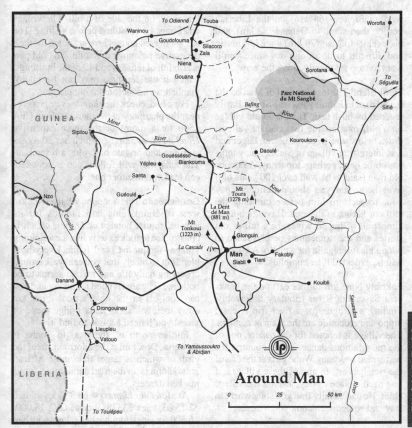

Around Man

0   25   50 km

The foot of the Dent is at Glonguin, 14 km away, so you'll probably want to take a taxi. If you're walking, continue north-east on Rue du Commerce straight out of town. By car, you may find a second route going two km east on the old airport road, then north-east to Gouapoloulé, then to Glonguin.

Find a kid at the latter (not in Man) to act as your guide. Without one, you're sure to lose the jungle path. I did even with a guide. The hike up and down takes three to four hours from the village. If anyone demands a 'ticket de passage' during the hike, you can be sure it's a hoax. Carry lots of water as the

trip is rather gruelling and the weather is usually hot and humid. The first half is gradual but the last section is very steep. A panoramic view on top awaits you – superb if it's not the harmattan season. For a bigger challenge, try Mt Nimba (1752 metres) on the Liberian border via Danané.

Local Villages

The main attraction of Man is the villages in the surrounding area. For travellers with wheels, an interesting itinerary is the following circular route: north from Man to Biankouma and Gouéssésso (49 km), then west to Sipitou (63 km) on the Liberian border, then south to Danané (82 km), and back (east) to Man (79 km) – a 273-km trip and difficult to do in one day since you'll want to stop frequently along the way.

Tieni-Siabli Thirteen km east of Man on the paved road to Fakobly is Tieni-Siabli. Easily reached by bush taxi, Tieni is an old village on a cliff overlooking two verdant valleys; down below you'll see the newer, larger and less interesting village of Siabli. Many tourists come here, perhaps too many. A famous old man (said to be well over 100 years old) lives here, and you should definitely pay your respects to him before climbing the cliffs or hiking in the area. Having outlived almost all of his 36 wives, he's full of old stories and can sometimes be persuaded to put on his full regalia for a photo. A good tip will be expected if he complies.

Fakobly Nine km further east on the banks of a Sassandra River tributary is Fakobly. Finding a pirogue for a river trip is easy; hippo and crocodile are the main attractions. The village is reputed for the *tematé*, one of the most famous dances in the country. It's performed by young Wobé girls at the end of the rice harvest. In any of these villages, if you need a place to stay, just ask the village chief. He can usually find you somewhere to stay and someone to cook you a meal.

Biankouma Some 44 km north of Man on the paved road to Touba, Biankouma is famous for its acrobatic Goua dances, which reportedly can be seen every Sunday. The new part of town on the main highway is of no interest, so head for the old section several km away, on the side of a hill. The village chief must be consulted before visiting. The straw-covered houses here are noted for their decorative paintings in kaolin. The old part is also full of fetishes and 12 of the buildings, which house fetishes, may not be photographed, so ask before taking pictures.

For a bed, check the *chambres de passage* near the pharmacy at the market (about CFA 1500 for a room) or the more expensive *Hôtel du Mont Sangbé*, which has 20 rooms with fan and private bath plus a restaurant. The kids who will follow you everywhere can lead you to either one.

Gouéssésso This Yacouba village is 12 km west of Biankouma and famous for its unusual tourist hotel, *Les Lianes*, which is constructed to look exactly like the adjoining village – unique in Côte d'Ivoire. Everything blends in so nicely that you can walk around observing daily life and no one seems to be bothered. The area is good for hiking and you can cool off in the hotel's pool. Four km away there's a short liana bridge made of vines; you'll need a guide to find it.

Further north on the road to Touba is **Gouana**. Don't miss the enormous tree, the girth of which is larger than most African huts. **Niena** is up the road and famous for its masked dancers.

At *Motel des Lianes* (☎ 63 33 95, Abidjan 32 75 03, telex 23328) it costs CFA 18,000/26,500 for single/double bungalows with half board (obligatory), less in July and August.

TOUBA
This Malinké town 115 km north of Man is of no great interest except on Saturday when there's a wonderful market with lots of local

---

The Stilt Dancers
Tourist brochures of Côte d'Ivoire almost all have a photo of masked dancers doing incredible feats on their three-metre stilts. This is a speciality of a very select group of young Yacouba men in the mountainous area of Touba. During the three to five years of training, the dancers must tell no one, not even their wives, what they're doing. Once initiated, they become empowered to communicate with the spirits who, during the dancing, direct their elaborate acrobatic stunts, all to the sounds of chanting and drums – and the crowds' delight. ■

colour. However, the area just to the south is famous for its stilt dancers, well publicised in tourist brochures. Three villages most notable in this respect are **Goudofouma**, which is 10 km or so south of Touba along the main highway, **Zala**, which is 15 km south of Touba, then east a bit on a dirt track, and **Booni**, which is nearby. Because of its location on a scenic rock overlooking a 500-metre rock, Zala is a hang-gliding centre for Africa. In early January, when the strong harmattan wind is blowing off the savannahs, there is a hang-gliding festival for aficionados.

Places to Stay & Eat
Hôtel Mahou has closed but *Hôtel l'Escale du Port* (☎ 70 70 63), near the market and the gare routière, is still going strong. It has 10 air-con rooms and an excellent restaurant, the *Star Maquis*.

Getting There & Away
There are one or two minibuses a day to Touba from Man, departing from the gare routière on the northern outskirts of Man. You can also get here on the daily courrier postal from Man or Odienné.

DANANÉ
If you're coming from Guinea or Liberia, Danané (79 km west of Man) is the first major town you'll come to. The two gares routières (*est* for Man and *ouest* for the Liberian border) are at opposite ends of town, about two km apart, so you may want to take a taxi (CFA 125) from one to the other. When arriving or leaving, be sure to get your passport stamped by the police in the centre; otherwise you'll be sent back.

The principal attractions are the *ponts de lianes* (liana bridges) crossing the Cavally River which runs north-south to the east of Danané. The major ones are near three villages south of Danané – Drongouineu (14 km), Lieupleu (22 km) and Vatouo (30 km). The one at Lieupleu is the easiest to see; it's two km east of the road to Toulépeu, with a sign thereon. The cheapest way to get there is to catch a minibus (CFA 600) towards Toulépeu and have the driver drop you off at the appropriate point.

Otherwise, you'll have to pay for a taxi (about CFA 3500 to Lieupleu). There's an entry fee to the bridge of CFA 500.

If you're here in late December, enquire about the little-known carnival in Zéale, six km further south of Vatouo; it's reportedly quite fascinating.

Places to Stay & Eat
A highly recommended place is the *Hôtel Tia Étienne* on the road to Man, half a km east of the gare routière est. Rooms cost about CFA 3000 (CFA 500 more with fan and double with air-con) and the restaurant is quite good with meals for CFA 1500, even wine. If it's full and price is your major concern, try the *Bar de la Frontière*, where rooms cost about CFA 3000.

Simon, of La Paillote fame in Man, owns the *Hôtel des Lianes* and his restaurant is quite good. Rooms there cost about CFA 5000. Two other possibilities are the *Hôtel Le Marquis*, which has rooms for about CFA 2000; and the *Hôtel Le Refuge*, which has tiny doubles for about CFA 3000.

Getting There & Away
Minibuses and bush taxis (CFA 1500) to Man go from the gare routière est on the eastern side of town. A minibus to the Liberian border leaves from the gare routière ouest and takes 1½ hours (CFA 700); there are bush taxis on the Liberian side.

For Guinea there are several vans every morning to Nzo or Sipilou at the border (about CFA 1700 plus baggage) and others from there to Nzérékoré (about GF 7000). The trip is very slow because of the many baggage searches en route, and you may have to wait up to five hours or so to catch another vehicle at the border. You must also pay a CFA 500 fee there. If you get caught in Sipilou, there are two inexpensive hotels.

GAGNOA
Gagnoa, which is Bété country and surrounded by cacao plantations, is a major crossroads, lying halfway between Abidjan and Man and between San Pédro and Bouaké. There's nothing of interest, but it is

Gagnoa

0   250   500 m

See Inset

*To Sinfra &
Bouaflé*

*To Hôtel
Beau Séjour*

*To
Soubré &
San Pédro*

Rond-
Point
du
Centre
Ville

*To Divo &
Abidjan*

*To
Oumé &
Yamoussoukro*

Market

0   125   250 m

OTHER
3   Elf Station
4   SGBCI Bank
5   Sous-Préfecture
6   Commissariat
7   BICICI Bank
8   Gare Routière d'Abidjan
    & Texaco Station
9   Mairie
10 Post Office
11 BIAO Bank
14 Gare Routière
15 Mobil & Elf Stations
16 Hospital
17 Toyota
18 Club de Ténis La Cabosse
20 Lycée de la Paix
21 Church
23 Agip Station

PLACES TO STAY
1   Hôtel du Lac
2   Hôtel Le Refuge
13 Hôtel Le Cottage
19 Hôtel Calvas
22 Hôtel Le Fromager &
    Bourgeois Nightclub

24 Hôtel du Vallon
25 Hôtel Le Progrès
26 Hôtel La Gazelle
27 Hôtel Le Flamboyant

PLACES TO EAT
12 Chawarma Restaurant

a convenient place to break the journey.
The market and gare routière border the
city's only roundabout, the Rond-Point du
Centre Ville, the commercial core being
between there and the commissariat.
There's also a lake on the northern outskirts of town.

Places to Stay – bottom end

Gagnoa has a number of good cheap hotels;
almost none of them have restaurants.

Three of the cheapest are all on the road
east to Oumé and Yamoussoukro and are
well marked. Coming from the heart, after

several blocks you'll come to the single-
storey *Hôtel Calvas* on your right. It has
clean rooms with fresh sheets and shared
baths for CFA 2000 (CFA 2500 with fan
and CFA 4000 with air-con) and greenery
all around. About one km further out on
your left is *Hôtel du Vallon*, which is one
block off the highway. Hard to beat for
value, it has small clean rooms with fans
and full attached baths with cold showers
for CFA 2000. About 700 metres further,
at the edge of town, is *Hôtel Le Progrès*
(☎ 77 26 47), which has slightly larger
rooms with fans for CFA 2000 (CFA 3500

with air-con). The exterior is a bit shabby but the rooms are fine.

If you'd rather be on the northern side of town, check *Hôtel du Lac* (☎ 77 20 42), which is several km from the centre on the road to Sinfra and Bouafflé and well marked. Fairly new and well maintained, it has spotless rooms with fans and full attached baths for CFA 2500.

Other possibilities which are more expensive and no better are *Hôtel Le Refuge*, which is one km closer to town, off the same highway, and *Hôtel La Gazelle* on the opposite side of town, about 1.5 km out. The poorly marked Refuge is two km from the centre and several blocks off the highway and thus is not easy to find without instructions. It has clean rooms with fans and full attached baths for CFA 3000 (CFA 4500 with air-con). La Gazelle is well marked and is the only cheap hotel with a restaurant. The menu is African and there are a number of selections. The rooms are clean and have fans and attached baths, but they are also tiny and slightly overpriced at CFA 3500 (CFA 5000 with air-con).

Places to Stay – top end

The city's top address is the old French-run *Hôtel Le Cottage* (☎ 77 21 73) in the heart of town. There's no pool but the restaurant, which is not cheap, is the best in town. Air-con singles/doubles with shared baths cost CFA 6500/7500 (CFA 7600/9200 with attached bath and CFA 8400/10,000 with TV and phone).

Le Fromager (☎ 77 20 36) offers excellent value. This tranquil modern place has spacious air-con rooms for CFA 4000 (CFA 6000 with TV and phone), a long pool and a restaurant which is good for breakfast. The new two-storey *Hôtel Le Flamboyant* (☎ 77 20 35), much further out on the same road, has air-con rooms with large beds, TV and tile baths for CFA 7000, but it's even less lively.

A better alternative to the Fromager is *Hôtel Beau Séjour* (☎ 77 20 74), several km north of the heart and well off the main highway. It has spotless new-looking rooms with air-con and tile floors for CFA 4500 to CFA 6000.

Places to Eat

For cheap chawarma sandwiches (CFA 400), head for the central area between the taxi stand and the roundabout. You'll find a typical Lebanese chawarma place there. For maquis food, a good place is the *Hôtel La Gazelle*. It has braised fish, for example, for CFA 1000 a plate. Two other places that have been recommended are *La Terrasse*, a pleasant open-air place with meals for CFA 500 to CFA 1000, and the small *La Cachette*. For European fare, the best place by far is *Hôtel Le Cottage*. It's not cheap however.

Getting There & Away

Buses all leave from the gare routière at the market. Bush taxis leave from there and from the taxi stand in the centre near the post office. The main bus company, UTB, provides connections to Yamoussoukro, Bouaké, Man and San Pédro. Two others are Sabé, which serves Abidjan and San Pédro, and Tramoci, which serves Abidjan and Man. Bus fares from Gagnoa are CFA 1500 to Abidjan, CFA 2000 to Yamoussoukro and San Pédro, and CFA 2500 to Bouaké. Fares to Gagnoa are often quite higher if Gagnoa is not the final destination, which is usually the case. If you take the San Pédro to Bouaké bus, for example, the fare from San Pédro to here will be CFA 3000.

The Centre

YAMOUSSOUKRO

Yamoussoukro became the official capital in 1983, but it's the capital in name only and probably will remain that way for many years. Starting in the 1960s, Houphouët-Boigny began spending lavishly on his native village of 30,000 inhabitants (now 100,000). The result is a wasteful, bizarre site. You'll find almost deserted, eight-lane highways lined with over 10,000 lights and avenues that end right in the jungle. There are virtually no traditional African houses left; Houphouët-Boigny replaced them with concrete middle-class (for Africa) structures.

CÔTE D'IVOIRE

There's no city like it in Africa. This small version of Brasilia hardly appears bustling but the city is fascinating and the core centre is a lot livelier at night than the town's grandiose, impersonal appearance suggests.

Yamoussoukro has an amazing array of facilities for a town of its size. The dazzling centrepiece is the huge post-Renaissance basilica; from several km away it looks like a giant pearl-grey dirigible hovering over the African bush. It is, however, only the culmination of a 20-year building boom.

Basilique de Notre Dame de la Paix

The Basilica is a sight to behold but what is truly most spectacular, and unforgettable, are the 36 immense stained-glass windows, all hand-blown in France by the best stained-glass makers in the world. Brilliantly conceived by an Ivoirian architect of Lebanese descent, they cover 8000 sq metres, splashing hundreds of colours across the nave in patterns that change throughout the day. They are so magnificent that the basilica needs no paintings, statues, tapestries, wood panelling or carvings. But some prominent members of the Ivoirian church were so embarrassed by the project's exorbitant costs that they tried to convince the Pope not to consecrate it; but he reluctantly agreed in 1989 upon the president's promise to build a hospital there.

The entrance is on the south side. It's open every day from 8 am to noon and 2 to 5 pm except on Sundays mornings when it's open only for mass, which starts at 10 am. Seeing the basilica while the choir performs is unforgettable. Entrance is free unless you want a guided tour, which costs CFA 500 and is the only way to get a visit to the top.

INSET & ENSTP Colleges

Don't miss the two colleges, INSET (the teachers' institute) and ENSTP (the engineering school), both well maintained and architecturally interesting. Coming from the West, they may not seem so special, but if you've travelled around West Africa a bit, you'll be impressed, especially with ENSTP. They're some distance apart on rolling green hills on the far eastern side of town, several km from the centre.

The main buildings at ENSTP are surrounded by huge marble arches – an impressive site. There's a huge outdoor pool, a well-maintained soccer field, and an attractive modern cafeteria constructed entirely of local wood. If you ask at the gate, the proud student guards will give you a free guided tour.

Presidential Palace

Like many official buildings here, Houphouët's huge walled home (five km around), where he is now buried, can be seen only from a distance. An arm of the city's main lake runs along the southern side of his house, forming ponds. They are full of crocodiles *(caïmans)* that supposedly lend

---

Facts about the Basilica

Some of the facts about the famous Basilica of Our Lady of Peace are startling. It was built in only three years (ending 1989) compared to more than 100 years for St Peter's in Rome, to which it bears a striking resemblance. Although the cupola is slightly lower than St Peter's dome (due to a papal request), it's topped by a huge cross of gold, making it the tallest church in all Christendom.

While it seats about 2000 fewer worshippers than St Peter's (ie 7000 people), it is air-conditioned and as many as 300,000 pilgrims can fit into the 7.4-acre plaza, which is slightly larger than St Peter's and paved with granite and marble. (There are only about one million Catholics in the entire country.)

The price tag was roughly US$300 million, a sum matching half the national budget deficit, and annual maintenance costs will be about US$1.5 million – which will probably be picked up by the Houphouët-Boigny Foundation. There's nothing African about the cathedral; even the figures depicted in the stained-glass windows are White except for a lone Black pilgrim who bears a remarkable resemblance to Houphouët-Boigny and is shown kneeling at the feet of Christ. ∎

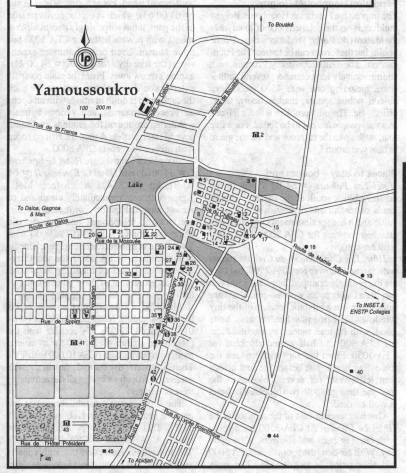

PLACES TO STAY

4 Hôtel La Résidence
10 Hôtel Las Palmas &
   Maquis Le Jardin
11 Hôtel Akwaba
21 Hôtel Le Bélier
23 Hôtel Le Caméo
24 Hôtel Le Bonheur II
25 Motel Agip
26 Hôtel de la Paix
27 Hôtel Le Bonheur I
32 Hôtel Les Confidences
   du Ciel
33 Hôtel Waka Waka
40 Hôtel Akraya
45 Hôtel Président

PLACES TO EAT

9 Restaurant Tchong Fa
12 Le Printemps &
   Maquis Le Molokai
13 Maquis Les Cocotiers
14 Maquis Street
16 Cheap Foutou Place
17 Maquis Le Loisir
31 Chez Valentine
34 Maquis Tanti Adjoua
35 A La Belle Pizza

OTHER

1 Basilica
2 Presidential Palace
3 Feeding Spot for
  Crocodiles
5 Commissariat
6 Score Supermarket &
  Texaco Station
7 Marché de Kossou
8 Market
15 Le Chateau (Tower)
18 Lycée Mamie Adjoua
19 Mairie
20 Gare de Burkina
22 Mosque

28 Gare Routière &
   Motel Shell
29 Post Office
30 Gendarmerie
36 BIAO Bank
37 Marseille Nightclub &
   Cinéma Mofeta
38 BICICI Bank
39 Air Ivoire
41 Fondation
   Houphouët-Boigny
42 SGCBI Bank
43 Maison du Party
44 Lycée Scientifique
46 Golf Course

Yamoussoukro

0   100   200 m

To Bouaké

Lake

To Daloa, Gagnoa & Man

Route de Daloa

Rue de St France

Route de Daloa

Route de Bouaké

Route de Mamie Adjoua

Rue du Chateau

Rue de la Mosquée

Boulevard-Boigny

Rue de la Fondation

Rue de Sopim

Rue de

To INSET &
ENSTP Colleges

To Daloa &
Man

Route d'Abidjan

Rue du Lycée Scientifique

Rue de l'Hôtel Président

To Abidjan

CÔTE D'IVOIRE

protection. Every day at 7.30 am and 6.30 pm the guardian gives them 15 kg of beef. In years past, they lived on sacrifices of live chickens but that practice has ceased. If you want to have your photo taken with the crocs, you'll have to give the guardian some money plus a tip so that he can attract the animals out of the water. Otherwise, unless you come at feeding time, there will probably be little to see.

Fondation Houphouët-Boigny

The impressive Fondation Houphouët-Boigny building is on the southern side of town, near the **Maison du Party**. The latter is closed to the public, but the former can be toured. The Foundation is a beautiful four-storey structure, with an impressively long entrance, several auditoriums including one with 4500 seats, huge air-con public spaces, marble floors, travel offices, etc. The only problem is that's it like a morgue; people are not to be found. For a free tour, walk up to the entrance and ask the guard to take you around.

Places to Stay – bottom end

Hôtel Las Palmas (☎ 64 02 73) is in the centre, a block south of the market, with all kinds of restaurants nearby. It's very good value and it has spotless rooms with fans and attached showers for CFA 2000 (CFA 4000 with air-con).

Hôtel Les Confidences du Ciel has rooms with fan and shower for CFA 2500, but they are exceedingly cramped. For CFA 3500 you can get a larger room with air-con. Units are quite clean but a bit dark because of the tiny windows. The maquis here is also quite good, with African sauces, eg agouti sauce, for CFA 900 and half grilled chickens for CFA 1050. From the gare routière take the main drag north; just before the first bridge turn left (west) for several blocks to the mosque, then go south two blocks. The hotel is well marked.

One block south-east of the mosque is the *Hôtel Le Caméo*. At CFA 3500 for a room with fan, big beds and showers, it's a good buy. With air-con, the rooms cost CFA 5000 but that price is negotiable. The only

problem is that it's also the pick of every bug in town. The attractive bar-restaurant under a big paillote is a plus as is the friendly woman owner who is a wonderful cook. Meals cost around CFA 1000.

Places to Stay – middle

Most of the mid-range hotels are conveniently located in the centre near the gare routière. Two of the best are at petrol stations. The best for the money is the well-maintained French-run *Motel Agip* (☎ 64 00 64), which is on the northern side of the gare. It has surprisingly decent air-con rooms with private baths for CFA 5000 but no restaurant. Even better but more expensive is the friendly *Motel Shell* (☎ 64 00 24), a stone's throw away. From the plain no-frills exterior you'd never know that out the back the ambience is quite inviting, with an open-air French restaurant, and various animals wandering around on the grounds, including several large turtles. A modern air-con room with private bath costs CFA 8000.

Two places opposite are *Hôtel Le Bonheur I* (☎ 64 00 61) and *Hôtel Le Bonheur II* (☎ 64 00 31, fax 64 09 42), which faces Motel Agip. Both are immaculately clean and of almost identical quality, with carpeted air-con rooms, telephones and private tile bathrooms for CFA 8000 (CFA 9000 with TV). You can also get excellent French meals at either place (CFA 3500 for the three-course menu), and on Saturday afternoons you can go on one of their guided tours of the city provided enough people sign up.

About half a km north on the same road is the long-standing *Hôtel La Résidence* (☎ 64 01 48, fax 64 22 22). It's popular with the French and charges CFA 8000 for an air-con room with private bath (CFA 10,000 with TV). There's also an active bar and a restaurant, with a terrace in front for viewing all the activity on the main drag.

The city's newest establishment is the modern four-storey *Hôtel Akraya* (☎ 64 11 31/2). This place is very clean and the rooms, CFA 10,000 to CFA 12,000, have TV and video. However, the ambience is very sterile and if you don't have a vehicle, you're likely to find the hotel's location, several blocks south of the mairie, to be a major drawback.

Places to Stay – top end

The town's finest is the *Hôtel Président* (☎ 64 01 58/9, fax 64 05 77), now an Intercontinental. This once grand establishment is going downhill fast and room rates have dropped accordingly – to CFA 20,000. Meals at the panoramic restaurant on top are also now more affordable: most main dishes are in the CFA 2300 to CFA 3500 range, eg CFA 2700 for lasagne. You'll probably be their only customer, so expect 1st-class service.

Places to Eat

African For cheap African food during the day, head for the small Marché de Kossou on Rue du Château, two blocks east of the Score supermarket. There are several shacks on the north side where women sell dishes, such as sauce graine, riz sauce, etc, typically for CFA 250 a plate. One of them is the *Restaurant Spécial Manger Africain*.

A short block or two south of the Chateau is an open-air place serving foutou, with rock-bottom prices. These places are a lot better for African sauces than the gare routière, where you'll find mostly snack food and brochettes.

Maquis Yamoussoukro has some excellent maquis, most of which are open only in the evenings. They're not particularly cheap, however; a half braised chicken can easily cost CFA 1700 or more. Most of the best maquis are in the Habitat district between the two arms of the lake. *Maquis Le Jardin* (☎ 64 14 22), facing Hôtel Las Palmas, has a two-page menu, interior seating and a breezy atmosphere.

Most maquis in this district, however, are a block or two south, along the east-west road running along the southernmost arm of the lake. The furthest east along this road, about 400 metres east of the main drag, is *Maquis Le Loisir*, which is largely enclosed by a hedge. Poulet braisé costs CFA 2400. A block or two further west along this road is

Maquis Les Cocotiers, which is another good place. Two new ones further west along this road are *Maquis Pharmacie du Garde* and *Maquis La Paillote*.

For a fancier maquis with both maquis food and Continental selections and slightly higher prices, you may prefer *Chez Valentine*, which is 2½ blocks east of the gare routière.

Miscellaneous Along the main drag, Ave Houphouët-Boigny, are at least two non-African restaurants. The *Restaurant Tchong Fa*, just south of the market, is an unpretentious Chinese-run restaurant that has a wide selection of Chinese dishes, mostly for CFA 1500. Heading south, there's *A La Belle Pizza*. The French owner offers pizzas for CFA 1400 to CFA 2600; it's closed on Monday.

Entertainment

At night, the liveliest area of town besides the gare routière is along Rue du Château leading eastward from the market. The best place for dancing in this area is *Le Printemps*, a block before the Château. Other places along this street, such as *Maquis Le Molokai*, a rustic bar next door, are also for working people. Upmarket places include *Marseille Nightclub*, a fancy disco on the main drag between Hôtel Président and the gare routière, and *Kotou* at the Président. The latter is often crowded on weekend nights and sometimes on Thursday, which is jazz night; the rest of the week it's dead.

Because the restaurant at the *Hôtel Président* overlooks the city, it's a great place to come just for a drink. The cinema here is the best in town, with showings at 6.30 and 9 pm every evening (CFA 1000), but few people go there or to the hotel's nightclub except on weekends.

Getting There & Away

Getting rides in all directions is easy from Yamoussoukro because of its central location. Buses tend to be the best, quickest and cheapest form of transport; day or night you can catch one of the many buses heading to Man (CFA 2500), Abidjan (CFA 2000), Bouaké (CFA 1500) or Korhogo (CFA

CÔTE D'IVOIRE

3500). Bush taxis are more expensive, eg CFA 3500 to Abidjan and CFA 4000 to Man.

All of these vehicles leave from the gare routière on the main drag except those to Burkina Faso, which leave from the Gare de Burkina on Rue de la Mosquée. Two of the better bus companies with comfortable large *cars* serving Bobo-Dioulasso are Sans Frontières and Sogebaf. They have departures every day and charge CFA 9000 one way. The Sans Frontières bus leaves every day around 6 pm and arrives at Bobo around 5 pm the following day, with a seven-hour stopover in Bouaké.

Getting Around
Because the city is so spread out, covering it on foot is difficult. Except for the two colleges, most places of interest are, fortunately, along the major north-south drag or within a block or two of it. By the hour, taxis cost about CFA 2500.

MARAHOUÉ NATIONAL PARK
Parc National de la Marahoué, 80 km west of Yamoussoukro, is one of the country's more obscure parks; most Ivoirians have never heard of it. However, it is fairly accessible, at least by car. One-third of the 10,100-sq-km park is savannah woodland and the rest is dense forest, including some mahogany trees. The Marahoué River runs through here, and there's a footpath and several watch-towers to allow visitors to see hippo. Many people stay in an area called Bandama Rouge, which is not easy to get to and return from in one day if you're walking.

In addition to hippo, baboons are fairly plentiful, so you'll probably see some of them, maybe elephants as well, of which there are about 50. Other animals that you might see include monkey, chimpanzee, buffalo, waterbuck, hartebeest and various species of antelope. Nearly 300 species of birds have been recorded here as well.

Unlike Comoë National Park, this one is open year-round and you can walk around because there are no lions. There's no accommodation but you can camp at the entrance. Previously, food was not available and water was available only at Gobazra, which is on the main highway, six km south of the park entrance, or from a spring one km before the park entrance. However, there's a new centre d'accueil at the park entrance, so you can probably get drinks there; but bring food in case none is available.

In Gobazra, you must register with the park rangers, who are reportedly not particularly friendly, and pay the park fee (CFA 2000 a day) and the compulsory guide fee (CFA 3000). Because of these fees and the six-km walk from the main highway to the entrance, some travellers find a visit here not worth the hassle and cost.

Getting There & Away
Take any bus or bush taxi from Yamoussoukro towards Man on the Yamoussoukro-Man highway and get off at Gobazra, 25 km west of Bouafflé. The dirt road leading north from Gobazra to the park entrance is well marked but six km long – a long round-trip walk if you don't have a car.

BOUAKÉ
Situated in the heart of Baoulé country, 106 km north of Yamoussoukro, Bouaké is the country's second-largest city. There's little to see other than the huge sprawling market next to the main gare routière, so many travellers give the city a cursory look and pass on.

Bouaké is a better place to meet Africans, however, than Abidjan. For starters, there's much less crime, which means that unlike in Abidjan, you may be able to walk around at night if you're on your guard. Also, with only the market as a 'must see', you can concentrate on simply enjoying the people and the city's vibrant African quarters, particularly Koko which is where the Baoulé are concentrated.

The city is big – about half a million people – but the core centre can still be covered on foot if you don't mind walking a little. The main north-south highway through town is the wide Ave Houphouët-

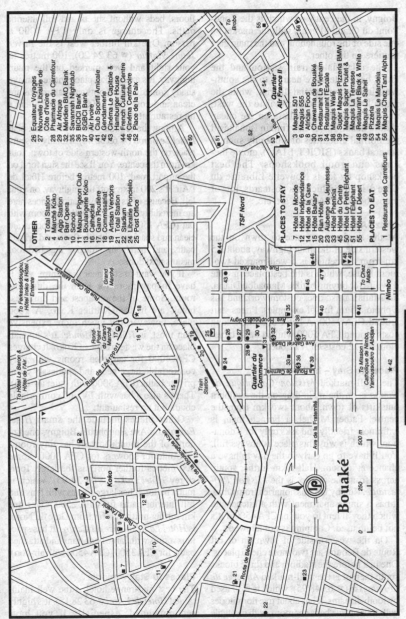

CÔTE D'IVOIRE

Bouaké

0   250   500 m

To Ferkessédougou,
Hôtel Irako & Hôtel
Entente

To Hôtel Le Baron &
Hôtel de l'Air

To Brobo

Quartier
Air France II

TSF Nord

Grand
Marché

Rond-Point
du Grand
Marché

Rue du Camp Militaire

Rue de l'Aéroport

Rue de Boundiali Koko

Rue de l'Avenir

Koko

Train
Station

Rue Jacque Aka

Ave Houphouët-Boigny

Ave Gabriel Dadié

Route de Cannes

Quartier du
Commerce

Ave de la Fraternité

Route de Béoumi

To Mission,
Cathédrale de
Yamoussoukro & Abidjan

To Chez
Mado

Nimbo

PLACES TO STAY

7   Hôtel Le Monde
12 Hôtel Independance
14 Hôtel de la Gare
15 Hôtel Bakary
20 Ran Hôtel
23 Auberge de Jeunesse
33 Hôtel Phenicia
45 Hôtel du Centre
50 Hôtel Le Petit Eléphant
51 Hôtel Eléphant
55 Hôtel Le Désert

PLACES TO EAT

1   Restaurant des Carrefours
3   Maquis 501
6   Maquis 555
8   African Food
30 Chawarma de Bouaké
31 Restaurant Le Vietnam
34 Restaurant l'Escale
38 Maquis Walé
39 Super Maquis Pizzeria BMW
47 Maquis Super Poulet &
    Restaurant Yvonne
48 Maquis La Terrasse
49 Maquis Bleu & White
49 Maquis Le Sahel
53 Pizzeria
54 Maquis Le Mandela
56 Maquis Chez Tanti Alpha

OTHER

2   Total Station
4   Marché Koko
5   Agip Station
9   Bar Opera
10 School
11 Maquis Pigeon Club
13 Boulangerie Koko
16 Cathédrale
17 Gare Routière
18 Commissariat
19 Gendarmerie
21 Artisan Vendors
22 Total Station
24 Librairie Ponciello
25 Post Office
26 Equateur Voyages
27 Nouvelle Librairie de
    Côte d'Ivoire
28 Pharmacie du Carrefour
29 Air Afrique
32 Méridien BIAO Bank
35 Savannah Nightclub
36 BICICI Bank
40 SGBCI Bank
41 Air Ivoire
42 Club Sportif Amicale
43 Cinéma Le Capitole &
    Hamburger House
44 French Cultural Centre
46 Cinéma Centrivoire
52 Place de la Paix

Boigny, in the centre of which is the Rond-Point du Grand Marché, with the market on one side of the roundabout and the main gare routière on the other.

The dilapidated train station and the city's best hotels are nearby to the south-west in the commercial district, while the much livelier Koko district is to the west, and this is where travellers on the cheap should head. You'll also find in Bouaké all the normal amenities of a big city such as several banks (BICICI, BIAO), movie theatres and good bookshops. The best bookshop by far is Nouvelle Librairie du Côte d'Ivoire, which has postcards, lots of maps, books on African art, etc.

Chez l'Artiste du Batik

At the southern entrance to town on the western side of the main highway, about 2.5 km from the centre, is a well-marked two-room house, which is the best place in Côte d'Ivoire for buying batiks. Mamadou Diarra, the Malian artist, does custom work and has a photo album full of examples. Prices start around CFA 1500. A batik one metre long costs around CFA 5000 while a batik table-cloth for 12 costs CFA 22,000.

Places to Stay – bottom end

The well-marked *Mission Catholique de Nimbo* is on the main drag on the southern outskirts of town, about two km from the centre. Father Michel, a French man, is extremely friendly and asks only for a donation, which is why this place is always full. You'll have to go early in the day to have a chance at a room. Half a km further south, across from the mairie, is the *Mission Protestante*. Run by US missionaries from Ohio, it has a single apartment with a kitchenette which they'll rent to you for CFA 4500 if it's not being used. Camping is not allowed.

On the western side of town on or off Route de Béoumi are two more cheap places. One just before the stadium and three blocks south thereof is the well-marked *Auberge de la Jeunesse* (☎ 63 48 95), which is well used by football teams. It has about five dormitories with four or five beds per room, with clean tile

floors, beds without sheets and full interior baths. The charge is only CFA 1000 a person. One km further west is the *Foyer Jeune Viateur* (☎ 63 24 20), 100 metres to your right and well marked on the main highway. It's a Christian place with extensive shady grounds. The rooms and bathrooms are clean and cost CFA 2000 a person; there's no restaurant.

Among the regular hotels, you can't beat *Hôtel Le Baron* (☎ 63 58 44), a totally obscure place on the north-western side of town, four km from the centre. You'll see the sign for it on the airport road, 100 metres before Hôtel de l'Air. It's 200 metres off the highway, on your left. Because of its remote location, prices here are incredibly low – CFA 1000 for a room with fan (CFA 1500 with air-con). The rooms are clean and spacious, with tile floors and private baths, and there's an attractive thatched-roof maquis next door.

If you want to stay near the centre, you'll have to pay more for even the dumpiest room. Some of the cheapest and dumpiest hotels are in the Quartier Koko. A good place, however, but much more expensive than most, is *Hôtel Le Monde*. It's a small place on the western edge of Koko. It charges CFA 4000 for carpeted rooms with very comfortable large beds and spotlessly clean private baths (CFA 5000 with quiet air-con). There's also a bar with TV and comfortable chairs but no restaurant.

Other places include the small *Hôtel Entente* on Ave Houphouët-Boigny, one km north of the roundabout. It has tiny rooms with interior showers for CFA 3000. Some 200 metres further north is the large, four-storey *Hôtel Iroko* (☎ 63 34 95), which is much better. It has large rooms with fans and full interior baths for CFA 2500. Over one km further north, not far from Gare du Nord, is *Hôtel La Résidence du Centre*. It has spacious rooms with large beds, fans and attached baths for CFA 3500 (CFA 4500 with air-con).

Places to Stay – middle

The best mid-range hotel is the well-maintained *Hôtel de l'Air* (☎ 63 28 15). It's highly recommended, especially if you have wheels, and is superior to the city's only top-end establishment, the Ran. It has a French restaurant, with most dishes in the CFA 1600 to CFA 2200 range, and is a superb deal for the money – CFA 7500 for an excellent air-con room with a large bed (CFA 9000 with two beds). The only drawback is the location, four km north-west from the heart of town on the highway to the airport.

If it's full or you'd prefer to be closer to the centre, try *Hôtel du Centre* (☎ 63 32 78), which charges CFA 7000-7500/8000-8500 for singles/doubles with air-con; there's also a restaurant and a disco.

Hôtel l'Éléphant (☎ 63 25 28) is very reasonably priced at CFA 6500 for a clean air-con room with TV and full bath (CFA 8500 with twin beds). The restaurant looks good and the plat du jour costs CFA 2000. It's one km to the east of the centre, and 70 metres north of Place de la Paix. It also has an unmarked annexe, *Le Petit Éléphant*, two short blocks north. An air-con double with private bath costs CFA 4000; excellent value.

Places to Stay – top end
The modern *Ran Hôtel* (☎ 63 20 16, fax 63 40 32; cards AE, D, V, CB), in the centre next to the train station, still has the reputation for being the city's top hotel, but it's going downhill quickly and developing a seedy ambience. It has singles/doubles for CFA 14,800/16,800, vendors of cheap African crafts everywhere, and a long clean pool (CFA 900 for nonguests). You'll do much better staying at Hôtel de l'Air.

Places to Eat
Cheap Eats & African For chawarma sandwiches (CFA 400) and other inexpensive Lebanese fare, head for *Restaurant l'Escale* on Ave Houphouët-Boigny, one km south of the roundabout, or *Chawarma de Bouaké*, a block north on the same avenue. Next to Cinéma Le Capitole near the northern end of Rue J Aka, you'll find *Hamburger House*, where you can get hamburgers (CFA 1300) and other fast food.

A great place for African food is *Chez Mado*, which is at the southern end of the street just east of Ave Houphouët-Boigny and parallel to it, about two km south of the roundabout. Popular for lunch or dinner, it's far too rustic to have a menu; the selections include excellent sauce agouti (bush rat) for CFA 600 and poulet braisé for CFA 1700.

For African sauces during the day, try the Koko district. Just south of Koko market, if you go south-west from the Agip station for half a block, you'll find some no-name shacks on your right where, during the day, various women make a number of excellent sauces to be eaten with pâte or rice; prices here are rock bottom, about CFA 250 for a meal. Also, on Rue de l'Aéroport, several blocks east of Koko market, you'll find *Restaurant des Carrefours*. It doesn't have quite as many sauces but it's an actual restaurant and prices are low.

Maquis The maquis in Bouaké are less expensive than those in Abidjan and Yamoussoukro; quite a few are open for lunch as well as dinner. The best maquis are in Quartier Air France Deux.

For one that is a cut above the rest, head for the well-known and ever-popular *Maquis Le Sahel* (☎ 63 38 59). Open for lunch and dinner, it charges CFA 1800 for a whole braised chicken with attiéké, CFA 1000 for couscous or beef brochettes, and CFA 800 to CFA 1000 for its other selections. Going south along Ave Houphouët-Boigny, take the second left after passing Air Ivoire and walk for two blocks.

Two other places on Rue Jacque Aka worth checking are *Restaurant Black & White* next door and *Maquis Super Poulet* a block north. *Maquis Walé* on Ave Houphouët-Boigny, opposite the Savannah nightclub, is another in this area.

Heading east on Rue 18 you'll find several more maquis. The first, just before Place de la Paix, is *Maquis Le Fouquet* (☎ 63 49 04). Prices here are very reasonable, eg CFA 1000 for agouti sauce and CFA 1800 for chicken braisé or kedjenou style, but the place has a run-down appearance. The fanciest maquis, the attractive *Maquis Le Mandela* (☎ 63 59 59), is just beyond Place de la Paix. The menu is quite large and includes some French selections. You can get various African sauces for around CFA 1500 and poulet braisé or beef brochettes for CFA 2500.

If you head two blocks further east along Rue 18 and take a right (south) just before the train tracks and go four blocks, you'll come to *Maquis Chez Tanti Alpha*. Open every day, it's one of the largest maquis in town but very basic, with low prices.

In the Koko district, half a block east of the Agip station is the shady, open-air *Maquis 501*, which is fairly rustic and one of the best maquis in that area. West a block from the Agip station is the *Maquis 555*, which is also reputedly good. Both places are open in the evening and are as popular for drinking as for eating.

Miscellaneous The best restaurant in the commercial centre is *Restaurant Le Vietnam* (☎ 63 33 21) on Ave Gabriel Dadié, three blocks south of the train station. All selections on the extensive menu are in the CFA 1400 to CFA 1600 range, including bamboo pork and ginger chicken. For cheaper Vietnamese fare such as nems and shrimp beignets, try *Maquis La Terrasse* on Rue Jacque Aka.

Entertainment

For a drink in the commercial district, the street-side terrace of the *Hôtel Provençal* is as good as you'll find. It's shady but the atmosphere is seedy. For more rustic African bars, head for Koko; there are several in the area.

For a disco, the ever-popular *Savannah* on Ave Houphouët-Boigny, one km south of the roundabout, charges about CFA 2000 (closed Tuesday). For a change, check *Le Monica* nightclub at Hôtel du Centre.

Getting There & Away

Air Air Ivoire (☎ 63 33 93) has a flight every day to/from Abidjan (CFA 16,250) and several times a week to/from Korhogo (CFA 12,550). It's also possible to catch international flights in Bouaké headed for Ouaga (about CFA 30,000 with Air Ivoire or Air Burkina), Bamako and Conakry, but connections are not very frequent.

For information on international flights, contact Air Afrique (☎ 63 37 45), several blocks south of the Ran Hôtel or, nearby, Equateur Voyages (☎ 63 13 52), the city's top travel agency.

Bus & Bush Taxi Buses and bush taxis all leave from either of two stations: Gare Routière du Grand Marché in the centre at the roundabout and Gare du Nord three km north. The former serves all points east, south and west, eg Abidjan, San Pédro, Man, etc; the latter serves all points north, eg Korhogo, Odienné, Ferkessédougou, Burkina Faso and Mali.

UTB has big luxury buses leaving every 30 minutes from the former; the first and last buses in either direction are at 6 am and 11 pm. The trip takes five hours. UTB is also the main company serving San Pédro. There is also direct service to Man, but in some cases it may be faster to catch a bus or bush taxi to Yamoussoukro and one of the luxury buses from there to Man.

Express Bouaké-Korhogo has fives buses every day to/from Korhogo; they leave in either direction at 8.15 and 11 am and at 2 and 9 pm. For Korhogo and Ferké, you could also catch one of the buses from Abidjan, provided there's space. San Frontières has pre-dawn departures every day for Bobo-Dioulasso, arriving around 5 pm. Standard fares are CFA 2500 to Korhogo (four hours), CFA 3000 to Boudiali, CFA 3500 to Odienné, CFA 4000 to Tingéla, CFA 4000 to Abidjan, CFA 6000 to San Pédro, CFA 7500 to Bobo and CFA 12,500 to Ouaga.

Peugeot 504 bush taxis serve all of the same routes and charge about 50% more.

Train The *Express* train departs Abidjan and Ouaga on Tuesday, Thursday and Saturday mornings, arriving Bouaké at 3.05 pm headed north to Ouaga and at 2.05 am the following day headed south to Abidjan. The 1st/2nd-class fare is CFA 4800/2600 to Abidjan and CFA 11,800/8400 to Ouaga. Those with student IDs can get reductions, eg CFA 1500 in 2nd class to Abidjan. There is also the slower and slightly cheaper *Rapide* which does the Abidjan-Bouaké trip once a day.

TANOU-SAKASSOU

Some 12 km east of Bouaké on the road to Brobo, Tanou-Sakassou is one of several obscure villages in the Bouaké area where the women specialise in pottery making. The village is on the left and marked by a small artisans' co-operative sign. The bisque work here is in the form of animals or women's heads and is exquisitely done, with a wonderful balance of form and decorative line. You can get a beautiful pot here for around CFA 2500.

KATIOLA

Just 54 km north of Bouaké on the major north-south route to Burkina Faso, Katiola is the take-off point for the southern entrance to Comoë National Park some 170 km to the east.

The town is nothing special but it does have one attraction – a huge pottery co-operative on the eastern outskirts of town. The pottery is heavily glazed and tourist quality; however, stopping here may still be worthwhile if you're interested in seeing pottery made. As elsewhere in the region, only the women make pottery, and it's possible to see them at work. The jugs are shaped without the aid of wheels, but still come out symmetrical.

Places to Stay

For a cheap room in the centre try *Hôtel Makarwa* or *Hôtel de l'Amitié* (☎ 65 43 63). *La Paillote*, two km from the centre, has clean individual huts with showers and mos-

quito nets. The top hotel is the modern *Hôtel Hambol* (☎ 65 47 25) on the main highway on the north side of town. It's has modern rooms for about CFA 9500, a bar and restaurant, pool and nightclub.

The North

KORHOGO

A nine-hour bus ride north from Abidjan, Korhogo is the capital of the Senoufo and dates from the 13th century. The Senoufo are best known for their wooden carvings and Korhogo cloth (*la toile de Korhogo*) – coarse raw cotton, like burlap, with painted, mud-coloured designs. It's sold in Korhogo and in several surrounding areas where the weavers live. The Senoufo are also renowned for their skilled *forgerons* (blacksmiths) and *potiers* (potters), so seeing them at work and picking up some crafts are what make the Korhogo area one of the most popular in Côte d'Ivoire. One of the best times to come is during the first week of December when there are funeral celebrations every night during the week, with lots of music and dancing.

The heart of town is the bustling market, near which the various bus companies all have their offices, and also the BIAO bank, which will cash travellers' cheques if you have your purchase receipt. The city's top hotel is named after Mt Korhogo, which is on the south-western outskirts of town and

The Lô Association

The secret Lô association of the Senoufo, which is divided into the Poro cult for boys and the Sakrobundu cult for girls, is essentially a system whereby children are prepared for adulthood. The goal is to preserve the group's folklore, teach them about their tribal customs so that they can take over the various social duties of the community and, through various rigorous tests, enable them to gain self-control. Their education is divided into three seven-year periods ending with an initiation ceremony involving circumcision, isolation, instruction and the use of masks. Each community has a 'sacred forest' where the training takes place. Many of the rituals involve masked dances, and the uninitiated are never allowed to see them or the tests which they must undergo in the forests. However, some ritualist ceremonies, such as the dance of the leopard men, occur in the village itself when the boys return from one of their training sessions, and these can be witnessed by everyone. ■

PLACES TO STAY

1 Hôtel Le Tisserin
2 Hôtel Le Pacific
3 Hôtel Les Avocats
4 Hôtel Kadjona
10 Hôtel Pèlerin & Express Bouaké-Korhogo
11 Motel Agip & Vehicles to Ferké
12 Hôtel Le Palmier
19 Hôtel du Centre Ville
23 Hôtel Mont Korhogo & Artisan Stalls
25 Mission Catholique & Public Fax
29 Hôtel Gon
41 Hôtel La Rose Blanche
42 Hôtel Le Méridien

PLACES TO EAT

20 Maquis 2000
26 Maquis Zougmore
28 Maquis Les 6
30 Super Maquis Le Lys & Pâtisserie
31 La Bonne Cuisine
36 Good Maquis
37 Foutou Place
38 Crémerie Donald

OTHER

5 Maison de Coulibaly Kassim
6 Maison des Fetisheurs
7 Mosquée
8 Cinema
9 Taxis
13 Pharmacie du Nord
14 BIAO Bank & Alimentacion Générale
15 SGBCI Bank
16 Photo Shop
17 STVF Bus Station
18 SWTK Bus Terminal
21 CTK Bus Station
22 BICICI Bank
24 Post Office & Buses to Odienné
27 Musée Péléforo Gbon Coulibaly
32 Commissariat
33 Préfecture
34 Mairie
35 Palais de Justice
39 La Co-operative Artisanal
40 Municipal Pool

Korhogo

0   100   200 m

To Koni & M'Bengue

To Ferkessédougou

Petit Paris

Koro Nord

Servil Kaha

Quartier des Sculptures

To Boundiali & Odienné

Route de Boundiali

Route de Koni

Koro Sud

Dem

Marché

To Boundiali

Sinistre

Place de la Paix

Residential

To Hôtel de la Montagne, Kaplélé, Foro & Mt Korhogo

To Waraniéné & Sirasso

Route de Sirasso

To Napié, Dikodougou, Farkaha & Old Airport

Route de Dikodougou

To New Airport, Karakoro & Badikaha

Rue de Air France

CÔTE D'IVOIRE

can be hiked in half an hour or so. Going from the market towards the mountain, you'll cross a large roundabout, the Place de la Paix, where you'll find most government offices including the police.

Musée Régional Péléforo Gbon Coulibaly

This museum, which opened in 1992, has six exposition rooms with a good collection of old photographs, chiefs' chairs and, most of all, wooden statues and masks. Built between 1938 and 1950, the building was once the house of the famous Senoufo chief, Péléforo Gbon Coulibaly, who lived here until his death in 1962. The museum is open Tuesday to Saturday from 8.30 am to noon and 3 to 6 pm; donations are accepted.

La Co-operative Artisanal

Korhogo cloth is recognisable by the bold figures (traditionally dark brown or black) painted on rough, plain, cotton material (usually off-white). The weavers use a natural vegetable dye (made from leaves and mixed with black mud) and a knife with a thick curved blade to paint the animal motifs and geometrical figures. There are many imitations. If the dark dye fully penetrates the back side of the material, it is genuine and probably from Farkaha. The material was originally used for those being initiated and for hunters and dancers, but today it's made primarily for the tourist market.

Portable and inexpensive, this material makes a good souvenir wall-hanging; a metre-long piece can cost as little as CFA 3500 to CFA 5000. Vendors will tell you it's washable but the untreated ones will fade after the first wash.

The best quality Korhogo cloth and other Senoufo weavings is found at the Maison de l'Union des GVC d'Artisans du Nord, more commonly called La Co-operative Artisanal, three blocks west of the Place de la Paix. The selection is quite extensive and varied and includes pottery from Kanioraba (beyond Sirasso). Prices are reasonable considering the excellent quality; a large cloth from Farkaha

costs about CFA 12,000. The centre is open from 8 am to noon and 2.30 to 6 pm daily.

Quartier des Sculptures

The small district just north of the mosque is where most of the city's woodcarvers live and work. The heart is the *maison des fetisheurs*, a small building dating from 1901 which is full of fetishes. For a price, the old man who guards this place might agree to let you see inside; he will also ask for money just to take a photograph of the exterior. All around this place you'll find woodcarvers at work and buildings where they store their work, which is mostly souvenir quality.

Dances

Be on the lookout for opportunities to see Senoufo dancing. The Senoufo hold animals in high regard, and each clan has its own animal totem. When they die they transform into the clan's animal totem, so some of the dances are associated with animals. In Natiokabadara (five km from Korhogo), for example, on special occasions they perform *la dance des hommes-panthères* (dance of the leopard-men), an unforgettable experience if you should be so lucky to see it. It's typically performed throughout the Senoufo area when the boys return from one of the secret *Poro* – initiation-training sessions. In all of these dances, masks, often of animal heads, play a critical role in reaching the gods and driving away bad spirits.

Municipal Pool

The pool, open every day from 8 am to 6 pm, costs CFA 500. It's clean and one of the nicest municipal pools in West Africa (longer and larger than those at most hotels).

Organised Tours

From December to May, Touraco Tours at Hôtel Mt Korhogo offers tours of Comoë National Park, and also a 'Découverte de la Pays Senoufo' excursion throughout the year when there's enough demand. A one-day excursion of the park from Korhogo costs CFA 60,000 per person, departing at 3 am and returning around 6 pm. It's better to

CÔTE D'IVOIRE

extend this to two days, which costs only CFA 12,000 more, including a night and meals at the Safari Lodge.

Places to Stay – bottom end

For rock-bottom prices, try the friendly quiet *Mission Catholique*, five blocks south-east of the market. It charges CFA 2000 per person for a poorly ventilated room with no fan. The units have bare mattresses and shared baths without soap or towels. It's on Ave Coulibaly leading south to the Place de la Paix. Cheaper still is the unmarked two-storey *Hôtel Gon* (☎ 86 06 70), a block east of the museum. It has large rooms with grubby shared baths for CFA 1500 (CFA 2000 with fan). The popular and noisy *Hôtel Le Pélerin*, facing the market's eastern side, has a bar and also charges CFA 2000.

A better place in the centre is *Hôtel Le Palmier*, south of the Agip station. Rooms with fan cost CFA 2500 (CFA 3500 with air-con that operates very poorly). Units are spacious and have dirty tile floors, uncomfortable sagging mattresses, fresh sheets, and decent private tile baths with flush toilets.

If you insist on air-con, head for the *Hôtel du Centre Ville* (☎ 86 13 34), 3½ blocks south-east of the market. It has a restaurant and spacious rooms with air-con, comfortable mattresses, relaxing reading chairs, and private baths for CFA 4000 (CFA 6000 for larger rooms), which is excellent value.

Equally good or better is *Hôtel Le Tisserin*, at the north-eastern entrance to town on the road to Ferkessédougou, two km from the centre. For a medium-sized room with air-con, small tile attached bath and comfortable bed, it charges CFA 4000/4500 (one/two people), CFA 1000 more with TV/video. There's no restaurant but a maquis is nearby and transport to the centre is easy to find. On the same side of town is *Hôtel Le Pacific*, which charges CFA 5000 for an air-con room and is often full. This attractive place serves breakfast and features a small courtyard full of greenery and very decent air-con rooms for CFA 5000.

If you prefer more remote, tranquil places with no foreign travellers, try *Hôtel de la Montagne*, three km south-west of the centre. Its small rooms with fan and bath are immaculately clean and excellent value at CFA 3000 (CFA 3500 with air-con).

Places to Stay – middle

The most popular mid-range place remains the long-standing French-run *Motel Agip* (☎ 86 01 13) in the heart of town, 300 metres north-east of the market on the road to Ferké. Almost always full, it has high-quality air-con rooms for CFA 5800 and one of the best French restaurants in town.

If a relaxing ambience is more important than a central location, check *Hôtel La Rose Blanche* (☎ 86 06 13), which is equally good. It's on the south-western outskirts of town, one km from the centre, and has rooms for CFA 6000. They are fairly small but have carpets, air-con, TV and fine baths. There is also a good restaurant here. Another possibility is the brand new *Hôtel Le Méridien* (☎ 86 05 76), which is about the same distance from the centre but on the south-eastern outskirts of town, behind the hospital. It has a restaurant and spotless medium-sized rooms with air-con, TV-videos and one/two beds for CFA 6500/7500.

If you like tranquil places with an African ambience and don't mind being in a slightly remote location, try *Hôtel Les Avocats* (☎ 86 05 69) or the similarly priced *Hôtel Le Recueil* (☎ 86 05 02) nearby. The former has a restaurant and large, comfortable air-con rooms with decent tile baths for CFA 7000, which is definitely negotiable because business here is very slow. For the Avocats, take the Ferké road and turn left on a dirt road just before the *Hôtel Kadjona*, go about 300 metres and ask. To get a taxi from the hotel, you'll probably have to walk a few blocks.

Places to Stay – top end

The best buy among the top-end establishments is *Hôtel Kadjona* (☎ 86 06 14), which is one km north of the centre on the highway to Ferkessédougou. It has well-maintained air-con rooms for CFA 6500/8500 one/two people, a pool and two very decent restaurants including a maquis.

Most tours groups stay at *Hôtel Mont Korhogo* (☎ 86 04 00, fax 86 04 07; cards AE, V, CB), which by reputation remains the city's top hotel. This quiet, overpriced place is three blocks south of the market, and has small singles/doubles with air-con and TV-videos for CFA 11,000/13,500. There's also a large pool, a pleasant restaurant with frequent pool-side buffets (CFA 2800 for the plat du jour and CFA 4000 for a three-course meal), the Air Ivoire office, and a travel agency with guided tours and good deals on car rentals. Even if you don't stay here, you can swim in the long pool for CFA 800.

Places to Eat

For Ivoirian food at low prices, there are many choices; most places are very basic and some are open only during the day. One is the long-standing *La Bonne Cuisine*, one km south-east of the market. It has dishes such as sauce aubergine, sauce graine, sauce gombo and sauce claire, each for CFA 300. At night this place becomes a maquis with poulet braisé for CFA 1500 and poisson braisé for CFA 800 to CFA 1500.

Others include the unmarked *Maquis Les 6*, a block east of the museum (various selections including foufou and rice), *Maquis Zougmore*, on the same block closer to the museum on Ave Coulibaly and has a sign, *Maquis 2000*, five blocks south next to Hôtel du Centre Ville, *Maquis La Paillote* behind the Catholic Mission (fish soup at lunch or dinner for CFA 250 plus other dishes by special order), and several more places nearby, on or near the short Rue de Air France.

For a more upmarket maquis with braised dishes, try the maquis at *Hôtel Kadjona* or *Super Maquis Le Lys* (☎ 86 09 57) on the eastern side of town near the popular *Crémerie Donald*. The Lys serves traditional maquis food (poulet braisé), also chicken kedjenou, aloco and Senoufo specialities, while the Donald features Lebanese chawarma sandwiches (CFA 400) and steak and chips (CFA 1500).

The best French restaurant is at the *Motel Agip*; it offers a fixed three-course meal for CFA 3000 plus à la carte dining. *Hôtel Mont Korhogo* has pool-side buffets at least once a week. For pastries, try the *pâtisserie* around the corner from the Lys.

Getting There & Away

Air Air Ivoire offers service between Abidjan and Korhogo on Friday, Saturday and Sunday, usually with a stop en route at Bouaké; the one-way fare is CFA 18,150 (CFA 12,550 from Bouaké).

Bus To save money, take a night bus; the cost from Abidjan is CFA 4500 and they take from eight to 10 hours. If you arrive here before dawn you can sleep on the bus. Buses depart Korhogo from the individual bus companies' offices, none more than three blocks south of the market. There are at least three companies serving the Korhogo-Abidjan route with six departures daily. To/from Bouaké (CFA 2500), the best connections are provided by Express Bouaké-Korhogo, which has four daily departures in either direction. The trip takes about four hours.

To Odienné, the best way to go is with the courrier postal van, which leaves from the post office every day between 7 and 9 am. Otherwise, you'll have to look around the market for a minibus, which often takes half a day to fill up.

For Burkina Faso or Mali, you'll find transport, especially large buses, much more readily in Ferké, 55 km and one hour away.

Bush Taxi Ivoirians prefer buses to bush taxis because they're slightly cheaper, more comfortable and leave at set times. So you'll only find a few bush taxis, mostly around the market. A minivan costs CFA 1000 to Ferkessédougou and CFA 2000 to Boundiali, plus CFA 200 or so for baggage.

Getting Around

Taxi There are taxis all over town. By the hour, you should be able to get one for between CFA 2000 and CFA 2500 if you bargain hard.

You can save money on car rental by

renting a taxi for the day; a typical rate is CFA 20,000 per day for the taxi plus CFA 5000 a day for the driver plus petrol, less with hard bargaining.

Car Touraco Tours at Hôtel Mont Korhogo offers good deals on car rental. A Peugeot 505, for example, costs about CFA 30,000 a day plus petrol (CFA 20,000 plus petrol for a mini-car just for Korhogo and surrounding areas).

The Délégation du Tourisme (☎ 86 05 84) also rents cars with guides or minibuses for groups, and makes arrangements to see some of the dancing for which the Senoufo are famous.

AROUND KORHOGO

The villages around Korhogo have become quite touristy and prices are generally no lower than in Korhogo. What's most interesting is seeing the artisans at work. The major villages of interest are Waraniéné for weavers (*tisserands*), Farkaha for painted Korhogo cloth (*toiles peintes*), Sinématiali and Kanioraba (kah-nee-YOR-ah-bah) for potters (*potiers*), Koni and Kasoumbarga for blacksmiths (*forgerons*), Niofouin for tradi-

tional Senoufo architecture, and Torgokaha for basket makers (*vanniers*).

Waraniéné

The most touristy village is Waraniéné, in part because it's so accessible, only four km south-west of Korhogo on the route to Sirasso. As in all Senoufo communities, men do the weaving while the women do the spinning and spooling of the threads. You'll see weavings spread all over the place, including tablecloths, bedspreads and African-style clothes. The weavers' co-operative there has set prices, which are about half those in Abidjan.

Farkaha

The sleepy town of Farkaha (FAK-ha) is 35 km south-east of Korhogo and is famous for its Korhogo cloth. Most of the top-quality Korhogo cloth comes from here; much of the rest is an inferior imitation thereof. As in Waraniéné, there's a co-operative, but bargaining is possible. To get here, take the old airport road to Napié (19 km) where you take the left fork on to Farkaha, 16 km further. For more of the same material, stop en route at Katia, which

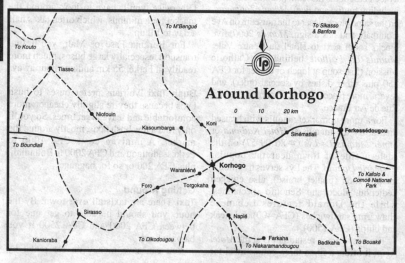

Around Korhogo

To M'Bengué · To Kouto · To Sikasso & Banfora · Tiasso · Niofouin · Kasoumbarga · Koni · To Boundiali · Sinématiali · Ferkessédougou · Waraniéné · Korhogo · To Kafolo & Comoé National Park · Foro · Torgokaha · Sirasso · Napié · Kanioraba · To Dikodougou · Farkaha · To Niakaramandougou · Badikaha · To Bouaké

0   10   20 km

is about halfway between Korhogo and Napié.

Sinématiali & Kanioraba

For pottery, head east for Sinématali (30 km on the paved road to Ferkessédougou) or, better, south-west for Kanioraba (50 km) via Sirasso. Kanioraba, which is much more difficult to reach, is a village of traditional round houses while Sinématiali, which once was similar, now has ugly modern structures with metallic roofs.

Koni

Some 17 km north-west of Korhogo on the dirt road to M'Bengué, Koni is where you can see Senoufo blacksmiths making agricultural implements. If you're very lucky, you might see parts of the entire process in one visit, from mining the ore to making iron to making implements. What's most fascinating is how they drop men down into deep wells (up to 20 metres deep!) to collect the ore. Like all Senoufo smiths, they don't work on Friday, the holy day of rest.

Kasoumbarga

Kasoumbarga is another blacksmith centre, but it also has an unusual 17th-century mosque in ruins that may be of interest. It is round with a thatched roof and there is a barely recognisable monastery next door. The village is 23 km west of Korhogo. Take the paved Boundiali road for 14 km until you come to the dirt road turn-off to your right (north) for Kasoumbarga and proceed a further nine km.

Niofouin

Those interested in traditional Senoufo housing are likely to find Niofouin interesting. Many of the mud-walled buildings with thick straw roofs are in good condition. While some of the oldest structures may not be in good shape, they are less altered by incongruous modern features, such as metal roofs, than those in some other villages. Take the Boundiali road west for 45 km, then left (north-west) on a dirt road for another 12 km.

Torgokaha

Torgokaha is seven km south of Korhogo on the road to Dikodougou and is noted for its basket and mat weavers.

Places to Stay

The only inexpensive hotel in the towns near Korhogo is the *Hôtel Le Womadeli* in Sinématiali. It has 10 air-con rooms and a restaurant.

Getting There & Away

Without a vehicle, it's difficult to see all but the closest villages. The easiest solution is to get a group together and rent a taxi. CFA 15,000 to 18,000 for the day (or CFA 2000 to CFA 2500 by the hour) plus petrol is a fair price. If you negotiate a price that includes petrol, the driver will balk every time you make the slightest detour. If you do have a vehicle, consider getting a guide (they're everywhere in Korhogo), in part to avoid getting lost.

BOUNDIALI

Some 98 km west of Korhogo, this Senoufo town in the heart of the country's cotton belt offers little of interest to travellers other than the market. It is, however, a good point of departure for visiting traditional Senoufo villages to see their artisans at work. And 31 km north of Boundiali is **Kouto**, which has a

CÔTE D'IVOIRE

Blacksmiths & The Senoufo

Blacksmiths hold a special position with the Senoufo. Their relationship with the earth invests them with power, and their caste presides over funerals. When someone dies, the corpse is carried through the village in a long procession, while men in enormous grotesque masks chase away the soul. Immune to evil spirits, the blacksmiths dig the grave and carefully position the corpse inside, after which they present a last meal to the dead, then feast and celebrate. ■

beautiful 17th-century mosque with mud walls (and a Catholic mission to stay at). On the way here, you'll pass **Kolia**, noted for its pottery crafts centre. Both towns are also noted centres for **blacksmiths**, and watching them haul the iron-filled dirt from deep vertical shafts and wash it in the river before being processed into iron can be interesting.

Places to Stay & Eat
Hôtel Record, not far from the market, has clean rooms with attached baths for CFA 2500. There's no restaurant, but you can get good cheap food at *Maquis de l'Indenie* (Chez Tanty Viane), which is on Ave Jean-Baptiste-Mockey and not easy to find.

Getting There & Away
Bush taxis leave from the gare routière for Korhogo (CFA 2000) and, much less often, Odienné. You could also try hopping on the courrier postal van, which passes through town in the late morning, one headed for Korhogo and the other for Odienné.

ODIENNÉ
Odienné (population 35,000) is Malinké country and a major centre for the country's Muslims. Historically the town is important because of its strong support for Samory Touré, whose empire in this area was famous for the incredibly strong resistance it gave the French, who finally conquered it in 1893. Near the large mosque here is the grave of Vakaba Tourié, the Malinké warrior who founded the city.

Today, most of the town's traditional houses have been replaced by unattractive modern buildings. However, the setting in a valley, 12 km east of the 800-metre-high **Massif du Dinguélé**, is nice. You could hire a taxi to the foot of the mountain and then hike up. It will take all morning but the spectacular view from the summit makes the effort worthwhile.

Also, the French manager of Hôtel Les Frontières can give you information about, and possibly arrange a tour of, the nearby Zievasso and Diougoro **gold mines**, where

you can pan for gold. Or head north to **Samatiguila** (38 km) for a visit to the town's well-preserved 17th-century mosque and the adjoining museum, which has a small display of weapons from the time of Samory Touré.

Places to Stay & Eat
The cheapest place to stay is the *Mission Catholique*, behind the préfecture and near the post office; it has inexpensive dormitory rooms for about CFA 1500 per person and slightly more expensive private ones with attached baths. Nearby, close to the post office, is *Le Campement*, which is a bit dirty and has simple ventilated rooms with showers for CFA 4000 (CFA 5000 with air-con).

Also check the friendly *Hôtel de la Savane*, not far from the centre. It has 13 decent rooms with private bath for about CFA 4000 (CFA 500 more with fan and CFA 1000 more with air-con) plus a restaurant with Ivoirian food. For even cheaper African fare, try *La Bonne Auberge* facing the market, *Le Yancadi* near the SGBCI bank or, best, the *Maquis Bar* opposite the Campement, which is not as expensive as it looks.

The top hotel is the attractive, French-run *Hôtel des Frontières* (☎ 80 04 05). This three-star place has a pool surrounded by 30 bungalows. Singles/doubles with air-con, TV and private bath cost about CFA 9000/10,000. It also has the best restaurant in town, but the French food here is fairly expensive. For a change of cuisines, try *Le Maquistade*, an inexpensive African restaurant not far away on the same road, or *Le Wara*, relatively expensive.

Getting There & Away
Air Air Ivoire offers connections between Abidjan and Odienné every Wednesday, Saturday and Sunday; the fare is CFA 21,000.

Bus & Bush Taxi Buses and bush taxis all leave from the gare routière; after mid-morning finding a ride anywhere is extremely difficult. There are daily buses to

Abidjan via Man and to Korhogo. You should also find at least one bush taxi a day headed to Bougouni (Mali). If you're headed for Kankan (Guinea), good luck – very few vehicles travel that route. Finally, you can catch an old vehicle, the courrier postal, at the post office every day around 7 am or so headed for Man and another for Korhogo. The trip to either town takes five or six hours.

FERKESSÉDOUGOU

Ferké is on the major road north from Abidjan to Mali and Burkina Faso, and 231 km north of Bouaké, between Korhogo and Comoë National Park. If you're here on a Thursday, check the market; it's particularly vibrant then. Otherwise, you won't find much of interest as it's basically just a transit point. Quite surprisingly, Ferké has one of the two best hospitals in the country; it's run by Baptist missionaries and attracts patients from as far away as Ouaga and Bamako.

The heart of town is the carrefour du centre and the market nearby. If you need to change money, try SIB bank; it reportedly takes foreign currencies but you may have to show your purchase receipt to cash a travellers' cheque.

Places to Stay – bottom end

Hôtel La Muraille II is on the main drag, about half a km south of the main carrefour. Dumpy on the outside, it has small rooms with fans and passably clean exterior baths for CFA 2000 (CFA 2500 for a larger room with attached bath).

On the northern side of town are two places with rooms for CFA 2500. Hôtel Welcome, which is a block west of the Agip station, is not so great. It has 10 cramped rooms with fans, fresh sheets and attached showers. Four blocks further north is the well-marked La Paillote, which has round bungalows; each has a fan, beds with two fresh sheets and tolerably clean attached baths. There is also a maquis nearby for food and drinks.

Hôtel La Muraille I, four blocks behind the top-end Réserve, has spotlessly clean rooms with fans, comfortable wide beds, tile floors, closets and nice tile baths for CFA 3000; CFA 4500 with air-con. There's also a small restaurant. If you'd prefer to be in the centre, try its sister Hôtel La Muraille III, 100 metres or so east of the main carrefour. Rooms also cost CFA 3000.

On the northern side of town you'll find Hôtel Senoufo (☎ 88 03 23), well located on the main drag, a block north of the Agip station. Its drawing card is not the rooms, which are OK (CFA 4500 with air-con), but the restaurant. The menu includes breakfast for CFA 450, plain omelettes for CFA 1000 and steak with potatoes for CFA 1700.

Hôtel Le Refuge (☎ 88 01 45) is nearby. It has friendly staff and nice rooms with private baths (CFA 4000 with air-con) and a popular restaurant.

Places to Stay – top end

For years, the town's best hotel was the sprawling and shady L'Auberge de la Réserve (☎ 88 01 85) at the southern entrance to town, however, it has gone downhill considerably; an air-con room costs only CFA 5000. The restaurant is still fairly decent, with most dishes in the CFA 1500 to CFA 1800 range. Dishes include poulet kedjenou and braised fish.

The spotless new Hôtel La Pivoire (☎ 88 03 90), 100 metres to the east off the main highway, is now the top hotel. It has a restaurant and charges CFA 6000 for a fairly small room with air-con and a tiny TV. If it's full, try the new Hôtel Le Chantier, a block further east on a dirt road. It has very clean small rooms with fan for CFA 3000 and similar rooms with air-con and TV for CFA 5000.

Places to Eat

For good inexpensive African food, you can't beat La Concorde, a block north of the Agip station, just off the main drag. It's a relaxing open-air place with lots of chairs and is good for drinks, especially at night. The menu includes sauce claire de boeuf for CFA 300 and sauce foutou graine for CFA 300.

CÔTE D'IVOIRE

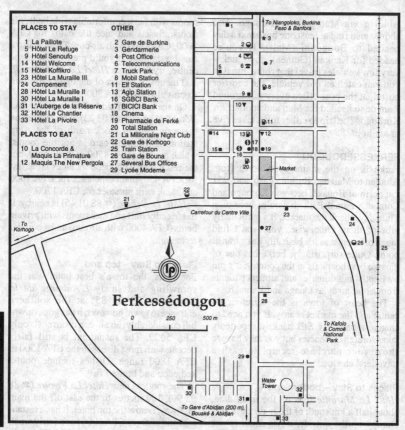

PLACES TO STAY
1 La Paillote
5 Hôtel Le Refuge
9 Hôtel Senoufo
14 Hôtel Welcome
15 Hôtel Koffikro
23 Hôtel La Muraille III
24 Campement
28 Hôtel La Muraille II
30 Hôtel La Muraille I
31 L'Auberge de la Réserve
32 Hôtel Le Chantier
33 Hôtel La Pivoire

PLACES TO EAT
10 La Concorde &
    Maquis La Primature
12 Maquis The New Pergola

OTHER
2 Gare de Burkina
3 Gendarmerie
4 Post Office
6 Telecommunications
7 Truck Park
8 Mobil Station
11 Elf Station
13 Agip Station
16 SGBCI Bank
17 BICICI Bank
18 Cinema
19 Pharmacie de Ferké
20 Total Station
21 La Millionaire Night Club
22 Gare de Korhogo
25 Train Station
26 Gare de Bouna
27 Several Bus Offices
29 Lycée Moderne

To Niangoloko, Burkina Faso & Banfora

Carrefour du Centre Ville

To Korhogo

Ferkessédougou

0   250   500 m

Market

To Kafolo & Comoë National Park

Water Tower

To Gare d'Abidjan (200 m),
Bouaké & Abidjan

CÔTE D'IVOIRE

For maquis food, try *Maquis La Primature* next door. It's also relaxing and a good place for lunch or dinner. The menu includes various sauces for around CFA 350, also poulet braisé for CFA 1800 and large beers for CFA 375. *Maquis The New Pergola*, a block away behind the Elf station, has a single large paillote and is more rustic. The selections include braised fish/chicken for CFA 800/2000 and a whole chicken kedjenou-style for CFA 1600.

Good for dancing is *La Millionaire* on the western side of town beyond the Gare de Korhogo.

Getting There & Away

Bus & Bush Taxi The big modern buses are much faster than the train. Most of the buses from Abidjan to Korhogo leave in the morning or early evening, stopping in Ferké en route. The fare is CFA 4000 to Abidjan (eight or nine hours), CFA 5000 to Bobo and CFA 8000 to Ouaga. Peugeot 504 bush taxis are more expensive, particularly those headed north to Burkina Faso.

There are four gares routières. Vehicles headed for Burkina and Mali leave from Gare du Nord (or Gare du Burkina) just beyond the post office. To Sikasso (Mali), the cost is CFA 5000 and the trip can take all day because of the numerous police stops along the way. Gare de Korhogo is about 0.75 km west of the carrefour du centre; minibuses to Korhogo cost CFA 1000 and leave regularly throughout the day. The Gare d'Abidjan is at the southern entrance to town, almost two km from the centre.

Minibuses headed east for the Comoë National Park area – Kong (CFA 1500), Kafolo (CFA 2800) and Bouna (CFA 4800) – leave in the morning from Gare de Bouna on the eastern side of town, about one km from the centre.

Train The *Express* trains from Ouaga and Abidjan are scheduled to arrive here at 8.25 pm and 8.30 pm, respectively, but they usually arrive about two hours late. The 1st/2nd-class fare is CFA 8800/5600 to Abidjan, CFA 4000/3000 to Bobo and CFA 7600/5400 to Ouaga. There is usually a bus waiting in the evening at the train station to take passengers from Burkina on to Abidjan, as the bus is considerably cheaper and faster than the train.

BOUNA
Travellers headed from Ferké to Ghana should count on spending 12 hours in the minibus to Bouna. If you stay at least a day here, you may be able to visit some nearby Lobi villages; they are noted for their unique adobe architecture, called *soukala*, which are castle-like structures with inner courtyards. The most attractive soukala can be found at Puon, a small village to the north of Bouna which can only be reached during the dry season.

In Bouna, you can stay at *Hôtel Eléphant* (CFA 3500 a room) or the small *Bar* (CFA 2500 a room) across the street; prices at both places are negotiable. You need to stop at customs, which is in town. A taxi to the border at the Black Volta River takes 1½ hours and costs CFA 750. Crossing the river costs CFA 500 or C 1000. On the other side are minibuses headed for Bole (C 1000), and also moneychangers. From Bouna to Bole (78 km) by minibus takes an entire day

counting waiting time! In Bole, there's a cheap grubby *motel* (C 1200) with no electricity or running water and a bus every day for Tamale at 6 am.

Exchange rates at the border are about 10% lower than the official rate but you should change enough money to get to Tamale because there's only one bank en route (at Damongo), and you can't change money there unless the bank's phone is working (to find the rate), which usually isn't the case.

OUANGOLODOUGOU
Some 44 km south of the Burkina border, Ouangolodougou is a possible overnight stop if you can't make it to the border by 6.30 pm when it closes.

The top hotel is *Hôtel Le Tenin* on the southern side of town. It has a restaurant and rooms with fan for CFA 3000 (CFA 4000 with air-con). Cheaper places nearer the centre include *Hôtel du Nord* and *Hôtel de l'Amitié*, which have singles/doubles for about CFA 2500/3000 and CFA 2000/2500, respectively. For cheap food, try *Gesco Modern*, a kiosk at the southern end of the gare routière. It serves ragout (CFA 200), oats and milk (CFA 175), good French expresso (CFA 100), etc.

If you proceed to the border, the only accommodation you'll find is a *chambre de passage* next to customs. The small bare rooms, which cost CFA 2000, have beds with sheets and shared toilets. There is also a bar (large beers for CFA 325) and a restaurant (chicken kedjenou for CFA 1300 and chicken soup for CFA 400).

KONG
Kong is an old Dioula village dating from the 12th century and may be of interest to architectural buffs. The village's Sudanese architecture and flat-roofed buildings are reminiscent of Mali. Much of the town was burned to the ground in the late 19th century by Samory, the famous Malinké warrior, during a military battle with the French. The most impressive building standing today is the mud-built Friday

CÔTE D'IVOIRE

mosque with protruding wooden beams, built originally in the 17th century. You'll also find an old Koran school and traditional mud houses with roof terraces.

Kong is a few km west of Comoë National Park, and 34 km south of the Ferké-Kafolo road. If you're caught here for the night, the only hotel you'll find is the *Campement*, which has rooms for about CFA 3000.

COMOË NATIONAL PARK

In the north-east corner of the country, Comoë is 567 km from Abidjan (to the southern entrance to park) and is the largest game park in West Africa (11,500 sq km). Those who haven't been spoiled by the parks in East Africa usually find it interesting. As you ride through the park, you'll pass through savannah, forest and grassland.

One of the most popular tracks passes alongside the Comoë River, which runs from the north-west corner at Kafolo to Gansé in the south. Going all the way from Kafolo to Gansé, with frequent stops along the way, takes virtually a full day. In the dry season, most of the game is in this middle to western section of the park where there's more water.

Lions tend to be more abundant in the southern section, particularly in the *triangle de Kakpin* area, the top of which is roughly 30 km north of Kakpin, so staying at the southern end does have advantages. The best bet, however, is to ask the guides as they always know where the various animals have most recently been spotted.

There are an estimated 100 elephants in the park, so there's an excellent chance of seeing them. Other animals in the park include 21 species of pig, green monkey, hippo, Anubis baboon, black and white colobus, waterbuck, kob, roan and other species of antelopes. Leopards also exist, but are rarely seen. Birds, on the other hand, are abundant; over 400 species have been recorded here and one couple reported spotting 130 species in three days.

There are various entrances to the park; the most widely used are Kafolo (also called Petit Ferké) in the north, and Gansé and Kakpin in the south. The park is open from December to May. The best viewing time is at the crack of dawn and the late afternoon before 6 pm (when the park closes).

At all three hotels bordering the park, you'll find guides, although it's not obligatory to hire one, despite what they may say. However, without one your chances of seeing the animals will be far less. The cost is negotiable; you should be able to get one for about CFA 5000 for the day.

Places to Stay & Eat

Budget travellers should plan on staying at the southern end of the park because there is no cheap lodging at the northern end around Kafolo. While some travellers have managed in years past to find Africans to put them up, the owner of the lodge there reportedly puts pressure on the locals not to do this. Also, you cannot camp inside the park; however with a little cajoling the guards will sometimes let you pitch a tent by their office at the entrance.

At the southern entrance to the park, if you cannot find Africans to put you up, you can always stay at the *Campement* in Kakpin, 15 km east of Gansé. It has 17 traditional huts with private bathrooms but no air-con for about CFA 7000, and a thatched-roof bar-restaurant with minimum camp-like food such as spaghetti and canned tomato sauce.

For those with money, the park has two good tourist hotels of equal quality, both with pools in working condition. The 25-room *Comoë Segetel* (Bouaké ☎ 63 31 95) is at the southern entrance in Gansé near the Comoë River and has modern Sudanese-inspired cabins. The 40-room *Comoë Safari Lodge* (Abidjan ☎ 32 70 73) is at the northern entrance near Kafolo, overlooking the Comoë River. The cost at either place for a small but clean air-con room is about CFA 19,000 (about CFA 35,000 for two people with half board, which is sometimes said to be obligatory).

Getting There & Away

Air Flying from Abidjan to Korhogo costs

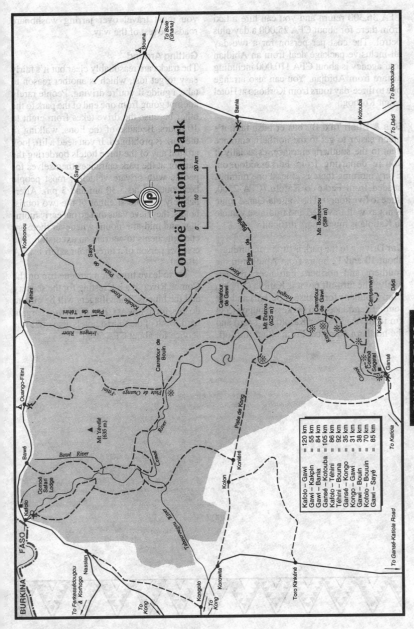

Comoë National Park

To Bole (Ghana)

To Bouna

To Bania

To Bandoukou

To Kotouba

To Dédi

Mt Boutourou (589 m)

Piste de Bania

Iringou River

Carrefour de Gawi

Mt Potrou (625 m)

Carrefour de Gawi

Campement

Dédi

Kakpin

Gansé

Comoë Segetel

Comoë River

Carrefour de Bouin

Piste de Kong

To Katiola

To Gansé-Katiola Road

Konéfé

Kolon

Korowita

Toro Kirkéné

Piste de Téhini

Kolodio River

Iringou River

Piste de Ouango-Fitini

Comoë River

Mt Vévélé (635 m)

Bawé River

Comoë Safari Lodge

Kafolo

Bawé

Ouango-Fitini

Téhini

Sayé

Sayé

Piste de Sayé

Kobbonou

Korowita

Kongolo

To Kong

To Toro Kirkéné

Nassian

To Ferkéssédougou & Korhogo

BURKINA FASO

Kafolo – Gawi	= 120 km
Gawi – Kakpin	= 55 km
Gawi – Bania	= 84 km
Gansé – Kotouba	= 105 km
Kafolo – Téhini	= 86 km
Téhini – Bouna	= 92 km
Gansé – Kongo	= 35 km
Kongo – Gawi	= 31 km
Gansé – Bouin	= 38 km
Kofolo – Bouin	= 70 km
Gawi – Sayé	= 85 km

0   10   20 km

CÔTE D'IVOIRE

CFA 36,300 return and you can hire a taxi from there for about CFA 25,000 a day plus petrol. The cost per person for a two-day all-inclusive package deal from an Abidjan tour agency is about CFA 110,000 including airfare from Abidjan. You can also arrange one to three-day tours from Korhogo at Hôtel Mont Korhogo.

Bus & Bush Taxi By bus or bush taxi, it's much easier to get to the northern entrance than to the southern entrance, especially if you're departing from Ferkessédougou. Every morning there is at least one minibus headed from Ferké to Kafolo (CFA 2500, three to five hours). The Katiola-Gansé route is not as well travelled and finding a vehicle in Katiola is much more difficult.

Car Driving to the park is time-consuming – about 10 and 12 hours from Abidjan to the southern and northern entrances, respectively. The turn-off point is Katiola (407 km from Abidjan) for Gansé (160 km) and the southern entrance, and Ferkessédougou (584 km from Abidjan) for Kafolo (121 km) and the northern entrance. From either turn-off, you must travel over jarring washboard roads the rest of the way.

Getting Around

The tracks are reasonably clear but it's fairly easy to get lost, which is another reason to take a guide if you're driving. People rarely attempt going from one end of the park to the other because the drive takes from eight to 10 hours. Because of the lions, walking in the park is prohibited. If you need a lift, look around any of the three hotels bordering the park or at the park entrances themselves for people with private vehicles; most people head out around 5.30 am and 3 pm. Alternatively, enquire at either of the two tourist hotels; they have vans that go out early mornings and mid-afternoons whenever there are enough clients to warrant an excursion. The cost per person of a three-hour safari is CFA 10,000.

Try to leave time for a pirogue trip on the Comoë River; it's interesting for the scenery and the hippos. The villagers will be glad to do this, for as low as CFA 1000 if you bargain hard. Both of the tourist hotels also offer this service for about CFA 5000.

The Gambia

Every year, thousands of European visitors come to The Gambia, attracted by a peaceful environment, vast beaches and guaranteed sunshine for nine months of the year. Another attraction is the abundance of cheap package tours and flights. Some people also come for the cultural experience, particularly to visit Juffure, the village featured in Alex Haley's famous novel *Roots*. Bird-watchers are in for a real treat too – over 400 species have been recorded here. You can also visit wildlife reserves, see African-style wrestling matches or take a cruise up the Gambia River. Compared to other countries in the region, adventure here is with a small 'a' but if you want to see a bit of Africa with the minimum of hassle, The Gambia may be perfect.

Facts about the Country

HISTORY

In the 13th century, the area around the Gambia River was part of the ancient Empire of Mali, which stretched between the modern-day states of Senegal and Niger. Mandinka traders migrated into the area, and introduced Islam, which remains the principal religion of The Gambia.

The first Europeans to reach The Gambia were Portuguese traders who arrived in 1455. They introduced groundnuts (peanuts) – now the mainstay of the economy – and cotton, but in 1581 they sold their trading rights to Britain. By 1661, the British had established Fort James, on an island 25 km upstream from the mouth of the Gambia River. Twenty years later, the French built a rival fort at Albreda on the nearby north bank. During the 17th and 18th centuries these two forts were the scenes of periodic battles between the French and British for control of the region's trade. With tobacco and gunpowder the European traders purchased ivory, gold and slaves from local

REPUBLIC OF THE GAMBIA

Area: 10,690 sq km
Population: 956,000
Population Growth Rate: 3.1%
Capital: Banjul
Head of State: Lt Yaya Jammeh
Official Language: English
Currency: Dalasi
Exchange Rate: 9D = US$1
Per Capita GNP: US$240
Inflation: 9%
Time: GMT/UTC

chiefs. In 1783, Britain gained all rights to trade on the Gambia River and Fort James became one of West Africa's most infamous slave trans-shipment points.

The Colonial Period

When the British abolished slavery in 1807, they were not content with letting others continue on the wicked path. Royal Navy ships began capturing slave vessels of other nations headed for the New World, and Fort James was converted from a dungeon to a haven. The British also decided that the mouth of the Gambia River was a better place from which to patrol the slave trade so, in 1816, they leased Banjul Island from a

329

Suggested Itineraries

The Gambia's small and dusty capital, **Banjul**, has little in the way of 'sights', so you only need a day to see what there is and get a feel for the place. You should allow another two to four days if you want to visit some of the places near Banjul, such as the **Bijilo** and **Abuko** wildlife reserves, **Serekunda** market, **Juffure** (the *Roots* village), or the mangrove creeks. Also allow extra days if you simply want to lie on the beach at one of the **Atlantic** coast resorts.

The Gambia is a very thin country, only a few km either side of the Gambia River, so your choice of route is limited to either going along the south bank of the river (quick and easy), or along the north bank (slower and harder, but possibly more interesting). A third option is to travel on the river itself, by the public boat which runs weekly between Banjul and Georgetown.

From Banjul your first stop may be at **Mansa Konko** (on the south bank) and **Farafenni** (on the north bank), both of which have lively markets and are worth a day's visit. If you go by the southern route, you could consider stopping at **Tendaba Camp** and the nearby **West Kiang National Park** (two to three days).

From Mansa Konko or Farafenni you can leave The Gambia and head north towards Dakar or south towards Ziguinchor on the Trans-Gambia Highway (see the Senegal chapter for more details). Or you can continue eastwards to **Georgetown**, once an important trade and administrative centre, now somewhat sleepy, but still a pleasant place to spend one or two days. From here you can visit **Wassu Stone Circles** (one day) and the **River Gambia (Baboon Island) National Park** (one day). Further upstream you reach **Basse Santa Su** (one or two days), from where you can return to Banjul, by road or boat, or continue heading east into Senegal. ■

local chief and founded a settlement which was named Bathurst. Fort James was finally abandoned in 1829.

In Bathurst, the British laid streets and planned MacCarthy Square, but the settlement was never prosperous. As an economy measure, the territory was administered from Sierra Leone until 1888, when Gambia became a crown colony, completely surrounded by French Senegal except for a small section of coastline. For the next 75-odd years of colonial rule, the British did virtually nothing to develop the area, and by the 1950s, there was one hospital, one school and no paved roads outside Bathurst.

Independence

In 1960, when the rest of West Africa was gaining independence, one Dawda Jawara, an upcountry Mandinka who had trained as a veterinary surgeon, founded the People's Progressive Party (PPP). However, there was little else in the way of a local political infrastructure and Britain doubted that complete independence was feasible. Federation with Senegal was considered but came to nothing, so in 1965 Gambia became independent, and Jawara became the first president. Without any official explanation, Gambia was renamed The Gambia. More understandably, Bathurst was renamed Banjul.

Few observers thought the country had a

viable economic future, but during the next 10 years, the world price for groundnuts increased significantly, raising the country's GNP almost threefold. The number of tourists grew even more dramatically – from 300 in 1966 to 25,000 a decade later. By the early 1970s, and for the rest of that decade, The Gambia was doing fine: Jawara and the PPP remained popular and in control. Opposition parties were tolerated and there were no political prisoners.

Everything seemed relatively calm until 1981 when some disaffected soldiers staged a coup while Jawara was in London. Pursuant to the mutual defence pact between Senegal and The Gambia, Jawara asked the Senegalese government to oust them, which it did. Acknowledging this debt, Jawara announced that the Gambian and Senegalese armed forces would be fully integrated. In 1982 the Senegambian confederation came into effect, with both countries working closely together whilst maintaining their independence and sovereignty.

The Gambia Today

Although the Senegambian Federation seemed a good idea, through the rest of the 1980s it encountered several problems. Cultural differences were a major impediment: people in Senegal, a former French colony, simply don't think the same way as the Gambians, even though the ethnic composition of the two countries is similar. Smuggling was another problem: high duties in Senegal made some imported goods there more expensive, while prices for groundnuts in the two countries always varied. Periodically, tensions flared: at a football match in Banjul, rioting provoked the Senegalese ambassador to call in Senegalese troops to protect the players. The Gambia responded by asking Senegal to recall him.

By August 1989, things were so bad that the confederation was suspended and, a month later, dissolved. Both The Gambia and Senegal imposed severe border restrictions, and tensions ran high well into 1990, although after a year relations between the countries improved again, and a treaty of

friendship and co-operation was signed in 1991.

In April 1992 President Jawara was re-elected for a sixth term, winning almost 60% of the vote, and his government retained their majority in the House of Representatives. As African presidents go, Jawara seemed to remain popular. It came as some surprise, therefore, when he was overthrown in a reportedly bloodless coup led by young military officers in July 1994. The coup leader, Lieutenant Yaya (also spelt Yahya) Jammeh, announced a new government headed by the Armed Forces Provisional Ruling Council and composed of several military men, most of whom had trained in Britain and the USA, and several civilian ministers who had served under the previous government. Ex-president Jawara was granted asylum in Senegal. Jammeh promised that the Ruling Council would be back in the barracks in September, but this never materialised, and an attempted counter-coup in November further delayed the return to civilian rule. In response, aid donors such as the European Union, the USA and World Bank threatened to cut their support. But despite this, the situation outside State House remained calm, and for most Gambians life continued as normal.

However, these events hit The Gambia's tourist trade, with the major British tour companies cancelling their package flights. But through the second half of 1994 tourists from other European countries, plus independent

Ex-president Dawda Kairaba Jawara – overthrown in a coup in July 1994

visitors, or those with smaller specialist operators, continued to arrive.

In March 1995, the British Foreign Office advised visitors that The Gambia was safe once again, with a proviso that the political situation was still uncertain and could change again. Following this announcement things picked up, and for some holiday companies it was pretty much business as usual, although it will take a while for The Gambia's good reputation to recover completely. Just how easy the future will be for the tourist trade, new government, and the country itself, remains to be seen.

GEOGRAPHY

The Gambia's shape and position epitomises the absurdity of the national boundaries carved by the European colonial powers. About 300 km long, but averaging only 35 km wide, the country follows the course of the Gambia River, and is entirely surrounded by French-speaking Senegal, except for 48 km of coastline.

The Gambia River winds through dense mangrove swamps bordered by cotton trees, bamboo forests and salt flats, with saline waters extending far upstream during the dry season, making it unsuitable for irrigation.

Banjul, the capital, is at the mouth of the river. On the opposite bank is the small town of Barra and 25 km upstream is the *Roots* village of Juffure. Further up the river are many more villages, but the only towns of any size are Farafenni, Mansa Konko, Georgetown and Basse Santa Su.

The Gambia lies at the southern edge of the Sahel, and the vegetation consists of savannah and open woodland with tall grasses and shrubs. A fifth of this perfectly flat country is saline marsh which hinders agricultural development. Other problems include deforestation and overgrazing.

CLIMATE

The rainy season is short: from July to September. Temperatures are high (the average daytime maximum is around 35°C) in October and November, and again from mid-February to the end of June. The climate is dry and pleasantly warm (the average daytime maximum is around 24°C) from December to mid-February and this is the peak of the tourist 'high' season. Temperatures in the coastal areas are generally lower than these averages, while in upcountry areas they are higher.

The low season is from May to September and some travellers say this is the best time to visit The Gambia because hotels are cheap and there are far fewer tourists. Rain during that period is not really a problem because it often comes at night.

GOVERNMENT

The Gambia is a republic and (until the coup of 1994) a political paragon in Africa. In addition to having one of the best human rights records in Africa, it had several political parties, and free and open elections for the presidency and members of the House of Representatives were held every five years by universal adult suffrage. In fair elections, President Jawara won between 50 and 60% of the vote in 1987 and again in 1992. The coup has changed all this, showing that the military still has a strong hand in political affairs. If Jammeh relinquishes power as he promises, the country's civilian-controlled democratic form of government will, presumably, be re-established. Until then, however, the government must be labelled a military dictatorship.

ECONOMY

The Gambia's balance of trade has been negative for every year since 1975 and continues to decline. During the 1980s, in an attempt to combat this downward move, the International Monetary Fund (IMF) granted loans to The Gambia on the condition that subsidies were eliminated and the groundnut trade was opened up to private traders. The Gambia found the loans hard to repay, as harvests were hit by several droughts during this period, but they kept to the conditions and by the early 1990s the IMF-supported Economic Recovery Programme (ERP) was showing small signs of improvement and was replaced by a Programme for Sustained

Recovery (PSR). However, despite the somewhat cosmetic reclassifications, The Gambia remains pretty much a one-crop economy, and recent attempts at diversification have met with only limited success. Groundnuts still account for some 80% of all export earnings, and world prices have not been favourable.

The Gambia's other main economic activity is tourism. The number of visitors from Europe (mainly Britain, Germany and Scandinavia) grew considerably during the 1980s. It peaked in the 1989/90 season, with more than 110,000 visitors, but the figure fluctuated between 70,000 and 100,000 per year through the early 1990s. Numbers fell due to the recession in Europe, reports in the European media about political instability in the region, and competition from neighbouring Senegal.

Although tourism contributes more in percentage terms to export earnings than in other West African countries, this figure is only between 10 and 15% of the total. And less than 10,000 local people are employed directly or indirectly in the tourist industry, mostly in low-earning jobs which only last for the six-month tourist season, although it is estimated that five times this figure (10% of the population) is actually dependent on the money tourism provides.

Virtually all tourists are on package tours, paid for in their home countries, so they spend very little money in The Gambia itself. And those who do venture outside their hotel grounds, rarely go beyond the Banjul area. Yet the government continues to spend a significant portion of its capital-development budget on tourist-related projects, thus diverting funds from those sectors directly benefiting Gambians, such as agriculture.

POPULATION & PEOPLE
Current estimates put The Gambia's population at nearly one million. This is in an area of just under 11,000 sq km, making it the fourth most densely populated country in Africa.

The main ethnic group is the Mandinka (also called Mandingo and Malinké), traditionally farmers, comprising about 40% of the total population. Other groups include the Fulani (about 20%), traditionally herders found throughout West Africa, and Wolof (about 15%), mainly traders inhabiting the Banjul area and some other larger towns.

There are several other ethnic groups, and intermarriage is not uncommon. The common denominator is religion – over 90% follow Islam. In West Africa, only Mauritania has a higher percentage of Muslims.

Non-Africans (mainly from Lebanon and Western Europe) account for less than 1% of the total population.

ART & CULTURE
The Mandinka have strong musical traditions. Islamic feast-days, such as the end of Ramadan, and family celebrations, such as a wedding or circumcision, or even the arrival of a special guest, are seen as good reasons for some music and dancing. Traditional instruments include the *kora*, something like a lute, the *balafon*, like a xylophone, and the *tama*, a hand-held drum. Mandinka dances are based upon common movements in everyday life such as cultivating and fishing.

Amongst the Wolof, weddings are also important, and celebrated with great enthusiasm. On the day of the marriage, the legal and religious ceremonies are performed as early as possible so that the day can be spent singing, dancing and feasting. In a traditional wedding, the grandmother, great aunts and so on take the bride to the marriage chamber, lecture her, then undress her, summon the husband and wait in an adjoining room. As soon as the girl screams they all rush in, the husband retires, and they take away the sheet and exhibit it the next morning to the guests, after which the bride is smothered with gifts.

Knife used in juju ceremonies

For Wolof men, the circumcision rite is equally important. Boys are circumcised shortly after reaching puberty. Before the operation the candidates are dressed like women, with shells and jewels in their long hair. Afterwards, still wearing their costumes, they stay away from people and live in special huts until healed. Then there's a big feast and they are given a magical potion which renders their bodies immune to knife blows.

Christmas-time in The Gambia is yet another excuse for celebration, even though most of the population is Muslim. Crowds of people carry around large lanterns called *fanals* which they have made themselves from local materials. Some of these lanterns are very impressive: made in the shape of boats or houses, brightly painted with intricate decorations, and illuminated at night. The tradition originated on Gorée Island and in St-Louis in Senegal, and dates from the time when wealthy inhabitants going to midnight mass would be led by slaves carrying decorative lamps. Today in The Gambia, the people sing and chant as they parade their fanals around the streets, while onlookers donate a few coins to the group as a sign of appreciation.

At the same time of year, groups of younger children also do the rounds, singing and playing home-made drums and instruments, with one of their number wearing a mask and performing the role of jester. Once again, a few (small) coins are appreciated.

The best place in The Gambia (and one of the best places in West Africa) for a 'hands on' experience of African art and craft is the Kololi Inn & Tavern in Banjul, where the friendly staff organise one-day 'cultural workshops' for visitors to learn how to dance, play drums, paint, make pottery and tie-dye, or even cook an African meal. (For details see Places to Eat in the Banjul section.)

The Baobab Tree

Along with the acacia, the baobab tree (*Adansonia digitata*) is an instantly recognised symbol of Africa. Its thick, sturdy trunk and stunted root-like branches are featured on countless postcards and brochures. Baobabs grow in The Gambia, as well as in Senegal, Mali and in many other many parts of the continent (there are, in fact, several different species), usually in savannah zones where rainfall is limited. Many cultures, including those in The Gambia, have their own version of a story that involves the tree displeasing a deity who plucked it in anger and thrust it back into the ground upside down. Hence the root-like branches.

However, despite the misdemeanours of its ancestor, today's baobab is held in high regard by local people. Because of its wizened appearance, combined with its ability to survive great droughts and live for many hundreds of years, the baobab is often revered and believed to have magical powers. In some parts of West Africa, when a griot died, he was reputedly 'buried' inside the hollowed-out trunk of a dead baobab.

The baobab also has many practical uses. The wood can be used as fuel or as a building material. It is also suitable for building boats. The tree's large pods (sometimes called 'monkey bread') contain seeds encased in a sherbert-like substance which can be eaten or made into a drink. The pods themselves are used to make cups or bowls (often for drinking palm wine). Any not suitable for this purpose are used as fuel. They burn slowly and are especially good for smoking fish. The leaves of the baobab can be eaten when chopped and boiled into a sauce. They can also be dried and ground into a paste to use as a poultice for skin infections and joint complaints. Even the flowers are used for decoration at ceremonies. ∎

LANGUAGE

English is the official language. A number of African languages are spoken, the principal ones being Mandinka, Wolof and Fula.

Expressions in Mandinka

Good morning.	*ee-SAM-ah*
Good evening.	*ee-wou-RAH-rah*
How are you?	*EE-bee-dee?*
Thank you.	*ah-bah-RAH-kah*
Goodbye.	*AH-lah-mah*,
	nee-ah-JAH-mah-lah

Expressions in Wolof

Good morning.	*ya-MAN-gah fah-NIN*
Good evening.	*ya-MAN-gah YEN-lou*
How are you?	*nang-gah-DEF?*
Thank you.	*jair-ruh-JEF*
Goodbye.	*mahn-gah-DEM*

Facts for the Visitor

VISAS & EMBASSIES
The Gambia Visas

Visas are not needed by most nationals of the British Commonwealth, Belgium, Canada, Denmark, Finland, Germany, Iceland, Ireland, Italy, Luxembourg, the Netherlands, Norway, Spain and Sweden. All other nationalities need them.

In West Africa, you can get visas for The Gambia in Abidjan (Côte d'Ivoire), Accra (Ghana), Lagos (Nigeria), Dakar (Senegal) and Freetown (Sierra Leone). For details, see Visas & Embassies in the relevant country chapter.

Outside of West Africa, some British high commissions may still have authority to issue visas to The Gambia in countries without Gambian representation. The Gambian embassy in Washington, open weekdays from 8 am to 2 pm, issues three-month multiple-entry visas on the spot for US$8.

The Gambian embassy in London requires two photos and charges UK£20 for a three-month single-entry visa and UK£40 for a six-month multiple-entry visa. It processes visas in 48 hours. Britons do not need tourist visas.

If you arrive in The Gambia at the airport without a visa, you'll probably be issued one if you look like a tourist and have a good excuse. However, if you come direct from Europe, most airlines won't let you on board without a visa.

If you arrive at the border without a visa you may be able to get one on the spot (for about CFA 2500). This is only possible (and not guaranteed) if you come from southern or eastern Senegal. If you come from Dakar you should get a visa there.

Visa Extensions

Visa extensions are easily obtained from Immigration (☎ 228611) at the Ministry of Interior in Banjul.

Gambian Embassies

Belgium 126 Ave Franklin-Roosevelt, Brussels 1050 (☎ (02) 640-10-49)

France (consulate) 57 rue de Villiers, 92200 Neuilly-sur-Seine (☎ (1) 47-57-31-60)

Germany Mergenthalerallee 1-3, 65760 Eschborn/Ts (☎ (06196) 450-45)

UK 57 Kensington Court, London W8 5QG (☎ (0171) 937-6316/7)

USA 1155 15th St, NW, Washington, DC 20005 (☎ (202) 785-1399)

The Gambia also has embassies in Frankfurt and Zürich, plus consulates in Lisbon, Montreal, Stockholm, Toronto and Vienna.

Other African Visas

Ghana The consul issues 'visas' on the spot for 25D, which seems a real bargain. But these are only 'Requests for Passage'; when you actually get to Ghana you pay US$18 for an entry stamp.

Guinea The consulate issues visas for CFA 10,000 in 48 hours.

Guinea-Bissau The embassy issues one-month visas for 100D. The process takes a few hours. It's just as easy, but more expensive, to get Guinea-Bissau visas in Ziguinchor (Senegal) where the consulate issues them on the spot for CFA 5000.

Mali The consul routinely issues seven-day visas, but getting a visa for one month is not difficult if you ask. The cost is CFA 5000 or 250D (although some travellers have paid 25D). The process can be completed in one morning if you come early.

Senegal The embassy takes 24 hours to issue one-month multiple entry visas for 230D. (Warning: we've had many reports that New Zealanders can wait up to six months for Senegalese visas. See the Senegal chapter for more details.)

THE GAMBIA

Sierra Leone The embassy issues visas in 48 hours. Costs vary: 320D for Britons; 250D for other Western nationalities; and free for Americans. You need a return ticket and proof of sufficient funds.

Mauritania The embassy issues one-month visas on the spot for 50D.

Liberia Single-entry visas, valid for six months, are issued in three hours for 500D, although this depends on the situation in Liberia.

Other Countries There is a Nigerian embassy in Banjul, but visas are issued only to Gambian residents.

Foreign Embassies

See Information in the Banjul section for the embassy addresses.

DOCUMENTS

Everybody needs a passport. Officially, an International Vaccination Certificate for yellow fever is required only if you have arrived from an infected or endemic country. But situations can change, so carrying a certificate is recommended.

CUSTOMS

There are no restrictions on the import of local or foreign currencies, or on the export of foreign currency. You cannot export more than 70D in local currency.

MONEY

1FF	=	1.60D
UK£1	=	13.50D
US$1	=	9.00D

The unit of currency is the dalasi (da-la-see), divided into 100 bututs. The exchange rate has been amazingly stable during the past few years.

Banks in The Gambia include Banque Internationale pour le Commerce et l'Industrie du Senegal (BICIS) and Standard Chartered. There are banks in Banjul, Bakau, Serekunda and Basse.

Changing money (cash or travellers' cheques) is fairly quick and straightforward. You cannot draw cash on a Visa card. There's a bank at the airport; if it's closed, the police will help you find a moneychanger.

Black market dealers offer about 5% more than the banks. In Banjul, you'll find moneychangers around the post office, Gambia

Airways and MacCarthy Square. You'll also find them at Bakau (at the stalls near the CFAO supermarket), Serekunda (although there's a chance of being ripped off here), and at the towns on the Trans-Gambia Highway.

Many items can be paid for in CFA bills. However, since 1994, when the CFA was suddenly devalued, rates are poor, so this is only recommended if you're stuck with no dalasi. (If you're travelling between north and south Senegal on the Trans-Gambia Highway, everything – ferry charges, drinks, snacks, etc – can be paid for in CFA.)

BUSINESS HOURS & HOLIDAYS

Business hours are Monday to Thursday from 8.30 am to 12.30 pm and 2.30 to 5.30 pm; Friday to Saturday from 8 am to noon. Government offices are open Monday to Thursday from 8 am to 3 pm; Friday to Saturday from 8 am to 12.45 pm. Banks are usually open Monday to Friday from 9 am to noon and either 2 to 4 pm or 4 to 6 pm. In Banjul and Bakau some banks open on Saturday from 8 to 11 am.

Public Holidays

1 January, 18 February (Independence), Good Friday, Easter Monday, End of Ramadan, 1 May, Tabaski, 15 August, Muslim New Year, Mohammed's Birthday, 25 December.

POST & TELECOMMUNICATIONS

The post service out of the country is quite reliable; most cards and letters arrive at their destination. The poste restante at the main post office in Banjul is also reasonably good.

Banjul is one of the best places in West Africa for making international calls. The cost is about 20D per minute to the USA and slightly less to Europe. At Gamtel (the state telephone company) offices you can buy phonecards which make international calls even cheaper. You can also call reverse charge (collect). Most Gamtel offices are open evenings and also offer telex and fax services which are cheaper than those offered by the major hotels.

All telephone numbers in The Gambia now have six figures. An extra digit should be added to the front of any old five-figure number: for numbers in Banjul add 2, in Serekunda add 3, in Fajara and Bakau add 4, for numbers in Basse and the surrounding area add 6, and for numbers in Farafenni and the surrounding area add 7.

PHOTOGRAPHY

No permit is required, but as in most African countries, taking photos of military installations, airports, ferries, harbours and government buildings could get you into trouble.

HEALTH

In the Banjul area, the best place is the British-run clinic at the Medical Research Council on Atlantic Rd in Fajara. Also good are the private Westfield Clinic (☎ 292213) in Serekunda, and the Lamtoro Clinic (☎ 460934) in Kololi. The Royal Victoria Hospital (☎ 228223) on Independence Drive in Banjul centre was completely renovated in 1993, and the service has also improved, although it still lags behind the private establishments. For a doctor, some of the tour companies recommend a Dr Senghore at 74 Gloucester St, Banjul (☎ 226941 or (home) 495251). If you're upcountry, the hospital at Bansang is the only one outside the capital.

DANGERS & ANNOYANCES

Petty thefts and more serious muggings have increased in the Banjul area over the last few years. Tourists are occasionally robbed in broad daylight in Banjul, Serekunda and on the beaches around Bakau and Fajara, but the major problem is walking in these areas at night. Don't do it.

Many visitors also complain about the beach boys (known locally as 'bumsters' or 'bumsas') who wait outside hotels and offer tourists anything from souvenirs and postcards to drugs and sex. Most bumsters are very pushy, and (presuming you don't want any of their services) it's best to ignore them completely: don't even shake hands or try to explain that you want to be on your own. Verbal abuse is the usual response, but it's all hot air and after a few encounters of this kind you'll think nothing of it. If you get hassled in the market, complain to a stallholder that it's preventing you buying. The bumster will soon be chased off!

Some visitors, however, find that hiring a bumster as a guide is a good way to avoid trouble and still meet the locals. For about 20 to 60D a day, he can show you around, ward off other hustlers, and maybe introduce you to his friends and family. We've heard from several people who have hired a guide in this way and become genuine friends after a day or two. Have no illusions though: such friends are providing a service and most are with you only for the money.

Once you leave the Banjul area to travel upcountry, security is a much lesser concern, and there's no need to hire 'friends'.

Drugs

A combination of tourism and urban deprivation around Banjul means grass and some harder drugs are available. If this is your scene, be careful: the police will be severe if you're caught with even a small amount as they're looking for a bribe from you to avoid arrest. Tourists have been busted recently at the airport and on the beach.

ACCOMMODATION

In Banjul and the nearby Atlantic coast resorts of Bakau, Fajara, Kotu Strand and Kololi, there's a very wide range of places to stay, from simple guesthouses to international-standard hotels. Upcountry there are a few smart tourist lodges or 'camps', but your choice is usually limited to basic local-style rest houses.

FOOD

If you're travelling on a tight budget you'll find cheap restaurants called *chop houses* in Banjul and other large towns where prices are sometimes as low as 5D for a plate of rice and sauce. Many of the chop houses are nameless; they can usually be identified by coloured plastic strips hanging in their doorways. In Serekunda and the towns on the Trans-Gambia Highway some chop houses go by their Senegalese name: *gargotte*.

Even if you're not strapped for cash, it's well worth making the effort to try some local cooking during your visit, especially as all you'll seem to find in the resort areas around Banjul are European meals like steak and chips. Traditional Gambian food is similar to Senegalese food, with the same ingredients and cultural background, although names and spellings may differ. Chicken *yasser* and *mafay* feature on some menus (for details see the Food section in the Senegal chapter). Other Gambian dishes worth searching for include *domodah* (peanut stew with rice), *plasas* (meat and fish cooked with vegetable leaves in palm oil) and served with *foufou* (mashed cassava), and *benechin* (fish and rice).

Getting There & Away

AIR
To/From Europe & the USA
Airlines from Europe with scheduled flights to The Gambia include Swissair (via Zürich) and Sabena (via Brussels). Gambia Airways and Air Gambia have direct flights between London and Banjul, with one-way fares starting at about UK£350 (US$470). From the USA Air Afrique flies from New York to Dakar (there are also more flights from Europe to Dakar), from where you can fly to Banjul on a regional airline, or travel overland.

One of the cheapest ways of getting from Europe to The Gambia is on a charter flight. Several companies in Britain offer deals from around UK£200 (US$300) return, sometimes with accommodation included, and you can get last-minute bargains for less than UK£100. Most of these deals are for fixed-date two-week holidays, although many travellers use them to get to The Gambia and simply don't use the return half of the ticket. (Unused tickets are sometimes advertised for sale on the noticeboard at the CFAO supermarket in Bakau.)

Another option for a cheap seat back to Europe is to contact a tour operator in Banjul, through the reps in the major hotels. One-way flights cost about UK£200, but this is still one of the cheapest places in West Africa to find a ticket back to Europe.

To/From West Africa
Within West Africa there are flights between Banjul and Dakar (Senegal), Nouakchott (Mauritania), Conakry (Guinea), Bissau (Guinea-Bissau), Freetown (Sierra Leone), plus several other cities including Lagos (Nigeria) and Accra (Ghana). Regional airlines include Gambia Airways, Air Gambia, Air Senegal, ADC Airlines, Sierra National Airlines, Nigeria Airways, Ghana Airways, Air Guinée and Air Bissau. (For office addresses see the Banjul Getting There & Away section.) Some sample one-way fares are: Banjul to Dakar US$55 on Gambia Airways, and Banjul to Conakry one-way US$150 on Air Guinée; but wherever you're going, it's worth shopping around, as airline fares can vary considerably.

LAND
The Gambia is completely surrounded by Senegal (except for 48 km of coastline), which you can reach by travelling either north to Dakar, south to Ziguinchor or east to Tambacounda. All land journeys by public transport involve changing vehicles at the border. Only vehicles travelling between north and south Senegal on the Trans-Gambia Highway can cross the border, although passengers are not allowed to end their journey in The Gambia.

Bush Taxi
To/From Dakar If you're headed from Banjul north to Dakar, take the ferry across the river to Barra (3D). There you'll find transport to the Senegalese border post at Karang: the bus costs 3D (but you have to be quick to get a seat); a pick-up is 9D; and a private taxi 50D. All vehicles stop at the Gambian border post so you can complete formalities, but you might have to walk (or get another taxi) the last one km to the Senegal side. From there, you can get to Dakar by Peugeot 504 (CFA 2900), minibus (CFA 2550) or bus (CFA 1500). With frequent transport changes, passport checks and customs searches, this section of your journey can be frustrating. Stay cool! From Dakar, transport to Karang leaves from the

main *gare routière* (bus/taxi park). Costs are the same. If you use a 504, the whole Banjul to Dakar journey takes about six hours depending on your luck with the ferry. Minibuses and buses take longer. If you're in a hurry and the ferry isn't leaving soon, you could take a *pirogue* (small boat) across. The fare is 3D per person.

To/From Ziguinchor Bush taxis headed south for Ziguinchor leave from the *garage* (taxi park) in Serekunda, and also from Brikama. From Serekunda to the border costs 25D (payable in dalasi or CFA), and from there to Ziguinchor it costs CFA 1400. Going the other way, Ziguinchor to the border is CFA 1500, and from there to Serekunda it's 20D. This is because transport always takes you to the far side of the border. The 159-km trip takes three to five hours, depending on connections.

To/From Tambacounda From Basse (the last town in The Gambia) you can take a pick-up to Velingara (the first town in Senegal) for CFA 300. In Velingara, you'll find 504s to Tambacounda (CFA 1200) at the petrol station on the south side of town. From Velingara to Basse, transport leaves from a taxi park on the north side of town. The road between Tambacounda and Velingara (110 km) is tarred, and between Velingara and Basse (25 km) it's good dirt. The Basse to Tambacounda journey takes between two and six hours depending on connections. Crossing this border (coming or going), you must report to the immigration official at Basse police station.

Car

Between Banjul and Dakar there are two routes. The most direct way (320 km) is via the Banjul-Barra ferry, Karang (the border) and Kaolack. The road is tarred all the way, but in bad condition between Karang and Kaolack. Once you've crossed on the ferry, the drive takes about four hours. The second option is longer (480 km) but more interesting: east from Banjul to Soma, then across the Gambia River by ferry to Farafenni, and then north on the Trans-Gambia Highway

to Dakar. The route is paved all the way but badly potholed in Senegal.

Between Banjul and Ziguinchor, the 135-km road is paved and in good condition. Driving time is about two to three hours.

Heading eastward, the road between Basse and Velingara (25 km) is reasonable dirt, and between Velingara and Tambacounda (110 km) it's tarred.

The borders between The Gambia and Senegal are open from 6 am to 9 pm.

SEA

There is nothing in the way of public ships to/from The Gambia, although you can ask around the harbour for information about freighters headed north to Europe and eastward along the West African coast. Some travellers find sea-going pirogues sailing between Banjul and Dakar or Ziguinchor (Senegal), or to Cacheu in Guinea-Bissau, but these don't run to a set timetable and are notoriously unsafe.

LEAVING THE GAMBIA

If you leave Banjul by air, there's a US$20/UK£15 departure tax, payable in any hard currency. This tax is included in some charter flight tickets. We've also heard that volunteers and aid workers don't have to pay.

Getting Around

AIR

There are no internal flights between Banjul and the upcountry towns.

BUS & BUSH TAXI

The Gambia is a very thin country, so getting around it means going east from Banjul along the river – going north or south takes you into Senegal within a few km!

There are two routes: the tarred road along the southern edge of the river, and the dirt road along the north bank. Most travellers take one of the comfortable government (GPTC) buses along the southern route, which leave at least six times daily from the GPTC station in Banjul. Fares are cheap: for

THE GAMBIA

example, across the country from Banjul to Basse (362 km by road) costs 60D on the ordinary bus and 84D on the express.

Bush taxis (usually Peugeot 504s or minibuses) on the southern route leave from the garage in Serekunda, but only go as far as Soma (about halfway up the country), where you must change to another vehicle. Bush-taxi fares are about the same as the ordinary bus. Wherever you go by bush taxi there's usually a baggage charge: 5D for short journeys; 10D for longer trips.

There are few buses along the northern route, mostly basic bush taxis, as the road is full of potholes and washed away at a few points, although it's usually repaired every dry season. To reach the northern route from Banjul, take the ferry to Barra and find a vehicle there, or cross the river upstream between Mansa Konko and Farafenni, or at Georgetown, Bansang or Basse.

CAR, MOPED & BICYCLE

There are various car rental agencies in the Banjul area, and many hotels rent bicycles and mopeds. (See the Banjul Getting Around section for details on vehicle and bicycle rental.) Several travellers have recommended hiring a bike for a few days or a week to get around the country: the north bank road is particularly good. And you can always put your bike on top of a bush taxi if you get tired.

HITCHING

Hitching is quite feasible on the south bank road, but it's more difficult on the north bank road because traffic is light.

RIVER BOAT

There is no longer a regular public service on the Gambia River. However, a company called Gambia River Excursion Ltd, also called Samba River Venture (☎ 495526), runs a service between Lamin Lodge (southeast of Serekunda) and Jangjang-bureh Camp at Georgetown, via several places of interest along the river. The upstream boat leaves Lamin Lodge every Wednesday at 8 am and arrives at Georgetown on Friday afternoon. The downstream boat leaves Georgetown on Saturdays at 7 am and arrives at Lamin Lodge on Sunday evening. Overnight stops are at Tendaba Camp and Sofin Yama Camp. The entire one-way trip costs 800D per person. Or you can leave the boat at any of the 10 or so intermediate stops: Lamin to Tendaba Camp costs 275D, to Farafenni it's 375D, and to Kuntaur (near Wassu Stone Circles) it costs 700D. Downstream prices are the same. The large wooden boat has a bar, toilet and sun deck, but no cabins. Simple meals are available. Passengers can sleep in bungalows at each camp or on the deck (mattresses, nets and blankets are provided) which costs 50D extra. The timetable might alter, so phone to check the latest information.

TOURS

Nearly all places of interest in The Gambia can be reached by public transport, but several companies (based in the Banjul area) run organised tours and 'safaris' lasting from a few hours to several days. Most cater for groups of tourists staying at the beach-front hotels, but anyone can join a tour, and it can be a good way to get around if time is short or money is not a primary concern. However, before joining a tour, check if the price is all-inclusive or if there are any extras.

Of the larger companies, West African Tours (☎ 495258, fax 496118) is reckoned to be one of the best, although they mainly arrange things for groups rather than for individuals. They offer about 10 trips including a morning 'Birds and Breakfast' outing for UK£23 per person, and a one-day Gambia River Cruise for UK£30. They also do a two-day trip to Georgetown for about UK£75, including a canoe ride into the creeks of the Gambia River, a visit to Wassu Stone Circles and some local villages, and an African night (food, dances and stories) in a lodge where you spend the night. Other companies with similar tours and prices include Gamtours (☎ 392359) and Five-Star Tours (☎ 371110).

Competing with the big operators are many small independent companies, from where you can sometimes get good bargains.

They include United Tours (☎ 464629), Crocodile Safaris (☎ 496068) and Gambia Tours (☎ 228963). For something a bit more imaginative and authentic, try Kinkiliba Tours, a small company running longer tours around The Gambia and into Casamance, who describe themselves as a co-operative venture promoting self-motivated development through small scale, environmentally sensitive tourism. You can contact them through Bayo Kunda Camp in Gunjur (PO Box 219, Serekunda), listed in the South Coast section of this chapter, or through their European base in the UK (☎ (0181) 880-1090).

It's also possible to make arrangements through the tour desk at one of the major beach hotels (you don't have to be a guest). They either have their own in-house agency or they can contact a tour company for you. Recommended are Damel Travel Services at the Atlantic Hotel in Banjul (☎ 228601) and Village Tours, based at the African Village Hotel in Bakau (☎ 495384).

You can also arrange a tour with one of the 'bumsters' (see Dangers & Annoyances, earlier) who lurk around the hotels. He'll be able to find you a car and driver for a tour at a much lower price than those quoted by the companies listed above. However, on this type of tour you always get what you pay for. We've heard plenty of stories about cars breaking down, drivers having no money to buy petrol, extra charges such as ferry fees, and even things being stolen. Be warned.

Banjul

Banjul is the country's major metropolis, with all of 50,000 inhabitants. It lies on the tip of a peninsula at the mouth of the Gambia River, separated from the mainland by a narrow creek. The city has been stagnant for years, giving it a somewhat depressing ambience, although the area around Albert Market and the main thoroughfares of Wellington and Buckle Sts are lively and colourful

during the day. At night the streets are pitch black, making them dangerous.

Because Banjul is locked on an island with nowhere to grow, the nearby towns of Bakau, Fajara and Serekunda are where most of the action takes place these days. While Banjul city centre can support only one tourist-class hotel, there are over a dozen (and many more guesthouses) in the Bakau and Fajara areas, plus several embassies and many expatriate residences. Serekunda is a thriving boom town and a major hub of activity for Gambians.

Orientation

The focal point of Banjul is MacCarthy Square, the city's one public park. From here run two main streets of shops and offices: Buckle St, and Russel St, which leads into Wellington St. The main market (Albert Market) is off Russel St, just east of MacCarthy Square, while the port for the ferry to Barra is at the southern end of Wellington St. (Some streets in Banjul have been renamed, although the old names are still commonly used by locals: Cameron St is now Nelson Mandela St, while Leman St has become OAU Blvd.)

Independence Drive runs west from MacCarthy Square and is the main road out of Banjul. On the edge of the city it turns into a major highway and after about four km crosses Oyster Creek on Denton Bridge to reach the mainland proper. After another two km the road splits: the right fork goes to Bakau and Fajara; straight on goes to Serekunda, the airport, Abuko Nature Reserve and everywhere else along the southern bank of the Gambia River.

In Bakau and Fajara, the main drag is Atlantic Rd, running parallel to the coast, and linking Saitmatty Rd (formerly Cape Rd) and Kairaba Ave (formerly Pipeline Rd). A major landmark on Atlantic Rd is the CFAO supermarket. Just south of Atlantic Rd is Garba Jahumpa Rd (formerly New Town Rd). Kairaba Ave connects Fajara with Serekunda, and the road to the hotel/beach areas of Kololi and Kotu branches off at the Fajara end.

Information
Tourist Office The tourist office at the Craft

Market behind Albert Market was closed after the market was partially destroyed by fire. However, market rebuilding was completed in 1994 so the tourist office may soon reopen too.

Money Banks in Banjul include Standard Chartered (☎ 228681) and Meridien BIAO (☎ 225777) both on Buckle St, and BICIS (☎ 228145) at 11a Wellington St. In Bakau, there are branches near the CFAO supermarket. (For opening hours see Money, earlier.)

Foreign Embassies The following countries have embassies in the centre of Banjul:

Guinea Wellington St, above Marché Juboo shop, next to Gambia Airways
Guinea-Bissau Wellington St just south of Picton St, upstairs next to the African Heritage Restaurant (☎ 228134)
Mali The Mali consul works at the VM Company Ltd, in the part of town called Halfdie, about 50 metres from the bus station on Cotton St (☎ 226947)
Senegal On the corner of Nelson Mandela (formerly Cameron) and Buckle Sts (☎ 227469)
Sierra Leone Hagan St between Hill and Anglesea Sts (☎ 228206)

In Fajara the following countries have embassies:

Liberia Garba Jahumpa Rd (formerly New Town Rd) (☎ 496775)
Mauritania Just off Kairaba Ave (formerly Pipeline Rd), on a minor road between Weaso's Nightclub and the Afro Bar (☎ 496518)
Nigeria Garba Jahumpa Rd (formerly New Town Rd) (☎ 495803)
UK 48 Atlantic Rd, opposite the Medical Research Council (☎ 495133, fax 496134)
USA Kairaba Ave (formerly Pipeline Rd) (☎ 492856, fax 492475)

The consul for Ghana can be found at 18 Mosque Rd, Serekunda, behind a pharmacy opposite a shop called International Traders.

Honorary consuls with limited powers, mainly there to assist holiday-makers with problems, include: France (at the CFAO supermarket on Wellington St, Banjul); Belgium (at the Kairaba Hotel, Kololi); and Sweden and Norway (above The Point Restaurant, Saitmatty Rd (formerly Cape Rd), Bakau).

Germany and Denmark also have consuls – usually an expatriate connected with the tour industry who can change from year to year. If you need either of these consuls, you can get information about them from one of the holiday reps working for the German and Scandinavian tour companies, usually contactable through one of the larger hotels.

Travel Agencies For international flights on African and European airlines, it's easier to deal with the airline office directly but, if this is not possible, the Banjul Travel Agency (☎ 228473) on Buckle St has been recommended.

Bookshops & Supermarkets The Methodist Bookshop, on the corner of Buckle and Nelson Mandela Sts in central Banjul, has a reasonable range of religious and general books. Also try the unnamed bookshop next to the Oasis Snack Bar on Clarkson St near MacCarthy Square. The CFAO supermarkets in Banjul and Bakau also sell paperbacks. Many of the large beach hotels have small bookshops or run book exchanges (where paperbacks can be swapped) which are officially only for guests.

The best supermarkets are the CFAO branches in central Banjul, on the corner of Wellington and Picton Sts, and in Bakau. Others include St Mary's Supermarket, near the Sunwing Hotel at the eastern end of Bakau, and the mini-markets near the Bungalow Beach Hotel at Kotu Strand and near the Senegambia Hotel in Kololi.

All these supermarkets stock local and imported food, simple medicines, toiletries, suncream, sunglasses, swim gear, books, newspapers (local and foreign), toys and some sports equipment.

Gambia National Museum

The museum is on Independence Drive, and many visitors find it well worth a short visit. Some of the more interesting items are the wooden carvings and the old maps and photos. The entrance fee is 10D. It's open from 8 am to 4 pm Monday to Thursday, and from 8 am to 1 pm on Friday and Saturday.

Markets

The principal market in Banjul, Albert Market, is near MacCarthy Square at the northern end of Wellington St. All kinds of items, including fabrics, clothing and food, are sold here. Artisan goods are sold at the Banjul Craft Market (sometimes called the tourist market) next to Albert Market and behind the post office. Both are interesting to browse around, but watch your pockets!

Bakau has a traditional fruit and vegetable market, handy if you're self-catering, and a small tourist market selling carvings and clothing.

Straw hat

Activities

For **swimming**, all the major beach hotels have pools, but only those at the Senegambia and the Bungalow Beach are big enough for doing lengths (laps). Most of the major hotels also rent **sailboards**; the typical charge is about 35D an hour. At the Senegambia you can get a 10-lesson deal for about 300D. Learning in the surf, however, is difficult: try the early morning when it's calmer. At the Watersport Centre near the Sunwing Hotel you can also hire sailboards, plus jet skis for 125D per 15 minutes.

The Fajara Club near the Fajara Hotel has a pool, snooker tables and courts for **tennis**, **squash** and **badminton**. Temporary membership is 75D per day or 300D per week.

Beaches

Beaches in The Gambia are relatively safe, with little undertow. However, drownings still occur every year, so inexperienced swimmers should check conditions locally before plunging in. The beaches in Bakau are OK, but those in Fajara are better. At Kotu Strand and Kololi, further west, they are better still.

Yacht Cruises

Day cruises through the mangrove creeks around Banjul are a popular excursion. They are arranged by major hotels and tour companies (listed in Tours, earlier) and are recommended especially for those who don't get a chance to travel up the Gambia River. The scenery along the way is wonderful, and you might spot a monkey or two as well as numerous birds, such as herons, hawks, grass warblers, doves, swallows and kingfishers. Most cruises go from Denton Bridge down Oyster Creek, stopping for a picnic lunch and a swim at Mandinari, and cost about UK£30.

Longer cruises are also available on the Gambia River. Some companies arrange two or three-day trips to Tendaba Camp, or to Georgetown. These companies include Gambia Safari (☎ 495299), which runs the MS *Beatrice*, a 30-metre motor cruiser with cabins and many facilities. Another is Gambia River Excursion Ltd (☎ 495526) which runs more straightforward craft and also offers day trips.

Canoe Trips

For a less elaborate (and cheaper) ride around the mangrove creeks, find a local boatman with a canoe. Ask at the river bank along Wellington St between Albert Market and the ferry pier, or at Denton Bridge. To get to Denton Bridge by public transport, take any minibus running between Banjul and Bakau or Serekunda and ask the driver to let you off at the bridge. If you go in a motorised canoe, the price will be quite stiff, so it's best to get a group together. A trip in a hand-paddled canoe will be cheaper, but shorter.

Travellers have recommended the boat trips organised by the Atlantic Guesthouse in Bakau (see Places to Stay). Rates are reasonable, and vary depending on where you go and what you do (fishing, bird-watching etc).

Places to Stay

Most hotels catering for tourists have high and low season rates. High season (November to

Mangroves

The mangrove is a tropical evergreen plant that grows on tidal mud flats and inlets all along the coast of West Africa. It is one of very few plants which can survive in saltwater. In fact, it positively thrives in it, and will quickly colonise areas of mud where no other plant would have a chance. The mangrove is also remarkable, and fairly unique, in its capacity to actually create more land for future plants to grow on.

One of the best places to see mangroves is in The Gambia; here you can get deep into the mangrove 'forests' by taking a boat trip through the creeks around Banjul or up the Gambia River.

In The Gambia, there are two types of mangrove which can be seen and easily identified. The red mangrove (of which there are three species – although to the untrained eye they all look the same) is most prominent. It's easy to recognise by its leathery leaves and dense tangle of stilt-like buttress roots. The seeds germinate while the fruit still hangs on the tree, growing a long stem called a 'radical'. When the fruit drops, the radical lodges in the mud and becomes a ready-made root for the new seedling. The seed can survive in sea water for up to a year, so if the tide happens to be in when the seed drops off it will float around, with radical down, ready to start growing as soon as it's washed ashore.

The white mangrove is less common, and is found mainly on ground that is only covered by particularly high tides. It does not have stilt roots. It's most recognisable characteristic is the breathing roots, with circular pores, that grow out of the mud from the base of the tree.

Mangrove trees catch silt, vegetation and other floating debris in their root systems. The mangrove's own falling leaves are added to the pile. As this mire becomes waterlogged and consolidated, it forms an ideal breeding ground for young mangroves. In this way the mangrove creates new land and can quickly colonise new areas. As the mangrove forest expands on its seaward side, the older trees on the landward side gradually get further and further from the water. Eventually they die, leaving behind a rich soil which is good for cultivation.

The mangrove has many other uses. Oysters and shellfish cling to the roots as the tide comes in. When it retreats, they are left exposed and easily captured by local people who cruise the creeks in pirogues or wade through the mud and water. Larger fish also like the darkness between the roots, and the mangroves are popular fishing grounds for locals and visitors. ■

April) rates are quoted throughout this section. Low season rates are between 25 and 50% cheaper, and you can get rooms for even less if you're prepared to negotiate, although some hotels close completely at this time.

Some hotels also offer rooms without air-con at a discount (even in the high season). This can be a good deal, as the high season is also the cool season, so air-con is not necessary, and because the electricity is frequently cut off at night, it's often irrelevant anyway (although most large hotels have a generator). The blackouts mean that it's a good idea to have some candles too, especially in the hotels with no generator.

In the area around Banjul, new hotels are built while old ones close or change names, so keep this in mind when looking for somewhere to stay. The list here is not complete.

Places to Stay – bottom end

Banjul The cheapest place is the *Teranga Hotel* (☎ 228387) at 13 Hill St where filthy rooms (for one or two people) cost 90D. Much better is the friendly *Duma Guesthouse* (☎ 228381) near the corner of Oxford St and Sam Jack Terrace where clean doubles with fans cost 125D, or 150D for a self-contained room. Food can be ordered every day except Sunday.

Best value in this range is the *Kantora Hotel* (☎ 228715) on Independence Drive with clean singles/doubles for 165/200D including breakfast. Rooms with air-con are 215/250D but if you promise not to use it they'll charge the 'without' price. The rooms on the right side of the hotel are quieter and lighter. The nearby *Carlton Hotel* (☎ 227258) has recently gone downhill. Its tatty doubles are bad value at 200D (290D with air-con).

The *Apollo Hotel* (☎ 228184) on Orange St near Buckle St, is a bit rambling and gloomy, but perfectly adequate, with self-contained air-con singles/doubles for 220/330D. Couples can share a single. The

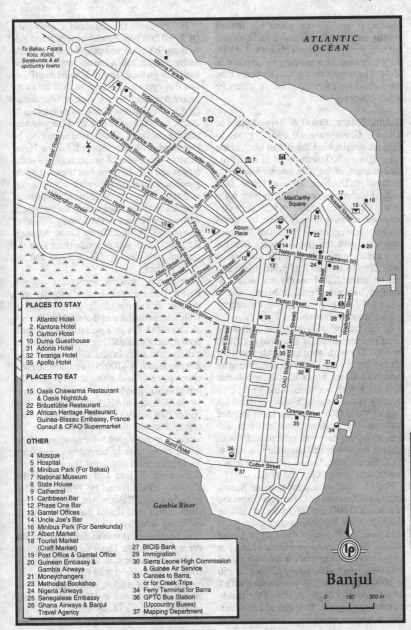

ATLANTIC
OCEAN

To Bakau, Fajara,
Kotu, Kololi,
Serekunda & all
upcountry towns

MacCarthy
Square

Albion
Place

Nelson Mandela St
(Cameron St)

Picton Street

Anglesea Street

Hill Street

Orange Street

Bund Road

Gambia River

Cotton Street

PLACES TO STAY

1 Atlantic Hotel
2 Kantora Hotel
3 Carlton Hotel
10 Duma Guesthouse
31 Adonis Hotel
32 Teranga Hotel
35 Apollo Hotel

PLACES TO EAT

15 Oasis Chawarma Restaurant
& Oasis Nightclub
22 Bräustüble Restaurant
28 African Heritage Restaurant,
Guinea-Bissau Embassy, France
Consul & CFAO Supermarket

OTHER

4 Mosque
5 Hospital
6 Minibus Park (For Bakau)
7 National Museum
8 State House
9 Cathedral
11 Caribbean Bar
12 Phase One Bar
13 Gamtel Offices
14 Uncle Joe's Bar
16 Minibus Park (For Serekunda)
17 Albert Market
18 Tourist Market
(Craft Market)
19 Post Office & Gamtel Office
20 Guinean Embassy &
Gambia Airways
21 Moneychangers
23 Methodist Bookshop
24 Nigeria Airways
25 Senegalese Embassy
26 Ghana Airways & Banjul
Travel Agency

27 BICIS Bank
29 Immigration
30 Sierra Leone High Commission
& Guinée Air Service
33 Canoes to Barra,
or for Creek Trips
34 Ferry Terminal for Barra
36 GPTC Bus Station
(Upcountry Buses)
37 Mapping Department

THE GAMBIA

Banjul

0   150   300 m

restaurant has a long menu but there's usually only one dish available and even it is not very good. The *Adonis Hotel* (☎ 228262) on Wellington St was being refurbished in 1994. The owner says it will be better than the Apollo for a similar price, so it may be worth checking out.

Bakau, Fajara, Kololi & Serekunda The *Atlantic Guesthouse* (☎ 496237), set in gardens overlooking the ocean on Atlantic Rd in Bakau, 500 metres west of the CFAO supermarket, is the only budget hotel right on the coast. Double rooms cost 150 to 200D (shared bathroom) and 250D (private bathroom). Occasional problems with the water pressure mean you may have to take a bucket shower, and even more frequent problems with the electricity account for the candles in the rooms. In the low season rates drop to around half-price. Breakfast can be ordered, and nearby are some reasonable bar/restaurants, a bakery and a small food shop. Boat trips on the nearby creeks are also available.

In the 'centre' of Bakau, just east of the CFAO supermarket, is the *Romana Hotel* (☎ 495127) with singles/doubles at 150/200D. The rooms are quite attractive with fans, brick floors, big beds, sofas and decent tiled baths with hot water. Also worth considering is the large four-storey *Friendship Lodge* (☎ 495830) next to the Independence Stadium. The spotless rooms have fans, air-con, mosquito nets and private baths with reliable hot water, and the price is a steal at 200D for a double. Guests can use the tennis courts, ping-pong tables and gym.

For cheaper accommodation in Bakau, some travellers stay with families. Expect to pay about 100D per night for a double, although with bargaining you may get a reduction. Dr Ngum (☎ 495400) at 5 Saul Samba St has been recommended. For longer stays you can rent a whole compound with bedroom, bathroom and kitchen for 750 to 1000D per month. If you do stay with a family, consider engaging one of the family members as a guide; they can add considerably to your experience.

In Fajara, the *Malawi Guesthouse* (☎ 393012) is popular with travellers and aidworkers. It's clean and peaceful, with double rooms at 100 to 180D, and has very good value meals. To get there, turn off Kairaba Ave (Pipeline Rd) opposite the mosque. Not far away, nearer the beach, is the *Fajara Guesthouse* (☎ /fax 496122 or 495294), with doubles at 200D, or 300D with fan, mini-bar and teamaking facilities. (This place is not to be confused with the top-end Fajara Hotel nearby.) The owner often meets flights at the airport and will give you free transport to the guesthouse. You can even phone from abroad so that he meets your flight (worth doing as an international call is cheaper than the taxi ride!). Also recommended is the friendly *Newtown Guesthouse* (☎ 496930), off Garba Jahumpa Rd (New Town Rd) in a side street near the stadium, with clean doubles at 200D, and use of the kitchen.

In Kololi, between Serekunda and the Palma Rima Hotel, is the friendly and popular *Kololi Inn & Tavern* (☎ 463410) with singles/doubles in thatched bungalows at 150/200D. Set in a pleasant shady compound, there's a small bar, restaurant and art gallery attached. In the same area is the *Keneba Hotel* (☎ 470093), a quieter, slightly tattier place with doubles at 150D, and the remarkably good-value *Bakadaji Hotel* (☎ 462307; cards AE, V) with rooms (for one or two people) at 250D and bungalows (up to four people) for 400D. At the far southern end of Kololi is the *Montrose Hotel* where clean homely bungalows cost from 350D per person with breakfast.

Between Fajara and Serekunda, the *Kenifeng YMCA Hostel* (☎ 392647), on 5th St to the east of Kairaba Ave, has simple but clean rooms with shared bath for 80/124D, including breakfast.

In Serekunda, if you're desperate, try the dreary *Jalakunda Hotel* overlooking the market, with rooms at 125D. Better is the *Green Line Hotel* (☎ 394245), about 100 metres from the market, with clean self-contained air-con rooms at 150/225D including breakfast. It has a cheap snack bar and hot showers. Also worth trying is the *Gambisarra*

Motel, at the main Serekunda intersection, where singles/doubles cost 150/ 225D.

Places to Stay – middle

Banjul The centre has nothing in this range. Nearest is the *Wadner Beach Hotel* (☎ 228199, telex 2219; cards AE), four km out of town on the main highway. Air-con rooms cost 475/575D with breakfast, and the hotel has a pool, tennis court and nightclub. Next door is the better value *Palm Grove Hotel* (☎ 228630, fax 296218) where doubles cost 400D (450D with air-con)

including breakfast. Other meals are excellent plus there's a pool, a private beach, and free nightly entertainment.

Bakau You'll have a hard time beating the attractive *Cape Point Hotel* (☎ 495005) at the far eastern end of Atlantic Rd. It's open year-round, with doubles for 300D, or an apartment for 400D, with breakfast. Almost next door is the popular *Amies Beach Hotel* (☎ 495035, fax 296-218; cards AE) with rooms for 380D (450D with air-con). Another good deal is the *African Village*

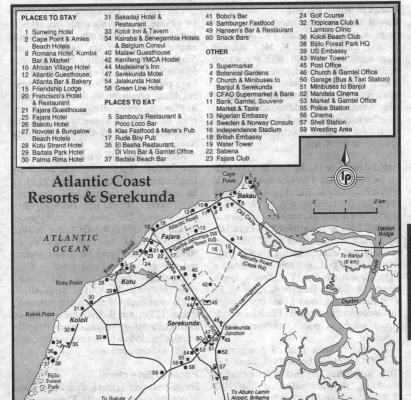

PLACES TO STAY

1 Sunwing Hotel
2 Cape Point & Amies Beach Hotels
8 Romana Hotel, Kumba Bar & Market
10 African Village Hotel
12 Atlantic Guesthouse, Atlanta Bar & Bakery
15 Friendship Lodge
20 Francisco's Hotel & Restaurant
21 Fajara Guesthouse
25 Fajara Hotel
26 Bakotu Hotel
27 Novotel & Bungalow Beach Hotels
28 Kotu Strand Hotel
29 Badala Park Hotel
30 Palma Rima Hotel
31 Bakadaji Hotel & Restaurant
33 Kololi Inn & Tavern
34 Kairaba & Senegambia Hotels & Belgium Consul
40 Malawi Guesthouse
42 Kenifeng YMCA Hostel
44 Madeleine's Inn
47 Serekunda Motel
54 Jalakunda Hotel
58 Green Line Hotel

PLACES TO EAT

5 Sambou's Restaurant & Poco Loco Bar
6 Klas Fastfood & Marie's Pub
17 Rude Boy Pub
35 El Basha Reataurant, Di Vino Bar & Gamtel Office
37 Badala Beach Bar

41 Bobo's Bar
48 Samburger Fastfood
49 Hansen's Bar & Restaurant
60 Snack Bars

OTHER

3 Supermarket
4 Botanical Gardens
7 Church & Minibuses to Banjul & Serekunda
9 CFAO Supermarket & Bank
11 Bank, Gamtel, Souvenir Market & Taxis
13 Nigerian Embassy
14 Sweden & Norway Consuls
16 Independence Stadium
18 British Embassy
19 Water Tower
22 Sabena
23 Fajara Club

24 Golf Course
32 Tropicana Club & Lamtoro Clinic
36 Kololi Beach Club
38 Bijilo Forest Park HQ
39 US Embassy
43 Water Tower'
45 Post Office
46 Church & Gamtel Office
50 Garage (Bus & Taxi Station)
51 Minibuses to Banjul
52 Mandela Cinema
53 Market & Gamtel Office
55 Police Station
56 Cinema
57 Shell Station
59 Wrestling Area

Atlantic Coast Resorts & Serekunda

THE GAMBIA

Hotel (☎ 495034, fax 496042; cards AE, V, M) overlooking the ocean on Atlantic Rd near the CFAO supermarket. It has a good bar and restaurant, a pool, its own beach and nightly entertainment.

Fajara *Francisco's Hotel & Restaurant* (☎ 495332) has very nice air-con rooms at 350/450D including a full English breakfast and 10% discount in the restaurant. In the Kotu Strand area, the modern *Bakotu Hotel* (☎ 495555, fax 495959) is recommended: singles/doubles cost 365/470D, with breakfast. It's near the beach and opposite the Novotel, where you can take advantage of the facilities.

Places to Stay – top end
Banjul The best (and only) place in this range is the *Atlantic Hotel* (☎ 228601, fax 227861; cards AE, D, V, MC). Air-con singles/doubles cost 910/1190D. It has good facilities, including a pool, tennis, squash, sailboards, sail boats and water-skiing, but the beach is not too clean. If you fancy a change of scene, most restaurants and nightclubs (and all the other major hotels) are between 12 and 20 km away in the coastal resorts of Bakau, Fajara, Kotu Strand and Kololi.

Coastal Resorts The *Kairaba Hotel* (☎ 492-940 or 462717, fax 492947; cards AE, D, V, MC) at Kololi, about 20 km from Banjul, is one of the best hotels (along with the Novotel) in terms of the quality of rooms and vibrancy of nightlife. It has air-con singles/doubles, including breakfast, from 1070/1210D. Facilities include a pool, tennis, squash, gym, volleyball, archery, mini-golf, billiards, sailboards, a nightclub and car hire. The *Kombo Beach Novotel* (☎ 465466, fax 495490; cards AE, D, V) at Kotu Strand, about 17 km from Banjul, has air-con doubles for 955D. Facilities include a pool, tennis, sailboards, surfboards and a nightclub.

The older, more relaxed *Senegambia Hotel* (☎ 462718/9, fax 461839; cards AE, D) in Kololi has singles/doubles including breakfast, showers only, for 770/910D (895/1035D with air-con). It has a pool, tennis, squash, mini-golf, volleyball, a night-

club and offers car hire. Nearby is *Kololi Beach Club*, a 'club-share' complex.

Down slightly in quality is the four-star *Palma Rima Hotel* (☎ 463380, fax 493382; cards AE, V) in between Kotu Strand and Kololi. Air-con singles/doubles, including breakfast, cost 840/1050D. It has a pool, tennis and squash facilities, and a nightclub. A notch down again, in quality and price, is the large *Fajara Hotel* (☎ 495605, fax 495339; cards AE, D, V) at the far western end of Atlantic Rd. It has singles/doubles with breakfast but without air-con for 475/575D. Guests can use the tennis and squash facilities at the nearby Fajara Club (see Activities, earlier).

The smaller *Bungalow Beach Hotel* (☎ 495288, fax 496180; cards AE, D) is in Kotu Strand, just on the other side of the golf course (about three km round by road). Singles/doubles, including breakfast, cost 660/865D (about 75D extra for air-con). It has a pool, tennis facilities and a supermarket. Many people prefer this hotel because its prices are lower, all rooms have kitchenettes, the restaurant is one of the best, and you can take advantage of the facilities at the Novotel next door.

Also at Kotu Strand is the rather run-down *Kotu Strand Hotel* (☎ 465609; no cards). Singles/doubles with breakfast cost 450/550D. Its facilities include a pool, mini-market and tennis courts; sailboards are available next door at the Novotel. The newer, reasonably priced *Badala Park Hotel* (☎ 460400, fax 460402; cards AE, V, M) has singles/doubles for 500/575D. If offers a pool, jacuzzi, acupressure and massage clinic, and a nightclub.

The cheapest top-end place is the *Sunwing Hotel* (☎ 495428, fax 496102; cards AE, V) in the most lively of the coastal 'suburbs', Bakau (12 km from Banjul). Air-con singles/doubles, including breakfast, cost 420/550D. Facilities include a pool, tennis courts, sailboards and catamarans.

Places to Eat – cheap
Banjul has several chop houses where plates of rice and sauce start at 5D. There are a few cheap restaurants around the Sam Jack

Terrace area. The cheapest place of all may be Albert Market, which has stalls where food is served all day. The *Oasis Chawarma Restaurant* on Clarkson St between Dobson and Hagan Sts serves good chawarmas (grilled meat sandwiches) for 14D and is open from noon to late evening.

In Bakau and Fajara, finding cheap food is more difficult. Try *Chez Awa* in the market. Other than that, the cheapest you'll find are the snack bars catering mainly for tourists. These include *Klas Fastfood* on Old Cape Rd, and the lively *Kumba Bar* on Atlantic Rd, where meals like burgers or fish & chips cost around 35D. The quieter *Atlanta Bar* next to the Atlantic Guesthouse has cold beer, a pool table, and meals such as grilled chicken and chips for 40D.

In Kotu and Kololi, near the big hotels, it's even harder to find cheap food. Your best option is the *Kololi Inn & Tavern* which serves good African meals for between 30 and 60D. The people here run art and craft workshops and short African cookery courses: if you come early, you can help prepare your own evening meal.

In Serekunda, there are several cheap eating houses around the market. Two basic but good places are directly opposite the taxi-park entrance, where you can get bread and eggs, or bowls of rice and sauce. Smarter is *Hansen's Bar & Restaurant*, near the main intersection, which has a garden and good-value meals from around 30D. Nearby is *Samburger Fastfood* with snacks from 20D.

Places to Eat – middle & top end

African The *Carlton Hotel* in Banjul has an African meal of the day for 40D but it's nothing special. Better for Gambian and European food is the *African Heritage Restaurant* on Wellington St, just south of Picton St, open every day except Sunday until 6 pm. Snacks are around 30D, meals cost from 50 to 90D, and a small beer is 13D.

In Bakau, *Sambou's Restaurant* on Old Cape Rd has a varied menu that includes a few Gambian dishes in the 45 to 65D price range. The unpretentious *Cape Point Restaurant* next to the Sunwing Hotel is in the same price range and serves Gambian specialities as well as European fare.

Between Kotu and Kololi *The Bakadaji*, near the Palma Rima Hotel, is the top African restaurant, although it's not cheap. The best value is the Thursday and Saturday night buffets which cost 80D. European food is also available. Mr Njie, the owner, comes from the upcountry village of Bakadaji and donates some of the restaurant profits to the school there. The rather exclusive *Dolphin Bar & Restaurant* (☎ 460929), near the Senegambia Hotel, has British and Gambian dishes starting at 50D.

European In Banjul, the Austrian-style *Braüstüble Restaurant* on OAU Blvd, half a block south of MacCarthy Square, is highly recommended. In the attractive 'biergarten' there's relatively inexpensive fare, including cold draught beer (13D for a small glass) and sandwiches. Meals in the inside dining room, including German selections, are mostly in the 35 to 75D price range.

In Fajara on Kairaba Ave (Pipeline Rd) is *Bobo's Bar*, a pub popular with Britons. Every day they have two specials, such as shepherd's pie and fish & chips, for about 45D. Nearby is the *Malawi Guesthouse*, which serves good home-cooked English-style food, with a Sunday roast for 50D and an evening buffet with some African dishes twice a week for 40D.

Also on Kairaba Ave, at the junction with Atlantic Rd, is *Francisco's Hotel & Restaurant* (☎ 495332), with a great atmosphere and good meals from 50 to 85D. It's open every day until midnight. Nearby is the *Bull & Bush Steakhouse* (☎ 496853), which also brews its own British-style beer. Further down Kairaba Ave is the *Athina* (☎ 392638) – a Greek restaurant open every evening until midnight.

If you want French cuisine, and if money is of no concern, head for *Yvonne Class* in Bakau near the Sunwing Hotel; the meals are reportedly fabulous. They ought to be, with prices from 150 to 300D and a three-course *menu* (daily special) for 130D.

THE GAMBIA

Chinese On Kairaba Ave, half a km south from the junction with Atlantic Rd, is *Le Lotus Restaurant* and nearby the *Bamboo Restaurant*. Open daily except Mondays, the Bamboo serves good Chinese food at moderate prices, but the portions are small. You can eat inside or in the garden. Several hundred metres further south is the *Yellow Gate* which serves Chinese and Malaysian food but some people feel that it lacks certain critical Asian seasonings and ingredients.

Miscellaneous For Indian food, *The Clay Oven* (☎ 496600) on Old Cape Rd in Bakau is highly recommended. It's open every day, and meals cost between 50 and 150D. For Lebanese and European cuisine try the *Al Basha* (☎ 463300) near the Senegambia Hotel in Kololi.

All the up-market hotels have their own restaurants where nonguests are welcome. Most also serve all-you-can-eat evening buffets in the 100 to 150D price range. The Senegambia, for instance, does an excellent African buffet every Tuesday night for 120D. Some travellers make the most of this deal by forgoing breakfast and lunch and then stuffing themselves silly at the buffet. Breakfast buffets are also available: those at the Senegambia and the Novotel are first rate and cost 65D.

Entertainment

Bars For a cheap drink in Banjul try *Uncle Joe's* at the north-eastern corner of Nelson Mandela and Clarkson Sts. The bar is only open during the day. They serve JulBrew for 6D a bottle and the atmosphere is tranquil. For louder lowlife after dark try the *Phase One Bar* on Long St, or the *Caribbean Bar* at the junction of Allen and Ingram Sts, but don't carry anything you wouldn't mind losing, or go with a streetwise Gambian friend. For more salubrious surroundings try the *Braüstüble* (see Places to Eat).

In Bakau, near the Atlantic Guesthouse, is a clutch of bars (most also serve food), including the *Atlanta Bar*, with bottles of JulBrew for 10D and a pool table, *Goldfinger Bar* with similar prices, and the smarter, more expensive *Dublin Bar*, decorated like

an Irish pub. Near the CFAO supermarket is the *Kumba Bar* and the *Tropic Smile*, both also serve food and are popular with tourists and locals. There's also *Sambou's Restaurant* on Old Cape Rd, with happy-hour prices from 5 to 7 pm. Next door, the *Poco Loco Bar* is similar. For cheap drinks, try *Marie's Pub* just across the street: it's a popular shanty-like bar with Gambian clientele and reggae music. On Garba Jahumpa (New Town) Rd is the *Rude Boy International Pub*, open from 7 pm. The Danish-Gambian management state that single women can drink here in a hassle-free environment. In the Bakau back streets are several more local bars, including the *Bar Podium*, which require some searching out and are not for the faint-hearted.

In Fajara, a popular place, especially with Britons, is *Bobo's Bar* on Kairaba Ave, where you can eat, play darts and drink big draught beers for 20D. The more refined bar at nearby *Francisco's* (see Places to Eat) is also popular. Or try the *Bull & Bush*, a steakhouse which brews its own beer. Also on Kairaba Ave is *Madeleine's Inn* a Swiss-run bar and restaurant.

In Kotu Strand, *Dominoes*, between the Novotel and the Bungalow Beach Hotel, has a nice view of the ocean from the terrace and friendly staff. The *Kotu Bendula Bar* has similar prices but no view. The *Paradise* is on the beach, on the other side of the Bungalow Beach Hotel, where beers and sandwiches cost about 10 and 15D.

At the far end of the coastal strip, on the beach beyond the Kololi Beach Club and near Bijilo Forest Park, is the *Badala Beach Bar*, a rustic and surprisingly cheap place (considering its proximity to the major hotels) with beers for 8D.

Nightclubs In Banjul, the *Oasis Nightclub* on Clarkson St between Dobson and Hagan Sts is one of the liveliest places, particularly on weekends or when there's a band playing, although visitors can get hassled here and it's worth going with a Gambian friend to avoid this. It's open from 10 pm to 6 am, entrance costs 10D.

Serekunda and Brikama are livelier at night

than Banjul, and have a number of clubs catering for locals, such as *City Disco* in Serekunda, and *Safari Club* in Brikama. *Hansen's Bar* in Serekunda has live bands some evenings.

Some tourists and expatriates prefer the discos catering to them, which tend to be more European in style and more expensive. In Bakau, one of the hottest places in the high season is *Club 98* at the African Village Hotel (see Places to Stay). Open every day during the winter season, with a cover charge on Saturday, it's very active.

For a place simply mobbed with tourists, head for the ever-popular *Bellingo* disco at the Novotel, where the cover charge alone is 30D. At Kololi, the *Tropicana Club* has live bands and discos featuring reggae and international pop, and a lively mix of tourists and locals.

Casinos For roulette, blackjack and slot machines, the *Kololi Casino* in Kololi near the Senegambia Hotel is the place to be. Open every evening from 9 pm, the Casino also has a bar, coffee shop and an Italian restaurant.

Cinemas In Banjul, the Banjul Cinema on Lasso Wharf, just beyond New St, shows mainly Indian flicks. There are videos open to the public at the Novotel every day; the programme is posted at reception.

Things to Buy
Artisan Goods In Banjul, the best place for art and African materials is Albert Market on Wellington St. The most popular souvenir items are the batik prints, tie-dyed cloths, colourful 'gambishirts', gold and silver filigree jewellery, wooden carvings and leather

Gambian crafts

Traditional Wrestling
Traditional wrestling matches are great spectacles that attract crowds of locals and tourists. The preliminaries can be as entertaining as the actual fights: wrestlers enter the arena in full costume, a loincloth in bright patterned materials arranged with a tail falling behind and their bodies and arms smothered in *gris-gris* (charms), before slowly strutting around the ring, always performing with an eye to the audience. True champions are showered with gifts from their admirers and some may even be preceded by their griots with a roll of the drums.

Between matches there's a cacophony of sounds – drums, flutes, whistles and girls chanting like cheerleaders. And for the fight itself – anything goes: biting, kicking, punching. No fancy hand-locks, technical throws, or points. Just get him down.

You can see matches in the late afternoon (from 5 to 7 pm) on most weekends (except during Ramadan) in Serekunda (two km east of the market). The entrance fee is 10D. All the major hotels have buses leaving around 4 pm or so; the cost is about 150D. Taxis do this trip for the same price, including waiting time. Or you can get there by shared taxi for about 5D. If you need directions, the Wolof word for wrestling is *boreh*, although many local people use the French-Senegalese word: *les luttes*. Occasionally, matches are held at the big stadium in Bakau, but the atmosphere is not so good here. ∎

goods. When the Banjul Craft Market next door reopens it will probably sell more of the same stuff. For silver filigree, try the Mauritanian shop next to the Braüstüble restaurant on OAU Blvd.

In Bakau, there are stalls on Atlantic Rd, near the CFAO supermarket; the quality is the same as in Banjul but the selection is more limited. Nearby, the snappily titled Gambia Black African Arts Club Art Gallery (open Monday to Saturday from 9.30 am to 12.30 pm and 2.30 to 6.30 pm), sells batiks, pottery, paintings, sculpture, and graphics. For up-market tie-dyed cloths, batiks and leatherwork visit Gena Be's on Garba Jahumpa (New Town) Rd.

In Kotu Strand, there's a craft centre next to the Novotel, and in Kololi the gallery at the Kololi Inn & Tavern sells local crafts.

Also try the markets in Serekunda, which are particularly good for antique Venetian beads, and in Brikama, which is renowned for woodcarvers, although their work is generally souvenir quality, not for serious collectors, and lots of bargaining is required.

Music For cassettes of African music, the best place may be Kerewan Sound at shop No 5 in Albert Market. Senegalese music is popular, and there are only a few Gambian recording artists. Two singers currently popular are Ismael Issac and Abdd Kabir; others include Jaliba Kayateh, Framboling, Ifang Bondi and Magadan.

Getting There & Away

Air For details of regional flights between Banjul and the rest of West Africa, and international flights to/from Europe, see the main Getting There & Away section, earlier in this chapter.

For reservations, most airline offices are in Banjul centre: Gambia Airways (☎ 227463) is on Wellington St, while Air Gambia (☎ 227824) is nearby on Nelson Mandela St. Ghana Airways (☎ 228245) and Nigeria Airways (☎ 227438) are both on Buckle St, and may offer student discounts. Guinée Air Service is on Hagan St and Air Guinée is nearby on OAU Blvd. ADC Airlines (with flights to Freetown, Monrovia and Lagos) are represented by Score Travel Agency

(☎ 224195) on Anglesea St. Sabena's office (☎ 396301) is on Kairaba Ave in Fajara.

Bus Government buses run between Banjul and Basse, via Georgetown and other upcountry towns south of the river. They go from the GPTC bus station on Cotton St in Banjul centre. Ordinary buses leave at 6, 6.30, 7.30, 9 and 10 am and at 1 pm (the fare to Basse is 60D and the journey time is around eight hours); the express bus leaves at 8 am and costs 70D. The super-express bus (with reclining seats) costs 84D and leaves at 11 am, stopping only at Serekunda, Brikama, Soma and Bansang. Reservations are not possible but the buses are rarely full.

Bush Taxi Bush taxis and minibuses to upcountry destinations south of the river, and to the southern border with Senegal (see the main Getting There & Away section) leave from the garage in Serekunda, which you can get to by minibus from Banjul or Bakau. Taxis to the northern border with Senegal (from where you get transport to Dakar) and bush taxis along the north side of the river leave from Barra which you get to by ferry from Banjul (see below).

Boat Ferries run between Banjul and Barra every hour from 8 am until the last ferry leaves from Barra at 7 pm. The trip takes about 30 minutes. Car space is limited as two trucks fill about half the deck. You can buy tickets at the pier on the Banjul side and at the public weigh-bridge (about one km from the ferry dock) on the Barra side. People with Senegal registered vehicles must pay in CFA. For passengers, the fare is 3D or CFA 200. For more information, call the ferry office (☎ 228205).

For boat service along the Gambia River, see the main Getting Around section.

Getting Around

To/From the Airport A taxi from the airport to Serekunda is 100D. To the beach area (Bakau, Fajara and Kotu Strand) and to Banjul (27 km) is 120D. Most drivers will quote you the official rate, painted on the wall at the taxi rank, so bargaining is usually not required. Going to the airport you should be able to negotiate at least 30% off this price, although only certain taxis are allowed into the airport. On my last visit I got a taxi from Serekunda to the airport for 50D, but this involved a short stop while the driver removed his yellow number plates and fixed on some black ones, neatly turning his taxi into a 'private' car!

There are no buses to/from the airport but regular minibuses run along the main road between Brikama and Serekunda, passing the airport turn-off. It's a three-km walk between the airport and the turn-off, but you may be lucky and get a lift.

Minibus & Shared Taxi All public transport vehicles (including private taxis and shared taxis) have yellow number plates. For getting around town, minibuses and shared taxis run regularly between Banjul, Serekunda, Bakau, Fajara, and the other outer suburbs. From Banjul, vehicles to Bakau leave about every 15 minutes between 6 am and 8 pm from the stand opposite the Shell station on Independence Drive. If you're going to Fajara, take a minibus to Bakau and either walk from there or take an onward shared taxi to Serekunda and hop off in Fajara. Vehicles from Banjul to Serekunda and Brikama leave from the taxi park off Albion Place, a block from both Clarkson St and Independence Drive. Shared taxis also run from the Serekunda taxi park to the beach hotel areas at Kotu Strand and Kololi. Fares are as follows:

from	to	fare
Banjul	Bakau	3D
Banjul	Serekunda	3D
Banjul	Brikama	6D
Serekunda	Brikama	4D
Serekunda	Fajara/Bakau	2D
Serekunda	Abuko	2D
Bakau	Fajara	2D

Private Taxi For a taxi to yourself (known as a 'town trip') around Banjul city centre, a short ride should cost about 5D, but you'll be lucky to get it for under 20D. From Banjul it costs about 40D to Bakau, 60D to Fajara, and 75D to Kotu Strand. Check the price before getting in: bargaining is definitely required. A taxi by the hour should cost around 40D if you stay within the city limits. Hiring a taxi for the day will start at about 350D, although for a tour out of the city most drivers charge by the destination. A trip to Juffure, for example, will cost 600D, including waiting time. Taxis are plentiful during the day but difficult to find at night except at the major beach hotels.

Car Holiday Car Rental, based at the Senegambia Hotel (☎ 463393), has small saloon cars for 750D per day and Suzuki 4WDs for 800D per day, unlimited mileage. Village Tours, at the African Village Hotel in Bakau (☎ 495384), has small saloon cars for 450D per day. A driver is available at no extra charge. Madeleine's Inn (☎ 391464) in Fajara has a couple of small basic runarounds for 360D per day. Land Rovers, seating up to eight people, are available from Village Tours for 550D per day, and from Crocodile Safaris (☎ 496068) in Serekunda for 600D per day. This includes a driver. For all cars, the prices do not include petrol. Also worth trying are Spot Car Hire (☎ 392657) and Black & White Safaris (☎ 393174).

Bicycle & Motorcycle Mountain bikes and more traditional roadsters (of varying quality) can be hired from several hotels in Bakau, Kotu and Kololi, or from private outfits nearby, for about 40D for half a day and 80D for a full day. Try the Sunwing, the African Village, the Fajara or the Bungalow Beach hotels. With negotiation you can reduce these rates to at least half-price.

Mopeds can be hired from outside the Novotel at Kotu Strand or from the Atlantic Hotel in Banjul for around 200D per day. Suzuki 125cc and 350cc trail bikes can be hired from outside the Senegambia Hotel for around 600D per day, although don't sign anything that makes you responsible for all theft and damage.

THE GAMBIA

AROUND BANJUL
Abuko Nature Reserve

Abuko is unique among West African wildlife reserves in that it's fenced and easy to reach. It is also one of the best managed reserves in the region, established largely due to the work of Mr Eddie Brewer – an active conservationist and director of the Wildlife Conservation Department during the 1970s – with the positive support of President Jawara and the Gambian government. (Mr Brewer's daughter, Stella, wrote *The Chimps of Mount Aserik*, which describes her attempts to reintroduce orphaned chimpanzees into the wilds.)

Abuko has amazingly diverse vegetation for a park of only 102 hectares because a stream runs through the centre, allowing both riverside and savannah species to flourish. You can see up to 50 tree varieties along the two-km-loop walk. In the middle of the park, there's a small zoo with spacious pens for hyenas, lions, bushbuck, duiker and a tame baboon. Other animals include sitatungas, green vervet monkeys, red colobus monkeys, patas monkeys, ground squirrels and a lonely crocodile. There are also pythons and three species of poisonous snake: puff adders, green mambas and cobras. Don't worry about the snakes – they keep well away from the paths.

Over 200 species of birds have been recorded here, making this one of the best reserves in West Africa for bird-watching, particularly in the winter when numerous species migrate from Europe. Stars of the show include the violet-and-green crested turaco, Senegal parrot, lily trotter, pelican, pied kingfisher, amethyst and glossy starling, plus several types of colourful flycatcher and sunbird.

The reserve is open every day from 8 am to 6 pm; allow two hours for the walk. To avoid the heat, most tourist groups go in the early morning or late afternoon. They ruin the tranquillity of the reserve, which is why you should consider going during the middle of the day. It's hotter then but the thick vegetation makes it tolerable. If you've got the time and inclination, take a packed lunch and plenty to drink,

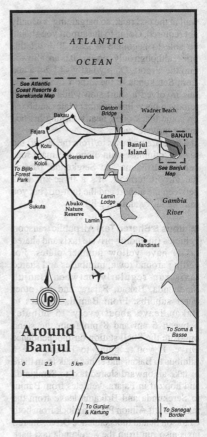

and spend all day in one of the comfortable hides, simply watching at your leisure.

The entry fee during the high season is 15D (10D during the summer rainy season). Leaflets on the trees and animals in the reserve can be bought at the ticket office. To cool off after your walk, there's an expensive refreshment stand at the entrance, or you can visit the small and shady Ningke-Nangka Bar on the other side of the road.

Getting There & Away A private taxi from one of the beach hotels costs about 300D, including two hours waiting time. You can

THE GAMBIA

The Monkeys of Abuko

Most visitors to Abuko find the monkeys fascinating to watch, especially in the morning or evening when they are most active. There are three types of monkey commonly found here: the green (or vervet) monkey, the red colobus monkey and the patas monkey (sometimes called the red patas).

The green monkey has grey underparts and a light green-brown back (which sometimes even looks golden when the sun shines on it), with a black face surrounded by white fur. The tail is long and the same colour as the back, although lighter towards the tip. Perhaps the most recognisable feature is the male's bright blue scrotum. Green monkeys are adaptable, and move around the reserve in troops, feeding either in the woodland savannah or the riverine forest areas. They often sleep in the oil palms that grow between these two vegetation zones. Their diet is mixed: leaves, roots, fruit, insects, birds' eggs and even small birds all get gobbled up.

The red colobus is, not surprisingly, red in colour, usually tending to dark brown on the back and a lighter russet on the underparts, although shades vary between individuals. They are larger than the green monkey, although their head seems small in proportion to the body. The back legs are larger than the front legs; the tale is long and thin, and darker towards the tip. Red colobus monkeys prefer the higher parts of the riverine forest, where they sleep and feed, and can often be seen jumping from branch to branch. They form troops which are generally 'resident' in nature, and do not stray far from their territory. They eat fruit and, occasionally, leaves.

The patas monkey is about the same size as the red colobus, although more slender, with longer legs and tail. They are light brownish-red on the back and top of the head, with very light grey underparts and face. A prominent feature is the dark bushy eyebrows. These monkeys inhabit the savannah parts of the reserve and are more 'terrestrial' than the other two species, feeding on the ground and only using trees for sleeping. They are by nature far-ranging and often go beyond the reserve to raid crops and fruit trees near the surrounding villages.

Even to the untrained eye, it is apparent that the three monkey species of Abuko live in relative harmony and do not compete for territory or food. There are also instances where one species indirectly helps another. For example, when the patas return from a raid their droppings contain seeds. These seeds grow into fruit trees and provide tasty food for the less adventurous colobus.

You may even notice different monkey species deliberately co-operating with each other. Young colobus and green monkeys can be seen playing together, while their adult counterparts help each other groom. The green monkeys are also the most alert and their warning cries in times of danger are recognised by the other species. You may also see single colobus monkeys feeding within a troop of green monkeys, who seem quite happy to have a 'stranger' in their midst. It is apparently not unusual for colobus nearing maturity to leave their own troop in this way (the females seem happy to go, but the males are forced out) and team up with a group of green monkeys for a while before rejoining a new colobus troop to mate. Researchers believe that by joining up with the wide-ranging green monkeys, the usually 'resident' colobus can explore a wider area and meet with other colobus troops some distance from their own. ■

---

avoid this cost by taking a minibus for Brikama from Banjul (7D) or Serekunda (5D; 15 minutes). The reserve entrance is on the main road; ask to be let off here.

Lamin Lodge

Beyond Serekunda, near Lamin village, Lamin Lodge is a unique restaurant built on stilts overlooking a mangrove creek. The surrounding swamps and rice fields are great for bird-watching or simply strolling. The lodge is where tour groups come for their 'Birds and Breakfast' trip (some people more for the breakfast than for the birds!). The restaurant serves African and European meals in the 50 to 80D price range and snacks for around 25D. You can hire small motor boats (150D per hour) or paddle your own canoe for less, and even get a ride back to Banjul for 250D. The owners plan to build a few rooms and even a couple of houseboats. For more information call ☎ 495526.

Lamin Lodge can be reached by private taxi; most drivers know it and will charge about 120D each way. Alternatively, you can take any minibus towards Brikama, get off in Lamin village, then follow the dirt road for about three km. Look for the small sign.

Bijilo Forest Park

This small reserve is on the coast at Kololi, near the Senegambia Hotel, and easy to reach by private taxi, minibus from Serekunda or hired bike. You follow a 4.5-km footpath through the forest to see monkeys and numerous birds. On weekdays a guide is available. Entrance is 15D, and the reserve should be supported as it helps prevent more hotel development down the coast.

The South Coast

The Gambia's southern coastline, between the resorts of Kololi and the border with Senegal, is only about 30 km long, but remains surprisingly seldom-visited.

GUNJUR

Gunjur is a fishing village, about 15 km south-west of Brikama, a long way in *feel*, if not in actual distance, from the touristy areas around Banjul. The beach is large, but sun-bathing seems inappropriate here as there's a lot of activity: boats going in and out, nets being mended and fish being gutted. This is a place to sit down quietly and just watch what's going on. Keep your camera out of sight to avoid upsetting the locals.

For a place to stay, try *Bayo Kunda Camp*, a locally run enterprise on the beach about two km south of Gunjur village centre. Clean rooms cost 100D per person, with breakfast. Other meals are available, but you'll need to order them in advance. To get here, there's usually at least one bush taxi per day to/from Brikama. There may even be a vehicle running down the coast road from Serekunda.

KARTUNG

This sleepy village is about eight km south of Gunjur, just north of the border between The Gambia and Senegal. You can cross the border here and, if you're not in a rush, this can be an interesting way to go to/from Casamance, travelling the small dirt roads that run along the coast. For a place to stay (likely due to transport connections) there's a basic *guesthouse* here which also serves food. The beach is big and deserted, however, sun-bathing in view of the villagers is considered bad form. If you head north up the beach a small way, it's easy enough to find seclusion. You can reach Kartung by bush taxi from Brikama via Gunjur, or from Kafountine in Senegal.

The Interior

JUFFURE, ALBREDA & JAMES ISLAND

Juffure is a small village that Alex Haley, the African-American writer, made famous with his novel *Roots*, in which he describes how Kunta Kinte, his great-great-grandfather, was captured as a slave some 200 years ago. Today Juffure is a tourist trap, as it's easily reached from Banjul, although it's not as busy as it was in the 1980s when Haley's book was still fresh. Critics have pointed out (quite reasonably) that Kinte is a common Senegambian family name, and even Juffure is not an unusual name for a village, and although the story of Alex Haley's ancestor may well be true, it's exceedingly unlikely that he actually came from here. In reality, Juffure is no different or any more interesting than other traditional villages, and some people who have travelled elsewhere in The Gambia or Africa are disappointed with it.

If you do decide to visit, Juffure's ageing chief *(alkalo)* will tell you about the history of the village followed by a request for a small donation. Many others will also ask for hand-outs. Binta Kinte, an old lady who purports to be a direct descendant of Kunta Kinte, will ask for about 15D to let you come inside her compound and talk. You'll also be offered a tour to see Kunta Kinte's own compound, and the ruins of the slave trading station. If you refuse to take the tour, local youths will give you a hard time.

Near Juffure is **Fort Albreda** and **Fort James** (for details see History in the earlier Facts about the Country section). Fort James can be reached by dugout canoe for about 100D return (an hour each way). Some people find this disappointing too, because all that remains are some walls, arches and an old cannon, although the river trip itself can be interesting.

Getting There & Away

Juffure and Albreda are on the north side of the Gambia River, about 25 km upstream from Barra. To get here you can take a tour organised by one of the companies listed in the earlier Tours section: a day trip costs around UK£30. If you want to go independently, take the ferry from Banjul across to Barra, dodge the touts who will try to get you into a private taxi, and find a shared taxi to Juffure which should cost about 10D per person. (To make it there and back in one day, you'll have to catch the first ferry at 8 am.) A third option, if you have lots of money to spare, is to hire a motorised canoe to take you directly from Banjul.

TENDABA CAMP

Tendaba Camp is on the southern bank of the Gambia River, 165 km upstream from Banjul and 35 km west of Soma and Mansa Konko. It was the country's first inland tourist hotel, constructed to look like an African village, with traditional-style huts plus a restaurant, bar and swimming pool. There are sometimes local dance shows. Most of the clients staying here are on short trips organised by the big hotels in Banjul. One traveller wrote to say they enjoyed Tendaba 'although it isn't very authentic (whatever that means) – like a slice of Fajara teleported into the bush'.

Several tour companies run two-day trips to Tendaba starting at around 850D which includes transport, room, food and side trips. If you make your own arrangements, it costs 140D per person to stay here plus 35D for breakfast, about 50D for lunch and 90D for a buffet dinner.

The side trips are Tendaba's major attraction. You can go to the nearby West Kiang National Park and to local African villages by Land Rover, motor boat or dugout canoe. Bird-watching in this area is excellent.

The camp is about five km north of the main highway, and easy to reach by car. If you're without your own vehicle, buses will drop you at the junction from where you'll probably have to walk.

WEST KIANG NATIONAL PARK

Also called Kiang West, this area of bush and riverine forest on the south bank of the river, some 150 km from Banjul, has not been settled or farmed due to tsetse flies. It's a refuge for bushpig and several species of monkey and antelope, plus of course, many types of bird. The park's status is unclear: you may be allowed to visit independently, but most people stay at Tendaba Camp and reach the park on an organised trip.

SOMA

Soma is a junction town where the main road between Banjul and Basse crosses the Trans-Gambia Highway, and where you change transport if you're heading upcountry (unless you're on a GPTC bus). Going to/from southern Senegal, the Gambian customs and immigration post is also here. Nearby is the market town of Mansa Konko, and the ferry across the Gambia River to Farafenni. A pick-up between Soma and the southern border is 5D or CFA 250, and costs the same between Soma and the ferry. The ferry itself costs 2D or CFA 200. If you get stuck in Soma the *Travellers Lodge* (also called the *BP Motel*), near the petrol station, has dirty rooms for 50D. The *Government Resthouse* in Mansa Konko also charges 50D per person and is reported to be in better condition.

FARAFENNI

Farafenni is on the Trans-Gambia Highway north of the Gambia River. It's a busy little town and a good place to sample upcountry 'urban' life, although it feels more like Senegal than Gambia here: CFA is used more than dalasi, and more French than English is spoken. The market is especially lively on Sundays.

Places to Stay & Eat

Many travellers are fond of *Eddie's Hotel & Bar* (☎ 731259) which has self-contained single/double rooms with fans and nets for

125/250D. Couples can share a single. There's cold beer, meals for about 30D (order at least an hour in advance), and discos at weekends.

For cheaper accommodation, try the *Fantasia Hotel*, one km south of the town, where basic rooms with a fan and shower cost 50D. For cheap food, try the chop houses on the main street where meals start at about 5D.

Getting There & Away

A pick-up or minibus between Farafenni and the northern border (from where you can get onward transport to Dakar) is 2D. Between Farafenni and the ferry it costs 3D or CFA 200. The ferry itself is 2D or CFA 200.

PAKALIBA

This is a small village on the main road between Soma and Georgetown. Nearby is *Sofin Yama Camp* run by the same people who own Jangjang-bureh Camp in Georgetown. It was under renovation in 1994, but facilities and prices are expected to be the same as Jangjangbureh when complete. Phone Samba River Venture (☎ 495526) in Banjul for details.

WASSU STONE CIRCLES

Wassu is on the northern side of the river, about 25 km north-west of Georgetown. Nearby are several stone circles believed to be burial sites constructed about 1200 years ago. Each consists of about 10 to 24 massive, reddish-brown stones between one and 2.5 metres high and weighing several tonnes. Similar structures are found in Guinea and the Sahara, but this is the largest concentration. If possible go on a Monday and visit Wassu's weekly *lumo* (market). If you can't make it there and back in a day, camping is reported to be possible. Regardless, the old caretaker who lives here will ask you to sign the visitors' book and pay 10D.

Getting There & Away

The easiest way to get to Wassu is from Georgetown, by taking a bush taxi along the north side of the river towards Farafenni. The stone circles are about 500 metres north-east of Wassu. In Georgetown, buses which leave every day at 9 am and 2 pm will drop you near the stone circles; they leave from the dock on the north side of the river. The last return bus from Kuntaur passes this point between 5.30 and 6.30 pm. Tours from Banjul or from the camps at Tendaba or Jangjang-bureh also visit the stone circles.

RIVER GAMBIA (BABOON ISLAND) NATIONAL PARK

Beyond Farafenni, the character of the Gambia River changes: mangrove swamps virtually disappear, thick forest grows down to the water's edge, and there are more islands. South of Kuntaur are five such islands, protected as a national park. The largest is Baboon Island, and the park is often known by this name. This is the site of a project that takes chimpanzees from labs, zoos and poachers, and rehabilitates them to live in the wilds. Casual visitors are not allowed, especially since a chimp was stolen in 1992. However, you don't need permission to cruise past the island in a boat from which you may see chimps and monkeys in the trees. In Kuntaur you can hire a boat (several people provide the service). The going rate is about 200D for a five-hour trip, after some bargaining. The police will give you a map showing where you are allowed to go.

GEORGETOWN

Georgetown is on the northern edge of MacCarthy Island in the Gambia River, about 300 km by road from Banjul. The island is 10 km long and 2.5 km wide, covered with fields of rice and groundnuts, with ferries on both sides linking it to either bank.

An important administrative centre during colonial times, Georgetown is now tranquil, with a very pleasant ambience. There's rarely a tourist in sight – unusual for The Gambia – although it is becoming more popular as the several new lodges built in the area try hard to attract customers.

Nearby places to visit are the River Gambia National Park and the Wassu Stone Circles. The single stone circle of Lamin Koto is only one km away, and historians of exploration may want to head for Karantaba village, about 10 km from Georgetown, where an obelisk marks the spot where Mungo Park started on his journey to trace the course of the Niger River.

Places to Stay

The *Government Rest House* charges 50D per person: rooms are clean and quiet and have hot water, and there's even a lounge. For the key, enquire at the police station facing it. For food, ask the caretaker; he'll find someone to cook you a meal. Better value is the friendly *Alakabung Lodge* at the other end of the main street, where a double thatched hut with its own shower and clean shared toilets costs 50D per person. Nearby is *Dreambird Camp* with similar facilities for 100D per person.

On the eastern side of town is the large *Baobolong Camp*, in a pleasant spot near the river, with self-contained chalets for 80D per person.

On the north side of the river, opposite MacCarthy Island, is the peaceful *Jangjangbureh Camp*. Good self-contained bungalows cost 110D per person. River cruises and trips to Wassu are arranged, and canoes can be hired for 75D per hour. For more details ring Samba River Ventures (☎ 495526) in Banjul.

Places to Eat

All the places to stay listed above have restaurants serving reasonable Western and African meals and snacks for 15 to 60D. There are also a few cheap local eating houses in town. If you're self-catering the market is small but has a good selection.

Getting There & Away

MacCarthy Island is reached by ferry from either the south or north bank of the river. The main road between Banjul and Basse does not go directly past the southern ferry, and only the ordinary buses turn off the main road and go to the ferry itself. On the express bus you have to drop at Bansang, and take a bush taxi back to the southern ferry ramp (8D). Crossing on the ferry is free for passengers. On the far side pick-ups take people across the island to Georgetown for 2D. Georgetown can also be reached by the weekly boat from Lamin Lodge near Banjul (see the main Getting Around section).

BASSE SANTA SU

Basse Santa Su, more commonly called Basse, is The Gambia's easternmost town (although there are villages further upstream) and the largest and liveliest of the upcountry settlements. It is also the last major ferry-crossing point. The most interesting section of the town is the waterfront with its many old shops and riverside market, the main hub of activity. If you've come in from Senegal and need to change money, there's a Standard Bank branch in the town and several moneychangers around the market or at the border. The main market day is Thursday.

Places to Stay

The best place is the *Government Rest House*, about two km from the centre, with rooms for 50D a person but no restaurant. In town, the basic but clean *Apollo Hotel* on the main street has singles/doubles from 25/50D with ceiling fans and running water. Or try the *Plaza Hotel* which overlooks the main square, where doubles with fans cost 50D. On the other side of the square is the *Basse Guesthouse* with doubles at 60D. It's in slightly better condition but lacks the ambience of the Plaza. The *Linguere Motel* on the edge of town has clean self-contained doubles for 150D (120D with shared bath). Other possibilities include the clean and quiet but less convenient *Agricultural Rest House* on the far outskirts of town and the new *Jem Hotel* (☎ 668356) near the centre.

Places to Eat

Most of the eating places in Basse are grouped around the centre of town. There are several small tea shacks opposite the taxi park and there's cheap street food in the market, especially on Thursday. The *No 1 Fast Food Restaurant* is somewhat optimistically named, although coffee, egg and bread comes quickly enough and costs 15D. *Ebrima's Restaurant* opposite is marginally cheaper. Other places to try are the *Baubab Restaurant*, under the Basse Guesthouse, and the *No Flie Restaurant* near the police station which serves chicken and chips for 30D or meat and rice for 20D. The *Linguere Motel* has a restaurant, where prices are only slightly higher.

The coldest beers in town are at the endearing *Uncle Peacock's Bar* behind the taxi park, a hang-out for local volunteers.

Getting There & Away

GPTC buses between Banjul and Basse leave throughout the day (see the Banjul Getting There & Away section for departure times from Banjul). From Basse, the express bus leaves at 8 am; the super-express bus at 11 am. You can also get to Basse from Senegal via Tambacounda and Velingara (see this chapter's Getting There & Away section). Don't forget to report to the immigration official at the police station if you come into Basse from Senegal, or if you are leaving The Gambia.

Ghana

If an award were given for the country with the friendliest people in West Africa, Ghana would probably win. One of the best educated peoples in Black Africa at independence, Ghanaians are a proud, open people and they like to do things their way. Accra may not be the most beautiful city in Africa, but it's their city – not a city catering to tourists or Western expatriates. And they like to have fun. Accra and Kumasi on Saturday night are jumping – there's usually a choice of at least four or five live bands. Ghana is, after all, the place where the somewhat passé 'highlife' music got its start. Ghana also has some of the most beautiful fabrics in West Africa; the most well known are the expensive and colourful *kente* cloth made by the Ashanti.

Ghana is the old 'Gold Coast', where Europeans came 500 years ago searching for gold – and found it. Along the coast, you'll see a string of forts and castles that the Europeans left behind. Inside, your spirits will sink when you see how slaves were branded with hot irons, then crammed into wet dungeons and chained, waiting to be shipped to the New World.

Ghana also has one of the real 'in' spots in West Africa – Dixcove – where you can sleep on one of the most beautiful beaches in West Africa, or in one of the old forts, for a song, and eat giant crayfish and shrimp for the price of a cheap beer. Those travelling on the cheap come away raving about Ghana. Chances are you will too.

Facts about the Country

HISTORY

There is evidence of settlements along the Ghanaian coast dating back 30,000 to 40,000 years, but according to one widely held theory which today is largely discounted, the ancestors of today's Ghanaians may have

REPUBLIC OF GHANA

Area: 238,305 sq km
Population: 17 million
Population Growth Rate: 3.2%
Capital: Accra
Head of State: Flight Lt Jerry Rawlings
Official Language: English
Currency: Cedi
Exchange Rate: C 940 = US$1
Per Capita GNP: US$420
Inflation: 10%
Time: GMT/UTC

migrated from the north, starting around the 12th century, after the fall of the Empire of Ghana. This was a kingdom to the north-west which incorporated parts of Mali, Mauritania and Senegal and was in no way related to present-day Ghana.

The Portuguese arrived in the late 15th century looking for gold. They found enough golden artefacts among the Ashanti and other tribes to justify building several forts along the coast, starting in 1482. Gold was shipped back to Europe as ingots. By the 17th century, the currency had become gold-based.

The real wealth, however, turned out to be in slaves. It was the fortunes earned in the

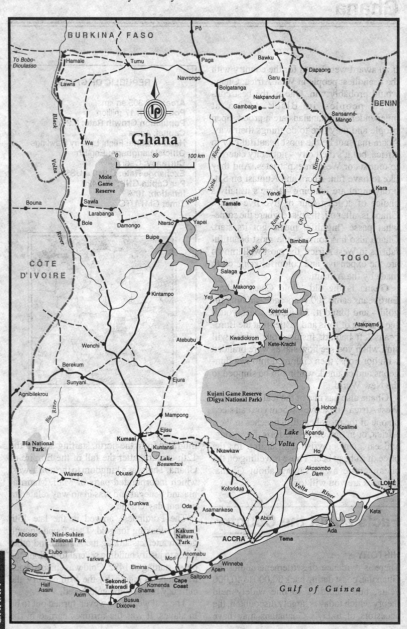

Ghana

0   50   100 km

Gulf of Guinea

Suggested Itineraries

Ghana's capital, **Accra**, is one of the liveliest cities along the West African coast, so plan on staying at least a few days there, checking out the museum, arts centre, the major markets and the city's fabulous nightlife, which is as lively as you'll find anywhere in West Africa. Potential day trips include ones to the university at **Legon**, the **Aburi Gardens** and **Akosombo Dam**, but you also have the option of staying overnight at the latter two. Then, you'll want to head either west along the coast or north towards **Kumasi**. Touring many of the various **forts** and fishing villages along the coast can easily take a week or more, especially if you take in the new **Kakum Nature Park** north of Cape Coast. Beach lovers should add a few days.

From **Takoradi** you could take the over-night train to Kumasi. The city has several points of interest including a fabulous arts centre and a huge market, but the surrounding area is just as interesting, so count on a few days for that too. The majority of travellers never make it to the far north except to visit **Mole Game Reserve**, which requires at least two days to see. However, if you're looking for true adventure, the far north is probably the best area to visit. ■

slave trade that were to attract the Dutch, British and Danes in the late 16th century. During the next 250 years, all four nations competed fiercely for this trade, building forts and capturing those of their rivals. The average yearly 'take' in slaves was 10,000. When it all ended in the 19th century, they left 76 forts and castles along the Gold Coast, an average of one every six km.

After slavery was outlawed in the early 19th century, the British took over the forts to use as customs posts along the coast, and they signed treaties with many of the coastal chiefs. They also stayed to make sure that no one revived the slave trade. The Ashanti, for example, profited handsomely from it. Kumasi, the Ashanti capital city, had many of the trappings of a European city, even employing Europeans in the late 19th century as military trainers and economic advisors. The Ashanti weren't about to give this up, so the British attacked Kumasi in 1873. It took the British well over a year to sack the city, and immediately afterwards they declared the area a crown colony.

Ashanti resistance continued until 1900. When the British governor demanded the Ashanti's golden stool – the equivalent of asking for the golden ark – the Ashanti unsuccessfully attacked the British fort at Kumasi, but the city was almost totally destroyed in the process. You can see many photographs of this famous war in the Armed Forces Museum in Kumasi.

Colonial Period

The British set out to make the Gold Coast a showcase. It was to be an African country, not dominated by outsiders. So they allowed few Europeans to settle or even be employed there. The British administrators never numbered over 4000.

Cocoa soon became the backbone of the economy, and in the 1920s, the colony's most prosperous decade ever, the Gold Coast overtook Equatorial Guinea as the world's leading producer. Gold was the only ore exported – only about UK£20,000 worth in 1900. To increase production, the British built railroads in all directions from Sekondi, the sole commercial port. Kumasi, the cocoa and timber centre, was linked to Sekondi in 1903. By WW I, cocoa, gold and timber made the Gold Coast the most prosperous colony in Africa. By independence, the Gold Coast was also the world's leading producer of manganese, as well as exporting diamonds and bauxite. It also had the best schools and the best civil service in Africa, a cadre of enlightened lawyers, and a thriving press.

Until 1948, when the British established University College of the Gold Coast at Legon, now the University of Ghana, they sent Africans abroad for advanced study. One of these students was Kwame Nkrumah, who spent from 1935 to 1945 in the USA studying and teaching at Lincoln University in Pennsylvania. There he read and was influenced by Black literature and Marxist writings.

GHANA

In 1947, Nkrumah broke away from the country's leading political party, the United Gold Coast Convention, which advocated independence within 'the shortest possible time', and formed the Convention People's Party (CPP) aimed at the common person, with the slogan 'Self Government Now'. Two years later he called a general strike. The British responded by putting him in prison. While he was there, the CPP won the general elections of 1951. The British were so impressed by how efficiently the CPP had gained votes despite Nkrumah's absence, that they released him and asked him to form a government.

Independence

Nkrumah agreed to abandon the party's slogan in order to work with the colonial administrators, thereby gaining their confidence and enabling him to learn the ins and outs of government. In 1957, the strategy paid off when Britain granted independence. Nkrumah cast aside the name Gold Coast in favour of that of the first great empire in West Africa – Ghana – even though the country had only a tenuous connection with that kingdom. For Africa, it was a momentous occasion: Ghana was the first Black African country to gain independence. For Ghana, it was the beginning of an economic nightmare, and 25 years of almost continuous decline followed.

Nkrumah borrowed heavily to finance grandiose schemes. Many of his projects were wasteful – US$16 million was spent on a conference centre to host a single meeting of the Organisation of African Unity (OAU). At independence, Ghana had almost half a billion US dollars in foreign-exchange reserves; by 1966, the country was a billion dollars in debt. World prices for cocoa didn't help matters; they went tumbling from UK£247 a tonne at independence to below UK£100 a tonne by 1966.

Nkrumah's most grandiose project, though, was Akosombo Dam, to be financed by the World Bank, other international banks and Valco, a US aluminium company. Although Ghana was to lose about 10,000 sq km of land to be covered by Lake Volta,

Nkrumah desperately wanted the prestige from the project; Valco wanted the dam to fuel its plants for smelting bauxite. Revenue from the projected sale of electricity was to permit Ghana to electrify its rural areas and finance the irrigation of the Accra plains, Ghana's potential breadbasket. However, in accepting Valco's offer of the dam in return for the right to all the electricity it needed, virtually at cost, Nkrumah short-changed his country. With a steadily deteriorating economy, the projected private sector demand never materialised, and the electrification and irrigation programmes were shelved for over a decade.

To a continent of new nations desperate for political unity, Nkrumah was a hero. Handsome, charismatic and articulate, he espoused the cause of African unity on every occasion. He even sent soldiers off to the Congo to help keep the peace, though he could hardly afford it. When Nkrumah talked, people and nations listened. At home, however, he became ruthless. Within a year following independence, Ghana had become virtually a one-party state. In 1958, he had approved a law providing for up to five years detention without trial or appeal. Four years later, an estimated 2000 to 3000 people were held in jail without trial. In 1962, a coup attempt led to a wide-scale purge.

Nkrumah alienated the business community by turning over a large portion of the economy to state-run enterprises, very few of which became profitable. He alienated the West by his never-ending denunciation of imperialism and neocolonialism, the heavy accumulation of debts, and the rapid growth of commercial ties with the Soviet Bloc. Perhaps worst of all, he alienated Ghana's army by setting up a private army answerable to him alone. The public, which appreciated the significant improvements in infrastructure and social services, became disillusioned by conspicuous corruption among the party's leaders. In 1964, there were food shortages for the first time ever.

It was all too much. In 1966, while the president was on a mission to Hanoi, the army staged a coup. There was rejoicing in

Ghana. Exiled to Guinea, Nkrumah died of cancer six years later.

The Great Decline

Between 1966 and 1981, Ghana suffered through six governments, all corrupt or incompetent except for one which lasted three months.

Probably no ruler was worse than Colonel Acheampong, who 'redeemed' the country in 1972, and thereafter dissolved parliament. He considered a previous devaluation of the cedi an affront to the country's honour, and did the unheard of – he revalued the currency upward by 44%, even though the currency was already grossly overvalued.

Acheampong had a simple solution to all of Ghana's problems – print money. In 1976 alone, he increased the cedis in circulation by 80%. Inflation reached 12% a month. Prices went up every week. When he left office, the cedi was overvalued by 20 times the market value. Travellers, unless they changed money on the black market, had to pay the equivalent of US$1.50 for an orange. Little wonder they began to avoid Ghana.

As the cedi became increasingly worthless, more and more cocoa – up to 50,000 tonnes a year – was smuggled across the borders to Togo and Côte d'Ivoire. Meanwhile, production was falling, from 430,000 tonnes in 1965 to 265,000 tonnes in 1978. Staple goods became scarce. Everybody in those days periodically took a bus to Lomé (Togo) to buy essentials like detergent, oil and milk. At the airport in Accra, custom officials inspecting the suitcases of passengers coming from London often found them 100% filled with detergent.

In 1978 the army requested Acheampong to step down. The military stayed in power, however, continuing its pilferage while promising new elections. Two weeks before the promised elections, due in 1979, a group of young military officers led by Flight Lieutenant Jerry Rawlings, not content to let their corrupt military bosses retire in a state of luxury, staged a coup. The elections proceeded as planned and a new president was elected. Before turning over the government,

the coup leaders, relenting to pressure from the lower ranks, publicly executed three former heads of state, among them Acheampong, who was accused of embezzling US$100 million in foreign accounts. In addition, hundreds of other officers and business people were tried and convicted by impromptu 'peoples' courts and given long sentences. Then, after only three months in power, Rawlings bowed out as he had promised – to everyone's amazement.

Adopting very conservative economic policies and austerity measures, the new president was unable to arrest the economy's downward spiral. Rawlings on the other hand remained enormously popular with the people with his warnings of the need for vigilance against corruption. At the end of 1981, after the new leadership had demonstrated its inability to halt economic decline, Rawlings staged another coup. He became the only modern-day African ruler to gain power a second time after having previously given it up. This time he stayed.

The Rawlings Era

Rawlings did the seemingly impossible. By 1986, articles in Western newspapers were appearing with titles such as 'Ghana: Black Africa's Economic Showcase'. Since 1983, the economy has grown by more than 5% a year in real terms, the highest growth rate in Africa, while inflation has gone down from 122% in 1983 to 25% in 1990. Between 1983 and 1990, export earnings averaged 10% annual increases and manufacturing went from 3.6% of GDP to over 10%. Ghana now exports corn to Togo, Niger and Guinea.

What did Rawlings do? He did exactly what the International Monetary Fund (IMF) and the World Bank said he should. Between late 1983 and mid-1986, he devalued the currency 33-fold; now the exchange rate floats. He also raised payments to cocoa farmers fourfold, laid off 28,000 civil servants in one year alone, removed price controls on all but 23 essential commodities, and started getting rid of some of the unprofitable state enterprises. The government also renegotiated its agreement with Valco, raising electricity rates by 200%. In return, the World Bank and the IMF have given some hefty loans. By 1988, the government budget was in surplus.

The changes have been visible, particularly in infrastructure. Major new hotels and other buildings have been constructed, the government has rebuilt roads from one end of the land to the other, telecommunications and electricity cover the country, and ports have been rebuilt. In addition, farmers have replanted cocoa trees and reclaimed abandoned farms. Most noticeably, consumer goods are everywhere.

Not everything has been a success, however. Many companies in the industrial area in Accra, for example, have had to curtail or stop production because they can't compete with the avalanche of foreign goods descending on Ghana.

Rawlings is not only a man with guts – he is a maverick. Instead of fostering the cult of personality, he ordered all pictures of him removed from public places. He rides around in a jeep, not a limousine. In other ways, he's not so different. He tolerates little dissent – when newspapers are even mildly critical, he closes them down. Those caught for corruption, like two Ghanaians and a Lebanese charged in 1985 with embezzling US$1.3 million, get the firing squad. In a more recent incident, a top football star, Sarfo Gyambi, refused to shake Rawlings' hand and was fined C 25,000 for 'breach of protocol'.

One might think that with Ghana's free-market revolution, Rawlings would be the darling of the West. He isn't. The problem is his leftist politics. When Libya's Gaddafi speaks, Rawlings applauds. When the USA votes one way in the UN, Rawlings votes the other. When the West talks about human rights, Rawlings talks about anti-imperialism. More importantly, he has lots of Ghanaian political enemies. During his first decade in office, there was a major coup attempt about every other year.

Ghana Today

Rawlings was one of the last West African leaders to submit himself to the polls. In the

late 1980s he introduced popularly elected district assemblies, claiming they were a better basis for genuine grass-roots democracy than a multiparty system. In reality, these were merely an imposition from above. In 1990 he made a further small concession by allowing multiparty advocates to hold press conferences lambasting his party's position, which is that Ghanaians don't want many political parties. However, with support for multiparty government gathering across the board, Rawlings in late 1991 acceded to elections within a year.

Following a referendum approving a new constitution in early 1992, political parties were given complete freedom to organise. The public feuding amongst rival groups played directly into Rawlings' hands. To keep the suspense up, Rawlings' party, the National Defence Council (NDC), waited until only a few weeks before the presidential elections to put forward Rawlings as their candidate. The main challenge came from the New Patriotic Party (NPP) led by professor Albert Boahen. Other parties included the People's National Convention (PNC), the National Independence Party (NIP) and the National Convention Party (NCP). Boahen had a substantial following but failed to form an opposition coalition. As a result, he lost the elections to Rawlings by a wide margin: 59% to 39% on a national turnout of 48% of the electorate.

Although the election was deemed fair by international observers, Boahen refused to accept the results and the NPP boycotted the parliamentary elections the following month. Consequently only 29% of the electorate bothered to vote and the NDC won in a landslide, collecting all but 11 of the 200 seats. This was not exactly what Rawlings wanted, however, as it seemed to add legitimacy to the opposition's claim that the system under the NDC was democratic in name only. Regardless, the elections left Rawlings' government in a stronger position than before, with a reasonable semblance of being democratic.

Since then, the NPP and other parties are sorry they boycotted the elections because it has put them out of the political debate until the next elections, resulting in a relatively calm political scene. Ethnic clashes in the far north-east in early 1994 between Konkombas, settlers from Togo, and Nanumbas resulted in over 1000 dead. That problem has subsided, however, leaving the economy to continue growing fast by sub-Saharan Africa standards.

GEOGRAPHY

Ghana is about the size of the UK, and relatively flat. The dry coastal region consists mostly of low-lying scrubland and plains. Starting 20 to 30 km inland, thick rainforests take over and continue to the northern third of the country, a plateau area of about 500 metres elevation which is predominantly savannah and open woodland – ideal for cotton. Most of the cacao, which is refined into cocoa, is grown in the central and southern area, home of the Ashanti, who have always cultivated it.

Except for some low mountains in the eastern Volta region, Ghana has no mountains to break up the landscape. Instead, it has Lake Volta – the world's largest artificial lake, about twice the size of Luxembourg. It's fed from Burkina Faso by the Black Volta and White Volta rivers.

CLIMATE

Ghana has three rainfall zones. Along the coast including Accra, the rainfall is light, the season being April to June and October. In the rainforests, the rains become heavier and last longer. In the north, the weather becomes drier again, with one rainy season – May to September.

GOVERNMENT

After over two and half decades, military rule finally ended with the inauguration of the Fourth Republic on 9 January 1993. This was preceded by the adoption of a new constitution in April 1992, allowing political parties complete freedom to organise. Under the constitution, the government is headed by an elected president and an elected 200-member parliament. Parliament is currently dominated by Rawlings' party, the NDC, which holds 189 seats. The rest are held by the NCP and independents. New presidential and parliamentary elections are scheduled for 1996, and Rawlings has promised to compile a new voters' register in time for it.

ECONOMY

Gold has recently replaced cocoa as the country's leading export. In a typical year, they both earn over US$300 million. Ghana is the world's second-largest producer of cocoa, after Côte d'Ivoire, but the quality of Ghanaian cocoa is considered to be superior. Prices in recent years have not been favourable, however, so production is not increasing. One of the main stimulants for economic growth has been the expansion of the national electricity grid. Since Rawlings

---

The Environment

Overgrazing by livestock (due to increased animal populations in response to improvements in water availability), coupled with the expansion of land under cultivation, is decreasing vegetation all over the country. This process is causing progressively larger areas of the northern savannah to resemble the arid lands to the north. In the south, savannah is encroaching on areas which were previously forested. Cacao is a forest-zone crop and growing it in cleared forests has contributed to this process in the central zone. The timber and mining industries have also helped devastate the forests, in part as a result of their cutting and clearing practices. There are no longer any productive forests outside of government reserves.

On the brighter side, farmers and fisher people in the north who evacuated the banks of Ghana's Sissili and Kulpawn rivers are now returning because the World Health Organisation has controlled the humpback black fly which causes river blindness. The amazingly successful US$340-million project has essentially eliminated new cases of river blindness not only in Ghana but also in Burkina Faso, Mali, Niger, Benin, Togo and Côte d'Ivoire. ■

came to office in 1981, access to electricity nationwide has expanded fourfold, from 12% to around 50% today. After almost 30 years, all district capitals have been connected to the national grid from Akosombo.

The country's rural water supply and sanitation programme are now in full swing and are expected to increase access to drinkable water in the rural areas from around 57% to 75% when completed in 1996. In all of Africa, only Egypt and The Gambia have higher percentages in this area. Roads are continuing to be improved. To strengthen the private sector, the government finally abolished an old law forbidding manufacturers from setting free-market prices for their goods. State-owned enterprises are also being sold; among those advertised for divesture are Ashanti Goldfields (the largest gold mine in Ghana), Kumasi Brewery and several major banks. However, what may have the most major long-term impact is the country's new stock exchange. International mutual funds are beginning to take a keen interest in Ghana. If the economy continues to grow and the political situation remains calm, foreign capital could begin to flow in, potentially giving birth to an African tiger.

POPULATION & PEOPLE

Ghana's population of 17 million makes it one of the more densely populated countries in West Africa. Some 44% of the people are Akan, which includes the Ashanti (also spelled Asante) whose heartland is around Kumasi. Another 16% are Mole-Dagbani, mainly in the north, 13% are Ewé, mainly in the east, followed by the Ga (8%) in the south around Accra, and various other tribes, including the Guan, the Gurma and, in the north, the Gonja and the Dagomba.

Because of fairly enlightened government policies over the decades, the divisive tendencies which might be expected in a country with 60 different languages have not occurred. Rather, most Ghanaians have a strong national consciousness which Nkrumah encouraged.

Because they had so much gold and profited from the slave trade, the Ashanti developed one of the richest and most famous civilisations in Africa. Their fame in pre-colonial days came largely from the legendary splendour and wealth of their rulers; today it also comes from their craft work, in particular their kente cloth, fertility dolls, stools and other wooden carvings.

When the first Europeans arrived, they found the Ashanti's use of gold far exceeded anything elsewhere in West Africa. A portion of all the gold went to adorn the ruling group. The king's stool, for example, was entirely cased in gold and displayed under a splendid umbrella, with drums, horns and other adornments also cased in gold. The king (Ashantihene) was covered in gold; his bracelets were a mixture of gold and beads and his fingers were covered with gold rings. He wore a necklace of gold cockspur shells and a silk cord was draped over his shoulders, suspending three ornaments cased in gold. His ankles had a string of gold ornaments around them, and his sandals were embossed with small golden ornaments as well. So be on the lookout for Ashanti festivals or other special occasions; you might get to see some of this splendid regalia.

CULTURE

One of the more interesting aspect of Ghanaian culture is that of the clan. A clan includes all people who hark back to a common founding ancestor, and is headed by a chief. Chiefs do not have absolute power; those

Fertility
doll

GHANA

who have committed crimes can be deposed by the council of elders and replaced by another member. Moreover, unlike in European royal families, the eldest sons never have any specific right to succession because in every lineage there are several possible candidates, and it's up to the elders to decide who is best fit to lead.

Clan organisations of the Akan are unique. They are different from those of other ethnic groups in two basic ways. First, filiation within the clan, or *abusua*, is via the women, not via the men. In the election of a new chief, for example, candidates are chosen not from the deceased chief's sons but from amongst the mother's relatives. Thus, the queen mothers enjoy a special status in the community and retain a great influence over the choice of the pretender to the stool. The father's influence is through his spirit; in the view of the Akan, while people get their blood from their mothers, their spirits come from their fathers. Alongside the abusua therefore, a second clan grouping, the *ntoro*, establishes filiation via the spirit, from the father back to the initial founder.

Second, all Akan clans are members of confederations of villages and towns whose chiefs, for political reasons, recognise the authority of a paramount chief and form amongst themselves a council of subchiefs to assist and advise him. As a result, all Akan people belong both to one of eight abusua, such as the Oyoko, and to one of eight recognised ntoro. One result of these confederations is that they give weight to the

---

The Juju Priest

By tradition, spirits are thought to be everywhere in West Africa, causing the fortunes and misfortunes of everyday Africans. Only the fetish, or juju, priest can hold back the tide of spirits. An intermediary between the deities and mortals, the juju priest can help his patients by conjuring up a favourite god to consult on future events and by warding off evil spirits, bad health, failed crops, even impotence. Part doctor, part psychic, the juju practitioner does this with the aid of herbal medicine, magic fetishes, charms and positive thinking. A wide array of medicinal plants, roots and barks are all used for everything from diarrhoea to cuts and bruises and muscle pains. Even more important, perhaps, are the fetish, or juju. In animist belief, spirits embody and convey influence through fetishes. Just about anything can be a fetish so long as it is imbued with the spirits. A fetish can be as large as a tree or as small as a pin but it must have magical powers. Skulls, antelope horns, pieces of leopard skin and bones of horses, pigs, monkeys, crocodiles, hyenas, even lions, are all frequently used. One of the juju priest's duties is to preside over these items.

The job of being a fetish priest is often passed down from one generation to another. While the calling can happen at any time, perhaps causing the person to fall down and go into a trance, would-be priests must first learn their trade, undergoing at least several years of training in the art of healing and the worship of gods. The following is a description of how some priests operate. The priest sits on a stool in a coloured robe and holds a regal staff. A young man enters, falling prostrate before the priest, then several more people enter and do the same. A serious illness has occurred in the family. The lesser priests begin to drum and chant, then start dancing in earnest, eventually going into a frenzy. They jump and gyrate, arms flailing and bodies flopping like marionettes. The head priest joins in and there's dancing around him in a circle. Things ebb a bit. The priest receives gifts, including gin, which he drinks. After several rounds, the music, chanting and wild dancing resume, sometimes well into the night. Eventually, the people make their way home, but not without offering more gifts – alcohol, chickens, cats, dogs, money and the like are all accepted.

If you're interested in witnessing a session, ask around any fetish market for where to find a priest. The largest fetish market in West Africa is said to be in Akodessewa, Togo. In Accra, ask around for Torgbui (chief fetish priest) Mawutayo, better known by the unlikely name of '41 No1', or Torgbui Afatsawo Aheaku Kukubor, another well-known fetish priest who lives about 18 km outside of Accra. ∎

traditional Akan rulers in their dealings with the government.

RELIGION

Christians outnumber Muslims about two to one, with the Muslims concentrated mostly in the north and the Christians in the south. The rest of the people (about 35%) practise traditional ancestral religions. The ancestors, who are invisible but constantly present, ensure vital protection for the clan, and one must perform certain rites to ensure that the ancestors enjoy a proper existence in the afterlife. Ancestors remain the true owners of land and need to be placated before it can be sold.

LANGUAGE

English is the official language. You'll hear Ga (gah) around Accra and Ewé (ev-vay) in the east as well as in Accra. The most widely spoken language, however, is Twi (chwee), the language of the Ashanti (which is part of a larger language group called Akan) and the Fanti; it's spoken all over Ghana, particularly in the southern half.

Expressions in Ga

Good morning/ good evening.	meeng-gah-bou
How are you?	toy-yah-tain?
I'm fine.	ee-oh-joh-bahn
What's your name?	toh-cho-boh-tain?
My name is...	ah-cho-mee...
Thank you.	oh-gee-wah-dong
Goodbye.	bye-bye

Expressions in Twi

Good morning.	mah-CHEENG
Good evening.	MAH-joe
How are you?	AY-tah-sein?
I'm fine.	AY-yah
Are you going to...?	yah-coh...?
Let's go.	YEN-coh
Safe journey.	nan-tee yee-yay
Thank you.	may-DAH-say
Goodbye.	mah-KROW

Facts for the Visitor

VISAS & EMBASSIES
Ghana Visas

Visas are required by all travellers and are usually valid for three months, permitting at least a one-month stay. In London, the Ghanaian high commission requires UK£15 and four photos and takes two days to process visas. Multiple-entry visas are available to those who have previously travelled to Ghana. In Washington, the Ghanaian embassy requires four photos, a copy of your round-trip ticket and US$20 (US$50 for a multiple-entry visa). Visas take three days to process and are good for visits of 30 days.

Ghana has embassies in eight West African countries but most of them take two or three days to issue visas. Visas cost CFA 10,000 in Togo and CFA 14,000 in Benin.

The Ghanaian embassy in Burkina Faso is open every day of the week, takes two days to issue visas and, reportedly, has reduced the fee to CFA 6000. It has been known, however, to refuse visas to travellers who put down as their place of residence a country with a Ghanaian embassy. Visas are not issued at the borders, all of which close promptly at 6 pm.

In years past, it was necessary to register with immigration upon arrival in Accra but this is no longer required for stays of 14 days or less. This exemption period may be extended, so ask around. The process takes five minutes and requires no money or photos. Registration is at the 3rd-floor immigration branch office next door to, and east of, the Ministry of Interior on Kinbu Rd, north-west of Independence Square.

Visa Extensions

Getting visa extensions is time consuming; re-entry permits even more so. They are processed at immigration's head office (☎ 223243/1047) south-west of Sankara Circle. You'll need two B&W passport photos, C 1000 (more if your visa has already expired), a currency declaration form if you received one upon entering, and a typed letter explaining why you want to stay longer. Go to the post office in the city centre to get letters typed. The process takes about a week and usually involves no fuss.

Ghanaian Embassies

Belgium 7 General Wahisin Iaan, Brussels B-1030 (☎ (02) 705-82-20)

France 8 villa Said, 75116 Paris (☎ (1) 45-00-09-50)

Germany Rheinalle 58, 53173 Bonn (☎ (0228) 35-20-11/3)

UK (high commission) 104 Highgate Hill, London N6 5HE (☎ (0181) 342-8686)

USA 3512 International Drive, NW, Washington, DC 20008 (☎ (202) 686-4520)

Ghana also has embassies in Abidjan, Addis Ababa, Algiers, Berlin, Berne, Brasilia, Cairo, Conakry, Copenhagen, Cotonou, Freetown, Harare, Hoofdorp, Lagos, Lomé, Monrovia, Moscow, New Delhi, Ottawa, Ouaga, Prague, Rome, Riyadh, Sofia and Tokyo.

Other African Visas

Burkina Faso The embassy is open weekdays from 8 am to 2 pm and gives same-day or 24-hour service. You'll need three photos and CFA 20,000 or US$40 (no cedis) for three-month visas.

Benin The embassy is open weekdays from 8 am to 3 pm. Two-day transit visas cost C 2000; issued in 24 to 48 hours (less if you're pressed for time).

Côte d'Ivoire Open weekdays from 8 am to 1.30 pm, the embassy issues visas in 48 hours (two photos and C 18,000 required). Australians and New Zealanders must wait from one to two weeks for a telex to go to Abidjan before getting a visa (consider getting one from the French embassy in Lomé). Visas issued in Accra are normally valid for 15 days.

Guinea Open weekdays from 8 am to 2 pm (1 pm on Fridays) the embassy issues visas in 24 to 48 hours. The receptionist may tell you that you need US$40 or CFA 20,000 (no cedis), three photos and a typed letter of introduction from your embassy. One traveller reported, however, that it was US$10, not US$40, so check.

Liberia The embassy is open from 9 am to 2 pm on Monday, Wednesday and Friday. Single/double-entry three-month visas cost C 8000/12,000. Two photos required; five days to process.

Mali The embassy is open weekdays from 7.30 am to 3 pm; same-day service. Two photos and US$20 (no cedis) required; valid for 15 days (persist and you may get a one-month visa).

Niger The embassy, open weekdays from 7.30 am to 2 pm, requires four photos and issues visas the same day; CFA 15,000 plus 2000 cedis.

Nigeria The embassy is open weekdays from 8 am to 3 pm; two to three days to issue. Visas are issued only to residents (Ghanaian or expatriate) but if you're from a country without a Nigerian embassy, you still may get one. Two photos required. The cost depends on your nationality: free for Americans, C 8030 for New Zealanders and C 20,180 for Britons.

Togo Open weekdays from 7.30 am to 2 pm and 3 to 4.30 pm, the embassy requires three photos and C 3000; it takes one to three days to issue 15-day visas. If the Ghana/Togo border is closed, you'll need a *laissez passer* request from your embassy approved by the Togo embassy to cross into Togo.

Other Countries For visas to The Gambia, Kenya and other Commonwealth countries without high commissions in Accra, go to the Ghana Immigration Service at Immigration Headquarters. From Sankara Circle it's one block south on Independence Ave and 100 metres west. It's open weekdays from 8.30 am to noon and 2 to 4.30 pm and requires C 7500, two photos and a typed letter of request directed to Ghana Immigration Service, Immigration Headquarters, Private Mail Bag, Ministries Post Office, Accra. The process takes a week.

Foreign Embassies

See the Accra Information section for details. If asked, the Canadian embassy will represent Australians.

DOCUMENTS

You'll need a passport with a Ghanaian visa and an International Vaccination Certificate with proof of having received a yellow fever vaccination within the past 10 years and, sometimes (when there's a cholera outbreak), a cholera shot.

You should carry your passport at all times. In town, carry the passport or at least a photocopy of it as police occasionally ask travellers for their papers. In theory, you must produce proof of onward/return transport, but in practice the rule is rarely enforced.

CUSTOMS

Upon entering and leaving, you will almost certainly be asked by customs officials to show your money; they may also search you. Importing or exporting more than C 500 is illegal. There are no limits on importing foreign currency.

GHANA

Be sure to get a currency declaration form for recording official transactions. Without this form, you may be hassled by customs officials when you leave. However, they sometimes do not ask to see the declaration form. Stamps showing at least several official exchanges are usually enough to satisfy them. At Accra Airport, on the other hand, customs officials will usually frisk you, so hiding money can be risky.

Travellers with video cameras or portable computers are required to pay a refundable deposit of 17.5% of their value upon entry into Ghana. However, this rule may be relaxed, so ask around. To receive the refund you must apply to the customs and excise office in central Accra two days before departure.

MONEY

CFA 1000	=	C 1800
UK£1	=	C 1400
US$1	=	C 940

The unit of currency is the cedi (cee-dee). For travellers' cheques and small bills, exchange rates are less favourable – typically about 5% less – than for cash in large denominations. The dollar follows inflation so expect prices to be somewhat higher again. The best currencies to bring are US dollars, German marks, UK pounds and French francs; other currencies, including the Canadian dollar and Japanese yen, exchange at extremely unfavourable rates.

In the early 1980s, Ghana was one of the most expensive countries in Africa, but the country now has a floating exchange rate, so prices are reasonable. The currency is floated on a weekly basis. Even many expensive hotels now accept payment in cedis. Major credit cards are also widely accepted.

Since 1988 Ghana has had privately operated foreign exchange bureaus; these 'Forex' are scattered all over Accra and the country. They usually offer a much better rate than the banks and about as good a rate as the black market.

Moneychangers hang around Makola market, the Arts Centre and near the corner of Zongo Lane and Selwyn Market Rd in Accra, at the borders and in Lomé (exchanging money at the border and in Lomé, however, tends to be much more expensive than in Accra, where the rates are generally more favourable). The rates they offer are rarely better and usually worse than those offered by the Forex. The one exception is the CFA; moneychangers offer significantly better rates for these than the Forex. If you declare all your money upon entering the country and then change money on the black market, you won't be able to show on your currency declaration form that you changed all your money at official outlets. These days however, customs officials don't generally pay much attention to minor discrepancies.

It pays to check several Forex before changing any money because their rates can vary significantly. As for travellers' cheques, not all Forex accept them and of those that do, the independent Forex tend to give much worse rates than the banks. Barclays in Accra, and possibly others as well, will advance money (cedis only) on Visa and MasterCard but if you have a US card, you'll get hit with two exchange rates – dollars to UK pounds and UK pounds to cedis. You can get up to UK£100 worth of cedis, or more if you're willing to wait while they telex London. Also, American Express cardholders can get money through the company's Ghanaian affiliate, Scantravel, which will give you a form that you take to Barclays to get US dollar travellers' cheques. Those with French travellers' cheques will find it difficult exchanging cheques outside Accra and Kumasi. In Takoradi, for example, only Barclays will accept such cheques and their rates are bad.

Other banks that change money include: Ghana Commercial, Standard Chartered, Ecobank and Meridien BIAO.

BUSINESS HOURS & HOLIDAYS

Business hours are weekdays from 8 am to 12.30 pm and 1.30 to 5.30 pm, Saturdays from 8.30 am to 1 pm. Government offices are open weekdays from 8 am to 12.30 pm and 1.30 to 5 pm.

Banking hours are weekdays from 8.30 am to 2 pm (3 pm on Fridays). A few bank branches are also open on Saturdays from 8.30 am to 1 pm.

GHANA

Public Holidays

1 January, 6 March (Independence), Good Friday, Easter Monday, 1 May (Labour Day), 4 June, 1 July (Republic Day), 25-26 December, 31 December (Revolution Day).

POST & TELECOMMUNICATIONS

The poste restante at the main post office in Accra is free and quite reliable. The post office offers express mail which in theory should arrive in a third of the time. Locals say that it is often no faster than regular mail and that the fastest way is to post your letters at Accra Airport.

Area dialling codes are:

Aburi	081
Accra	021
Akosombo	0251
Bawku	0743
Bolgatanga	072
Cape Coast	042
Elmina	024
Ho	091
Kumasi	051
Mampong	0561
Takoradi	031
Tamale	071
Tema	0221
Sunyani	061
Winneba	042

There is a public telephone office at Extelcom House, High St, Accra (open Monday to Saturday from 7 am to 9 pm). Phone and fax rates per minute are C 2600 to the UK and most of Europe, C 3000 to France and the USA, C 3200 to Canada and C 3500 to Australia. You can also direct dial 24 hours a day with phonecards purchased there. C 22,500 will buy you 120 units or eight minutes to the UK. AT&T cardholders with 'USA direct service' can call the USA reverse charge (collect) or with their cards. In Ghana, the AT&T access phone number is 0191. For reverse charge and card calls to the UK, the access number is 0194. Reverse charge and card calls to other countries, however, are still not possible. To send a fax or cable, go to the post office or, more expensive, any major hotel.

MAPS

The best map of Ghana is the KLM/Shell map; one side shows Accra and the other is a road map of Ghana. It costs C 1500 at any Shell station, the KLM booking office, Omari and some major hotels. For more detailed maps of Ghana, Accra, Kumasi and other cities go to the Survey Department near the airport. From No 37 Roundabout, it's one km east on Burma

---

Ghanaian Literature

Ghana has one of the longest written literary traditions in Africa, stemming from the introduction of formal education in West Africa by missionaries in the 18th century, but it wasn't until independence that the literary movement really took off.

One of the first post-independence novels, *The Beautiful Ones Are Not Yet Born* (Heinemann, London, 1988) by Ayi Kwei Armah, is a sharp, sardonic observation of post-independence politics daring to criticise Nkrumah's socialist régime and the country's new elite. Kofi Awoonor's first and best-known novel, *This Earth, My Brother* (Heinemann, London, 1972), tells of a young African lawyer trained abroad who must work within the confines of a judicial system inherited from the British. Even more polemic is Amu Djoleto's *Hurricane of Dust* (Longman, Harlow, 1987); a petty thief and supporter of the revolution falls foul of the régime and, following torture and imprisonment, ends up at their mercy. Kojo Laing's major work, *Search Sweet Country* (Picador, London, 1987), is an exuberant explosion of imagery and free-wheeling prose attempting to convey a country in the process of change.

Among the most interesting nonfiction works about Ghana are: *African Traditional Theatre in Ghana*, about concert parties, by Kwabena Bame; *Sharing the Same Bowl*, a sociological study of the food sellers of Accra, by Claire Robertson; *The Shadows of Laughter*, a collection of melancholic love poetry, by Kwesi Brew, set in northern Ghana; *Uhuru*, a monthly arts, culture and entertainment guide; and *Okyeame*, an occasional literary magazine. ∎

GHANA

Camp Rd. The sales office is open weekdays from 8.30 am to noon (to 9 am on Fridays) and 1.30 to 4 pm; the map of Accra costs C 3600.

PHOTOGRAPHY

Photo permits are not required, but many Ghanaians are suspicious of people taking photographs, so as a general rule you should always ask permission first.

You should also be particularly cautious in Accra as the numerous coup attempts against Rawlings keep soldiers wary. There are important government installations in the area around the old castle in Accra. Taking photos here will land you in jail, as will taking photos of any government buildings, dams, airport, TV and radio stations, etc. Ports and harbours are also not to be photographed.

HEALTH

Vaccinations are required for yellow fever and cholera. The best hospitals in Accra are private. Foreigners generally prefer the North Ridge clinic, near the Immigration Department in North Ridge. The police hospital not far from the US embassy is another, but you may not be allowed to use it.

Two of the best pharmacies in Accra are Kingsway Chemist on Knutsford Ave near TCU Motors, and Ghana Drug House on Asafoatsee Nettey Rd opposite the ice company.

DANGERS & ANNOYANCES

For such a large city, Accra has relatively few pickpockets, perhaps because very few foreigners walk around the city centre. Many women who have travelled around West Africa consider Ghana to be one of the safer countries.

Still, one must take the normal precautions in large cities. In Accra, the worst areas for pickpockets are the hotels, the beaches and the old Jamestown area.

Travellers should also definitely avoid the area around Osu castle, which is the seat of Rawlings' government. The guards in that area are suspicious and are likely to view you as a spy or, worse, a journalist.

Outside of Accra, pickpockets are most often found wherever tourists are, especially on the beaches and at festivals.

ACCOMMODATION

Hotels in Ghana have vastly improved in recent years. Cheap accommodation averages around C 4000 or C 5000 a night even in Accra, and for that you can get a very decent room with a fan, shared baths with running water and a reliable supply of electricity. Sleeping anywhere along the beach is definitely not advisable because the chances of being robbed are very high. However, in very remote spots, such as in Princes Town on the far western coast, this can be done.

Mid-range hotels are available in every major town in the country, and many are quite decent. Rooms usually have air-con and private baths with running water. There's almost always a bar-restaurant, although maybe not the best in town. Top-end hotels are available only in Accra and Kumasi and two of them rate five stars. There are also some first-class beach hotels at Biriwa, Busua and Ada.

FOOD

Soups, which are really sauces, are the mainstay of the Ghanaian diet; they're usually fairly thick broths eaten with a starch such as *fufu*, *kenkey* or *banku* (see below). Four of the most popular soups are *nkatenkwan* (groundnut soup prepared with peanut butter, onions, tomatoes and fish or meat), *abenkwan* (made with pounded palm fruit and fish), *shito* (pepper soup) and *nkita* (garden egg soup with fish and beef).

Stews include groundnut, garden egg, fish, bean leaf and *forowe* (fish stew with tomatoes). There's also paella-like *jollof rice* (rice with meat), *palaver* sauce (meat with spinach, akatewa, efan and bitter leaves), *kyemgbuma* (crabs with cassava dough, meat and tomatoes), *mboteleba* (fish or meat with crabs, tomatoes and corn dough), *gari foto* (eggs, onions, dried shrimp and tomatoes accompanied by *gari*, or coarse manioc flour), *agushie* (pumpkin seed sauce, typically served with cooked yams) and *omo tuo* (mashed rice balls with vegetable stew).

Boiled foods include *emo dokon* (beef with rice flour), *akapinkyi* (green plantains with smoked fish and palm oil), *garri jollof* (gari with tomatoes and onions), egg curry (with rice, tomatoes and groundnuts) and *oto* (yams with eggs and palm oil).

Starches include fufu (mashed cooked cassava, plantain, manioc or yam with no liquid added and shaped into a ball), banku and kenkey (both are a sour fermented corn mash which is wrapped in plantain leaves and boiled), *ampesi* (made with yam, plantain, cassava, sweet potato or cocoyam), gari, *abolo* (steamed corn dough), *kokonte* (boiled cassava cooked to a paste), *kyekyirebetu* (mashed plantains with palm oil), *ametse* (mixed cassava and corn dough), *akla* (pounded beans with palm oil) and *apapransa* (dried corn meal).

The least expensive restaurants are called 'chop bars', but the cheapest food of all is sold on the streets by women. They'll typically have a mound of rice on a wooden table along with several sauces to choose from. One of the most popular street foods is *kelewele*, a popular spicy dessert of fried plantains in long chips seasoned with ground chilli pepper and ginger. Another is *ntomo krakro* (fried sweet potato cakes). If you like the food, tell the cook it's 'sweet' (ie delicious).

DRINKS

A popular nonalcoholic beverage sold on the streets is a cool milky-white corn drink, *askenkee* (as-KEEN-key). Among the alcoholic drinks, *pito* (millet beer) is the drink of choice in the north while palm wine is more popular in the south.

THINGS TO BUY

The Ashanti are best known today for their kente cloth (metre for metre, probably the most expensive material in Africa), their *adinkra* cloth, their stools, which are among the finest in Africa, and their fertility dolls. For all of these, the Kumasi area is a bit better than Accra. The best place for glass beads is Koforidua, which has a huge bead market. If you buy any wooden artefacts (masks, etc) and they are not obviously new, upon leaving at the border or airport you'll have to present a certificate from the National Museum in Accra or the Arts Centre to prove that they aren't of historic value. This isn't a problem as either place will issue you one in a minute or two for a nominal fee.

Stools

Stools (*gua* in Twi and *dwa* in Ashanti) are used all over Africa but those of the Ashanti are among the most elaborate. Historically, certain designs, such as those in which the seat is supported upon the image of a leopard or elephant, were restricted to particular ranks within Ashanti society. The higher up in Ashanti society, the larger and more elaborate the stools; those of major chiefs are still carried in public by the chief's stool-bearers. Stools play a greater role in Akan culture than they do elsewhere in Africa. In social affairs they act as symbols of authority, but they are also objects of worship and are even 'fed' and 'given drinks', usually annually during the Ashanti's Odwira Festival in the Kumasi area and during the Ga's Homowo festivals in the south. The first gift that a father gives to his son, and the first gift bestowed by a man on his future bride, is a stool. Everyone has their favourite; it would be heresy to sell it or give it away. When a person dies, the relatives use the stool to sit the corpse on and bathe it, after which they place the stool in the room for ancestral worship. Chiefs consider stools to be their supreme insignia. The most famous is the *Sika Gwa Kofi*, the Golden Stool, which is said to have been captured from heaven by Okomfo Anokye, the chief priest of Osei Tutu, king of the Ashanti. It's the only gold one ever to exist. Not even the supreme Ashanti king may sit on this stool, which is brought out only on rare occasions. There are as many stool designs as there are chiefs, and the symbols are infinite. You'll undoubtedly see these stools for sale as you travel around Ghana. If they weren't so bulky, they'd make great souvenirs. ■

Getting There & Away

AIR

From Europe there are direct flights from London, Amsterdam, Geneva, Zürich, Düsseldorf, Rome and Moscow.

The cheapest way to get to Ghana is with a ticket from a bucket shop in London or Amsterdam. From West Africa to Europe, Balkan Airlines usually has the lowest rates. Aeroflot is also cheap; its Accra office accepts only US dollars cash, however. The same is true of many other airlines, including Ethiopian Airlines and Ghana Airways, and converting, say, UK pound-denominated travellers' cheques into dollars cash can be expensive. On international flights only, Ghana Airways offers a 25% student discount but only with a student ID and a letter of introduction from your school. From the USA, you can take Ghana Airways or Air Afrique. With the latter you must transfer in Dakar or Abidjan.

Within West Africa, Ghana Airways is one of the better airlines but even it receives many complaints. Fares must be paid for in hard currency unless you're travelling only inside Ghana. There are connections with Abidjan, Lagos, Monrovia, Dakar, Conakry and Freetown; most of these flights are on Ghana Airways or Nigeria Airways.

For direct links with eastern and southern Africa, you have two choices: Ethiopian Airlines to Addis Ababa (connecting to Nairobi) or Ghana Airways flights to/from Harare (Zimbabwe). The former requires that you purchase a round-trip ticket to Addis or, if you argue persistently, an onward ticket from Addis. Flights are not cheap. A one-way ticket to Nairobi via Addis, for example, is US$618.

LAND

Bus & Bush Taxi

To/From Burkina Faso The government's STC bus company has big buses providing the fastest and cheapest transport to Ouagadougou. The buses depart twice weekly in either direction; from Ouaga on Monday and Friday mornings and, in the opposite direction, from Kumasi on Wednesday mornings and from Accra on Saturday mornings. The fare is C 10,500 from Kumasi and C 13,100 from Accra (CFA 6700 from Ouaga to Kumasi). The buses are in average condition and the trip takes at least 24 hours. Taking the bus the entire distance in one sitting is virtually unbearable so consider breaking the trip.

To/From Côte d'Ivoire The STC buses between Accra and Abidjan leave Accra from the main STC bus terminal daily at 6 pm and from Abidjan at 8 am; the trip takes about 14 hours, sometimes longer if the delay at the border exceeds the normal two to three-hour wait. In Accra, the bus to Abidjan rarely leaves on time. The cost is CFA 5000 plus CFA 1000 at the border.

To/From Togo STC buses leave twice daily from Accra east to Aflao/Lomé, departing at 7 am and 12.30 pm and taking four hours. The buses leave from Accra's second STC station in the centre, just north of Makola market.

Most people do not take the bus to Lomé, however, because it's quicker to take a taxi or *tro-tro* (minivan); C 3000 and C 1800 respectively. You won't make it to Lomé unless you're on the road by 2.30 pm as the border closes at 6 pm sharp. The trip is three hours in a bush taxi. Bush taxis and minibuses leave Accra from before dawn to 2.30 pm from the main lorry park on Kinbu Rd.

Car

The major roads in Ghana are generally in good condition except for the potholed stretch in the far north between Tamale and Bolgatanga. The drive from Accra to Abidjan (556 km) can be done in as little as 10 hours. Accra-Lomé takes three hours while Accra-Kumasi takes 3½ hours. If you don't have a *carnet de passage*, you can leave a returnable deposit at the border of entry, but the deposit is high (about US$500 in cash) and you may never get it back at all.

Petrol in Ghana is C 1900 a gallon, which is slightly more expensive than in Benin and Togo but considerably cheaper than in other nearby countries. Police will stop and interrogate anyone with foreign licence plates driving after 6pm.

SEA

Ghana is a bit cheaper than most countries along the West African coast for shipping vehicles to Europe. Black Star Lines, for example, charges about US$500 to ship a motorcycle to Europe without a container. Its freighters also take passengers; the normal fare including meals is US$445 to Rotterdam and US$545 to the UK. See the Tema section for more details.

TOURS

One of the best ways to experience Ghana is with Insight Travel (☎ (01995) 606095, fax 602124), 6 Norton Rd, Garstang, Preston, Lancashire PR3 1JY, UK. This agency, whose motto is 'Don't be a tourist, be a guest', offers host-based trips every month to Kumasi with the opportunity of living with a Ghanaian family, seeing a traditional Akan ceremony (which could include a funeral) in a local village, bird-watching, touring craft villages around Kumasi, visiting a nearby game park, and taking lessons in dance, music or weaving. The cost of a two-week trip is about UK£550 plus air fare; the price includes accommodation, half board and all local activities.

LEAVING GHANA

The airport tax in Accra is C 8000/US$10.

Getting Around

AIR

Airlink flies three times a week to Kumasi and Tamale. The fares are low, eg C 28,000/52,000 one way/round trip from Accra to Tamale (C 18,000 one way from Kumasi). Nonresident foreigners are apparently supposed to pay in hard currency at much higher rates, but this rule isn't strictly enforced. From Accra to Kumasi, however, it's about as quick to travel overland.

BUS

Ghana used to be famous for its government-run STC buses – big, comfortable, fast, inexpensive, with fixed schedules. In recent years, however, the buses have been going down in quality and punctuality and sometimes take on more passengers than there are seats. Also, express service has been discontinued. There are a total of 57 destinations, including some very remote towns.

Tickets are mostly sold only on the day of departure but you may be able to get one the day before. Otherwise get to the station early because the queues can be long. It sometimes makes sense to take bush taxis for short trips and the STC buses for long ones. Ghana also has lots of big private buses, many better and more frequent than the STC buses. Since their condition can vary from new to dilapidated, check your bus before buying a ticket. Their offices are at the main motor parks.

TRO-TRO & BUSH TAXI

Apart from large buses, you have a choice between taxis (also called bush taxis) and the much cheaper tro-tro, which are minivans or small buses, often called mammy trucks when they operate between cities. Taxis (usually seven-seater Peugeot 504s) and tro-tro operate on all the major routes, usually involve less waiting time than the large private buses or the STC buses, and cover many minor routes.

Tro-tro are extremely crowded and uncomfortable and generally make slow progress, and only slightly cheaper than the large buses. Most, however, are in reasonable shape and for short trips they're fine. Taxis normally charge roughly 50% more than tro-tro or large private buses but they (and the buses) are also about 50% faster.

TRAIN

The government purchased some used German trains in 1986, almost instantly converting their passenger train service from one of the worst in West Africa to the best. There are three train lines in Ghana: Accra to Kumasi and Accra to Takoradi both have a morning train and a night train; Kumasi to Takoradi has three departures daily. On the

GHANA

western line between Kumasi and Takoradi, the difference in travel times between bush taxis and the train is not great, so this is the line that is most popular with travellers, especially the overnight train. It is also the only line with bar-restaurant service. The eastern line (Accra-Kumasi) through the Kwahu and Akim highlands is more scenic, while the Accra-Takoradi line passes through a heavily forested area on the way to Huni Valley where you must change trains. On these two routes the train takes about three times as long as a bus.

Fares are low, about 10% less than the STC bus in 1st class and about 40% less in 2nd class. First-class tickets are limited to the seats available while 2nd-class tickets are not; consequently 2nd-class coaches tend to be overcrowded. All night trains have four-berth sleepers in 2nd class, but only the Kumasi-Takoradi train has two-berth 1st-class sleepers as well. A sleeper adds roughly 50% to the fare.

CAR

Major car rental agencies are located in Accra, including Hertz, Avis and Europcar. Europcar, which is at the Golden Tulip Hotel, seems to have the lowest rates but you must make a US$1000 deposit. It charges US$38 per day and US$0.15 per km (unlimited milage for Accra-only rentals) for its cheapest model without air-con; Visa and MasterCard are accepted.

BOAT

For a real adventure, take a steamer up Lake Volta. The *Bupei Queen* plies the entire length of the lake to Yapei, stopping en route at Kpandu, Kete-Krachi and Yeji. For more information see the Akosombo section.

TOURS

There are now a number of travel agencies in Accra providing all-inclusive tours to virtually all sections of the country (see Information in the Accra section). Popular destinations are Kumasi and the surrounding area, Akosombo Dam, Mole Game Reserve, Kakum Nature Park, and the coastal forts.

Accra

Accra (ah-KRAH) is a lively city that is beginning to attract travellers again. In the late 1970s and early '80s life there simply became too difficult to enjoy; those days are long gone. The city is now much cleaner and busier, with new taxis crowding the streets, painted buildings, two new five-star hotels, affordable restaurants, and a nightlife second to none in Africa. It also has a striking new National Theatre which should not be missed. Ultramodern Abidjan may on the surface appear more prosperous but it's dead compared to Accra, which is now the most vibrant city in West Africa and far safer than most as well.

With 1.7 million people, Accra is big and sprawling. It is still possible to spend the day in the centre and see few Westerners. That's because in Ghana, like Nigeria, the local people run the show.

Orientation

Accra city has two major arteries which are used to get from one side of the city to the other: Ring Rd, a broad semicircular four-lane highway, and Burma Camp and Achimota Rds which are further out towards the airport. Much of the commercial district is along the two streets parallel to each other, Nkrumah Ave and Kojo Thompson Rd, which run north-south from the Nkrumah Circle area to the city centre. From the heart of town there are also three finger-like major arteries leading out of town: from east to west, Independence Ave which leads north-east from Makola Market to No 37 Roundabout and the airport, eventually linking with the toll road, a 30-km superhighway heading eastward to Tema and Lomé; Nkrumah Ave, the extension of Nsawam Rd leading north-west to Kumasi; and Graphic Rd, which becomes Winneba Rd leading west to Cape Coast.

Information

Tourist Office The tourist information office, open weekdays from 8 am to 5 pm, is in the Ministry of Trade & Tourism

(☎ 665421) on Kinbu Rd. The staff are friendly but they have no maps and little to offer other than directions to various places.

Money Barclays (☎ 664901) sells and cashes travellers' cheques and accepts Visa and MasterCard for drawing money. It's in the city centre on Nkrumah Ave, 100 metres north of Cocoa House and is open weekdays from 8.30 am to 2 pm. Standard Chartered (☎ 664491) has several branches in Accra.

A hundred or so Forex are scattered over town, although not all accept travellers' cheques. Their rates vary only slightly for cash, more considerably for travellers' cheques. In the centre, the greatest number are found around the main post office (eg Ladans) and along Kojo Thompson Rd (eg Sunkwa near British Airways). Amex Forex on the corner of Nkrumah and Selwyn Aves gives the best rates and has good air-con. In the Cantonments area, the best is Efoshi Forex behind Trust Hospital.

Foreign Embassies Some of the countries represented include:

Algeria 82 Tito Ave, north of Ring Rd (☎ 776719)

Benin 19 Volta St, 2nd Close, airport residential area (☎ 774860)

Brazil 5 Volta St, 2nd Close, airport residential area near the Benin embassy (☎ 774908)

Burkina Faso 772/3 Asylum Down, west of Mango Tree Ave (☎ 221988)

Canada 46 Independence Ave at Sankara Circle (☎ 228555, telex 2024)

Slovakia Kanda High Rd, No 2, House C260/5 (☎ 223540)

Côte d'Ivoire 9 18th Lane, 700 metres south of Danquah Circle (☎ 774611)

Ethiopia 6 Adiembra Rd, East Cantonments (☎ 775928)

France 12th Rd, off Liberation Ave north of Sankara Circle (☎ 228571)

Germany Valdemosa Lodge, 7th Ave Extension, North Ridge (☎ 221311, telex 2025)

Guinea 11 Osu Badu St, Djorwulu district (☎ 777921)

Italy Jawaharlal Nehru Rd, north of Ring Rd (☎ 775849)

Japan 8 Tito Ave, off Jawaharlal Nehru Rd (☎ 775616, telex 2068)

Liberia 10 West Cantonments Rd, off Jawaharlal Nehru Rd (☎ 775641)

Mali 14 Agostino Neto Rd, airport residential area (☎ 775160)

The Netherlands 89 Liberation Ave, Sankara Circle (☎ 773694, telex 2128)

Niger House No E104/3 Independence Ave, 600 metres south of Sankara Circle (☎ 224962/9011)

Nigeria Tito Ave, one km north of Ring Rd (☎ 776158/9)

Poland 2 Akosombo St, airport residential area (☎ 775972)

Romania North Labone Ward F, Block 6, House 262 (☎ 774076)

Russia F856/1 Ring Rd East (☎ 775611)

Spain Lampty Ave Extension, airport residential area (☎ 774004/5)

Switzerland 9 Water Rd, North Ridge (☎ 228125)

Togo Cantonments Rd, one km north of Danquah Circle (☎ 777950)

UK Cantonments Rd, one km north of Danquah Circle (☎ 221665/1715, telex 2323)

USA Ring Rd East, 100 metres east of Danquah Circle (☎ 775347/6601, telex 2579)

Travel Agencies Three of the best travel agencies in the centre are: Akuaba Tourist Travel Agency (☎ 228020) on Tudu Rd just east of Nkrumah Ave; Universal Travel & Tourist Services (☎ 222813) just around the corner; and Scantravel (☎ 663134) further south on High St, a block before Barclays. Scantravel is the representative for American Express and can issue travellers' cheques to cardholders through Barclays. It also carries a list available to the public of all shipping companies and agents in Tema. All three travel agencies make airline reservations and can also arrange in-country tours. Further north along Kojo Thompson Rd, two blocks north of Castle Rd, is Doorstep Travel Services (☎ 223719).

One of the major companies specialising in tours of Ghana is Silicon Travel & Tours (☎ 228520, fax 662680) at 321 Coplan House on Kojo Thompson Rd. Others include M&J Travel & Tours (☎ 776081) on Station Rd opposite the train station, Vanep Tours (☎ 226365, fax 224648) at 46 Farrar Ave south-east of Nkrumah Circle, and Sunseekers Tours (☎ 225393, fax 667533) at the Novotel.

Bookshops The best bookshop is Omari on Ring Rd half a km east of Danquah Circle. It carries a lot of interesting Ghanaian books in

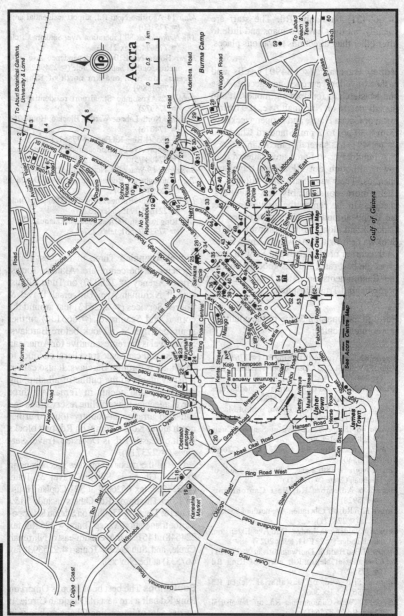

Accra

0   0.5   1 km

GHANA

PLACES TO STAY		34	Afrikiko Bar-Restaurant & Ice-Cream Parlour	32	British High Commission
3	Hotel Shangri-La	58	Hinlone Chinese	33	Japanese & Algerian
4	Granada Hotel		Restaurant		Embassies
10	Golden Tulip Hotel			35	The Netherlands
16	Goklen Hotel	**OTHER**			Embassy
17	Apex Guest House			37	Burkina Faso Embassy
22	Princeway Hotel	1	Guinean Embassy	38	Danish Embassy
23	Sadisco Hotel	5	Benin Embassy	39	German Embassy
24	King David Hotel	7	Spanish Embassy	41	Ghana Immigration
28	Mariset International	8	Kotoka Airport		Service
	Hotel (Cantonments)	9	Mali Embassy	42	Canadian Embassy
36	North Ridge Hotel	12	Taxi Park	43	Police Headquarters
40	Sunrise Hotel	13	Survey Department	44	Nigerian Embassy
55	Penta Hotel		(Maps)	45	EEC Office
60	Labadi Beach Hotel	14	Italian Embassy	46	Cantonments Hospital
61	Mariset International	15	Peace Corps, Liberian		& Togo Embassy
	Hotel (Osu)		Embassy &	47	UNICEF
			US Recreation	48	UN Office
PLACES TO EAT			Centre	49	Austrian Embassy
		18	Carnation Market	50	Swissair & USAID
2	La Chaumière	19	Carnation Motor Park	51	Lufthansa
	Restaurant		(for Cape Coast,	52	Conference Centre
6	Bella Napoli		Takoradi & Côte	53	Stadium
11	Round Gidda		d'Ivoire Border)	54	State House
	Restaurant (Vittorio's)	20	STC Bus Station	56	US Embassy
29	Boajin Chinese	21	Post Office	57	Omari Bookshop
	Restaurant	25	Zoo & Ghana Films	59	International Trade Fair
30	African Heritage	26	French Embassy	62	Independence Arch &
	Restaurant & Du Bois	27	Awak Stadium		Independence
	Centre for	31	International School		Square
	Pan-African Culture			63	James Fort

addition to British and American novels. In the centre of town, your best bet is the large UTC department store on Nkrumah Ave. For foreign magazines and newspapers, the bookshops at the major hotels are one source but you can get them more cheaply from the supermarkets along Cantonments Rd. Many of them carry the *Sunday Times* (C 2500) and the *International Herald Tribune*. The bookshop at the University of Legon is excellent but before spending the time and tro-tro fare to get there, check to see whether they're on strike, which occurs fairly often these days.

If you just want to read, try the British Council on Liberia Rd or the USIS Library on the corner of Castle Rd and Independence Ave. Both have well-stocked libraries and a wide selection of magazines and newspapers. The air-con is also wonderful.

Supermarkets For the best supermarket in Accra, head for the British-run Four Flowers, north-east of Sankara Circle off Nima Ave. It has all sorts of imported goods. Most of the better supermarkets, however, are more conveniently located along Cantonments Rd, south of Danquah Circle. The two closest to the circle are Kwatsons and Afridom, which are full of Western groceries and quite good, but the best on this street is Lightsbridge further south at the intersection with Mission Rd. It has a better selection and better prices. The Tops, near the corner of Cantonments Rd and Abrebrensem St, is where most Lebanese families shop. In the centre, two large stand-bys are Kingsway and UTC, both on lower Nkrumah Ave.

National Museum
The National Museum is on Barnes Rd, just south of Museum Circle. It is open every day from 9 am to 6 pm and is one of the best museums in West Africa. The main floor houses an assortment of royal stools, superb

GHANA

examples of kente cloth, wooden carvings, historical regalia, drums including a superb female drum used on special occasions, swords, implements, old photographs, masks, and numerous items not of Ghanaian origin. Some of the exhibits show how the crafts are made. Upstairs are archaeological relics, including stone tools dating back 10,000 years and some of the famous Ashanti gold weights. The entrance fee is C 500 (C 500 more to take photos), and there's a pleasant airy restaurant with various Ghanaian dishes, each for C 2500.

Markets

The city's major market, **Makola Market**, has shrunk in size since soldiers blew up a major portion of it during revolutionary days and, more recently, a fire in 1993 which destroyed a large section. It's still good for beads and fabrics, some of the better places being the shops around the market and along Kojo Thompson Rd and Selwyn and Derby Aves. The market spreads over several blocks between Kinbur Rd to the north, Kojo Thompson Rd to the west, and Barnes Rd/High St Junction to the south.

The city's second major market, **Kaneshie Market**, is on the western side of the city on Winneba Rd leading towards Cape Coast, half a km west of Obetsebi Lamptey Circle. It's much more orderly than Makola Market. The first level is reserved for foodstuffs while the upper level is where all the textiles are. Nearby you'll find the city's major motor park for Takoradi.

Another interesting place to shop is the **Obruni Wao Market** near the train station. It's not easy to find. Just ask around UTC on Nkrumah Ave; it's around the corner and through some hardware sellers. It's probably the largest used-goods store you've ever seen. You can buy a used

Ritual sword

T-shirt here for less than it costs you to clean a filthy one. Saturday morning, when the new shipments of clothes arrive, is the best but most crowded time to shop here.

Even more interesting is **Timber Market** on Hansen Rd in the industrial area of Ushertown. If you can find someone to show you the fetish section, you're in for a treat: animal skulls, live and dead reptiles, strange powders, charms, bells, shakers, leopard skins, teeth, porcupine quills and juju figurines. People are very friendly but they'll also be curious as to why you're there. Finding this place is difficult at best and impossible without assistance from locals.

Independence Square

Independence Square, sometimes called Blackstar Square, with the Independence Arch, is to Accra what Red Square is to Moscow. It's a huge parade ground backed by the sea with a capacity for 30,000 people. Here three ex-servicemen in colonial times were shot while attempting to present grievances to the governor in a peaceful demonstration. Nkrumah built it in 1961 along with the huge stadium across the street; behind is the State House built in 1965 for the OAU conference – all examples of his extravagant spending habits.

From the square Osu Castle is visible in the distance near the ocean. Built by the Danes around 1659, it is Accra's most historic structure, but is now the seat of government and off limits to the public.

Arts Centre

The Arts Centre is on 28 February Rd, between Independence Square and the centre. Here artisan goods are sold and people congregate inside from Thursday to Sunday afternoons (particularly Saturday) for entertainment of all kinds including music, traditional dance and theatre. There's a schedule of activities. This is the largest crafts market in Accra, with kente cloth, Ashanti sandals, beads, wooden carvings, brass work and leather work, and a favourite place for purchasing cassettes of African music. Inside on your right, is an art gallery

Necklace of 108 beads

(closed Saturday) selling oils and water-colours by local artists.

If you buy any wooden objects that might be mistaken for an antique, you can save yourself lots of hassles at the airport by having them examined beforehand at the National Museum; they'll give you a certif-icate of exemption.

Other Attractions

Heading west from the Arts Centre you pass, on your right, **Parliament House**, which has been closed since 1981, and the **High Courts**. On the left is the Anglican Holy Trinity Cathe-dral. From here, if you carry on along High St for another km you will arrive in the old area of **James Town** which includes many dilapi-dated houses and **James Fort**, now a run-down whitewashed prison and hardly worth visiting. Next to it is an old **lighthouse**, 31-metres high and still in use.

Activities

Beaches Ghana boasts beautiful sandy beaches and lagoons but swimmers must be very careful because of the strong undertow and rip-tides. Labadi Beach stretches eastward for several km starting at the Labadi Beach Hotel. Just west of the hotel is a section open to the public. A bit further east is the well-marked main public beach. It's protected with a well-guarded

entrance, but crime is still a problem. Joggers have been accosted at gunpoint, and leaving bags unattended is foolish. The entrance fee is C 500, and there are several shaded places for eating and drinking plus showers and a lifeguard. If you like quiet beaches, go during the week.

A lot of foreigners 'in the know' prefer Coco Beach in Nungua, which is a few km further east on the road to Tema and easily accessible by tro-tro. It's rarely crowded and you can get food, drink and lodging at the Coco Beach Resort, which overlooks the beach (see under Places to Stay). Watch your belongings because thefts on the beach occur fairly frequently.

If you have wheels and want more secluded beaches, head west of Accra to the unmarked beaches at mile 13, mile 14 and mile 16 near AAMAL (see Around Accra).

Swimming Many of the top-end hotels have pools. The Labadi Beach and Novotel, for example, charge visitors about C 3500 for the use of their pools while the Shangri-La charges C 3000. Those at the North Ridge and Sunrise hotels are undoubtedly cheaper but they're also quite small.

Places to Stay – bottom end

The friendly *YMCA* (☎ 224700) and the nearby *YWCA*, both in the city centre on Castle Rd near Museum Circle, are the cheapest places. The YMCA, which has a Forex and accepts only men, charges C 1500 per person for a bed in a four-bed dormitory. It's a good place to meet Africans. There are also clean bathrooms with showers, good locks on the doors and a cheap restaurant, but buy a good padlock to lock your possessions in the box near your bed. Rooms are usually available if you arrive early and there's not a course going on. The facilities at the YWCA are worse. Its four-bed dormitory rooms are bare except for the beds, the shared baths are very dirty and there's no restaurant.

Two other possibilities are the unmarked *Methodist Church Headquarters* on Liberia Rd, 200 metres east of Standard Chartered, and the *University of Ghana* (☎ 275381) at Legon.

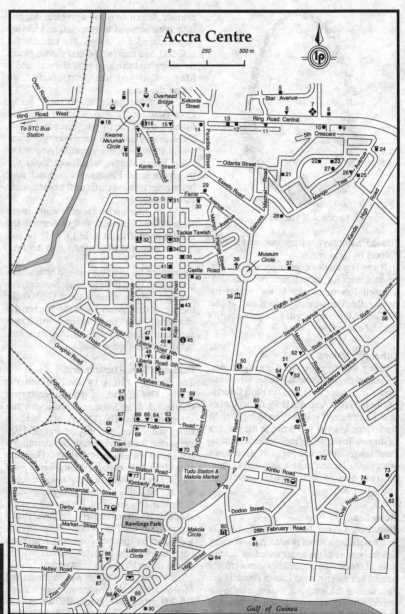

Accra Centre

0   250   500 m

PLACES TO STAY

2   Aam's Hotel
5   New Haven Hotel
8   Adeshi Hotel
12   Kob Lodge Hotel
13   Marymont Hotel
21   Asylum Down Hotel
22   Lemon Lodge
23   Korkdam Hotel
25   Mavis Hotel
28   Time Square Lodge
29   President Hotel
35   St George's Hotel
37   YMCA
40   YWCA
41   Crown Prince Hotel
42   Hotel de California
43   Avenida Hotel
46   Nkrumah Memorial Hotel
54   Methodist Church Headquarters
59   Bellview Hotel
60   Ambassador Hotel
64   Hotel Tropicana
70   Station View Hotel
71   Novotel
87   Take Care Lodge & Taxi Stand (for Korle Bu)

PLACES TO EAT

4   Street Food Area & Taxi Stand
6   Joysco Restaurant
11   Bus Stop Restaurant
15   Blow Up Restaurant & Tro-Tro Park
17   Street Food & Terra Nova Bar
24   Astella Bar-Restaurant
26   Little Wood's Restaurant
31   White Bells
48   Annabelle's
51   Good Chop Bar
52   Best Cuisine
53   Good Chop Bar

56   Renovation Works Restaurant
58   Cosmos Restaurant
65   Harvester's Restaurant, Universal Travel, Akuaba Travel Agency & Handicrafts Emporium
76   Kinbu Gardens Restaurant
86   Deotali Restaurant & Casan-Casan Fast Foods
88   Wato Bar

OTHER

1   Neoplan Motor Park & Tro-Tro Park (for Kumasi, Tema & Takoradi)
3   Taxi Park (for Labadi, Airport, Osu & Keshi) & Tip Toe Gardens Nightclub
7   Paloma Shopping Mall
9   Alitalia
10   Volvo Dealer
14   Apollo Theatre
16   Barclays Bank
18   The Loom
19   Container Spot Nightclub
20   Piccadilly Circle & Kilimanjaro Nightclubs
27   Burkina Faso Embassy
30   Miracle Mirage Nightclub & Vanef Tours/Europcar
32   Standard Chartered Bank
33   Ghana Airways (Branch) Booking Office
34   Doorstep Travel Services
36   Church
38   Lufthansa
39   National Museum & Edvy's Restaurant

44   Nigeria Airways
45   Ministry of Tourism
47   Eden Travel
49   British Airways & Aeroflot
50   Standard Chartered Bank
55   Goil Station
57   Barclays Bank & Kingsway Department Store
61   British Council
62   National Theatre
63   Standard Chartered Bank
66   KLM
67   Air Afrique, Ethiopian Airlines, Ghana Airways, Forex, Snack Bar & Cocoa House
68   CNB Motor Park (for Cape Coast, Swedru & Winneba) & La Nyanteh Communications Centre (Telephones)
69   Police Station
72   Various Ministries
73   Foreign Ministry
74   Ministry of Interior & Immigration Branch Office
75   Tema Station
77   M & J Travel & Tours
78   Taxi Park, EgyptAir & Liberty House
79   Local Bus Park & UTC Department Store
80   Parliament House
81   Arts Centre
82   Stadium
83   Independence Arch & Independence Square
84   Labadi Lorry Park
85   Main Post Office
89   Barclays Bank Headquarters
90   Scantravel

The former has only one room, for C 4500; the guardian, James, lives at the back and can make the arrangements. At the latter, student dormitory rooms become available from 10 July to the end of September; the cost is about C 5000 a person. Enquire at the office of student affairs.

Another place near the YMCA that has been warmly recommended is the *Cavalry Methodist Church* on the eastern side of Barnes Rd. Very popular and often full, it has excellent cheap rooms. (Men and women sleep separately.)

For a really cheap hotel in the city centre, check the decrepit *Take Care Lodge* (☎ 667064) close to the post office. This place is not so bad although the sheets are a little grubby. Rooms with one/two beds and shared baths cost C 3300/4400.

GHANA

About halfway between the post office area and Nkrumah Circle, five km to the north, are several good hotels on or just off Kojo Thompson Rd. The long-time favourite of many is the popular and recommended *Hotel de California* (☎ 226199) on the corner of Kojo Thompson and Castle Rds. Singles/doubles with fans cost C 4400/6600; the shared baths are clean with good showers and you can hang out on the front porch or in the reception area which has a TV and bar. As in many of these places, a couple can have a single room if the bed is large enough.

Across the street, the friendly *Crown Prince Hotel* (☎ 225381) has similar singles/doubles for C 4400/5500, but the rooms are smaller and the ambience is zero.

Further south is the *Nkrumah Memorial Hotel*, which is also good for the price. The rooms have thin walls but its spacious singles/doubles with fans and shared baths (but no basins) are still a good deal at C 4400/6600; the front bar and the restaurant, which serves surprisingly good food, are other pluses.

Another hotel in the heart of the city is the *Station View Hotel*, on Kinbu Rd facing the main lorry park. Rooms at this run-down place, which cost C 4500, are fairly clean and have fans and shared baths plus there's a restaurant with cheap African food.

A better place for the price is the nearby *Hotel Tropicana* (☎ 666245) on Tudu Rd. It charges C 4400/6600 for singles/doubles with fans and decent attached baths (C 8800 with air-con) and has a central lounge.

A much quieter area for cheap hotels is Asylum Down, halfway between Nkrumah and Sankara circles, just south of Ring Rd. This area is less convenient but it's only one km from the lively Nkrumah Circle area and two to three km from the city centre. A long-standing favourite of travellers is the *Lemon Lodge* (☎ 227857), which is two blocks south of the Adeshi Hotel on Ring Rd. Singles/doubles with fans and shared baths, which are not always clean, cost C 4400/5500 (C 6600 with air-con) including a full breakfast with eggs.

I much prefer the nearby *Asylum Down Hotel*. The rooms (C 5000) are large and

quite nice, with overhead fans, comfortable armchairs, desks and clean shared baths. The thatched-roof bar out the back serves cheap beer and good Ghanaian meals (C 500).

Several blocks south is the dreary three-storey *Time Square Lodge*, which charges C 5500. The *Mavis Hotel* (☎ 225426), which is further east and a bit better, has ventilated singles/doubles with shared baths for C 4400/5500.

Just east and north of Nkrumah Circle there are several hotels. My favourite is *Aam's Hotel*, which is just a block north of the circle. It has a good bar and a lively atmosphere. Spacious doubles with a comfortable bed, clean sheets, fan, basin, tile floor and shared bath cost C 4950 (C 6600 with private bath). Avoid the rooms facing the patio as this area is noisy at night.

The *Princeway Hotel* (☎ 228568), a block or two east off New Town Rd, is presentable, has low lights and a large tranquil drinking area, and charges C 6000 for a clean room with fan and shared bath.

Marymont Hotel (☎ 221011), on Ring Rd, 600 metres east of Nkrumah Circle, has rooms with shared baths for about C 5500, and a porch.

Further east is the *New Haven Hotel* where singles/doubles with bath cost C 5500/6000 (C 7000 for a double with hot water). It serves decent inexpensive food. The beds are so large that a single suffices for two people. From the Marymont go about 200 metres further east to the Bus Stop Restaurant, then north on Silver Cap Rd for one block, and turn right at the first corner (Star Ave).

If you head much further east along Ring Rd to Nima Highway and then head north for a block or two you'll find the *Emperor Hotel*, a Peace Corps favourite. A room with a double bed costs only C 4500; you can stuff as many people in a room as you like.

Camping The best place for camping is the *Coco Beach Resort* (see below). You can also camp at *Labadi Pleasure Beach*, which is on the same road (the coastal highway to Tema) slightly closer to Accra. It charges the same but there are no facilities. The guard strictly enforces the regulations, so you're safe here.

Places to Stay – middle

There are only two mid-range hotels near the centre. The best for the price is the new *Bellview* (☎ 667730) on Tudu Crescent Rd. Highly recommended, it has a nicely decorated air-con lobby with a shady open-air terrace. Its ventilated rooms are excellent value at C 7500 for a single with shared bath and C 9500 for a double with attached bath (C 15,000 with air-con).

If you can afford to pay a bit more, you may prefer *St George's Hotel* (☎ 224629, telex 2236), which is one km to the north on Amusudai Rd. It has a restaurant and carpeted rooms with large beds, air-con, refrigerators, comfortable chairs and decent private baths for C 17,000.

East of Nkrumah Circle is the well-known *Korkdam Hotel* (☎ 226797) in Asylum Down, next door to Lemon Lodge. Singles/doubles with fans cost C 8800/13,200; C 11,000/15,400 with air-con. Two winning features are the cable TV with CNN in the lobby and the shady terrace outside, which is a good place for drinks and excellent kebabs. There's also a decent restaurant inside. The Korkdam is a lot better than the run-down *Kob Lodge Hotel* (☎ 227647) on Ring Rd near the well-known Bus Stop restaurant. Popular and often full, singles/doubles cost C 9900/11,000 (C 12,100/14,850 with air-con).

The modern new *Apex Guest House* (☎ 229456) is roughly 1.5 km north-east of Nkrumah Circle and a little difficult to find (behind Caprice St and off Nsawan Rd). Its rooms, C 22,000, have air-con, refrigerators, TVs and new tile baths. There is also a restaurant but breakfast is overpriced.

If you don't mind being eight km north of the city centre, head for the well-managed *Dimples Inn* out on Achimota Rd on the edge of the quiet Djorwulu residential area near the motorway. With air-con singles/doubles with refrigerators for C 16,000/18,000, it may be the best deal of any mid-range hotel. Breakfast is about C 1600 and during the day snacks are available from the bar; the restau-

rant is open in the evenings. The well-maintained *Sanaa Lodge* (☎ 220443, fax 227494), which is not far away on 15th Ave in Tesano, is in the same price range. Popular with tour groups, it has a pool, business centre and satellite TVs.

Even further out but to the east is *Coco Beach Resort* (☎ 712887), clearly marked on the western outskirts of Nungua, seven km east of the Labadi Beach Hotel on the coastal road to Tema. It's busy on weekends. Singles/doubles with fans cost C 16,200/18,000 (C 27,000/31,500 with air-con). You can also camp here for C 1500. The hotel has a squash court, decent restaurant and, most importantly, a beach. Draught beers will cost you C 500, cheese omelettes C 3000 and pepper steaks C 4000. On weekdays, many dishes aren't available and service can be extremely slow. Tro-tro from Tema Station in Accra cost C 150 and are plentiful.

Places to Stay – top end

By far the best and most expensive hotel is the new five-star *Labadi Beach Hotel* on the eastern outskirts of town overlooking the ocean. However, it's ridiculously expensive (US$210 for a double) as is the remodelled *Golden Tulip* out near the airport.

The French-managed *Novotel* on Barnes Rd near the heart of town is almost as expensive and pales in comparison. Nevertheless, it still does good business and has all the amenities of a top-class hotel.

The next best, and a far better deal, is the *Hotel Shangri-La* overlooking the polo grounds. It's more informal with a relaxing atmosphere, 36 rooms with kitchenettes and the best pizza in town. In the mornings, clients can go horse riding. The only problem beside its being fully booked much of the time is its remote location on the northern outskirts of town just beyond the airport, eight km from the city centre. Next door is the much less expensive *Granada Hotel*, a small, well-managed hotel with a good restaurant.

The *North Ridge Hotel* is a well-managed establishment with big rooms, a pleasant ambience and a good restaurant. It's three km from the city centre on Seventh Ave Exten-

GHANA

sion in a quiet residential area near Sankara Circle. The *Sunrise Hotel*, 100 metres south on the same street, is very similar.

There are also several good *Mariset International* hotels: one in the north-western Cantonments area near Burma Camp Rd, another in the south-western Osu area several blocks west of the intersection of Labadi Beach Rd and Ring Rd East, and another in the airport residential area on the northern outskirts of town. One third of the price of the city's poshest hotels, they are all modern, comfortable and exceptionally well maintained with excellent service.

The *Gye Nyame Hotel* in Asylum Down, several blocks south of Ring Rd and near the Adeshi Hotel, and the *Penta Hotel* are both overpriced. The Penta, however, is popular with those more concerned with location than quality and some travellers have succeeded in bargaining down the price after the first night. It's one block south of Danquah Circle on a lively stretch of Cantonments Rd, with lots of restaurants, supermarkets and nightclubs nearby. The new *Secaps Hotel* two km north of the airport is way overpriced with a huge disco and nothing else. The modern and well-marked *Goklen Hotel* at 1 Switchback Crescent is near No 37 Roundabout and not expensive; it's a homy two-storey place with a porch, friendly staff, lounge with TV, and large rooms with fine carpets, air-con, work areas and tiled baths.

Labadi Beach Hotel (☎ 772501, fax 772520), C 162,000/189,000 singles/doubles, satellite TV, pool, tennis, health centre, Avis, private beach, business centre, shops, casino; cards AE, D, V, MC.

Golden Tulip (☎ 775360, fax 775361), C 161,500/ 180,500 singles/doubles, satellite TV, pool, tennis, health club, casino, Hertz, Europcar, nightclub, business centre; cards AE, D, V, MC.

Novotel (☎ 667546, fax 667533), C 144,000/153,000 singles/doubles, satellite TV, pool, tennis, travel agency, bookshop, car rental, shops; cards AE, D, V, MC.

Hotel Shangri-La (☎ 776993/4, fax 774873), C 85,500/99,000 singles/doubles, TV, pool, tennis, travel agency, car rental; cards AE, D, V, MC.

Granada Hotel (☎ 775344, fax 774880), C 44,000 per room, TV, mini-bars, pool, travel agency, gift shop.

North Ridge Hotel (☎ 225809, fax 221417), C 39,600/44,000, singles/doubles, pool, business centre; AE, V, MC.

Sunrise Hotel (☎ 224575, fax 227656), C 39,600/ 49,500 singles/doubles, small pool, tennis, car hire, shops; cards AE, D, MC.

Mariset International hotels – both Osu & Cantonments areas (☎ 777998, fax 773154), C 45,000/ 49,500 singles/doubles with breakfast, cable TV, mini-bars.

Penta Hotel (☎ 774529, fax 773418), C 39,500 a room, travel agency, Forex; cards AE.

Gye Nyame Hotel (☎ 223321), C 45,000 to C 65,000 per room, cable TV, mini-bars.

Secaps Hotel (☎ 773209, fax 773206), C 62,100 per room, pool, well-known nightclub

Goklen Hotel (☎ 774061), C 36,000/40,500 with breakfast.

Places to Eat

Cheap Eats If you're staying at the YMCA, check the stands outside. You can get a local breakfast for C 200. And throughout the day all over Accra you'll find road-side stands with coffee, hot chocolate, omelettes and bread.

Many of the cheapest eats are African. Of the non-African restaurants, a cheap place in the centre but open only during the day is the *Kingsway* department store on Nkrumah Ave. It has a peaceful café with Western snacks such as sandwiches and cakes, plus good toilet facilities. You can get delicious hot or cold cocoa drinks for C 60 at the tiny café at *Cocoa House* nearby, and jollof rice with beef for C 700.

About six blocks further south along Nkrumah Ave you'll come to three more inexpensive restaurants, all around Lutterodt Circle. Come here during the day as at night the area is not the safest and most restaurants are closed. Just north of this open area is *Deotali Restaurant*. It has hamburgers for C 600 and African dishes, such as okra soup with bako, starting at C 1000, also more expensive selections including spaghetti for C 2000 and beef kebabs for C 2800. A stone's throw away on the same road you'll find *Casan-Casan Fast Foods*, which may be better for the price. The menu includes burgers, meat pies and some Ghanaian dishes; a filling lunch with a soft drink usually costs less than C 2000. And just south of the circle and the post office is the seedy-looking *Wato Bar*, on the 2nd floor of a triangular building. You can get a decent meal of chicken curry and rice for C 2000 and watch the crowds, or buy rice, chicken and sauce in a banana leaf on the street and bring it up to the terrace.

If you're near the Novotel try *Kinbu Gardens* on Independence Ave, half a block south of the hotel. This open-air bar-restaurant serves cold beer and snacks, such as meat kebabs, and chicken and rice.

Annabelle's is one of the most popular places because it's in the centre and one of only two roof-top restaurants in Accra, but it's not cheap. The views are great and there's good music, mostly reggae. Open from noon to 11 pm except Sunday when it's closed, Annabelle's offers Lebanese selections, vegetarian dishes, Continental dishes and fancy concoctions, eg Irish coffee, with prices ranging from C 950 to C 5000. Even the soft drinks (C 400) and large beers (C 800) are not cheap. Poorly marked and a bit difficult to spot because of its roof-top location, it's in Adabraka on the corner of Liberia Rd South and Jones Nelson Rd, south of the British Airways office on Kojo Thompson Rd. A block west is *Renovation Works*, a new modern restaurant worth checking.

The other roof-top place is *White Bells*, which is on Farrar Ave just south of Nkrumah Circle. One floor up, it's quite breezy but protected from the sun. The selections here, which are more reasonably priced than Annabelle's, include hamburgers for C 800, sandwiches for C 800 to C 1600, various African dishes for C 1200 to C 2000, and large beers for C 650. Some 800 metres east of the circle along Ring Rd you'll find the long-standing *Bus Stop Restaurant*, which has good music and attracts a friendly young Ghanaian crowd. Large beers cost C 600 and draught beer C 400, and you can get simple fare here including good ice cream, meat pies, sausage rolls, sandwiches, kebabs, fish, chicken and, on Sundays, a few cheap Ghanaian dishes. It's open every day from 9 am to 10 pm. Across the street you'll find the

Joysco Restaurant, which features inexpensive full meals, and, slightly further east, *Paloma Snack*. The latter is in a new shopping mall with expensive shops and has an open-air setting and live music on weekends. Most dishes are between C 1500 and C 3000, including burgers, chicken and rice, Lebanese food and very good pizza.

North of Sankara Circle and behind the well-known *Afrikiko* bar-restaurant (follow the signs down the side road) you'll find *Fish'N'Chips*, which serves real fish & chips and English breakfasts at reasonable prices.

On Danquah Circle, *Number One Snacks* facing the south-eastern corner is in the open air and is popular for draught beers and snacks in the C 600 to C 700 range. Southward along Cantonments Rd you'll find three more fast-food places. After 3½ blocks you'll come to the popular *Ramec*. It's a 24-hour joint with inexpensive food for between C 200 and C 1400. Vegetarians may prefer *Dollys*, which is two blocks further south and open every day until 1 am. The menu includes good egg fried rice and falafel sandwiches (C 500), also kebe sandwiches (C 500), burgers and chips (C 950) and fish & chips (C 1500). *Papaye*, which is one block further and provides takeaway service, features the best charcoal-grilled chicken in Accra. It's seasoned with red pepper, ginger and garlic and is accompanied by either chips or rice and coleslaw (C 1900). You can also get burgers for C 700 and fish & chips for C 1900.

African For street food, it's hard to beat the vendors on the north-east side of Nkrumah Circle. During the day, you'll also find a good selection of vendors in the centre just north of the Arts Centre between the Superior Law Courts building and Accra Library. In the Danquah Circle area, try the stalls on either side of the Penta Hotel, two blocks south of the circle. A popular place starting around dusk is near the California and Crown Prince hotels, a block to the west thereof. You can get a full meal of rice, yams, beans and plantains for about C 300. At night, head for Nkrumah Circle, both north and south thereof.

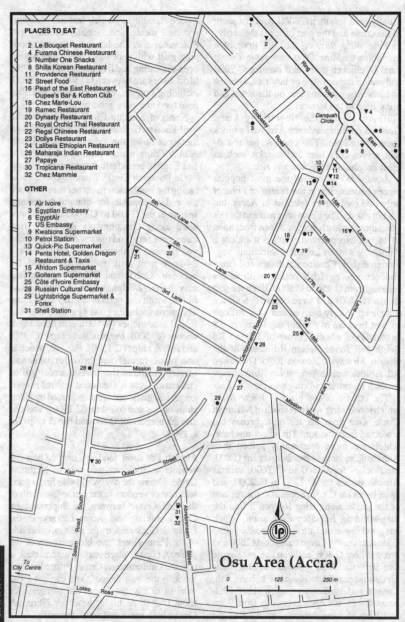

PLACES TO EAT

2 Le Bouquet Restaurant
4 Furama Chinese Restaurant
5 Number One Snacks
8 Shilla Korean Restaurant
11 Providence Restaurant
12 Street Food
16 Pearl of the East Restaurant,
   Dupee's Bar & Kotton Club
18 Chez Marie-Lou
19 Ramec Restaurant
20 Dynasty Restaurant
21 Royal Orchid Thai Restaurant
22 Regal Chinese Restaurant
23 Dollys Restaurant
24 Lalibela Ethiopian Restaurant
26 Maharaja Indian Restaurant
27 Papaye
30 Tropicana Restaurant
32 Chez Mammie

OTHER

1 Air Ivoire
3 Egyptian Embassy
6 EgyptAir
7 US Embassy
9 Kwatsons Supermarket
10 Petrol Station
13 Quick-Pic Supermarket
14 Penta Hotel, Golden Dragon
   Restaurant & Taxis
15 Afridom Supermarket
17 Goiteram Supermarket
25 Côte d'Ivoire Embassy
28 Russian Cultural Centre
29 Lightsbridge Supermarket &
   Forex
31 Shell Station

Danquah
Circle

Ring
Road

Embassy
Road

East

6th
Lane

5th
Lane

Lane

Cantonments Road

3rd Lane

15th
Lane

16th
Lane

17th Lane

18th
Lane

Mission Street

Mission
Street

Karl
Quist
Street

Salem Road
South

Lokko Road

Abrebrensem
Street

To
City Centre

Osu Area (Accra)

0   125   250 m

GHANA

A good place in the centre of Accra is the *Harvester's Restaurant* across from Cocoa House and behind Akuaba travel agency. It's a simple place but spotless, with ice-cold air-con. Most dishes are Ghanaian and in the C 1500 to C 2000 range. It's open until 6 pm.

If you'll be visiting the National Museum on Barnes Rd, consider going around noon and having lunch at the museum's breezy *Edvy Restaurant*, which is a great place for sampling Ghanaian cuisine, the speciality here. Open only for lunch, the menu features daily specials, also apapransa and palava sauce, palm soup, red-red (fish), snail soup, seasoned crab and a special buffet on Wednesday which includes fufu, jollof rice, fried red plantains and red bean stew. All dishes are C 2500. If this is too expensive, try *Best Cuisine*, which is not far away, several blocks south-eastward on the corner of Sixth Ave and Morocco Rd, both dirt roads. It's a cafeteria on the 2nd floor and most Ghanaian dishes are C 800 (C 1200 for Chinese dishes). Don't confuse it with the more expensive restaurant on the 3rd floor which has Ghanaian lunch specials for about C 2500 and other dishes closer to C 4000. A great *chop bar* featuring mainly rice dishes is just to the south closer to Liberia Rd, and facing it is a similar place with banku and fufu.

Another place with good prices is the *African Heritage Restaurant* at the Du Bois Centre (☎ 776502) on 1st Cantonments Rd, some 250 metres south of Burma Camp Rd. All dishes are in the C 800 to C 1500 range including fufu and groundnut soup (C 1000) and yams with palava sauce (C 800). It closes at 9 pm.

In the Danquah Circle area, the best place for Ghanaian food is *Providence Restaurant* (☎ 773696), conveniently located a block to the south of the circle. There are six Ghanaian selections, all C 2900, including ampesi and fufu, plus various slightly more expensive European dishes. It's open until 6 pm every day except Sunday when it's closed. At night, a more fun place to go is *Blue Gate*, which is almost one km south of the circle on the corner of Mission St Extension and Okodan Rd. The speciality is grilled tilapia fish and banku. It's very lively especially on weekend nights. A meal with beer shouldn't exceed C 2500.

For Ethiopian food, head for *Lalibela Restaurant* (☎ 776343), five blocks south of Danquah Circle on 18th Lane facing the Côte d'Ivoire embassy. There are over one dozen selections, including doro wat (spicy chicken) and lamb stew, all in the C 3500 to C 4000 range, and some vegetarian dishes. They're served in traditional style on large pieces of Ethiopian injera bread in a shared round basket. It's open for lunch and dinner and don't arrive early because it takes a long time if you're the first customer.

If you want simply the best Ghanaian restaurant in Accra, head for the undisputed champ, *Country Kitchen* (☎ 229107), in 2nd Ringway Estate (south-east of Sankara Circle); all the taxi drivers know it. Open from 9 am to 11 pm and closed on weekends. The service is good, the food is fresh, and it's excellent value.

Asian Accra has the best Chinese restaurants in West Africa, and all are open every day. If price is your major concern, try *Pearl of the East* (☎ 774907) behind the Penta Hotel, which is on Cantonments Rd. Most dishes are in the C 1200 to C 1800 range. There's also an outside section which has music and a more rustic, casual ambience. Afterwards, you can have a drink at Dupee's, a popular pub next door.

Boajin (☎ 775847) to the north-east in the Cantonments area, and *Lam's Restaurant* at the Granada Hotel are too remote to recommend for travellers without wheels. The best is the attractive *Hinlone Restaurant*, where most dishes are in the C 2200 to C 2800 range. Anything with black bean sauce is terrific, especially the lobster, and the wonton soup and home-made bean curd are superb. It's on the east side of Danquah Circle on Orphan Crescent Rd in the Labone area. From the circle, go south-east for one km and take your first left (Sithole Rd), then first left again for 30 metres.

The two other strong contenders for the best Chinese restaurant are *Dynasty Restaurant* (☎ 775496) on Cantonments Rd, about half a km south of Danquah Circle, and the *Regal Chinese Restaurant* (☎ 773386), around the corner on 5th Lane near Salem Rd South. The Dynasty is the fanciest and features Peking cuisine while the attractive Regal has mostly Chinese clients, which is always a good sign. The Regal's prices are the same as Hinlone's and there's a big menu as well.

Thai & Vietnamese For Thai cuisine, from the Regal head 50 metres eastward to Salem Rd South, then southward for a block to the new and attractive *Royal Orchid Thai Restaurant* (☎ 662993). Run by a friendly Thai woman, it's a bit more expensive, with most dishes in the C 2500 to C 3800 range, but this place is well worth the price. The lemon grass soup and the pad Thai are among the house specialities. For Vietnamese fare, your only choice is *Chez Lien* (☎ 775356), a new place in the airport residential area which is a hotel and also serves reportedly better French food.

Korean The *Shilla Restaurant* on Ring Rd East, 100 metres south-east of Danquah Circle, serves excellent Korean food in attractive surroundings at moderate prices.

Italian The best Italian restaurants are all out towards the airport. *Round Gidda Restaurant*, also known as Vittorio's or 'the 37', gives the best value. It's nestled in the woods behind the taxi park and opposite a Mobil petrol station, just north of No 37 Roundabout. You can get excellent pasta with pesto, lasagne or fresh fish for about C 4000, which includes a salad and garlic bread.

Further north, one km beyond the airport, is the *Shangri-La Hotel*, which has the best pizza in town. Nearby in the airport residential area, on the corner of Volta and Akosombo Rds, is *Bella Napoli* (☎ 773389), the city's finest restaurant of any kind; expect to pay C 10,000 a person with drinks.

Indian The long-standing *Maharaja Restaurant*, conveniently located on Cantonments Rd, about 600 metres south of Danquah Circle, is pleasant enough but it's not great.

German If you have a hankering for German food, check the *Aquarius Restaurant* on Osu Crescent, just south of Labone Junction and about one km north-east of Danquah Circle. It has an extensive menu and good food, especially the potato salad and sausages. Expensive German bottled beer is available, and there's a pool table plus pinball and table football. It's closed Monday.

French The city's five French restaurants are all expensive and all closed on Sunday. The best is apparently *Le Bouquet* (☎ 772417), a new restaurant on Ring Rd East near the Russian embassy and Danquah Circle. Two others are *La Chaumière* (☎ 772408), which is in the airport area and well marked, just beyond Hotel Granada, and the previously listed *Chez Lien* in the same residential area.

For most travellers, the two best options are the more conveniently located *Chez Mammie* (☎ 775670) and *Chez Marie-Lou* (☎ 227975), both on Cantonments Rd south of Danquah Circle. Chez Mammie, which is one km south, charges C 3000 to C 4500 for most dishes (but bouillabaisse for C 7400!). It's a small cosy place and reservations are essential on Friday and Saturday nights. About halfway between Chez Mammie and the circle you'll pass the Swiss-run Chez Marie-Lou (☎ 227975), which has similar fare and prices but is not so intimate.

Entertainment
Around Ghana is a bimonthly information and entertainment guide to Accra. The cost is C 1000 and most hotel bookshops carry it.

Bars One of the best places for a drink is *Annabelle's* (listed under Places to Eat). Beers are C 800. For a real dive, day or night, head for the cheap *Wato Bar* in the centre at the intersection just east of the post office. From the 2nd-floor terrace, it's like being on a ship. At night however, the area is not safe.

The highly popular *Afrikiko* is an outdoor beer-garden 200 metres north of Sankara Circle. Draught beers, snacks and full meals are all available. Much better, however, is the

Afrikiko Garden Amusement Centre next door, a bar and ice-cream shop.

Another institution, the small *Bus Stop Restaurant*, has good music. It has a bar-like atmosphere and is good for a drink (draught beers for C 400) and snack food.

Number One Snack Bar (see Places to Eat) is a good inexpensive place for draught beer and light meals. Nearby, around the corner from the Penta Hotel is *Dupee's*, a pub-like bar with music, darts and beers for C 800. At night, a great place for drinking and viewing the much wilder activity around Nkrumah Circle is *Terra Nova*, just south of the circle.

If you're at Independence Square, don't miss chatting with old George at *George Attoh's Bar* on Ashanti Blohun St, a short north-south road 800 metres to the east. It's open from noon to 10 pm every day except Sunday.

Nightclubs Accra is one of the best places in West Africa for dancing, especially on Saturday night. The wildest spots are around Nkrumah Circle. Some 80 metres south of the circle is *Piccadilly Circle*, colloquially known as 'Pick-a-Lady'. It's open-air, fun and vibrant, usually with a nightly reggae band and no cover charge. *Kilimanjaro* next door has a C 500 cover charge and is a darkly lit modern disco with more prostitutes. If you're wearing sandals, you'll be refused entrance at Kilimanjaro's, but you can often rent shoes from the prostitutes outside. Just across the street is the popular *Container Spot*. All three places are open every day from 8 pm and start getting lively from about 10 pm. At any one of them you may be offered cocaine, gold smuggling, marriage, prostitutes and lots of other deals best refused.

Two other open-air places worth checking are *Tip Toe Gardens* a block north of the circle and *Apollo Theatre* 400 metres east of the circle on Ring Rd. Both are popular long-standing dancing places with small covers (about C 500) and occasional live bands. For the truly brave, there's *The Caribbean*, a Rasta bar with lots of ganja and interesting people. It's north of Nkrumah Circle in Kokomlemle and anyone with a Rasta hairdo should be able to give you

directions; otherwise walk up Nsawam Rd, turn right at the Shell station, left on the first major street and keep walking north.

For great dancing places which are a bit tamer, head for Cantonments Rd in Osu. Most of them have cover charges, typically around C 2000. The best is the loud *Kotton Club* around the corner from the Penta Hotel. It's cool, comfortable and nicely furnished. Almost equally good but a bit more unusual is *La Cave du Roi* on Salem Rd South near Third Lane. Cave-like with stalactites hanging from the ceiling and tables, and chairs resembling giant fungus, it's dimly lit and so tiny that if you don't get here by 11 pm, you'll have no chance for a seat. Also try *The Matador* and *Mapees*, both widely advertised in local newspapers.

Cinemas The best cinema is Ghana Films on a street behind (west of) Afrikiko. It shows the latest Ghanaian films (C 700) and is often packed. Next door the Executive Film House shows mostly recent US films (C 1000). Both places have air-con and showings every night at 6.30 and 8.30 pm (also 10.30 pm on Saturday).

Two large, central public theatres are the Orion at Nkrumah Circle and the Rex behind Parliament House. Show time is usually around 8 pm. In addition, every Thursday is film night at the Goethe Institute.

Cultural Performances Check *Around Ghana* for what's going on at the W E B Du Bois Centre for Pan-African Culture (☎ 776502) at 22 1st Circular Rd in the Cantonments area, some 250 metres south of Burma Camp Rd. Du Bois, an African-American, was raised in the USA and died in Ghana. He was very critical of the treatment of African-Americans in the USA. His tomb and that of his wife are on the premises. In addition to public lectures on Africa, you'll see jazz concerts and other musical performances, and you can dine at the centre's *African Heritage Restaurant*.

Things to Buy
Artisan Goods Outside the Arts Centre

(open every day) you'll see a wide assortment of wooden carvings, masks, brass, baskets, blankets, paintings (not all Ghanaian) plus a wide assortment of materials, including the famous kente cloth. Asking prices are often high, so expect to bargain hard. The musical instruments here are cheap imitations; the prices and selection of carvings and cloth are better in Kumasi; and Koforidua has a more varied bead market.

Makola Market is OK for glass beads although they're not particularly cheap. You can also find lots of fabrics here including batiks and tie-dyes, particularly at the shops surrounding the market as well as those on Kojo Thompson Rd, and Selwyn and Derby Aves. Expensive wax cloth from Holland is everywhere, but you can also find almost identical cloth made by Akosombo Textile Co that is virtually as good and much cheaper. Another street to check is Zongo Lane, which has rows of small shops offering colourful prints. That lane is not far from the post office; ask someone to show you the way. You might also try The Loom, a few blocks west of Nkrumah Circle, which has fabrics and clothes as well as wooden carvings and statues.

One of Ghana's top artists, Glover, owns a gallery on the road to Tema, a few km past the Labadi Beach Hotel; it's worth visiting.

Music For cassettes of Ghanaian music, try the music shop outside the Arts Centre. Open daily until 6.30 pm, it has an extensive collection and can be helpful in selecting recordings. There are also lots of music stores on Nkrumah Ave south of Nkrumah Circle where you can ask to record a specified selection of tracks (the cost is little more than that of a pre-recorded tape). Street vendors selling tapes are another source; the standard price is C 1800.

Getting There & Away

Air For flight arrival/departures, call the airport (☎ 776171). The following airlines have their offices along Kojo Thompson Rd: Nigeria Airways (☎ 223749), British Airways (☎ 667800/7900) and Aeroflot (☎ 225289).

Others have their offices along Nkrumah Ave at or near Cocoa House: Ghana Airways (☎ 221151/0), Air Afrique (☎ 666256/9557) and Ethiopian Airlines (☎ 222657) at Cocoa House, KLM (☎ 224050/4370) and, further north, Balkan Airlines (☎ 220491). Swissair is on Independence Ave. EgyptAir (☎ 777826/6586) on Ring Rd just off Danquah Circle will pay for overnight lodging in Cairo if you're flying to Europe with them. Air Ivoire (☎ 224666) is nearby at Trinity House on Ring Rd, 350 metres west of Danquah Circle.

Airlink (☎ 773498) has flights on Sunday, Tuesday and Friday at 5 pm for Kumasi and on Monday, Wednesday and Friday at 9.15 am for Tamale (C 28,000). For tickets and information, see M&J Travels & Tours (☎ 773498) across from the train station.

Bus There are two STC bus stations in Accra. The main one (☎ 221912 for information) is on the western side of town just east of Lamptey Circle; the second one, which serves Aflao (bordering Lomé) and Akosombo, is in the city centre at the north-eastern corner of Makola Market, next to Tudu Station. STC buses fill up quickly, so most people buy tickets well in advance. There are departures hourly for Kumasi and Takoradi between 5 am and 5.30 pm. Late departures are quite common. The trip from Accra takes 4½ hours and costs C 2600. The bus for Tamale costs C 6200 and leaves at 7 am while those for Aflao/Lomé (C 1500) leave at 7 am and 12.30 pm. The one for Ho departs at 1 pm.

Frequent good private buses leave for points north and west from Neoplan motor park on Ring Rd, 100 metres west of Nkrumah Circle. Private buses for Tema, Ho and Aburi leave from Tema Station a block east of the Novotel. The buses for Takoradi (C 1600) leave from Kaneshie motor park on the western side of town, half a km west of Lamptey Circle. To get to Kaneshie motor park, take a tro-tro from Neoplan for C 100.

Bush Taxi & Tro-Tro Bush taxis and minibuses for Tema, Ho and Aburi leave from Tema Station. Those for Aflao/Lomé (C 1800) and Akosombo (C 800) leave from Tudu Station, which is part of the north-east corner of Makola Market, 600 metres west of the former motor park. For details on getting to Lomé, see To/From Togo in the main Getting There & Away section.

Private buses, tro-tro and shared taxis for Kumasi, Tema and most destinations northward, leave from Neoplan motor park. For Winneba, Cape Coast, Takoradi and Abidjan they leave from Kaneshie motor park on the western side of Accra on Winneba Rd, half a km west of Lamptey Circle. You can also catch tro-tro to Winneba, Swedru (C 700) and Cape Coast (C 1350) at the small CNB motor park in the centre on Kinbu Rd just north of the train station.

Train The train station is in the city centre on the corner of Nkrumah Ave and Kinbu Rd. There is one train a day to Takoradi at 7.25 pm and another to Kumasi at 8.30 pm, arriving both cities about 10 to 12 hours later. The fare to Takoradi/Kumasi costs C 1400/2200 in 2nd class (C 2200/3200 with sleeper) and C 2400/2800 in 1st class (no sleepers). Neither train has a bar or restaurant. Advance ticket purchase is usually not required.

Getting Around

To/From the Airport Accra's Kotoka Airport has a post office, DHL courier service, a business centre, a restaurant, a bank which is not always open, and a bar.

In front of the terminal is a small taxi park to your left. You can get a fairly cheap shared taxi to any part of the city. For a dropping (unshared) taxi, you'll have to pay considerably more, typically about C 2000 if you bargain well.

For public transport into town, walk to the main highway (Liberation Ave) 250 metres west of the airport to catch a tro-tro or shared taxi. You may not find one going exactly where you're headed, so count on changing vehicles en route. Alternatively, look for other travellers to share a cab with.

Taxi Finding a taxi is usually fairly easy except during rush hours (7 to 8.30 am and 5 to 7 pm). Late at night, you can find them outside the Penta Hotel on Cantonments Rd, and outside the Novotel.

There are three types of taxis in Accra: line taxis, dropping taxis and charter taxis. Line taxis are shared and thus the cheapest; they usually run from major places or between circles. Most line taxis connect the various neighbourhoods to one of the main circles, most commonly Danquah Circle, No 37 Roundabout and Nkrumah Circle. From these circles there are other line taxis to the heart of Accra. So to get to virtually any outlying neighbourhood from the centre, you will probably have to take two taxis, one to a circle and another from there. You're more likely to get to your specific destination if you go to one of the major taxi parks like Neoplan Station, Tema Station and the one at No 37 Roundabout. The taxis there have placards on top indicating their destinations. If you're in the centre, walk over to Nkrumah Ave where many of the taxis heading out from the centre run north along that avenue from the UTC department store to Nkrumah Circle and then branch off from there.

To hail one on the street, point your pointer finger into the air in the direction you want to go and make a circular motion. If you enter a taxi with other passengers, you shouldn't have to worry about the fare. However, if you enter an empty taxi, you'll be quoted the dropping fare unless you say 'no dropping, shared taxi'. Even then, some drivers will refuse and ask you to get out; if this happens, look for another. Fares are fixed. The rate is C 120 from circle to circle and up to C 200 if you pass through several circles. At night, fares go up slightly but they do not double.

A dropping taxi is a taxi to yourself (you are allowed to pick up friends en route however) and is thus more expensive. Rates are negotiable and start at C 400. No destination within the city limits should cost more than C 1000. For longer distances such as from Kaneshie motor park to the university just outside the city (about 14 km), you should pay from C 1500 to C 2000. To hail a dropping taxi, point your finger to the ground in the direction you want to go but don't make a circle. Charter taxis, which are similar, are generally hired for multiple destinations or for a fixed amount of time and are hailed in the same manner. They cost about C 2500 by the hour if you bargain well.

Tro-Tro The Accra-area tro-tro are cheaper than line taxis and they ply the same routes. The main tro-tro parks in the centre are Tudu Station and Tema Station; some of the destinations they serve include Legon, Nungua, Tema, Asylum Down, New Town, Medina and Aburi. CNB motor park just north of the train station serves areas on the western side of Accra as well as Winneba, Swedru and Cape Coast. Neoplan at the north-west corner on Nkrumah Circle serves virtually every area of the city. The park on Ring Rd, 150 metres east of Nkrumah Circle on the southern side, serves Labadi Beach, the airport and Teshi. The park further east at Sankara Circle (northern side) serves points north along Liberation Ave, including the airport and Legon.

Car Vanef Tours (☎ 226365 or 229554, fax 224648) on Farrar Ave near Nkrumah Circle is the Europcar representative. Compared to elsewhere in West Africa, its rates are low. It also has an office at the Golden Tulip Hotel as does Hertz. Avis' head office is at Speedway Travel & Tours (☎ 227744, telex 2134) at 5 Tackie Tawia St in Adabraka, with a 24-hour branch office at the Labadi Beach Hotel (☎ 772501, fax 772520). Two less expensive ones are Graneeda (☎ 772048) and City Car Rentals (☎ 666158).

AROUND ACCRA
University of Ghana

The university, on the northern fringes of Accra in Legon, five km or so beyond the airport, is definitely worth a visit. It is the oldest in Ghana and has one of the prettiest and best maintained campuses in Africa.

Ask for directions to the Balme Library which has a rich collection dating from the colonial era. Some works contain interesting, yet sometimes frightening, views of Africa. Also on campus are a couple of museums and some smaller libraries worth visiting, in particular, the library of the Archaeology Department. The university also has the best bookshop in the country. In the evenings there's quite a few movies showing and various theatrical and musical performances. Look for the announcements pinned to the trees.

Places to Eat For delicious Ghanaian chop at rock-bottom prices you can't beat the campus *Bush Canteen* and the *New Market*, near the tro-tro stand and overhead bridge on Legon Rd. Meals at both cost about C 225. Prices are similar at Legon, Akuafo and Volta halls where you can get kente, banku, fufu, omo tuo, palavar and jollof rice.

The 'in' place is the *Campus Lifeline* at Akuafo Hall. Meals here are more expensive (C 700 to C 2500) so most people just come to drink. Poor quality meals at *The Basement* and *The Rooftop* are also overpriced. Other popular campus restaurants are *Central Cafeteria*, *Premier Palace* and *Sarbah Loggia*.

Getting There & Away For a tro-tro from Accra, head for Tudu Station on Kinbu Rd or, better, the tro-tro stop on the north side of Sankara Circle. If someone yells 'old road' or 'new road', hop on that one because those are neighbourhoods just beyond Legon.

Aburi Botanical Gardens

Aburi is perched on a ridge 20 km beyond Legon and 32 km north of Accra; on a clear day you can just see Accra in the plains below. A few km before Aburi you'll pass **Peduase Lodge**, a weekend house for the president since Nkrumah's time. The famous botanical gardens, just beyond Aburi, provide a popular retreat on weekends. They are well maintained, with majestic trees and a large variety of plants from around the world, including two tall 'monkey pot' trees from Brazil and a quinine tree; the former supposedly trap monkeys. The oldest tree, approximately 150 years old, is a huge kapok tree facing the beautiful headquarters building.

Aburi Botanical Gardens

It's the only tree the British didn't cut down when they were planting the gardens, which opened in 1890. Ask for the caretaker, Emmanuel Obese; he's very knowledgeable and will be glad to show you around. The entrance fee to the gardens is C 500 and taking photos is free except for videos (C 2000 extra).

Places to Stay & Eat Coming from Accra, some 200 metres before the entrance to Aburi, near the girls' school, you'll pass the well-marked *Restaurant May & Lodge*. It's a relaxing breezy place with decent meals at reasonable prices, eg C 1200/1650/2500 for breakfast/lunch/dinner and C 650 for a large beer. There are only four guest rooms. Often full on the weekends, they cost C 6700 and have private baths but no fans.

One hundred metres up the hill from the turn-off for the gardens is *Olander Guest House*, a nicely decorated homy establishment with wonderful family-style meals. The C 5500 rooms are attractive and have fans, carpets and clean shared baths. There are also larger rooms for C 8800 with private baths.

You can also stay at the headquarters building (☎ 22) inside the gardens. It has large clean guest rooms (C 5500) upstairs with wide beds, fans and decent shared baths. Those in front have beautiful views of the gardens. There are modern ventilated self-contained bungalows in back from C 8000 to C 10,000. In both types of rooms, there is sometimes no running water, thus necessitating bucket baths. Not many people stay here; it's peaceful and you can get meals at *Rose Plot Restaurant* in the gardens (C 2500 plus drinks) or, much cheaper, in town.

Getting There & Away Coming from Accra, pass the first entrance into town and continue around to the eastern side where you'll find a second entrance, which is also the entrance to the gardens. For a tro-tro to Aburi, try Tema Station in Accra.

Academy of African Music & Arts Ltd

The AAMAL (☎ (027) 554042), 30 km west of Accra in Kokrobite, is a beach-side resort where you can hear free concerts on weekends, take courses in traditional African music and dance, or simply swim at the sandy palm-fringed beach. Set up by Mustafa Tettey Addy, a master drummer, and his German wife, it currently offers lessons given by Amano and Freddy, two students of his, at their house about 1.5 km from AAMAL on the road into Kokrobite proper. They are highly skilled and know lots of different rhythms, however, the teaching is sometimes slow, and one-on-one instruction in drumming or dancing is not cheap – about C 3000 an hour and C 5000 for two hours. If you get a group together, however, the price per person will be less. On Saturdays and Sundays from 3 to 6.30 pm, the teachers drum for free while people dine.

There's also a good restaurant with freshly squeezed juices and grilled seafood, but it's not cheap. Singles/doubles/triples with shared baths and no fans cost C 5500/6600/7700 including tax (C 8800 with private bath). You can sleep on the beach for C 1500 a person. While the hotel itself is lovely, there are increasing complaints about the staff, the service and the water – or lack of it. Perhaps try finding a family in town that will rent you a room. Ask some of the younger foreign 'students' or people on the beach. Whatever you do, don't camp on the beach; you'll be robbed of everything.

Getting There & Away There is no transport directly to Kokrobite. You can get a tro-tro or bush taxi at Kaneshie motor park in Accra and get off 22 km west on the Accra to Takoradi coastal highway at the turn-off for Kokrobite (look for the 'AAMAL' sign). The fare is C 500. From there you can walk or hitch a ride (there's little traffic, however, except on Sundays) for eight km south to Kokrobite and the well-marked AAMAL just beyond. Or arrange for a private taxi at Kaneshie motor park or elsewhere (there are lots around the Novotel) to take you there and pick you up at a set time.

The Coast

Travellers rave about the coastal area west of Accra, particularly Winneba, Biriwa, Cape Coast, Elmina and Dixcove. Things that make the area extra special are the old slave-trading forts, the fishing villages, a new nature reserve and the low prices. Where else can you see 15 forts and castles along a 250-km stretch of beach, actually sleep in several of them for about US$2, and feast on cheap seafood?

For years, the beach at Dixcove has been one of the most 'in' places on the West African coast for budget travellers; Elmina was not far behind. Today, the upgraded hotel at Dixcove is usually full on weekends, as is the increasingly popular tourist hotel at Biriwa, which has an excellent beach. However, relatively cheap options still exist at Dixcove and Elmina but not at Biriwa. The major coastal city, Takoradi, and its sister city, Sekondi, hold little interest besides the port, but they are transport hubs to Accra, Kumasi and Côte d'Ivoire.

COASTAL FORTS

The major forts and castles, east to west starting with Accra are:

Osu Castle – Accra; now the seat of government and off limits to the public

Fort Good Hope – Senya Beraku, 50 km west of Accra; sleeping at the fort is possible

Fort Patience – Apam, 10 km west of Winneba; it's a guesthouse

Fort William – Anomabu, 18 km east of Cape Coast

Fort Nassau – Mori, nine km east of Cape Coast

Cape Coast Castle – Cape Coast, 165 km from Accra

St George's Castle & Fort St Jago – Elmina, 13 km west of Cape Coast

Fort Vredenburg & Fort English – Komenda, 10 km west of Elmina

Fort Sebastian – Shama, 25 km east of Takoradi; one basic small room where travellers can stay

Fort Orange – Sekondi, next to Takoradi, 237 km from Accra

Fort Metal Cross – Dixcove, 42 km south-west of Takoradi

Fort Princes Town – Princes Town, 50 km west of Takoradi; sleeping at the fort is possible

Fort St Anthony – Axim, 69 km west of Takoradi

Fort Apollonia – Beyin, 65 km west of Axim and 20 km east of Half Assini

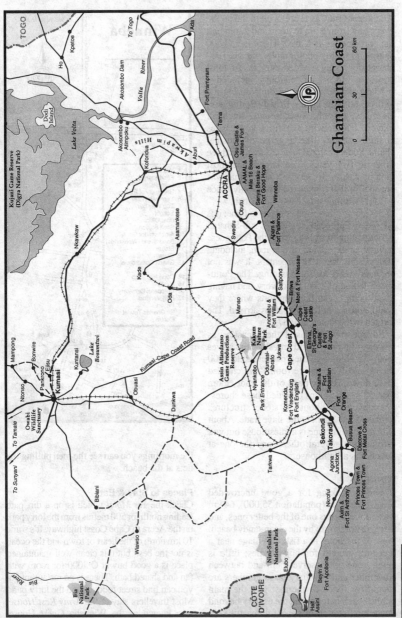

Ghanaian Coast

All except Osu Castle are open to the public every day from 8 am to noon and 2 to 6 pm; the entrance fee is C 600. There is a C 500 charge for taking photographs and a C 1000 charge for using a video camera. At most castles and forts a guided tour is included.

Many of the forts were built during the 17th century; the Danes, British, Portuguese, Germans, French, Swedes and Dutch all played a role, with the forts and castles changing hands like a game of musical chairs. Some changed hands as many as three times in five years. The largest and most famous castle, St George's at Elmina, was unusual in that it changed hands only twice – from Portuguese to Dutch to British.

St George's has another claim to fame; it is the oldest European structure in sub-Saharan Africa, dating from 1482 when the Portuguese brought an expedition of 600 men, including 100 masons and 100 carpenters. It was not originally used for slave trading. The Portuguese, looking for gold and ivory, and having found both, began building forts where they could store it until trading ships arrived. The fort fell to the Dutch in 1637.

Europeans later used these castles as places to literally brand and store the slaves ready for shipping. They packed up to 2000 slaves into four or five rooms and chained them down. By the peak of the trade, more than 50 fortifications crowded these shores.

Today, only about 30 stone structures remain as testament to the slave trade. About half are in ruins; one is a guesthouse but you can sleep at several others; and the one at Sekondi is a lighthouse.

WINNEBA

If you're looking for a good uncrowded beach, Winneba (population 55,000), 64 km west of Accra, has one of the better ones, and there's a hotel right by the clean sandy beach. West of the hotel is a fishing village near a breeding ground for huge turtles; little is being done to conserve them and between November and February large numbers are caught for food. To the east past the main public beach in town and the estuary beyond lies a long stretch of peaceful coastline. In

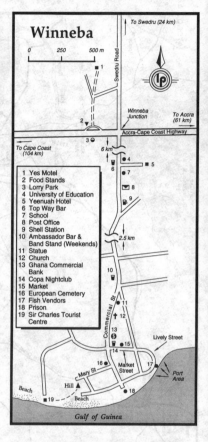

Winneba

1 Yes Motel
2 Food Stands
3 Lorry Park
4 University of Education
5 Yeenuah Hotel
6 Top Way Bar
7 School
8 Post Office
9 Shell Station
10 Ambassador Bar & Band Stand (Weekends)
11 Statue
12 Church
13 Ghana Commercial Bank
14 Copa Nightclub
15 Market
16 European Cemetery
17 Fish Vendors
18 Prison
19 Sir Charles Tourist Centre

the mornings you can see the men pulling the nets at the beach.

Places to Stay & Eat

Check the *Yes Motel* which is on a dirt path leading north for 500 metres from the lorry park on the Accra to Cape Coast highway. It's some 10 km north of the heart of town and the ocean is not the best, but this clean well-maintained place is a good buy at C 3000 for room with fan and shared bath. There is no restaurant but you can find street food around the lorry park. Most travellers stay at the *Army Rest House*, also known as the Winneba Guest House, which is closer to the centre, near the University of Education (or Advanced Teacher Training College). A large ventilated room with a fan, a wonderful view of the ocean and bucket baths with flush toilets costs C 2500 and the woman who runs the place will cook you a meal if you ask ahead. Ghanaians take precedence if only a few rooms are available. Closer to the centre is the *Flamingo Motel*. Cramped doubles cost C 2750, and they serve food if you order in advance.

Next in line is the *Yeenuah Hotel* (☎ 161), a nice and breezy place on a hill some four km from the centre of town. Poorly marked, this white two-storey structure is between the University of Education and post office; take the dirt road leading east from the small Top Way Bar. Singles/doubles cost C 5000/8500 (C 10,000 with private bath).

The city's 'top' hotel is the large *Sir Charles Tourist Centre* (☎ 189), right on the beach and one km west of the port. It has numerous buildings including cement cabins; the rooms are breezy (C 6200/7700 without fans). The C 6200 units are fairly decent with wide beds, fresh sheets, colourful curtains and private baths with running water. There's also a restaurant with selections in the C 1200 to C 2400 range.

Getting There & Away

Tro-tro, buses and bush taxis headed for Winneba and points further west leave Accra from CNB motor park near the train station and from Kaneshie motor park. The cost is C 500. Get off at the 61-km Winneba-Swedru Junction; Winneba is about nine km south. A shared taxi from the junction into town costs C 200 (C 800 if chartered); you could also take a less frequent STC bus.

AROUND WINNEBA
Senya Beraku

Some 20 km east of Winneba, Senya Beraku

Deer Hunt Festival

Winneba is the site of the most famous festival in Ghana – the Deer Hunt Festival (the 'Aboakyer') – which has been celebrated for more than 300 years and is held on the first weekend in May. By legend, Penkye Otu, a tribal god, demanded an annual sacrifice from his people. The main event, therefore, is a competitive hunt in which two *Asafo* (companies) of men, the *Tuafo* (No 1 company) and the *Dentsifo* (No 2 company), go looking for an antelope to sacrifice. The first Asafo company to capture one alive with their bare hands and bring it back to the village chief (*Omanhene*), wins.

Each company has its own colours, emblems and flags, so it's easy to tell them apart. The Tuafo men wear clothes made from blue and white materials and are led by their captain who carries a cutlass and rides on a wooden horse; the Dentsifo dress in red and gold and their captain, who is carried in a chair, wears an iron helmet and carries a sword and cutlass. Early on the Saturday morning the young men put on their traditional battle dress and go to the beach to purify themselves, then to the Penkye Otu's residence to be 'baptised' with herbs, then to the Omanhene's palace to greet the royal family, and finally to the adjacent hunting grounds. Each group, singing war songs along the way, and carrying sticks and cudgels, is equipped with gongs, rattles, bells, bugles and whistles to scare the antelope from hiding. The man who catches one alive rushes with his company to the Omanhene's dais, singing and dancing along the way and hurling taunts at their opponents. The Omanhene is then borne in a palanquin and paraded through the streets amidst drumming and much shouting. The villagers continue celebrating throughout the night.

At 2 pm on the following day, the companies assemble before the Penkye Otu god to question the oracle. For this, the chief priest draws four parallel lines on the ground, one in white clay, one in red, another in charcoal and a fourth in salt. A stone is allowed to roll down from the fetish. If the stone falls upon the white clay line, there will be a great drought. If it falls upon the charcoal lines, it portends heavy rains. Landing on the salt line indicates that there will be plenty of food and fish, while settling upon the red line augurs war and strife. The animal is then sacrificed and cooked, the chief priest taking some of the hot deer soup mixture with his bare hands and placing it on the Penkye Otu fetish. This offering is the *raison d'être* of the hunt and the festival is then over. ■

itself is a dirty place with little of interest, though the people are friendly and will take you fishing if you ask, plus the beaches are isolated and great for relaxing. A fantastic place to stay is **Fort Good Hope**. The fort was built by the Dutch starting in 1706 for purposes of the gold trade, was temporarily captured in 1782 by the British, and finally ceded to them in 1868. This stolid building was originally triangular but was expanded in 1715 when the Dutch converted it into a slave prison and later surrounded it with a wall (barely visible today). Overlooking the sea, the fort offers superb views of all the fishing activity below. It's not a guesthouse, but extremely basic rooms with broken beds and bucket showers are available for about C 1500. The caretaker may cook you a meal; otherwise try the market.

About five km east of Senya Beraku by dirt road is **Fete**, one of the two best surfing spots along the Ghanaian coast (the other is Dixcove).

To get here from Winneba, take a taxi or tro-tro east from Winneba Junction to the tiny Senya Junction (20 km) on the Accra to Takoradi highway; the sign says 'Gomua'. The road south from there to Senya Beraku (13 km) is paved and tro-tro (C 200) and shared taxis (C 300) are usually waiting at the junction.

Apam

Some 15 km west of Winneba, Apam is a small fishing village whose main attraction is also a fort. **Fort Patience** (or Fort Leyd-saemheyt) was originally nothing more than a small two-storey house flanked by two bastions which nevertheless took the Dutch five years to build starting in 1697, hence the name. Later, they added some rooms, lost the fort to the British in 1782, regained it, and lost it again in 1868. Serving as a guesthouse, it has bare rooms, with bucket showers and proper toilets, costing about C 1000 per person. There's a well for water and kerosene lanterns for light. The market has food.

To get to Apam from Winneba, take a taxi or tro-tro west on the coastal road for 15 km or so to the large well-marked Apam Junction (also a second, more western junction for Swedru) and change for Apam, which is about 12 km to the south, facing the ocean.

CAPE COAST

Cape Coast (population 110,000) is noted for having the oldest and best schools in the country, including **Mfantsipim**, the first school on the West African coast.

The major landmark is **Cape Coast Castle** in the heart of town overlooking the sea. In the late afternoon you can watch the fishers as they land their boats at the beach below the castle. Better beaches are west of town at Elmina and Biriwa.

At the western end of town just north of the bypass highway is the **University** of Cape Coast. You could combine a trip to the university with a swim, as the beach is only 200 metres to the south.

Cape Coast Castle
Built with slave labour by the Swedes starting in 1652, Cape Coast Castle changed hands five times during the next 13 tumultuous years, starting with the Danish and ending with the British. For the next 211 years the castle was the headquarters of Britain's operations in West Africa, until 1876 when they moved the capital of the Gold Coast to Accra.

The castle was not originally well-built. Despite being strengthened and greatly enlarged from 1673 to 1694, walls collapsed and roofs leaked until an overhaul in the mid-1700s. Part of the triangular-shaped castle (closed to the public) still serves as a prison. Just inside the entrance is a small museum displaying historical photographs, documents, Ghanaian cultural artefacts and muzzle-loading muskets, and shackles and chains used during the slavery period. It has books of Ghanaian culture and history for sale. The trapezoidal courtyard facing the sea is impressive but the dungeons below are shocking. Several metres underground at the bottom of a ramp are the four dark stale-smelling rooms on whose stone walls you can see the scratchings made by desperate inmates. From here no escape was possible for the 1500 slaves the castle held when full. ■

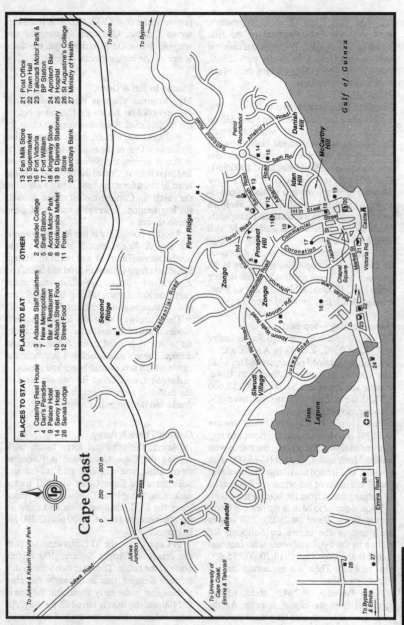

Cape Coast

GHANA

If you visit Cape Coast in September, don't miss the **Fetu Festival** on the first Saturday of the month. It's a raucous carnival and is highlighted by an all-day parade with chiefs from surrounding villages decked out in their finest garments.

Places to Stay – bottom end
A good place for the price is the *Palace Hotel* on Aboom Rd, one km north-west of the centre. This popular well-maintained place, which is frequently full, has clean singles/doubles with fans, basins and shared baths for C 4000/5500 (C 8000 with private shower). Don't leave valuables in your room as a number of travellers have had their belongings stolen. There's a bar on the ground floor and a restaurant upstairs which isn't bad; the area is quite lively with street food nearby.

It is sometimes possible to get a room at the *University of Cape Coast*. Enquire at the residence hall. There are usually a few student rooms for C 1800 available for visitors. Or talk to the students; they may find a bed for you.

Places to Stay – top end
The town's best is the modern *Sanaa Lodge* (☎ 2570 or 2392; 220443 in Accra), a tranquil well-maintained place perched on a hill near the westernmost entrance to town. Rooms are expensive at US$40/C 37,600 (US$50 for a family room) but have TV, mini-bar, carpet and phone.

The tranquil *Catering Rest House* (☎ 2594) is more reasonably priced and recommended if you have wheels. Big rooms with fans and bath cost C 13,000 (C 16,000 with air-con). You'll need a taxi to get here because it's 2.5 km north of the centre off Residential Rd; getting a taxi from the hotel is not easy.

If you'd prefer to be near the heart of town, try the *Savoy Hotel* (☎ 2805), 750 metres north-east of the centre on Saltpond Rd leading to the bypass. Rooms with fans and shared bathrooms cost C 13,200 (C 15,400 with air-con). There's a restaurant but it's relatively expensive.

Dan's Paradise (☎ 2942), about 1.5 km north-east from the centre, is better for the price. Air-con rooms with king-sized beds and

private baths cost C 13,200. The restaurant serves Chinese, Ghanaian, Continental and seafood dishes. On Saturday night, the disco is one of the hottest places in town.

Places to Eat & Drink
My favourite place is the *Adasada Staff Quarters* out on Jukwa Rd half a km before the bypass road. It serves excellent chop for C 300 to C 400 a plate, often accompanied by kenkey. One of the reasons it's so popular is that it adjoins the *Solace Spot*, an active and relaxing bar. One of the best places in the heart of town for street food is half a km from the castle up Commercial St at the Ashanti Rd intersection. It serves a variety of good cheap sauces.

Another possibility is the *New Metropolitan Bar & Restaurant*, 2½ blocks to the north-east on Tantri St just north of Sarbah Rd; it has cheap Ghanaian food and beer. You might also try the *Saraggy Restaurant* in the centre on Kotokuraba Rd near UTC. It serves both Ghanaian and Continental food.

The Kingsway store on Intin St several blocks north of the castle has a small cafeteria which is a good place for snacks and drinks. There's also *Stockwell Bar* near the castle which serves cold beers and meals.

Aprotech, on Elmina Rd one km west of the castle, is a breezy beach-front place for drinks but no longer has rooms.

Getting There & Away
In Accra, the principal lorry motor park serving the Cape Coast road is Kaneshie motor park; you can also find tro-tro and bush taxis for Cape Coast at CNB motor park. Comfortable STC buses from Accra leave the STC station at 8 am and again in the afternoon and cost C 2400 plus C 200 for baggage.

In Cape Coast, the STC bus terminal is in the centre at Chapel Square, 100 metres north of the castle. There are two buses a day to/from Kumasi, one in the early morning and another in the early afternoon; the fare is C 2400 and the road is tarred all the way. All other vehicles (buses, tro-tro and bush taxis) for Accra and Kumasi leave from Accra motor park, which is further north on the corner of Sarbah and Tantri Rds. The tro-tro fare to Accra is C 1350. Takoradi motor park is on the western side of town on Elmina Rd, some 750 metres west of the castle.

AROUND CAPE COAST
Mori
About nine km east of Cape Coast, Mori is the site of **Fort Nassau**, which is in total ruins. Built in 1612 and enlarged during the 1620s and '30s, it was temporarily captured twice by the British, once in 1664 and again in 1782, before being ceded to Britain in 1868. It was the first fort constructed by the Dutch on the Gold Coast and shows almost total lack of adaptation to the African environment. Even the bricks used for the walls were brought from Holland.

Biriwa
Some 13 km east of Cape Coast, Biriwa (bee-ree-WAY) has one of the best **beaches** around and is a popular spot on weekends.

The sandy beach and the modern sprawling *Biriwa Beach Hotel* (☎ (042) 33444 or 33555, fax 2122), on a bluff overlooking the sea, are responsible for Biriwa's growing popularity. Rooms with fans and cold-water showers cost C 15,000 (C 18,000 with sea view and C 25,000 with air-con and telephone). The 10% tax is extra. You can camp here for about C 1000 a person. The specialities of the restaurant, which is the best in the area, are seafood and German dishes; a meal costs C 4000 and above. The well-marked hotel is on the western edge of town and only about 150 metres off the main coastal highway. For reservations, call before 9 am or after 5 pm when it's easier to get through. Getting a reservation on a weekend is extremely difficult.

Anomabu
Anomabu is about five km east of Biriwa and is the site of a second **Fort William**. The original fort here was built by the Dutch in 1640, then changed hands several times before being abandoned in 1730. Starting in 1753, the British began constructing the present fort, renaming it Fort William and using it for trading. Bombarded by the French in 1794 and later attacked by the Ashanti, it was purchased by Britain in 1872 and restored in 1954. It's one of the most handsome and best built forts on the coast and, despite being a prison, can be visited, although there are no tours.

Don't miss the **asafo shrine**. These edifices, generally folk art sculptures, symbolise proverbs or notable events in a village's history. The one here is in the form of a large brilliantly painted ship. Ask the villagers for help in finding it.

Saltpond
Some 25 km east of Cape Coast, Saltpond (population 15,000) also has an asafo shrine; again, ask the villagers for directions.

At Saltpond Junction on the Accra to Takoradi highway are three places to stay, all within 200 metres of each other near the junction to town and well away from the ocean. The cheapest is the *Briefing Course Flats* of the Ghana Educational Services, which has a small sign on your left, 150 metres south of the junction leading into town. It has basic rooms for between C 1500 and C 2000 but the place is often deserted, especially at night when you may have trouble locating the caretaker. Next in quality is the *Hotel Palm Beach*, a well-marked two-storey hotel on a hill on the main highway, just east of the junction. Rooms cost C 4000 and have large beds, clean sheets, fans and attached bathrooms.

The best place to stay is the *Nkubeim Hotel*, an obscure unmarked place on the south-western side of the junction. It's very clean and has guest rooms with comfortable chairs and beds, attached baths and running water for C 5500. The friendly manager will offer you a drink but food is not available.

KAKUM NATURE PARK
Some 30 km north of Cape Coast is the country's newest park, Kakum Nature Park and the adjoining Assin Attandanso Game Production Reserve. It's a tropical, semi-deciduous rainforest that has been developed

for eco-tourism. The park area is 357 sq km but only about 14 sq km of pure virgin rainforest remains; the rest has undergone selective logging in years past. A striking feature of the park is the large number of hanging creepers and climbers.

The diverse and dense vegetation supports forest elephant, bongo, diana monkey, olive colobus monkey, red river hog, duiker and antelope. In all, some 40 species of larger mammals including seven species of primates and over 200 species of birds are found here. The *Field Guide to the Kakum Nature Park*, available at the park headquarters, makes identification much easier. The park has a two-km-long nature trail. Come during the rainy season, May to October, for the best chance to spot elephants.

The park has some rustic wooden structures for camping. They are at Antwikavaa Camp, 20 km north of the park entrance.

Getting There & Away

In Cape Coast, go to Jukwa Junction on the bypass highway and head north-west from there on Jukwa Rd past Jukwa to Abrafo (30 km) and then 1.5 km further to the park entrance. Antwikavaa Camp is on the western border of the park. The park fee is C 1000 and the park trail begins at the entrance. For tro-tro to Jukwa and points further north, look around Takoradi motor park and around Jukwa Junction.

ELMINA

Elmina, a small vibrant fishing village west of Cape Coast, has both a **fort** and a **castle** and it's a wonderful place to pass time with Ghanaians. Just before the castle is the crowded Mpoben fish landing where fishers unload their catch in the afternoon and mend their nets. It's an animated sight and the smells can be overwhelming. The fishing co-operative charges C 100 for the opportunity of experiencing all the activity close-up. Unfortunately the locals use the beach as a public latrine, so don't expect to swim here.

If you're here on the first Tuesday in July, don't miss the **Bakatue Festival**, which is a joyous thanksgiving feast held before the harvest has been brought in. The chiefs parade through town in their finery, each walking under an ornately decorated umbrella and accompanied by members of the family carrying his stool and staff. Singers, dancers and men on huge stilts follow. One of the highlights is watching the priest in the harbour waters casting a net to lift a ban on fishing in the lagoon.

St George's Castle & Fort St Jago

Perched high up on the end of a rocky peninsula, St George's Castle in Elmina is clearly visible from a distance, and is more majestic and imposing than the one in Cape Coast. A double moat (now dry) guards the entrance to the vast castle. The Portuguese built it in 1482 after discovering that the area was full of gold. For the next 150 years they brought beads, metals and hardware to exchange with the Africans for gold and ivory. The exterior was rebuilt between 1580 and 1589 and during that time the French gained control of it for a few months. The Dutch captured the castle in 1637, then between 1652 and 1662 constructed Fort St Jago, several hundred metres away, to help protect it. From then until 1872, when the Dutch ceded it to the British, the castle served as the African headquarters of the Dutch West Indies Company. Both the castle and fort were expanded when slaves replaced gold as the major object of commerce, and the storerooms were converted into dungeons. By the 18th century the Dutch had exported over 65,000 slaves to European and US markets.

You'll leave with a deep impression of just how badly these people were treated – it's amazing any of them survived. The guide here, Charles Adu-Arhin, is enthusiastic and knowledgeable, and during his one-hour tour you'll see the slave quarters, the quarters of the condemned people, the slave auctioning rooms and the governor's quarters. The castle is open every day. Entrance costs C 600, which includes a guide. It's C 500 more if you want to take photographs. ∎

Places to Stay – bottom end

At *Fort St Jago* there are 10 self-contained double rooms. Although not cheap, staying here would be worth it as the fort is wonderfully located on a hill overlooking the castle and the fishing village below. The cheapest place to stay is the *Hollywood Hotel*, or Nyansapow Hotel (☎ 23, operator 20), on the northern edge of town, about six blocks north of the fort and well away from the ocean. Look for the hotel's sign on the road into town from Elmina Motel. Clean guest rooms cost C 4500 (C 6000 for a triple). Some have mosquito nets and all have fans and cold showers and open on to a pleasant courtyard. There's no restaurant but somebody may offer to get you a drink, and direct you to one of the nearby street corners where you can get good chop.

Places to Stay – top end

The 62-room *Elmina Motel* (☎ 2699, ext 20), on the eastern outskirts of town, one km from the centre, has simply furnished bungalows for C 15,000 (10% reduction for more than three nights) for two people, but during the week when there are virtually no guests some travellers have bargained the price down by a third. All have twin beds, fans and individual terraces that receive the ocean breeze. Meals inside are limited and relatively expensive (C 1500 to C 2500) and service is slow. On weekends during the dry season, it is frequently full, so try to make a reservation. If you have problems calling direct, ask the operator for the post office in Elmina, which will then connect you.

Places to Eat

Just across the bridge on the northern side, between the castle and the fort, is the *Castle Bridge Bar*, a good place for drinks and perfectly located overlooking the harbour. *Gramsel J Bar* looks fun from the outside, but inside it's grim, with ordinary food. *Aggie's Video Chop* near the church is reportedly good.

Getting There & Away

In Cape Coast, try the main motor park near Kotokuraba Market for a tro-tro or a shared taxi to Elmina (C 300 by taxi; half that by tro-tro). Or hire a private taxi; it shouldn't cost more than C 1000. If you're coming from Takoradi, have the bus driver let you off at the turn-off for Elmina, about 11 km west of Cape Coast; the town is only several km south. Returning to Accra, you might be able to hitch a ride back with a guest at the Elmina Hotel, especially on Sundays. Otherwise, take a lorry; the fare is C 1450.

KOMENDA

If you're really into old forts, visit the two nearby in Komenda. The Dutch built **Fort Vredenburg** on the left bank of the Komenda River starting in 1688, and five years later the British built **Fort English** on the opposite bank. The former was taken and destroyed by the British in 1782, then restored three years later by the Dutch, who finally ceded it to Britain in 1872. In near total ruin, the forts are still testimony to the fierce rivalry between the countries.

Getting There & Away

To get there from Cape Coast or Elmina, take a bus towards Takoradi and get off about 10 km west of Elmina Junction at the first entrance to Komenda, where there's a small sign 'Ft Komenda – 5 km' pointing down a dirt road. If you're without a vehicle, it may be easier to go two km further west to Kissi Junction where you'll find a tarred road to Komenda; taxis from there cost C 120.

SHAMA

The small fort here, **Fort Sebastian**, which is in the heart of Shama near the ocean, is in good condition and well worth visiting. Built by the Portuguese in 1590 on the site of a former Dutch lodge and abandoned just 10 years later, the fort was in near ruins by the time the Dutch captured it in 1638. After restoration it was taken away from them in 1664 by the British. A few months later, the Dutch regained control, rebuilt it and then held on for over two centuries. Like most Dutch forts it was ceded in 1872 to Britain, which restored it during the mid-1950s. The entrance fee is C 600; don't pay any more if asked.

Less than half a km away on the eastern outskirts of town, where the Pra River joins the ocean, there's a colourful **fish market** along a stretch of beach lined with palm trees. It starts up around 9 am and lasts until 6 pm except on Tuesdays. Nearby on the long peninsula created by the bend in the river there's a beautiful sandy beach, the best area for swimming. Boaters on the town side will ferry you across for a small fee and can take you on longer excursions up the river.

The only place to stay appears to be the fort. For a small donation, the caretaker has allowed travellers to use a room here with bare walls, a hard floor and no bed.

Getting There & Away

Shama Junction, which is not well marked, is about 18 km east of Takoradi off the Accra to Takoradi highway; the town is four km south via a tarred road. You can get a tro-tro from Takoradi to the junction for about C 200 and a taxi fairly easily into town for C 100.

SEKONDI-TAKORADI

The twin city of Sekondi-Takoradi (population 270,000) is as lively as any city in Ghana but it's often skipped over by travellers.

Sekondi (see-con-DEE) is the older of the two cities and the regional administrative centre. The large market next to the motor park is interesting, as is the old '**European Town**' section which has many British colonial-style houses in disrepair. **Fort Orange**, nearby, was built by the Dutch in 1640, seized by the Ahantas in 1694 and abandoned in 1840 before being taken over by the British in 1872, who turned it into one of their main trading posts. Today, it's a lighthouse and open to visitors. The British also built a fort here, Fort Sekondi, but few traces of it remain.

Takoradi was just a fishing village until it was chosen as Ghana's first deep-water seaport; since then it has prospered. The centre is 10 km west of the heart of Sekondi; the road closest to the ocean connects the

two. It's a younger, more vibrant city; the main train station and most of the hotels are here. The heart of town is **Market Circle**; the motor parks are nearby as are most of the cheap hotels and restaurants. The **Artisan Centre**, at the eastern end of Liberation Rd, is one km away. Run by some very friendly people, it's open every day except Sunday from 8 am to 5 pm. There's a wide selection of crafts at fixed prices.

The **port** area is south-west, about two km away; that's where you'll find the main post office, the train station and several banks and large department stores. The better hotels and restaurants are nearby.

The city's main **beach** is two km south of Market Circle.

Places to Stay – bottom end

The three-storey *Embassy Hotel* (☎ 2309) at the western end of Liberation Rd, facing Airport Roundabout, has a grassy area in front with chairs – a good place for sunning and for drinks at night. There's also an active bar-restaurant on the ground floor, but noise can be a problem. Tiny rooms with a large bed and shared bath cost C 3300 (C 4400 with fan and C 5500 with two beds and fan).

The popular and well-maintained *Amenlah Hotel* (☎ 2543) on John Sarbah Rd, about 200 metres west of Market Circle, has equally good rooms with fans and fresh sheets. It has a bar but no restaurant. Singles/ doubles with shared baths cost C 3000/4000 (C 6500 with attached bath).

The place with the best ambience is the *Zenith Hotel* (☎ 2359), an old well-maintained building with a central courtyard several blocks east of the market in an area with good bars and street food. Rooms with one/two beds cost C 3000/4000; the rooms have fans, clean sheets and decent shared baths. There is also a restaurant open on weekdays. On a Sunday morning you'll hear some great singing from the gospel service upstairs.

Another possibility is the *Hotel de Star* a block north of Market Circle. It has rooms on a par with the Embassy's but

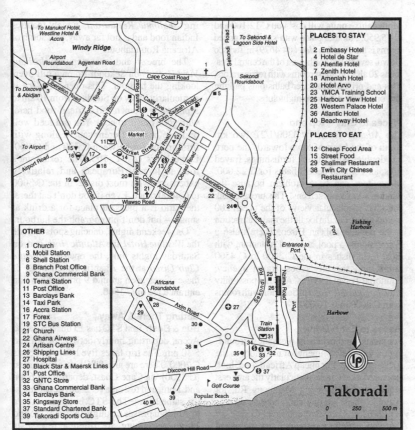

PLACES TO STAY
2 Embassy Hotel
4 Hotel de Star
5 Ahenfie Hotel
7 Zenith Hotel
18 Amenlah Hotel
20 Hotel Arvo
23 YMCA Training School
25 Harbour View Hotel
28 Western Palace Hotel
36 Atlantic Hotel
40 Beachway Hotel

PLACES TO EAT
12 Cheap Food Area
15 Street Food
29 Shalimar Restaurant
38 Twin City Chinese Restaurant

OTHER
1 Church
3 Mobil Station
6 Shell Station
8 Branch Post Office
9 Ghana Commercial Bank
10 Tema Station
11 Post Office
13 Barclays Bank
14 Taxi Park
16 Accra Station
17 Forex
19 STC Bus Station
21 Church
22 Ghana Airways
24 Artisan Centre
26 Shipping Lines
27 Hospital
30 Black Star & Maersk Lines
31 Post Office
32 GNTC Store
33 Ghana Commercial Bank
34 Barclays Bank
35 Kingsway Store
37 Standard Chartered Bank
39 Takoradi Sports Club

Takoradi

there's no bar or restaurant. Singles/doubles with fans and clean shared baths cost C 4400/5500.

Places to Stay – middle

The *Ahenfie* (ah-HEEN-fee-ay) *Hotel* (☎ 4272 or 2966) on John Sarbah Rd across from the Shell station has clean singles/doubles with fan and bath for C 8800/11,000 (C 15,400 for a double with air-con and hot-water baths). The hotel features a disco which is one of the liveliest in town, and an attractive air-con restaurant with carpeting.

For a room with a balcony facing the sea,

head for the *Beachway Hotel*, at the southern end of Axim Rd, near the golf course and 100 metres from the city's major beach. It's a nice laid-back place with large ventilated rooms and clean shared baths for C 6600. There's also a bar with TV, and you can order food on the verandah.

The *Western Palace Hotel* (☎ 3601) at Africana Roundabout, one km to the north, has a TV with CNN in the reception and ventilated rooms with single beds and shared baths for C 5500 (C 9900 with private bath); a similar room with a large bed, air-con, refrigerator and shared bath costs C 9900.

GHANA

More deluxe units will cost you C 12,100 and C 15,950. Another place with similarly priced rooms is the *Westline Hotel* (☎ 4679) in Tadisco Down, several km north-west of the central area. It has 20 air-con guest rooms with refrigerators, TVs and private hot-water baths plus parking and one of the city's top nightclubs.

Places to Stay – top end

The *Atlantic Hotel* (☎ 3300/1/2), two km south of the heart of town towards the port, has doubles with shabby furnishings, frayed rugs, air-con and decent baths for C 22,000. Mosquitoes can be a problem because the windows have no screens. The breezy back patio has spectacular views of the ocean 200 metres away. For the locals the major attraction is the popular Pelican Disco. There's also a Forex, shops, a pool, a decent restaurant with most main dishes in the C 3000 to C 4500 range, and the city's best travel agency, Equitorial Travel Services. Another possibility is the *Lagoonside Hotel* in Sekondi, with rooms from C 8000 to C 16,000.

Places to Eat & Drink

For snacks and drinks in pleasant surroundings, try the refreshment bar next door to the Artisan Centre. For cheap African food, look around Market Circle, particularly the area east of the circle. All along Mampong Rd, for example, there are tiny chop houses, such as the *Ebenezer Chop Bar*, and street food.

If you'd prefer a restaurant, try the one at the nearby Zenith Hotel; it's fairly inexpensive but only open weekdays.

For a more up-market place with air-con near the centre, try the *Ahenfie Hotel*. There are three Ghanaian dishes on the menu, all around C 2500, plus a wide selection of other foods. At the *Takoradi Sports Club* most selections are around C 1000 but you can also get hamburgers for C 600.

Of the city's top restaurants, the best is probably the well-marked *Twin City Chinese Restaurant* (☎ 2516) on the 2nd floor of a building on Dixcove Hill Rd in the port area. Most dishes are in the C 1500 to C 3500 range.

Another top restaurant is the long-standing *Shalimar Restaurant*, which features Indian food and is not far away, just south of Africana Roundabout.

The breezy and ever-popular *Harbour View Hotel* is on Sekondi Rd on a hill overlooking the harbour. This open-air place is particularly lively on Sundays from 10 am to 3 pm when women sell African food here, with good music to boot. You can feed well on three or so different sauces along with fufu or rice for between C 400 and C 800. Large beers cost C 700. The restaurant's food is largely European and relatively expensive, with most dishes in the C 3000 to C 4000 range. Even if you don't eat there, the patio is a pleasant place for a drink at sunset – but don't photograph the harbour.

On weekend nights, dancing spots include the *Westline Hotel*, the *Atlantic Hotel* and, on Saturday nights only, the open-air *Ahenfie Club Disco* at the Ahenfie Hotel. Most of these places open around 9 pm and have an entrance fee of C 1500.

Getting There & Away

Bus & Bush Taxi STC has 15 buses a day to Accra, departing hourly between 4 am and 5.30 pm. The trip takes five hours and costs C 2000. There are also STC buses to Kumasi (C 3000) via Cape Coast, departing at 6 am and 1 pm, and to Tema (C 2200) departing at the same hours. The STC bus from Accra to Abidjan passes through Takoradi around 11 am and there are often a few seats available; the cost from Takoradi is C 6600. The STC station (☎ 3351 for information) is on Axim Rd at the intersection with John Sarbah Rd.

The city's main lorry park, Accra Station, is a block away to the north. Tro-tro and Peugeot 504s depart at all hours of the day and night for Accra; the fare is C 1800 and C 2800, respectively. Those for Cape Coast, and Kumasi via Cape Coast, also depart from here but not nearly so frequently. If you're headed west to Dixcove or Côte d'Ivoire, go to Tema Station, which is about 150 metres further north on the same street. The fare is C 300 to Agona Junction (the turn-off for Busua Beach and Dixcove) and C 1800 to

Elubo (the border) by tro-tro and CFA 5000 to Abidjan by Peugeot 504. The border is open from 6.30 am to 6.30 pm.

For taxis to Sekondi, head for the small taxi park on the south-western side of Market Circle. The fare to Sekondi is C 200 by shared taxi and C 1000 by private taxi.

Train The easiest way to get to Kumasi is by train. There are three trains daily, departing at 6 am, noon and 8 pm and arriving 8¼ hours later. On Sundays however, only the 8 pm train operates. The cost is C 2700/1900 for 1st/2nd class. On the night train you can take a sleeper for C 3900/2900 in 1st/2nd class. There is also a daily train for Accra, departing Takoradi at 7.15 pm, but it's very slow, taking about 12 hours (C 2800/2200 in 1st/2nd class). Sleepers on this train are available only in 2nd class (C 3200 for a berth) and there's no bar or restaurant.

DIXCOVE & BUSUA

Dixcove and Busua, 32 km west of Takoradi, have for years been a Mecca for beach lovers and travellers on the cheap. Busua has only a beach and a hotel (also a tiny settlement) but they're the best in this area. Dixcove, which is a 25-minute walk to the west (12 km by road), has a **fort** and a vibrant **port** and is one of the most colourful fishing towns along the Ghanaian coast.

Those interested in sun and surf should head for Busua beach. A blight killed many of the coconut palms which used to line the long, white sand beach here. Nevertheless, it's still a scenic spot with safe swimming and an island in the distance.

On the shore of a little rocky cove, Dixcove has a harbour deep enough for small ships to enter and partly for this reason it became the site of **Fort Metal Cross**, which overlooks the bay and is now being renovated.

Dixcove is renowned for its **lobsters**; the waterfront and local market are good places to look for them. The village is quite lively and interesting, especially around the port, and the people are friendly.

Places to Stay

Virtually all travellers stay at the *Busua Beach Resort*, directly on the beach in Busua. It has 72 new or remodelled units, all with air-con, telephones and private baths. Each chalet has two rooms and a common kitchen for about C 30,000. The Ghanaian owners are also building 50 dormitories with two beds per room; they will cost C 4000 when completed. You can also camp here for C 1000. The restaurant here is a bit expensive, with beers for C 800 and full meals for much more. Budget travellers can ask the nearby villagers to supply them with food, especially lobster which they will cook for you.

If you prefer to stay with the villagers in Busua, ask for *Sabina's*, *Mary's* or *Elizabeth's*; all the villagers know where these guesthouses are. Sabina's is just to the left of the church on the way to the hotel; she

---

Fort Metal Cross

The British commenced work on Fort Metal Cross in 1683 but disputes with the Germans prevented construction by Captain Dixon until 1691. The fort was on a hill in the village of Fuma, which had over 1000 inhabitants. Over the years, Dixon's Cove became shortened to Dixcove. Dixon made a cross of gold at the fort where he used to pray, hence the name.

Built originally for trading purposes, the fort was besieged for eight years starting in 1748 and converted to a place for storing slaves in 1775. At least two of the slaves, including a 15-year-old girl, were even buried alive as sacrifices to appease the African gods. Both are buried in the courtyard. The Dutch held the fort briefly from 1868 to 1872, and it was restored in the mid-1950s. Conditions were always overcrowded; moreover there was no distance between the quarters of the captors and the captives. The building itself, however, is elegant, with arched doorways flanked by columns and a large open courtyard. ■

charges about C 2500 per room and has a bar as well. Elizabeth has very clean doubles with mosquito nets for C 3000, and Mary charges as low as C 1500 for one of the best rooms in Busua, with a terrace facing the ocean. These places will also prepare you a meal or make arrangements for such.

If you'd like to stay in Dixcove, away from the crowds, head for the *Quiet Storm Hotel*, a well-marked two-storey house on the main drag leading into town. The rooms cost C 5500 and are spacious, carpeted, ventilated and have shared baths with bucket showers. Meals are available.

Places to Eat

In Busua, one of many young locals who prepare meals for travellers is Kofi Saki; ask for him at the two-storey white building on the left, just before entering the Busua Beach Resort. Like others, he needs a minimum of one to two hour's notice. Also try *Frank's Place*; his famous banana pancakes are the main attraction. West of Sabina's, *Frank's Restaurant* has tasty fish and rice for C 700.

In Dixcove, even if you're not staying at the *Quiet Storm Hotel*, the owner will probably be delighted to make you a meal – order in advance. Otherwise, look around the harbour, where there's smoked fish and other street food.

Getting There & Away

Coming from Takoradi, take the main coastal highway west for 20 km to Agona Junction, then south for six km to where the road splits. The left fork leads to Busua and the right one to Dixcove, both six km further. The trip to either one takes 45 minutes from Takoradi.

In Takoradi, tro-tro for Agona Junction or Dixcove leave from Tema Station. Drivers of chartered taxis ask C 8000 one way or round trip, much more if you ask them to wait all day. During the day, you can catch a tro-tro (C 250) from Agona Junction to Dixcove or Busua fairly easily.

If you're headed to Busua, don't wait at that junction for a vehicle to Busua because you may have to wait for hours. Better, take the first one to Dixcove and walk the three km from there to Busua.

WEST OF DIXCOVE
Princes Town

For those looking for a secluded unspoilt beach, Princes Town is a good choice. There is also a fort here, open to visitors. Originally called Gross Friedrichsburg by the Prussians who built it in 1683, **Fort Princes Town** was luxurious by the standards of the day and had a monumental gateway with an impressive bell tower. Within 35 years the Prussians had abandoned it, leaving it in the hands of a crafty African gold trader, John Conny, who was the village chief. The Dutch seized it from him in 1725 and renamed it Fort Hollandia, after which it became a minor trading station until 1872 when it was ceded to Britain. Today, the fort seems half destroyed but it is still quite interesting.

The fort is not a guesthouse but the caretaker still lets people sleep here. Camping on the beach is also possible, but safety might be a problem.

Getting There & Away Getting here is not easy. Princes Town Junction on the coastal road is about 10 km west of Agona Junction. From there it's 20 km or so south to the town (ie about 50 km in all from Takoradi) and the road is very sandy. Taxis will come here only during the dry season. During the rainy season, a 4WD vehicle is necessary. Otherwise, be prepared to walk.

Axim

In Axim, 69 km west of Takoradi, there's **Fort St Anthony**. It was built by the Portuguese in 1515 and is the second-oldest fort on the Ghanaian coast (St George's Castle in Elmina is the oldest). In 1642, it was taken by the Dutch, who subsequently rebuilt the internal structure. Some 22 years later it was captured for a few months by the British and, much later in 1872, ceded to them. It's been in fairly good condition since the mid-1950s. Today, it houses government offices but visitors can take a look. While you're there, you might ask for directions to the nearby village of **Nkroful**. Nkrumah was born there and he's buried in a small mausoleum.

Beyin & Half Assini

Some 65 km further west is Beyin and **Fort Apollonia**. Built by the British between 1750 and 1770, it was abandoned in 1830, temporarily reoccupied by them in 1836 to facilitate confrontation with one of the local kings, then transferred to the Dutch in 1868 and ceded back to the British four years later. It's the newest and sturdiest of the coastal forts and has the oddest shape, with the bastion closest to the sea much larger and stronger than the others.

Half Assini is nearby. It has a bank and the *Captain Williams Hotel*. From here you can catch a boat over to the Côte d'Ivoire side, but it's a hassle as this old route is not well travelled.

The East

TEMA

Some 25 km east of Accra, Tema is Ghana's fourth-largest city and the country's major port. It's a fairly sterile city, so most travellers avoid it. However, if you are leaving Ghana by ship, this is the place to come.

Tema has grown faster than any other city in Ghana (from 35,000 inhabitants in 1961 to about 240,000 now), thanks to the construction of the Akosombo Dam. As a result of that mammoth project, Tema became the site of a huge aluminium smelter, but many of the country's other major industries (oil refineries, cocoa processing plants, cement plants, etc) have their headquarters here too, mostly in the industrial zone near the port.

The most interesting area is the fishing port just behind the main port.

Orientation

The core of the city stretches from the port northward for about six km to the huge roundabout on the lightly travelled express Accra to Tema autoroute (or Toll Rd), one of Nkrumah's extravagant projects which people are still paying for. The city's com-

mercial centre is Community 1, the heart of which is about one km north of the port. You'll find the market there, the post office, various shipping companies and the city's best restaurants. A livelier area of town, however, is Community 8, about four km further north and one or two km before Toll Rd Roundabout. This is where most hotels are located and, unlike in much of Tema, finding a place to eat here is not difficult.

Information

Money To change money, try the Ghana Commercial bank next door to the old Meridien Hotel or look for a Forex in the area around the market.

Travel Agency For airline reservations, try Special-T Travels (☎ 6221 or 4030) at the Abronkase-C9 shopping centre.

Shipping Companies Ghana's major shipping company is the Black Star Line (☎ 2088 or 2888), just north of the port. If you want to ship something or hop on a freighter, enquire here weekdays from 8 am to 5 pm.

There are various other shipping companies. The best for shipping motorcycles is Ewald because it's the only one which will sell you space in a container. The agent for Grimaldi Lines is Umarco Ghana Ltd (☎ 4031), also in the greater port area. For other lines, enquire at the Ghana Port-Harbour Authority (GPHA) near the port entrance.

Places to Stay

The only hotel near the port area appears to be the *Friends Hotel Annexe* (☎ 6575), which is 1.5 km to the west of the defunct Meridien. This one-storey house-like establishment is very clean and has spacious rooms with shared baths and fans/air-con for C 6500/10,000. Food is not available but just behind there's a small restaurant. It's in a residential area, so anticipate walking a bit before finding a taxi to go anywhere.

Most hotels are in Community 8, all of similar quality and fairly respectable in appearance, with two or three floors of rooms. One of the newest is *Hotel Lucia* (☎ 6134), which has rooms on a par with the Friends' for C 6600 (C 10,050 with air-con). Some 250 metres away in the very heart of Community 8 you'll find the *Page Hotel* (☎ 6244). It has air-con rooms for C 13,000; there's a good restaurant next door and an open-air nightclub and a casino a stone's throw away. About four long blocks further north you'll come to the *Hotel du Planet* (☎ 2613), which has singles/doubles with fans for C 7700/8800 and air-con for C 9900 to C 13,000. Just across the street is the *Satellite Hotel* (☎ 2402), which has rooms

with fans/air-con for C 6600/9900, more expensive units with TVs and refrigerators for C 15,000, and a restaurant.

Places to Eat

For inexpensive fare in the port area, head for the popular *Cottage Grove Restaurant*, about 500 metres west of the port gates. The menu includes banku (C 1000), sandwiches (C 800), jollof rice with chicken (C 1200), fufu chicken (C 1500), large beers (C 600) and cold soft drinks (C 300). It's a breezy place with wooden picnic-type tables and closes at 6 pm. Sailors should try the

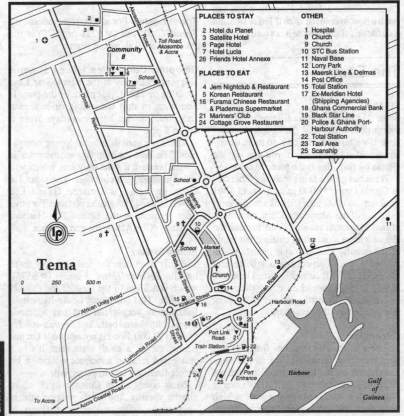

PLACES TO STAY	OTHER
2 Hotel du Planet	1 Hospital
3 Satellite Hotel	8 Church
6 Page Hotel	9 Church
7 Hotel Lucia	10 STC Bus Station
26 Friends Hotel Annexe	11 Naval Base
	12 Lorry Park
PLACES TO EAT	13 Maersk Line & Delmas
	14 Post Office
4 Jem Nightclub & Restaurant	15 Total Station
5 Korean Restaurant	17 Ex-Meridien Hotel
16 Furama Chinese Restaurant	(Shipping Agencies)
& Plademus Supermarket	18 Ghana Commercial Bank
21 Mariners' Club	19 Black Star Line
24 Cottage Grove Restaurant	20 Police & Ghana Port-
	Harbour Authority
	22 Total Station
	23 Taxi Area
	25 Scanship

Tema

0   250   500 m

Mariners' Club, which is just north of the port facing Black Star Line.

The city has lots of Asian restaurants. In the centre you might try the *Furama Chinese Restaurant*, at the southern end of Baba Fara St, behind the Meridien and next to the tiny Plademus supermarket, or the *Mermaid* (☎ 2221), which is also in Community 1 as is the long-standing *Chopsticks* (☎ 6424). Another place on a par with some of Accra's finest Asian restaurants is the *Atlantic Chinese Restaurant* (☎ 6966), which is further north in Community 5.

If you're out in Community 8, eating at one of the hotels there is a possibility. The *Korean Restaurant*, next to the Page Hotel, is highly regarded. For a less expensive and more relaxing open-air place to eat, try the *Jem Nightclub & Restaurant* behind it. Afterwards, you could try your luck at the *Club Vegas Casino* next door. For dancing, in addition to Jem there's the *Alcazar Disco*, which is closer to the city centre.

Getting There & Away

Bus & Tro-Tro STC has large buses serving the Accra-Tema route, departing Tema hourly from just north of the central market and Accra from the STC station. Tro-tro for Tema, which depart more frequently, leave Accra from Tema Station and from Neoplan motor park 100 metres west of Nkrumah Circle. The fare is C 280. In Tema, you'll find them at the lorry park on Torman Rd and around the central market.

ADA

The only noteworthy thing about Ada, a small river town 70 km east of Tema, is the attractive 51-room *Paradise Beach Hotel*, a 1st-class beach resort on the outskirts facing a protected beach. Otherwise, try one of the cheap guesthouses in town; there are reportedly several to choose from. Driving here from Accra takes a good hour. On the way you might stop in the fishing village of **Prampram** to watch the fishers repair their nets. Fort Yernon and Fort Kongensten, both dating from around 1800, are in complete ruins.

AKOSOMBO

The Akosombo Dam, 104 km north-east of Accra, is responsible for the world's largest artificial lake – the 402-km-long Lake Volta. It's also the starting point for cargo ships north to Kete-Krachi, Yeji and Yapei (near Tamale).

The town of Akosombo, two km before the dam and six km before the port, was built to house the workers who built the dam; resident engineers and other Volta River Authority (VRA) employees are still there. Five km to the south is **Atimpoku**, where you'll find the main lorry park and several cheap hotels and chop bars. If you're interested in fishing or just taking a canoe ride out through the tall grass to the lake, go to **Kpong**, which is south of Atimpoku. The villagers there have canoes and will take you for a small fee. There's also a clean public pool near the tourist hotel in Akosombo; it costs about C 500.

To visit the dam, you must get permission from the VRA authorities at the administration building just down the hill from the Volta Hotel. You'll need a vehicle and if you're without one, the administration building is the best place to look for a lift, which you are likely to find only on weekends. A very touristy thing to do is to take the modern *Dodi Princess* on a cruise to nearby Dodi Island. The trip takes six hours altogether with two hours on the island. Departures are on Sundays at 10.30 am. The fare is C 6500 (bring a picnic). On Saturdays it departs at 4 pm for a two-hour trip to the nearby dam.

In general, it is prohibited to take photos of dams in Ghana; they are considered as military sites. However, if you go to the Volta Hotel, you'll find tourists taking photos of the dam without hassle. Elsewhere around the dam, you could run into big problems with the military.

Places to Stay & Eat

Akosombo has no hotels, so you'll have to stay in Atimpoku. The best value is the *Benkum Hotel*, which is a good clean place with rooms sleeping three people for C 3600 (C 4800 with fan). If it's full, enquire at the motor park whether the nearby *Delta Queen Hotel* is still in business; if so, its rooms

Akosombo Dam

Back in 1915, a far-sighted engineer, Albert Kison, realised that the Kwahu plateau was a rich bauxite deposit and that if the Volta River at Akosombo could be dammed, there would be more than enough electricity to generate a huge foundry, and that Tema was suitable for converting into a deep-water port to export the aluminium. He submitted his report to the British governor, Guggisberg, who dismissed the idea as too expensive. Some 40 years later, Nkrumah picked up on the idea. Obsessed with industrialising the country as fast as possible, he felt it was necessary to go forward with the project at all costs. However, at that time the country was exporting only about UK£25 million worth of gold, manganese, bauxite and diamonds. While impressive by African standards at the time, this was far too little to carry out the project, so he had no option but to accede to the exceedingly harsh terms of Valco, the US company most interested in the project. Valco's terms were that in return for constructing the dam, it would receive over two-thirds of the electricity generated for its aluminium smelter at Tema, that the price it paid for the electricity would be at cost, and that these generous terms would extend far into the future.

The project was so costly that the plans for extracting bauxite from the Kwahu plateau had to be shelved. The necessary raw material would be imported instead. Work began in 1961 and costs immediately began escalating. Young Ghanaians who would operate the dam had to be sent abroad for training, and 84,000 displaced people had to be relocated, mostly to the Kete-Krachi area, plus at Tema a completely new port and town had to be constructed. Meanwhile, as work progressed, the price of cocoa slumped sharply on several occasions. The drain on the economy was simply too much, so just a month after Nkrumah inaugurated the dam in 1966, the army ousted him. For the next 17 years, the economy spiralled downward and because the terms with Valco allowed very little potential for earning money from power generation, there was never any chance to realise the dam's potential for electrifying the country or irrigating nearby farmland. Indeed, by the early 1980s, while blackouts were occurring almost nightly in Accra, in Benin and Togo, where the government was forced to sell electricity to earn foreign exchange, electricity was plentiful. With Rawlings in command, the country is just now beginning to really benefit, but the dam's full potential is still far from realised.

The statistics regarding the dam and lake are impressive. The dam is 124 metres high and 368 metres wide and can generate 912,000 kilowatts. Except when there are back-to-back droughts, as in 1983-84, there's enough electricity to power all of Ghana and even a good portion of neighbouring Togo and Benin. Because of potential earthquakes, the dam is not built of solid concrete but, rather, has a central nucleus of clay covered by a layer of crushed rock and outer walls covered with huge rocks. As for Lake Volta, the world's largest artificial lake, it stretches 402 km and has 4830 km of shoreline. However, it floods 850,000 hectares of land – 7% of Ghana's land surface – and virtually nothing is being done in terms of fishing, commerce or irrigation to compensate for that loss. On this account alone, in many circles the dam is viewed as a colossal disaster. All over the world, however, huge dams like Akosombo have run into massive problems, so the country's experience with it is perhaps closer to the norm than the exception. ■

should cost about the same. The motor park is also the best place for street food. The speciality of the region is fried shrimp; they're sold in plastic bags around the motor park and are quite tasty.

For more up-market accommodation, try the *Lakeside Motel* (☎ 310) south of Atimpoku in the direction of Kpong. It has a pleasant setting and rooms with fan for C 8800 (C 11,000 with air-con which doesn't always work).

The only top-end hotel is the modern single-storey *Volta Hotel* (☎ (0251) 1731, Accra ☎/fax 663791), which is ideally perched on a hill with sweeping views of the lake, dam and surrounding Akwamu highlands. Run by the VRA and recently completely renovated, it has 34 rooms, four suites and a terrace restaurant overlooking the lake; the shrimp and fresh lake perch are their specialities. Rooms (C 60,000) have air-con, bars, safes, TV and private baths. Even if you don't stay here, a drink at the restaurant is a must; the views are spectacular. In the evening, guests are sometimes taken to see a traditional dance. Most credit cards are accepted.

Also check the *Maritime Club*, 300 metres beyond the port. It has relatively cheap drinks and kebabs and lots of expatriates go

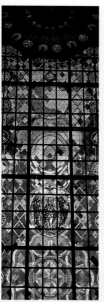

Top Left & Right: The Basilica, Yamoussoukro, Côte d'Ivoire (AN)
      Bottom Left: Fetish temple, Korhogo, Côte d'Ivoire (AN)
   Bottom Right: Modern African painting, Grand-Bassam, Côte d'Ivoire (AN)

Top: Fishing boat, Elmina, Ghana (DW)
Middle: Children in Shama, Ghana (AN)
Bottom: Fishing boats & St Georges Castle, Elmina, Ghana (DW)

there on weekends. They have been known to offer travellers lodging in their homes.

Getting There & Away

Bus, Bush Taxi & Tro-Tro Buses for Akosombo leave from Tudu Station in Accra, near Makola Market. The best buses are those of STC. You can also find private ones (C 800; two hours) and tro-tro and bush taxis there. Those for Ho and Kpandu also stop in Akosombo but they leave from Tema Station nearby.

In Atimpoku, you'll find lots of taxis at the lorry park headed for Akosombo. In Akosombo, the cheapest way to get to the dam (six km) is to hop on one of the yellow workers' buses that leave every 30 minutes during the day from the lorry station there; they stop in front of the administration building, just below the Volta Hotel.

Steamer The steamer presents a great alternative to travelling upcountry by road. Some travellers find it a wonderful adventure, quietly drifting between green hills with tiny fishing villages on the banks and lots of canoes floating by. Others find the trip a nightmare (most would not do it more than once), however, it's an excellent opportunity to get off the tourist track and meet the locals.

These days, the only ships plying Lake Volta are cargo boats which means that you'll almost certainly have to sleep on deck. Most passengers sleep on straw mats which are sold just outside the port in Akosombo. Be prepared to sleep on a stack of fertiliser bags and share filthy squat toilets. The toilets get worse as the journey progresses, so try to use them early on. Be sure to bring mosquito repellent. Food and drink can be purchased at every stop.

The principal steamer is the *Buipe Queen*. It departs Akosombo on Tuesdays around 4 pm, arriving at Kpandu around 10 pm and Kete-Krachi early the next morning. After several hours at Kete-Krachi it leaves at 11 am, arriving at Yeji around 4 pm and Yapei before midnight. From Yapei it goes southwards in the wee hours of Thursday morning to Yeji, arriving mid-morning, and then reaches Kete-Krachi by mid-afternoon. It leaves Kete-Krachi at 5 pm, arriving in Kpandu about 11 pm and Akosombo on Friday around 7 am. The one-way fare is C 2600 to Kete-Krachi, C 3800 to Yeji and C 5000 to Yapei. Advance bookings are not required but try to buy your ticket in Akosombo on Tuesday before 2 pm as this is when everyone rushes on board to get the good spots.

There are also other cargo boats which ply the lake, such as the *Yapei Queen*, but their schedules are very erratic and getting any information on them is extremely difficult. You'll have to wait around for several days to get one of them.

Since there are stops en route, it isn't necessary to take the boat the entire distance. At both Kete-Krachi and Yeji, for example, you can take an east-west ferry to the other side of the lake. Between Kete-Krachi and Kwadiokrom there is one every morning in either direction, while between Yeji and Makongo there are two daily crossings in either direction. There are also bus connections between Kete-Krachi and Tamale as well as between Yeji and both Tamale and Kumasi.

You may find that the schedule has completely changed, that there are additional cargo departures, or that the principal steamer is out of order. Check with the Lake Volta Transport Co in either Akosombo (☎ 686) or Accra (☎ 665300).

HO

Ho (population 65,000), the eastern regional capital and Ewé country, is 80 km beyond Akosombo (184 km north-east of Accra) and is a transit place for those on their way to Kpalimé (Togo). You can get a good view of the town and surrounding area from the TV relay station; there's a path leading up the hill. The two main points of interest are the **market** in the centre and the **Volta Regional Museum** (closed Monday) behind the hospital on the western side of town.

Many people find the area around Ho to be one of the most interesting in Ghana and village hopping in the area is a lot of fun. A popular destination is **Amedzofe**, a mountain village with a small guesthouse. The people are friendly and you can hike in the rainforests here. Another place to check is

GHANA

Kpetoe, 25 km to the south-east near the Togo border. It's one of the country's major centres for kente cloth making. The Ewé cloth is beautiful and sells for much less than Ashanti kente cloth. Toga-size pieces can be found for under C 15,000.

Places to Stay & Eat

One of the best places is the *E P Church Social Centre*, which has rooms for around C 2500 and cheaper dormitory beds. It's at the church's headquarters near the historic Basel Missionary monuments, one km from the centre. If rooms there aren't available, try the *Hotel de Tarso*, which is just south of Ghana Commercial bank and close to the TV tower. It's a good place with decent rooms for C 4000. Another place in the same price range is the *Alinda Guest House* near the museum. Also good is the *Freedom Hotel*, down the street from the lorry park, on the road towards Kpalimé: C 3300 for a clean comfortable single that has a fan and shared bath. There is also a bar and restaurant.

A little more up-market is the *Peace Palace Hotel* (☎ 567) on the south-western side of town off the road to Accra. It has eight air-con rooms and food on request. The two best places in town are the attractive *Catering Rest House* (☎ 418), which sprawls over a large area, and the *Premier Hotel* (☎ 534). Both have air-con rooms and restaurants.

For Ghanaian food, try the lorry park or, better, the well-regarded *Doris Day Restaurant* on Housing Rd.

Getting There & Away

STC (☎ 325 for information) has one bus a day from Accra, departing Accra at 1 pm. Private buses and tro-tro for Ho depart from Tema Station off Kinbu Rd in Accra. The tro-tro fare to/from Accra is C 1500.

KPANDU

Kpandu (population 18,000) is the first major stop for ferries headed north from Akosombo. There are also ferry crossings from here to the western side of the lake and Kujani Game Reserve (see the later Kumasi section for details).

The *Lucky Hotel* in town and about six km from the port, charges C 2000 for a single without fan and about twice that for a double with private bath, but prices are often negotiable. You can eat here or at the very friendly *Rose's Restaurant* on the eastern side of town at the beginning of the road to Golokuati.

Getting There & Away

Buses and tro-tro for Kpandu leave from Tema Station in Accra. If you're headed for Kpalimé you can catch a taxi in Golokuati direct to Kpalimé, but as these are rare many travellers prefer to catch a taxi to the border and walk to the other side. It's eight km by car to the Togo border post, but there's a well-trodden, 1.5-km footpath. The boat fare from here to Kete-Krachi is C 2300.

KETE-KRACHI

An eight-hour boat ride north of Kpandu, Kete-Krachi is roughly the halfway point on the eastern route from Accra to Tamale. Despite being on the lake, it is without running water. The pleasant *Education Guest House* charges about C 1700 for a room with fan and bucket showers. There is also the *Simon Hotel*, about two km from the lake. Rooms with fan cost around C 4000.

Getting There & Away

STC buses ply between Tamale and Kete-Krachi, departing Tamale on Monday, Wednesday and Friday after 10.30 am and arriving about 12 hours later. The fare for this hot and dusty ride is about C 3300. Alternatively, you can cross over any morning to Kwadiokrom and take a bus west to Kumasi (256 km) via Atebubu and Mampong. If you take a tro-tro, the trip will take at least two days, starting with a tro-tro to Kpandai (C 1500).

The Centre

KUMASI

Kumasi is a sprawling city of over 800,000 people. It's the heart of Ashanti country and the site of West Africa's largest cultural centre, the palace of the Ashanti king; it also has an old fort which is now a museum, and one of the country's three major universities. The rolling green hills add to the city's aesthetic appeal and the vast central market is as vibrant as any in Africa.

Don't miss Kumasi; it's becoming increasingly popular because of the region's rich cultural heritage. There are, for example, numerous colourful festivals in the summer and authentic Akan religious ceremonies held at 42-day intervals year-round. There are also interesting Ashanti villages specialising in crafts such as goldsmithing, kente cloth weaving, adinkra cloth printing and the carving of Ashanti stools. It's also possible to take classes in traditional dance and drumming at the National Cultural Centre.

Orientation

The city's layout is confusing because of the hilly environment, but the city is ringed by Bypass Rd, which helps with getting around. There are various major roundabouts on Bypass Rd including Airport Roundabout (for the airport and Bonwire) and Suame Roundabout (for Mampong and Tamale) on the northern side, and Ahodjo Roundabout, also known as Georgia Roundabout (for Lake Bosumtwi) on the southern side.

The heart of town is the market. The train station is just to the south while Kejetia Circle, a large roundabout, and Kejetia motor park, the city's main lorry park, are just to the west. Adum is the modern commercial district and its major landmark is the Prempeh II Roundabout at the intersection of Prempeh II Rd, Stewart Ave, Bank Rd and Harper Rd. The major supermarkets and department stores, eg A-Life, Kingsway and UTC, are nearby.

Information

Tourist Office The very informative Ghana Tourist Board (☎ 6243) is near the centre at the National Cultural Centre. Its very friendly staff have maps of Kumasi (C 500), postcards, hotel listings and points of interest outside Kumasi. For C 5000, they'll organise a one-day guided tour to the three nearby craft villages as well as to the local market. Ask them about

upcoming festivals in surrounding villages (most are held from July to October) including the Adea Festival, which is celebrated every 42 days at the Asantehene's Palace. If a local wrestling match is coming up, they may also have information on that as it's a big sport in Kumasi and can be quite entertaining.

Money Barclays, in the commercial centre at the Prempeh II Roundabout, is open weekdays from 8.30 am to 2 pm. Strangely, it won't change foreign notes but it does accept travellers' cheques and charges no commission. However, the service is slow. You can also get money with a Visa card here. Standard Chartered across the street will change both foreign notes and travellers' cheques and its service is faster, but you can't obtain cash here with a Visa card. Some travellers also recommend the Social Security bank.

The Forex, however, are better for changing money. There's one next to the Hotel de Kingsway, and another on Antoa Rd near the central market, between Kejetia Circle and Manhyia Palace. The best, however, is Oregon Forex on Asomfo Rd between Nsenie Rd Roundabout and Kejetia motor park. It changes all kinds of currencies plus travellers' cheques in numerous denominations.

Post The main post office is on Stewart Ave one block north-west of Prempeh II Roundabout. It's open weekdays from 8 am to 5 pm. The poste restante is reliable and free, but the parcel office is a mess. You can also make international calls here 24 hours a day.

Travel Agencies The best area for travel agencies is along 24 February Rd just east of Mensah Memorial Hotel. One of the best is Aeroplane House (☎ 2217 or 4613), which represents Lufthansa, KLM, British Airways, Swissair, Alitalia and Ghana Airways and may handle other airlines as well. Also good are Johnson's Travels & Tours and Kumasi Travel Agency (☎ 3348) next door.

Supermarkets The best grocery store is the new A-Life, a block from the STC bus station.

GHANA

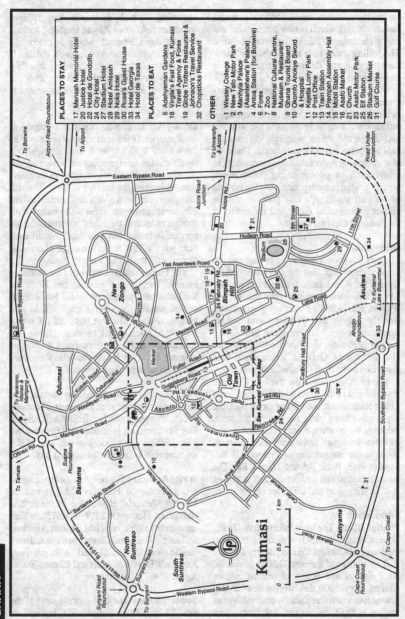

PLACES TO STAY

17 Mensah Memorial Hotel
20 Justice Hotel
22 Hotel de Gondolfo
24 City Hotel
27 Stadium Hotel
28 Hotel Amissah
29 Noks Hotel
30 Rose's Guest House
33 Hotel Georgia
34 Hotel de Texas

PLACES TO EAT

5 Adehyeman Gardens
18 Virgile's Fast Food, Kumasi
   Travel Agency & Forex
19 Globe Trotters Restaurant &
   Johnson's Travel Service
32 Chopsticks Restaurant

OTHER

1 Wesley College
2 New Tafo Motor Park
3 Manhyia Palace
   (Asantehene's Palace)
4 Antoa Station (for Bonwire)
6 Forex
7 Zoo
8 National Cultural Centre,
   Museum & Restaurant
9 Ghana Tourist Board
10 Okomfo Anokye Sword
   & Hospital
11 Kejetia Lorry Park
12 Post Office
13 Train Station
14 Prempeh Assembly Hall
15 Mobil Station
16 Asafo Market
21 Church
23 Asafo Motor Park
25 Elf Station
26 Stadium Market
31 Golf Course

Kumasi

National Cultural Centre

The city's major attraction is the National Cultural Centre, a 10-minute walk west of the market. This sprawling complex is open Tuesday to Sunday from 8 am to 5 pm. There's a museum of Ashanti history, a decent well-used library with books and magazines on Ashanti culture and history among other topics, a craft shop and exhibition hall; the Ghana Tourist Board is nearby. Local bands perform at the hall on the occasional Sunday afternoon. There's also a restaurant (see Places to Eat).

The small Prempeh II Jubilee Museum of Ashanti history contains a collection of rare Ashanti items including the king's war attire, clothing, jewellery, personal equipment for bathing and dining, furniture and royal insignia. It's constructed to look like an Ashanti chief's house, with a courtyard in front and walls adorned with traditional carved symbols. If you're in Kumasi during a major Ashanti festival, head for the museum because the courtyard here is where the Asantehene sits to receive homage.

The museum has a good B&W photo of the king's golden stool, which is at Manhyia Palace and brought out only on special occasions. It's so sacred that even the king isn't allowed to sit on the stool; indeed, it is never allowed to even touch the ground. The museum also contains the fake golden stool made by the Ashanti elders which they used to fool the British in 1900 when as a final humiliating blow, the British governor, who had been tipped off that the strength of the Ashanti was in the royal stool, demanded the stool itself. The British, who had never seen the real stool, fell for the trick. The real stool wasn't found until over 20 years later.

Don't miss the interesting craft shop. It has an assortment of inexpensive crafts which make good gifts and souvenirs. You can see potters and woodcarvers at work and the 'lost wax' method of making brass weight figurines. You can also see crafts people weaving kente cloth and making adinkra dye-print cloth; some of the items are for sale.

Zoological Gardens & Okomfo Anokye Sword

If you're looking for a shady place to escape the heat, head for the zoological gardens next door. Open weekdays from 9 am to 5 pm and on weekends and holidays from 8.30 am to 5.45 pm, the combination gardens and zoo has common tropical plants and birds. Some travellers find the zoo depressing, however, as most of the animals live in smelly cages and the chimps are often seen playing with broken beer bottles. Feeding time for the lions and other carnivores is 4 pm. Porcupines, and crocodiles which live in a stream, walk around freely.

One long block (half a km) to the west you'll find the city's best hospital, the Okomfo Anokye Teaching Hospital, and the Okomfo Anokye Sword (oh-KOM-foh ah-NOH-chee) behind Block C of the hospital. The sword, partially visible, enclosed in broken wood planks, has been in the ground for three centuries and has never been pulled out. By legend, it is where the Golden Stool descended from the sky to mark the beginning of the Ashanti people, and if anyone ever pulls the sword out, the Ashanti kingdom will disappear.

Market

The centre of Kumasi is the huge, 10-hectare market, which has some 10,000 traders. Vultures perched on top of the rusty stalls add an ominous touch. The market sprawls over such a large area that it's very confusing, but with a little patience you can find almost anything, from bicycle parts and sandals and leather goods to fruits and vegetables. Cotton materials, particularly wax cotton prints, are plentiful. If you have time, have one of the many tailors sew you something; they can make you a colourful African shirt, skirt or trousers in an afternoon.

Kente cloth is also a good deal here. It's usually sold only in huge pieces sufficient to make an elaborate toga. The price, typically US$100 to US$200, varies according to the material (cloth containing a mixture of cotton, silk and rayon is more expensive than all-cotton material) and weave (double weave is naturally more expensive than single weave).

GHANA

Armed Forces Museum

Old Kumasi Fort and the museum inside is another attraction well worth a visit. The fort dates from 1820 but the major attraction is the museum, which focuses primarily on the British-Ashanti war of 1900. In this war the Ashanti, led by their queen Yaa Asantewa, temporarily besieged the fort, starving the British residents.

The museum has an interesting display of military regalia, old maps and fascinating old photographs of the war taken by Lord Baden-Powell. You'll also see the detention cells where serious criminals were kept; many of them went blind from lack of light. A guided tour takes about an hour and is well worth the C 500 fee.

The fort/museum is on Stewart Ave, a block north-west of Prempeh II Roundabout, and is open Tuesday to Saturday from 10 am to 5 pm.

Asantehene's Palace

The Manhyia Palace, better known simply as the Asantehene's Palace, dates from only 1926 when Prempeh I returned from exile in the Seychelles to resume residence in Kumasi. The Ashanti kings have never lived in luxury, and visitors are often surprised or disappointed by its unpretentiousness. Today's king lives in an attractive, more recent, palace directly behind the old one. The entrance fee, which allows you to walk around the grounds, is C 1000 and the photo permit costs another C 3000, which is a complete rip-off. The palace is one km north of the market on the corner of Antoa and Kotoko Rds.

While you are here or at the Ghana Tourist Board you might enquire about seeing the Ashanti king. Appointments to see him in private must normally be made one or two days in advance; the best time is on Monday and Thursday mornings when he presides over his court. If you bring a gift, you may get to shake his hand and take a photograph. In addition, the **Adae Festival** is celebrated at the palace. It's an Ashanti religious festival based on their 42-day, nine-month calendar. On that day from about 10.30 am to 1 pm, the king receives homage from his subjects and if you pay the photo permit, you can take photos.

Places to Stay – bottom end

Campers should check with the friendly

The Adae Festival

The Ashanti calendar is divided into nine cycles of 42 days called *adae*, which means resting place. There are two adaes every 42 days, one on a Sunday and another 17 days later on a Wednesday. (The ninth or final adae, the Odwira Festival, is a state festival lasting a week and marking the end of the year.) Each adae is a special day of worship when no work is done, and on this day the chief and his elders go to the stool house. This is a single dark room where the sacred stools are kept; the stools, which are thought to harbour the souls of the departed chiefs, are laid on their sides and are often preserved with a coating of soot and egg yolk. The chiefs go there to ask their deceased forefathers for guidance and to offer them drinks and food.

On the day before the adae, horn-blowers and drummers assemble at the chief's house and play until late at night. Early the next morning the chief's head musician goes to the stool house and drums loudly. Eventually the chief arrives. The only people allowed inside are those who perform the rites and a few of the chief's relatives. Ritual food of mashed yam, eggs and chicken is then brought into the room; the chief takes it and places portions on each of the sacred stools inside, beginning with the first stool of the dynasty. An attendant brings in a sheep on his shoulders. Its throat is cut, and the blood is collected and smeared on the seats of all the stools. The chief and his entourage then go outside to the courtyard where the sheep is roasted and bits placed on each stool. The queen mother simultaneously prepares fufu and places some of it on the stools; the spirits do not eat salt, so none is used. When the final course is placed upon the stools, a bell is sounded indicating that the spirits are eating. Then rum is poured on the stools and the rest is passed around to all present. With the ritual over, the chief retires to the courtyard and the merrymaking begins; drums beat and horns blast. The chief dons his traditional dress with regalia to sit in court, receiving the homage of his subjects. On some occasions, he is then borne in public in a palanquin shadowed by a huge canopy, and accompanied by lesser chiefs. ■

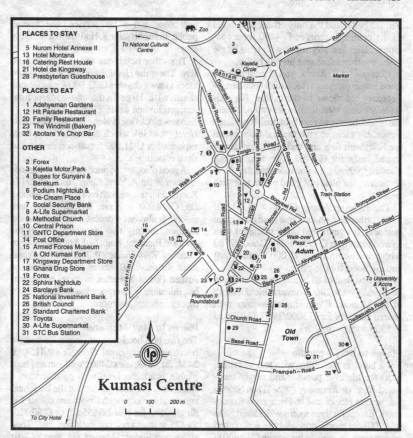

PLACES TO STAY
5 Nurom Hotel Annexe II
13 Hotel Montana
16 Catering Rest House
21 Hotel de Kingsway
28 Presbyterian Guesthouse

PLACES TO EAT
1 Adehyeman Gardens
12 Hit Parade Restaurant
20 Family Restaurant
23 The Windmill (Bakery)
32 Abotare Ye Chop Bar

OTHER
2 Forex
3 Kejetia Motor Park
4 Buses for Sunyani & Berekum
6 Podium Nightclub & Ice-Cream Place
7 Social Security Bank
8 A-Life Supermarket
9 Methodist Church
10 Central Prison
11 GNTC Department Store
14 Post Office
15 Armed Forces Museum & Old Kumasi Fort
17 Kingsway Department Store
18 Ghana Drug Store
19 Forex
22 Sphinx Nightclub
24 Barclays Bank
25 National Investment Bank
26 British Council
27 Standard Chartered Bank
29 Toyota
30 A-Life Supermarket
31 STC Bus Station

Kumasi Centre

0   100   200 m

To City Hotel

owner of *Rose's Guest House* listed under top-end hotels as she has been known to allow people to camp there.

In the heart of town in Adum, there are three choices. The best is the two-storey colonial *Presbyterian Guesthouse* on Mission Rd, conveniently located 2½ blocks east of Barclays. Known locally as Presby's, it is a great place to meet other travellers. Rooms cost C 2000 per person and have twin beds. It's often full but they sometimes allow travellers to sleep in the library (C 1000). If not, you can at least reserve for the following night. You can use the kitchen for free or buy fried egg sand-

wiches and other food at several small places nearby. Overland expedition trucks often stop here to camp on the lawn, so you could also camp here or at the National Cultural Centre.

The conveniently located *Hotel Montana* (☎ 2366) charges C 4500/5500 for rooms with fans/air-con and shared baths. Do not take a room without checking the lock. To get there, from Prempeh II Rd, turn left onto Odum Rd and after a few metres take another left down a small alley for a further 40 metres.

The smaller *Nurom Hotel Annexe II*, which is three blocks north on Nsenie Rd, is

GHANA

a notch better and the only other cheap hotel in the centre. It charges C 4400 for a spacious, clean and airy room with twin single beds, overhead fans and private baths.

Coming from Accra, you'll pass several good hotels on Accra Rd, which becomes 24 February Rd closer to the centre. The old-style *Mensah Memorial Hotel* (☎ 6432) near the roundabout is an excellent deal. It has large reasonably clean rooms (the 2nd-floor rooms are best) with fans and wide beds and decent shared baths for C 4400. Two men are not allowed to share the same room and there's no restaurant, but plenty of good places to eat are nearby.

The 39-room *Justice Hotel* (☎ 2525) half a km further east on the same road does good business. It's ventilated singles/doubles with shared baths cost C 4950/5500 (C 6600/7700 with private bath and C 11,000 with air-con) and are good for the price.

The best deal of all in this area is the *Hotel de Gondolfo* (☎ 2866), several blocks south of the Mensah. Clean singles/doubles with shared showers for C 3000/3800 (C 4400 to C 5500 with twin beds).

Places to Stay – middle

For a hotel in the centre with lots of action, head for the ever-popular and newly renovated *Hotel de Kingsway* (☎ 2441) on Ntomin Rd, several blocks east of Prempeh II Roundabout. Except for three rooms with shared baths (C 9900), its rooms now all have air-con and private baths, ranging in price from C 12,400 to C 19,800. The old-style bathrooms are in good condition but the water is not always reliable. In the centre of the hotel there's a big area for drinking and dancing; in the evening it often becomes a nightclub. You can also eat here, but the food is not cheap.

Several of the better mid-range hotels are near the stadium off Hudson Rd, about three km south-east of the centre in a quiet residential area called Asukwa. At the *Stadium Hotel* (☎ 3647, fax 3731) just south of the stadium, singles/doubles cost C 11,000/13,200 with fans and private baths (C 16,500 with air-con). They are good for the price which is why this place is often full. There's also a tiny grocery store

next door and a fax service, and finding public transport along Hudson Rd is fairly easy.

The other hotels are much more expensive. The quiet *Hotel Amissah* (☎ 5601) two blocks away, charges C 22,800 for an air-con room with large beds, plush carpeting, refrigerator and cable TV with CNN.

A few blocks south along Hudson Rd is *Noks Hotel* (☎ 4438), which is better and no more expensive at C 21,600 for air-con rooms and similar facilities.

A good place for the price on the opposite side of town is the *Ashford Court Hotel* (☎ 2917). Rooms with private bath cost C 11,000 without fan, C 14,000 with fan, and C 19,000 with air-con. It also has a decent restaurant and the location, roughly two km north-west of the centre in Bantama, is not bad. The old state-run *Catering Rest House* (☎ 3656), on Government Rd only 300 metres or so west of the Armed Forces Museum, is more convenient but ridiculously overpriced at C 22,000 for a mediocre bungalow room.

Places to Stay – top end

The two best hotels are on Harper Rd and are both fairly new. *Hotel Georgia* (☎ 4154 or 2434, fax 4299, telex 2480), well-run and hospitable, is a larger hotel with good service, a small attractive beer garden out the back, and comfortable rooms with air-con and colour TV. Singles/doubles cost US$55/65, or C 50,325/59,475 at their very fair exchange rate. They also accept Visa and MasterCard. *Rose's Guest House* (☎ 3500 or 4072, fax 3500) is much better value at C 35,200 a room; the friendly owner has been known to lower her price. Credit cards are not accepted. It's a small hotel with a garden setting, 10 air-con rooms with cable TVs and a delightful cosy ambience. The service here is tops and there is a good bar and restaurant. Even if you don't stay here, the garden is a good place to come for a drink.

Those who like grand old hotels may prefer the state-owned *City Hotel* (☎ 3293) on a verdant hill one km south of the centre just off Harper Rd. The air-con rooms, all with balconies and cable TVs with CNN, cost C 24,200. In addition to an excellent

Chinese restaurant, the hotel has a casino, numerous shops, beauty parlour, small grocery store, magazine stand, gift shop and Forex. The Nsadwase Nightclub here is quite popular on weekends.

Places to Eat

Cheap Eats For good street food, try the women outside the Hotel de Kingsway and along Prempeh II Rd starting at Prempeh II Roundabout. A few metres from the hotel, below the Family Restaurant is *Burger Queen*, a fast-food place with principally American selections. At that same intersection on Prempeh II Rd you'll find a cheap place on the street for breakfast; bread, eggs, tea, coffee and Milo are all served. If you walk north-eastward along Prempeh II Rd and take a sharp left as soon as you reach the GNTC pharmacy, you'll find *Jerry's Chicken Americana*, which serves superb jollof rice with chicken for C 1000. At the National Cultural Centre, the thatched-roof *Kentish Kitchen*, across from the Tourist Board, is open until 10 pm. It's one of the few places in town where you can get draught beer. It also serves about a dozen different Ghanaian dishes, mostly around C 1000 a plate.

Two good new places in this area are *Baboo's Cafeteria* opposite Hotel de Kingsway and *The Windmill*, just north-west of Prempeh II Roundabout off Stewart Ave. Baboo's serves good beef burgers (C 550), also vegetarian burgers and chips. The Windmill, a restaurant and a bakery, has a spacious open-air setting and is best for drinks, pastries and snacks. The service is fast and friendly. You can also get excellent Ghanaian and European meals here, including several vegetarian dishes and outstanding English breakfasts, but they are not cheap.

If you're in the lively area near the Mensah Hotel on 24 February Rd, you'll find several fairly inexpensive places to eat including *Virgile's Fast Food*, 100 metres east of the hotel. Open until midnight, this sidewalk café does good business day and night. The selections include hamburgers for C 1000, chicken fried rice for C 1200, chicken and chips for C 2200 and large beers for C 700.

Much cheaper beef skewers (C 200) are grilled separately at night. A few metres further is the *Globe Trotters Restaurant*. It has a nice African ambience and a lively bar to boot. The food is nothing special but prices are slightly lower, most dishes being in the C 1100 to C 1600 range. Not far away in the stadium area, you'll find several small restaurants under the stands, including a Chinese one which serves huge portions.

Ghanaian There is good Ghanaian food at the popular *Abotare Ye Chop Bar* at the southern end of Odum Rd in Odum, just south of A-Life supermarket and the STC station. A block from the Kingsway department store is the *YMCA*, which serves good cheap Ghanaian meals but it's open only for lunch.

For a more up-market Ghanaian restaurant, try the wonderful *Adehyeman Gardens* (ah-DESH-eh-mans) just north of Kejetia motor park. Popular day and night, it has an enclosed area for eating and a shady outside area for drinks. The selections here are reasonably priced, eg C 880 for jollof rice, fufu with mutton or red-red (fish) with beans, C 800 for ampesi with palava sauce, and from C 1200 to C 1900 for most European selections including various fish and chicken dishes.

Other Cuisines The city's top restaurant remains the ever-popular *Chopsticks*, which is two km south of the centre on Harper Rd, 150 metres beyond Rose's Guest House. Closed Mondays, it serves delicious Chinese food, with most main dishes in the C 2000 to C 3000 range. In the gardens behind you can also get draught beer. The Chinese restaurant at the City Hotel, *Sweet Gardens*, is also quite good as is the one at Hotel Georgia. The former has lots of selections, most cost from C 1800 to C 3000.

Slightly cheaper and more central is the well-marked *Family Restaurant*, on the 2nd floor of a building next to Hotel de Kingsway and open daily until 9.30 pm. This popular Lebanese-run establishment features Middle Eastern specialities, mostly in the C 1000 to C 2000 range, however the portions are quite small. The extensive menu also includes numerous European selections such as spaghetti for C 1200 and omelettes for C 1000.

Entertainment

Bars One of the best places for a drink, day or night, is *Adehyeman Gardens* (see Places to Eat). Also try *Virgile's Fast Food* (large beers C 700) or the garden at *Rose's Guest House*. If you're dying for draught beer, head for the restaurant at the National Cultural Centre; it's open until 10 pm.

Nightclubs Anyone in Kumasi on a Saturday night should visit the *Old-Timer's Club* at the Hotel de Kingsway in the heart of town. It attracts huge crowds of people, many in traditional gowns, and the dancing starts early, around 6 pm, lasting until 2 am. Since the 1950s, this legendary nightclub has been the home of Kumasi's major highlife bands, but unfortunately those days are now gone and there's rarely live entertainment there or anywhere in town. One exception is *Adehyeman Gardens*, listed under Places to Eat. A local band performs there every Sunday from 6 to 11 pm. Entrance is free and drinks and good food are available.

The top flashy places are the *Podium Nightclub* (Wednesday is ladies' night) three blocks north just beyond Nsenie Rd Roundabout, the *Fox Trap* on 24 February Rd just beyond the Mensah Memorial Hotel, *Masarati* (ex-Star Nite Club) near the stadium, and the *Nsadwase Disco* at the City Hotel. Many of these places are open only from Thursday to Sunday. Still another is the *Sphinx Nightclub* opposite Hotel de Kingsway. It's not open on a regular basis.

Working Ghanaians frequent small bars called 'spots' marked with fences painted in white, pink and blue. At many of them you can get the local brew *akpeteshie*, which makes you more high than drunk. The best places to meet people, however, are at small bars on the outskirts of town where people sit all afternoon and drink palm wine. Chances are you'll eventually be invited into someone's house for a meal.

Cinemas One of the most convenient cinemas is the Odeon near the Cultural Centre. Two others not far from the centre are the Rex and the Rivoli.

Getting There & Away

Air Airlink (☎ 6234) has flights at 6.30 am on Monday, Wednesday and Friday (also at 6.15 pm on Friday) to Accra and at 5 pm on Tuesday, Thursday, Friday and Sunday from Accra to Kumasi. There are also several flights a week from Kumasi to Tamale. The fare to either is C 17,000. Don't forget to reconfirm your flight several days in advance. For information and reservations, go to M&J Travel & Tour (☎ 6243).

Bus The STC bus terminal (☎ 4282 for information) is on Prempeh II Rd half a km south of the train terminal. There are 12 buses a day to/from Accra, departing almost hourly on the hour between 4 am and 5 pm (between 7.30 am and 4 pm on Sundays). STC buses depart at 4 am and 6 pm for Tamale and at 4 am for Bolgatanga (possibly other destinations as well) and at 6 am and 1 pm for Cape Coast and Takoradi. There are also several departures daily for Wa (C 4400). Express service has been dropped on all routes, leaving only regular buses which leave when full. The trip takes 4½ hours to Accra, six hours to Tamale and eight hours to Wa and tickets go fast, so get there early. There is also an STC bus to Ouaga (Burkina Faso) twice a week, leaving Kumasi on Wednesday at 8 am and Accra on Saturday at 8 am. STC bus service from Kumasi to Abidjan, however, has been discontinued. STC's fares are C 2400 to Cape Coast, C 2600 to Accra, C 2800 to Tema, C 3000 to Takoradi, C 3600 to Tamale and C 10,500 to Ouaga. Baggage is C 200 extra per bag.

STC is not the only company with large buses. On the Tamale and Bolgatanga route, for example, OSA has equally good buses, with one bus a day to/from Kumasi. City Express also serves Bolgatanga and Tamale, with several departures a day, but its buses are in much worse condition.

Bush Taxi & Tro-Tro The largest lorry park

is Kejetia motor park on Bantama Rd between the central market and the cultural centre. It's where you catch tro-tro for most small towns near Kumasi as well as for Sunyani, Berekum and the Côte d'Ivoire border. If you're headed for Abidjan, get here by 7 am, otherwise you may not get a seat. You must change vehicles at the border. The trip to Abidjan takes about 12 hours.

Vehicles for Accra and Takoradi leave from Asafo market motor park, which is 1.5 km to the south on Fuller Rd, past the train station on the same street. Tro-tro for Kuntansi/Lake Bosumtwi also leave from here. Vehicles for Tamale leave from New Tafo motor park on the northern side of town.

Examples of tro-tro/Peugeot 504 fares are: C 2500/3500 to Accra, C 2800/3800 to Takoradi, C 1100/1400 to Sunyani, C 1400/1700 to Berekum and C 3900/5000 to Tamale. Tro-tro are somewhat slower, eg 4½ hours to Accra compared to 3½ hours in a Peugeot, and they break down more frequently. The last departures are around 5.30 or 6 pm. Vehicles for Accra, however, leave well into the night.

Train The train to Takoradi is much more popular than the one to Accra because it's faster, leaves at night and offers 1st-class sleepers. The Kumasi-Takoradi train departs punctually at 6 and 11.45 am and 8.10 pm in either direction and takes 8¼ hours, while that for Accra, which is painfully slow, departs at 8.30 pm and arrives at 6.20 am according to the schedule but closer to 8.30 am in practice. First and 2nd-class fares are C 2700/1900 to Takoradi and C 2200/1400 to Accra. Only the night trains have sleepers. On the Takoradi train a berth costs C 3900 in a two-bed 1st-class sleeper and C 2900 in a four-bed 2nd-class sleeper. On the Accra train, which has no bar or restaurant, sleepers are available only in 2nd class; a berth costs C 2400.

The train station, which is in disgraceful condition, is in the centre just south of the central market.

Getting Around
Taxis There's no inner-city bus line, so

shared taxis take their place. They adhere to fixed routes but you can be dropped off anywhere along the way. The fare is C 130. Most taxi lines start at Kejetia motor park and across the street at the intersection of Prempeh II and Guggisberg Rds. Two more lines, all headed south along Harper Rd, start from Ntomin Rd, behind the post office, serving the sections of town beyond Ahodjo Roundabout called Naiyaeso, Dakodwom, Ahodwo and Daban.

AROUND KUMASI
Owabi Wildlife Sanctuary
If a walk through a quiet forest sounds appealing, consider a short trip to Owabi, a very small sanctuary 16 km north-west of Kumasi, just off the Sunyani road.

The Owabi is a river flowing past Kumasi that has been dammed for water, making it an ideal home for birds and some animals. There are no tracks, so you'll have to walk. It's popular on weekends.

Bonwire
If you're interested in seeing kente cloth being made, or buying large quantities, head for Bonwire (BONE-wee-ray), 26 km north-east of Kumasi. The village, like others in the area, exists almost entirely from kente weaving. It receives lots of tourists and, as a result, prices here are no better than you'll find in Kumasi. However, if you bargain with the weavers, you can get good prices. While you're here, have a look at some of the traditional Ashanti housing compounds with enclosed inner courts.

Getting There & Away Buses for Bonwire leave from Antoa (ANN-twah) Station on Antoa Rd in Kumasi, one km north of the market across from the Asantehene's Palace. They depart throughout the day between 6.30 am and 8.30 pm and the cost is C 240.

Lake Bosumtwi
Bosumtwi is a crater-lake 38 km south-east of Kumasi via Kuntansi, and is very popular on weekends with people from Kumasi. They come here to swim, canoe, fish, or

rest and admire the lush green surrounding hills.

It's possible to hire someone to take you across the lake; it's about eight km. The asking price for a boat ride is C 5000 by the hour and C 20,000 by the half-day, so expect to do some hard bargaining to get a more reasonable price. Or walk along the banks, as there are some 30 small villages around the lake. If you're fit, you can make it round the lake in one day; the distance is 24 km.

Swimming here is safe and the water is checked periodically. In the hot season, however, the water is too warm to be refreshing. You could, instead, persuade a local fisher to take you out on their boat to fish for tilapia, the local catch. The traditional fishing canoes are of solid wood and paddled either by hand or with a wooden paddle.

Not only is Bosumtwi the country's largest and deepest natural lake (78 metres in the centre), but it is also sacred. The Ashanti believe that their souls come here after death to bid farewell to their god Twi. There's also a tale about the hunter and the antelope; the caretaker at the rest house will be glad to recount it for you.

Places to Stay & Eat The only place to stay at the lake is the tranquil *Sabon de Lac Hotel*. In addition to a nice covered patio overlooking the water, it has eight large rooms with electricity and fans, wide beds and modern private baths for C 4400. There's no running water and you must bring your own soap, towel and toilet paper. If this place is renovated as they say it may be, expect to pay more. The caretaker is very friendly and will serve you a meal if you ask. The menu includes fresh fish from the lake (C 1200), jollof rice (C 1400), roast chicken (C 1400) and chicken and yam chips (C 2400). On weekends you might find the hotel full. If so, you could also camp here or outside one of the nearby villages. If you do the latter, make sure the villagers know, and don't take pictures without their permission.

Getting There & Away There are no tro-tro direct from Kumasi to the lake, so you must take one to Kuntansi (27 km) and look for transport headed to Abono (11 km) on the lake's edge. In Kumasi, tro-tro for Kuntansi, which are generally dilapidated, leave from the Asafo market lorry park. The trip costs C 240 and takes about an hour. The last tro-tro leaves Kumasi around 6.30 pm and Kuntansi around 7.30 pm. Finding a tro-tro or truck from Kuntansi to Abono (C 250) can involve a long wait; hiring a private taxi (C 1500) is an option. The road is paved all the way to the lake.

Pankrono, Ahwiaa & Ntonso

These three villages lie north-east of Kumasi on the road to Mampong, and all are on the tourist trail. The first two are on the outskirts of Kumasi, five km and six km respectively, beyond Suame Roundabout. Pankrono is a major **pottery** centre and all along the highway through town you'll see pots for sale. They're too large for travellers to carry but stopping here to see the various stages of making the pots can be very interesting.

One km further is Ahwiaa, which is one of the major **woodcarving** centres in the Ashanti region. All along the highway you'll see men carving the famous Ashanti stools, sculptured figures and other wooden objects. The artisans may have lost some of their inspiration but prices are lower here than elsewhere. Two types of wood are used; their prices are the same. The lighter ones, which Ghanaians tend to prefer, are made of sesée, the darker ones of mahogany. Most are dyed with shoe polish; verify that it won't rub off on your clothes. You can have a stool made to order if you wish; a large one takes only about three days to make. (If termites later become a problem, soak the stool with lighter fluid or put it in the freezer.)

Ntonso, some 15 km further on the same tarred road, is the centre of **adinkra cloth** production. The cloth is made with black cotton and has hand-printed designs. It's traditionally worn at funerals and other special occasions.

Getting There & Away You could consider hiring a private taxi to these towns but it's

The Odwira Festival

The Odwira Festival, which is the last or ninth adae of the Ashanti calendar, is the principal annual festival of the Ashanti and it's celebrated all over the Ashanti region, including Akropong, Akuapem, Akim, Akwamu and Assin-Manso but sometimes under a different name (eg *Apafram* in Akwamu). Most are week-long celebrations and each is quite different. In Akuapem, for example, which is north-west of Kumasi, outside Akropong (20 km), the celebration usually takes place in September and lasts five days.

On Monday, the path to the royal mausoleum is cleared. On Tuesday, the day the ban on eating the new yam is lifted, tubers are paraded through the streets while the chief sexton proceeds to the royal mausoleum with sheep and rum to invoke the Odwira spirit. He then returns to the chief and is blessed; drumming follows well into the night. Wednesday is a day of mourning and fasting; the people wear sepia-coloured attire and red turbans. There is also lots of drinking and drumming all day.

Thursday is for feasting; food is provided in all houses for everyone, even at the chief's palace. Ritual food, including yam fufu, mashed yam and hard-boiled eggs, is borne in a long procession to a shrine where they are given to their forefathers. The food carriers start from the royal house and are impressively covered by umbrellas. That night with the strike of the gong, everyone must go indoors because no one except the privileged few may see the procession of the dead whereby the sacred stools are borne to the stream for their yearly ceremonial cleansing.

The climax is Friday, when the chief holds a great durbar at which all the subchiefs and his subjects come to pay their respects. The highlight is a great procession all around town, ending at the palace, of elegantly dressed chiefs, the principal ones being borne on palanquins and covered by multicoloured umbrellas. This is accompanied by lots of drumming and dancing. It lasts late into the evening. ■

cheaper to take a tro-tro from Kejetia motor park; they cost only C 120 to either Pankrono or Ahwiaa.

Fiema-Boabeng Monkey Sanctuary

For a little adventure, you might consider a visit to the monkey sanctuary in the twin villages of Fiema and Boabeng, 165 km north of Kumasi via Nkoranza (which is 20 km to the south). The forest here is so open that you can easily spot the black and white colobus and mona monkeys feeding, playing and sleeping; you can walk around without a guide. Fiema and Boabeng are part of this largely unknown sanctuary and the villagers will gladly arrange a place for you to stay or put your tent, and they'll supply you with home-made food as well. Otherwise, ask Mr D K Akowuah, the sanctuary's originator, to let you use the room he has for visitors. The sanctuary's entrance fee is C 1000.

MAMPONG

With the development of Lake Volta, Mampong, 50 km north-east of Kumasi on the road to Yeji, has declined in importance but it's still a fairly lively medium-sized town. It is perched on an escarpment and the surrounding area is beautiful, so for **hikers** and **bikers** it might make a good stop. There's a guy in town who rents bicycles for C 75 an hour. The road to Ejura has been much improved recently.

Rooms with two beds at the friendly *Midway Hotel* (☎ 240) cost C 660. It's on the edge of town but only a short walk to the centre. The *Hotel Video City* is nicer and costs twice as much, but it lacks character.

YEJI

Some 216 km north-east of Kumasi on the old Tamale road, Yeji is one of the principal port towns on Lake Volta. There's a great **market** here with lots of fresh catch from the lake. If you like fishing, this would be a good place to catch your own.

The best place to stay is the *Alliance Hotel* (C 2200 double). The shared baths have no running water but there is electricity from 6.30 to 10.30 pm. If it's full, try the *Volta Lake Hotel*, just down the street. It is similarily priced but reportedly inferior.

GHANA

Getting There & Away

The 45-minute ferry over to Makongo on the other bank costs C 600 and leaves at 9 am, connecting with an STC bus to Tamale. When you arrive in Makongo be prepared to really run to the bus otherwise you won't get a seat and you'll have to stand for the four-hour journey. This connection with the STC bus isn't always reliable, however, so it may be necessary to take a tro-tro. There's another ferry in the afternoon. The steamer from Akosombo passes by at around 4 pm on Wednesdays, headed for Yapei. For details, see the Akosombo section.

OBUASI

Some 70 km south of Kumasi on the Kumasi to Takoradi train line, Obuasi (population 70,000) lies in a steep valley surrounded by hills and is the gold-mining centre of Ghana. On Sundays, the Lonrho mining company conducts tours of the **gold mines**. The shafts go down very deep and trips through them can be fascinating. You can also buy gold items such as bracelets, earrings and so on.

For a cheap room, try the modest *Black Star Hotel*, the *Adansiman Hotel* (☎ 90) or the *Hotel de Sennet* (☎ 63). *Ceci's Lodge*

Pollution from Gold Mining

A new law passed in 1989 encouraging small-scale mining saw a surge of unregulated mining operations (over 50 new ones in the western region alone). An almost immediate consequence was the environmental impact of the gold refineries. The already lifeless waters of the local rivers have been poisoned by mercury and other chemicals used in mining, and the air is polluted by smoke containing arsenic and sulphur dioxide. It is impossible to grow crops around Obuasi, Tarkwa and Mpohor. However, the Ghanaian government has turned a blind eye to the resulting pollution and, either because of the government's inaction or because protest would be useless, the residents of the major gold-mining centres seem to accept the risks. ■

(☎ 43) and the *Silence Hotel* (☎ 80) both have restaurants and rooms with fans.

Getting There & Away

The Kumasi-Takoradi train passes through town three times a day in either direction, twice in the morning and again in the evening (see the Kumasi section). You could also take a bus or taxi from Kumasi; the trip takes from one to 1½ hours.

SUNYANI

Sunyani (population 80,000), 127 km northwest of Kumasi on the highway to Abidjan, has little of interest to travellers but it is the capital of the Brong Ahafo region. There's a GNTC store, Ghana Commercial bank, airport, and various hotels with restaurants.

For the cheapest accommodation, try the modest *Tata Hotel* or the *Hotel de Nimpong*. The *Ebenezer Hotel* has rooms with fans. All of them serve food.

The best hotel in town is the government-run *Catering Rest House* (☎ 7280). It has the most expensive accommodation, about C 18,000 for an air-con room with private bath, and the city's best restaurant, with most main dishes around C 3000. The two next-best hotels are the *South Ridge Hotel* and the *Tropical Hotel*, both with rooms for around C 11,000.

Getting There & Away

Peugeot cars and tro-tro travel between Kumasi and Sunyani throughout the day starting around 6 am, with the last departure around 6 pm. The cost is C 1100 by tro-tro and C 1400 by Peugeot. In Kumasi, vehicles for Sunyani leave from the southern side of Kejetia motor park near Bantama Rd. There are also STC buses connecting the two cities, but they leave far less frequently.

NATIONAL PARKS
Kujani Game Reserve

Kujani, which is also known as Digya National Park, is Ghana's largest park with some 3120 sq km of land bordering the western shore of Lake Volta. It's in a transitional zone between the savannah and forest belt, with lots of savannah woodland and forested river banks. Few foreigners ever come here because it is not easily accessible.

Some of the animals that you might see are baboon, various species of monkey, elephant, hippo, buffalo, antelope, waterbuck, bush pig and crocodile.

There are no facilities or tracks in the park, so you'll have to walk. You should be able to find a guide at either of the park's two entrance points – Ejura and Atebubu. From Kumasi, head north-east on the old Tamale road past Mampong to Ejura (110 km). The main entrance is at Atebubu, 61 km further north-east towards Yeji.

Bia National Park

Bia is about 260 km west of Kumasi between the Côte d'Ivoire border and the Bia River. It's a small park, only 308 sq km, and protects the headwaters of the Panabo, Sukusuku, and Tawya rivers. Bia is Ghana's major rainforest park and it's one of the few places in West Africa where you can see virgin rainforest. Palm trees, orchids and moist evergreen trees abound.

While the park is most interesting for its rainforests, it also has fauna including a herd of forest elephant. You might also spot chimpanzee and other species of monkey, buffalo, duiker, giant forest hog and lots of birds.

To get here from Kumasi, the best route is south by paved road to Dunkwa (99 km), then west on a dirt road past Wiawso to the Bia River. The park has no facilities or roads, so be prepared to hike and camp.

Bui National Park

About 160 km north-west of Kumasi near the Côte d'Ivoire border, Bui park is not developed for tourists but plans are being made to add facilities. It's in a woodland area with forests along the numerous small tributaries of the Black Volta River. Some of the animals that you might see, if you're very lucky, include hippo, waterbuck, duiker, monkey, baboon, buffalo and the few remaining elephant if the poachers haven't killed them all. Birds are also plentiful.

From Kumasi, take the paved highway north to Wenchi; a dirt access road leads from there into the park. There's a shelter for those staying overnight.

The North

TAMALE

Tamale (population 275,000), 611 km north of Accra, is the capital and transport hub of the northern region, an area that produces most of the country's rice and cotton. The city is pleasantly spread out with tree-lined avenues. The heart of town is the tall radio antenna which can be seen from a long distance. That's where you'll find the market, STC station and main lorry park.

Tamale is not exactly a swinging town, except on Saturday nights, but there are stores such as Kingsway, UTC and GNTC, major banks, a market with cheap leather goods and handmade cotton items, and several decent bars and restaurants (pito, the local millet brew, is good). You should also check the **National Cultural Centre**, which is near the centre and has a tiny craft shop and a restaurant but little else. On occasion, however, local musical groups play here, so enquire if anything special is coming up.

The **market** here is the best place for finding Ghana's northern cloths, particularly those woven by the Gonja and Dagomba. It's already tailored – into men's smocks and women's dresses – making it more practical than kente cloth. A large man's smock should cost about C 15,000 or so, which is a lot less than you'll pay in Accra.

A good way to see Tamale and the surrounding areas is by bicycle. Many people will gladly rent you one; the main market is the best place to enquire. One of the more scenic areas is north-west from the market, out along Education Ridge Rd to the ridge and villages beyond.

If you need to change money, there are several banks in the centre including Standard Chartered, which is open weekdays until 1 pm. It accepts travellers' cheques but the net exchange rate is not as good as in Accra; there's a 1% commission with a C 2000 minimum.

Places to Stay – bottom end

The city has at least five hotels with rooms under C 5000. The cheapest rooms are those at the *Alhassan Hotel* (☎ 2834), which has singles/doubles with fans and shared baths for C 2200/3300 (C 4400 with attached bath) and video movies every night. There's no running water and bucket showers are the norm. The hotel is run-down and the manager has been known to say only the more expensive self-contained rooms are available when that is not the case. However, he's usually friendly and the city centre location is unbeatable, plus the restaurant here is surprisingly good though not cheap.

The well-marked and slightly less decrepit *Macos Hotel* has ventilated rooms for C 3300

that are larger and a bit cleaner, and the bathrooms are relatively clean. There's no restaurant and being one km north of the central area it's not as convenient. Another km further north along Bolgatanga Rd is the peaceful African-run *Christian Services Guest House* (or CCPO Guest House), which has ventilated rooms and shared baths of similar quality for C 3850. No food is available but guests are allowed to use the kitchen.

On the opposite end of town off Salaga Rd are two more places, both about 1.5 km from the centre. The place with the best ambience is the friendly and highly recommended *Atta Essibi Hotel* (☎ 2569), which is a very neat and well-maintained place on a dirt side street (St Charles Seminary Rd) with clean ventilated rooms for C 4500 (C 5500 with private baths). The water supply is fairly reliable and food is available upon request plus the yard can be used for having drinks and parking. The nearby *Mirihu* (ex-America) is more modern and has similar quality rooms with

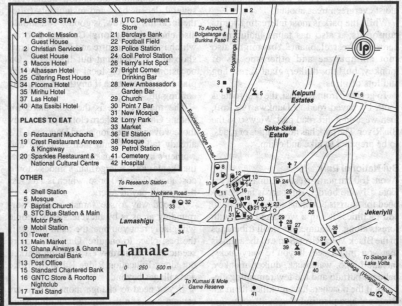

PLACES TO STAY	18	UTC Department Store
1	Catholic Mission Guest House	21	Barclays Bank
2	Christian Services Guest House	22	Football Field
		23	Police Station
3	Macos Hotel	24	Goil Petrol Station
14	Alhassan Hotel	26	Harry's Hot Spot
25	Catering Rest House	27	Bright Corner Drinking Bar
34	Picorna Hotel	28	New Ambassador's Garden Bar
35	Mirihu Hotel	
37	Las Hotel	29	Church
40	Atta Essibi Hotel	30	Point 7 Bar
		31	New Mosque
PLACES TO EAT	32	Lorry Park
		33	Market
6	Restaurant Muchacha	36	Elf Station
19	Crest Restaurant Annexe & Kingsway	38	Mosque
		39	Petrol Station
20	Sparkles Restaurant & National Cultural Centre	41	Cemetery
		42	Hospital
OTHER		
4	Shell Station		
5	Mosque		
7	Baptist Church		
8	STC Bus Station & Main Motor Park		
9	Mobil Station		
10	Tower		
11	Main Market		
12	Ghana Airways & Ghana Commercial Bank		
13	Post Office		
15	Standard Chartered Bank		
16	GNTC Store & Rooftop Nightclub		
17	Taxi Stand		

To Airport, Bolgatanga & Burkina Faso

To Research Station

Nyohene Road

To Kumasi & Mole Game Reserve

To Salaga & Lake Volta

Kalpuni Estates

Saka-Saka Estate

Jekeriyili

Salaga (Hospital) Road

Lamashigu

Tamale

0   250   500 m

double beds, fans and decent shared baths for C 4500 (C 6500 with twin beds and private bath). There's no restaurant.

Places to Stay – top end

The city has three top-end hotels, but most travellers prefer the friendly and well-maintained *Catholic Mission Guest House* (☎ 2365), well marked on the northern side of town just off Bolgatanga Rd. It's unbeatable at C 5500/8800 for singles/doubles including breakfast. Rooms have twin beds, fans and showers. You can also get lunch and dinner here, but you must order in advance. If it's full, they'll put you in a less attractive guesthouse about eight km away.

Of the three hotels, the most popular is the *Las Hotel* on Salaga Rd, over one km southeast of the centre. Often fully booked, it has rooms for C 11,000/22,000 with fans/aircon, which are fairly spacious with tiled floors, clean sheets, work tables and private baths. It also has one of the city's best restaurants. Chinese food is the attraction and most dishes are in the C 2000 to C 4000 range.

The new *Picorna Hotel* (☎ 2672), on the western side of town not far from the centre, has equally good facilities but a moribund ambience. The most expensive units, which cost C 22,000, have air-con, carpets, TVs, refrigerators, telephones, comfortable chairs and modern baths, while the cheaper C 15,000 units are similar but without TVs, refrigerators or telephones. There is also a restaurant, bar and a rustic 'garden' for drinks.

A third possibility is the long-standing *Catering Rest House* (☎ 2978), an attractive sprawling complex in a quiet shady area some 750 metres east of the centre. The cost is C 11,000 for a round bungalow with a fan and attached bath, and C 16,500 for a large air-con room in the hotel's more modern section. However, some travellers have managed to negotiate a 25% reduction. There's running water only in the evening and occasionally none at all. You can also eat here.

Places to Eat & Drink

For cheap Ghanaian food, check out the street food around the market; it's delicious. Food typical of the area is stewed guinea fowl, vegetable soups (stews) and barbecued beef, all usually served with rice.

The most popular restaurant with travellers is the *Crest Restaurant Annexe*, in the centre on the 2nd floor of the building next to the Kingsway. It offers a choice of dining inside or outside on a breezy covered patio. The menu is fairly extensive with many selections in the C 800 to C 2000 range.

Another good place is *Sparkles Restaurant*, nearby at the National Cultural Centre. Attractive and well-ventilated, it offers numerous Chinese selections for C 2000 to C 3000, and also some cheaper dishes including Chinese rice for C 800 and beef/chicken foufou for C 1100/1600.

Other possibilities include the small outdoor *Cowrie Restaurant* in the Kalpuni Estates area, several km north-east of the central area, the excellent Chinese restaurant at the *Las Hotel*, the restaurant at the *Alhassan Hotel* in the centre, which has good meals for around C 1500 to C 2000, and the *Catering Rest House*, which has mostly European fare in the C 3000 range.

The most popular drinking place for travellers is the *Crest Restaurant Annexe*, which features good music. You'll find cold beer at the rustic *Point 7 Bar* across the street, and at *Bright Corner Drinking Bar*, which is another small outdoor bar in the centre, as well as pito at various places around the market.

The most popular nightclub is the *Rooftop Nightclub* in the centre on top of GNTC, followed by the *Picorna Gardens* at the Picorna Hotel and *Harry's Hot Spot*, just beyond the Catering Rest House. Most are open every night but lively only on weekends.

Getting There & Away

Air The airport is some distance north of town. Airlink (☎ 2428), which uses the Ghana Airways office in Tamale, has flights on Mondays, Wednesdays and Fridays to/from Accra, departing Accra at 9.15 am and Tamale at 11.15 am. The one-way cost is C 28,000. Remember to reconfirm your flight several days in advance.

Bus & Bush Taxi There are STC buses every day to Kumasi and Accra; the road is in excellent condition. The six-hour trip to Kumasi costs C 3600 (C 6200 to Accra) and tickets go fast, so get there early. The scheduled departure times are 6.30 am and 5.30 pm to Kumasi and 5 pm (two buses) to Accra, but buses usually leave half an hour late. The STC station (☎ 2444 for information) is a block north-west of the city's main intersection. There are also STC buses daily at 2 pm to Mole Game Reserve, at least one a day to Wa (C 3800) via Mole, and others north every day to Bolgatanga (C 2000), Navrongo (C 2400) and Bawku (C 2600), also one on Monday, Wednesday and Friday for Kete-Krachi (C 3300) via Yendi, departing at 10.30 am and arriving 12 hours later.

STC is not the only company with large buses to Kumasi and Bolgatanga. OSA has equally good buses, with several departures a day to Bolgatanga, but they leave when full rather than by a schedule. Its daily bus to Kumasi should leave around noon but a 2 pm departure is typical. City Express also serves Bolgatanga and Kumasi, with several departures a day. Its buses are in much worse condition. Both companies have their offices at the STC station.

Buses for Ouaga (Burkina Faso) pass through Tamale headed north around midnight every Wednesday and Saturday. They are usually full so it's not worth waiting for them; instead, take a City Express or some other bus to Bolgatanga where your chances of getting on are increased. Tro-tro, bush taxis and private buses for Kumasi and points north all leave from the main lorry park, usually in the morning. For a little adventure, take the older route via Salaga to Lake Volta at Makongo and cross over to Yeji. The STC bus to Makongo takes four hours and costs about C 1000. From there you can catch a 45-minute ferry over to Yeji twice daily. From Yeji, you could continue on to Kumasi or take the Thursday ferry to Akosombo.

Ferry Once the port is finished at Yapei, 32 km to the south-west of Tamale on the Kumasi road, you can take a ferry all the way

to Akosombo (see that section for details). Otherwise, catch one at Buipe further south off the Kumasi road or at Makongo on the old Kumasi road via Salaga.

AROUND TAMALE
Daboya

Daboya, 60 km west of Tamale via Tolon, is a wonderful little village and well worth visiting. It's the centre for all *gonja* **cloth weaving** and dyeing. Ask to see the chief, Wasipewura Takora II, who will find someone to show you the village including where they dye and weave the cloth, as well as to interpret for you. Take kola nuts to show your respect and appreciation because he's an important person and meeting with him is not to be taken lightly. For C 4000, you can also take a two-hour canoe ride up the river. There's no restaurant or bar, so take food and water with you. Taking photographs is free and not a problem.

Getting There & Away The bus leaves Tamale at 6 am and drops you by the river opposite Daboya, as the bridge connecting the village was destroyed long ago. You must catch a canoe to the village. The last bus leaves Daboya around 3.30 or 4 pm.

Yendi

Some 97 km east of Tamale, Yendi is notable for its **palace** of the paramount Dagomba chief. The *Ya-Na*, as he is called, has 22 wives all marked by shaven heads. Once a week there's a ceremony where his elders come with talking drums and praise singers. It's a memorable sight but to see such an event you'd have to make friends with a prominent Dagomba in Tamale or Yendi, who could make arrangements for you to be introduced to the Ya-Na.

Yendi (as well as Tamale) is also a good place to see the **Damba Festival** of the Dagomba. The exact day is not announced until several weeks before the festival, but it's always in September or October. It's a wild, fun day; the chiefs parade on horseback in full regal attire and there are dances all day.

There are no hotels in Yendi but if you're

friendly with the locals at the chop bars, they will show you a house with accommodation.

Getting There & Away STC buses leave Monday, Wednesday and Friday for Kete-Krachi via Yendi, departing Tamale at 10.30 am. The trip takes two hours and costs about C 1200. You can also catch tro-tro every day in Tamale headed this way; they charge about the same. Instead of returning to Tamale, you could continue south by tro-tro or STC bus to Kpandai and Kete-Krachi and catch a ferry there south to Kpandu and Akosombo.

Kpandai

If you're going from Tamale to Kete-Krachi, you can make it here by tro-tro in one long day if you leave early from Tamale and find a tro-tro in Yendi headed this way. Tro-tro cost about C 2000 between Yendi and Kpandai and another C 1500 on to Kete-Krachi. The road is in pitiful condition, especially the section between Kpandai and Kete-Krachi, which takes the better part of a day. Kpandai may look forsaken but you'll find both food and cheap lodging here.

MOLE GAME RESERVE

Roughly one-third the size of nearby Comoë National Park in Côte d'Ivoire, Mole, which has accommodation and tracks for vehicles, is the only game reserve in Ghana that has been developed to receive visitors. The best viewing time is the November to May dry season when the animals tend to congregate around water holes. The park is open year-round. (If you go during the rainy season, see the grasses will be high and you won't see as much, although spotting elephants and some other animals is still possible.) The dirt tracks are dry then and vehicles can be used. You can also view it on foot if you take a guard; the fee is about C 700 a person but the safari usually doesn't last more than a few hours unless you promise to tip well.

Some of the animals you might see beside antelope include elephant, baboon, buffalo, waterbuck, wart hog, kob, oribi, hyena, wild dog, jackal, various species of monkey and crocodile. The few lion here are rarely seen.

Over 300 species of birds have also been recorded here. To improve your chances of seeing fauna, hire one of the park wardens as a guide, and go in a vehicle so as to cover more territory. However, regardless of what park officials may tell you in Accra, don't count on using their vehicles because they haven't been working for years. Many people find the walking safaris much more exciting. Walks leave twice a day, at 6.30 am and 3.30 pm, and last 2½ hours. A guide is mandatory and groups may not exceed six people. The park entrance fee is about C 800 (C 200 for students) and the guide's fee is about C 700 an hour.

If you pass through **Larabanga** on the way here, check out the picturesque old mosque; it's of traditional mud construction and painted white. Originally built centuries ago, it's one of the older mosques in West Africa and reportedly has a Koran about as old as the mosque itself.

Places to Stay & Eat

Travellers can camp at the park or stay at the park's *Mole Hotel* (☎ (071) 2563, Tamale 3028). The 30 rooms are surprisingly nice and spacious. All have private bath, but there's usually no running water. Rooms with fans and shower cost C 5000; more expensive for bath and/or air-con (however there's no electricity after 10 pm). The most expensive accommodation here is in one of the five bungalows. There is also a swimming pool and a restaurant (you must order in the morning). A meal of chicken and yam or rice costs about C 2000. There's little variety and the service is very slow. It may be better to bring some food with you as anything other than dinner can be difficult to arrange.

The motel is on a hill overlooking a water hole; from there you can watch the animals gather in the early morning and late afternoon during the dry season. At night you may hear elephants trumpeting. Reservations are advisable only on weekends during the dry season. Contact one of the major travel agencies in Accra. If you camp near the motel, bring

GHANA

all of your food as the nearest village, Larabanga, is seven km away.

Getting There & Away

The reserve is 626 km north of Accra and 135 km west of Tamale. The turn-off for the park is on the Kumasi to Tamale highway at Nteso, 298 km north of Kumasi and 60 km south-west of Tamale. From Nteso, head west over a dirt road another 60 km to Damongo. The main entrance is 15 km beyond Damongo at Larabanga.

The best way by far to get here from Tamale is by taking the daily 2 pm STC bus which leaves from Tamale and goes directly to the park motel. You need to get to the STC station not later than 12.30 pm otherwise your chances of getting a seat will be very poor. This same bus leaves the reserve at 6 am, returning to Tamale. If you take a private bus or tro-tro to Damongo, you may have to walk to the park (22 km) as traffic from Damongo onward is very light. Another option is taking one of the more frequent STC buses to Wa and getting off at Damongo Junction. If you take a Wa bus, you'll have to pay the Wa price.

BOLGATANGA

'Bolga' (population 55,000), the fast-growing capital of the upper eastern region, is the major town between Tamale (161 km) and the Burkina Faso border (45 km).

This is also the craft centre of the north, and the central **market** is definitely worth checking. Leather and baskets are the main items. In the leather line, you can get sandals, handbags, wallets, briefcases, satchels, etc – mainly reddish brown and black with traditional designs. Best are the multicoloured baskets, which are closely woven from raffia, and range from minute to enormous; they're strikingly beautiful. Place mats and the famous Bolga straw hats, which are made in the market area, are also available. Also try the stand next to the STC bus station. Items there have fixed prices, eg C 1200 for sandals and C 2200 for woven bags. If you want to see where they're made, look along Bazaar Rd near the market as there are some leather workers in that area.

Orientation

The heart of town is the roundabout where the roads from Navrongo, Tamale and Bawku converge. The commercial centre, however, is along Commercial Rd, where you'll find several restaurants, banks, the post office and a hotel among other establishments, and along Bazaar Rd which runs roughly parallel to it a block to the east. You'll find the market and artisans here.

Activities

Take a tro-tro to Tongo (16 km) if you want to **hike** or **bike** into the surrounding hills. You should have no problem renting a bike or hiring a guide there but you might check first with the village chief as these scenic hills are sacred. To get there, go south for eight km to Winkogo on the Tamale road, then eight km east to Tongo.

Places to Stay – bottom end

The best place to stay for the money is the *Catholic Mission*, on the northern side of town; it charges C 3300/5500 for clean singles/doubles with shared baths. The *Hotel Bolco* behind the police station has probably

---

Kraals

The area east of Bolga is famous for its delightful *kraals*, particularly the villages of Zebila and, further on, Amkwalaga (both just off the Bolga to Bawku road). The kraal, which has different local names, is an impeccably clean compound of round straw-roof houses. These houses are connected by high walls around the perimeter and low walls around the inner courtyards, to keep out livestock. The curving design and the soothing ochre colour of the walls and, most unusually, the dark brown geometric designs painted on them, make an arresting sight. ■

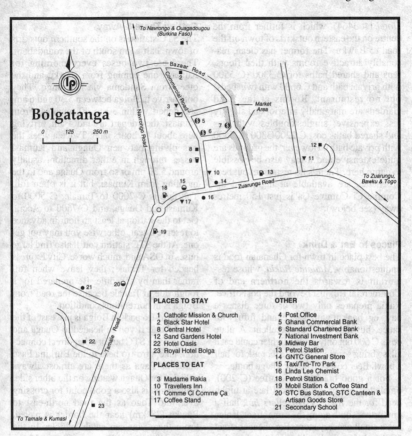

Bolgatanga

0   125   250 m

To Navrongo & Ouagadougou
(Burkina Faso)

Bazaar Road

Commercial Road

Navrongo Road

Market
Area

Zuarungu Road

To Zuarungu,
Bawku & Togo

To Tamale & Kumasi

PLACES TO STAY

1 Catholic Mission & Church
2 Black Star Hotel
8 Central Hotel
12 Sand Gardens Hotel
22 Hotel Oasis
23 Royal Hotel Bolga

PLACES TO EAT

3 Madame Rakia
10 Travellers Inn
11 Comme Ci Comme Ça
17 Coffee Stand

OTHER

4 Post Office
5 Ghana Commercial Bank
6 Standard Chartered Bank
7 National Investment Bank
9 Midway Bar
13 Petrol Station
14 GNTC General Store
15 Taxi/Tro-Tro Park
16 Linda Lee Chemist
18 Petrol Station
19 Mobil Station & Coffee Stand
20 STC Bus Station, STC Canteen &
     Artisan Goods Store
21 Secondary School

the cheapest rooms in town and you'll see why. Two places on the opposite side of town on the road to Tamale you might try are the *Royal Hotel Bolga*, which is one km south of the roundabout, and the *Hotel Oasis*, which is about 250 metres closer to town and 150 metres west of Tamale Rd down a dirt road. The former has doubles with fans and private baths for C 4000 but it suffers blackouts at night. Singles/doubles at the Oasis, which have fans and attached baths, cost C 3300/ 4400.

If you want air-con, the *Central Hotel* may be your only choice. It's a somewhat run-down two-storey building in the heart of

town on the main drag, Commercial Rd, but not well marked. Singles/doubles with air-con and private baths cost C 5500/6500. The rooms are quite large and the air-con is quiet, but the water pressure is so bad that they'll probably have to bring you a bucket of water to take a bath.

Places to Stay – top end

The city's top hotels, which are only marginally more expensive than the others, are the old two-storey *Black Star Hotel* (☎ 2346), which is on the northern side of town near the Catholic Mission, and the *Sand Gardens*

GHANA

Hotel (☎ 3464), which is further from the centre on the eastern outskirts of town off the road to Bawku. The former has clean, reasonably attractive rooms with tiled floors, fans and shared baths for C 3300 (C 5500 with private bath and C 6600 with twin beds) but no restaurant. Rooms at the Sand Gardens are marginally inferior and slightly less expensive; singles/doubles with fans and shared baths cost C 2200/3300 (C 5500 with private bath). However, the grounds are quite extensive and it may also be possible to camp here. There's no restaurant but beef brochettes are available at night and the Comme Ci Comme Ça is just 150 metres away (see below).

Places to Eat & Drink

The best place in town for Ghanaian food is unquestionably *Madame Rakia*, whose restaurant is towards the northern end of Commercial Rd, just beyond the post office. Rakia prepares only two or three dishes a day, eg banku with sauce and fufu with sauce, but they'll all be excellent. A plate costs C 600 but only a prize-fighter could eat it all, so bring someone to share it or ask for half a bowl. Beer costs C 700 for a large bottle.

For a good breakfast of coffee (C 200), omelettes, etc or a light meal late at night, head for the friendly *Travellers Inn*, half a km further south along the same street. It also has a small grocery store. For cheaper street food and pito, the local brew, try the market area nearby.

The only place for European cuisine is *Comme Ci Comme Ça*, a block east of the market area. Most European dishes cost around C 2500, but you can also get cheaper Ghanaian food here for C 1000. The tranquil shady garden is a good place to come just for a drink.

For a drink in the centre, head for the lively *Midway Bar*, across from the Travellers Inn. It's a rustic outdoor place facing the street with music at a tolerable volume and grilled-meat vendors nearby. You can also get a drink at the STC station's lively canteen, which is not so rustic.

Getting There & Away

The STC station is on the southern outskirts of town, half a km south of the roundabout. There are two buses every morning for Kumasi, one coming from Bawku and the other from Sandema via Navrongo. They both arrive in Bolga between 5.30 and 6 am, and depart within 30 to 40 minutes. From Kumasi, they depart around 4 am, arriving here about 12 hours later. Twice a week the bus plying between Ouaga and Kumasi passes through in either direction, usually around 5.30 pm or so from Ouaga and in the morning from Kumasi, but it is often full. The fare is C 2000 to Tamale, C 5000 to Kumasi and Ouaga, and C 7600 to Accra. Get to the station at least an hour in advance to reserve a seat, otherwise you may not get one. At the STC station you'll also find large buses of OSA and, much worse, City Express headed for Tamale; they leave when full rather than by schedule. Be prepared for a rough ride to Tamale because the road from Bolga is in horrendous condition.

The tro-tro park in Bolga is just east of the roundabout. If you're headed to Ouaga and can't find an STC bus or other direct connection, take a tro-tro here to the Burkina Faso border at Paga as there are almost always vehicles for Ouaga waiting on the other side. Bolgatanga is also a good point for crossing over into Togo as the road north-east to Bawku (78 km) near the border is paved. From there you can catch vehicles to the border (30 km) and Dapaong (Togo), 15 km further east, as well as to Nakpanduri to the south. Especially in the mornings you can find vehicles every day at Bolga's tro-tro park for Paga (C 750), Bawku (C 800), Tamale (C 1500) and Wa, and on Tuesday, Friday and Sunday direct to the Togo border (C 2000).

NAKPANDURI

Hikers and those looking for a tranquil village to relax in should consider a trip to Nakpanduri, a small village perched on the **Gambaga Escarpment**, 128 km east of Bolga via Bawku. The village is very traditional with huts neatly thatched and well maintained. You can go for walks along the edge of the escarpment and down to the forest floor where you may spot elephant droppings and numerous birds. In the dry season the animals gather at a watering hole by the bridge three km down the hill.

Places to Stay & Eat
The *Government Rest House* on the edge of the escarpment offers fantastic views. It's fairly basic with no cooking facilities but the rooms are clean, large and cost about C 750 each.

Your other option is to stay at the *Assemblies of God Rest House*. It has no views but better facilities. It has three spotlessly clean doubles and a waterbed no less, and an equipped kitchen. The cost is about C 1700 a person. You can buy essential food items in the village; bring everything else with you. Another possibility is the guesthouse at the Agriculture Rehabilitation Centre for the Blind (ARB) in Garu, which is on the road from here to Bawku. It has clean rooms with showers for C 3500, and for a bit extra the caretaker will arrange for you to use the centre's cooking facilities.

Getting There & Away
Public transport from Bawku south to Nakpanduri (50 km) is best on market day in Bawku (which is also Bolga's market day), every three days.

NAVRONGO
Navrongo (population 11,000) is 16 km south of the Burkina Faso border and the last major Ghanaian town on the road to Ouagadougou. In the centre you'll see several large half-built structures. They are hotels begun in the mid-70s by Acheampong as a gift to this small village. Construction on this insane project stopped when he was deposed and today it's just an eyesore. Check out the Catholic **cathedral** too. It's unusual in that it was constructed of mud in the traditional Sudanese style (French colonial architectural style in the Sahel), and the colourful interior decorations likewise reflect the local influence.

If you're interested in a side trip, visit the large dam and **lake** eight km away in Tono. The lake is six km long and provides irrigation for the entire valley, making the area verdant when everything else is dry. From a distance you can see the Chiara Hills.

There are no hotels, but the *Catholic Mission* on the south-east side of town rents out clean, cheap rooms for about C 2000 a person.

For cheap food and pito, try the market area and *Tiko's* near the STC bus stop.

Getting There & Away
There are STC buses every day to Kumasi, departing around 4.30 am. Coming from Kumasi they depart around 4 am and arrive here in the late afternoon or early evening. If you're headed only to Bolgatanga, take a tro-tro from the market as they depart more frequently and the trip only takes an hour.

PAGA
The Burkina Faso border town of Paga has one major attraction, a **crocodile pond** very near the village. You pay C 1000 to C 2000 (negotiable, plus other miscellaneous fees) to have the crocodile summoned on land so you can be photographed with it; for about C 600 more, something live, such as a chicken, can be sacrificed to the crocodile. The typical photo is that of a foreigner sitting on the croc's back just before the sacrifice.

Travellers stuck here for the night can get a basic room at the *Paga Motel* for C 3500.

WA
Wa, capital of the upper western region, and the nearby town of Lawra in the north-west corner of the country are completely devoid of tourists and for this reason worth a visit. The best time to come is the first week in October when both towns have festivals. During Wa's **Durbar Festival**, as at all durbar festivals, the king, always elaborately dressed, sits in state to receive the homage of his subjects, on whom he showers hospitality and gifts. The ritual here, however, is truly unique because by tradition the king must jump over a cow or he will be slain! Wa has a small **market**, which is really

GHANA

quite good. Another sight is the town's imposing **mosque**, which is a superb example of traditional Sudanese-style architecture found more commonly in Burkina Faso and Mali. The dazzling white traditional-style residence of the Wa-Na (the king) is also worth checking.

The area is renowned for its pito, smocks and xylophone players – all reputedly the best in Ghana. Sitting around drinking pito is a great way to meet people. The numerous government agricultural development workers here are all very friendly and chances are they'll be happy to take you out into the surrounding area where they work.

If you're in nearby **Lawra**, try arranging your trip to coincide with the **Kobinah Festival**, which takes place in October. It features about 30 dancing groups which come from all over northern Ghana and Burkina Faso. Otherwise, Lawra may seem a bit dead unless you meet the chief, a former agriculture secretary who loves to talk. His palace is also an interesting place to visit.

Places to Stay & Eat

Wa has several hotels and some great street food. The cheapest place to stay is the *Residency*, which has OK rooms with double beds, fans and shared baths. The best place for the money, however, is the *Kunateh Lodge* (☎ 102) on Zongo St. The manager is very helpful and charges C 4400/6600 for clean singles/doubles with fans and showers. There's a small bar with balcony and a flat roof where you may be able to sleep for a small fee. Just across the street you'll find a woman who cooks excellent cheap street food. For a place with air-con rooms, try the overpriced *Upland Hotel*. Still another option is the *Hotel du Pond*.

Getting There & Away

The STC bus from Accra costs C 7000 (C 4400 from Kumasi) and the trip takes 12 hours if you're lucky (eight hours from Kumasi). From Kumasi, you also have the option of taking a tro-tro. They're often a bit faster but cost slightly more; the Wa tro-tro station in Kumasi is quite difficult to find but most taxi drivers know it. You can also get to Wa by bus from Tamale (C 3800), Bolgatanga and Damongo (near Mole Game Reserve).

Guinea

Guinea (sometimes called Guinea-Conakry to distinguish it from neighbouring Guinea-Bissau) used to suffer under one of the most oppressive regimes in Africa. But since the death of president Sekou Touré in 1984, it has changed radically: you can almost feel the new liberty and economic vitality.

One of Guinea's major attractions is the vibrancy of the culture. Across the country, there's a strong tradition of live music, and Conakry has more night spots than you can count. Any evening, too, you can find a musical celebration in the streets. Added to this is Guinea's spectacular landscape: the Fouta Djalon hill region, in the west of the country, has a relatively cool climate and some of the most striking scenery in West Africa, and is an excellent area for hiking.

Despite these attractions, Guinea is not prepared for tourism. Outside Conakry, most accommodation is quite basic (although cheaper than comparable places in, say, Senegal) and journeys by road can be long and hard. If you insist on creature comforts you may not enjoy Guinea. But if you're prepared to rough it, a visit here can be very rewarding.

REPUBLIC OF GUINEA

Area: 245,855 sq km
Population: 6.5 million
Population Growth Rate: 3%
Capital: Conakry
Head of State: President General Lansana Conté
Official Language: French
Currency: Guinean franc
Exchange Rate: GF 960 = US$1
Per Capita GNP: US $500
Inflation: 7%
Time: GMT/UTC

Facts about the Country

HISTORY

Guinea was part of the Empire of Mali, which dominated most of the Sahel region between the 13th and 15th centuries; descendants of the Mali rulers, the Malinké, still live in Guinea. Around the 15th century, Fulani herders started migrating into the area and, as a result of the Holy Islamic War of 1725, gained hegemony over the mountainous Fouta Djalon area.

In the 19th century, the Guinean hero, Samori Touré, led the fight against French colonialists. He was captured in 1898 and resistance gradually dried up. Once the railway from Conakry to Kankan was com-pleted, France began serious exploitation of the area, by then part of French West Africa.

The most famous Guinean of all was Sekou Touré, born into a poor Malinké family and a descendant of the legendary Samori Touré. After becoming the foremost trade unionist in French West Africa he led the fight for independence; in 1956, while still holding communist views, he led a breakaway movement from the French parent union to form a federation of African trade unions.

Independence

In 1958, Charles de Gaulle offered the French colonies a choice between autonomy

GUINEA

Guinea

0   100   200 km

~~~~~~

Suggested Itineraries
There is no obvious 'circuit' around the country so travel in Guinea usually means following the main roads that link Conakry to the other large towns. If you can visit only one part of Guinea, it should be the **Fouta Djalon** hill region, where you can spend between three days and a week in **Pita** (from where you can reach the **Chutes de Kinkon** waterfall) and **Dalaba**, where the scenery is particularly pleasant. If you're heading north overland, from Labé you can get transport to Koundara and on to Senegal, or to Gabú in Guinea-Bissau.

Of the other towns in Guinea, **Faranah** is worth staying at for a day or two: many travellers rate it as the nicest in the country, with some lively streets and a good market. From here (with patience and determination) you can reach the **Source of the Niger** in two to three days. Other interesting towns are: **Kankan**, the regional capital of the north, from where you can find transport into Mali; **Guéckédou**, which has a very large market, with traders and goods from Mali, Liberia and Côte d'Ivoire; and **Nzérékoré**, Guinea's 'gateway to the east'. ∎

~~~~~~

as separate countries in a Franco-African community or immediate independence. Sekou Touré, declaring that Guinea preferred 'freedom in poverty to prosperity in chains', was the only leader to reject de Gaulle's proposal. Thus, Guinea became the first French colony to gain independence. Sekou Touré became an African legend in his own time, and since he was the leader of Guinea's only viable political party, also the country's first president.

De Gaulle, infuriated, immediately withdrew the French colonial administration – but not before they had destroyed all military equipment and civilian archives, leaving nothing behind. They even ripped out the telephones. French private citizens fled with massive amounts of capital, thus assuring Guinea's economic collapse.

Wanting nothing more to do with the CFA franc, which was linked to the French franc, Touré introduced a new currency, the syli. But with French economic assistance gone, the new country badly needed foreign aid. Touré turned to the Russians, but the link with the USSR was short-lived – in 1961, the Soviet ambassador was thrown out for 'interfering in the internal affairs of the country'.

The government continued on a socialist road, however, and in 1967 commenced a campaign of cultural revolution on the Chinese model, with state-run farms and weekly meetings of each revolutionary unit. It was an unmitigated disaster. As many as one million Guineans fled into neighbouring countries looking for work. The remaining farmers were able to work only one-quarter of the country's cultivable area. The USA had to give tonnes of food aid every year to keep people from starving.

The Reign of Terror
Sekou Touré appointed Malinké to virtually every major government position and treated his political opponents cruelly. Following an unsuccessful Portuguese-led invasion of the country in 1970, he became paranoid, staying in Guinea for the next five years, and he often spoke of a 'permanent plot' against his regime. Waves of arrests followed. Prisoners were sentenced to death, and torture

became commonplace. Every year, Guinea was near the top of Amnesty International's list of the worst human rights offenders. In 1976, Touré charged the entire Fulani population with collusion in an attempt to overthrow the government. The alleged Fulani leader of the plot was starved to death in prison. A quarter of the country's population, mostly Fulani, went into exile.

A historic revolt by market women in 1977 turned the tide. As part of its programme to discourage private trade, the government had decreed that all agricultural produce was to be delivered to the state-run co-operatives. For the market women, many of whom had been among Sekou Touré's most ardent supporters, this was too much. Riots started in Conakry, where the women destroyed various police offices, then spread to most of Guinea's towns, where they killed the governors of Kindia, Faranah and Boké. On hearing their complaints directly, Sekou Touré was deeply moved and again legalised petty trade. The day the revolt began, 27 August, is now a national holiday.

The riots seemed to alter Sekou Touré's thinking in other ways as well. Soon afterwards, he stepped up his *rapprochement* with France, with whom diplomatic relations had been resumed the year before. In 1978, Giscard d'Estaing became the first French president since independence to set foot in Guinea. Touré then went on a 16-country tour of Africa, making amends with Senegal and Côte d'Ivoire.

Touré died of heart failure in 1984, only months before a scheduled conference of the Organisation of African Unity (OAU) that he was to chair in Conakry. His death was followed by one of the most spectacular funerals in modern-day Africa, attended by numerous heads of state from Africa and elsewhere. Three days later, however, the people's real feelings came to light. A military coup was staged by a group of colonels, including Lansana Conté, who became president and Diarra Traoré, who became prime minister. They denounced Touré and released a thousand political prisoners, promising an open society and the restoration of free enterprise.

The change of government certainly opened up Guinea and returned it to the Western fold, but ethnic tension amongst the leaders (Conté is a Susu, Traoré a Malinké) and within the government led to more problems. In July 1985 Traoré staged another coup while Conté was out of the country. The attempt failed, as Traoré did not enjoy sufficient support, but it forced Conté to face the urgent matter of reforming the economy. He introduced austerity measures to secure funding from the International Monetary Fund (IMF), and a new currency, the Guinean franc (GF), replaced the syli.

Guinea Today

Since the mid-1980s, incomes of many Guineans have risen slightly or, in some cases, quite a lot. The Susu and Lebanese communities are doing particularly well, evidenced by an estimated fivefold increase in the number of expensive cars and new villas around Conakry. Many exiles have returned and free enterprise is encouraged. Main roads and telecommunications throughout the country have been improved, and rural tracks in several areas are being rebuilt so that local farmers can get their produce to market. People can now watch the news on colour TV and talk freely and, while the press is still not completely uncensored, reporters can at least express themselves. Also, presidential elections have been held, so the government can now be labelled as one in 'transition to democracy'.

The problem is that the quality of life for most Guineans remains miserable. Under the UN's quality of life index, Guinea has ranked last in the world (or next to the last) every year since at least 1990. That's because life expectancy at birth (45 years) and the rate of adult literacy (25%) are among the two or three lowest in the world in both categories. This is because from 1986 to 1990, health and education received an average of just 3% and 11% of the national budget, compared with 29% for defence.

In October 1991, after considerable pressure from within his government and from Western donor-nations (particularly France), Conté agreed to proposals for a multiparty political system. In April the following year, the system was formally introduced and 17 parties were legalised. By July this number had doubled. The plan was to hold presidential and parliamentary elections after a six-year 'introductory' period, but pressure for reform remained strong and in October 1993 it was announced that presidential elections would be held in December the same year. Eight candidates stood for the post, including Conté. In the run-up to voting, the actual date of the election was changed several times, giving rise to unrest in Conakry and some other towns. The situation became increasingly tense and in mid-December the country's land borders were closed while voting and counting took place. They remained closed into early 1994 – some weeks after the election, which Conté won comfortably with over 50% of the total. His main opponent, Alpha Condé, polled 20%. There were accusations of vote-rigging (which may have been true), but it is likely that a divided opposition allowed Conté to remain in power. Plans are still on course for general elections to take place in 1998 or 1999. It remains to be seen if the Guinean people are prepared to wait that long.

GEOGRAPHY

Guinea has an area of about 246,000 sq km (slightly larger than Britain) and can be divided into four zones: the coastal plain (with Conakry, the capital, on a narrow peninsula jutting out from the plain); the north-western Fouta Djalon hill region; the northern dry lowlands; and the forests of the south-east.

The Fouta Djalon hills are Guinea's best known geographical feature and the source of much of the Niger River (although the source of the Niger lies to the south on the Guinea-Sierra Leone border). It is a beautiful plateau rising in the central west of the country to over 1500 metres, with the town of Labé in the centre. The hills were popular with the colonial administrators before independence because of their cool climate and splendid scenery.

The remote south-east corner of the country, along the Liberian border, is also hilly with dense tropical forests and, during the rainy season, some of the muddiest roads this side of Zaïre.

Environmentally, Guinea's problems are less immediate and threatening than those of its northern neighbours because of its benign climate and generous natural resources. The far eastern area is heavily vegetated, though because of fires and cultivation very little of it is virgin rainforest. Exploitation has been mostly small scale due to limited mechanisation, but this is changing. The vastly improved road system in the east is great for travellers but it's bad for the forests, as the wood can now be shipped out more easily.

There are no national parks in Guinea, which means that the few remaining forest elephants and other fauna have to fend for themselves.

CLIMATE

Guinea is one of the wettest countries in West Africa. Rainfall along the coast is particularly high. Conakry, for example, receives about 4300 mm in a normal year, about half of it in July and August. While the central mountainous region receives less than half this amount, the rains there are more evenly distributed throughout the rainy season, from May to October.

ECONOMY

Although the economic situation has improved since President Conté took control of the country, Guinea is still a long way from losing its place amongst the world's 25 poorest countries. The economy is still based on agriculture, much of it at subsistence level. However, Guinea is a country which could be built around mining, particularly bauxite (to manufacture aluminium), as everything about this mineral here is statistically impressive. Guinea has the third-largest known reserves of bauxite in the world, with an estimated 30% of the world total, and it's the second-largest producer of bauxite in the world. It also has the world's largest bauxite mine, which is in Boké and owned by CGB, a company which is 51% owned by Halco, an international aluminium consortium, and the remainder by the gov-

ernment. The next largest mines are in Kindia and Kimbo and are partially owned by Russia.

Guinea also has impressive reserves of diamonds, iron, copper, manganese and uranium, so it's not surprising that it is counting on its mineral wealth to lift it out of poverty. However, its second-largest export, diamonds, has declined in recent years and most of what is discovered is smuggled out of the country, escaping the government coffers. Some 80% of the gold output is similarly exported illegally. Smartly positioned traders and government officials stand to profit handsomely.

Most of Guineas's huge iron ore deposits are around Mt Nimba, which is on the southwestern edge of the country and practically made of iron. A quarter of the mountain is in Liberia; that alone justified foreign companies in Liberia building a railway to the coast. Guinea, however, has not been able to arrange a hook-up with this railway line because of the civil war in that country and has, therefore, shelved plans at least temporarily to expand mining there. Regardless, international donors are reluctant to assist in this effort because of the serious environmental damage that would result.

In the public sector many hard decisions have already been made. In the early 1990s, almost half of the government's 70,000 civil service bureaucrats were fired. At the same time, 16 state-run enterprises were liquidated and another 41 were privatised. About half of those privatised, however, either have not reopened or have subsequently closed down.

Meanwhile, the country's economic growth rate, which was strong during the late '80s, has declined while imports of food, particularly rice, have doubled since the early '80s due to trade liberalisation. As a result, the outlook for the overall economy is less rosy than it was five years ago.

POPULATION & PEOPLE

The population is estimated at 6.5 million. The main groups are the Malinké (or Mandingo), the Fula (or Fulani) and the Susu. Together they constitute about three-quarters

Music

As in Mali, the Malinké of northern Guinea are best known for their musical talents: their kora traditions are particularly rich and influential, and continue to provide inspiration for many modern artists.

Today, Guinea's most famous star is Mory Kanté. He was born in the early '50s in Kissidougou into a Malinké family of musicians and griots, and now lives in France, where he is one of the most popular musicians in the country. His distinctive music combines the kora with brass and electric piano to produce a modern sound which fuses rock and soul with traditional African music. Other Malinké musicians combining traditional kora and modern electric sounds, and rivalling Mory Kanté's international fame, include Kanté Manfila and Jali Musa Jawara (also written Djeli Moussa Diawara). The rhythm of their exhilarating but subtle music is more of a pulse than a beat, like the sensation of being on a rocking boat.

Other Guinean artists, less well-known internationally, include Sékouba Kandia Kouyaté (son of the late Kouyaté Sory Kandia – one of Guinea's most popular and influential artists in the early years of independence), and the female singer Djanka Diabaté. If you're buying cassettes, apart from the artists listed above, names to look out for include Bembeya Jazz National (another influential band from early post-independence days), Kaloum Star (the backing band for South African singer Miriam Makeba when she lived in Guinea), Fodé Kouyaté, and the Super Boiro Band.

Some places where you can buy cassettes, or sample live Guinean music, are listed in the Conakry section. ■

of the total population; 15 other ethnic groups make up the rest. The Susu generally inhabit the coastal region, while more Malinké and Fula live in the north and centre.

ART

Despite their heritage and large numbers in Guinea, Mali, Senegal and elsewhere, the

Nimba mask
(the Nimba represents fertility)

Mask, Simo society

Malinké produce very little art – quite the opposite of the Bambara in Mali, to whom they are closely related. If you find any Malinké wooden carvings, they are likely to be in the form of antelopes, a favourite subject. Sculptured human figures are almost nonexistent.

RELIGION

About 75% of the people are Muslims. Christians constitute less than 1%, and the remainder practice traditional religions.

LANGUAGE

French is the official language. Many African languages are spoken: Malinké by 40% of the people, especially in the north around Kankan and Faranah, Fula by 30%, particularly in the Fouta Djalon region, and Susu by 23%, mainly in the south around Conakry.

Expressions in Susu

Good morning.	*tay-nah mah-ree*
Good evening.	*tay-nah mah-fay-yen*
How are you?	*oh-REE toh-nah-moh?*
Thank you.	*een-wah-lee*
Goodbye.	*une-GAY-say-gay*

Expressions in Fula

Good morning/ evening.	*JAR-ah-mah*
How are you?	*tan-ah ah-lah-TON?*
Thank you.	*JAR-ah-mah*
Goodbye.	*an OUNT-tou-mah*

Facts for the Visitor

VISAS & EMBASSIES
Guinea Visas

Visas are required by all visitors. From embassies in Africa they are usually valid for only one or two weeks; you have to state clearly on your form, and maybe plead with the officials, to get more time, although one month is normally the maximum. Some embassies may require a letter of introduction from your own embassy, or proof of 'sufficient funds', although this is rare.

In West Africa you can get visas for Guinea in Dakar (Senegal), Bamako (Mali), Bissau (Guinea-Bissau), Banjul (The Gambia), Abidjan (Côte d'Ivoire), Freetown (Sierra Leone), Accra (Ghana), Monrovia (Liberia) and Lagos (Nigeria). For details refer to the Visas & Embassies section of the relevant country chapter.

Outside of Africa, the embassy in Washington issues them free and gives two-day service. It requires three photos, a copy of your international health certificate, a copy of your round-trip ticket and a letter explaining the purpose of your visit and where you intend to travel. Visas are valid for two months and multiple-entry visas are available on request. There is no Guinean embassy in London, but there is one in Paris and in Bonn.

Wherever you get your visas, tell the embassy if you intend travelling overland, otherwise your passport will be stamped 'Voyage (Aller et Retour) en Guinée Aeroport Gbissa', which means you must fly in and out of Conakry. However, once there you can change it at Immigration (☎ 44 14 39) in central Conakry on the corner of 1st Blvd and Ave Tubman (8th Ave). You can also get visa extensions from Immigration.

Guinea Embassies

Belgium 75 Ave Vandendriessche, Brussels 1150 (☎ (02) 771-01-90)
France 24 rue Emile-Meunieur, 75016 Paris (☎ (1) 45-53-72-25)
Germany Rochusweg 50, 5300 Bonn 1 (☎ (0228) 23-10-97/8)
USA 2112 Leroy Place, NW, Washington, DC 20008 (☎ (202) 483-9420)

Guinea also has embassies in Addis Ababa, Brazzaville, Cairo, Dar es Salaam, Kinshasa, Maputo, Nairobi, Ottawa, Rabat, Rome and Tokyo; plus consulates in Duisburg, Madrid and Geneva.

Other African Visas

Ghana The embassy is open weekday mornings and issues visas in 24 hours for US$50 or equivalent in Guinea francs. The form asks for an onward ticket, sufficient funds, and referees in Ghana, but they don't ask for proof and if you don't have a referee it doesn't matter.
Guinea-Bissau The embassy is open weekdays from 8 am to 1 pm, and issues visas the same day, often on the spot, for GF 20,000.
Liberia The embassy should start issuing visas again once the turmoil in Liberia subsides.
Mali The embassy issues one-month visas for in 24 hours for GF 15,000.
Nigeria The embassy is open weekdays from 10 am to 2 pm. Visas take 24 hours. The cost varies

according to nationality, from about US$1 for Americans to about US$40 for Britons.

Senegal The embassy is open from 8.30 am to 2 pm Monday to Thursday and until 1 pm on Friday and Saturday. Visas cost GF 2500, and are issued in 24 hours.

Sierra Leone The embassy is open weekdays from 8 am to 3 pm (to 1 pm on Fridays) and gives same-day service for visas up to one month. You need a letter of introduction from your own embassy. The cost is US$30 for Britons, US$15 for Americans and US$10 for most other nationalities, or the equivalent in Guinea francs. However, prices seem fairly arbitrary (some Aussies have got free visas, and we heard from another traveller who paid nothing 'because Americans are good'), and staff do not always know the current exchange rates.

Other Countries The French embassy issues visas to Togo, Burkina Faso, Chad and the Central African Republic in 24 hours. The cost of each is approximately 50FF.

Foreign Embassies

See the Conakry Information section for embassy addresses.

DOCUMENTS

All visitors need a passport and an International Vaccination Certificate.

CUSTOMS

You may not import or export local currency, but there is no limit on foreign currency, although declaration forms are used at the airport. To export art objects, you need a permit from the Musée National on 7th Blvd and Corniche Sud.

MONEY

1FF   = GF 165
UK£1 = GF 1350
US$1 = GF 960

The unit of currency is the Guinean franc (GF). Prices have been rising by around 25% a year but in dollar terms they are fairly stable. Banks that change money include: Banque Internationale pour le Commerce et l'Industrie de la Guinée (BICIGUI), Société Général des Banques en Guinée (SGBG), and Meridien BIAG. Service in Conakry banks is usually quite swift, although in banks upcountry changing money can be a long process.

The exchange rate offered by black-market dealers is at best 5% better than the bank rate, but only for cash. In Conakry the dealers operate at the airport and in the city centre next to the post office on 4th Blvd.

Currency declaration forms are reportedly no longer required. However, if you fly into Guinea, this requirement may still exist. If so, when you change money in a bank get the form stamped as it's checked at the airport when you leave. The officials here just love it if there's a discrepancy, as it gives them a chance to put the thumbscrews on and scare you into paying a large backhander. There's a bank at Conakry Airport but the rates are low for travellers' cheques. Neither this bank nor any other in Guinea will change back Guinea francs into hard currency (such as US dollars) when you leave, even if you retain your bank receipts. However, the money-changers will help you out. It all seems fairly open, but it's worth being as discreet as possible. At land borders, currency forms are not issued or asked for.

BUSINESS HOURS & HOLIDAYS

Government office hours are Monday to Thursday from 7.30 am to 3 pm and Friday and Saturday from 7.30 am to 1 pm. Some businesses work government hours. Others are open Monday to Saturday from 8 am to 12.30 pm and 3 to 6 pm except Friday, when shops close at 12.30 pm. Banking hours are Monday to Friday 8.30 am to 12.30 pm; some open from 2 to 4 pm and Saturday mornings; all close Sundays.

Public Holidays

1 January, 1 April, End of Ramadan, Easter Monday, 1 May, Tabaski, 1st Monday in August (Freedom Day), 27 August (Market Womens' Revolt), Mohammed's Birthday, 1 October (Independence Day), 1 November (Armed Forces Day), 25 December. The biggest holidays are 1 April, the day the present regime came to power, and Independence Day.

POST & TELECOMMUNICATIONS

To make an international call go to the

Top: Butterflies, Guinea (CB)
Bottom: Abandoned statues at Cacheu Fort, Guinea-Bissau (DE)

Top & Left: Ireli, Dogon country, Mali (DW)
Right: Timbuktu doors, Mali (DE)

Novotel. If you have no money to spare and time to waste, go to the post office.

MAPS
The French Institut Géographique National (IGN) produce a good map of Guinea at a scale of 1:1,000,000. It is unavailable in Conakry, but is occasionally seen in Dakar bookshops.

PHOTOGRAPHY
The situation on photo permits is unclear: they are available from the Ministry of Tourism, although they may not be obligatory. Whatever, even with a permit, you should be very careful when taking photographs. As in all African cities you should not snap government buildings, airports, bridges etc, but it's best not to use a camera at all in cities and towns unless you're sure the police aren't watching and the locals have no objection. Otherwise, save your film for rural areas.

HEALTH
In Conakry, the Hôpital Ignace Dean, in the centre at the northern end of Ave de la République, is recommended only for dire emergencies. Pharmacies in Conakry are fairly well stocked.

DANGERS & ANNOYANCES
Outside the capital, Guinea is a safe country, but most travellers agree that Conakry itself is one of the worst cities in the region. Street crime is a big problem (you should be particularly careful in markets and bus stations) and guests have even been robbed in their hotel rooms. Don't be put off visiting Guinea though – just avoid Conakry if you can.

ACCOMMODATION & FOOD
In Conakry, budget hotels are limited. But outside Conakry, most towns have at least one place to stay, often with quite basic, but cheap, facilities.

In most towns, street food (such as brochettes, grilled fish, peanuts and cakes) is available, and there are usually one or two basic eating houses doing cheap meals of rice and sauce. Only the larger towns have anything like

a restaurant where you might also find meat, chicken or chips. Conakry has several smart pâtisseries selling coffee and cakes, pizzas, burgers and other Western-style food.

Getting There & Away

AIR
To/From Europe & the USA
Airlines from Europe serving Guinea include Air France (via Paris), KLM (via Amsterdam), Sabena (via Brussels) and Aeroflot (via Moscow). Return flights cost between US$600 and US$700, depending on the season and your length of stay. Ghana Airways (via Accra) and Air Afrique (via Dakar) also have flights to/from Europe. From the USA you can take Air Afrique from New York, transferring to a regional airline in Dakar or Abidjan. Otherwise you'll have to go via Europe.

To/From West Africa
Within West Africa, Conakry is connected to Bamako, Niamey and all the capital cities along the West African coast, primarily by Air Afrique, Gambia Airways, Ghana Airways, Nigeria Airways, Air Guinée and Guinée Air Service. Some sample prices and schedules are: Conakry to Freetown, twice a week on Gambia Airways for GF 65,000 or twice a week on Ghana Airways for GF 58,000; and Conakry to Banjul/Dakar three times a week on Gambia Airways for GF 100,000/136,000. For airline office addresses see the Conakry Getting There & Away section.

Warning Some of the police officers at Conakry Airport are notorious tricksters; they offer to assist you through passport control and customs, but their conversations on your behalf with the officials usually results in you being last out of the airport. Then they demand a large tip. Be calm and polite, and follow the other passengers rather than accept this kind of 'assistance'.

LAND
Bush Taxi & Minibus
To/From Côte d'Ivoire Most travellers going overland from Guinea to Côte d'Ivoire take the route through Guéckédou, Macenta, Nzérékoré, Danané and Man. It's easy to get from Conakry to Macenta by bus, and on to Nzérékoré by bush taxi (for more details see the Macenta Getting There & Away section). From Nzérékoré bush taxis run to Man for CFA 5000.

An alternative route goes via Kankan and Odienné, passing through Mandiana and Tindila, but this is in poor condition and infrequently travelled. Bush taxis run between Kankan and Mandiana; for the rest of this route you'll probably have to hitch a ride with a truck. Allow two days.

To/From Guinea-Bissau Most travellers going overland to Guinea-Bissau take the route via Labé and Koundara to Gabú because the roads are in better condition and there's more traffic. Getting between Conakry and Koundara is straightforward (see Conakry Getting There & Away for details on the bus to/from Labé, and the Labé section for details on transport to/from Koundara), and between Bissau and Gabú is also easy (see the Guinea-Bissau chapter).

Catching rides between Koundara and Gabú, however, is difficult: it can take at least a day to cover this 100-km stretch. You may be lucky and find a truck or pick-up going direct, for which the charge will be around GF 10,000 .

Alternatively, you can do it in stages: chang-

Crossing the Border

As well as the main routes between Guinea-Bissau and Guinea that are described in this chapter, we've heard about another crossing point that seems to be very rarely used by travellers. Alex and Bridget, two Antipodean mountain bikers, sent us this story.

We collected our visas from the Guinea embassy in Bissau and aimed for the border at Kandika, between Gabú and Koundara. Leaving Guinea-Bissau was no problem: the officials were nice, and cheerfully stamped us out. But when we got to the Guinea border it was closed. We couldn't go into Guinea and were unable to go back into Guinea-Bissau, because we now had exit stamps in our passports. We were stuck in no-man's-land. With us were four other travellers, who had already been there for two days, and had been making trips back into Guinea-Bissau to buy food. The Guinea-Bissau officials knew they were there when we came through. Shame they forgot to mention it.

It turned out that the borders had been closed for a few weeks because presidential elections were due and the situation was potentially volatile. Shame they hadn't told us about this at the embassy.

We camped in no-man's-land for a week, but the Guinea border remained well and truly closed, even after the election (and counting of results) had taken place. By this time, we were nine travellers, as the Guinea-Bissau officials continued to stamp people out across their border.

After ten days, there was still no sign of the border opening. Even if it had, by this time our Guinea visa was already half expired. So we had to go back into Guinea-Bissau. The eternally cheerful border guards gave us new visas, with surprisingly little bureaucracy and, even more surprising, no request for cadeaux.

We returned to Bissau, and went back to the Guinea embassy to get another visa. The ambassador seemed completely unaware that the border was closed. In fact, he insisted it had been open for weeks. But we weren't going to risk getting stuck again, so we decided to try one of the border crossings in the south.

Finally, almost a month after first trying to make it, we crossed into Guinea on a narrow track near the coast, to reach the village of Kandiafra. The track is marked on the Michelin map, but we wouldn't advise anyone to take it unless they were on foot or a sturdy mountain bike. It was very very rough, and so badly rutted that most vehicles simply wouldn't get through. There were swamps where we had to carry our bikes, while some local people helped by carrying our panniers on their heads. There was also a major river crossing where we managed to get ourselves and the bikes ferried across by pirogue.

We eventually arrived in Boké then headed north to Koumbia on a relatively good dirt road. Koumbia was like an oasis for us! ■

ing at Seréboïdo, the last village in Guinea, and maybe walking between there and the border. In Guinea-Bissau, there's usually at least one pick-up a day between Gabú and the border. Your best chance of good connections is to tie in your travels with Seréboïdo's weekly market (Sunday): vehicles go there from Gabú and from Koundara on Saturday and return to both places on Sunday or Monday.

An alternative route between Conakry and Bissau goes via Boké, but this is slow and strenuous. See Getting There & Away in the Guinea-Bissau chapter for more details.

All these routes are slow or impassable in the rainy season.

To/From Mali The usual route from Conakry to Bamako is via Kankan and Siguiri. From Kankan, there's a bus most days to the border at Kourémalé, via Siguiri, for GF 10,000. If the bus isn't running, bush taxis go this way for about the same price (although many drivers who say they're going to Bamako are actually going *towards* Bamako and only go as far as the border). On this route, you cross the Niger River twice, each time on a decrepit ferry. If they're broken, you have to cross by *pirogue* (dugout canoe) and find a vehicle on the other side. If you stop off at Siguiri, bush taxis go to the border for GF 4000 and occasionally all the way to Bamako for GF 9000.

On the Mali side, there's a bus three times a week each way between Bamako and the border at Kourémalé for CFA 1500 (which sometimes goes all the way to/from Siguiri). Bush taxis travel this route on the days when there's no bus.

It seems that the road east of Kourémalé, via Bankan (also called Banko) and Kangara is in better condition and many bush taxis now go this way. The border checkpoint is north of Bankan.

If you go by bus or bush taxi across the border the baggage charge may be higher than usual; this goes towards a *cadeau* (bribe) for the border guards, so the search is quick and easy. If you get stuck at the border, there's a campement with rooms for CFA 1500. The roads on both sides of the border are rough.

An alternative route goes from Kankan to Bougouni via Mandiana. It's likely that you'll have to do the trip in stages, but the road is being renovated and more transport will run this way in the future.

To/From Senegal The main route between Guinea and Senegal goes via Koundara. From here (and from Labé) vehicles head for Tambacounda or Velingara most days. Some go all the way to Dakar (CFA 25,000) or Ziguinchor. You can also find trucks between Labé and Tambacounda: the fare is about CFA 9000. On the section between Koundara and Kaliforou (the border town) the scenery is beautiful but the road is pitiful. The whole trip between Labé and Dakar takes between 25 and 35 hours. During the rainy season the stretch between Labé and Koundara is very slow or impassable as the trucks tear up the road, causing other vehicles to get stuck. Occasionally, travellers have had to wait several days in Koundara or Sambailo looking for onward vehicles. For more details on transport from Dakar to Guinea, see the Senegal chapter.

To/From Sierra Leone There are plenty of minibuses and bush taxis running directly between Conakry and Freetown via Pamelap (the border). Alternatively, you can take a bush taxi to Pamelap and connect with vehicles on the other side. Either way, the trip takes from 10 to 12 hours but can be done in a day if you leave early. The border crossing is easy or difficult, depending on your luck, but there are numerous police checks on this route (in both countries).

You can also enter Sierra Leone from Faranah: a good dirt road (with little traffic) goes south-west to the border town of Gberia-Fotombu, from where you may find a truck heading for Kabala. (If you're heading north, see the Kabala section in the Sierra Leone chapter for more details.) Or you can go from Guéckédou, by taking the 30-km road west to the border town of Nongoa, then cross the river in a canoe to reach Koindu, from where buses and bush taxis go to Kenema and Freetown.

It's also possible to reach Makeni in western-central Sierra Leone from Kindia, via the border at Medina Dula (shown as Medina Oula on the Michelin map) and Kamakwie (near Outamba-Kilimi National Park). Bush taxis run between Kindia and the border. Trucks and pick-ups also go to the border or all the way to Kamakwie. On the Sierra Leone side, vehicles run between the border and Kamakwie, from where there's a daily bush taxi to Makeni. If you get stuck at the border, the police will let you camp.

Car

To/From Côte d'Ivoire The major route between Conakry and Abidjan is via Nzérékoré and Man. During the dry season this route poses few problems, except the section of road between Macenta and Nzérékoré which is in bad condition, although it's due to be tarred by 1996. It's also possible to drive from Kankan to Odienné, but the route is rarely travelled and in fair condition at best. If you want a little adventure or the most scenic, mountainous route possible, you can combine these routes by driving from Nzérékoré north to Kankan, but during the rainy season this stretch is usually impassable.

To/From Guinea-Bissau The better route between Conakry and Bissau is via Labé and Koundara, not via Boké to the south. See the details on route conditions in the earlier Bush Taxi & Minibus section.

To/From Mali The usual route from Conakry to Bamako is via Kankan. Conakry to Kankan via Faranah takes from 16 to 20 hours nonstop; the route is tarred all of the way and mostly in reasonable condition. Then, from Kankan to Bamako, you have a choice of three routes: via Siguiri and Kourémalé; via Siguiri and Kangara; or via Mandiana and Bougouni. See the earlier Bush Taxi & Minibus section for more details.

To/From Senegal The main route is via Koundara. The drive from Conakry to the border takes two long days in the dry season, with a stopover in Labé. The road is paved to Labé; the

unpaved 300-km section from there to the border is poor, the worst stretch being the last 150 km. This is a major truck route, however, and quite passable during the dry season. During the rainy season, trucks continue to pass, but they churn up the road sometimes making it impassable for smaller vehicles.

To/From Sierra Leone The 330-km drive from Conakry to Freetown, via the border at Pamelap, takes six to eight hours; a little longer in the rainy season. The road is tarred except for a 70-km stretch near the border.

You can also drive from Faranah to Kabala, or from Macenta to Voinjama in Liberia (although the borders are likely to be closed until the war ends) then west to Koindu. (There is no car ferry over the river north of Koindu to Nongoa.)

RIVER

To/From Mali You can travel between Kankan and Bamako by river boat which runs weekly when the river is high enough. See Getting There & Away in the Mali chapter for more details.

To/From Sierra Leone A fast luxurious hydrofoil service was operating twice a week between Conakry and Freetown until the end of 1993. Fares were US$40\70 one way\ return. It may start running again, so make enquiries at a travel agency in Conakry.

LEAVING GUINEA

If you're flying to another country, there's no airport departure tax. For domestic flights, it's around GF 5000.

Getting Around

AIR

For details on flights around the country see the Conakry Getting There & Away section.

BUS

SOGETRAG, the government bus company, runs between Conakry and all the main towns in the country, except Nzérékoré (although services may start when the road from Macenta is tarred). Its large 'Transguinée' buses are comfortable and good value. Some sample prices: Conakry to Labé is GF 11,500; Conakry to Kankan is GF 23,000; and Conakry to Macenta is GF 17,000, with services between once and three times per week. To Mamou (via Kindia) they leave every day and cost GF 6300. For more details see the Conakry Getting There & Away section.

There are also private buses running on some of these routes, usually for around the same price, but generally these are not as reliable as the government buses. You have to go to the main gare voiture in Conakry to check the schedules. (In Guinea, the term *gare voiture* is used, rather than gare routière, for the bus and taxi park.)

The main road from Conakry to Macenta via Mamou, Faranah, Kissidougou and Guéckédou is tarred and in good or reasonable condition. The tarred roads from Mamou to Labé and from Kissidougou to Kankan are also mostly fine.

BUSH TAXI & MINIBUS
Bush taxis in Guinea are usually Peugeot 504s, made for six people but often carrying up to 12 adults, plus children, goats, luggage, huge bunches of bananas and a few more people on the roof. Some bush taxis are standard saloon cars (carrying six or seven people) and slightly more comfortable.

Because long-distance buses are so cheap and reliable, bush taxis tend only to cover the relatively shorter runs between major towns. They are frequent, but no faster than the government buses. Sample fares (in GF) include:

from	to	fare
Mamou	Labé	6000
Mamou	Faranah	7000
Faranah	Kissidougou	5000
Kissidougou	Kankan	8000
Kissidougou	Guéckédou	3000
Guéckédou	Macenta	2500
Macenta	Nzérékoré	8000
Guéckédou	Nzérékoré	10,000

Minibuses cover the same routes as bush taxis. They are cheaper, more crowded, significantly more dangerous and best avoided unless there's absolutely no alternative.

TRAIN
Despite the train lines shown on most maps, trains no longer run anywhere in Guinea. In towns where the railway used to go, however, you can still find rooms in the hotel-buffet at the old station. There are reports that the line may be reopened between Conakry and Kindia or Mamou, so make enquiries locally.

Conakry

After being run down by Sekou Touré for a quarter of a century, Conakry (KON-ah-kree) is definitely on the upswing. Although new visitors may not be impressed, old-timers certainly are. Once a city of tight-lipped people, Conakry is now open and vibrant. Streets in the core central area have all been paved and, unusually for Africa, the main drag has been attractively landscaped with brick benches. Glitzy new shops, restaurants and nightclubs are constantly popping up.

The city has a lot of African flavour too. If you walk around the side streets on a Sunday, chances are you'll see a street celebration or two. Onlookers form a circle, and on one side three or four men play koras and the balafon, while women dance.

On the down side, street crime in Conakry has increased considerably, particularly around the central Marché du Niger, so you always have to be on your guard. You might consider not visiting Conakry at all: for budget travellers, there's little in the way of cheap accommodation, and for any visitor there's not much of interest to see or do in the city. The rest of Guinea has beautiful landscapes and friendly people, and is well worth a visit. But, unless you really need to come for some reason, such as getting a visa, Conakry itself is well worth avoiding.

Orientation
The city's location on a narrow peninsula is

Greater Conakry

PLACES TO STAY

- 3 Hôtel du Golfe
- 16 Hôtel Camayenne
- 18 Hôtel Le Triangle & Coléah Cinéma
- 22 Hôtel Casa Alu & Chez Maman
- 27 Hôtel de l'Unité

PLACES TO EAT

- 4 Le Rustique
- 29 Le Petit Bateau

OTHER

- 1 King's Club
- 2 Marché de Taouyah, Cinéma Rogbané & Post Office
- 5 Mali Embassy
- 6 Guinea-Bissau Embassy
- 7 Sierra Leone Embassy
- 8 Gare Voiture de Madina
- 9 Stadium
- 10 Marché M'balia
- 11 Swiss Embassy
- 12 British Consul
- 13 Japanese Embassy
- 14 Senegalese Embassy
- 15 Donka Hospital
- 17 Grande Mosquée
- 19 Nigerian Embassy & Benin Embassy
- 20 Italian Embassy
- 21 Congo Embassy
- 23 La Paillote Arts Centre
- 24 Canadian Embassy
- 25 American Cultural Centre
- 26 Cinéma 8 Novembre
- 28 Palais du Peuple
- 30 Marché du Niger
- 31 Hôpital Ignace Dean

a mixed blessing. The good part is that the ocean is so visible. The bad part is that the city has nowhere to expand except north-ward, making it longer every year and increasingly difficult to travel from one end to the other – sometimes up to an hour in heavy traffic, which is every day until 11 pm.

The main north-south drag is the Auto-route, which, as you move south and closer to the centre, becomes the Route du Niger and, in the heart, the Ave de la République. On or around this main street are banks, airline offices and several restaurants.

Ten km north of the centre are the lively Rogbané and Taouyah quartiers (suburbs), centred around the Marché de Taouyah and the Cinéma Rogbané (still called Cinéma M'Balia by some people). At night, these areas are livlier than the city centre.

Further out again is the quartier of Ratoma, where you'll find some up-market hotels and restaurants, and beyond here are the quartiers of Kipé and Kaporo.

Information
Conakry has no tourist office, but for details on local events find a copy of *Dyeli*, a listings magazine available free at large hotels, airline offices and some restaurants. It also has phone numbers of government depart-ments and embassies, local tide tables and even a horoscope page.

Money Banks for changing money include the SGBG and the BICIGUI on Ave de la République, or the BIAG round the corner on Blvd de Commerce. Rates and commis-sions vary for cash and travellers' cheques, for the number and even for the type of cheques you change, so it's worth doing a quick comparison. All banks in Conakry are reasonably quick and efficient.

Foreign Embassies Embassies in the centre of Conakry:

Algeria On the corner of 5th Ave and 1st Blvd (☎ 44 15 05)
Côte d'Ivoire On 4th Ave, half a block west of Blvd de Commerce

France On the corner of Blvd de Commerce and Ave Tubman (☎ 44 16 55)
Ghana Off Ave de la République, behind Sabena (☎ 44 15 10)
Germany On the corner of 2nd Blvd and 9th Ave (☎ 44 15 06)
Morocco Near the southern end of Corniche Nord (☎ 44 37 10)
The Netherlands In the offices of KLM, Ave de la République (☎ 44 31 07)
USA On the corner of 2nd Blvd and 9th Ave (☎ 44 15 20)
Zaïre Ave de la Gare near the train station (☎ 44 15 02)

Embassies and consuls in the Corniche Sud area, north of the Place du 8 Novembre:

Benin Corniche Sud, near the Nigerian embassy
Canada Corniche Sud, near the American Cultural Centre (☎ 44 23 95)
Egypt Next to the Nigerian embassy (☎ 46 14 25)
Japan Corniche Sud, two km beyond the Nigerian embassy (☎ 46 14 38)
Nigeria Corniche Sud, 750 metres beyond the Place du 8 Novembre (☎ 46 13 43)
Senegal Corniche Sud, 1.5 km beyond the Nigerian embassy (☎ 46 28 34)
Switzerland Corniche Sud, one km north of the Jap-anese embassy (☎ 46 13 87)
UK In the offices of SODEGUI, clearly signposted between Corniche Sud and the Route National (☎ 44 29 59)

Embassies along or near Route Donka:

Congo Half a km north-west of Place du 8 Novembre (☎ 46 24 51)
Guinea-Bissau Route Donka, half a km beyond Car-refour Bellevue (☎ 46 21 36)
Italy In the Camayenne quartier, 200 metres south of the Hôtel Camayenne (☎ 44 35 88)
Liberia Near the Italian embassy (closed until the war in Liberia ends)
Mali In Rogbané, near the Restaurant Le Rustique
Sierra Leone Route Donka, just south of Carrefour Bellevue (☎ 46 14 39)
Tanzania Cité des Ministres in Donka (☎ 46 13 32)

Travel Agencies For flights to Europe or elsewhere in West Africa, there are several travel agencies on Ave de la République and Blvd de Commerce who can explain the choices and save you walking round all the airline offices. Recommended is Karou Voyages (☎ 44 20 42) on Ave de la Répu-lique. They also have a branch at the

Novotel. For tours, a Mr Coza (contactable through Karou Voyages) runs day trips to the nearby islands (for around GF 20,000) or to Kindia, Bridal Falls and Le Chien Qui Fume Mountain for around GF 50,000.

Bookshops & Supermarkets For books (mostly in French), try the Soguidip bookshop in the street off Ave de la République, behind the Sabena office. English-language newspapers and magazines are available at the Novotel shop, or you can buy from the hawkers outside the main post office.

Supermarkets with imported items are Superbobo, near the Camayenne Hotel, and Super V near the Coléah Cinéma.

National Museum
The Musée National has a modest collection of masks, statues and musical instruments on display in one large room. It's on 7th Blvd, just north of the Corniche Sud. It's supposed to be open Monday to Saturday from 9 am to 2 pm, but often it isn't. Entrance is free.

Things to See
The **Palais de l'OUA** near the Novotel was to be the venue for the OAU conference in 1984, which was cancelled when Sekou Touré died; it now serves as the office of the president. It is forbidden to come here at night, and the soldiers on guard are reported to be trigger-happy. Facing the palace are 50 identical Moorish-style villas, built to house the African presidents during the week-long meeting. They are now used as offices by international organisations such as the World Bank, IMF and UNICEF.

The **Palais du Peuple** is a huge Chinese-built auditorium at the north end of Route du Niger. Renovated in 1988, it is a centre for ballet groups; the two national troupes have toured Europe and the USA. The performances tend to be long but worth the effort.

Beaches
The Îles de Los are a group of small islands five to 10 km south-west of Conakry, popular on Sundays and holidays. Expatriates prefer the Île de Roume, which has a tranquil side

good for youngsters and a rougher side with waves. To get there, hire a motorised pirogue from the beach near the Novotel. A round-trip *déplacement* (boat to yourself) should cost about US$25 for the boat plus GF 1000 per person tourist tax. If you ask, the captain will wait on the beach and guard your belongings. The Guineans prefer Kassa Island: the beach is crowded every Sunday and a real scene. There's a boat which leaves Sunday at 9 am from the port and returns at 5.30 pm (GF 1000 for the round trip).

Another possibility is to take one of the regular, relatively inexpensive pirogues over to the small village of Soro. They leave from the beach just north of the Novotel.

Places to Stay – bottom & middle
City Centre The homy *Pension Doherty* (☎ 44 17 64) on 5th Ave between 8th and 9th Blvds, near Hôpital Ignace Dean, has clean self-contained singles/doubles with a fan for GF 23,000/28,000 (GF 6000 extra for air-con). There's a bar, a decent restaurant, and an attractive garden area.

Your other choice is the *Hôtel du Niger*, one block south of the Marché du Niger, which has large self-contained rooms with a fan for GF 25,000/35,000 (GF 10,000 extra for air-con) including an excellent breakfast. You could also try the *Hôtel Kaloum* (☎ 44 33 11) on Ave de la République near Blvd de Commerce, charging GF 35,000/40,000 for large apartments, although these rates may be negotiable.

Outside the City Centre The *Casa Alu*, a few hundred metres north-west of Place du 8 Novembre (about three km north of the centre), is quiet and pleasant with spotless self-contained air-conditioned rooms for GF 25,000/30,000.

Further from the centre (10 km), in the Rogbané-Taouyah area, and up several grades in quality and price, is the friendly and good-value *Hôtel du Golfe* (☎ 46 43 10) charging GF 30,000/38,000 for immaculately clean singles/doubles with air-con. It's well signposted, just off Route Donka, about one km before Cinéma Rogbané.

Beyond Rogbané you come to the Ratoma area. The old but good-quality *Hotel Mariador Park* has singles/doubles for GF 53,000/ 69,000. Just down the road is the new top-end Mariador Residence (see below). In between the two Mariadors, a sandy track leads to *Hôtel-Restaurant Cesar* where clean self-contained doubles with nets and air-con are GF 36,000.

Even further from the centre, in the Kipé area, is the active and ever-popular *Hôtel Mixte*, a classier whorehouse with a tranquil garden setting, music and clean ventilated rooms with red lights and fairly dirty toilets for GF 10,000 to GF 15,000. It's about three km beyond the Cinéma Rogbané on the paved highway (the extension of Route Donka); look for the small sign on the left. The 'C' or 'Kaporo' bus passes on this route. Look for the bus stop with *Kipé* written on it. If the Mixte is full, ask around for the *Hôtel Diguila*, one of the few alternatives in the greater Rogbané area, where rooms are similar but slightly more expensive. It's off Route Hamdalaye and not easy to find.

Places to Stay – top end
The best hotel is the *Hôtel Camayenne* (☎ 44 40 89; cards AE, D, V) in the area of the same name, about one km north-west of Place du 8 Novembre. A standard room with break-fast costs GF 130,000. It has all the facilities of a top-class international hotel, plus an excellent setting on the edge of the ocean. The open-air restaurant is tasteful with the menu du jour at GF 12,000.

Next best is the *Novotel* (Hôtel de l'Indépendance) (☎ 44 50 21, telex 2112; cards AE, D, V) in the centre, also over-looking the ocean. To compete with the Camayenne, room rates are now negotiable (singles/doubles including tax and breakfast are GF 100,000/120,000) although the hotel has reportedly gone downhill. Ask for one of the older rooms with a balcony. The restaurant is expensive and not very good.

The *Hôtel Mariador Residence* (☎ 44 27 50; cards AE, D) in the Ratoma area, beyond Rogbané, is a new up-market place with most facilities. Doubles cost GF 95,000. The *Hôtel de l'Unité* (☎ 44 31 37, telex 2139), 2.5 km from

the centre, is cheaper (doubles including tax and breakfast GF 90,000) but also reported to be getting worse. It has a long pool and a lively disco on weekends. All top-end hotels accept local or foreign currency.

Places to Eat – cheap
Street food is available in and around Marché du Niger. Here you'll find grilled meat and maize, bread and cakes.

For bowls of rice and sauce at lunchtime for around GF 500 to GF 1000, there are two recommended places, especially popular with taxi drivers: one is in the centre at the intersection of the Corniche Nord and Blvd de Commerce; the other is in the Rogbané area on Route Donka just past Carrefour Hamdalaye and 250 metres south of the Cinéma Rogbané. At lunchtime, just look for the taxis; you'll see up to 40 parked outside.

For cheap African food in a restaurant, try the *Bar Café au Bon Coin* on 4th Ave just east of Blvd de Commerce, where rice and sauce is around GF 1500, or the friendly *Gargotte Lamp Fall*, on 8th Blvd two blocks south of Route du Niger, where you sit in armchairs to eat good filling meals for around GF 2500. Other fairly cheap places include *Le Djoliba* on 9th Ave, between 5th and 6th Blvds, and *Café Nunez* on 7th Ave between 4th Blvd and Blvd de Commerce.

In the centre of Conakry there are also several inexpensive Lebanese restaurants serving chawarmas, kafta sandwiches and hamburgers for around GF 1300 and meals like grilled chicken and chips for GF 2500, plus ice cream, pastries, etc. These include *Oriental Snack* on 8th Blvd near the junction with Route du Niger, and *Akwaba Snack* near the Hôtel du Niger.

Places to Eat – more expensive
City Centre At the *Pâtisserie Centrale*, on the corner of Ave de la République and 6th Blvd, burgers and pizzas start at GF 2300. They also do ice cream, cakes and coffee. At *Pâtisserie Le Damier* on Route du Niger facing the market, prices are slightly lower. More expensive is *Pâtisserie Le Gondole*, on

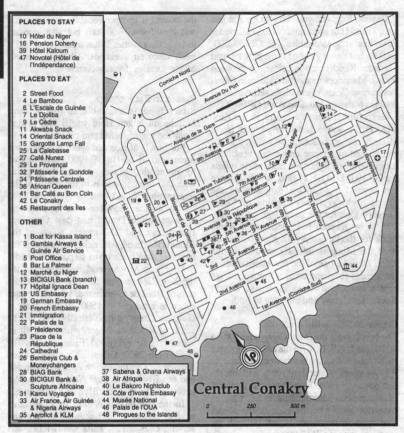

PLACES TO STAY
10 Hôtel du Niger
16 Pension Doherty
39 Hôtel Kaloum
47 Novotel (Hôtel de
l'Indépendance)

PLACES TO EAT
2 Street Food
4 Le Bambou
6 L'Escale de Guinée
7 Le Djoliba
9 Le Cèdre
11 Akwaba Snack
14 Oriental Snack
15 Gargotte Lamp Fall
25 La Calebasse
27 Café Nunez
29 Le Provençal
32 Pâtisserie Le Gondole
34 Pâtisserie Centrale
36 African Queen
41 Bar Café au Bon Coin
42 Le Conakry
45 Restaurant des Îles

OTHER
1 Boat for Kassa Island
3 Gambia Airways &
Guinée Air Service
5 Post Office
8 Bar Le Palmer
13 Marché du Niger
13 BICIGUI Bank (branch)
17 Hôpital Ignace Dean
18 US Embassy
19 German Embassy
20 French Embassy
21 Immigration
22 Palais de la
Présidence
23 Place de la
République
24 Cathedral
26 Bembeya Club &
Moneychangers
28 BIAG Bank
30 BICIGUI Bank &
Sculpture Africaine
31 Karou Voyages
33 Air France, Air Guinée
& Nigeria Airways
35 Aeroflot & KLM

37 Sabena & Ghana Airways
38 Air Afrique
40 Le Bakoro Nightclub
43 Côte d'Ivoire Embassy
44 Musée National
46 Palais de l'OUA
48 Pirogues to the Islands

Central Conakry

0   250   500 m

Ave de la République, with pizzas at GF 2500 and ice creams at GF 1200.

In the centre, *Le Provençal*, on 4th Blvd, one block from Ave de la République, is open every day except Sunday from noon to 3 pm and 8 to midnight. The upstairs terrace (above the bar) has a relaxing informal ambience, great for talking and drinks, but the service is painfully slow and the menu is often quite limited. *La Calebasse* on 7th Ave, around the corner from the post office is primarily a French restaurant, and also serves African specials, with main meals in the GF 4500 to GF 7000 range. *Le Cèdre*,

between 5th and 6th Blvds, is more professional with prices for good Continental or Lebanese meals in the same range.

Among Conakry's pricier places, the *Restaurant des Îles* (☎ 44 27 64) on 2nd Ave near 4th Blvd gives perhaps the best value for money, with main meals from GF 6000 to GF 9000 range, although the small antelope tied up in a corner may put you off your dinner. Nearby, on 4th Ave, is the ever-popular *Le Conakry*, a roaring success since the day it opened, with a pleasant atmosphere, a popular bar, air-con and good service. The menu of the day costs GF 9000.

It's especially full at midday when they do a three-course lunch for GF 7000 (closed Sundays). The *African Queen* is two blocks away on 5th Ave between 4th and 5th Blvds. It has air-con and is open from 10 am to 5 pm. Its speciality is pizza (GF 6000), and the plat du jour is GF 10,000.

Another good French restaurant and a Conakry institution is *L'Escale de Guinée*, on 5th Blvd, a block south of Ave de la Gare (10th Ave). The garden setting is quite attractive, without being fancy. Jumbo shrimp has long been one of the specialities. *Le Bambou*, on the same street on the corner of 9th Ave, is also French, but expensive. The Indian restaurant *Natraj* in the centre near Sabena has also been highly recommended.

Outside the City Centre To the north of the city centre, the restaurant with the nicest setting is *Le Petit Bateau*, 300 metres out in the water on a tiny stretch of land with a great view of Conakry, although the food is nothing special. The only problem other than the slow service is that the bugs like it here too. Further north, just beyond Place du 8 Novembre, is the friendly and unpretentious *Chez Maman*, which does French and Zaïrois specialities: meals are GF 5000 and the menu du jour is GF 9500. Next door is *La Paillote* (see Live Music, below).

In the Rogbané area is *Le Rustique*, 100 metres to the left off Route Donka, two km before Cinema Rogbané. It's one of Conakry's best and most expensive restaurants, with elegant décor, air-con, and French, German and African specialities starting at GF 9000. (Open evenings only, closed Mondays).

In the Ratoma area is Conakry's best Vietnamese restaurant, *Délices d'Asie*, where your money goes on the good food and not the ambience, which is ordinary. Nearby is the *Jardin de Chine*; also recommended. In both places, meals start at around GF 9000. Also in Ratoma is the Italian-run *Hôtel-Restaurant Cesar* (see Places to Stay) where oven-baked steaks and pizzas are the house speciality. Meals are in the GF 5000 to GF 8000 range, and on Sunday afternoons

boule (pétanque) tournaments are often held. The only thing that spoils this place is the sad old baboon tied to a tree in the garden.

Entertainment

Bars Bars are not one of Conakry's strong points. In the city centre, the street-level bar of *Le Provençal* is fairly cheap and pleasant, as is *Le Palmer* on the same street. For more up-market surroundings try the air-con bar at *Le Conakry* on 4th Ave. In the Rogbané area, there are some popular African bars; a very lively one is just beyond Cinéma Rogbané at the junction with Ave Taouyah.

Nightclubs Conakry has lots of good nightclubs, although most are in the suburbs. None of them get lively before 11 pm, and the cover charges are usually around GF 1500, or GF 3000 on Thursday, Saturday and Sunday – the biggest nights. Except for the Bembeya Club, all are appropriate for women accompanied by men.

One of the most popular with the locals is *King's Club*, just beyond Cinéma Rogbané. To get there, take your first left after passing the cinema and go 100 metres down Route Taouyah. Also popular is *Eden Park*, one km or two beyond Cinéma Rogbané.

There are several nightclubs in the airport area, including *Le Balafon* which attracts a big Lebanese crowd and plays a wide variety of Western, African and Cuban music, and the aptly named *Privilege*, just before the Hôtel Gbessia, which is popular with Conakry's middle class. Closer to town on the Corniche Nord is the *Cotton Club*, an expat hang-out; look for a bright red gate on the sea side of the Corniche.

In the centre itself is *Le Bakoro*, on 4th Ave just south of 4th Blvd. It is small, smoky and popular, and open every night with a GF 1000 cover charge. A seedy place with plenty of action is the crowded and always lively *Bembeya Club* in the centre on 4th Blvd, a block south of the post office. Out the back there's an open-air courtyard and lots of drinking and dancing. Be very careful – at night the area is known for thugs and thieves.

GUINEA

Live Music To hear live Guinean music, check out *La Paillote*, 100 metres north-west of the Place du 8 Novembre, a local arts centre for Guinea's rising young stars, providing an opportunity for stage experience. There seem to be no set times or days for concerts: just turn up and see what's happening. Even if there's nothing going on, the centre has a good, reasonably priced bar-restaurant. Alternatively, try the *Cyrkano*, a smarter restaurant-bar in Ratoma between the two Miriador hotels, which has live Guinean music most evenings and jazz every Thursday.

Cinemas The air-con Cinéma Rogbané, 10 km from the centre on Route Donka, is the best in town, with shows at 6 and 9 pm. Cinéma 8 Novembre, at the southern end of the Autoroute, is the next best: it has the same hours but no air-con. Le Palais on Ave de la République is cheap and cheerful. Cinéma Coléah on Route du Niger is similar

Things to Buy

Artisan Goods Guinea is the best place in West Africa to buy the harp-like kora. The regular ones are very bulky, but some smaller versions are available.

You'll find artisan goods of mediocre quality at various stalls along Ave de la République. For higher quality crafts, try Sculpture Africaine on 4th Blvd, just off Ave de la République.

For African print material, the Marché du Niger is best. The women's co-operatives, Les Centres de Promotion du Pouvoir Feminin, have several outlets in Conakry; they sell tie-dyed cloth, tablecloths and napkins.

Gold & Silver Many jewellers have shops near the Marché du Niger. Two among many are Bijouterie Art et Moderne and Bijouterie de la Nation, both two blocks from the market. The general level of craft is not as high as in Mali, Senegal and Côte d'Ivoire, but prices tend to be lower.

Music Guinea is a good place to buy cassettes of African music as they are significantly cheaper than in CFA countries. The stalls in the Marché du Niger stock tapes of the current

stars. For recordings of older performers, enquire at Enima inside the Palais du Peuple (open Monday to Saturday from 8 am to 2 pm). They have a good selection, though Sory Kandia, Fodé Kouyaté and others may be considered a little passé today. (For more details on Guinean artists, see the earlier boxed story on Music.)

Getting There & Away

Air For domestic flights inside the country, Air Guinée, Guinea Inter Air and Guinée Air Service all go from Conakry to Boké, Kissidougou, Kankan, Siguiri, Labé and Koundara. There are usually one or two flights per week, although the schedule changes constantly.

For details on regional flights between Conakry and other West African cities, and intercontinental flights to/from Europe (and departure tax), see the main Getting There & Away section in this chapter.

For reservations or reconfirmations in Conakry, most airline offices are on Ave de la République, including Aeroflot (☎ 44 41 43), Air Afrique (☎ 44 44 70), Sabena (☎ 44 34 40), Ghana Airways (☎ 44 48 13), Air France (☎ 44 36 57), Nigeria Airways (☎ 44 40 82), Air Guinée (☎ 44 46 14) and KLM (☎ 44 31 07). Gambia Airways and Guinée Air Service share an office at the northern end of Blvd de Commerce (☎ 44 17 47). Guinea Inter Air (☎ 44 37 08) is near the junction of 4th Blvd and 4th Ave.

Bus All SOGETRAG long-distance buses leave from Gare Voiture de Madina on the Autoroute, six km from the city centre. (To get here it's GF 3000 by taxi, or take an 'A' city bus from Ave de la République.) Buses from Conakry to Pita (via Kindia and Mamou) go every day except Thursday, and cost GF 11,000. On Tuesday, Friday and Sunday they do the same route and on to Labé for GF 11,500 (ie an extra GF 500). There's a bus every Saturday to Kissidougou (via Mamou and Faranah) for GF 14,500, every Thursday to Macenta (via Mamou, Faranah, Kissidougou and Guéckédou) for GF 17,000, and every Sunday to Kankan (via

Faranah and Kissidougou) for GF 23,000. If you get off at an intermediate stop the fare is proportionately less. Big bags cost GF 3000 regardless of where you get off. All long-distance buses depart at 8 am. For most buses, reservations are not possible; you have to go early (around 6 am) to the office at the gare voiture on the day of departure. At this time of day, get a taxi and make the driver drop you right by the ticket office (GF 200 extra to go into the gare voiture) as it's still dark at this time and this place is a favourite haunt for thieves. Only for the Kankan bus can you buy tickets the day before, at Gare Voiture de Matoto, several km beyond the airport.

Private buses direct to Freetown leave from Gare Voiture de Matoto. They take all day and are supposed to leave around 8 am but often leave an hour or two later.

Bush Taxi Bush taxis and minibuses for destinations such as Kindia and Mamou leave from Gare Voiture de Madina. Long-distance bush taxis from Conakry to places beyond Mamou are rare because the buses are so popular. Bush taxis and vans for Sierra Leone leave from Gare Voiture de Matoto.

Note All bush taxis going into Conakry no longer enter the city at night, but stop on the roadside and wait until dawn before finishing their journey.

Getting Around

To/From the Airport Taxis from town to the airport cost between GF 3000 and GF 5000 depending on your bargaining powers. Going from the airport into town (13 km) the drivers start with outlandish figures like US$50, then show you the 'official tariff sheet' which says GF 10,000. After you've walked away a few times you should get it for GF 5000.

Alternatively, it's very easy to catch a bus or shared taxi from the airport to the centre; just walk across the road and hail a cab (heading left, if you've got your back to the airport) or take the 'A' bus (marked Port or Ville) into the centre for GF 200.

Bus SOGETRAG has two main bus lines in

the city : the 'C' line (marked Kaporo) from the centre to Kaporo out beyond Cinéma Rogbané, and the 'A' line (marked Matoto) from the centre to Matoto out beyond the airport. Fares vary according to the distance, from GF 120 to GF 200. In the centre, both lines start at the roundabout next to the port and pass along Ave de la République and Route du Niger until they reach Place du 8 Novembre, where the C bus takes Route Donka and the A bus either continues on the Autoroute or takes the parallel Route Nationale to the east.

Taxi Taxis are yellow, and plentiful along the main streets. For a seat in a shared taxi around town just stand at the side of the road in the direction you want to go and shout your destination as the taxi passes. If it's going your way, it'll stop (cost is about GF 200 per three km or so). When you hire a taxi to yourself instead of sharing, the minimum is GF 600; taxis outside the big hotels charge about double this. A taxi by the hour should cost about GF 2500 if you bargain well.

Car Europcar at the Novotel (☎ 44 50 21) charges GF 33,000 per day for its cheapest car plus GF 350 per km, plus GF 10,000 per day for insurance, GF 10,000 per day for a chauffeur (obligatory for driving outside Conakry), and 15% tax. If you don't pay with a credit card, you'll have to put up a GF 500,000 guarantee. Avis at the Novotel (☎ 44 46 83) and the Camayenne (☎ 44 40 89) are about the same. For cheaper rates, try Guinée Cars (☎ 44 39 26) on Ave de la République near Route du Niger, or Locagui (☎ 44 35 24) on Route du Niger near the Coléah Cinéma.

AROUND CONAKRY
Coyah
Coyah is a small town about 50 km from the centre of Conakry on the main road which leads to all the large towns in the country. It's also where Guinea's bottled mineral water comes from.

If you're coming into Conakry from upcountry, and want to avoid arriving in the capital at night, you could stay here and

GUINEA

continue in the morning. The *Hôtel Mariana* has reasonable rooms for GF 12,000 and there are some basic eateries around the bus park area. If you're coming in from Freetown, and want to avoid Conakry altogether, you can change transport here: buses and bush taxis go regularly to Kindia or Mamou, where there are more places to stay, and onward transport to the rest of the country.

Alternatively, if you want to escape Conakry for the day and you have wheels, you can come to Coyah to eat at *Chez Claude* – a very decent French restaurant which is open every day except Friday. People come for pre-lunch drinks and don't go home until evening. The six or seven selections on the menu include wart hog and couscous, and cost GF 7000 to GF 10,000. As you come into Coyah from Conakry, look for the restaurant sign on your left.

Also in Coyah are two other restaurants: *Kinsy*, on the right as you come in from Conakry, where meals are in the GF 5000 range; and the similar *Bananarie*, in Maneah, on the left before Coyah, on the site of an old plantation.

Mt Kaloulima

Heading towards Coyah, 36 km from Conakry a road branches off left towards this mountain, clearly visible from the main road, which is also called Le Chien Qui Fume, as it's supposed to resemble a smoking dog. The dirt road is drivable to Dubreka village, which has a small restaurant called *Le Chien Qui Fume*, and from there it's a 12 km walk to the summit, although some of this may be drivable in the dry season. This place is easily reached if you've got your own wheels. Alternatively, take a bush taxi or minibuses from Conakry towards Coyah and get off at the Dubreka junction, from where you can get a bush taxi to Dubreka itself. Another option is an organised trip with Mr Coza of Conakry (see Travel Agencies in the Conakry Information section). Also worth a look is another nearby hill where there's a telecommunications mast. It's called Wonkyfon. Really.

Kindia & the Bridal Falls

Kindia is about 140 km from Conakry: a good one-day excursion for those with

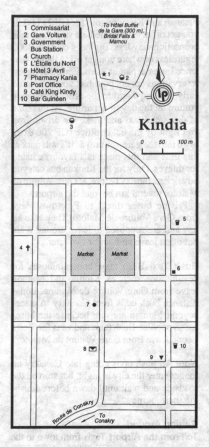

1	Commissariat
2	Gare Voiture
3	Government Bus Station
4	Church
5	L'Étoile du Nord
6	Hôtel 3 Avril
7	Pharmacy Kania
8	Post Office
9	Café King Kindy
10	Bar Guinéen

To Hôtel Buffet de la Gare (300 m), Bridal Falls & Mamou

Kindia

0   50   100 m

Market   Market

Route de Conakry

To Conakry

wheels, and a possible stopover if you're on public transport. Places to visit include the Institut Pasteur de Kindia, a research centre (open every day except Sunday) with an interesting collection of snakes and monkeys. Also worth a look is the work area of the strip-cloth weavers, on the northern side of town behind the old train station. Nearby is an indigo dying centre and cloth market; one of the largest in Guinea.

The main attraction of Kindia is the Bridal Falls. These are 12 km beyond town, two km off the road to your right. There's a sign at the junction announcing Le Voile de la

Mariée. The falls are interesting only during the rainy season when the flowing water resembles a bridal veil. There's a small restaurant here, where meals costs GF 5000, and a bungalow can be rented for GF 20,000 per night. Camping is also allowed. To get here from Kindia, any bush taxi for Mamou will drop you at the junction.

Kindia has a new bypass: coming in from Conakry, signposts to Mamou direct you round the town, missing the centre.

Places to Stay & Eat The cheapest place is the *Hôtel 3 Avril*, which is a filthy dump. The only thing positive other than the low prices (GF 3000 per room) is that it has electricity and is in the town centre, one block directly east of the market. Another cheapie worth trying is the *Hôtel Vietnam*, about four km south of town on the road to Conakry, charging GF 4000 for clean rooms, although there's no electricity or running water. A smarter and more central alternative is the recently renovated *Hôtel Buffet de la Gare* north of the town centre on the road to Mamou, where rooms are GF 10,000, although prices may increase as renovation continues. *Restaurant Sam*, on the south-west edge of town near the hospital, has a few adequate rooms for GF 10,000 and reputedly the best food in Kindia.

Also worth trying is the *Hôtel Phare de Guinée* two to three km south of the centre on the road to Conakry, which charges GF 8000 for a room with electricity but no fans or, despite the private showers, running water. The ambience is better than the accommodation facilities: the restaurant serves reasonable food, and at weekends the nightclub is popular. It gets going around 10 pm, after which you should abandon all hope of sleep until dawn.

For street food, look around the market in the centre on the main drag and the gare voiture. For coffee and snacks, visit *Café King Kindy* two blocks south-east of the market, an expat and volunteer hang-out. For a drink, go to the popular *Bar Guinéen* nearby, or try the bar/nightclub, *L'Étoile du Nord*, in the centre a block east of the market.

The Fouta Djalon

One of the most interesting areas of Guinea is the Fouta Djalon plateau, which includes the towns of Labé, Pita, Dalaba and Mali. This is the heartland of Guinea's Fula population; an area of green rolling hills, with many 1000-metre peaks, where the temperature is cooler than the lowlands. It is one of the better hiking places in West Africa, with many options.

The best time to visit the Fouta Djalon is from November to January when the weather is cooler. The skies become progressively dustier during December, tarnishing the view until the first rains in April or May.

Labé, Pita and Dalaba are easy to reach by public transport. To avoid backtracking, you might fly to Labé and travel from there by bush taxi, first to Pita to see the Kinkon Falls, then on to Dalaba for some hiking, then to Kindia and the Bridal Falls. For a remote trip, try Mali (often called Mali-ville to distinguish it from the country), a small town 120 km north of Labé by dirt road. This area is beautiful; particularly the Massif du Tamgué.

The towns are listed below in order of distance from Conakry.

MAMOU

Mamou, sometimes called 'the gateway to the Fouta Djalon', is a small lively town, about 220 km from Conakry (five to six hours by bus/bush taxi), where the road into the hills branches off the main road to Faranah and the country's other major towns. For amusement, check the open-air Cinéma Almamya two long blocks from the market. At night, it's the liveliest place in town and good for street food.

Places to Stay & Eat

The cheapest place is *Hôtel Luna* on the north side of the town centre. Basic but clean rooms with nets and fans are GF 6000. Cheaper rooms cost GF 4000. The shared toilets are filthy. Alternatively, go to the *Hôtel-Buffet de la Gare*, on the main road through town, between the Luna and the gare voiture, where quiet clean self-contained rooms cost GF 10,000. There's usually

GUINEA

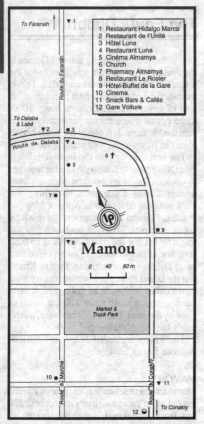

To Faranah

1 Restaurant Hidalgo Marca
2 Restaurant de l'Unité
3 Hôtel Luna
4 Restaurant Luna
5 Cinéma Almamya
6 Church
7 Pharmacy Almamya
8 Restaurant Le Rosier
9 Hôtel-Buffet de la Gare
10 Cinema
11 Snack Bars & Cafés
12 Gare Voiture

Route du Faranah

To Dalaba & Labé

Route de Dalaba

To Dalaba & Labé

6 †

7

Mamou

0   40   80 m

Market & Truck Park

10

Route du Marché

Route du Conakry

11

12   To Conakry

electricity and running water, but candles and bucket showers are also provided.

For cheap food, there's a row of cafés near the gare voiture and a couple of basic eating houses near the truck park in the market. Or try *Restaurant de l'Unité*, a popular cheapie 50 metres west of the main junction, on the road towards Labé.

More up-market is the *Restaurant Luna*, opposite the Hôtel Luna, where filling meals cost GF 1000.

Getting There & Away

The government buses from Conakry go twice a day for GF 6300. Heading to Conakry you can wait for the bus, but it's easier to take a bush taxi (GF 6000). Going upcountry, bush taxis cost GF 6000 to Labé and GF 7000 to Faranah.

DALABA

On the main route from Mamou to Labé, Dalaba is the next town you reach, and an excellent base for day hikes in the surrounding area. During the colonial period it was a theraputic centre, because of its 1000-metre altitude and scenic rolling hills. The colonials have gone but the **Centre d'Accueil** is still intact; it's on the outskirts of town overlooking the hills. The president sometimes holidays here, but at other times you can stay in the rooms used by his entourage, and have fantasies of grandeur.

For an idea of hiking routes, go either to the Centre d'Acceuil or to the large boulders on the edge of the escarpment to the west of the Hôtel Tangama, where you get good views of the surrounding area and from where paths lead down into the valley. You can also follow the dirt track that leads along the edge of the escarpment from the Centre d'Accueil.

Places to Stay & Eat

All the places to stay are on the south-western edge of town, reached by turning off the main road towards Labé at a sharp bend. The cheapest place is the *Étoile de Fouta*, a dingy bar-restaurant-nightclub with a few rooms of varying quality for GF 4000. Nearby is the new *Hôtel Tangama*, about one km from the sharp bend, where clean double rooms are GF 7000. Some rooms are self-contained and even have hot showers, although this may require a negotiable extra fee, and the manager may say the hotel is full to bump up the price. If you can deal with this nonsense, the hotel is very good value.

Further down the road is the *Centre d'Accueil*, also called Les Villas, Le Villa Presidential and Villa Syli. The main villa must have been very fine once, but the chandeliers, embroidered curtains and furniture are now broken and covered in dust. The adjoining large bungalows each have four

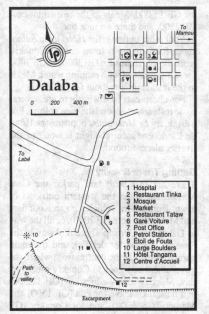

Dalaba

0   200   400 m

To Mamou

To Labé

Path to valley

Escarpment

1 Hospital
2 Restaurant Tinka
3 Mosque
4 Market
5 Restaurant Tataw
6 Gare Voiture
7 Post Office
8 Petrol Station
9 Étoil de Fouta
10 Large Boulders
11 Hôtel Tangama
12 Centre d'Accueil

PITA

As you travel between Dalaba and Labé you'll pass through rolling hills. Roughly halfway is the small town of Pita, where the major attraction is the **Chutes du Kinkon waterfalls**. To get here, take the main road north out of town for one km then left down a dirt road which you follow for 10 km to reach the falls. Hitching opportunities are rare but it's a very nice walk, through villages and hills, and easily done there and back in a day.

The setting is not ideal as the falls are below a hydroelectric plant but it's still worth a visit. Camping is definitely prohibited. You'll see where a number of African presidents have etched their names into the rock. You are supposed to get permission from the police to go to the falls, as the power station is nearby, but they try and charge GF 5000 for a *laissez passer* (permit). Some people don't bother and plead ignorance if they're stopped by guards. Others refuse to pay for the permit. It's up to you.

Places to Stay & Eat

You can stay at the rustic *Hôtel Kinkon* for GF 4000 a room, on the north side of town in a leafy 'suburb' behind the public gardens. Excellent meals cost GF 2500. Or there's the smarter but characterless *Centre d'Accueil* on the other side of the main road, under an archway and down a drive, where singles/doubles are GF 5000/6000 (couples can share a single). You can eat at either of the hotels, or try one of the cheap restaurants along the main street, or the snack stalls where the buses and bush taxis stop.

LABÉ

Labé is around 400 km from Conakry, at the end of the tar road through the Fouta Djalon. It's Guinea's third-largest town and a major stopping point for traffic going to/from Senegal and Guinea-Bissau. The town is fairly unattractive but if you've spent several long days coming in from Gabú or Tambacounda, it may seem better than if you've arrived from Conakry.

The heart of Labé is on a hill; the market and most of the town's few stores are there. At the foot of the hill is the gare voiture, and

self-contained rooms opening onto a central lounge. The caretaker charges the same price as the Hôtel Tangama, but rates are negotiable. There's no restaurant, so you'll have to bring your own food, walk into town (two km), or arrange with the caretaker for his wife to prepare you something.

In the centre of town *Restaurant Tinka* and *Restaurant Tataw* do cheap meals, and near the gare voiture are several simple cafés. For a drink try *Bar Le Relais 55* nearby.

Getting There & Away

The gare voiture is next to the market. Government buses between Labé or Pita and Conakry pass through Dalaba six times per week in each direction. You may also find a bush taxi to Conakry for GF 10,000. They leave early in the morning and will pick you up at your hotel if you make arrangements the night before. Bush taxis also go to/from Mamou and Labé (both GF 2000) every day.

GUINEA

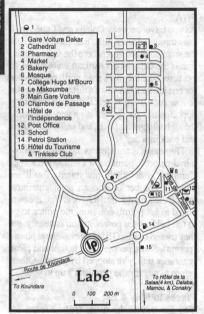

1 Gare Voiture Dakar
2 Cathedral
3 Pharmacy
4 Market
5 Bakery
6 Mosque
7 College Hugo M'Bouro
8 Le Makoumba
9 Main Gare Voiture
10 Chambre de Passage
11 Hôtel de
   l'Indépendance
12 Post Office
13 School
14 Petrol Station
15 Hôtel du Tourisme
   & Tinkisso Club

Labé

To Hôtel de la Salaa (4 km), Dalaba, Mamou, & Conakry

Route de Koundara

To Koundara

0   100   200 m

for GF 15,000. Meals in the restaurant cost GF 2500, and there's a nice bar.

Your other option is the *Hôtel de la Salaa*, about four km from town on the Conakry road. Simple rooms are GF 3000, or GF 7000 for self-contained with running water. Meals in the restaurant are about GF 2000.

For cheap eats in town, there are several basic restaurants around the gare voiture. For a drink, try *Le Makoumba* opposite the Hôtel de l'Indépendance: at night it's one of the livelier places around.

Getting There & Away

There are two bush taxi parks: the Gare Voiture Dakar on the western outskirts of town, from where vehicles go to Koundara and Mali-ville (both GF 7000), or all the way to Dakar (see Getting There & Away in the Senegal chapter for details); and the main gare voiture near the centre, from where the government bus goes to Conakry on Saturday, Monday and Wednesday (GF 11,500) and bush taxis leave for Pita (GF 1500) and Mamou (GF 6000), and for Conakry (GF 12,000) if there's no bus that day.

MALI

Not many travellers make it to Mali (Mali-ville), 120 km north of Labé via a rough dirt road. It's the highest town in the Fouta Djalon, with cool temperatures and wonderful views, making it ideal for hiking. Points to head for include: **Mt Loura** (1538 metres), seven km north of town; the legendary rock, **La Dame de Mali**, a few km further; and the **Massif du Tamgué** to the north-west.

For a place to stay, *La Dame de Mali* has rooms for about GF 3000. To get here, bush taxis leave from the central gare voiture in Labé. Intrepid travellers can find transport in Mali-ville heading northward to Kédougou (Senegal).

KOUNDARA

For those on their way to or from Senegal or Guinea-Bissau, Koundara is a junction town 50 km from the Senegalese border.

For a cheap hotel, try the *Hôtel Chez Adja* on the main street or the *Hôtel Koundara* on

some hotels and cheap eating houses. Labé has a bank, but changing money can be a long-winded affair. For a swifter service, some of the shops near the Hôtel de l'Indépendance may be able to help.

Places to Stay & Eat

For GF 2000, you can get a bed at the dingy *chambre de passage* near the main gare voiture. Ask for directions. If you want luxuries like sheets and windows try the old *Hôtel du Tourisme* on the southern side of town, 500 metres from the main gare voiture, which has clean rooms with showers and double beds for GF 5000 or two single beds for GF 8000, although the shared toilets are dirty. There's a restaurant which is OK, with meals for around about GF 2000. If there's a disco in the nightclub downstairs, don't expect an early night. The *Hôtel de l'Indépendance* near the main gare voiture has been completely renovated, with good quality rooms the main square. Both charge about GF 4000 for a room with no electricity or running water. The *Mission Catholique* no longer takes guests. The best place in town is the *Hôtel Mamadou Boiro*, where clean decent rooms cost GF 8000, and there's also a pleasant bar.

Getting There & Away

There are lots of vehicles headed for Senegal; some going direct to Dakar. There are also trucks that ply the 80-km route between Koundara and Pitche in Guinea-Bissau (where the asphalt road to Bissau begins) and the much longer route between Koundara and Basse in The Gambia. Expect to pay about CFA 4000 for the latter trip. By bush taxi or truck, Koundara to Labé (244 km) costs GF 7000. If you're headed south from Koundara to Boké (317 km), trucks charge about GF 8000 for the slow-going, 16-hour trip.

The East

The main road from Conakry swings east at Mamou, running parallel to the borders of Sierra Leone and Liberia. It leads towards the lowlands and forest of the interior, where there are several large towns (listed below in order of distance from Conakry). At Kissidougou another road branches off northwards through low dry country, to the towns of Kankan and Siguiri.

FARANAH

Faranah is about 200 km east of Mamou, a major stopping point for long-distance transport running between Conakry and Kankan or Macenta. At night the town comes alive with several cafés and restaurants serving drinks and cheap meals for the passing trade. President Sekou Touré was from this region and the town seems to have benefited from his patronage: it has wide boulevards and even street lighting (now broken). He also had built a conference centre (now hardly used), a large **mosque** (still in use), and a villa (now used as a hotel). The large **market** is lively, especially on Mondays. Faranah is also the highest point on the Niger River

which can be easily reached, and only 150 km from its source. For a view, follow the main road towards Mamou for about two km until you get to a bridge over the river.

Places to Stay & Eat

The best place in town, and one of the most interesting places to stay in the whole country, is Sekou Touré's former villa, which has been turned into the *Hôtel de Ville* (not the town hall). Apart from being opened to the public, nothing else has changed: the four-storey house is full of kitsch furniture, Persian rugs and mammoth sculptures, all part of the former president's garish art collection that has been left intact. You'll feel that history stopped when Sekou Touré died.

A huge room with private bath, sumptuous double bed, refrigerator, built-in wardrobes and plush carpeting will set you back about GF 9000 – worth every franc. An added bonus is the balcony which runs the whole perimeter of the hotel and affords a splendid view of the town. Meals are available if you arrange them in advance with the caretaker (who lives with his family in the hotel lobby). The hotel is opposite the mosque in

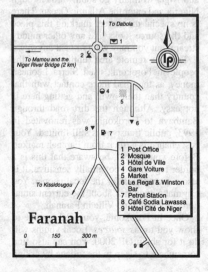

1	Post Office
2	Mosque
3	Hôtel de Ville
4	Gare Voiture
5	Market
6	Le Regal & Winston Bar
7	Petrol Station
8	Café Sodia Lawassa
9	Hôtel Cité de Niger

To Dabola

To Mamou and the Niger River Bridge (2 km)

To Kissidougou

Faranah

0   150   300 m

the centre of town (there's no sign). If you're short of cash ask about the basic rooms in the annexe for GF 5000.

Your other choice is the *Hôtel Cité de Niger*, on the edge of town, built more recently, but lacking the bizarre character of the Hôtel de Ville. Fairly clean rooms in modern bungalows cost GF 12,000.

The town centre is full of street food, especially in the evening. There are several cafés and cheap restaurants on the road towards Mamou. More up-market, and recommended, is *Le Regal*, a clean and friendly Senegalese restaurant behind the market, where meals are around GF 3000. Next door is the pleasant Winston Bar.

THE SOURCE OF THE NIGER

Halfway along the main road between Faranah and Kissidougou, a dirt road branches off south, through the villages of Bambaya and Kolikoro, to reach the remote settlement of **Forokonia** (72 km from the main road), just north of the border between Guinea and Sierra Leone. Only seven km from here is the source of the Niger, from where the river flows north to Bamako before curving in a giant arc through Mali and Niger to finally go southwards through Nigeria and enter the Atlantic Ocean. There is no special monument marking this place and the source looks like any other muddy stream, but you may want to visit anyway.

This is a remote area (until recently, the people in Forokonia used Sierra Leonean money, as they had more contact with that country than their own) and getting here is not easy. Although the dirt road through Bambaya to Forokonia was renovated in 1993, public transport is still limited. Your best chance is a truck from Faranah market. Before you set out, be aware that this is a border region and potentially sensitive. It is also a sacred area for the local people. You can make enquiries about the current situation at the Hôtel de Ville in Faranah.

Once in Forokonia, you need a guide to show you to *les sources*. Local youths will do it for about GF 2000. You can also find somewhere to sleep in the village by asking

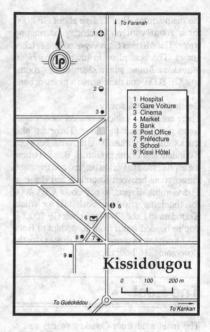

around: expect to pay GF 5000 for a bed in a hut and a simple meal.

KISSIDOUGOU

Kissidougou (often called Kissi) is a junction-town, where the main road from Conakry divides: one road heads north to Kankan, the other heads south to Guéckédou, Nzérékoré and onward to Côte d'Ivoire.

For a place to stay, the *Kissi Hôtel* has fairly decent doubles with electricity and bucket baths for GF 6000. You can get meals here for around GF 3000, or for less at any of the eating houses around the market and gare voiture.

For onward travel, bush taxis go from the gare voiture to Faranah for GF 5000, Kankan for GF 8000, Mamou for GF 14,000 and to Guéckédou for GF 2500.

GUÉCKÉDOU

Guéckédou is 95 km south of Kissidougou, one hour by bush taxi on a good tar road. It's near

1 Hôtel Gazelle
2 Gare Voiture & Market
3 Post Office
4 Gendarmerie
5 Hospital
6 Hôtel Mafissa

To Kissidougou
River

To Macenta

3

4 ★   +
5

Guéckédou

0   250   500 m

6 ■
To Sierra Leone

the borders of Sierra Leone and Liberia (which can both be reached from here) and so it's a major smuggling centre. The town itself is quite unattractive, but the weekly **market** (Wednesdays) is huge, with traders from all over Guinea, plus many more from Sierra Leone, Liberia, Mali and Côte d'Ivoire. You can buy anything here, and change several types of currency. Guéckédou market is also remarkable as it's the only place in Guinea with a clean, functioning public toilet.

The best place to stay is the *Hôtel Mafissa*, on the south-western edge of town, one km along the road between the hospital and the gendarmerie, heading towards Sierra Leone. It's fairly clean and friendly, with single/double rooms for GF 3000/6000, although often full on market day. There are a few other places around the market, all rough dens catering to passing truck drivers.

For onward travel, bush taxis cost GF 2500 to Macenta, where you change for Nzérékoré, and GF 3000 to Kissidougou, where you change for Kankan or Faranah.

MACENTA

Macenta is in the south-east of the country between Kissidougou and Nzérékoré, at the

end of the tar road from Conakry. Beyond Macenta, the road to Nzérékoré is in bad condition, although there are plans to tar it sometime in 1995 or 1996.

In town, your choices for somewhere to stay are limited. At the *Hôtel Palm* (also called Chez Le Vieux Libanais) dirty rooms with a stinking toilet are GF 10,000 for one bed and GF 15,000 for two beds. Meals are available on demand, and the bar may be able to sell you a warm beer. Near the gare voiture on the main street is the *Hôtel Magnetic* where rooms with shared bathrooms which are no dirtier than the Palm's cost GF 5000.

For cheap food, go to the unnamed restaurant up the hill from the Palm, on the left, where bowls of rice and sauce are GF 1000. About four km outside town, along a bad dirt road (which leads to the airport and Liberia), is the very clean and smart *Hôtel Balaki* where simple rooms are GF 10,000 and self-contained doubles are GF 25,000. Meals (starting at GF 4000) are available.

Getting There & Away

Macenta has two gares voitures: on the west side of town, on the road to Guéckédou, for

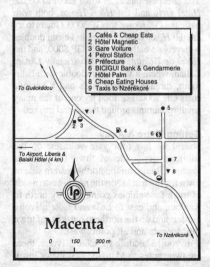

1 Cafés & Cheap Eats
2 Hôtel Magnetic
3 Gare Voiture
4 Petrol Station
5 Préfecture
6 BICIGUI Bank & Gendarmerie
7 Hôtel Palm
8 Cheap Eating Houses
9 Taxis to Nzérékoré

To Guéckédou

▼ 1
2 3   ■ 4   ● 5

6 ⊕

To Airport, Liberia & Balaki Hôtel (4 km)

■ 7
9 ▼ 8

Macenta

0   150   300 m

To Nzérékoré

bush taxis and buses in that direction; and on the east side of town for bush taxis to Nzérékoré (GF 8000). Because the road between Macenta to Nzérékoré is so bad, there are no buses on this route. A government bus to Conakry leaves once a week and private buses on other days. Bush taxis from Macenta cost GF 2500 to Guéckédou and GF 3000 to Kissidougou.

NZÉRÉKORÉ

In the far south-eastern corner of Guinea near iron-ore rich Mt Nimba and the Liberian border, Nzérékoré is the major city in Guinea's forest country. It's an active place, with lots of smuggling going on with Liberia. It's also a vital transportation hub, which will become even busier when the last section of the 954-km main road from Conakry is tarred (which should be in 1995 or 1996). From here there are connections to both Liberia and Côte d'Ivoire. The weekly market is on Wednesday. Around the market you'll find black-market moneychangers: most travellers use them, but there is a bank if you want one.

Places to Stay & Eat

The cheapest places in town seem to be the *Hôtel Orly* and the *Hôtel Hanoi*, both with basic but OK rooms for GF 3000. Others to try are the *Hôtel Biafra*, which has clean doubles with private baths for about GF 8000, and the *Hôtel de l'Unité*, run by the friendly Oularé Ballan, where a very clean double with bathroom, running water, towels and a veranda costs GF 5000. For food try one of the many small restaurants around the central market.

Getting There & Away

Nzérékoré has four gare voitures: on the south-western side of town for vehicles toward Liberia; on the north-western side of town for big trucks; on the north-eastern side of town for vehicles going directly north to Kankan, and east to Lola and Côte d'Ivoire border; and on the northern outskirts of town for Macenta and all points west.

If you're heading for Côte d'Ivoire, there are two routes to Man, the first major town.

The more well-travelled route is via Lola (market day Monday), Nzo and Danané. It's possible to make it to Danané in one long day if you leave early. A bush taxi costs GF 8000. One advantage of this route is that you can get off in Nzo to climb Mt Nimba (1752 metres). Or you can go via Sipilou (just inside Côte d'Ivoire, one km from the border), passing through some of the most spectacular scenery in all of West Africa.

Early every morning, the Syndicat des Transports Guinéens in Nzérékoré has Land Rovers going to Sipilou. The ride typically takes six hours and costs CFA 3000. From Sipilou you'll find minibuses for Biankouma and Man. If you get caught in Sipilou, there's a cheap hotel on the road entering town from Nzérékoré.

If you've come from Côte d'Ivoire, and are heading into Guinea, a bush taxi is GF 8000 to Macenta, where you can get a bus or bush taxis on to Guéckédou and Kissidougou (from where you can go to Faranah or Kankan). But if you're heading for Kankan and looking for adventure, you could take the road that goes directly north, via Beyla. Few travellers go this way – it's slow, and in miserable condition during the rainy season – but the scenery is good.

If conditions settle in Liberia, transport to the border town of Ganta (79 km) should recommence. There used to be a Liberian consul in Nzérékoré. If you need a visa it may be worth asking if he's still around.

KANKAN

On the banks of the Milo River (a large tributary of the Niger), Kankan is Guinea's second city. However, the infrastructure is quite limited despite the fact that it's a university town and the site of the former palace of president Sekou Touré. The capital of the ancient Mali Empire (see the History section in this chapter) was near here, and today it's still something of an unofficial 'capital' for Guinea's Malinké people. Nearly every Malinké (Mandinka) you meet, even in places as far away as Senegal and The Gambia, regards Kankan as a spiritual home, and may still have family there.

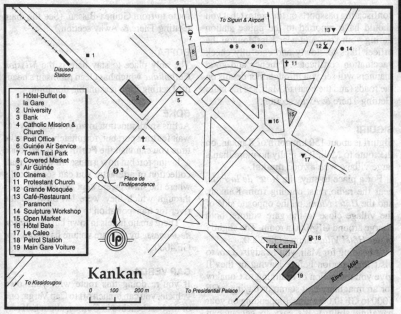

1 Hôtel-Buffet de
   la Gare
2 University
3 Bank
4 Catholic Mission &
   Church
5 Post Office
6 Guinée Air Service
7 Town Taxi Park
8 Covered Market
9 Air Guinée
10 Cinema
11 Protestant Church
12 Grande Mosquée
13 Café-Restaurant
   Paramont
14 Sculpture Workshop
15 Open Market
16 Hôtel Bate
17 Le Caleo
18 Petrol Station
19 Main Gare Voiture

To Siguiri & Airport

Disused
Station

Place de
l'Indépendence

Kankan

To Kissidougou   0   100   200 m   To Presidential Palace

Park Central

River Milo

The town seems to be on the up these days (there's a new hotel, several banks and a supermarket) but it's still a lot quieter than, say, Faranah. The principal sights are the **open market** with its large arched entrances, the covered market, and the **Grande Mosquée**. To visit the mosque, ask the caretaker; he'll be glad to show you around for a small fee. There's a small sculpture workshop opposite the mosque (on the south side). Also worth a visit (no photos!) is the old presidential palace overlooking the river.

Places to Stay & Eat

The *Hôtel-Buffet de la Gare* in the centre next to the defunct train station has half-decent rooms upstairs for GF 10,000 and rooms out the back which are worse for GF 5500. Meals are available if you order them in advance. The *Catholic Mission* no longer takes guests. Your only other option is the new up-market *Hôtel Bate* where small but good quality self-contained rooms are GF

22,000, or GF 29,000 with air-con. Meals in the restaurant are around GF 5000, and you can get snacks for GF 2000. At *Le Caleo* restaurant down a side street on the other side of the open market, you can get meals from GF 3500 and snacks from GF 1500. Down a notch from here is the friendly *Café-Restaurant Paramont*, just east of the mosque. Nearby is the smaller *Café Tropicana*. For cheaper fare, there's a row of coffee and bread stalls near the open market.

Getting There & Away

Kankan has two gare voitures: the main one by the bridge over the river, for all southbound traffic; and a smaller one, near the Grande Mosquée, for vehicles to Siguiri. A bus from Conakry to Kankan costs GF 23,000. Or, if you come here in stages by bush taxi, Kissidougou to Kankan is GF 8000. For some reason, the police on the Kankan to Kissidougou road are the worst in the country: the officer at the road block outside Kankan has a trick of confiscating passports on the pretext that you should have reported to the police station during your stay, and near Kissidougou the officer likes to slowly and carefully check vaccination certificates. Patience and good manners will see you through. For details on the roads (and the boat) to Mali, see the main Getting There & Away section.

SIGUIRI

Siguiri is about 150 km north of Kankan, on the route to Mali. It is really no more than a large village with a good **market**.

For a place to stay, the *Hôtel de la Paix*, near the radio mast coming from Kankan, and the *Hôtel Niani*, on the opposite side of the village close to the gare voiture, both charge around GF 4000 a room. The slightly better *Hôtel Villa* charges GF 8000.

If heading for Mali, you're advised *not* to visit immigration before leaving or they'll give you the option of returning to Conakry for an imaginary exit stamp or paying a GF 5000 to GF30,000 'fine' (depending on your haggling ability). It's easy to get an exit stamp at the border (Kouremalé).

The West

You may pass through this low-lying corner of the country if you're travelling the coast

route to/from Guinea-Bissau. (See the main Getting There & Away section.)

BOFFA

The only place to stay here is the *Mission Catholique* which has clean rooms in a beautiful setting for a reasonable donation.

BOKÉ

At this small junction town you may have to wait for transport but, fortunately, to pass the time you can visit the **Fortin de Boké**, once a slaving fort but now a museum with a small collection of artefacts. You can see the cells where the slaves were kept and the passages through which they were led down to the river for transportation to the coast.

There are no hotels in town but the *Maison de Jeunesse* by the gare voiture has rooms for GF 4000.

CAP VERGA

If you're doing this route with your own vehicle, you can branch off to Cap Verga, one of the best beaches in Guinea, about halfway between Boffa and Boké. It's popular at weekends with expatriates working at the bauxite mines inland, otherwise it's deserted.

You can rent beach huts here for GF 1000 per day. Meals can be arranged with local people at reasonable prices (seafood and chicken). The nearest place for provisions is **Koukadie**, a fishing village about five km along the beach.

Guinea-Bissau

For travellers, Guinea-Bissau is a joy. It has some of the friendliest people on the continent, small clean towns with wide streets and flowering trees, and rarely a tourist in sight. Bissau, the capital, witnessed an economic renaissance in the past few years but still has a pleasant feel, with pastel-coloured buildings, Mediterranean-style verandas, bars where you can meet people, and a selection of lively nightclubs. It is also one of the safest cities in Africa. South of Bissau is Bubaque Island, with some of the best beaches in the country.

But Guinea-Bissau is certainly not for everybody. If you insist on having your creature comforts and are looking for vibrant markets, interesting things to buy, unusual sights and historic edifices, pass on. You won't find them here.

Facts about the Country

HISTORY
The Empire of Mali, which flourished between the 13th and 15th centuries, included part of present-day Guinea-Bissau. In the late 15th century, over 50 years before Columbus discovered America, the Portuguese sent ships to Guinea-Bissau and other areas along the coast to seek slaves, gold, ivory and pepper.

The Portuguese built forts along the coast of present-day Guinea-Bissau and elsewhere in West Africa. Their trade monopoly ended in the late 1600s when the British, Spanish, French and Dutch captured most of their forts and entered the slave trade with great enthusiasm. The area was popular with slavers because it was on the coast and closer to Europe and the Americas than most other part of Africa.

But the effects of the slave trade, particularly the social disintegration, were devastating. Local tribes were encouraged to declare war on their neighbours, and the losers of any battle were sold into slavery.

REPUBLIC OF GUINEA-BISSAU

Area: 36,125 sq km
Population: 1 million
Population Growth Rate: 2.4%
Capital: Bissau
Head of State: President João Bernardo Vieira
Official Language: Portuguese
Currency: Guinea-Bissau peso
Exchange Rate: 12,000 pesos = US$1
Per Capita GNP: US$180
Inflation: 50%
Time: GMT/UTC

Content to exploit the coast, Portugal didn't lay claim to the interior until 1879, when European powers carved up the continent. Even after being 'given' what became known as Portuguese Guinea, Portugal was unable to gain full control of the entire area until 1915, after a long series of wars with the Guineans. In the process, Portuguese Guinea ended up with the most repressive and exploitative of all the colonial powers.

Colonial Period
By the late 19th century, the abolition of slavery was enforced by British navy patrols, and so the export of agricultural products to

GUINEA-BISSAU

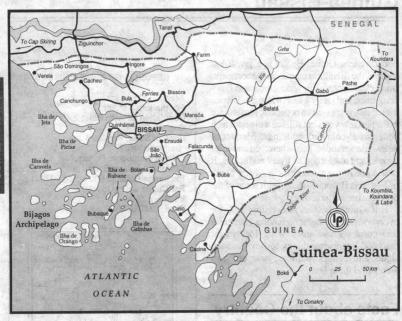

Europe became the main interest of the colonial powers in West Africa. But because Portugal was not a wealthy country and had few resources, it did not develop its colonies. The republican government in Portugal was so weak that it allowed non-Portuguese European companies to control and export the crops, mainly peanuts and palm oil.

This changed in the Lisbon coup of 1926 when the dictator Salazar came to power and imposed restrictive customs duties on foreign companies, forcing them to sell out to Portuguese interests. Portuguese colonial power resumed and their rule was simple: if you were a peasant, you planted peanuts, like it or not.

In the late 1950s and early 1960s, many countries in Africa were gaining independence from their European colonial rulers, but Portugal refused to relinquish its hold on

Guinea. The reasons for this were based on Portugal's own weaknesses. When Britain and France gave up their African colonies, they merely changed from being colonials to neo-colonials. They still profited considerably from trade with their former colonies. But the Portuguese realised that if their colonies were liberated, neocolonialism could not be imposed. So, while other countries became free, the grip on Guinea tightened further.

War of Liberation

The result was the longest liberation struggle in the history of Africa: a guerrilla war waged by the African Party for Independence in Guinea and Cape Verde (PAIGC) with significant help from the Soviet Union and Cuba.

From its inception in 1956, the PAIGC was committed to the joint liberation of both Portuguese colonies. The better educated Cape Verdeans provided many of the leaders, including the head leader and co-founder of the party, Amilcar Cabral, one of Africa's modern-day heroes. But it was in Portuguese Guinea that the mass movement was strongest.

In 1961, the PAIGC entered Portuguese Guinea from independent Guinea and started arming and mobilising the peasants. At first, they numbered only a few hundred courageous and resourceful young villagers, but as their numbers grew to about 10,000 the Portuguese

responded by increasing their troop strength to 25,000 plus some 10,000 conscripted African troops. Yet within five years, half the country was liberated. Internationally, Portugal became isolated. Foreign politicians, journalists and photographers all visited the liberated area, and the struggle became front-page news during the early '70s.

The Portuguese continued to hold out in refugee-swollen Bissau, a few smaller towns, and pockets in the north-east where some of the more prominent Muslim Fula collaborated with the Portuguese in an attempt to preserve their social privileges. Their agents in Conakry even assassinated Amilcar Cabral. But the movement was too strong. In 1973, the PAIGC organised nationwide elections in the liberated areas and proclaimed independence, with Amilcar Cabral's half-brother, Louis (also a Cape Verdean), as president. Eighty countries quickly recognised it as the legitimate government, but it still took Salazar's overthrow the following year for Portugal to call it quits and recognise Guinea-Bissau as an independent state.

Independence

Once in power, the new PAIGC government had more than a handful of problems. The Portuguese had seen Guinea as little more than a cheap source of peanuts and palm oil, and had done almost nothing to develop the

GUINEA-BISSAU

PAIGC & Independence

Now viewed as a model, the African Party for Independence in Guinea and Cape Verde was successful largely because of its political strategy during the war. As they liberated each part of the country, they built schools, provided medical services and encouraged widespread political participation to help people realise the promise of a better life. Cabral had insisted on a war of revolution, not of revolt, and he realised that society had to be completely reorganised if the people were ever to be genuinely free.

Thus, from the very start of the war, the people of Guinea-Bissau believed in what they were fighting for. The meaning of independence for Guineans is eloquently summed up by the military officer's comments in David Lamb's *The Africans*:

'You ask what the difference between colonialism and independence means to me', the 36-year-old Miranda said, filling my glass with wine. 'Well, I will tell you. The difference is great. Now I go to bed at night and I sleep comfortably. I do not worry about the secret police. And I do not tip my hat to the *Tuga* (Portuguese).

'Now I speak to a White man without fear. Before, White and Black did not talk. But now at this moment I have the pleasure of sitting with you, a White, and I speak to you like a man. That is all we fought for, the right to respect. We did not hate the Portuguese people, only the Portuguese government. Even if you were Portuguese, I would still be happy to sit with you, because now we are equals.' ∎

country. They left behind a grand total of one brewery built for the Portuguese troops, a few small factories for hulling rice and peanuts, 14 university graduates, and not a single doctor. Only one in 20 people could read, life expectancy was 35 years, and 45% of the children died before the age of five. During the war, rice production had fallen 71%, and many of the rice polders (areas of reclaimed land) were ruined and would take years to rebuild. Rice had to be imported for the first time ever.

Politically, the PAIGC, led mainly by Cape Verdeans, wanted a unified Guinea-Bissau and Cape Verde. However, they abruptly dropped the idea in 1980 when President Cabral was overthrown in a coup while he was visiting Cape Verde to negotiate the union. João ('Nino') Vieira took over and became president.

Despite the change of leader, Guinea-Bissau continued to follow a socialist path. The state controlled most major enterprises, Marxist literature was everywhere and political dissent was banned. Hordes of Soviet advisors came but were rarely seen – mixing with the locals was taboo. However, despite the dogma, Vieira encouraged pragmatism and political neutrality. Private citizens continued to own most of the small shops. The Soviets provided military aid (as they had during the liberation war) while the West provided the nonmilitary aid.

But life remained hard for most people. The shops were almost empty except for uninteresting items from Eastern Bloc countries. Whenever potatoes and wine from Portugal arrived, they remained on the shelves all of 30 minutes. Conditions were so bad that finding food was almost a clandestine activity; housewives spent four or five hours a day searching for food, relying on friends and relatives for tip-offs, sometimes paying by barter. In the interior, foreign products were so scarce that matches made a welcome gift.

By the mid-1980s Guinea-Bissau was making no progress under Marxism. Apart from the Soviet advisors, the country received very little economic aid from the USSR. So in 1986, after a serious coup attempt the year

before, the Vieira government completely reversed its policies, devalued the currency and began selling off almost all the state enterprises.

Guinea-Bissau Today
Nino Vieira has proved to be a shrewd and deft politician, surviving three coup attempts while keeping the PAIGC party in power, and remaining generally popular. For Guineans, things have improved: the electricity supply is fairly regular and blackouts are now rare, while local produce and foreign goods can be bought in shops and markets. Bottled beer is easy to find, and various clubs have opened bringing Bissau's nightlife into line with other African capital cities.

The mood of the country continues to be upbeat. Roads are in relatively good condition and the trip time to southern Senegal has been dramatically reduced by an improved ferry system on that route. Trade with the outside world is increasing and the importation of foreign goods is continuing to increase.

GEOGRAPHY
Guinea-Bissau has an area of 36,000 sq km (about the size of Switzerland) making it one of Africa's smaller countries. The country can be divided into three main zones.

The coastal zone is flat with meandering rivers, tangled trees, rainforests and deep estuaries; it isn't easy to distinguish mud, mangrove and water from solid land. The major environmental problem in this area is the rapid destruction of the mangroves – some of the most important in Africa – due to the growth of rice production. Inlets indent the coast, and high tides periodically submerge the lowest areas, sometimes covering up to a third of the land surface. Consequently there are only a few rudimentary roads in this zone.

Inland, the landscape is still flat, with the highest ground (near the Guinea border) just topping 300 metres above sea level. The natural vegetation is lightly wooded savannah, but much of it is under cultivation. You'll see rice fields, most of it in polders; also peanuts, manioc, maize and other subsistence crops. What you won't find are large towns: Gabú, Bafatá, Canchungo and Cacheu (with little more than a market, a main street, and a few places to stay and eat) are as big as they get.

The third zone is the Bijagos Archipelago, consisting of 18 main islands. The most important, and easiest to reach, is Bubaque. The other islands are lightly populated, where some inhabitants have never come into contact with Westerners.

CLIMATE

The rainy season is from June to October; the rainfall is almost twice as heavy along the coast as it is inland. Conditions are humid most of the time, especially in the months before the rains. The most pleasant time is from November to February.

GOVERNMENT

Progress towards democracy in Guinea-Bissau has been slow. Multiparty democracy was approved in principle by the government in early 1991, thereafter opposition leaders began returning from exile. A year later the PAIGC agreed to set up a multiparty commission which would organise pluralist elections. Early in 1993 there was an unsuccessful coup attempt against Vieira. João da Costa, leader of the opposition – the Party for Renovation & Development (PRD) – was accused of masterminding the attempt and arrested under Vieira's orders. A few weeks later, however, the Vieira government, bending to pressure from foreign aid-donor countries and from inside Guinea-Bissau, finally legalised a multiparty political system and set up an electoral commission. It then released da Costa from prison.

Presidential elections were due to be held in March 1994, but were postponed at short notice until June. The official reasons given were lack of government revenue to fund the election and incomplete registration of voters. Elections were finally held in July 1994: Vieira won with 52% of the vote. As a result, Vieira legitimised his rule, and the country is now clearly on the road towards democracy. However, there is still only one newspaper, the government-owned *Nô*

Pintcha, and the number of radios in the country is only one for every 25 people, the third lowest in the world. Whether favourable trends will develop regarding these and other important elements of a democratic society remains to be seen.

ECONOMY

Guinea-Bissau is one of the world's 10 poorest countries according to the UN's human development index, but six other West African countries are in the same group and lower still on the index. Guinea-Bissau differs from the others in that people are surviving relatively well in rural areas, which employs 90% of the workforce. Rainfall is more dependable than in many African countries, and scarcity of land isn't yet a major problem. Agriculture is the economy's most dynamic sector, growing at 6% a year since the early 1990s, and production of rice, the country's main crop, has doubled since 1983. As a result, Guinea-Bissau is now self-sufficient in rice and it's one of only five countries in Africa in a position to export food. The bulk of foreign earnings presently come from the agricultural sector, specifically the export of peanuts, fish and, above all, cashew nuts.

POPULATION & PEOPLE

Current estimates put the population at just over one million, made up of 23 ethnic groups. The main groups are Balante (30%) and Fula (20%); other large groups are the Manjaco and Mandinga (also known as *Maninka* and *Malinké*). There's also a minority of *mestizos* (people of mixed European and African descent). Most Lebanese and Portuguese traders left in the 1970s following independence, although some have since returned.

CULTURE

Folk dancing is as strongly preserved here as anywhere in Africa, so if you go upcountry, be on the lookout for a celebration. The harp-like *kora* and the xylophone-like *balafon* are played, while women dance frantically in a circle of onlookers.

GUINEA-BISSAU

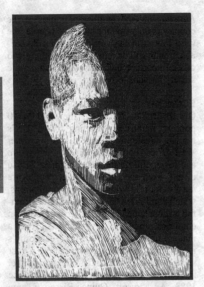

GUINEA-BISSAU

In Bubaque, a typical men's group might be wearing masks depicting animals with horns, along with a variety of arm and leg bands, frequently with green leaves stuck into them. Some costumes make use of dry grass, giving a much more jungle-like appearance than those in, say, the Sahelian countries. But costumes change from area to area and dance to dance. In Bafatá, for example, you might see dancers with their faces painted white, and simple costumes made primarily of thick pieces of rope with dangling bells for sounds.

If possible, try to hit Bissau at carnival time in February or March; the assortment of masks is incredible. Spirits are also high then and it's perhaps easier to meet people.

In traditional music, Guinea-Bissau's influences come from the Malinké and Diola people of neighbouring Guinea and Senegal. Modern music shares the same roots, and the Portuguese colonial legacy has given some sounds a Latin edge. One of the most popular singers these days is Dulce Maria Neves; she occasionally sings at some of the nightclubs. Others are the group Super Mama Djombo and singers Mario Cooperante and N'Kassa

Cobra. Singers from Guinea-Bissau who have made records in Europe include Ramiro Naka and Kaba Mane.

RELIGION
About 40% of the people are Muslims, mainly Fula and Mandinga; both groups are concentrated more upcountry than along the coast. Except for a few Christians in the towns, the rest are ancestral worshippers and follow traditional animist beliefs.

LANGUAGE
Portuguese is the official language, but no more than a third of the people in town can speak it, and then not fluently. Virtually everyone speaks Crioulo on a daily basis. Quite a few people understand French.

Expressions in Crioulo
Good morning.	*bom DEE-ah*
Good evening.	*bow-ah NO-tay*
How are you?	*ou-KOR-poh*
	ees-tah BON?
I'm fine.	*tah-BON*
Thank you.	*ob-ree-GAH-doh*
Goodbye.	*NAH-buy*

Facts for the Visitor

VISAS & EMBASSIES
Guinea-Bissau Visas
Visas are required by everyone, except citizens of Cape Verde and Nigeria. In West Africa, you can get visas for Guinea-Bissau in Dakar (Senegal), Banjul (The Gambia) and Conakry (Guinea). There's also a consulate in Ziguinchor (Senegal). For details refer to the Visas & Embassies section in the relevant country chapter. In Washington, the embassy charges US$15 and requires two photographs for single or multiple-entry visas valid for one month (or up to three months if you so request). Visa processing takes two to three days. In London, the embassy issues tourist visas on the spot, for UK£30 and three photos. Visas are typically valid for a month unless you ask for a longer period, which is often approved.

Visas may also be available at the airport in Bissau (if you pay with hard currency) but don't rely on this.

Visa Extensions

Extensions are easy to obtain at the central police station in Bissau. The process is straightforward, but costs seem to vary between 100,000 and 300,000 pesos. If you're staying for more than a month, check if you need an exit visa.

Guinea-Bissau Embassies

Belgium 70 Ave Franklin-Roosevelt, Brussels 1050 (☎ (02) 647-08-90/647-13-51)

France 24 rue du Gant da Lalouette, 75013 Paris (☎ (1) 43-36-99-90)

Germany (consulate) Am Wall 142, 2800 Bremen 1 (☎ (0421) 15-122)

USA 918 16th St, NW, Mezzanine Suite, Washington, DC 20006 (☎ (202) 872-4222)

Guinea-Bissau also has embassies or consuls in Algiers, Lisbon and Stockholm.

Other African Visas

The Gambia The embassy is open weekday mornings, and charges 52,000 pesos for a one-month visa – issued on the same day if you come early.

Guinea The embassy charges US$25 (payable in hard currency) for a standard 15-day visa. The process requires endless patience but should take no more than three days. Getting a one-month visa may take even more determination. However, if you bring a letter of introduction from your embassy, you may get the visa the same day. Dress neatly, especially if your embassy is not present in Bissau and you have to plead for a visa. 'Tourism' as a reason to visit occasionally causes a problem. If that seems the case you may need to tell another story. The embassy's hours are from 8.30 am to 3 pm Monday to Thursday, to 1 pm on Friday, and sometimes to noon on Saturday.

Senegal The embassy charges CFA 3000 to CFA 5000, depending on your nationality. Visas are issued in 48 hours.

Other Countries The French embassy issues visas in 24 hours to Burkina Faso, Côte d'Ivoire, Togo, Chad, Central African Republic and (possibly) Mauritania. The cost is between 50 and 100FF (US$10 to US$20).

Foreign Embassies

See the Bissau Information section for a list of embassies found in the capital.

DOCUMENTS

All visitors need a valid passport. An International Vaccination Certificate for yellow fever is mandatory if you come within six days from an infected area and you're staying for more than two weeks.

CUSTOMS

The import or export of local currency is illegal. Occasionally, customs officials do a thorough search. If you're found carrying pesos when entering or leaving the country, they will be confiscated. The import or export of foreign currencies is not prohibited but it is probably better to declare large amounts on arrival so as to avoid any hassle when leaving.

You used to have to change a set amount at the border, but this rule has been dropped. If border officials say otherwise, a polite but firm refusal should see you through without problems.

MONEY

1FF	=	2,100 pesos
UK£1	=	18,000 pesos
US$1	=	12,000 pesos

The unit of currency is the Guinea-Bissau peso. Inflation is rampant, so expect prices much higher than indicated here.

Banks include the Banco International de Guinea-Bissau (BIGB) and the Banco Central de Guinea-Bissau (BCGB). In Bissau banks change cash and travellers' cheques but the process is slow, and upcountry there are few banks, so most travellers change on the black market. In Bissau the rate is virtually the same as the banks, but the process is quicker. Moneychangers hang out at the central market and near the post office. It seems to be semi-legal, although if the police see you they could give you problems. To avoid any trouble, there's also a small moneychanging bureau near the central market. You can also buy pesos at the border, when you enter Guinea-Bissau, but rates are lower than in Bissau.

All hotels will accept payment in hard currency and CFA. The Sheraton and Hotel 24 de Setembro in Bissau accept hard currency only. They are also the only places accepting credit cards – see Places to Stay in the Bissau section of this chapter.

BUSINESS HOURS & HOLIDAYS

Businesses and government offices are open weekdays from 8 am to noon and 3 to 6 pm, and Saturday from 8 am to noon. Banks are open weekdays from 7.30 to 11.00 am or noon, and closed weekends.

Public Holidays

1 January, 20 January, 8 March, Good Friday, End of Ramadan, 1 May, Tabaski, 3 August, 24 September (Independence Day), 14 November, 25 December.

POST & TELECOMMUNICATIONS

The postal service out of the country is good, but travellers report that the poste restante is unhelpful and unreliable. We heard from one traveller who couldn't collect his mail because the clerk in charge of the poste restante had been arrested for stealing letters!

You can make international phone calls from the post office. Connections are quite good. The Sheraton hotel is more efficient, but more expensive.

PHOTOGRAPHY

Photo permits are not required. As in most African countries, do not take shots of the Presidential Palace, public buildings, the port, bridges, ferries and anything military.

HEALTH

The Hospital Simão Mendes (☎ 212816) is the better of the two hospitals in Bissau, and there are several pharmacies in the city centre. Gabú and Bafatá each have a hospital and pharmacy. Canchungo also has a hospital – reportedly the best in the country.

DANGERS & ANNOYANCES

Walking around Bissau at night is safer than in just about any African capital city. Nevertheless, crime is slowly increasing, so take the usual precautions. Avoid side streets and the port area at night.

ACCOMMODATION

In Bissau, up-market hotels are on the increase, but the choice of budget places to stay has shrunk, as most cheapies have shut their doors for the last time. For this reason, many travellers head upcountry or to the islands, where accommodation is more reasonably priced, and usually good value.

FOOD & DRINKS

In Bissau and other towns, street food such as brochettes or roast corn is hard to find. Even coffee and bread stalls, which are much more common in neighbouring countries, take some determined tracking down. However, in the last few years, Bissau's choice of pâtisseries and smart restaurants has grown considerably, ideal if you want some good living after a long time on the road.

Beer is plentiful too, and relatively cheap (see below). For more than a beer, sample some *căna rum*; it's 60% proof. Or try palm wine, a milky-white and slightly bitter drink that's 4% proof when fresh and 8% when aged.

You may also come across *căna de cajeu* (cashew rum), made not from the nuts, but from the fruit that surrounds them.

Beer Bottles

In Guinea-Bissau, the cheapest bottled beer is the locally brewed Pampa (costing around 7000 pesos a bottle) while Sagres and Superbock are better-quality Portuguese imports (around 10,000 pesos). Unfortunately, Sagres and Superbock bottles cannot be reused. This leads to two problems: Guinea-Bissau wastes money and energy by manufacturing or importing bottles for Pampa; and there are discarded Sagres and Superbock bottles *everywhere* you go. ■

Getting There & Away

AIR
To/From Europe & the USA
Airlines from Europe serving Guinea-Bissau include Portugal's TAP (with flights via Lisbon), Aeroflot (via Moscow), and the French company EAS (flying from Paris via Lisbon). Return flights from Europe on TAP start at the equivalent of around US$750, depending on the season and your length of stay. However, a one-way flight from Bissau to London on TAP is US$960. On Aeroflot it's half that, or even less if you pay US dollars (cash). Most visitors arriving from Europe by air fly to Dakar and then change to a regional airline such as Air Bissau (TAGB) or Air Senegal (see below for details). From the USA you can take Air Afrique from New York, transferring to a regional airline at Dakar or Abidjan. Otherwise you'll have to go via Europe.

To/From West Africa
For flights between Guinea-Bissau and other West African destinations, your choice is not large, but planes are often full, so you should reserve and reconfirm as far in advance as possible, preferably in person. Air Senegal and TAGB between them have four flights a week between Bissau and Dakar (US$186 one way); those with Air Senegal stop in Ziguinchor. TAGB also has a weekly flight to Conakry (US$120) and to Banjul (US$108). Guinée Air Service also flies weekly to/from Conakry, and Air Mauritanie has weekly flights to Casablanca via Banjul and Nouakchott. All tickets purchased in Guinea-Bissau must be paid for in hard currency. For airline office addresses see the Bissau Getting There & Away section.

LAND
Bush Taxi
To/From Guinea Most travellers heading overland to Guinea take the northern route via Gabú, Koundara and Labé. Getting between Bissau and Gabú is easy (see

Getting Around) and between Conakry and Koundara is also straightforward (see the Guinea chapter), but catching rides between Gabú and Koundara is slow and difficult: it takes at least one day to cover this 100-km stretch. You may be lucky and find a truck going all the way (for around US$10 in pesos, Guinea francs or CFA), otherwise you'll have to do it in stages, changing at the border town of Sereboïdo and maybe walking between there and the border post itself, although there's normally one bush taxi per day between Gabú and the Guinea-Bissau side of the border. It's best to tie in your travels with Sereboïdo's weekly market (Sunday). On Saturdays trucks or pick-ups go from Gabú and Koundara to Sereboïdo, and on Sundays or Mondays they return. Although transport on this route can be tricky, the winding road through Guinea's Fouta Djalon foothills is beautiful.

We've heard from travellers who went from Bissau to Conakry on the southern route via Boké. Public road transport is virtually nonexistent and it can take up to a week to go this way between the two capitals.

You can also combine these two routes, by travelling from Gabú or Koundara to the border village of Kandika, then going south to Koumbia and on to Boké. From Kandika to Boké takes two to four days, depending on connections and the condition of the roads. Occasionally, trucks from Gabú go direct to Koumbia or Boké.

All these routes are slow or impassable in the rainy season.

To/From Senegal The main route between Senegal and Guinea-Bissau goes between Ziguinchor and Bissau via São Domingos, Ingore and Bula. This 140-km route is tarred all the way, but there are two ferry crossings which can make the total journey anything from three to six hours. The northern rivercrossing at St Vincent has a small ferry carrying one vehicle with a 20-minute turn-around time, and a larger ferry carrying six cars (only running at high tide) with a two-hour turn-around. The southern ferry at Joalande carries 12 vehicles and has a one-hour turn-around.

From Ziguinchor, bush taxis leave the *gare routière* (bush taxi stand), mostly before 9 am, and go all the way to Bissau for CFA 2000. Each passenger also has to pay 2000 pesos for each ferry crossing.

From Bissau, direct bush taxis leave the main *garage* (bush taxi/bus park – see Getting Around, later) usually between 8 and 10 am. After that you're unlikely to find direct transport, so you'll have to do it in stages, using local bush taxis to shuttle between the ferries (ask for the *embarcado*), but don't bank on reaching Ziguinchor in a day this way.

The coastal route between Ziguinchor and Bissau, via Canchungo, is not viable. Since the new road via Ingore was completed, the ferry between Cacheu and São Domingos no longer runs.

Another route – via Tanaf (100 km east of Ziguinchor) and Farim – is rarely used because of the improved connections via São Domingos. Irregular bush taxis run between Tanaf and Farim for about CFA 400 and there's a short river crossing at Farim.

Car
To/From Guinea Bissau to Conakry is about 1000 km and typically takes three days – one to Koundara (Guinea), another to Labé, and another to Conakry. About 70% of the total Bissau to Conakry route is paved but the big question is always the condition of the 285-km section between the border and Labé; it gets so muddy during the rainy season that getting stuck or taking more than one day on this stretch are real possibilities.

Petrol is readily available in Bissau, Koundara and Labé. The chances of finding petrol in Gabú or Bafatá are often poor.

To/From Senegal The principal route goes via São Domingos and Ingore; tar all the way. See the previous Bush Taxi section for details of ferry crossings, etc.

From Ziguinchor you could also drive about 100 km eastward to Tanaf (Senegal), then south to Farim. This 250-km route is paved all the way except for the 33-km section between Tanaf and Farim. The advantage of this route is that there's only one short ferry crossing at Farim compared to two longer ones on the main route.

SEA
It may be possible to find a freighter in Bissau heading for Dakar or Conakry. All international shipping is controlled by an organisation called Guinema. The office is in Bissau, near the port, and information on ships is usually posted in its windows. Typical fares are CFA 20,000 to Dakar and CFA 28,000 to Conakry.

Adventurous travellers can go from Cacheu to Banjul (The Gambia) in large sea-going *pirogues* (dugout canoes). There's no schedule, no fixed fare and a high degree of risk, as these notoriously dangerous boats are often overloaded and have been known to sink without trace.

LEAVING GUINEA-BISSAU
Leaving by air, departure tax is US$15, but may be included in the cost of some tickets. For details on getting to/from the airport see the Bissau Getting Around section.

Getting Around

AIR
There are no internal flights on the mainland. For details on the plane to Bubaque Island see Getting There & Away in that section.

BUSH TAXI & MINIBUS
The main roads between Bissau and the towns of Gabú, Cacheu and Farim, and to the border at São Domingos are all tarred and in good condition. Other roads are not so good and can be impassable in the rains. There are no bridges in Guinea-Bissau, so most road journeys require at least one ferry crossing.

Public transport around the country consists of minibuses, bush taxis and pick-ups called *kandongas*, and they serve virtually every town of any size in the country. In

Bissau, they leave from the main garage on Avenida de 14 Novembro, about two km from the Mercado (market) de Bandim. During the morning, there's a minibus every hour or so to Bafatá and Gabú, and two or more bush taxis to Ziguinchor and São Domingos, and to Canchungo. Pick-ups serve the smaller towns and villages off the main routes. There are fewer vehicles in the afternoon, and the waits are longer. Fares are cheap. For example, across the country from Bissau to Gabú is 30,000 pesos (less than US$3). On any trip, baggage is between 5 and 10% extra.

FERRY

From Bissau port there are ferries once a week to Bubaque Island (80 km to the south-west), twice a week to Bolama (40 km to the south), once a week to Catio, on the coast near the southern border with Guinea, and every morning (except Sunday) to Enxudé just across the bay from Bissau. They all leave from the port in Bissau. Fares are cheap. For more information, see the Getting There & Away sections for each town.

Bissau

Until the mid-1980s, Bissau had spotlessly clean streets, few cars and a low noise level. On the down side, the commercial area was lifeless, food was scarce, bottled beer was hard to find, and there was a blackout nearly every night. But recently Bissau has become increasingly like other African cities or, as some say, more 'Senegalised'. Now there's activity in the air, with cars and taxis on the streets, stores full of foreign goods, and thriving bars and nightclubs. TV has been introduced, plus beer from Portugal and canned soft drinks all the way from Europe! In the process, Bissau has lost some of its uniqueness, but the locals aren't complaining.

Some things haven't changed – yet. It's unlikely you will be hassled by hawkers trying to sell you what you don't need; there's little danger of being robbed or falling into an open sewer; the police don't set up road blocks; and the old central area still has charm.

Orientation

Bissau's main drag is the wide Avenida Amilcar Cabral, running from the port to the Praça dos Heróis Nacionais (a large square) and the Presidential Palace. Along it you'll find most banks, the cathedral and the cinema. A block to the west on Avenida Domingos Ramos is the small central market and Praça Ché Guevara, around which there are several popular bars and restaurants. On the north-western edge of the city centre is the Mercado de Bandim market. From here Avenida de 14 Novembro leads west to the main garage (two km) and the airport (another 10 km). This is also the main road out of town towards Bafatá, Gabú and Ziguinchor.

Information

Tourist Office There's a small tourist information office on Rue Guerra Mendes, south of the fort, with limited information on accommodation and tours around the country.

Money The large banks (BIGB and BCGB) are both on Avenida Amilcar Cabral, just south of the post office. Moneychangers also operate in this area. See the main Money section for details. The new Banco de Totto is in the narrow streets near the port.

Post The post office on Avenida Amilcar Cabral across from the cathedral is open from 8 am to 1 pm Monday to Friday.

Foreign Embassies The following diplomatic missions are in Bissau:

Algeria Rua 12 (☎ 211533)
Belgium Avenida Amilcar Cabral, next to Pensão Centrale
Brazil At the junction of Avenida Francisco Mendes and Avenida do Brazil
France Avenida de 14 Novembro, near the Sheraton (☎ 251031)
The Gambia Avenida de 14 Novembro, about one km from Mercado de Bandim
Guinea On the corner of Rua 12 and Rua Osvaldo Vieira (☎ 212681)

GUINEA-BISSAU

The Netherlands Represented by the Dutch Co-operation Service, Rua Justino Lopes

Nigeria Avenida de 14 Novembro, facing Mercado de Bandim (☎ 212782)

Mauritania Avenida de 14 Novembro, opposite the Gambian embassy

Portugal 6 Rua 16 (☎ 212741)

Senegal Praça dos Heróis Nacionais facing TAP Air Portugal (☎ 212636)

Sweden Avenida Domingos Ramos, north of Praça Ché Guevara (☎ 214422)

UK Avenida Pansau Na Isna

USA At the southern end of Avenida Domingos Ramos (☎ 201139 or 212816)

Cultural Centres The French Cultural Centre on Praça Ché Guevara has a library and good selection of magazines (mostly in French), and a small snack bar.

Travel Agencies For international flights there are several travel agencies, including Agencia Sagres (☎ 213709), on Avenida Amilcar Cabral below Pensão Centrale; and Guinea Tours (☎ 212409) on the corner of Avenida Amilcar Cabral and Rua Eduardo Mondlane. However, neither can confirm existing reservations. More efficient is Bijagos Tours, at the southern end of Avenida Pansau Na Isna. They also handle bookings for upcountry hunting and fishing camps.

Bookshops There are two bookstalls on the Praça Ché Guevara, selling mostly Portuguese periodicals and cheap postcards. International magazines and papers are available at the Sheraton and Hotel 24 de Setembro.

Markets For local produce try the Mercado Centrale, in the centre on Avenida Domingos Ramos, and Mercado de Bandim, at the beginning of Avenida de 14 Novembro. Fresh produce is usually plentiful, especially in season (January to May), but there's very little in the way of arts and crafts. On the outskirts of town is Feira Popular, an open-air market with expensive goods from neighbouring countries, especially Senegal.

Things to See & Do
The **Presidential Palace** at the northern end of Avenida Amilcar Cabral, overlooking Praça

dos Heróis Nacionais, is probably the closest thing to a 'must see' that Bissau has to offer. But no photos are allowed here, and it is forbidden to walk up the streets on either side of the palace. The **port** at the southern end of Avenida Amilcar Cabral is quite interesting, as are the narrow streets of Portuguese-style buildings just to the north. The old **fort** is still used by the military and not open to visitors. Keep your camera out of sight.

The **Museu Nacional** (national museum) is at the Complex Escolar on Avenida 14 de Novembro; it has a very small collection of art from Guinea-Bissau and is open daily from 9 am to 2 pm. More interesting is the **Centro Artistico Juvenil**, a training centre for young local artists, also on Avenida de 14 Novembro, near the bush taxi park. The fixed prices here are reasonable, some pieces are very good, and there's no pressure to buy (closed Sundays).

For **swimming** there are excellent pools at the Sheraton and Hotel 24 de Setembro; neither accepts nonguests but the 24 de Setembro isn't very vigilant in enforcing this rule.

Places to Stay – bottom end
A big change in recent years has been the increased reliability of the electricity supply, so you probably won't spend every night in darkness. A backup torch (flashlight) or candle is still worth having though. Running water is also more reliable. However, finding a cheap room is difficult, certainly more so than in other West African capitals.

The old *Pensão Luar* in the centre on the east side of Rua Mbana, 30 metres south of the junction with Avenida Pansau Na Isna, has been open only for food and beer in the last few years, although it might be worth checking in case the rooms reopen. Expect to pay about 100,000 pesos.

Your other option is to ask around at the bus park. Some travellers have found locals to stay with, paying about 100,000 pesos for a room and a meal.

Places to Stay – middle
Cheapest in this range is the *Grande Hotel* (☎ 213437), on Avenida Pansau Na Isna two

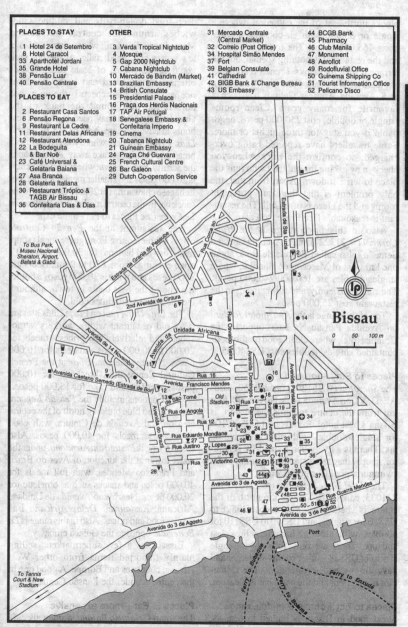

PLACES TO STAY
1 Hotel 24 de Setembro
8 Hotel Caracol
33 Aparthotel Jordani
35 Grande Hotel
38 Pensão Luar
40 Pensão Centrale

PLACES TO EAT
2 Restaurant Casa Santos
6 Pensão Regona
9 Restaurant Le Cedre
11 Restaurant Delas Africana
12 Restaurant Atendona
22 La Bodeguita
   & Bar Noé
23 Café Universal &
   Gelataria Baiana
27 Asa Branca
28 Gelateria Italiana
30 Restaurant Trópico &
   TAGB Air Bissau
36 Confeitaria Dias & Dias

OTHER
3 Verda Tropical Nightclub
4 Mosque
5 Gap 2000 Nightclub
7 Cabana Nightclub
10 Mercado de Bandim (Market)
13 Brazilian Embassy
14 British Consulate
15 Presidential Palace
16 Praça dos Heróis Nacionais
17 TAP Air Portugal
18 Senegalese Embassy &
   Confeitaria Imperio
19 Cinema
20 Tabanca Nightclub
21 Guinean Embassy
24 Praça Ché Guevara
26 Bar Galeon
29 Dutch Co-operation Service

31 Mercado Centrale
   (Central Market)
32 Correio (Post Office)
34 Hospital Simão Mendes
37 Fort
39 Belgian Consulate
41 Cathedral
42 BIGB Bank & Change Bureau
43 US Embassy

44 BCGB Bank
45 Pharmacy
46 Club Manila
47 Monument
48 Aeroflot
49 Rodofluvial Office
50 Guinema Shipping Co
51 Tourist Information Office
52 Pelicano Disco

GUINEA-BISSAU

To Bus Park,
Museu Nacional
Sheraton, Airport,
Bafatá & Gabú

Estrada de Granja de Pessube

Estrada de Sta Luzia

Rua Corça 80

2nd Avenida de Cintura

Avenida da Unidade Africana

Rua Osvaldo Vieira

Avenida de 14 Novembro

Avenida Caetano Semedo (Estrada de Bor)

Avenida Domingos Ramos

Avenida Pansau Na Isna

Bissau

0   50   100 m

Avenida Francisco Mendes

Rua 16

Avenida Amilcar Cabral

Rua de São Tomé

Old Stadium

Rua 16

Rua de Angola

Rua 12

Rua Eduardo Mondlane

Rua do Brazil

Rua Justino Lopes

Rua Diaz

Victorino Costa

Avenida do 3 de Agosto

Rua Mouta

Rua Guerra Mendes

Avenida do 3 de Agosto

Port

Avenida do 3 de Agosto

To Tennis
Court & New
Stadium

Ferry to Bubaque

Ferry to Bolama

Ferry to Enxude

blocks north-east of the cathedral, where a single or double with air-con and shower costs 165,000 pesos. The toilets are filthy, and the restaurant is nothing special, but the terrace is nice for drinks. French is spoken.

Nearby, the *Pensão Centrale* (☎ 213270), at 8 Avenida Amilcar Cabral, has been a favourite for many years. Clean rooms (single or double) cost 250,000 pesos, negotiable if you stay for three nights or more. Some travellers have reported being overcharged, so confirm the price when you check in by asking the old lady who runs the place to write it down. Apart from that, the only problem is that there are just eight rooms and the place is often full. The restaurant is reasonable (see Places to Eat).

Also in this price range is the *Hotel Caracol* (☎ 213227), at 25 Avenida Caetano Semedo (also called Estrada de Bor), about one km west of Mercado de Bandim, where singles/doubles are 160,000/240,000 pesos. The staff are friendly, and filling meals in the restaurant cost 25,000 pesos.

Top of this range is the *Aparthotel Jordani* on Avenida Pansau Na Isna, opposite the Grande Hotel, where clean good quality self-contained singles/doubles cost US$40/55.

Places to Stay – top end

The *Sheraton* (☎ 251251, fax 251152; cards AE, D, V), on Avenida 14 de Novembro, four km from the centre towards the airport, is Bissau's best hotel. Rooms cost US$90/100 for singles/doubles with air-con including tax. There is a lively bar, a stand-by generator, shops, magazine stand, car rental, and a swimming pool (for guests only).

The *Hotel 24 de Setembro* (☎ 221026, fax 221033; cards AE, V), one km north of the centre, is a better deal. Rooms cost US$28 to US$80 for singles, and US$70 to US$110 for doubles with air-con, including breakfast and tax. There are only four cheap single rooms at US$28 – other rooms are larger and have air-con and refrigerators. The restaurant is excellent and the patio bar is pleasant.

Places to Eat – cheap & middle range

Street food in Bissau is limited to peanuts,

deep-fried dough-balls and sardine sandwiches around the central market and Mercado de Bandim, where there's also a few coffee and bread stalls. At the bus park you'll find a couple of basic eating houses offering coffee, bread and cheap bowls of rice and sauce. Also cheap is the un-named hole-in-the-wall round the back of the Grande Hotel; you may need to order a few hours in advance here. Nearby is *Confeitaria Dias & Dias*, a bakery where you can buy fresh bread and pastries to take away. Also cheap is the scruffy *Pensão Luar* where beef and chips is 20,000 pesos and smaller meals half that. For Lebanese chawarmas at 20,000 pesos go to the snack bar by the central market or to *Restaurant Le Cedre* (see Places to Eat - more expensive).

The restaurant at the *Pensão Centrale* offers a three-course Portuguese meal (soup, main dish and banana) for 30,000 pesos. It's open evenings from 7.30 to 9 pm. Beers are 8000 pesos and wine is 30,000 pesos a bottle. It's one of the best deals in town, although the meals are sometimes cold.

The *Café Universal* on Praça Ché Guevara is an old restaurant with a workers' atmosphere and relatively low prices – meals for 20,000 to 30,000 pesos and beers for 10,000 pesos. Nearby, the *snack bar* at the French Cultural Centre does breakfast for 10,000 pesos, or coffee and cake for 15,000 pesos.

Other options include the *Pensão Regona*, an unmarked blue building north of the central area on 2nd Avenida de Cintura, with good three-course meals for 40,000 pesos. Also worth trying is *Restaurant Atendona*, under the water tower at the junction of Aves do Brazil and Francisco Mendes, with full meals for 40,000 pesos and snacks such as omelette for 20,000 pesos. Nearby, on Avenida de Unidade Africana, *Restaurant Delas Africana* has similar food and prices. Also in this range is *La Bodeguita* opposite the Guinea embassy.

Bissau has a few supermarkets, selling mainly imported items from other West African countries and Europe. A good one is in the centre is under the Pensão Centrale.

Places to Eat – more expensive

The smart *Gelataria Baiana*, a sidewalk café

on Praça Ché Guevara, serves ice cream, sandwiches, pastries and coffee. Nearby, the even smarter *Bar Galeon* serves Western-style meals such as hamburger and chips for around 40,000 pesos. For full-scale meals try *Restaurant Trópico* on Rua Osvaldo Vieira, which has a pleasant garden setting, main dishes around 40,000 pesos to 50,000 pesos, and beers at 10,000 pesos. During the day the indoor snack bar serves cheaper meals, such as omelette and chips for 35,000 pesos. With similar prices but better food is *Asa Branca* on Rua Justino Lopes.

The *Bate Papo* at the western end of Rue Eduardo Mondlane has coffee and croissants for 15,000 pesos, snacks for around 30,000 pesos and meals from 45,000 pesos. Similar in choice and price is *Gelataria Italiana* at the southern end of Avenida do Brazil.

Another place to try is *Casa Santos*, which has air-con and main dishes in the 50,000 to 60,000 pesos range. It's a white unmarked house, just off the road to the Hotel 24 de Setembro, about 200 metres south of the hotel, near the Arab-Libyan Cultural Centre, and open to 11 pm every day except Sunday. Also out of the city centre is *Restaurant Le Cedre* on Avenida Caetano Semedo, between Mercado de Bandim and the Hotel Caracol, where excellent meals start at 50,000 pesos.

The most expensive place in town is *Restaurant Orango* at the Sheraton where main dishes start at 100,000 pesos, but the all-you-can-eat breakfast for 50,000 pesos is worth the splurge. The *Hotel 24 de Setembro* has an excellent fancy restaurant with air-con and an elaborate menu. Most main dishes are in the 70,000 to 90,000 pesos range. For French food, try *Restaurant Franco* on Avenida de 14 Novembro about 500 metres east of the Sheraton, where dishes start at 70,000 pesos.

Entertainment

Bars One of the cheapest bars in the city centre is *Bar Noë*, an unmarked dive opposite the Guinean embassy. Much better, and only slightly more expensive, is the *Café Universal* at the other end of the same street, where beers are 8000 pesos. Another in the same category

is the terrace of the Grande Hotel on Avenida Pansau Na Isna. Or try the *Bar Je T'aime*, almost opposite the Grande, next to the Aparthotel Jordani. The best place for a reasonably priced beer, coffee or snack and some decent people-watching is the *Confeitaria Imperio* on the Praça dos Heróis Nacionais.

The most up-market bar in the heart of town is *Bar Galeon*, on Praça Ché Guevara, near the Café Universal. It's like a smart British pub, and sometimes has live music. Those with money to spare seem to head for the lively piano bar at the *Sheraton*, or the shady patio of the *Hotel 24 de Setembro*, which probably has the nicest outdoor setting for a drink.

Nightclubs City centre nightclubs include: *Club Manila* on Avenida Domingos Ramos, a block south of the US embassy, which is reckoned to be the best, not least because it has air-con; the *Pelicano Disco*, on the eastern end of Avenida 3 de Agosto; and the *Tabanca*, on the corner of Rua 14 and Rua Osvaldo Vieira. Here the speciality is Cape Verdean music. Other places worth checking are the *Gap 2000* and *Verda Tropical*, both on 2nd Avenida de Cintura, and the *Cabana* near the Hotel Caracol.

One good choice for music, dancing and drinks is *Ponta Neto*. You'll need wheels to get there, however, because it's eight km from the centre. There's usually dancing after dinner starting around 11 pm. Bring bug repellent because the mosquitoes like to dance too.

Cinema The main cinema is in the centre on Avenida Amilcar Cabral, 100 metres south of the Praça dos Heróis Nacionais.

Things to Buy

Artisan Goods Woodcarvings are sold at pavement stalls around the central market and outside the Pensão Centrale. Most stuff is souvenir-quality, but there are a few nice pieces to be had.

Music Cassettes are not easy to find; try looking around Mercado de Bandim. Some artists to look out for are listed in the earlier Culture section of this chapter.

Clothes For colourful casual gear, take a look at Jimmy's Shop, probably Bissau's first boutique for a long time, in the narrow streets near the port.

Getting There & Away

Air There are no flights between Bissau and upcountry towns. Details on flights to/from Bubaque Island are in that section. For details on regional flights between Bissau and other West African destinations, and international flights to/from Europe (and departure tax), see the main Getting There & Away section in this chapter

Airlines represented in Bissau include: Air Bissau (TAGB) (☎ 212801), on the corner of Ruas Vitorino Costa and Osvaldo Vieira, it also represents Air Senegal and EAS; Aeroflot (☎ 212707), on Rue Mbana; and TAP Air Portugal (☎ 213993) on Praça dos Heróis Nacionais.

Bush Taxi & Bus All bush taxis and minibuses out of Bissau leave from the main garage on Avenida de 14 Novembro, about two km west of the Mercado de Bandim. During the morning, there's a minibus every hour or so to Bafatá (20,000 pesos) and Gabú (30,000 pesos), and two or more bush taxis to São Domingos and Ziguinchor in Senegal (see the main Getting There & Away section).

Car Tupi Rent-A-Car (☎ 211070, fax 21-5413) at the Sheraton is the only car-rental agency in Guinea-Bissau. For its cheapest vehicle, a Peugeot 205, you'll pay US$50 per day plus US$0.50 per km, or US$72 per day with unlimited km, plus US$7 per day for insurance and 10% tax.

If you need a car for a day or more, instead of renting one, consider negotiating an all-day rate with a taxi driver; it's likely to come out much cheaper. This may take some talking because few drivers have experience hiring themselves out on this basis. Those hanging around the Sheraton may have done this but they're sure to charge more. It'll be easier for the driver to calculate the price if you agree to pay separately for the petrol.

Boat Guinea-Bissau's ferries are operated by Rodofluvial. Sailing days and times are posted in their office near the port on Avenida do 3 de Agosto. For more details on the ferries to Bubaque, Enxudé, Bolama and Catio, see Getting There & Away in the relevant sections.

Getting Around

To/From the Airport Taxis meet all scheduled flights, and charge anything from US$5 to US$40 into town (10 km). To get a shared taxi or bus into town, walk 700 metres from the airport to the roundabout at the start of Avenida de 14 Novembro, the highway into the city. Going to the airport, a private taxi is 50,000 pesos, a shared taxi is about 10,000 pesos, or the bus is 2000 pesos.

Bus The Bissau city bus company is called Paragem. All rides cost 2000 pesos. Most useful for visitors are the buses running along Avenida de 14 Novembro between the airport and city centre, passing the bus park and the Mercado de Bandim.

Taxi Taxis are painted blue and white, and are plentiful. A private hire should cost about 10,000 pesos for a short ride across town, but check the price with the driver before getting in. Some negotiation may be necessary.

Shared taxis are relatively cheap and easy to use: stand by the side of the road in the direction you want to go and shout your destination as the taxi passes. If it's going that way it'll stop. Fares vary according to the distance: about 2000 pesos for every one or two km, so a shared taxi from the centre to the Sheraton should cost 5000 pesos.

AROUND BISSAU
Quinhámel

Those with transport might consider a trip to the village of Quinhámel, west of Bissau along a reasonable dirt road. Some people in Bissau will tell you there's a great beach there. There's no such thing; just a river estuary and hectares of mud. But if you wander around the pathways, you'll see people living in traditional huts whose lifestyle has been almost totally untouched by the 19th century, let alone the 20th. If you come here, please do not take photographs.

When you've finished wandering around, call in at the village's only bar and restaurant. The village is right out in the sticks but the restaurant, run by a remarkable Portuguese couple (who lived here in colonial times and returned after the war of liberation), can put on the most delicious meal of oysters, fish & chips and salad you've ever tasted. And all for far less than you'll pay in Bissau. They also have cold beer and wine at reasonable prices. It's rare to come across a gem like this but good to see that some people positively prefer to forgo the 'wonders' of modern society and opt for life in the bush.

The Islands

The Bijagos Archipelago is the group of islands off the coast of Guinea-Bissau.

Several are uninhabited, while others are home to small fishing communities that are rarely, if ever, visited by foreigners. The islands that are easiest to reach are: Bubaque, which has some wonderful beaches and a fledgling tourist infrastructure; Galinhas, where facilities are more limited; and Bolama, where they're nonexistent.

BOLAMA

Bolama Island is near the mainland about 40 km south of Bissau. The island's main town, also called Bolama, was the country's capital during early colonial days, but it has been slowly crumbling away since 1941 when everything was transferred to Bissau. Architecture buffs will find the **old buildings** interesting, and the island is reported to be a great place to bring a bicycle as you can travel from one end of the island to the other and enjoy the nearly deserted **beaches** along the way. Other travellers have managed to hire mobylettes in Bolama. The closest

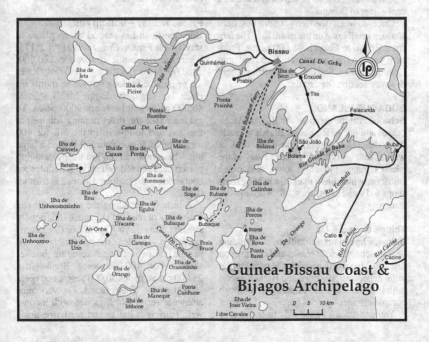

Guinea-Bissau Coast & Bijagos Archipelago

beach is about four km south of Bolama, but the best beaches are along the far south-western end of the island, about 20 to 25 km from Bolama. You'll have to try hitching a ride to get to them unless you want to take a long hike. On your way, you'll realise that Bolama is fairly isolated. For some residents, you may be the first foreigner they've met.

There's no place to stay. Some travellers camp out, but if you're friendly with the locals, you may be invited to stay with someone. If you're given food and lodgings you should pay the going rate (ie what you'd pay in a basic hotel).

Getting There & Away

The ferry for Bolama leaves Bissau every Tuesday and Saturday and returns the following day. For times, check at the Rodofluvial office on Avenida do 3 de Agosto, opposite the port. The fare is 30,000 pesos each way. If you miss it you can catch the ferry to Enxudé every day (except Sunday) from where you can catch a bush taxi to São João 32 km away and then a canoe over to Bolama.

Once a week the ferry continues onto Catio, a small town on the mainland. The fare from Bissau to Catio is 45,000 pesos. From here you can find transport to Buba and onto Boké in Guinea. See the main Getting There & Away section for details.

BUBAQUE ISLAND

Bubaque is at the centre of the Bijagos Archipelago and one of the easiest islands to reach. It's a delightful place to pass a few days or weeks, with a choice of places to stay in the island's main (and only) town, also called Bubaque, which has a market, a bakery, some shops and small cafés, a post office and a police station.

Things to See & Do

Bubaque has an **art exhibition**, in a building near the church, with masks and carvings on display. Also worth a look is the **president's villa**, in between the town and Hotel Bijagos, built in an adventurous offset style, although completely incongruous here.

You can take a canoe ride to the nearby

islands, or walk through the forest, palm groves and fields around the town. But most visitors come for the **beaches**: there's a little one near the Hotel Bijagos that's fairly quiet. Much better is Praia Bruce (Bruce Beach) at the southern end of the island, about 18 km from Bubaque town. The hotel provides a shuttle bus to this beach when there's sufficient demand and nonguests can take it if they pay. The return fare is 20,000 pesos per person (with a minimum four people). Otherwise you'll have to walk or negotiate a ride with drivers in the village. Some travellers have managed to hire bikes. The road to the beach is rideable with a hard surface of shells and cement. Expect to pay around 50,000 pesos a day.

Before you go to any beach, check the tides. When it's low the sea is miles away and you'll have to wade through thigh-deep mud to get a swim. The Pension Cadjoco (see below) has a tide-table. Also be on the lookout for stingrays; coming in contact with their blade-like tails can be extremely painful.

Places to Stay – bottom end

Bubaque town has several cheap places to stay. One is *Pensão Cruz Pontez* (☎ 821135) where single/double rooms are 120,000/ 140,000 pesos, including breakfast. Rates are negotiable for long stays. The rooms are clean but strangely damp. Meals start at 40,000 pesos and beers are 9000 pesos. To get there take the street running south from the port and follow it up the hill for 400 metres or so. It's on your left behind a large hut. The owner Paulino is a happy outgoing person, and can tell you about schedules for boats back to the mainland as well as to other islands.

A little further along the same street (by now dusty or muddy) you reach the friendly *Pension Cadjoco* (☎ 821192), or Chez Patricia, where very clean rooms (for one or two people) with nets and separate bucket showers cost 100,000 pesos. Breakfast is 25,000 pesos, meals 50,000 pesos, and beers 10,000 pesos. This place has a very nice ambience set in a lush garden with its own well. Patricia is Italian and her home-made

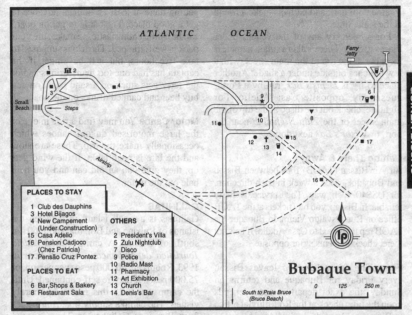

PLACES TO STAY

1 Club des Dauphins
3 Hotel Bijagos
4 New Campement
    (Under Construction)
15 Casa Adelio
16 Pension Cadjoco
    (Chez Patricia)
17 Pensão Cruz Pontez

PLACES TO EAT

6 Bar, Shops & Bakery
8 Restaurant Saia

OTHERS

2 President's Villa
5 Zulu Nightclub
7 Disco
9 Police
10 Radio Mast
11 Pharmacy
12 Art Exhibition
13 Church
14 Denis's Bar

Bubaque Town

0   125   250 m

*South to Praia Bruce
(Bruce Beach)*

ATLANTIC   OCEAN

Ferry
Jetty

Small Beach   Steps

Airstrip

GUINEA-BISSAU

seafood pizzas are the best! Boat trips to neighbouring islands can be arranged for the day, or longer if you have camping gear. The only minus point: there's a monkey tied to a tree in the garden.

Another place in the same price bracket is *Casa Adelio* (☎ 821126/7). It's near the church, and run by Luis Paulo Ines (known as Cacho), but was closed in 1994. It may reopen and be worth checking if the other places are full.

Places to Stay – top end

The *Hotel Bijagos* (☎ 821144) has single/double rooms in self-contained bungalows with fans for 155,000/180,000 pesos (an extra 65,000 pesos for air-con), including breakfast, which is good value for what you get. Meals range from 35,000 to 50,000 pesos and beers are 10,000 pesos. In quiet periods, rates are negotiable. We heard from two travellers who got their own air-con bungalow with breakfast and evening meal

for 100,000 pesos. The hotel is about two km from the town near the airstrip. If the hotel knows you're coming, they'll send a car to pick you up.

Places to Eat

Apart from the hotel and pensãos, try *Restaurant Saia*, a French-Senegalese operation on the street between the port and the police station. Meals are in the 40,000 to 70,000 pesos range. For cheaper fare, in the town centre is a shop selling bread and coffee, which will serve evening meals of fish and rice if you order during the day. You'll also find fresh food and bread in the market, and a limited supply of tinned food in the shops.

Entertainment

It's no joke – there are things to do on this island besides lounge in the sun. For starters there's a football field near Casa Adelio. If you turn up in the late afternoon, you can join a game until dark and perhaps make a friend at the same time.

For a beer, try any of the venues under Places to Stay. There's also a small, nameless local bar at the top of the main street, with a few benches outside under a shade. Another place to try is *Denis's Bar*, run by a Portuguese guy, opposite Casa Adelio. For nightlife, check out the disco at the top of the main street or the *Zulu Nightclub* near the port, or *Victor's Bar* next door.

Getting There & Away

Air Air Bissau (TAGB) flies between Bissau and Bubaque, once a week in each direction, for US$40 each way. The service is fairly reliable. In Bissau, you buy tickets at the TAGB office on Rua Osvaldo Vieira. In Bubaque the TAGB rep lives next to Casa Adelio. If he's not there, check in Denis's Bar opposite.

Ferry The ferry *Sambuia* leaves Bissau every Friday for Bubaque and returns on Sunday; the exact departure time depends upon the tide: check at the Rodofluvial office in Bissau on Avenida do 3 de Agosto, opposite the port. The one-way cost is 40,000 pesos on the lower deck, where you sit on the cargo under a large tarpaulin, or 50,000 pesos on the upper deck, which has benches and a proper sunroof. Tickets are sold from a small booth at the port gates. It's worth getting there at least an hour in advance to get a good place. The battle to get on board can be a little enthusiastic, so make sure your pack is well strapped. The trip is supposed to take five hours, but it'll be longer if the captain has had one too many drinks and/or the ferry gets stuck on a sand bar. You can buy beer and canned drinks on the boat.

Motor Canoe You may find a ride in one of the large motorised dugout canoes which occasionally make the trip. These are slow and the fare is negotiable. If the wind gets up, they give you an old can and you help bale out the water.

GALINHAS

Galinhas is a small island in between the islands of Rubane and Bolama, about 60 km south of Bissau. A camp called *Aldeia Touristica de Ambancana* opened here in 1993. Rooms are 50,000 pesos per person, or 75,000 pesos if they're self-contained. Until the camp was built this island was rarely visited. The camp's supply boat *Amor* goes from Bissau to Galinhas on Thursday and returns Sunday. The boat is small and you'll get wet from the spray in choppy conditions. Sometimes it meets the big boat going to/from Bubaque and you have to transfer from one to the other: quite an effort in a swell. The camp relies on the supply boat for

---

Other Islands

If you could get to some of the other islands of the Bijagos Archipelago, you would find them almost completely untouched by modern civilisation: even tin cans and plastic containers are a rarity. Some sailing-boat operators who cater for tourists have caught on to these islands and head towards them from The Gambia. Foreigners descending on them would surely destroy their culture.

These islands are beautiful, and the people's customs are also very interesting. On one island they are superstitious about the dead and the cadaver is put into a canoe and sent to another island, so that no dead are buried on the island and the spirits do not haunt them. The deceased's family is expected to make regular trips to the spirit island with supplies to nourish the dead.

On Canhabaque and several other islands, as soon as a young girl reaches puberty the young men venture forth with as much cãna and as many sacks of rice as they can afford in hope of buying their way into her favour. She chooses one suitor, but if she's not pregnant within a year, or if she tires of him, or if a well-stocked successor makes a better bid, she can get rid of him and choose another. When she does get pregnant the man usually stays around only until she gives birth, and then he returns to his home and becomes eligible again for other liaisons. Children take the mother's name, and are rarely able to identify their father. ■

everything. There are no shops or markets on the island, so occasionally they run out of things. But it's a very friendly and interesting place: we've heard from people who went for a few days and stayed for 10. More details are available in Bissau from the Electrodata photocopy shop near the Shell station, 100 metres from the port.

The Mainland

BAFATÁ

Outside the capital, Bafatá is one of Guinea-Bissau's largest towns with about 10,000 inhabitants. It's a quiet place on a hill by a river, with some narrow streets of old Portuguese-style houses and shops. Don't miss the **bookshop** with its window full of dusty Marxist tomes. For a place to stay, your only choice seems to be *Apartmento Gloria*, near a bar and disco of the same name, a few streets back on the right side of the main road as you come in from Bissau. Basic rooms are 50,000 pesos. Facilities include bucket showers and oil lamps. For food, there's a snack bar at the empty swimming pool *(piscina)* near the

market, or try *Restaurant Cassumai* next to the church. Buses to Bissau (20,000 pesos) or Gabú (10,000 pesos) depart from the garage at the bottom of the hill, near the market. Several go in the morning and a few in the afternoon. One traveller apparently hired a bike in Bafatá and cycled through fields, villages and 'beautiful jungle' to reach a ruined Portuguese outpost called Géba.

BULA

Bula is a small 'junction town' where the road to Canchungo and Cacheu branches off the main road between Bissau and São Domingos. There's a market, some shops and one bar-restaurant on the main street which has simple rooms for 50,000 pesos. If you switch transport here, note that the junction itself is about one km outside the town towards Bissau: it's a big triangle of grass with trees in the middle. Make sure you stand in the right place or you'll miss half the traffic going your way.

CACHEU

Cacheu (CASH-ay-you) is a small coastal town about 100 km north-west of Bissau. From the 16th to 18th centuries, this was the centre of Portuguese slave-trading operations on the West African coast. More recently, the town was an important ferry-crossing point on the main route between Ziguinchor and Bissau, but since the new road was built via Ingore, the ferry to São Domingos no longer runs, and the town seems to be fading into insignificance. Nevertheless, its quiet and friendly ambience makes it worth a visit if you've got a few days to spare.

On the shore there's a ruined **fort**, dating from the slave-trade era. Sir John Hawkins and Sir Francis Drake were repulsed by the Portuguese in 1567 during their attempt to capture slaves here. You can visit the fort and see the cannons still in place. There's also some large **bronze statues** of figures, possibly including Lenin and Prince Henry the Navigator, with snapped limbs and torsos, stacked in a corner and seemingly forgotten.

1 Swimming Pool & Bar
2 Bus Park & Market
3 Correio (Post Office)
4 Petrol Station
5 Church
6 Restaurant Cassumai
7 Hospital
8 Pharmacy
9 Apartmento Gloria
10 Stadium

To Gabú

To Bissau

Bafatá

0   125   250 m

GUINEA-BISSAU

Places to Stay & Eat

The relatively modern, and rarely used, *Hotel Baluarte* has very decent self-contained double rooms for 108,000 pesos, although prices seem negotiable. For food, there's a small eating house with a thatched shelter next to the port office. Meals have to be ordered in advance but are very good value. They also sell beer.

Getting There & Away

To reach Cacheu from Bissau, take a minibus to Canchungo (30,000 pesos). There are normally one or two minibuses from Bissau to Canchungo between 7 and 9 am, and the journey takes between three and five hours depending on the ferry. From Canchungo to Cacheu (29 km) pick-ups charge 6000 pesos. Going the other way, pick-ups leave very early from Cacheu to connect with the first minibus from Canchungo to Bissau.

If you want to avoid backtracking you can charter a motor boat at the fish factory to take you to São Domingos. This costs about 750,000 pesos and the trip takes from one to two hours depending on the tide. Alternatively you can try hiring a dugout canoe. The

asking price is half that of a motor boat, but with hard bargaining you should be able to get it lower.

You other option is a sea-going pirogue to Banjul. See the main Getting There & Away section of this chapter for details.

CANCHUNGO

If you're travelling between Bissau and Cacheu by bush taxi or minibus, you'll have to change vehicles here. The centre of everything is the praça (square), ringed by shops, cheap restaurants and market stalls. It's also the transport hub of this part of the country: as well as minibuses to/from Bissau (30,000 pesos) you can get Senegalese Peugeot 504s to/from Ziguinchor (90,000 pesos or the equivalent in CFA). For lodging, one of the restaurants (nameless) has basic but adequate rooms for 25,000 pesos. The Banco Central is the only bank in Canchungo, and will change money, but they prefer cash and are very slow. Drivers in the praça will also change money.

ENXUDÉ

For a glimpse of rural village life with little evidence of the 20th century, take a short trip

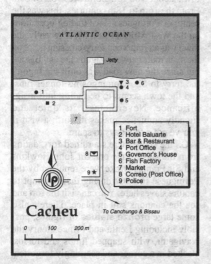

to Enxudé (en-SHOU-day), just across the river from Bissau. The ferry runs daily except Sundays, stays an hour then returns; the one-way fare is 20,000 pesos. For information on the times, enquire at the Rodofluvial office. If you miss the ferry back, negotiate with a canoe owner to take you across. For onward travels, it's possible to catch a bush taxi from here to Buba, where you can try your luck at finding a vehicle to Boké in Guinea. (See the main Getting There & Away section.)

FARIM

Farim is near the border with Senegal, to the north-east of Bissau. If you get caught here try the *Casa Miranda* or the unmarked pensão on the main street. There's usually a minibus from Bissau to Farim, leaving between 7 and 9 am, and the journey takes about three hours. If you're headed for Tanaf (Senegal), bush taxis go from the market place in Farim, on a fill-up-and-go basis, although you've got more chance of the vehicle filling in the morning. The border closes at 6 pm.

GABÚ

Gabú is in the east of the country, a 200-km four-hour bush taxi ride from Bissau. It's a lively town, with a decent market and electricity virtually 24 hours a day. It's also a major transport hub for the eastern part of the country and for the neighbouring parts of Guinea and Senegal.

Places to Stay & Eat

One of the best deals is the *Pensão Miriama Sago*, in the centre near the market, where fairly basic rooms cost 65,000 pesos. Meals need to be ordered in advance. A step up in quality is the French-run *Hotel Suigt* (☎ 511255), a hunting camp also called Bissau-Caca or Campement Réné, where clean basic rooms cost 125,000 pesos. There is also the pleasant *Hotel Madina Boé* (☎ 51236), set in a shady palm grove on the edge of town, with double self-contained bungalows with a tin roof (hot in the dry season and noisy in the rain) for 100,000 pesos or with thatch

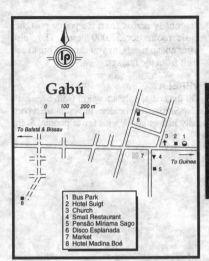

Gabú

0   100   200 m

To Bafatá & Bissau ←

To Guinea →

1 Bus Park
2 Hotel Suigt
3 Church
4 Small Restaurant
5 Pensão Miriama Sago
6 Disco Esplanada
7 Market
8 Hotel Madina Boé

(cool but leaky) for 150,000 pesos, although room rates are negotiable. The hotel has a restaurant with meals from 40,000 pesos and beers at 7500 pesos. Apart from the hotels already listed, you can get street food around the market. There's also a small nameless restaurant between the market and Pensão Miriama Sago. For a drink and a meal (and a dance at weekends) try the *Bar-Restaurant-Disco Esplanada* near the market.

Getting There & Away

The garage is on the east side of town. Minibuses to Bissau (30,000 pesos) go about once an hour between 7 am and noon. There may also be one or two afternoon departures. If you're aiming for Guinea, ask around here or the market for trucks or pick-ups to Koundara and, less frequently, to Koumbia and Boké (see the Getting There & Away section at the start of this chapter for details). You can also find vehicles to Kolda and Velingara in Senegal.

SÃO DOMINGOS

Most travellers pass through the border town of São Domingos without stopping overnight, but if you are stuck here the *Hotel Yal*, diagonally across from the police post, has basic rooms for 55,000 pesos. They also offer cheap meals, or you can buy bread and fruit from the market.

VERELA

On the coast, only a few km from Senegal's Cap Skiring, the beaches in Verela are reportedly just as good, with fewer people. Some travellers camp on the beach. Others find a room with a local person or splash out at the new *Aparthotel Jordani*, owned by (and the same price and style as) its namesake in Bissau. There's a small restaurant, and bread and fruit are available in the village. A bush taxi comes here from São Domingos most days. There are plans for more small hotels here, so be prepared for changes in the future.

Liberia

REPUBLIC OF LIBERIA

Area: 111,370 sq km
Population: 2.9 million
Population Growth Rate: 3.4%
Capital: Monrovia
Head of State: Prof David Kpomakpor, Chairman of Transitional Council of State
Official Language: English
Currency: Liberian dollar
Exchange Rate: L$1 = US$1
Per Capita GNP: US$200
Inflation: 100%
Time: GMT/UTC

During the 1980s, Liberia seemed to be on a path of self destruction. In 1990, it did self-destruct, with the biggest blood bath in its history. While civil war raged, some 750,000 refugees fled to neighbouring countries. In the end, the corrupt president, Samuel Doe, received exactly what he had given to the president of Liberia, and 13 members of his cabinet, 10 years before – an ignominious execution; rebel troops then paraded his dismembered body through the streets of Monrovia. By 1994 with two rebel factions vying for control, the country was still in a mess, with no prospect of the conflict being resolved – and no travellers. However, at the end of that year the government and rebel factions led by Charles Taylor signed a peace agreement. A similar accord in 1993 didn't hold. If this one does, visiting the country may once again become possible.

When travel to Liberia revives, you may hear that there is nothing of interest to see or do here, that it rains all the time, and that there are blackouts almost daily in Monrovia. Only the last point is entirely true. Liberia has some beautiful old mansions built during the first part of the 19th century which resemble those in the southern USA. In the north, hills reaching up more than 1000 metres provide a refreshing climate for hiking and weekend excursions. If it's adventure in the tropical forests you're seeking, there's nothing to beat travel in upcountry Liberia. You may have your first taste of bush rat, see an adolescent's initiation rite, or wander upon a pygmy hippo, about the size of a pig and unique to Liberia and western Côte d'Ivoire. Liberia also has its fair share of precious masks and other wooden carvings as well as some of the best baskets in West Africa.

Still, even before the horrible events of 1990, Liberia, a relatively small country, had less markets, traditional music and costume, and transport (especially upcountry) than

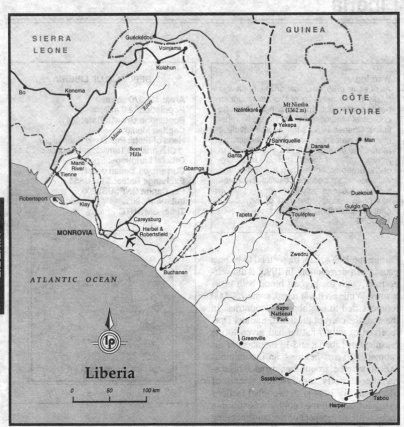

Liberia

0   50   100 km

Suggested Itineraries
The people in **Monrovia** are known for their friendliness, so while the city itself may not have any sites of great interest, it's a good place to explore for a few days and get to know Liberians. When the country's political situation returns to normal, it should be possible once again to travel around the country. Certainly the most interesting excursion would be to **Sapo National Park** and if the Peace Corps should return to Liberia, the volunteers are likely to re-establish the logistical links for making this possible. A few days at **Robertsport,** sun bathing on the beach, going out with the fisher people and exploring the village, can be interesting. The same is true of **Harper** but getting there takes several days. Afterwards you'll want to spend a few days exploring the interior, especially the area around **Mt Nimba**, which has always been the best area for hiking. ■

many other African countries. It also does get very wet from May to October, with about 4650 mm of rainfall a year.

What makes Liberia special is the people. Many foreigners find Liberians easier to meet than other Africans, perhaps because of their historical ties with the USA. Liberians are known for their zest for living and sense of humour, plus food and beer (look for the Club label) unsurpassed in West Africa. So maybe it's not surprising that Liberia has produced a wide spectrum of opinions, from 'It's a screwed up country with no traditions and nothing of interest to see', to 'I never had a better time in Africa'. Lately, no one could really expect to say the latter, but that may change if conditions improve. Certainly they can't get any worse.

Facts about the Country

HISTORY

Liberia is unique. It is one of only two African countries (the other being Ethiopia) that did not suffer from the yoke of colonialism. Traditionally, it has had the freest press in West Africa, a number of opposition political parties, and the largest commercial fleet of ships in the world (almost all foreign-owned, but registered in Monrovia). And it's the wettest capital city in Africa. Since 1980, it has achieved another distinction – the worst economic nose dive in Africa.

Before 1822, when the first group of Black American settlers arrived, only a few Africans lived in the area because the tropical forests covering almost the entire country were simply too inhospitable. Consequently, no great metropolises had developed.

The settlement of Liberia was sponsored by the American Colonization Society (ACS), which was supported by James Madison and Thomas Jefferson. The project brought together strange bedfellows – Whites who wished to correct the injustices done to Blacks, joining with Whites who just wanted to get rid of them. The Congress enacted legislation designating the ACS as the custodian of Africans who had been rescued by slave-patrolling ships. President Monroe, who couldn't give direct financial aid because of the controversy surrounding the society, instead interpreted this legislation imaginatively to justify funding a 'transit camp' in Africa.

In 1820, two ships with free American Blacks arrived in Sierra Leone but disease killed so many that the expedition failed. A year later, another ship followed. The expedition leaders negotiated with the Bassa chiefs for a 100-km strip of coastal land in present-day Liberia. The price tag came to about US$300 in beads, tobacco, cloth, rum and gunpowder. Proceeding down the coast in early 1822, they took possession of Providence Island, a tiny island between what is now the city centre and the port. Fever and attacks by hostile Africans decimated the original group and many others returned to the USA. Nonetheless, some managed to survive, in part with the assistance of the US navy, and within two years had enacted a constitution.

Independence

The success of the venture prompted several colonisation societies in several states to sponsor similar settlements at present-day Harper and Greenville. After quarrels amongst themselves these eventually merged. By 1846, they wanted independence from the ACS, whose governors were mostly Whites. Liberian leaders drafted a Declaration of Independence and asked a Harvard law school professor to draft a new constitution. He modelled it after the USA's, with an elected president and bicameral legislature. Only citizens of Liberia could own real estate and vote; until 1904 'natives' were not considered to be citizens. The leaders declared independence in 1847 and Joseph Roberts was elected president. Every successive president until 1980 was of American ancestry.

By the mid-19th century, of the 5000 Black Americans who had migrated to Liberia, 2000 had died from tropical diseases; several hundred others returned to the USA. The Americo-Liberians, as they came to be known, though constituting only a tiny fraction

LIBERIA

LIBERIA

of the total population, came to dominate the indigenous peoples – ironic in view of the fact that the colonising societies had intended for the settlers to be a 'civilising' influence.

Curiously enough the Masonic Order, established in the country in 1851, came to be a symbol of Americo-Liberian solidarity, and many political issues were discussed and decided upon in the lodges. Five presidents, starting with Roberts, were grand masters.

Between independence and 1926, when the tyre company Firestone started its plantation at Harbel, Liberia floundered politically and economically, losing 40% of its territory to the British and French during the scramble for colonies in the late 1800s. Economically, Liberia was in sad shape. Its primary exports, coffee and palm oil, were no longer attractive on the world market. Nearly everything, including food, was imported.

Firestone Era
Looking around the globe for a cheaper source of rubber, Firestone ended up with a real coup in Liberia in 1926. It secured one million acres of land at an annual rent of only US$0.06 per acre, with gross income taxed at only 1%. The company employed 20,000 workers, 10 to 15% of Liberia's labour force, though elevating few to management positions. It also built a port and a railroad, and helped to develop the country's hydroelectric potential. Today, this is still the world's largest rubber plantation.

A scandal in the 1930s put Liberia on the front pages. Spanish colonials in Equatorial Guinea had been looking for labourers for their cocoa plantations. Starting in 1905, Liberia had supplied the workers on contract. Village chiefs rounded up young men and supplied them to the contractors; the labourers received no salary until they returned to Liberia. Publishing a scathing report, the League of Nations equated the system to slavery and implicated both the president and vice-president of Liberia as part of the syndicate of Americo-Liberians receiving a cut in the lucrative venture.

Liberia's 'Watergate' ended with both the president and vice-president resigning.

Liberian-American relations were solidified by WW II. The USA built air bases and Black Africa's first truly international airport at Robertsfield, next to Firestone. About 5000 Black American troops were stationed in Liberia during the war and antisubmarine patrols were flown by sea planes based at Lake Piso, near Robertsport. Even Roosevelt landed there, and the US dollar was made official currency. Today, a Voice of America transmitter near Monrovia, a satellite tracking station, landing and refuelling rights for military planes, as well as private investment, strongly motivate the USA to maintain good relations.

The Era of Prosperity & the Coup
For 20 years following the war Liberia sustained the highest growth rate in Black Africa, raising per capita incomes to the highest in West Africa by the early 1960s. Twenty-four American companies joined Firestone in making major investments in Liberia and the total amount rose to US$800 million. Much of the credit went to Liberia's most famous president, William Tubman, president for 27 years and the 'Maker of Modern Liberia'. Nonetheless, the road network was primitive and until 1945 it was not possible to travel by road from Monrovia to Liberia's three neighbouring countries. Only in 1967-68 were Robertsport, Greenville and Harper, all major towns on the coast, connected to Monrovia. Monrovia grew from a sleepy town of 12,000 in 1940 to around 250,000 by 1980.

The 1960s saw the establishment of iron-ore mining operations in the north near Yekepa by Lamco (the Liberian-American Swedish Minerals Company); Yekepa grew from next to nothing to over 20,000 people, and the company became the largest private enterprise in Black Africa. It also built a railroad from Yekepa to Buchanan and a port in Buchanan. Today, Lamco accounts for about half of Liberia's annual iron-ore output; Bong Mining Company, 70 km north of Monrovia, is number two. By the early 1980s, the Lamco ore deposit under exploitation was nearing depletion. Production fell and employees were fired. Still, Liberia remained the largest iron-ore producer in Africa.

The economic boom came to an end in the mid-1970s after Tolbert took over as president from Tubman. While he initiated a series of reforms, the upper levels of government continued to be controlled by about a dozen related Americo-Liberians. Tolbert's brother, brother-in-law and son-in-law were all senators as well as prominent business people. Corruption continued unabated. Officials appropriated government vehicles for their own use, contractors had to pay kickbacks to various levels of government not only to win contracts but just to get paid; the governing Americo-Liberians used the money to enrich themselves and buy support. Extravagant public works projects blew out the budget deficit.

The rice riots in early 1979 were an ominous event. For decades, the government had subsidised rice prices to appease city dwellers. This policy made rice growing unprofitable and brought thousands of people into Monrovia looking for work. Strapped for money, the government decided to raise rice prices by about 20% (from which the Tolbert family, with large-scale rice farms, stood to profit handsomely). As the people rioted, the government closed the university and suspended due process.

In April 1980, a small group of noncommissioned officers led by an unschooled backwoods master sergeant, Samuel Doe, staged a successful coup, killing Tolbert. For the first time Liberia had a chief-of-state who wasn't an Americo-Liberian, giving the indigenous population their first taste of political power, and their first opportunity for vengeance. The 28-year-old Doe shocked the world by ordering 13 ex-ministers to be executed by firing squad on a public beach before TV cameras.

The Doe Decade

Liberia almost immediately went into further decline and Doe did little to halt it. Corruption continued at the same level as during the

Tubman-Tolbert years, except that the government could no longer afford it. For instance, it was alleged that US$900,000 was embezzled by Charles Taylor. Taylor, who headed the government's procurement agency and later became a rebel leader, fled to the USA after being accused. During the '80s, Liberia recorded the worst economic performance in Africa; real incomes fell by half. While the originally slim president got fatter by the day, unemployment in Monrovia rose to 50%. Blackouts became so frequent that only hotels with generators had electricity. Bankrupt and no longer able to repay its debts, the government reduced salaries by a full 25%. By the mid-1980s, the World Bank and the IMF halted their lending programmes.

The only significant donor remaining was the USA, which Doe outfoxed at every turn. He promised to turn the government into a civilian government, but did not. He promised to hold free elections, then rigged them. He promised to get his financial books in order, and faked the reports. And each time he made a promise, the USA, keenly aware of its valuable interests such as the Voice of America transmitter, rewarded him handsomely. During the '80s, the USA gave more aid per capita to Liberia than to any other African country – US$500 million.

Doe held elections as promised in late 1985. During the campaign, he declared ineligible two major opposing political parties. He also threw Amos Sawyer, a well-known former university dean, into jail as a dissident. When one party put up Jackson Doe, a political unknown, and spectators surmised that it was a ploy to confuse the voters, the unknown still polled more than Doe. Ignoring mounds of burnt presidential ballots that were discovered outside the capital, the government declared Samuel Doe the winner. The Reagan administration concurred, the US assistant secretary of state for African affairs telling Congress that the election was 'the beginning, however imperfect, of a democratic experience...' A subsequent coup attempt was foiled by Doe's soldiers who, with Doe nodding approval, cruised around

Monrovia displaying the coup leader's severed testicles. The allegation that Doe's men then proceeded to eat him, as is widely reported, remains unproven. Prince Johnson, a Liberian army lieutenant who had joined the coup attempt, escaped this fate; five years later Johnson would parade around the dismembered Doe.

Soon after the coup, members of Doe's small Krahn tribe, which constitutes only 2% of the country's population, began killing and torturing rival tribespeople, particularly the Gio and Mano in Nimba county. Travellers weren't immune. Undercover police roamed the streets of Monrovia, throwing them in jail on trumped-up charges. By the end of the decade, Doe was being compared to Idi Amin. Even the USA cut him off almost entirely, reducing aid levels to US$10 million a year. Years before, Bethlehem Steel had thrown in the towel and sold its 25% interest in Lamco, but most US companies stuck it out, their investments in Liberia (approximately US$500 million) representing about half of the total foreign investment. Firestone, with around 10,000 workers, remained the largest employer.

Civil War

Charles Taylor, accused in 1984 of stealing US$900,000, while awaiting extradition sawed through the bars of his US jail cell and escaped. As reported in the *International Herald Tribune*, he later bragged to associates that he managed it by bribing prison guards with US$30,000. In the late '80s Taylor ended up in Côte d'Ivoire where, with the secret support of Houphouët Boigny, he began assembling troops (many of whom were of the Gio and Mano tribes) for an invasion. The Ivoirian president's aid was no surprise as he and Tolbert (executed by Doe) were brothers-in-law through the marriage of their children. At the same time, Amos Sawyer, who had escaped the country in 1986, became an exile leader in Washington.

The 'Nimba Revolt' began on Christmas day 1989 when several hundred rebels led by Taylor invaded Nimba County in northeastern Liberia from Côte d'Ivoire. Doe's troops arrived shortly thereafter and indiscriminately killed up to 500 unarmed civilians, raped women and burnt villages. Thousands of civilians began fleeing into Côte d'Ivoire and Guinea; within a month the refugee numbers had swollen to 250,000. Others joined the rebel army, while Doe's troops began to desert. The rebel army numbered an estimated 4000 by May, almost equal to Doe's. Not surprisingly, Doe's tribe became their main target; thousands of Krahn, heading for Sierra Leone to escape the rebel advance, flooded the roads travelling in the opposite direction.

Shortly after the invasion, Prince Johnson of the Gio tribe broke away from Taylor and formed his own rebel forces. Johnson was erratic and volatile, ruling his men by intimidation and fear. But they were potent militarily, more so than Taylor's larger forces. By July 1990, Taylor's 10,000-strong force controlled most of the country, Johnson's 1000 guerrillas had seized most of Monrovia, and Doe was defending himself with his most loyal troops and two hungry lions in a cliff-top mansion. Only 40,000 people remained in Monrovia. Johnson's troops drove through the city spraying bullets and dumping corpses all along the beach. Anybody who didn't speak the right dialect was shot, beheaded or set on fire with fuel oil. Meanwhile two US ships, waiting offshore with a force of marines, did nothing.

In late August, six ECOWAS (Economic Community of West African States) countries sent 3000 troops to Monrovia to try to establish and monitor a cease-fire. Two weeks later, Doe went to their headquarters with less than 100 troops, intending to hold discussions and thinking the peace-keeping forces would protect him. But as Johnson's forces raided the headquarters and killed most of Doe's entourage, the heavily armed peace-keeping troops ducked for cover and watched. As the crowning insult to ECOWAS, Johnson's men drove out of the port with Doe, who was wounded in the leg but still alive. Johnson's troops proceeded to cut off his ears. He died a day later, probably after further torture. The troops then cut up his body and paraded the pieces around the streets of Monrovia, just as his own troops had done to the leader of the 1985 coup.

Liberia Today

After Doe's death both Johnson and Taylor claimed the presidency. But ECOWAS, trying to prevent either rebel movement from achieving absolute power, named as provisional president the exiled dissident, Amos Sawyer, who commands high respect in Liberia and abroad for his integrity. However, the fragile interim government, headed by the erudite Sawyer and backed by ECOWAS, could only control Monrovia and surrounding areas. The rest of the country remained in the hands of Charles Taylor's National Patriotic Front of Liberia (NPFL) troops, with small pockets near the Sierra Leone border in the hands of the United Liberation Movement of Liberia for Democracy (ULIMO), a faction primarily encompassed by former supporters of Samuel Doe. Taylor even set up a 'government' in Gbarnga, which issued its own currency. His army was kept at bay outside a 50-km buffer zone surrounding Monrovia by the 15,000 troops, primarily Nigerian, from the West African intervention force ECOMOG (ECOWAS Monitoring Group). What remained of Johnson's troops were in Monrovia, guarded by the six-nation ECOMOG troops which patrolled the streets. Some 30 nonprofit organisations were working in Monrovia, providing food and health care to the residents. Few refugees returned from neighbouring countries. There were also some 250,000 refugees who had been driven into the northern rain forests by the bloodshed, and it was they, especially the children, who were most at risk of starvation. An estimated 500 children died weekly.

Despite occasional victories by the Nigerian-led ECOMOG forces, Taylor's highly effective but irregular troops were initially able to keep control of the hinterland. The uniform of the average NPFL fighter was a pair of shredded trousers, tennis shoes and a soiled T-shirt. They were not paid and mainly lived off the land. All they needed was a constant supply of bullets and morale. Some soldiers, members of the Small Boy Unit, mostly orphans, were as young as nine years old, with their AK-47 automatic rifles nearly as tall as they were.

However, by late 1992, when Taylor attacked Monrovia, his forces were driven into retreat by the larger and better armed ECOMOG forces, which had Swedish-made artillery and even jet bombers. Thereafter ECOMOG went on the offensive and by early 1993 had taken the key port city of Buchanan, a major blow to Taylor's flagging rebellion. By then more than 150,000 Liberians had been killed in the conflict. A cease-fire agreement was signed later that year and, following elections in early 1994, a transitional government was sworn into office. It failed to last. Despite an agreement, Taylor's troops did not disarm, and the horrors continued. One of the worst was at Carter Camp, an abandoned rubber plantation some 50 km east of Monrovia serving as a refugee camp. Taylor's troops massacred 600 refugees there, mostly women and children, and strewed their dismembered body parts over the grounds. Whether the new peace agreement signed at the end of 1994 will stop all of this is what remains to be seen.

GEOGRAPHY

Liberia is one of the last West African countries with significant rainforests. They can be found all over Liberia and cover an estimated 44% of the total land area. Sapo National Park in eastern Liberia, bounded on the west by the Sinoe River, has some 1250 sq km of virgin forests, making it one of the largest primal rainforests in West Africa. There's also Lofa-Mano National Park on the border with Sierra Leone; it too is predominantly rainforest with significant fauna.

In the far north around Yekepa, you'll find the huge Lamco iron-ore operations and the Nimba mountains, reaching up to 1752 metres. Eleven major rivers empty into the Atlantic Ocean, the biggest being the St Paul, which passes through Monrovia. The water flow on the St Paul can be tremendous, on occasion exceeding one million litres per second in

---

Destruction of Liberia's Forests

With only 2.9 million inhabitants in an area the size of New York state, Liberia hasn't had to worry about the destruction of its forests until now. But shifting cultivation and slash-burn farming methods are wiping out 1% of the country's rainforest annually. As logging concessions build roads to haul out the timber, they give farmers ready access to the cleared areas; the farmers then cut more trees and plant fields of upland rice. After several years, they leave and the area becomes permanent scrub land. Some Liberian conservation experts recommend that farmers be trained in techniques for swamp rice farming. The logging companies also share the blame, having been given over 70% of the total forest area to work in; fortunately, half of this area has not yet been worked. Some environmentalists are now intensifying international pressure to ban the importation of logs from tropical rainforests including Liberia's. ■

August – more than twice the normal flow of the Colorado River in the Grand Canyon.

Large parts of Liberia are still uninhabited or have very scattered populations, especially large sections in the south-east. The narrow coastal plain is intersected by marshes, creeks and tidal lagoons. There's little farming in this area. Five major towns line the coast: Harper, Greenville, Buchanan, Monrovia and Robertsport. Only the last three are connected by a coastal road. To get to the others, you must fly or travel several hundred km inland. Both national parks are also hard to get to.

CLIMATE

Liberia is in the heart of the tropics and Monrovia, on the coast, is one of the two wettest capital cities in Africa (Freetown is the other). Monrovia averages 25 mm of rain a day during the six-month rainy season, May to October. Inland, the average rainfall drops to about half this. The best time to visit is obviously in the dry season. The temperature never gets over 33°C in Monrovia; inland it gets a little hotter.

GOVERNMENT

The government is modelled after that of the USA. It is organised around a popularly elected president and his or her appointed ministers. The popularly elected, American-style Senate and House of Representatives are not presently operating but the independent judiciary theoretically is. The latest interim government was formed in March 1994, replacing a previous one headed by Amos Sawyer. It carefully includes representatives not only of the old government but also of the NPFL and ULIMO. Since joining the government, many former guerrillas have disowned – or been disowned by – the factions they are meant to represent. Some have turned on their former friends and switched sides altogether. Two of Taylor's lieutenants, for example, joined the government with his blessing; since then they have turned around and called for his execution.

The interim government is totally ineffective because of squabbling amongst the various factions. Ministers scarcely talk to one another. Real power is thought by some observers to lie not with the interim government, which controls little outside Monrovia, but with the Nigerian commanders of ECOMOG, whose hatred of Taylor borders on paranoia. Under the new peace accord signed in late 1994, this government may be replaced by still another.

ECONOMY

The economy is in a shambles. Per capita incomes, which were around US$380 before the present rebellion began, have fallen to around US$200, amongst the very lowest in Africa. Also, because of the conflict, starvation by refugees in the countryside is a major problem. Traditional mainstays of the economy besides subsistence agriculture, particularly cassava and rice, have been iron ore, rubber and timber, which represent 60%, 20% and 5%, respectively, of external exports. Liberia is one of the world's largest producers of iron ore, but that sector accounts for only 5% of the workforce. Most Liberians are involved in agriculture and even though foreigners own the largest rubber plantations, smallholders are responsible for over half the total acreage.

POPULATION & PEOPLE

Except during the recent civil war, ethnic groups in Liberia have not put as strong a stamp on the country as they have in other African countries. None of them clearly dominates numerically. The groups most frequently mentioned, ie the Gio and Mano groups in north-eastern Nimba county and Doe's Krahn people in the south-east, constitute only a tiny portion of the population. The Kpelle in the centre and the Bassa around Buchanan are the most numerous, with 19% and 15% of the population, respectively; the Vai in the south-west, the Mandingo in the north, and the seafaring Kru along the coast are also well known. There's been too much intermarriage for any of these tribes to be culturally homogeneous or united into a single political unit.

Americo-Liberians have received most attention because of their political and economic dominance, but they account for less than 3% of the total population (2.9 million). A further disproportionate share of economic power, residing in the hands of Lebanese and Indians, has also been the cause of considerable resentment in the past. Some 5000 or so Lebanese traders used to own shops in Monrovia, vying with Indians for control of the retail trade, but many fled Liberia during the conflict.

RELIGION

Adherents of non-indigenous religions constitute roughly half the population and are split fairly evenly between Christians and Muslims. The settlers, primarily Baptists and Methodists, did little missionary work among the indigenous peoples, leaving that to foreigners. Even within a given denomination, the Americo-Liberian and indigenous congregations did not mix and had separate churches. Membership in a recognised church was related to social position. Before the

Female statuette

Secret Societies

One of the most distinctive features of Liberian culture is the secret societies. Called Poro for men and Sande for women, and centred primarily in the north-west, these are particularly fascinating. Nonmembers cannot attend meetings nor partake in the rituals; decisions are often executed in secrecy. Each has rites and ceremonies whose purpose is to educate young people in the customs of the tribe, preserve the group's folklore, skills and crafts, and instil discipline. Their contribution in preserving traditional ways has been significant.

These societies are not restricted to one particular tribe and, in principle, everyone in the community should be initiated, as uninitiated people would not be able to engage in political and ritual activities. The initiations, which used to involve as much as four years of training, now usually less, take place when the children approach puberty. The initiates are easily recognised by their white painted faces and bodies and their shaved heads, but what they actually do is anybody's guess.

Hierarchies prevail; the most extreme example are the Poro among the Vai, which traditionally had 99 levels. Lower ranking members cannot acquire the esoteric knowledge of higher ranking members or attend their secret meetings. Ascending in the ranks depends on birth (the leadership is frequently restricted to certain families), seniority, and the ability to learn the societies' beliefs and rituals.

The role of these societies has traditionally gone beyond religion and the education of the young. They control the activities of indigenous medical practitioners, and they often judge disputes between members of high-ranking families. A village chief who doesn't have the support of the Poro on important decisions can expect trouble enforcing them. They may even punish people for such things as theft, incest and murder, sometimes by execution. Today, while secret societies are still fairly important among some tribes, modern customs and institutions are undermining them. ■

LIBERIA

1980 coup, some church leaders charged that the typical Americo-Liberian tended to regard the church as if it was a club. Politics and religion were closely meshed and if a person lost political office, they were likely to lose their church office as well. The 1980 coup broke, perhaps forever, this tie between the church and politics.

LANGUAGE

English is the official language while Kpelle and Kru are two of the major African dialects. Almost everybody speaks English but some travellers have difficulty understanding the local version. The following will help you to get started:

dash	bribe
hard to spend	stingy
sweet	delicious (sweet soup)
weak	lazy
straight	immediately
waste	discard (waste the milk)
eat money	embezzle

Facts for the Visitor

As already mentioned, the situation in Liberia is far from stable at the time of writing, and it is impossible to predict whether the peace accord of late 1994 will stop the fighting. In Monrovia the infrastructure in the suburbs was all but destroyed during the fighting, but life in central Monrovia has taken on an air of normality, as many hotels, restaurants and shops have reopened.

The listings given are for places which existed prior to the major upheavals. Expect things to be vastly different – and let us know how it is!

VISAS & EMBASSIES
Liberian Visas

Visas are required of everyone except nationals of some West African countries. In most countries where Liberian embassies are present, embassies charge about US$10 for visas, but for Americans they are free. Regardless of how long your visa is valid for, the exact length of your stay will be determined in Liberia upon entry. In London, the Liberian embassy charges UK£30 for a single-entry visa (UK£60 for a multiple-entry visa) which is valid for 90 days from the day of delivery and good for stays of 30 days (which may be reduced to a lesser duration upon entry). The embassy requires two photos and gives 24-hour service. In addition to two photos and your international health card, the one in Washington may ask for a doctor's certificate proving your good health.

Upon entering Liberia you must report to the Bureau of Immigration on Broad St in Monrovia; the length of your stay will be determined there or at the airport. Bring photos. The immigration office in Monrovia also handles visa extensions. To leave the country you may have to get an exit visa from immigration; if so, bring photos for this too.

From the moment you enter Liberia, you will be asked for 'gifts'. If a military officer escorts you through customs, for example, he'll expect a tip. The immigration office people in Monrovia may want money for their service. One traveller reported some years ago that border officials even charged him US$5 to inspect his luggage! Another was charged the same at the border for an exit stamp in his passport. Hopefully all this will change when the conflict ends.

Liberian Embassies

Belgium (consulate) 336 Ave van Volxem, 1060 Brussels (☎ (02) 344-49-90)

France 8 rue Jacques Bingen, 75017 Paris (☎ (1) 47-63-58-55/47-63-23-85)

Germany Hohenzellerstrabe 73, 5300 Bonn 2 (☎ (0228) 35-23-94)

UK 2 Pembridge Place, London W2 4XB (☎ (0171) 221-1036)

USA 5201 16th St, NW, Washington, DC 20011 (☎ (202) 291-0761)

Liberia also has embassies in Abidjan, Accra, Addis Ababa, Berlin, Cairo, Conakry, Freetown, The Hague, Kinshasa, Lagos, Nairobi, Rome, Stockholm, Tokyo, and Yaoundé. There are also consulates in Madrid, Milan, Montreal, Ottawa and Zürich.

Other African Visas
Because of all the recent turmoil, Liberia is not a good place to get visas to other African countries. When normality returns, you should be able to get visas in Monrovia to all three neighbouring countries as well as Ghana, Nigeria, Burkina Faso and Togo. The French embassy issues visas to the latter two countries. You may also be able to get visas to Mali if the Malian consulate returns.

Foreign Embassies
See the Monrovia Information section for a list of embassies in the capital.

DOCUMENTS
You need a passport and International Vaccination Certificate (showing proof of having a yellow fever vaccination) to enter the country. On arriving in Liberia, you must report to immigration. There may be new or additional requirements, so ask officials upon entering the country. If you plan on taking photographs, you'll also need a permit for this.

Be sure to carry your passport with you at all times because, with so few foreigners in the country, you will stand out and will undoubtedly be asked to produce it everywhere you go. It might also be a good idea to leave a photocopy of it and all other important documents back in your hotel as security is uncertain.

CUSTOMS
There is no restriction on the import and export of local or foreign currency, and there are no currency declaration forms.

MONEY
CFA 1000 = L$4.17
UK£1 = L$1.50
US$1 = L$1.00

The US dollar and the new Liberian dollar are both legal currency. Their official value is identical, but not on the street, where the exchange rate is well over eight Liberian dollars to one US dollar. The US dollar has virtually disappeared as people hoard them when they get their hands on any. Merchants offer discounts to those paying with US dollars. At most hotels, only US dollars are accepted although some of them may allow you to pay for meals with Liberian dollars. You can exchange the two at whatever rate you can get since they're both legal tender. Most people change their money with one of the many Indian or Lebanese shop owners. It is difficult to find small coins, and the five dollar coins and bills aren't helping matters any. Upcountry, a new currency issued by Charles Taylor's 'government' circulates widely but that may soon end.

As of early 1995, many banks in Liberia were still closed so travellers' cheques are virtually useless; bring plenty of cash.

All prices quoted in this chapter are in US dollars.

BUSINESS HOURS & HOLIDAYS
Business hours are weekdays from 8 am to noon and 2 to 4 pm; and Saturday from 8 am to noon. Government offices are open weekdays from 8 am to noon and 1 to 4 pm.

Banking hours are Monday to Thursday from 8 am to noon, and Friday until 2 pm.

Public Holidays
1 January, 11 February, Decoration Day (2nd Wednesday in March), 15 March, Easter Friday, 7 April, 14 May (National Unification Day), 25 May, 26 July (Independence), 24 August, 24 October, 29 October, Liberian Thanksgiving Day (first Thursday in November), 29 November, 25 December.

POST & TELECOMMUNICATIONS
The post in Monrovia has traditionally been fairly reliable.

Long distance calls are by satellite and fairly reasonably priced if you dial station to station. Calling reverse-charges (collect) is also possible. For telexes, try the post office or the Ducor Palace Hotel.

PHOTOGRAPHY
Taking photographs is more problematic in Liberia than in any other West African country. Don't take photos unless you're sure it's OK.

Under Doe, a photo permit was definitely required. In Monrovia, the police questioned anyone seen taking photographs. Those who didn't have permits were escorted immediately to headquarters; some were put in jail for several days and then thrown out of the country.

Traditionally, permits were issued by the Ministry of Information, Cultural Affairs & Tourism (☎ 222229, telex 44249) on Capitol Hill near the presidential palace, and this practice is likely to be resumed whenever conditions normalise. Find out what the current regulations are.

HEALTH

Vaccinations for cholera and yellow fever are both required. The best hospital in Monrovia for emergencies is Elwa Hospital (☎ 271512) in Paynesville.

DANGERS & ANNOYANCES

As of early 1995, travelling overland in Liberia was still impossible. Until Taylor's troops disband, travelling outside Monrovia will continue to be impossible except for those involved in international relief operations whom Taylor allows to pass. Even they, however, meet serious suspicions from the predominantly stoned adolescent rebels who control checkpoints out of Monrovia.

Until conditions change, do not enter the country overland.

Even when Liberia returns to normality, security may continue to be a problem. Pickpockets in Monrovia and the police everywhere were causes for concern in the past.

ACCOMMODATION

Accommodation in Liberia is now extremely limited. In Monrovia, only a few of the former hotels are back in operation. Most are reasonably decent but not cheap, and one, Hotel Africa, used to meet international standards. Outside of Monrovia, the situation is unclear but many of the hotels are undoubtedly closed. Once travel throughout the country becomes possible, it is likely that many places will reopen and that finding a place to stay won't be difficult. However,

virtually all of them are in the lower-end category.

Getting There & Away

AIR

Both Air Ivoire and Air Guinea provide regular services to Monrovia, with four flights a week from Abidjan and two from Conakry. If the peace accord holds, direct flights from Europe may resume.

The airport at Robertsfield (50 km east of Monrovia) is the main international airport but as of early 1995 the old Spriggs-Payne airfield just beyond the Sinkor area was being used for all flights. It's not clear whether the normal US$20 airport tax is being charged there.

LAND
Bush Taxi

Bush taxis are the principal means for getting to Liberia from Côte d'Ivoire, Sierra Leone and Guinea. The routes are outlined in the following Car section.

From the Côte d'Ivoire border you'll have to change in Ganta and maybe Sanniquellie as well.

Car

The road north from Monrovia to Ganta is paved but in bad condition, as is the road east from Monrovia to Buchanan and west from Monrovia towards the Sierra Leone border.

To/From Côte d'Ivoire There is no road east of Buchanan to the border, so the best route in is the road via Man (Côte d'Ivoire), Sanniquellie and Ganta. The road from Monrovia to Abidjan is asphalted for all but the 190-km stretch between Man and Ganta, which is an all-weather dirt road. Monrovia to Man takes about 12 hours.

The other option is to travel west along the coast of Côte d'Ivoire until Harper, and then north from Harper to Ganta via Zwedru. This route is much longer and more difficult. You will almost certainly get stuck on the Harper to Zwedru section in the heavy rainy season from June to October. Monrovia to Harper takes about 15 hours in the dry season.

To/From Guinea It's possible to travel on the coastal route via Sierra Leone, or from the northern border town of Ganta to Nzérékoré (Guinea), only 79 km away. This latter route from Monrovia to Conakry is paved for all but 200 km and is preferable during the rainy season when the eastern stretch in Sierra Leone becomes extremely difficult if not impassable. Monrovia to Nzérékoré takes eight hours.

To/From Sierra Leone During the dry season, you can drive from Monrovia to Freetown in one long day. The coastal road to the border has been largely paved but the onward section in Sierra Leone to Kenema is nearly impassable from July to October. The border closes at 6 pm.

Getting Around

AIR
There are presently no flights within Liberia.

BUSH TAXI & MINIBUS
Virtually all transport was commandeered by the various troops during the fighting.

When conditions return to normal, cars should once again be the most common kind of bush taxi but there may also be pick-up trucks converted into cabs, and a few buses. Bush taxis going north from Monrovia and east towards Buchanan should become plentiful and there may also be several every day from Monrovia to Robertsport and the Sierra Leone border. Heading towards Man, you'll find no taxis going to the border; you'll have to change in Ganta.

The frequent roadblocks are annoying and soldiers are often looking for a bribe.

Monrovia

During the 1980s, travellers rarely had good things to say about Monrovia (population 450,000), which is one of the rainiest capital cities in the world. Now it's a total mess, especially the section south beyond the Executive Mansion (Sinkor etc), as that area was totally thrashed by Taylor's troops. However, since they never reached past the Executive Mansion, the central area is largely intact. Waterside market is again vibrant with lots of goods, and numerous hotels and restaurants have been spruced up and reopened. Bars, cinemas and dancing places on the famous Gurley St and elsewhere have returned to normal. Because of a 7 pm curfew, daytime discotheques have sprung up, belting out rap music. Even school children, in neatly pressed uniforms, make their way to newly reopened schools.

Nevertheless, the scars of battle remain. Shell-pocked tower blocks, in danger of collapse, are home to hundreds of refugees, who continue to flee the dangers of the countryside. They have had no electricity or running water for years. Even when conditions were better, most buildings were in shoddy condition and there was a lack of any interesting stores and very few artisan goods for sale. Its no wonder that for years many travellers have been inclined to strike Monrovia off their list of places to visit.

But if you've come to see and experience the real Africa, Monrovia is certainly that. If you like places with a seedy character don't cross Monrovia off your list. Throughout the older part of town, especially between Broad St and the water, there are three-storey mansions like those in *Gone with the Wind* and all seem to be inhabited by four or five families. The houses have broken window panes, shutters falling off, rusty tin roofs, paint (what little there is) peeling off and clothes strung out everywhere, but if you look carefully you'll see that many of them have doorways and columns as fine as those in the southern USA.

LIBERIA

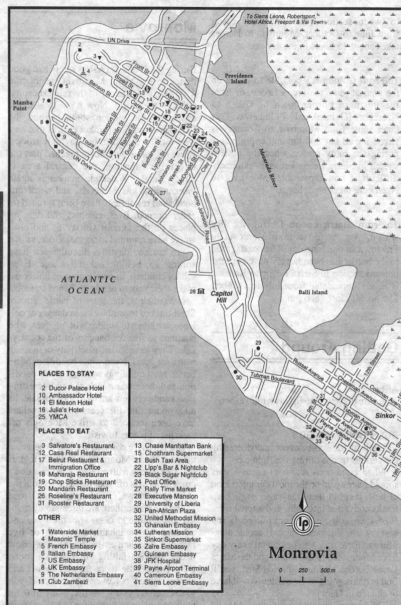

PLACES TO STAY

2 Ducor Palace Hotel
10 Ambassador Hotel
14 El Meson Hotel
16 Julia's Hotel
25 YMCA

PLACES TO EAT

3 Salvatore's Restaurant
12 Casa Real Restaurant
17 Beirut Restaurant & Immigration Office
18 Maharaja Restaurant
19 Chop Sticks Restaurant
20 Mandarin Restaurant
26 Roseline's Restaurant
31 Rooster Restaurant

OTHER

1 Waterside Market
4 Masonic Temple
5 French Embassy
6 Italian Embassy
7 US Embassy
8 UK Embassy
9 The Netherlands Embassy
11 Club Zambezi

13 Chase Manhattan Bank
15 Choithram Supermarket
21 Bush Taxi Area
22 Lipp's Bar & Nightclub
23 Black Sugar Nightclub
24 Post Office
27 Rally Time Market
28 Executive Mansion
29 University of Liberia
30 Pan-African Plaza
32 United Methodist Mission
33 Ghanaian Embassy
34 Lutheran Mission
35 Sinkor Supermarket
36 Zaïre Embassy
37 Guinean Embassy
38 JFK Hospital
39 Payne Airport Terminal
40 Cameroun Embassy
41 Sierra Leone Embassy

Monrovia

0   250   500 m

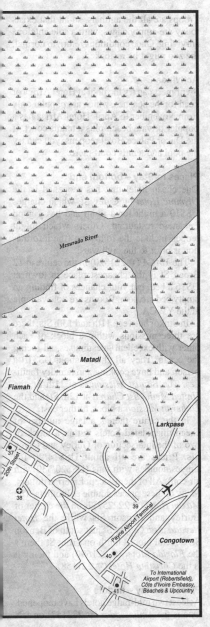

Information

Post & Telecommunications The post office is near the centre of town on Broad St at Warren St. Traditionally the post has been fairly reliable. It is also the cheapest place to make international phone calls (reverse charge (collect) available).

Foreign Embassies The following embassies are near the centre on UN Drive: France (☎ 221122, telex 44360), Italy (☎ 224580, telex 44438), the Netherlands (☎ 221155), the UK (☎ 221055, telex 44287) and the USA (☎ 226370, fax 222450).

The embassies of Nigeria (☎ 261093) and Japan (☎ 262468, telex 44209) are on Tubman Blvd between the centre and Sinkor, while those of Ghana (☎ 261477 at 11th St), Guinea (☎ 261711 at 19th St) and Zaïre (☎ 261326) are in Sinkor.

Several km further out in Congotown, there are four more embassies: Cameroun (☎ 261516), Côte d'Ivoire (☎ 261284), Germany (☎ 261516, telex 44230), Sierra Leone (☎ 261301) and Switzerland (☎ 261-065, telex 4559).

Travel Agencies One or more of the following travel agencies, all in the centre and within several blocks of each other, might reopen: Brasilia Travel (☎ 222378) at 67 Broad St, Morgan Travel (☎ 223586) at 70 Ashmun St and Doukor Travel (☎ 221104) on Randall St at Chase Manhattan Plaza.

Bookshops & Supermarkets Check to see if the National Bookstore, on the corner of Carey and Mechlin Sts, has reopened. In the past, it was the best and offered English novels, books on Liberia, including one of the most entertaining novels by a Liberian on Liberia, *Red Dust on the Green Leaves*, magazines of all sorts, maps of Liberia, etc.

For international newspapers and magazines, try the Ducor Palace Hotel and the Pan-African Plaza on Tubman Blvd. The bookshop at the Ducor may still have a fair selection of English novels.

For a supermarket, try Choithram's on the corner of Carey and Gurley Sts. There's also one on Randall St and one on Tubman Blvd in Sinkor.

Waterside Market

Waterside market near the centre at the northern end of Mechlin St is back in full action and should not be missed. Surrounded by slums and old buildings in the old port area, it has returned to life and even has some artisan goods for sale. If you look hard behind the basketball shoes and mountains of cigarettes, you'll find some vibrantly coloured batiks, beads and carvings.

Providence Island

This is where the first expedition of freed American slaves landed. It is beneath the bridge connecting the centre of town and the port. It's a cultural park and once conditions return to normal in Monrovia, you may be able to see traditional dancing, concerts and special programmes. Even if there's no performance, it may be worth a trip as there may be groups practising.

Masonic Temple

Now in ruins, the Masonic Temple was Monrovia's major landmark until the 1980 coup. Since most of the Masons were Americo-Liberian descendants of the original settlers, the Temple was the most prominent symbol of the previous regimes. It was vandalised after the 1980 coup, when the Masonic Order was banned. Photographs were not allowed during the Doe era and shouldn't be taken now unless you're sure it's OK. During Doe's time, more than one traveller was put in jail for several days for taking photos of it.

Museum

The new national museum on the corner of Broad and Buchanan Sts had a modest collection of Liberian artefacts before the events of 1990. It may reopen if its contents have not been totally looted.

Zoo

The city's tiny zoo, which is in the area of Payne Airport Terminal, is in total disarray.

Troops ate all the animals, so all that exists today are empty cages, with a sole antelope surviving. Once conditions return to normal, the zoo might be restocked.

Activities

Swimmers can try the pool at Hotel Africa or head for the beaches, which are popular only from November to April. Hotel Africa has a popular private beach plus a tennis court. If the Ducor Palace Hotel reopens, you can try the pool and tennis court there.

Places to Stay – bottom end

One cheap hotel that has reopened is the *Olympic Hotel* on Carey St, which charges US$10 a night for a room and has a good Lebanese restaurant. Others which might reopen include the following (the information is prior to the civil war):

The *YMCA* (☎ 221520) in the centre at 12 Broad St is the cheapest place in town at US$6 a bed, but your chances of finding an empty bed are poor. Rooms are not available at the YWCA.

In Sinkor between 11th and 13th Sts, there are three missions within a block of each other with excellent guesthouses, all facing the ocean. They all charge about US$10 a person and have cooking and laundry facilities. The *Baptist Mission* is at 11th St, the *United Methodist Church* at 12th St, and the *Lutheran Mission* a block further east.

In the centre there's a large number of cheap dilapidated hotels within a block or two of the intersection of Gurley and Carey Sts. Prices are all about US$14/20 for singles/doubles with fans (US$20/$30 with air-con). All of them accept Liberian dollars. Many of these places double as brothels. The *Maxim Hotel* (☎ 222252) is on the corner of Gurley and Benson Sts while the *Hotel Nevada* is on Gurley St just south of Benson St. Several blocks north on Front St there's the *Florida Motel* (☎ 221690) and facing it is the *Christina Hotel* (☎ 221158).

Places to Stay – middle

At least two mid-range hotels have reopened. One is the *Ambassador* (☎ 223147) on UN

Drive, near the UK embassy and 10 to 15 minutes' walk from the centre. It used to be the best deal in this range, but the area is not safe at night, there's little light and the neighbourhood is boring. It has renovated wood-panelled rooms, a saltwater pool (undoubtedly empty) and a decent pizzeria. It is less expensive than *El Meson* (☎ 222154) on Carey St, which has reopened and is the most popular place to stay. It has a generator, air-con and reliable water, and charges US$60 for a room.

There are two other hotels with similar prices that might reopen. *Julia's* (☎ 222432), two blocks away on Gurley St south of Benson St, used to be comparable to El Meson and the Ambassador and had a popular tranquil bar and a good restaurant. Even if the *Carlton Hotel* (☎ 221245) on Broad St reopens, it's unlikely to be worth checking as it was overpriced and full of young prostitutes.

Places to Stay – top end
Of the top-end hotels, only the ocean-front *Hotel Africa* (☎ 224519 or 223951, fax 223732, telex 44223) has reopened its doors. Built for the Organisation of African Unity (OAU) summit in 1979, it charges between US$100 and US$150 a room depending on your influence. Only US dollars are accepted. It has the liveliest mirrored disco in town, tennis courts and a good private beach club past the bungalows but the horses were all eaten during the civil strife. Its major drawback is the 10-km, 15-minute taxi ride from the centre which is necessary to get there. Finding a cab can be a problem.

Two other hotels in this category which might reopen are the *Ducor Palace* (☎ 224200, telex 44268), perched on a hill in the heart of town, and *Robertsfield Hotel* (☎ 224200, telex 44268) at Robertsfield Airport, an hour's drive out of town. Even before the civil war, guests rarely had good things to say about the Ducor. The rooms are small and musty, the restaurants expensive and the area too dark and unsafe for walking at night. Its facilities include a pool, car rental, tennis courts and a generator.

The three-star Robertsfield Hotel was never a good place to stay for the money as it was way overpriced for the mediocre quality of the rooms.

Places to Eat
Many places in the city centre have reopened. Most foreigners eat at the newly reopened hotels. The pizzeria at the *Ambassador* is reportedly decent while the restaurant at *El Meson* is reported to be disappointing with dreadful service. *Chicken Inn* on Carey St sometimes has chicken and always has good local dishes. For the money and atmosphere, there's no beating the cooking of a Bassa woman near the House of Muscle beer shack on the corner of Benson and Gurley Sts. Many other chop houses in the centre have also reopened and since other restaurants are likely to reopen, the following information is given for what it's worth on eateries as they existed before mid-1990.

Chop Houses There are 'chop houses' everywhere serving local fare for US$1.50 to US$2. In the centre, try the one across from Julia's Hotel; it's open until midnight. The *Rooster* offers fast-food-style fried and barbecued chicken and delicious cassava chips with hot sauce. A dinner costs US$3.50. It's in Sinkor on the corner of 9th St and Tubman Blvd.

Liberian *Roseline's* in the centre on the corner of Carey and Warren Sts is the best known and one of the more expensive Liberian restaurants. In Sinkor near the ACS, you can try *Angi's*, a small restaurant with good food. It may still have a Friday luncheon special – all you can eat from a large variety of African dishes for US$15.

Silver Spoons, at the Pan-African Plaza near the Presidential Palace, is good only at lunch time. It offers a few African selections plus non-African dishes. *Arlene's*, in the centre on Warren St near Carey St, offers some African dishes but mostly Continental food. *Chicken Nest*, on Mechlin near Carey St, has half chickens for US$4. *King Burger* on Broad St near Randall St, is open every day until 11 pm and is something like Burger King, but more expensive.

LIBERIA

Lebanese *Beirut*, on Center St near Broad St, is the best Lebanese restaurant in town, plus it offers many non-Lebanese dishes. *Geege*, on Gurley St, is open every day. The *Gondole Restaurant* on Broad St at the Paradise Hotel has inexpensive Lebanese sandwiches and has been recommended.

Indian *Maharaja's*, on Center St near Carey St, has excellent food and quite a few selections. The *Tandoor Restaurant*, on Broad St near Randall St, is open every day and has Indian selections plus some American and Liberian dishes.

Italian *La Villa* has good Italian selections, excellent steaks and numerous fish dishes. It's on 14th St in Sinkor, a 10-minute ride from the centre, and is closed on Sunday. *Salvatore's* is a popular restaurant on Broad St just down the hill from the Ducor, with an extensive menu and a pleasant atmosphere.

Chinese The *Mandarin* is a well-known restaurant in a restored old house in the centre on Broad St. *Chop Sticks*, in the centre on the corner of Carey and Lynch Sts and closed Monday, is also good.

French In addition to the restaurant at *El Meson*, there's a restaurant at *Julia's* which has well-prepared food but few selections (closed Sundays).

The expensive *Casa Real*, in the heart of town on Carey St near Mechlin St, has well-prepared food, including seafood and some Portuguese specialties.

Entertainment

Bars The most popular with expatriates is the bar at *El Meson*. Another bar that has reopened is *Lipp's Bar & Nightclub*, in the centre on Lynch St. For years the downstairs bar has been lively and popular with locals and foreigners.

The *Executive Pub* at the foot of the Ducor Palace Hotel served as Sawyer's seat of government and is a meeting spot for young intellectuals fleeing the prostitution markets further down on Broad St. For really cheap places, look along Broad St.

Nightclubs In addition to Lipp's Bar & Nightclub, a long-time favourite that has reopened is *Black Sugar* near the central area on Warren St. It has a back-up generator, good sound system and spacious dance floor. The cover charge may be negotiable. The upstairs disco has also been quite popular. The flashy, elitist nightclub *Bacardi* at the Hotel Africa is also back in business. For years it has been popular with wealthy locals and foreigners; on weekends it is likely to be very crowded.

In addition, the numerous nightclubs on Gurley St are back in business, as are the prostitutes. When the 7 pm curfew is in effect, many of them operate during the day. Rogueries at night have always been common here, including muggings, but aggression seems less common – a strange side-effect in a city with many assault weapons beneath its beds (no one is ever quite sure who they're stepping out of line with). Nevertheless, take the maximum precautions.

Cinemas The Relda Theatre on Tubman Blvd in Sinkor used to be the best cinema in town, but it's in an area that suffered huge destruction by Johnson's troops. There are, however, cinemas in the town centre that are back in business, mostly with kung fu flicks.

Things to Buy
Artisan Goods Liberia has traditionally been a good place to buy masks, baskets, soapstone carvings, 'country cloth' and tie-dye materials, and African dresses and shirts. Three popular materials for African dresses and shirts include patterned Fanti cloth which is sold by the *lappa* (two metres), tie-dyes and wax prints, and country cloth, a thick, durable, hand-woven cotton material, sold in strips of ready-made outfits. None of these materials are colourfast. The best place to look for these materials is the Waterside Market; also check the shops on Randall St between Carey and Broad Sts as well as on Benson and Mechlin Sts.

There are some very fine masks made of sapwood and used in the Sande and Poro

Gunyege-type mask

rituals. The styles vary; one used in initiation ceremonies has tubular eyes beneath a horn. Finding them is a problem but, again, Waterside Market is the place to look. The few for sale are hidden behind the clothes and shoes as the tourist market for these items has entirely dried up.

Music For recordings of Liberian and African music, bring your own high quality blank cassettes because the cassettes sold in Monrovia are of poor quality. Enquire about Sam Music Shop in the centre on the corner of Carey and Center Sts, and Soul Sound on the corner of Broad and Gurley Sts; they used to be two of the better places. Some of the local stars are Morris Dorley, who mixes merengues, rumbas and highlife with his Sunset Boys, and the groups Music Makers and Voice of Liberia.

Getting There & Away
Air Air Conakry and Air Ivoire are the only two commercial airlines presently serving Monrovia.

Bush Taxi There are no buses in Liberia, just minibuses and cars. There are two motor parks. Most bush taxi cars leave from the centre of town next to the bridge. Those for the Sierra Leone border leave from Water St next to the Waterside Market. All vehicles leaving Monrovia are subject to extensive searches by Taylor's troops starting about 50 km outside Monrovia. Not including the time taken for these searches, the normal driving time from Monrovia is about three hours to Buchanan or the Sierra Leone border and five hours to Ganta.

Getting Around
Taxi Taxis are yellow; you share them, and there's a zone system for fares. Traditionally taxi drivers have been honest and bargaining with them was not required. However, it is not clear if this is still the case. Cabs waiting outside the major hotels naturally charge more because you rent the entire cab.

Car Some of the agencies that, in the past, rented cars are Morgan Travel Agency (☎ 223586) in the centre at 70 Ashmun St, International Automobile Co (☎ 222486) on Front St, Brazilia Travel Agency (☎ 222378) on Broad St, and Yes Transport Co (☎ 222970) on Camp Johnson Rd. There's also an Avis agency on Randall St.

AROUND MONROVIA
Cooper's Beach
In addition to the private beach at Hotel Africa, Cooper's Beach (or Kenema Beach) just out of town is still lovely, safe and quiet. It's protected from the large breakers and is thus fairly safe for swimming, even for children. Bring your own refreshments as the vendors haven't yet adjusted to the cease-fire. It's about 15 km from the central area towards Robertsfield Airport, about three km beyond Elwa junction and the new stadium. Look for the sign on your right. It can be reached by shared taxi.

Caesar's Beach
Caesar's Beach is a 45-minute ride from Monrovia in the direction of Robertsfield

Airport. It's no longer behind Taylor's lines and you may find it more tranquil than Cooper's Beach.

Firestone Plantation

The Firestone plantation is an hour's ride east of Monrovia, near Robertsfield Airport, and is now back under government control. During the week, they used to conduct tours of the plantation, so ask to see if they've been resumed.

The Coast

ROBERTSPORT

The information on Robertsport and all other places outside Monrovia is pre-1990. The beach town of Robertsport is a good place to spend a few days away from the bustle of Monrovia. Not that it's full of historical monuments or sights of interest, it's just that Robertsport doesn't have much competition. It's a sleepy town of about 3000 people with no seeming destiny other than to exist in tranquillity surrounded by a tropical green hill with the surf pounding nearby. Most of the locals exist off the only thing keeping the town alive – fishing.

Before arriving at Robertsport, you'll pass by a peaceful lake. It's the best spot for campers seeking a little tranquillity. Its saltwater is free of bilharzia, so you can swim there. During WW II, this area was used as a seaplane base by the Allies.

Robertsport itself is a good place to walk around and get to see and know the locals. You can walk from one end of town to the other in 20 minutes. Most important for those who don't like to rough it too much, there is, surprisingly, a fairly decent ocean-front hotel only a 10-minute walk from the centre.

Places to Stay & Eat

The *Wakorlor Hotel* (☎ 601060), with singles/doubles for US$15/20 (US$25/40 with air-con), is surprisingly large for such a small town. There's a breezy dining area

overlooking the ocean, as well as a run-down tennis court. There's also an airstrip. Chances are you'll have the place to yourself. *Josephine's Hotel*, with very basic rooms for US$8 to US$15, is in the centre one block from the water. It is not very clean and doesn't have a restaurant.

Those who can't afford the hotel might try *Benisab's Coffeehouse*, a hole-in-the-wall drinking place in the centre.

Entertainment

For night entertainment, there's *The Zoe Bush*, a nightclub in the central area which is open only on the weekends. Bring your dancing shoes.

Getting There & Away

Robertsport is a two-hour ride west of Monrovia, off the main trunk route to Sierra Leone. About half the distance is paved. There are several bush taxi minibuses a day connecting the two; about US$5. They leave Monrovia at the main lorry park just south of the bridge over to the port.

BUCHANAN

Buchanan, 100 km south-east of Monrovia, is a three-hour bush taxi ride east along the coast from Monrovia. It is Liberia's second major port and stopping point for the Lamco train from Yekepa. Except for the **port** itself and the many **old houses** in the older section of town, there's not much of interest. There is, however, an excellent **beach**, Silver Beach, south-west of town. It's a little tricky to get to, so ask the locals for directions.

The best place to stay is at the *Louiza Hotel*, which is nothing special but it does have air-con. Another is the *Sabra Hotel* on Atlantic St. There may also still be a good Chinese restaurant here.

SAPO NATIONAL PARK

Greenville is the starting point for trips to Sapo, the country's major park, which is north-east of Greenville, bounded on the west by the Sinoe River and in the north by the Putu mountain range. The vegetation is partly swamp but mainly virgin rainforest. There is very little primal **rainforest** remaining in West Africa and Sapo is one of the best places for viewing it. So a trip here would undoubtedly be the highlight of any visit to Liberia.

Of the fauna, the major attraction is the **pygmy hippo**. Other animals that you might see include forest elephant, various species of duiker, hippo, monkey, chimpanzee, buffalo and giant forest hog. From January to March the park staff, including Peace Corps volunteers, used to run canoe trips on the Sinoe River to raise money for the park. These trips may be resumed once conditions normalise in Liberia and if the Peace Corps returns. They present an excellent chance to travel into the interior with a minimum of hassle, and to experience adventure to boot. The trips are three to four days, and the fee (US$80) covers all your needs. Reservations are necessary and can be made through the National Park Office in Sinkor, Monrovia or at the Peace Corps.

In Greenville be prepared to eat only in chop houses and sleep in a private dwelling as there may be no hotels.

Getting There & Away

As the crow flies Greenville is only about 250 km south-east of Monrovia, but to get here you must first travel upcountry to Ganta and then south to Zwedru and Greenville, a distance of about 600 km. The straight driving time from Monrovia is about 15 hours during the dry season, so it's normally a two-day trip overland. During the rainy season you'd have to have a 4WD as the roads can become incredibly muddy.

HARPER

This remote port town of 11,000 people is almost on the Côte d'Ivoire border. There are some sites of historical interest, including the residence of the late President William Tubman and the Tubman **Library** & **Museum**. Nowadays, its primary reason for existence is to serve as an outlet for the rubber plantations, though it also has a small fishing industry.

If the town seems particularly pleasant, part of the reason may be excellent **beaches** nearby and the tasty seafood for which Harper is renowned. The other reason is that the overland trip to get here is so arduous that anything resembling civilisation may seem like paradise. The trip is so exhausting, because of the bad roads, that it's not recommended unless you're on your way to or from Côte d'Ivoire via the slower coastal route, or you want to see some real tropical rainforests.

Places to Stay & Eat

The *Cape Motel*, with singles/doubles for about US$20/30, is one of the nicest hotels outside Monrovia. There's no air-con, but it's not really needed with the sea breeze. Nets hang everywhere and there are turtles in a pool and you can eat excellent seafood on the hotel's patio as the waves lap nearby in the bay. The hotel is outside the central area, on the peninsula and beyond the lighthouse. For cheaper chop bars, look around the market area and Green St in the centre of town.

Getting There & Away

Access is difficult because there is no coastal road. As with Greenville, you must go way upcountry and then back south. The route from Monrovia is via Ganta, Tapeta and Zwedru with an overnight stop usually in Tapeta or Zwedru. Straight driving time from Monrovia is 15 to 17 hours during the dry season. During the rainy months, a 4WD is an absolute must, and even then you can expect to get stuck. The road passes through some of the thickest rainforests in all of Africa and this is a large part of what makes the journey interesting. It's another day and a half to Abidjan.

The Interior

GBARNGA

Gbarnga, where Taylor has established his headquarters, has become virtually the second capital of Liberia. It is 196 km north-east of Monrovia. Cuttington College is on the southern outskirts of town; its **museum** is worth checking.

On the southern end of town, just off the main Monrovia to Ganta highway, is the *Dafal Motel*. It's fairly grubby and over-priced even at US$13 a room. If you'd like to meet students from the nearby college, one advantage of this place is that it's not far from the well-known casino where they hang out. Otherwise, try the more expensive *Hillcrest Hotel* on the northern side of town on the main drag.

GANTA

Virtually everyone travelling overland through Liberia stops in Ganta as it's the country's major northern hub. So it's fairly active with lots of chop houses and other establishments. The main attraction here is the **craft shop** of the leper institution where lepers make some of the most interesting baskets in West Africa. Don't miss it. The baskets vary considerably in design, some being quite large and colourful.

The town's major hotel is the *Travellers' Inn* on the main drag. It has rooms for about US$15 and a good chop house next door. For cheaper accommodation try *Toe's Motel* or the *Kinta Motel*.

YEKEPA

Normally you wouldn't think that a mining town would be a place of interest. Yekepa, a town of some 20,000 in the mountains of north-east Liberia, is one of the exceptions. It is best known for being the company town of **Lamco**. It was not until 1965 that some of the world's biggest and richest iron-ore deposits were discovered here.

At about 350 metres above sea level, Yekepa has the best climate in Liberia. This, plus the view of the lush surrounding mountains attracts most people, especially those tired of the flat lands elsewhere in Liberia.

The area also offers some of the best light hiking in West Africa.

November to March is the best time for visiting and **hiking** as it's cooler then and there's little rain. The main attraction is **Mt Nimba**, 1752 metres high. The starting point is about 10 km east at the border with Côte d'Ivoire. If you pass into Côte d'Ivoire or Guinea on the way to the summit, it's usually no problem as no one is around to stop you. There is also the possibility of taking a tour of the mines.

Places to Stay

Your only choice besides the several missions here may be the *Traveller's Inn* in the centre of town. If there's no electricity, you can bargain them down to US$6 for a double, otherwise expect to pay more.

Getting There & Away

A bush taxi from Monrovia takes about seven hours and costs US$10.90 plus a baggage fee. The taxi or van will drop you off at the first camp village, about seven km from town. From there you must catch any vehicle to Yekepa itself. The road from Monrovia is in excellent condition and is paved all the way to Ganta. Bush taxis leave Monrovia from the main lorry park just south of the bridge, but you'll probably have to change in Ganta.

Coming from Côte d'Ivoire, you can make it from Man to Yekepa in six to nine hours depending on your luck with taxi connections as well as your luck at the border. The trip must be done in five separate stages: Man, Danané and the border, then on to Kamplay, Sanniquellie and Yekepa. If you stay in Sanniquellie, look for *Evangeline's Motel*. It's a 10 to 15-minute walk from the taxi park and is the only hotel in town. A single room costs about US$10.

Mali

Timbuktu is that place you always heard about, but could never find on the map. But now you know: it's in Mali, where you can see the great Niger River, nomads on camels crossing the desert, and ancient mosques dating from medieval times, when the trans-Saharan trade routes dominated West African economic life. Other highlights include Mopti, a busy Niger River port and the centre of Mali's fledgling tourist industry. Nearby is Djenné, Mali's best preserved city from the medieval period. Also on the river is Bamako, Mali's lively capital, large enough to have amenities and small enough to cover on foot, with some of the best markets in the region. Away from the cities, adventure seekers can travel down the Niger by boat, or go trekking along the spectacular Dogon Escarpment. All these are just some of the attractions that make Mali a jewel in the crown of West Africa.

Unfortunately, there's a flip side to the story. Mali is one of the world's five poorest countries. Part of this reality is evident in the considerable number of beggars in Bamako, but there are other aspects not so readily visible – a life expectancy of 44 years, an average calorie intake about 30% below the required minimum, a literacy rate of about 32%, and a mortality rate of about 15% among children less than one year old. Poverty is nothing new to Malians, but their fortitude despite the hardships, their friendliness, and the vibrancy of their city life and local markets are, ultimately, what leave the most lasting impressions for visitors.

Facts about the Country

HISTORY

Strategically located on the southern edge of the Sahara and at the top of the Niger River's 'Great Bend', Timbuktu was (and still is) the terminus of a camel caravan route across the

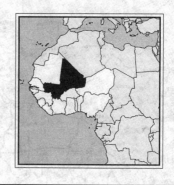

REPUBLIC OF MALI

Area: 1,240,140 sq km
Population: 10.4 million
Population Growth Rate: 2.4%
Capital: Bamako
Head of State: President Alpha Oumar Konaré
Official Language: French
Currency: West African CFA franc
Exchange Rate: CFA 500 = US$1
Per Capita GNP: US$300
Time: GMT/UTC

Sahara that has linked Arabia with Black Africa since ancient times. Gold, ivory, kola nuts and slaves from the central part of West Africa were transported north, eventually making their way to Europe and the Middle East. In return, the West Africans wanted salt which, as incredible as it may seem, traded pound for pound with gold. Tuareg nomads carried this salt in slabs on the backs of their camels from an oasis in northern Mali south to Timbuktu, from where it was ferried along the Niger River to Mopti. Timbuktu became an influential centre of trade and Islamic learning, and between the 9th and 16th centuries its fame was

MALI

Mali

further enhanced by the rise of three great empires in the region.

Empire of Ghana

The first empire to flourish was the Empire of Ghana, which covered much of today's Mali and parts of Senegal (and had no geographic connection with the present-day country of the same name). The capital, Kumbi, was built 200 km north of modern Bamako. Although Islam had taken a firm hold in the regions north of the Sahara, the Empire of Ghana did not fully embrace the new religion. The empire was destroyed in the late 11th century in battle against the better armed Muslim Berbers from Mauritania and Morocco.

Empire of Mali

In the middle of the 13th century Sundiata Keita, leader of the Mandinka people (also called the Malinké), founded the Empire of Mali in the region between mid-Senegal and the modern-day country of Niger, and converted to Islam as a gesture of friendship to his northern neighbours and trading partners. By the next century the Empire of Mali stretched from the Atlantic to present-day

Suggested Itineraries
You can easily spend a day or two in Bamako wandering around the lively streets and markets, or longer if you plan day trips to **Koulikoro** or other nearby places along the banks of the Niger. From Bamako, most travellers follow the 'river route' (alongside the Niger) to **Ségou** (worth visiting for a day or two, if you've got time), and on to **Mopti**. This town, with its market, mosques, active waterfront and pleasant surrounding fields and villages, easily takes a few days to see, but most travellers stay even longer as Mopti makes a good base for visits to **Djenné** (which can be visited in one day, although two is better), **Timbuktu** (which you can visit for anything between one day and one week, plus up to a week each way to travel overland by boat or vehicle to/from Mopti), and **Dogon Country** (where you can trek for between two and 10 days, plus a day at each end of your trek for travel to/from Mopti).

Onwards from Mopti, if you're travelling east overland, you can reach **Gao** (worth a visit of one or two days), from where transport heads towards Niamey (Niger) or north across the Sahara into Algeria.

A popular option for the 'river route' between Bamako and Goa, via Mopti and Timbuktu, is to go by boat. This takes time (up to a week for the whole journey, not counting the days you spend in the various stopping-off points), but is an excellent way to travel.

If you're heading south from Bamako, Ségou or Mopti you can reach **Sikasso**, and there find transport into Côte d'Ivoire or Burkina Faso. If you're heading west into Senegal you can go direct by express train all the way to Dakar, or take a slower 'local' train, stopping off at the rarely visited towns of **Kita** and **Kayes** (one or two days each) on the way. ■

Nigeria and controlled nearly all trans-Saharan trade. The empire originally derived its revenues from levying taxes on gold, silver and ivory traders within its territory, but it eventually expanded and gained ownership of the gold and silver-mining areas.

When the Emperor of Mali, Mansa Musa, visited Mecca via Egypt in the early 14th century, he went with an entourage of 60,000 people and 150 kg of gold. His lavish gifts of the precious metal all over Egypt caused the value of gold to slump for several years. As if this weren't enough, wherever he stopped on Friday to pray, he had a mosque built – or so the story goes.

During this period, the trans-Saharan trade reached its peak, allowing Timbuktu and Djenné to become major centres of finance and culture. New mosques, designed by Arabian architects, were built and the two Islamic universities had over 2500 students. By the 16th century Timbuktu was an important commercial city with about 100,000 inhabitants – it now has about 15,000.

Empire of Songhaï

Although Timbuktu and Djenné were at the height of their powers, to the east the people of Songhaï had established their own city-state around Gao. They became powerful and well organised, and by the middle of the 15th century had eclipsed the Mali Empire and embarked on their own conquest of the Sahel (for more details about the Sahel, see Geography in the introductory Facts about the Region chapter). A hallmark of the Songhaï Empire was the creation, for the first time in Mali, of a professional army and a civil service with provincial governors. The government of the day even subsidised Muslim scholars, judges and doctors in places such as Timbuktu.

This golden period ended with the invasion, again, by Berber armies from Morocco in the late 16th century. At the same time the European maritime nations began circumventing the Saharan trade routes by sending ships down along the coast of West Africa. They not only broke the Muslim monopoly on trade but destroyed the base of the Sahel's wealth. Timbuktu was sent into oblivion.

The Colonial Period

Mali became a French colony in 1883 and part of the territory of French West Africa which by the turn of the century stretched from the Atlantic to present-day Niger. Remnants of the colonial period include the

MALI

largest irrigation works (the Office du Niger, near Ségou) and the longest railway span (1200 km between Dakar and Bamako) in West Africa. However, French Soudan (as Mali was then called) always remained the 'poor relative' of other colonies such as Senegal and Côte d'Ivoire. France's chief interest was in developing the colony as a source of cheap cash crops, especially cotton and rice, for export to France.

Independence

Mali became independent in 1960 (although for a few months it was federated with Senegal) and the first president, Modibo Keita, embarked on an unsuccessful period of socialism, employing hundreds of Soviet advisers while maintaining close political and economic ties with France. The advisers went for politically popular projects, building a large bridge over the Niger at Bamako, as well as a sports stadium and hospital. Even more politically important was the Soviet assistance to the Malian military.

Fired by a sense of nationalistic pride, Mali left the franc zone in 1962 and established its own currency. Newly formed state corporations without foreign assistance took control of the economy, down to the level of supermarkets. Almost all of the corporations began losing money except the cotton enterprise, which benefited from French advisors and a fairly reliable world market. Ambitious planning schemes went awry, resulting in unpopular austerity measures. Eventually, in 1968, Keita was overthrown when a group of army officers, led by Moussa Traoré, staged a bloodless coup.

Politically, things were calm during the 1970s and '80s – at least by African standards. Still, there were four coup attempts during the two decades and a well-publicised student strike in late 1979 that, according to Amnesty International, resulted in 13 young people being shot or tortured to death. Also in 1979, the country was officially returned to civilian rule, although the single party permitted to exist was very much influenced by senior military figures. Traoré remained head of state.

Another major political event occurred in

late 1985 when Mali and Burkina Faso declared war over a long-standing border dispute. Burkina even dropped a small bomb on Sikasso. But the war ended after five days – in part, perhaps, because neither side had the resources to continue.

A greater cause for concern were the continual food shortages. These were conveniently blamed on the droughts suffered by many Sahel countries at the time, but were due largely to government mismanagement.

During the 1980s Soviet influence in Mali waned, with the country moving steadily towards the West, and a free enterprise system was reinstalled. In 1984 Mali re-adopted the CFA franc, several state-owned companies were dismantled or sold, and the government withdrew from the business of buying and selling grain, long a recommendation of the Western donor countries. By 1987, Mali had an estimated grain surplus of 150,000 tonnes – more than the deficit during the great 1983-84 drought. Adequate rainfall was the main reason, but policy change may have helped.

Mali Today

During the droughts and food shortages of the 1980s the Tuareg people of northern Mali had suffered more than most. There were calls for an independent Tuareg state and in 1990 a small group of Tuareg separatists attacked some isolated army posts in the Gao region. The soldiers' heavy-handed retaliation led to further fighting: hundreds of people were killed on both sides and a full-scale civil war seemed imminent. The north of Mali was off limits for foreigners, and the city of Gao was briefly under siege.

Meanwhile, there was also unrest in Bamako. Talk of multiparty democracy had begun in 1989 and became increasingly open, mainly through *Les Échos*, an opposition newspaper which had frankly criticised the Traoré government. In mid-1990, the push grew stronger when a group of officials and intellectuals wrote an open letter to the president calling for political pluralism. In late 1990, a peaceful demonstration in support of multiparty democracy drew some 30,000 people into the streets of Bamako.

In January 1991 the trade union organised a general strike for higher salaries; it paralysed Bamako for two days. Later that month the movement for pluralism turned violent. Riots in Bamako resulted in four people dead, cars and shops in ashes, and tanks on the streets. Several days later, when another march was announced, police beat up and arrested association members, including one of the principal leaders. In response, hundreds of students rampaged through the city. All schools were closed indefinitely, but that gave students more time to hand out underground newspapers calling for democracy.

Traoré was reportedly willing to liberalise the government but his powerful wife, Mariam, persisted in encouraging the army hardliners. Massive strikes and demonstrations continued through February and early March of 1991, during which protesters continued to demand a national conference to discuss multiparty democracy and freedom of the press. On March 17 the students declared a national day of martyrs, followed by a huge demonstration calling for the resignation of the Minister of Education. The students were joined in the streets of Bamako by tens of thousands of people calling for multiparty democracy. The security forces met them with machine-gun fire, triggering three days of rioting and looting during which government troops killed nearly 150 people and injured 1000.

That three-day slaughter finally provoked the army, led by Lt Col Amadou Toumani Touré, to once again take control. Moussa Traoré was arrested, and about 59 others were killed in the overnight coup, including the Minister of Education and the president's brother-in-law who were burned alive.

Amadou Touré established a National Reconciliation Council (Conseil de Réconciliation Nationale) but, stating that 'the army will no longer meddle in politics', he appointed Soumana Sacko, a civilian, and senior official with the United Nations Development Programme (UNDP), to oversee a transitional government until multiparty elections could be held.

Touré (or ATT as he became known) gained considerable respect and support from the people of Mali, especially when he carried through with his promise to hold multiparty elections. In June 1992, following the elections, Touré formally resigned and the winner, Alpha Konaré, was invested. By then, 'a national pact' had been signed with the Tuareg rebels, which allowed more Tuareg representation in the army, civil service and government. Since then, hundreds of former rebels have been integrated into the army. Peace returned to most areas in the north where they operated, but some sporadic outbreaks of violence continued through 1992 and into 1993 as some rebel factions (largely based upon clan lines) disagreed with some of the pact's conditions.

During this period, ex-president Traoré went on trial and, in February 1993 he was sentenced to death, along with three of his senior aides, for killing citizens in the March 1991 riots. But his execution has been delayed, perhaps permanently, pending his co-operation in restoring to Mali the huge sums of money he and his colleagues reportedly amassed in foreign bank accounts.

Throughout 1993 and early 1994, sporadic fighting between Tuareg rebels and government forces continued in the north of the country. Negotiations in Algeria in May and June of 1994 struggled to find common ground to please all sides in the dispute, but without any great success. It seems that hardline Tuareg groups are demanding an independent homeland, while the army sees some factions as 'bandits' simply exploiting the anti-government unrest in the area.

In early 1995 both Timbuktu and Gao could be reached by visitors, although foreign embassies in Bamako were warning visitors not to go there, and vehicles on the roads around Gao were still travelling in armed convoys. The area remains volatile and you should check the latest situation if you are travelling north or east beyond Mopti, or heading to Gao from Niger.

GEOGRAPHY

Mali is the largest country in West Africa, measuring about 1.3 million sq km (more than twice the size of France, although with only about one-seventh as many people). It can be broadly divided into three main areas. In the north, the Sahara covers 58% of the country, and rainfall is minimal or nonexistent. In the south, near Côte d'Ivoire and Guinea borders, the rainfall is adequate for natural forest or cultivation without irrigation. In between these two areas is the relatively flat Sahel zone where fluctuations in rainfall (between 200 to 800 mm per year) often cause great havoc.

The Sahel zone is the part most often seen by visitors. This is where the Niger River winds slowly through Mali, passing Bamako, Ségou, Mopti, Timbuktu and Gao on its way to Nigeria and the ocean.

Environmentally, Mali's most urgent problem is desertification which threatens virtually all parts of the country which are not desert already. Particularly affected are the Mopti and Gao areas but even in the well-watered south, forests have been cleared. The multiple causes of desertification stem, ultimately, from excessive population pressures. The demand for wood, for fuel or charcoal production, is high. Overgrazing is another contributing factor, despite the droughts in the 1970s and '80s which severely cut Mali's livestock herds.

CLIMATE

The rainy season is from June to September: however, rainfall is rare in the north, variable in the Sahel and heaviest in the south. The hot season is from March to May, when temperatures frequently exceed 40˚C. The best time to visit is October to February. The harmattan (a hot, dry, dusty wind from the north – ie from the Sahara) blows from December to February, which is not a major problem but does obscure the views. November is therefore the absolute best time to visit, but it's also the peak of Mali's 'high' tourist season.

GOVERNMENT

In August 1991 the country's constitution was changed to allow a multiparty political system, and presidential elections were held in 1992. Turn-out was low, but voting passed

peacefully, and the election was regarded by international observers as fair and representative. Alpha Oumar Konaré, a 46-year-old scientist and a former director of the company publishing *Les Échos*, was elected president. There were also elections to the newly resurrected 82-member National Assembly (Assemblée Nationale) whose members are elected by universal suffrage every three years. Younoussi Touré became prime minister.

However, although the old president has been replaced, Mali still has its problems. The people's expectations were high following the coup, but by early 1993 Konaré was seen as having done little to build on Touré's improvements. In April 1993 serious anti-government rioting, led by students, again broke out in Bamako. The Assemblée Nationale was attacked, as well as several ministries, and even the offices of *Les Échos*. The government's immediate response was to close the university and put army patrols on the streets, but later the same month several opposition figures were included in a reshuffled coalition government.

It seems that these changes pleased nobody. In December 1993, five army officers were arrested, accused of plotting to overthrow the government, and in February 1994 there was more unrest in Bamako, this time with students protesting about the previous month's CFA devaluation (see the Money section in this chapter). Also, the prime minister resigned and two opposition parties withdrew from the coalition government. In response, Konaré took the by now familiar step of reshuffling his cabinet of ministers, closing all secondary schools and universities, and banning student meetings.

ECONOMY

In 1960 Mali was a net exporter of food and even embarked on a limited programme of road improvement for the purpose of increasing its export potential. Within a few years, however, as a result of bad management, it became a net importer of food. The droughts in 1973-74 and 1983-84 only worsened the situation. Even in years of good rainfall, cereal production became insufficient to meet demand. Nearly everyone blamed the weather, saying a permanent climatic change had occurred. In fact, the droughts were only repeating a pattern that has continued over the centuries. With an annual population growth of about 2.5% the government had, and continues to have, its hands full just trying to keep conditions from deteriorating further.

The low prices paid by the government to farmers certainly contributed to the per capita decline in food production. During the period from the time of independence until the early 1980s government prices were 25% less than those on the open market. Farmers either stopped growing more than they needed, switched to cash crops, or smuggled grain across the border to neighbouring countries where prices were better.

One result is that since independence, the government has had a chronic financial deficit. Revenues barely cover the cost of the bureaucracy and officials are often paid their salaries four or five months late. The national budget shortfall has always been covered by France, while other Western nations are major donors of development aid. In 1990 aid funds amounted to 20% of the country's GNP. The average per capita income is only US$300 and growing slowly.

One of the brightest spots in the economy is gold. Mali is now regarded by international mining companies as having gold deposits potentially as huge as those in Ghana. Today, gold output from the open-cast Syama mine in the south, which began output in 1990 and is run by Australia's BHP Minerals, accounts for 10% of GDP. Meanwhile, the French are looking at a concession in Loulo in the west. For the moment, however, cotton remains the major export followed by livestock.

POPULATION & PEOPLE

Mali's population is estimated at about 10.4 million people. With a birthrate of 2.9%, this is projected to grow to 24 million by 2025 – a disastrous trend for a country whose arable land is being reduced by desertification. Mali also has the world's second highest infant mortality rate (164 per 1000 live births) and an adult literacy rate (32%) which ranks among the 10 lowest in the world. With these demographics, Mali faces an uphill battle just to maintain existing socio-economic conditions.

Ethnically, Mali is a fascinating country with three main groups standing out: the Bambara, the Tuareg and the Dogon.

The Bambara

The Bambara (BAM-bah-rah), concentrated in the area around Bamako and Ségou, are the largest group in Mali, comprising about one quarter of the population. Many senior positions in the government are occupied by Bambara people. The Bambara are also noted for their art. Indeed, there is no piece of African art more well known than the *chiwara*, a headpiece carved in the form of an antelope used in ritualistic dances. Air Afrique even uses the chiwara as its company logo.

Tyiwara crest (Beledougou region)

The Tuareg

The Tuareg (TWA-reg) men are known as the 'blue men of the desert' because of the indigo robes and turbans they wear to protect them from sun and sand. Concentrated in the area around Timbuktu, the Tuareg people are fiercely proud of their Caucasian descent and feel themselves to be superior to the Black Africans, such as the Bambara with whom they have a history of conflict. The Tuareg

MALI

were famous for their fighting abilities and artwork which, not surprisingly, adorns mostly swords and other metal objects.

Tuareg lives have been totally altered in recent years as droughts have killed off most of their sheep and goats, and their camel caravans cannot compete with trucks for the transport of salt and other produce from the north.

Forced to retreat south in search of water and vegetation for their animals, many have set aside their nomadic ways and become farmers or even urban residents. Others have not made the transition and live in camps outside Timbuktu where food is distributed to them by relief organisations during the droughts. It's a pathetic sight and yet one can only admire their resilience.

The Dogon

The Dogon (DOH-ghon) are incredibly

industrious farmers living on the rocky Bandiagara Escarpment some 100 km east of Mopti. They are also famous for their artistic abilities; and their homeland, the Pays Dogon (Dogon Country), has been designated a World Heritage site for its cultural and natural significance. The Dogon first settled around the escarpment during the 15th century. The original inhabitants of this area were the Tellem who were expelled or absorbed by the Dogon. Remains of old Tellem granaries and burial caves can still be seen high on the cliff walls. Dogon art and religion, including the use of ceremonial masks, is thought to be derived from Tellem beliefs. (See the Dogon Country section.)

Other Groups

Three other groups of people in Mali are: the Peul, the Bozo and the Songhaï. The Peul (also

---

Music

The musical tradition of Mali is based on the songs of the jalis (often referred to as griots), who have been a distinct caste in the social structure since the days of the Mali Empire. Today, many of Mali's modern singers are members of the griot caste. Major clans within the caste include the Diabates and the Kouyatés; you'll see and hear many musicians with these names.

In Mali's early days of independence, it was official government policy to reject European influences (including modern music) and encourage African traditions. Several state-sponsored cultural groups were founded, whose members were technically employees of the civil service or nationalised industries. Hence, musicians and singers with the legendary Rail Band were actually employed by Chemins de Fer Du Mali (the Mali Railway Corporation). This band was (and still is) a very fluid organisation with many musicians 'passing through' and a constantly changing line-up.

The most famous ex-member of the Rail Band, and one of the most famous West African musicians in Europe, is Salif Keïta. He has a stunning high-pitched voice, and his albums *Soro* and *Ko-Yan* were landmarks in the world music explosion that swept across Europe in the late 1980s. He is now based in Paris, but is reported to play in Bamako occasionally. Legend has it that he sometimes turns up unannounced to jam with the Rail Band of today, who still play regularly at Bamako's station hotel on Saturday nights.

Other names to look out for if you're browsing for cassettes include: Les Ambassadeurs (Salif Keita also played with them, after he left the Rail Band); the Super Biton National de Ségou (another state-sponsored band whose music was influenced by Bambara traditions); and Orchestre National Badema (whose lead singer, Kasse Mady Diabaté, went on to be a solo star).

Worthy of mention is Sidiki Diabaté, a traditional kora player, and Toumani Diabaté who is probably best known in Europe for being part of Songhaï, a 'world-combo' comprised of a Malian jali on kora, a British jazz musician on double bass and a trio of Spanish guitarists.

Mali also has many women singers, some of whom are jalis. These include: Tata Bembo Kouyaté, Ami Koita and Fanta Damba. Other (non-jali) artistes include Oumou Sangaré, whose combination of Bambara-influenced music and contemporary urban lyrics has made her a big star all over West Africa.

Mali's most unusual musician, Ali Farka Touré, is more popular abroad than at home. His free-style music is the closest thing on the African continent to American blues, and he has in fact played with legendary blues musician John Lee Hooker. However, the music is very much African in origin. Purists point out that African music originally inspired the blues anyway, so Ali Farka Touré is just bringing things back full circle. He would probably agree. ■

known as Fulani) are widely spread across West Africa, from Nigeria to Senegal, and are traditionally herders and semi-nomadic. In return for rice or other goods, they take care of cattle owned by farmers. The Bozo (BOH-zoh) are traditionally fishers, found all along the Niger River, from Bamako to Timbuktu. Mopti and Djenné are major Peul and Bozo towns. The Songhaï (SONG-guy) are fishers, farmers and herders, and are concentrated in the desert area around Gao.

RELIGION

Approximately 75% of the population is Muslim. The remainder of the people, including most notably the Dogon, who have strongly resisted the Muslim faith for centuries, hold traditional beliefs and a few are Christian. The Muslim religion here is quite strong and the fact that only 16% of the women are in the labour force (the lowest in West Africa), compared to 49% in neighbouring Burkina Faso (which is mainly non-Muslim), may be a reflection of its cultural impact.

LANGUAGE

French is the official language. The most widely spoken African language in Mali (especially around Bamako) is Bambara, which is almost identical to Dioula (the market language in much of West Africa). Songhaï is spoken widely in the north around Gao and Timbuktu. The Dogon people speak some 48 dialects, Sangha being a major one, but even this dialect is not understood by many Dogon.

Greetings in Bambara

Good morning.	*e-nee-SOH-goh-mah*
Good evening.	*e-nee-WON-lah*
How are you?	*e-koh-kay-nay-WAH?*
I'm fine.	*ah-HON kah-kay-NAY*
Thank you.	*e-nee-chay*
Goodbye.	*khan-bee-ah-FOH*

You should always answer each Bambara greeting (which can last up to five minutes) with *mba* (for men) or *ntze* for women. Both mean 'everything is OK'.

Greetings in Sangha Dialect

Good morning.	*ah-GAH-poh*
Good evening.	*dee-GAH-poh*
How are you?	*ou SAY-oh?*
I'm fine.	*SAY-oh*
Thank you.	*bee-ray-POH*
Goodbye.	*ee-eye-EE WAY-dang*
Have a safe journey.	*day-gay-day-YAH*

Facts for the Visitor

VISAS & EMBASSIES
Mali Visas

Visas cannot be obtained at the border, but if you arrive in Bamako by air without a visa, the chances are you'll be issued one (at twice the usual price), or told to get one at the main immigration office (*sûreté*) in Bamako. (This only works if you're flying from elsewhere in West Africa; from Europe you won't be allowed on board without a visa.) In addition, travellers coming by train from Senegal have sometimes been issued visas at the border. However, since obtaining visas to Mali is usually easy, there's little reason to take these risks.

During the early 1990s only one-week visas were issued, but most embassies now issue visas for up to one month without any hassles.

In West Africa, you can get visas for Mali in Abidjan (Côte d'Ivoire), Accra (Ghana), Banjul (The Gambia), Conakry (Guinea), Dakar (Senegal), Freetown (Sierra Leone), Lagos (Nigeria) and Niamey (Niger). For details refer to the Visa & Embassies section in the relevant country chapter. In Algeria you can get them from the embassy in Algiers and the consulate in Tamanrasset.

Outside West Africa, the Malian embassy in Washington issues visas for US$17. They require two photos and a return airline ticket or an itinerary if you are arriving in your own vehicle. Visas are issued in three days and are valid for one-month stays.

In Europe, there's a Malian embassy in Paris which issues visas for 100FF.

MALI

We heard from some travellers in Sweden who sent their passports to the Mali embassy in Paris for a visa. The money, the completed forms and even the passports were mislaid for so long that they had to use a courier service to bring them back to Stockholm, paying more than US$100, plus the cost of several frantic international phone calls.

Visa Extensions

Visa extensions are easy to get at the sûreté on Ave de la Nation in Bamako, or at the police stations in Mopti or Gao. They cost CFA 5000 and are issued in 24 hours or less.

Malian Embassies

Belgium 487 Ave Molière, Brussels 1060
France 89 rue du Cherche-Midi, 75006 Paris (☎ (1) 45-48-58-43)
Germany Basteistrabe 86, 5300 Bonn 2 (☎ (0228) 35-70-48)
USA 2130 R St, NW, Washington, DC 20008 (☎ (202) 332-2249)

Mali also has embassies in Cairo and Ottawa, plus consulates in Hamburg and Munich.

Other African Visas

Algeria The embassy is open from 9 am to 2.30 pm daily, except Sunday (CFA 3500; 24 hours).
Burkina Faso The embassy is open weekdays from 8 am to 2 pm; CFA 40,000. If you come between 8 and 9 am, you can often get a visa by 1 pm.
Guinea The embassy is open from Monday to Saturday from 8 am to 2.30 pm (closes at 12.30 pm on Friday). Visas cost CFA 15,000 and are issued within 24 to 48 hours.
Mauritania The embassy has the same hours as Guinean embassy. Visas cost CFA 3900 and are issued on the same day.
Nigeria The embassy is open weekdays from 8 am to 2 pm. Visas, issued in 24 hours, are free for Americans, US$12 for Australians and UK£20 for UK citizens.
Senegal Open weekday mornings, the embassy charges CFA 2500 for visas, and issues them in 24 hours or less.
Other Countries The French embassy in Bamako issues visas to Côte d'Ivoire, Togo, Chad and the Central African Republic. Visas for Morocco are available from the Moroccan embassy, although not required by Americans, most Europeans (including Britons), Australians and New Zealanders. Visas to Niger cannot be obtained in Bamako or Ouagadougou.

Foreign Embassies

See the Bamako Information section for a list of foreign embassies in the capital.

DOCUMENTS

All visitors must have a valid passport and International Vaccination Certificate. Those driving must also have a *carnet de passage en douane*, a *laissez passer* (issued at the borders for CFA 2500) and insurance (which can also be purchased in Mali).

Registration

Foreigners may be required to register with the police in the tourist towns of Mopti, Gao and Timbuktu. This involves filling in a form, while the police put a stamp and some illegible scrawl in your passport, for which you pay a CFA 1000 'fee'. Things are changing, however. In an effort to encourage tourism, it seems that the government does not require tourists to register any more. Also, there are fewer roadblocks and a more relaxed attitude towards tourists from the police. However, some police officers either don't know about the change of rule or pretend not to, so that they can still get the fee. If you're stopped without a stamp in your passport, just telling the police it's no longer obligatory for tourists seems to be accepted, as long as you are polite.

If you come into Mali from Senegal on the train, you're supposed to register with the police at Kayes, the first large town; no fee is payable, and the process seems completely arbitrary, so most travellers don't bother. In the same way, if you come into Mali from Niger, you're supposed to register in Gao. Because the region is still slightly tense following the Tuareg uprising it's not clear if the requirement to register is still in force. It might be more important if you're leaving Mali this way, as the border guards on the road to Niamey may insist on a police stamp from Gao. If you go through Bandiagara, on your way to Dogon Country, you're supposed to register here, but no fee is asked for.

Registration in other towns is not required, but in remote villages where you'll be staying overnight it is often a good idea to pay your respects to the village police officer (if there is one), or to the chief.

CUSTOMS

Currency declaration forms are not used, and visitors rarely have problems at customs. Theoretically there is a limit on the amount of CFA that you can take out of the country but whatever the rule (no one seems to know the exact limit), it's rarely enforced.

If you want to take a Dogon mask or other artefact out of the country, you'll need an export permit, if it looks the least bit old. The national museum in Bamako issues permits for 10% of the price of the artefact. The process typically takes two days.

MONEY

1FF	=	CFA 100
UK£1	=	CFA 775
US$1	=	CFA 500

The unit of currency is the West African CFA franc, which is pegged to the French franc at 100:1. In January 1994 the CFA was devalued overnight from a rate of 50:1, and other hard currency rates also increased by a similar amount. In Mali, and throughout the CFA zone, prices everywhere went up by 120 to 200%, and are likely to fluctuate more in the future, but because the exchange rate has doubled, Mali is cheaper overall for visitors.

Banks that change money include Meridien BIAO, Banque de Dévelopement du Mali (BDM), and Banque Malienne de Crédit ét Depôt (BMCD). There are branches of these banks in Bamako and other large towns. Exchange commissions vary between banks (and according to the currency you change) but are invariably high; sometimes up to CFA 5000. If you're coming from Burkina Faso, Niger or Senegal, change your money into CFA in those countries, as commissions are usually lower.

At all banks in Mali changing cash takes a long time, and changing travellers' cheques even longer. Bank staff prefer dealing in French francs, as this makes the process less complicated for them. In banks outside Bamako they often refuse to deal in anything other than

French francs cash at all, although with constant pleading (or a demand to see the manager) you might get a change of mind.

When changing travellers' cheques in Bamako (and some other towns) you need to show your purchase receipts, supposedly to prove that the cheques are not forged. The staff are strict about this, although anyone able to forge a travellers' cheque probably wouldn't have too much difficulty doing a receipt as well.

Some large hotels in main towns will change cash or travellers' cheques, sometimes charging no commission at all, sometimes charging even more than the banks. It all depends who's on duty.

You can get cash with a Visa card at BDM and BMCD in Bamako, but the process can be very time consuming.

There is usually no black market for CFA, although demand was high just prior to the 1994 devaluation. If the CFA is devalued again, or floated, a black market may be established.

BUSINESS HOURS & HOLIDAYS

Business hours are from 8 am to noon and 3 to 6 pm (approximately) on weekdays, and from 8 am to noon on Saturdays. Banking hours are Monday to Friday from 8.30 to noon (for cash transactions). Some banks are open Saturday mornings but won't change money at this time. Government offices are open from 7 am to noon and 2 pm to 4.30 pm on weekdays, except Fridays when they're closed (or as good as) after noon.

Public Holidays

1 January, 20 January, Easter Monday, End of Ramadan, 1 May, Tabaski, 25 May, Mohammed's Birthday, 22 September (Independence Day), 25 December.

POST & TELECOMMUNICATIONS

Letter and parcel post out of Mali (posted in Bamako or Mopti) is reasonably reliable. The poste restante in Bamako is OK for letters but not reliable for packages, and you should avoid having letters or parcels sent to the poste restante in any other town. In Bamako you can send telexes or make international phone or fax calls at the post office, and at one of the many private *télécentres* where the service is prompt and rates are only slightly more, although at all places international calls are expensive: CFA 3000 per minute to Europe, and about CFA 4300 to the USA. You can also make international calls from big hotels in Bamako, and other large towns, but these are even more costly. Reverse-charge (collect) calls cannot be made from anywhere in Mali.

PHOTOGRAPHY

Photo permits are no longer required but you still cannot take pictures of bridges, airports, military installations, radio stations, etc. As throughout West Africa, whenever you want to photograph someone, ask permission first. This is particularly true in the Dogon area.

HEALTH

Most large towns have a hospital and pharmacy, although standards are low and supplies sometimes limited. In Bamako, the Hôpital Gabriel Touré (☎ 22 27 12) is perhaps better for emergencies; otherwise the Hôpital du Point G (☎ 22 50 02) on the plateau overlooking Bamako is better. One of the best pharmacies in Bamako is at the Hôtel de l'Amitié, but there are several other cheaper ones around the city centre.

DANGERS & ANNOYANCES

Crime in Bamako is on the increase. We've heard from several travellers who were mugged at the train station or near the Maison des Jeunes. If you arrive on the train at night, either stay in the station building until dawn or get a taxi to your hotel. Bamako also has its share of pickpockets and bag snatchers: normal security precautions are definitely advisable.

Another danger to watch out for is the men who engage you in conversation about Malian politics, who then turn out to be secret police and threaten to arrest you for subversion. They of course settle for a large 'fine'. There are other similar scams – be careful what you say to strangers.

Problems may also occur if you are invited to stay with a family: the local police may attempt to fine your hosts for having an unauthorised guest.

The civil war around Gao and Timbuktu (see Mali Today in the earlier History section) seems to be worsening, so before travelling north or east beyond Mopti, or heading to Gao from Niger, check the latest situation.

ACCOMMODATION

Places to stay in Bamako and large towns frequented by tourists (Ségou, Mopti and Timbuktu) range from backstreet brothels to smart hotels. In between these two extremes are *campements* – there's one in most towns – where accommodation in bungalows or huts is simple but adequate, and sometimes good value. Some hotels add a tourist tax of CFA 500 per person per night onto the cost of the room. In Dogon Country, where many travellers go trekking, it's usual to sleep on the flat roof of a hut in a village, and a blanket or light sleeping bag may be required.

FOOD

Food in Mali is generally similar to that found in Senegal, with *poulet yassa*, *riz yollof* and *couscous* featuring on many menus. (For more details see the Food & Drink section in the Senegal chapter). All along the River Niger, restaurants also serve *capitaine* (Nile perch), which is usually either grilled or deep fried, although more imaginative methods (such as baked or stewed) are occasionally employed.

Getting There & Away

AIR
To/From Europe & the USA

European airlines serving Bamako include Air France, Sabena and Aeroflot. Return flights range from the equivalent of about US$600 to US$800, depending on the season and your length of stay. There are also flights from Europe on Air Afrique (from Paris and Marseilles, sometimes via Abidjan or Dakar), Ethiopian Airlines (via Addis

Ababa), Air Algérie (via Algiers), and Air Maroc (via Casablanca). Many travellers go overland from Europe through Morocco and fly to Bamako from Casablanca on Royal Air Moroc; fares start at US$300. From the USA, you can take Air Afrique from New York, transferring to a regional flight in Dakar or Abidjan. Otherwise you'll have to go via Europe.

To/From West Africa

Within West Africa, there are flights every day between Bamako and Abidjan, five days a week to/from Ouagadougou, four days a week to/from Dakar and twice a week to/from Niamey (all on Air Afrique or Ethiopian Airlines). There are also three flights a week to/from Conakry (on Air Guinée, Guinée Air Service and Air France), plus flights to Cotonou and Lomé (on Air Afrique), Lagos (Nigeria Airways), and once a week to/from Banjul (Air Guinée). Some sample Air Afrique fares (from Bamako) are: CFA 81,500 one way to Abidjan; CFA 77,000 one way to Conakry; and CFA 64,800 one way to Ouaga. Bamako to Conakry one way is around CFA 53,000 on Guinée Air Service and around CFA 62,000 on Air France. For airline office addresses, see the Bamako Information section.

LAND

Bush Taxi & Bus

To/From Burkina Faso The main route between Mali and Burkina Faso goes via Ségou and Bobo-Dioulasso. There are direct buses three or four times per week between Bamako and Bobo for CFA 10,000; they leave from the Sogoniko *gare routière* (bush taxi/bus park) in Bamako and the trip takes 12 hours. Many travellers do it in stages, breaking the trip at Ségou. There's a bus from Ségou to Bobo twice per week for CFA 5000, and more expensive bush taxis on most other days. It's also possible to go via Sikasso, and break your journey there. Daily buses between Bamako and Sikasso cost CFA 3000, and there's a bus every two days between Sikasso and Bobo for CFA 5000.

Bush taxis from Mopti head for Bobo-Dioulasso most days for about CFA 5000. These can take all day to fill and an overnight stop at the border is likely, as it closes between midnight and 6 am. (The nearby campement has rooms for CFA 2500.) Many travellers do this trip in stages: a bush taxi from Mopti to Bankas is CFA 3000, from Bankas to Koro is CFA 2250, and from Koro to Ouahigouya is CFA 2500.

To/From Côte d'Ivoire The main route between Mali and Côte d'Ivoire is via Sikasso and Ferkessédougou. Direct buses go three times per week from the Sogoniko gare routière in Bamako all the way to Abidjan for CFA 15,000. The 1200-km trip is supposed to take 1½ days but breakdowns and other delays are common. One traveller called it 'the most broken-down, over-packed, sweaty, dirty, dusty, smelly, sweltering bus trip I have ever taken'. His bus took over four days! It's much more pleasant to do the trip in stages: daily buses between Bamako and Sikasso cost CFA 3000. There's at least one bus per day between Sikasso and Ferkessédougou for CFA 6200, and a weekly bus between Sikasso and Abidjan for CFA 10,000. You can also go via Bougouni and Odienné, but traffic is light on this route.

To/From Guinea The main route between Mali and Guinea is via Kankan. Between Bamako and Kankan there are two choices: via Kourémalé (the border) and Siguiri, or via Bougouni and Mandiana. There's a bus run by a company called Sahel Transport going three times per week from Bamako (leaving from the small gare routière – a dusty dead-end street – near the Maison des Jeunes) to Kourémalé for CFA 1800. This bus may go on to Siguiri, although you're more likely to have to take a bush taxi towards Kankan from the border (see Getting To/From Mali in the Guinea chapter for more details). There's a possibility that the road between Bougouni and Kankan may be improved. If this is true, more traffic will start using this route.

MALI

To/From Mauritania The main route between Mali and Mauritania is via Nara (north of Bamako) and Néma, although public transport on this route is light, especially between Nara and Néma when you'll probably have to resort to one of the trucks or pick-ups that go this way. It's also possible to go into Mauritania from Kayes or Nioro (north-west of Bamako). See the later Kayes section for more details.

To/From Niger On this route, your only choice is the bus between Gao and Niamey. See the Gao section for details.

To/From Senegal Travelling by public transport between Senegal and Mali involves a lot of short truck or bush taxi rides, often on bad roads, and takes a very long time. Therefore most travellers take the train.

Train

To/From Senegal Express trains run between Bamako and Dakar twice per week in each direction, departing each city on Wednesday and Saturday mornings. The journey is scheduled to take 30 hours, but it's more like 35. The fare from Bamako to Dakar is CFA 52,900 to CFA 72,330 in a *couchette* (sleeping berth) or CFA 37,300/24,600 in 1st/2nd class. The trains have dining cars or you can buy food at stations along the way.

Some travellers do the trip in stages, by taking the slower, cheaper (by about 40%) 'local' train between Bamako and Kayes, then the express or 'omnibus' to Tambacounda and then a bush taxi from there to Dakar. See the Bamako Getting There & Away section and the Getting Around section in the Senegal chapter for details.

Car

To/From Senegal Between Bamako and Dakar, drivers have two options. The better route is via Nioro and Kayes (not the road following the train line), however, the section between Bamako and Kayes is terrible (taking at least two days) and it is next to impossible to drive from Kayes to Tambacounda during the wet season, and difficult

at other times. Many motorists put their cars on the train and ride with them between Bamako and Tambacounda or Dakar.

The cost of transporting a vehicle on the freight train is sky-high – about CFA 70,000 from Bamako to the border and CFA 61,000 from the border to Tambacounda. On to Dakar is about another CFA 62,000. Bribes at customs can easily amount to CFA 25,000. Moreover, you may have to purchase a seat on the train, even if you plan on travelling the entire distance in your car, and the train workers often demand sizeable amounts to tie down the vehicle and unload it.

Another problem is that it often takes a week or longer to get a reservation from Dakar but, as the train returns to Senegal fairly empty, in Bamako you can sometimes get permission to go the same day. The freight train is scheduled to leave every day around 9 pm. Coming from Senegal you can put the car on in Tambacounda and take it off in Kayes or Bamako; coming from Mali, it is apparently more difficult or impossible to put your car on in Kayes.

To/From Mauritania The main route between Mali and Mauritania goes north from Bamako via Kolokani and Nara to Néma. (You can also get to Senegal this way via Mauritania, which is longer but easier than going via Nioro and Kayes, as described above.) The Bamako to Nara section has been improved and is in good condition all the way. The Nara to Néma stretch is sandy in the dry season and muddy in the wet (July and August), but from Néma the road (the Transmauritanienne) is paved all the way to Nouakchott and Dakar. It's difficult to get petrol in Néma but no problem on the Transmauritanienne.

An alternative route from Bamako to Néma goes via Ségou. The road is tarred between Bamako and Niono, but the last 168 km between Niono and Nara is terrible, sometimes impassable from July to August, and worse than the Nara to Néma section.

To/From Burkina Faso & Côte d'Ivoire The routes in the earlier Bush Taxi & Bus section can be easily covered by car. Bamako to Abidjan via Sikasso takes from 20 to 24 hours nonstop; Bamako to Ouagadougou via Ségou and Bobo, 12 to 14 hours.

To/From Guinea Either of the routes via Kankan described in the Bush Taxi & Bus section earlier can be covered by car.

RIVER
To/From Guinea
A barge carrying passengers goes roughly once per week between Jukuroni (upstream from Bamako) and Kankan from July to November, or when the river is high enough. The trip costs CFA 5000 and takes four days. For details in Bamako ask at the CMN office (see the following Getting Around section).

TOURS
Most of the US and European companies listed under Package Tours and Adventure Trips in the introductory Getting There & Away chapter offer tours of Mali, and most itineraries include visits to the Dogon area, Mopti, Djenné and, with less frequency, to Timbuktu, which is less accessible. You can also come to Mali and hook up with a local tour operator. For their addresses, see Travel Agencies under Bamako.

LEAVING MALI
There are three types of airport departure tax payable at Bamako: CFA 1250 for flights within Mali; CFA 3750 for flights to other African countries; and CFA 5000 for all other international flights. At other Mali airports (Mopti, Timbuktu, etc) the tax is CFA 1250.

Getting Around

AIR
For getting around the country by air, domestic flights are operated by Air Mali and handled by an agency called Malitas (Mali Tombouctou Air Service). There are flights three times per week in each direction between Bamako and Timbuktu, stopping at Mopti and Goundam

each way. Once per week the flight goes on to Gao, although this may be increased. Flights usually depart Bamako around 7 am, arriving Mopti at 8.30 am and Gao at 11 am, then depart Gao at noon, Mopti around 2 pm and arrive at Bamako around 4 pm. There are also two flights a week between Bamako and Kayes, via Nioro. The flight days vary, and delays and cancellations are not uncommon, so you should enquire locally for more details. In Bamako reservations are handled by Air Afrique, but there are Air Mali or Malitas offices in the other touch-down towns. Flights (with one-way fares) most often used by visitors are: Bamako to Mopti (CFA 42,000); Bamako to Timbuktu (CFA 60,000); Mopti to Timbuktu (CFA 30,000); Gao to Timbuktu (CFA 18,750); Mopti to Gao (CFA 43,500). Fares are the same in either direction and returns are double.

For private plane charter, contact STA Mali (☎ 32 99 32, telex 454) or Mali Air Service (☎ 22 45 30, telex 418), or enquire at a travel agency.

You may even be able to hitch on a plane. I once got a ride to Timbuktu by going out to the airport in Bamako around 6 am and seeing if anyone was chartering a plane with an unoccupied seat. Two reporters let me join them for free. It's worth trying and you won't waste much time as private planes almost always leave before 7 am to avoid the heat.

BUS & BUSH TAXI
Getting around Mali by road is a lot more pleasant than it used to be. In recent years large buses have become commonplace, with several private companies running safe and comfortable vehicles on the routes between the main towns (particularly on the Bamako to Ségou, Mopti and Gao routes). They are cheaper than bush taxis (usually by around a third), and many buses travel at night, also saving you the cost of a hotel. Some sample bus fares are: Bamako to Sikasso CFA 3000, Bamako to Mopti CFA 6000; and Bamako to Gao from CFA 12,000 to CFA 15,000. You can normally buy tickets in advance which reserves your seat. Fares are fixed, and vary only very slightly

MALI

between the various companies. To attract passengers some companies offer a free drink, and one company (Bamabus) even has an in-flight raffle – with prizes! Other companies hire local youths to tout for custom around the bus park (more details in the Bamako section). On most routes there's at least one bus every day, except to Gao which is twice per week, to link up with the convoys running through the 'bandit territory' north of Hombori (more details in the Gao section). If the situation becomes calm, daily services to Gao will probably start running.

Because buses are cheaper and better (in comfort, speed, reliability and safety), there are very few bush taxis on the main long-distance routes; they can no longer compete with the buses. However, on shorter routes bush taxis are usually the only option. They are either Peugeot 504 seven-seaters (*sept-places*) with around 11 people inside, or pick-ups (*bachés*) carrying about 16 passengers. Bachés are slower but about 25% cheaper than 504s, eg Mopti to Djenné CFA 2250 by 504, CFA 2000 by baché; Mopti to Bandiagara CFA 1500 by 504. Luggage usually costs between 5 and 10% of the fare.

TRAIN

The only journey within Mali that can be done by rail is between Bamako and Kayes, in the west of the country. This is on the main line running between Bamako and Dakar in Senegal. For details see the main Getting There & Away section in this chapter.

CAR

If you're driving around Mali in your own vehicle, your Green Card (see Vehicle Documents in the introductory Getting There & Away chapter) is not valid; you will have to buy insurance in Bamako (or Gao if you're coming across the desert), such as at the Assurances Générales de France. A carnet de passage is also required. Petrol is expensive in Mali (CFA 400 a litre) but usually available in all major towns (although not always in Timbuktu). If for some reason it is not available, you can almost always obtain it on the black market at a slightly higher price.

BOAT
Passenger Boat

Large passenger boats, operated by the Compagnie Malienne de Navigation (CMN), ply the Niger River between Koulikoro (60 km east of Bamako) and Gao, stopping at Mopti, Kabara (for Timbuktu) and several other riverside towns. They run usually from August to November, when the river is high. In December and January the service may run only between Mopti and Gao or be suspended. In theory, one boat heads downstream from Koulikoro every Tuesday and arrives in Gao the following Monday, while another boat heads upstream from Gao every Thursday and arrives at Koulikoro a week later. The journey from Koulikoro to Mopti should take three days and from Mopti to Gao should be four days, but schedules are very unreliable and each section can take twice as long.

Most travellers find this journey fascinating as they get a close look at life along the Niger: particularly interesting is all the activity at the small ports along the way. But this trip is not for those who dream of sipping piña coladas lounging in deck chairs: it can be uncomfortable and is only for the more adventurous. There's a story about a couple from New York who read about the Niger river boats and pictured a small Caribbean cruise ship. What they found was a floating village, with sweltering cabins, loud music blasting away in the bar, dirty toilets and cargo spread everywhere with people on top. Another traveller's tale relates how the boat was once stuck on a sandbank for two days, during which time that water pump broke and the restaurant started running out of food. But don't let this put you off: it's not essential to do the whole trip. A two-day section between Mopti and Timbuktu (about 400 km), for example, is quite enough for some people.

There are three boats, although one always seems to be out of action: the *Kankan Moussa* is the best; the *Tombouctou* and the *Général Soumaré* are more basic. All boats have the same three-deck configuration, with the top two decks for the cabins and bar-restaurant and the lower deck for cargo and 4th-class passengers. The *Kankan Moussa*, however, has less upper deck space and hence it is not as good as the other two boats for 3rd-class passengers. On the other hand, only the *Kankan Moussa* bar has air-con. Despite their differences, all the boats have the same fare structure. Fares (in CFA) for the sectors (in either direction) most used by travellers are:

route	luxe	1st	2nd	3rd	4th
Koulikoro to Mopti	60,000	40,000	28,000	16,000	6000
Mopti to Kabara	46,000	31,000	22,000	13,000	4000
Mopti to Gao	94,000	63,000	45,000	27,000	9000

The 'luxe' cabins are either single or double (about 30% more, split between the two passengers). The 1st-class cabins have bunk beds, toilet and washbasin (luxe also has a fridge and air-con – sometimes broken); 2nd class is a four-berth cabin with a washbasin and outside toilets and showers; 3rd class is either an eight-berth or 12-berth cabin (although you can also sleep on the upper deck, and hang out there during the day); and on 4th class all you get is space on the extremely crowded lower deck, which many travellers find to be the absolute pits, with filthy shared toilets, although you're allowed into the bar on the upper deck, as long as you buy a few drinks.

Each boat has a restaurant and a bar with TV and music blasting away. Except in 4th class, meals are included in the fare. The food is bland, and in 3rd class you need your own bowl and fork. Extra food can be bought

from traders on board, from the kitchen or at stops en route. Beers, soft drinks and bottled mineral water can be bought on the boat, but they sometimes run out. Water is drawn from the river and 'purified' by the addition of bleach, but it's best to purify your own or bring your own supply of mineral water.

You can buy tickets at the CMN offices in Bamako, Mopti, Timbuktu and Gao. At Bamako tickets often sell out, except for in 4th class where space is seen as infinite. At offices in other towns they never sell out, which means you can always get a ticket although there may not be a berth when you actually get on the boat and you end up in 4th class anyway. However, during the trip, you may be able to pay a supplementary fee for a bunk in 3rd class.

Some people take the boat from Mopti to Gao, hoping to visit Timbuktu on the way. However, Timbuktu is nine km from the river, so the only way you can visit is to charter a taxi in Kabara (Timbuktu's port) and make a mad dash round the city during the boat's stop. For more details, see the Timbuktu section in this chapter.

Pirogues & Pinasses

If you don't want to take a large passenger boat (or can't because of gaps in the timetable, or the water level), there are other, more traditional, boats carrying passengers up and down the river. *Pirogues* are small canoes, either motorised or paddled by hand. *Pinasses* tend to be larger, motorised, and with extra features such as simple cabins or

Pirogue, Mopti *(from photograph by Ann Porteus)*

a reed mat rigged up to keep off the sun. Pirogues are usually the slowest form of river transport, but are OK for short journeys or if you're not in any kind of a rush. Pinasses are generally faster than pirogues, but still are not as fast as the large passenger boats (unless a large boat breaks down or runs aground – which is often). The most popular pirogue and pinasse routes for travellers are between Mopti and Djenné, and between Mopti and Kabara (for Timbuktu).

A pinasse between Mopti and Djenné takes all day and costs CFA 4500. It's also possible to go by non-motorised pirogue: this takes two days and costs CFA 3000. Between Mopti and Kabara, a trip in a large pinasse costs about CFA 7500, with hard bargaining. The journey varies from three days to two weeks depending on the amount of cargo carried, the size of the boat, and the water level. Expect delays when the boat owner goes off to see friends and family on the river bank – often for up to half a day at a time. There's very little food for sale on the way. Take enough for your own needs or arrange to pay the boat owner in advance for a share of the daily communal bowl of fish and rice. (On-board cooking conditions are very basic and some travellers have reported getting sick from the meals provided.)

TOURS

If you have no car and are wary of public transport, it is also possible to get around the country on an organised tour. You should note, however, that the set up in Mali is very different to the safari scene in East Africa (where you can choose from a range of trips for all tastes and budgets), and even less developed than in Senegal, where some outfits at least run excursions with set departure dates and prices. Many tour companies in Mali act as ground agents, running trips for European agents who send out ready-made groups. Independent travellers cannot usually join these. So, if you want a tour, it will be made to your own specification: you'll get good service, but it doesn't come cheap.

In Bamako, one of the most reputable tour companies is ATS Voyages (☎ 22 44 35, fax 22 94 50) on Ave du Fleuve, just north of Square Patrice Lumumba. They are the American Express agents and also deal in international flights. Other companies include: Sahel Tours (☎ 22 69 49) on Rue Rochester, also with an office in Mopti; Savanna Tours, with an office at the Grand Hôtel in Bamako (☎ 22 38 73) and also in Mopti (see below); and Timbuctours (☎ 22 53 15), near the Maison des Artisans in Bamako, with an office in Sanga and an agent in Mopti (☎ 42 00 92). Malitas (☎ 22 23 24, fax 22 23 49) on Ave de la Nation, used to operate internal flights, but they've now gone into general tours and car hire. They have English-speaking staff.

From Bamako, all these tour companies run tailor-made tours for individual clients and do not have set departure dates or prices, although rates are high, based usually on the cost of a hire vehicle. Rates for a five-seater Landcruiser start at CFA 60,500 per day with driver-guide, plus petrol (an extra CFA 12,500 to CFA 25,000 per day). Food and hotel rooms, plus any side trips such as mosque visits, boat rides or local guide fees, are all extra. Typical trips from Bamako include four days to Dogon Country, via Mopti and Djenné; and 10 days to Timbuktu, via Ségou, Djenné and Mopti.

From Mopti, Sahel Tours (☎ 43 00 56) runs trips to Sanga, in Dogon Country, or to Djenné, costing CFA 62,500 for one to three people for a one-day trip, or CFA 20,000 per person for groups of four to six. Two-day trips cost about double this. Trekking in Dogon Country can also be arranged, for about CFA 6200 per person per day, on top of the two-day Sanga trip. Sahel's Mopti office is on the street north of the pâtisserie.

Also in Mopti, Savana Tours (☎ 43 05 00) runs half-day trips around the town or to surrounding villages for CFA 10,000, day trips to Djenné for CFA 22,500, or two-day trips to Sanga for CFA 41,000 (with all prices based on a group of four people). Savana's Mopti office is in the Kananga Hôtel, or you can contact their European office: 117 bis rue d'Estienne d'Orves, 93110 Rosny Sous Bois, France (☎ (1) 48-54-21-70).

Timbuctours have an office in Sanga, offering a series of guided day walks from CFA 2500 to CFA 4300 for groups of one to four, and longer treks for CFA 2500 per person per day, plus meals and village taxes (see the Dogon Country section).

For more adventurous tours in Mali, by 4WD through the desert and private pinasse on the Niger, contact Nomadis Expeditionen, run by the friendly and multilingual Juan Dobler. He mainly operates for European agents, but can set things up for private groups, or may be able to fit you in with a group already booked. A two-week all-inclusive trip is US$1700, which is not cheap, but worth considering if your time is short and you want to get well off the beaten track. The company's address is BP 252, Ségou 1260 (telex 0985), or BP 01 2989, Cotonou, Benin (☎/fax 31-5041).

If you're into riding, a company called Cheval Savane runs horseback tours out of Ségou to Timbuktu, Djenné or through Dogon Country. A 10-day trip starts at CFA 375,000. Less elaborate 'pioneer' trips, exploring the country between the Niger and Bani rivers, cost CFA 287,000 for 10 days. Addresses: BP 342, Ségou (☎ 32 04 69); or 15 route de Louye, 27650 Le Mesnil sur l'Etrée, France (☎ 37-82-98-47).

Bamako

Mali is such a poor country that many visitors expect the pace of life in Bamako to be pretty slow. Nothing could be further from the truth. The city centre is like one big market, still small enough to cover on foot, with metalworkers bashing out pots and pans, music blasting away in shop doorways, and traders selling everything under the sun. The streets are full of cars and people, and it seems like everybody and their aunt has a motorbike. Bamako can provide hours of entertainment, even if you can't speak the language or don't like shopping. Bamako has buzz!

Orientation

Bamako city centre is on the north bank of the River Niger. The core city centre area, where you'll find the main markets, shops, restaurants and some hotels, is the triangle formed by Ave du Fleuve, Blvd du Peuple and, to the north just across the railroad tracks, Ave van Vollenhoven. The Grand Marché is in the centre of this triangle.

Blvd du Peuple is a busy street of small shops and market stalls. About halfway along is Dabanani intersection (a major taxi stand) and at its northern end is the artisan centre and Grande Mosquée. North of the mosque, two major roads extend eastward: Route de Sotuba, which begins at the artisan centre and leads out to the smart suburbs of Niaréla; and Route de Koulikoro, which leads to the hippodrome, the Hôtel Les Hirondelles and, beyond, to several embassies.

Ave du Fleuve is a wide street of shops, banks and offices. At its northern end is Place de la Liberté, and about halfway down a major junction with Ave de la Nation, which meets the wide Blvd de l'Indépendance at the Rond Point de la Nation. If you head south on Ave du Fleuve you reach Square Lumumba and, just beyond, cross the river on Pont des Martyrs to reach Route de Ségou (also called Ave de l'Unité Africaine), the main highway to all major towns in the country. This area is called Badalabougou. On this road are more embassies, and the main Sogoniko gare routière is after about six km. The airport is a further nine km, past a major road junction where the routes to Ségou and Sikasso divide. Alternatively, you can reach the airport by crossing the new Pont de Roi (to the west of Pont des Martyrs) and taking the new highway which runs parallel to Route de Ségou.

Information

Tourist Office The government tourist agency, SMERT, until recently controlled all tourism in the country with an iron grip. Thankfully this organisation has been disbanded and the office, where the people were only ever interested in squeezing fees from visitors, has closed for good.

Money Banks for changing money include

Bamako

To Plateau (Point G) & Kati

To Hôtel Lido

Route de Lido

0 250 500 m

To Hôtel Lido

To Guinea

New Highway to Airport (17 km)

Route de Guinée

Rond Point de la Nation

Boulevard de l'Indépendance

See Central Bamako Map

Avenue de la Liberté

Avenue du Fleuve

Boulevard du Peuple

Route de Sotuba

Rue Enseigne Ruge

Niaréla (Quartière)

To Canadian & Mauritanian Embassies

To Route de Koulikoro

To Submersible Bridge & La Savanne Restaurant

Avenue Kassa Keita

Route de l'Ancien Aéroport

Avenue de la Nation

Pont des Martyrs

Pont du Roi

Niger River

To Route de Ségou, Sogoniko (Gare Routière), Airport & Ségou

MALI

PLACES TO STAY

6	Hôtel Les Hirondelles
15	Hôtel Rabelais
17	Hôtel Dakan
18	Hôtel Le Tennessee
21	Maison des Jeunes

PLACES TO EAT

4	Restaurant Le Djenné
5	Salon de Thé Relax &
	Restaurant Le Petit Saigon
9	Salon de Thé l'Express
14	Restaurant Asia

OTHER

1	Parc Zoologique
2	Musée National
3	Stadium (Stade Omnisport)
7	Hippodrome
8	Burkina Faso Embassy
10	La Paysanne Weaving Co-operative
11	Cinéma Babemba
12	Mosquée de Mali-Libye
13	Guinean Embassy
16	Malibu Nightclub
19	Russian Embassy
20	French Embassy
22	Sahel Bus (to Guinea Border)
23	Compagnie Malienne de Navigation (CMN)
24	BCEAO
25	Palais de Congrés

the BIAO at Rond Point de la Nation, BDM and BMCD (which also give cash advances with a Visa card) both on Ave du Fleuve. See the main Money section in this chapter for details on commissions, and special requirements for travellers' cheques. If you want to avoid banks, or they're closed, you can change money on the black market with a local who hangs out at the taxi park near the cathedral. Rates are the same as at the bank, but there's no commission and the process is quick. A lot of unsavoury characters lurk around this part of town so it's no place to be seen with wads of money in your hand.

Foreign Embassies The following countries have diplomatic representation in Bamako:

Algeria In Badalabougou, on the west side of Route de Ségou, about four km south of the bridge over the Niger River (☎ 22 51 76)

Burkina Faso North-east of the centre, just beyond the hippodrome, 300 metres (three blocks) north of Route de Koulikoro (☎ 22 31 71)

Canada On Route de Koulikoro, about five km from the centre (☎ 22 22 36, telex 2530)

Egypt In Badalabougou, on the south side of the Niger River bridge (☎ 22 35 03)

France In the centre, on Square Lumumba (☎ 22 62 46 or 22 31 41, telex 2529)

Germany On Ave de Farako in Badalabougou, south of the Niger River bridge (☎ 22 32 99, telex 2529)

Guinea On the western side of town, one block south of the Route de l'Ancien Aéroport at the end of the first turn-off to your left after the small bridge (☎ 22 29 75)

Morocco In Badalabougou, on the west side of Route de Ségou, just south of the Niger River bridge (☎ 22 21 23)

Mauritania About six km out of the centre on Route de Koulikoro to Fina Video (on your right), then left on a dirt road for one block (☎ 22-4815)

Nigeria In Badalabougou, on the east side of Route de Ségou, one km beyond the Niger River bridge (☎ 22 46 96)

Saudi Arabia In Badalabougou, on the east side of Route de Ségou, about two km beyond the Niger River bridge

Senegal Just south of the centre, three blocks west of Square Patrice Lumumba and 50 metres south of Ave de l'Yser

USA In the centre, on the corner of Rue de Rochester New York and Rue Mohammed V (☎ 22 56 63 or 22 54 70, fax 22 39 33, telex 2448)

Honorary consulates include: Belgium (☎ 22 21 44) on Place du Souvenir, Italy (☎ 22 34 35) in Niaréla, the Netherlands (☎ 22 59 43) on Route de Koulikoro, Switzerland (☎ 22 32 05) on Route de Koulikoro and the UK (☎ 22 67 79).

Cultural Centres The US Information Centre, on Rue Baba Diarra near the train station, has English-language newspapers, magazines and books in its air-con library. It's open from 8 am to 12.30 pm and 3 to 6 pm. The French Cultural Centre on Blvd de l'Indépéndance near the Rond Point de la Nation also provides an interesting array of activities, including films.

Travel Agencies There are several agencies dealing in international and regional flights. These include Express Voyages (☎ 22 41 59) on Rue Mohammed V, one block south of the Salon de Thé La Phoenecia, and ATS Voyages (☎ 22 44 35), on Ave du Fleuve, just north of Square Lumumba, where the staff are helpful and speak English. (ATS also arrange tours around Mali – see Tours in the main Getting Around section of this chapter.) Fares vary between the agencies and the airlines so it's worth checking at a few places.

Bookshops The bookshop at the Hôtel de l'Amitié sells *Time*, *Newsweek* and the *International Herald Tribune*, although the mark-up is stiff. The bookshop at the Grand Hôtel is better and also has a small selection of books in English. For Malian literature try the bookshop at the National Museum. There's also a bookshop on Ave du Fleuve, south of the Hôtel Lac Debo and on the other side of the road, selling mainly school books (in French) and stationery. For second-hand books you could try browsing at the stalls on Rue de Rochester near the junction with Blvd du Peuple. The stalls outside the main post office sell good postcards, stationery, and a few books.

Markets

The Grand Marché, at the junction of Ave de la République and Rue Mohammed V, sadly

MALI

burnt down in 1993. It's due to be rebuilt, but until it is all the stalls have moved to the surrounding streets and the area is still very busy, and well worth a visit. There's everything from beads, blankets, indigo cloth, gold and brass to incense, African spices and medicines. The merchants here are not pushy like those in Dakar and Abidjan. In Bamako they will take 'no' for an answer. Malians have a reputation for being very pleasant and you can take your time wandering around without people pulling at you. Just finding out what most of the food items are at the Petit Marché nearby could easily take all day.

National Museum

The Musée National, on Ave de la Liberté, is one of the best ethnographic museums in West Africa and certainly one of the best in terms of its architecture – modern Sudanese inspired by the old mud brick architecture of Djenné. It has over 4000 exhibition pieces, all well displayed. The tapestry section is particularly good; it has some extraordinary Mopti blankets and Fulani wedding blankets. There are also masks, funeral objects and weapons on display. The museum is doing a commendable job of trying to keep the country's cultural treasures within its borders, but with ancient terracotta figures from Djenné selling illegally for around US$5000, the museum is fighting an uphill battle. The entrance fee is CFA 500, and hours are 9 am to 6 pm every day except Monday. French and English-speaking guides can be hired.

Zoo

The Parc Zoologique is half a km beyond the museum. Although the pens are more spacious than in some other zoos, it's pretty sad-looking these days and obviously lacking funds. Some animals have died and a few of the monkeys have escaped; they now sit on top of their cages instead of inside. The zoo is open every day until sundown (entrance is CFA 50), but the sooner it's closed the better.

Plateau Viewpoint

The Presidential Palace and other government buildings are on the huge plateau overlooking Bamako, known as Point G. The road to the top of the plateau starts near the museum. About halfway up this road, you'll see a sign, 'Point de Vue Touristique', pointing to the left down a dirt track. Follow it for about one km. The panoramic view of the city is superb, especially at dusk.

Biennal

If possible, try to be in Bamako in early September in an even year. That's when the 'Biennal', a biannual national sport and cultural festival, takes place. Lots of regional bands enter the competitions. A major venue for music nearly every day is the cinema opposite the train station. It's the best opportunity to hear live Malian music.

Places to Stay – bottom end

If you arrive late at night at the Sogoniko gare routière, and don't fancy walking the dark streets of central Bamako, it might be worth staying at one of the nearby *chambres de passage* where a dirty mat on the floor costs around CFA 625.

In the city centre, the cheapest place is the *Maison des Jeunes*, just west of Square Lumumba, where it costs CFA 1250 for a bed in the dormitory or CFA 2500 for a partition room, which could take a couple. Bathrooms are only just bearable, but the main problem is theft, as rooms are shared or cannot be locked. We've also heard from several travellers who have been mugged in the surrounding area. Camping is allowed but would be suicidal. Another cheapie is the *Carrefour des Jeunes* on Ave Kasse Keita, facing Place de la Liberté, but the rooms are filthy, the atmosphere heavy and the chance of having your gear stolen (even while you are with it) is extremely high.

Much safer and better quality is the *Centre d'Accueil des Soeurs Blanches* on the corner of Rue 133 and Rue 130, west of the centre, where a bed in the dorm (which sleeps six) costs CFA 2500 and private doubles cost CFA 6250. The rooms are clean, with fans and mosquito nets. Missionaries have priority here, and the French nuns who run the place take no nonsense from travellers. You

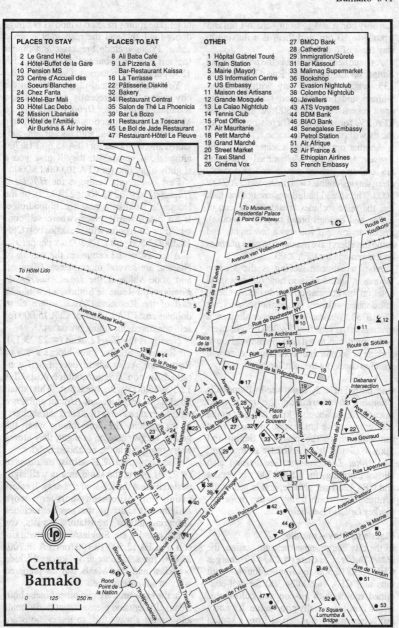

PLACES TO STAY
2 Le Grand Hôtel
4 Hôtel-Buffet de la Gare
10 Pension MS
23 Centre d'Accueil des
     Soeurs Blanches
24 Chez Fanta
25 Hôtel-Bar Mali
30 Hôtel Lac Debo
42 Mission Libanaise
50 Hôtel de l'Amitié,
     Air Burkina & Air Ivoire

PLACES TO EAT
8 Ali Baba Café
9 La Pizzeria &
     Bar-Restaurant Kaissa
16 La Terrasse
22 Pâtisserie Diakité
32 Bakery
34 Restaurant Central
35 Salon de Thé La Phoenicia
39 Bar Le Bozo
41 Restaurant La Toscana
45 Le Bol de Jade Restaurant
47 Restaurant-Hôtel Le Fleuve

OTHER
1 Hôpital Gabriel Touré
3 Train Station
5 Mairie (Mayor)
6 US Information Centre
7 US Embassy
11 Maison des Artisans
12 Grande Mosquée
13 Le Calao Nightclub
14 Tennis Club
15 Post Office
17 Air Mauritanie
18 Petit Marché
19 Grand Marché
20 Street Market
21 Taxi Stand
26 Cinéma Vox

27 BMCD Bank
28 Cathedral
29 Immigration/Sûreté
31 Bar Kassouf
33 Malimag Supermarket
36 Bookshop
37 Evasion Nightclub
38 Colombo Nightclub
40 Jewellers
43 ATS Voyages
44 BDM Bank
46 BIAO Bank
48 Senegalese Embassy
49 Petrol Station
51 Air Afrique
52 Air France &
     Ethiopian Airlines
53 French Embassy

To Museum,
Presidential Palace
& Point G Plateau

Route de Koulikoro

Avenue van Vollenhoven

To Hôtel Lido

Rue Baba Diarra

Rue de Rochester NY

Rue Archinard

Avenue Kasse Keita

Rue Karamoko Diaby

Route de Sotuba

Place de la Liberté

Rue de la Fosse

Avenue de la République

Dabanani Intersection

Place du Souvenir

Rue Gouraud

Rue Laperrive

Avenue Pasteur

Avenue de la Marne

Avenue de Verdun

MALI

Central Bamako

0   125   250 m

Rond Point de la Nation

Avenue Ruault

Avenue de l'Yser

To Square Lumumba & Bridge

Boulevard de l'Indépendance

Avenue Moussa Travélé

Avenue de la Nation

Rue Enseigne Froger

Rue Poincaré

can only come and go from 7 am to 1 pm and from 4 to 10 pm, and there is a maximum stay limit of four nights.

A friendlier alternative is the nearby *Chez Fanta*, on the corner of Rue 130 and Rue 135, where you can stay with a Malian woman and her extended family in large open rooms for CFA 2800 per night, plus CFA 250 for breakfast. There's no sign, but locals will point out the house.

Another option in the cheap range is the *Pension MS*, on Rue Mohammed V near the US embassy, where secure and reasonably clean singles/doubles with fans cost CFA 6000/8000. The shared bathrooms are not too bad, and the price includes breakfast (one cup of coffee and enough bread to feed a mouse). Prices are lower if you stay a few nights, and some travellers have managed to get a mattress on the veranda for CFA 2500.

Also worth considering is the *Mission Libanaise*, an old mission now run as a small hotel, on Rue Poincaré off Ave du Fleuve. Clean, safe doubles with nets, fans and hot showers cost CFA 8750. You can also camp or sleep on a mattress in the yard for CFA 2000. Some overlanders with cars to sell base themselves here as parking is secure, and local buyers often call round to check out the merchandise.

Camping The only camp site in Bamako is *Camping de Patriot* on the main road towards Ségou about 15 km south-east of the centre, some five km beyond the major road junction where the roads to Ségou and Sikasso divide. It's marked by a large sign. The *Hôtel Les Colibris* (see below) also allows camping, for CFA 2500 per person and CFA 1250 per vehicle, and is nearer the centre. Also worth trying is the more up-market *Le Lido* (see below).

Places to Stay – middle

In the city centre, near the train station, the *Hôtel-Buffet de la Gare* (☎ 22 54 60) charges CFA 7500/12,500 for singles/doubles with fans and CFA 16,800/24,300 for self-contained rooms with air-con and cold baths, which is not especially good value. It's noisy but better than you'd expect from a station

hotel. The rooms have no windows but huge doors for light, and the restaurant is good value. Prices include breakfast and dinner (dessert is extra!), but you may get a CFA 1550 per person reduction if you don't eat.

Your only other mid-range option in the city centre is the recently renovated and renamed *Hôtel Lac Debo* (formerly the Majestic), at the junction of Ave du Fleuve and Ave de la Nation, with decent self-contained air-con rooms for CFA 15,600/18,700 although, if you insist, they'll give you a slightly older one for CFA 10,000/15,000.

East of the city centre is the *Hôtel Les Hirondelles* (☎ 22 88 40 or 22 49 29), on the Route de Koulikoro near the hippodrome. It's a plain, sterile place, where self-contained air-con rooms with breakfast cost CFA 18,300/22,500 plus CFA 500 tax per person.

Also east of the centre, in the suburb of Niaréla, are several more places. Cheapest and good value is the *Hôtel-Auberge du Kombori*, on Route de Sotuba, a few blocks east of the Restaurant Asia, where clean doubles cost CFA 12,500, or CFA 15,000 for self-contained, including breakfast.

Nearby is the *Hôtel Dakan* (☎ 22 23 15), off Route de Sotuba, three blocks south of Restaurant Asia, where decent self-contained air-con singles/doubles cost CFA 12,500/15,600 with breakfast. This small hotel has a very pleasant African ambience with several *paillotes* (thatched sun shelters) in the garden. The only minus: when the garden lamps come on at night, they attract every mosquito in the neighbourhood.

The homy *Bed & Breakfast de Bamako* (☎ 22 01 04) in the same area is well signposted behind the Russian embassy. It caters mainly for visitors on short-term work assignments. Part of the service includes arranging guides, translators, typists, car rental, laundry, etc. Singles/doubles with air-con are CFA 12,500/18,700 (or CFA 18,700/25,000 for self-contained). Prices include breakfast and tax. Meals can be prepared without advance notice.

In the same area are two other hotels: both clean, efficient and pleasant, but fairly small and almost always full, so reservations are advisable. The *Hôtel Rabelais* (☎ 22 52 98 or 22 36 37, fax 22 27 86) is on Route de Sotuba, a block beyond Restaurant Asia, with rooms at 21,000/23,000 and breakfast at CFA 2500. *Hôtel Le Tennessee* (☎ 22 36 77, fax 22 61 26) is four blocks to the south of Restaurant Asia on a dirt road with rooms at CFA 22,500/27,500. Guests get free transport to/from the airport. If you would rather have a view of the Niger River, it might be worth checking the *Hôtel Mande*, which is about three km further east and along the river, on the outskirts of town. It's a very peaceful place with a good restaurant.

South of the centre, just off Route de Ségou, about three km from the Niger River bridge, is the relaxed and popular *Hôtel Les Colibris* (☎ 22 66 37) with self-contained air-con rooms at CFA 12,500/15,000. Meals are available. For getting to/from town, shared taxis and buses run regularly nearby.

Places to Stay – top end

The *Hôtel de l'Amitié* (☎ 22 43 21 or 22 43 95, fax 22 43 85), on Ave de la Marne, just off Square Lumumba, is the city's best. Part of the Sofitel chain, it has most amenities of a typical four-star hotel, including a cinema, mini-golf course and jogging track. Rooms cost CFA 40,000 plus CFA 500 tax per person.

Le Grand Hôtel (☎ 22 38 73, fax 22 26 01), on Ave van Vollenhoven, on the north side of the centre, is a colonial-era hotel but a major renovation destroyed much of its charm, although it still has a better ambience than the Amitié. Self-contained rooms are CFA 23,100/26,800 (plus CFA 500 tax per person, CFA 2250 for breakfast, and CFA 3750 extra if you want a bath instead of a shower).

Places to Eat – cheap & middle range

For street food, beef brochettes are sold all over town and, eaten with bread and fried plantains, make a safe and very economical meal. At the train station you'll find a row of stalls serving coffee and bread throughout the day. Just outside the station, in a tiny smoke-filled room on Rue Baba Diarra, you can buy freshly cooked meat. Bamako also has several bakeries selling good cheap bread, straight from the oven; the one near the station is open 24 hours. The *Pâtisserie Diakité* on Blvd du Peuple serves bread and a good selection of reasonably priced cakes.

If you're staying at the Centre d'Accueil des Soeurs Blanches or nearby, try the small *Escale des Jeuneaux* run by a hip dude called As, where breakfast is CFA 250 and other meals cost CFA 375 to CFA 625. In the same area, next to the Bar Mali on Rue Bagayoko, is a small shack run by a friendly old Senegalese man, where meals are in the same price range. Nearby, on Ave Mamadou Konaté, a block south of Bar Mali, is *Restaurant Joal-Fadiouth*, where a decent meal costs CFA 1000 to CFA 2000 and large beers CFA 500. On the opposite side of the street there's a small stall serving plates of hot bean sauce and manioc for around CFA 250. At the taxi park near the Cinéma Vox try *Gargot Dunkuta*, where you can get rice and sauce at rock-bottom prices.

Up a few grades from these places, but still relatively cheap, is the pleasant *Ali Baba Snack Bar*, on Rue Mohammed V opposite the US embassy. They serve chawarmas for CFA 600 and good coffee for CFA 300, plus pizzas, sandwiches, milkshakes, cakes and ice cream. Also on Rue Mohammed V, south of the Grand Marché, is *Salon de Thé La Phoenicia*. This is a popular hang-out for travellers and serves hot croissants for CFA 125, snacks in the CFA 600 to CFA 3500 range, other meals from CFA 1250, plus pastries and ice cream. Their beers, however, are expensive – CFA 850 for a big beer and CFA 550 for a small one. Another place to try is the *Restaurant Central*, between Ave du Fleuve and Rue Fabolo Coulibaly, where the special menu du jour, which has attracted visitors for years, varies from CFA 1500 to CFA 2000. It also has a limited à la carte menu, excellent yoghurt, sandwiches for CFA 1000, and quick service. All three places are open every day until midnight. Another good place for a cheap drink or meal is *La Terrasse*, upstairs on the corner of Ave de la République and Ave du Fleuve.

If you're looking for a decent meal for around CFA 1600, the restaurant at *Hôtel*

Buffet de la Gare is a good choice: it has some authentic African selections such as fonio. At the nearby *Bar-Restaurant Kaissa* on Rue Mohammed V (close to Pension MS) the prices are similar and the food is good. *Bistro 104*, next to the Kaissa, is in the same range, with music at weekends.

On the western edge of the centre, along Ave de la Nation, is *Bar Le Bozo*. It's clean, but seems to attract some disreputable characters. However, the food is quite good, and the prices are reasonable.

There are three popular snack bars on Route de Koulikoro: *Salon de Thé Relax* is near the Hôtel Hirondelles; about one km further is *La Cigalle*; and *Salon de Thé l'Express* is about another 500 metres along. All have similar fare and prices: chawarmas for CFA 600, meals like steak and chips from CFA 1250 to CFA 2500, ice cream for CFA 250 and pastries around CFA 650.

Places to Eat – more expensive

African The best up-market African restaurant is *Chez Kadia* in Badalabougou, on a side street west off Route de Ségou about one km south of the bridge. You can get great stuffed pigeon, excellent Niger perch (capitaine), and superb chips. If price is of no concern, don't miss *Restaurant Le Djenné* (☎ 22 30 82) which is very luxurious and open evenings only (closed Sunday). It's one of Bamako's fanciest restaurants, with most main courses in the CFA 3750 to CFA 4300 range. They also serve European food but no alcohol. To get there, turn left on the first paved road off the Route de Koulikoro after the intersection with Blvd du Peuple. Look for the signposts. Nearby on Route de Koulikoro, three blocks east of the sign for Le Djenné, you'll find the new *Restaurant San Toro*, which serves equally good and expensive food. The capitaine kebabs are wonderful as are the lamb dishes. You can listen to live kora music while you dine and buy crafts afterwards at the gallery here.

If you've got wheels, try *La Savanne*. It offers only grilled chicken and chips, but they are well prepared and inexpensive. The open-air ambience and late-night dancing on weekends are as much attractions as the good food. The problem is that it's a 25-minute ride east of Bamako. If you go by taxi it must remain with you.

Italian *Restaurant La Toscana* (☎ 22 52 23) on Ave de la Nation is a long-time favourite and one of Bamako's oldest restaurants. Pizza is the speciality but there are many selections. The lunch menu is CFA 4650 and the restaurant is closed Mondays. Cheaper is *La Pizzeria* on Rue Mohammed V, near the US embassy, with small pizzas at CFA 1600 to CFA 2000, and other meals in the CFA 2000 to CFA 4000 range.

Asian Near the corner of Ave du Fleuve and Ave Ruault, *Le Bol de Jade* (☎ 22 63 03) is very good, and relatively inexpensive with authentic Vietnamese cuisine. Open every day, it's two blocks west of Square Lumumba on Ave Ruault.

On the eastern side of the centre, on Route de Sotuba, is *Restaurant Asia*, reputedly the best and fanciest of the Asian restaurants, which also has seafood dishes. In the same area, on Route de Koulikoro is the reasonably priced *Le Petit Saigon* (☎ 22 66 49) and, half a km further out, the *Restaurant Hong Kong* (☎ 22 75 68). Still another good place for Vietnamese food is the new *Hong Mai*, which is near the Peace Corps office and has prices similar to those of other Asian restaurants, ie CFA 3750 to CFA 6250 for a two-course meal with a beer.

French The best French restaurants in town are *Le Dougouni* at the Hôtel de l'Amitié and *Le Bananier* at the Grand Hôtel, both with meals between CFA 4000 and CFA 10,000, and a menu du jour around CFA 7500. Every Friday evening, the CFA 6250 buffet and grillade at the Grand, which includes an orchestra, attracts a lot of people.

More reasonably priced is *Restaurant Le Fleuve*, just south of Ave de l'Yser, next to the Senegalese embassy, which has French and Lebanese meals in the CFA 2500 to CFA 4300 range. If you're looking for a relaxing way to spend an afternoon at a quiet place overlooking the Niger River, head for the *Hôtel Mande* which is on the eastern outskirts of town via the Route de Sotouba. The restaurant is very decent and offers views of the river which are particularly stunning in the late afternoon.

Entertainment

Bars In the city centre, try *Salon de Thé La Phoenecia*, which has a mixed crowd and a terrace for watching people, although drinks are a bit pricey with big beers at CFA 850. For cheaper drinks (big beers at CFA 650) but less salubrious surrounding go to *Bar Kassouf*, just off Ave du Fleuve. More sleazy is *Bar Le Bozo* on Ave de la Nation which attracts prostitutes and closes around 3 am. It's clean and serves some of the best-value eats in town. Even sleazier is *Bar Mali*, on the corner of Ave Mamadou Konaté and Rue Bagayoko, which attracts the same clientele and is also open late. For more tranquillity and up-market surroundings, visit the *Manantali* bar at the Grand Hôtel or the *Faguibine* at the Amitié, where beers are CFA 1600 and there's sometimes live music.

Nightclubs Your best chance of hearing a Malian band is at the *Hôtel Buffet de la Gare*. Various artists, sometimes including the famous Rail Band, play here on Saturday nights for a cover charge of CFA 1250. Other places in the city centre where you might hear a band are the *Bar Bozo*, *L'Escale* (next door), and the *Carrefour des Jeunes* near Place de la Liberté, although this place has a rough reputation.

Outside the city centre, the *Palais de la Culture*, on the south side of the river, sometimes has live bands – look out for adverts and posters. Other places with live music include: *La Cigalle* on Route de Koulikoro, about one km past the Hôtel Hirondelles, with bands on Sunday nights; *Rive Gauche*, also on Route de Koulikoro, with bands on Saturday nights; and *L'Equelle* on Route de Sotuba, which has live music on Saturdays and sometimes Thursdays, an open-air setting, good food, moderate prices and chaotic service.

Most discos are in the centre and don't get going before 11 pm. Thursdays to Sundays are the lively nights. On Mondays they're either closed or dead. Cover charges are mostly in the CFA 1250 to CFA 2500 range and usually include a drink. Your choices include the intriguingly named *37.2*, diagonally opposite the US embassy, with music most nights and a CFA 2500 cover charge, or the smarter *Evasion*, just off Ave du Fleuve, the 'in' place for rich hip Malians, which is why it can get away with its stiff CFA 3750 cover charge.

Slightly less pretentious are the *Colombo* on Ave de la Nation and *Le Calao* on Rue de la Fosse, west of Place de la Liberté, both with a mixture of African and disco music. Very smart but frequently dead midweek are *Le Dogon* at the Hôtel de l'Amitié, and *Le Village Kilimandjaro* at the Grand.

Cinemas The cinema at the Hôtel de l'Amitié has air-con and daily showings at 9 pm. Entrance is CFA 1600. Films are sometimes shown at the Palais de la Culture just across the river. For karate flicks and Indian movies try the Vox on Rue Bagayoko, the Ciné Soudan on Ave Kasse Keita, and the Rex near the station.

Horse Racing For Sunday entertainment, go to the hippodrome (horse track) on the Route de Koulikoro. You'll see Malians in their finest threads and, between races, wrestling matches and singing by a local star. The first race is at 4 pm.

How's this for some unusual entertainment? We heard from a traveller called Martin Bottenberg (Holland), who was approached by a 'guide' in the streets of Bamako, offering to arrange a visit to see former president Moussa Traoré, who is being held in a military prison on the outskirts of Bamako. The guide claimed to know an officer who could easily be bribed into getting Martin and his friend past the guards, provided they were prepared to pose as Red Cross workers. The offer was declined.

Things to Buy

Artisan Goods For all kinds of fabrics, tie-dyed cloth, Mopti blankets, Fulani wedding blankets and rugs, brass and beads, visit the stalls in the streets around the ruins of the Grand Marché in the centre of town. The choice is one of the best in West Africa. Another place to go is the Maison des Artisans, also known as the gold market or the artisan centre, on Blvd du Peuple next to the Grande Mosquée. It's open every day until 6 pm. Leather goods and wooden carvings are made and sold here.

The women's co-operative, La Paysanne (☎ 22 31 42), which has been around for many years, primarily sells fabrics, including tie-dyes, mud cloth (see the Djenné section for more details) and great ready-made clothes that are guaranteed to be washable. Prices are slightly higher than at the market, but the clothes are more adapted to Western tastes. To get there take Route de Lido (Ave Kasse Keita) from Place de la Liberté, then take your first right (after about one km) over the train tracks. It's open Monday to Saturday, 9 am to 4 pm; to noon on Saturdays. The Centre for the Blind also has a limited selection of handmade items, such as tablecloths. It's near the centre just north of the Pont des Martyrs river bridge.

Gold & Silver The Maison des Artisans (see Artisan Goods above), is one of the best places to buy gold and silver in West Africa. Both metals are sold by weight and bargaining is usually not possible. Gold sells at CFA 5000 per gram and silver at CFA 625. There are also reputable gold shops on Ave de la Nation. You need not worry about getting cheated at any of these places, but if you do, just go to the police and they will help you get your money back.

Music Cassette vendors are everywhere, especially along Blvd du Peuple and around the market. Once you've decided what to buy, try and listen to it before paying. Or at least remove the cellophane to check that the tape inside is not broken. There are also some places with original discs and tapes that record onto blank cassettes. Bring your own cassettes as most of theirs are terrible quality.

Getting There & Away
Air Airlines with offices in Bamako include: Air Burkina, Air Guinée, Air Gabon, Air Maroc and Air Ivoire, all at the Hôtel de l'Amitié (☎ 22 43 21 or 22 43 95); Air Afrique (☎ 22 58 02),

dealing with Air Mali flights, Air France and Ethiopian Airlines, all on Square Lumumba; Air Mauritanie at the junction of Ave du Fleuve and Rue Fabolo Coulibaly; and Aeroflot (☎ 22 56 93) on Rue Loveran, off Ave du Fleuve.

For flight details, see the earlier Getting There & Away and Getting Around sections in this chapter.

Bus Nearly all long-distance buses go from the gare routière at Sogoniko (sometimes written Soko Niko), about six km south of the city centre along Route de Ségou, and all the bus companies have ticket offices there. The main companies are Bamabus, Gana du Nord, N'Ga, Sahel, COMATRA, Coulibaly, Djedje, Rudycar, and SENTRAC. Another company, SOMATRA, has its yard on the other side of the main road from the gare routière. (Most companies also have yards and offices elsewhere in the city, where you can sometimes buy tickets or get on the bus, but these usually take some searching out, so it's easier to go to Sogoniko where you can compare routes, times and prices all in one place.)

To get to Sogoniko catch a crowded pick-up from Square Lumumba along Route de Ségou for CFA 75, or take one of the smart white and blue 'Taba' minibuses on the same route for CFA 100. A taxi from town costs CFA 750. It's advisable (but not essential) to visit the gare routière the day before you travel to check departure times and buy your ticket (which reserves your seat). This also helps you avoid the touts whose enthusiasm to get you onto 'their' bus can be a little rough and involve such tricks as grabbing your bag and loading it onto the roof before you've even had a chance to say where you're going. If you come by taxi, get dropped on the road outside and walk into the gare routière to escape notice.

From Sogoniko, there are buses two or three times per week to Bobo-Dioulasso for CFA 10,000 and to Abidjan for CFA 15,000 (for more details see the main Getting There & Away section of this chapter). There are about six SOMATRA buses per day to Ségou for CFA 2250; some go on to Mopti. Most buses for long-distance destinations (eg

Mopti and Gao) go overnight, leaving Sogoniko between 4 and 8 pm (arriving at Mopti the next morning, and Gao the following afternoon/evening), although a few go during the day. There are several buses to Mopti every day; the fare is CFA 6000. Buses to Gao cost between CFA 12,000 and CFA 15,000, going twice per week to link in with the convoys at Hombori (see the Gao section for details). Fares from Bamako to other destinations include: Djenné CFA 6700; Sikasso CFA 3750; San CFA 4500.

Overnight buses arrive at Sogoniko in the very early morning. If it's still dark, you may be allowed to sleep on the bus for a few hours until dawn. Otherwise, go and find a coffee stall or *chambre de passage* (see Places to Stay) where you can wait a few hours before going into town. Unless you plan to stay in one of the better hotels, there's no point going in any earlier, as all the cheap places to stay will be locked up and you don't want to be wandering the streets in the dark.

Transport for Kourémalé (on the border with Guinea) and Siguiri (in Guinea) leaves from a small gare routière (in a dusty dead-end street) just south of the city centre, to the west of Square Lumumba. Sahel Transport has their ticket office here, and runs buses to Kourémalé three times a week (CFA 2200).

There's also a small gare routière near the Grande Mosquée, with vehicles for destinations north of Bamako, including Nara and Nioro (on the way to Kayes and Mauritania).

Train The train station (☎ 22 55 66) is on Rue Baba Diarra, in the city centre. The ticket office is officially open daily from 6.30 to 11 am and 3 to 6 pm but the clerk doesn't know this, so you have to go along and hope for the best. The service most used by travellers is the express train to Tambacounda and Dakar, which goes twice weekly in each direction. You may purchase a ticket no earlier than a day before departure. Only 1st-class seats can be reserved, so if you're going 2nd class, board several hours in advance to be assured of getting a seat.

Other train services to/from Bamako include the 'local' to Kayes which leaves

Bamako most mornings, with an extra service on Friday evenings. It costs CFA 9600 in 1st class and CFA 5700 in 2nd class, which is about 40% less than the express.

Boat For details on the river boat service between Koulikoro (60 km east of Bamako) and Gao, via Mopti and Timbuktu, see the main Getting Around section in this chapter. To make bookings in Bamako, go to the CMN office (☎ 22 38 02), a small two-storey building on the river bank a few hundred metres to the west of the Pont des Martyrs (open weekdays to 2.30 pm; Saturdays to noon). The people there can also tell you about the barges that ply between Bamako and Kankan in Guinea (see the main Getting There & Away section in this chapter).

To get to Koulikoro, bush taxis leave from the market at Medina Koura, near the start of the Route de Koulikoro in central Bamako. Ask the CMN staff for directions. Or take the train which leaves Bamako train station daily at 6 pm. The trip takes 1½ hours and costs CFA 750; bring a torch as there are no lights on the train. If you're coming into Bamako, the train leaves Koulikoro early each morning.

Car Avis has an office at the Hôtel de l'Amitié (☎ 22 43 21, fax 22 43 85). You can also hire a car at the Grand Hôtel (☎ 22 24 81, fax 22 36 26), or check with one of the tour agencies listed earlier in this section. Rates for the cheapest saloon (sedan) car start at about CFA 12,500 per day, plus CFA 125 per km, tax at 15%, insurance at CFA 2500 per day, and petrol. For a Landcruiser or similar, expect to pay at least four times this.

Getting Around
To/From the Airport Bamako's airport is 15 km south of the city centre. A bus meets most international flights and goes into town for CFA 1500, which is good value as taxis between the airport and city centre cost at least CFA 4500 and more usually CFA 7500. If you're coming from the city centre, you can avoid taxis by taking a Taba city minibus to the major road junction at the southern end of Route de Ségou, from where you can get

MALI

a taxi the last five km to the airport for CFA 750. Alternatively, Taba city minibuses run between town and the airport via Pont de Roi and the new highway.

Minibus & Pick-Up The best city buses are those of Bamabus, which has clean, fast, convenient and reliable buses plying the city's major routes. The standard fare is CFA 150. In addition, a new network of Taba blue and white city minibuses serves most parts of Bamako. Bus stops are clearly marked, and most journeys cost CFA 100 (up to CFA 300 to the far suburbs). If you want to save money, battered pick-ups cover the same routes for CFA 75 to CFA 150 per ride.

Taxi Since the introduction of the Taba buses, shared taxis around town are very difficult to find (they were never easy). If you're in the centre, head for the taxi station at the Dabanani intersection on Blvd du Peuple, or the one in front of Cinéma Vox on Rue Bagayoko, where you'll find shared taxis headed, among other directions, out to the gare routière in Sogoniko.

For a private hire (*charter* or *déplacement*), the minimum charge for a short trip across the city centre is CFA 750 (CFA 1000 for longer trips across town), although with bargaining you can pay the same price for a ride between the centre and the Sogoniko gare routière. If you want a taxi for longer, it will cost you about CFA 3000 per hour or about CFA 20,000 plus gas by the day (bargaining definitely required). You can find taxis for private hire along Ave du Fleuve, near the cathedral, at the station or at any of the major hotels (although the cabs at the Hôtel de l'Amitié or the Grand Hôtel always charge premium rates).

AROUND BAMAKO

For a break from hectic city life, consider a day or two in **Koulikoro**, 50 km east of Bamako, on the north bank of the River Niger. This is the port for the passenger boats to/from Mopti and Gao, and it was an important town in French colonial days (the Atlantic-Niger train from Dakar actually ended here, not Bamako). Around the harbour you can still see the grand old buildings and sunken boats. There are two cheap hotels in town, and the *Refuge Hippo* is a good place for a meal or drink. You can get here by bush taxi or train (see the Bamako Getting There & Away section). By car it's less than an hour's drive.

Those with wheels might also consider the drive to **Selingue Dam** which is an hour or so south of Bamako. The lake behind the dam is popular on Sundays. You can rent a two-bedroom furnished villa for about CFA 12,500. It has a pool and you can play tennis, volleyball or go fishing.

Another interesting place is **Sibi**, a one-hour drive on the road to Guinea. There are massive cliffs in the area; great for climbing. It's also a nice place to hike and picnic.

The Niger River Route

For most people, a journey through Mali means following the Niger River, either by road or by boat. The towns and cities along this route are listed here in order of distance from Bamako.

SÉGOU

Ségou is a large town about 230 km east of Bamako, on the south bank of the Niger. Though often overlooked by visitors, it's an interesting place to stop for a night or two. This was an important centre in colonial days. Today, with several large old buildings and abundant trees on the main streets, you can get an idea of how French West African towns looked at that time. You can also get a better feeling of real life today on the Niger River; Ségou is quieter than Bamako, and less touristy than Mopti or Djenné.

Orientation & Information

There's only one main drag running roughly north-east to south-west, parallel to the river. Coming from Bamako you'll pass the Office du Niger headquarters on your right in the western outskirts. Continuing towards the

Office du Niger

The headquarters of the Office du Niger, an organisation founded in the 1920s by the French colonial government to develop Mali's agricultural output, is in Ségou. It was hoped at the time that the scheme would provide food crops for the whole of French West Africa and cash crops for export to France. Vast areas of land along the Niger River were cleared and irrigated, and in the early 1930s a dam was built to increase the supply of water. Groundnuts and cotton were planted but the soil was found to be unsuitable, so production was switched to rice. As this could not be exported, France lost interest in the scheme, and it's been trundling along in a half-hearted manner ever since.

In many areas, the plots of land are owned by bureaucrats, soldiers, teachers – anybody but the sharecroppers who actually till the land. Management is also a problem: for the system to operate successfully, the land must be flat and water must enter each plot at just the right moment, otherwise some crops get too much water and others not enough. The required degree of co-ordination is often lacking and, as a result, the system has been a failure from the beginning, with yields 25% of similar schemes in Asia. You can catch a glimpse of these fields by travelling north of Ségou towards Niono. For fields closer to town, enquire at the Operation Riz Ségou offices. The rice-growing season is from June to October. ∎

centre for about two km you'll come to a crossroads with the commissariat on your left. The left turn here goes towards the Grand Marché and the main commercial area; the right goes south on Ave du Président Konaté towards the Nieleni rug co-operative and the Medina area. Continuing straight ahead, you pass the BDM bank on your left after about 600 metres, then you come to a major five-ways intersection by a large water tower. Nearby is the local bush taxi gare routière and the hospital. Just to the northwest, at another five-ways junction, is the landmark Snack Bar Golfe. Eastward from here, the main road leads past the main bus and minibus gare routière, several restaurants and a few hotels, continuing through the outer suburbs towards Mopti.

Nieleni Rug Co-operative

Rugs of all sizes are made to order at the Nieleni Rug Co-operative. It's about 1200 metres south of the commissariat via Ave du Président Konaté and one block east. Closed Sundays.

Market

The Grand Marché at Ségou is open all week but is especially good on Mondays, when you can find Bambara pottery and Ségou strip cloth and blankets at very good prices.

Places to Stay – bottom & middle

The cheapest place to stay is *Le Campement* (☎ 32 00 78), also called the Centre d'Accueil, on the western edge of town near the Office du Niger headquarters, where rooms with fan and mosquito nets cost CFA 3750 (one or two people) and CFA 5000 with air-con. If they're full (which they frequently seem to be), you may be able to sleep in the yard for CFA 1750. The restaurant does breakfast (expensive at CFA 750) and straightforward meals like riz sauce (good value at CFA 650). Cleaner and quieter is the *Mission Catholique* (also called the Centre Gabriel Cisse) with double rooms at CFA 5000. It is about halfway between the campement and the town centre, two blocks south of the main road, next to the church.

Hôtel de France (☎ 32 03 15), formerly Hôtel Bakari Djanna, is in the centre one block south of Snack Bar Golfe, with decent self-contained air-con rooms for CFA 10,000, and simple rooms for CFA 5000 (one or two people), all set around a courtyard which becomes a restaurant and lively bar at night.

Your other cheap option is *La Maison du Peuple* on the east side of town, about three km from the centre near a small market and opposite a water tower. Clean rooms with fans cost CFA 3750.

MALI

Cattle Crossing at Diafarabé

This is unquestionably the most captivating event in Mali and one of the most interesting in West Africa. Every year during December, in a rite that goes back more than 160 years, the sleepy village of Diafarabé is transformed into a centre of activity and celebration as hundreds of thousands of cattle (about one-third of the total cattle population of Mali) are driven southward across the Niger River to greener pastures. It's a happy time for the herders, who have been up in the Sahara for months on end. The crossing means reunion with their families and a time to celebrate. On the first day, a festival of music and dance is held.

A little known aspect is the democratic process preceding the crossing that determines when and in what order the herds will cross and where the herds will graze once they are on the other side. This is accomplished at a council of the local chiefs or elders. Cattle begin converging on the area well in advance of the crossing and must remain spread out to prevent complete destruction of the grazing grounds.

The major crossing is at Diafarabé because it's at one of the narrowest places along the river. This is an event not to be missed. Diafarabé is 187 km east of Ségou, on the western bank of the Niger River, about a six-hour drive from Bamako. A 4WD is not required.

The exact date is not set until November by the government's livestock agency (Ministère d'Élevage); the water level is an important determinant. The second weekend in December, give or take a week, is the approximate date. If you can't make the crossing at Diafarabé, enquire about the dates of the others; they continue throughout December. ■

Places to Stay – top end

In the centre, just south of the river, is the good value *L'Auberge* (☎ 32 01 45) with clean single/double rooms for CFA 7500/8750, or CFA 11,250/15,600 with air-con and hot showers. There's a nice café in front and a pleasant garden at the back. The restaurant is the best in Ségou, with meals like capitaine and braised chicken for around CFA 2000, a menu du jour for CFA 4000, and large beers for CFA 875. Even if you don't stay here, visit the bar. It is a meeting place for well-off locals and foreigners, and the management is a source of good humour and information.

Another choice in this price range is the *Hôtel du 22 Septembre 1960* (☎ 32 04 62), in the eastern outskirts, on the road towards Mopti, about five km from the town centre. Rooms are new and reasonably priced: CFA 6800 with fans and CFA 10,600 with air-con (for one or two people). Decent food is available in the air-con restaurant. The owner, Pierre Saadé, offers a 10% discount to those who show him this guidebook.

In the same part of town, about 3.5 km from the centre, is the *Hôtel Miverna* (☎ 32 03 31). This place is clean, verging on sterile, with excellent self-contained air-con rooms, but still a bit pricey at CFA 15,000/30,000.

Places to Eat

Most of the hotels listed in Places to Stay have restaurants, but Ségou has a surprisingly wide range of other places to eat. There's a choice of cheap eating houses on the road just east of the centre, at the place where minibuses leave for Bamako and Mopti, and all the long-distance buses stop. These include *Restaurant Bon Coin* and *Tanti J'ai Faime*, both with riz sauce for CFA 200, and other meals up to CFA 500. Or try the *Regal*, just east of the Snack Bar Golfe, where meals start at CFA 250, or the *Chez Madame Halima*, nearby, where decent riz sauce is CFA 200 and large beers CFA 500.

If you're staying at the Mission Catholique, the nearby *Café Surprise* has meals like meat and chips for CFA 1250 and beers at 500. If you're staying at La Maison du Peuple, there's a small restaurant just behind it with very good inexpensive food. Some travellers have recommended *Restaurant Lat Dior*, very much a locals' place, in the Medina area about one km south of the centre, where meals and beers are cheap, and there's music some evenings.

In the town centre the long-established *Snack Bar Golfe* is easy to find (and in a good position for people-watching) between the market and the gare routière. It has tables

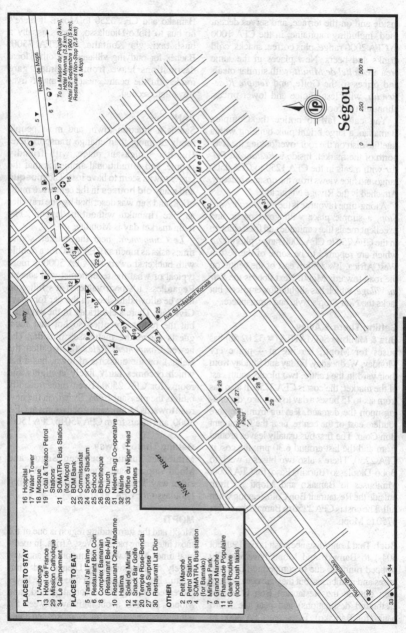

Ségou

MALI

PLACES TO STAY
1   L'Auberge
13 Hôtel de France
29 Mission Catholique
34 Le Campement

PLACES TO EAT
5   Tanti J'ai Faime
6   Restaurant Bon Coin
8   Complex Bamanan
    (Restaurant Bel-Air)
10 Restaurant Chez Madame
    Halima
12 Soleil de Minuit
14 Snack Bar Golfe
20 Temple Rose-Berdia
27 Café Surprise
30 Restaurant Lat Dior

OTHER
2   Petit Marché
3   Petrol Station
4   SOMATRA Bus station
    (for Bamako)
7   Minibus Park
9   Grand Marché
11 Pharmacie Populaire
15 Gare Routière
    (local bush taxis)
16 Hospital
17 Water Tower
18 Mosque
19 Total & Texaco Petrol
    Stations
21 SOMATRA Bus Station
    (for Mopti)
22 BDM Bank
23 Commissariat
24 Sports Stadium
25 School
26 Bibliotheque
28 Church
31 Nielení Rug Co-operative
32 Mairie
33 Office du Niger Head
    Quarters

To La Maison du Peuple (3 km),
Hôtel Minerva (3.5 km),
Hôtel l22 Septembre 1960 (5 km),
Restaurant Non-Stop (2.5 km)
& Mopti

Route de Mopti

Medina

Ava du Président Konaté

Niger River

Jetty

Football
Field

Route de Bamako

500 m
250
0

inside and on the terrace, and serves decent food, including capitaine, in the CFA 1000 to CFA 2000 range, plus coffee, snacks, cold drinks and beers. New places in the same area are *Soliel de Minuit*, with similar meals and prices to the Golfe, and *Temple Rose-Bendia*, with less choice and lower prices, although the food is good.

You can't fail to notice the Complex Bamanan, a large bright pink building with a satellite dish on the roof, overlooking the river north of the market. Inside is *Restaurant Bel-Air* with meals in the CFA 1250 to CFA 2500 range and nice views from the upstairs balcony. Attached is the Rivage Nightclub.

A long-time favourite is the *Restaurant Non-Stop*, a simple place with good music and excellent meals like capitaine and fried chicken in the CFA 750 to CFA 2000 range, plus pizzas which are reported to be some of the best in West Africa. It's 2.5 km east of the centre on the road towards Mopti. Next door is the *Soir au Village*, which has slightly lower prices, but lacks the Non-Stop's style and atmosphere.

Getting There & Away

Bus & Minibus SOMATRA (☎ 32 02 66) has buses for Mopti, leaving at 4 pm every Monday, Wednesday, Friday and Sunday from their yard in the centre, two blocks south-east of the market; the cost is CFA 3750. It also has from six to 15 buses a day to Bamako, depending upon the demand, leaving from the gare routière east of the centre, near the Restaurant Bon Coin. The first bus usually leaves around 7 am and the last around 6.30 pm; the cost is CFA 2250. There's also two buses a week to Bobo-Dioulasso (Burkina Faso) for CFA 5000. Minibuses to Bamako and Mopti go from outside the Restaurant Bon Coin, leaving when full. The cost is CFA 2250 to Bamako and CFA 3750 to Mopti.

Bush Taxi Long-distance bush taxis (Peugeot 504s) to Bamako and Mopti have virtually stopped running, due to competition from the buses and minibuses, but they are occasionally seen outside the Restaurant Bon Coin (for eastbound destinations) and near the BDM bank (for Bamako). Fares are CFA 3000 to Bamako and CFA 5250 to Mopti. If there's no bus to Bobo-Dioulasso, there's usually a bush taxi, via Koutalia, for CFA 7500. Bachés for outlying villages and other local destinations leave from the small gare routière in the centre, near the major five-ways intersection.

SAN

San is a junction town, and most people rarely do more than change transport here. But it's a pleasant place, with friendly people, and a traditional ambience that the larger towns seem to have lost. The **mosque** and many **old houses** in the centre are mud-brick, and San was described by one traveller as 'like Timbuktu without the legend'. The main market day is Monday.

Le Campement, near the market, sometimes asks as much as CFA 7500 for a double with bucket showers but CFA 5000 is more typical of what the receptionist will accept. Regardless, it's poor value. If it's full, you may be allowed to sleep in the bar for about CFA 750. There's electricity in the evening, but the rooms are often so hot that most guests move the mattresses outside. The newer *Campement Relax* (also called the Relais), on the outskirts of town, has a bar which becomes fairly lively at nights and rooms for CFA 2500. Even more recently built is the pleasant *Hôtel Teriya*, on the new road towards Mopti, with good rooms at CFA 3000, and meals from CFA 750 to CFA 1500.

Getting There & Away

Minibuses running between Ségou and Mopti stop in San. The fare is CFA 2250 either way. There are also bush taxis to Bobo-Dioulasso for CFA 5000.

MOPTI

Mopti and the surrounding region is one of the most interesting parts of West Africa. In medieval times Mopti was not important, and was largely overshadowed by Djenné and Timbuktu. But commerce on the Niger River increased during the colonial period, and Mopti's position, about halfway between the administrative centres of Bamako and Gao, gave it a distinct advantage. Today, with over 40,000 inhabitants, Mopti has four times Djenné's population, and is a very active place, with a large market, a beautiful mosque and the most vibrant port on the Niger River.

Mopti lies at the junction of the Niger and Bani rivers (Mopti is technically on the Bani River) at the centre of the vast inland delta region, formed where the rivers divide and subdivide into numerous streams and seasonal lakes or swamps.

Within a day's journey of Mopti is the ancient city of Djenné and the fascinating Dogon Country, and many travellers pass through here on the route to Timbuktu. Mopti is also a good place to meet locals and other travellers, and has a good choice of bars and restaurants suitable for all budgets. Whatever you do, there's enough to keep you fully occupied for quite a few days.

Orientation

The town stands on an area of high ground, surrounded by swamp and water every rainy season, and linked to the mainland proper by a 12-km causeway (dyke) constructed by the French in colonial times. Today, this causeway is still the only road approach to Mopti, reached by turning off the main road between Bamako and Gao at Sévaré. On either side of the causeway are rice fields that are inundated half the year.

As you enter Mopti you'll pass on your right the commissariat, the campement, and the gare routière serving Sévaré and Djenné. Between the campement and the waterfront are most of the small shops, restaurants and the Marché des Souvenirs. The old town is to your left (south), across another causeway, where you'll find the Grande Mosquée, the Grand Marché and the Hôtel Bar Mali.

Information

Money Mopti has two banks: the BDM in the centre and the BIAO on the waterfront to the north of the centre. Hours are Monday to Friday from 8.30 to 11.30 am and from 2.15 to 3.15 pm. At both, the service is slow and the commission varies according to the currency you change, although it's usually high, and the staff often refuse to accept all but French francs anyway.

Police On your day of arrival you must register with the police at the commissariat, and pay a 'fee' of CFA 1000 (see Documents under Facts for the Visitor). You may also be able to get visa extensions here.

Dangers & Annoyances Mopti is the centre of Mali's tourist industry, and your visit can be ruined by local youths continually pestering you, offering their services as guides or trying to sell you postcards and souvenirs. Just ignore them completely.

Beware that some of them are tricksters. We've heard stories from travellers who were told by a 'guide' that he could find them a lift to Gao or Timbuktu with an aid-worker, and needed some money to rent a mobylette (moped) to go and find the driver. Of course, the lift had gone and the money was never seen again.

Guides If you do want a guide, either for Mopti or Dogon Country, it is worth asking other travellers who have been in town for a few days, or have come back from Dogon Country, for their recommendations. Two guides that have been recommended are Al Haj (whose street name is 'Bouctou') and Ismael (street name: 'Le Vieu'). Both are quiet, well mannered, knowledgeable and speak English well. They're often hired by the overland tour companies who pass through Mopti. If they're not around, some other guides may pretend to be one of them – so make sure you get the right guy. Other Mopti guides recommended by travellers include Abdulaye Sangare, Assou Faradj, Aldiouma Iongoiba and 'Pascal Falaise'. Other recommended guides based in Bandiagara and Bankas are listed in the Dogon Country section. But, like restaurants, good guides can go bad so get a personal recommendation if you can.

Mosque

Approaching Mopti you'll see the large

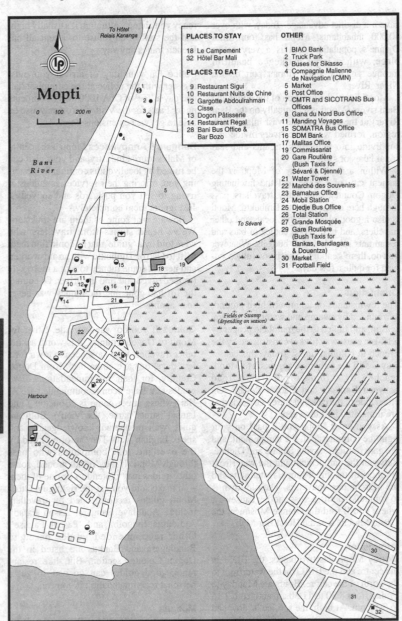

Mopti

0   100   200 m

To Hôtel Relais Kananga

Bani River

To Sévaré

Fields or Swamp (depending on season)

Harbour

PLACES TO STAY
18 Le Campement
32 Hôtel Bar Mali

PLACES TO EAT
9 Restaurant Sigui
10 Restaurant Nuits de Chine
12 Gargotte Abdoulrahman Cisse
13 Dogon Pâtisserie
14 Restaurant Regal
28 Bani Bus Office & Bar Bozo

OTHER
1 BIAO Bank
2 Truck Park
3 Buses for Sikasso
4 Compagnie Malienne de Navigation (CMN)
5 Market
6 Post Office
7 CMTR and SICOTRANS Bus Offices
8 Gana du Nord Bus Office
11 Manding Voyages
15 SOMATRA Bus Office
16 BDM Bank
17 Malitas Office
19 Commissariat
20 Gare Routière (Bush Taxis for Sévaré & Djenné)
21 Water Tower
22 Marché des Souvenirs
23 Bamabus Office
24 Mobil Station
25 Djedje Bus Office
26 Total Station
27 Grande Mosquée
29 Gare Routière (Bush Taxis for Bankas, Bandiagara & Douentza)
30 Market
31 Football Field

MALI

mud-brick mosque, built in 1935, towering above the city's old section on your left. It's style was inspired by the mosque in Djenné and, if you're lucky (or a Muslim), the guard will let you go in and climb the stairs for a view of the city. Otherwise, the local man who lives next to the mosque will let you onto the roof of his house (for a small fee) so you can look at the mosque from there.

Market

The Grand Marché is in the old town about 10 blocks beyond the mosque on the same road. Thursday is market day. Bozo fishers converge on the city to sell their dried fish. If you see huge white slabs looking like tombstones, it is salt from northern Mali brought down by the camel caravans. It's the same rock salt you'll see in most of the markets throughout West Africa.

Pirogue Trips

Dusk is a good time to hire a pirogue for a small river trip. The going rate is about CFA 1000 per hour, especially if you go straight to the boat owner, rather than arrange things through a guide (although the harder you bargain, the shorter the trip). If you've got the time and money, a good destination is the Bozo village of Kakalodaga. At dusk, the village is active, with women cooking, kids playing and men repairing their nets and building boats. There's also an abandoned Tuareg village nearby. Pelicans, ibis and herons may contribute to the tranquillity of the ride back. At the Bar Bozo, which has a beautiful view of the river scene at sunset, there's no lack of boat owners offering to take passengers. You can also go for longer trips, further down the river, to villages where the people are less used to tourists.

Places to Stay – bottom end

The Peace Corps rest house no longer accepts visitors (unless you're a volunteer), so most travellers on a budget stay at the *Hôtel Bar Mali*, on the southern side of the old town. This is a dirty brothel but it has a kind of sleazy charm. Singles/doubles with fans cost CFA 3500/4000. Upstairs is a corridor with a nice balcony at one end, and tourists generally get put in rooms along here. If these are full, choose carefully: some of the hotel's other rooms have no windows and those on the top floor get hot (although they are cheaper). The shared showers and toilets are not too bad, and there always seems to be water. The bar serves cheap beer, and food is available if you order several hours in advance. If you want to travel light to Djenné or Dogon Country, you can leave baggage at the hotel.

If you've got a tent, you can pitch it in the car park at *Le Campement* (see below) for CFA 2000 per person per night, although it's usually only overlanders with vehicles who do this.

In Sévaré, *Camping Toguna* charges CFA 2000 per person for camping and CFA 2500 per person for a bed in a simple room with nets and shared bucket showers. The restaurant is cheap and decent. From the main intersection in Sévaré, head west for several blocks towards Mopti. You'll see a sign pointing to your left (south). Follow that dirt road for about 800 metres.

Places to Stay – middle

The only mid-range hotel in Mopti is *Le Campement*. It's well patronised and a good place for meeting people but the basic rooms with nets, fans and dirty shared bathrooms are bad value at CFA 8000 (one or two people), or CFA 15,000 with air-con. Prices go up in the high season (mid-November to early March).

The other mid-range hotels are in Sévaré. Cheapest and relatively good value, is *Hôtel Oasis* (☎ 42 01 06), in the backstreets a few blocks off the main road, not far from the bush taxi gare routière, with clean singles/doubles at CFA 6250. Bathrooms are also very clean. Breakfast costs CFA 625. The restaurant serves meals in the CFA 1200 range, and has a useful map of the surrounding area (including Dogon Country) on the wall. On the main road itself is the old run-down *Motel de Sévaré* (☎ 42 01 11), gloomy and way overpriced at CFA 7000/9000 with fans and CFA 12,500/16,200 with air-con. Prices include breakfast. Much better is the new *Hôtel Débo* (☎ 42 01 24) nearby which is frequently full and charges CFA 12,500 to CFA 15,600 for singles and CFA 15,600 to CFA 18,100 for doubles, all self-contained with air-con, plus CFA 500 tax. Meals cost from CFA 1500 to CFA 2500.

Places to Stay – top end

The *Hôtel Relais Kananga* (☎ 43 05 00 or 43 05 48, telex 8002) is next to the river, about one km north of the centre. It charges CFA 27,500/35,000 plus CFA 500 tax per person. Groups can get doubles for CFA 22,500. The hotel used to be part of the Sofitel chain, but it's privately run now. There's a back-up generator but no pool.

Places to Eat

Most of the places listed in Places to Stay also serve food, but Mopti has several other places to choose from. For cheap street food, such as brochettes, nuts, fried plantain and small cakes, check the stalls around the gare routière near the campement. There are also a couple of reasonable *gargottes* (basic eating houses or stalls) around the gare routière near the harbour. A bit more expensive, but a real travellers' favourite, is the *Dogon Pâtisserie*, in between the campement and the river, with excellent coffee (CFA 250) and pastries (CFA 150 to CFA 450). Round the corner is the simpler *Gargotte Abdoulrahman Cisse* where you sit on a bench in the street; coffee is CFA 125 and omelettes and bread CFA 300. Slightly more expensive, but good value, is the nearby *Restaurant Regal* (also called Chez Mama) where the *patron* is very friendly and meals such as meat and chips cost around CFA 1000, and riz sauce is CFA 500. Next door, but up a few notches in quality, is *Restaurant Nuits de Chine* with well-prepared meals (including five capitaine selections, riz Cantonnais and nems) in the CFA 1500 to CFA 2500 range, and big beers at CFA 650. A block to the north is *Restaurant Sigui* which has a less elaborate menu and a very nice garden setting, with good food and cold beer in the same price range. Similar, and with

better views of the river, although a few more mosquitoes, is *Bar Bozo* on the harbour.

Things to Buy

Mopti is famous for blankets. There are two types: the 'standard' models, and the much more ornate (and expensive) Fulani wedding blankets. Look for sellers outside the Nuits de Chine and Sigui restaurants, and at the Marché des Souvenirs. (Although they're more likely to find you.) The 'standard' Mopti blankets can be all-wool, a wool-cotton mix, or all-cotton. With hard bargaining, you can get all-wool blankets with six or seven bands for CFA 3750 to CFA 5000, wool-cotton mix for CFA 6250 to CFA 7500, all-cotton ones with simple coloured squares for CFA 5000 to CFA 10,000, and all-cotton ones with complex designs for CFA 10,000 to CFA 12,500. The five-metre-long Fulani wedding blankets can cost CFA 62,500 or more, depending on the material.

Getting There & Away

Air The airport is in Sévaré. Air Mali has flights to/from Bamako, Timbuktu and Gao. For details see the main Getting Around section in this chapter. Schedules change all the time, so check at the Malitas office near the campement or the Air Mali office in the campement itself.

Bus Several bus companies serve Mopti, with ticket offices in various parts of town. Djedje Transport and Gana du Nord have offices on the waterfront, SOMATRA is near the post office, and Bamabus is near the Marché des Souvenirs. For transport to Bamako, Djedje and Gana du Nord buses leave every day between 3 and 5 pm, arriving Bamako at daybreak, while SOMATRA and Bamabus leave every morning, typically around 10 am. Another company serving this route is Bani Bus; its buses, which are a bit run-down, depart Mopti around 5 pm. The cost on all of these large buses is CFA 6000. For transport to Gao, most of these companies have a twice-weekly service for CFA 6000, linking in with the convoy between Hombori and Gao. If this area becomes safe, daily services are likely. Transport to Sikasso departs daily from the gare routière north of the centre. All companies charge CFA 6000. Several companies also serve Bobo-Dioulasso (Burkina Faso), but departure days and times vary, so you need to ask (and buy your ticket) in advance. The fare is CFA 7500. One possibility is to take a Somtrie bus to Sikasso and get off in Koutiala (CFA 2750) and then continue on from there to Bobo by bush taxi (CFA 3600). Somtrie buses depart Mopti at noon and 5 pm and take about nine hours to reach Koutiala. For more information, see Getting There & Away under Bobo-Dioulasso.

Bush Taxi Because buses cover all long-distance routes, bush taxis only serve nearer destinations. Bachés cover the 12 km between Mopti and Sévaré throughout the day for CFA 225, departing Mopti from the small gare routière near the campement. Bush taxis to Djenné also go from here, charging CFA 2000 in a baché and CFA 2250 in a 504. See the Djenné Getting There & Away section for advice about chartering a taxi from Mopti to Djenné. Bush taxis to other destinations go from the gare routière south of the harbour. To Bandiagara is CFA 1500 by 504, to Bankas is CFA 2500, and to Douentza is CFA 3000. For information on the routes to Timbuktu, see the Getting There & Away section for that city.

Car Rental & Tours Some people rent a vehicle to reach Djenné, Timbuktu or Dogon Country. Savana Tours (office at the Hôtel Kananga, ☎ 43 05 00) rent a Peugeot 504 for CFA 18,750 per day, and a Land Rover for CFA 56,000 per day, plus petrol (both with driver). You can also hire a car and driver-guide through the campement at slightly cheaper rates.

Savanna Tours also arrange excursions for groups from Mopti to Djenné, Timbuktu and Dogon Country, as do Sahel Tours (☎ 43 05 61), also based in Mopti, and Timbuctours (☎ 42 00 92) based in Sévaré and Sanga.

Boat It's possible to go to/from Mopti by river. For details of the passenger boats run by the CMN see the main Getting Around

section in this chapter. Mopti's CMN office is on the waterfront, 200 metres north of Restaurant Nuits de Chine.

Pinasses from Mopti to Djenné usually leave on Friday, Saturday and Sunday, to tie in with Djenné's Monday market, and return to Mopti on Monday evening or Tuesday morning. The 12-hour trip by motorised pinasse costs CFA 3500 to CFA 4500 per person and rice and sauce are provided. Non-motorised pirogue take two days and cost CFA 3000.

Many travellers go by large pinasse between Mopti and Kabara (for Timbuktu), or do the section between Mopti and Diré by pinasse and between Timbuktu and Diré by road. For more details see Getting There & Away in the Timbuktu section.

DJENNÉ

Djenné is sometimes missed by travellers pressed for time, as it's just off the main route between Bamako and Mopti. This is a pity because Djenné is unquestionably one of the most interesting and picturesque towns in West Africa. Little has changed here for centuries: almost all of the houses are of mud with thatched roofs, making for an aesthetically pleasing town that blends in with the environment. The town is built on an island in the Niger River Delta, about 130 km south-west of Mopti and 30 km off the Mopti to Ségou highway. It's worth coming to Djenné on market day (Monday), when this otherwise sleepy town comes alive, but even on other days it's still worth a visit.

History

Founded in the 9th century, Djenné is one of the oldest towns in West Africa and was in its prime during the 14th and 15th centuries when it profited, like Timbuktu, from the trans-Saharan trade. This wealth existed for many centuries: when the French explorer René Caillié visited here in the early 19th century, he reported that the inhabitants enjoyed a good standard of living and had plenty to eat, most could read, no one went barefoot, and everyone seemed to be usefully employed.

Djenné was surrounded by a wall until the end of the 19th century, when parts of it were

MALI

Fulani Earrings

Djenné is a good place to see well-to-do Peul (Fulani) people, particularly at the Monday market. Many women, having inherited gold and jewellery, are financially independent of their husbands. You'll see them dressed very elaborately, with earrings and neck pendants of gold, large bracelets of silver and necklaces of European glass beads. Most spectacular, however, are the huge 14-carat gold *kwotenai kanye* earrings worn by the wealthiest women. They are so heavy that the top of each earring is bound with red wool or silk to protect the ear. Most Peul women inherit them from their mothers or receive them at marriage from their husbands, who have to sell off some of their cattle to afford them. Note also their voluminous brightly coloured head scarves; they too are objects of glamour and signs of opulence and often conceal elaborate hairstyles. ■

---

destroyed by the French and much of the rest dissolved in the rain. Other parts were incorporated into houses and other buildings. You can see remnants of the wall if you walk along the edge of the old part of the town near the river.

Mosque

The elegant mosque in Djenné, built in 1905, is renowned as a classic example of Sudanese (or Sahelian) mud architecture; photographs of it are shown in exhibits worldwide. It's design is based on that of the previous mosque, dating from the 11th century, which was famous even in Europe, and demolished in the 19th century because of political and religious strife. Just to keep the mosque from disintegrating during the rains is a major task and each year the mud structure must undergo considerable repair. Inside, there is a forest of a hundred or so massive columns, taking up almost half of the floor surface. Non-Muslim visitors cannot go inside (after somebody let in a photographer and group of models for a fashion shoot), but an excellent view of the outer walls can be had from the roof of the Petit Marché opposite the mosque.

Walking Tour

Leave at least a few hours to walk around. The narrow streets allow the sun to penetrate only rarely, making the town cooler than most. Late afternoon is especially pleasant, and you can finish with a stroll along the river side at sunset.

Guides are not essential in Djenné but you'll be pestered all day by local youths offering their services, so hiring one will keep the others at bay. You'll also see a lot more than you would on your own. Your guide will be able to take you onto the roof of a private house to get a view of the town, ask permission from the locals to take photos, and show you where the various artisans (such as goldsmiths, woodcarvers and mud-cloth artists) work. (A recommended guide is Oumarou Gogo Thiokary – but a lot of guides seem to have this name, so ask for his ID!)

The **Grand Marché** is the wide area between the Grande Mosquée and the Petit Marché. Most of the time it's quiet, but on market day (Monday) the place is packed with traders and customers.

As you go through the narrow streets and alleyways, you'll pass between the walls of

---

Jenné-Jeno

Three km from Djenné are the ruins of Jenné-Jeno, an ancient settlement that dates back to about 250 BC. It is now only an archaeological site. Iron implements and jewellery have been discovered there which suggest that it may have been one of the first places in Africa where iron was used. In the 8th century Jenné-Jeno was one of the two oldest fortified cities in West Africa with walls three metres thick. Around 1400 it was abandoned; nobody knows why.

Jenné-Jeno is also spelt Djenné-Djeno. Either way, it means Old Djenné but for some reason the anglicised spelling is more commonly used. Perhaps because most of the archaeologists involved in uncovering the site were American. ■

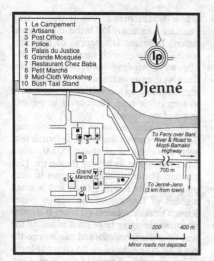

1 Le Campement
2 Artisans
3 Post Office
4 Police
5 Palais du Justice
6 Grande Mosquée
7 Restaurant Chez Baba
8 Petit Marché
9 Mud-Cloth Workshop
10 Bush Taxi Stand

Djenné

To Ferry over Bani
River & Road to
Mopt-Bamako
Highway

700 m

To Jenné-Jeno
(3 km from town)

Grand Marché

0   200   400 m

Minor roads not depicted

mud-brick houses. Many have more than one storey; traditionally the top part was for the masters, the middle floor for the slaves and the bottom floor for storage and selling. The porches of the houses are lined with wooden columns, while the wooden window shutters and doors are decorated with paint and metal objects. In one part of town, the houses are decorated in a Moorish style, dating from the period when Moroccan traders lived here and dominated the trade.

You will also pass a few **madrassa** schools (where young Muslim children learn the Koran). There are more madrassa in Djenné than in any other town in Mali. With the help of a guide, you can see the old well, the old prison, and the house of the traditional chief. His role today is mainly as an adjudicator in local disputes (eg when Fulani cattle eat Bambara crops) and he commands considerable respect from the citizens.

Your guide may also want to show you the place where young girls were buried alive in the sand to protect the town from floods. Don't go; only the story is interesting.

Places to Stay & Eat

Other than finding a room in someone's house, the only place to stay is *Le Campement*, near the Grande Mosquée, where single/double rooms with nets cost CFA 3000/4000, or you may be allowed to sleep on the roof for CFA 1500. The bar serves beers for CFA 800. Meals, such as rice and sauce for CFA 625 and a full chicken for CFA 2500, should be ordered in advance. For better food, and service with a smile, search out *Restaurant Chez Baba*, run by the former cook at the campement, in a courtyard off a backstreet near the small market, where rice and chicken, with a dessert, costs CFA 1000. You can also stay overnight here for CFA 1250 a person but no mattresses or lanterns are provided. In the evening (especially on Sunday and Monday) you may find cheap street food around the market.

Things to Buy

Djenné is famous for 'mud cloth' – traditional or abstract designs painted onto sheets of rough cloth using various types of soil for colour. These works of art are sometimes called batiks although the process is not the same. However, the organic effect is pleasing to the eye, and some of the artists (nearly all women) in Djenné are very skilled. Most famous is Pama Sinatoa, whose work was featured in the book *Africa Through the Eyes of Women Artists* (Africa World Press, USA, 1991). Her workshop is a few blocks away from the small bridge where the road from the ferry enters the town. There are several other workshops and places selling mud cloth in the same area.

Getting There & Away

Bus & Bush Taxi From Bamako, there are direct buses to Djenné on Saturday and Monday from the Sogoniko gare routière. The fare is CFA 6700. (They return to Bamako on Sunday and Tuesday departing from the square across from the mosque). The road to Djenné is now tarred all the way. From Ségou, there are minibuses and bush taxis to Djenné on Sunday and early Monday morning. If you don't get transport direct, you can get dropped off at the junction where the road to Djenné branches off the main road

MALI

between Ségou and Mopti. However, you may have a long wait here, as traffic is light and most bush taxis will be full by the time they reach you. If it's not market day (Monday), you're better off going to Mopti and finding transport back to Djenné from there.

In Mopti, bush taxis for Djenné leave from the gare routière near the campement. They go most days, and there may be two or more on Monday mornings, when the first one goes at about 7 am. Bachés cost CFA 2000 and 504s CFA 2250. The trip takes three to four hours. From Mopti you can get to Djenné and back in a day by bush taxi, as long as you leave early, although this only gives you about four hours for looking around. Some travellers get their own small group together and charter the whole bush taxi. This may be a bit more expensive (CFA 25,000 for the car) but it saves lots of time. Except when the river is low enough to drive across, bush taxis reach Djenné by a small ferry. Passengers pay CFA 150.

For leaving Djenné, the best time to find transport back to Mopti, or onwards to Ségou or Bamako, is Monday afternoon or early evening, following the market.

Car From February to June, vehicles pass over the submersible causeway crossing the Bani River, which flows alongside the town. During the rest of the year, they must be put on the ferry, which costs CFA 3750 plus CFA 150 per person.

Pinasse Large pinasses ply the Bani River, connecting Djenné and Mopti. See Getting There & Away in the Mopti section for details. On Tuesday mornings there is always one leaving for Bamako. On other days the chances of finding one headed for Bamako are slim. The pinasse leaves anywhere from dawn to 8 am so you may have to leave the town before dawn to catch it as the loading point is four km away.

TIMBUKTU (TOMBOUCTOU)
In Timbuktu sand is everywhere. Even when you bite into a loaf of the city's famous whole-wheat bread, you'll detect tiny particles. Seemingly lost in the middle of the desert, Timbuktu is a sprawl of low, flat-roofed buildings with narrow streets and alleyways winding between the houses. Sand is piling up on the outskirts, and the city itself is filling up too, so that you now have to step *down* from street-level to go into many of the houses.

Once a great centre of art and learning, Timbuktu is now a shadow of its former self, with a population of about 15,000, down from 100,000 in its heyday during the 15th century. The only thing that seems to keep people here is tourism, trade and a small amount of farming on the nearby Niger River. Occasional camel caravans still come into town, bringing huge slabs of salt all the way from the Taoudenni salt mines in northern Mali to be shipped up the river to Mopti.

For centuries, Timbuktu has been a byword for an inaccessible place and, even today, it's still hard to reach – although this seems to make people want to come here more than ever. However, when they arrive, some visitors find Timbuktu disappointing; like the early European explorers, maybe they expect the streets to be paved with gold. But most are glad they came; even if Timbuktu didn't have a magical name, it would still be a fascinating place to visit, with a 'feel' and atmosphere quite unlike any of the other towns along the Niger.

History
Timbuktu dates back to around 1100 AD when a group of Tuareg nomads settled here. The settlement was put in the charge of an old woman while the men tended to the animals. Her name was Timbuktu, meaning 'mother with a large navel', possibly meaning she had a physical disorder. The settlement was named after her.

In 1494, Leo Africanus, a well-travelled Spanish Moor, visited Timbuktu and recorded in his *History & Description of Africa* that Timbuktu had 'a great store of doctors, judges, priests and other learned men, that are bountifully maintained at the king's expense'. But by the time the first

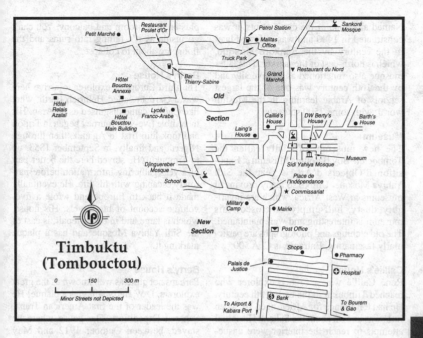

Timbuktu
(Tombouctou)

0   150   300 m

Minor Streets not Depicted

MALI

European explorers arrived in the early 19th century, Timbuktu, after centuries of repeated invasions and the ravages of time, was a changed city and more like it is today.

Orientation & Information

The focus of Timbuktu is the Place de l'Indépendance. Nearby is the commissariat, the *mairie* (town hall), and the all-important post office that stamps your postcards. South from here the main road leads past the New Section of town (with several streets of houses, the bank and the hospital) and out towards the airport and Kabara, on the Niger River, nine km away. The part of town north of the Place de l'Indépendance is the Old Section, where you find the Grand Marché, the museum, three old mosques, a few restaurants and Timbuktu's two hotels.

Police You must register with the police at the commissariat upon arrival. A 'fee' of CFA 1000 is required (see Documents under

Facts for the Visitor). You must do this even if you're on your way between Gao and Mopti by boat and are merely taking a brief tour of the city by taxi while the boat is unloading its cargo at Kabara.

Mosques

Timbuktu has three of the oldest mosques in West Africa. They're not large, architecturally impressive, or in good repair – just old. **Djinguereber Mosque** (the Grande Mosquée), 250 metres west of the Place de l'Indépendance, is the oldest and the only one that can be visited inside. (The guard asks for an entrance fee of CFA 1000, but seems to be open to negotiation). You may also be allowed to climb the minaret for a view over the city. The mosque dates from the early 14th century when Emperor Kankan Moussa, having taken control of the city from the Tuareg, commanded its construction.

About 250 metres north of the roundabout is the **Sidi Yahya Mosque** on your right.

Named after one of the city's saints, it was constructed in 1400 and was followed later in the century by the **Sankoré Mosque**, which is north-east of the market. This latter mosque also functioned as a university and by the 16th century was one of the largest schools of Arabic learning in the Muslim world, with some 2500 students.

Museum

The new museum, officially called the Tombouctou-Boy Batouma Museum et Exposition d'Objects d'Art, is near the Sidi Yahiya Mosque. Unlike so many provincial museums in West Africa, which are invariably dusty, half-empty or closed, this museum is interesting and well maintained. The old etchings and photographs are particularly fascinating. Entrance is CFA 500.

Caillié's House

René Caillié was a French explorer who reached Timbuktu in the early 19th century. He had left France for Africa, aged 16, when little was known about the Sahara. His initial attempts to reach the interior were unsuccessful, but in 1824 he travelled through the desert disguised as a Moor, and learned all about the Arab culture. In 1828 he finally fulfilled his ambition and became the first European both to reach Timbuktu and live to tell the tale. His account of the trip and the cultures he encountered is one of the most fascinating pieces of historical literature relating to Africa. The house where he stayed is in the backstreets, south of the Grand Marché and west of Sidi Yahiya Mosque. It is unoccupied and in tumbledown condition, but a plaque remains on the wall.

Laing's House

Caillié was not the first European explorer to reach Timbuktu. That honour went to a Scot called Gordon Laing, but he never made it back to Europe. He was killed on his way to Ségou by one of his Arab escorts on the order of the sultan, who had no tolerance for infidels. The house where he stayed is west of Caillié's on the same winding street. It's very small, with one lower room and front terrace

plus an upper room and balcony. You can't go inside as it's falling into ruins and the floors are about to collapse.

Barth's House

The third European explorer to arrive here was a German called Heinrich Barth, who, like Caillié, came disguised as an Arab. His incredible five-year journey began in Tripoli and took him first to Agadez, then through Nigeria and finally, in September 1853, up to Timbuktu. He stayed here the better part of a year gathering information before narrowly escaping with his life. He eventually made it back to Europe and wrote a five-volume account of his travels. His house, which is large and in better repair, is east of the Sidi Yahiya Mosque and has a plaque marking it.

Berty's House

Perhaps not quite as well known as the great explorers, D W Berty still gets a plaque! He was the leader of the first American Trans-Saharan Expedition. The house where he stayed, between October 1912 and May 1913, is almost opposite the museum.

Markets

The Grand Marché is a large covered building in the north-east part of the Old Section. It's not particularly grand: there are a few merchants selling cloth and other goods, some tailors and a man mending pots and pans. There's so little food being sold there that you'll think people must be starving. Some reporters visiting during the droughts have been fooled into thinking the situation is bordering on catastrophic. In reality, commerce in Timbuktu is somewhat unusual; most staples are sold in bulk at merchants' homes.

At the Petit Marché, to the west of the centre, north of the Hôtel Bouctou, you can buy meat, vegetables and other goods. Artisans also work and sell their handicrafts here.

Timbuktu used to have a supermarket, part of the government-owned Somiex chain. It's now closed and empty, except for the part which has been turned into a bar.

Desert Wells

Near the Hôtel Bouctou are some large, funnel-shaped wells, about 50 metres across at the top, with a line of steps leading down to a small pool at the bottom. They have to be this shape because of the sandy soil; a conventional well would soon collapse. Each well is surrounded by a small ring of vegetable plots; the tiny patches of vivid green seem strangely incongruous in this grey city of sand. The best views of the wells are from the roof of the hotel.

Tuareg Camps

The most touristy thing you can do in Timbuktu is to take a short camel ride out to one of the Tuareg camps that surround the city. The going rate is CFA 6000 per camel (two people can ride one camel but this is so uncomfortable it's a false economy) and you can sometimes bargain the price down. Even if you do, this is still a bit expensive but it's an enjoyable trip. If you've come to Timbuktu by plane or boat, a camel trip also gives you a taste of the desert. The best time to go is early morning or late afternoon. You may be entertained by a sword fight and energised by the strong, sweet Arab tea offered inside a Tuareg tent. You'll undoubtedly also be offered some knives or leatherwork to buy. Some travellers have complained about being taken to tents that were set up as a tourist trap (not a real camp at all) where they were charged extra for tea and submitted to an hour of souvenir hardsell. The only way to avoid this is to make it clear right from the start that you will not pay any extras or buy anything, or to go with someone who's been recommended by other travellers. To sample the desert by moonlight, some people manage to stay overnight in one of the Tuareg camps. This is prohibited (partly for security reasons, and partly because the hotel owners complain to the police) but, with discretion, it can be done.

Places to Stay & Eat

There are only two hotels in Timbuktu, both on the west side of the Old Section. Most expensive is the *Hôtel Relais Azalaï* (☎ 92 11 63) where self-contained air-con singles/doubles cost CFA 22,100/26,300 plus tax (CFA 500 per person). The menu du jour in the restaurant costs CFA 6250 and beers are CFA 1250. Nearby is the old *Hôtel Bouctou* (usually called Le Campement) where ordinary rooms cost CFA 6250/8750 (or CFA 5000 extra for self-contained), plus tax. Breakfast is CFA 1000. Other meals are expensive and made to order. Beers are CFA 1000. If you want to economise, ask to sleep in the older annexe, which has more character and double rooms on the ground floor with nets and fans for CFA 6800. Upstairs rooms with a mattress on the floor cost CFA 2500 but the manager will tell you that foreign tourists can't stay there. With persistence you'll probably be allowed.

Cheap street food is hard to find, but a few stalls around the markets sell brochettes, and you can buy bread at the *Restaurant du Nord* near the Grand Marché, which also does tea, coffee, and meals such as eggs or rice and sauce for around CFA 500. Near the Petit Marché is the friendly *Restaurant Poulet d'Or* with better food at slightly higher prices.

For a beer, colder than the Bouctou's and cheaper than the Azalaï's, visit *Bar Thierry-*

MALI

Île de Paix

If you can get a ride, go to the Île de Paix (Isle of Peace), a privately run Belgian organisation which sponsors an irrigated rice scheme of several hundred hectares just outside town towards the river. It's a successful project in terms of producing food, but the technology (huge pumps) is too complex, making it impossible for the Belgians to leave without the system breaking down. Thus, without further training, it cannot be duplicated elsewhere by Malians and is not useful as a development model. Still, the project is doing exactly what it's supposed to do – produce rice at a cost considerably less than shipping it in from Asia or the USA. That's no mean accomplishment. ■

Sabine in the old supermarket building on the main street, west of the centre.

Things to Buy

The Tuareg artisans of Timbuktu have formed an association, and set up a shop, to sell direct to the public and to promote high quality artistry. The Federation des Artisans Tuareg is on the main street, near the post office. Knives and swords (all made by men), with engraved blades and inlaid handles are popular, and you can also buy various leatherwork items (all made by women). A leading member of the association is Ayouba Ag Moihar. He can also help you find a reliable guide for the town or surrounding area if required.

Getting There & Away

Air Timbuktu is served by Air Mali flights between Bamako and Gao (see the main Getting Around section in this chapter for details). If you're really pushed for time you can fly from Bamako or Mopti to Timbuktu and back in a day, as the plane goes on to Gao or has a long turn-around time in Timbuktu, allowing you about three hours to see the city. The airport is about five km from the town. A bus meets all flights. Between the airport and the town centre is CFA 750. If you want to go all the way to/from your hotel the driver charges an extra CFA 750. If you're on a lightning visit you can arrange a tour by taxi from the airport. Prices start high, but you should get it down to a slightly less extortionate CFA 15,000 for the car (not per person) for a few hours.

Land The Djedje bus company runs a weekly service during the dry season between Bamako and Timbuktu, via Ségou and Niono along the north-west side of the Niger River. The trip takes three very hard days and costs CFA 15,000. Another option (if you have time and fortitude in good measure) is to go the same way in stages. From Ségou you can get a bush taxi to Niono, and from there trucks and pick-ups go to Nampala and Léré (about 200 km south-west of Goundam), especially on Thursdays, as there's a big market in Léré on Fridays. From

Léré (after the market) you should be able to find a truck heading for Timbuktu, or to Goundam or Niafounké, from where you can get another lift to Timbuktu.

From Mopti, battered old Land Rovers run to Timbuktu a few times per week during the dry season for CFA 15,000. The trip should take two days (and two nights) although it can take four. One of these Land Rovers is the weekly Courier Postal, carrying mail as well as passengers. Breakdowns are common and you should carry plenty of water for this trip. By asking around, you can also find one of the trucks that run irregularly between Mopti and Timbuktu. It costs between CFA 10,000 and CFA 15,000 to ride on the back, and 50% extra to go in the cab. Trucks are just as uncomfortable as the Land Rovers, but can take longer.

The usual land route from Mopti is east to Douentza and Gossi, then north to Gourma-Rharous where there's a ferry. This breaks down quite often, so you may have to wait a day (or cross by pirogue and find something on the other side). An alternative route from Mopti goes to Douentza then north to Ngouma, but it's difficult to do from June to September. There is also a third route north from Mopti to Korientze and Saraféré, then west to Niafounké and north to Timbuktu, but this route is only open from about March to May when the river is low.

If you're driving your own vehicle, you can take any of the routes outlined above. Many drivers prefer going via Mopti, Gossi and Gourma-Rharous as it's open year-round and less problematic. There are marker posts every so often on the road to Gourma but to be on the safe side you might want to pick up a local in Gossi who knows the way. If you decide to take the route via Ségou, Niono, Nampala, Niafounké and Goundam, allow three days for this 1000-km trip (half of it paved, half of it sand) and don't schedule yourself too tightly as the unexpected frequently happens. This route can become impassable north of Nampala at times between mid-July and the end of August.

To travel between Timbuktu and Gao, those without vehicles can catch a truck.

MALI

They are frequently stationed near the Grand Marché in Timbuktu. You may have to wait a day or two to find one. The trip usually takes about 24 hours. Those driving should be aware that the Gao to Timbuktu route is worse than anything on the Reggane (Algeria) to Gao route, and it can become impassable at times between mid-July and the end of August.

Boat Between late July and late November, the large passenger boats stop at Kabara, nine km south of Timbuktu (see the main Getting Around section in this chapter). The boat stops for about two hours in Kabara, so if you're travelling between Gao and Mopti, it's possible to make a mad dash to Timbuktu for a brief tour. You'll have to charter a taxi as there's no time to take a shared one. The going rate for a round-trip tour is CFA 15,000. The most aggravating part is that you must register and pay CFA 1000 to the police which often leaves no more than 15 minutes to see the town.

Alternatively, you can go to/from Timbuktu by pinasse. There are no schedules: between Mopti and Kabara (Timbuktu's port) a good pinasse should take about three days, although it can take much longer (see the main Getting Around section of this chapter). Expect to pay CFA 6500 to CFA 10,000 (after some hard haggling). You may have to change pinasse at Diré or Niafounké, which can add a day or two to the trip. Some travellers go by pinasse from Mopti to Diré or Niafounké and then travel on to Timbuktu by truck or pick-up.

There are some very large pinasses running between Mopti and Kabara, which leave on set days and run as close to schedules as anything else does on the river. Look out for the powerful 80-metre-long *Baba Tigamba*, going once per week in each direction, and taking only two days. It has proper seats, a roof, and even a small upper deck which the owner calls the 'cabine luxe'. Fares start at a ridiculous CFA 37,500, but after negotiation you should get a ride for about CFA 15,000 or even less.

There are also very occasional pinasses running between Gao and Timbuktu. These tend to be even slower and less reliable than those on the Mopti route, but cost the same.

Some tour companies charter a pinasse to carry groups from Mopti to Timbuktu. They rarely take independent travellers, but ask around at the campement or along the waterfront near the Hôtel Kananga.

AROUND TIMBUKTU
Diré
This is a small town on the river between Timbuktu and Mopti that is rarely visited by outsiders. Market day is Tuesday; if you're travelling between Mopti and Timbuktu, organise your transport around this day to speed up connections, as you may have to change boats here, or switch to road transport for part of the journey. The campement has closed, but the owner of the café on the main square will find you a room for CFA 1250.

Goundam
Goundam is a small town, about 100 km west of Timbuktu, and about 30 km north-west of Diré. Travelling by road along the north bank of the Niger you may pass though this way. There are reports of a campement here, but it may have closed.

To the north and south of Goundam are some small lakes, and the area between here and Diré is the only place in West Africa where wheat is grown, made possible by the cool winter nights and plentiful supply of water. The famous Timbuktu bread is made from this wheat. Other crops such as millet and rice are also grown. Late November to March is the growing season. From December to February, you can watch farmers lift the water up several metres by swinging gourds over their shoulders.

Lake Faguibine
Lake Faguibine is about 50 km to the north of Goundam. It dried up completely in the 1984 drought, but in years of normal rainfall it's the largest natural lake in West Africa, as long as you put Lake Chad (some 2000 km to the East) in Central Africa. A few villages line the southern shore, and this is one of the

MALI

three best places in the Sahel for seeing migratory birds.

For around CFA 100,000, SMERT used to take travellers on a one-day trip to Goundam (about three hours by car) and on to Lake Faguibine. If you ask at either of the hotels in Timbuktu, the people there would probably know of private individuals with 4WDs willing to do the same.

Araouane

Araouane, over 250 km north of Timbuktu, is a small oasis village (with about 150 inhabitants) completely surrounded by sand dunes, and a major staging post on the camel caravan route between Timbuktu and the salt mines of Taoudenni, in the far north of the country. In Araouane the local people have started a project called Arbres pour Araouane (Trees for Araouane). With help from a guy called Ernest Aebi, and a solar pump to bring water to the surface, the people have built vegetable gardens, planted trees, and – believe me – built an eight-room hotel, using all local materials: the shelves, for instance, are made of salt bars.

The hotel charges CFA 10,000/15,000 for singles/doubles. Breakfast is CFA 1500 and an evening meal, with various Tuareg specialities, is CFA 6250. These prices may seem a bit stiff, but remember Araouane is a long way from anywhere, and all profits go towards funding the project. If you want to stay in Araouane for more than a few nights, local people are happy to take guests, at rates lower than the hotel. And, as long as tourism is creating income for the local people, the hotel doesn't seem to mind if you come to such a private arrangement.

Getting There & Away You can get to Araouane from Timbuktu by car or camel. The best time is between October and March; at other times it's too hot even for the Tuareg. By car, the drive takes one long day. If you don't have your own wheels, you can hire a 4WD vehicle (seating up to six people) for CFA 150,000. This rate has been agreed between drivers and the people of Araouane, and is for a two-way journey allowing for

one night in Araouane. If you want to stay longer, you must pay extra for the driver's time, food and lodging. If you go by camel, this takes about one week, riding (or walking) for seven to eight hours each day. The cost is CFA 12,500 per day (which includes food – typical Tuareg fare of rice, goat and camel meat, and litres of tea). You also need a sleeping bag or blanket, something to keep off the sun (a Tuareg turban, not surprisingly, does the job well), a large bottle (*bidon*) and something to purify the water. It takes a bit of preparation, and is not something to enter into lightly, as the trip can be hard, but anyone who's done it rates it as absolutely fantastic. You can, of course, go one way by camel and the other way by 4WD, although you'll still have to pay the two-way cost for the car.

In Timbuktu, contact the project's representatives for information on camels, vehicles and so on. These are Salah Baba, Malik Alkady (who both speak French) or Drahman Alpha (who speaks English as well). To find any one of them, ask at either of the hotels and they'll get a local kid to take you. Or you can write in advance to Malik Alkady (Arbres pour Araouane), Magasinier du PAM (World Food Programme), Timbuktu. For more information you could also contact Trees for Araouane at 460 West Broadway, New York, NY 10012, USA (☎ (212) 473-8114) or at Am Seeli, 9044 Wald/AR, Switzerland (☎ (071) 95 22 03).

Another man to contact for advice and information about joining a caravan is Ayouba Ag Moihar, who is also a leading member of the Tuareg Artisan Federation, and general all-round fix-it man. Several professional travel writers and photographers have used Ayouba to set them up on a caravan trip. If you want to sort things out in advance write to him (in French) at Boite Postale 49, Timbuktu.

If you are going to join a caravan during your trip, you will probably need more than the standard one-month visa. Get a longer one before you leave your home country, or get it extended in Bamako or Mopti.

HOMBORI

Hombori is on the main road between Mopti and Gao. What stands out about this place, quite literally, is a huge rock formation called **Mt Hombori Tondo**, that rises straight up from the flat plains to 1155 metres. The village is picturesquely situated at the base and you can get drinks and food there at *La Belle Sénégalaise*. If you are on public transport between Gao and Mopti, you may have to stay overnight here. If you don't go to the small hotel in the village, coffee sellers rent out mats on the sand for CFA 125.

Rock Climbing

Twelve km to the south-west of Hombori, the road to Mopti passes just to the south of **La Main de Fatma**, a major rock formation. The name comes from the needle-like rocks which look like fingers. It may be the single best place in West Africa for technical rock climbing and occasionally attracts climbers from Europe. Some of the routes are extremely difficult, and should only be tackled if you have experience and the right equipment. There are also some relatively easier ways up, where you might be able to scramble to the top. You can get guides from Hombori, but you could easily get killed here if you don't know what you're doing.

GAO

Gao gets mixed reviews. If you come from Bamako or Mopti, you may think Gao is Dullsville. If you come across the desert from Algeria, you'll think it's the liveliest town in the Sahara. In either case, you won't be amused by the local youths who fight to be your 'guide' or 'car guard'; they can become thieves if you don't keep a watchful eye on them. Another minus: Gao is hot – up to 48°C in the desert sun.

The **markets** and waterfront, however, are interesting, and the river is picturesque: you can rent a pirogue around dusk and watch the dunes turn orange as you drift along. Gao also has a small ethnological **museum** (near the SNTN bus station). The only other thing coming close to a 'sight' is the **Tomb of the Askia** (a 16th-century ruler), now

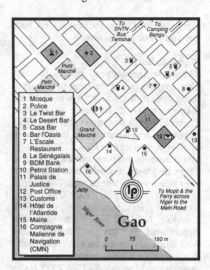

1 Mosque
2 Police
3 Le Twist Bar
4 Le Desert Bar
5 Casa Bar
6 Bar l'Oasis
7 L'Escale Restaurant
8 Le Sénégalais
9 BDM Bank
10 Petrol Station
11 Palais de Justice
12 Post Office
13 Customs
14 Hôtel de l'Atlantide
15 Mairie
16 Compagnie Malienne de Navigation (CMN)

Gao

used as a mosque, with the exposed beams typical of Soudanese mud-brick buildings sticking out even further than usual. And there's some lively outdoor night spots with music, occasional dancing and – that essential so difficult to find in Algeria – a cool beer.

Information

Money Gao's only bank, the BDM, is open only from 8 to 11 am, Monday to Friday. Processes here are extremely slow and the staff do not usually accept travellers' cheques of any kind. (Although after much pleading, some travellers have persuaded them to accept US dollar travellers' cheques: the commission was an outrageous CFA 5250.) Change elsewhere if you can.

Police All visitors are supposed to report to the police and pay a fee of CFA 1000. In the past, travellers failing to do this have been sent back to Gao from the Niger border. More recently, several people have not reported, and have had no problems. (See the advice on registration in Documents under Facts for the Visitor in this chapter.) The police office, opposite the mosque, closes for passport business at noon. You can also get

MALI

visa extensions there; the cost is CFA 5000 and you'll need one photo.

Places to Stay

There are three cheap places to stay. *Camping Bangu* has the great advantage of being closest to town: 1.5 km north of the market on the direct route to Tessalit. Thatched double bungalows cost CFA 3750, or you can rent a mattress on the terrace or pitch your own tent for CFA 1250, although you'll have to keep an eye on your gear. There are plenty of showers and you can get your laundry done here as well. The bar-restaurant serves beers for CFA 750 and decent food, with prices starting around CFA 1250. *Camping Tizi-Mizi* is 2.5 km along the airport road, and has good double rooms with fans and showers for CFA 5600, basic doubles for CFA 3000, or you can sleep on a mattress on the terrace for CFA 2000. If you pitch your own tent, the cost is CFA 1250. The outdoor bar-restaurant is good but not cheap, and the disco can be noisy. *Camping Yurga* is an older, more basic place near the river about three km from the town, on the road to the ferry and Mopti, making up for its lack of facilities by having a friendly manager. It costs CFA 1250 per person in one of the mud-brick huts, and the same if you sleep outside or pitch your own tent. There are showers, the food is good for the price, and you can borrow the camp bicycle to get into town. (It is illegal to camp within 10 km of Gao except at one of these places.)

The only hotel in Gao is the *Hôtel de l'Atlantide*, near the Grand Marché. This old place has become very run-down over the years, charging from CFA 3750 for a single with shared bath to CFA 8300 for a double with private bath and up to CFA 18,500 for rooms with air-con. Prices include breakfast and tax, but are still bad value as there is frequently no water or electricity and even the best rooms are dingy. However, rates are negotiable, and you can usually get away with putting three people in a double. You can sleep on the roof for CFA 2500 and the caretaker may let you take a shower in one of the rooms for a small extra fee. Even if you don't stay here, it's a pleasant place for a drink (big beers for CFA 1000 – but even the price of these is negotiable!) and a good place to meet other travellers. Also, the restaurant can sometimes serve a fairly decent meal, from about CFA 2500.

Places to Eat & Drink

The food in the market, particularly the grilled meat, is good. In addition to the places to stay listed above, there are several other restaurants around the market area and also around the Palais du Justice. *Le Camerouni* is cheap and *Le Sénégalais* is slightly more expensive, but both are recommended. For eats with drinks, try *Bar l'Oasis*, a popular meeting place for overland travellers, or the *Casa Bar*, where you can also buy brochettes and other snacks. For drinks only, try the *Twist Bar* or the *Café Sportif*, which has a nice garden and decent music.

Getting There & Away

Air Gao has a dusty airstrip and the Air Mali plane flies once per week to/from Bamako, via Timbuktu and Mopti. For details of the schedule see the main Getting Around section in this chapter.

Bus Several bus companies, including Gana du Nord and Transport Coulibaly run services between Gao, Mopti and Bamako. The fare to/from Bamako is CFA 15,000, or CFA 9000 to/from Mopti. While transport around Gao is restricted, all buses were going in armed convoy twice per week in each direction. They go from Mopti on Tuesdays and Fridays to arrive at Hombori that evening. You must spend the night in Hombori (see the Hombori section for more details) then the convoy departs at dawn on Wednesday and Saturday, arriving at Gao around noon. Going from Gao to Mopti the convoy leaves early on Thursday and Sunday mornings, arriving in Mopti around evening the same day. If the situation around Gao improves, daily bus services are likely to start.

MALI

Rice-Growing Near Gao

Taking a pirogue ride to one of the outlying villages around Gao is a good way to observe rural life, particularly the peculiarly West African methods of rice-growing. The river starts rising around early July (from the rains in Guinea, the source of the Niger). Rice is transplanted or scattered as the river rises, the plants growing just fast enough to keep their heads out of the waters. Dykes have been built to keep the river from flooding the plants too soon; maintaining them is no small job, even more so because they are eventually covered by the river each year. From November to January, this 'floating' rice is harvested from pirogues.

As the river recedes, sorghum is planted on the wet banks and reaches maturity using only the residual moisture. Agriculture may not be your bag, but you're likely to find this interesting if you get the chance to talk to some Songhaï farmers or others knowledgeable on the subject. Crop-farming is, after all, a critical matter in this area of the world.

Even when the rice and sorghum crops are decent, the area around Gao imports about half of its grain requirements. In a bad year, this can be 90% of the total consumed. And getting grain from the USA to Gao and the outlying areas can be very expensive. One million dollar's worth of grain costs another US$2.5 million to transport here. ■

Between Gao and Niamey, you can take the SNTN bus, which should run three times per week in each direction, although until the region is declared safe, there's a bus only once per week, currently Saturday. In Gao the bus goes from the SNTN office on the eastern side of town, about 1.5 km from the centre. For details of departures from Niamey, see the Niger chapter. In either direction, you'll be told to report at 8 am, but the buses usually don't leave until two to four hours later. They stop overnight at the border and arrive the following day around sunset. The fare is CFA 8000 plus a baggage fee. During the peak of the rainy season in July and August, the trip often takes two full days. Seats for the next bus go on sale as soon as a bus leaves. They sell very quickly, so reserve your seat far in advance. The journey is long and hot, so take plenty of water.

Truck If you're heading to Algeria, there are trucks almost every day, except from July to September, when the temperatures are high and traffic very light. Expect to pay about CFA 25,000 to Adrar. To find a truck, ask any of the 'guides' to enquire on your behalf (and pay them an agreed fee after they've found you a lift). There are very few trucks to Niamey; hitching is not recommended.

Car The driving time between Gao and Mopti is six to eight hours. This involves a ferry crossing a few km south of Gao. If petrol is scarce, don't panic; you can always get it on the black market if you're willing to pay a premium. If you're headed to Algeria, see Crossing the Sahara section in the introductory Getting There & Away chapter.

The 443-km stretch between Gao and Niamey can be done in as little as 12 to 15 hours, but it takes much longer in the July to August rainy season. Be prepared for some difficult sections south of Ansongo, occasionally impassable in the rainy season. About 55 km south of Ansongo is *Chez Fafa*, a very pleasant campement with clean rooms for about CFA 4700, possibly closed from July to August. There's also the possibility of taking a pirogue ride to see the hippos.

Boat For details on the large passenger boats that ply the river between Gao and Koulikoro (near Bamako) via Timbuktu, Mopti and several other towns, see the main Getting Around section. Below Gao, there are some rapids, so it's not possible to travel to Niamey by river, although we heard from two intrepid travellers who made it down as far as Ansongo by leaky pinasse. It's also rare to find a pinasse headed for Timbuktu.

MALI

Dogon Country

On everybody's list of the top 10 places to see in West Africa, this area is worth all the extra effort it takes to get here. The Dogon people live on and around the huge Bandiagara Escarpment (*Falaise*) that extends some 135 km from Douentza in the north to near Bankas in the south, in the area east of Mopti. What makes the Dogon special is their complex and elaborate culture, their art forms (among the best known in Africa), their multistorey houses and granaries, seemingly clinging to the sheer rock faces of the escarpment, and their unique vegetable plots on ledges in the cliffs.

The best way to see Dogon Country is to trek along the escarpment, for anything between two and 10 days, walking slowly from village to village, giving yourself plenty of time to see and appreciate the people and the landscape. Distances are short, and it's usual to walk from one village to the next during the morning, rest during the heat of the afternoon, then explore the village itself and its nearby cliff dwellings in the early evening. You can find food and lodging in the villages, for which you pay a small charge, and guides are available.

DOGON CULTURE & ART

The Dogon people migrated to the Bandiagara Escarpment from the surrounding plains in around 1300, to take refuge from the more bellicose Muslims. Today they remain mostly animist: about 35% of the Dogon follow Islam, and only a few of the villages, such as Kani-Kombolé, have mosques.

Architecture

The villages the Dogon built on the high cliffs of the escarpment resemble those of cliff-dwelling Indians in the south-west of the USA, and are very photogenic. The houses are of mud with flat roofs supported by beams. The granaries are smaller, with a conical roof. These were assembled on the ground and then hoisted into position. Some of the houses are multistorey and quite old. The better ones have elaborately carved doors that art collectors are forever seeking. In recent times, many of the cliff dwellings have been abandoned, and the people have moved onto the plains at the foot of the escarpment, although usually only a short distance from their former village. (See the boxed story on Dogon Villages.)

Masks

Masks are very important in Dogon culture, and play an important role in religious ceremonies (see the boxed story on Dogon

---

Dogon Villages & Houses

Religion permeates not just Dogon art but everything they do, including the design of their villages and homes. Dogon villages extend from north to south, traditionally laid out in the form of a human body. The head is the *togu-na* (the men's shelter and meeting place) with eight wooden posts supporting a thick roof of dried millet stalks. The pillars are frequently carved into figures representing the eight mythical Dogon ancestors (four men and four women created by the Dogon God Amma). It's a cool place where the men lounge, smoke, tell jokes, take naps and discuss matters of the village. Women are banned. Instead, they have special houses where they stay during menstruation; these two outlying houses form the hands of the 'body'.

The design of Dogon houses is unique. Each house, collectively built and made of rock and mud-brick, consists of a number of separate rooms with flat roofs, surrounding a small yard and interlinked with stone walls. The granaries, with their conical straw roofs, stand on stone legs to protect the maize or other crops from mice.

The villagers' houses represent the arteries and veins of the 'body' and are also in the form of a body themselves: the circular kitchen represents the head, the central area is the torso, the bed chambers on either side are the arms, and the entrance way is the genitals. ■

Dogon Masks

Masks are the most important symbol of Dogon culture. The most famous ceremony is the Sigui, performed every 60 years (most recently during the 1960s) when the Dogon carve and bring out a large mask called the *iminana*, which is in the form of a prostrate serpent and can sometimes reach a height of 10 metres. During the Sigui, the Dogon perform dances using the iminana to help recount the story of the origin of the Dogon. According to legend, the Dogon's first ancestor took the form of a snake when he died. After the ceremony, it's stored in one of the caves high on the cliffs.

The iminana is also used during funerals. According to Dogon tradition, when a person dies their spirit wanders about looking for a new 'residence'. Fearful that the spirit might rest in another mortal, the Dogon bring out the iminana and take it to the deceased's house for a ceremony which entices the spirit to reside in the mask. Later, dances with other masks are performed.

There are various other types of mask including the bird-like *kanaga* which protects against vengeance (of a killed animal), and the house-like *sirige* which represents the house of the *hogon* who is responsible for passing on Dogon traditions to younger generations.

Other Dogon festivals where you may see masks include: Agguet, around May in honour of the ancestors; Ondonfile, three weeks before the first rains; or Guinam Golo, around January. ■

Masks). Like Dogon doors, masks are continually sought by collectors and visitors looking for an authentic souvenir. If you're in a village, you may be led secretly to some outlying house where the owner purports to have some very old masks and doors for sale. They are rarely old but the quality of Dogon art remains fairly good compared to that being produced in other areas of Africa; just don't be surprised to find your piece coloured with shoe polish.

Marriage

The Dogon are obsessed with raising children. Marriages are arranged by the parents, sometimes even before the birth of their children. A young man usually learns the name of his wife when she is circumcised around the age of 12. Sexual relations begin almost immediately, even before the girl's first menstruation. Until a man has produced a child, he is not really considered to be a man. Considering the difficulty of growing things in the rocky cliff, it is not difficult to understand why procreation is also a common theme in

Female ancestral figure

Dogon statues and plays a strong role in Dogon mythology.

Burial Caves

Above the villages the cliffs are stippled with older granaries and burial caves built by the Tellem, a people who lived on the escarpment before the Dogon arrived. The Tellem were obviously some of the finest climbers in the world as these caves are virtually inaccessible today. Some still hold valuable pottery, bracelets and rare finger bells.

The Dogon bury their own dead in the same area, occasionally appropriating a Tellem cave. When a Dogon dies, masked dances are held following which the body is run head-high through the village. It is then lifted up with ropes to one of those caves. Watching a young Dogon man risking his life by climbing up a long rope to one of these caves high up on the cliffs, then hoisting up the body of the deceased, is quite memorable.

Agriculture

Extensive cereal agriculture is impossible along the rocky cliffs so the Dogon have developed a unique agricultural system, which in some areas involves bringing topsoil from the flat land below to the water trapped in pools in the rocks. In other areas the women draw water from the deep wells and carry it in large pots to irrigate the onion fields. The system works well and is very productive – Dogon onions, introduced by the French after WW I, make their way all over the country. Foreign technicians trying to provide assistance have found little to improve upon except the water catchments, which can be made more watertight with cement.

Market Day

The Dogon week has only five days, and in most villages along the escarpment every fifth day is market day, which is always a lively and interesting event. Dogon markets usually don't get going in full force until around noon and women dominate the scene. A successful market always ends with lots of drinking. Millet beer (kojo or chakalow), still fermenting, is usually poured into a large earthenware pot and then served in the shade to the men. It's an occasion to tell jokes and catch up on the news and the men can get fairly drunk.

Souvenirs

Because the number of people visiting the Dogon region has the potential to destroy this unique culture, travellers need to be particularly sensitive to local customs and do as little as possible to intrude into the locals' lives. You should also think hard about what you buy, as everything (old tools, carvings, masks, fetishes, even the doors off houses) in Dogon Country is for sale. You can't blame the Dogon – it's no different to somebody from the West selling a family heirloom – especially when the buyer offers an amount worth several years' salary. But to stop the whole place turning into a supermarket, and the Dogon culture disappearing completely, you might consider only buying new *objets d'art*, specially made for tourists. In this way, you still get your souvenir, the culture stands a chance of remaining intact for a bit longer, and the locals still make a bit of cash.

WHEN TO GO

The hottest part of the year is March to May – too hot for hiking. The high tourist season is late July to early September and mid-December to the end of January. This leaves February, June to mid-July and mid-September to mid-December as the ideal times to visit. Mid-December to early February is the worst time for taking photographs as the harmattan is at its peak then and skies are usually very hazy.

If you come in April or May, however, you may be able to see the spectacular five-day Fête des Masques, which is the Dogon's major festival. The festival is celebrated in all Dogon villages. Tireli is a particularly good village for seeing the fête because the older people, who are the real pros, do most of the dancing. In other villages the younger dancers predominate. The exact dates of the fête are not set until about a month prior to it. If you are visiting the area at this time, your guide will know the exact dates.

GETTING THERE & AWAY

There are three main starting points for a trek in Dogon Country: Bandiagara, Bankas and Sanga (also spelt Sangha). At each place you can find accommodation and guides. In Bankas and Bandiagara you can also arrange transport to the escarpment, either by horse-cart or mobylette, and buy some supplies.

These starting points are all linked to Mopti by reasonable roads, and are best approached from that direction (although Bankas can also be approached from Koro, if you're coming into Mali from Burkina Faso). Bandiagara and Bankas are easily reached from Mopti by bus and bush taxi. There's no public transport to Sanga, so it's a more popular starting point for tour groups or people with their own vehicle.

If you don't have your own vehicle, you might be able to get a lift with someone who does by asking around at the campement or Hôtel Kananga in Mopti. You can also catch a truck from Mopti or Bandiagara to Sanga on market day (every five days).

More information on getting to/from Bandiagara, Bankas and Sanga, plus details on places to stay and eat, are given later in this section.

Tours

If you're short of time, or if money is not a problem, you can join an organised tour. This can be arranged in Bamako (see Tours in the main Getting Around section of this chapter) or in Mopti. The usual destination is Sanga, but most groups only spend one or two days there. As a loner or couple you may be able to join another party. During the high season it is sometimes possible to arrange a lift to Sanga with one group, returning with another group a few days, or even a week, later. In Mopti contact Savanna Tours, Sahel Tours or Timbuctours (see the earlier Mopti section for addresses). Timbuctours also has an office at the campement in Sanga and arrange excursions from there (see the later Sanga section for details).

TREKKING PRACTICALITIES
Guides

Guides in Dogon Country are not essential, but you'll find things much easier if you do take one. Guides will show you the route, help with translation (since few Dogon speak French), make all the arrangements with the villagers for sleeping and meals, and take you to abandoned cliff dwellings. They will also help you avoid being overcharged by village chiefs and hassled by local youths, and can explain something of the history and the culture of the Dogon as you go along. Without a guide, you'll undoubtedly miss many points of interest and you stand a good chance of doing something to cause offence, such as touching one of the many sacred objects. In short, a good guide will ensure that you actually enjoy your trek, and the fee you pay one should be at least partly offset by the money you save with their help. (For details of guide fees see the Costs section below.) Nevertheless, a few trekkers do manage to go without a guide, especially in the more remote parts of the escarpment which are rarely reached by visitors.

Some travellers have had bad experiences with guides. A major complaint is that there are always undiscussed expenses that pop up during the trip. Another is that some guides don't know the area very well. When choosing a guide, write down all the expenses together as this aids memory on both sides, and ask lots of questions about market days, history, festivals, or anything else you can think of, then verify their answers with someone else. Also ask if they have any relatives in the villages, where you might be able to stay or visit. If possible, talk to other travellers who have done a trek and ask them for recommendations (or warnings) regarding guides, as well as information on logistics, prices and routes.

It is usual (and easier) to hire your guide at Bandiagara, Bankas or Sanga, but many of the guides from these places come to Mopti to look for work. It does not really matter *where* you find your guide, as this does not affect the fee you pay them (and all other trekking costs are more or less fixed), but there are some other important factors you should check before hiring them:

- It is essential that they have an official guide's identification card, which permits them to work in Dogon Country: these have been issued since late 1993, and any guide without one may be arrested.
- Your guide should be a Dogon: guides from other groups have less freedom to show you around the villages, and will have to subcontract a genuine local (who you pay for). The ID card will show their place of birth.
- You should like and trust your guide. Particularly in Mopti there are many who may be cheap but they can quickly become unpleasant and unhelpful. Some recommended guides, and places to hire them, are listed in the earlier Mopti section and in the later Bankas and Bandiagara sections.

Accommodation & Food

At each village where you stop for the night, your guide will arrange a place for you to sleep and eat. In the larger villages, a special *case de passage* is reserved for visitors. In smaller villages you'll stay with a family. It's usual to unroll your sleeping bag on the flat roof of one of the houses and sleep under the stars. This is a wonderful experience: particularly in the early morning, as the sunlight hits the top of the giant cliffs and you listen to the sounds of the village stirring around you.

At the place where you sleep, a bowl of food (usually rice with a sauce of vegetables, meat or chicken) will be provided. In the morning, you'll be given tea and possibly 'Dogon porridge' made from millet. You should bring all your other food with you. Biscuits, crackers, cheese and tins of sardines or meat can be bought in Mopti and Bandiagara, and maybe in Bankas. Fruit can be bought in Bandiagara and Bankas. In some of the larger villages along the escarpment, an enterprising local sells cold drinks.

When arranging things with a guide make sure it's clear who will be paying for their meals and lodging. It is usual for a guide's own costs to be covered by the fee you pay them.

Equipment

The general rule is to travel as light as possible as paths are steep or sandy in places. Special footwear is not required. Essentials include a good hat and a water bottle, as it can get extremely hot on the escarpment and trekkers are at risk of heatstroke and serious dehydration. You should carry at least one litre of water with you while walking. If you don't have a bottle, buy one in Mopti market (ask for a bidon). Each village has a well, but you should filter and purify water before drinking. A sleeping bag is useful but not essential during the dry season, as nights are warm, although a light blanket (available in Mopti) will keep off the pre-dawn chill. Dogon villages are dark at night, so it's useful to have a torch. Wearing shorts for trekking is OK, as they do not offend Dogon culture, although women will feel more comfortable with a wraparound skirt or long trousers when staying in a village, especially in the more remote areas. Tents are not required as all visitors are expected to stay at the cases de passage or hut in the village.

Costs

Visitors to Dogon Country must pay for the privilege. Fees are reasonable, and provide the local people with a much-needed source of income. Despite what you may be told by some guides, these fees are fixed. It costs CFA 500 per person to enter a village; this allows you to take photos of houses and other buildings (but *not* people – unless you get their permission) and to visit nearby cliff dwellings. If you decide not to look around, but simply walk through on your way to the next place, you do not have to pay this fee.

To sleep at a village costs CFA 500, on top of your visit fee. Food costs are variable: around CFA 500 per person for lunch or dinner, and CFA 300 for breakfast.

Fees for guides are not fixed, and range from CFA 2000 to CFA 6000 per day depending on the size of the group, the length of the trip and the quality of the guide. The guide fee for two trekkers on a three-day trip might be around CFA 10,000 but some friendly negotiation is essential. This fee includes the guide's own food and accommodation costs. (Guides hired in Mopti pay their own transport costs to the start of the trek.) If you want to travel really light, your guide can arrange for a porter to carry your pack: expect to pay about half the daily guide fee. Some guides put together all-in packages, setting up everything (transport, food, fees, etc) for about CFA 12,500 per day.

Your only other cost is getting to the actual escarpment. In Bandiagara, you can hire a mobylette (without a driver) for about CFA 4500 a day, plus petrol, although with haggling you might find one cheaper. Alternatively, if you're trekking for more than two days, or not doing a circular route, you can arrange to hire a moped and driver to drop you off at the start of your trek.

From Bandiagara, a drop off in Djiguibombo (20 km) by moped is CFA 7500. This fee includes the driver and petrol and covers the whole trip (out and back). A horse-cart from Bandiagara to Djiguibombo is the same price as a mobylette, although slower, and can take four people and their gear. From Bankas to the escarpment at Endé (12 km) by horse-cart is CFA 3000, shared by up to six people. (The track is too sandy for mopeds.) Of course, you can save money by walking these sections, but you need to allow for the extra days this requires.

In some villages where water is scarce, you may be charged a 'water tax' of around CFA 125. Also in some villages, you may be taken to see the *Hogon* (spiritual leader). It's usual to give him a small gift of around CFA 300. Alternatively, give about five kola nuts as they are what the Dogon use for gifts. These can be bought in Mopti or Bandiagara (but not in Bankas or Sanga). As a general rule, other gifts should be discouraged.

Hiking & Trekking Routes

The walking route you choose depends on your time, money and energy. The best information is always from other travellers, so ask around in Mopti before finalising anything.

When planning a route, you should consider the locations of the cases de passage, although in virtually every village there will be someone willing to let you sleep on their roof for the usual fee. Villages with a case de passage include Djiguibombo, Kani-Kombolé, Teli, Endé, Begnimato, Dourou, Nombori, Tireli, Ireli and Banani, but more are being planned in other villages as the

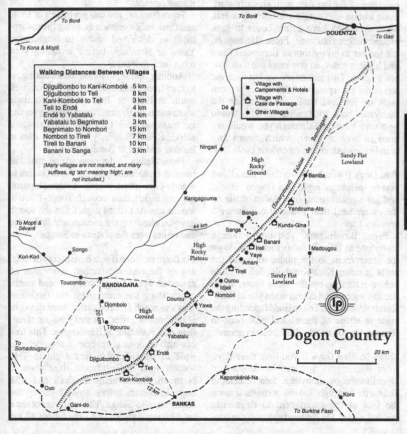

Walking Distances Between Villages

Djiguibombo to Kani-Kombolé 5 km
Djiguibombo to Teli 8 km
Kani-Kombolé to Teli 3 km
Teli to Endé 4 km
Endé to Yabatalu 4 km
Yabatalu to Begnimato 3 km
Begnimato to Nombori 15 km
Nombori to Tireli 7 km
Tireli to Banani 10 km
Banani to Sanga 3 km

(Many villages are not marked, and many suffixes, eg 'ato' meaning 'high', are not included.)

Village with Campements & Hotels
Village with Case de Passage
Other Villages

Dogon Country

0   10   20 km

MALI

number of visitors to Dogon Country continues to increase.

One Day If you are very short of time, the best place to be is Sanga, as there are three routes starting and ending here that can all be done in a day (although, without your own vehicle, you can easily take two or three days just getting to/from Sanga): the seven-km Petit Tour (to Gogoli) taking three hours, the 10-km Moyen Tour (to Gogoli and Banani), taking four hours, and the 15-km Grand Tour (to Gogoli, Banani and Ireli) taking six to seven hours.

From Bankas, it is possible to visit the escarpment for the day, with an early start, using a horse-cart to take you to Endé or Teli, where you can have a few hours to look around before returning. From Bandiagara, it's too far to go by foot or horse-cart there and back in a day, so you must use a mobylette to get to Djiguibombo (two km from the top of the escarpment), from where you can walk to Teli and back, and then ride the mobylette back to Bandiagara. This would be a very long day, although you would not need to take a driver, which means two people could share the mobylette costs.

Two Days If you have two days, this allows you to spend one night in a Dogon village, and get a much better impression of life on the escarpment than you ever can during a one-day trip.

From Bandiagara, you could take a mobylette to Djiguibombo, then walk down the escarpment to the plain, to spend the night in either Kani-Kombolé, Teli or Endé before returning by the same route. From Bankas a nice short circuit takes you to Kani-Kombolé, through Teli to Endé (spending the night at either of these) and then back to Bankas. Or you can do this circuit in reverse.

Three to Five Days If you have three days, from Bandiagara you can be dropped at Djiguibombo by mobylette, then descend to Teli for the first night and trek northwards along the foot of the escarpment to Begnimato (second night). On the third day you can continue on to Yawa, then up the escarpment to Dourou, where you can either stay and walk back to Bandiagara on day four, or arrange for a mobylette to come and pick you up. You can add an extra day to this by diverting northward from Begnimato to Nombori. An easier three-day trip from Bandiagara would be Djiguibombo, Teli, Endé, and then return by the same route. Another alternative is Bandiagara, Kani-Kombolé, Gani-Do, then either retracing to Bandiagara or going across the plains via Ouo, but this is a very long stage (30 km). This route is rarely travelled, so you're less likely to see other tourists, but the escarpment tends to be less dramatic west of Kani-Kombolé.

From Bankas, you can get to Teli or Endé and then walk northwards along the escarpment as described above to Begnimato, Yawa or Nombori, before retracing your route back to Bankas.

Another option, to avoid backtracking, is to start from Bandiagara, go to Dourou, trek south to Endé or Teli and then continue southwards to Bankas, from where you can get transport back to Mopti or on towards Burkina Faso. Similarly, you could start in Bankas and end at Bandiagara.

From Sanga, a four-day route that has been recommended goes north via Banani to Kundu-Gina (first night), Yougo-Dogorou (second night), then through Yougo-Pilou to Yendouma-Ato (third night). On the fourth day you climb up the escarpment at Tiogou and return over the plateau to Sanga.

Six Days or More If you have plenty of time, any of the routes described above can be extended. From Sanga, you can head southwards along the escarpment via Tireli and Yawa to reach Dourou (after three days) or Djiguibombo (after another two or three) then end your trek at Bandiagara. This trek can also be done in reverse: a mobylette or walk to Djiguibombo, first night in Teli, second night in Begnimato, third night in Nombori, fourth night in Tireli and fifth night in Banani before going back up the escarpment to Sanga. This route involves a total hiking distance of 62 km (about 12 km a day) between Djiguibombo and Sanga. If you do this route, it's generally better to hike northward towards Sanga because you get better views of the villages up the escarpment. Also, if you don't have your own vehicle, it seems easier to find lifts coming out of Sanga rather than going in, and Sanga is a nicer to place to wait for a lift than Bandiagara anyway.

Another long route from Sanga would be north through Yendouma-Ato and Bamba along the foot of the escarpment all the way to Douentza, a week-long 75-km trip. Finding food is more difficult on this route, so you need to take extra provisions, but it's a real adventure. The cliffs end about 10 km south of Douentza. From Douentza you can find transport along the main road back to Mopti.

Other Routes Travellers with their own 4WD may consider driving the route from Bandiagara east over the rocky plateau to Dourou, then down a pass to Yawa at the bottom of the escarpment, then further east over the sandy Gondo Plain to Kaporokénié-Pé, then north to Madougou, Diankabo, Bamba and on across the plain to Douentza. It's a difficult route but by no means impossible during the dry season and, once on the plain, you'll be passing through villages that are relatively untainted by tourism. The people are friendly and more curious along this route, and you can get food, water and accommodation if you ask.

Intrepid backpackers could also sample the plains villages by trekking from Sanga to Madougou via Banani. There's a weekly market in Madougou, and on the evening of this day you should be able to find vehicles heading north to Douentza or south to Bankas. There's also a chance of transport out of Madougou on Saturday (market day in Koro), Sunday (market day in Douentza), or Monday (market day in Bankas).

Things to See

If you are still trying to decide which route to take, the following information may be helpful. Of all the villages, **Tireli** is one of the most picturesque. In **Teli**, which is also picturesque, there are some waterfalls and rock paintings (*peintures rupestres*). **Songo** also has some interesting rock paintings as well as a cave where numerous musical instruments used on special occasions are stored. **Begnimato** has one of the best cases de passage. In **Tégourou** check the German-financed dam outside of town. You'll also see nearby some of the onion fields for which the Dogon are famous. **Kani-Kombolé** has an interesting mosque, and near **Banani** there's a fascinating natural tunnel and a small waterfall. **Bongo** and **Dourou** have spectacular views of the plains and Bongo is a good place to watch Dogon artisans at work as well as purchase Dogon art.

BANDIAGARA

Bandiagara is a small dusty town, some 70 km east of Mopti, and about 20 km from the top of the escarpment. In the heart of town is the **market** and bush taxi park. The main market day is Monday, and Fridays are also busy. This is a good place to buy the famous Dogon indigo cloth. (You can also buy it in some of the escarpment villages but it's cheaper in Bandiagara.)

The main street heading through the market leads south to the bridge, towards the gendarmerie and the road to Djiguibombo, and north to a roundabout at the junction of the main road to Mopti. There are several Dogon *togu-nas* (traditional shelters) in town; one is a block north-west of the market. Also check **Artisanat Napo** on the north-western side of town, a block north of the Mopti road. Someone will have to point it out to you as it's just a tiny room full of Dogon art, which is OK but nothing unusual. There's another tiny **artisan shop** half a block south of the market on the main street.

At the **Centre for Traditional Medicine** on the north-eastern outskirts of town (on the road to Sanga) mentally ill people are treated. The building itself is worth a look: financed by the Italians, it was built in 1988 out of stone and brick with a somewhat experimental Arab-inspired design.

Visitors staying the night in Bandiagara must report to the police at the gendarmerie

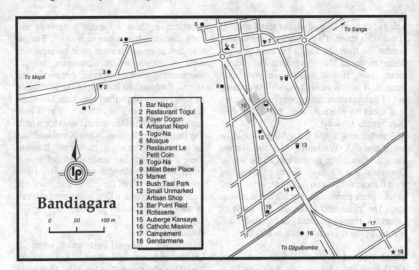

1	Bar Napo
2	Restaurant Togui
3	Foyer Dogon
4	Artisanat Napo
5	Togu-Na
6	Mosque
7	Restaurant Le Petit Coin
8	Togu-Na
9	Millet Beer Place
10	Market
11	Bush Taxi Park
12	Small Unmarked Artisan Shop
13	Bar Point Raid
14	Rotisserie
15	Auberge Kansaye
16	Catholic Mission
17	Campement
18	Gendarmerie

Bandiagara

0   50   100 m

on the southern outskirts of town; no fee or photos are required and the process is quick although, as regulations change throughout Mali, it might not be necessary at all in the future.

Boss of the guides in this town is Abdoulaye Touré (☎ 42 00 05): he's straight and will make sure you get good service if you make arrangements through him, although the town is full of freelance guides who offer cheaper prices. Guides recommended by travellers in the past include Boubacar Ouologuem, 'Togo', Dibo Ibrahim ('Moustique') and Nouhoum Toumounté.

Places to Stay & Eat

The best place to stay is the *Auberge Kansaye* (kahn-SAY) off the southern end of the main street, just before the bridge. The rooms are spartan but the beds have clean sheets and the price is reasonable at CFA 2000 per person. There are only six rooms; everybody else sleeps on the patio for the same price. Food can be prepared to order. The friendly old owner, Mamadou Kansaye, is an *ancien combattant* (WW II veteran) who now leaves running the hotel to his family. You can store excess baggage, and

also arrange a guide. Many travellers stay here, so it's a good place for information. At the *campement*, just across the bridge and up the hill, tatty doubles cost an outrageous CFA 5600, or you can camp for CFA 1250.

Other places to stay include *Bar Napo*, west of the centre, one block south of the main road towards Mopti, which has single/ double rooms for CFA 2500/3750. Also worth trying is *Chez Daniel*, which has clean beds with nets for CFA 2500/3750 including breakfast. It's on the north side of town, several blocks north of Restaurant Le Petit Coin. There's no sign, but most guides know the house.

Your only other alternative is to solicit the help of one of the guides; they seem to know everything and everybody and may be able to find you a room or a place to pitch a tent, particularly if they want your business.

For food, in addition to the Kansaye there's a good street-side *rotisserie* (selling roast meat), just a block east of the Kansaye. For a restaurant your only choice may be *Le Petit Coin*, a few blocks east of the roundabout, which serves simple fare including steak and bread for CFA 750, riz sauce for CFA 625, Cokes for CFA 300 and big beers for CFA 650. Two other places to try are the *Restaurant Togui* and the *Foyer Dogon*, both west of the centre on the main road towards Mopti.

For a drink, go to the *Bar Point Raid*, just off the main street, two blocks north of the Kansaye. Big beers are CFA 650, and the upstairs terrace is pleasant. It's also a good place to meet guides and other travellers. For millet beer, there's a well-known place in the heart of town, a block east of the bush taxi park. There's no sign, so you'll have to ask.

Getting There & Away

Bush taxis and minibuses to Bandiagara go every day from the gare routière by the harbour in Mopti or from the gare routière at the major intersection in Sévaré. The trip takes 1½ to two hours and costs CFA 1500 in a 504. Getting a ride is easiest on market days in Bandiagara (Mondays and Fridays) when there's also a bus to/from Sévaré.

SANGA

Sanga (also spelt Sangha) is about 40 km to the north-east of Bandiagara, very close to the top of the escarpment and one of the largest Dogon villages in the region. The people here are very used to visitors, so don't expect them to be too curious. They resisted the Muslims for 600 years and their resistance to tourists is just as strong. Nonetheless, the government is concerned that tourism may spoil the place, so you are not supposed to walk around without a guide, one of whom can be hired through either of the places to stay listed below.

Organised Tours

Timbuctours has an office in the campement and runs short day walks or longer treks from there. A guided walk on the Grand Tour (see Trekking Routes) costs CFA 4500 for groups of one to four. The Moyen Tour costs CFA 3000, and the Petit Tour CFA 2500. For longer treks the charge is CFA 2500 per person per day for the guide, plus all other charges (see Costs).

Places to Stay & Eat

The *campement* is among the best in Mali. It is clean with showers and washbasins in the room, mosquito nets, and bucket flush toilets outside. The food is good and the beer is cold. Singles/doubles with breakfast cost CFA 3500/5000, or CFA 8500 per person with full board. If it's hot you can take your mattress outside.

Some travellers prefer the *Hôtel Femme Dogon*, at the end of the village near the church, which is slightly more rustic. It costs CFA 2000 per person in a room or on the terrace. Bathrooms are basic but clean and there's always plenty of water. Cold drinks are available and meals can be provided: they're good, although a bit steep at CFA 1750 (but where else can you go?).

Getting There & Away

You first need to get to Bandiagara (see above). From there, you may find a truck or pick-up going to Sanga, especially on the morning of Sanga's market day (every five days, so you have to ask), or on the evening of Bandiagara's market day. On other days finding a ride is often impossible: you just have to wait by the side of the road and hope something comes along. The easy alternative is to pay someone in Bandiagara with a mobylette to drop you off in Sanga; the going rate is CFA 9000 (including petrol). If you're driving, getting from Bandiagara to Sanga is straightforward: the road was graded in early 1994 and the journey takes about an hour.

BANKAS

Bankas is about 100 km from Mopti, and about 10 km from the southern end of the escarpment. Because it's easy to reach and near the cliffs, this is one of the best starting points for a trek in Dogon Country. The guides are also less pushy than in Bandiagara (although this may change as more visitors come here). Market day is Monday, and this is a good place to buy indigo Dogon cloth.

Places to Stay & Eat

The most popular place for travellers is *Campement Hogon*, a few hundred metres from the main street where all transport stops. Basic rooms cost CFA 3000 per person, and camping is also allowed. The

MALI

shared bucket showers are clean and there's always plenty of water. The place is run by Issa Guindo, the son of a Dogon elder, and boss of all the guides in Bankas. He speaks French and English (and Russian!), and is very friendly and helpful. Cheap local-style meals are available to order. Issa is also planning to build a second site, called *Camping Hogon*, with bungalows and a good camp site, nearby.

A smarter place to stay is *Hôtel les Abres*, a Holland-Mali joint enterprise, where rooms cost CFA 10,000 (for one or two people), plus tax at CFA 500 per person. Breakfast is CFA 750 and meals are in the CFA 750 to CFA 1250 range. The hotel incorporates Ben's Bar, which for many years was the only place in Bankas where you could find a guide. Ben himself is still around and worth talking to. With his Dutch business partner he has founded the Organisation des Guides de Bankas; guides working out of the hotel are all members and have to be good quality.

If you're looking for a low-cost place, the *Hôtel-Bar Faïda* is cheap but very basic: rooms have mats on the floor and no doors. Security might be questionable although you should check to see how things look.

For cheap eats, there are a couple of basic gargottes near the market. Otherwise your only choice is the campement or the hotel.

Getting There & Away

Bankas is on the main dirt road from Mopti to Ouahigouya in Burkina Faso, so getting a truck or bush taxi from Mopti is not difficult. They leave Mopti from the gare routière by the harbour and the trip takes about five hours. It cost CFA 3000 from Mopti to Bankas in a 504, and CFA 2250 from Bankas to Koro, 52 km further east.

KORO

This town is not really in Dogon Country, but you may pass through here before or after your trek if you're going to/from Burkina Faso. The friendly *campement* near the gendarmerie charges CFA 2500 a room and serves decent food while the *Tolo Bar* at the

market is even cheaper. Market day is Saturday: your best chance of quick transport connections. Bush taxis between Koro and Bankas cost CFA 2250; this road is very sandy and worse than the route between Mopti and Bankas. Bush taxis to Ouahigouya charge CFA 3000; this road is also in terrible condition, especially between Koro and the border and between Thiou and Ouahigouya. Travellers sometimes have to wait for up to two days for the pick-up to Ouahigouya to fill up, so don't expect to make quick connections. In Koro it's also possible on occasion to find vehicles headed north over the Gondo Plain to Douentza.

The South

SIKASSO

Sikasso is in the far south of Mali, 373 km from Bamako. It is the gateway to Ferkessédougou (Côte d'Ivoire) and Bobo-Dioulasso (Burkina Faso) . The only notable 'sight' is the **Palais du Dernier Roi** on the western side of town; guided tours are available. If you've a got a day to kill, and a torch, check out the caves at **Grottes Missirikoro**, 10 km to the south of town: they contain the relics of an old tribe. Those with wheels might visit the **Cascades de Farako** waterfalls some 30 km to the east; they are most interesting during the rainy season.

Sikasso has three hotels. The cheapest place to stay is the *Hôtel de l'Autogare* at the gare routière. It has very basic but tolerable rooms for about CFA 1250 with shared toilets and bucket showers. If it's too grubby for you, try the nearby *Hôtel Solo-Khan*, which has simple but clean rooms for CFA 2500. Up a grade is the *Hôtel Lotio*, on the Bamako Rd with rooms at CFA 3750/5000, and the *Hôtel Tata* with singles at CFA 3750 and self-contained doubles at CFA 6250. Up again is the *Hotel-Bar Ouassalou*, also on the Bamako Rd, with rooms at CFA 11,250, and a decent restaurant. Sikasso's top address is the *Hôtel Mamelon*, in the town centre, which has air-con rooms for CFA 12,500/15,000.

Getting There & Away

Buses run daily between Sikasso and Bamako; the fare is CFA 3000. You can also go to/from Mopti by bus for CFA 6000, or to/from Ségou for CFA 5250. For details of transport to/from Burkina Faso or Côte d'Ivoire see the main Getting There & Away section in this chapter.

KOUTIALA

Koutiala is the country's cotton-growing capital, at the junction of the main roads between Ségou, Bobo-Dioulasso, Mopti and Sikasso. Few travellers do more than change bus here, but if you're looking for a place to stay there is the *Hôtel Cotonnier*, on the main road at the eastern end of town, with a pleasant bar-restaurant and small but functional singles/doubles for CFA 3750/5600.

The West

KAYES

Kayes (pronounced Ky, to rhyme with 'eye') is near the border with Senegal and Mauritania, and all that most travellers see of this town is the train station, as they pass through on the train between Bamako and Dakar. However, Kayes is a pleasant place; there's plenty of activity but not the hassle tourism has created in some of Mali's other towns. There's a thriving **market**, an interesting waterfront, and several **old buildings** dating from the time when Kayes was a major port on the Senegal River and an important colonial administrative centre.

The town has a Malitas office (☎ 52 12 54), a post office and four banks. (Changing travellers' cheques is always hard, but least problematic at the BCD.)

Foreigners are supposed to report to the police here. No fee is required and the process seems fairly arbitrary. Go to the commissariat, opposite the train station, as soon as you get off the train. Even if you are staying in town for a few days, the police will presume you're taking the train on to Dakar or Bamako and give you a stamp without any hassle. (See the advice on registration in the Documents section under Facts for the Visitor in this chapter.)

Places to Stay & Eat

For cheap accommodation, the best place is the *Hôtel Amical* a few blocks south of the market, where basic rooms with fans cost CFA 3750/5000 for singles/doubles. Breakfast is CFA 1000 and meals CFA 1000 to CFA 1250. Cheaper is *Bar-Restaurant Harlem* (also called Chez Ben), between the centre and the station. A room is CFA 2000 to CFA 2500. Another cheapie is *Le Campement*, next to the Carefour des Jeunesse (a youth centre), just round the corner from the train station, where basic singles/doubles are CFA 3750/5000. Directly opposite the train station is the Moorish-style *Hôtel du Rail* (☎ 22 55 86), supposedly the city's best, but old and run-down. Air-con rooms cost CFA 11,250/17,500, including breakfast and either dinner or lunch (but no discount if you don't eat). The bar-restaurant is nice for a drink, even if you're not staying, and a good place to wait for trains.

Getting There & Away

Air Air Mali has flights twice a week between Kayes and Bamako. See the main Getting Around section in this chapter for details. Flights stop in Nioro.

Bush Taxi & Truck The road to/from Bamako is long and indirect (via Nioro) which is why most people use the train. However, there are trucks and bush taxis every day to Nioro, charging about CFA 6000 to CFA 7500. If you're heading for Mauritania, most trucks go via Nioro, but you might find one headed to Sélibabi; they charge CFA 6500 (or CFA 10,000 to ride in the cab). The road is good for the first few hours to the customs post but from there to Sélibabi there are several river crossings. Moreover, the road can become extremely muddy during the rainy season, making the trip take two full days.

It's also possible to reach Tambacounda (Senegal) by taking one of the occasional

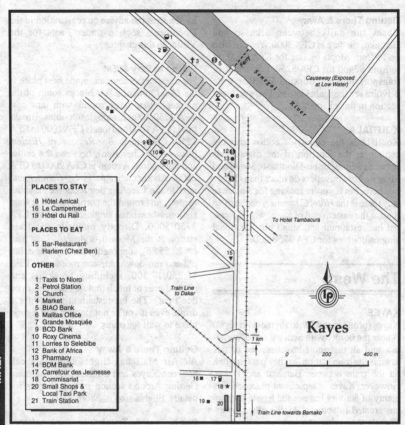

Causeway (Exposed at Low Water)

Senegal River

Ferry

To Hotel Tambacura

Train Line to Dakar

Kayes

0   200   400 m

1 km

Train Line towards Bamako

PLACES TO STAY

8   Hôtel Amical
16 Le Campement
19 Hôtel du Rail

PLACES TO EAT

15 Bar-Restaurant
    Harlem (Chez Ben)

OTHER

1   Taxis to Nioro
2   Petrol Station
3   Church
4   Market
5   BIAO Bank
6   Malitas Office
7   Grande Mosquée
8   BCD Bank
9   Roxy Cinema
10 Lorries to Selebibe
11 Small Shops &
12 Bank of Africa
13 Pharmacy
14 BDM Bank
17 Carrefour des Jeunesse
18 Commisariat
20 Small Shops &
    Local Taxi Park
21 Train Station

trucks which go to the border at Diboli. There's no bridge for vehicles across the river, but you can walk across the railway bridge then find a vehicle going from Kidira to Tambacounda. However, this journey is for real adventurers: it's long, hard and exceedingly slow. Even if you go 2nd class on the local train and end up sleeping in the gangway, it will still be quicker and a lot more comfortable than going by road.

Train You can catch the express train to Bamako, or to Dakar or Tambacounda in Senegal (twice per week in each direction).

For details see the main Getting Around and Getting There & Away sections in this chapter or the Senegal chapter. Most days there's also a slower and cheaper 'local' train between Kayes and Bamako. It leaves Bamako most mornings, arriving in the late afternoon, with an extra service on Friday evenings (arriving Kayes on Saturday morning). The fare is CFA 9600/5700 in 1st/2nd class; about 40% less than the express. From Kayes to Bamako the 'local' leaves at around 7 am, plus an extra train on Sunday evening, which arrives in Bamako at dawn. There's also a weekly 'omnibus' service to/from Dakar which terminates in Kayes (see the Senegal chapter for details).

Getting Around

The train station is about 2.5 km from the town centre. A taxi costs CFA 300. On the north side of the river is Kayes Ndi (Petite Kayes) a large traditional village. A pirogue across is CFA 25 per person, or at times of low water you can walk over the causeway (at high water times, a decrepit car ferry steams back and forth at irregular intervals). Pirogue rides are available if you ask around at the waterfront: expect to pay about CFA 1500 per hour.

To get to the Chuttes de Felou, an impressive set of rapids and waterfalls on the Senegal River (about 15 km from Kayes) you may be able to find a baché at the train station. Otherwise you can get a taxi there and back for CFA 9000.

KITA

This charming little town, with a lively **market**, is on the train line about halfway between Kayes and Bamako. For a place to stay the *Hôtel Relais Touristique* (also called the Kita Karou), opposite the station, has clean self-contained doubles with fans for CFA 5750. Meals are available and there's even a swimming pool! This is an excellent place to rest up or slow down for a while. Getting to/from Kita is easy as most days there's at least one train in each direction, heading towards Bamako or Kayes and Senegal.

NIORO

Nioro is to the north-west of Bamako, and you may pass though here on your way to Mauritania, or travelling by road to Kayes.

There's a *campement* in town which reportedly charges foreigners CFA 7500 and Malians CFA 1250.

Mauritania

Mauritania is the only country in West Africa controlled by people who are traditionally nomads. The Moors are the dominant ethnic group and give Mauritania its special character. In other countries, nomads tend to be looked upon as people not in step with the 20th century and a 'problem'. In Mauritania, however, they are in the majority and their settled descendants call the shots. It is also the only country in sub-Saharan Africa where Islam is the official religion.

Race plays a significant role in everyday life in Mauritania. The Moors look down upon the Blacks, who predominate in the south, and regard them as uncivilised, while the Blacks, primarily of Senegalese origin, perceive the Moors as racist and cruel.

In 1989 the delicate balance between Moors and Blacks broke with the eruption of a series of bloody riots. The initial riots occurred in Senegal, after which the Bidan Moors, reportedly supported by Mauritanian security forces, committed atrocities, even genocide, against the Blacks. Hundreds died and tens of thousands of Senegalese fled the country with the aid of an international airlift. As a result, the borders between Mauritania and Senegal were closed for several years. They are now open again.

Ethics aside, you'll enjoy Mauritania if you like venturing through towns half blanketed in sand, sipping tea with nomads under their colourful tents, crossing plateaus that resemble the moon, and looking at prehistoric rock drawings and ancient Saharan architecture. Even people who have lived in this 'Godforsaken place' and would never do so again agree that it's a truly exotic and unforgettable place to visit.

Mauritania is one of the best bird-watching areas in the world. There's nothing quite like the 200-km-long Arguin Bank; it's the mating place for hundreds of thousands of sea birds, squashed side by side on islands of sand as far as the eye can see. If you're lucky you might get to see Imragen fishers using dolphins to round up the fish.

ISLAMIC REPUBLIC OF MAURITANIA

Area: 1,030,700 sq km
Population: 2.2 million
Population Growth Rate: 3.0%
Capital: Nouakchott
Head of State: President Colonel Maaouya Sid'Ahmed Ould Taya
Official Language: Arabic
Currency: Ouguiya
Exchange Rate: UM 130 = US$1
Per Capita GNP: US$500
Inflation: 11%
Time: GMT/UTC

Facts about the Country

HISTORY

It is hard to imagine that thousands of years ago Mauritania had large lakes, rivers and enough vegetation to support an abundance of elephants, rhinos and hippos. There is also evidence of early human habitation; you can find prehistoric rock drawings, arrowheads and the like all over Mauritania. This came to an end when the Sahara started spreading about 10,000 years ago.

Around the 3rd century the camel was introduced to the Berbers from Morocco. For

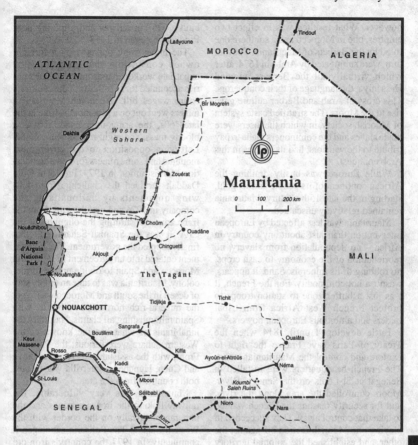

Mauritania this significant event also meant the arrival of the nomads. With the camel, the Berbers could cover long distances and they established trading routes all over the Western Sahara. Salt was the primary commodity; in those times it was traded on a par with gold. Later, gold and slaves were traded as well, giving rise in the 9th and 10th centuries to the first empire in all of West Africa, the Empire of Ghana, the capital city of which is believed to have been in south-east Mauritania at Koumbi Saleh. The Berbers in Mauritania were reduced to vassals.

Islamic Beginnings
Islam began spreading throughout the area about this time. One Muslim group stood out – the Almoravids. They gained control over the Berbers and established their capital in Marrakesh (Morocco), from where they ruled the whole of north-west Africa as well as southern Spain. In 1076 they pushed south and, with the assistance of Mauritanian Berber leaders, destroyed the Empire of Ghana. That victory led to the spread of Islam throughout the Western Sahara – their most important legacy to Mauritania.

The Almoravids did not run a tight ship,

however. What resulted was in effect two empires, one in Morocco and a southern one ruled by the Berbers of Mauritania. They, in turn, were subjugated by Arabs in 1674, after which virtually all the Berbers adopted Hassaniya, the language of their conquerors. This cross of Arab and Berber culture gave rise to the Moors. The stratified caste system of Moorish society, in which the losers were made slaves and the commoners made to pay tribute to the warriors, had its origins in this Arab conquest.

While Europe was busily draining the African continent of its people and its gold, starting in the late 15th century, Mauritania remained relatively unscathed.

Mauritania was less affected by European intervention than just about any country in Africa – no depopulation from slavery, no reorientation of the economy to cash crops, no robbing of its minerals. Sand, it appears, wasn't a hot commodity. For the French, it was just a buffer zone to station troops to protect French West Africa from tribal raiders and ambitious European powers.

Little developed until 1814 when the Treaty of Paris gave France the right to explore and control the Mauritanian coast. The French headquarters were installed in Senegal at St-Louis on the Senegal River. Moors controlled the area along the river, and for security reasons the French wanted to take that control away. They succeeded in playing one Moorish faction off against the other, and established the colonial territory of Mauritania in 1904.

It took the French another 30 years to subjugate the stubborn Moors in the northern areas. Yet the French, with their attention focused elsewhere, did not even discover the huge iron ore deposits there until just before independence.

Independence

With independence in 1960, the Moors declared Mauritania an Islamic republic and set about building a new capital, Nouakchott. Mokhtar Ould Daddah was the new president. To take advantage of the country's sizeable iron-ore deposits in Zouérat, they built a 675-km railway and a mining port. Production began in 1963.

The mines were operated by a foreign-owned consortium that paid its 3000 expatriate workers handsomely – their salaries accounted for two-thirds of the country's entire wages bill. When the Mauritanian miners went out on a two-month strike in the late '60s, the army intervened. It was a bloody mess, and eight miners were killed. Left-wing opposition to the government mounted and some miners formed a clandestine Marxist union in 1973. President Ould Daddah survived the challenge from left-wing opponents by nationalising the company in 1974 and withdrawing from the franc zone, substituting the ouguiya for the CFA. It was the Spanish Sahara issue that finally toppled the government. The government entered into an agreement in 1975 with Morocco and Spain to divide up the former colony. Mauritania was to take an empty slab of desert in the south and Morocco was to get the mineral-rich northern two-thirds, with Spain relinquishing all claims. Naturally the inhabitants of what became known as the Western Sahara were furious; the Polisario Front, with the assistance of Algeria, Libya and Cuba, launched a guerrilla war to oust both countries from the area.

Mauritania was very vulnerable; the railway linking the iron-ore mines and the port ran practically on the border with the Western Sahara. The Polisario sabotaged it continually. In 1977 the country's iron-ore exports were down by 18% due to the disruptions of the train service. A year later, exports were down 36% from the pre-war level. Twice the Polisario units travelled 1000 km from their base camps to lob mortars at Nouakchott.

At great expense the government increased its troops from 1800 to 17,000, but experience and morale were lacking. The Moors were more concerned with the danger of drought than that of an independent Western Sahara. To the Black Africans of southern Mauritania, the war was meaningless. They were more concerned with the government's racial policies, inequitable political representation, and attempts to compel all school children to study in Arabic (lessening their opportunities for university education in French-speaking countries).

A successful coup in 1978 brought in a new government that, with difficulty, extricated Mauritania from the conflict within a year by renouncing all territorial claims to the Western Sahara. (Today, a UN-supervised referendum is in process to hopefully end that conflict for good.) Despite promises to get the economy back on the rails, the new government was unable to do so. The military wanted a change; so in 1984, there was a palace coup, called 'the restructuring' by the new government, which brought in the present military ruler, Colonel Maaouya Sid'Ahmed Ould Taya.

The Race Riots of 1989

In 1989, bloody riots broke out in both Mauritania and Senegal between Moors and Black Africans, the majority of whom were of Senegalese origin. The riots were touched off by a familiar dispute: Mauritanian-owned camels were grazing on land that the black Soninké farmers of Senegalese origin believed to be theirs. Mauritanians killed two Soninké peasants, after which riots broke out in Senegal. The Senegalese looted hundreds of Mauritanian stores throughout Senegal. Mauritanians who feared for their lives and their property began fleeing to the sanctuary of mosques or went into hiding with Senegalese friends.

In Mauritania, the Moors retaliated with genocide, rape, brutal maiming and Gestapo-like raiding of homes and confiscation of property as well as forced deportation and expulsion of tens of thousands of Blacks from towns and villages all over the country. Senegalese nationals were the first targeted, but Black Mauritanians of Pulaar descent were fair game as well. The targeted ethnic groups took shelter in embassies and the UN office; the government rounded them up in mosques and fairgrounds. In rural southern areas, government troops rounded up entire Black African villages and put them in the desert without food or water. Morocco, France, Algeria and Spain sent planes for their rescue; in a surreal air brigade, they

ferried out an equal number of victims from both countries. Bewildered deportees were divested of meagre clothing and family valuables and 'returned home' to Senegal, a country most of them had never known. Tens of thousands of others voluntarily fled by road. In all, some 50,000 to 70,000 Senegalese nationals were expelled and some 20,000 Black Mauritanians were forced into exile – far greater than the number of Mauritanians who had to leave Senegal.

The climate of the Taya government became more ethnocentric and xenophobic as international condemnation rained in. Numerous international aid organisations packed their bags while aid poured in from Islamic border nations. Senegal and Mauritania closed their joint border. The impetus for all this was Taya himself, who had become an Islamic extremist. He alienated more moderate Muslims, particularly the Algerians, and his closest ally became Iraq, but at the same time he and his followers conveniently rid themselves of their long-time political rivals, the Black Africans. Fifty prominent Mauritanians, including several former government officials, signed an open letter denouncing 'in all its horror, the extent of the repression against Negro-African civilians and soldiers during the last few months of 1990'.

Mauritania Today

To thwart criticism, Taya pushed through a new constitution permitting multiple parties, and in early 1992, in the country's first open presidential elections, he fought Ahmed Ould Daddah, a former finance minister and political exile, and won the re-election with 63% of the vote.

GDP had dropped nearly 11% the year before. With the country's economy severely crippled and more focus towards development and investment being given to the agricultural sector, the question of landownership became an issue of increasing importance, further straining the ethnic relations between Moors and Black Mauritanians. The haunting question of repatriation persists as a result of the deportation of Black Mauritanians in order for traditionally nomadic

White Moors to obtain land and eliminate Toucouleurs, the most outspoken group on the issue of civil and land rights. Although the attacks and violence against Black Mauritanians has ceased, they continue to have difficulty getting jobs, identity cards and bank loans, and recovering their land. They live in fear and are denied their civil rights. Many refugees have been returning since 1992 but few have been repatriated.

Meanwhile, the Taya régime refuses to address or comment on the problem. Moreover, many high ranking government officials who were responsible for the abuses and linked to the crimes committed by the security forces have gotten off scott-free by the government's declaration of amnesty in 1993. For Black Mauritanians living along the Senegal River valley, the future will be a long and bitter struggle for social justice and land, even with the Human Rights Watch working to bring this issue to the forefront in future negotiations between foreign aid-donors and Mauritania. Pitted with the forces of nature, unemployment, growing slums, poverty, malnutrition and increasingly scarce resources, Mauritania's future rests on its ability to amend these ethnic and territorial problems, reorganise its priorities and focus on a solid socioeconomic plan.

GEOGRAPHY

Although twice the size of France (1,030,700 sq km) the northern two-thirds of Mauritania, including Nouakchott, is primarily desert, with huge expanses of flat plains broken by occasional ridges and cliff-like overhangings. Moreover, the desert is expanding southward, leading to a major exodus in recent years of nomads into the urban areas.

The south is fairly flat land with scrub, but as you move northward into the Sahara ,there are more sand dunes and the scrub begins to disappear. The rocky plateaus of this desert region offer the most spectacular sights in Mauritania. Most of the plateaus have been eroded, so that only isolated peaks remain. One of the highest and most well-known plateau areas, over 500 metres, is the Adrar, 450 km north-east of Nouakchott. This is where you'll find the 'must see' towns of Atâr, Chinguetti and Ouadâne.

These plateaus are often rich in iron ore, especially at Zouérat about 200 km north of Chinguetti. The highest peak is Kediet Ijill (915 metres) near the city of Zouérat. The other two major plateau areas are Tagant, 400 km east of Nouakchott, and Assaba, to the south of the Tagant plateau.

Mauritania also has some 700 km of shoreline. The fishing town of Nouâdhibou in the extreme north is the second-largest city. Between there and Nouakchott is the Arguin Bank National Park, a bird-watchers' paradise where hundreds of thousands of birds migrate from Europe in the winter. It is one of the world's natural major breeding grounds and is listed by UNESCO as one of the World Heritage natural sites on the globe.

The new Diawling National Park in the flood plains of the Senegal River is helping to attract additional birds, including some

---

The Chemana
Even in the south, which forms part of the Sahel, there are only a few areas that receive enough rainfall in good years to grow sorghum and millet. The country's total arable land consists of a 400-km strip up to 25-km wide, called the *chemana*, on the northern bank of the Senegal River which separates Mauritania from Senegal. The completion in the late 1980s of the huge Manantali Dam further up the river increased significantly the country's potential irrigated land area. While the causes of the violent ethnic clashes of 1989 are rooted in centuries-old cultural practices, there may have been some more immediate reasons why the clashes broke out when they did. According to one theory, since few Moors are farmers, the increased value of land in and near the chemana due to its potential for irrigation stood to benefit primarily the Black farmers; this, in turn, contributed to increased tensions which eventually erupted in violence. ∎

Desertification
As the desert continues to expand southward, it is pushing with it people in search of food, water and habitation. The desertification process is the country's major environmental problem; approximately three-quarters of the country is desert or near desert. It's especially severe around settled areas. Certain developments, mostly attributed to population pressures, are aggravating the problem. They include the expansion of agriculture to marginal lands formerly reserved for grazing, the growth of livestock herds (which in many cases has been due to the drilling of new wells) and the ensuing overgrazing, and deforestation resulting from foraging for firewood or clearing of new agricultural land. ∎

endangered ones. With the exception of a precious few gazelles and bustards, not much is left of the wildlife in Mauritania.

CLIMATE
Mauritania experiences extremes in temperature and insufficient, sporadic rainfall. In the Sahara region, rainfall is usually less than 100 mm or absent. Southward in the Sahelian zone, rainfall increases to about 600 mm per year. There is a short rainy season in the south from July to September, which enables the 400-km strip of arable land to support sheep, goats, cattle, and crops of millet and sorghum. This strip, which represents only 1% of the country's land area, is the only area which receives enough rainfall to support cultivation. In the north, vegetation is insufficient to graze even a camel.

It is extremely hot from April to October, but especially between June and the end of August when average maximum temperatures are 40°C and above. However, along the coast, including Nouakchott and Nouâdhibou, the trade winds called the *alizé* blow from the ocean, causing average highs in those areas to be about 5°C lower.

The best weather is from December to March; the highs and lows in Nouakchott are typically 29°C and 13°C, respectively. You'll need a heavy sweater in Nouâdhibou (generally much cooler than Nouakchott).

GOVERNMENT
Mauritania is in the process of what has been called 'controlled democratisation'. President Taya was returned to power in 1992 in multiparty elections, making Mauritania the first member of the Arab League to have elected a head-of-state by direct universal suffrage. However, the elections were marred by serious inconsistencies and fraud. Moreover, there is no constituent assembly and there has been no formal transition to civilian rule, plus the government continues to rely heavily on military support.

The country's new constitution of 1991 declared Arabic the sole official language, introduced *Sharia* (Islamic law), and legalised political parties but forbid them to be organised on racial or regional lines or to be opposed to Islam. Thus, it has only fuelled tensions between the White Moors and the

The Jefhya & Irifi Winds
Between December and March, the country is frequently blasted by the cold *jefhya* winds from the Sahara which periodically blow south. If you're camping during this period, you'll get surprisingly cold unless you are very warmly clothed.

During the summer and the harmattan season, very hot and sandy winds called the *irifi* blow throughout the country. These dreaded and blinding sandstorms are most frequent in March and April, and can easily blow your tent away. The fine sand will sandpaper your face and permeate everything, including valuable electronic equipment. Be sure to bring some zip-lock plastic bags and fluid for your eyes. You can buy a large headwrap locally. ∎

MAURITANIA

Black community – reflected by the growing number of political parties.

Often labelled as one of the most openly racist countries in the world, Mauritania is ripe for government manipulation of the ethnic conflict. Taya's régime has been hoping to attract foreign aid once again, while shunning any responsibility for the extraditions, violent abuses and killings during the 1989-1992 conflict with Senegal. Taya's main draw card is that he will have difficulty pre-empting the spread of Islamic extremists from Morocco and Algeria unless he can overcome the country's economic problems – with assistance from the West.

ECONOMY

A series of developments during the past two decades has left Mauritania's economy staggering and made this country one of the most deeply indebted in the world. The devastating and persistent years of drought, the decimation of livestock, and the relentless stalking by Mauritania's greatest enemy – desertification – have resulted in a mass exodus of nomads from the desert and rural areas to the cities, primarily to the slums of Nouakchott. Today, only about 10% of the population is officially nomadic, compared with 83% in the late 1960s! The economic situation is further exacerbated by the large sums of debts from the '80s used to finance questionable projects, the diversion of funds into the military budget during the Gulf War, and the high population growth rate (3%).

The present GNP per capita is just over US$500, which is relatively high for West Africa. However, life expectancy is only 47 years, which is less than the West African average, and there is only one doctor per 12,093 inhabitants. All of this suggests that the quality of life here is quite low. Agricultural production from the narrow strip of land along the Senegal River contributes to one-third of the GNP, making this land a governmental focal point for development and expansion. While irrigation in this area is possible, the government considers herding, not agriculture, to be its most important resource, and tends to encourage traditional rain-fed farming methods, to the detriment of the Black farmers in that area.

For several decades fishing has been one of the mainstays of the economy, representing over half of the country's total export earnings. The waters off Mauritania are said to be the richest in the world in terms of fish but over-fishing in recent years has devastated stocks. Profits and foreign investors have decreased significantly due to underinvestment, insufficient monitoring of stock and the poor condition of Mauritania's fleet. While this industry still brings in 25% of the government's revenues, much of the profit from fishing bypasses the national economy by being paid straight into foreign accounts.

Mauritania has one of the largest reserves of iron ore in the world, mainly around Zouérat, and the iron-ore industry accounts for over 40% of the country's foreign earnings. But in recent years exports have been declining because of falling world demand and lower prices. As a result, the largely state-owned mining group Société Nationale Industrielle et Minière (SNIM) now has huge debts. Operations began in 1992 to extract gold from the mines in Akjoujt, a joint venture with an Australian company, and there is talk of a possible venture to exploit old copper mines in the area.

Mauritania's current major problem is its huge external debt, which is the highest in West Africa (as a percentage of the country's GNP). The World Bank and International Monetary Fund (IMF) are working with the government to solve this. As part of the structural adjustment programme the government devalued the ouguiya by 28% in 1992 and plans to privatise numerous state enterprises.

POPULATION & PEOPLE

Of Mauritania's 2.2 million inhabitants, three-quarters are commonly said to be Moors (or Maurs) of Arab and Berber descent. However, lack of reliable demographic data and a long tradition of interracial marriage have blurred ethnic boundaries. Until the mass expulsion of Blacks in 1989, the actual figure for Moors was closer to about 40%. Today, it may be slightly higher. The other major ethnic group are Black Africans, ethnically split into two groups. The Haratin, or Black Moors, the descendants of Blacks enslaved by the Moors, have assimilated the Moorish culture and speak their language, Hassaniya. Culturally, they have little affinity with the southerners: the Black Africans living in the south along the Senegal River. The southerners are mostly Soninké, Pulaar or Toucouleur (sedentary Fulani), Peuls (cattle-raising Fulani) plus a few Wolof – the same ethnic groups found across the border in Senegal.

Population densities and way of life have been controlled by climatic factors which recently have ended a way of life for the traditionally nomadic Moors, who once made their livelihood from raising camels, cattle, sheep and goats and from commerce, particularly transport with camel caravans. For some, this came to an end during the severe droughts of the '70s and early '80s when most of their animals died and they had no choice but to come to Nouakchott and live in shanty towns. But many had long ago given up their nomadic existence for life in the city as traders; indeed, Moorish merchants are a common sight all over West Africa except Senegal. They're easy to spot. If you see a merchant with coffee-coloured skin and Arab facial features, wearing a long light blue African robe, he's probably a Moor.

Women are in a particularly disadvantaged position. For example, only a third as many women as men are literate. There is, however, a National Women's Movement in Mauritania working towards equality.

EDUCATION

Since the arrival of the French colonial administration, an education system began developing slowly. While formal education is not compulsory, Mauritanian families are opting for public schools in lieu of the traditional Islamic education based on rote learning of Arabic, teachings of the Koran, and simple mathematics – disciplines which prepare them little for the changing world. An estimated 51% of school-age children attend primary school (six years) and about 15% go on to secondary school. However, the

---

Caste System of the Moors

The Moors have one of the most stratified caste systems in Africa. The system, however, is based more on lineage, occupation and access to power than simply skin colour. This division hampers any attempt to unify the people. With the inevitable tagged superficialities accompanying racism, colour has become a popular but inaccurate measure to determine status. At the top are the upper classes, the typically light-skinned Bidan Moors descended from warriors and men of letters. Below them are commoners, mostly of Berber-Negroid stock. The lowest castes traditionally consisted of four groups: the Haratin Moors, artisans, bards, and slaves with no rights of any kind. The Haratin do all the house and field work; they are as lean and sinewy as the palm trees they tend. The Bidan women, on the other hand, tend to be plump; fat for them is beautiful. They even feed their daughters a special diet of milk and peanuts so that they will grow up desirably colossal. Socially, the rate of divorce among the Moors is higher than in any other country in West Africa, and divorce is not a social stigma for either party. Women usually divorce in order to find a man with more money, and while Islamic law allows a man to have up to four wives, few men have more than one.

In 1980, there were an estimated 100,000 Haratin slaves in Mauritania. It wasn't until then that Mauritania declared slavery illegal, the last country in the world with slaves to do so! But it's one thing to declare slavery illegal; it's another for it to happen. In fact slavery had been declared illegal three times before this. Yet, in the Adrar area north-east of Nouakchott, people are reportedly still being bought and sold. For one thing, freeing the slaves was conditional on the owners being compensated. Also, most slaves have been attached all their lives to Bidan families and have agreeable relationships. Once they walk out the door, they lose all their financial security. So it's not surprising that most continue living and working for their Bidan families while at the same time being part of, and cared for by, the greater family itself. ∎

MAURITANIA

adult literacy rate is still only 34%, which is well below the sub-Saharan average (51%).

ART & CULTURE

The traditional music of Mauritania (Arabic in origin) is very different from other traditional West African music. To unaccustomed ears, it can often be nerve-shattering. It's characterised by the four-string lute (*tidnit*), sometimes a harp (*ardin*) and usually a soloist wailing praises to Allah.

There is virtually no literature or theatre in Mauritania, but you may get to learn one of the traditional Mauritanian sand games while having tea or waiting for a taxi.

The Moors' social activities often revolve around the traditional glass of Arab tea (green tea imported from China) with mint. Traditionally, it's not one but three glasses that are served over an hour or so. The sweet tea is like a liqueur and has the punch of a strong cup of coffee.

RELIGION

Brought to Mauritania by Berber Muslim traders and crafts people from northern Africa, Islam plays an intricate part in the people's daily lives. Over 99% of the population are Sunni Muslims, and their adherence to the religion provides a superficial unity of the Moors and the Blacks. Women are allowed to attend the mosques but they pray separately from the men and their attendance is often discouraged. Islamic fundamentalists, who were apparently responsible for a brutal attack on two Catholic priests during a Sunday mass in Nouakchott in 1993, are growing in numbers but they are still a decided minority.

LANGUAGE

In 1991, Arabic was declared the official language, but in all government sectors, French is still spoken and all government documents are written in French. In business circles, French is also widely used.

The everyday language of the Moors is a Berber-Arabic dialect called Hassaniya. The Black Africans in the south have their own languages; the principal ones are Pulaar, Wolof and Soninké.

Expressions in Hassaniya

Good morning.	*sa-LAH-mah ah-LAY-koum*
Good evening.	*mah-sah el-HAIR*
How are you?	*ish-TAH-ree?*
Thank you.	*SHOE-kran*
Goodbye.	*mah-sah-LAM*

Expressions in Wolof

Good morning.	*yah-MAN-gah fah-NIN*
Good evening.	*yah-MAN-gah YEN-lou*
How are you?	*nang-gah-DEF?*
Thank you.	*jair-ruh-JEF*
Goodbye.	*mahn-gah-DEM*

Facts for the Visitor

VISAS & EMBASSIES
Mauritanian Visas

Only French, Italian and certain African nationals do not need visas. The standard visa is valid for three months and good for a single-entry one-month stay, but visas good for stays of up to three months are sometimes available (ask). The embassy in Washington, for example, issues visas valid for stays of one to three months depending on your request. It requires US$10, four photos and proof of your yellow fever vaccination, and processes applications in two to three days.

In Europe, visas are just as easy to get at the Mauritanian embassies in Paris, Bonn, Brussels and Madrid and the consulate in Geneva. (Travellers in the UK should consult the French embassy as it may have authority to issue Mauritanian visas.) While they do not insist upon seeing your airline ticket, they usually issue visas only to those indicating that they'll be arriving by air. Travellers who indicate that they'll be going overland seriously risk having their applications rejected.

Because of the ease of getting visas in Europe, try to get your visa there. This is especially true if you'll be arriving overland via Morocco and possibly Algeria as well. While there are Mauritanian embassies in Rabat (Morocco) and Algiers (Algeria), getting Mauritanian visas in Rabat is problematic. The embassy there requires a *note verbale* (letter of introduction) from your embassy and a return airline ticket (plus the application fee and photos). Moreover, some embassies in Rabat, such as the Dutch embassy, refuse to write introduction letters for Mauritanian visas, and others, such as the Belgium embassy, are reluctant to do so. Without the letter and ticket, you will not get a visa. If you bring both, they'll issue the visa on the spot. It is common practice for an overland traveller purchasing an airline ticket in Rabat for the purpose of obtaining a visa to sell the ticket once the visa is issued. The visa will indicate that it's valid for entry at Nouakchott Airport but border officials reportedly ignore this, so you probably shouldn't worry about this if you'll be travelling overland.

Note too that while you can get a visa to Mauritania in Las Palmas (Canary Islands) at Pêcheurs Mauritaines on Calle Raffael Cabrera, don't count on it unless you'll be there quite a while as visa applications must be sent to Madrid and therefore take quite some time to process.

If you wait until arriving in West Africa to get your visa, you should have no problem as Mauritania has embassies in the capital cities of Côte d'Ivoire, The Gambia, Mali, Nigeria and Senegal plus a consulate in Niger. In most, you can get visas on the spot or within 24 hours and without any hassles. In other African countries, there is a good chance that the French embassy has authority to issue them. The only requirements are usually the application fee and photos. The typical cost in CFA countries is between CFA 6500 (eg in Senegal) and CFA 20,000 (at most French embassies).

Visa Extensions

For visa extensions in Nouakchott, see Immigration at the Ministry of Interior (☎ 52020, fax 53661).

Mauritanian Embassies

Belgium 6 Rue de Colombie, Brussels 1050 (☎ (02) 672-47-47)
France (consulate) 89 rue du Cherche-Midi, 75006 Paris (☎ (1) 45-48-23-88)
Germany Bonnerstrasse 48, 5300 Bonn 2 (☎ (0228) 36-40-24)
USA 2129 Leroy Place, NW, Washington, DC 20008 (☎ (202) 232-5700)

Mauritania also has embassies in Abidjan, Algiers, Bamako, Banjul, Dakar, Lagos, Madrid and Rabat; consulates in Düsseldorf, Geneva, Las Palmas, Niamey and Vienna.

Other African Visas

The Senegalese embassy issues visas without hassles. If you'll be travelling overland to Morocco, stop by its embassy in Nouakchott to register even if you don't need a visa. The French consulate issues three-month visas to Burkina Faso, Chad, Côte d'Ivoire and Togo in 24 hours; bring two photos and UM 5200 (less for five-day visas). In Nouakchott you can also get visas to Zaïre (delivered on the spot; about UM 2850 for single-entry visas good for 30-day stays, more for multiple entries or longer stays), Nigeria and Algeria, but not to Mali.

Foreign Embassies

For a list of foreign embassies, see the Nouakchott Information section.

DOCUMENTS

The only documents required are a passport and an International Health Certificate. Those driving need a *carnet de passage en douane* and will have to purchase insurance in Nouakchott or, better yet, in Senegal. An International Driving Permit (IDP) is not required; your own licence will suffice.

CUSTOMS

It is illegal to bring any alcohol into the country. In Nouakchott, the only place besides the private clubs where you can get alcohol is the Hôtel Oasis, while in Nouâdhibou there are several places that serve it.

Mauritania also takes its currency laws very seriously. It's one of the few countries

MAURITANIA

in West Africa which still issues currency declaration forms. There is no restriction on the amount of foreign currency that you may bring in, just be sure to declare it, regardless of where and how you enter. Officials at the border or airport may physically check to verify you're not smuggling in anything undeclared, including alcohol. If you make mistakes in adding your money and they find out, you may end up having to offer a sizeable bribe to avoid detention.

Without your declaration form, changing money, buying airline tickets and exiting the country can be very difficult. In addition, don't rule out being thoroughly searched by police while you're travelling around.

Finally, if you should lose your currency form or fail to receive one, ask the head of customs at the airport to issue you another one. He's usually only there during flight arrivals and departures.

MONEY

CFA 1000	=	UM 260
UK£1	=	UM 200
US$1	=	UM 130

The unit of currency is the ouguiya (ou-GUEE-yah). Between 1991 and 1994 it lost about 50% of its value to the US dollar, going from 78 to 119 ouguiya to the dollar. Even with this marked devaluation, Mauritania is still the most expensive country in West Africa. There is a black market and many local taxi drivers know where the money-changers operate. However, this market is very hush-hush and finding someone to guide you to the dealers may not be easy. The banks give slightly lower rates but they're much more convenient. Between Thursday afternoon and Saturday evening the bank at the airport in Nouakchott is closed. Your only hope for exchanging money during this period is at a top-end hotel. The Novotel offers slightly better rates than the others, but often runs out of ouguiyas on weekends; check Hôtel Marhaba.

There are banks in Nouakchott, Nouâdhibou, Néma and Rosso but nowhere else, and only those in Nouakchott and Nouâdhibou

accept travellers' cheques. Hotels usually don't accept travellers' cheques, but if it's your last resort, they'll take them. Don't make the common mistake of not taking enough ouguiya when travelling upcountry. Mauritania is a very expensive country and you'll spend money faster than you'd expect. Moreover, outside Nouakchott, foreign currencies, including the US dollar and UK pound, will get you nowhere. (The CFA and French franc may be accepted in a pinch.)

Banks for changing money in Nouakchott include: Banque Al Baraka Mauritanienne Islamique (BAMIS), Banque Mauritanienne pour le Commerce International (BMCI), Banque Arabe Libyenne en Mauritanie (BALM) and the Banque Arabe Africaine en Mauritanie (BAAM). BALM doesn't take travellers' cheques; BMCI does and charges no commission. Travellers frequently experience difficulty cashing American Express travellers' cheques, so consider bringing other types or, best, French franc travellers' cheques. Credit cards are accepted only at the Novotel and Hôtel Halima.

BUSINESS HOURS & HOLIDAYS

Business hours are Sunday to Thursday from 8 am to noon and 3 to 6 pm; closed Friday and Saturday. Some businesses such as Air Afrique and Air Mauritanie are open on Saturday mornings. Government offices are open Saturday to Wednesday from 8 am to 3 pm; Thursday from 8 am to 1 pm.

Banking hours are Sunday to Thursday from 7 am to 1 pm (closed Friday and Saturday).

Public Holidays

1 January, Eid-ul-Fitr (end of Ramadan), 26 February, 8 March (Mauritanian women only), Tabaski, 1 May, 25 May (African Liberation Day), 10 July, Matouloud (Mohammed's Birthday), 28 November (Independence), Islamic New Year.

POST & TELECOMMUNICATIONS

The post office in Nouakchott is open seven days a week. You can also make international phone calls from there. The telephone system is connected to satellite and you can dial direct to almost anywhere. The cost is about US$5 a minute to the USA and US$3 to US$4 a minute to Europe. When calling Mauritania, after the country code (222), add another 2 (the code for all cities).

FILM & PHOTOGRAPHY

Taking photos reportedly requires a permit. The rule is rarely enforced, but a police officer might cause you problems if he sees you photographing something other than a tourist site. Taking photographs of government buildings including post offices, airports, ports, radio antennas and military installations is strictly forbidden.

The only places where you can purchase film are in Nouakchott at the Novotel, Dipal and other smaller boutiques.

HEALTH

A yellow fever vaccination is mandatory for those arriving from an infected area or staying more than two weeks, as is a cholera shot for those arriving within six days from an infected area. Nouakchott hospital has French doctors for emergencies. For any serious emergencies, contact your embassy.

DANGERS & ANNOYANCES

Despite a slight rise in crime, particularly petty thefts, Nouakchott remains one of the safest capital cities in Africa. Elsewhere, it's not a bad idea to check in with the police if you'll be staying overnight in a village as that may help alleviate their suspicions and, ultimately, help you if you have any problems.

Be aware of how you dress. Here, more so than in other West African countries, local people, particularly Islamic fundamentalists, are very rigid about the dress code. Miniskirts, shorts and swimsuits are offensive to many Mauritanians, especially outside Nouakchott. There have been reported attacks in Nouakchott; one is believed to have been provoked because of the manner in which a young foreign woman was dressed. Also, avoid open discussions or comments on religious issues.

With Mauritania's long and ugly history of discrimination passed down by the Arabs,

Black Africans are still frequently subjected to unnecessary hassles as well as verbal and sometimes physical harassment by the police and Moors. Often mistaken for Black Africans, Black foreigners could very well receive this same treatment and should be aware of this possibility before visiting.

An unstable area you need to be aware of is the frontier of the Western Sahara. It still has thousands of land mines buried along the Mauritanian frontier. People have been killed there, so avoid it, including the area just west of Nouâdhibou. If you're planning to travel overland to Mali, check first with your embassy or with government officials for the latest information. Since the early '90s, the border near Néma has been closed because of disturbances, some violent, near the Malian border involving ethnic conflicts, cattle rustling and weapons trade.

ACCOMMODATION

Hotels are generally more expensive in Mauritania than anywhere else in West Africa. Finding a room for less than US$20 is impossible in Nouakchott and extremely difficult elsewhere. The hotel tax (10%) is usually included. For camping in Nouakchott and Nouâdhibou you need a vehicle; the only place to camp is well out of town in the open desert.

FOOD

The desert cuisine of the Moors wins no culinary awards. Dishes are generally bland and limited to lamb, goat, rice and yoghurt-millet preparations. Street food is neither as cheap nor as varied as in other countries of the region. However, Mauritanian couscous, similar to the Moroccan variety, is delicious.

A real treat would be attending a *méchui* (MAY-shoe-ee) where an entire lamb is roasted over a fire and stuffed with cooked rice. Guests tear off cooked bits of meat with their hands. It is an event followed by the ritualistic three glasses of tea.

THINGS TO BUY

The Moors are known for being good crafts people. In years past, the silver was of the highest quality. It's still around but becoming very rare. Nothing is more sought after than the wooden chests with silver inlay, but there are also earth-tone rugs of camel and goat hair from Boutilimit, hand-woven carpets, hand-painted Kiffa beads, hand-dyed leather work, cushions, saddles, silver daggers and jewellery. The quality was once excellent; imitations are now the norm. In the southern town of Kaédi, artists continue to make colourful batik cloth.

Getting There & Away

AIR
To/From Europe & the USA
There are four direct flights a week between Paris and Nouakchott on Air France and Air Afrique. From Paris a one-way economy fare is ridiculously high at 6720FF; special fares are better value. From Nouakchott, regular fares (UM 75,520 or US$580 one-way economy class) are over 50% cheaper than the same class ticket purchased in France.

You can also fly via Casablanca (Morocco). There are flights in either direction between Casablanca and Nouakchott on Monday, Wednesday and Friday on Royal Air Maroc, Air Algérie and Air Mauritanie; the one-way fare is UM 42,460 (about US$325). The Air Algérie flight (Wednesday) originates in Algiers. Reconfirm flights carefully, especially during Ramadan.

To/From West Africa
Within West Africa, there are direct flights to Nouakchott daily (except Sunday) to/from Dakar on Air Mauritanie, Air Afrique and Air France; twice weekly to/from Bamako on Air Afrique and Air Mauritanie, and Banjul on Air Gambia and Air Mauritanie, and Abidjan on Air France and Air Afrique. Typical one-way fares are UM 10,500 (CFA 69,400) to Dakar, UM 15,900 (CFA 105,350) to Banjul, UM 29,700 (CFA 196,800) to Bamako, and UM 42,580 (CFA 282,000) to Abidjan. Prices go down by as much as 10% during the low season (October to March) except around Christmas.

Purchasing tickets in CFA countries costs approximately 75% more than in Mauritania. Never purchase a return ticket to Nouakchott from a CFA country – purchase two one-way tickets.

Air Mauritanie also flies Nouakchott-Las Palmas (Canary Islands) round trip, stopping in Nouâdhibou; reconfirmation is necessary in Las Palmas. Flights are often full for weeks, but if you try standby and go to the airport, your chances of getting on are not bad.

One of the quirks about air travel to Mauritania is that there are occasional flight cancellations due to sandstorms. This occurs most frequently during the December to March harmattan season. One of these storms resulted in an airplane crash in 1994.

LAND
Bush Taxi
From Dakar (Senegal) to St-Louis (268 km) and then on to Rosso (93 km) the trip overland by bush taxi takes from 11 to 13 hours depending on the wait at Rosso. At Rosso, you must cross the Senegal River by ferry or *pirogue* (dugout canoe). If you have lots of baggage, you must use the ferry unless you're willing to pay extra for your baggage. The ferry, which is free for passengers, operates from 7 am to 12.30 pm and from 4 to 5 pm. The pirogues, which charge a minimal fee, depart as soon as they fill up. You may also need to change a small amount of CFA to ouguiyas at this border to pay for the taxi from Rosso to Nouakchott.

Bush taxis for Nouakchott cost UM 800 and are always waiting in Rosso near the ferry dock. There are frequent police stops on the road to Nouakchott, but if there's a sandstorm, your vehicle won't be stopped much. Regardless, keep your passport handy as you will be asked to present it at all stops. Fortunately, baggage checks are much less frequent these days. Black foreigners may be treated more suspiciously by police, particularly about their nationality or the validity of their passports. If this happens to you, remain cool and co-operative.

Car
To/From Morocco Crossing the desert

begins at Dakhla, 1703 km south of Casablanca. The road is tarred all the way and there are good bus connections. In Dakhla, the army leads a convoy every Tuesday and Friday to the Mauritanian border, where you must wait at least several days to pass through customs. Waits of up to 10 days are not unheard of, so bring lots of water and food just in case. From there, vehicles are escorted by Mauritanian police to Nouâdhibou. (This is now the preferred trans-Saharan route. For a detailed description see the introductory Getting There & Away chapter.)

To/From Algeria As the Sahara crossings via Niger and Mali have become increasingly complicated in recent years because of the armed conflicts in northern Niger and Mali, the rarely travelled route via western Algeria down into Mauritania is becoming increasingly attractive. (See the introductory Getting There & Away chapter.)

To/From Senegal The most well-travelled overland route is from Dakar to Nouakchott via St-Louis and Rosso. It involves crossing the Senegal River by ferry which operates from 7 am to 12.30 pm and from 4 to 5 pm. It costs UM 1700 per vehicle. There is, however, a new border crossing which involves branching off northward from Diama (halfway between St-Louis and Rosso) and passing over the Senegal River via a new dyke (85 km from St-Louis), then heading eastward to Rosso. This route takes about an hour longer, but it avoids planning your trip around the ferry schedule. Procedures for obtaining car insurance and for passing through police and customs are very efficient on the Senegalese side; less so on the Mauritanian side.

To/From Mali The border with Mali at Néma, the main crossing point, has been closed since the early '90s but it's possible to cross at other points, such as south of Kiffa. For the latest information, consult with officials in Nouakchott or Bamako.

Getting Around

AIR

Air Mauritanie, one of the better airlines in West Africa, flies twice-daily to Nouâdhibou (UM 6120 one way), three times a week to Atâr, twice a week to Néma (UM 8900), Zouérat and Tidjikja, and once a week to Kaédi (UM 4600), Ayoûn-el-Atroûs and Kiffa. Flights are not always reliable because there are a limited number of planes and the president is given first priority to use them. Flight departures and arrivals are punctual (weather permitting) and short. Because of the poor road conditions most people fly. Make your reservations in advance as most flights are fully booked.

BUSH TAXI & TRUCK

Peugeot 504s (station wagons) and *bachés* (pick-up trucks), which are slightly cheaper, are the two types of public overland transport. Taxis go to all the major towns daily, but finding a taxi to take you to smaller villages is more challenging and costly. Travellers also have the option of taking large trucks, which transport food supplies, construction materials, sheep and people. Needless to say, travel by large truck is more uncomfortable and time consuming, but it's also at least one-third cheaper. Even the Peugeot 504s are fairly uncomfortable because the passengers are crammed in.

Unless you are going to one of the towns in the south-east, expect a long and hot trip. Take along plenty of water and something to munch on. If you choose a baché or large truck, be sure to bring something to cover your head, nose and mouth; a bottle of eye drops is also recommended. The driver usually provides food such as couscous and goat meat but most travellers find the quantity insufficient. Count on frequent stops en route for prayer and tea.

From Nouakchott to Nouâdhibou you have two choices. Either take a bush taxi to Atâr (10 hours) and on to Choûm (three to four hours), where you can catch the train to

Nouâdhibou. Or take a large truck (UM 2500) or Land Rover direct between the two cities. There are trucks every day in either direction; a typical trip (which passes along the coast) takes from 20 hours to two days.

TRAIN

The train is only for those looking for adventure, and really want to rough it. It was never meant to be a passenger train but has become one for many Mauritanians because of the lack of good alternatives. There are two trains every day between Nouâdhibou and Zouérat, with scheduled departures around noon and 3 pm in either direction. They often leave an hour or two late, and while the trip is supposed to take 17 hours, 20 hours is more typical. Both trains have a passenger car at the rear including berths; a seat for the entire distance costs around UM 1050. The first train is very dirty and the few windows are sealed. The passenger car attached to the second train is more comfortable as it is for the staff engineers. If space is available, travellers should be able to take it.

The ride on these trains is far from comfortable and surprisingly cold. Ore dust settles on just about everything, and because you travel mostly at night, you won't see very much. Nevertheless, many travellers recommend taking it.

From Nouakchott there are bush taxis to Atâr and on to Choûm, where you can catch the train either to Nouâdhibou or Zouérat. It's also possible to ride free on one of the iron-ore wagons. If you do, you'll see almost nothing because the dust is so thick that you'll have to wrap your head in cloth and huddle in the corner of a wagon for the entire journey. In the passenger car, on the other hand, you can chat with the locals and brush up on your Hassaniya; they may even offer you some tea. If you chat with the engineer you may end up with a free ride in the cab.

Some travellers have attached their car to the top of the freight cars but this is not really necessary as the road between Nouâdhibou and Zouérat is in reasonably good condition. Check with officials of SNIM (☎ 53337) in

Nouakchott or the train company SNTFM (☎ 45174) in Nouâdhibou.

CAR

The sands of time have deteriorated much of the once asphalted Nouakchott-Atâr road (450 km). Now it's better to take the desert path parallel to the lacy road. The nonstop driving time to Atâr is eight to 10 hours. The 120-km stretch from Atâr to Chinguetti and Ouadâne is very sandy and difficult. Unless you're an expert desert driver, you'll need a 4WD. The road is not as bad from Atâr to Choûm (the northern limit of permitted travel). For the rest of Mauritania, you'll need a 4WD and sand ladders.

The overland trip from Nouakchott to Nouâdhibou takes at least two days and the road is so awful that virtually no one attempts it except truckers. The first 155 km of the 525-km seaside road are on the beach itself, a risky route, especially if you break down. After the beach, you run into dunes. It can be done, but for safety reasons you must go with at least one other vehicle, and study the tide schedule carefully before setting out. A 4WD is essential, and getting lost is almost guaranteed without a guide.

Nouakchott

Nouakchott, meaning 'the place of the winds', is one of the newest capitals in the world, created in 1960 at the beginning of independence. Prior to then, it was a grassy fertile plain governed by the French from St-Louis.

When Senegal and Mauritania separated at independence, St-Louis ended up on the Senegalese side, leaving Mauritania without a major city. The site for a new city was chosen 200 km north of the Senegalese border and near the ocean, many days' walk from the Sahara. During the next 30 years the Sahara moved in – part of the desertification process that is occurring all along the 6000-km southern border of the Sahara. Now the city is in the Sahara surrounded by rolling sand dunes, with sand piling up against walls and fences like snow drifts.

The city was planned with wide streets, an adequate water supply and some space around public buildings and houses – quite unlike the typical African city. Some say that because the city is new and planned, the atmosphere is artificial and uninteresting, but if you find the desert intriguing, you are less likely to agree. While some of the locals may seem reserved, the trades people in particular are easy to meet; browse around the souk and you'll be invited for tea.

Following the race riots, Nouakchott lost some of its energy – not that it had much in the first place. Today, the two main markets are again lively and the beaches are superb for jogging, surf-casting and picnicking. Watching the artisans at work is fascinating. Petty thefts, however, are increasing.

Nouakchott's major problem is that it was designed for about 200,000 inhabitants but has now nearly triple that number because of the hordes of nomads attracted to the city during the recent droughts. Accordingly, the outskirts of Nouakchott are the antithesis of what the designers intended – a shanty town of tiny metal shacks and tents cluttered one against the other. Thin goats and old women in ragged black robes wander along the streets. The conditions here are far worse than those in other African cities because in the rest of Africa, people migrating to the city usually end up living with relatives. In the case of Nouakchott, there were more displaced nomads descending on the city than there were inhabitants. There was no way the city could absorb these numbers.

In 1990, in order to free some of the city's marginal land for middle-class Moors, the government moved the poorest renters from some of the city's poorest areas to new settlements far from town, leaving these displaced people with impossible hikes to the few jobs in town, and with no public transport, no electricity, and steep fees for water hauled in by trucks.

Orientation

The main street is Ave Abdel Nasser, which runs east to west through the heart of the city.

Along it are three major hotels, most banks and travel agencies, the post office, several restaurants and artisan dealers. The ocean is five km west along this road. If you go east and then left on the major route north, you'll quickly come to the old Ksar district and the airport, only three km from the centre of the city. Perpendicular to Ave Abdel Nasser is Ave Kennedy, near the intersection of which is the Marché Capital. In the north of the city is the Peace Corps office, the Novotel and the new stadium, while to the south is the Cinquième district, which is the major shanty town and a long walk from the centre.

Information

Money The BALM (☎ 52469) has probably the lowest charges for exchanging money but it doesn't accept travellers' cheques. It's in the centre on Ave Abdel Nasser. Another good place to change money and travellers' cheques is the BMCI (☎ 52826, fax 52045) also on Ave Abdel Nasser.

Post & Telecommunications The post office, which isn't clearly marked, is in the central area facing the Hôtel Marhaba on Ave Abdel Nasser. Buying stamps here is a bit of a free for all and requires a combination of pushiness and patience. This is the cheapest place to make international phone calls and send faxes. You can also place calls and send faxes at the Novotel, Hôtel Marhaba and Hôtel Halima. For information on telephone numbers or codes, call ☎ 12.

Foreign Embassies The following countries are represented in Nouakchott:

Egypt (☎ 52192)
France Rue Ahmed Ould Mohamed (☎ 51740)
Germany Rue Abdalaye (☎ 51032 or 51729)
Morocco South of Rue Abdalaye (☎ 51411, telex 550)
Nigeria (☎ 52314)
Senegal Rue Mamadou Konaté, north of Rue Abdalaye (☎ 57290)
Spain (☎ 52080)
Tunisia (☎ 52871)
USA Rue Abdalaye (☎ 52660/3, fax 52589, telex 558)

Travel Agencies Unitours (☎ 53816, fax

MAURITANIA

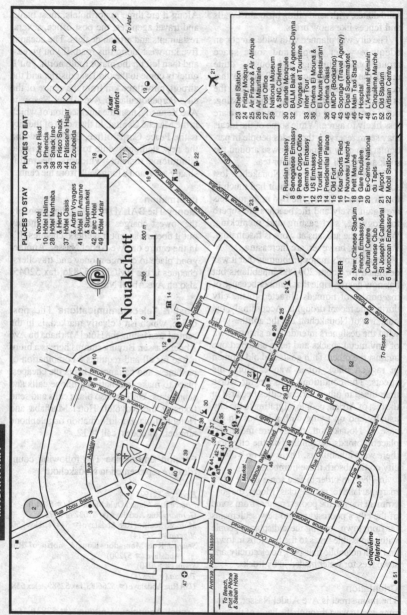

Nouakchott

PLACES TO STAY
1 Novotel
10 Hôtel Halima
28 Hôtel Marhaba & Hertz
37 Hôtel Oasis
41 Hôtel El Amane & Adrar Voyages & Supermarket
42 Parc Hôtel
49 Hôtel Adrar

PLACES TO EAT
31 Chez Riad
34 Phenicia
38 Snack Inac
39 Frisco Snack
44 Pâtisserie Hajjar
50 Zoubeïda

OTHER
2 New Chinese Stadium
3 French Embassy & Cultural Centre
4 Lebanese Club
5 St Joseph's Cathedral
6 Moroccan Embassy
7 Russian Embassy
8 Senegalese Embassy
9 Peace Corps Office
11 German Embassy
13 US Embassy
14 Tourist Information
15 Presidential Palace
16 Old Fort
17 Ksar Sports Field
18 Nouveau Marché
19 Petit Marché
20 Gare Routière
21 Airport
22 Mobil Station
23 Shell Station
24 Friday Mosque
25 Air France & Air Afrique
26 Air Mauritanie
27 Post Office
29 National Museum & SNC Cinéma
30 Grande Mosquée
32 BALM Bank & Agence-Dayna
33 Voyages et Tourisme
33 Inter Tour
35 Cinéma El Mouna & El Mouna Restaurant
36 Cinéma Oasis
40 IMDP (Bookshop)
43 Soprage (Travel Agency)
45 Dipal Supermarket
46 Main Taxi Stand
47 Hospital
48 L'Arsenal Féminin
51 Cinquième Marché
52 Old Stadium
53 Artisan Centre

53225, telex 5801), on the main drag near the turn-off for the hospital, specialises in tours to the Adrar area (Atâr, Chinguetti, Ouadâne) and the Parc du Banc d'Arguin. It charges about UM 8300 a day plus UM 40 per km, 16% tax for a 4WD Toyota Landcruiser and UM 1200 a day for the chauffeur/guide. Lodgings and meals, which are extra, are usually arranged with local families.

Two of Unitours' leading competitors are the long-standing Adrar Voyages/Sodetour (☎ 51717, fax 53210, telex 531) on Ave de Gaulle north of Hôtel Oasis, and Atlas Voyage (☎ 52092, fax 57570) on Ave Abdel Nasser, both of which rent vehicles with drivers. Adrar also provides weekend packages to Air Afrique's fishing resort hotel in Nouâdhibou. Others to consult, all along Ave Abdel Nasser, include Morel Caravane (☎ 51350, fax 54755), Agence-Dayna Voyages et Tourisme next to the BALM bank, Inter Tour (☎ 53217, telex 847) about 100 metres from Hôtel El Amanne, Agence Mauritanie de Voyages et des Transports (☎ 52298, telex 590) near the hospital, and Soprage.

Bookshops & Supermarkets Hôtel Marhaba and the Novotel have small bookstalls where you'll find postcards, French publications and, frequently, *Time* and *Newsweek*. The best bookshop, however, is IMDP (☎ 52684) on Ave Kennedy across from Frisco Snack; it has information and literature on Mauritania. For a place to relax and read during the day, head for the French Cultural Centre.

For imported grocery items, including bottled water, check the two supermarkets next to Hôtel El Amanne; Dipal has the better selection and the more reliable supply.

Markets
The Marché Capital, or Grand Marché, in the centre south of the intersection of Ave Abdel Nasser and Ave Kennedy, is interesting and has an array of items for sale. The northern half of the market is housed in a two-storey building while the southern half consists of open stalls. Among the potential souvenirs you'll find here are silver jewellery, wooden boxes with silver inlay, traditional teapots

and smoking pipes. If you go past the small buildings at the end of the section of stalls you'll find a small vegetable market with fairly reasonable prices.

The colourful Cinquième Marché on the southern outskirts in the 5th Arrondissement has less merchandise but it's a good place to go if you're interested in just walking around and observing the culture. It's also the best place to buy vegetables, cloth and house ware. It's a long walk from the centre, so you may want to take a taxi. On Ave Kennedy just west of the Marché Capital are green minivans (about UM 25) headed south to the market; just ask for 'le cinquième'. If you're walking from Marché Capital, go a few blocks southward along Ave Kennedy, turn to the right then back again south and continue for five or six more blocks. When you see a road on your left where there are lots of mattresses and long rolls of carpet standing on end, you have reached the market. To return, walk to the street on the east end of the market and look for a green van.

National Museum
This is definitely worth checking, especially before travelling outside Nouakchott. The exhibits focus on the life and culture of the country's nomads, totally excluding that of the Black southerners.

On the first level is a prehistoric gallery displaying various ancient tools and artefacts, showing the evolution of human kind. The second level has a display of beauty aids used by nomadic women, local games, fishing gear, camel saddles and other artefacts reflecting the daily cognitive, pastoral, agricultural and musical activities of the Moors. The museum is at the Maison du Parti et de la Culture, built by the Chinese. It's open Saturday to Wednesday from 9.30 am to 2.30 pm and 4 to 6 pm, and on Thursday from 9.30 am to 12.30 pm. Admission is UM 300. (You'll only be supplied with a guide if you are in a group.)

Mosques
The Grande Mosquée (better known as the Mosquée Saudique) in the centre on Rue

Mamadou Konaté was donated by Saudi Arabia, while the Friday mosque on Ave Abdel Nasser just before the major intersection with the road to Rosso was donated by Morocco. Both are quite attractive and can be visited.

Port de Pêche

One of the more interesting activities is visiting the small wharf and fish market, Port de Pêche, every afternoon between 4 and 6 pm when the fishing boats return with the day's catch. You'll see teams of strong men and boys dragging in metre upon metre of heavy hand-knotted seines. Small boys hurry back and forth with trays of fish which they sort, gut, fillet and lay out on large trestles to dry. You'll find a wide selection here, including tuna, mullet, flounder, rock lobster and sea bass; all are relatively cheap.

It's a great place to take photos and one of the few places where you'll find people who generally don't mind being photographed. The fisher people, mostly Wolof and Pulaar, are very friendly and will explain techniques, the different types of fish they catch and the going prices.

The cheapest way to get here is by shared taxi or 'route' taxi. At the taxi stand at Marché Capital, you'll find a route taxi to take you to the south-west edge of town (UM 30). Get out at the stoplight and walk west for eight or 10 blocks, where you'll find taxis parked under some trees on the left side of a roundabout. The drivers will try to get you to take a 'course', which is the local name for a taxi to yourself and more expensive, but if you insist on a route taxi, they'll show you which one to get in. Route taxis at this roundabout usually fill up within five minutes or so. The fare from here to the fish market is another UM 30. A course taxi from the centre of town to the fish market can be negotiated for about UM 300.

Ksar

This old Moorish settlement, which was once destroyed by a flood and has been only partially rebuilt, is fast becoming a slum, with growing numbers of tin shacks for recently displaced nomads. You'll have to ask around for the beautiful rugs for which Ksar is famous (try along Rue Ghary).

Swimming

Pools The Novotel and Hôtel Marhaba have pools. The Novotel's is open only to guests. The Marhaba's pool can be used by non-guests if they order a meal at the restaurant.

Beaches The closest beach to Nouakchott is about five km from the centre. Men can swim and sunbathe without problems, but women must use discretion because locals consider it offensive for women not to be covered. (Look for spots further down the beach where there are no locals.) If you have a 4WD, head for the unmarked Tanit beach, 61 km to the north. It's much better because of the clean white sand, and it's a more secluded spot for camping.

Places to Stay – bottom end

Decent, reasonably priced hotels are few in Nouakchott. *Hôtel Adrar* (☎ 52955) is smelly and has poor lighting, but it's cheap – UM 1500/2000 for singles/doubles with shared bath and UM 2000/3000 upstairs with private bath and window.

Hôtel Oasis (☎ 52011) charges UM 4500/5000 for singles/doubles. The restaurant has reasonable prices and an open terrace. The lively Oasis is notable for being the only hotel in town which serves alcohol, both beer and hard liquor. It's on Ave de Gaulle next to the Cinéma Oasis. *Hôtel Chinguetti*, on the same block but facing Rue Mamadou Konaté, is barely functioning these days.

Camping The beach is five km from town, far enough away so as not to be pestered by intruders if you camp here. It is relatively safe now but be sure to enquire about current safety conditions beforehand.

Places to Stay – middle

The *Parc Hôtel* (☎ 51444) is good value, with large singles/doubles for UM 5700/7100. It has air-con, good lighting, balconies, a relatively good restaurant, and is in the heart of the city on Ave Abdel Nasser.

Many recommend *Hôtel El Amanne*

(☎ 52178) near the Parc. Singles/doubles cost UM 7000/8000. The pleasant open-air terrace is a popular meeting place, and the restaurant is one of the best in town.

The *Sabah Hôtel* (☎ 51552/64, telex 821) is right on the beach, but is quite run-down and virtually deserted. Singles/doubles with air-con cost UM 4000/5000. Because it's five km from the city, finding a taxi is difficult, especially at night.

Places to Stay – top end

The best top-end hotel is *Hôtel Marhaba* (☎ 51686, fax 57854) on Ave Abdel Nasser facing the post office. Singles/doubles cost UM 10,000/12,000 with air-con, satellite TV and decent baths. The facilities include a bar with video TV and a pool which nonguests may use if they have a meal here.

The city's top hotel, however, is the *Novotel* (☎ 53526, fax 51831, telex 866). Rooms are pretty expensive at UM 15,900/18,700 for singles/doubles, and although 1.5 km north of the centre on Rue Abou Baker, it has a good pool (guests only) and a decent but expensive restaurant.

Hôtel Halima (☎ 57920/1, fax 57922), in a residential area 500 metres from the Presidential Palace, has small and unimpressive rooms, overpriced at UM 13,000/15,000 for singles/doubles. There's a decent restaurant and credit cards are accepted.

Places to Eat

Cheap Eats For non-African cheap eats, you can't beat the many Lebanese places around town. *Snack Irac* is a decent place for chawarmas (grilled meat sandwiches). It's sort of a walk-up window place with a few scattered chairs in the front. The *Phenicia*, in the centre on Rue Mamadou Konaté, half a block north of Ave Abdel Nasser, is a great lunch place with Moroccan and Lebanese dishes, a loud TV, and healthy servings for low prices. The Lebanese chawarma sandwiches, yoghurt and fruit salads are excellent. *El Mouna*, directly across the street, serves slightly cheaper meals but offers few choices. The American-run *Welcome Burger*, on Ave de Gaulle towards

the Peace Corps office, serves burgers, chips, fried chicken, ice cream, Lebanese chawarma sandwiches and full meals.

For brochettes, try the friendly *Beyrouth* on Ave Abdel Nasser. The best bakery is *Le Délice* at the northern end of Ave Kennedy. *Pâtisserie Hajjar* a block behind the Parc Hôtel is closer to the centre but has no seating.

African The highest concentration of cheap Mauritanian restaurants and street vendors is south and west of Marché Capital, particularly along Ave Kennedy. The standard fare of these nameless hole-in-the-walls is lamb, goat, rice and occasionally yoghurt-millet concoctions. Street food is generally limited to grilled meat of unknown origins.

Lebanese One of the best restaurants in town is *Frisco Snack*, on Ave Kennedy, a block north of Ave Nasser. It has an American and Lebanese menu. Although not cheap, they have good hamburgers and pizza and it's the only place that sells pita bread.

There's also the old standby, *Chez Riad*. Prices are quite reasonable (about UM 900 for the fixed price menu) plus there's a wide à la carte selection. The main restaurant is at the back; the front section serves a wide variety of sandwiches for only UM 150. It's in the centre of town on Ave Abdel Nasser, two blocks east of Hôtel El Amanne, and is open every day.

Moroccan The best and most expensive Moroccan restaurant is the *Mamounia* on Rue Abdalaye, between the French and German embassies. The tagine (baked vegetables and meat or fish) is good although the portions are a bit small. An alternative is *Zoubeida*, which serves tagine and other Moroccan specialities. If price is of no concern, special order beforehand; they'll serve you upstairs in the Moroccan room where cushions are arranged around low tables. For the money, the separate dining area in front is a much better deal. You can get cheap fare, such as couscous, for about UM 250. It's on Rue Ely Ould Mohamed.

Chinese The *Dragon d'Or* is one of the better restaurants and serves good but expensive Chinese food. They've also added French food to their menu, and it's one of the few place you can get ice cream. It's in the centre on a side street facing the Grande Mosquée.

French Two of the better places for French food are the *Hôtel Marhaba*, which has the best chef in town, and *Hôtel El Amanne*. The latter has excellent service and large portions. Another good place is the new *Hôtel Halima*; the restaurant there has an impressive menu and prices to match.

Entertainment

Bars Nouakchott has no nightclubs or places with live music. There is presently only one hotel, the *Oasis*, which serves alcohol. It attracts overland travellers and a slightly disreputable local crowd. Both *Le Racing Club* and the *Lebanese Club* have bars and sometimes dancing, but it's by invitation only.

Cinemas Cinéma Oasis, in the centre on Ave de Gaulle, and Cinéma El Mouna, a block to the east, show a variety of Hindu and karate flicks. The best selection of films is at the government-operated SNC Cinéma, south of the post office. See the billboard next to the post office for showings. The French Cultural Centre shows French films on a regular basis and posts a calendar there and at the embassy listing upcoming films and cultural programmes, including occasional concerts.

Things to Buy

Artisan Goods The womens' co-operative, L'Artisanal Féminin, on Ave de Gaulle facing the central market, sells tablecloths, clothes, purses, pillows, camel-hair rugs, colourfully painted leather cushions, huge decorated nomad tents, and fine straw mats at fixed prices. Except Friday, it's open daily (8 to 11 am and 4 to 6 pm).

The Marché Capital and the cheaper Cinquième Marché offer a bit of everything, including leather sandals (*les samaras*) and the popular but bulky Moroccan brass kettles for hand washing at meal times. There are good bargains from Moor and Hausa trading-bead sellers as well as vendors of *gris-gris* (charms) who stock dried frogs, bird claws etc. You can buy Soninké tie-dyed material and Senegalese batiks along Ave Abdel Nasser near Hôtel El Amanne. Only Wolof and Soninké women wear and sell this colourful cloth. Most Moor women wear the crinkly voile called a *malafa*; it's used by them as a facial cover. You can buy it at both markets and it is relatively inexpensive.

Silver For years, Mauritania has been famous for its silver, particularly its wooden boxes with silver inlay, daggers and jewellery. Today you can still get some authentic pieces at surprisingly reasonable prices because so few tourists are coming to Mauritania and traders need money. The most convenient place to look and to bargain with the Moor traders is in front of Hôtel El Amanne, but the prices are high. You'll find much better bargains and a wider variety at the nearby Marché Capital. If you look around behind the market, you'll find some Moor gold and silversmiths. Observing them at work can be very interesting, but don't expect their prices to be any lower.

Silver Moor pendants

Rugs Mauritanian rugs are traditionally made of white, beige or chestnut-coloured wool with geometrical designs, and are less complex and colourful than those in northern Africa. Although the Centre National du

Tapis is closed, you might find one or two for sale along Rue Ghary in the Old Ksar district or at the Cinquième Marché. Because they are rarely made these days, their price and value have increased.

Getting There & Away

Air Air Mauritanie (☎ 52211), on Ave Abdel Nasser, has flights every day except Sunday to/from Dakar (UM 10,460 or CFA 69,400); daily flights in the morning and afternoon to Nouâdhibou (UM 6100); flights on Monday, Thursday and Saturday to Atâr (UM 5400); and once or twice a week to Kaédi (UM 4600), Kiffa (UM 5500), Ayoûn-el-Atroûs (UM 7100), Tidjikja (UM 5300), Zouérat (UM 7900) and Néma (UM 8900). Air Afrique (☎ 52081/4, fax 51487) and Air France (☎ 51802) are further east on the same street.

Bush Taxi There are no buses connecting towns, only Peugeot 504 bush taxis, bachés and Land Rovers. The *gare routière* (bush taxi park) is opposite the airport. Mauritania is not noted for its fast and frequent public transport, but you should be able to find taxis and bachés to all the major towns (Atâr, Kaédi, Néma, etc) as well as to the Senegalese border at Rosso. The one exception is Nouâdhibou. The sand tracks to it are so diabolical that only large trucks ply this route.

Traffic is so light in Mauritania that there may be only one vehicle a day headed to your intended destination. For this reason, it's best to go early in the morning to the gare routière to make sure you don't miss it or, better, go there the day before to enquire about the expected departure time. Taxis designed to carry a maximum of six people are invariably crammed with at least nine passengers, so don't expect the ride to be comfortable.

For a large truck, the best place to look is the market in the Cinquième district. Typical fares by truck from Nouakchott are UM 1500 to Atâr, UM 1800 to Choûm, UM 2100 to Néma and UM 2500 to Nouâdhibou. Bush taxi Peugeot 504s cost at least 50% more.

Car Nouakchott has numerous car rental agencies, all on Ave Abdel Nasser, including Hertz (☎ 53686, telex 335), Europcar (☎ 51136, fax 52285, telex 546) at Hôtel Marhaba, Avis (☎ 51713, telex 851), Morale Caravane (☎ 51350, fax 54755), Adrar Voyages (☎ 51717, fax 53210, telex 531), Unitours (☎ 53816, fax 53225) and Amal-Rep (☎ 56480).

Europcar's prices are typical: UM 7056 a day including driver and insurance plus UM 32 per km plus 16% tax for a Renault 12 or air-con Peugeot 504 in town (UM 1384 a day more for use out of town). For a 4WD Toyota Landcruiser it's UM 10,624 a day including driver and insurance plus UM 40 per km plus 16% tax. For rentals of six days or more, the per-day cost is about 10% less. Bold-print per-day prices are about 25% lower as driver and insurance are not factored in.

Getting Around

To/From the Airport The airport is on the city outskirts in the Ksar district, only three km from the centre.

There are taxis waiting at the airport and they charge considerably more than the normal fare. The asking price for a taxi in to town is UM 1000 but you should be able to get one for not more than UM 500 if you bargain. To cut costs, share a taxi or simply walk over to the main road 100 metres away and hail a taxi or minibus.

Bus The green and yellow public minibuses run throughout the city. The fare, UM 20, is uniform regardless of the destination. If you're headed to the Cinquième Marché, you'll find a green van if you stand along Ave Kennedy across from the Marché Capital.

Taxi The taxi system in Nouakchott is a bit complicated. Taxis, unlike the buses, can be found in all colours. The main taxi stand is on Ave Kennedy, at the north-west corner of Marché Capital and near Ave Abdel Nasser. Fares are UM 200 for a short taxi trip in town, and UM 20 to UM 30 for a 'seat' in a shared taxi to go anywhere in town. However, you must clearly specify whether you want a course or a route because there's a big difference in price. Saying route indicates you want a taxi that operates like a bus, with a specified route. You alight at the place nearest to your destination. Virtually all routes start at the main taxi stand at the market. If you're headed inward towards the market, a seat costs only UM 20, but if you get a taxi at that stand or near the market and are headed outward, the fare will be UM 30.

A course, which costs UM 200 anywhere in town including from near the airport, is when the driver takes you exactly where you want to go and you usually have the taxi to yourself. Taxis do not have meters but the drivers are fairly honest about fares. Their French, however, is often no better than that of many travellers, so anticipate having great confusion in communicating with them. The word 'route' or 'course' may be adequate. If you specify a destination, eg the French embassy, it's equivalent to asking for a course. To get the route fare, you must indicate simply the general area or direction.

Taxis leaving the stand in the centre are invariably full, so you cannot hail one near the market area. At the stand you'll find a bunch of parked taxis and one will pull up to the front and people will jump in. They leave as soon as they're full, rarely more than a couple of minutes except at night. Sometimes a taxi that has route passengers but is not full will take on course passengers. They will leave the route to take these passengers to their destinations and then return to the route, so hold tight.

The Coast

NOUÂDHIBOU

Fishing continues to be the principal activity of Nouâdhibou and a major contributor to Mauritania's economy, even though the waters are now in danger of over-exploitation. The city, named Port-Étienne during colonial days, is on the Bay of Lévrier which has one of the highest densities of fish in the world.

The town (population 45,000) is 525 km north of Nouakchott on Cap Blanc, the end of a 35-km-long peninsula which runs

roughly north-south, overlooking the Bay of Lévrier to the east. The eastern half of this narrow peninsula is Mauritania and the western half is Morocco, facing the Atlantic Ocean. There are many mines planted in the sands on the western side, relics of the Western Saharan conflict. As a result, this area is strictly off limits. Three French men were killed crossing it in 1988, so don't even think about wandering over there.

The Cape Canarian Tcherka district is near the centre, while the Cansado district six km to the south is one of the major residential areas. Most inhabitants, however, live in the

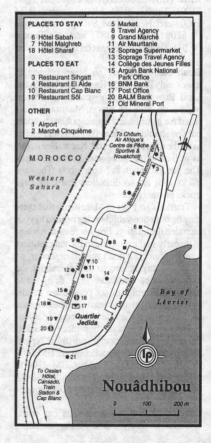

PLACES TO STAY	5 Market
	8 Travel Agency
6 Hôtel Sabah	9 Grand Marché
7 Hôtel Malghreb	11 Air Mauritanie
18 Hôtel Sharaf	12 Soprage Supermarket
	13 Soprage Travel Agency
PLACES TO EAT	14 Collège des Jeunes Filles
	15 Arguin Bank National
3 Restaurant Sihgatt	Park Office
4 Restaurant El Aide	16 BNM Bank
10 Restaurant Cap Blanc	17 Post Office
19 Restaurant Sôl	20 BALM Bank
	21 Old Mineral Port
OTHER	
1 Airport	
2 Marché Cinquième	

MOROCCO

Western Sahara

Bay of Lévrier

Quartier Jedida

To Châum, Air Afrique's Centre de Pêche Sportive & Nouackchott

To Oasian Hôtel, Cansado, Train Station & Cap Blanc

Nouâdhibou

0   100   200 m

The Coast – Arguin Bank National Park 607

shanties surrounding town. Port Minéralier, four km further, is where the train line ends and iron ore is loaded onto the ships. Some five km further south is Cap Blanc, the southern tip of the peninsula.

Travellers interested in catching a ship might try their luck at the port. Regardless, look for some of the crew; they might invite you on board for food and brew.

Places to Stay – bottom end

For really cheap lodging, ask around the market and at the beach. To camp on the beach or anywhere around town, consult the police as this could be dangerous and possibly illegal.

There are only two cheap hotels in town. The large 44-room *Hôtel Sharaf* (☎ 45522) is excellent value. Singles/doubles cost UM 2500/3500. It has a restaurant and bar (with alcohol). *Hôtel Malghreb* charges UM 4000/5000 for tiny singles/doubles. The quality is no better, but when the sun sets, this drab-looking place takes on a whole new face. There is a bar, with beer, music and lots of very lively people. For meals you may have to go to the Sharaf as the chef here often fails to show up for work.

Places to Stay – top end

Least expensive is the old 60-room Hôtel Sabah. It's the best hotel in the central area, which isn't saying much. Singles/doubles cost about UM 6500/9000 and come with air-con and hot-water private baths. The restaurant has good service with bland, uncreative dishes.

If you have the wheels and the cash, head for the new *Oasian Hôtel* (☎ 49042, fax 49053) in Cansado, roughly seven km south of the central area. It's a class act, with tennis courts, fishing boats for charter, videos and a shopping boutique. The lavish air-con rooms are the best in Mauritania and the prices, UM 9500/11,500 for singles/doubles, reflect this. A course taxi from the centre of town shouldn't cost more than UM 300.

Places to Eat

The cheapest restaurants, all small hole-in-the-walls such as *Restaurant El Aide* and *Restaurant Sihgatt*, are on the northern side

of town. You'll also find food around the market, particularly around noon.

Restaurant Sôl has Euro-Korean selections and excellent fish dishes, priced from UM 1000 to UM 1300. Further down the road *Restaurant Cap Blanc* has reasonably priced sandwiches, spicy rice dishes and the renowned Cap Blanc cake.

Getting There & Away

Air There are twice daily flights to/from Nouakchott (UM 6120) with Air Mauritanie. There are also connections once a week to Paris and Las Palmas.

Train There are two trains every day in either direction between Nouâdhibou and Zouérat (see under Train in Getting Around, earlier in this chapter). For Nouakchott, get off in Choûm; taxis will be waiting to take you to Atâr, a trip which takes from three to four hours (UM 1100 by bush taxi including baggage). For more information, call SNTFM (☎ 45174). In Nouakchott, call SNIM (☎ 53337).

Truck A ride to/from Nouakchott gives you a good impression of what a desert trip is like if you don't have the opportunity to cross the Sahara. The road is only tracks in the sand, so driving takes considerable time and getting stuck is almost guaranteed. The trip from Nouakchott usually takes from 24 to 30 hours, but can take up to two days; the cost is UM 2500. Heading to Nouakchott the trucks usually have little or no load and can make the trip in as little as 20 hours, bouncing all the way. It's also possible to find someone making the journey by Land Rover, but the cost will be higher. Remember to take a head wrap, eye drops and plenty of water.

Car Do not attempt driving to/from Nouakchott without a guide. The 525-km route over the sand is not marked. A high-clearance vehicle is imperative.

ARGUIN BANK NATIONAL PARK

The Banc d'Arguin is an important crossroads for multitudes of **aquatic birds** migrating between Europe and northern Asia

MAURITANIA

and most of Africa. Over two million broad-billed sandpipers have been recorded in the winter. Other migrants include black terns, flamingos, white pelicans and spoonbills. Some species breed here as well. During the mating season, they need lots of fish and seclusion from humans. The park itself is some 260 km from Nouakchott and 235 km from Nouâdhibou (but much harder to get to from there). The Banc d'Arguin extends some 200 km north from Cape Timiris (155 km north of Nouakchott) and provides an ideal breeding environment. The sea is crystal-clear and shallow (only several metres deep even 25 km from shore), so fish are easy to find. Most of the birds are found on islands of sand and the only way you can get to see them is by small shallow boats.

You can only take this trip with permission from the national parks service, and a guide. The Parc National de Banc d'Arguin office (☎ 45851 or 48051) in front of the BNM bank in Nouâdhibou sponsors trips to the park if there is a large enough group. There is a resort there where you can camp. The opening dates and travel within the park are regulated. During the mating season, April to July and October to January, you may not get close to the birds because the slightest disturbance will apparently cause them to fly away and abandon their eggs. So the best viewing time may be August and September and (cooler) February and March.

Even in Nouakchott it's difficult to find anyone who has made the trip. Bird-watchers come from Paris on organised trips. Explorator (16 Place de la Madeleine, 75008 Paris, France; ☎ (01) 42-66-66-24) is a good agency to contact about such excursions.

Getting There & Away

This is one trip for which you'll need to prepare. A 4WD vehicle equipped for desert driving is required, and it's better to go in convoy with a guide. You start at the Sabah Hôtel in Nouakchott and drive on the beach 155 km to Nouâmghâr, the fishing village at Cape Timiris. Avoid the soft beach sand or it could put an early end to your trip – study the tides carefully before setting out. Since you'll need a boat to get to the islands where the birds are, this village may be the best place to rent one.

From Nouâmghâr northward, there are metal poles every five km to mark the way, but they will not keep you from getting lost if you have no guide. It's another 50 km on a good sand track to a point where the track returns to the sea, with Tidra, the main island, across the way.

CAPE TAGARIT

A very interesting alternative to, or continuation of, a trip to see the birds at Arguin Bank is a visit to Cape Tagarit north of Tidra. Here you can fish, snorkel and camp without getting government permission or a guide, but it involves some serious desert driving.

The view from the cape is magnificent and the water is crystal clear; you can see turtles and huge fish swimming around the rocks even from the cliff. A good catch of trout, sea bass and sea bream is almost guaranteed; just

---

Dolphins of Nouâmghâr

From the outset, Nouâmghâr may look like a tin-shack city with nothing special to offer, but it is a fascinating place. This is the major fishing village of the Imragen, a people numbering only 300 or so and totally unlike those in the rest of Mauritania. What's unique is the way they catch the fish with the help of dolphins.

During certain seasons of the year, when a migrating school of yellow mullet (*mulets jaunes*) is spotted, a man hits the water with a long stick and the sound waves induce the dolphins, sometimes two km out in the sea, to drive the mullet toward shore and the nets. The Imragen can't fish every day – only when schools are spotted, which can be many days apart – and it all happens very quickly. Your chances of seeing this event are very poor unless it's the right season and you're prepared to stick it out for a week or two. It is not a place for the idle tourist, so if you are planning on hanging out, don't do it alone. There's no potable water in the area, so you must bring water or purifying tablets. ■

don't let the eerie wailing of jackals, or their presence near camp, bother you.

Getting There & Away

A journey to Cape Tagarit is not to be undertaken lightly. You should talk to someone who has made the trip for detailed instructions, and there aren't many who have.

Go north from Nouâmghâr for 70 km on a good sand track marked every five km by poles towards Nouâdhibou until it divides; take the left track for 10 km, then go directly north by compass over sand dunes for 15 km until you regain the track. At 106 km north of Cape Timiris, you'll reach two low rocky hills bisecting the track; at this point head directly west by compass over sand dunes for 25 km. Your trip ends at the edge of a cliff, 100 feet above, called Cape Tafarit. The smaller Cape Tagarit is five km to the north, and a good camping spot.

The North

It is the beauty of the north that attracts tourists to Mauritania. If you have time to visit only one area outside of Nouakchott,

head for the Adrar region encompassing Atâr, Chinguetti and Ouadâne. This is where you'll see oases, nomads in their natural habitat, spectacular plateau areas with deep canyons and ancient rock paintings, the most historic sites in Mauritania, and towns seemingly about to be buried under the encroaching desert. An example of how people are contributing to this desertification process are the deteriorating palm groves around Atâr; many farmers are improperly irrigating with overly saline water.

ATÂR

Atâr (population 18,000), situated in a lovely oasis, is the major market centre for the nomads of northern Mauritania. It's a minimum eight-hour drive north of Nouakchott, more by bush taxi. The asphalt road to **Akjoujt** (the site of a former copper mining industry) is in deteriorating condition, after which the road is not paved. Atâr is the starting point for several interesting side trips. It also is a good place to buy food for a trip to Chinguetti as it's a lot cheaper here. Bring lots of ouguiya – there are no banks.

The town is divided into two sections, a large new section with wide rectangular streets, and the more interesting smaller Ksar area with

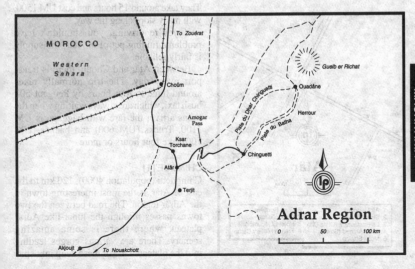

Adrar Region

The Guedra
In the Adrar region, a real treat would be seeing a performance of the *guedra*, a ritual dance of love performed by women for the men. Sometimes the dancer stands, but more often she squats, covered in a black veil. The dance is a ballet of complex movements of the hands and feet on which the women paint intricate designs with henna to draw attention to them. The dancers' hair is sumptuously decorated; every plait is embellished with pendants, talismans, carved shell discs and green and red glass beads. ■

---

narrow winding streets. Between the two is the **market**, an entire section of which is given over to the smiths and their workshops. This is one of the best places for purchasing Moorish sandals. You'll also see brilliantly coloured saddle bags and *girbas* (water bags), the nomads' most precious piece of equipment. Always hang the girbas up; if you leave them on the ground, the water will run out quickly. Other items in the market include leather goods, silver jewellery and rugs.

Places to Stay & Eat

The best place to stay is *Hôtel El Mourabitine*, a picturesque old colonial hotel. Singles/doubles cost about UM 3500/5000, and you can stay for 24 hours regardless of when you enter. There's also a restaurant serving three meals a day.

For cheaper accommodation ask around for *Le Restaurant*. It's on the same street as Air Mauritanie. There is no sign, but most people know the place. Pasta or rice costs about UM 100 a plate (about UM 325 with meat). If you eat here, you may get to sleep here for free.

If you need help looking for cheaper lodgings or are in need of a guide, ask for Salima; everybody knows him and he has been a guide for this region for many years.

Getting There & Away

Air Mauritanie has flights twice a week from Nouakchott; the one-way fare is UM 5400.

In Nouakchott, bush taxis for Atâr leave from the gare routière across from the airport. The trip normally takes about 10 hours and costs UM 2300. For a large truck, look around the market in Nouakchott's Cinquième district. They take around 15 hours and cost UM 1500, with many stops along the way.

If you're driving, you shouldn't have problems finding petrol in Atâr; the supply is fairly reliable.

Between Atâr and Choûm there is transport every day. The trip normally takes around three to four hours by Peugeot 504 bush taxi, which are always waiting when the trains arrive; the fare with baggage is UM 1100. Trucks (UM 600) and bachés (UM 700) take four hours or more.

CHINGUETTI

Chinguetti (population 4000), 120 km to the east of Atâr, is the most interesting town in the Adrar region. The road between the two towns passes through the lunar-like Adrar plateau, where there is some amazing scenery. There are various gorges leading into the plateau. One of these deep inhospit-

To Choûm
To Chinguetti
To Market
Airport ✈

Atâr

0   50   100m

1	Air Mauritanie	6	Gare Routière
2	Street Food	7	Old Building
3	Le Restaurant (Chez Dia)	8	Hôtel El Mourabitine
4	Chez Ahmed (Store)	9	French Military Camp
5	Mobil Station		

MAURITANIA

able gorges leads up to the **Amogar pass** and, at about the 70-km point, the summit of the Adrar plateau, which is reminiscent of Colorado. The panoramic view on top is particularly beautiful at sunset. Near the point where this highest plateau begins, there is a tall, easily recognisable rock formation on your left, a very short walk from the road. Amongst them are some prehistoric *peintures rupestres* (rock paintings). The painted objects, no longer easily discernible, are apparently giraffe, cows and people in a green and grassy landscape – all obviously long since gone.

Chinguetti is the seventh holy city of Islam, but is now threatened on all sides by encroaching dunes some 10 to 20 metres high. Once reputed for its poets and Muslim scholars, it was the ancient capital of the Moors, and some of the houses and mosques in its fascinating stone-built quarter date from the 13th century when it was founded. Each year this was where the pilgrims from all over Mauritania assembled to join the caravan to Mecca, sometimes taking several years. The town once boasted 11 mosques and witnessed huge *azalais* (caravans) of 30,000 camels laden with salt. Even up to the 1940s raiders from the north periodically came hunting for their camels; huge battles ensued. Today there are only 40 or so camels left in Chinguetti; a Haratin picks them up from each owner's house before sunrise and drives them far out into the plateau to feed. From noon to 3 pm all life stops.

Around the perimeter of the oasis there are numerous nomad tents pitched in the sand among the scrub; they are pyramid-shaped and made of thick goat's wool. Straw mats serve as floors. The nomads used to own camels but over half of their animals died in the last drought and the remainder had to be sold to pay off debts.

These people, once renowned for their independence, are entirely sedentary and live off their goats and date palms. After the date harvest in August, many leave the tents and move into their shelters in the palm groves. If you go out to where they live, you may get invited to drink tea, or zrig, a Moorish drink of

dried milk, sugar and water. If you're exceptionally lucky, you might be offered some delicious oval bread; it's cooked in a shallow pit and covered lightly with sand.

Things to See & Do
An ocean of dunes and amber-ivory colours cascade down to the wadi where palm trees grow, cutting the oasis neatly into halves. The only two notable things about the modern section are a solar demonstration **pump** (no longer working) and, dominating the town, an old **fort** that was renovated and converted into an air-con hotel for the actors in *Fort Saganne*, a French film shot here in the early 1980s.

Despite the depredations of time and desert raiders, the town's old quarter, the Ksar, is remarkably well preserved. Dominating it is the often-photographed 16th-century **mosque** (no entry to non-Muslims). More than half the houses in the outlying residential district are in ruin and many more are in a poor state. The residents will proudly show you their **library** housing some 1300 ancient manuscripts, some of them dating from the 3rd century, which have passed for centuries through the hands of prestigious Muslim theologians.

Most interesting of all would be renting some camels and taking a ride in the hills; something Adrar Voyages can organise.

Places to Stay & Eat
There is a guesthouse called the *Maison de Bien Être de Chinguetti* where most travellers stay. It's a white house with a green door on the left of the big cylinder in the old section of town. Everybody in town knows where it is. It's spartan but nice with mattresses on the floor. The cost is UM 800; the flies come free. There's a kitchen where you can prepare food, and a lovely garden complete with a nomad tent where you can recline and drink tea. You can find food around the market. There's a new hotel, the *Hôtel de Caravanes* at the entrance to town. The location away from the old section is not as nice, and it lacks the authentic desert ambience of the Bien Être.

Specify which hotel you want to be dropped at, otherwise you may end up at the wrong one.

Getting There & Away

There are bachés and one Land Rover every day to/from Atâr (UM 900). Getting to Ouadâne from Chinguetti, however, is a major problem. If you aren't lucky in finding someone passing through, you'll probably have to backtrack to Atâr and look for a vehicle.

OUADÂNE

Founded in 1147 by a tribe of Berbers, Ouadâne sits on the edge of the Adrar plateau 120 km north-east of Chinguetti. It was once a prosperous camel caravan centre, the last stopover for caravans undertaking the perilous crossing toward Tichit and Oualâta. Having suffered irreparable damage, it is now an imposing fortress of stone buildings in ruin set on a cliff overlooking an oasis and a wadi rich in palms.

The best view is from the minimally furnished *rest house*. It was shelled by the Polisario, so you'll probably have to enquire elsewhere for a place to stay. Towards the west are the oasis and a derelict looking wadi with **dated palms**. If you camp at the wadi, be prepared for an onslaught of ragged children with their packets of arrowheads for sale. Towards the east is a cliff covered with ruins, in particular the **mosque**, which is in disrepair, and the **Ksar el Klali** with its formidable stone walls. Other sites include a small museum and a library.

More than half the **stone houses** are in ruin. The only place where people are still holding out is the tiny 'modern' section on top of the cliff; even there the houses are crumbling.

Getting There & Away

Finding transport to Ouadâne is not easy. Atâr (240 km) is usually a better place to look than Chinguetti (120 km), as trucks and Land Rovers go between Atâr and Ouadâne (UM 1500) on a fairly regular basis though not every day. Arrange for the driver to take you back, otherwise you may have a long wait until the next vehicle arrives. Hitchhiking is always possible, but from Chinguetti it is very difficult because vehicles are so scarce. Taxi drivers in Atâr have a good idea when trucks make their runs to Ouadâne.

From Chinguetti, those driving have two routes to choose from: the southerly Piste du Batha which passes through sand dunes and definitely requires a guide, and the northerly Piste du Dhar Chinguetti, which is better but still requires a 4WD and a local guide.

F'DÉRIK & ZOUÉRAT

F'Dérik (population 18,000) is connected to Zouérat by a 30-km paved road. Both towns are important **iron-ore** centres and have little to offer the visitor. The mining company in Zouérat supports an expensive hotel, *The Oasian*, for employees. Rooms cost about UM 10,000 and there's a restaurant as well. It's possible to hitch a ride on a truck from Zouérat all the way up to Bîr Mogreïn in the far north, but only the occasional traveller attempting to cross the Sahara by this little-used route makes the effort. It's on the principal route to Tindouf (Algeria).

For trains to/from Nouâdhibou, see the main Getting Around section of this chapter. You can fly once a week to/from Nouakchott on Air Mauritanie, the fare is UM 9900.

Le Guelb er Richat

Those with a day or two to kill might try renting camels for a 40-km trip to Le Guelb er Richat, a mysterious crater-like volcano with a 38-km diameter. The round trip takes one or two days. From a distance you'll see a sheer wall of silver-grey stone rising out of the desert. It looks like the shell of an extinct volcano, though there is no evidence of volcanic activity in the area. Some believe that an enormous meteorite crashed here in prehistoric times. Don't bypass **Tin Labbé**, seven km north-west of Ouadâne, a small village of troglodyte houses. There are apparently some rock paintings and Arabic scripts of ancient Tuareg. ∎

The East & South

Like the Adrar region, the Tagant area east of Nouakchott offers impressive views from the plateau, prehistoric rock paintings, historical sites including old forts and fortresses, decaying towns such as Tidjikja and Tichit with mountains of sand about to consume them, as well as the opportunity to look for Neolithic items in the sand. Getting there is slightly more difficult.

BOUTILIMIT

If you'd like to see the real desert with large rolling **sand dunes** in all colours and have access to an all-terrain vehicle, head for Boutilimit. It's 154 km to the east of Nouakchott via the Road of Hope and is easily reached in two hours. Other than being the birthplace of Mokhtar Daddah, Mauritania's first president, there's not much of significance here.

TIDJIKJA

Tidjikja (610 km from Nouakchott) is the capital of the Tagant region. They don't see many visitors these days, so it's best to present yourself to the police on arrival to avoid suspicion. From the moment you enter town until you leave, you'll be followed by children; yet even they will disappear in the searing noon heat when everything closes and the streets clear as if by magic.

Founded in 1680 and now surrounded by sand dunes threatening its existence, the town supports a population of 6000, one of the country's more important **palm groves** from the 18th century, a relatively busy **market**, **Fort Coppolani** (the fort for the military who participated in colonisation), and an old **mosque** reconstructed many times. What's particularly interesting about the old section are the numerous **traditional houses**, some vacant and easily visited. Notice the decorative niches with geometrical designs, the flat roofs serving as terraces with gargoyles to keep the water from stagnating, the double-panelled doors in place of windows, and the elevated outdoor latrines

made of stone – built 10 steps up because the rock is too hard to dig through!

There is a 12-room *guesthouse* with mattresses. For food, you'll need to check around the market area.

Getting There & Away

The easy way to get here is with Air Mauritanie, which has flights from Nouakchott on Monday and Tuesday (UM 5300). In Nouakchott, you might check with the people at Oxfam and World Vision; they have projects in this area and may be able to give you a lift if their project vehicle is headed this way. By public transport, it's easy to get as far as Sangrafa (20 km beyond Magta-Lahjar) on the Transmauritanienne (Road of Hope) but from there you'll probably have to hitchhike. Be prepared to sit for long hours in the sun because the traffic is extremely light.

If you're driving, the first leg – 425 km south-east on the Transmauritanienne to Sangrafa – takes four or five hours. The remaining 205-km leg north-east to Tidjikja is well-packed sand dunes virtually blocking the entrance to Moudjéria. If you see huge tanker trucks stuck in the sand, you'll know you're there. For this reason finding petrol in Tidjikja can never be guaranteed, so carry plenty and be prepared with sand ladders.

It's possible to drive from Chinguetti to Tidjikja (350 km) as well. Vehicles are rarely seen on this route, so it's not advisable to go with only one vehicle. Quite a few unprepared foreigners have died on this route.

TICHIT

If you're exceptionally adventurous and want to see a ghost town in the making, head to the isolated ancient town of Tichit, 255 km east of Tidjikja. It lies in the centre of the **Baatin**, a massive fault of rock stretching almost the entire length of the desert between Tidjikja and Oualâta near the Malian border. Set on the edge of a sandstone promontory overlooking a desolate Saharan landscape, it used to furnish water and precious supplies to desert caravans. At its zenith, it boasted over 5000 people and 1500 houses. Only 286 houses exist today, and less than half are

MAURITANIA

habitable. The impressive **old houses** and **mosques** are the most developed in the Tagant because of their sedentary lifestyle. Architecturally they are more beautiful than those in Tidjikja with many rooms, stairs leading out to terraces and decorative motifs on the exterior. It is like the Arctic, except sand rather than snow blankets everything.

The tracks frequently disappear and there are few obvious landmarks along the way, so you'll definitely need a guide and enough petrol for a round trip. You'll pass through deadly landscape; the trees are bare, the scrub is twisted, and the ground is littered with bleached bones of camels and goats. If you see any desert dwellers without camels, they may be Nmadi – sedentary desert people who traditionally lived entirely by hunting. Now there's virtually no game and the few that remain are herders. Upon entering town you must report immediately to the gendarmerie; they'll probably stare at you, wondering what brings you here, and then scribble something in your passport.

ROSSO

Rosso, 203 km south of Nouakchott, has a population of about 28,000. This busy little town has a distinct Senegalese flavour but there's not much to see and little to do. Most travellers simply cross the border and head on. Fortunately, the border crossing is fairly straightforward, with no hassles. Only the ferry, which closes around noon for a long lunch, poses a problem and even then only for those with their own vehicles as others can cross the narrow river in a pirogue.

For changing money, customs officials act as the local bank and can assist you. When you cross over from Senegal, they will issue you a currency declaration form; staple it into your passport so that you don't lose it. When you depart Mauritania, they'll ask for it because exporting ouguiya is strictly illegal. The searches here used to be very thorough but these days customs officials are often more lax.

If you're trapped here for the night, head for *Le Restaurant Marie*. It has 12 rooms and a restaurant that is reputed to be quite good.

Getting There & Away

A taxi to Rosso from Nouakchott costs UM 800 and though the road is paved, it takes three to four unscenic hours of blinding sand and police checks.

KEUR MASSENE

Keur Massene is a small town some 60 km west of Rosso at the mouth of the Senegal River, on the northern side thereof and practically on the ocean. In years past, it was famous as a centre for small-game hunting. Contact Air Afrique or one of the travel agencies in Nouakchott to find out if the campement has reopened.

KAÉDI

South-east of Nouakchott on the Senegal River, Kaédi is a large town of 30,000 inhabitants, mostly Toucouleur. It has become a site for development projects, including SNIM's extraction of high-grade ore from a nearby reserve. There are also a couple of Peace Corps agricultural projects there. The **market** is a 'must-see' for Toucouleur crafts, sandals, boots and authentic Senegalese batik cloth. Prices here are much lower than in Nouakchott and in most cities in Senegal. If you're tempted to cool off in the river, don't do it as it's infested with bilharzia.

The United Nations Development Programme (UNDP) has a *guesthouse* here with air-con rooms (UM 5000) and a pool. There are plans to sell it.

Getting There & Away

The cheapest way to get here from Nouakchott is overland. Peugeot 504s (UM 1700) and bachés depart every day in either direction. Large trucks cost about UM 1000. Travel by car is relatively painless as the 437-km road from Nouakchott is tarred the entire distance. If you drive yourself, you can refuel at the petrol station here. You can also fly. Air Mauritanie has flights on Monday and Wednesday (UM 4600).

KIFFA

After a lifeless 607-km trip getting to Kiffa from Nouakchott, it's easy to appreciate the city's bustling vibrancy. With some 50,000 inhabitants, Kiffa is the capital of the southern Assabe region and an important regional trading centre and crossroads.

Much of the activity of this vibrant town centres around the **market**, which is very active and distinctly Black African in ambience. The city is famous throughout West Africa for its glass beads, so don't fail to check them out in the market, where they're both made and sold. Purchasing a few of these world-renowned beads could later prove to be a wise investment. Also check the nearby oases and escarpments as they offer an interesting change of scenery.

Places to Stay & Eat

The cheapest place to stay is the Peace Corps' *Maison de Passage*, which any kid in town can direct you to. While you must be invited to stay, the volunteers virtually never see travellers passing through, so the chances of their extending you the offer are excellent. If you can remember beforehand, try to reciprocate by bringing something that might interest them, such as recent foreign newspapers and magazines or good books.

The only hotel is the *Hôtel de L'Amitié et du Tourism*, in front of the police station. It has very basic singles/doubles with shared showers for UM 2000/3000 (negotiable). Each unit has a bed and table plus a fan which doesn't work until night when the battery is turned on. In the middle of the courtyard is a big TV blasting away at night. For a meal, ask the friendly Ghanaian woman here to cook you something, such as rice and sauce.

Another good place to eat is *Brahims*. It's run by an elderly man who specialises in couscous and sheep meat. Guests eat Mauritanian-style, on mattresses and without utensils. Just ask for him around town. Even though Kiffa has no electricity, it's possible to buy moderately cool drinks around town as many tiny shops have butane refrigerators.

Getting There & Away

Getting here from Nouakchott costs UM 2300 by Peugeot 504 (10 hours) and UM 1400 by truck (15 hours). Air Mauritanie has flights on Monday from Nouakchott (UM 5500).

If you're headed to Mali, you cannot get there by way of Néma, the traditional route, as the border there is closed. However, you can get there by heading south from Kiffa to Kayes as this border is open (conditions could change). For the latest information, check with authorities in Nouakchott.

AYOÛN-EL-ATROÛS

Ayoûn-el-Atroûs (population 30,000), better known simply as Ayoûn, is 210 km further east. While you won't see much life along the highway, you'll see signs pointing to villages that are far beyond the eye's range. There are no roads or even tracks leading to them. Ayoûn has **houses** made of beautiful blocks of local stone.

As in Kiffa, the cheapest place to stay is the Peace Corps' *Maison de Passage*. It's reportedly open to all travellers and all the kids in town know where it is. The only alternative is *Hotel Ayoûn* (☎ 90079), which is in the centre and a surprisingly nice place for such an out-of-the-way town. The rooms have balconies overlooking the city, fans and private baths and cost UM 2000/3000 for singles/doubles. Across the street is a restaurant that serves omelettes, steaks, vegetables and the Mauritanian standby – couscous.

Getting There & Away

A Peugeot 504 bush taxi costs UM 3000 from Nouakchott while large trucks charge about UM 2000; there are departures every morning in either direction. Drivers can refuel at the petrol station here. You can also fly here on Monday from Nouakchott on Air Mauritanie; the one-way fare is UM 7100.

KOUMBI SALEH

The legendary capital of Ghana, West Africa's first medieval empire, Koumbi Saleh is the most famous **archaeological site** in Mauritania. Traces of the town were first uncovered in 1913. Several digging campaigns have been carried out since then; an imposing mosque has been partially excavated, attesting to the large number of people, estimated in the

MAURITANIA

tens of thousands, who once lived here. There were few other cities that populated anywhere in the world at that period. Lack of funds has halted excavation work since the early '80s, but plans have been formalised to complete the work. It's about 60 km south of Timbedgha (halfway between Ayoûn-el-Atroûs and Néma).

NÉMA

Néma (population 6000) is the last town on the Road of Hope from Nouakchott (1113 km). You'll find a market, hospital, petrol pump and bank.

Néma was once the major departure point for Bamako (Mali), 555 km to the south. Since the early 1990s, the border here has been closed.

There's no hotel but as in all the towns along the Transmauritanienne, the police may be helpful in finding you a mat to sleep on. Otherwise, be prepared to camp and bring food if you don't like dry goat meat.

Getting There & Away

Getting here from Nouakchott costs UM 2100 by truck (20 hours) and UM 4000 by Peugeot 504 (30 hours). Air Mauritanie has flights every Monday and Friday from Nouakchott; the fare is UM 8900.

OUALÂTA

If you're really adventurous, you could head 90 km north from Néma to Oualâta (population 1500). Unless you're a truly intrepid traveller, you'll need wheels because, otherwise, you'll have to wait days to find a vehicle headed this way from Néma. That's because most trading takes place in Néma, not Oulâta, which has no market.

Dating from 1224, Oualâta used to be the last resting point for caravans heading to Timbuktu. Having been ransacked on several occasions, the town has suffered considerably; its mosque is in lamentable shape, the minaret practically in ruin. The narrow, winding streets resemble the traditional medinas found in North Africa.

Oualâta Architecture

What's special about Oualâta is its architecture. It's an unusual synthesis of Arabic and Black African traditions. The most extraordinary feature is the decorative painting on both the exterior and interior of the houses. The women in town paint geometric designs on them with dyes, typically red or indigo, and likewise decorate the windows and doors with delicate white arabesque designs, all unique but similarly inspired. Unfortunately many of the newer houses lack it. ■

Niger

Niger is one of the most fascinating countries in West Africa. The capital, Niamey, has a distinctive character, with camels walking down the wide new boulevards and interesting modern buildings seemingly out of place in the Sahel. Even the sand has a role in giving the city its desert charm, but despite being on the edge of the Sahara you'll find almost as many trees in Niamey as in Dakar, Bamako and Ouagadougou, its sister Sahelian capitals, although the climate is noticeably drier. For travellers flying in from the humid coast, the change is dramatic – and a treat.

Today, the camels seem to be leaving town for good. Their numbers have dropped from 20,000 in Niamey at independence to less than 1000 today. There are other signs of change as well. The construction boom of the 1970s, financed by Niger's uranium mines, ground to a halt in the 1980s when collapsing world prices sent the country's economy into a tailspin. Today, some of these once-fine buildings are looking a bit on the shabby side. The recession has hit the people too. Poverty is commonplace and begging is no longer confined to the handicapped.

Outside Niamey, you'll find plenty more of interest. North of the capital is the famous Sunday cattle market in Ayorou, and to the south is one of the better wildlife reserves in West Africa – Parc National du W.

In the northern part of Niger (pronounced nee-JAIR in French) is the city of Agadez; it's actually more interesting than Timbuktu, which similarly teeters on the Sahara's southern edge. For travellers who've just crossed the desert from Algeria, it's a paradise. And in September, west of Agadez, you can observe one of the great spectacles in Africa – the Cure Salée, the week-long reunion of the Wodaabé people when the unmarried men participate in a veritable beauty contest, make-up and all, wooing the opposite sex.

But it is the beauty and wonder of the Niger desert itself that has long brought curious and intrepid travellers from around the

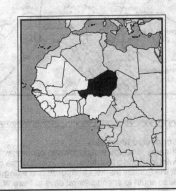

REPUBLIC OF NIGER

Area: 1,267,000 sq km
Population: 8.8 million
Population Growth Rate: 3.4%
Capital: Niamey
Head of State: President Mahamane Ousmane
Official Language: French
Currency: West African CFA franc
Exchange Rate: CFA 500 = US$1
Per Capita GNP: US$300
Time: GMT/UTC + 1

world. To the north-east of Agadez lie the incomparable Aïr Mountains (Aïr Massif). An excursion there would probably be your most lasting memory of this starkly dramatic country.

Facts about the Country

HISTORY

If you could step back to about 6000 years ago, you would find rivers running through grassy plateaux in the parts of northern Niger that are now pure desert. You would also meet hunters and herders, some of whom

NIGER

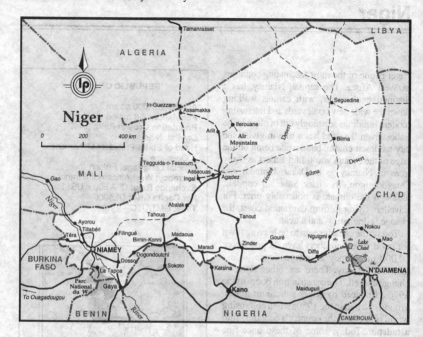

Niger

ALGERIA

LIBYA

Tamanrasset

In-Guezzam · Assamakka

Seguedine

Iferouane · Arlit · Aïr Mountains

Bilma

Teggida-n-Tessoum

Assaouas · Ingal · Agadez

Bilma

MALI

Gao

Abalak

CHAD

Ayorou · Tahoua · Tanout

Nokou · Mao

Téra · Tillabéri · Filingué · Birnin-Konni · Madaoua · Maradi · Zinder · Gouré · Nguigmi · Diffa · Lake Chad

NIAMEY · Dosso · Dogondoutchi

BURKINA FASO

Parc National du W · La Tapoa · Gaya

Sokoto · Katsina · Kano

Maiduguri

N'DJAMENA

To Ouagadougou

BENIN

NIGERIA

CAMEROUN

0 200 400 km

Suggested Itineraries

Niamey is an interesting town to explore, with a good market and museum, so you'll definitely want to spend a few days here. Possible one-day excursions include those to **Bourbon, Namaro,** or the Sunday markets at **Ayorou** and **Filingué**. From Niamey (during the dry season) you could head south to spend several days at **Parc W**, viewing the wild game and birds.

You could then head east along the main southern highway towards **Zinder**, with a possible stop at **Birnin-Konni** or **Maradi**. None of these towns along this route have any unusual sights, but they can be easily covered on foot, and are good places to meet people.

The most fascinating region is in the north, in particular Agadez and the nearby Aïr Mountains. During the Tuareg rebellion, travel in this area was difficult and expeditions in the Aïr Mountains off limits. However, a peace treaty was signed in May '95, and travel in these regions may become possible again. If this is the case, count on spending at least a few days in **Agadez** as it's a fascinating town, possibly taking a camel ride into the surrounding areas for a day or more followed by a major expedition into the **Aïr Mountains**. The latter can take anywhere from several days to several weeks, depending on how much time and money you have. ■

---

might be painting pictures of local animals – giraffe and rhino – on cave walls. As the Sahara became drier these people migrated southward. Towards the end of the 1st millennium BC, some of them had learnt the skills of metal work and developed elaborate social organisations and complex forms of trade.

Empires were founded, with wealth and power based on the control of the trans-Saharan trade in gold, salt and slaves. The first was the Kanem-Bornu Empire, which flourished between the 10th and 13th centuries AD, and again briefly in the early 16th century, in the eastern part of modern-day

NIGER

Niger, around Lake Chad. Around the same time, the large Hausa population expanded into southern Niger, from the north of present-day Nigeria. They were followed, in the 17th century, by groups of Djerma people, descendants of the great Songhaï Empire (see the Mali chapter for details).

Just 100 years ago, the slave trade (which had been abolished in most other parts of West Africa) was still going strong in Niger and Chad. The sultans and chiefs were determined to keep it alive, and with an army of 12,000 soldiers the Sultan of Zinder had little trouble attacking villages in his own kingdom, to capture the inhabitants and sell them into slavery whenever debts mounted.

The slave trade was the only way the sultan could support his 300 wives and numerous children, especially as the trade in gold had diminished. Agadez, once a great gold-trading centre, was also hit; its population shrank from 30,000 in 1450 to less than 3000 by the early 20th century.

As gold declined, the value of salt rose. Mined at remote oases in the desert, salt was the prerogative of the Tuareg nomads; it was so rare in the Sahel that markets often traded it ounce for ounce for gold. It was salt that kept alive the huge Saharan camel caravans, and as late as 1906 a 20,000-camel caravan left Agadez to collect salt at Bilma, an oasis some 610 km to the east.

Islam came via the trans-Saharan trade, but the rural people stuck entirely to their traditional religions until the 19th century. Today, about 85% of the people are Muslim. Europe's first intruder was a Scot, the celebrated Mungo Park, who disappeared on the Niger River in 1806. Although the French didn't arrive until 1890, their conquest was rapid and savage with bloody massacres in 1898 and 1899. By 1901, Niger was a military territory and the slave trade was over. Tuaregs in the north kept resisting until the '20s when Niger became a colony. Thereafter, the French did very little for the area, except perhaps for the introduction of groundnuts in the '30s.

Independence

In 1958, Charles de Gaulle offered the 12 French colonies the choice between a plan for self-government in a French union, or immediate independence. Guinea shocked de Gaulle and made history by becoming the only colony to reject his plan. Unofficially, Niger may have voted the same way. As Basil Davidson says in *Modern Africa*, 'There seems little doubt that the true voting returns were falsified by administrative action'.

The French-supported administration claimed that 370,000 people voted for the union, 100,000 against – and 750,000 didn't vote! It was clear, however, that nothing could stop Niger and the other 10 colonies from eventually gaining full independence. Djobo Bakari and the Sawaba Party campaigned for complete independence, and the infuriated government banned the party and sent Bakari into exile. This left Hamari Dori, leader of the Niger Progressive Party (PNN), in complete control and the only candidate for president when full independence arrived in 1960.

Dori maintained unusually close ties with the French and, despite several unsuccessful coups, survived until the great Sahelian drought of 1973-74. Niger was probably the worst hit country of all; over 60% of the livestock was lost. Stocks of food were discovered in the homes of several of Dori's ministers. Soon thereafter, Lt-Col Seyni Kountché (KOUNT-chay) overthrew Dori in a bloody coup. Most people were jubilant.

Kountché Era

The new military government took a hard line on morality. In his early years, Kountché was known for sensationalism. If a ministry's books didn't add up, he would surround it with troops and demand an immediate accounting. He also kicked out the French troops but still maintained good relations with France. Twice, in 1975 and 1976, members of his government attempted coups; neither succeeded.

Kountché was lucky in other ways. From 1974 to 1979, world prices for uranium quintupled. Production in Niger, which began in

1971, more than tripled and made Niger one of the five biggest uranium producers in the non-socialist world. Revenues rose to US$200 million. No longer needing the traditional French budget subsidy, the government set out on a number of ambitious projects, building deluxe ministry headquarters all over Niamey, roads all the way from Niamey to the Chadian border, and the 'uranium highway' to Agadez and Arlit, the centre of operations of the majority French-owned Somair mining company. Not everyone was smiling, however; prices rose dramatically, almost 25% in 1976 alone. The poorest of the poor were worse off than ever.

Kountché's luck ran out in the early 1980s. Antinuclear protests around the world contributed to a collapse in world uranium prices. Government revenues from uranium took a nose dive – from US$200 million in 1980 to US$20 million in 1985. The construction boom was over. In 1983-84, another great drought hit. For the first time in recorded history, the Niger River stopped flowing. Then the expulsion of 'illegal aliens' from Nigeria sent foreign remittances tumbling and landed thousands of dispossessed deportees in Niger. The country is still feeling the shock: second to Bamako (the capital of Mali), Niamey reputedly has the most beggars of any city in the Sahel.

Kountché's honesty helped him weather the storm, including an unsuccessful coup attempt in 1983. But in 1987 he died after a long illness and was replaced by his chosen successor, Colonel Ali Saïbou.

Saïbou Era

Saïbou immediately began a process of constitution-making. In 1989, he formed a new political organisation called the Mouvement National de Société de Développement (MNSD), but at the same time upheld the ban on political parties which Kountché had introduced after the 1974 coup. He then stood for presidential election, but with himself as the sole candidate in the interests of 'national unity'. The following year an elected general assembly met for the first time, but all its members belonged to the MNSD, and several army figures remained prominent in the government. It became evident that Saïbou's movement towards democracy was not genuine; and the country remained to all intents and purposes a one-party military state.

Keenly aware of the profound political changes sweeping across West Africa, the people weren't satisfied with Saïbou's cosmetic alterations. Students went to the streets in mass demonstrations and several were killed. Hardly contrite, Saïbou accused 'a small group of malcontents' of plotting to pitch the country into chaos. Meanwhile, political, industrial and ethnic unrest was flaring up everywhere. The government, and the whole country, was beginning to fall apart.

The promise of political reform, seriously needed, failed to pacify the people. In February 1990, students boycotting reforms again went took to the streets in mass demonstrations, and again several were killed. At the same time, the Union of Niger workers were demonstrating and striking against a two-year salary freeze.

Outside the capital, things were also far from peaceful. In May 1990, a band of armed Tuareg launched a violent attack on the gendarmerie (police post) at Tchin Tabaraden, in north-eastern Niger. This was precipitated by the lack of assistance given to Tuaregs recently returned from Algeria and the misappropriation of funds promised to them following Saïbou's accession to power. (For details see the boxed story on the Tuareg Rebellion in the Population & People section.) More than 100 people were killed in the raid and the incident brought more instability to Niger. But it also brought the country international attention, and was the final straw that led to Saïbou's downfall. Several Western countries, including France, put pressure on the president and the government to introduce genuine political reforms.

Delegates from throughout the country met for a national conference in 1991 to draft a new constitution facilitating political pluralism. Saïbou was stripped of power and a transitional government was set up with a remit to run the country until multiparty elections could be held. The prime minister of this government was Amadou Cheffou.

Niger Today

Multiparty elections were held in 1992, with delegates from several groups gaining seats in the new National Assembly. Nine of these parties formed a coalition called the Alliance des Forces de Changement (Alliance of Forces for Change, or AFC), which had a majority in the national assembly and therefore became the government. Then followed presidential elections, in March 1993, which were won by Mohamane Ousmane, a 43-year-old economist and former government adviser with French and Canadian university degrees. (Ousmane is a Muslim from Zinder – the first Hausa head of state since independence.) He won with the backing of the AFC, overcoming Mamadou Tanja of the MNSD, the former ruling party. Another AFC figure, Mahamadou Issoufou, was appointed as prime minister.

Although peace returned to the capital, unrest continued in the Tuareg areas, despite attempts by the new government to reach a settlement by peaceful means. Several Tuareg groups regarded the new government as untrustworthy, saw no benefit in negotiation, and wanted to continue fighting for their freedom. The situation was exacerbated by various clashes between the Tuareg and groups of Arabs, their traditional enemies (who also inhabit parts of eastern Niger). In an attempt to control the Tuareg, the former MNSD government had covertly armed the Arabs and now there were local scores to settle, quite separate from the conflict between the Tuareg and the central government in Niamey.

The problem was further complicated by armed bandits (possibly Tuareg, Arab or from other groups) taking advantage of the general breakdown of control, attacking and stealing vehicles, often killing drivers and passengers in the process. However, by June 1993, a truce was agreed with prominent Tuareg rebel groups, including the Front de Libération de l'Aïr et de l'Azawak (FLAA) and the Front de Libération Tamouist (FLT). Thereafter, the government re-opened negotiations and dropped the state of emergency which had prevented foreigners from travelling in the region.

Negotiations continued and the government agreed to address many of the Tuareg's concerns, but despite another cease-fire agreement signed by the government and Tuareg rebels at talks in Burkina Faso in October 1994, sporadic outbreaks of rebel activity and banditry continued, and the northern part of the country remained unsafe.

President Ousmane also had problems in Niamey. Parliament's smooth run was disrupted in 1994, when Prime Minister Mahamadou Issoufou (and several of his supporters) defected to the MNSD, removing the AFC's majority and forcing another election. These were held in January 1995. Surprisingly, the MNSD won a majority in the National Assembly, obliging President Ousmane to appoint Hama Amadou (of the MNSD) as the new prime minister, thus creating a divided, weak and ineffectual government. Mahamadou Issoufou, whose defection had led to Amadou's appointment, was promoted to the prestigious position of President of Parliament (Speaker).

Niger is still a very fragile democracy, struggling to maintain stability both inside and outside the capital. However, a truce was signed in May 1995 between the new government and l'Organisation de la Résistance Armée (ORA) which represents six of the main Tuareg groups. Mohamane Ousmane, still president of the country (although without any legislative power) was influential in brokering the new deal. However, although disarmament (of Tuaregs and Arabs) is part of the peace deal, it is unlikely that all the weaponry will be quickly removed from the volatile northern areas, where skirmishes and banditry have been a way of life for centuries. Although the new peace accord has more chance of holding than any of the previous cease-fires, according to local observers, nothing is certain, and you should check the latest situation carefully before travelling.

NIGER

GEOGRAPHY

Today, two-thirds of Niger is desert; the rest is in the Sahel (the semi-desert zone south of the Sahara). Over half of the country is uninhabitable – even by nomads.

Niger is West Africa's second-largest country, over twice the size of France, and is land-locked more than 650 km from the sea. The southern region receives just enough rainfall from July to September to grow crops, but the harvests are no longer sufficient to support the country's population. Much of Niger's food supply comes from grains (mainly rice) grown along the banks of the Niger River, which flows for about 300 km down the western side of the country. Sorghum is grown near Lake Chad, which is at the opposite end of the country, straddling the countries of Niger, Chad and Nigeria (although now mostly dry on the Niger side).

Just west of the Niger River south of Niamey, in the country's south-western corner, is W Park, home to various large mammals including hippo, giraffe, elephant, buffalo and leopard.

Niger's most remarkable area is the Aïr Massif in the north-east, which you can see from the tallest buildings in Agadez. Rising over 2000 metres and comprising dark volcanic formations culminating in the Bagzane peaks, the mountains afford some breathtaking sights. Beyond the massif is the Ténéré Desert, with some of the most spectacular sand dunes in all of the Sahara.

CLIMATE

The hottest part of the year is March to June, the worst month being April when day-time air temperatures reach 45°C (115°F) or more, with heat becoming so intense that rain evaporates before reaching the ground. December to February is the coolest period where temperatures in the desert can drop to freezing at night. This is said to be the preferred period for crossing the Sahara and visiting Niger. The harmattan winds, however, usually come before the rains and blow a fine dusty fog that envelops everything. Visibility is cut to less than one km. In late May, the rains come to the southern parts of the country, averaging around 50 mm in that month. The annual total in the south is usually 550 mm (although 1994 enjoyed an exceptionally high 800 mm). In contrast, the northern parts receive less than 150 mm of rainfall annually, even in the best of years. In the worst years it may not rain at all.

Do not underestimate the desert heat, especially during the hot seasons. Desert travel can be extremely harsh, with air temperatures way over 50°C (making sand and

---

The Environment

Desertification is Niger's greatest environmental problem; mostly due to deforestation, as people cut wood to use as fuel for cooking. Fortunately, there have been some successful reafforestation schemes, particularly the community forestry project at Guesselbodi, outside Niamey, which has encouraged villagers to build windbreaks and establish nurseries.

Overgrazing is the other major cause of desertification. Animal health and well-digging programmes have resulted in increases in herd sizes beyond the land's carrying capacity, although herds were severely depleted by the droughts in the early 1990s. To help rebuild stocks and generate income, one aid scheme 'loans' young goats to farmers who then must tend the animals until they mature and reproduce. The young are then 'repaid' to the aid scheme.

But this can lead to its own problems. When you're travelling upcountry, look at the areas around the wells; they are frequently denuded by the large herds of cattle and goats that come to drink there. Thus, while more wells may seem at first glance what this dry country needs, they can have disastrous environmental consequences, so it is important that stocks are only rebuilt to sustainable levels.

There are few agricultural projects in northern Niger. According to studies, and contrary to popular belief, lack of water is not the only limiting factor to growing food. The pure quartz sands of this desert region lack sufficient nutrients to produce high crop yields. ■

rocks hot enough to burn skin). Most people spend the majority of their day under the shade of rocks, trees and bushes, drinking up to 14 pints (eight litres) of water a day.

GOVERNMENT

With the adoption of the new constitution of the Third Republic following the elections of January 1993, Niger witnessed a remarkably smooth transition to a multiparty democracy, something few African countries have succeeded in doing. The president is elected by universal suffrage and serves for a five-year term; elections are next scheduled for early 1998. The president appoints the prime minister, who heads the National Assembly, which has 83 members elected by popular vote for five-year terms.

ECONOMY

Niger's economy is doing very poorly. Per capita GDP has been declining almost every year since 1989. The country would be economically lost without uranium. It owns 16% of the world's total uranium deposits, and despite the devastating collapse in world prices during the 1980s, uranium still accounts for about 75% of export earnings. The country may also have untapped deposits of gold and oil. Meanwhile the economy limps along, unable to support the government's bloated bureaucracy. Government workers frequently go many months without being paid. The government has acquired such an enormous debt that it desperately wants to sell its unprofitable state enterprises. Predictably, buyers are not pounding down the door.

While only 3% of the land is arable and rainfall is unpredictable, subsistence farming and stock rearing contribute around 47% of GNP and nearly 70% of the labour force is employed in this sector. Exports include cotton, cowpeas and groundnuts. Principal subsistence crops, with the aid of a few irrigation projects, are millet, sorghum, cassava and rice, all of which help to make the country self-sufficient during the non-drought years. Smuggling with Nigeria (where goods are cheaper and more available) is advantageous for those living along

Niger's southern border, but it distorts the economies of both countries.

POPULATION & PEOPLE

An area of 1,267,000 sq km and 8.8 million people gives Niger one of the lowest population densities in West Africa; about six people per sq km. (In contrast Nigeria is three-quarters the size of Niger and has 17 times more people.) However, 90% of Niger people live in the south of the country. Drought and heat have made it increasingly difficult for people to thrive in the northern regions.

The population is extremely diverse, with numerous ethnic groups. The main group is the Hausa, who make up over 50% of the population. The second-largest group is the Songhai-Zarma, with 22%, followed by the Tuareg (less than 10%) and the Fulani (8.5%). Other groups include: the Kanouri (4.3%) in the eastern part of Niger between Zinder and Chad; and the Toubou (1.2%) in the north. Niger also has a minority of Arabs in north-eastern parts of the country, related to the groups in Libya and Chad.

The population is growing at 3.4% annually. This is combined with a very high infant mortality rate. Life expectancy is an estimated 47 years.

Hausa

Making up over half of the population, is the group commonly misnamed the Hausa (HOW-sah). Hausa is actually a linguistic term as opposed to the ethnicity of this group of people. Hausa-speaking people are identified by their language and further by the similarities in culture that extend beyond any particular geographical place. Hausa, a composite language, is spoken by over 20 million people as a first language and by nearly as many as a second language, making it one of the most widely spoken indigenous languages in sub-Saharan Africa.

The ancient Hausa culture originated in the heartland of northern Nigeria, and began to spread with the establishment of other Hausa states in the region. The traditional caravan trade was also an important vehicle in facilitating the expansion of Hausa

NIGER

culture. Commerce was and still is one of the most important activities during the dry season. You'll find Hausa traders all over West Africa. But they are more frequently known for being skilled farmers with much of their time revolving around agriculture in their villages during the rainy season.

Songhai-Zarma

Descendants of the prestigious Songhaï Empire, the Songhai-Zarma (Son-GUY ZAR-mah) were once known as traditional administrators and warriors. About 400 years ago, they migrated south and settled along the Niger River. Today, they constitute over half the population of Niamey. Along the river you'll see them cultivating rice and fishing. There are also many Zarmas in the government because during colonial times the French concentrated their educational efforts in Niamey, the Songhai-Zarma being the primary beneficiaries.

Tuareg

In the north are the famous Tuareg (TWAH-reg) nomads, who make up less than 10% of the population. Before the arrival of the French colonial army, they were the lords of the desert, for whom robbery was an honourable occupation. They were renowned for their bravery, and their fierce raids on camel caravans. They would also attack the villages of other tribes, stealing crops and livestock

and enslaving the inhabitants. The French destroyed much of this activity by restricting nomadic movement and abolishing slavery (although in remoter parts of Niger it persisted until the 1960s). Without their slaves, the Tuareg eventually turned to herding and had to move south to the desert's rim in search of greener pastures. Today, only a few still inhabit the true desert to the north.

You can recognise Tuareg by their light-coloured skin and grey or blue eyes, often the only features showing through the long *taguelmoust* (shawl or scarf) worn as head-gear by the men. Still proud and warlike in character, many carry swords.

Camels are the focus of their lives. They give them names, write songs about them, settle arguments with camel races, go courting on camels, measure a man's wealth by the size of his herds and judge his nobility by how well he rides.

The Tuareg are Muslim, yet their customs are distinct from the Arabs. (They are also one of the few groups in Africa who traditionally eat with utensils – a large wooden spoon – rather than hands.) While celebrating most Muslim holidays, they ignore the annual Ramadan fast. Women, too, play a totally different role and enjoy a freedom and status unheard of in the Muslim world. Tuareg are one of the few matrilineal ethnic groups in West Africa, and the women do not wear veils. Tuareg women can also own

The Tuareg Rebellion

During the devastating drought of the 1970s, many Tuareg migrated to Algeria looking for work, but political strife there in the early 1990s forced many to return. The government of Niger promised to help them resettle, but due to drastically falling uranium prices, the economy took a nosedive. As a result, the government did nothing, causing widespread discontentment among the Tuareg, who are now claiming autonomy. Moreover, the uranium was being mined in the north of Niger – considered Tuareg land – but any money generated wasn't being spent to develop these areas. Anger led to the formation of rebel groups who carried out a number of violent attacks against government targets.

The government must give serious attention to the demands of the Tuareg, whose quality of life has been declining for years. Numerous factors are coming together, including the constant threat of drought, leading to an end to their traditional way of life. Life expectancy among the Tuareg remains very low and infant mortality is high. Access to medical facilities, education for their children and the availability of affordable food are now high on the list of demands of these once highly independent nomads. ∎

property, maintain it separately from the husband's during marriage, keep their social status even if marrying into a lower caste, and divorce their husbands (whereas a husband cannot divorce his wife). However, in company, women still tend to be deferential to men and keep quietly in the background at social gatherings.

In Tuareg society, as a sign of respect men must cover their faces. You are unlikely to see a Tuareg man remove his shawl to expose the lower half of his face in company. When the men drink tea, they are supposed to pass the glass under their shawl so as not to reveal the mouth. The taguelmoust is the symbol of a Tuareg's identity, and the way it is wrapped changes from tribe to tribe. Typically five metres long and made of blue or black cotton, it helps keep out the desert winds and sand. Tuareg are often called the 'blue men' because the indigo colouring from their robes and turbans dyes their skin.

Fulani

The Fulani (also called Peul) are the second-largest nomadic group in Niger. They have been influenced greatly by the sedentary population that they have come into contact with, yet they retain many of their customs. The most well known are the Bororo Fulani, or Wodaabé, from the Dakoro-Tanout region west of Agadez. They take great pride in being beautiful and, during festivals, wear lots of jewellery and have intricate hairstyles.

Their annual Cure Salée festival in September, known as the *gerewol*, is famous Africa wide. (See the Around Agadez section.) Young men make themselves exceptionally attractive in order to seduce

women into becoming their wives. If the woman agrees, the man arranges to have her kidnapped from her family and together they set off for a nomadic life, settling down only after the woman bears children. The Wodaabé dress, customs and festivals are covered brilliantly in *Nomads of Niger*.

RELIGION

Islam is a dominant force in the daily lives of the people of Niger, practised from birth until death. Nearly 85% of the population is Muslim and only a small percentage of urban dwellers are Christian. A few rural communities continue to practise the traditional animist religions.

LANGUAGE

French is the official language. The principal African languages are Hausa, spoken mainly in the south, and Zarma, which is written Djerma (pronounced JER-mah) in French and spoken mostly in the west including around Niamey. Other languages include Fulani and Tamashek (also spelt Tamachek and Tamasheq), the language of the Tuareg.

Expressions in Hausa

greeting	*say-NOH*
(response)	*YOW-way say-NOH*
Good morning.	*ee-nah KWAH-nah*
(reply)	*lah-PEE-yah-low*
Good evening.	*ee-nah-EE-nee*
(reply)	*lah-PEE-yah-low*
How are you?	*BAR-kah?*
I'm fine.	*LAF-ee-ah*
Thank you.	*nah-GOH-day*
Goodbye.	*SAY-goh-bay*

Expressions in Zarma

Good morning.	*mah-teen-keh-NEE*
Good evening.	*mah-teen-HEE-ree*
How are you?	*BAR-kah?*
Thank you.	*foh-foh*
Goodbye.	*kah-LAH ton-ton*

Expressions in Tamashek

How do you do?	*met-al-ee-khah* (polite)
	oh-yeek (informal)
I'm fine.	*eel-kharass*
How's the heat? (a	*min-ee-twixeh*
traditional greeting)	
Good/Fine	*ee-zott*
How much?	*min-ee-kit?*
Thank you.	*tan-oo-mert*
Goodbye.	*harr-sad*

Facts for the Visitor

VISAS & EMBASSIES
Niger Visas

Visas are required by everyone except nationals of Belgium, Denmark, Finland, France, Germany, Italy, Luxembourg, the Netherlands, Norway and Sweden. For stays of more than three months everyone needs a visa.

If you're travelling overland, note that Niger has only a few embassies in West Africa, none in Central Africa and only one in East Africa (Addis Ababa), so getting a visa requires careful planning. You should either get a visa in your home country before you leave, or make sure you remember to get it in one of the few West African countries where they are available.

Getting a visa in Europe or North America is fairly straightforward if you're arriving by air, but not by land. In Washington DC, for example, the Niger embassy requires US$35, three photos, your health card with proof of a yellow fever vaccination and a copy of your airline ticket proving onward or return transportation. If you're arriving by land and don't have an airline ticket *out* of the country, the embassy requires a letter from your bank showing US$500 in your account.

Other embassies outside Africa have similar requirements and charge up to US$40 for visas. The Niger embassy in Brussels, however, does not ask to see your airline ticket. In France, the Niger embassy, open weekdays from 9 am to 12.30 pm, charges the same for multiple-entry visas as single-entry ones, requires three photos and usually gives 24-hour service even though officially the turn-around time is 48 hours.

In West Africa, most embassies do not impose the onward ticket requirement on overland travellers. Visas are easy to obtain: in Algeria, both from the embassy in Algiers and from the consulate in Tamanrasset (100FF (no other currency accepted) to issue a 30-day visa); in Cotonou (Benin); and in Nigeria from the embassy in Lagos and from the consulate in Kano. Fees vary (normally between US$30 and US$40, but see the Benin and Nigeria chapters for details), but there's a 24-hour no-hassle service in all five cities.

You cannot get Niger visas in neighbouring Mali, Burkina Faso or Chad. You can, however, get them in Accra, Abidjan and Dakar from the Niger embassy in those countries, in Liberia and Tunisia from the Côte d'Ivoire embassy, and in Sudan from the Chadian embassy. French embassies do not have authority to issue visas to Niger.

For a visa extension, go to the Sûreté in Niamey; it requires CFA 7000 and two photos and takes 24 hours to issue.

Niger Embassies

Belgium 78 Ave Franklin-Roosevelt, Brussels 1050
(☎ (02) 648-61-40)
France 154 rue de Longchamp, 75116 Paris (☎ (1)
45-04-80-60)
Germany Dürenstrabe 9, 5300 Bonn 2 (☎ (0228)
356057/8)
USA 2204 R St, NW, Washington, DC 20008 (☎ (202)
483-4224)

As well as those listed above, Niger also has embassies in Cairo, Moscow, and Ottawa.

NIGER

Other African Visas

Visas for the following countries are available in Niger. For each visa you need between one and four photos.

Algeria The embassy is open weekdays from 10 am to 1 pm, charges CFA 15,000 for visas and usually gives same-day service. For Britons, however, it's a different game: you need an air ticket out of Algeria even to get the application form, then they charge you CFA 50,000 and must send a fax to Algiers, for which you may be charged another CFA 7500. The process takes at least two weeks and even then there's no assurance of getting a visa. There's also an Algerian consulate in Agadez (see the Agadez section for details) that issues visas routinely for most nationalities, but for Britons the process is no better and may take even longer.

Benin The embassy is open weekdays from 8 to 10 am and issues visas in 48 hours. A two-week visa costs CFA 10,000 (CFA 15,000 for multiple entry). You may also be able to get a visa at the northern border of Benin in Malanville but it's good only for 48 hours (though renewable in Cotonou).

Chad The embassy charges CFA 6000 for a two-week visa (extendible in Ndjamena) and takes several days to process applications. It opens Monday to Thursday 8 am to 3 pm, Friday to noon. A Niger exit visa may be required if you're travelling overland to Chad via Nguigmi. You can get one at the Ministry of Interior branch office in Zinder but you must also get a stamp en route at Diffa.

Mali The consulate is open weekdays from 9 am to noon and 4 to 6 pm. It requires CFA 25,000 and usually gives same-day service. Visas are good for stays up to 30 days, and you can have up to three months before this 30-day period begins. Malian visas are also available in Tamanrasset (Algeria); they cost 150FF (about US$30), payable only in French francs, and are processed in 24 hours.

Mauritania The consulate is open weekdays 9 am to noon, and charges CFA 6000 for visas valid up to one month.

Nigeria The embassy is open Monday to Thursday 10 am to 1 pm but will *not* issue visas to anyone who is not a resident of Niger. On occasion, travellers have been successful in getting around this requirement but you shouldn't come here counting on it. If you do manage it, costs for a one-month visa vary according to nationality: around CFA 1000 for Americans, around CFA 8000 for Canadians and Dutch, and around CFA 35,000 for Brits.

Senegal The Senegalese consul is a very laid-back lady who lives in a private house out in the suburbs of Niamey. A visa costs CFA 10,000 for up to one month, CFA 20,000 for two months. The consulate is 'open all the time' according to the consul, but it's best to call during normal office hours.

Other Countries The French consulate in Niamey is open Monday to Saturday from 7.30 am to noon. It issues visas to CAR, Côte d'Ivoire, Gabon, Togo and Burkina Faso, and usually gives a no-hassle 24-hour service. If you need a visa to more than one country, you can get all of them at the same time. The cost is CFA 20,000 for visas up to 90 days (CFA 6000 for five days or less).

Foreign Embassies

For a list of diplomatic missions in the capital, see the Niamey Information section.

DOCUMENTS

To enter Niger you need a passport and an International Health Certificate showing that you've had both yellow fever and cholera vaccinations. If you fly into Niger, you must show your certificate at the airport. Entering overland, a check usually depends on the mood of border officials.

Those entering overland from Algeria must also pay a CFA 1500 tourist tax at the Assamakka border post. If you don't have CFA to pay the tax, you can exchange Algerian dinar for CFA at the border. Formalities are usually quick and hassle-free but occasionally can take up to a day if the officials don't like your looks.

Those with their own vehicle need a driver's licence (preferably international) and a *carnet de passage en douane*. If you don't have a carnet, you can buy one at the border for CFA 12,000. However, a *laissez passer* (CFA 2500), which all drivers must purchase at the border, is all that's usually required. Even if you have vehicle insurance, you must buy Niger vehicle insurance (*la carte brune*) at the border or, cheaper, at the nearest major town near the border. In Arlit, for example, you can buy a three-month carte brune valid for most countries in West Africa from the Société Nigérienne d'Assurances et

Registration

It is necessary to register with the police in several towns and cities in Niger. In Niamey, the registration is done at the Préfecture in the centre, 100 metres south of the Hôtel Rivoli. Travellers arriving in Niamey by air no longer need to do this, as the airport stamp in the passport serves the same purpose; however, it wouldn't hurt to ask on arrival as rules can change.

If you pass through Arlit or Agadez, register with the police (and get the *vu au passage* stamp in your passport) whether or not it's officially required. This will save you a lot of hassle at police checks further along the road, and at the border or airport when you leave the country.

For most other towns, registration rules are vague, but the process takes only five minutes. It's usually done upon leaving the town. If you register on arrival and then stay some days in a town, you may have to do it again on departure.

Wherever you register, you don't need to pay but you may need a few visa-size photos.

CUSTOMS

Searches by customs officials vary greatly, but extensive searches are becoming increasingly rare except in the north where, due to the problems with the Tuareg, you'll be stopped constantly, especially if you're travelling in your own vehicle.

There is no limit on the import of foreign currencies. If you plan to export large amounts of foreign currency, declare it upon arrival. You are not supposed to export more than CFA 125,000 but the rule is generally not enforced, particularly if you are continuing on to another CFA country.

If you fly into Niamey, there's a security check between the health check and customs. It's usually hassle-free, but ignore demands for 'special taxes' to cover cameras etc. If such taxes do exist they'll be asked for at customs.

Also beware of enthusiastic porters at the baggage reclaim who will 'help' you load your trolley then demand a tip.

MONEY

UK£1	=	CFA 775
US$1	=	CFA 500

The unit of currency is the West African CFA franc. As in all other CFA countries, this is linked to the French Franc at a rate of 100:1.

Banks that change money include the Banque Internationale pour l'Afrique Occidentale (BIAO), the Bank of Africa Niger (BAN) and the Banque de Développement de la République du Niger (BDRN).

In Niamey, it's quicker and easier to change cash. At all banks, staff find French francs easiest to deal with, although US dollars are generally no problem. UK pounds and some other hard currencies are also accepted in the BIAO, but not at the BAN. Usually, no commission is charged when you change cash.

Banks in Niamey will also change travellers' cheques, but commissions can be high (compared to some other West African countries) and rates often extremely variable. At the BIAO in Niamey they charge between 1 and 2% to change travellers' cheques, plus a CFA 600 handling charge per cheque. They give quick service, and also handle Visa and MasterCard cash advances (but not always, so don't rely on it). At the BAN, the commission on travellers' cheques is 1.5% and there's a 600FF (about US$120) minimum limit. However, all rates and commissions continually vary, so before you change money, it is worth checking at all the banks in town, although you may end up walking around for a whole morning just to save a dollar or two.

Outside Niamey it is much easier to change cash (especially French francs) than travellers' cheques, but finding a bank, especially one that accepts travellers' cheques, is sometimes difficult. Also, banks outside Niamey often give bad rates and levy ridiculously high commissions, typically a flat rate of around CFA 4000 but sometimes a percentage. With French franc travellers' cheques, bank commissions vary considerably, from zero to the standard CFA 4000. Moreover, the branch of a bank in one town may have vastly different rates to another branch of the same bank in another town. There is no logic at all and the only way is to check around. To avoid all this hassle, change in Niamey. Or, if you're coming in from another country, bring enough cash, preferably French francs, to cover your trip from the border to Niamey.

This is particularly important if you're coming from Algeria, as the banks in Arlit and Agadez may be closed. Even if they're open, they are not always willing to accept travellers' cheques other than those in French francs, and even then you should expect to pay at least CFA 4000 commission. Sometimes they limit (per visit) the amount that you may change to US$100. (However, you can change privately – see the Agadez section for details.) When leaving Niger, and heading for a non-CFA country, you can change back surplus cash easily. You need to show all your previous change receipts, and may also be asked for your airline ticket and passport.

And one last point: wherever you change, put your money away before leaving because all banks have petty thieves lurking around the entrances ready to snatch the cash of unwary travellers.

BUSINESS HOURS & HOLIDAYS

Business hours are weekdays from 8 am to 12.30 pm and 3 to 6.30 pm; Saturday from 8 am to 12.30 pm. Government offices are open weekdays from 7.30 am to 12.30 pm and 3.30 to 6.30 pm, closed Saturday and Sunday.

Banking hours are weekdays from 8 to 11.30 am and 3.45 to 5 pm.

Public Holidays

There are holidays on 1 January, Feast of Ramadan, Easter Monday, Tabaski, 1 May, 3 August (Independence), Mohammed's Birthday, 5 September (Settlers' Day), Islamic New Year, 18 December (Republic Day), 25 December.

POST & TELECOMMUNICATIONS

Post

Postal services outside the capital are reported to be slow and unreliable, so you should do everything in Niamey. The city has two post offices (the old Grande Poste – also called the Hôtel des Postes, and not to be mistaken for a place to stay – and the modern Poste du Plateau, which is near the Sûreté), both with a reliable service. For an example of rates, a 10-gram letter to Europe costs CFA 390. The poste restante is at the Poste du Plateau; it's quick and reliable and costs about CFA 300 per letter. It will also keep letters for up to four months or more.

If you need to send something urgently, DHL have an office at the Gaweye hotel.

Telephone, Fax & Telex

Cheap telephone calls (and telexes) can be made from either of the post offices in Niamey; service is efficient. Three minutes (the minimum charge) to Europe costs CFA 4650, plus 1500 per subsequent minute. To send a fax, the first page costs CFA 3000, subsequent pages CFA 1500. The Grande Post also operates a 'fax restante' service; you can have faxes sent to you (☎ 73 44 70) and pick them up free of charge. The easiest place for international phone calls and faxes is the Gaweye hotel in Niamey, but the cost is high: CFA 3700 per minute/page to Europe or the USA.

PHOTOGRAPHY

A photo permit is not required. Nevertheless, you still can't take photos of government buildings and personnel, airports, banks, TV stations or bridges, including Kennedy Bridge in Niamey or people bathing in the river. It is also important to use discretion when taking pictures of people or even better – ask. You will need authorisation to film.

HEALTH

Vaccinations for yellow fever and cholera are required, and border officials do ask to see a certificate. A meningitis vaccination is strongly advisable. By early 1995, meningitis had become a very serious problem, attacking over 15,000 people in Niger and claiming more than 1500 lives in just a few months. A major vaccination campaign is under way to control this killer virus. Check with your embassy or the nearest Niger embassy for the latest update.

As the climate here is very dry, especially in the hot season (March to May), you'll consume far more water than normal. For this reason, it's particularly important that you drink only treated water. Some city supplies are treated. Also, bottled drinking water is available, but can become expensive over time, so bring enough purification tablets to cover your trip. They are generally unavailable in Niger.

The best hospital is Clinique de Gamkallé (☎ 73 20 33), in Niamey on Corniche de Gamkallé, about one km south of Kennedy Bridge. But it's expensive; the standard fee is CFA 20,000 per consultation and CFA 10,000 per test. A cheaper and highly recommended service is available at the new Centre Médical Pro Santé (☎ 72 26 50), at 10 Rue de la FAO, in the Plateau area of Niamey. The charge is CFA 10,000 per consultation. Staff and facilities are very good, and there's also a pharmacy.

The government hospital (☎ 72 25 21) is cheaper still, but you should use it only if you have no other choice. Also keep in mind that embassies can be helpful in recommending doctors for medical assistance.

DANGERS & ANNOYANCES
Crime & the Tuareg Rebellion
Crime has become a significant problem in Niamey, in part because of attacks by newly urbanised, dispossessed Tuareg. The most dangerous areas are the Petit Marché (where pickpockets are also a problem), Kennedy Bridge and the two Corniche roads running parallel to the river on the city side including the area around the Gaweye hotel. There have been frequent muggings and even knife-slashings in these areas, which should be avoided after sunset, especially if you are alone and walking. Crime is also a serious problem in the northern areas of Niamey,

including Yantala where the major camp site is located. The Grand Marché is relatively free of crime because it has its own security guards for protecting merchants from theft.

Travel in northern Niger has been dangerous since 1991 due to attacks by Tuareg rebels and bandits taking advantage of the general lawlessness. In the Agadez region, for example, lorries and tankers have been attacked and set on fire, but many 4WD cars (driven by aid workers or visitors) have also been hijacked and stolen. Tour companies ceased excursions into the north and many embassies issued travel warnings. The US embassy, for example, recommended avoiding travel beyond Tillabéri, Tahoua and Zinder.

At the end of May 1995, the travel warnings were still in effect although the peace accord signed that month between the government and the rebels may end the fighting in this area. However, there are still a lot of guns and a lack of any kind of real control in the north, so bandit attacks may continue for some time, making the area still unsafe for travellers.

You can check at any US embassy around the world for an update.

Dress
There have been incidents of foreign women being abused or attacked for wearing what was seen as improper clothing. It is important to be aware that as this is a Muslim country, where dress is taken very seriously. Women should wear only clothes that are 'modest' (ie covering the knees and shoulders, and fairly loose fitting). Shorts or singlets for women or men show a lack of sensitivity and are not advised.

ACCOMMODATION
Bottom-end places are relatively expensive in Niger, with the cheapest single rooms costing around CFA 3000, and the quality is often very low. However, camping (which normally costs about CFA 1500 per person) is possible in Niamey, Arlit, Agadez, Tahoua, Maradi and Birnin-Konni.

Mid-range hotels in Niger are more expensive than in neighbouring Nigeria, Benin and Togo, although on a par with Mali, with prices ranging from CFA 5000 to CFA 8000 for a double with fan, and another CFA 4000 to CFA 5000 if you want air-con. There are decent mid-range hotels in Niamey, Zinder, Maradi, Tahoua, Ayorou and Parc W but nowhere else.

Niamey, and a few other towns, have up-market hotels, where rooms are CFA 10,000 to CFA 20,000 or more, but the country's only international-standard deluxe hotel is the Gaweye, also in Niamey.

FOOD

The traditional food of Niger is nothing to write home about. In the north, dates, yoghurt, rice and mutton are standard fare amongst the nomadic Tuareg. In the south, rice and sauce is the most common dish. Couscous and ragout are also popular. Nevertheless, you're likely to enjoy mealtimes because in most instances you'll probably be eating in some open-air place, with your feet in the sand and, at night, with the star-lit heavens above you. Standard fare at restaurants is usually braised fish and chicken with chips, or beef brochettes and rice.

Getting There & Away

AIR
To/From Europe & the USA
The only European airline serving Niger is Air France (all flights via Paris), with a twice-weekly service. Return economy fares from Paris start at about 6000FF (about US$1000), or a little more from other European capitals, and vary according to season and length of stay. From Niamey, a one-way/return to Paris is CFA 522,000/577,800.

There are also twice-weekly flights from Europe to Niger on Air Algérie (via Algiers). London to Niamey return is about UK£500 (about US$750), although cheaper fares are often available, and students under 29 can get significant reductions. If you're heading

straight from Europe to Niger, to save even more money you could travel overland to Marseilles in southern France and take a ferry from there to Algiers, where you can pick up the Air Algérie flight on to Niamey. A one-way economy fare from Algiers to Niamey is about US$450 when purchased in Algeria (but CFA 409,000 (US$800) Niamey-Algiers when purchased in Niamey).

Note that Algeria may be unsafe for visitors travelling overland, although transiting at the airport should be OK – see elsewhere in this book for details.

Ethiopian Airlines also links Europe and Niger, with London-Niamey returns about the same price as Air Algérie. It has better service but a longer flight (via Addis Ababa).

Your other option is Air Afrique, who have flights from London and Paris, and several other French cities, going via Dakar or Abidjan. Wherever you buy the ticket, returns between Paris and Niamey are about US$750 (slightly higher to/from London), and may involve an overnight stop in Abidjan.

From the USA, you could take Air Afrique to Dakar or Abidjan and catch a connecting flight to Niamey, or fly to Paris and transfer there.

To/From East & North Africa
The only flights to/from East Africa are on Ethiopian Airlines, which has a weekly flight (currently Saturday) to/from Addis Ababa. From Addis you can fly to Nairobi and several other East African capitals. Niamey to Addis is CFA 419,100 one way. A one-month return is CFA 527,300.

Royal Air Maroc fly weekly from Niamey to Casablanca for CFA 285,000 one-way. An economy return to Paris is CFA 372,000, but the student fare is CFA 309,500.

To/From West Africa
Within West Africa, most flights from Niamey are on Air Afrique: four times a week to/from Abidjan (CFA 584,000 return) and Ouagadougou (CFA 105,000 return, CFA 52,600 one way), twice a week to/from Cotonou (CFA 194,000 return, CFA 105,200

one way), Bamako (CFA 271,000 return) and Ndjamena (CFA 366,000 return, CFA 183,600 one way), and once a week to/from Dakar (CFA 456,000 return, CFA 228,600 one way).

You can also fly on Ethiopian Airlines once a week from Niamey to Bamako (CFA 146,900 one way) and Dakar (CFA 248,500 one way).

And you can fly between Niamey and Ouagadougou, Bamako and Abidjan on the Air France service to/from Paris.

LAND
Bus
Long distance buses operate on the Niamey to Ouaga (Burkina Faso) and Niamey to Gao (Mali) routes. The government-operated SNTN buses are large, seating between 50 and 70 people. The private buses are about the same size, but on some routes if demand is slack the private companies run smaller buses too. These small buses do cross the border (unlike the minibus bush taxis). SNTN buses are generally in better condition, and quicker than the private buses, but cost about 25% more. Both types of bus are more comfortable than bush taxis but leave much less frequently.

To/From Benin & Nigeria There are SNTN and private buses from Niamey to the border towns of Gaya, Birnin-Konni, Maradi and Zinder, but none cross the border. Across the border from all these towns, bush taxis take you to points further south.

To/From Burkina Faso Only big buses (or minibuses operated by the big bus companies) can cross the border, making direct connections between Niamey and Ouagadougou.

SNTN and two Burkina bus companies, Faso Tours and X9, all run between Niamey and Ouagadougou, with five departures per week each way between them. The SNTN fare from Niamey is CFA 7500, private buses CFA 7000, although it seems it might be cheaper on the private buses if you're going the other way.

Departures are from the SNTN bus station in Niamey and from the Faso Tours office in Ouagadougou, except for X9, which has a separate office in Ouaga. The buses are reasonably comfortable and fairly punctual, departing at 7 am and arriving 12 to 14 hours later, with over two hours at the border for several laborious luggage checks. Tickets must be purchased a day or more in advance.

Buses also go between Niamey and the Burkina border at Foetchango. The cost is about CFA 2500 and the waiting time at the border for a bus or bush taxi on the other side can be short or long depending on your luck. If you don't have to wait long, you have a reasonable chance of making it from Niamey to Ouaga in a same day. Otherwise, you'll have to sleep at the border.

On the Burkina side, Sans Frontières provides a good service between Ouaga and the border (CFA 4000), departing either end around 9 am in the morning. In Ouaga, the Sans Frontières office is on Ave Coulibaly and advance reservations are required.

To/From Chad There is no public transport across the border. On the Niamey side, the farthest you can get is Nguigmi, about 100 km from the border. Nguigmi is linked to Zinder most days by bush taxi and minibus, which cost CFA 8500 and take 16 hours. (Diffa to/from Zinder is CFA 6000, and about 12 hours.)

On the Chad side there's no public transport, although trucks and pick-ups trundle between Nguigmi and Nokou once every few days and take passengers for about CFA 10,000. After more waiting you can find something between Nokou and Mao for about CFA 3000, and from there you might be able to find something on to Ndjamena, probably after another few days of waiting.

Apart from the waiting, you also need to be prepared for little in the way of accommodation. Most often you'll be allowed to sleep in the yard at a police post, but don't bank on it. For food, take some supplies with you – and expect to get thin.

One last thing – whichever way you go, don't forget to get your passport stamped in Diffa.

To/From Mali

SNTN has a bus (actually a truck with a cabin on the back) plying between Niamey and Gao, but service is occasionally suspended or reduced because of disturbances in the northern areas caused by Tuareg rebels. According to the schedule, they leave in either direction on Mondays, Wednesdays and Fridays, but until the situation settles it's once a week only.

The fare is CFA 10,400. On this route they don't leave punctually. The schedule shows an 11 am departure, but the buses usually don't leave until after noon. On a typical trip the bus gets to the border around 9 pm and crosses over the next morning, arriving in Gao or Niamey around 6 pm, but sometimes there's a second overnight stop at Ansongo. The road is paved from Niamey to Tillabéri, and is fairly decent to Ayorou; from there it's sandy all the way to Gao. It's a hellish trip but even more so from July to September when the route is quite muddy, often extending the journey time considerably. If the rain is unusually heavy, the road can become impassable.

Even in the dry season you should consider breaking your journey. See the Around Niamey section for ideas.

To/From Togo & Ghana

There's a weekly service from Niamey to Lome (Togo) for CFA 10,500, and then onto Accra (Ghana) for another CFA 1000.

Bush Taxi

There are two types of bush taxi in Niger: Peugeot 504 seven-seaters (station wagons) and minibuses.

To/From Benin

A minibus from Niamey to Gaya costs CFA 3500 and a 504 is CFA 4500 and takes four to six hours. A minibus between Dosso and Gaya is CFA 1600. You'll be let off at a junction 10 km before Gaya, where motorcycle-taxis will take you to the Benin border town of Malanville. From there to Parakou it's CFA 3000 by 504 (CFA 2000 by minibus, but

several hours longer). With good connections, you can make it from Niamey to Parakou in one long day.

To/From Burkina Faso

Despite what drivers may tell you, bush taxis do not cross the border and you must always change here. By bush taxi, Niamey to the border at Foetchango is about CFA 2000. You can do Niamey to Ouaga by bush taxi in a long day, if you leave early and make fairly quick connections at the border.

Coming from Ouaga, it's also possible to make the entire trip to Niamey in one long day if connections at the border are good, but 1½ days is more typical, as departures seem to be later and you lose an hour en route because of the time change. Most bush taxis from Ouaga do not reach the border by the 6.30 pm (Niger time) closing, so most travellers end up sleeping at the border.

The situation is confused as some minibuses are officially bush taxis, which cannot cross the border, while other minibuses are officially long-distance buses which can cross the border. Bush taxi drivers take advantage of this and swear that they'll be driving the entire distance between Niamey and Ouaga, and even collect the 'full' fare (up to CFA 10,000), then drop you at the border. When this happens, passengers become infuriated and sparks begin to fly, but the drivers always win. They may try to find you another vehicle (often in much worse condition) to take you on your journey, but that vehicle may have to wait long hours to fill up.

To/From Mali

There are no bush taxis ploughing the entire distance between Niamey and Gao. Only the SNTN bus provides direct connections. If you're headed for Gao and can't get a seat on the SNTN bus, try the gare routière next to Camping Touristique in Niamey. Trucks for Gao leave from there on an irregular basis.

To/From Nigeria

The cheapest way to get from Niamey to Nigeria is via Gaya (see To/From Benin above). At the junction 10 km before Gaya, motorcycle-taxis will be waiting to whisk you across the border to Kumba for only about CFA 500. From Kumba, you can catch bush taxis (which are much cheaper than in Niger) almost immediately for Sokoto.

You can also cross over into Nigeria from Birnin-Konni, Maradi and Zinder. From Konni, you can take a motorcycle-taxi (moto-taxi) to the border, while from Maradi and Zinder you must take a taxi. Once you're in Nigeria, at all of these points the waiting time for onward vehicles to Kano or Sokoto is minimal. Don't be surprised if Nigerian customs officials give you a hard time, especially if you're driving.

Car

Driving time to Niamey from the coastal cities of Lomé and Lagos is about 17 hours, and about 13 hours from Cotonou; each route is paved all the way. The Niger-Benin border closes at 7.30 pm. The Ouagadougou to Niamey road is also sealed; the trip usually takes about 10 hours. The Niger-Burkina border closes at 6.30 pm Niger time. (Niger is one hour ahead of Burkina Faso.) While it is sometimes possible to cross later if you offer a tip for the off-hours service, it's best not to take the risk. To get off the beaten path, try the route starting west from Farié (62 km north of Niamey) over the river by ferry towards Dori and Ouaga; the road is in good condition all the way.

Zinder to Ndjamena via Lake Chad takes three to five days. The all-sand stretch between the Chad border and Ndjamena is worse than anything on the Tamanrasset to Arlit route and it's far less travelled, making it much more dangerous. The border officials may even insist you take a guide (not really necessary) for part of the distance. Regardless, come prepared and travel with another vehicle if you can.

LEAVING NIGER

Airport tax is CFA 2500 for flights within West Africa, although this may rise in future. Some long-haul flights have the tax included (it should say in the bottom right corner of your ticket) although this depends on the airline.

Getting Around

AIR

For getting around the country by air, there is no scheduled public service. A company called Air Sonita used to fly between Niamey and Agadez but they have suspended operations, although it might be worth asking around in case they start up again in the future. Check properly though – we heard about a traveller who actually paid for an Air Sonita ticket, only to find out later that no flights existed.

A much more reliable option is the mining company in Arlit which regularly charters planes from a company called Nigeravia, with spare seats sold to the public. There's usually two flights per week. One-way fares from Niamey are CFA 187,000 to Agadez, and CFA 205,000 to Arlit.

You can also charter an entire plane from Nigeravia if the need arises: their 10 to 15-seater can land anywhere with an airstrip, and their five-seater can land just about anywhere. For an example of charter fares, Niamey to Agadez is CFA 1,852,000 (about US$3000) and Niamey to Ndjamena is 3,308,200 (about US$6500). Spare seats on these charter flights are often sold to the public, so it might be worth stopping by at the Nigeravia office, on the Rond Point near the Grand Hôtel (☎ 73 30 64, fax 74 18 42), to see if there's anything going in your direction.

BUS

The government's large SNTN buses are the best way to travel around Niger because they cover all the major routes, are comfortable, relatively fast and punctual. However, they are the most expensive form of public transport. As a sample, Niamey to Birnin-Konni (440 km) costs CFA 7950, and Niamey to Zinder (950 km) costs CFA 14,350. Seats must be reserved in advance, and the buses usually fill up fast, starting from the moment the previous one leaves. When reserving a seat, you'll be asked to show your passport, but you may actually pay only on the day of departure. In each town, SNTN has its own bus station.

You can save about 20% by taking a private bus. They tend to have more frequent departures from the gares routières (also called *autogares* in Niger), although later departure times. Depending on your luck they can be as comfortable as the SNTN buses or in very bad condition with frequent breakdowns. Even if they don't break down, the driving time is typically 50% longer.

BUSH TAXI

Because buses in Niger are fast and comfortable, many travellers prefer them to bush taxis, which tend to be neither. But bush taxis are cheaper, and leave more frequently than the buses, though they are often very crowded. There are two types of bush taxi: Peugeot 504 seven-seaters (station wagons), which normally carry about 12 people; and minibuses, which carry 30 people or more.

Remember that baggage is always charged extra, usually about 5 to 10% of the passenger fare, but this depends on the size of your bag and what the driver thinks he can get away with.

Bush taxis head in all directions: along the big roads between Niamey, Agadez and Zinder, and to the borders of Nigeria, Benin and Burkina Faso, as well as to many smaller places off the main routes. In rural areas you can also find converted trucks and pick-ups, called *fula-fulas*. These are cheap, but slow and terribly uncomfortable.

CAR

Main roads in Niger are excellent. From Niamey to Agadez and Arlit, from Niamey to Zinder and Nguigmi, and from Niamey to the Burkina border the roads are all tarred. The road between Zinder and Agadez still had a long section of dirt in May 1995, but were to be completed soon after. Niamey-Agadez and Niamey-Zinder (both about 900 km) take 12 to 14 hours straight driving time, but you'll encounter countless police checkpoints between Niamey and Agadez which will slow you down a bit. Police stops are more relaxed than in past years, though the

police are still sometimes gruff but only occasionally rude. If they are impolite, getting mad will only make matters worse.

At the height of the Tuareg rebellion, private vehicles (and public transport) had to join military convoys on the main road between Tahoua and Arlit. Following the May 1995 peace accord these had been suspended as far as Agadez and you could go as you please, although there was still an element of risk as bandits are active along this stretch. Convoys may still be operating between Arlit and the border at Assamakka, and between Agadez and Zinder. If you do have to join a convoy, you may have to wait several days to go with one and protection is not guaranteed. If you have a flat tyre en route, for example, they'll just continue without you.

Petrol costs about CFA 310 a litre, and diesel CFA 265, which is significantly cheaper than in Mali and Burkina Faso but more expensive than in Benin and Nigeria. You can also buy black market Nigerian petrol for about half this price in towns near the southern border such as Gaya, Birnin-Konni and Maradi. Look for the guys waving red plastic funnels as you drive by, but inspect the fuel first to make sure it's real.

Private cars must pay a toll (*péage*) to use the main routes. You buy a ticket before travelling from a checkpoint on the edge of each town, either for a whole trip (eg Niamey to Agadez CFA 1000) or in sections (eg Niamey to Tahoua CFA 500, then Tahoua to Agadez CFA 500). If you don't have a ticket when it's asked for at a check point, you're fined on the spot by police.

Niamey

Since becoming the capital, Niamey has experienced fantastic growth – from around 2000 people in the 1930s to over 650,000 today. However, it's a fairly spread out and uncongested city, although this means getting around requires a little more walking than in other Sahelian capitals.

The Grand Marché is one of the best in West Africa, with a big selection of artisan goods from all over the country. The new building is also architecturally interesting and even has several fountains – a first for West African markets. Indeed, if you've arrived from Ouagadougou or Bamako, you may be struck by the number of smart new government buildings in the centre, although their exteriors blend in with the environment far better than most modern structures. They are a reminder of the country's glorious past – the 1970s – when uranium prices were sky-high.

Yet despite the modern buildings, tarred roads and street lights, Niamey still has a traditional African ambience that gives the city its charm. It sits on the eastern bank of the Niger River, spanned by the Kennedy Bridge. Dusk is the time to have a drink nearby and watch the activity. If you wait long enough, you are bound to see a camel or two crossing over it. At night, finding a place to eat, drink and chat outside under the stars is easy; and, as with everywhere in the desert, that's when you'll most appreciate being here.

Orientation

As in many African cities, street names in Niamey are virtually useless as nobody knows them, even though most have signs. The street pattern, however, is easier to understand than it looks. The two principal arteries intersect at the Grand Marché: Rue de Kalley running roughly east-west towards the Niger River and Blvd de la Liberté running roughly north-south.

Rue de Kalley is the main commercial drag, stretching roughly westward from the Grand Marché to Kennedy Bridge, becoming Rue du Gaweye along the way. The city's top hotel, the Gaweye, is just before the bridge, overlooking the Niger River. A few hundred metres before the bridge is the Hôtel Rivoli, one of the city's principal landmarks. Between it and the bridge is a large triangular block on which there are three modern commercial build-ings, including the Sonara I and II buildings, with airlines offices, banks, etc.

The other major axis, Blvd de la Liberté, runs alongside the market, heading roughly southward towards the airport and out of town (to Agadez, Zinder, Benin, etc.) and northward towards the equally wide Route de Tillabéri (also spelt Tillabéry). The latter route, also called Blvd de l'Indépendance, leads out though the smart Plateau quartier (suburb) to the Rond-Point Yantala on the north-western edge of town where there's a camp site and, eventually, to Tillabéri and the Malian border.

The two Corniche roads (Corniche Yantala and Corniche de Gamkallé) also run roughly north-south, along the eastern bank of the river. The government's SNTN bus station is on the former. Most of the embassies, the better residential areas and the Presidential Palace are on the northern side of town, while the gare routière and many of the hotels and restaurants are on the southern half. Just across the bridge is the university, which has a large campus; the students are delighted to talk to foreigners, and can often speak several languages.

Information

Tourist Office The Office National du Tourisme (ONT; ☎ 73 24 47, fax 72 33 47, telex 5467) is in the centre on Ave Luebké between the Rivoli and the Grand hotels. It has a good map of Niamey for CFA 500 and one of all the market days around the country. The ONT also arranges trips to Parc W, the riverside villages north of Niamey and to the Aïr Mountains (from Agadez). Other-wise, their travel material is outdated and the ONT is not very useful.

Some tour and travel companies advertise in *Le Sahel* newspaper, which also publicises events such as films and shows at the cultural centres.

Money, Banks, Post & Telephone Details on all these facilities in Niamey and around Niger are listed in the Facts for the Visitor section of this chapter.

Foreign Embassies The following embassies and consulates issue visas:

Algeria Two km north-west of the centre, just north of Route de Tillabéri (☎ 75 30 97)

Belgium Sonara II building, Rue du Gaweye (☎ 73 33 14 or 73 34 47)

Benin On Rue des Dallois, two km north-west of the centre, near Route de Tillabéri (☎ 72 39 19)

Canada Sonara II building, Rue du Gaweye (☎ 73 36 86/7)

Chad Just off the western end of Rue de Mali Bero, behind the ambassador's residence, which is signposted (☎ 75 34 64)

France (consulate) Corner of Ave Mitterrand and Blvd de la République (☎ 72 27 22)

Germany Ave de Gaulle (☎ 72 25 34, telex 5223)

Mali (consulate) One block north of the market and 1½ blocks east of Blvd de la Liberté (☎ 73 23 42)

Mauritania Two km north-west of the centre, near Route de Tillabéri, just north of the Algerian embassy (☎ 75 38 43)

Nigeria On Blvd de la République, one km past the US embassy (after which the road becomes dirt) (☎ 73 24 10 or 73 27 95)

Senegal The consul lives in a private house, in a street off Ave de l'Entente, in a quartier (suburb) called Poudrière, east of the centre, near the Wadata Autogare, one block beyond the remains of the Hôtel Sabka Lahiya. There's no sign so you'll need to ask for directions (☎ 73 57 44)

Switzerland (consulate) Opposite L'Oriental Restaurant, in the city centre (☎ 73 39 16)

Tunisia Ave de Gaulle (☎ 72 26 03)

USA Four km north-west of the centre on Blvd de la République (☎ 72 26 61, telex 5444)

The honorary consul of the UK (☎ 73 25 39 or 73 20 51, fax 73 36 92) is a Nigerien businessman, director of Elf Oil (formerly BP – the British connection!), whose office is at the Elf headquarters, about five km out of town on the left side of the road to the airport. The consul has very limited powers and speaks very little English. Other honorary consulates include Italy (☎ 72 32 91 or 73 20 00) and the Netherlands (☎ 73 27 34 or 72 29 29).

Travel Agencies Most companies run tours to Park W (and other destinations fairly close to Niamey), and to the north of Niger. In the early 1990s many tour companies ceased operations because of the Tuareg situation.

New ones will inevitably start up whenever conditions improve; ask at your hotel for details.

One the best and most expensive agencies (who continued operating despite the Tuareg situation) is Nigercar Voyages (☎ 73 23 31) at the Gaweye hotel. They run tours to Park W and to the area just north of Niamey (Boubon, Ayorou and Tillabéri). They will also start up their trips to the north again when the area is safe. Their prices for a two-day (one night) trip to Park W, including simple accommodation, lunch and breakfast, range from CFA 122,000 per person for two people to CFA 851,500 per person for groups of six or more. If you stay in the smart Tapoa Lodge it costs an extra CFA 4000 per person. A day trip to Boubon (including lunch and a boat ride) costs CFA 55,000 each for two people, CFA 23,000 each for six or more. This company also rents cars – see the Niamey Getting Around section later in this section for details.

Other places to try for tours and car hire include the ONT office and NCA Voyages et Tourisme (☎ 73 25 22) on Ave de la Grande Mosquée.

Bookshops The two best bookshops are Indrap, on Rue de Martin Luther King, and Ascani, on a side street behind the Score supermarket. The latter is better for newspapers and magazines and is open Monday to Saturday from 8 am to 12.15 pm and 3.45 to 6.45 pm. You can also get slide film, batteries and camera equipment. Also try Papeterie Burama between Ave de Kalley and the Hôtel Maourey.

The *tabac* shop behind the Rivoli sells *Time*, *Newsweek* and the *International Herald Tribune* as do the bookshops at the Gaweye and Terminus hotels. For maps of Niger, try the tourist office and the Service Topographique et du Cadastre located in front of the Minister of Finance bureau.

Supermarkets The largest supermarket is Score, in the heart of town facing the Petit Marché. Closed on Sunday, it's large and loaded with groceries from France. While you're there, check out Perrissac next door; it's also quite large. There are smaller Lebanese-owned stores in the city centre area that carry many products from the Arab world. Also try the Mini Market, a small grocery next to Air Algérie.

For fresh produce, the best place is the Petit Marché. There are little shack-like boutiques all around Niamey which sell basic canned goods, toilet paper, flashlights and cheap quality batteries. You hardly find bottled water anywhere but at Score.

Pharmacies There are plenty all over town. One of the best pharmacies is Pharmacie du Grand Marché on Blvd de la Liberté. Another good one is Pharmacie Nouvelle in the centre between the Hôtel Rivoli and Air Afrique; it's open Sundays and closes late. Also recommended is the Pro Santé clinic; see under Health in the Facts for the Visitor section in this chapter for details.

Grand Marché

The Grand Marché is one of the city's major attractions and is one of West Africa's best markets. It has been completely rebuilt since it burned down in the mid-1980s and is quite impressive, with its modern architecture and even fountains. Good times to visit are in the early morning and at the end of the noon siesta when activity is calmer. You can buy anything from vegetables and fabric to bicycle parts and toys. The Petit Marché is mainly a food market and closer to the river.

Grande Mosquée

The impressive new mosque financed by Libya is 1.5 km east of the Grand Marché. Open to both male and female visitors, it has workers and guards who, if shown a little politeness, are often glad to give a short tour. A tip to your guide will be expected.

Musée National du Niger & Zoo

Built in 1959, the 24-hectare national museum is one of the better ones in West Africa and well worth a visit. You'll find life-size model dwellings of the Tuareg, Hausa, Djerma, Fulani and Toubou along with life-sized models in typical dress – a quick way to train the eye for detecting the differences in ethnic groups as you travel around the country. In addition, there is a series of pavilions, each with a different theme, eg handicrafts, weapons and costumes.

The most interesting area is the artisans centre, where you can see how the various crafts are made. If you buy something that seems overpriced (usually the case), you'll at least be supporting the centre. You can also get custom-made sterling silver rings, bracelets, earrings and, most unique, toe rings, which make great souvenirs. And don't miss the famous Arbre du Ténéré; for its significance, see the section on Bilma.

The zoo is part of the museum and is depressing because of the small cages in which the animals, including hippo, crocodile, monkeys, lion, hyena, snakes and birds, are kept.

The museum and zoo are open from 8 am to noon and 4 to 6.30 pm every day except Monday, and are in the middle of town, less than a five-minute walk from the Score supermarket. Entry is free but you may be asked to donate CFA 100.

Cultural Centres

Centre Culturel Franco-Nigérien The CCFN (☎ 73 47 68) faces the northern side of the museum. The library is open to everyone (but only members can check out books) and there's a busy schedule of lectures, exhibits, dance and theatre. Programmes are available from the ticket windows, open Monday to Saturday from 9 am to 12.30 pm and 4.30 to 7.30 pm It has excellent French, American and African films almost every night at 8.30 pm; the cost is CFA 500. Consult *Le Sahel* newspaper for movies and events.

American Cultural Centre The American Cultural Centre is on Ave de Gaulle, just west of the Plateau post office. It shows CNN every day, the ABC news summary on Saturday at 10 am, movies every Wednesday, and a large variety of cultural programmes.

Niamey

0   250   500 m

Minor streets not depicted

PLACES TO STAY
1 Camping Touristique
14 Hôtel Gaweye
17 Mission Catholique
22 Hôtel Maourey
34 Hôtel Rivoli
45 Grand Hôtel
57 Hôtel Ténéré
58 Hôtel Terminus
60 Hôtel Le Sahel &
   Restaurant-Bar
   Piscine Olympic

PLACES TO EAT
2 Les Canaries &
   Food Stalls
10 Bar-Restaurant Grenier
18 Poele Blue
23 Lion D'or
24 Restaurant Caramel
25 La Cascade
26 Score Supermarket
32 Niamey Club &
   Hi-Fi Nightclub
35 Maquis 2000
36 Bar Terenga
40 L'Oriental Restaurant
44 La Réserve & Le Viet-Nam
46 Au Quatre Paillotes
47 Oasis
48 La Bamba
50 Zouzou Beri
56 Le Karami
59 Restaurant Le Tattassey
61 Le Diamangou
   Restaurant & Les
   Tropiques

OTHER
3 Benin Embassy
4 Algerian Embassy
5 Presidential Palace
6 American Cultural Centre
7 Place Nelson Mandela
8 Hospital
9 SNTN Bus Station
11 French Consulate
12 Post du Plateau
13 Centre Culturel
   Franco-Nigérien
15 Rond-Point Monteil
16 Cathedral
19 La Grande Mosquée
20 Grand Marché
21 Rond-Point Maourey
27 Ascan Bookshop
28 Sonida Garage
29 Musée National
30 Air Afrique &
   Pharmacie Nouvelle
31 BIAO Bank
33 Sûreté
37 Grande Poste
38 Sonara II Building
39 Sonara I Bldg (Air France)
41 Préfecture
42 Tourist Office (ONT)
43 Rond-Point Kennedy
49 La Grande Mosquée
51 Muslim Cemetery
52 Senegalese Consulate
53 Wadata Autogare
54 Rond-Point du
   Nouveau Marché
55 L'Ermitage
62 Clinique de Gamkallé

To Ayrou & Gao (Mali)

To Filingué

Boulevard de Mali Béro

Avenue du Canada

Avenue de Gamkallé

Route de l'Aéroport

To Airport (12 km),
Maradi & Agadez

Rue du Mali

Blvd de l'Indépendance

Gamkallé

Avenue de l'Amitié

Corniche de Gamkallé

Avenue de l'Afrique (Route de Gamkallé)

Avenue du Sahel

See Inset

Boulevard de la Liberté

Rue de Kabokoira

Rue des Écoles

Avenue de la Mairie

Niger River

Kennedy Bridge

To University
& Ouagadougou

Avenue du
Président Carsten

Avenue Mitterrand

Plateau

Avenue de Gaulle

Route de Tillabéri

Rue des Dallois

Yantala

Boulevard de La République

Corniche de Yantala

To US Embassy
(500 m), Nigerian
Embassy (1.2 km)
& Hôtel Les Rôniers

Rond-Point
Yantala

To Ayrou & Gao (Mali)

0   125   250 m

NIGER

There's also an impressive library and regular exhibitions.

Centre Culturel Oumara Ganda Situated opposite the Grand Mosque, the CCOG sponsors a variety of African cultural activities including wrestling, dancing, films by local film makers, concerts and art exhibits. Activities are frequently advertised in *Le Sahel* newspaper and posted in store windows.

Swimming
The cheapest place to swim is at the public Olympic-size pool next to Hôtel Le Sahel; the fee including dressing room is CFA 500. It's closed on Fridays. On other weekdays it's virtually empty, while on weekends it's packed.

The top five hotels also have pools, with fees ranging from CFA 500 to CFA 2000 at the Gaweye. At the Ténéré, you can use the pool for free if you buy a drink and look presentable. The pool at the Grand Hôtel is small but secluded, with a pleasant ambience. It costs CFA 1000.

Organised Tours
Boat Rides Nigercar Voyages and ONT can arrange pirogue rides along the river, to see Niamey at sunset. Rates start at about CFA 3000 per person for an hour-long trip. Or you can arrange your own trip, by going direct to the *pirogeurs* at the waterfront near the SNTN bus station. These boats only take four people in safety, but the boatmen will fit in five or more if they think they can earn extra money, so it's best to take two boats if necessary; around CFA 3000 for a boat would be very reasonable.

Places to Stay – bottom end
Camping The popular *Camping Touristique* (also called Camping Yantala; ☎ 73 42 06) is 200 metres beyond Rond-Point Yantala. It costs CFA 2000 a person plus the same for a vehicle (less for motorcycles). It's dusty and fairly unattractive with few trees, but it has reasonably clean showers and toilets. Many travellers have been robbed here and even the night-guard will tell you to lock every-

thing. Thieves always seem to know when to come and even if you're there, they can cut through a tent or mosquito net and remove your clothes without waking you.

There are no rooms but there is a cheap restaurant open throughout the day with cold beers plus sandwiches and meals. There are also plenty of stalls outside where the food is better. The price of a shared taxi into town is CFA 250 to CFA 3000, and finding one is easy.

Hostels If you meet some Peace Corps volunteers, they may invite you to stay at the *Peace Corps Hostel*, a block or two southwest of Autogare Wadata, although this is not normally open to non-volunteers. Visitors must pay a CFA 1000 overnight fee.

Open to all, and highly rated, is the safe and peaceful *Mission Catholique*, near the cathedral, on the north-western side of the city centre, in between Ave de la Mairie and Rue de Kabekoira. Clean rooms cost CFA 3000 per person and there's a kitchen for guests. In other parts of West Africa, Catholic missions have stopped accepting travellers, because the hospitality and facilities have been abused. Make sure it doesn't happen here.

There are a handful of cheap hotels in town, but they are noisy and dirty and some double as brothels.

Places to Stay – middle
For years, the ageing and noisy *Hôtel Rivoli* (☎ 73 38 49, telex 5205) has been a favourite with travellers. It's so central as to be a landmark, but you pay for the location: CFA 8100/10,100 for singles/doubles with air-con. It has decent beds but toilet facilities that are badly in need of repair.

Much better value is the *Hôtel Maourey* (☎ 73 28 50 or 73-2054), in the heart of town at Rond-Point Maourey, charging CFA 12,000/15,000 for air-con singles/doubles. It's also the only mid-range hotel that has a predominantly African clientele and ambience.

Prostitutes are also a feature at both hotels, although things are fairly low-key.

Places to Stay – top end

Niamey's finest, most impressive hotel was erected during the uranium boom. Hôtel Gaweye, well managed and part of the Sofitel chain, overlooks the Niger River and is a 10-minute walk to the centre of town.

For half the price, however, the city offers a wide range of hotels that are quite pleasant and highly recommended. The long-standing Grand Hôtel is the most popular because it is comfortable, has a pool and pleasant terrace overlooking the river and is also only a 10-minute walk from the centre. The restaurant is popular but has unimpressive meals.

A far superior deal for the money is Hôtel Les Rôniers, which has an excellent restaurant and top quality bungalows. Prices here are among the lowest of the top-end hotels because it's on the northern outskirts of town, seven km from the centre and overlooking the river. The hotel can make arrangements for you to be taken into town in the mornings if you don't have wheels.

The Hôtel Ténéré is near the centre. Part of the PLM chain, it has rooms on a par with the Grand's and a pool. It's one km south of the market in the direction of the airport, and getting a taxi is easy because it's on a main drag, Blvd de la Liberté.

A better choice for the money and convenient location is the Hôtel Terminus. Very popular with tour groups and often fully booked, it's a tranquil hotel near the centre, close to the Grand. The rooms are about as good as the Ténéré's and even the best ones are slightly less expensive. There's a jazz club on Thursdays, satellite TV, and the restaurant is outstanding.

If it's full, one option is Hôtel Le Sahel, several blocks south on the same street. It's less expensive and quite nice. The restaurant is decent and specialises in pizza, and the night-club is still one of Niamey's most popular. One problem is that it's a 15 to 20-minute walk from the centre, with few taxis in the area, which is noted for robberies. There is a decent public Olympic-size pool next door.

Gaweye Sofitel (☎ 72 34 00, fax 72 33 47, telex 5367) from CFA 60,000 to CFA 65,000 for singles and doubles, pool, tennis, TV/video in rooms, travel agency, car hire, nightclub, casino, photocopying, DHL; cards AE, D, V, MC.

Grand Hôtel (☎ 73 26 41, telex 5239) CFA 22,500/28,500 plus 5% tax for singles/doubles; pool; cards AE, D.

Hôtel Les Rôniers (☎ 72 31 38, telex 5428) CFA 15,000/18,000 for single/double bungalows, pool, tennis; cards AE, D.

Hôtel Ténéré (☎ 73 39 20 or 73 20 20 telex 5232) about CFA 15,000/18,000 for singles/doubles, pool; cards AE, D.

Hôtel Terminus (☎ 73 26 92/3, fax 73 39 74, telex 5425) CFA 23,100/27,300 including tax for singles/doubles bungalows, pool, tennis; cards AE.

Hôtel Le Sahel (☎ 73 24 31/2, telex 5330) CFA 15,000/18,000 for singles/doubles

Places to Eat

Cheap The best place for really cheap food is around the market. Street stalls and basic eating houses serve riz avec sauce (rice with sauce of meat or chicken) for around CFA 500, plus Nescafé, bread and fried-egg sandwiches in the morning until around 9.30 am and again in the evening starting around 6.30 pm. The lait caillé (milk curds) at the market takes getting used to, but with bread it makes a safe, healthy and cheap meal.

There are similar stalls out the front of the Hôtel Moustache on Ave Soni Ali Ber near the mosque with men serving Nescafé, etc. There is a good bakery around the corner and the friendly Zouzou Beri bar, which has excellent chicken curry (CFA 2000), on the same block to the south. At the Yantala camp site, there are vendors outside the gate (Nescafé, egg sandwiches, etc) and a wider variety of street food at Rond-Point Yantala, 200 metres away.

From the market, west along Rue de Kalley towards the bridge, there are a number of cheap and popular places to eat on or just off the street. On Rue Copro, between Rue de Kalley and the Hôtel Maourey, is the animated Lion d'Or. It serves food until around 10 pm and drinks until midnight or later. The ambience is 100% African – bare tables and loud music – and the food is basically steak and brochettes, plus lots of beer. On the same street is Restaurant Caramel (☎ 73 40 40), also called Pâtisserie

NIGER

Chez Michel. It has great pastries, a basic menu with omelettes, chips for CFA 400, riz sauce for CFA 600, steak for CFA 550, and a strictly enforced no smoking policy.

Just behind Hôtel Le Sahel is *Ziggy's*, a popular hang-out for Peace Corps volunteers. It's right along the river and though there's not much of a breeze, it offers a soothing view and excellent fish fillet brochettes for CFA 600. Close to the Hôtel Rivoli is *Le Croissant d'Or*, which is good for bread, pastries and snacks.

The *Niamey Club* is on the same street facing the Hôtel Rivoli. It's a rustic open-air place with shade trees that's good for drinks and food. It's also a bar and night-club, which can get lively after dark. The selections include steak au poivre, omelettes, Nile perch (capitaine) and other non-African dishes, mostly in the CFA 1500 to CFA 2000 range.

The excellent *Poêle Bleu*, on Rond-Point Liberté, has fast friendly service, and an enormous range of inexpensive meals, such as steak for CFA 1000, hamburgers for CFA 500, plus chawarmas, fries and other snacks. It's open after 6 pm.

The Gaweye is hardly cheap, but if you have a craving for pizza, at night head for *La Potinière*, the hotel's informal pool-side restaurant. It's the least expensive of this hotel's restaurants and the pizza is the best in town.

There are also several cheap places in the Petit Marché area. One is the *Restaurant Mam* on Ave Luebké across from the craft stalls. The Senegalese owner serves large portions of rice/couscous/spaghetti with chicken/beef/mutton for CFA 500 a plate.

On Blvd de la Liberté is *L'Ermitage*, which is mainly an outdoor drinking place with shade trees but it also has simple food such as brochettes and steak frites.

Highly recommended is the *Restaurant-Bar Piscine Olympic*, very near (you guessed it) the swimming pool, behind Le Sahel hotel, serving brochettes for CFA 200, and cheap meals between CFA 500 and CFA 1000. Beers are cheap too, and this is a wonderful place to watch the sunset over the Niger River.

African For good but inexpensive African food, it's hard to beat *Les Canaries* (☎ 75 25 63) on the western side of town at Rond-Point Yantala, near the camp site. The menu includes grilled fish couscous, sauce de mouton and other African specialities, plus grilled chicken and pepper steak.

Just off Rue de Maroc are some more good places. *Bar Teranga* is open from around noon to 11 pm, with a pleasant outdoor eating area under some shade trees, and rock-bottom prices, eg CFA 200 for couscous (CFA 500 with meat). Nearby is *Maquis 2000* (☎ 73 56 56), a pleasant Ivoirian-style 'maquis' (eating house), with dishes such as poisson braisé, crevette grillé, poulet citron braisé and couscous d'igname for around CFA 2500.

A few blocks to the east, on Ave de la Liberté, is *Le Karami*, an open-air bar-restaurant, serving dinner only, with good brochettes, steak and chips, and a few pasta dishes.

Also recommended is *Restaurant La Tattassey*, a few blocks south-east of the Hôtel Terminus. It has an attractive garden setting and a good menu but business seems slow. Most dishes are in the CFA 2200 to CFA 2800 range.

Near the Hôtel Terminus are three more places worth a try, all doing African and European dishes: *La Bamba*, with meals starting at CFA 1500, and *La Réserve* and *Au Quatre Paillottes* where meals are much better but more expensive, between CFA 3000 and CFA 5000.

Asian Two of Niamey's better restaurants are Vietnamese, both with dishes in the CFA 2200 to CFA 3000 range. *Le Viet-Nam* (closed Mondays) on Rue Terminus, a 15-minute walk from the Rivoli, gets slightly better reviews from local expats than the *Lotus Bleu*, a block away (closed Tuesdays). Both are open evenings only and offer a choice of dining outside on a terrace or inside with air-con.

Le Dragon d'Or, serving more Chinese food, is also good but a bit more expensive than the others. It's opposite the Grand Hôtel, with a pleasant garden setting and lots of Chinese lanterns (also inside air-con dining) and over 100 Chinese and Vietnamese selections, mostly in the CFA 2500 to CFA 3000 range. It's open every day for lunch and dinner. *Chez Chinn* on Route de Tillabéri near the Pharmacie Yantala has meals starting around CFA 3000. Try the nems and don't miss the ice cream!

Another place to check is the *Gomni-Bar* across from the Hôtel Ténéré on Blvd de la Liberté. It has inexpensive Vietnamese food and is open all day. There's a pleasant garden out the back for drinks and light snacks.

Lebanese One of Niamey's most popular restaurants for years has been *L'Oriental* (☎ 72 20 15), near Rond-Point Kennedy. It has moderately priced daily specials around CFA 1500 to CFA 2500, plus an expensive à la carte menu, with fairly small portions and prices from CFA 3000 to CFA 4000. It's open evenings every day except Wednesday.

Italian Apart from the pizzas at the Gaweye hotel, there's *Restaurant Le Pilier* (☎ 72 24 86), in the Plateau area on Rue d'Oasis between Route de Tillabéri and Ave de Gaulle. This place is highly rated, but not cheap, with meals such as ravioli starting at CFA 1500, and poisson capitaine à la Sicilienne around CFA 2500.

French Three of the top French restaurants are at hotels. The food at the Gaweye's *La Croix du Sud* (closed Sunday), the Terminus' *Toukounia* (closed Monday) and *Hôtel Les Rôniers* is about as good as you'll find anywhere. The restaurant at the Rôniers is slightly less expensive and is the only one open at lunchtime. If you go on a Wednesday or Saturday night, you can eat fresh mussels and snails from France. However, if you don't have wheels, forget it.

For something less formal try *Le Diamangou* (☎ 73 51 43; also known as Le Bateau, because it has its own boat moored alongside, where some guests dine), along the Corniche road, about 1.5 km south of Kennedy Bridge; or *Bar-Restaurant Grenier* (☎ 73 32 62) north of the bridge near the SNTN station. Both are open evenings only

and are fairly expensive. Their main attraction is a pleasant setting overlooking the river, although the food, mainly French and Continental, is good. The Diamangou also serves African food, although service can be painfully slow.

Another possibility is *La Cascade*, in the heart of town a block from the Score supermarket. The food is quite good and the owners are very friendly but prices are on the high side.

The *Oasis*, near the Hôtel Terminus, is a bit shabby but has excellent meals with a French/European flavour, such as steak and beef stroganoff, for around CFA 1500 to CFA 3500.

Closer to the bridge is the *Damsi* in the Sonara I building. It's far from cheap but has good hamburgers, sandwiches, milkshakes and expensive French meals, particularly the capitaine basilique, which is outstanding. Service is usually quick except on Sunday evenings.

Entertainment

Bars The bar at the *Hôtel Rivoli* has for years been the most popular watering hole for foreigners. It's an excellent place for meeting other travellers, but its central location is the attraction, not the relatively expensive drinks. Much better is the lively *Niamey Club* opposite the Rivoli, which is good for cheap drinks, popular with foreigners and locals, and occasionally has live music at night.

The *Gas Camel*, south-west of Restaurant Le Viet-Nam, is a great place to go for live music. It features a blues band on the weekends and a good mix of people, but you'll have to wait until around midnight for it to get really lively.

For a bar with a rustic African feel and a central location, it's hard to beat the lively open-air *Lion d'Or*, between Rue de Kalley and the Hôtel Maourey. Still another is *Le Rendez-Vous Restaurant*, near the stadium and the Mercedes dealership.

The pool-side terrace at the *Grand Hôtel* provides the best views over the river, plus you can buy inexpensive brochettes and other snacks. Views from the Gaweye are obstructed and drinks very expensive. The

NIGER

views are just as good, though the ambience is less formal and the beers are cheaper at the *Restaurant-Bar Piscine Olympic*, listed under Places to Eat above.

Another place for a beer at sundown on the riverside is *Le Diamangou* (also listed under Places to Eat).

Nightclubs A long-time favourite is the rustic and breezy *Niamey Club*. Other good places include *L'Ermitage*, on Blvd de la Liberté two blocks beyond the Hôtel Ténéré, which has a huge beer garden and also serves brochettes and other inexpensive food. The clientele is almost entirely African, and the dancing, which starts around 10 pm and continues to around 3 am, is accompanied by a live band except on Sunday. Admission costs CFA 500. *Le Flamboyant*, across from the Hôtel Ténéré, is similar. The smarter *Les Tropiques* (☎ 73 31 04), next to Le Diamangou, is open-air with decent music, and drinks that are only slightly more expensive than at the Grand Hôtel.

For a really fancy disco, try the *Fofo Club* at Hôtel Le Sahel. Open only on weekends, it has an interesting décor. Three other discos in the centre are the old-style, mirrored-wall *Hi-Fi Club*, a stone's throw west of the Hôtel Rivoli, *Le Satellite*, a block away in the El-Nasr building, and *Kakaki*, two blocks away at the Gaweye.

All of these places (except Club Niamey) have similar prices (usually CFA 1500 to CFA 2000 for the cover charge which includes a drink) but are only open (or worth going to) at weekends.

If you're looking for an inexpensive place with local feel, head for *Akalan*, between the stadium and Blvd de la Liberté, a strobe-lit nightclub with cover/drinks for only CFA 500. The music is a mixture of African and Western. Open every night, it's a respectable place and livens up around midnight.

Cinemas The air-con *Studio* cinema, in the centre on the street behind Score, is the best in town. The *Vox* is a block away and worth checking too. Films are also shown at the *Centre Culturel Franco-Nigérien*, and at the *American Cultural Centre* which has freezing air-con and free films weekly in the afternoon.

Wrestling On some Sundays, you may have the opportunity to see African-style wrestling matches at *Le Stade de la Lutte Traditionelle*, an arena with a covered viewing stand a block from the new autogare on the same street, three km west of the Grand Marché. The crowds are very enthusiastic and the matches are definitely worth seeing. In one afternoon you'll see about 30 matches, each usually lasting one to six minutes. The men employ lots of ritualistic hand movements, trying to get both knees of the opponent on the ground. After each match, the winner prances around the arena as people toss him money. Consult *Le Sahel* newspaper for details of events.

Horse Racing Races are held almost every Sunday from 3 to 5 pm at the *Hippodrome* out near the airport.

Things to Buy
Artisan Goods At the Grand Marché there's an amazingly wide selection of products, enough to keep you busy for hours, including Tuareg and Hausa leather work, silver jewellery, imported goods from Europe and China, clothing, crafts, batiks and tie-dye cloth. What's truly spectacular are *les couvertures Djerma* – large bright strips of cotton partially sewn together which make great wall hangings and are unique to Niger.

Other markets include Marché Wadata, near the autogare, although this has a less extensive selection, or the nearby (and well-signposted) Co-operative Village Artisanal, which has a very wide range of high-quality merchandise, such as leather, carvings, cloth, paintings and jewellery, at reasonable prices. Outside the hall are 50 or more busy but friendly craft-workers, so you can see the stuff being made on the spot. Another attraction is the complete absence of hustlers and touts.

Along Ave Luebké between the Hôtel Rivoli and Score supermarket, there's a long row of artisan stalls with fabric, leather work, blankets, swords, calabash bowls, silver jewellery and unusual necklaces, some with the famous cross of Agadez. The museum nearby has a shop and workshops where you can see artisans working. The shop has fixed prices whereas bargaining is possible with the artisans.

Music Cassettes of local and Western music (originals and bootlegs) can be bought from several of the stalls in the Grand Marché, where you can also get tape-to-tape recording done (buy blanks here too, or bring your own). Other places to try include Le Chant du Monde at Rond-Point Maourey. It has an extensive selection and is open from 8.30 am to 1 pm and 4 to 9 pm. They are also involved in recording local groups and traditional artists and have copies of their recordings for sale. They also know where local bands are likely to be performing. Even better is Nous Les Jeunes, a block north of Photo Guida, where the friendly manager will help you choose some of today's most popular music artists. He has a large selection and will play samples for you. It's open Monday to Saturday from 8.30 am to 1 pm and 4.30 to 11.30 pm.

Niger has numerous traditional musicians but few noted performers of Sahelian pop music. Some of the leading modern groups/singers are Les Ambassadeurs du Sahel, Orchestre Assocé and Mamaré Garba.

Getting There & Away

Air Airlines with offices in Niamey include: Air Afrique (☎ 73 30 11, ☎/fax 73 33 75 at the airport), 3 Ave de Pont Luebké; Air France (☎ 73 31 61, fax 73 55 83), in the Sonara building I; Royal Air Maroc (☎ 73 28 85 or 73 28 53), Ethiopian Airlines (☎ 73 55 52), and Nigeria Airways, all in the El-Nasr building; and Air Algérie (☎ 73 30 11) nearby in the Hôtel Rivoli building.

Bus The SNTN bus station (☎ 72 30 20) is on the Corniche Yantala river road, north of the Kennedy Bridge. The ticket office is open weekdays from 7.30 am to 12.30 pm and 3.30 to 6.30 pm, Saturday from 8 to 9 am and Sunday from 8 am to noon. Schedules are constantly changing, and some services temporarily suspended by the Tuareg rebellion, so always enquire about current departure times and days.

SNTN has two buses a week to each of the following destinations. Prices (in CFA) are for one-way fares.

destination	cost
Arlit	21,150
Agadez	17,650
Tahoua	10,750
Zinder	14,350
Maradi	10,850
Birnin-Konni	7950

Large private buses leave from the autogare in the Wadata area on the east side of the city centre. If you ask for directions, note that it's called the autogare, as opposed to gare routière. In fact, its full name seems to be ECO-Autogare Wadata. Private buses are about 20% cheaper than the SNTN buses and serve most of the same towns, but can be slower and have more breakdowns. And whereas SNTN buses leave punctually early in the morning, private buses don't leave until they fill up, frequently not before noon.

Bush Taxi There are bush taxis to all the major towns. Most of them leave from Autogare Wadata on the eastern side of the city centre. Generally speaking they are slower than buses.

Bush taxis to Gaya are frequent because there are few large buses on this route. The 504s charge CFA 4500, and minibuses cost CFA 3500 (a four to six-hour trip). If you do this trip in stages, Niamey to Dosso costs CFA 1850, and Dosso to Gaya is CFA 2500.

To Birnin-Konni, 504s charge CFA 5000 and minibuses CFA 4000 (although by minibus this trip can easily take up to nine hours). To Tahoua, minibuses cost CFA 7700 and can take up to 14 hours!

Bush taxis are also popular on the route between Niamey and the Burkina Faso border. The 130-km trip takes about two hours and costs about CFA 1500 (or CFA 2500 between Niamey and Kantchari). Bush taxis on this route leave Niamey from a small gare routière just west of Kennedy Bridge.

Getting Around

To/From the Airport A taxi from the airport to Niamey city centre (12 km) costs between CFA 3000 and CFA 4000, depending on your bargaining powers and the time of day. It may be cheaper the other way. Luggage is extra. If you fly into Niamey and have no CFA (the airport bank is usually closed), you can pay for the taxi with French francs cash.

No buses serve the airport, but shared taxis run along the highway nearby; a seat costs CFA 500 into the centre.

At the airport you may also see hotel buses waiting to pick up guests from flights. You can get a ride for a price somewhere between the shared and private taxi rate if you speak to the driver. There's often also a member of the hotel staff on the bus with whom you can bargain for room prices.

Taxi Taxis around town don't have meters and are mostly shared, following set routes. Since it is rarely obvious where they're headed, the system is a bit confusing. You'll probably find that none are headed to exactly where you're going, so you'll have to take a taxi for part of the distance, then hop another or walk part of the way. If you wait for another cab, hoping it'll go closer to your destination, you'll probably be wasting your time. Fares for shared taxis are around CFA 200 per 'stage' (about 2.5 km), and this rate doubles at night.

A taxi to yourself *(déplacement)* will cost about CFA 1000 to CFA 1500 for a short ride across town, say from the centre to the Wadata Autogare, or about CFA 2500 by the hour and CFA 18,000 plus petrol by the day. You can find them at the Grand Marché, the Petit Marché and at the big hotels (although they charge higher rates). Around 10 pm, the taxis turn into pumpkins and are nowhere to be found, even at the Gaweye, unless you have arranged to be picked up.

Car The major car rental agency is Nigercar (☎ 73 23 31, telex 5327; cards AE, D, MC), with offices at the Gaweye hotel and at the airport. For its smallest car, a Toyota Starlet without air-con, Nigercar charges CFA 11,685 a day, plus CFA 1700 per day insurance, plus CFA 120 per km, plus tax (about 20%). This can only be used around town.

Outside Niamey, the cheapest car is a Toyota Corolla, which costs CFA 13,740 per day, plus CFA 1700 insurance, plus CFA 130 per km, plus obligatory chauffeur (at CFA 5750 a day) plus tax. This comes to almost CFA 50,000 a day plus petrol if you average 200 km a day. Air-con costs CFA 2700 a day extra. All other rental companies closed in the early 1990s, but some may re-open in the future.

One of the best garages for vehicle repair is Sonida (VW, Peugeot; ☎ 73 30 81) on Ave de la Mairie (the eastward extension of Ave du Général de Gaulle), opposite the BIAO bank. Others include Agence Centrale (Toyota) or Niger Afrique (Renault).

AROUND NIAMEY

Boubon

Boubon is 25 km north of Niamey on the paved road to Tillabéri. If you have your own wheels (and most of the people who stop here do) it's a 30-minute drive. It's west of the road a bit and easy to miss; look for the small sign.

The best time to come here is on Wednesday, when there's a marvellous market. But even more attractive is simply being so close to the Niger River. You can hire a *pirogue* (canoe) for a trip along the river, observing people as they go about their daily tasks. During the rice harvest season, November to January, you may see farmers in their pirogues paddling around, cutting down the 'floating' rice with their machetes. Most visitors, however, come just for a meal at the outdoor restaurant on the small island 200 metres from the village (you'll find someone with a pirogue to take you over).

While you're here, check out the clay pots in the village; this is one of the major pottery centres in Niger.

Places to Stay & Eat *Le Campement Tour-*

istique (☎ 73 24 27) is on the island and open year-round. It has a restaurant, a clean pool in good working order and eight new thatched-roof cabins for about CFA 2500. Although you can get a meal any day of the week, you're unlikely to find other guests except on Wednesday, which is market day, or on Sunday when expats from Niamey come here for lunch; things can be lively then. The capitaine fish here is excellent, and on Sunday you'll probably be entertained by a group of young drummers.

Namaro

About 30 km north of Boubon on the Tillabéri road, you come to a sign pointing to the *Complexe Touristique de Namaro* (☎ 73 21 13), a fairly popular weekend spot for expats wanting to escape Niamey. The complex is on the west side of the river on a hill overlooking the village, but it's easy to find a pirogue to take you across. Simple cabins with double beds, air-con and filthy toilets are about CFA 8000 to CFA 10,000 (CFA 12,000 to CFA 16,000 for rooms with four beds). There's also a fairly decent bar-restaurant, pool, ping-pong and games room.

From October to May it's open daily; December to February is the most popular period. From June to September it's less active and open only on weekends.

To get there you should be able to get a taxi from Niamey to drop you off there for CFA 4000 plus 10 litres of petrol. The hotel also has a bus for those needing transportation. To get back to Niamey, you might be able to hitch a ride with another guest.

Kollo

Kollo is about 40 km south-east of Niamey, on the east bank of the River Niger, linked to the capital by a good tarmac road. It's a good place to visit if you want to see life in a village near Niamey that isn't a weekend spot for expats. The day to come here is Friday, which is market day. The market isn't large but it is lively and colourful, with local people from various tribes dressed in their traditional garb. You'll probably be the only foreigner here.

Say

Say is south of Kollo, on the west bank of the Niger River, 60 km from Niamey. During the first or second weekend in December, there's an interesting festival here. Friday is market day.

West & North of Niamey

From Niamey, one main road leads northwest, alongside the Niger River, towards Gao and the Mali border. Beyond the villages of Boubon and Namaro are the larger settlements of Tillabéri and Ayorou, which see very few visitors except those hurrying to and from Gao. Even less frequently visited is Téra, some 100 km west of the river, on the 'back road' to Burkina Faso. The landscape and atmosphere is different here to the rest of the country, and that alone might be reason enough to come.

TILLABÉRI

On the way to Ayorou, Tillabéri (also spelt Tillabéry) is one of Niger's biggest rice growing areas. Sunday is market day. If you're driving to Mali, get your passport stamped here. You might also enquire about the local giraffe herd, which hangs out along the river bank, usually several km south of Tillabéri, during the dry season. These are the last giraffes living wild in West Africa. Ask the local kids; they'll take you to where they were last spotted.

Places to Stay & Eat

The 15-room *Relais Touristique* is along the river on the northern side of town. It has a restaurant and charges CFA 1500 a person for camping and about CFA 5500/6500 for singles/doubles with fans (CFA 1000 more with air-con).

AYOROU

The major attraction of Ayorou (ah-you-rou) is the famous livestock **market** (for cattle, camels, sheep and goats) held here every Sunday. It is particularly vibrant from

November to April. It's the people who make this an unforgettable place: you'll see Africans of various ethnic groups – including Tuareg, Peul, Bella, and Moors – all wearing their best garb, including elaborate head gear, swords and costumes. The market doesn't really warm up until around noon, so if you're there in the morning, go to the river to watch the cattle swimming across.

And leave time afterwards to take a trip on the river. You can rent pirogues in Ayorou or, cheaper, in **Firgoun**, a small, rarely visited fishing village 11 km to the north. Around CFA 3000 for the boat is a fair price. At Firgoun, you're virtually guaranteed to see hippo – the piroguers know where.

Places to Stay & Eat
Le Campement has some dirt-cheap huts where you can sleep on the floor, or you may find lodging with a local. For an inexpensive meal try *Restaurant à la Pirogue*, run by a local Tuareg. Otherwise bring some food with you, as there's little in town, especially if you're not here on a Sunday.

At the other end of the scale, you can stay at the *Hôtel Amenokal* on the riverbank. This good hotel has a pool, bar, restaurant and 24 air-con singles/doubles for CFA 13,000/19,000 on weekdays and CFA 18,000/26,000 on weekends. It's open only from November to April. You can reserve through Nigercar Voyages (☎ 73 23 31) in Niamey.

Getting There & Away
Ayorou is served by the SNTN bus running between Niamey and Gao, and by minibus bush taxis from Niamey which cost CFA 3200 each way. If you're hitching, either to Gao or Niamey, tie in your visit with the market: the best time to reach Ayorou is Saturday, and the best time to leave is Sunday or Monday.

If you have a car, or can rent one for the day, Ayorou is an interesting one-day excursion from Niamey and highly recommended during the dry season. Driving takes three hours each way. From July to September, the 88-km unpaved stretch north of Tillabéri

becomes muddy, increasing the total Niamey to Ayorou drive (208 km) by an hour or more.

TÉRA
Some 175 km north-west of Niamey, Téra receives few visitors. Those that do come here are on their way to/from Ouagadougou on the alternate route via Dori, 90 km to the west in Burkina Faso. The market is next to the autogare and is used only on Thursday. Be sure to get your passport stamped by the police; they'll try to keep it until you leave but if you stay and chat for a while, they may give it back.

Places to Stay & Eat
The only place is the *Campement de Téra*, which charges about CFA 1200 per person for a big room. It has no running water or electricity, but the friendly manager provides kerosene lanterns and buckets of water. You can also get warm beers and soft drinks and relatively expensive meals here. For colder drinks and better food, try the bar-restaurant on the other side of town. There are also some street stalls on the main drag.

Getting There & Away
Private buses from Niamey charge about CFA 2500; the trip takes eight hours or more, depending on the delay with the ferry crossing at Farié. You can also take a SNTN bus every Wednesday and Saturday; the fare is about 50% more.

If you're heading on to Burkina, the road from Téra to Dori is in bad condition and best attempted only in the dry season. During the rainy season vehicles are very scarce and getting stuck is probable. The total driving time to Dori in the dry season is only five hours, but the trip can easily take several days as vehicles are so scarce. Regardless, those without vehicles usually walk the 10 km from the last village, Fono, to the first village in Burkina Faso. At villages along the way, the people will usually find you a place to stay.

FILINGUÉ
Filingué is 185 km north-east of Niamey by paved road, and another interesting place for

an excursion (easily possible in one day if you have wheels). The market on Sunday is surprisingly active for such a small town. Inhabited primarily by Fulani and Songhai-Zarma, with examples of traditional architecture, it's at the base of a hill which you can climb to get an excellent view of the town and the Dallol Bosso, the valley of a dried-up river.

If you come on a Sunday, don't fail to stop in **Baleyara**, roughly halfway to Filingué. It too has a very picturesque market on that day under a canopy of neem trees, and the animal bartering, which takes place on the town side of the market, is particularly interesting.

Places to Stay
In Filingué, the *Campement* is on your right as you enter town from Niamey, next to the military fort. Singles cost about CFA 3000 and the beds are big enough for two people. There's also a shower but no fans.

Getting There & Away
Bush taxis for Filingué leave from the Wadata Autogare in Niamey every day in the early morning. The cost is CFA 2500.

The South

Niger's main arterial road leads from Niamey eastward along the bottom edge of the country, skirting Nigeria and aiming towards Chad, passing through several major towns and cities. The strip of territory along this road has been loosely termed the south, and the towns are listed here in order of distance from Niamey.

DOSSO
Some 140 km south-east of Niamey, Dosso is the first major settlement reached on the main road through the south. The name comes from 'Do-So', a Djerma spirit; this was once an important Islamic centre and the home of the Djermakoye, the most important Djerma religious leader (his Sudanese-style compound can be visited with permission). Today Dosso is a crossroad town, as the main road south to Benin and western Nigeria branches off here.

If you're in Niger on 3 August, come to

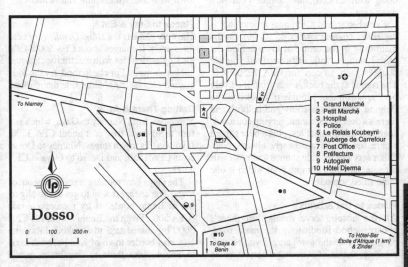

1 Grand Marché
2 Petit Marché
3 Hospital
4 Police
5 Le Relais Koubeyni
6 Auberge de Carrefour
7 Post Office
8 Préfecture
9 Autogare
10 Hôtel Djerma

To Niamey

Dosso

0   100   200 m

To Gaya &
Benin

To Hôtel-Bar
Étoile d'Afrique (1 km)
& Zinder

Dosso to celebrate the country's annual Republic Day celebration. There's a famous cavalry parade where the riders dress in outstanding finery, with colourful cotton quilts (once used to conceal weapons) and elaborate feathered headpieces for both the men and the horses.

Places to Stay

The cheapest place to stay in Dosso (and possibly in the whole of Niger) is the *Hôtel-Bar Étoile d'Afrique* on the road to Birnin-Konni, on the edge of town between one and two km from the autogare. It's cheap because the rooms are small and dirty with no fans. But what do you want for CFA 1000? As well as the bar, there's a basic restaurant serving cheap brochettes, and loud music. Only slightly better is *Le Relais Koubeyni*, signposted just off the Niamey road on the edge of the town centre, with basic grubby rooms with fans for CFA 3200, and a cheap restaurant.

Up again in quality is the newly renovated and good value *Auberge du Carrefour* (☎ 65 00 17), well situated on the right as you enter town from Niamey, not far from the autogare, with doubles for CFA 4500 (CFA 6000 with air-con), and a nice courtyard restaurant.

Even better, and also under renovation, is the *Hôtel Djerma* (☎/fax 65 02 06), on the main drag in the centre of town behind the Mobil station, with self-contained singles/doubles with air-con for CFA 7950/8950. The rooms at the back, away from the lively bar, are quieter. Monsieur Markito, the Belgian owner, is friendly and helpful, and there's a decent restaurant, serving couscous, spaghetti and steak frites, plus a beer garden where the drinks are nearly always cold. Other services include stamps and postcards for sale, and a swimming pool which is due to be filled someday...

Places to Eat & Drink

All the hotels serve meals, but there's cheaper good food along the main road, particularly at the autogare. If you're self-catering, the *Mini-Bazaar* grocery store on the main east-west drag sells yoghurt, milk, butter, coffee, jam, etc.

Near the Grand Marché is *Chez Rita* where the meals are good and cheap, but star attraction is Rita herself. You can't miss the four nearly poster-size photos of her on the walls.

There's also *Sous la Palmière*, which offers cheap rice and sauce, steak, fried fish, chips and green peas; most dishes are in the CFA 900 to CFA 1200 range.

For a drink try *La Dossolaise*, near the Étoile d'Afrique, or the bar at the *Jardin Publique*; both serve cheap beers in unpretentious surroundings.

Getting There & Away

Dosso sits at the junction of the main roads between Niamey and Zinder, and the main road south to Gaya (for Benin and Nigeria), so there's always plenty of bush taxis. Minibuses to/from Gaya cost CFA 2500 and to/from Niamey CFA 1850.

GAYA

Gaya is the only border town for Benin and one of four major ones for Nigeria. Most travellers cross the border as quickly as possible, and move on, but Gaya is a nice little town with some interesting Hausa houses.

Places to Stay & Eat

The only place is the *Hôtel Dendi*, very near the market. It charges about CFA 3000/4500 for singles/doubles with electricity, fans and bucket showers. For cheap food, try the *Restaurant La Joie d'Été* alongside the market.

Getting There & Away

Minibuses from Niamey to Gaya, which is a four to six-hour trip, cost about CFA 3500. If you do this trip in stages, Niamey to Dosso costs CFA 1850, and Dosso to Gaya is CFA 2500.

The Gaya gare routière is some way out of town. The cheapest way to get to the Nigerian or Benin border is by motorcycle-taxi (CFA 500). From the Benin border it's CFA 3000 by shared taxi to Parakou. From the Nigerian border town of Kamba, bush taxis to Sokoto take three to five hours, while minibuses to Niamey take four to six hours and charge CFA 3000.

W NATIONAL PARK

The Parc National du W, or Parc W for short, is on the western bank of the Niger River in an area of dry savannah woodland, a transition zone between the Sahel and moister savannahs to the south. The W (pronounced dou-blay-vay) in the name comes from the double bend in the Niger River at the park's northern border. The park actually straddles the territory of three countries: Niger, Benin and Burkina Faso, although most people

only visit the Niger section as it's the easiest to reach.

It's one of the better game parks in West Africa, with a wide variety of carnivores including lion, leopard, cheetah, hyena and jackal. Other animals you might see are elephant, crocodile, hippo, buffalo, antelope, duiker, baboon and wart hog, as well as a wide assortment of birds. Migratory aquatic birds arrive between February and May. While the variety of game is large, their total numbers are very small except for the antelope. Elephants number around 100 or less. The best viewing time is towards the end of

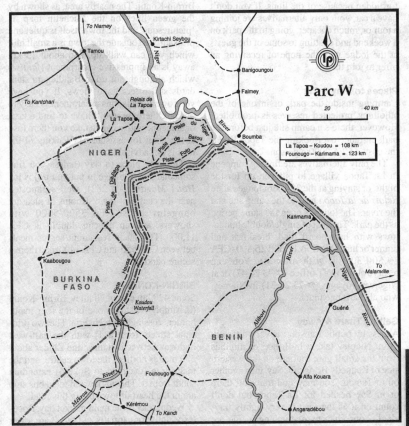

the dry season (ie March to May) when the animals are desperate for water and congregate around the water holes, especially at the crack of dawn and in the late afternoon. This is also the time of year when the park is most barren-looking. In the dry season, one of the favoured haunts of the park's elephants is the river near the park lodge.

The park is open from 1 December to late May, and the entrance is at La Tapoa, 145 km south of Niamey. The entrance fee is CFA 3500, and a map is available. A guide costs CFA 3000 to CFA 5000.

The only way in is by car. Motorcycles are not allowed, and walking around the park is forbidden because of the lions. If you don't have a car, your only alternatives are joining a tour or, much cheaper, going to the park on a weekend and chatting to some of the guests at the lodge with the hope of receiving an offer to join them.

Places to Stay & Eat

Camping inside the park or in one of the adjoining protected reserves is prohibited. However, there's a camp site just before the park entrance overlooking the Tapoa River; the cost is CFA 2000 a person.

The only alternatives are finding someone in La Tapoa village to put you up for the night, or staying at the 35-room lodge called *Relais de la Tapoa* next to the camp site and the river. The lodge is open the same period as the park. The cost of single/double bungalows with half board (bed, breakfast and dinner or lunch) is CFA 17,000/26,800 (CFA 19,500/30,500 with air-con). You can reserve at the ONT office (☎ 73 24 47) or at Nigercar Voyages (☎ 73 23 31) in Niamey, who also arrange tours.

Getting There & Away

Access by public transport is very difficult. From Niamey take a bush taxi or minibus from the small gare routière on the western side of Kennedy Bridge for Say, then another on to Tamou. You may find transport there or in Say headed for La Tapoa but don't count on it as the road is very lightly travelled. Your chances of hitching a ride are

much better on weekends, but be prepared to walk the 4.7 km from Tamou to the lodge.

If you're going by car, from Niamey take the conversation-stopping washboard road south to Say (50 km) and on to Tamou (55 km) at the Burkina Faso border, then 40 km further south to La Tapoa. The driving time is about two to three hours.

Most people without cars arrange tours with Nigercar Voyages or through the ONT (see above).

DOGONDOUTCHI

Dogondoutchi is a small town on the main road, about halfway between Dosso and Birnin-Konni. The nearby area, as shown by the green lines on the Michelin map, is 'picturesque' and the town itself is quiet and pleasant. Just outside the town is a small hill, which you can walk up, and about 15 km away is an impressive escarpment (*falaise*) which although not up to Bandiagara standards still offers good views. If you have your own wheels, this escarpment is easy to reach. Otherwise you'll have to find a taxi, or someone with a car, to take you there (ask at the hotel for assistance). Walking in the heat is not advisable.

The only place to stay (unless you find someone in the village to put you up) is the *Hôtel Magama* (☎ 282), well signposted near the centre of town. Rooms in pleasant bungalows cost CFA 3500/5000 with showers, and an air-con double is CFA 11,000. The shady restaurant serves meals between CFA 650 and CFA 1400, and there's secure parking.

BIRNIN-KONNI

Some 420 km east of Niamey, Birnin-Konni (or simply Konni) is one of the four major border crossings with Nigeria. The two principal streets form a T, with the east-west highway between Niamey and Zinder about 500 metres north of the town centre, and the main drag (the road to Sokoto) extending south from it. The market and main bus stop are in the heart of town along this road.

Wednesday is the main market day. Prices (especially for car parts and tyres) are lower here because cheap goods are smuggled in from Nigeria. You can also buy black market petrol, plus mineral water and Coke in large plastic bottles. The bank has closed, but moneychangers are everywhere, mostly offering good rates. (Which is probably why the bank closed.)

Places to Stay & Eat

There's a friendly *Relais-Camping Touristique* (☎ 208) on the western outskirts of town on the Niamey road, about two km from the centre. The sign is much easier to see when you're coming out of Konni. Double rooms with fans cost between CFA 3500 and CFA 5200, and camping is CFA 1500 per person plus CFA 1000 per vehicle.

In the centre of town on the main north-south drag is the *Hôtel Wadata*. They used to have basic rooms for about CFA 1500 but latest reports indicate this place is closed, although it might be worth trying in case business picks up again.

About 100 metres further north at the city's main intersection is *Le Campement*, behind the Gazelle nightclub sign, with aggressive prostitutes and depressing rooms with fans and showers, at CFA 3500 a double. The market is nearby and good for finding street food.

The *Hôtel Kado* (☎ 364), across the street at the same intersection, is the best hotel and has friendly helpful staff. It's an attractive place with air-con singles/doubles at CFA 8100/9500, and singles with fans at CFA 5700, which can be shared by couples. All rooms are self-contained. The mosquitoes come free. The shady restaurant is the best in town, with tables where you can put your feet in the sand, although meals are on the expensive side.

Getting There & Away

The SNTN bus to Zinder, which departs Niamey twice weekly, charges CFA 7950 from Niamey to Konni. Between Zinder and Konni it costs CFA 8500. There are also large private buses from Niamey to Konni every day; they charge about CFA 6000 but are slower. Cheaper still, but even slower (up to nine hours), are 504 bush taxis from Niamey to Konni for CFA 5000 (or CFA 4000 for a minibus).

TAHOUA

Tahoua, 122 km north of Konni, is the country's fourth-largest city and a major stop on the Niamey-Agadez road. The main attraction is the market, which is quite large and lively. Market day (Sunday) attracts a big crowd from outlying areas. For changing money, the BIAO bank usually accepts travellers' cheques (although don't count on it) charging a 2% commission on travellers' cheques in all currencies, including French francs.

The police may stamp your passport as you're entering town. This is no longer required but if you're travelling in your own vehicle instead of by public transport, getting your passport stamped would be wise so as to prevent hassles down the road.

Worth a visit is the new Centre Artisanal

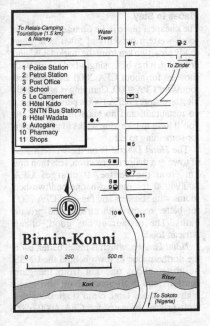

To Relais-Camping Touristique (1.5 km) & Niamey
Water Tower
★1
✉2
To Zinder
✉3
●4
■5
6■
◎7
8■
9⏾
10● ●11

1 Police Station
2 Petrol Station
3 Post Office
4 School
5 Le Campement
6 Hôtel Kado
7 SNTN Bus Station
8 Hôtel Wadata
9 Autogare
10 Pharmacy
11 Shops

Birnin-Konni

0   250   500 m

Kori

River

To Sokoto (Nigeria)

in the town centre, particularly good for Tuareg jewellery. A recommended trader is Ghissa (pronounced Risa) Habibou.

Places to Stay & Eat

The *Camping Touristique* on the north-western outskirts of town charges CFA 1500 per person for camping. If you want a room, go to the *Hôtel Galabi Ader*, north-west of the autogare, where air-con doubles cost CFA 7500, or CFA 5000 with a fan. There's also a restaurant and bar, and a safe and well-shaded camp site for CFA 1200 per person, plus CFA 500 per car.

The city's top hotel is *Les Bungalows de la Mairie* (☎ 61 05 53) across from the Mairie (mayor's office). It has air-con bungalow rooms for around CFA 8400 and a restaurant which serves good-value Continental food.

Also worth checking is the clean and well run *Hôtel L'Amitié* (also known as Le Galaxy – the attached nightclub; ☎ 61 01 53) on the main highway, 200 metres past the SNTN bus station on the way out of town towards the Niamey-Agadez fork. It charges around CFA 8000 for air-con rooms, and there's a friendly bar and restaurant with meals from CFA 1500. You can also camp for CFA 1500 a person but there's no shade.

For snacks and drinks, the best place is the shady *Jardin Publique* in town. For traditional African food, head for the popular *Chez Fatima* at the roundabout just east of the BIAO bank. Fatima is extremely popular and everyone knows her.

The airport has a small bar-restaurant that is busy primarily in the evenings.

Getting There & Away

The SNTN buses between Niamey and Agadez stop here, twice weekly. The fare between Tahoua and Niamey is CFA 10,750. Bush taxis to/from Niamey charge CFA 7700 and if you choose a decrepit one, the trip can easily take 14 hours.

MARADI

With a population of about 60,000, Maradi is the country's third-largest city. It was destroyed by floods in 1945 but rebuilt on higher ground. Outside of Niamey it remains the administrative capital and commercial centre for agriculture. It used to be the country's peanut capital but production in Niger has fallen drastically, leaving Maradi with only one operating oil press.

To change money, try the BIAO bank on the main drag in the centre; as everywhere in Niger, commissions on travellers' cheques are outrageously high. For black market naira, try the gare routière two blocks away.

Don't miss the **market**; it's in the heart of town on the main north-south drag. Cheap Nigerian goods are smuggled across the nearby border, which is the main reason the market is so active, especially on Monday and Friday, the main market days. Good buys are the Hausa blankets and Fulani cloth.

Also check the **Maison des Chefs** which is a fine example of Hausa architecture with traditional geometric designs. It's at Place Dan Kasswa on the western side of town, one km from the centre.

Places to Stay

The cheapest place is *Le Campement* on the south-western outskirts of town in a green shady area, two km from the market. Old and decaying, it has basic single-bed rooms with showers for about CFA 2000 and twin-bed rooms for CFA 4000. Camping is also possible; the charge is CFA 1000 a person. There's no restaurant, and no taxis in the area, so you'll have to take long walks to get to town for something to eat.

The *Hôtel Liberté* is on the western side of town at a major intersection, less than one km from the centre. It charges CFA 3000/4000 for run-down one-bed/two-bed rooms with showers and fans and CFA 7000 for better rooms with air-con and private baths. The restaurant has good, cheap African food.

Hôtel Larewa, which is much better, is on the northern side of town behind the CNSS building, about one km from the gare routière and well marked on the main highway. It has large clean singles/doubles with private showers for CFA 4000/6500

PLACES TO STAY
10 Hôtel Jangorzo
13 Hôtel Liberté
17 Le Campement

PLACES TO EAT
7 Supermarket
9 Berolina Bar &
  Restaurant
14 Chez Naoum

OTHER
1 Hirondelle Bar
2 Gare Routière
3 BIAO Bank
4 Sûreté
5 Market
6 Sonibank
8 SNTN Bus Depot
11 Ludo Club Nightclub
12 Pacific Bar
15 Hospital
16 Post Office

Maradi

0   100   200 m

To Hôtel Larewa (800 m),
Niamey & Zinder

Rue de la Sûreté

Route de l'Aéroport

To Airport

Rue de l'Hôtel

Race-
course

To Kano
(Nigeria)

NIGER

(plus an extra CFA 1000 for air-con), secure
parking and a restaurant. If it's full, enquire
about the *Hôtel Niger*, which is reportedly
better but costs twice as much.

The sprawling *Hôtel Jangorzo* (☎ 41 01
40, telex 8235), on the eastern side of town
on the Route de l'Aéroport, half a km from
the centre, is the nicest hotel but the standards here are slipping. Air-con singles/
doubles cost CFA 12,000/13,500 (smaller
rooms cost CFA 6000) but the plumbing is
not the best. If the hotel seems fairly empty,
bargaining down the price may be feasible.
On the plus side, the atmosphere is quite
pleasant, especially if there are numerous
guests, and the hotel's Palace Bawa Jangorzo
Nightclub is the hottest place in town on
Friday and Saturday nights. The three-
course menu costs CFA 3000, and breakfast
is CFA 1000.

Places to Eat & Drink
At night you'll find delicious grilled chicken

and other snacks on the streets at the Jardin
Publique (public gardens) facing the south-
western corner of the market. Another place
where the chicken is excellent is the Lebanese-run *Chez Naoum*, one of the city's
better known restaurants, about one km
south-west of the centre, several blocks
south of the Hôtel Liberté; meals are around
CFA 1500. If you'd prefer an attractive place
with a relaxing ambience, try the new well-
marked *Relais Saharien* (☎ 41 02 48) at the
western entrance to town. Guests dine under
paillotes and the food is good.

For cheap food in the centre, head for *Le
Cercle de l'Amitié* on the main drag, 200
metres north of the gare routière; it's tranquil
and not expensive. Another possibility is the
Hirondelle Bar (☎ 41 00 85) facing Cinéma
Dan Kassawa on the northern side of town,
though it's mainly for drinking. Also worth
a try is *Berolina*, a garden bar-restaurant with
African music and meals for CFA 1500.

Other places for drinks, music, dancing

and lively ambience include the rustic *Pacific Bar*, which sometimes has a live band, and the *Ludo Club* a block away and several blocks from Hôtel Liberté. Street food is sold in front of both these places.

Unusual for West Africa, the airport has a booming restaurant and the ambience is relaxed and friendly. The speciality is pizza but you may have to order in advance. You can also get brochettes and a few other items.

Getting There & Away

SNTN buses between Niamey and Zinder, via Maradi, go twice weekly in each direction. Niamey to Maradi is CFA 10,850.

Private buses do the Niamey-Maradi trip every day for around CFA 9000. Bush taxis to/from Niamey charge CFA 8700, and CFA 6300 to/from Dosso.

In Maradi you'll also find bush taxis heading for the border with Nigeria (50 km). On the other side are plenty of cheap 504s with maniac Nigerian drivers ready to whisk you away at life-threatening speeds to Katsina and Kano. The whole Maradi to Kano trip takes four to five hours by bush taxi.

ZINDER

When the French arrived in Niger at the end of the 19th century, the only significant city they found in the area was Zinder (zen-DAIR), a city on the old trans-Saharan caravan route. So they made it the capital until 1926, when the administrative offices were transferred to Niamey. Zinder was founded two centuries before by Hausa emigrating from the Kano area. They were soon joined by the Kanouri from the north. By the mid-19th century, Zinder was in its prime. The importance of this old Hausa trading town was due solely to its location on the trade route between Kano and Agadez. Most of the traffic now uses the 'Uranium Highway' via Tahoua, but that may change with the completion of the Agadez-Zinder road and the end of Tuareg disturbances. It's also the home of President Ousmane, who may push some business this way.

Zinder is still the country's second-largest city with 80,000 people, and one of the live-

liest markets in Niger; the big day is Thursday (which is also the best day to find trucks to Kano). Look for leather goods at the market; the best *artisans de cuir* in Niger are here.

Be sure to get your passport stamped at the Commissariat in the heart of town. To get naira, look for moneychangers around the gare routière; you'll need some for a taxi to Kano. But if you've got US dollars, however, don't change too much as the moneychangers in Kano (Nigeria) generally give better rates.

Things to See

The city has two old sections: the **Zengou Quarter** on the northern side of town, which has lots of commercial buildings and mudbrick houses; and the picturesque **Birnin Quarter** to the south-east. They are separated by the modern area with its hotels, banks, markets, the gare routière and wide streets.

A stroll through the narrow streets of the Birnin Quarter is highly recommended. You'll find small gardens, friendly people, an old French fort on a hill dominating the area and, most importantly, some fine examples of traditional Hausa architecture. Even in Nigeria you won't see an area with traditional Hausa building so intact. The old *banco* houses are everywhere, easily identified by the geometrical designs in relief, usually colourfully painted. A good place to start is the **Grande Mosquée**, as there are some fine examples nearby. Behind it is the **Sultan's Palace**, built in the mid-19th century. People from all around come to see the highly respected Muslim Sultan, a Kanouri, seeking his advice on marriage, divorce, debts, inheritance matters, etc. To make an appointment, visit the Mairie. There is also, reportedly, a museum up the hill from the fort.

Places to Stay – bottom end

Camping Camping at the *Hôtel Central* is CFA 1500 per person. There is a good camp site called *La Caféteria* on the northern outskirts of town on the Agadez road. It's run by a friendly local who understands travellers'

Top: Camel market, Nouâdhibou, Mauritania (AS)
Middle: Fish wharf, Nouakchott, Mauritania (AS)
Bottom: Goat herd in a remote village near Kiffa, Mauritania (AS)

   Top: Jewellery vendor, Niamey, Niger (AS)
Middle: Clothes washers on Niger River, Niamey, Niger (AS)
Bottom: Market near Tanout, Niger (DW)

needs and is eager to please. The charge here is CFA 1500 also per person and there's a restaurant with good service.

Hotels One of the cheapest places is the homey *Hôtel Malem Kal Ka Danu* (☎ 51 05 68) on the main drag on the northern side of town, 700 metres north of the central area. The friendly owner, Ali, charges CFA 2500/3000 for clean singles/doubles with fans and shared bucket showers (CFA 4500 with full attached bath). Cheap meals are available. You could enquire about other cheap places around the autogare.

The lively but deteriorating *Hôtel Central* (☎ 51-2047) has been the favourite hotel of British overland trucks for years. Recently, however, it has become a meeting place for prostitutes, making it somewhat less pleasant than previously. It's in the centre of town. Large doubles with fans go for about CFA 5500, and CFA 8000 with air-con (which doesn't always work). The pleasant outdoor

terrace is the city's most popular rendezvous in the evenings for expatriates and Africans, and the food here is not bad either. If you're really lucky, you might get entertained by some local musicians.

Places to Stay – top end
Zinder has two good quality hotels. The more central and active is *Hôtel Le Damagaram* (☎ 51 03 03 or 51 06 19, telex 8223), which has 50 very decent air-con rooms, a shaded patio, and a modern nightclub at weekends with a CFA 1500 cover charge and CFA 1200 drinks. It's in the heart of town on the main north-south drag. It has a restaurant and nice singles/doubles for about CFA 9000 to CFA 13,000.

Zinder's most prestigious hotel, and almost identically priced, is the newer, more tranquil *Amadou Kourandaga* (☎ 51 07 42) on the western outskirts of town on the Niamey road. It has 47 attractive rooms with air-con, a good restaurant and a pleasant

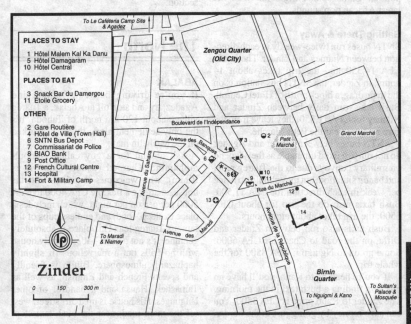

PLACES TO STAY
1 Hôtel Malem Kal Ka Danu
5 Hôtel Damagaram
10 Hôtel Central

PLACES TO EAT
3 Snack Bar du Damergou
11 Étoile Grocery

OTHER
2 Gare Routière
4 Hôtel de Ville (Town Hall)
6 SNTN Bus Depot
7 Commissariat de Police
8 BIAO Bank
9 Post Office
12 French Cultural Centre
13 Hospital
14 Fort & Military Camp

To Le Caféteria Camp Site & Agadez

Zengou Quarter (Old City)

Boulevard de l'Indépendance

Avenue des Banques

Avenue du Sahara

Petit Marché

Grand Marché

Rue du Marché

Avenue de la République

Avenue des Maradi

To Maradi & Niamey

Zinder

0   150   300 m

Birnin Quarter

To Nguigmi & Kano

To Sultan's Palace & Mosquée

NIGER

terrace bar. As at the Damagaram, the water is often cut off during the day.

Places to Eat

Some of the best street food can be found in the square in front of Hôtel Central and on Blvd de l'Indépendance by the gare routière. Or try the *Snack Bar du Damergou* almost opposite the Hôtel Le Damagaram. For good cheap meals, try *Restaurant Dan Kasina* in the centre, a block or two north of Hôtel Central. It serves simple fare such as omelettes and steak and chips.

Chez Emmanuel is a Peace Corps favourite and known for its chicken. It's near the centre, next to the cinema and not far from the *Étoile grocery* (which is good for shopping if you're self-catering).

For some of the best African food in town, including brochettes, pâte, and chicken in gumbo sauce, head for the *Scotch Bar*. It's on Rue du Marché, a 10-minute walk from the market and next to *Le Moulin Rouge*, a popular Camerounian nightclub with the latest African pop sounds.

Getting There & Away

SNTN buses run twice-weekly in each direction between Niamey and Zinder. The fare is CFA 14,350 and the trip takes about 14 hours. In Zinder, the SNTN bus station is on the main drag, a block north of Hôtel Central. Bush taxis run daily between Zinder and Niamey for CFA 11,350; they leave from the gare routière near the Petit Marché.

SNTN buses between Zinder and Agadez do not run to a fixed timetable as they depend on military convoys due to the Tuareg rebel and bandit situation, but they should go twice per week in each direction for CFA 11,500. Bush taxis also do the trip for about CFA 6500; the trip takes about eight hours.

Bush taxis also run between Zinder and Diffa, on the road to Chad, for CFA 6000. Some go on to Nguigmi; CFA 8500 for the whole trip.

If you're heading to Kano, you'll have no problem finding a bush taxi in the morning. The Zinder to Kano price is CFA 3500. You can save money by going just to the border, from where Nigerian bush taxis take you to Kano for the equivalent of about CFA 800. With 504s you can do Zinder to Kano in five hours but with minibuses six to eight hours is more typical.

NGUIGMI

Nguigmi is a small town in the far east of Niger, the end of the tarmac road, and the last settlement of any size before you reach Chad. The town has no hotels, but you can camp at the police station if you ask permission politely. There is a lively market area to the south of town where you can buy brochettes and nearby is a periodically stocked bar. By asking around at the market, you can change west-zone CFA into east-zone CFA (or visa versa), and also buy/sell naira. It is also reportedly possible to change travellers cheques, but at a very bad rate.

For transport to/from Zinder see the Zinder section above. For transport to/from Chad, see the main Getting There & Away section.

The North

ABALAK

If you're driving between Tahoua and Agadez, try and stop off at Abalak, a Tuareg village about 120 km north of Tahoua. It's the only settlement along this road marked on the Michelin map.

Ask around for a guy called Abdoulmohamine Khamed (usually known as Bihim), who welcomes travellers into his house, charging a flexible CFA 4000 to CFA 5000 per person per night, which includes a place to sleep, food, and endless cups of the famous Tuareg tea. This place is absolutely genuine. It's not a hotel – it's a family house with no frills but a marvellous (if slightly haphazard) atmosphere. Bihim is friendly and speaks French and English, as well as Tamashek, Hausa and a handful of other languages. His house is up a dirt street, west off the main road, near the bush taxi stop, behind the chief's house. You'll probably have to ask for directions.

AGADEZ

Warning We researched this section on Agadez in May 1995. At that time the whole city was very quiet. Due to the presence of Tuareg rebels and bandits in the surrounding area no overland travellers had come in across the Sahara for more than a year, and only a few local trucks and tankers were travelling between Agadez, Arlit and Tamanrasset in Algeria. Most embassies (including the USA) advised against foreigners travelling north of Tahoua, so even visitors arriving from other parts of Niger were very thin on the ground. Most of the hotels and restaurants were closed, and none of the tour companies were operating. Even the hustlers, for which Agadez is fabled, seemed to have given up and gone home.

However, there was a definite feel that Agadez was 'on pause', simply hibernating until the situation improved once again. In fact, a new peace accord between the government and the Tuaregs was being finalised while we were there, and optimistic observers reckon it's got more chance of bringing peace back to the region than any of the previous agreements.

So when you get to Agadez, be prepared for either situation. You may find the town buzzing, full of people and vehicles, with busy hotels, camp sites and bars. In the hope that peace (and travellers) will return, we've written about this lively version. But if the unrest continues, many of the hotels and bars we mention will still be closed, and Agadez will be a ghost town. ∎

With its sandy streets, excellent examples of Sudanese/Sahelian mud architecture, and Tuareg nomads, Agadez is one of the most interesting towns in Niger. Like Timbuktu, it was a great city in medieval times due to its strategic position on the trans-Saharan trade routes. Today, camels no longer carry gold and slaves across the desert but, unlike Timbuktu which seems to be dying, Agadez continues to thrive because of its important location on the 'Uranium Highway', and as a supply stop for trucks and overland travellers crossing the Sahara. If you're coming into Niger from Algeria, on the Route de Tamanrasset, Agadez is the first city you come to after crossing the desert.

In the 1990s Agadez hit a slump (see the box) but the city has seen the good times come and go before. In the 16th century, with a population of 30,000 people, it thrived off the gold caravans between Gao and Tripoli. As the gold trade waned, so did the city's population: down to about 3000 by 1900. Now, it's back up to 20,000, with uranium, the Trans-Saharan highway and travellers all contributing.

Unfortunately, the success of this trade also gave rise to tribes of hustlers bent on making money from travellers one way or another. You'll be pestered all day by people in traditional costumes trying to sell you swords, wallets, and jewellery, or by other hustlers trying to buy your car. If that doesn't work, others will offer to help you find a taxi, tour, camp site or spare part, then demand a large tip for their help. If you've come in from Algeria, don't confuse these men with the rest of the people in Niger. Most locals scorn them as well. You'll just have to learn to recognise them, then avoid them.

Whichever way you're travelling, don't forget to get your passport stamped at the Commissariat in town, not far from the tourist office. If you neglect to do this and continue on to Arlit, Niamey or Zinder, you may be forced to return to Agadez for the stamp.

Information

Tourist Office The tourist office (☎ 44 00 80) is on the city's main drag, just before the turn-off for Arlit, and open weekdays from 7.30 am to 12.30 pm and 3 to 6 pm and Saturday mornings. You may be able to get a free map of the city there and approval of your itinerary for travelling in the Aïr Mountains. This is obligatory, as is a guide.

Many travellers have recommended a local guy called Boubacar Moussa Tibilo (known to all as Moussa, and easy to find just by asking around) as the town's best source of information and general all-round fix-it man. He knows everything that's going on, and is reliable. For a small fee, he can help you find anything from camel rides to car parts.

Money Agadez has two banks, but they were closed during the Tuareg disturbances, and may never open again. Even if they do re-open, travellers' cheques may not be dealt with, or commissions may be very high. However, the town has many money-changers, although some of these guys are a bit on the shifty side. For security, most travellers, change money with store owners, where rates for cash are better than the bank, although travellers' cheques come in for a hefty 5% commission.

Foreign Consulates The Algerian consulate (☎ 44 01 17), open weekdays from 8 am to 2 pm, is about one km east of the central area. They issue visas in 24 hours except to Britons, who may have to wait several weeks for authorisation to come through. Agadez also has a Libyan consulate.

Travel Agencies All tour operations were suspended during the Tuareg disturbances, but will pick up again when peace returns.

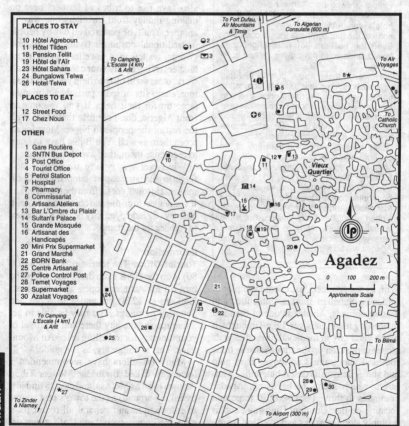

PLACES TO STAY
10 Hôtel Agreboun
11 Hôtel Tilden
18 Pension Tellit
19 Hôtel de l'Aïr
23 Hôtel Sahara
24 Bungalows Telwa
26 Hotel Telwa

PLACES TO EAT
12 Street Food
17 Chez Nous

OTHER
1 Gare Routière
2 SNTN Bus Depot
3 Post Office
4 Tourist Office
5 Petrol Station
6 Hospital
7 Pharmacy
8 Commissariat
9 Artisans Ateliers
13 Bar L'Ombre du Plaisir
14 Sultan's Palace
15 Grande Mosquée
16 Artisanat des Handicapés
20 Mini Prix Supermarket
21 Grand Marché
22 BDRN Bank
25 Centre Artisanal
27 Police Control Post
28 Ternet Voyages
29 Supermarket
30 Azalait Voyages

To Fort Dufau, Aïr Mountains & Timia
To Algerian Consulate (600 m)
To Camping, L'Escale (4 km) & Arlit
To Air Voyages
To Catholic Church

Vieux Quartier

Agadez

0   100   200 m
Approximate Scale

To Camping L'Escale (4 km) & Arlit
To Zinder & Niamey
To Bilma
To Airport (300 m)

Excursions range from a short camel ride on the Agadez outskirts, through trips to the Aïr Mountains (starting at CFA 50,000 per person per day for groups of four), to major expeditions into the Ténéré Desert or beyond. Names to look out for include Aligouran Voyages (☎ 44 00 94), east of the centre on the road towards Bilma. For other listings, see Getting There & Away in the Aïr Mountains section.

Grande Mosquée & Sultan's Palace

The Grande Mosquée dates from 1515 but it was totally rebuilt in 1844. Its 27-metre pyramid-like minaret with wooden scaffolding is a classic of Sudanese architecture and affords a view of the Aïr Mountains. If you're not sporting lots of camera equipment, a CFA 200 *cadeau* (gift) is often sufficient to persuade the guardian to let you climb to the top for a look.

The three-storey building to the north of the mosque is the Palais du Sultan, the residence of the city's traditional ruler.

Grand Marché & Tuareg Marché

The Grand Marché near the mosque is the most animated place in town. The variety of people here, many dressed in traditional desert costumes, is at least as interesting as what's for sale. You can find just about anything here including a variety of artisan goods, rugs and Tuareg leather-work. Some travellers are driven crazy by the aggressive young hawkers; if you're buying gold, silver or bronze, you're less likely to be cheated dealing direct with the artisans.

There is also a Tuareg Market on the outskirts of town and the Tuareg there will trade you just about anything.

Vieux Quartier

After being hassled to death by the never-say-no vendors in the market, you'll need to escape. Head for the slightly more tranquil Vieux Quartier, the old section of town which surrounds the market, particularly the district facing the mosque. With its small crooked streets, tiny shops and interesting old Sudanese houses with Hausa-inspired designs, it's the best place to go roaming around. Just ask for the houses with *les belles façades*. You'll also find all kinds of artisan shops here, including silversmiths making the famous cross (*croix*) d'Agadez (see Things to Buy), leather-workers producing Tuareg *samaras* (sandals), *coussins* (cushions) and magnificent *selles de chameau* (camel saddles), and bronzesmiths making a variety of objects including jewellery.

The bargaining is intense but not disagreeable. You can usually take photographs of the artisans at work as well. The early morning around 7 am is the best time for taking outdoor photographs, catching the multitude of soft colours on the walls.

Camel Market

The marvellous camel market on the north-western outskirts of town is another 'must see'. It has wonderful colours, and not so wonderful smells emanating from the camels, goats and other animals sold here. You must get here early as the activity is over by 10.30 am.

Camel Racing

Camel racing is a favourite sport of the Tuareg. The usual routine involves a champion rider taking an indigo scarf from a woman and heading off into the desert. The other riders try to catch him and grab the scarf. Whoever succeeds is the winner. During the race, the women, decked out in their best silver jewellery, cheer on the riders by singing and clapping to the sound of drums.

The best time to be in Agadez is during one of the Muslim holidays, especially Tabaski. Following the feast, you can see one of the great spectacles of the desert – the 'cavalcade', a furious camel race through the narrow crowded streets to the square in front of the Sultan's palace. ■

Camel Ride

For a bit of adventure, you can take a camel ride into the surrounding area for several days. Any number of Tuareg guides will do this. Moussa (listed under Information) can lead you to a Tuareg guide who offers this service. The price is often quoted for the camel and the guide, and starts at CFA 5000 per day (although there seems to be no distance limit). Just make sure your arrangements are absolutely clear before you start because unexpected extra charges always creep in. Permission from the Commissariat is also required before you leave. Here's how one traveller described his ride:

My guide took me on a three-day camel trek up into the Massif de Tarouadji, just east of Agadez. It was an unforgettable experience and not nearly long enough. My price included camel hire, food and water for me and the guide, and permission from the authorities. I was also able to lock up most of my gear safely at the Hôtel Agreboun.

We were fortunate to have well-behaved camels. Some can be quite homicidal, walking deliberately under low branches and trying to shake you off into thorn bushes! I would strongly recommend you take a good soft pillow. The wooden Tuareg saddle nearly crippled me.

The scenery consisted of barren rolling hills covered in rocks, like the surface of the moon, but the valleys and plains among the hills were often filled with thousands of trees, peach coloured sand, and dried stream beds, evidence of flash flooding.

It was most pleasant to be out in the middle of nowhere swaying gently back and forth in the saddle. The only sounds are the wind and the soft crunch of the camel's feet. Sometimes my guide would get too far ahead and I would lose sight of him. Then, just for a moment, I would be completely alone, following a barely discernible track. Being up on a camel means you catch all the cool breezes, and the landscape just goes on and on and on, magnificent!

The evenings in the villages were something special. The temperature cools to a bearable level as we sat around the glowing embers of a fire drinking hot, sweet Tuareg tea. I slept under the stars surrounded by the vast expanse of the Sahara, listening to the soft flow of Tuareg conversation in the background.

Neil McTaggart, Aberdeen, Scotland

Places to Stay

When the Paris-Dakar motor rally comes through Agadez (usually in January) hotel prices jump to three or four times the normal.

Places to Stay – bottom end

Camping As in all of Niger, you can't camp 'near' town. Travellers who have camped as far away as 15 km from Agadez have suffered fines over CFA 20,000. There is also a security risk.

Agadez has two camp sites. The most popular and closest to town is the large and shady (in parts) *Camping L'Escale* (☎ 44 05 22), on the north-western side of town on the road to Arlit near the road block. It charges CFA 3500 for a mattress in a decrepit room, or CFA 1500 per person to camp, plus CFA 500 per vehicle. The staff are usually friendly and there is a reliable supply of water for showers, plus a decent bar-restaurant. There are supposedly two night guards, but you should keep a close eye on your gear here.

Hotels For the friendly ambience and good vibes, it's hard to beat *Hôtel Agreboun* (☎ 44 03 07), on the western edge of town, several blocks from the mosque. Run by a friendly Tuareg man, it has nine clean singles/doubles with fans and showers for CFA 3000/3500 (more with air-con), a restaurant and a courtyard where you can have cheap beers, park your car and, to be a bit cooler, drag your mattress out for sleeping.

If the Agreboun is full, try the equally friendly *Hôtel Tilden*, which has similar rooms and prices. Or check the long-standing and shabby *Hôtel Sahara* (☎ 44 01 97) opposite the Grand Marché, where basic singles/doubles with fans cost CFA 3000/4000, and a double with air-con is CFA 8000. An extra bed costs CFA 1000, or you can sleep on the terrace for CFA 1500. Even if you don't stay here, the patio bar round the back is a good place for a drink. The restaurant, which is barely open, serves good meals with copious servings, but meals are fairly expensive and service is slow.

Places to Stay – top end

If you're into history and atmosphere, the best place to stay is the famous and once-elegant *Hôtel de l'Aïr* (☎ 44 01 47), located in the centre of town with a perfect view of the Grande Mosquée. Architecturally fascinating with metre-thick walls, the Aïr was formerly a Sultan's residence. Today, its rooms are not so grand, costing CFA 8500 for one or two people with fan and shared bath or CFA 13,500 for a self-contained air-con double. Older rooms, actually in the palace itself, are a bit cheaper. There's no hot water but near the Sahara, who needs it? The restaurant has little to recommend it other than the architectural splendour, but a drink on the rooftop terrace, with its great views of the city, is a real treat.

If you're into comfort, and money is not a big problem, head for the friendly *Pension Tellit* (☎ 44 02 31), opposite the Aïr, which has an excellent staff and a friendly Italian manager, Vittorio Gioni. All four rooms have air-con, fans, small refrigerators and private baths with hot water. Rooms for one to four people range from CFA 10,000 to CFA 20,000. Meals in Vittorio's restaurant (the most exclusive in Agadez, and probably the best outside Niamey) cost around CFA 3500. Worth a splurge – and don't miss the Italian ice cream!

Another possibility is the *Hôtel Telwa* (☎ 41 01 64), one block west of the Hôtel Sahara. It lacks the Aïr's charm, but it's a decent government-run hotel with more comfortable rooms, costing from CFA 4000 to CFA 9000; the more expensive ones have air-con. Nearby are the smart and secure *Bungalows Telwa* (☎ 44 02 64), connected to the above establishment, where singles/doubles with TV and fridge cost CFA 12,000/14,000, and an extra bed is CFA 1500. There's also a restaurant with standard meals at mid-range prices.

Places to Eat & Drink
As well as the hotels, Agadez has a number of interesting watering holes and decent restaurants catering mainly for the trans-Saharan tourist trade. When the Tuareg uprising put an end to the tourist trade, most of them closed. However, if the trade picks up, many will probably open again.

For street food, check the open-air vendors on the main drag, opposite Hôtel Agriboun, or around the market; the food at both places is quite good and varied.

Chez Nous is near the market and run by a Togolese woman who serves good food at reasonable prices. Her riz-sauce for around CFA 500 is an excellent buy, and for about CFA 200 you can help yourself to unlimited coffee. Or visit *Tafadek* in the heart of town, near the mosque and Hôtel de l'Aïr, where you can try some real Tuareg specialities such as hurwa (curdled milk with millet and sugar) or something less exotic like couscous and sauce.

Other places to try for food and drinks include the *Restaurant Islamique*, in the centre on the main drag opposite the Mobil station, the nearby *Restaurant Sénégalais*, *Bar Le Ténéré* near the water tower, *Café Guida* facing Hôtel de l'Aïr, *Bar La Belle Etoile* on the east side of town, and the nearby pleasant *Restaurant Orida*, where main meals are in the CFA 600 to CFA 1200 bracket. *Bar l'Ombre du Plaisir*, just off the main drag, has also been recommended.

Things to Buy
The most popular souvenir by far are the famous croix d'Agadez in silver filigree, which the Tuareg believe are powerful talismans, to protect against 'the evil eye'. Those with phallus designs are fertility symbols for both sexes while others are for good luck and protection. Inspect them closely; each desert town (Ingal, Tahoua, Zinder, Bilma, etc) has a slightly different design. The Tuareg men use the crosses as a form of currency to buy cattle, and between trades the crosses are worn by their wives as a sign of wealth. Men used to wear them, passed down from father to son when the boy reached puberty, but now only the women wear them.

For buying jewellery and seeing silversmiths at work, check the Centre Artisanal on the south-western edge of town, or the Artisana des Handicapés, in the heart of town on the main drag, where they specialise in straw hats and leather-work. At both places, some bargaining is required.

Getting There & Away
Air For details of flights to Agadez, see the Niamey Getting There & Away section.

NIGER

Bus & Bush Taxi SNTN services on the Agadez route were suspended during the Tuareg uprising, and SNTN buses from Niamey only go as far as Tahoua (CFA 10,750). When they start again the fare between Niamey and Agadez will be CFA 17,650. They also go from Niamey to Arlit for CFA 21,150. The SNTN terminal is next to the gare routière on the north side of Agadez on the road to Arlit.

Private buses and bush taxis were running on this route in May 1995, with fares from Niamey to Agadez at about 16,300, and Tahoua to Agadez about CFA 7000, although these may stop if the security situation worsens again.

The private buses from Niamey to Agadez run on to Arlit for about CFA 4000 more.

For details on the route between Agadez and Zinder, see the Zinder Getting There & Away section.

Truck For trucks to Tamanrasset (Tam), you'll do better going to Arlit and looking for one there. If you want to look for one in Agadez, check the area just west of the market. They bring dates from Tam to Agadez and take camels from Agadez to Tam. Other places for catching trucks are the gare routière and customs nearby. All truckers expect payment, typically CFA 50,000 from Agadez to Tam. Getting them to accept a lower price is very difficult but possible. The price often includes food and water, as most truck drivers expect to 'cater' for their passengers, but check first. Most trucks do the crossing in about four days; some drive day and night and reduce the trip to about 48 hours.

Car If you have car problems, you risk having your vehicle butchered if you don't use a real garage. Garage de l'Aïr facing the Hôtel Telwa, Garage Franco on the road to Zinder, and Garage Yahaya Ango, 300 metres from the Hôtel Agreboun on the same path, have all been recommended as has Garage Wadata.

Hitching Hitching across the desert for free is quite possible with other foreigners in their own vehicles. This is not hitching in the normal sense – you have to ask around at camp sites and bars, rather than stand at the roadside with your thumb out – but numerous lucky travellers have been offered free lifts. You may improve your chances if you have mechanical skills or even if you say how willing you are to help dig them out of soft sand (especially if there's only one or two people in the car). You should bring your own food, or offer to contribute to the vehicle's own supply. An offer to help towards petrol costs is also usually appreciated. Getting a ride is easier during the busy winter months – when many more people make the crossing – but you still may have to wait several days. Hitching free rides with local truckers is not possible.

AROUND AGADEZ

> **Warning** During the research for this book, we were unable to reach much of the area described in this section, as the region was officially off limits for tourists. Therefore most of the information is reproduced, with very few changes, from the earlier edition. The area could reopen quickly if the May 1995 peace accord with the Tuareg is effective, so be prepared for changes. ∎

If you tire of Agadez altogether, head for **Ingal**, 120 km to the west, a peaceful oasis of date trees, irrigated gardens and a market, and the site of the annual Cure Salée event. Or try **Elméki**, a tiny Tuareg oasis village about three hours from Agadez. You will see a beautiful lake, meet Tuaregs who have settled down to harvest dates and perhaps encounter a camel caravan and have lunch with Tuareg under the shade of an acacia tree.

AÏR MOUNTAINS & TÉNÉRÉ DESERT

Agadez is the main jumping-off point for expeditions into some of the most spectacular desert and mountain scenery in Africa. There are three principal zones: the Aïr (eye-AIR) Mountains starting immediately to the north and north-east of Agadez, the Ténéré Desert beyond and, further north-east, the

La Cure Salée

If you're in Niger during early September, don't miss the Cure Salée (kure sal-AY), an annual event of the herders in Niger. The location of the Cure Salée, or 'salt cure', is in the vicinity of Ingal, where the land and water are especially salty, particularly around Tegguidda-n-Tessoum.

The Cure Salée of the Wodaabé (woh-DAH-bay), a unique sect of Fulani (Peul) herders, is famous Africa-wide. When the Fulani migrated to West Africa centuries ago, possibly from the Upper Nile, many converted to Islam and intermarried; some even left herding to become sedentary farmers. For the Fulani who remained nomads, cattle retained their pre-eminent position. Valuing their freedom, they despised their settled neighbours and resisted outside influences. Many called themselves 'Wodaabé' meaning 'people of the taboo' – those who adhere to the traditional code of Fulani, particularly modesty. The sedentary Fulani called them 'Bororo', a name derived from their cattle and insinuating something like 'those who live in the bush and do not wash'.

The Wodaabé men have long, elegant, feminine features, and they believe they have been blessed with great beauty. To a married couple, it is of upmost importance to have beautiful children. Men who are not good-looking have, on occasion, shared their wives with more handsome men to gain more attractive children. The men are also playful and don't shy away from showing their friendship to one another. Wodaabé women have the same features and, before marriage, enjoy unusual sexual freedom, sleeping with unmarried men whenever they choose.

During the year, the nomadic Wodaabé are dispersed, tending to their animals. In very saline areas in the vicinity of Ingal, the fresh grass contains a high salt content and the animals need the salt to remain healthy. So at the height of the rainy season when the grass can support large herds, the nomads bring their herds to graze in the salty areas. During the Cure Salée, you'll see men on camels – like cowboys – trying to keep their herds in order as well as racing their camels. The event serves above all as a social gathering – a time for wooing the opposite sex, marriage and seeing old friends. Afterwards, some of the cattle are driven to Nigeria for sale. The Wodaabé need the money to buy certain things (eg jewellery and leather items) because for them all work other than tending animals is demeaning.

For the Wodaabé, the Cure Salée is the time for their *gerewol* festival. To win the attention of the eligible women, the single men participate in a virtual beauty contest. The main event is the *yaake*, a late afternoon performance in which the men dance, displaying their beauty, charisma and charm. In preparation they will spend long hours decorating themselves in front of small hand mirrors. They then form a long line and are dressed to the hilt with blackened lips to make the teeth seem whiter, lightened faces, white streaks down their foreheads and noses, star-like figures painted on their faces, braided hair, elaborate hats, anklets, all kinds of jewellery, beads and shiny objects. Tall, lean bodies, long slender noses, white even teeth and white eyes are what the women are looking for. After taking special stimulating drinks, the men dance for long hours, sometimes well into the night. Their personal charm is revealed in dancing, and charm can greatly increase the man's popularity. Eventually, the women, dressed less elaborately, timidly make their choices. If a marriage proposal results, the man takes a calabasse full of milk to the woman's parents. If they accept, he then brings them the bride price – three cattle which are slaughtered for the fête that follows.

Rivalry can be fierce, and to show their virility the Wodaabé men take part in the *soro*, an event where the young men stand smiling while others hit them with huge sticks, trying to make them fall over. At the end of the festival, the men remove their jewellery, except for a simple talisman. All of this is magnificently recorded in *Nomads of Niger* by Carol Beckwith & Marion Van Offelen.

Each group of herders has its own Cure Salée. The Tuareg equivalent of the gerewol is the *illoudjan*. Top government officials attend only that of the Wodaabé. Around August, the government sends out a team to select the site. It lasts a week, usually during the first half of September, and the big event happens over two days. ∎

Djado Plateau, about 1000 km from Agadez via Bilma.

The Aïr Mountains are close enough for travellers with wheels (or the money for a tour) and a few free days to visit. The other two destinations are extremely remote and require a lot more time and effort. A guide (or driver) and government authorisation are required for all trips.

Aïr Massif

The Aïr Massif is one of the most spectacular

sights in West Africa. Covering an area the size of Switzerland, these mountains are of dark volcanic rock capped with unusually shaped peaks, the highest being Mt Bagzane at 2022 metres, 145 km from Agadez. They aren't as bare as the Hoggar Mountains, and many different trees, plants and animals can be seen, including goats, camels, antelope and birds.

The major route is rough but compacted and fairly well marked on the Michelin map. From Agadez the road goes north-east 45 km to a fork in the road, called Téloua. The left fork takes you to the hot thermal springs at **Tafadek**. After about 15 km along this left fork there's another fork; the left one goes to Tafadek, the right goes to Elméki some 65 km further north-east. The right fork at Téloua takes an anticlockwise route that rejoins the main road just before Elméki.

The next stop past Elméki is Kreb-Kreb, then the lovely green oasis of **Timia**, some 110 km from Elméki. Timia is the second major destination on many tours and the waterfalls near town are a 'don't miss' attraction. The next oasis further north is Assodé, then **Iferouâne**, 180 km north of Timia and 160 km east of Arlit. This would be a good place to stop as the oasis

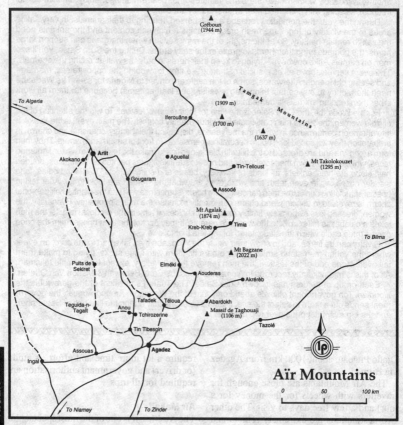

Aïr Mountains

0   50   100 km

is quite lovely and there are some interesting prehistoric sites in the area. You could then backtrack or head west to Arlit.

Ténéré Desert

The Ténéré Desert, some 500 km as the crow flies north-east of Agadez, is an area of sand dunes and monotonous flat areas of hard sand. The desert is reputed to have some of the most extraordinarily beautiful sand dune areas in the entire Sahara. You'll need several days to reach them, so it's a minimum one-week trip, preferably more. A minimum of two vehicles is required for safety reasons. There are two principal routes, both notoriously difficult – east towards Bilma then north, or north to Iferouâne and Tadéra, then east.

Bilma

Heading east from Agadez towards Bilma, you'll come to Tazolé after 100 km. To the south is a **dinosaur cemetery** – one of the world's most important ones. The fossils are spread over a belt 150 km long; you might even see one at the top of a dune. Continually covered and uncovered by the sand, they are silent witness to the fact that the whole Sahara Desert was once green and fertile. You may see a number of species, maybe even fossilised crocodiles.

After another 179 km, you'll pass the famous **Arbre du Ténéré**, the only tree in Africa marked on the Michelin map – except it no longer exists. This sole tree in the middle of the desert, over 400 km from the next nearest tree – the last acacia of the once great Saharan forests – was hit in 1973 by a Libyan truck driver. Incredible. All you'll see is a metal replica; the remnants of the real thing are in the museum in Niamey.

Some 171 km further east is the salt-producing oasis of Fachi and, 610 km from Agadez, Bilma, which is truly the end of the earth. Years ago, there were caravans (*azalai*), 20,000 camels long, that did the trip from Agadez to pick up the salt. Today, they still come but not nearly as frequently and only a fraction the size. You'll see how salt is dug out of the earth and then dissolved in

a pan and left to evaporate. Salt crystals are left at the top and heavier impurities at the bottom. This process is repeated until the salt is pure, after which it's poured into moulds made from large palm trunks, giving the salt its loaf-like aspect (in contrast, for example to the door-like slabs from Mali).

Djado Plateau

If you continue on to the Djado Plateau (a 10 to 14-day round-trip from Agadez), you'll see some of the prehistoric cave paintings of antelope, giraffe and rhino for which the area is noted.

Organised Tours

Most of the tour companies providing all-inclusive tours of the Aïr Mountains have closed or gone into remission. If conditions return to normal, many are likely to resume business, so the following list may be useful.

The best known one in Agadez is Temet Voyages (☎ 44 00 5 1, telex 8241, BP 178), which also has offices in Niamey. Niger Ténéré Voyages (☎ 44 01 47) is reportedly cheaper. Other agencies include Tamzak Voyages (☎ 44 00 29), which also has offices in Arlit (☎ 45 22 78), Aligouran Voyages (☎ 44 00 94, BP 205) and Aïr Voyages (BP 186). In addition, the Office du Tourisme (☎ 44 00 80) in Agadez helps to arrange tours. Tamesna Voyages (☎ 45 23 31/2) in Arlit is another place to try.

The price per person can be very high if you take an all-inclusive tour with tents, food, guide, etc. For example, Aligouran's seven-day excursion that includes most of the Aïr Massif and the dunes at Temet, and 12-day excursion that includes much of the Aïr Massif and the Ténéré Desert all the way to the Djado Plateau, both start at CFA 50,000 per person per day, but could easily rise to CFA 70,000 per person per day or more in the future.

Getting There & Away

Car Renting a vehicle is a lot cheaper than an all-inclusive tour; ask at the above agencies or the tourist office. If you bargain well, a five-passenger Land Rover and driver plus a guide (compulsory), all food and petrol will cost about CFA 70,000 a day. Getting the required government authorisations can easily take several hours, so don't plan on starting off the same day you make arrangements.

If you leave one day at 4 pm and return the next at 3 pm you'll be charged two full days. Discuss how much time the driver will have off for lunch; otherwise he is likely to take from 11 am to 2 pm for siesta. Also discuss the itinerary in detail and, best of all, put something in writing or draw a map so the driver can't claim a misunderstanding.

Also write down what he will provide. Some drivers are shifty and if you don't do these things, the chances are very high you'll experience problems. Some drivers have even been known to blackmail travellers on the last day of their trip by holding their passports until they've paid for an extra day. So make sure your arrangements are perfectly clear; don't leave any matter unsettled. And keep hold of your documents.

ARLIT

Before reading this section, see the warning on page 659 (under Agadez). Much of the information there concerning the uncertain situation following the May 1995 peace accord applies here too. Be prepared for changes. ∎

Uranium was discovered here in 1965. Six years later, Somair, the uranium mining company, created Arlit, Niger's northernmost major town. Since then, this dusty mining settlement has grown considerably and it's now amazingly vibrant. If you've been weeks in Algeria, where people are less than exuberant, you'll particularly appreciate Arlit's atmosphere – people laughing, unveiled women – and the beer.

Arlit is also the number one barter-town in Africa. Immediately on arrival you will be accosted by hustlers wanting to sell you souvenirs of every sort and buy everything you own. Vehicle parts (especially engines, tyres and wheels), freezers and Walkmans are the hottest items, also water canisters. Everyone wants to sell or buy something. The camp sites are more like used car lots – foreigners trying to sell their vehicles and locals coming up to you all day long, asking what you have to sell and offering ridiculously low prices. If you want to do business, have everything closed off except what you want to sell, otherwise some of your things may take a walk.

There's a tourist office (☎ 45 22 49), a French-run hospital, a colourful market bustling with activity, numerous places to stay and eat, a number of petrol stations and water so clean that many travellers don't bother purifying it.

Whether you enter town from Agadez or Assamakka, police at the checkpoints will take your passport and return it only when you're ready to leave. You must collect it from the Commissariat, which is a good place to look for a ride if you're hitching since everyone leaving town must pass by here first.

Even in the best of days, the BIAO and BDRN banks were next to useless and rarely had any cash. If things improve, you may still have to wait several days to change travellers' cheques, for which they give bad rates and charge high commissions. Better, look around for a prosperous store owner to change your money; just don't be surprised if he wants a healthy cut.

Places to Stay & Eat

Campers have a choice – one camp site three km north of town and a similar but smaller one three km south of town. They both charge about CFA 1500 a person and another CFA 1500 per vehicle, but neither is anything special. At both places you can pay just to use the shower (CFA 250 at the northern one and CFA 500 at the southern one), although the water supply is erratic. For a meal, you can get a fairly expensive one at the camp site on the northern end; otherwise you'll have to come into town.

A better place to camp is in town at the *Hôtel l'Auberge la Caravane* (☎ 45 22 78), in the centre west of the main street. You can camp here or sleep on the roof for CFA 2000 a person, as there's secure parking as well (CFA 1500 per vehicle). It also has double rooms with fans for around CFA 6500 (CFA 9000 with air-con). Around the corner is the *Hôtel Tamesna* (☎ 45 23 30/2), with similar rooms and prices. The terrace bar has cold beers and is a popular watering hole, and there's a pleasant roof-top restaurant as well, with meals around CFA 1000.

Behind the Tamesna you'll find the *Café des Arts* doing meals for around CFA 1000. The food is excellent and the waiter is friendly but service is slow. Or try *Restaurant Trottaria* next door; it's a bit more expensive, however.

For cheap fare, you can't beat the *Ramada*, in the centre of town near the post office, where a filling meal costs about CFA 600. Two other relatively cheap places, both on the main drag, are *Restaurant de l'Aïr* and *Bar Le Sahel*, although the latter is mainly for drinking.

At night, one of the most popular places for drinks is the open-air *Cheval Blanc*. It charges about CFA 650 for a cold beer, which is the going rate, but prices rise when there's music.

Getting There & Away

See the Agadez Getting There & Away section for details of buses between Niamey, Agadez and Arlit.

If you're in your own vehicle it may be necessary to travel in convoy. Ask at the police posts in Assamaka, Arlit, Agadez or Tahoua for the latest regulations. There are plenty of police checks along the Agadez to Arlit stretch, but if you're polite and patient there should be no major hassles.

Whatever form of transport you're on, make sure you get your passport stamped by the police in Agadez and Arlit.

ASSAMAKKA

Assamakka (200 km north-west of Arlit) consists of a border checkpoint, a military post with a nice shade tree (off limits to travellers), a few houses, a tiny market, and a small restaurant near the border post where

the soldiers drink and where you can eat while border officials stamp your passport.

Whether you're heading north from Agadez or south from Tamanrasset, you should be prepared for a fairly long border crossing at Assamakka on the Niger side and at In-Guezzam on the Algerian side.

The border officials on the Niger side are often gruff and indifferent, but most travellers pass through with no problems at all. Others experience great problems, especially when the soldiers are drunk, which is often the case. If you dress discreetly, have your papers in hand, and cooperate with the inspection, including offering to open boxes, the chances are good you'll have no trouble. Occasionally travellers are still asked to show proof of sufficient funds, but that's getting rarer. If you don't have CFA 1000 to pay for the tourist tax (more if you have a car), you can change dinar and sometimes other currencies at the market.

Getting through each border station normally takes one to two hours, more if there's a long line of people. The border closes at 6 pm. The soldiers take a two-hour siesta at noon, and if you arrive in Assamakka after 4 pm, you may have to wait until the next day. The bar charges CFA 850 for a big beer, CFA 500 for rice and sauce and CFA 300 for coffee and bread. You can also get chips there. For travellers heading south who have been in Algeria for a while, the beer here is frequently all that's needed for entertainment.

Border formalities at In-Guezzam, 30 km to the north, are usually even more relaxed than at Assamakka although even here travellers occasionally have had bad experiences. The soldiers usually make only cursory searches and, for those heading to Niger, occasionally don't even check the currency forms. If they do check and your Algerian currency declaration form and bank receipts don't match up, you may have to come to some arrangement to get through. The town has several stores (basically bread, biscuits and tins) and two terrible restaurants (basically soup or couscous), all rather expensive, but at least you won't die if you're hitchhiking and have to stay here a day or two.

NIGER

Getting There & Away

From Assamakka to Agadez, a seat in a pick-up truck can cost as much as CFA 8000 (CFA 6000 between Assamakka and Arlit); ask the price before entering. If you're driving between Assamakka and Agadez, it's possible to take the old camel train route via Tegguidda-n-Tessoum, and many truckers actually prefer it. Travellers with their own

vehicles have occasionally been turned back by soldiers but this is fairly rare.

From Assamakka to Tamanrasset a seat in a truck can cost as little as CFA 9000 but the drivers usually demand double that amount. Normally, once or twice a week there's public transport available, which makes the trip to/from Tamanrasset in one long day.

Nigeria

Nigeria is to Africa what China is to the world. It is home to one out of five Africans; every 12 months, new births equal the populations of Gabon, Mauritania, Cape Verde, The Gambia, Equatorial Guinea and São Tomé combined. Nigeria leads Africa in oil production, has six of the seven vehicle assembly plants in the region, and more kinds of beer than the rest of West Africa combined.

Lagos, however, has given Nigeria's reputation a black eye. It is West Africa's largest city and, by many criteria, Africa's worst, with one of the highest crime rates.

The trick to enjoying Nigeria is to avoid Lagos and the sprawling, congested cities of Ibadan, Port Harcourt, Enugu or Onitsha. If you spend most of your time in places such as Kano, Katsina, Zaria, Jos, Sokoto, Calabar, Ife and Maiduguri, in villages, or in the mountains in the far east along the Cameroun border, the chances are you'll enjoy Nigeria.

Facts about the Country

HISTORY

Northern and southern Nigeria are like two different countries, and their histories are equally disparate. Before the time of Christ, the Nok people around Jos were producing terracotta and casting iron. By the time Marco Polo set out for China, the first great kingdom in northern Nigeria – the Islamic Kanem-Borno Empire around Lake Chad – was already in decline. It had acquired its wealth through the trans-Saharan trade, particularly the slave trade.

Around 1000 AD, Islamic Hausa states rose in the north at Kano and nearby areas. Like the Kanem-Borno, they had powerful armies with imperial ambitions but no link with the outside world except through the trans-Saharan trade. The arrival of the Portuguese in the late 15th century on the southern coast had little effect on them. They

---

FEDERAL REPUBLIC OF NIGERIA

Area: 924,000 sq km
Population: 105 million
Population Growth Rate: 3.4%
Capital: Abuja
Head of State: General Sani Abacha
Official Language: English
Currency: Naira
Exchange Rate: N25 = US$1
Per Capita GNP: US$310
Inflation: 70%
Time: GMT/UTC + 1

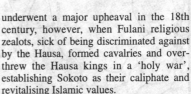

---

underwent a major upheaval in the 18th century, however, when Fulani religious zealots, sick of being discriminated against by the Hausa, formed cavalries and overthrew the Hausa kings in a 'holy war', establishing Sokoto as their caliphate and revitalising Islamic values.

In the south, powerful pagan kingdoms arose in Ife, Benin and Oyo. The Empire of Benin was particularly powerful. The king's palace occupied one-sixth of the huge walled city and virtually all artists worked for the court, producing the finest bronze work in Africa.

In the south-east, land of the Ibo, there were

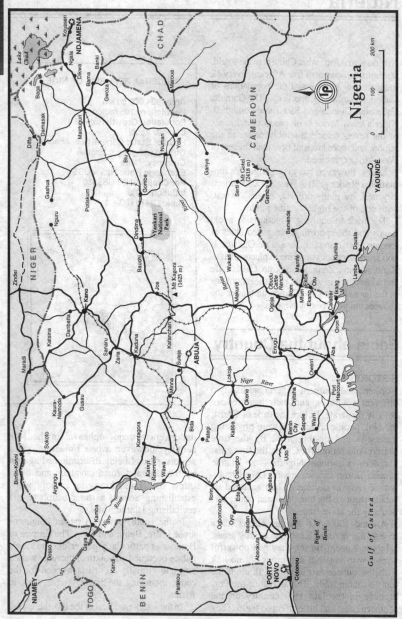

Suggested Itineraries
Most people would advise getting out of Lagos as soon as possible and bypassing Ibadan on your way out. In general, that's probably good advice.

However, for the brave, **Lagos** should not be overlooked, in part because one of the major highlights of any trip to Nigeria is an evening at Fela's or Sunny Ade's nightclub. Regardless, after Lagos, a good place to head for is Ife or Oshogbo, both north-east of Ibadan, a sprawling ugly city that has little to recommend. **Ife** has the country's major university and a good museum while in **Oshogbo**, the nation's modern art capital, you can walk through the Sacred Forest and view the various Yoruba shrines, or visit the artists' studios in the centre of town.

While **Benin City** has an interesting museum and the nearby **Okomo rainforest sanctuary**, and **Onitsha** has a fascinating market, cities in the southern half of the country have little to offer travellers. However, if you head to the far eastern section, you'll find some interesting parks and the country's best hiking area, especially along the eastern border. You could easily spend a week or more in this area which includes **Cross River National Park** north of Ikom, **Obudu Cattle Ranch** nearby and **Gashaka Game Reserve** north of Gembu. Towns in this remote eastern region, including **Calabar** which is one of the most pleasant in the area, are a bit smaller.

Heading north, you'll find **Kaduna**, the northern capital; **Jos**, which has a fabulous sprawling ethnographical museum; **Yankari National Park**, which is the country's best game reserve; and **Zaria**, which has an interesting old quarter. These are all worth stopping at for a day or two.

Nigeria's main attraction, however, is **Kano**. Allow at least three days to explore this fascinating old city, more if you'll be here during Muslim festivals when Kano, nearby Katsina, and Sokoto really come alive. ∎

no great kingdoms. People depended on agriculture for a living; a strong military wasn't needed. In the late 15th century, the Portuguese began trading in ivory and pepper, turning later to slaves. They were followed by the British who confined slaves temporarily in ships rather than in forts as they did in Ghana.

Colonial Period

After the British had outlawed slavery in 1807, they began looking for other ways to exploit Africa, financing the exploration of inland waterways and other means of opening up trade. During the scramble for Africa in the late 19th century, Britain sent armies to gain political control over Nigeria, storming Kano in 1902. By then, tin was a well-organised industry in the north. The British were intent on finding the sources, artfully concealed by the Nigerians. They found them in the central plateau area around Jos and over 50 foreign companies took over the Jos mines, employing nearly 40,000 tin miners by 1928. Thus, the British destroyed the thousands of independent tin producers, converting them into wage earners with no other means of livelihood.

Worse, the British replaced food crops with export crops; eventually – for the first time ever – there wasn't enough food to go around. A 1947 report to the British parliament said that malnutrition had become widespread in Nigeria. Cocoa farmers were the only Nigerians who prospered.

To their credit, the British were intent on keeping Nigeria a Black colony, allowing no White settlers and denying temporary work permits to foreigners who could not show that their presence was absolutely necessary. Rather than taking direct political control, the British administered Nigeria – as they did their dominions throughout Africa – by indirect rule, delegating authority to village chiefs, thereby preserving local culture. In 1938 all of Nigeria was governed by only 380 British officials.

There were two problems, however. In the south-east, where many Ibo communities had no chiefs, the British appointed them. These 'invented chiefs' and the people got on like cats and dogs. The second problem was that the British system of colonial rule did nothing to unify Nigeria or prepare it for independence. It isolated north from south, strengthening inter-regional rivalry. Years later, Nigeria was to pay a huge price – the Biafran War.

Independence

The cry for independence rang loud during the '50s. The northerners began worrying that the south's educational advantages would enable the southerners to dominate the country. The British reacted by giving the northerners even more regional autonomy. In the hard-fought elections of 1959, the Northern Peoples Congress party came out ahead but failed to win a majority. Its leader, Sir Abubakar Tafawa Balewa, a moderate well-spoken northerner and former school teacher, was asked by the British to form a government. This he did with the Ibo-dominated National Council for Nigeria and the Cameroun's party, thus isolating the Yoruba. When independence finally came in 1960, he became the country's first prime minister, to be joined in power three years later by Dr Nnamdi Azikiwe, an Ibo, who became president when a republic was declared in 1963. The British solution to the country's regional political conflicts was to divide the country into three regions, each governed by a party representing the majority in that region – the Hausa-Fulani in the north, the Yoruba in the south-west, and the Ibo in the south-east. It didn't work. Each region began governing itself as though it were a separate country, and tensions arose over who was to dominate the federal parliament in Lagos.

The coalition government of the First Republic was a disaster. Competition for civil service jobs became fierce, corruption was widespread, the gap between the haves and have-nots was wider than ever and major strikes became an annual event. The elections of 1965 were so outrageously rigged that protesting groups went on a rampage. In early 1966 the military staged a bloody coup, assassinating Tafawa Balewa, the premiers in the north and west and most of the senior army officers. An Ibo general took over, declaring soon after that the public service was to become nationwide – an advantage for the better educated Ibo. Northerners staged anti-Ibo riots and killed hundreds. This was followed by a counter-coup that reinstated northern control. A second wave of killings in the north followed; an estimated 10,000 to 30,000 Ibo were massacred.

In 1967, unable to take the abuse any longer, the Ibo declared an independent republic of Biafra. Civil war began. Seeing an opportunity to secure drilling rights in oil-rich Biafra, France threw its support behind Biafra. So did Côte d'Ivoire, South Africa, Portugal and Rhodesia, all of which wished to see Africa's giant split up. Washington supported the federal government, but the press was pro-Biafra, showing scenes of mass starvation. The world responded with donations of food, much of which rotted in the harbours. Biafra printed its own money, issued its own stamps and had its own TV station – on the back of a truck. After 2½ years and the death of one million people, federal Nigeria won. Africa's worst post-independence tragedy was over.

Oil Boom

Within several years, the war had virtually been forgotten, eclipsed by the oil boom. Oil production jumped sevenfold between 1965 and 1973, and world prices skyrocketed. Overnight, well-placed people became millionaires. By 1975 Nigeria found itself with a US$5 billion surplus. The military government went on a spending spree. New construction projects began sprouting like plants after the first rains. Foreign contractors with their pockets stuffed with *dash* (bribe) money rushed to Lagos, and were shocked to find that driving from the airport to the city centre took four hours – at six km/h. Crime was rampant. People were advised not to abandon their vehicles for any reason as a car would be a mere skeleton within hours.

The chaos became unbearable. When the president went away for a conference in 1975, a group of military officers took over power. A year later, military malcontents assassinated the leader, but the coup attempt failed. The spending spree continued. The five-year plan called for seven new universities, a new federal capital at Abuja, 13 new TV stations, 34 new prisons, 20,000 km of new paved roads and FESTAC, a Black arts festival that won world acclaim but reportedly cost a staggering US$200 million.

Politically, Nigeria was, as it still is, in

constant flux. In 1979 its military leaders proclaimed that they would adopt a US-style constitution. Thus Nigeria became the world's third-largest democracy, behind India and the USA. The new constitution provided for presidential elections, a vice president, two chambers of representatives and a supreme court. A northern Hausa-Fulani, Shagari, was sworn in as president.

In 1981 the world recession sent commodity prices tumbling. Oil revenues fell from US$25 billion in 1980 to US$5 billion in 1986. Prices and salaries were frozen, new construction projects curtailed and imports of nonessentials banned. Construction at Abuja slowed to a snail's pace. Only the brewing industry prospered.

Within four years the Second Republic had fallen. With rising crime, soaring inflation, mass unemployment and widespread corruption, Shagari had failed miserably. Amid rioting in the south following the announcement of electoral victory by a party perceived as northern, the military staged yet another coup. Most Nigerians welcomed the new régime.

Shagari's successor, Bahari, handled the economy no better, refused to deal with the International Monetary Fund (IMF), and tried to silence government critics. Totally inept, he lasted 20 months. The people celebrated again when the military ousted him in its sixth coup since independence – an African record. This coup, led by General Ibrahim Babangida, was bloodless.

The Babangida Years
Babangida, the new head of state, gained instant popularity by releasing political prisoners, including Nigeria's most popular singer, Fela Anikulapo Kuti. He also lifted press controls, making Nigeria's press among the most liberal in West Africa. Babangida also started a virtual economic revolution. Going further than the IMF dared recommend, he reopened the borders, devalued the naira fourfold, dismantled many of the major marketing boards, and privatised unprofitable public enterprises.

As a result of the devaluation, the black market virtually disappeared and prices decreased by about two-thirds. Labour became cheap, particularly in comparison to countries with the overvalued CFA. When economies in the French showcases (Côte d'Ivoire and Cameroun) began to decline, foreign investors, notably the French, began pulling out of the CFA zone. With the encouragement of the French government, some of this money went into Nigeria.

But devaluation and the West's other magic remedies bore little tangible fruit. Oil revenues dropped again and the debt rose up to US$20 billion. Crime increased; police and soldiers were often the worst culprits. Nigeria Airways had eight operational aircraft, down from a high of 27 in the 1970s. Roads emptied as car costs rose. Even the mail system deteriorated as postal workers routinely pilfered letters that appeared to contain money.

The country was broke, the annual budget deficit up to an astonishing US$4 billion a year. Quite simply, Babangida had supported too many projects: the largest aluminium smelting project in sub-Saharan Africa, a 13-year-old Soviet-designed steel plant at Ajaokuta on the Niger River, a new federal capital at Abuja, nine new regional governments, and the stationing of thousands of troops in Liberia in support of the peacekeeping mission there.

Despite the financial chaos, Babangida's liberal politics were, for a time, popular. In 1989, in the 'Abuja Declaration', he lifted the ban on political parties, declaring that there could be two political parties. Some 13 parties vied for the honour and submitted applications but Babangida rejected them all, instead forming two completely new political parties, the Social Democratic Party (SDP) and the National Republican Convention (NRC). Supposedly left-wing and right-wing respectively, they are really quite similar. Babangida then opened the road to Nigeria's Third Republic by setting 1992 as the year for returning the country to civilian rule and moving the federal capital to Abuja. A coup attempt in 1990 by disgruntled soldiers failed. State elections were held in December 1991, with the NRC winning 16 of the 30 governorships and the SDP winning a majority in the Houses of Assembly.

Spring of 1992 found Babangida dealing with one crisis after another in a climate of dwindling support and continued economic difficulties. None was greater than that of fuel shortages, which caused heavy riots throughout the country; in spite of Nigeria's wealth of oil there was an acute gasoline shortage, with three out of four refineries closing down. Large-scale smuggling of fuel to neighbouring countries further added to the scarcity. The devaluation of the naira by almost 50% doubled prices for food and consumer goods.

Keeping to his promise of returning the government to civilian rule, Babangida allowed the first legislative elections in 12 years, with the SDP winning a majority of the seats in both the Senate and the House of Representatives. These were followed in September by the first presidential primaries. Babangida then voided the results. Giving electoral fraud as the reason, he dissolved the leadership of the parties and disqualified all 23 candidates, postponing new presidential elections and the transition to civilian rule until June 1993. His only proactive gesture was to appoint an official Transitional Council (TC), led by Earnest Shonekan, to guide the return to civilian rule.

Both parties selected candidates and the elections were held in the summer. The SDP candidate, Moshood Abiola, a wealthy Yoruba Muslim from the south, was the apparent winner. The High Court, however, quickly nullified the elections, causing widespread rioting.

Had the election results been allowed, Abiola would have become the first member of the Yoruba tribe to beat a Hausa-Fulani candidate and become president. For the first time in Nigeria's history, people voted across ethnic and religious lines – a momentous break from past elections. The military, on the other hand, continued to be dominated by the Hausa-Fulani, and their resistance to Abiola was viewed by many Yoruba as indicative of the Hausa-Fulani's reluctance to share political power. For the fourth time in three years the transition to civilian rule was suspended; again, Babangida promised he would step down from power soon.

After annulling the election results, Babangida issued two new rules for candidates: presidential candidates had to be more than 50 years old (Tofa was 46), and they needed to have belonged to their party

for more than a year (Abiola had not). Public dissatisfaction swelled. At least 30 high-ranking military officers also retired in protest, declaring that the military's rule was the largest obstacle to the development of democracy. Campaign for Democracy, a coalition of 40 human rights, trade and labour groups organised a nationwide strike. The results of the election, published by the same organisation, showed Abiola had won 19 of 30 states and captured 58.4% of the 14.3 million votes cast.

Immediately following the elections and amidst deepening turmoil, Babangida scurried to schedule new elections for August 14. The SDP refused to participate, saying Abiola's right to the presidency was being denied. Babangida then shut down radio stations and five newspapers in a desperate attempt to quell the chaos. Various religious, ethnic and military leaders added their voices and condemned the election nullification. His last days were spent empowering the TC, which was unelected and did not represent civilians. Then in late August 1993, Babangida stepped down, ending his eight-year rule.

Nigeria Today

Earnest Shonekan, chairperson of the TC and now president, inherited a US$34-billion debt and a country in economic and political upheaval. His first priority, he claimed, was to hold 'democratic' elections. He and newly appointed Vice President General Sani Abacha urged Nigerians to be patient. Despite his immediate act of releasing three political prisoners, violent rioting around the country broke out, resulting in scores of deaths. The chaos continued. Abiola, who by this time had fled the country, denounced the puppet government and called upon the international community to do the same.

Shonekan lasted three months. Several days after announcing that fuel prices would increase sevenfold, he was ousted in a bloodless coup by his vice president, Abacha, who had played key roles in the 1983 and 1985 coups. It was the seventh coup since Nigeria gained independence. Abacha immediately made plans to dissolve all national, state and local assemblies, once again subjecting the country to military rule. He also vowed to dissolve the two political parties and ban all political activity and meetings.

Establishing a Provisional Ruling Council and appointing himself chairperson, Abacha created a tightly constructed power base from which he could rule. In a surprise move, he chose a primarily all-civilian cabinet that included Abiola's running mate. But it has not been smooth sailing for Abacha.

Strikes and protests by students and oil workers have been a constant since he assumed power. Striking oil workers have been particularly damaging, seriously reducing the output of Nigeria's economic lifeblood. In a country that receives more than 90% of its foreign-exchange income from oil, the results are disastrous. The strikes have caused oil prices on the world market to fluctuate and proved to be a substantial embarrassment to Abacha.

The average Nigerian is no better off today than at the end of the civil war in the late 1960s. Population growth and neglect of the agricultural sector are two reasons; government mismanagement and corruption are others. Beside the obvious economic difficulties, the most significant pain in Abacha's side was Abiola, who'd returned to Nigeria to claim the presidency. The presumed president-elect went so far as to take the presidential oath and declare his intentions to set up a rival government. Naturally, Abacha quickly ordered Abiola's arrest. After several weeks' search, Abiola was found and charged with treason. Abiola's incarceration continues to spark riots, with oil workers' and university teachers' unions, students and other groups demanding he be sworn in as president.

Even dissent among the military is gaining strength as larger numbers of personnel, opposed to Abacha's hard-line positions, find their pay and prestige diminishing. Approximately one-third of the armed forces also happen to be Yoruba. In August 1994, Abacha replaced the commanders of the army and navy and openly threatened to punish all opponents of the government.

In his attempt to maintain a grip on power, many leading Nigerian politicians, intellectu-als, labour leaders, politicians, pro-democracy leaders and retired military leaders have been arrested. Crackdowns on the opposition has also resulted in dozens of newspapers, like the *Guardian*, being shut down – this in a country once known for having one of the most liberal press in Africa. Perhaps Abacha's most distressing act has been the suspension of habeas corpus – the right of an arrested suspect to appear before a judge.

Among the victims is one of Nigeria's most prized authors and the first African to win the Nobel Prize, Wole Soyinka. An outspoken critic of the Abacha régime and a driving force in the pro-democracy movement, Soyinka fled Nigeria in November 1994 to avoid arrest. He is now calling for an international boycott of the country; his argument is that while an economic boycott would be painful, it is the only medicine for Nigeria's present disease. Several of Soyinka's books have been banned and his office raided. An author who was not fortunate enough to escape arrest is Kenule Saro-Wiwa, president of the Movement for the Salvation of the Ogoni People. The Ogoni homeland of Kidere, where much of Nigeria's oil comes from, has been irremediably polluted, but the Ogoni themselves have received none of the oil's benefits.

The single fear shared by all the many critics of the government is the potential that still exists for widespread factional fighting and bloodshed along ethnic and religious lines – something Nigeria experienced during the Biafran War.

The question remains whether Abacha can withstand this storm of protest, maintain support among the military and manipulate the public like Babangida – whose fancy manoeuvring won him the nickname Maradona – or whether the military will step down, or even be forced down.

GEOGRAPHY

Over three times the size of the UK, Nigeria occupies 15% of West Africa (but has 56% of its people). The topography is unexciting. The only mountains are in the far east along the Cameroun border, affording some spectacular scenery but too far off the beaten path for most. In the centre around Jos is a plateau area in the 1500-metre range, with the most pleasant climate in the country. With short grass and open scenery, this central savannah area offers some fairly impressive sights. The north borders the Sahel and is largely savannah, with a drier climate. Cutting north-west to south-east is the Niger River, Africa's third-longest river. The Benue flows west from Cameroun, emptying into the Niger near Lokoja.

The coastal oil-producing region is almost a different country, with lagoons, mangrove swamps, sandy beaches, innumerable streams and, as you move inland, thick forests. Before malaria tablets, the hot muggy coast, the Bight of Benin, was infamously hostile to foreigners: 'Beware, beware, the Bight of Benin, where one comes out though forty go in.'

Nigeria has extraordinary biological diversity. Most of it, however, is on a swift path to destruction. Nigeria's major environmental problems stem in large part from the rapidly increasing population. One consequence of this is deforestation. During the 1980s, the average annual deforestation rate in Nigeria was 2.7%; in West Africa only Côte d'Ivoire had a higher rate. Moreover, very little land in Nigeria is protected – less than one-third of the all-Africa average, which isn't very high. In Nigeria, the failure to protect forests has allowed the destruction of animal habitats by human activity to go unabated. The number of mammal species threatened with extinction here is the second-highest in the world.

CLIMATE

Nigeria's weather pattern differs substantially between the north and the south. In the north, the climate is like that of the Sahel – hot and dry, with one long rainy season from late May to the end of September. Between March and May, temperatures reach 45°C. Along the coast, temperatures average 5 to 10°C less, but the humidity can be unbearable. There, it rains most heavily between April and July, peaking in June; September to October is a second, minor rainy season.

FLORA, FAUNA & NATIONAL PARKS

While Nigeria doesn't have a huge population of large mammals, one can still see a number of animals and the bird-watching is excellent.

The **Yankari National Park** is the most famous of the parks in Nigeria and the most developed. While one can expect to see waterbuck, elephant and baboon, the real pull here is birds. Yankari, a stopover for migratory birds, is an ornithologist's dream. There are approximately 600 species of birds that call Yankari home for a time; savannah, wetland, river and raptor species are all found here.

The **Cross River National Park** (in the far east near Obudu Cattle Ranch) is an exciting place to visit as gorillas, which were previously believed to be extinct here, have been spotted; camping and hiking possibilities also exist. The World Wildlife Fund (WWF) has an office in Obudu; check there before starting out. The park entrance is approximately 30 km north-east of Ikom on the Ikom-Obudu road.

The **Gashaka Game Reserve** near Yola is the largest national park in Nigeria and has the most diverse wildlife and terrain – areas of guinea savannah, pockets of gallery and mountain forest, and Chapal Waddi, the highest mountain in Nigeria. You might see primates, chimps, hippos and a staggering number of birds. Very basic accommodation is available. The entrance to the reserve is about 50 km north of Gembu on the Gembu-Serti road, 16 km south of Serti. The park is mostly to the east of that north-south road.

The **Okomo Sanctuary** is less than one hour from Benin City and home to a patch of real rainforest. It is also host to the endangered white-throated monkey and the forest elephant, and various birds including cranes and hornbills. There is a fantastic tree house 65 metres up with a commanding view of the lake. To get to Okomo, head due west from Benin City (not the north-west route to Lagos) for 30 km to Udo; it's nearby. **Kamuku Wildlife Reserve**, west of Kaduna, not far from Birnin Gwari (122 km west of Kaduna), is another great place for bird-watchers, as is the **Hadejia-Nguru Wetlands**. Located near the town of Nguru, about 200 km north-east of Kano, this project is supported by the Nigerian Conservation Foundation (NCF).

Another group involved in national parks and environmental matters is the British Vol-

untary Service Overseas (VSO). Their main
office is in Kano at 9B Myohaungu Rd, and
although they are quite busy, they can provide
travellers with information on current programmes. The volunteers working in the field
also enjoy the occasional visitor – especially
when they bring magazines – and are a good
source of local information.

GOVERNMENT

Nigeria's current military dictatorship is supposedly a stepping stone to the country's
return to democracy. Nigeria drafted a constitution in 1979 that provided for a
president, vice president, two chambers of
representatives and a supreme court. That
may change, since a constitutional delegation has been convened to 'determine the
future constitutional structure of Nigeria'.
The military government insists on vetting
any such proposals. Almost a constant of the
political scene, however, are the distrust,
apathy and resignation of the people, after
years of waiting for civilian rule. For a
picture of the Nigerian political climate, see
Nigeria Today earlier in this section.

ECONOMY

With such a turbulent government, Nigeria's
economy has suffered. The country is frighteningly dependent on oil. As the world's
10th-largest producer of black gold, oil
accounts for 90% of Nigeria's foreign
exports and 80% of foreign earnings. Contrast this with the fact that in 1960 food
accounted for 70% of its exports and it was
the largest producer of palm kernels and
palm oil. Nigeria now imports cooking oil
and food imports cost billions of dollars.

As finance minister under Babangida,
Earnest Shonekan set a budget plan in 1993
which, by 1995, projected to reduce inflation
from 46% to 5% and lower the budget deficit
from 12.4% to 3.3% of GDP; this was intended
to stabilise the exchange rate, fortify the private
sector and thus attract foreign investors. Addi-
tionally, in an effort to appease the IMF and
World Bank he attempted to boldly raise fuel
prices fourfold and cut government subsidies.
The resulting public outcry, and Shonekan's
overthrow, killed any chance for progress
towards these goals.

By mid-1994 Nigeria's foreign debt had
grown from US$20 billion to a shocking
US$34 billion, while the price of oil had
dropped by more than one-third. With fraud
and mismanagement running rampant in the
oil industry and frequent oil strikes, there is
little hope that the country can soon shrug off
its debts. The government, trying to stimulate industry (now running at about 35%
capacity), reintroduced foreign exchange
controls, but for companies needing foreign-
sourced components the shortage of foreign
currency has made matters worse. Because
local petrol is so heavily subsidised (the real
price is thought to be the lowest in the
world), over 100,000 barrels are smuggled
out of the country every day with the collusion of government officials and the army.
Meanwhile the US government, angry with
Nigeria's slow progress towards democracy,
has refused Nigeria Airways permission to
land in the USA.

In sum, the situation is spiralling virtually
out of control. Inflation is rampant; real
incomes are at least one-third less than in
1974, and per capita incomes have dropped

from US$860 in 1982 to US$290 in 1994. By some estimates, this is lower than it was in 1965, before Nigeria's oil began flowing in. While Nigeria has numerous breweries, autoplants, oil and a highway system that is the envy of the region, there are so many obstacles that the future looks very grim.

POPULATION

Nigeria has a population of roughly 105 million according to World Bank statistics. Almost one in two West and Central Africans is a Nigerian. Most importantly, the population is increasing by 3.4% annually (the fifth-highest growth rate in Africa) and doubling every 19 years. By 2025, with an estimated 285 million people, Nigeria will be the third most densely populated place, behind India and China but just ahead of the USA! From a different perspective, in just 19 years Nigeria will need twice the amount of food and double the number of hospitals and schools it has now just to maintain present standards.

It is a grim scenario that bodes tragically for the country's future. Efforts to curb the population growth aren't working. During the late 1980s, the US government poured more money into population-control programmes in Nigeria than in any other country in the world. Unlike similar programmes in Asia and Latin America, the effort has had minimal impact. The number of couples using contraception is less than 10%. In Kenya and India it is 18% and 35%, respectively; literacy, often a major constraint, doesn't appear to be a factor in this. Nigerians are as literate as Indians, and the literacy rate is higher than in any other country in West Africa apart from Ghana and Cape Verde.

PEOPLE

Nigeria has over 250 ethnic groups, most with their own language, but three stand out

Elaborately carved door panel from a Yoruba dwelling

– the Hausa in the north, the Ibo (or Igbo) in the east and the Yoruba in the west around Lagos and Ibadan. Nigeria's religions follow ethnic lines: the Muslims dominate the north, Catholics the east, and animists the west. These three groups constitute two-thirds of the country's population. Countless smaller linguistic groups (Ido, Nupe, Efik, etc) make up the other third. In some ways, these minorities help unify Nigeria as a nation; since none could be politically viable independently, they tend to forge alliances as it suits their interests, thereby blurring the tribal-political divisions.

Other than a recent past of rigged elections, Nigerians as a people have no common history, and ethnic rivalries are fiercer now than ever. In large part this is due to the scramble for national resources. The country's vast petroleum wealth is pooled at the centre and redistributed among the 30 states. The states compete for the federal government's favour, thus reinforcing the respective groups' strong community and ethnic identities. By insisting that individuals declare their towns of origin on all government forms, government policy actually formalises ethnic rivalry. And political patronage – the bedrock of Nigerian politics – has in turn fed off these regional rivalries, further undermining national solidarity.

Yoruba

The Yoruba historically have been Africa's most prolific artists. In museums, you may see the large helmet masks of the Epa cult, the most spectacular of the Yoruba masks. During festivals, the wearer must jump on to an earth mound one metre tall – no small feat since masks can be up to 1.5 metres tall and weigh 30 kg. Yoruba chiefs were treated royally. They wore beaded crowns; some had beaded umbrellas, cushions, sceptres and slippers as well. Elaborately carved house posts and doors from their dwellings can be seen in the local museums.

Hausa-Fulani

The Hausa-Fulani are mainly Muslim. Long the dominant group in the political arena, Hausa states before independence were ruled by family dynasties. The Fulani, who were primarily nomadic herders, led the jihads against corrupt Hausa rulers and enforced fundamentalist Islam. Today, the Emirs of the north continue to wield considerable political and religious power; and cattle, a common sight in the north, continue to be a source of pride and wealth among the Fulani.

Hausa is the dominant language of the north, with much of its vocabulary of Arabic origin. Because it is a tonal language, one word can have a variety of meanings depending upon the pitch, tone and intonation; for example *kashi* can mean 'heap,' 'fighting,' 'rain soaked,' or 'excrement'. The pastoral Fulani speak Fulfulde in addition to Hausa.

Ibo

The third-largest ethnic group in Nigeria is the Ibo. Pre-European contact saw the Ibo organised in clan affiliations. The Ibo flourished under the colonial system and quickly took advantage of missionary education. The result was that Ibo came to fill many administrative posts. While the lion's share of Nigeria's oil is in Iboland, not much of the wealth is ploughed back into the community and they remain disenfranchised and largely out of the circles of power.

ARTS

Ancient Africa's view of the universe was an all embracing and religious one, and acts, particularly acts of creation, were seldom, if ever, carried out without a reason, an intention, or appropriate ritual preparation...There was no division between the sacred and the profane...Pre-colonial African art is a form of religious participation in the forces of life, and a way of belonging to both the visible and the invisible worlds.
Introduction to African Art by Warren M Robbins

This art, finally recognised as some of the finest in the world, must be viewed from an occult or religious perspective which sees the living dynamic force behind all appearances. Each work had a purpose or a function (though interpretations are still controversial) and artists were thought only to be mediums for transmissions from the creator.

Nigeria's vast array of art forms attests to the diversity of cultures, yet they all maintain the underlying themes of respect for life, unity of life, and unity of all things.

Perhaps the most well-known arts in Nigeria are the sculptures of bronze, terracotta and wood; the great expressions of the Yoruba, Nupe, Igbira, and Igala. The third Oni Obalufon, an early chief, reputedly started metal casting. These early pieces use the lost-wax method of casting, producing very advanced forms, though despite the recovery of hundreds of sculptures in the Ife region, archaeologists have been unable to find evidence of a foundry.

Equally impressive are the bronzes of Owo and Benin. The largest bronze cast, that of the Gara figure of a divine king or warrior, is of Owo origin.

Bronze portrait head

Older and more numerous than the bronzes are the terracotta works. Archaeologists have unearthed exquisite examples of varied sculptures, often more abstract than the bronzes, that include representations of human and mythical figures used both in ceremony and daily practices.

There is also Yoruba appliqué cloth and some brilliant surviving woodcarvings from Dahomey. The soapstone figures from Esie in the Iloun, the pottery, metalwork and glass-making of Nupe, and the phenomenal beadwork of the Yoruba are just a few of the great reflections of pre-colonial Nigeria. Don't miss the museums here; they really help to understand the spiritual, political, and social fabrics of the cultures as they were.

LITERATURE

Nigeria seems to have as many writers as the rest of Black Africa combined. Chinua Achebe is Nigeria's most famous author, followed by Wole Soyinka, Ben Okri, Amos Tutuola and Cyprian Ekwensi. Some of their works are discussed under Books in the introductory Facts for the Visitor chapter.

In 1986, the Yoruba Wole Soyinka was awarded the Nobel Prize for Literature – only the fifth time that the prize has been awarded to a person from the Third World. Having written over 20 plays, four volumes of poetry and two novels, he is the most versatile of Nigeria's writers. He is best known, however, as a playwright. *A Dance of the Forests* written in 1963 for the independence celebration, *The Man Died, Opera Wonyosi* and *A Play of Giants* are some of his more well-known plays.

Most of the writings of this new Nigerian hero are devastating denunciations of the corrupt government and commercial establishment that has held power since independence, and all who service and benefit from it. As Soyinka says in his introduction to *Opera Wonyosi*:

Art should expose, reflect, indeed magnify the decadent, rotted underbelly of a society that has lost its direction, jettisoned all sense of values and is careering down a precipice as fast as the latest artificial boom can take it.

This one-time playwright for the Royal Court Theatre in London has also written popular satirical comedies, such as *The Trials of Brother Jero*. Some people find his denunciations too bitter, a charge which Soyinka replies to in *The Man Died*, written while he was in prison for 27 months during the Biafran War: 'The man dies in all who keep silent in the face of tyranny.'

Another major writer is Flora Nwapa, an Ibo teacher and administrator, who was the first Nigerian woman to have a novel published. Most of her stories focus on the problems women face in marriage and with children. Critics have praised her skill in presenting her women characters as individuals and dealing with their special burdens.

Her first book, *Efuru* (1966), deals with the role of women in Ibo society. *Idu* (1970) concerns the importance of children in the African family. She has since formed her own publishing company, Flora Nwapa & Co, and published 12 stories, seven of which she wrote. Her latest, *Once Is Enough*, is about a childless woman caught in a bad marriage. Buchi Emecheta has followed in Nwapa's footsteps, publishing seven novels and attaining some recognition as well.

MUSIC

Some of Africa's best known singers come from Nigeria. Foremost among them are Fela Anikulapo Kuti and Sunny Ade, followed by Sonny Okosun, the group Ghetto Blaster and Ebenezer Obey. Sunny Ade is king of the extremely popular juju music, a style unique to Nigeria. (He recently teamed up with Onyeka Onwenu to record *Choices* and *Wait For Me*, two songs encouraging family planning; both are hits, with royalties going to the Planned Parenthood Federation). Sonny Okosun plays a funk/highlife/Afro-pop synthesis called Afro-Soul, while Ebenezer Obey plays an older form of highlife.

Fela stands out as Africa's most famous musician. Immensely popular in Nigeria, he's also the most politically vocal, and various Nigerian governments have taken revenge. Travelling to Los Angeles in 1964, he met Malcolm X who stirred Black consciousness in him. On the musical front, James Brown influenced Fela greatly. Returning to Nigeria, he mixed Brown's soul music with the many cultural intricacies of Nigerian music to create Afro-beat. During the '70s, he formed the Kalakuta Republic, a commune for playing music. The government burned it down in 1977, resulting in his mother's death two days later. Exiled in Ghana from 1978 to 1980, he returned to Nigeria and continued playing music with lyrics critical of the régime. In 1985 he was put in jail on currency smuggling charges, then released a year later when the judge – under the present régime – admitted it was a frame-up. Fela was also accused in 1993 of killing a man whose body was found near his compound; Fela and his brother, a key figure in the group Campaign for Democracy, rebutted the charge as politically motivated. *Confusion Breaks Bones* is one of Fela's latest albums blasting at the military; he also targets international organisations such as the IMF.

RELIGION

There are three primary religions practised in Nigeria: Christianity, Islam, and animism. The Christians dominate the south, while the Muslims are most populous in the north. The Igbo, or Ibo, in the south are the principal people practising animism. In addition, there are countless cults and syncretic religions that combine, for example, Christianity with local spirits and guardians.

Islam expanded into Nigeria via the trans-Sahara trading caravans and various holy wars. Today, evidence of its influence is seen in every aspect of life in the north, from the soaring minarets sounding out the muezzin's call to the ritual ablutions and dress of the faithful. As with Muslims everywhere, Nigerians strongly uphold the five pillars of Islam and pray five times daily. If you happen to be in Kano on a Friday, the sacred day of prayer, you can witness the extraordinary scene of 50,000 people gathering in and around the Great Kano Mosque.

Christianity arrived much later with the colonial powers. There are both Catholics and Protestants as well as vast numbers of Christian sects throughout the south that have fused the Christian with traditional beliefs. The Aladura church is a unique result of the meeting between two distinct cultures and an original religion in its own right. Today, a Nigerian's choice of church often reflects their social class. Christianity is strongest along the coast.

Animism and traditional beliefs comprise the third type of religion in Nigeria. In a country with over 250 different languages, there are not surprisingly a tremendous number of cults, groups and religions. Two common threads are the notion of a Supreme Being who created all and the spiritual nature of every entity. A local river that floods its banks might be interpreted as the river god expressing anger. A spirit intermediary would be called upon to stop or prevent such

Islamic Architecture

Islamic life centres around the mosque, and while there are many differences in size, shape and opulence, mosques have a basic design common to all. Ablution chambers – where believers wash out the mouth and neck, hands to the elbows and feet – lead to a large enclosed courtyard divided into three aisles. The 'Mithrab', or prayer niche, faces Mecca and orients the faithful where they are led in prayer by the imam.

Since Islam prevents any 3-D representations of human or animal figures, calligraphy is heavily stressed in lieu of paintings. A great example of the wedding between mosque design and calligraphy can be found in the Zaria Friday Mosque. Concealed within its structural shape – pillars, columns and arches – are patterns based on the name of Allah. While entrance to a mosque is allowed only to the faithful, one may visit the informative replica of the Zaria Friday Mosque in the Jos museum complex. ■

a disaster. Ancestors worship is also strong due to the belief that ancestors can influence the spirit world and bring luck or prevent illness. Sacrifices are made to appease the various lesser deities, spirits and ancestors. Juju plays an important role in many peoples' lives; a stroll through almost any market in the south will reveal baskets of animal skulls, dried insects, bones and other accoutrements used in juju ceremonies.

LANGUAGE

English is the official language. The three principal African languages are Hausa in the north, Ibo in the south-east and Yoruba in the south-west around Lagos.

Expressions in Ibo

Good morning.	*ee-BOW-lah-chee*
Good evening.	*nah-NO-nah*
How are you?	*ee-MAY-nah ahn-GHAN?*
Thank you.	*ee-MAY-nah*
Goodbye.	*kay-MAY-see-ah*
White person	*bay-kay*

Expressions in Hausa

Greeting.	*soon-NEW*
(response)	*YOW-wah soon-NEW*
Good morning.	*ee-nah-EE-nee*
(response)	*lah-FEE-yah-low*
Good evening.	*ee-nah-WOH-nee*
(response)	*lah-FEE-yah-low*
How are you?	*BAR-kah?*
I'm fine.	*lah-FEE-yah-low*
Thank you.	*nah-GOH-day*
Goodbye.	*SAY-goh-bay*
White person	*bau-TU-ree*
Black person	*BUT-ying-bata*

Expressions in Yoruba

Good morning.	*eh-KAH-roh*
Good evening.	*EE-kou-roh-lay*
How are you?	*BAH-un?*
I'm fine.	*AH-dou-pay*
Thank you.	*oh-SHAY*
Goodbye.	*OH-dah-boh*
White person	*OYH-yee-boh*
Black person	*DOO-doo*

Colloquial English Expressions

don	past tense, eg 'I don chop'
go	future tense, eg 'I go chop'
buka	shanty restaurant
kiss	bump another car
quench	to break down
sabi	know, eg 'I sabi am' (I know it)
hear	speak/know, eg 'I hear Ibo'
moto	car
tay	to stay

Facts for the Visitor

VISAS & EMBASSIES
Nigerian Visas

Everyone needs a visa; they can be issued in four days (Africa) or two weeks (USA). Cameroun is a good place to get Nigerian visas as Nigeria has diplomatic representatives in Yaoundé, Douala (24-hour service) and Buea. Embassies in the USA and Europe issue visas valid for two to four weeks. The Nigerian embassy (☎ (202) 822-1500) in Washington, as well as the consulates in New York and San Francisco, issue single-entry visas valid for a month's stay free of charge and process applications in two days. Send two photos, a photocopy of your round-trip airline ticket, a letter of invitation from someone in Nigeria (if you don't know anyone, your travel agent can write one stating you are a tourist), an official bank account statement showing sufficient funds and proof of vaccination for yellow fever. You will also need to submit a confirmation of reservation from a hotel in Nigeria.

The Nigerian consulate in London (☎ (0171) 353-3776) requires one photo, a copy of your round-trip airline ticket, an official bank account statement showing sufficient funds or sufficient money in travellers' cheques, and a letter of invitation from someone in Nigeria addressed to the consulate assuming full financial responsibility for you. The fee varies according to nationality; for Britons and Australians it's UK£30 (UK£50 for multiple-entry visas).

Even though Nigeria has embassies all

over the African continent, including in all four neighbouring countries, getting a visa in Africa is becoming increasingly difficult as more and more Nigerian embassies issue visas only to residents of the country in which they are located. The embassies in Benin, Ghana, Niger and Senegal now require local residency. Moreover, some embassies request that you present a round-trip airline ticket or one with an onward destination. If you do get a visa in Africa, it may be valid only for a short stay; regardless, visas are easily renewable.

Historically, British consulates have acted for Nigeria in those countries where Nigeria has no representation of its own, but this practice is becoming increasingly rare. While visas were once free, many embassies now charge up to UK£80 – a tit-for-tat response to the British restriction on Nigerians entering the UK.

Visa Extensions

For visa extensions, see the Ministry of External Affairs (☎ 635 354) in Lagos at 23 Marina St. Visa extensions cost N 55, but you'll need a letter from a local citizen or resident vouching for you.

Nigerian Embassies

Belgium 3B Ave de Tervueren, Brussels 1040 (☎ (02) 735-40-71)
France 173 ave Victor Hugo, 75016 Paris (☎ (1) 47-04-68-65)
Germany Goldbergweg 13, 5300 Bonn 2 (☎ (0288) 32-20-71/2)
UK 76 Fleet St, London BC4Y (consulate) (☎ (0171) 353-3776, (0891) 600-199, telex 23665)
USA 2201 M St, NW, Washington, DC 20037 (☎ (202) 822-1500). Also in New York (☎ (212) 370-0856)

Nigeria also has embassies in the capital city of every West and Central African country except Cape Verde and São Tomé. In addition, there are embassies in Addis Ababa, Algiers, Athens, Berne, Cairo, Canberra, Dar es Salaam, Dublin, The Hague, Hong Kong, Lisbon, Madrid, Nairobi, New Delhi, Ottawa, Rabat, Rome, Stockholm, Tokyo

and Vienna. It has consulates that issue visas in Buea, Douala, Edinburgh and Liverpool.

Other African Visas

Benin The embassy is open weekdays from 9 am to 3 pm and gives same-day service if you come in the morning. Visas are valid for 15 days but are easily renewable in Cotonou. The cost is N 300 and you'll need one photo. Warning: some US embassy interns had their passports stolen here.
Cameroun The embassy is open weekdays from 9 am to 2 pm and issues visas valid for one month in 24 hours. Bring N 940 and three photos. You'll be asked to show your round-trip airline ticket but if you have one to elsewhere in Africa and plan to travel overland to Cameroun, that is sufficient. You can also get visas to Cameroun with much less hassle in Calabar in 24 hours. The cost is N 1875 and you'll need two photos.
Côte d'Ivoire The embassy requires N 800 plus your photo, a round-trip airline ticket and a photocopy of the first four pages of your passport. It issues visas in 48 hours.
The Gambia The high commission is open weekdays from 9 am to 3 pm and issues visas in 48 hours or less. It requires N 500 and two photos, and the visas are good for up to three-month stays.
Ghana The embassy is open weekdays from 8.30 am to 1 pm and gives same-day service if you arrive in the morning. Bring N 500 and four photos for a three-month visa; N 200 for a transit visa.
Guinea The embassy is open weekdays from 8.30 am to 2.30 pm and will issue the visa on the spot provided you bring three photos and pay N 1250.
Niger The embassy is open weekdays from 9 am to 2.30 pm and issues visas in 24 hours. The cost is N 2000 for visas valid for one month; it requires three photos. You can also get visas to Niger in Kano; the requirements and cost are the same.

Foreign Embassies

For a list of diplomatic missions in Nigeria, see under Information in the Lagos section.

DOCUMENTS

To enter Nigeria, you need a valid passport with a visa for Nigeria and an International Health Certificate showing proof of vaccination for yellow fever.

CUSTOMS

It is illegal to import or export any more than N 50. When leaving, customs officials search passengers fairly rigorously, hoping to confiscate any excess naira. While currency declaration forms are no longer required, you will be issued an immigration card that must be surrendered when you leave the country. Nigeria strictly enforces its laws against exporting Nigerian antiquities; anything that looks old is likely to be confiscated by customs unless you have a certificate (N 150) from the national museum in Lagos indicating that export is OK.

MONEY

CFA 1000	=	N 38
UK£1	=	N 34
US$1	=	N 25

The unit of currency is the naira (N). The official rate is creeping up only very slowly but the black market rate is increasing significantly. At the time of the above rates, the black market rates were US$1 = N 65, UK£1 = N 90 and CFA 1000 = N 105, ie well over double, which is why most travellers change money on the black market or try at a bureau de change, which sometimes gives the free-market rates.

In January 1994 the parallel market was declared illegal and the two-tier system was discontinued. The naira continues to be devalued against foreign currencies in an attempt to control inflation, which is 70% annually.

Many travellers regret bringing travellers' cheques instead of cash. Many bureaux de change won't accept cheques, and some banks won't either. If you're very lucky, you might get an exchange rate about 10% less than that for cash; more often the rate will be about 50% less and you may waste an entire morning at the bank. Among the banks, try the First Bank of Nigeria (FBN); it reportedly gives better rates and its commissions are very low. Credit cards are virtually useless except at major hotels in Lagos. Outside Lagos, no hotels accept them. Interbank transfers are well nigh impossible to accomplish. Bring dollars.

Changing money on the black market is a widespread practice, especially around the Bristol Hotel in Lagos, in just about every town of any size and in neighbouring countries, especially in Lomé (Togo). The obvious advantage is your money goes further, and it is convenient.

In Lagos, for example, you can drive by the Bristol Hotel in a taxi and do your transaction in the taxi quickly, but discretion is the key. Police do frequent Broad St to shake down tourists changing money illegally, so be alert and prudent. US dollars are the hot favourite, particularly US$100 bills, but UK, German and French currencies and the CFA are all readily accepted in Lagos; outside Lagos US dollars are best.

The major banks for changing money are: the FBN, the International Bank for West Africa (IBWA), the Société Générale Banque Nigeria (SGBN), the Union Bank of Nigeria (UBN) and United Bank for Africa (UBA).

Hotel Tax & Deposit
Hotel room bills are subject to a hefty 15% tax; prices quoted in this chapter include it. The top-end hotels and many mid-range hotels require a deposit, often as much as twice the room rate.

BUSINESS HOURS & HOLIDAYS
Business hours are weekdays from 8.30 am to 5 pm. Government offices are open weekdays from 7.30 am to 3.30 pm, and Saturday until 1 pm. Banking hours are Monday to Thursday from 8 am to 3 pm, and Friday until 1 pm.

Sanitation day (when people are theoretically required to go out in the morning and clean up) is the last Saturday of each month. Everything opens late (after 10 am) in order to give people time to clean up.

Public Holidays
1 January, Good Friday, End of Ramadan, Easter Monday, 1 May, Tabaski, Mohammed's Birthday, 1 October (National Day), 25-26 December.

Muslim holidays are observed even in the south. (For Muslim holiday dates, see Cultural Events & Holidays in the introductory Facts for the Visitor chapter.)

CULTURAL EVENTS
Sallah Celebrations
Of all the festivals in West Africa, the most elaborate are the Sallah celebrations in northern Nigeria for the two most important

Islamic holidays – the end of Ramadan and Tabaski, 69 days later.

The principal event is the Durbar, a procession of ornately dressed men mounted on gaily bedecked horses. The Hausa-Fulani horsemen wear breastplates and coats of flexible armour and, on their scarlet turbans, copper helmets topped with plumes. The Emir, draped in white and protected by a heavy brocade parasol embroidered with silver, rides in the middle of the cavalry in blue. He may be followed by traditional wrestlers flexing huge biceps, and lute players with feathered headdresses decorated with cowrie shells. The major Durbars are in the north – Kano, Zaria and, above all, Katsina. Don't miss them, but be prepared for every hotel in town to be booked.

Argungu Fishing & Cultural Festival

In mid to late February this famous three-day festival takes place on the banks of the Sokoto River in Argungu, 100 km southwest of Sokoto. It has acquired international status and attracts visitors from all over the world. The fishing people's customs and traditions are closely tied to Islamic religious practices. Several months before the festival, the Sokoto River is dammed. When the festival begins, hundreds of fishers jump into the river with their nets and gourds. Some come out with fish weighing over 50 kg. It's quite a sight.

Pategi Regatta

Around August, don't miss Nigeria's most photographed festival – the Pategi Regatta. Pategi is on the Niger River, halfway between Ibadan and Kaduna. There's swimming, traditional dancing, acrobatic displays and fishing. The highlight is a rowing competition.

Oshun Festival

On the last Friday in August, this well-known festival in Oshogbo, 86 km north-east of Ibadan, has music, dancing and sacrifices. It is well worth seeing. (Oshun is the water goddess and sacrifices to her help restore the bond between the goddess and the people of Oshogbo.)

Igue Festival

In December, this week-long festival in Benin City includes traditional dancing.

Mnonwu Festival

In December there's the week-long Mnonwu Festival in Enugu, during which there are all kinds of spectacular mask parades.

POST & TELECOMMUNICATIONS

Postal rates are low – N 30 a letter and N 20 for an aerogram – but the service is questionable. Alternatively, try the EMS service; the documents are insured and are almost guaranteed to arrive at their intended destination. The cost to Europe is N 600 per 100 grams.

Telephone services tend to be erratic. Lagos is in the process of digitising its system, but many areas have not been covered. International telephone, fax and telex facilities are generally quite good and efficient; they are available at Nigeria Telecom's (NITEL) principal office in Lagos (Necom House, 14 Marina St) and at NITEL's offices throughout the country. The charges are reasonable, eg N 235 for a three-minute call to North America. The major city (and state) telephone codes are:

Abeokuta (039), Abuja (09), Bauchi (077), Benin City (052), Calabar (087), Enugu (042), Ibadan (022), Ife (036), Ilorin (031), Jos (073), Kaduna (062), Kano (064), Katsina (065), Lagos (01), Maiduguri (076), Makurdi (044), Minna (066), Onitsha (046), Oshogbo (035), Owerri (083), Port Harcourt (084), Sokoto (060), Zaria (068).

BOOKS

Nigeria has produced many gifted writers who have written a number of award-winning books. From the vast sea of words, a few arbitrarily chosen gems include:

Things Fall Apart (Chinua Achebe, 1958) tells the story of the impact of colonialism and religion on a traditional Ibo village at the turn of the century.
The Famished Road (1991) by Ben Okri, an African Gabriel Garcia Marquez, is a winner of the Booker Prize for Fiction. In it modern Nigeria is seen through the magical realism of a young boy's daily experiences.

Yoruba: Nine Centuries of African Art & Thought (Henry John Drewal, John Pemberton III & Rowland Abiodun) is a must for the art enthusiast. It is a hefty tome that covers the art of this creatively fecund people in detail, and has excellent photos.

Nigeria: Giant of Africa (Peter Holmes, 1985) is excellent coffee-table material.

Enjoy Nigeria (Ian Nason, 1993) is good for information on less-travelled roads and little-known towns, natural wonders and celebrations; it's available in Lagos.

MAPS

WAPB Street Maps Lagos 1992 is the latest street guide to Lagos, though the older and in places out-of-date *Winnay Lagos Street Atlas* (1985) is easier to use. *Spectrum Road Map Nigeria* has full contour colouring with a scale of 1:1 500 000.

PHOTOGRAPHY

No permit is required, but use great caution; you may find lots of people who are offended by being photographed. Even when taking photos of crowd scenes, you should ask around to see if people would be offended. As usual, taking photos of bridges, airports, military personnel and installations, harbours, TV and radio stations is prohibited. Be careful: the police are often looking for ways to hassle travellers, sometimes extorting bribes.

HEALTH

A yellow fever vaccination is required of all visitors. There is cerebral malaria in Lagos and along the southern coast and precautions are advised.

For emergencies, the best hospitals in Lagos are St Nicholas Hospital (☎ 263 1739) at 57 Campbell St on Lagos Island and the clean, modern Medical Consultants Group at Flat 4, Eko Court Annexe, Kofo Abayomi St on Victoria Island.

Dr C O Da Silva (☎ 263 6997) is a general practitioner who accepts emergency cases without appointment. Dr Seeman (☎ 268 4125) and Dr B R Bahl (☎ 268 3127) are also recommended.

DANGERS & ANNOYANCES

Lagos is one of the two most dangerous cities in West Africa (Abidjan is the other); Port Harcourt is not far behind. In some areas of Lagos home-owners take turns guarding their neighbourhoods.

For travellers, armed thieves rather than burglars are the major problem. Taxi drivers seem to be involved in most of the thefts involving foreigners, so be careful in picking a driver at the airport, particularly if you are arriving at night (to be avoided if at all possible). Drivers who are well known at the airport are safer; ask the luggage handlers or dispatchers. Be conspicuous about writing down the number of the taxi's licence plate. Also, avoid taxis where there is a second

---

Avoiding Bribes

'Only a masochist with an exuberant taste for self-violence will pick Nigeria for a holiday.' If the Nobel laureate Wole Soyinka has that to say about his country, is it any wonder many travellers approach Nigeria in general and Lagos in particular as though entering a plague zone?

In reality, it isn't that bad. Lagos can indeed be profoundly frenetic, with officials asking for bribes and traffic jams that would test the patience of Job, but the Nigerians can be incredibly amiable and helpful. The police and their fondness for bribes are the main annoyance. Your attitude and how you approach the situation will greatly affect the outcome. Yelling and loudly stating that as a foreigner you should be treated with respect will not gain positive results. Don't scream or become agitated; maintain a calm exterior and keep your voice even. More often than not the situation will work itself out.

Be aware that confrontations with police are a game and you are a player. If you are walking along minding your own business and a police officer queries, 'What have you for me master?', you are not obligated to *dash*, ie give a bribe. A case in point: at the airport a customs official asked me that same question. I replied, 'A firm handshake and a smile'. He broke into a grin and wished me a safe journey. ■

Top: Market vendor, Misau, Nigeria (CBe)
Middle: Decoration on wall of Emir's Palace, Zaria, Nigeria (JK)
Left: Diviner's looking plate, Nigeria (GB)
Right: Nigerian bags (GB)

Top: Pirogues at Yoff Beach, Senegal (DE)
Middle: New Year celebrations, Kabala, Sierra Leone (DE)
Bottom: Bicycle repair men, Vogan, Togo (AN)

Commercial Fraud

Nigerians have made the news for a series of ruses which duped foreign business people. The variations are many but share a common thread; a letter or fax is sent to a business or corporation asking if they are interested in making a profitable amount of money in exchange for use of their bank account. If they show interest the hook is set. A second letter explains that there is a large amount – say US$25 million – of government funds that could be easily transferred by the corrupt Nigerian official if he had access to a foreign bank account. For use of the account the business would receive a 10% cut of the total amount. These Nigerian con-artists play on the lure of easy money and greed of foreign investors; by some accounts, more than US$200 million has been fraudulently collected.

Another ruse is to invite business people to Nigeria and tell them they don't need a visa. The visitor is met at the plane and never sees customs or immigration. After being wined and dined, he or she is asked to transfer $10,000 as a goodwill gesture. If the visitor doesn't make the transfer, the rough stuff begins.

Note: it is unwise and illegal to engage in any business activity in Nigeria on a tourist visa. ■

---

person riding along for some inexplicable reason. Carry your passport at all times – police stops are frequent – but keep it well hidden. Walking alone at night anywhere in Lagos is extremely risky and to be avoided, particularly around hotels and other areas frequented by foreigners.

Once you are outside Lagos and Port Harcourt the risk drops significantly. Leaving Lagos is like a breath of fresh air. Bribery, however, is everywhere. If the police stop you on the road and ask you to 'settle' the problem, they want money, not an explanation. They are empowered to shoot anybody on the streets who does not stop, and they can even arrest you for 'wandering'. Of course they'll be arresting you for nothing – they just want money. In Nigeria, there's one law for the rich and another for the poor. Money can 'settle' anything. The Nigerians know this all too well, which is one reason why Fela Kuti, the only one who dares to sing out against these injustices, is so popular.

ACCOMMODATION

Hotels in Nigeria are reasonably priced just about everywhere except Lagos. Even in Lagos, however, if you're willing to stay at the YMCA or YWCA or in one of the suburbs, you can sleep cheaply. Elsewhere, Nigeria's large cities have hotels to suit all budgets; you'll be able to get a room for under US$5. In some cities, such as Jos,

Sokoto, Ibadan and Kano, there are religious mission guesthouses with rooms at bargain prices. The only city with camping facilities is Kano. Do not expect to camp anywhere else except for in the far eastern region near the Cameroun border where hiking is possible. If you insist on 1st-class accommodation, you won't have much success outside Lagos and Abuja. In Kaduna, Enugu, Maiduguri, Benin City and Port Harcourt, for example, the quality of the best hotels is rather poor for what you pay.

FOOD

Soup is a very common food in Nigeria and it's generally eaten at lunch. Most Nigerians eat soup with their hands, scooping it up with a closed hand in the form of a spoon. As in most of Africa, you only eat with your right hand; indeed, you shouldn't even hand anyone anything with your left hand as it's considered to be the dirty hand. In the south, two favourites of the Yoruba are *egusi soup* and *palm nut soup*. The former is a fiery-hot yellow stew made with meat, red peppers, ground dried prawns and bits of green leaves. The latter is a thicker stew made with meat, peppers, tomatoes, onions and palm nut oil. Other favourites include *fish pepper soup*, *bitter leaf soup*, made with greens and various meats and usually eaten with pounded yams, *groundnut soup*, *ikokore*, a main course made with grounded yams and

---

Egusi

1½ lbs (675 grams) meat, chicken or fish
1/2 cup dried shrimp or crayfish
2-3 cups of fresh okra
1½ cups of tomato paste
2 cups of leafy greens (spinach, kale, etc)

2-3 chilli peppers
1 cup (1/4 litre) palm oil
1/2 cup sliced onions
1 cup egusi seeds (or melon seeds)
salt to taste

Cut the meat or fish into bite-sized chunks and add to 1 cup of water, 1/2 teaspoon salt and half the onions, then cook for 10 minutes. Meanwhile, heat the oil in a heavy pot. Separately, grind or crush the seeds, peppers and crayfish (or shrimp), and tear the greens into small pieces. Remove the oil from the heat and add the remaining onions and tomato paste along with the liquid from the meat, then reheat for several minutes and add all the remaining ingredients, including the meat. Cook for 10 minutes or until the meat is done. This dish serves from four to six people and can be eaten on its own or with rice. ■

---

various fish and popular in the west, *ukwaka*, a steamed pudding based on corn and ripe plantains, various okra-based stews, usually very spicy and tasty, brown beans, paella-like *jollof rice* and *moyin-moyin*, which is a steamed cake of ground dried beans with fish or boiled eggs eaten with *gari* (dried manioc flour) or yams.

You'll also find lots of snack food cooked on the street, including fried yam chips, fried plantains, boiled groundnuts, meat pastries, *akara* (a puffy deep-fried cake made with black-eyed peas and sometimes eaten with chilli dip), *kulikuli* (small deep-dried balls made of peanut paste), *suya* (a hot spicy kebab eaten in the north), and a few sweets such as *chinchin* (fried pastries in strips).

Getting There & Away

AIR

To/From the USA

There are no longer any direct Nigeria Airways flights to/from the USA. Travellers must pass through Europe, another West African country or through Addis Ababa, Cairo, Harare or Nairobi.

To/From Europe

There are direct flights to Lagos from Amsterdam, Brussels, Frankfurt, Geneva, London, Madrid, Moscow, Paris, Rome and Zürich.

Nigeria Airways' nonstop flights from London are nothing like those within West Africa. The service is quite respectable, and departures are reasonably punctual. However, according to Condé Nast, of the world's 50 largest airlines Nigeria Airways comes 47th for safety, ranked by records of fatal accidents.

The cheapest tickets from London are invariably those purchased at bucket shops, and flights with Nigeria Airways are usually the cheapest, starting at UK£350. Airlines Travel PLC (☎ (0171) 437-5555), for example, sells round-trip tickets on Nigeria Airways from London to Lagos for that amount, but there's a one-month return restriction. For a one-year return ticket, the price is UK£485. This special fare is year-round as is the £495 bucket-shop fare on EgyptAir. With most other fares there's a substantial difference between those in the high season (mid-May to mid-September and Christmas time) and the low season, and between those with a one-month return restriction and those with a much longer return restriction. With Air France, for example, the London-Lagos fare with London Student Travel is £489 in the low season and £694 in the high season. Also check with bucket shops about flying with Aeroflot; its fares are low but many bucket shops refuse to deal with them. If you're in Lagos looking for a one-way ticket back to Europe, Balkan Airlines is unbeatable.

British Airways has weekly flights from

London to Kano. This is a much more tranquil way to arrive in Nigeria and is recommended for the first-time visitor.

To/From West Africa

Within West Africa, Nigeria Airways flies all along the coast. The service varies between terrible and atrocious except when there aren't many passengers, which is very rare. At times, so many of the flights are full that you cannot reserve a seat for days. If you buy the ticket and later want a refund, keep dreaming. If you want to change your flight to another airline, Nigeria Airways may refuse to endorse the ticket. If the ticket was purchased with naira, other airlines will not accept it even if they do endorse it. For flights within West Africa, see under Getting There & Away in the Lagos section.

LAND
Bush Taxi

To/From Benin There are direct bush taxis to Cotonou from Lagos Island. You can also board a ferry on Lagos Island to Mile 2 (west of the Apapa district in Lagos), and catch Benin-bound vehicles from the motor park there. Bush taxis charge N 300 to Cotonou and the trip takes three hours in Peugeot 504s, and up to six hours in cheaper minibuses, which tend to be stopped more frequently by police. The coastal border with Benin is open 24 hours and moneychangers abound at the border.

To/From Cameroun You should have no problem finding a bush taxi in Ikom for the 25-km trip to the border (Mfum-Ekok) or in Ekok for other points in Cameroun.

To/From Niger There are four major entry points into Niger. From east to west they are Kano-Zinder, Katsina-Maradi, Sokoto-Birnin-Konni and Kamba-Gaya. The last route is usually the cheapest way to Niamey as you travel more in cheap Nigeria and less in expensive Niger.

Car

The road system is excellent, however,

driving is dangerous, especially on the expressway between Lagos and Ibadan where it's like playing bumper cars at the carnival. Drive only during the day and be aware of frequent police roadblocks – often consisting of a nail-studded board.

Typical driving times are three hours Lagos-Cotonou (longer during rush hour), one day Lagos-Enugu, one to 1½ days Lagos-Kano, 2½ days Lagos-Douala via Ikom, and three days Lagos-Agadez. Should you need help, contact the Automobile Club of Nigeria (☎ 296 0514) at 24 Mercy Eneli St, Surulere in Lagos.

SEA

You can travel to Cameroun by boat from Oron, which is a short ferry ride from Calabar. It's usually a two-day trip from Calabar to Limbe, including an overnight stay in Oron. Alternatively, you can take a bus from Calabar to nearby Ikang on the Cameroun border and then take a boat from there towards Limbe. For more information, see the section on Calabar.

LEAVING NIGERIA

There is a departure tax of US$35 for international flights from Lagos and Kano.

Getting Around

AIR

For air travel within Nigeria, the service on Nigeria Airways is sometimes good. You may find that you cannot book – buy your airline ticket at the airport, and anticipate wasting lots of time as the flight departure schedules are a joke. Any number of expediters will offer to get your ticket. Many are reportedly crooked (as mine was – he was beaten by the police for attempting to run off), so keep an eye on them. Flights are usually full because services have been cut back. In Lagos, flights for the interior do not go from Murtala Mohammed Airport but from an older domestic airport 10 km away.

Don't overlook the private airlines, which are superior and generally more punctual than Nigeria Airways. They include ADC which is the best for safety, Kabo Airlines (to Kaduna, Kano and Jos), Okada Air (to Port Harcourt, Benin City and Enugu), Gas Air (to Kano and Maiduguri), Express Airways (to Kaduna), Sky Power Express Airways (Katsina to Kaduna), Harco, Harka, Bellview and Concord Airlines.

Flights are cheap; for example, N 1950 (Lagos-Kaduna) and N 2000 (Lagos-Jos). Flights from Lagos to Sokoto and Kano cost about the same.

There is a N 50 airport tax for all domestic flights.

BUS

Travel by bus is safer, more comfortable (depending upon the condition of the bus) and cheaper on long-haul routes. There are lines connecting all the main cities. Each bus company has its own offices, often not at the motor park, so finding them isn't always easy. However, most companies tend to have their offices in the same general area. Large buses are typically slightly cheaper than minibuses and about 40% cheaper than bush taxis. Though not quite as fast as bush taxis, they are often more comfortable and seemingly much safer. The main advantage of bush taxis is that they leave at all hours.

BUSH TAXI

The bush-taxi system in Nigeria is unquestionably the fastest and most comfortable in Africa – but it's dangerous. There are two types of Peugeot bush taxis – the Peugeot 504 saloons that take only four or five passengers (more expensive) and the 504 station wagons that take eight. Minibuses are slower and generally at least 25% cheaper than Peugeot 504s. Taxis are cheaper in Nigeria than in any other country in West Africa, eg N 600 from Lagos to Kano (1028 km).

Because Nigeria has so many people, you may have to wait 10 minutes or more for bush taxis on some routes. Drivers try to

compensate by travelling at 140 km/h. Accidents are usually fatal

TRAIN

Trains in Nigeria are so slow that they're not worth taking except, possibly, for short trips such as Kano to Kaduna, typically about six hours. A trip from Ibadan to Kano can easily take 40 hours, at about 25 km/h. By bush taxi the same trip takes 12 hours. Either way the scenery is the same.

Don't let the schedules fool you as trains never arrive on time. Also, the schedules are rarely convenient. Between Ibadan and Kano, for instance, there are only two trains a week (and only one between Lagos and Kano). Moreover, the 1st-class air-con sleeper fare (eg N 528 Lagos to Kano) is barely less than the bush taxi fare. Even though a 2nd-class ticket is a good two-thirds less, the added discomfort on a long trip is hard to bear. The train might seem safer but, as all the derailed cars along the way show, accidents do happen. Rail services have been further sabotaged by railway workers whose wages are many months in arrears. Passenger services have also been suspended on many routes when engines and rolling stock are used to distribute fertiliser during planting seasons. It is conceivable that the Nigerian railways could grind to a halt altogether.

There are three railway lines, none of them particularly scenic. One line connects Lagos with Ibadan, Kaduna and Kano; the Port Harcourt-Maiduguri line passes through Enugu, Jos and Bauchi; the 200-km Kaduna-Kafanchan line connects the two. First-class coaches have sleeping berths, fans and shared toilets; bedding is N 25 extra. The air-con does not work but there is a dining car; it serves only stew and rice, warm beer and tea throughout the long trip.

HITCHING

Hitchhiking in Nigeria is relatively easy, especially in the north. However, unless you make it clear that you can't pay, chances are the driver will expect money – sometimes more than the public transport fare.

Lagos

Most travellers detest Lagos. The city's reputation for crime is worldwide. Its number of inhabitants – nine million – doesn't help matters; during the last 30 years, it has grown 20-fold, a world record for cities of more than one million people. About half of its inhabitants are under the age of 16. By 2025 Lagos is predicted to become one of the world's five-largest cities.

Wide expressways connect the airport with the city centre and encircle Lagos Island (the heart) and nearby Ikoyi and Victoria islands, where you'll find three of the four top hotels and many posh residences.

The city's main attraction is the music; Sunny Ade and Fela Kuti both have their own nightclubs. This hardly makes up for its other faults – hassles with the taxi drivers and police, a dearth of good restaurants, high prices and suspicious people. If you hear of people liking Lagos, chances are they stayed with Nigerians. This seems to be the only way to enjoy it.

Orientation

The heart of Lagos is Lagos Island, where the major banks, department stores and large commercial establishments are found. The major street is Broad St which passes Tinubu Square, a major intersection near the centre of the island, and ends at Tafawa Balewa Square, a large complex with many airline offices and travel agencies. The national museum is just beyond.

Running roughly parallel with Broad St is Marina St, which overlooks the harbour and has numerous large commercial establishments. The commercial heart of the island, however, is the Bristol Hotel on Martins St, just north of Broad St. Within several blocks of the hotel are most banks, the island's major restaurants, airline offices and black marketeers. The entire island is encircled by Ring Rd, a major expressway.

Most of the embassies and big houses are on Victoria and Ikoyi islands, both just to the south-east. At either end of Victoria Island

are the two leading central hotels – the Eko Meridien and the Federal Palace. On Ikoyi Island, the most notable street is the wide Kingsway Rd leading up to the Ikoyi Hotel, but the liveliest street is Awolowo Rd, along which are nearly a dozen major restaurants, the YMCA and numerous embassies.

Most of the city's living quarters are to the north in the direction of the airport and are connected to Lagos Island by three bridges: from east to west they are 3rd Axial Bridge, Carter Bridge and Eko Bridge. Yaba, about five km north of Lagos Island, and Surulere, north-east of it, are major nightclub areas with lots of inexpensive hotels and several markets. Two major expressways, Agege Motor Rd, which connects with both the international and domestic airports, and Ikorodu Rd along which you'll find Sunny Ade's nightclub and Ojota motor park (to Ibadan etc), intersect in Yaba. Ikorodu Rd eventually intersects with the Lagos-Ibadan Expressway, which leads to all points north. Both airports are some 22 km from Lagos Island in Ikeja, where the Sheraton and Fela's nightclub are also located.

Information

Money Lagos has over 50 banks; the three largest are the FBN at 35 Marina St, the UBN at 40 Marina St, and the UBA (a French bank) at 97 Broad St.

Two other major banks include IBWA at 94 Broad St and SGBN at 13 Martins St and 126 Broad St. Moneychangers hang out around the Bristol Hotel and along Broad St.

Post & Telecommunications The main post office is on Marina St on Lagos Island, roughly two blocks south of Tinubu Square. There are smaller branches on Ikoyi Island, about 200 metres east of the intersection of Kingsway and Awolowo Rds, and on Victoria Island, on Adeola Odeku St. They all close on weekends. For phone calls, try the NITEL offices on Marina St on Lagos Island and at the Falomo Shopping Centre on Ikoyi Island.

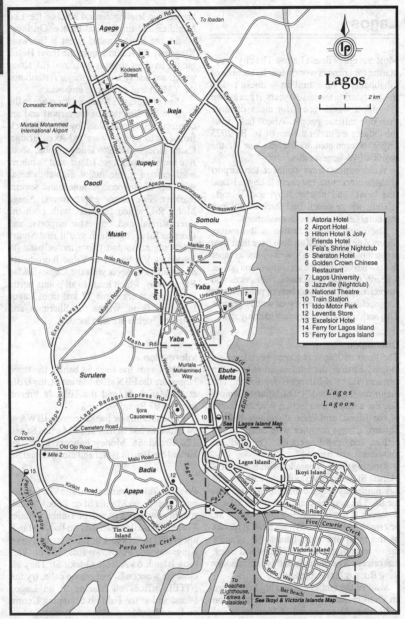

To Ibadan

Lagos

0   1   2 km

Agege

Awolowo Rd

Lagos-Ibadan Road

Oregun Rd

Allen Avenue

Kodesoh Street

Akinpobi St

Airport Road

Ikorodu Road

Expressway

Ikeja

Domestic Terminal

Murtala Mohammed International Airport

Agege Motor Road

Ilupeju

Osodi

Apapa

Oworonsoki

Expressway

Ikorodu Road

Musin

Somolu

Market St

Isolo Road

Lawe St

Expressway

Mushin Road

See Yaba Map

Yaba

University Road

Yaba

Masha Rd

Western Avenue

Ebute-Metta

Murtala Mohammed Way

Surulere

Lagos-Badagri Express Rd

Ijora Causeway

Cemetery Road

Old Ojo Road

Malu Road

Ixiwoya Owonronshi

Apapa Oworonshi Expressway

To Cotonou

Mile 2

Badia

Liverpool Rd

Apapa

Kirikiri Road

Creek Road

Tin Can Island

Porto Novo Creek

3rd Axial Bridge

Lagos Lagoon

See Lagos Island Map

Ring Rd

Lagos Island

Ikoyi Island

Ground Street

Kingsway Road

Awolowo Road

Five Cowrie Creek

Ahmadu Bello Way

Victoria Island

Bar Beach

See Ikoyi & Victoria Islands Map

To Beaches (Lighthouse, Tarkwa & Palasides)

To Ferry to Lagos Island

1	Astoria Hotel
2	Airport Hotel
3	Hilton Hotel & Jolly Friends Hotel
4	Fela's Shrine Nightclub
5	Sheraton Hotel
6	Golden Crown Chinese Restaurant
7	Lagos University
8	Jazzville (Nightclub)
9	National Theatre
10	Train Station
11	Iddo Motor Park
12	Leventis Store
13	Excelsior Hotel
14	Ferry for Lagos Island
15	Ferry for Lagos Island

Foreign Embassies Most are on Victoria Island, particularly the north-west quadrant:

Australia Plot 43, Nurses House, Ozumba Mbadiwe Ave (☎ 261 1020)
Benin 4 Abudu Smith St (☎ 261 4411)
Cameroun 5 Femi Pearse St (☎ 261 2386)
Canada Plot 8A, 4 Idowu Taylor St (☎ 261 2382, telex 21275)
Côte d'Ivoire 3 Abudu Smith St (☎ 261 0963)
Egypt 182B Kofo Abayomi Rd (☎ 261 0660)
Germany 15 Eleke Crescent (☎ 261 1011, telex 21229)
Guinea 8 Abudu Smith St (☎ 261 2206)
Italy 12 Eleke Crescent (☎ 261 2791)
Japan 24/25 Apese St (☎ 261 4929, telex 21364)
Liberia 3 Idejo St (☎ 261 8899)
The Netherlands 24 Ozumba Mbadiwe Ave (☎ 261 2989)
Niger 15 Adeola Odeku St (☎ 261 2300)
Senegal 14 Kofo Abayomi Rd (☎ 261 1722)
Sierra Leone 31 Waziri Ibrahim Crescent (☎ 261 1133)
Switzerland 7 Anifowashe St (☎ 261 3918)
Togo 976 Oju Olobun Close (261 1762)
UK 11 Eleke Crescent (☎ 261 1551, telex 21247, PMB 12136)
USA 2 Eleke Crescent (☎ 261 0078, fax 263 5397, telex 23616, Box 554).
Zaïre 23A Kofo Abayomi Rd (☎ 261 4799)

The following embassies are on Ikoyi Island:

Algeria 26 Maitama Sule St (☎ 268 3155)
Burkina Faso 15 Norman Williams St (☎ 268 1001)
Equatorial Guinea 7 Bank Rd (☎ 268 3717)
France 1 Queens Drive (☎ 268 4040, telex 23290)
Gabon 8 Norman Williams St (☎ 268 4566)
The Gambia 162 Awolowo Rd (☎ 268 2192)
Kenya 52 Queens Drive (☎ 268 2768)
Mauritania 1 Karimu Giwa Close (☎ 268 4439)

Three others elsewhere in Lagos include:

Central African Republic Plot 137, Ajao Estate in Osodi near the international airport (☎ 268 2820)
Ghana 23 King George V St, Lagos Island (☎ 263 0015)
Ireland 31 Marina St, Lagos Island (☎ 266 3371)

Cultural Centres The British Council (☎ 268 0008) at 11 Kingsway on Ikoyi Island carries various newspapers and magazines in its reading room; open from 10 am to 6 pm. The Maison de France at 2 Aromire Rd, roughly across and north from the Ikoyi Hotel, screens films every Thursday at 7 pm with English subtitles. The Goethe Institute is on Victoria Island on Maroko Rd, 200 metres beyond Adetokumba Ademola St.

Travel Agencies Transcap Travel (☎ 266 5063) at 1 Davies St, near the Bristol Hotel on Lagos Island, is the agent for Thomas Cook. Mandilas Travel (☎ 266 3339) nearby at 96 Broad St is the agent for American Express and Hertz. You'll find others at Tafawa Balewa Square, such as Beacon Travels (☎ 263 4526) at Shop 75. Bitts Travel & Tours (☎ 268 4550) and Range Travel Agency are both at Falomo Shopping Centre on Ikoyi Island.

Bookshops One of the best in town is Glendora at the Falomo Shopping Centre. It has lots of imported books, including the Lonely Planet series. The Bestseller Bookshop next door carries mostly Nigerian publications. The bookshop at the Eko Meridien Hotel is small but has a few good books, including some by Nigerian writers. The Bookworm, near Napex supermarket on Victoria Island, has US bestsellers.

The largest bookshop is CSS Bookshop on Lagos Island on the corner of Broad and Odunlami Sts. It carries primarily Nigerian publications including maps of Nigeria.

A couple of books to look out for are *Enjoy Nigeria* by Ian Nason (1993), an interesting guidebook to some obscure areas, and *Lagos Walking Tours* by Richard Amman (1994), a dandy little book full of eclectic information on the city and its neighbourhoods, buildings and history.

Supermarkets Try UTC on Lagos Island on Broad St near the Bristol Hotel, or Leventis nearby at 42 Marina St. On Ikoyi Island, head for Awolowo Rd, particularly the Falomo Shopping Centre, and the small Ace supermarket 350 metres further west at 99 Awolowo Rd. Jay-Jay's Meat & Frozen Foods is 20 metres further west at 115 Awolowo Rd and is well stocked, as is Bhojonsons supermarket at 77 Awolowo Rd. On Victoria Island there's Napex supermarket opposite the US embassy on Eleke

Crescent, and Payless 3 across from the Federal Palace Hotel on Ahmadu Bello Rd.

National Museum

This museum is definitely worth seeing. The star attractions are the Benin bronzes and ivory carvings. Equally memorable is the bullet-riddled car in which Murtala Mohammed, a former head of state, died. There is also an impressive display of masks and body-coverings, and terracotta antiquities from the Jos area. Architectural buffs will enjoy the numerous wooden doorways and house posts, and those interested in crafts should check out the craft shop here for a demonstration of *adire* cloth-making.

The museum is on Lagos Island south-east of Tafawa Balewa Square and is open every day from 9 am to 5 pm; the entrance fee is N 5. Come at lunchtime and take advantage of the museum's restaurant, which is famous for its Nigerian specialities.

National Theatre

Opened in 1976 for FESTAC, the National Theatre (☎ 283 0200) is the huge round

building you'll see as you come in from the airport. Call the theatre or consult the local newspapers for its programme, which may include dancing, film and drama. Even if no events are scheduled, a visit here can be worthwhile to see the three galleries (of modern Nigerian art, Nigerian crafts and Black arts and civilisation). The best times to visit are Tuesday to Saturday between 10 am and 3 pm, when all three galleries are open. The city's best *moin-moin* (bean-cake) is reputed to be found around the many kiosks outside.

The Oba's Palace

The residence of the traditional king of Lagos, built during the 18th century, is extremely modest and understandably attracts few visitors. The oldest part of 'Iga Idunganran', including a parlour, is built of mud, with bronze pillars; corrugated iron

sheets have replaced the original tile roof. It's near the northern tip of Lagos Island, roughly four blocks east of Carter Bridge. For appointments, call ☎ 265 6397.

Other Attractions

The **Tafawa Balewa Square** is a huge arena adorned by gargantuan horses. You'll find most of Lagos' airline offices and travel agencies on one side of the square and shops and restaurants on the other.

Remembrance Arcade, which is located here, features memorials to Nigeria's WW I, WW II and civil-war victims. The guard changes on the hour, and there's often a parade on Saturday from 9.30 to 11 am. Across the street on Campbell St just west of Tafawa Balewa Square is the 26-storey **Independence House**, constructed in 1963 to commemorate Nigeria's independence.

PLACES TO STAY		OTHER		31	Central Library
14	Bristol Hotel & Alitalia	1	Oba's Palace	33	Ferry Station (for Apapa & Mile 2)
23	Fantasy Hotel	2	Udumata Bus Stop		& CMS Bus Park
24	Ziena Hotel	3	Ebute Era Motor Park	34	Ministry of External
40	Hotel Wayfarers		(for Cotonou)		Affairs
48	YWCA	4	Jankara Market	35	Passport Photos
49	Ritz Hotel	5	Central Mosque	37	NAL Towers
		7	UPS (United Parcel	38	First Baptist Church
PLACES TO EAT			Service)	41	St Nicholas Hospital
		8	UTB Bank	42	NITEL House
6	Larry's Restaurant,	9	Transcap Travel		(skyscraper)
	Ghana Airways		(Thomas Cook)	43	Nigeria Airways,
	& Sabena	10	UK High Commission		Ethiopian Airlines,
13	Mr Bigg's (fast food		(Consular Section)		Balkan Airlines, Jet
	restaurant)	11	Lufthansa		Travels,
15	Tabriz Restaurant	12	Kingsway Department		Cameroun Airlines &
17	Zenith Water Chinese		Store		Iberia
	Restaurant	16	UBA Bank	44	Aeroflot & Air Gabon
	& Chicken George	18	Leventis Department	45	State House
19	Lady Samak		Store	46	Passport Photo Shop
21	Cathay Chinese	20	Foreign Exchange	47	Public Telephones
	Restaurant,		Bureau	50	Police Headquarters
	American Express,	22	Small Market	51	Plaza Cinema
	Hertz & KLM	25	Union Bank of Nigeria	52	Ghanaian High
32	Double 44 Restaurant		(UBN)		Commission
36	Winners Fast Food	26	Old House	53	National Museum &
39	Maharaja Restaurant	27	Post Office		Museum Kitchen
		28	Niger House		Restaurant
		29	NITEL Office	54	Yoruba Tennis Club
		30	Bus Stop & CSS	55	Onikan Swimming Pool
			Bookshop	56	Stadium

Beaches

The once popular Bar Beach on the southern end of Victoria Island has been largely washed away by a flood. Some weekend favourites are Palasides Beach, Lekki Beach, Tarkwa Beach (no undertow) and, nearby, Lighthouse Beach (strong undertow). The water is never very clear. At Tarkwa Beach you can get snacks and drinks at Bubbe's Bar and from vendors. The beaches are a delightful half-hour trip by water taxi through the port, across the lagoon and past fishing villages. Launches are available most readily on weekends and holidays. You'll find them on Victoria Island along Eleke Crescent, opposite the US embassy. The price is negotiable, with N 100 per person (return) the maximum. Make arrangements to be picked up in the afternoon and don't pay beforehand. Ilekki Beach, 50 km from Lagos off the Ilekki-Eppi Expressway, is also popular.

Places to Stay – bottom end

Downtown Islands An incredibly good deal for men is the *YMCA* (☎ 680 516) at 77 Awolowo Rd on Ikoyi Island. The cost is N 70 per person in reasonably clean four-bed rooms. It's also sometimes possible to pitch tents outside. Staying here offers an excellent opportunity to meet young Africans. The Y is in a relatively safe, convenient and lively area with a supermarket and fairly cheap restaurants nearby on the same street. Look for the YMCA sign on an eight-storey building; the offices are at the back.

The *YWCA*, for women only, is on Lagos Island on the corner of Maloney and George V Sts, a block east of Tafawa Balewa Square. The N 80 price of a dormitory bed includes breakfast but not the one-time N 10 fee.

Close by at 41 George V St is the very nice *Ritz Hotel*, where singles/doubles cost N 400/500. You can also get a mini-room for N 200. The rooms are small but OK.

Another option on Lagos Island is *Hotel Wayfarers* (☎ 263 011), roughly in the centre of the island at 52 Campbell St at the intersection with Joseph St. It's overpriced at N 437 for air-con singles with reasonably comfortable beds and private baths. The lively bar charges N 80 for lunch or dinner.

The *Ziena Hotel* is the cheapest place on the island at N 150 for a single with fan and shared bath; N 450 for a double with air-con and private bath. It's at 11 Smith St, several blocks north of Timbu Square. Close by at 25a Obe St is the *Fantasy Hotel*, with clean and pleasant singles/doubles for N 300/600. However, the area is not very safe at night.

Yaba Yaba, five km north of Lagos Island and easily reached by shared taxis, is livelier, safer and much cheaper than the central area.

The old *Majestic Hotel* at 14 Popo St, two blocks north of Yaba market, charges N 150 for a decent single with fan. The beds are wide enough for two people and there's electricity during the day. The building is dilapidated but the people are friendly.

Just east of Western Ave is the *Mullard Restaurant & Hotel* at 89 Oju Elegba Rd. Clean singles/doubles with fan cost N 200/400. The *Mayoa Hotel*, near the Stadium Hotel, at 8 Awonaike St charges similar prices for a quiet room. There are many chop bars in the neighbourhood.

Places to Stay – middle

Downtown Islands Most of the pricier hotels require deposits, usually double the cost of the room. On the islands, a nice mid-range hotel is the *Bristol Hotel* (☎ 661 204, telex 21144) on Lagos Island. It charges N 805/1035 for singles/doubles plus a deposit of N 500/700. It's in the heart of town but few travellers find that an advantage.

A better choice but way more expensive is *B-Jay's Hotel* (☎ 261 391), a small two-storey hotel in a quiet, safe residential area at 25 Samuel Manuwa St near the eastern corner of Victoria Island. Doubles with TV, shower and refrigerator cost N 2300.

Yaba As with the cheap hotels, you'll get better value here. The *Niger Palace Hotel* (☎ 800 010) is a bit pricey at N 920 plus N 580 deposit for a double with carpet and TV, but it is noisy at night. It's at 1 Thurburn Ave at the intersection with Commercial Ave, half a km south-east of Yaba market.

A better place and good value for the

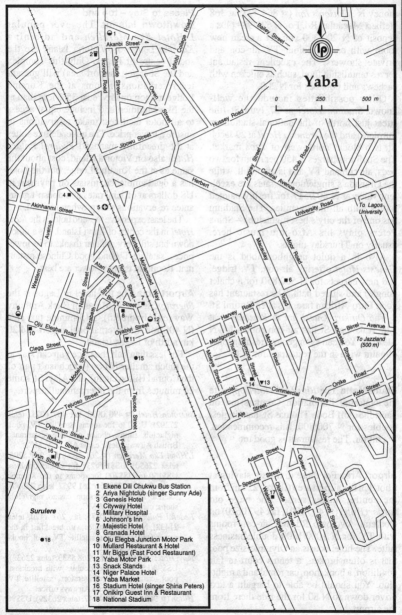

Yaba

0   250   500 m

To Lagos
University

To Jazzland
(500 m)

Surulere

1   Ekene Dili Chukwu Bus Station
2   Ariya Nightclub (singer Sunny Ade)
3   Genesis Hotel
4   Cityway Hotel
5   Military Hospital
6   Johnson's Inn
7   Majestic Hotel
8   Granada Hotel
9   Oju Elegba Junction Motor Park
10 Mullard Restaurant & Hotel
11 Mr Biggs (Fast Food Restaurant)
12 Yaba Motor Park
13 Snack Stands
14 Niger Palace Hotel
15 Yaba Market
16 Stadium Hotel (singer Shina Peters)
17 Onikirp Guest Inn & Restaurant
18 National Stadium

money is *Johnson's Inn* (☎ 864 475) at 368 Herbert Macaulay Rd. For N 690/989 plus a deposit of N 200/300 you get a clean new room with carpet, colour TV, air-con and private showers. The excellent restaurant serves tantalising food, such as chicken with cashews and potatoes for N 200.

Other possibilities include the well-known *Stadium Hotel* at 27 Iyun St (the street just north of the national stadium in Surulere) and the *Granada Hotel* at 29 Jacob St, two blocks north-west of Yaba market. The Stadium charges N 450 per room for two beds, air-con and TV, and is often full, while the Granada's single/double rates are excellent value at N 402/517 for freshly painted rooms with all the amenities. The Stadium has one of the city's best nightclubs – Shina Peters plays his Afro-juju music here, usually on Thursday nights.

Also in a quiet neighbourhood is the *Genesis Hotel* offering air-con, TV, fridge, and new carpets for N 500/850 for a chalet (single) and shared bath. The restaurant has good Euro-African fare. It's at 28 Rotimi St.

The *Onikirp Guest Inn & Restaurant* at 328 Wakeman St has air-con rooms for N 517/575. You can even get a refreshing glass of palm wine in the restaurant for N 15.

Ebute-Metta The *Rita Lori Hotel* opposite the National Population Commission on Taoridi St, off Bode Thomas St, has singles/doubles for N 700/800. It is recommended, if a bit far. The restaurant is good too.

Airport Area For those in transit, staying at a hotel in the airport area (Ikeja), 22 km from the centre, makes sense. The huge old *Airport Hotel* (☎ 490 1001, fax 497 0620) on Obafemi Awolowo Rd, has air-con rooms with TV for N 1000/1800 double/business suite. The hotel boasts an Olympic-size pool that is often broken, a tennis court in fair condition, a bookshop, car rental and a nightclub. You should be able to bargain a taxi driver down to N 80 for the ride there from the airport.

Places to Stay – top end
Downtown Islands The ever-popular *L'Hôtel Eko Meridien* and adjoining *Kuramo Lodge* on Victoria Island are the social centre of Lagos. Only this complex and the Sheraton (airport area) will guarantee reservations. Rooms at the Kuramo Lodge are top quality, cost 35% less than at the Eko Meridien and include equal access to all hotel facilities; make reservations to ensure a lower price. The huge, deluxe suites at the dreadfully managed *Federal Palace Hotel*, also on Victoria Island, cost about the same as at the Kuramo Lodge, but the hotel has a dead ambience, insists on payment in US dollars at official rates and doesn't guarantee reservations except when prepaid.

The least expensive top-end hotel is the *Ikoyi Hotel* in the centre of Ikoyi Island. It's a notch down but still very popular thanks to its lower prices, satellite TV and good Chinese restaurant. Rooms in the new tower are best.

Airport Area The top hotel in Lagos is the *Sheraton*. It's at 30 Mobolaji Bank Anthony Way (ex-Airport Rd), a 15-minute taxi ride (N 40) from the international airport and 20 km north of Lagos Island.

For less than half the price you can stay at the much smaller *Hilton* (which isn't part of the Conrad Hilton chain), at 2 Ajayi St, some 20 minutes from the international airport.

Sheraton Hotel (☎ 490 0930, fax 497 0321, telex 27202), US$236 for rooms, satellite TV, pool, nightclub, shops, choice of three restaurants, British Airways desk; cards AE, D, V, MC.
L'Hôtel Eko Meridien (☎ 261 5000, fax 261 5205, telex 22650), US$198/238 for singles/doubles, US$150 to US$200 for rooms in the *Kuramo Lodge* (☎ 261 2228, fax 261 9957, telex 22650), satellite TV, pool, bookshop, casino, nightclub, shops; cards AE, D, V, MC.
Federal Palace (☎ 261 0175, fax 261 1420, telex 21432), N 3300 for suites with breakfast in the newer 'suites' section, satellite TV, pool, bookshop, casino; cards AE.
Ikoyi Hotel (☎ 269 1522, fax 268 5833, telex 22632), US$98/156 for singles/doubles with breakfast, pool, casino, mini-refrigerators, satellite TV, magazine stand, Nigeria Airways office.
Hilton (☎ 960 601, fax 964 947, telex 26329), US$90 for doubles; pool, nightclub; no cards.

Places to Eat – cheap

On Ikoyi Island, head for Awolowo Rd; it is lined with restaurants in all price ranges. Among the cheapest is *Ace Supermarket & Fast Food*, 100 metres east of the YMCA at 99 Awolowo Rd. You can get Western groceries at the supermarket and hamburgers (N 35) at the fast-food section.

Across the street at 160 Awolowo Rd (the numbering system is confusing) is the popular *Les Amis Restaurant*. It has many Lebanese specialities, including felafel and kofta sandwiches for N 60 and hamburgers for N 80; you can eat in or take away. At the Falomo Shopping Centre *The Oasis* serves reasonably priced hamburgers and simple meals.

On Victoria Island, try *The Grill* on Akim Adesola St; it's a fancy snack bar and pastry shop. On Lagos Island, a good area for cheap food is around the busy intersection of Broad and Martins Sts. If you hanker for some fowl, try *Chicken George* on Abibu Oki St next door to the more up-scale *Zenith Water Chinese Restaurant*.

The snack bars at the large stores (*UTC* on Broad St, *Leventis* at 42 Marina St and *Kingsway* at the southern end of Martins St, for instance) serve snacks and Nigerian fare. The modern *Mr Bigg's*, next door to Kingsway, has hamburgers for N 45. *Larry's Restaurant*, two blocks north at 17 Martins St, has a wider range of choices and prices; it's closed on weekends.

For some inexpensive chicken and rice (N 50) try *Rita Lori* at 34 Nnamdi Azikiwe St. *Winners Fast Food* at 168 Broad St and *Bliss* at 6 Nathan St both have the usual burger and chips fare.

There is a *Mr Bigg's* restaurant in Yaba across from the Tejuosho market, and also many chop shops in this area.

African Nigerian specialities include gwaten doya (yam soup), ikokore (yams with seafood), bitter leaf soup, pepper soup and groundnut soup. On Lagos Island the *Museum Kitchen Restaurant* at the National Museum is probably the best place in town to sample these Nigerian foods; it offers palm wine and a different regional speciality each weekday lunchtime.

On Ikoyi Island, try *Josephine Restaurant* west of the YMCA at 10 Keffi St. Josephine serves basic fare such as rice and soup at low prices. Further west at about 38 Awolowo Rd is a tiny alley leading south towards the creek with good chop houses serving pepper soup.

On Victoria Island, there's good street food outside the Eko Meridien and one km to the north on Manuwa St near B-Jay's Hotel. In Yaba, try the area around Yaba market and around the corner from the Niger Palace Hotel on Raymond St.

Pastry Shops *Frenchies* is a pastry shop with good éclairs (N 40), bread, pizza (N 300) and sandwiches (N 120); it is at 29A Akim Adesola. *Big Treat*, a pastry shop that doesn't quite live up to its name, is just west of Jazz 38 on Awolowo Rd.

Places to Eat – more expensive

Ikoyi Island The area with the highest concentration of good restaurants in Lagos is a one-km stretch along Awolowo Rd. The street numbering system is confusing. The *Koreana Restaurant* at 81 Awolowo Rd, just before the YMCA, serves the best Korean and Japanese fare in town; expect to pay N 300 to N 400. For some goat-meat pizza (N 90) or shawarma (N 50) try the *Al-Bahsa* at 126 Awolowo Rd. The inexpensively priced *Sherlaton* at 108 Awolowo Rd has been around for years. It is the city's best Indian restaurant by reputation, with dishes for around N 150.

Further west is the good *Water Gardens Chinese Restaurant*, which charges N 300 to N 400 a plate. Just east of it, the popular *Bacchus Restaurant* (closed Sunday) at 57 Awolowo Rd is a dressy affair on Saturdays with a stiff N 250 cover charge. The dancing is the attraction; the Western food is fair and optional. Opposite the Burkina Faso embassy on Norman Williams St is the *Fazoc Restaurant* where a breakfast of pancakes costs N 90.

The popular *44 Restaurant* at 44 Awolowo Rd is an attractive up-market café with pizza (N 195) and Lebanese selections among others. The *New Yorker* at 59 Raymond

Ikoyi & Victoria Islands

PLACES TO STAY		27 Frenchies Bakery	14 British Airways
		30 The Grill	15 Swiss Embassy
2	Ikoyi Hotel		17 Zaïrean Embassy
10	B-Jay's Hotel	**OTHER**	18 Camerounian Embassy
23	Federal Palace Hotel		19 Sierra Leonean High
28	Hotel Eko Meridien &	1 Maison de France	Commission
	Kuramo Lodge	3 Equatorial Guinean	20 Chad Embassy
		Embassy & Belgian	21 Niger Embassy
PLACES TO EAT		Embassy	22 Beninese & Côte
		4 State House	d'Ivoire Embassies
8	Peninsula Jaws	5 British Council	24 Payless 3 Shopping
	Chinese Restaurant	6 Post Office	Complex
	& Calabash Restaurant	7 French Embassy	25 Air France
11	La Brasserie	9 Goethe Institute	26 Post Office
	Restaurant	12 Air Afrique	29 Moroccan Embassy
16	The Flamingo	13 Canadian High	31 Togolese Embassy
	Restaurant	Commission	

Njoku St is said to have the best hamburgers (N 300) in Lagos.

Victoria Island There is also a variety of restaurants on Victoria Island.

African The *Calabash* at 8 Maroko Rd serves a mean fish pepper soup for N 100 and has an all-you-can-eat buffet for N 350 on weekdays from noon to 3 pm.

European The popular *4 Seasons* on Akim Adesola St (across from the Didi Museum) serves quality Continental fare for around N 500. Two of the island's top restaurants are on Ozumba Mbadiwe Ave/Maroko Rd, on the northern end along Five Cowrie Creek. Aside from the food, both have patios overlooking the creek. The more westerly is the newer *Lagoon Restaurant*; it has European food and a cheaper section for takeaway pizza (N 400) and banana splits (N 100). For a splurge try the other restaurant, *After Hours* on Eleke Crescent; expect to pay N 1000 per person.

Asian At the *Peninsula Jaws Chinese Restaurant* at 8 Maroko Rd a meal with drinks costs between N 600 and N 800. The *Imperial Restaurant* at the Federal Palace is, unlike the hotel, maintaining its high standards, and the Chinese restaurant on the 14th floor of the *Eko Meridien* has good food, atmosphere and views; expect to pay N 800 to N 1000.

Indian Two places that combine Chinese and Indian food are the casual *La Brasserie* at 52 Adetokumba Ademola St, and *The Flamingo* at 10 Kofo Abayomi Rd which is more dressy, with dishes in the N 300 range.

Lagos Island There's also a good variety of places to eat on Lagos Island.

African For moderately priced informal restaurants, head for the Bristol Hotel area. The aptly named *Food* at 9 Nnamdi Azikiwe serves large portions for N 100 in a pleasant air-con setting and is open Sunday.

Asian The *Cathay Restaurant* at 68 Broad St

is slightly more expensive (N 190 to N 300), with good Chinese food, although the atmosphere can be dead. A few blocks away on Abibu Oki St is the *Zenith Water Chinese Restaurant* with a more upbeat ambience and comparable prices; both are closed Sunday. The *Victory Garden* is one of the more elegant expensive restaurants and serves excellent food. Located on the 19th floor of Western House at 8 Broad St, it has views of the harbour and dishes for as little as N 150, so splurge and take in the vista. Men should wear ties.

European & Indian Another elegant restaurant is the *Bagatelle Restaurant* at 208 Broad St on the 4th floor. It has been a Lagos institution for more than 30 years and has excellent harbour views. It's closed Sunday. Men need to wear ties here too.

Yaba & Airport Area The restaurant at *Johnson's Inn* has excellent European and African dishes for around N 200. The *Golden Crown Restaurant* at 177 Western Ave serves good Chinese fare.

For those staying at or near the Sheraton there is the *Taj Mahal Indian Restaurant* on Mojo Bank Anthony Way. The *Sheraton* itself has three different restaurants and two bars; the Italian restaurant is good and the prices range from N 200 to N 800.

Entertainment
Bars A fun watering hole at the water's edge is *Fiki's*, just off the Falomo Bridge on Victoria Island; this is also the only place in Lagos where you can hear a band from Zaïre play Francophone music. Nearby is *Cocos*, a 'respectable brothel bar' where a beer will set you back N 60; there is a live band on Friday and Saturday night.

Down the road on Eleke Crescent is *After Hours*, a decidedly more up-scale bar with a live band on the weekends. Further west on Eleke Crescent is the *Bush Bar*. Located near where the speedboats leave, this little bar at the water's edge serves food and drink and is worth the search. The major hotels also have bars with music.

Nightclubs Lagos probably has more nightclubs with live music than Dakar, Abidjan, Accra, Lomé and Cotonou combined. Among the numerous clubs, two are famous throughout West Africa and known by every taxi driver in Lagos. Neither has a telephone, so you can't call to see what's playing.

The star nightclub and an unforgettable experience is Fela's *The Shrine* in Ikeja. It's half a km east of Agege Motor Rd Expressway at the point where it intersects with the road from the domestic airport. The club's banner, 'Music Is The Weapon Of The Future', sets the tone. This is where the Afrobeat music of Fela's 35-strong band throbs. Fela, who makes rare appearances (generally on Fridays), won't come on stage until midnight or later, but he will often sing until dawn. It is dangerous to get a taxi at night so rest up and make it an event. The cover charge is just N 50.

The other club, where juju music reigns, is Sunny Ade's *Ariya Night Club* in Yaba. It's at 15 Ikorodu Rd (the major expressway towards the airport), a 15-minute ride north from Lagos Island. Most recently Sunny Ade was singing there on Friday nights, but this may change. It's open every evening except Mondays until dawn and the cover charge is N 50; don't arrive before 11 pm unless you're coming to eat.

Ikoyi The open-air *Jazz 38* (☎ 268 4984) is at 38 Awolowo Rd (half a km west of the YMCA), the main nightlife drag near the centre of Lagos. Tunde and Fela's niece Fran Kuboye run it; the star attraction is the Kuyobe Jazz Quintet, sometimes accompanied by Fela. The cover charge is N 100 and if you are a musician with an instrument, you can play with the band.

Victoria Island *Club Towers & Restaurant* at 18 Idowu Taylor St is popular with the

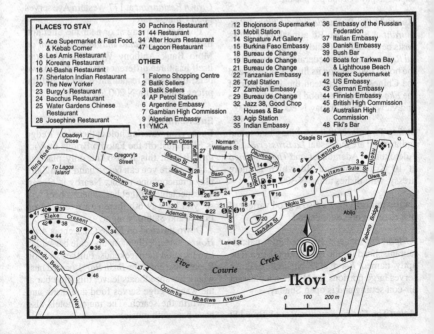

PLACES TO STAY

5   Ace Supermarket & Fast Food, & Kebab Corner
8   Les Amis Restaurant
10 Koreana Restaurant
16 Al-Basha Restaurant
17 Sherlaton Indian Restaurant
20 The New Yorker
23 Burgy's Restaurant
24 Bacchus Restaurant
25 Water Gardens Chinese Restaurant
28 Josephine Restaurant
30 Pachinos Restaurant
31 44 Restaurant
34 After Hours Restaurant
47 Lagoon Restaurant

OTHER

1   Falomo Shopping Centre
2   Batik Sellers
3   Batik Sellers
4   AP Petrol Station
6   Argentine Embassy
7   Gambian High Commission
9   Algerian Embassy
11 YMCA
12 Bhojonsons Supermarket
13 Mobil Station
14 Signature Art Gallery
15 Burkina Faso Embassy
18 Bureau de Change
19 Bureau de Change
21 Bureau de Change
22 Tanzanian Embassy
26 Total Station
27 Zambian Embassy
29 Bureau de Change
32 Jazz 38, Good Chop Houses & Bar
33 Agip Station
35 Indian Embassy
36 Embassy of the Russian Federation
37 Italian Embassy
38 Danish Embassy
39 Bush Bar
40 Boats for Tarkwa Bay & Lighthouse Beach
41 Napex Supermarket
42 US Embassy
43 German Embassy
44 Finnish Embassy
45 British High Commission
46 Australian High Commission
48 Fiki's Bar

young expat set; the music tends to be loud rap and the cover charge is N 250.

Yaba One of the newest recording stars in Nigeria is Shina Peters, who is particularly popular with the younger crowd. Recently returned from the USA, he calls his music Afro-juju. His forum is the *Stadium Hotel* (☎ 833 593) at 27 Iyun St. He usually sings on Thursday nights but you can call to check. For a blues fix try *Jazzville* (☎ 867 597) at 21 Majaro St. Jazz is also played here; they have an open mike and musicians are invited to join the band; there is a N 40 cover charge, and don't pass up the suya.

For a taste of Yoruba fuji music as well as juju, try the *Standard Hotel* at 13 Oloko Dahah St in Somolu, just north of Yaba. It has a well-organised schedule, with fuji music Monday to Thursday, juju music on Friday and Saturday and a different band each night. The door is often closed; knock to get in.

Surulere The *Woodhouse* plays jazz on Wednesday and there's no cover charge. In addition to having great fish pepper soup, it serves beer in pint glasses like an English pub. *The Falls* has pool tables and live music on most Wednesday and Friday nights; there's no cover charge and a Star beer costs N 35.

Airport Area There are a few clubs along Allen Ave, also known as 'Cocaine Alley'. One that stands out is *Pintos*; the atmosphere is good and it is packed. There is fast food downstairs and a jazz club upstairs. The cover charge is N 90. Bring your own whisky to avoid the high drink prices. Down the way is *Nightshift*, a disco good for dancing. The crowd here is mostly young and rich; the cover charge is N

100. *Daniels* on Old Kingsway has dancing, Western hip-hop and Wednesday is women's night; the cover charge is N 150.

Things to Buy

Traditional Arts & Crafts The best place for batiks (shirts, tablecloths, wall hangings) is Njoku St on the western side of the Falomo Shopping Centre on Awolowo Rd, Ikoyi. They are sold along the street and the selection is extensive.

The National Museum has a nonprofit crafts centre with batik, calabashes, woodcarvings and textiles at fixed prices. Most interesting of all, you can see see batik being made and woodcarvers at work.

Jankara market on Adeniji Adele Rd, half a km north of Tinubu Square, is the largest market in Lagos, but is nothing special by West African standards. You'll find traditional tie-dyed and indigo cloth, African prints by the yard, African trade beads, Nigerian-made jewellery and pottery, plus a fetishers' market where they sell juju beads and various medicines. Speaking a few words of Yoruba helps.

At the eastern end of Bar Beach on Victoria Island is a market where traders sell a variety of items, including batik, baskets, calabashes, old coins and antiquities. There are also stalls outside the Federal Palace and Ikoyi hotels. The wooden carvings are generally of low quality. For better quality work with prices to match, Quintessence at the Falomo Shopping Centre is best.

Music Quintessence is the best music shop. The Jazz Hole, another option, is just before the Falomo Bridge on Grillo St. For cheaper cassettes of lower quality, try Jankara market.

Aso Adire

Aso Adire is a broad term that means dyed cloth, a common handicraft found in many markets in Nigeria. One type that has become popular worldwide is *adire oniku*, or tie-dyed cloth. The second style, *adire eleko*, while less colourful, is very artistic; it's basically indigo cloth with a design in white. Designs, which are often named, are drawn on white cloth by applying cassava starch. When dried, this cloth is then dipped into vats of the ubiquitous indigo dye. The cassava starch repels the indigo dye and the design stands out. ∎

NIGERIA

Getting There & Away

Air International flights leave from Murtala Mohammed Airport and internal flights leave from the older airport 10 km away. Nigeria Airways (☎ 263 1002) is at 15/19 Tafawa Balewa Square. There are flights every day between Lagos and Abidjan, Accra, Lomé and Douala, and four flights to/from Dakar. Most of these flights are on Nigeria Airways or Ghana Airways.

Many other airline offices are at Tafawa Balewa Square, including Aeroflot (☎ 263 7223), Air Gabon (☎ 263 2827), Air Zaïre (☎ 263 5419), Cameroun Airlines (☎ 263 0909), Ethiopian Airlines (☎ 263 7655) and Iberia (☎ 263 6950).

Others are all within a block or two of the Bristol Hotel:

Alitalia 2 Martins St (☎ 266 2468)
EgyptAir 39 Martins St (☎ 266 1102)
KLM 96 Broad St (☎ 266 0032/1452)
Lufthansa 150 Broad St (☎ 266 4430)
Sabena 23 Martins St (☎ 266 4132)
Swissair 31 Martins St (☎ 266 2299)

The remaining international airlines are, with one exception, on Victoria Island:

Air Afrique 24 Amodu Tijani St (☎ 261 6467)
Air France 4th floor Icon Building on Idejo St (☎ 262 1456)
British Airways 1 Idowu Taylor St (☎ 261 3004)
Ghana Airways 130 Awolowo Rd, Ikoyi Island (☎ 266 1808)

Nigeria's major private airlines all have their offices at the domestic airport, including ADC (☎ 496 1942), Harco Air Services (☎ 933 911), Okada Airlines (☎ 963 881), Triax (☎ 493 7549), Gas Air (☎ 931 199), Concord Airlines, Express Airways Nigeria, Kabo Airlines, Bellview and Oriental Air.

Bus There are various bus companies connecting Lagos with major interior cities, and each has its own station. A major company serving the south (Benin City, Onitsha, Enugu) is Ekene Dili Chukwu, which has its station in Yaba on Ikorodu Rd, opposite Sunny Ade's Ariya Night Club. Many others,

including those to Kano (N 280 including baggage), are near Iddo motor park on the mainland, just north of Lagos Island.

Bush Taxi From north to south, the main motor parks are: Ojota motor park (Ibadan, Oshogbo, Ife) on Ikorodu Rd in Ojota, roughly 15 km north of Lagos Island; Oju Elegba Junction motor park in Yaba (Benin City, Onitsha, Enugu, Port Harcourt, Calabar) on Western Ave, at the intersection with Oju Elegba Rd; Iddo motor park (Kano, Kaduna, Jos, Sokoto) on Murtala Mohammed Way on the mainland; and Ebute Era motor park (Cotonou and Lomé) on the northern tip of Lagos Island just south-west of Carter Bridge.

Typical fares are Ibadan (N 70), Ife (N 150), Benin City (N 250), Onitsha (N 400), and Kano (N 600).

Train The train station (☎ 834 302) is on the mainland just north of Lagos Island near Iddo motor park. The train is scheduled to leave Lagos for Kano on Monday at noon, arriving in Ibadan at 5 pm, Kaduna at 1 pm on Tuesday and Kano at 6.15 pm. Late arrivals are normal and 35 to 45 hours to Kano is typical. The train leaves Kano on Saturday morning for Lagos (and Wednesday mornings for Ibadan).

The train to Jos leaves Lagos on Thursday at noon and theoretically takes about 30 hours. For Maiduguri you change at Kaduna and at Kafanchan. The train leaves Lagos on Saturday at noon and should arrive 48 hours later in Maiduguri; 60 hours is more realistic. The 1st/2nd-class fares are N 365/203 to Kano, N 245/263 to Kaduna, N 320/213 to Jos and N 483/322 to Maiduguri. Check whether these trains are actually running.

Getting Around

To/From the Airport At Murtala Mohammed Airport there is a restaurant and Hertz agency. There's no bureau de change so you'll probably have to negotiate a taxi fare in dollars.

At the airport, numerous drivers and porters will surround you, vying for your business. The situation is ideal for theft, so be careful. Taxis licensed to carry passengers will show you their identity cards; they are likely to be more reliable and safer. Haggle over the fare. A taxi from the international airport should cost N 500 – but you'll probably end up paying US$15 to Lagos Island (22 km) or nearby Victoria and Ikoyi islands, N 80 to the domestic airport and N 200 to the Sheraton.

There are no buses from the airport to the centre. Since flights from Europe arrive at night or early in the morning, your best bet is to grab a taxi and not worry too much about overpaying. For the intrepid penny-pincher, take a taxi to the nearby expressway, Agege Motor Rd (up to N 80), and hail a shared taxi from there to the city centre.

Taxi & Minibus Minibuses provide the cheapest transport around Lagos; most go on fixed routes. They can cost as little as N 3, and can be entertaining because boarding one along with seemingly hundreds of people vying for the same few seats is a great adventure. The CMS bus park is on Ring Rd in Lagos Island. There are no longer any shared cabs in Lagos so you must charter the cab and haggle like crazy. A good way to find out how much you should pay is to ask locals, who are generally helpful. A taxi costs N 20 to go anywhere on Lagos Island and N 50 to Victoria and Ikoyi islands.

Car Self-drive rental cars are virtually unavailable in Lagos. By the hour, expect to pay about N 400 with a driver. (Taxis by the hour are less than half this.) Hertz is handled by Mandilas Travel (☎ 266 3514, telex 21383), 96 Broad St, Lagos Island; Europcar by Cross Keys Travel (☎ 266 2572, telex 21089), 21 Broad St; and Avis by Nigerian Rent-a-Car (☎ 284 6336, telex 21324), 225 Apapa Rd, Inganmu.

Other agencies include Safedrive (☎ 844 615), 19 Adam St in Yaba; Intra (☎ 263 4884), 11 Martins St, Lagos Island; and Dilvy, which has a branch at the Bristol Hotel.

Ferry Ferries provide the cheapest and quickest transport from Lagos Island to Apapa and to Mile 2 on the western side of town. (Vehicles for Benin leave from Mile 2 as well as from Ebute Era motor park on Lagos Island.) The ferry fare is N 2. The Lagos Island-Apapa ferry leaves from Lagos at 7, 8 and 9 am, noon and 2, 3, 4 and 5.30 pm, and from Apapa half an hour later. A ferry leaves Lagos Island for Mile 2 at 6.45, 7.15, 8.30, 9, 10.15 and 11 am, noon and on the hour from 1 to 6 pm. The ferry terminal on Lagos Island is just south of Ring Rd on the southern side of the island.

AROUND LAGOS
Lekki
A mere 20-minute drive east from Lagos on the Lagos-Epe Expressway, opposite the Chevron Plant, is the Lekki Reserve. Run by the Nigerian Conservation Foundation, it has 78 hectares of wetlands which have been set aside for viewing the wildlife. Raised walkways enable you to see monkeys, crocodiles and various birds; early morning is the best time to view animals. There is also a conservation/visitors centre and a library open every day; admission is free.

Getting There & Away The easiest transport is to flag a bus on Victoria Island along Akim Adesola St; the cost is around N 20.

Abeokuta
Abeokuta, which means 'under the rock', is famous not only for being the birthplace of Fela Kuti and Wole Soyinka, but also for the Olumo rock. This huge chunk of granite is considered sacred and is used in various celebrations and rituals. There are caves and a shrine. Guides will take you to the top of the rock for commanding views of the city and surrounding country – be sure to wear boots as the route is steep and the rocks can be slippery. There is a market selling the traditional *adire* cloth and plenty of juju material.

Getting There & Away Bush taxis leave from Ojota motor park; the two-hour trip should cost N 100.

The South

IBADAN

Roughly half the size of Lagos, Ibadan (ee-BAH-dan) is an ugly, congested and sprawling Yoruba city. It's the second-largest city in West Africa and was the largest from the late 1800s to the 1960s, which makes it all the more surprising that there's so little of interest to travellers. The major sights are the huge sprawling Dugbe market, the University of Ibadan (UI) and the International Institute of Tropical Agriculture (IITA), a well-known research centre six km beyond UI on the northern edge of town.

Two interesting markets that are notably less hectic than Dugbe are Oje and Bode. Oje is full of produce and huge snails, as well as a few stalls selling Aso-Oke cloth (you can see kids weaving the cloth alongside the road, just north of the market) while the Bode market mainly has vegetables. Bode, however, is most fascinating because of its fabulous juju section with all kinds of animal heads, dried bats and piles of bones, herbs and twigs. At the university, in addition to an incredible bookshop, there is a good museum in the Institute of African Studies building with great woodcarvings.

Orientation

The commercial heart of town is the block-size triangle formed by Dugbe market, the train station (the post office faces it) and the 27-storey Cocoa House. Cocoa House and Bower Tower, on a hill 1.5 km to the east, are good reference points as it's easy to get disoriented in this sprawling city.

UI is on the northern outskirts of town and is connected to the centre (5.5 km away) by Oyo Rd, which leads south-west past the Premier Hotel to become Fajuyi Rd and, near the market, Dugbe Rd and, further south-west beyond the train station, Yaganku and Abeokuta Rds. Bodija Rd leads directly south from UI, becoming Ogumola St and eventually Lagos Rd.

Three major connecting roads running roughly east-west, are (from north to south): Queen Elizabeth II Rd, which connects the southern end of Oyo Rd with Bodija Rd; Lagos By-pass Rd, which connects the central triangle with Lagos Rd; and Ring Rd, which connects the southern end of Yaganku Rd with Lagos Rd. Further south on Lagos Rd is New Garage, which is the motor park for Lagos and points east (including Benin City, Onitsha etc).

Information

Money The National Bank of Nigeria, UBA, UBN and a bureau de change are all on Lebanon Rd next to Dugbe market, while FBN and the New Nigeria Bank are one and two blocks to the south, respectively.

Foreign Consulates An office of the British high commission is in the Finance Corp building on Lebanon St, while the German honorary consul is on Dugbe Rd in the Lufthansa building.

Cultural Centres The American Cultural Center is on Bodija Rd near the PI Hostel, while the Alliance Française is in the heart of town at 7 Lebanon Rd. The British Council is on Magazine/Jericho Rd, half a km north-west of the train station.

Bookshops The bookshop at UI is one of the best in West Africa. Opposite the entrance to UI is the Agbowo Shopping Complex where you'll find Syba's Books 'N' Things.

Places to Stay – bottom end

Excellent value for money is the *Cuso Guesthouse* (☎ 315 485), at 12 Adelabu Rd in New Gra, 150 metres north-east of Ring Rd. In a small shady compound with two buildings, it has a big clean room with four single beds, fan and shared bath. The cost is N 80 per person.

Nearby is the *Gbafe Guesthouse*, which has singles/doubles for N 150/200. The rooms have a fan and shower, and there's a bar. From the Mobil station on Ring Rd, take the paved road across the street heading north (parallel with Olaniyan Fagbemi Rd) and take the first left for about 70 metres.

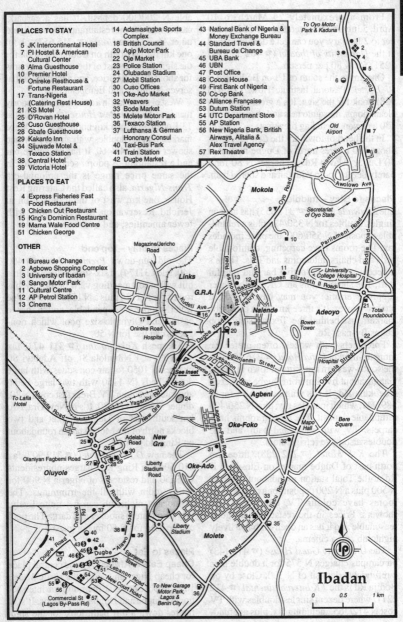

PLACES TO STAY

5 JK Intercontinental Hotel
7 PI Hostel & American Cultural Center
8 Alma Guesthouse
10 Premier Hotel
16 Onireke Resthouse & Fortune Restaurant
17 Trans-Nigeria (Catering Rest House)
21 KS Motel
25 D'Rovan Hotel
26 Cuso Guesthouse
29 Gbafe Guesthouse
34 Sijuwade Motel & Texaco Station
38 Central Hotel
39 Victoria Hotel

PLACES TO EAT

4 Express Fisheries Fast Food Restaurant
9 Chicken Out Restaurant
15 King's Dominion Restaurant
19 Mama Wale Food Centre
51 Chicken George

OTHER

1 Bureau de Change
2 Agbowo Shopping Complex
3 University of Ibadan
6 Sango Motor Park
11 Cultural Centre
12 AP Petrol Station
13 Cinema

14 Adamasingba Sports Complex
18 British Council
20 Agip Motor Park
22 Oje Market
23 Police Station
24 Olubadan Stadium
27 Mobil Station
30 Cuso Offices
31 Oke-Ado Market
32 Weavers
33 Bode Market
35 Molete Motor Park
36 Texaco Station
37 Lufthansa & German Honorary Consul
40 Taxi-Bus Park
41 Train Station
42 Dugbe Market

43 National Bank of Nigeria & Money Exchange Bureau
44 Standard Travel & Bureau de Change
45 UBA Bank
46 UBN
47 Post Office
48 Cocoa House
49 First Bank of Nigeria
50 Co-op Bank
52 Alliance Française
53 Dutum Station
54 UTC Department Store
55 AP Station
56 New Nigeria Bank, British Airways, Alitalia & Alex Travel Agency
57 Rex Theatre

Ibadan

From approximately 25 March to 10 April, 5 July to 15 September and 18 December to 2 January, you can get a dormitory bed at the *University of Ibadan* (☎ 462 550, ext 1251) for N 80 per person.

One km to the south of UI on Bodija Rd is *PI Hostel* (Pastoral Institute Hostel) (☎ 413 928); look for the sign. It's a great place with clean rooms, mosquito nets and showers for N 130 a person, including breakfast.

In the heart of town, try the *Central Hotel*, about 100 metres north of Dugbe market at 30 Dugbe Alawo Rd. It charges N 80 for a barely decent room with fan and shared bath.

Places to Stay – middle

The *Sijuwade Motel* (☎ 317 855) has air-con singles/doubles for N 350/425 plus a refundable deposit of N 550/600; the price includes tax. The rooms have carpeting, comfortable beds and chairs, intercoms and TVs. There's a decent restaurant, active bar and helpful staff. The shared baths are OK but the water supply is erratic; you may have to take a bucket shower. It's three km south of Dugbe market, just behind the Texaco station on Lagos By-pass Rd.

Foreigners with wheels often prefer the more up-market *Lafia Hotel* (☎ 316 555), on the south-western outskirts of town in Apata Ganga, about five km from Dugbe market on Abeokuta Rd. It has singles/doubles for N 589/941, which includes tax, plus N 250/400 refundable deposit. The air-con rooms have carpets, TV with cable and bath, and the doubles also have refrigerators.

The *K S Motel* (☎ 712 238), three km north-east of Dugbe market on Elizabeth II Rd at the Total station roundabout, charges N 500 plus a N 200 deposit for a double. The rooms have colour TV, telephones and showers. Prices in the restaurant are quite reasonable and it has an open-air bar, a lively nightclub and a cinema.

The *University Guest House* (☎ 413 143) on campus charges N 575 for a double plus a refundable deposit of N 300. Close by on Bodija Rd is the *J K Intercontinental* (☎ 412 221), where decent singles/doubles with TV cost N 412/765, including tax, plus a refund-

able N 200/300 deposit. It has a carpark, casino and decent restaurant. The small and quiet *Alma Guest House* (☎ 715 657), about one km further south on Bodija Rd (look for the sign pointing east of the road), has rooms for about the same price, and a restaurant that serves Nigerian and European fare.

West of the centre in a quiet area is the poorly managed *Onireke Rest House* (☎ 414 607) at 13 Kudeti Ave, one km north-west of Dugbe market. Singles/doubles with air-con, TV and shower cost N 345/460. It has an active bar and a restaurant. A poorer second choice in the same price range is the colonial-era *Trans-Nigeria*, also called the Catering Rest House, one km west of the train station in Jericho Reservation. It has rooms with fewer amenities, and a restaurant.

Places to Stay – top end

The old run-down *Premier Hotel* (☎ 400 340, telex 31174), a six-storey structure on a hill with a commanding view of the city, has rooms for N 1176 plus a N 1500 deposit. The water supply is dependable and it has a casino and Olympic-size pool which non-guests can use for N 50.

The posh *Kakanfo Inn* (☎ 311 471, fax 414 909) at 1 Nihinlola St, off Adebiyi St, charges N 1050 for air-con suites with large double beds (N 1150 with two large beds) and satellite colour TV. Breakfast costs N 80; dinner is around N 180. It's in New Gra, two km south-west of Dugbe market and two blocks north of the Mobil station roundabout on Ring Rd.

The new *D'Rovan Hotel* (☎ 312 907, fax 410 506) on Ring Rd charges nonresidents US$150 and residents of Nigeria N 900 for a tiny room with all the trimmings. The casino and nightclub can get quite lively; they also feature snooker and darts. The pool can be used for N 50 by nonguests.

Places to Eat

Cheap Eats & African A good central place for cheap Nigerian food is the rustic *Mama Wale Food Centre* at the northern intersection of Dugbe and Dugbe Alawo Rds. It's 30 metres down a dirt path; look for the sign.

This is also a good area for street food, as is the area to the south around Dugbe market.

Opposite Mama Wale is *King's Dominion Restaurant*, an inexpensive fast-food restaurant with fried chicken, chips etc. *Chicken George* nearby has similar food and prices (a quarter fried chicken, chips and Coke for N 72) and is a little fancier. It's on Lebanon Rd, a block east of Dugbe market.

A block or two away near Cocoa House is the *New Kokodome Restaurant*. It's pleasant and moderately priced, with Nigerian and European selections for N 180. There is also a snack bar by the pool; if you order food you can use the pool for free. The *Ring Rd Restaurant* is near the Cuso Guesthouse and serves inexpensive dishes.

In the UI area, try the UI *cafeteria*, the fancier *Staff Club*, or *Express Fisheries*, a fast-food restaurant just south of the Agbowo Shopping Complex on Bodija Rd. There's also *Chicken Out Restaurant* on Oyo Rd, a fast-food place down the hill from the Premier Hotel.

Chinese Two of Ibadan's best restaurants are Chinese. The best is *Fortune Restaurant* at 27 Kudeti Ave, 150 metres beyond the Onireke Guesthouse. Meals cost around N 180; it's open every day for lunch and dinner except Saturday lunchtime. The other is the *Dragon d'Or* at the Premier Hotel; it's also quite good and has similar prices.

Getting There & Away
Bush Taxi Bush taxis and minibuses for Lagos and points east leave from New Garage motor park on the southern outskirts of town off Lagos Rd. Vehicles leave every few minutes for Lagos (N 80), which is just over an hour away. Those east to Benin City (N 200), Onitsha and other points east take longer to fill. Oyo motor park on the northern outskirts of town, which also serves Lagos, has a greater variety of vehicles – Toyota vans (N 60), Peugeot 504s (N 70) and Peugeot 504 SR sedans (N 80).

Vehicles headed for Kaduna, Kano and other points north leave from Sango motor park on Oyo Rd. Peugeot 504s to Kano (N 550; 11 hours) and Abuja (N 450; 8 hours)

usually leave by 7 am. Bush taxis for Ife (N 50) and Oshogbo (N 50) leave from Gate motor park on the south-east side of town not far from Molete motor park on Lagos Rd, which is a major motor park for inner-city vehicles. You'll also find lots of inner-city minibuses and taxis on Dugbe Rd across from the market.

Train The train for Kano leaves Ibadan on Monday at 5 pm (leaving Lagos at noon), arriving in Kano the next day around 6.15 pm (usually much later, however). The cost is N 336 in 1st class.

There is also a twice-weekly train to Kaduna, leaving Ibadan on Thursday and Saturday at 5 pm and supposedly arriving in Kaduna 24 hours later. The train station is in the heart of town, one block west of Dugbe market.

OYO
This former capital of the Yoruba domain is now a small town that stands in quiet contrast to Ibadan, the present-day capital of Oyo State. One can wander around the various stalls of the **Akasen market**, which extends from the Town Hall to the **Alafin of Oyo's Palace**. Munch on a moin-moin and keep your eyes open for carved and blue-dyed *igba* (gourds) as well as pots and baskets. This is also a great place to buy 'talking drums'; there are several shops along Atiba Rd. To hear these drums played by professionals, visit the palace where several older men will announce your entrance by playing a short riff.

Places to Stay & Eat
The *Oyo Merrytime Hotel* is conveniently located by the Agip petrol station, which is where you will be dropped off by a bush taxi. A basic single with fan and bucket bath costs N 100; make sure the windows have a screen. The nearby and maintained *National Garden Hotel* is behind the National petrol station and is a better choice. A double with fan and bath is N 150; there is also a cheerful restaurant and bar. Folks with wheels can try the *Labamba Hotel* (☎ (038) 230 444) on the southern outskirts of town. A double with

air-con, TV and shower costs N 500, and the restaurant is reputed to be good.

Getting There & Away
Bush taxis leave for Ibadan (N 20) and Lagos (N 100) from Owode motor park, south of the Agip station.

ILORIN
Ilorin is a gateway city between the north and south both economically and culturally. Here, you can feel and see a strong Muslim influence – quite a change from other cities in Yorubaland. A huge blue-domed **mosque** and four towering minarets dominate the skyline of this busy trading centre. The Emir's bright white **palace** is next door and behind the two sprawls a vibrant **market** – full of basic plastic household items. The only other place of interest is the **Dada pottery workshop** in the Okelele district.

There's a NITEL office at 190 Lagos Rd which is open from 7 am to 9 pm and charges N 235 for a three-minute call to Europe or the USA. A shared taxi costs N 5 in town and to all motor parks.

Places to Stay & Eat
For cheap lodging, the centrally located *Layo Hotel* on Coca Cola Rd, just off the junction of Unity and Murtala Mohammed Rds, has singles/doubles with fan/air-con and bucket bath for N 210/262. The *Cucumba Hotel* on Lagos Rd has similar doubles for N 170 (N 219 with air-con).

Across the road at 183 Lagos Rd the *White House Hotel* (☎ 220 770) has singles/doubles with TV, bucket bath and fan/air-con for N 200/300. Doubles with TV, shower and phone at the *Kwara Hotel* (☎ 221 490), on Ahmadu Bello Ave, cost nonresidents/residents N 975/650 plus a deposit of N 1950/1300. The *Prince Garden Chinese Restaurant* is OK but, like the rest of the hotel, it's overpriced (about N 350 per dish). In addition to a video club, car hire and boutique, this is a good place to change money.

The better value *Circular Hotel* (☎ 220 490) on New Yidi Rd, just off Unity Rd, has doubles with air-con and TV for N 412 plus

a deposit of N 800. The location is good and there's an inviting restaurant and a carpark.

Getting There & Away
The Marara motor park for Kaduna (N 350), Kano (N 450) and Zaria (N 370) is on Murtala Mohammed Rd on the northern outskirts of town. Bush taxis to Lagos (N 150) and Ibadan (N 12) leave from Lagos motor park, 500 metres north of the White House Hotel on Lagos Rd. Transport to Oyo (N 80) leaves from Gerialimi Garage, one km south of Marara motor park. Offa Garage on the southern outskirts of town has vehicles to Oshogbo (N 80).

IFE
Ife – official name Ile-Ife – is the legendary home of the founder of the Yoruba, Oranmiyan. It has three major attractions besides its numerous colonial-era houses: the **Oni's Palace** and nearby **Ife Museum** at the eastern end of town, and five km away on the north-western outskirts, sprawling **Obafemi Awolowo University** campus. Brief tours around the Oni's Palace often include a recitation of the story of Oranmiyan. The museum (open daily) has interesting histor-

Benin bronze head

ical artefacts though it's small and the tours are poorly explained. Ife was one of the first areas in West Africa where the famous lost-wax technique of making bronze and brass objects and figurines was used. The museum has lots of these artefacts dating back many centuries. You can also see the **Oranmiyan Staff** – a five-metre-tall stone monolith carved and decorated with iron nails – in an unmarked plot off Omison St, one km south-east of the museum.

The university is the largest in Nigeria and meeting students and teachers is fairly easy, especially if you stay at or near the university. It also has a natural history museum and a small zoo; both are open every day. To get there from the centre, you can catch buses (N 10) or motorcycles (N 15), called 'machines', quite easily along the city's main east-west drag (Lager St and Iremo St).

Information

International phone calls can be made from the university's Conference Centre Guest House, but not from the NITEL tower. The main post office is just north of Enuwa Square and Tower, near the Oni. A ride in town costs N 3 by van and N 15 by taxi.

Places to Stay & Eat

The university's *Conference Centre Guest House* (☎ (036) 230 705), just east of the campus, is excellent and you don't have to be connected with the university to stay here. Clean doubles (no singles) cost N 520 plus a N 80 refundable deposit in advance. The rooms have hot showers, TV, air-con and balconies; the food and service are excellent. There are two bars, and the *Olokun Restaurant* serves Nigerian and European dishes for around N 185. The nearby Leventis supermarket is the best place for groceries, and the *Staff Centre* across the road prepares an excellent fish pepper soup and other inexpensive dishes. For even cheaper food *The Bukateria Complex* at the other end of campus has stalls with heaped portions of rice, pasta, plantains etc, for around N 33. Or try *Forks & Fingers* in the student centre.

Most hotels are on the western side of

town not far from the university's long entrance. Cheapest and furthest west is *Mayor King Hotel* on Ibadan Rd. A basic single with fan and shared bath costs N 150. Ask to be let off at the 7-UP depot; transport could be difficult at night.

About 200 metres further east on Ibadan Rd is *Hotel Diganga* (☎ 233 200), the best top-end option. Singles/doubles with air-con TV and shower cost N 450/600 plus a refundable deposit of N 100. You can eat there or at *La Cuisine*, 50 metres to the west and more reasonably priced.

The quiet *Trans Nigeria Motel*, off the same road and 300 metres or so closer to the centre, charges N 400 for a double with air-con and private bath. About 200 metres further east is the Ibadan/Ondu Rds junction, where you'll find the *Samtad Garden*, a pleasant place for a beer, and the run-down *Mayfair Hotel*. An air-con double (no singles) with bath costs N 450 plus a deposit of N 600.

Central Olympic Motel, on Ondu Rd just south of the junction, has singles with fans (N 200), shared baths with showers and lively music in the bar at night. If you're desperate, the *Green Tops Hotel* at 85 Eleyele St is a fairly clean brothel; N 150 will get you a room which has a semi-bearable shared bath and a sheet which serves as a door.

Getting There & Away

From Lagere motor park in the centre there are frequent bush taxis to Oshogbo (N 20), Ibadan (N 30) and Lagos (N 150). Transport to Benin City (N 200) leaves from Urbanday motor park, near Ibadan/Ondu Rds junction.

OSHOGBO

This town of half a million people is the cradle of Yoruba art and is without doubt the most creative art centre in Africa today. Oshogbo, along with Ife, has produced more vivid, experimental and purely enjoyable modern African art in the last 30 years than probably anywhere else in Africa. The best time to come is during the last week in August, particularly the last Friday, during the Oshun Festival. There's lots of dancing and sacrifices among other things. Be sure to see the **Oja Oba market** across

NIGERIA

from the Oba's palace, which is packed with stalls selling juju material and a number of shrines to various gods. The richly painted building decorated with intricate carvings facing the present palace is reputed to be the first Oba's palace in Oshogbo.

Oshogbo is also famous for its **Sacred Forest** on the outskirts of town, a half-hour's walk from the Oba's palace. It contains numerous monumental shrine complexes dedicated to the different Yoruba gods. Some shrines seem to be reverting to the forest as the cement and laterite mix crumbles and vines encroach into the inner sanctums. For a tour of the forests, ask the caretaker or enquire at the New Sacred Art Shop in town.

The Sacred Forest

Since the 1950s, the Austrian sculptor, Suzanne Wenger, has been working in the Sacred Forest to bring the shrines back to life through her imaginative 'restorations'. Called the 'adored one', or *Aduni Olosa*, by the locals, she is now so highly regarded that the local women have made her the priestess of two cults. With the help of local artisans she has been restoring the old shrines while adding her own touches. The result is a forest of spectacular, monumental and truly unique shrines. While they are totally different in style from that traditionally associated with African art, the inspiration is still Yoruba.

The principal shrine is that of the river goddess Oshuno, a grove enclosed by an imaginatively designed wall. Down by the sacred river, near the Iya Mapa grove where stunning huge new sculptures soar to the heavens, you can see a monumental and complex cement sculpture to Ifa, the divine Yoruba oracle; Suzanne has been working on it for over seven years. Another one, approximately five metres high, is the shrine of Onkoro, the mother goddess. ■

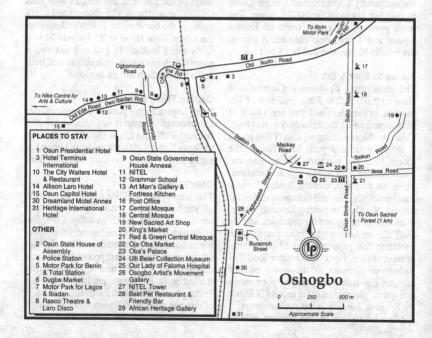

PLACES TO STAY

1 Osun Presidential Hotel
3 Hotel Terminus International
10 The City Waiters Hotel & Restaurant
14 Allison Laro Hotel
15 Osun Capitol Hotel
30 Dreamland Motel Annex
31 Heritage International Hotel

9 Osun State Government House Annexe
11 NITEL
12 Grammar School
13 Art Man's Gallery & Fortress Kitchen
16 Post Office
17 Central Mosque
18 Central Mosque
19 New Sacred Art Shop
20 King's Market
21 Red & Green Central Mosque
22 Oja Oba Market
23 Oba's Palace

OTHER

2 Osun State House of Assembly
4 Police Station
5 Motor Park for Benin & Total Station
6 Dugbe Theatre
7 Motor Park for Lagos & Ibadan
8 Rasco Theatre & Laro Disco

24 Ulli Beier Collection Museum
25 Our Lady of Faloma Hospital
26 Osogbo Artist's Movement Gallery
27 NITEL Tower
28 Best Pet Restaurant & Friendly Bar
29 African Heritage Gallery

Oshogbo

To Ilorin Motor Park
New Ikurin Rd
To Osun Sacred Forest (1 km)

Old Ikurin Road
Ogbomosho Road
Oke Fla Rd
To Nike Centre for Arts & Culture
Old Ede Road (Iwo Ibadan Rd)
Alakuwodo Road
Station Road
Sabo Road
Mackay Road
Ibokun Road
Ilesa Road
Osun Shrine Road
Fagbewesa Street
Buraimoh Street

0   250   500 m
Approximate Scale

Information

Post & Telecommunications The main post office, which has an EMS post, is on Station Rd near Dugbe market. International phone calls can be made quickly and efficiently from the NITEL office on Iwo Ibadan Rd (N 236 for three minutes to the USA or Europe).

Art Studios To see some of the artists' works, you'll have to visit their individual studios, as there is no central outlet for the sale of Oshogbo art other than the Nike Centre for Arts & Culture. All the studios are open to the public with pieces for sale and you can talk to the artists. Two galleries stand out: Twins 77's Art Man's Gallery, at 1 Old Ede Rd opposite the grammar school, and Jimoh Buraimoh's African Heritage Gallery at 1 Buraimoh St. There is also a small museum on Station Rd that houses the Ulli Beier collection, which is worth a quick visit.

Suzanne Wenger's New Sacred Art Shop at 41a Ibokun Rd sells copies of the informative *The Sacred Groves of Oshogbo* (N 350) as well as pieces of art.

Places to Stay & Eat

On Old Ede Rd, there are three relatively cheap hotels that charge N 150 for a single room with fan and shared bath. *The City Waiters Hotel & Restaurant* has a ping-pong table and great inexpensive food. The *Osun Capitol Hotel* (☎ (035) 230 396) is friendly and clean and the *Allison Laro Hotel* (☎ (035) 233 046) has an open bar, but the rooms are grimy.

Singles at the huge and run-down *Hotel Terminus International* on Old Ikurin Rd cost N225 with air-con and bucket bath.

The *Heritage International Hotel* (☎ 234 285) across from the 7-Up depot, one km south from town, has comfortable air-con singles with TV for N 250. There is a restaurant and nightclub. The city's best hotel is the *Osun Presidential Hotel* (☎ 232 399), where a double with air-con, TV and shower costs N 375 plus a deposit of N 450. The facilities include a cinema (open on weekends) and a nightclub, and an overpriced restaurant.

The *Fortress Kitchen* near the Art Man's Gallery is a great spot for Nigerian fare and for soaking up local colour. Those with a thirst might try the *Friendly Bar* which lives up to its name, and the nearby *Best Pet Restaurant* is a good choice for cheap chop.

Getting There & Away

Bush taxis leave throughout the day from the motor park near the town centre by the

---

The Oshogbo School of Art

This so-called 'school' got its start during the early 1960s when Ulli and Georgina Beier gathered together a creative band of young men and women to study theatre and art. The experimental workshop lasted several years and produced some outstanding artists of international renown, such as Rufus Ogundele, Jimoh Buraimoh, Twins 77 and Muraina Oyelami. Many now have compounds of their own, built with the proceeds of their art sales. Some have large studios and apprentices.

Other artists are having a more profound impact today. Muraina Oyelami, who previously directed the music department at the university in Ife, now runs an arts centre to which both international and local students flock. Nike Davies has broken free from the studio of her former husband, Twins 77, to become an internationally acclaimed batik artist. She and David Osevwe started the Nike Centre for Arts & Culture on Iwo Rd, the only organisation for promoting sales of Oshogbo art in general.

The creative diversification that took place during the Biafran War, when the school developed the surrealistic juxtaposition of beads and wool, plastic strips and wood for which it became famous, is gone but today's subject matter continues to be inspired by Yoruba legends. Second-generation artists, such as Adeneji Adeyemi and Labayo Ogundele, are now at the forefront and many of their prints and oils are being shown internationally. Some of the other young stars are batik artist Shangodare Gbadegbin, who makes extraordinary cloths using up to 32 colours; Buraimoh Gbadamosi, who works in stone and wood; and Kasali Akanbi, who produces stunning masks of the gods. All are without doubt among the elite of African artists today. ■

NIGERIA

railroad tracks on Oke Fia Rd; typical fares are N 50 to Ibadan (86 km), N 100 to Lagos (211 km) and N 200 to Benin City (222 km). Transport to Ilorin leaves from the motor park on the outskirts of town and costs N 80 for the 80-minute ride. If you're just travelling around town, expect to pay about N 5 for a shared taxi for a short drop and N 10 for a long one.

BENIN CITY

Until the British sacked it, Benin City was one of the great cities of West Africa, dating back to the 10th century. Human sacrifice was a part of Bini culture and was thought to appease the gods. When a British contingent arrived in 1897, a ceremony was held in an attempt to ward off the invaders. Upon entering the walled city, the conquering troops encountered a shocking, seemingly savage sight – countless decapitated corpses. However, what they carted back to Europe – 2000 bronze statutes from the Oba's palace – was hardly produced by 'savages'. The Western world was amazed by their quality and museums pounced on the work. The bronzes of Benin became one of the first styles of African art to win major worldwide recognition.

Today Benin City, capital of Bendel State, is a sprawling, undistinguished place. There are, however, several interesting sites that the locals (mainly Edo, Urhobo and Ibo) will proudly show you, including the **Okada's House** facing the Edo Hotel. It is opulent, with many interesting statues outside. Also check out the new **Oba market** across from the national museum. It burned down in 1983 but has been rebuilt since; explore the cloth merchants on the 2nd floor.

Portion of a 16th-century bronze plaque

Information

The post office on Airport Rd next to the hospital and the telephone company on Akpakpava Rd behind the FBN bank are conveniently on opposite sides of Ring Rd. A good place to change money is at the mosque – the blue building opposite the Oba market (be discreet) or at the Ibudor Arts Gallery. A good time to visit is December when the seven-day Igue/Ewere Festival as well as the nine-day New Yams Festival take place around Bendel State. Minivans are N 3, shared taxis are N 5 and a motorcycle N 5 to N 10 depending upon the distance.

National Museum

The museum, the city's major landmark built in 1973, is in the dead centre of town, encircled by Ring Rd. It's open every day from 9 am to 6 pm; admission is N 1. The star attraction is the bronze work for which the Bini were famous – virtually all produced for the king's court. The pieces on display are good but not spectacular: there are more notable pieces of Benin art in London than in Nigeria. Photographs make up a sizeable part of the collection. Upstairs there is an excellent Okokaybe dancers' costume and headdress as well as masks, stools, doorways, terracotta, pottery and ivory carvings.

Oba's Palace

The mud-walled Oba's palace, a block southwest of the museum, is quite spectacular. The palace contains sculptures, brass relics and other art depicting historical events during Benin's heyday. There is also an impressive array of traditional crafts, historic bronzes, ivory and other works of art. You need the secretary's permission to visit, but he's a busy man. Moreover, you're supposed to request permission a week or so in advance, so few travellers see it.

Idubor Arts Gallery

To see artisans at work on huge sculptures, or to purchase art, check the Idubor Arts Gallery (open from 8 am to 5 pm) at 2 Sakpoba Rd, 100 metres south of the museum. Crafts are also sold along Airport Rd north of the YWCA.

Places to Stay – bottom end

One of the cheapest places in town is *Talk of the City*, on Dawson Rd near the intersection with Lagos St, where N 100 buys you a hyper-basic room, yet still quite manageable. For the same price and still worse conditions try the *Daylight Hotel* at 7 Urubi St. *Tommy's Guest House* on 1st East Circular Rd, a block off Sapele Rd is a brothel with a lively bar that charges an outrageous N 200 for a dingy ventilated room for the entire night and filthy shared bath with bucket shower.

Much better is the *Goodwill Hotel* (☎ 245 690) at 23 Uribi St, which charges N 50 for a single with a huge shared shower. The Lily Restaurant next door has good inexpensive food. The *Edo Delta Hotel* at 128 Akpakpava St is overpriced at N 250 for a dingy single with no water or screens on the windows. Also check out the nearby *Jajat Hotel*, also on Akpakpava Rd and see if renovations are completed. Finally, women should check out the *YWCA* at 23 Airport Rd. Beds, if available, are N 50 and you're also allowed to sleep on the ground.

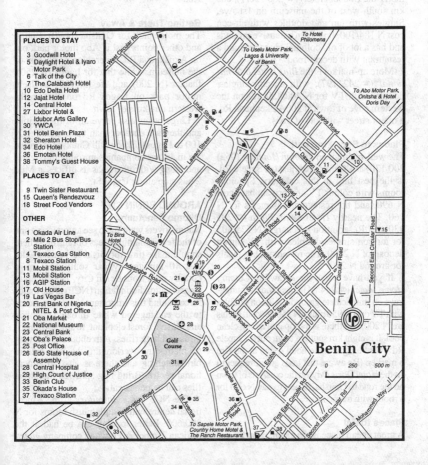

PLACES TO STAY

3 Goodwill Hotel
5 Daylight Hotel & Iyaro Motor Park
6 Talk of the City
7 The Calabash Hotel
10 Edo Delta Hotel
12 Jajat Hotel
14 Central Hotel
27 Lixbor Hotel & Idubor Arts Gallery
30 YWCA
31 Hotel Benin Plaza
32 Sheraton Hotel
34 Edo Hotel
36 Emotan Hotel
38 Tommy's Guest House

PLACES TO EAT

9 Twin Sister Restaurant
15 Queen's Rendezvouz
18 Street Food Vendors

OTHER

1 Okada Air Line
2 Mile 2 Bus Stop/Bus Station
4 Texaco Gas Station
8 Texaco Station
11 Mobil Station
13 Mobil Station
16 AGIP Station
17 Old House
19 Las Vegas Bar
20 First Bank of Nigeria, NITEL & Post Office
21 Oba Market
22 National Museum
23 Central Bank
24 Oba's Palace
25 Post Office
26 Edo State House of Assembly
28 Central Hospital
29 High Court of Justice
33 Benin Club
35 Okada's House
37 Texaco Station

To Hotel Philomena
To Uselu Motor Park, Lagos & University of Benin
To Abo Motor Park, Onitsha & Hotel Doris Day

West Circular Rd
Wire Road
Urubi Street
Lawani Street
Lagos Street
Mission Road
James Watt Road
Dawson Road
Lagos Road
Siluko Road
To Bins Hotel
Adesogbe Road
Ring Road
Airport Road
Reservation Road
1st Avenue
Akpakpava Road
Igbesanmwan Street
Agbado Street
Owina Street
Sakponba Road
Arusa Street
Ezoba Street
Circular Road
Second East Circular Road
Second East Circular Road
Country Home Road
First East Circular Rd
Central Road
Murtala Mohammed Way

Golf Course

Benin City

0   250   500 m

To Sapele Motor Park, Country Home Motel & The Ranch Restaurant

Places to Stay – middle

For convenience, you can't beat the *Lixbor Hotel* at 4 Sakpoba Rd. Expect to pay N 450 a room. It's part of the Idubor Arts Gallery building and at the back you can watch men carving.

The *Central Hotel* (☎ 200 780) at 76 Akpakpava Rd is a bit worn and costs N 200 for a room with fan or N 300 for a much nicer room with air-con. However, it is quite popular and one of the best places in town for hearing live music, especially on weekends when parties are held in the courtyard

Best for value is the old *Edo Hotel* (formerly the Bendel Hotel) (☎ 200 120/1), one km south-west of the museum on 1st Ave. Singles with fan and doubles with air-con cost N 184/100. It is set in extensive grounds and has a lot of old colonial character, and a restaurant with decent food.

More up-market is the *Bins Hotel International* (☎ 242 197), with air-con singles/doubles with TV for N 400/450. It's on the western edge of town at 200A Ekenhuan Rd, a major street with lots of taxis.

Places to Stay – top end

The well-maintained *Emotan Hotel* (☎ (052) 200 130) at 1 Central Rd, just off Sapele Rd, is the best buy in this category. Spacious rooms with colour TV and private bath cost N 690, and the restaurant has meals for N 160. The nearby *Hotel Benin Plaza* (☎ 201 430) at 1 Reservation Rd charges N 575/805 for air-con singles/doubles with TV plus a deposit of N 2000. The restaurant has meals for around N 250.

If you have a car, the sprawling *Country Home Motel* (☎ 244 641) has modern bungalows on immaculate grounds. Air-con doubles with TV cost N 950 plus a N 550 deposit. Meals are N 200, and there is a shop and a long clean pool. It is eight km south of town out on Sapele Rd – take a right at the hotel's sign at the Km 6 marker. (Be aware that taxis are infrequent.) At the *Hotel Doris Day*, on the outskirts of town on the road to Onitsha, expect to pay N 600 for a room with traffic noise.

Places to Eat

A great cheap place is the clean, friendly and ventilated *Twin Sister Restaurant* opposite the Edo Delta Hotel. It serves a generous portion of gari with eba and beer for N 85. The *Queen's Rendezvous* at 202 2nd East Circular Rd also has good inexpensive meals and snacks. The areas around the Oba market and the small Agbadan market near the Central Hotel are also good for street food.

For European food, the best places are the *Emotan Hotel* and the *Ranch Restaurant* at the Country Home Motel. For groceries, try Leventis on Sakpoba Rd near the Lixton Hotel or UTC on Sapele Rd beyond the Emotan Hotel.

Getting There & Away

The motor park for Onitsha (N 70), Enugu and other points east is Abo motor park out on Akpakpava Rd, several km north-east of the museum, while that for Lagos (N 250), Ibadan (N 200) and Ife (N 150) is Uselu motor park on Lagos Rd on the north-western outskirts of town.

Large buses also serve all of these cities and they are cheaper than bush taxis (eg N 100 to Lagos). Ekene Dili Chukwu is one of the main bus companies in southern Nigeria and along with others has its offices at Mile 2 bus stop along Urubi St.

AROUND BENIN CITY
Okomo Sanctuary

Nature lovers wanting to see animals and one of the few remaining areas of rainforest here should make time for this reserve near Udo, just 40 minutes by car south-west on a country road from Benin City. The Nigerian Conservation Foundation (NCF) is the major force behind this important sanctuary, home to the endangered white throated monkey and elusive forest elephant, to say nothing of birds and butterflies. A treehouse a dizzying 65 metres up overlooking the lake aids in bird-watching and there is also an educational centre. Bring bug spray as the sweat flies can be persistent.

The NCF has a *dormitory* at the educational centre with simple/plush rooms for N 200/600. Better lodging can be had at the African Timber & Plywood company *guest-*

house. For permission to enter the sanctuary and to book accommodation, contact the NCF (☎ (01) 268 6163) at 5 Moseley Rd, Ikoyi Island, Lagos.

ONITSHA

Onitsha, home of Premier and Masters beers, is in the heart of the most densely populated area in Africa after the Nile valley. Before the Biafran War, traders from as far away as Cameroun converged on its large market, but the fighting destroyed much of the city, including the market.

Today, this rebuilt city on the banks of the Niger River has regained its vitality. As Chinua Achebe explains, it has always attracted the 'exceptional, the colourful and the bizarre'. Nevertheless, it has little to offer travellers other than the new **market**, undoubtedly one of the most vibrant in Nigeria – the sounds alone are worth the experience.

Places to Stay – bottom end

One of the cheapest places in the heart of town is *Hotel Toma-Stab* (☎ 210 767) at 59 New Market Rd, west of Ogbomonanu Junction. Small rooms with private baths (with towels) cost N 190/250 a single with fan/air-con, N 300 a double with air-con and TV. Also cheap is *Eleganza Hotel* (☎ 212 256) at 4 O'Connor St near DMJ's Roundabout. It charges N 150 for a single with fan and shared bath or N 230 for a room with TV, air-con and private toilet and basin. There is also a bar and an inviting restaurant.

The *Travellers Palace Hotel* (☎ 211 013) at 8 Agbu Ogbuefi St has dirty rooms with grimy baths for N 315 plus a deposit of N 365. Two men are not allowed in the same room. The truly desperate could try the *Hotel de Pride* on Ojedi Rd, just off Oguta Rd; singles costs N 185.

Places to Stay – middle

Best and cheapest in this category is the *People's Club Guesthouse* (☎ 212 717). Air-con singles/doubles with TV, fridge and bath cost N 250/350. It's frequently fully booked, and there's a comfortable bar and a decent restaurant. To get there, cross the overpass from the motor park on the Lagos-Enugu Expressway and continue about 500 metres south on Owerri Rd; you'll come to the unmarked left turn-off for the hotel.

Onitsha Market Writers

Keep your eye out for Nigerian paperback novels as Onitsha is famous for its 'market writers'. Most works, really thin pamphlets, are short and often moralistic. The themes vary, but love and romance are popular, as are unsuccessful forced marriages. Titles include *How to Write Love Letters*, *My Seven Young Daughters Are After Young Boys* and, the largest seller of all, *The Nigerian Bachelors Guide*. Below is a conversation from a popular play called *Husbands and Wives Who Hate Themselves*:

Mark: I hate not marry you further you are a useless, hopeless, stupid, disobedient and nonsense wife.
Victoria: Bad man, bokom man, silly man, wicked man, bush man, I am packing quick quick and must move today. You could remember that I refused to marry you but my illiterate father forced me. You deceived and corrupted him with a bottle of White Horse.

It all began in the late 1940s when Onitsha was growing and people wanted books that were cheap and easy to read: books about their own country and problems. Eastern Nigeria had a relatively high literacy rate, so ordinary Onitsha people – taxi drivers, traders, farmers, as well as teachers and journalists – began writing part time and buying second-hand missionary printing presses to produce cheap books. By 1960 there were over 200 titles. Some famous writers, including Cyprian Ekwensi, started their literary careers here. They knew how to catch their readers' interest; one writer advertises: 'This book entertains more than two bottles of beer'. If you browse through the market, you may find a few of these books – they are highly entertaining and, for foreigners, educational. For further reading, see *Market Literature from Nigeria* (British Library, London, 1990). ∎

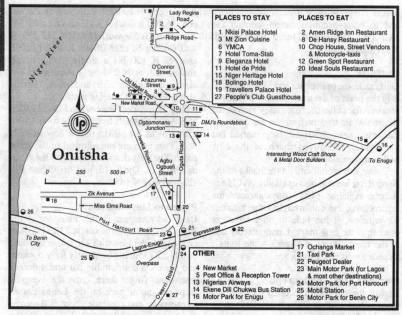

Lady Regina Road

PLACES TO STAY
1 Nkisi Palace Hotel
3 Mt Zion Cuisine
6 YMCA
7 Hotel Toma-Stab
9 Eleganza Hotel
11 Hotel de Pride
15 Niger Heritage Hotel
18 Bolingo Hotel
19 Travellers Palace Hotel
27 People's Club Guesthouse

PLACES TO EAT
2 Amen Ridge Inn Restaurant
8 De Hansy Restaurant
10 Chop House, Street Vendors
   & Motorcycle-taxis
12 Green Spot Restaurant
20 Ideal Souls Restaurant

Onitsha

Interesting Wood Craft Shops
& Metal Door Builders

To Enugu

To Benin City

OTHER
4 New Market
5 Post Office & Reception Tower
13 Nigerian Airways
14 Ekene Dili Chukwa Bus Station
16 Motor Park for Enugu
17 Ochanga Market
21 Taxi Park
22 Peugeot Dealer
23 Main Motor Park (for Lagos
   & most other destinations)
24 Motor Park for Port Harcourt
25 Mobil Station
26 Motor Park for Benin City

Places to Stay – top end

The best hotel is the small *Mt Zion Cuisine*, at 3 Lady Regina Rd, just off Ridge Rd. Air-con singles/doubles with colour TV and hot showers cost N 450/600 plus a deposit of N 500. The *Niger Heritage Hotel* (☎ 216 680) near the eastern outskirts of town, not far from the Lagos-Enugu Expressway, has singles/ doubles for N 1035/1150 plus a deposit of N 1203/1400. Travellers are not usually asked to pay the much higher non-resident rate.

At the *Bolingo Hotel* (☎ 210 962) an air-con single costs N 550 plus a deposit of N 600. It's on Zik Ave, 1.5 km north-west of the overpass. The *Nkisi Palace Hotel* (☎ 211 719) on Nkisi Rd charges N 575/750 for a single/double with a bucket bath.

Places to Eat

A great cheap place is the *De Hansy Restaurant* not far from Ogbomonanu Junction. A plate of rice or gari with fish or meat costs N 30; it's very popular and the goat pepper soup is delicious.

Another good place is the *Ideal Souls Restaurant* off Oguta Rd near the Travellers Palace Hotel. A supermarket, inexpensive restaurants and street food can be found at the junction of Old and New Market Rds. Another good place for street food is the *Green Spot Restaurant* just north of the Ekene Dili Chukwu bus station on Oguta Rd.

For those looking to spend N 200 a dish for excellent Chinese food, the *Amen Ridge Inn* at 3A Ridge Rd is the place to go (open until 10 pm); they serve breakfast too. The similarly priced *Mt Zion Cuisine* also serves good Chinese fare and the restaurant at the *Bolingo Hotel* comes a close third.

Getting There & Away

One of the largest bus companies, Ekene Dili Chukwu, is on Oguta Rd, 250 metres south of DMJ's Roundabout. A big bus to Abuja costs N 200, to Kano N 350 and to Lagos

N 250. Bush taxis cost N 60 to Enugu, N 130 to Port Harcourt and N 500 to Lagos. A seat on a J5 Peugeot van costs N 30 to Enugu and N 200 to Lagos. Bush taxis and minibuses for most cities (Lagos, Abuja, etc) leave from the motor park just north of the overpass on the expressway, while the motor park for Enugu is on the eastern side of town a little beyond the Niger Heritage Hotel.

OWERRI

After passing through so many huge, noisy, congested cities, you'll find Owerri's tranquillity delightful. Mid-range hotels worth trying are the *Ivory Hotel* (☎ 230 902), four km north-east of town on Okigwe Rd, the *Executive* and the *Modotel Owerri* (☎ (083) 233 333) on Okigwe Rd. Tops is the *Imo Concorde Hotel* (☎ 231 111), about 45 minutes from Port Harcourt Airport. It has a pool, tennis court, nightclub, casino, telex and bookshop. Next best is the *Pinewood Hotel* (☎ 230 135), with pool and car hire.

ENUGU

The centre of Nigeria's coal-mining region, Enugu in Anambra State is another sprawling Iboland city with little to interest travellers. However, trees along the streets provide shade and rolling green hills in the suburbs make it prettier than many cities. Visiting the **Ekulu mines** several km out of town is apparently permitted.

Orientation & Information

The city's main street, running roughly north-east to south-west, is Okpara Ave, along which you'll find many businesses, banks and, nearby, the post office. Another major artery, Zik Ave/May 27th Ave, runs roughly parallel with Okpara Ave but further to the east, with the train line and central station on Ogui Rd splitting them.

You can make international calls from the NITEL office at the Trade Fair Complex on Okpara Rd and send letters via EMS, whose office is near the NITEL tower at 23 Okpara Ave. There are moneychangers across the street; you can also change US dollars and travellers' cheques quickly and easily at Emerald Agencies at 8 Okpara Ave. There's a British Council office at the intersection of Chime Ave and Ogui Rd (open from 10 am to 6 pm). Shared taxis around town cost N 5 to N 10 depending upon the distance.

Places to Stay – bottom end

The state-run *Ikenga Hotel* (☎ 334 055), behind the Central Bank of Nigeria on Club Rd, has well-maintained chalets with air-con, TV, fan and bucket bath for N 250 a double, plus a deposit of N 250. If you really want to save money, try the *Garden City Hotel* at 7 Annang St. A less than clean single with shared bath and fan costs N 230.

Places to Stay – middle

One of the least expensive is the *Romas International Hotel* (☎ (042) 333 551) at 8 Aku St not far from the centre. Singles/doubles with air-con and TV cost N 350/554 plus a deposit of N 100/150. The nearby *Placia Hotel* (☎ 331 565) at 25 Edinburgh Rd has small air-con singles/doubles for N 460/575 plus a deposit of N 100/250 and a decent restaurant with meals for N 70. The *First Hotel* (☎ 330 301) at 17/19 Annang St has small but clean singles/doubles with air-con and TV for N 500/600. The restaurant is pleasant although the bar is slow.

The *Hotel Metropole* (☎ 334 553) at 13 Ogui Rd has comfortable singles/doubles with air-con and TV for N 518/644 plus a deposit of N 90. The *Quixotel* (☎ 332 565) at 41 Ogui Rd has singles/ doubles for N 345/ 650. Also good value is the *Panafric Hotel* (☎ 335 248) at 6 Murtala Mohammed Way, with singles/ doubles with fridge and TV for N 575/700 plus a deposit of N 225/300. You can also get decent Nigerian and European meals at the restaurant for N 150. The *Royal Palace Hotel* (☎ 334 082) at 301 Agbani is far from the centre but close to the Afor Awk motor park.

Places to Stay – top end

Three of the city's best hotels (and restaurants) are in the same residential area and have the usual facilities. The *Zodiac Hotel* (☎ 337 900, telex 51242) at 5 Rangers Ave has singles/doubles with TV and fridge for

N 603/845 plus a deposit of N 400/700. The *Gemini Inn Hotel* (☎ 331 286) at 19 Igboeze St has singles/doubles for N 690/885 plus a deposit of N 200. The state-run *Hotel Presidential* (☎ 337 274) has doubles between N 450 and N 950 plus deposits of N 500.

The more expensive *Modotel Enugu* (☎ 338 870, telex 51156) at 2 Club Rd has air-con singles/doubles with TV and showers for N 920/1035.

Places to Eat

For cheap chop, try *Bon Apetit* on Edinburgh Rd or *Ideal Cuisine* a few doors down at 15 Edinburgh Rd. *Genesis Restaurant* at 36 Zik Ave and *Raya Chinese Restaurant* at 36 Ogui Rd serve good Chinese dishes for around N 200. Many of the hotels have decent restaurants. For groceries, try Leventis at 38 Ogui Rd or Tonson at 3 Enugu Rd.

Getting There & Away

Bush taxis for Onitsha (N 60) leave from Afor Awk motor park on the southern outskirts of town and from Enugu's main motor park opposite the prison. Vehicles for Owerri (N 60) leave from Ogbete main motor park nearby, while those for Abuja (N 300) and Jos (N 400) leave from 9th mile motor park; to get to any of them, take a van from Enugu's main motor park. For vehicles to Lagos, check EDC at 44 Zik Ave; it charges N 300 for a bus and N 550 for a bush taxi.

OBUDU CATTLE RANCH

This unlikely but well-known resort is on the Cameroun border, 110 km east of Ogoja. On the way you'll pass through dense forests with trees so high that their branches form a canopy, shutting out the sun entirely. Driving up to the plateau, you'll see rolling mountain ranges. Built during the 1950s by Scottish ranchers, this was at one time a well-functioning ranch-resort. These days it's run-down but it is slowly being renovated and is still a good place for walking, as the climate is agreeable. It can be a little chilly at the top. At 1890 metres with no mosquitoes, you might think you're in Scotland.

The *Obudu Ranch Hotel* has 23 chalets,

tennis courts and horses. The rooms are not cheap, but you can always pitch a tent; at Easter and Christmas this place may be fully booked. For reservations, call the booking office in Bauchi (☎ 42174) or write: Obudu Cattle Ranch, Manager, Obudu Ranch Hotel, PO Box 40, Obudu, Cross River State.

Getting There & Away

By vehicle the 110-km drive east from Ogoja to the ranch via Obudu is straightforward and paved part of the way. If you take a bush taxi, you will probably have to hitchhike from Obudu, which is 44 km west of the ranch.

GEMBU

Hikers should check out Gembu on the Cameroun border. It's in a hilly area of tea estates and cattle ranches way off the beaten track. The walks are up to your imagination as there are few marked paths. If you head for the hospital at Waar Wa, you'll walk above, through and under the clouds. After Lagos, you won't believe how friendly the people are here; they love to show visitors around.

The only place to stay is the *Daula Hotel*, which has single/doubles with shared bucket showers for N 20/30 (N 50 to N 90 for large rooms with private showers). It has a generator and a restaurant.

Gashaka Game Reserve

Gashaka is Nigeria's largest national park and has the country's highest mountain, **Chapal Waddi** (2407 metres). Within its large area is a plethora of rivers and the most diverse ecology of any Nigerian park, including guinea savannah, grasslands and pockets of mountain (or gallery) forest. Hippo, waterbuck, buffalo, monkeys and big cats are all found here, and bird-watchers will be in their element. The hot springs are another attraction. There are several good hikes, so bring all your camping equipment; porters can be hired at or near the national parks office in Serti.

There is basic accommodation at the reserve, N 100 a room, but you will need to bring all your food (you can buy supplies in Serti). There is no electricity in the reserve.

To get there from Gembu, take a bush taxi to Serti. The entrance to the reserve is some 16 km south.

Getting There & Away

Gembu is a two-hour bush-taxi ride from Nguroje; non-4WD vehicles can make the trip only with great difficulty.

PORT HARCOURT

Built as a port for exporting coal from Enugu, Port Harcourt in Rivers State now has another *raison d'être* – oil. All around town you can see oil flares at night. Wealth has made it one of Nigeria's most expensive cities but not one of its most interesting. New market and the port, both in the central area, are the only places of interest.

Orientation & Information

Azikwe Rd is the main road in the central commercial area. In this vicinity you'll find the train station, major banks, the post office and stores such as Leventis and UTC.

The older area of town is south of the centre. Three of the major travel agencies are along Aba Rd within one km of each other. From north to south they are: Tamsaki at the Presidential Hotel, Ideal Travel Agency in the Nigeria Airways building and Benjosy Travel Agency (☎ 221 420).

Places to Stay – bottom end

Port Harcourt's cheapest hotels are not cheap compared to hotels elsewhere in Nigeria, Lagos excepted. For example, the *Continental Guest House* near Aba Rd offers nothing more than a bed and a light bulb in a bare room for N 300. At the *Alhaja Titilope* at 2 Rumuadaolu Rd a single with fan and shared bath costs N 350 while an air-con double goes for N 550. Slightly higher in price and not worth the difference is the *Tamsill Satellite Hotel* (☎ 331 684) at 4 Abuja Lane. Reasonably clean rooms and dirty baths cost N 400 for a ventilated single or N 700 for an air-con double. The best value is the *Anneta Guest House* at 4 Kalagbar St, where air-con singles with shared baths cost N 250. The

staff is super friendly and the little restaurant here offers basic fare for around N 30.

Places to Stay – middle

A good choice is the *Delta Hotel* (☎ 300 190), at 1-3 Harley St not far from the centre. Well-maintained singles/doubles with air-con, TV and telephone cost N 690/900. It has a decent bar and restaurant. At the *Labake Hotel & Restaurant* at 3 Odu St, singles/doubles cost N 450/750 with air-con, fridge and TV. In the same price range is *Biddy's Hotel* at 16 Rumuadaolu Rd, where a single with private bath, shower and air-con costs N 500 (N 600 for a double).

The *Seanel International* at 2 Okorodo St (☎ 332 141) has small dark rooms and charges N500/600 for singles with fans and doubles with air-con. The more expensive *Hotel Chez Theresa* at 23 Udom St has singles/doubles with air-con and TV for N 900/1500. At *Anon Lodge* at 157 Aba Rd a dingy single costs N 525.

The *Cedar Palace Hotel* on Harbour Rd in the central port area charges N 874/1270 for a single/double with colour TV, fridge and shower. The restaurant serves basic meals and the popular bar attracts sailors. This is also an easy place to change money.

Places to Stay – top end

The *Presidential Hotel* (☎ 236 260, telex 61308) on Aba Rd is the best. For nonresidents it has rooms which seem overpriced at N 4048 plus a N 5000 deposit; credit cards are not accepted. Both Lufthansa and ADC have offices here and you'll find it easy to change money. You can also swim in the pool for an extra N 40.

Places to Eat

For inexpensive food in the old area, try *Luna's Restaurant* at 157 Victoria St, which has strictly Nigerian fare, or *Black & White Restaurant* nearby at 54 Aggrey Rd. For fast food, try *Mr Bigg's* just north of Leventis on Azikwe Ave.

On Aba Rd are some better restaurants with a wider range of cuisines and prices. *Le Bistro* at 171 Aba Rd has fine French food

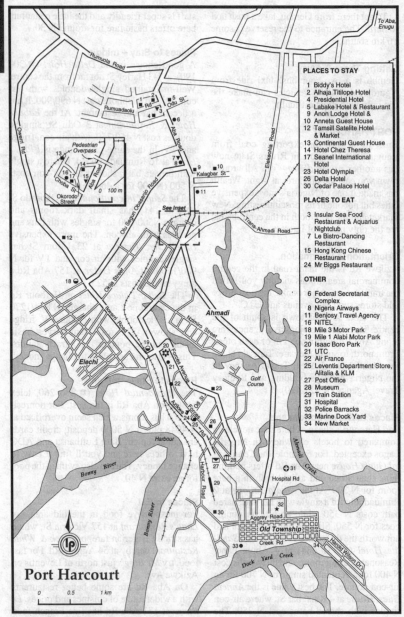

PLACES TO STAY

1 Biddy's Hotel
2 Alhaja Titilope Hotel
4 Presidential Hotel
5 Labake Hotel & Restaurant
9 Anon Lodge Hotel &
10 Anneta Guest House
12 Tamsil Satelite Hotel & Market
13 Continental Guest House
14 Hotel Chez Theresa
17 Seanel International Hotel
23 Hotel Olympia
26 Delta Hotel
30 Cedar Palace Hotel

PLACES TO EAT

3 Insular Sea Food Restaurant & Aquarius Nightclub
7 Le Bistro-Dancing Restaurant
15 Hong Kong Chinese Restaurant
24 Mr Biggs Restaurant

OTHER

6 Federal Secretariat Complex
8 Nigeria Airways
11 Benjosy Travel Agency
16 NITEL
18 Mile 3 Motor Park
19 Mile 1 Alabi Motor Park
20 Isaac Boro Park
21 UTC
22 Air France
25 Leventis Department Store, Alitalia & KLM
27 Post Office
28 Museum
29 Train Station
31 Hospital
32 Police Barracks
33 Marine Dock Yard
34 New Market

Port Harcourt

0   0.5   1 km

and dancing. The *Festival Restaurant* nearby serves delicious European fare. For reasonable Chinese meals, try the *Hong Kong Chinese Restaurant* on Aba Ave. There is also the *4-5-6 Chinese Restaurant* in the Presidential Hotel. The *Labake Hotel & Restaurant* serves great Nigerian food and the Delta has set meals for around N 175.

For elegant surroundings, try the *Insular Sea Food Restaurant*, a block off Aba Rd. Lobster is its speciality but meat dishes are also served.

Entertainment

Aquarius, next to the Insular Restaurant on the corner of Aba and Rumuadaolu Rds, is one of the city's most popular nightclubs. *Uncle Sam* nearby is one of the hottest, but with prostitutes galore. Both these places are basically male hang-outs. The nightclub at the *Presidential* is more comfortable for women; the hotel also has a casino.

Getting There & Away

Bus & Bush Taxi The main motor park for all destinations is on Owerri Rd at Mile 3. You'll probably arrive here. You can catch a taxi to the delta for about N 20 or a minivan for N 10. If you're headed to Owerri, you can take a Peugeot J5 van for N 50 while a Peugeot 504 saloon to Warri will cost N 150. The smaller Mile 1 Abali motor park on Azikwe Rd is better for certain destinations. From there, expect to pay N 40 to Aba, N 150 to Calabar, N 180 to Enugu (two hours), N 200 to Warri, N 250 to Benin City, N 450 to Ibadan and N 500 to Lagos.

Train The train for Jos, Bauchi and Maiduguri leaves on Monday at 7 am and according to the schedule takes 25 hours to Jos and almost twice that long to Maiduguri. It departs southward from Jos on Wednesday at 1 pm. To Jos it's N 189/130 in 1st/2nd class and almost double that to Maiduguri.

ABA

Only 65 km north-east of Port Harcourt, Aba, noted for its flourishing market, is a frequent stopover for those headed east to Calabar

(184 km). The city has a number of lower-end hotels; three on Pound Rd include *Voyage Guest House*, *Grace Guest Inn* and *City Guest Home*.

The top hotels, with singles/doubles around N 90/140, are the *Imo Hotel* (☎ 220 111), *Enitona Hotel* (☎ 220 200), and the *Crystal Park Hotel* (☎ 221 930).

Crosslines Bus offers services to Jos; the cost is N 200 and the trip takes 10 hours. Bush taxis east to Calabar charge N 80 (N 60 by minibus) and north to Enugu charge N 120 and take two hours.

ORON

Don't miss the excellent **museum** opposite the ferry wharf. Open daily from 9 am to 5.30 pm, it has a wonderful collection of wooden carvings – masks, puppets and funerary art – and the museum guide is well worth N 20. Immigration for Cameroun is at the beach and you must get your exit stamp there.

The basic *King Kong Motel* is 20 metres from the museum at 4 Ogoja St and charges N 70 for a room with fan. So does the *Peninsula Hotel* at 157 Oron Rd, about 1.5 km out of town; there are several food stalls nearby. Slightly nicer is the *Feeder Hotel* at 169 Oron Rd, where a single with fan and clean bath costs N 150. The best place is the *Namoba Hotel*, with air-con singles at N 100. However, it's about two km from the wharf and flagging down a motorcycle-taxi could be a problem. For food try the *Green Spot Restaurant* at the motor park or any of the numerous food stalls along the main drag.

A bush taxi to Aba costs N 70.

CALABAR

In the far south-east, with twice as much rainfall as Lagos, Calabar is popular with travellers passing through Nigeria, especially those headed to Cameroun, 25 km away. High on a hill, it commands a fine view of the Calabar River and the city on its eastern banks.

Calabar is small by Nigerian standards, which makes it livable and likeable. People are especially friendly and you will often hear the phrase 'you are welcome'. Even the immigration police, who pop up here now

NIGERIA

and then, are friendly. Also, walking around town is a pleasure and relatively safe at night. If you don't care to walk, motorcycle-taxis are everywhere and dirt cheap.

Orientation & Information

Marina Rd runs along the eastern banks of the Calabar River. Most of the port activity is along this road. Several blocks inland, running parallel with Marina Rd and the river, is Calabar Rd, the city's main drag. Watt market, the heart of town, is on this road, as is the post office and many major stores and banks. Proceeding northward, Calabar Rd eventually becomes Odu Kpani Rd, the main highway north out of town towards Ikom. At the southern end of Calabar Rd, Target Rd branches off to the north-east, eventually becoming Marian Rd and running parallel to Calabar Rd.

International phone calls can be made from the NITEL office at 2 Club Rd. Nigeria Airways has an office at 45 Bedwell St and is open weekdays from 8 am to 6 pm. Motorcycle-taxis are plentiful and cost N 5 per drop, and you might even be invited to drive!

Cameroun Visas The Cameroun consulate at 21 Marian Rd/Ndiden Iso Rd issues visas routinely and without problems. They cost N 1875 and you'll need two or three photos. It's open weekdays from 9 am to 2.30 pm, and visas are usually issued within 24 hours.

Calabar Museum

The beautiful old governor's residency on the hill overlooking the river has been converted into the city's museum. Open daily from 9 am to 6 pm, it has an entrance fee of only N 1 and is well worth a visit. This fascinating and impressive collection covers the pre-colonial days, the slaving era, the palm-oil trade, the British invasion in the late 19th century and independence. The view of the river from the bar is excellent.

Excursions

A good day trip is to the tranquil village of Creek Town, a short, relaxing trip up the river. You can meet people going about their

business as you wander along the dusty roads, try the local palm wine, sit, chat and soak up the tranquillity. Another place to visit while staying in Calabar is the Drill Ranch. Two expatriates here rescue drill monkeys and chimps (the former famous for their fluorescent genitalia and overtly sexual behaviour), and offer visitors free lodging in exchange for helping out.

Places to Stay

The most inviting place to stay for cheap accommodation is the family-run *Stardos Guesthouse* at 7a O'Dwyer St. A furnished room with fan and private bath with bucket shower costs N 140 (N 180 with air-con). The grimy *Rolson Motel* at 15 Yellow Duke Rd charges N 80/150 for singles/doubles, but you get what you pay for. *Andy Guest House* on Fosberry St has air-con singles/doubles with private bath for N 180/200. For N 100/200 a single/double, the *Nsibuk Sea-Side Hotel* at 45 Edem St has panoramic views from its 3rd-floor glassed-in bar, perfect for watching sunsets.

The *Ekunikpa Hotel* on Mayne Ave has air-con rooms with bucket baths and a noisy generator for N 200/270. The *Chalsma Hotel* at 7 Otop Abasi St charges N 300/400 for singles/doubles with air-con and TV.

Excellent value with great river views is the *Ellinah Guest House* at 20 Hawkins Rd. Clean singles/doubles with TV and fridge are very reasonably priced at N 270/300.

The *Vetas Guest House* at 41 Atu St has overpriced singles/doubles for N 350/400 with TV and shower. Further out, the *Paradise City Hotel* at 88 Atekong Drive has nicer rooms for N 400/600.

The city's finest hotel is the *Metropolitan Hotel* (☎ 220 913) on Calabar Rd. Doubles with TV, air-con and private bath cost about N 800 (plus N700 deposit); doubles with fan cost N 600 (plus N 600 deposit). Meals in the restaurant, mostly European fare, cost between N 175 and N 200.

Places to Eat

At *Mr Magik Restaurant*, 10 Atakpa, just off Inyang Rd, Mr & Mrs Magik will make you

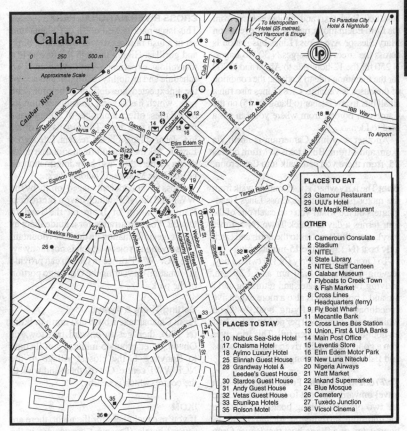

Calabar

0   250   500 m
Approximate Scale

Calabar River

Marina Road
Edem St
Nyua St
Beecroft St
Eket St
Lagos St
Egerton Street
Garden St
Calabar Road
Goldie Street
Nelson Mandela Street
Club Rd
Barracks Road
Akim Qua Town Road
Otop Abasi Street
Mary Slessor Avenue
Target Road
IBB Way
To Airport
Merian Road (Ndidem Iso Rd)
Etim Edem St
Basle Davis St
Duke St
Chamley Street
White House Road
Palm Street
Academy Street
Webber Street
Analima Street
O'Dwyer St
Fosberry Street
Inyang NTA Henshaw St
Atu Street
Hawkins Road
Calabar Road
Eyo Ita Street
Mayne
Palm St
Palm Avenue

To Metropolitan
Hotel (25 metres),
Port Harcourt & Enugu

To Paradise City
Hotel & Nightclub

PLACES TO EAT
23 Glamour Restaurant
29 UUJ's Hotel
34 Mr Magik Restaurant

OTHER
1   Cameroun Consulate
2   Stadium
3   NITEL
4   State Library
5   NITEL Staff Canteen
6   Calabar Museum
7   Flyboats to Creek Town
    & Fish Market
8   Cross Lines
    Headquarters (ferry)
9   Fly Boat Wharf
11 Mecantile Bank
12 Cross Lines Bus Station
13 Union, First & UBA Banks
14 Main Post Office
15 Leventis Store
16 Etim Edem Motor Park
19 New Luna Niteclub
20 Nigeria Airways
21 Watt Market
22 Inkand Supermarket
24 Blue Mosque
26 Cemetery
27 Tuxedo Junction
36 Vicsol Cinema

PLACES TO STAY
10 Nsibuk Sea-Side Hotel
17 Chalsma Hotel
18 Ayimo Luxury Hotel
25 Elinnah Guest House
28 Grandway Hotel &
    Leedee's Guest House
30 Stardos Guest House
31 Andy Guest House
32 Vetas Guest House
33 Ekunikpa Hotels
35 Rolson Motel

anything, but check the price before ordering. The Calabar soup with periwinkles (snails), and the native delicacy, ekpang nkukwo ikpong (coco-yam wrapped in coco-yam leaves), are delicious.

Other places to eat include the *Glamour Restaurant* at 77 Egerton St where gari costs N 50, and *UUJ's Hotel* on Chamley St, a chop bar with rock-bottom prices, eg gari with egusi for N 15. For groceries, try Inkand on Egerton St.

Entertainment
The *New Luna Nightclub* at 18 Nelson Mandela St has live music and also serves

food. *Tuxedo Junction* at 147 Calabar Rd, at the intersection with Chamley, is also popular for music. For a karate film, check Vicsol Cinema at 67 Ekpo Abasi St.

Getting There & Away
Air Nigeria Airways and ADC have three flights a week to Lagos; the fare is N 1670.

Bus & Bush Taxi Bush taxis to Aba cost N 80 (N 60 by minibus) and the trip takes two hours, while those to Ikang cost N 30. The trip to Ikom (217 km) costs N 50 by bus (2½ hours), N 70 by minibus and N 100 by bush taxi. Bush taxis and minibuses leave from the Etim Edem motor park next to Leventis on Mary Slessor Ave. Cross Lines bus station is across the street and charges N 300 to Lagos, N 250 for the 12-hour ride to Abuja and N 300 for the marathon ride to Kaduna; the condition of the buses is variable. Cross Lines also run a small bus from Calabar to Ikang (N 15) on the Cameroun border, from where you can get a boat to Idenao.

Another way into Cameroun is north via Ikom and Mfum. Bush taxis to Mfum cost N 25; from there you can walk into Cameroun.

Boat The ferry wharf is a 45-minute walk from the motor park. From the Cross Lines Headquarters on the wharf you can catch one of the four ferries a day to Creek Town (N 5; times vary), or walk 50 metres to the north and catch a fly boat (N 15) for the 15-minute ride.

To Oron there's a ferry (N 15) twice a day, leaving Calabar at 8.30 am and 1.30 pm, arriving two hours later and returning at 11 am and 4 pm. There is also a more expensive speedboat, called a flying boat, to Oron which costs about N 40 per person, takes half an hour and leaves when full. This trip gives you a good view of the river, mango swamps and fishing villages along the way.

To/From Cameroun From Oron you can travel onwards by boat to Cameroun. There are two options: fishing boats that leave in the morning, arriving in Idenao 12 to 14 hours later, or a flying boat that leaves Oron around 10 am and takes about four hours. The latter takes up to eight passengers and the cost varies according to the number of passengers; N 400 per person is typical. Don't let them drop you at the beach before Idenao unless you want to wait for another boat to town. At Oron you could also look for six other people and pay N 600 each for the five-hour ride to Limbe.

Either way, you will probably have to stay overnight in Oron because the boats to Oron usually arrive after all the fishing boats and flyboats have departed. You could also take a bus to Ikang before getting a boat from there to Idenao (see Bus, above).

CROSS RIVER NATIONAL PARK

This large park is well north of Calabar and set in a lush rainforest with waterfalls, birds and gorillas. Hiking through the forests is a marvellous experience, but having an open schedule and an ability to rough it and accept the unexpected are definitely helpful. The park, which has several divisions within its boundaries, offers a number of hiking trails from one to five days. The park has an office in Calabar at No 3 Ebuta Crescent, Ette Agbor Layout. Ask there for information and an introductory letter; they also have information on nearby Mbe Mountain National Park.

Cross River Park is managed jointly by the WWF and the NCF, which have a centre near Kanyang, north of Ikom on the road to Obudu. You can arrange for a guide there as well as get information on the Mbe Mountain Conservation Project, which is not far away. The NCF/WWF office in Obudu can provide information on visiting the Okwango portion of the park.

Getting There & Away

From Calabar take a bush taxi north to Ikom (N 100), then get an onward taxi towards Obudu. After about 45 minutes you'll come to Kanyang 1, the closest village to the NCF/WWF centre. Get off there and walk to the centre, which is nearby.

IKOM

If you're caught here for the night, there are several hotels. The most convenient is the run-down *Hotel Garden*, in the top right corner of the motor park as you enter from the main road. It charges N 120 for a single with fan and bucket showers. Facing the motor park is a place that serves good chicken, beer and ice cream. If the Garden is full, try the *Lisbon*, another cheap place, or the friendly *Castel Inn Hotel*, which also allows travellers to camp in the grounds. Some travellers have also been invited by the locals to camp at the forestry camp some 10 km from the border.

Getting There & Away

A bush taxi to Calabar costs N 100 (N 70 by

minibus, N 50 by bus) and takes less than two hours. Calabar to Mfum costs N 25 by bush taxi.

The Centre

ABUJA

During the oil-boom days of the 1970s, the government decided that Lagos was becoming too unmanageable and, worse, overly dominated by the Yoruba. It was decided to construct a new capital, like Brasilia, in an undeveloped central area supposed to be outside the control of any one ethnic group. Construction began in the early 1980s, which was the worst time possible, as oil revenues were then beginning to slide. As a result construction has proceeded at a snail's pace. The mosque, the *sharia* (Moslem law) courts and the presidential guesthouse are finished, but the wide boulevards have relatively few vehicles and many lots are still vacant. However, unlike Yamoussoukro (Côte d'Ivoire), which is a capital in name only, Abuja is slowly becoming Nigeria's actual capital; Abacha has in fact moved his government here. But while many official functions are now held in Abuja, many ministries are still in Lagos and the city remains unfinished.

Information

The NITEL office is on Faskari St in the Garki district; a three-minute call to Europe costs N 220. There is a post office and EMS in the Wuse Shopping Centre, and the Wuse hospital is nearby on Sultan Abakar St. Nigeria Airways has an office at the UTC Shopping Centre while the private airlines have theirs at the Sheraton (ADC and Okada) and Agura (Bellview Airlines) hotels. The European Community House (☎ 523 3144) at 63 Usuma St serves the diplomatic needs of citizens of Belgium, Britain, Denmark, France, Germany, Ireland, Italy, Luxembourg, the Netherlands, Portugal and Spain. Australian and Canadian citizens should call at Ghana St, opposite the Nicon Noga Hilton.

Places to Stay – bottom end

There are few 'cheap' hotels in Abuja. The cheapest appears to be the *Eddie-Vic Hotel*, which is off Muhammed Buhari Way and quite isolated. It charges N 350 for a single with a wretched shared bath. If you pay a little more, you'll get better value. A convenient place not far from the Wuse motor park (where you'll be dropped off by bush taxi) is the *Dubu Hotel* at 155 Bissau St. It has singles with air-con and shared baths for N 400 (N 450 with private bath). If you want a shower, be sure to take it at night; you'll have to use buckets in the morning. Another possibility is the *FAI Mini Guest House* behind

---

Abuja – City of Controversy

Few matters in Nigerian politics generate as much controversy as Abuja. The major issue until recently was statehood. As originally conceived, Abuja was to be run like Washington, DC – not as a state. But that issue has given rise to great debate, all of which is polarised along ethnic and religious lines. Until recently, northerners were arguing that it should be the 22nd state, that the area was too large to be run simply as a capital city. The Constituent Assembly resolved the issue several years ago in favour of the southerners by decreeing that it would be a mayoralty. The other major issue – what to do with the native Gwari inhabitants who were kicked off their land – remains unresolved. The original plan of relocating them has proven too costly.

Today, the major issue is simply whether the government can continue pouring money into this arguably 'luxury' project while refusing to pay its creditors' debts. When the Senate and House of Representatives were in existence, their members had to be housed, at great expense, in the city's two international luxury hotels. Abacha, on taking power, dissolved these bodies and returned the capital to Lagos, but since early 1994 he has moved his government, unencumbered by democratic institutions, back to Abuja. At the rate things are moving now, work on the city centre and the Maitama market, the two largest projects in progress, will take years. ■

the Garki Post Office at 560 Owo Close. A basic room with shared bath costs N 400.

The *Sonny Guest Inn* behind the old Garki motor park on 41 Areal St off Benue Crescent is slightly better but the location is less than desirable and finding a taxi entails walking out to Festival Rd. Pleasant and clean, it charges N 460 for a single with fan (N 750 with air-con).

Places to Stay – middle

The *Sharon International Hotel* off Bissau St at 220 Fortlammy St and the *Tamara Guest Inn*

at 2059 Abidjan St have singles for N 977 plus a deposit of N 273 and doubles for N 1207 plus a deposit of N 293. Both are very nice with friendly staff and have TV, fridge etc. They also have restaurants, with the Tamara offering European and Nigerian fare for around N 200 per plate. For slightly less there is the *New Rendezvous Hotel* (☎ 523 1195), also off Bissau St at 188 Makeni St. For N 700 plus deposit you get a room with air-con, TV and a decent private bath.

The *Ibro Hotel* in the same area has doubles at N 1000 for residents but a ridicu-

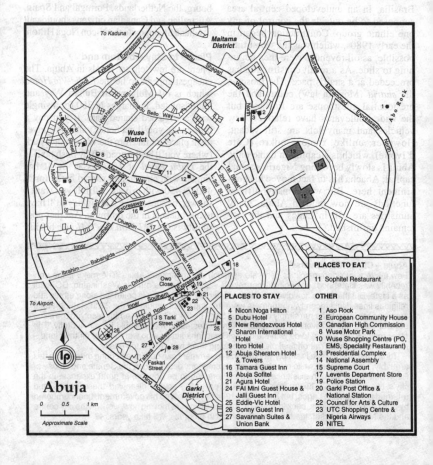

Abuja

```
0      0.5      1 km
Approximate Scale
```

PLACES TO STAY

4 Nicon Noga Hilton
5 Dubu Hotel
6 New Rendezvous Hotel
7 Sharon International Hotel
9 Ibro Hotel
12 Abuja Sheraton Hotel & Towers
16 Tamara Guest Inn
18 Abuja Sofitel
21 Agura Hotel
24 FAI Mini Guest House & Jalli Guest Inn
25 Eddie-Vic Hotel
26 Sonny Guest Inn
27 Savannah Suites & Union Bank

PLACES TO EAT

11 Sophitel Restaurant

OTHER

1 Aso Rock
2 European Community House
3 Canadian High Commission
8 Wuse Motor Park
10 Wuse Shopping Centre (PO, EMS, Speciality Restaurant)
13 Presidential Complex
14 National Assembly
15 Supreme Court
17 Leventis Department Store
19 Police Station
20 Garki Post Office & National Station
22 Council for Arts & Culture
23 UTC Shopping Centre & Nigeria Airways
28 NITEL

lous US$90 for nonresidents. Behind the
post office in the Garki district is the *Jalli
Guest Inn* (☎ 234 3950, fax 234 3956) at 561
Owo Close. It charges a steep N 1005 for a
single with TV, fridge and clean shower.

Places to Stay – top end
The best top-end hotel for the money is the
Savannah Suites in the Garki district off J S
Tarki St between the Union and Allied banks.
Comfortable, clean rooms cost N 1380 plus
a deposit of N 800.

All the other 1st-class hotels in town are
deluxe, with swimming pools, tennis courts,
free airport shuttle service, etc. Of these, the
best value is the *Abuja Sheraton Hotel &
Towers* (☎ (09) 523 0225, fax 523 1570, telex
91250) at Ladi Kwali Way, where singles/
doubles cost US$125/170 plus a deposit of
US$105. Less pretentious and more expensive
is the *Agura Hotel* (☎ 234 2753, telex 71496)
on Festival Rd. The nonresident rate is US$140
for a standard plus a deposit of N 3500. The
Nicon Noga Hilton (☎ 523 1811, fax 523 2417,
telex 91504) charges US$185/210 for singles/
doubles plus a deposit of N 4600.

Places to Eat
For cheap chop try one of the little stands
around Wuse motor park and head over to
Bissau St in the evenings for great slabs of
suya. The *Speciality Restaurant* in the Wuse
Shopping Centre prepares standard gari and
the *Sophitel Restaurant* near the Sheraton
serves large portions of jollof rice for N 50.
Luigi's is an Italian restaurant at the Sheraton
that has excellent food at an affordable price
including a salad buffet for N 90, fettucine
Alfredo for N 180 and an all-you-can-eat
buffet on Monday night.

Getting There & Away
Nigeria Airways, ADC, Okada Airlines and
Bellview Airlines have daily flights to
Lagos. The airport is 40 km west of town.
Bush taxis leave from Wuse motor park off
Herbert Macauley Way. The major routes are
to Kano (N 200; five hours), Kaduna (N 90;
two hours), Jos (N 150; two hours), Makurdi

(N 150; three hours), Onitsha (N 200; four
hours) and Lagos (N 450; eight hours).

AROUND ABUJA
One of Nigeria's more famous landmarks is
Zuma rock. This huge granite outcrop is
approximately 300 metres high and one km
in length. It's not exactly spine-tingling, but
it is somewhat impressive. To get there, from
Wuse motor park take a minivan to Suleja (N
15), a 50-minute trip. Heading south from
Abuja you can see the distinctive round
thatched-roof huts of the Gwari tribe.

JOS
Jos is one of the more popular destinations
in central Nigeria. The two major attractions
are the cooler climate and the unique Jos
museum complex. At 1200 metres above sea
level, the Jos plateau is noticeably cooler
than most other areas of the country. The
stone-covered rolling hills also make it more
scenic. While there are taxis everywhere,
covering the city on foot is possible as the
museum and many hotels and restaurants are
within 1.5 km of the central market.

Orientation & Information
The city has two main north-south drags.
One is Bauchi Rd, along which you'll find
the large new market, the Terminus Hotel,
the train station and some commercial
establishments. Southward it turns into
Bukuru Rd. Roughly one km to the west is
Zaria Rd, which becomes Gomwalk Rd
further south.

For a map of Jos, ask at the Ministry of
Information or the tourist office on the far
southern side of town. They may also be
sources of information on hiking in the area.

The post office and EMS centre is on
Ahmadu Bello Way in the city centre, while
the NITEL office is on the outskirts of town
on Yakubu Gowon Way, opposite the State
Library. Becay Bureau de Change at 21
Rwang Pam St and Farida Bureau de Change
opposite the post office will change
travellers' cheques but the souvenir stalls
across from the Lantana supermarket give
better rates.

For trips around town, expect to pay from N 5 to N 10 on a motorcycle-taxi and double that for a regular taxi.

Jos Museum Complex

The highly recommended museum complex is really four separate museums and a zoo. The Railroad Museum, Tin Mining Museum and zoo are not so exciting. The Jos National Museum and the Museum of Traditional Nigerian Architecture, however, are special. The pottery and much older terracotta collections at the former are superb. The latter museum is more unusual. Spread out over some 20 hectares are full-scale reproductions of buildings from each of Nigeria's major regions. You can see a reconstruction of the Kano wall, the old Zaria mosque with a Muslim museum inside, the Ilorin mosque, and examples of the major styles of village architecture, such as the circular *katanga* buildings of the Nupe people, with beautifully carved posts supporting a thatched roof. Many of the buildings are being refurbished and you can see how they use *tubali* – cone-shaped loam bricks of mud and straw, and *azara* – planks cut from the dulub palm and used in construction.

The museum is open every day from 8.30 am to 5.30 pm with an entrance fee of N 2 (check out the bat-infested tree at the entrance). There's a short cut via a path extending south from Rwang Pam St.

Jos Wildlife Game Reserve

This reserve, which is half zoo and half park, is starting to look run-down and depressing, and the animals are in cages. It's about 10 km south of town, west of the road to Bukuru, and is open from 10 am to 6 pm. You'll see savannah elephants, red river hogs, buffalos, hippos and two smelly and semi-catatonic leopards. The entrance fee is N 5.

To get here, take a minivan to Bukuru and tell the driver to drop you off at Miango Rd, after the NASCO plant; from there, grab a motorcycle-taxi or flag down a shared taxi for the four-km ride. Or you can hire a private taxi; they cost about N 70 to the reserve.

Organised Tours

The Rock brewery has tours of the facilities and charges N 50 for all you can drink. It also has an all-you-can-eat-and-drink buffet for N 200. The Guinness brewery has an all-you-can-eat-and-drink buffet for N 250, and for N 350 more you can stay overnight at their guesthouse, *Porter Cabins*.

Places to Stay – bottom end

One of the best places is the *Tekan Guest House* (☎ 53036), a Christian missionary centre at 6 Noad Ave. There are dormitory rooms with beds for N 50 a person, N 75 rooms with two beds and shared baths, and N 100 rooms with single wide beds and private baths. Good cheap European or African meals are available. Opposite, the cheery *Cocin Guest House* charges N 80 per bed in a two-bed room with private bath.

The tranquil *ECWA Guesthouse* (☎ 54482), another Protestant missionary centre 2½ blocks to the south, is similar. For a dorm room with shared bath (cold water only) it charges N 50 a person, N 75 with private bath and hot water and N 100 for a private room with bath. It offers filling meals for around N 30. It's well marked with a big sign. Across the street the *EYN* (☎ 52056), yet another Christian missionary centre, charges N 70 per person and also has a dining room.

The *Universal Hotel*, at 11 Pankshin Rd, has singles with fans, shared baths and towels for N 85 (N 155 with private bath) and they bring steaming buckets of hot water to your door in the morning! The restaurant serves good Nigerian food. There are also nearby chop shops where one can try goat's head soup. One block behind (west of) the Universal at 1 Nnamdi Azikiwe St, is the slightly more expensive *Varsity Hotel*. Immaculate self-contained singles/doubles cost N 125/150; there is also a restaurant and sedate bar. The nearby *El Duniya Hotel* (☎ 54294) at 12 Ibrahim Dasuki St charges N 100 for a single with grubby shared bath.

There are several hotels with the name Jubilee, but only one that gives cause for celebration. The *Jubilee Up* (☎ 55457) at 32 Adebayo has clean singles with shared and

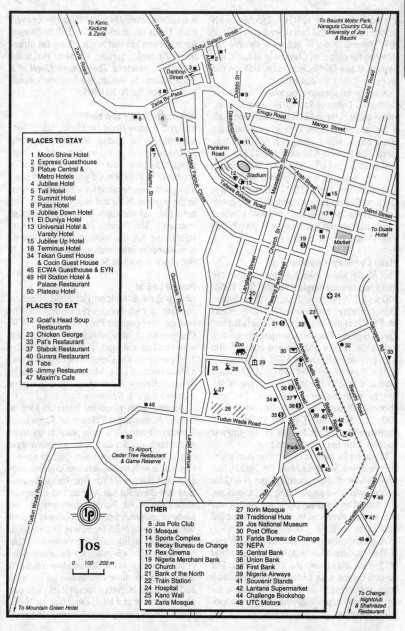

PLACES TO STAY

1 Moon Shine Hotel
2 Express Guesthouse
3 Platue Central &
   Metro Hotels
4 Jubilee Hotel
5 Tati Hotel
6 Summit Hotel
7 Paas Hotel
9 Jubilee Down Hotel
11 El Duniya Hotel
13 Universal Hotel &
   Varsity Hotel
15 Jubilee Up Hotel
18 Terminus Hotel
34 Tekan Guest House
   & Cocin Guest House
45 ECWA Guesthouse & EYN
49 Hill Station Hotel &
   Palace Restaurant
50 Plateau Hotel

PLACES TO EAT

12 Goat's Head Soup
   Restaurants
23 Chicken George
33 Pat's Restaurant
37 Stabok Restaurant
40 Gurara Restaurant
43 Tabs
46 Jimmy Restaurant
47 Maxim's Cafe

OTHER

6 Jos Polo Club
10 Mosque
14 Sports Complex
16 Becay Bureau de Change
17 Rex Cinema
19 Nigeria Merchant Bank
20 Church
21 Bank of the North
22 Train Station
24 Hospital
25 Kano Wall
26 Zaria Mosque
27 Ilorin Mosque
28 Traditional Huts
29 Jos National Museum
30 Post Office
32 NEPA
35 Central Bank
36 Union Bank
38 First Bank
39 Nigeria Airways
41 Lantana Supermarket
42 Challenge Bookshop
44 Souvenir Stands
48 UTC Motors
31 Farida Bureau de Change

Jos

0   100 200 m

To Kano,
Kaduna
& Zaria

To Bauchi Motor Park,
Naraguta Country Club,
University of Jos
& Bauchi

To Duala
Hotel

To Airport,
Cedar Tree Restaurant
& Game Reserve

To Mountain Green Hotel

To Change
Nightclub
& Shahrazad
Restaurant

NIGERIA

private baths for N 126/189. Doubles with private bath, TV and fan/air-con cost N 260/ 367. Moving down in quality is the *Jubilee Hotel* on the corner of Chojizang St and Zaria Bypass. It has fairly clean beds, sinks in the rooms and dirty shared baths.

A fairly inexpensive option is the *Platue Central* on Danboyi St. N 100 gets you a bed for the entire night and a fairly clean shared bath at this cheerful brothel. Two doors down is the *Metro Hotel*, which charges N 60 for a dirty room. The *Express Guesthouse* at 41 Mohammed Wada St, just off Abdul Salami, has singles with big beds, fans and private baths with bucket showers for N 115 (N 125 with TV). A block further on Enugu Agidi St is the good-value *Moon Shine Hotel* (☎ 55645), where rooms with shared baths go for N 100 (N 220 with TV and private bath).

Places to Stay – middle

The *Moon Shine Hotel Annexe* across the street has air-con singles/doubles for N 264/ 340 with TV, fridge and bath with hot water. The popular, more modern *Tati Hotel* (☎ 55897) at the intersection of Zaria Rd and Zaria Bypass has similar quality air-con rooms for N 310 with shared bath, N 400 with private bath, and N 517 for a suite.

The *Paas Hotel* (☎ 53851), at 42 Ndagi Farouk Close is the best mid-range hotel. Rooms with balconies, air-con, TV, telephone, bath and one/two beds cost N 300/ 400. The *Samoroa Hotel* (☎ 55516) at 18 Pankshin St, charges N 250/300 for singles/ doubles with fan and private bath.

If you prefer to be in the very heart of town, the run-down *Terminus Hotel* (☎ 54831), half a block west of the market, charges N 400 for a room with two single beds, fan, telephone, and bath. The water supply is not always reliable and the street can be noisy. It's on the 3rd floor of the building.

A good deal among the mid-range hotels is the modern *Daula International Hotel* (☎ 53340) at 41 Daula Rd, Dogun Dutse. For air-con rooms with fridge, TV and one/two beds, it charges N 288/346. The reason for the favourable price appears to be the isolated location, 1.5 km north-east of the

market and several blocks off the main paved road. From the market, take Dilimi St east for about one km and begin asking for directions. At night, getting a taxi at the hotel could be a problem. The *Summit Hotel* at 1 Jenta Adamu St has shabby singles/doubles with air-con for N 300/405.

Places to Stay – top end

The *Hill Station Hotel* (☎ 55398, fax 55394, telex 81130) on Tudun Wada Rd, is nicely perched on a hill on the western side of town. Singles/doubles cost N 1121/1380 plus a deposit of N 1079. Even if you don't stay here, it's a good place to come for a drink or to swim in the pool for N 20 and enjoy the view. The hotel also has the city's best known Chinese restaurant. The *Plateau Hotel* (☎ 55741) on Rest House Rd, just south of the Hill Station, is much better value with air-con doubles at N 690 plus a deposit of N 510.

Places to Eat

Cheap Eats & African For good Nigerian cooking at rock-bottom prices, it's hard to beat the ever-popular *Pat's Restaurant*, at 10 Gangare Rd. A large portion of pounded yam with chicken and egusi is N 50; it closes by 7.30 pm or so. On Constitution Hill Rd and a block north of UTC Motors is the similarly priced *Jimmy Restaurant* and nearby *Maxim's Café & Restaurant*.

Another great place for Nigerian food is *Gurara Restaurant* at 9 Beach Rd. Open from 7 am to 10 pm, it's a great place to try local dishes such as koko da kosat – a custard-style corn mash (N 20), super tasty fura da nano – cow's milk with millet, or tuwan shinkafa with egusi and chicken (N 70). The *Stabok Restaurant* at 8 Bank Rd has African and European dishes for N 80. For a hamburger try the *Lantana supermarket*. For coffee and peanut butter cookies at N 20, try *Tabs* at 13 Beach Rd.

If you're staying on the north-western side of town off Zaria Bypass, try the wood-panelled restaurant at the *Moon Shine Hotel*. It serves a decent three-course special for N 70 and has some Nigerian specialities. You can also get coffee and a full breakfast for N 40. There are also many chop houses in the area.

A wonderful place for lunch is the *Bight of Benin* restaurant at the museum. It offers an interesting variety of reasonably priced Nigerian dishes, and you get to eat in a replica of a chief's house.

Other Restaurants One of the best value restaurants is at the *Plateau Hotel*, where for N 200 you get a large three-course meal. A shared taxi there costs about N 5. One of the best restaurants is the Lebanese *Cedar Tree Restaurant* (☎ 54890), five km south of the market on Bauchi/Bukuru Rd, opposite Tilley Gyado House. A typical meal costs about N 250. The *Shahrazad* at 2 Bukuru Bypass and *Andalucia Restaurant* (☎ 56137) at 41 Yakubu Gowon Way also serve excellent Lebanese in the same price range. The former is also a nightclub and has 'Scottish dancing until 11' every Wednesday! The *Palace Restaurant* at the Hill Station Hotel is open from 11 am to 3 pm and 6.30 to 10.30 pm and gets mixed reviews.

Entertainment

For a disco near the central area, head for the *Tati Hotel*. It is one of the most popular places in town and has a cover charge of about N 50 on weekends. The run-down bar at the *Hotel Terminus* might offer something interesting in the heart of town.

For live music, try the ever-popular *Shahrazad* (see Places to Eat). It's one of the best nightclubs in town and often features local bands. *Change Nightclub*, half a km closer to the centre on the same road, also frequently has live music. At all of these places, the green label Rock Beer, brewed in Jos, is the most popular.

Getting There & Away

Air Nigeria Airways (☎ 52298) has numerous flights to Lagos (N 2000), but virtually none to other cities. Its office is on Bank Rd. Okada Airlines and Harka have several flights a day to Lagos and have their offices in the Hill Station Hotel. The airport is 40 km out of town and the taxi trip costs N 200. Flights rarely depart on time.

Bus On long-distance routes, you can save

slightly by taking a large bus instead of a Peugeot 504 bush taxi. The bus trip to Aba (893 km), for example, costs N 350 (N 240 by minibus) and leaves at 6 am, taking 10 hours. Buses to Lagos cost the same and take slightly longer; Platue Express and Assisted Mass Transit leave from the sports complex (on Tafawa Balewa Rd). Companies with buses east to Bauchi and Maiduguri, such as Yankari Express, and south to Aba and Calabar, such as Cross Lines, operate next to Bauchi motor park on Bauchi Rd.

Bush Taxi Bush taxis and minivans all depart from Bauchi motor park. Peugeot J5 minibuses charge N 100 to Abuja (245 km) and Kano (330 km); the trip to either one can take up to four hours. Bush taxis cost N 150 to Abuja (three hours), N 130 to Kaduna (3½ hours), N 150 to Kano (four hours), N 300 to Enugu (six hours) and N 450 to Calabar (nine hours).

Train Few travellers take the train, since Jos is on a branch line and you have to change trains at Kafanchan, approximately 100 km to the south-west. The Lagos-Jos train departs Lagos on Thursday at noon and Jos on Saturday at 3 pm. It is scheduled to take 41 hours, but it actually takes much longer. The fare is N 426/213 in 1st/2nd class. Jos-Kaduna costs N 103/50. The Port Harcourt-Jos train leaves Port Harcourt on Monday at 7 am and Jos on Wednesday at 1 pm, taking much longer than the scheduled 25 hours. The fare is N 393/152 in 1st/2nd class.

AROUND JOS

Tin Mines, Hiking & Excursions

The tin mines around Jos made the area extremely important to the British; building a railroad to Jos was one of their first major projects. There are some significant mines at Bukuru, 24 km south of Jos. For a tour, contact the tin mining company.

The area around Bukuru is good for hiking, especially around **Kurra Falls**. To get there, take a minibus from Bukuru to Barakin Ladi. As you go out of Barakin Ladi, turn right towards Bokkos, and right again after about 10 km towards Kurra village. At the village take the left fork (marked) towards the lake and falls. Swimming at the lake may be possible; ask for permission from the NASCO office in Bukuru.

Another area to visit, for those with time and transport, is the **Assop Waterfalls**, some 65 km south of Jos, just before the town of Gimi on the Akwanga road. Go during the rainy season for the best views. There are no facilities, but you could come prepared for a day hike or for a longer hike (camping may be possible) in the Ganawuri mountains. Near the town of Geji there are interesting rock paintings, and some of the older indigenous women of the area have coins embedded in their upper lips.

KADUNA

Kaduna is the antithesis of Kano. Intended by the British in the early 20th century to be the seat of power in the north, Kaduna has virtually no points of historical interest. Unless you enjoy visiting factories such as the local Peugeot plant, you probably won't want to stay long. On the positive side, large parts of Kaduna are relatively uncrowded. This can be a relief to travellers, especially those who have been through cities like Ibadan, Onitsha or Enugu.

Orientation

The main street running north-south through the centre of town is the wide Ahmadu Bello Way, which becomes Junction Rd further south towards the stadium. Most major banks and stores such as Leventis, UTC and Chellarams supermarket are along this road. In the heart of town and several blocks to the west on Market Rd are the central market and main motor park.

There are several hotels and restaurants along the east-west Constitution Rd just north of the stadium.

Information

The UK has a consulate (☎ 201 380) at 2 Lamido Rd. The NITEL office on the corner of Lafia and Kukawa Rds is open 24 hours. The post office and the British Council are on Hospital Rd as are many banks. For a travel agent, try Habis Travels between the Durbar and Hamdala hotels.

Things to See

The museum, at the northern end of the city on the road to Kano (Ali Akilu Rd) and across from the Emir's palace, has a little bit of everything – masks, pottery, musical instruments, brasswork, door posts, wooden carvings and leather displays; the entrance fee is N 1. It is open daily from 9 am to 6 pm, but closes if there is no electricity. There is a craft complex behind the museum with weavers, basket makers, leather workers and brass artisans. There is also a kitchen that serves local dishes.

If you're interested in pottery, it's a 20-km drive south-east on Kachia Rd to Jacaranda Restaurant & Pottery. Here you'll also find a craft shop and information on Maraba, another pottery centre.

Places to Stay – bottom end

The cheapest place in town is the *Kaduna Guest Inn* at 15 Ibadan St, which charges N 60 for a room with fan and shared bath and is often full. Bring a candle if you want to read as the light is poor.

The noisy *Central Guest Inn* at 182 Benue Rd charges N 120 for a single with a clean shared bath. Another cheap lively place is the *Safari Club* (☎ 211 838) at 10 Argungu Rd. It has singles with fans for N 80, clean baths with bucket showers and a huge active bar, but the rooms are quieter than at the Central.

A good choice is the *Nabor Hotel* at NK 4 Junction Rd. For N 130/200 a single/double you get clean rooms with separate baths in a good location. It also has a 2nd floor with a large open bar. Next door are *Fejeco Guest Inn* and *Fina White House*. Both charge N 150 for a single with air-con and shared bath.

The *Fina White House Guest Inn* (☎ 213 407) at 14 Constitution Rd (look for the large four-storey building with the 'Motor Oil' sign on top) has small singles for N 150/200 with fan and shared bath or with air-con and private bath. There is also an air-con restaurant with Nigerian dishes such as gari for N 30. The

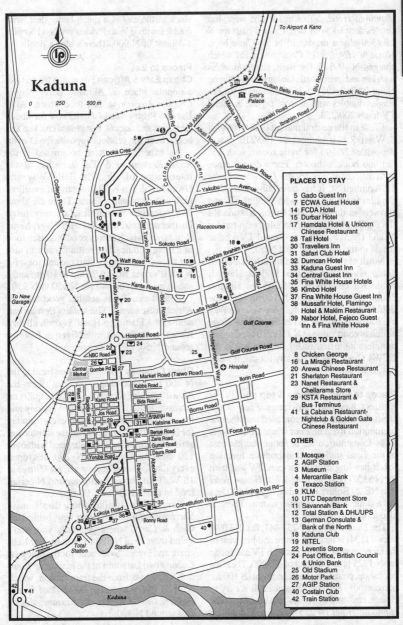

Kaduna

0   250   500 m

To Airport & Kano

To New Garage

To Total Station

PLACES TO STAY

5 Gado Guest Inn
7 ECWA Guest House
14 FCDA Hotel
15 Durbar Hotel
17 Hamdala Hotel & Unicorn Chinese Restaurant
28 Tati Hotel
30 Travellers Inn
31 Safari Club Hotel
32 Durncan Hotel
33 Kaduna Guest Inn
34 Central Guest Inn
35 Fina White House Hotels
36 Kimbo Hotel
37 Fina White House Guest Inn
38 Mussafir Hotel, Flamingo Hotel & Makim Restaurant
39 Nabor Hotel, Fejeco Guest Inn & Fina White House

PLACES TO EAT

8 Chicken George
16 La Mirage Restaurant
20 Arewa Chinese Restaurant
21 Sherlaton Restaurant
23 Nanet Restaurant & Chellarams Store
29 KSTA Restaurant & Bus Terminus
41 La Cabana Restaurant-Nightclub & Golden Gate Chinese Restaurant

OTHER

1 Mosque
2 AGIP Station
3 Museum
4 Mercantile Bank
6 Texaco Station
9 KLM
10 UTC Department Store
11 Savannah Bank
12 Total Station & DHL/UPS
13 German Consulate & Bank of the North
18 Kaduna Club
19 NITEL
22 Leventis Store
24 Post Office, British Council & Union Bank
25 Old Stadium
26 Motor Park
27 AGIP Station
40 Costain Club
42 Train Station

Flamingo Hotel, 50 metres to the west, has singles/doubles with fan, TV and bath for N 250/300 plus a deposit of N 50. Close by is *Mussafir Hotel* at 15 Constitution Rd which charges N 45/175 for basic singles/doubles with fan and shared bath. Going east the *Kimbo Hotel* (☎ 212 492) at 26 Constitution Rd has singles/doubles with air-con, private bath and TV for N 200/250.

Close to the central market is *Tati Hotel* at 3 Warri Rd. It charges N 190/210 plus a deposit of N 100 for basic rooms with TV, fan and bucket shower. For a decent place with air-con rooms, try the *Travellers Inn* at 19 Argungu St. It has quiet air-con singles/doubles for N 230/345 with satellite TV and showers in the bath. Not far on Katsina Rd the *Durncan Hotel* has doubles with fan for N 263 (N 315 with air-con and TV); basic meals in the restaurant cost N 50.

North of the centre, the slightly run-down *Gado Guest Inn* (☎ 215 339) at 11A Ali Akilu Rd charges N 245/365 for singles/doubles plus a deposit of N 160 and only the doubles have TV. Just off Independence Way on Kashim Ibrahim Rd is the *FCDA Hotel* which is good value at N 160/210 for singles/doubles; it's often full. Check to see if the *ECWA Guest House* has any rooms; it's at 8 Ali Akilu Rd.

Places to Stay – middle & top end

Kaduna has two mid-range *Fina White House* hotels, not to be confused with the one on Junction Rd. The *Fina White House Hotel* at 24 Constitution Rd is about one km east of the Total station roundabout on Junction Rd. It has singles with air-con, TV and bath for N 555. The other *Fina White House Hotel* is at NE 20 Bonny Rd and charges N 100 less for a double and has nicer rooms. There is also a restaurant and bar.

The *Durbar Hotel* (☎ 231 441, fax 213 097, telex 71134) is near the centre and just west of the racecourse. It has rooms with TV and fridge for N 1725 plus a deposit of N 3000. There's a bookshop, pharmacy, bank and pool (N 100 for nonguests); *The Grill* has snacks. It is easy to change cash and travellers' cheques here. The *Hamdala Hotel* (☎ 235 441, fax 235 449) a

block to the east is a much better deal, with doubles with TV and video for N 1150 plus a deposit of N 900. There's also a pool.

Places to Eat

Cheap Eats & African For non-African fare, a popular place on Ahmadu Bello Way is *Chicken George*, a fast-food chain. At 9 Katsina Rd try *Jovad Fast Food* for cheap meat pies and donuts. For grilled chicken and beef, check the vendors opposite the Durbar.

An experience not to be missed is the *KSTA Restaurant & Bus Terminus* at the intersection of Ahmadu Bello Way and Gwandu Rd. For N 22 you can get excellent gari with egusi and a Fanta. There are about five Nigerian specialities, all very tasty. Further north on Ahmadu Bello Way is *Nanet Restaurant* which serves good Nigerian food in a more middle-class setting; you can also get a breakfast of eggs, sausage and toast for N 80. It's open from 6.30 am to 10 pm and a sound meal can be had for N 150 to N 250.

Constitution Rd is another good area for African restaurants. The *Makim Restaurant*, next to the Flamingo Hotel, is open all day. It's a tiny restaurant with Nigerian food for around N 50; gari is the speciality.

Other Cuisines For an excellent meal in the N 200 to N 300 range, you can't beat the *Arewa Chinese Restaurant* (☎ 212 380) on Ahmadu Bello Way. It's open every day and has an all-you-can-eat buffet every Sunday for N 360. The *Unicorn Chinese Restaurant* at the Hamdala Hotel is quite good with over 120 choices for around N 200. It's open every day for lunch and dinner. *La Mirage* at 18 Waff Rd serves European and Nigerian food in the N 100 to N 200 range.

For superb Indian food don't miss *Sherlaton* on Ahmadu Bello Way, behind the Cash & Carry, where generally you won't spend more than N 380 for a feast. For Lebanese and French food, head for the fancy *La Cabana* two km south of the market on Junction Rd, across from the train station, which is open every evening. Next door is the *Golden Gate Chinese Restaurant*; dishes cost around N 300.

Entertainment

The weekend nightclub at *La Cabana* is for those looking for an up-market place with dancing and drinking. The disco at the *Durbar Hotel* and the nightclub next door to the Hamdala Hotel are others.

A far more interesting place, however, is the *Costain Club* on the south side of town, a wonderful rustic place with live music and a cover charge of N 50. To get here from Constitution Rd, walk 200 metres past the Fina White House Hotel then head south on a dirt road for 150 metres and ask around; everyone knows it.

Getting There & Away

Air Nigeria Airways (☎ 210 174) on Ahmadu Bello Way has, on average, two flights a day to Lagos (N 1907) and several flights a week to Port Harcourt. Kabo Airlines and Harco Air on Ahmadu Bello Way, two km north of the market, and Okada Air also have flights to Lagos.

Bush Taxi & Bus Bush taxis cost N 130 for the 3½-hour trip to Jos and leave from the Kawo motor park. New Garage is just south of Kawo on the Bypass Expressway and is the main motor park; bush taxis to Zaria cost N 25 and take one hour. To reach either motor park, catch a minivan from the motor park on Gombe Rd; the fare is N 5. The cheapest way to get to Lagos is on one of the large overnight buses.

Train Trains to Lagos and Ibadan are scheduled to pass through Kaduna on Wednesday and Saturday around 2 pm. The Monday train from Lagos to Kano and the Saturday train from Lagos to Maiduguri are usually many hours late. First and 2nd-class tickets cost N 245/163 to Lagos.

ZARIA

An old city and once one of the seven Hausa Emirates, Zaria retains its traditional character. A 14-km mud wall, now largely disintegrated, surrounds part of the old section of the city, which is on the southern side towards Kaduna, south of the Kubani River and behind an old gate. The old market

and the Friday mosque are both inside; the latter is modern but has the magnificent original interior vaulting. The streets of the old town contain fine examples of traditional Hausa homes with patterned mud walls. Among them the most notable is the Emir's palace, complete with colourfully garbed guards and the occasional blast on the ram's horn to announce the arrival of someone of importance at the *Babang Kofa*, the festively decorated main gate. The market is quite sedate. Look hard and you will find a few dye pits, blacksmiths and other crafts people at work; other artisans spin thread for the traditional *kaptani*, a knee-length embroidered shirt for men that costs around N 1500. Be sure to try a bowl of kunu, a typical Hausa meal of millet, water, sugar and peanuts served warm – delicious!

Places to Stay & Eat

Most hotels are in Sabon Gari, the new section north of the river. The first you'll come to is the friendly *Royal Guest House* at 8 Park Rd; it charges N 150 for a good air-con single with hot water. Across the street and 100 metres north you can get good cheap

A Zaria princess in a traditional post-wedding gown

Nigerian food and beer at *Queen Amina Restaurant*. The *Zaria Central Hotel*, 100 metres further north at 26 Park Rd, is similar to the Royal Guest House and the restaurant serves typical dishes for N 50. Restaurants in this area include the *Chummy Restaurant* at 3 Crescent Rd, *Prestige Restaurant* at 22 Rwaff Rd and *Ify Groove Restaurant* at 16 Park Rd; all serve inexpensive dishes such as moin-moin and gari.

The *Zaria Motel* (☎ 32451), opposite the High Court of Justice, has large rooms and the chalets are spread out and well maintained. There is also an attractive restaurant. The *Kubanni International Hotel* (☎ 34443), west at 33 Liverpool Rd, has spacious singles with air-con, fan and bath for N 200 plus a deposit of N 50. The *Efficient Restaurant* at F3 Kaduna Rd has good salads for N 40.

The old *Kuta Hotel* (☎ 33268) at 8 Aliyu Rd, 200 metres south of the bridge, has a central courtyard and is decent for the price (N 200 a double). There is a superb restaurant nearby called the *Shagarikun*, where you can eat local dishes (N 50) in a traditional setting – on the floor with shoes off; they also serve European dishes. Two km north of town by the golf course is the *Beauty Guest Inn* (☎ 34038) which has clean doubles with air-con for N 300.

The cities two nicest hotels are the *Zaria Hotel* (☎ 32875), on the northern edge of town, beyond the golf course, and the *Kongo Conference Hotel* (☎ 32872, fax 32875), in the centre of Sabon Gari. The latter charges N 1035 for a double. Both have air-con rooms and while the latter has a pool, the former has 'scintillating makosa music from 9pm to dawn' in the nightclub every Friday and Saturday.

Getting There & Away
The motor park is in Sabon Gari. To Kano it's N 40 by minibus (two hours) and N 60 by bush taxi. Bush taxis to Jos cost N 110 while a minibus costs N 80 (three hours).

BAUCHI
This is the most convenient place to stay on your way to or from the Yankari National Park. Bauchi is unpretentious and not terribly exciting for travellers. Definitely make time for the local **museum** (two km outside of town, across from the 11-storey Zaranda Hotel) which has a surprisingly diverse collection of art, artefacts, musical instruments and tools, or visit Tafawa Balewa's sparse and elegant **mausoleum**.

Places to Stay
The cheapest is the *Lido Hotel* behind the stadium; a single there costs N 80 and it's the cleanest of the town's cheap hotels. There is also the *Bauchi Terminus Hotel* near the Jos motor park. A self-contained single with fan costs N 170 plus a N 100 deposit. For N 157/210 a single/double, the *Segiji Hotel* offers a large bed with either a fan or air-con. The *CFA Hotel* near the Jos motor park has singles/doubles with air-con, private bath and satellite TV for N 287/487 plus deposit of N 100.

The *Zaranda Hotel* (☎ 43590) is several km out of town and charges N 575 plus a deposit of N 375 for very comfortable rooms with all the usual amenities, and a booking office for Yankari National Park. In town the *Horizontal Hotel* (☎ 42344, telex 83268) on Yandoka Rd has rooms equal in price and quality. The city's top hotel is *The Awalh* (☎ 42344, telex 83268)

Places to Eat
Terry's Chinese Restaurant on the Maiduguri Bypass by the Elephant serves a good meal with cold beer for around N 200. For cheap chop try *Ibom* at 6 Yandoka St, or *Chicken George* across from the Horizontal Hotel. If you'll be camping in the game reserve, *Leventis* has excellent fresh meat.

Getting There & Away
Bush taxis leave from Maiduguri motor park on Ningi Rd for Kano (N 150; 3½ hours), while those for Jos (N 60; 1½ hours) depart from Jos motor park on Jos Rd by Bauchi Terminus Hotel. Transport to Yankari leaves from Minivan motor park.

YANKARI NATIONAL PARK
Open for game viewing all year round, Yankari is 225 km east of Jos and 80 km from the nearest

town. Covering an area of 2244 sq km, it is definitely one of the better game parks in West Africa and is a good cheap place to visit.

There are around 600 elephants, by far the largest number in any West African game park. Bushbuck and horned waterbuck are the most common animals and too numerous to count, followed by approximately 200 buffalo, 40 hippos, 50 lions, monkeys, wart hogs, waterbucks, crocs and plenty of baboons. The vegetation is fairly dense, so seeing the animals is not easy.

Another great attraction of Yankari is the lake formed by the **Wikki warm springs**, near the park lodge. About 200 metres long and 10 metres wide, it's wonderful and scenic with crystal-clear mineral water at a constant 31°C and, most importantly, it's free of bilharzia. Baboons, and occasionally elephants, will come down to the springs; keep a sharp eye on your belongings as baboons are agile and daring thieves.

The best time to see animals is from late February to late April, before the rains, when the thirsty animals congregate at the Gaji River. Driving is permitted in the park, but most people take advantage of the park's 1½ to two-hour tours at 7.30 am and 3.30 pm in specially converted trucks and buses. The tours are excellent value at N 20 per person by truck, with a minimum number of five people required. Students pay half-price for the tours and the entrance fee (N 15 per person and N 20 for a camera permit). The warm springs are free and can be used at all hours. If you drive in the park, you must hire a guide (N 50). Arriving around 2 pm on the first day and leaving in the afternoon of the second will allow you to take an afternoon and morning tour and a few swims in the warm springs.

Places to Stay & Eat

Wikki Warm Springs Hotel (Bauchi ☎ 42174) in the park is often full on weekends, so reservations are advisable. It has circular bungalows that are ageing rapidly. They cost a quite reasonable N 172 per room plus a deposit of N 125 and have air-con and private baths. In addition to a family chalet that costs N 240, there is also an executive suite at the Marshall House that

costs N 1000, but you can put up to six people in it, which makes it quite affordable. The restaurant, too, is reasonably priced at N 80 for surprisingly good three-course meals, although you may have to eat by candlelight. If the hotel is full, you can camp for N 40 per person and get water from the lodge.

Getting There & Away

Minivans leave from Gombe motor park in Bauchi and charge N 10 to Dindima (80 km, 30 minutes). From there, flag a bush taxi and expect to pay N 15 for the 30-minute ride to the main gate. From the main gate wait for transport going into the park and cross your fingers; there is more traffic on the weekends. If you are stuck at the main gate, a bush taxi could be chartered from the nearby Yashi motor park for N 300. A park truck leaves the gate at 2 pm every Wednesday and you can catch a ride with them. If that all seems too iffy, a bush taxi can be chartered from Gombe motor park in Bauchi for N 400. Also, Yankari has a VW bus for charter; arrangements can be made at the Zaranda Hotel. If you are pressed for time, ask the driver to stay overnight with you as the nearest taxis are in Dindima. If you're in Kaduna, the travel agents at the Durbar Hotel occasionally organise bus trips.

The North

KANO

Dating back more than 1000 years, Kano is the oldest city in West Africa, and for centuries was one of the most active commercial centres in the region. Today, it is Nigeria's third-largest city and number one on most travellers' list of places to see in Nigeria.

Kano's main attraction is the old city, which has a huge wonderful market, an important mosque, an interesting museum, the Emir's palace and some centuries-old dye pits. The new section is also interesting, particularly just north of Sabon Gari market.

NIGERIA

Orientation

The centre of Kano is Sabon Gari market. Just to the north is Sabon Gari itself, where most of the city's cheap hotels and restaurants are. The city's modern commercial centre is south of the market, and major roads include E Bello Rd (not to be confused with Ahmadu Bello Way two km to the east) and Murtala Mohammed Way, which runs east-west along the southern side of the market.

The old city is about one km to the south-west of the market, the boundary being the old city wall, now largely destroyed. Some of the gates in the wall, however, are still intact; the main one is Kofar Mata Gate on Kofar Mata Rd which leads to the mosque and Emir's palace. At the heart of the old city is Kurmi market, the city's major 'must see'.

Information

Money Barclays is on Bank Rd, two blocks north-west of the post office. NBCI and UBA are on Bompai Rd; several others are nearby on Murtala Mohammed Way.

You can change money much faster at bureaux de change; one is on Bompai Rd across from the Central Hotel. The fastest way to change money and get the best rate is with the black-market dealers in front of the Kano Tourist Camp or at the Central Hotel.

Post & Telecommunications

The post office is at the eastern end of Post Office Rd. International calls can be made at the NITEL office opposite; open from 8 am to 10 pm.

Foreign Consulates The Niger consulate (☎ 645 274) is at 12 Aliyu Ave (which is just off Ibrahim Murtala Mohammed Way) on the north-western side of town near Airport Roundabout, about 1.5 km beyond (north-west of) the Akija Hotel (not south of the racecourse, which is the residence). It requires

three photos and N 2000 for 30-day visas. The British liaison office (☎ 646 420; open Monday to Friday from 8 am to noon) is at 6a Sab Bakin Zuwo Rd, near Governor's Roundabout which is on the south-eastern side of town at the intersection of Amadou Bellow Way and Maiduguri Rd. For consular matters ask for Mr H A Blackburne OBE at Nigerian Oil Mills (☎ (064) 632 429), 80-82 Tafawa Balewa Rd.

Cultural Centres The British Council is at 10 Emir Palace Rd, 200 metres north-east of Gidan Makama Museum. The Alliance Française is at 22 Magajin Rumfa Rd, south-east of the racecourse.

Travel Agencies A good travel agency is Habis Travels (☎ 631 258) at 15 Post Office Rd, 300 metres west of the post office.

Medical Services For medical treatment, the best place is the Doctors' Clinic, 2.5 km east of the centre out on Bompai Rd. It's open Monday to Saturday from 8 am to 10 pm and has an emergency room.

VSO The Voluntary Service Overseas organisation's office is at 9B Myonango Rd. They are involved in educational, health and environmental projects throughout Nigeria, and can give some information on outlying areas where volunteers are working.

Kurmi Market & Dye Pits

With thousands of stalls in a 16-hectare area, Kurmi market is one of the largest markets in Africa and the city's number one attraction. It's a centre for African crafts including gold, bronze, silver and all types of fabrics, from ancient religious Hausa gowns and a huge selection of hand-painted African cloth to the latest imported suits. Guides will approach you. As the market is crowded and confusing with many narrow passageways, you may find a guide quite helpful. Most importantly,

Benin figure

he will ward off other would-be guides. A tip is of course expected.

The market is two km south-west of Sabon Gari market via Kofar Mata Rd. The Kofar Mata Gate is unimpressive, but just beyond it are the famous dye pits, reputedly the oldest in Africa, where men with indigo-stained hands dip the cloth into pots in the ground filled with natural indigo dye. It's a fascinating sight.

Central Mosque

Not outstanding architecturally, the central mosque is nevertheless very important; the Friday prayers around 12.30 pm attract up to 50,000 worshippers – a sight to see. You may be able to enter and climb the minarets; ask for permission next door at the entrance to the Emir's palace.

Emir's Palace & Museum

The huge mud-walled Emir's palace is next door to the mosque. Visitors may enter only with the permission of the palace receptionist. Lucky ones get an invitation to meet the Emir; seeing him in his traditional dress at the centuries-old palace would certainly be the highlight of any trip to Kano.

Facing the palace's southern end is the attractive Gidan Makama Museum. Built in the 15th century for the 20th Emir of Kano, it is now completely restored and very interesting architecturally. On display are photographs of Kano architecture, a fascinating photographic history of Kano (including the taking of Kano in 1902 by the British) and various crafts – leather, baskets and fabrics. Open every day from 10 am to 4 pm, the entrance fee is a nominal N 2 and it's well worth an extended visit.

Gida Dan Hausa

An outstanding example of Kano's architecture, blending Hausa and Arab styles, is the Gida Dan Hausa. It's the remarkable centuries-old home of the first British administrator and is on the southern side of town just south of State Rd, near the Ministry of Works, which is on Bello Kano Rd. While you're in the area, check the Ministry of Culture nearby. It's another interesting colonial house, and you might get to watch a traditional dance rehearsal as well.

Zoo

On the southern end of town off Zaria Rd there's the zoo, open every day from 7.30 am to 6.30 pm. It's the largest city zoo in Nigeria and the only zoo in West Africa with kangaroos and wallabies. Over 50 other species, including rhinoceros, are represented.

Places to Stay – bottom end

At 11a Bompai Rd the Kano State Tourist Camp (☎ 646 309) charges N 57 in an eight to 12-bed dorm, and N 287 for your own double room with fans and shared baths. You can also pitch a tent for N 46 a person and use the communal baths, which are quite clean with good showers but inoperative sinks and erratic water supply. You can also park a truck and sleep in it for N 57 or likewise with a car for N 23. The friendly managers will get your clothes washed and change money (cash and cheques); ask them about their Kano city tour (about N 75). Group meals can be ordered in advance; otherwise, there's cheap beer and food across the street.

The quiet ECWA Guesthouse, which has much better accommodation, charges N 50 for dorm-style accommodation or N 100/200 for decent singles/doubles with fans and shared baths, N 20 for breakfast and N 50 for lunch or dinner. It's east of the market on Tafawa Balewa Rd; look for the small sign over the door. It's often full, however.

At the busy intersection of Ibrahim Taiwo Rd (No 114) and Murtala Mohammed Way, the Kano Guest Inn (☎ 632 717) charges N 145/310 for singles/doubles with air-con that have blankets on the beds instead of sheets. There is also a decent restaurant serving Nigerian food. It's often full, however.

Two of the cheapest hotels in Sabon Gari are the Universal Guest Inn, 86 Church Rd, and the Republic Hotel, at 10 New Rd. Both are clean and good value at N 100 for rooms with fans, showers and African-style toilets. At the Universal, be prepared for loud music

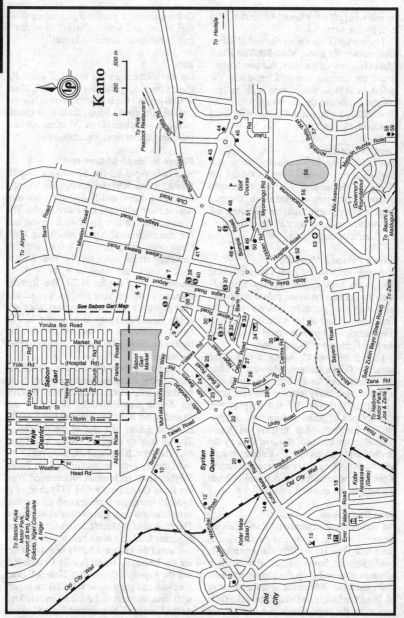

Kano

0   250   500 m

To Hadejia

To Pink
Peacock Restaurant

To Airport

See Sabon Gari Map

Yoruba Ibo Road

Market   Rd

Yola   Rd   (Hospital   Rd)

Enugu   New Rd   Church   Rd

Ibadan   St   Court Rd

Wale   District

Sani Giwa St

Illorin St

Weather

Head Rd

To Station Kuka
Motor Park,
Airport (6 km), Katsina,
Sokoto, Niger Consulate
& Niger

Sabon
Gari
Market

Murtali Mohammed   Way   (France Road)

Ibrahim

Taiwo Road

Syrian
Quarter

Wambai   Road

Kofar Mata
(Gate)

Kofar Mata   Road

Old City Wall

Old
City

Old City Wall

Club Road

Maganda   Road

Mission   Road

Bard   Road

Talawa Balawa Road

Airport   Road

Lagos Road

Bako Dandago   Ado Bayero Rd

Yolawa Rd

E Bello Road

Post Office   Niger Rd

Palmer   Rd

Bank   Rd

Bompai   Rd

Azikan Rd

Hospital Road

Abdu Bako Road

Civic Centre Rd

Beirut   Rd

Unity Road

Stadium Road

Bayero   Road

Abulia Road

Sabo Zubin Bayo (State Road)

Zaria   Rd

Buk   Road

Kofar Mata Road

Palace Road

Emir

Golf
Course

Racecourse Road

Myonango Rd

Ahmadu Bello Way

Magidin Rumfa Road

Alu Avenue

Governor's
Roundabout

To Bauchi &
Maiduguri

To Zaria

To Naibowa
Motor Park,
Jos & Zaria

Kofar
Nassarawa
(Gate)

To Bauchi &
Maiduguri

PLACES TO STAY		41	Galaxy Restaurant		16	Emir's Palace
		42	Empire Peking		17	Gidan Makama
1	Akija Hotel		Chinese Restaurant			Museum
4	ECWA Guesthouse	48	Chicken George,		18	British Council
11	Kano Guest Inn		Smarts Tandoor		19	Festival Stadium
45	Daula Hotel		Royal Indian		20	Plaza Cinema
49	Central Hotel		Cuisine & Exchange		21	Kori Cloth Market
51	Kano State Tourist		Bureau		25	UTC
	Camp & INCAR	54	Nasarawa Restaurant		27	Habis Travel Agency
	Staff Canteen	55	Palace Restaurant		31	Barclays Bank
52	Prince Hotel	57	Castle Restaurant &		32	Nigeria Airways
			Nightclub		33	NITEL
PLACES TO EAT		59	Kano Flying Club		34	Post Office
					35	Afro Nightclub
2	Akesan Foods	OTHER			36	Train Station
	Restaurant				37	First Bank
22	El Duniya Restaurant	3	Gidan Togo Nightclub		39	CFAO Bank
23	Pâtisserie & Restaurant	5	Church		40	Savannah Bank
	(Lebanese)	6	Church		43	Alitalia & EgyptAir
24	Bet Restaurant	7	KLM		44	Immigration
26	Arabian Sweets	8	United Bank of Africa		46	Kano Club
28	Toppers Restaurant	9	Leventis Department		47	UBA, NBCI & British
29	Jay's Exclusive		Store			Airways
	Restaurant	10	Wapa Cinema		50	VSO Office
30	Mallam Kato Restaurant	12	Orie Cinema		53	Nassarawa Hospital
38	Copper Chimney	13	Kurmi Market		56	Racecourse
	(Shangrila)	14	Dye Pits		58	Alliance Française
	Restaurant	15	Central Mosque			

until the early hours on weekends. The *Paradise Hotel* at 17/23 Agbomosho Ave charges N 70 per room and is anything but paradise. The *Challenge Hotel* at 87 Yoruba Rd charges N 90 for reasonably clean rooms with fans, and the showers and toilets work.

Around the corner from the Paradise on Ibadan St and a much better deal is the *Criss Cross Hotel*. Singles/doubles with fans are N 125/170, more with air-con. The nice courtyard and friendly staff make this place quite popular and it is often full.

The *Harmony Guesthouse* at 5 New Rd is a good choice at N 110 for ventilated rooms or N 130 for a room with air-con, plus it has the advantage of being on a block where you can get some excellent Nigerian street food.

Some people prefer the grubby *TYC Guest Inn* (☎ 647 491) on the corner of France and Ibo Rds because of its rooftop restaurant with views. It asks N 300 for its air-con rooms with TV and refrigerator. A better choice is the *Rolling Nigeria Hotel* at 82 Church Rd. It charges N 200 for a clean single with fan and self-contained bathroom.

Places to Stay – middle
The well-maintained *Remco Hotel* (☎ 628 600) at 61 New Rd has singles/doubles with air-con, TV and fridge for N 350/370. Another excellent choice in this area is the *Sky World Hotel* (☎ 647 622) at 95 Niger Ave. The rooms are new, clean and good value at N 350/450 for air-con singles/doubles.

For a livelier place, try the popular *Akija Hotel* (☎ 645 327) at 43 Murtala Mohammed Way, one km north-west of Sabon Gari market. It has singles/doubles from N 200/300 plus a deposit of N 700/1000; the more expensive rooms have TV and fridge. There's also a decent restaurant and a nightclub.

The *International Hotel* at 30 Enugu Rd is quiet, with singles/doubles with air-con and TV at N 275/350 plus a deposit of N 100; the restaurant is good and there is a big bar.

The *Tower Hotel* at 64 Aba Rd is overpriced at N 350/420 for singles/doubles with air-con and TV. The *Mairabo Hotel* at 25 Ogoja Ave is clean and comfortable, with singles/doubles with air-con, TV and private

NIGERIA

bath for N 250/330. A more expensive choice is the *Motel La Mirage* at 27 Enugu Rd. The rooms are small but good with air-con, fridge, TV and showers for N 430/520 per single/double. The restaurant is also good.

Places to Stay – top end

The *Central Hotel* (☎ (064) 630 000, fax 630 628) on Bompai Rd has rooms with noisy air-con and an erratic water supply for N 1092 plus a deposit of N 1000; facilities include a pool, tennis courts and a magazine shop with maps of Kano. The Euro-African restaurant has lunch for around N 250; dinner is more expensive.

The *Daula Hotel* (☎ 640 010, fax 640 017, telex 77241) has better rooms (with telephone, fridge and satellite TV) for the same price as the Central, but the restaurant is poor. It's at 152 Murtala Mohammed Way. The brand new *Prince Hotel* (☎ 639 402, fax 635 944) on Court Close charges N 2070 plus a deposit of N 1000 for a nice room with fridge, TV and

phone; it has an almost elegant restaurant with Euro-Afro cuisine for around N 300.

Places to Eat

Cheap The *INCAR Staff Canteen* is right by the Kano Tourist camp and serves large, inexpensive meals. There is a cheap chop house hidden behind the souvenir stands opposite the Central Hotel (N 20 for generous, tasty portions). Nearby is the fast-food *Chicken George* restaurant.

The *Galaxy Restaurant*, in an old colonial house at 139 Murtala Mohammed Way, has meals of variable quality for about N 50.

For pastries and the best ice cream in town (N 30), head for *Arabian Sweets* on Beirut Rd. At 7 E Bello Rd is the *Pâtisserie & Restaurant*, a similar Lebanese pastry shop with good takeaway meals.

African Sabon Gari is a good place for cheap Nigerian restaurants. *World Samankwe International Restaurant* is a small chop house on New Rd, which serves great pepper soup, chicken pepper soup and gari. For N 30 you can stuff yourself. Another cheap one at 37 Weather-Head Rd is the *Akesan Food Centre*, a rustic chop house open from noon to 5 pm; it serves beans, gari, fish, yams, rice and goat meat at rock-bottom prices. The *Bet Restaurant* at 12 E Bello Rd is similar. For a chop house under shade try *Nasarawa Restaurant* on Racecourse Rd, where you can eat out on mats for N 40.

Sabon Gari (Kano)

0   100   200 m

1	Tower Hotel
2	International Hotel
3	Motel La Mirage
4	Mairabo Hotel
5	Republic Hotel
6	Harmony Guesthouse
7	World Samankwe International Restaurant
8	Remco Hotel
9	Criss Cross Hotel
10	Paradise Hotel
11	Rolling Nigeria Hotel
12	Challenge Hotel
13	Universal Guest Inn
14	TYC Guest Inn

For a slightly more up-market Nigerian restaurant, try the *Mallam Kato Restaurant* on the corner of Palmer and Yolawa Rds. It's a popular open-air place with a pleasant, shady atmosphere and good rice and sauce. *El Duniya Restaurant*, at 63 Ibrahim Taiwo Rd is similar. Many of the cheap African restaurants close by 6 or 7 pm; hotel restaurants are open later. The restaurant at the *Remco Hotel* at the eastern end of New Rd in Sabon Gari is a moderately attractive place with decent, inexpensive Nigerian food.

Chinese The *Empire Peking Chinese Restaurant* at 2 Bompai Rd is one of the best expensive restaurants; a meal can easily cost N 600 or more. The *Pink Peacock*, to the north at 10 Dantala Rd, is much cheaper but lacks atmosphere. The *Palace Restaurant* on Race Course Rd has excellent food and the best prices, eg chicken and corn soup for N 18 and chicken with cashews for N 90 (open for lunch and dinner Tuesday to Sunday).

European *Toppers Restaurant* at 65 Ibrahim Taiwo Rd serves large portions of European and African fare for around N 85 in a pleasant air-con setting. The *Kano Flying Club* at 24 Magajin Rumfa Rd serves the cheapest European fare in town. Chicken and chips cost N 50 but you'll need to take out a temporary membership for N 50. For a pizza go to *Jay's Exclusive Restaurant* at 2b Niger St.

Indian For good, reasonably priced Indian food, the *Copper Chimney Shangrila Restaurant* at 9a Lagos St has soups, samosas and tandoori for reasonable prices. Opposite the Central Hotel, *Smarts-Tandoor-Royal Indian Cuisine* is more of a snack place.

Lebanese The long-established *Castle Restaurant* on Ahmadu Bello Way, just east of the stadium, is expensive and the food is ordinary at best. For excellent Lebanese in the N 280 to N 300 range, you can't beat *Al-Diwan* at 41D Hadejia Rd. There is also a great Sunday brunch for N 300.

Entertainment

Bars Many travellers rave about the rooftop bar of the *TYC Guest Inn* in Sabon Gari; the views of the city are the attraction. Nights are best because during the day it can be miserably hot.

Another popular bar is the terrace of the *Galaxy Restaurant* at 139 Murtala Mohammed Way, where a Guinness costs N 40.

Nightclubs The nightclub at the *Daula Hotel*, or the *Masters Club* at the Castle Restaurant, are two of the best discos in town and the cover charges are reasonable. If you want a true Hausa music experience *Gidan Togo* at 12 Sani Giwa St, off France Rd, is excellent. An open patio, live musicians, superb drumming, singing and snacks await you for a cover charge of only N 20.

Getting There & Away

Air International flights from Kano include Nigeria Airways and British Airways to London, EgyptAir to London via Cairo and KLM to Amsterdam. Sabena offers flights between Brussels and Kano. EgyptAir (☎ 630 759) and Alitalia (☎ 637 281) are on Murtala Mohammed Way. KLM (☎ 632 632) is on Airport Rd just north of Murtala Mohammed Way. Sabena is on Bompai Rd.

Nigeria Airways (☎ 623 891) at 3 Bank Rd has daily flights to Lagos (N 2000), as does Harka Air Services, Kabo Air, Harco Air Services and Okada. Okada has two flights a week to Yola (N 1600) and Harco flies to Sokoto (N 900) once a week and to Maiduguri (N 1390) three times a week.

Bush Taxi Station Kuka, near the army barracks out on the road to the airport on the western side of town, is the motor park for Sokoto and Katsina and, in Niger, Zinder and Maradi. Naibowa (nigh-BOH-ah) motor park, which serves points south (Zaria, Jos, Kaduna, Lagos, etc), is on Zaria Rd on the southern outskirts of town. You can get minibuses and shared taxis for both from Sabon Gari market. A third motor park on Murtala Mohammed Way east of the market serves points east, including Maiduguri.

Bush taxis to Sokoto (485 km; five hours) cost N 300. To Zaria (172 km), expect a two-hour ride for N 40. The three to five-hour ride to Maradi (time depends on the delay at the border) costs N 150, N 220 to Zinder, and N 70 to Katsina. A bush taxi to the border (145 km; 1¾ hours) costs N 90. The trip to Zinder takes about five hours (from six to eight hours by minibus).

From the Naibowa motor park Lagos is a 15-hour ride by bush taxi and costs N 600, or N 280 by Brazil Bus. Bush taxis go to Benin (eight hours; N 400), Zaria (1½ hours; N 40), Abuja (five hours; N 200), Jos (six hours; N 150), Maiduguri (six hours; N 250) and Kaduna (2½ hours; N 80).

Train The train station is a block south of the post office. If you're travelling 2nd class, get there at least two hours prior to departure as the 2nd-class queues are long. Trains leave on Tuesday at 7.30 am for Port Harcourt (arriving at 5.30 pm Wednesday), Wednesday at 8 am for Ibadan (arriving at 10 am Thursday) and for Lagos on Monday at 8.30 am (arriving at 3 pm Tuesday). Fares are low, eg N 365/203 in 1st/2nd class to Lagos, more for a sleeper. Make sure they are actually running before you front up ready to go.

Getting Around
The Mallam Aminu Kano International Airport is eight km north-west of Sabon Gari market. There is an airport tax of N 50 for all domestic flights. A motorcycle-taxi to the airport from town will cost N 20, a taxi from N 35 to N 45.

In town, taxis and motorcycle-taxis are everywhere and cost N 5 to N 10 depending upon the length of a drop.

AROUND KANO
If you'll be in Kano on a Sunday, consider going to **Danbatta**, 50 km to the north. The market here is very interesting, and the cattle market the largest in Nigeria. Minibuses leave from Sabon Gari market in Kano for the one-hour trip which costs N 20. About 35 km east of the town of Nguru is the **Hadejia-Nguru Wetlands Conservation Project**.

This area is an incredible place for the avid bird-watcher, as it is an important resting point for birds migrating from/to Europe as well as home for indigenous water birds. The intrepid ornithologist with interest in visiting this area should stop at the VSO office in Kano for further details; a mosquito net and binoculars are essential.

KATSINA
Some 174 km north-west of Kano, this old Hausa city has lost some of its old structures, but parts of the old city wall and gates, the Emir's palace, the Gobir Minaret (which can be climbed) and some old Hausa burial mounds outside town are still standing. Katsina's claim to fame is the spectacular **Durbar Festival** at the end of Ramadan, when the sight of horses charging in the Emir's honour makes for an unforgettable experience.

Places to Stay & Eat
The *Maikudi Hotel* on 3 Kano Rd has basic singles for N 100, and there's a good restaurant serving large portions (a large plate of delicious spaghetti with a salad costs only N 45). Also on Kano Rd is the *Abuja Guest Inn* where a basic single with shared bath costs N 120. Directly opposite is the basic but clean *Darma Annexe*.

Livelier is the *Luna Castle Hotel* which charges N 185/285 for singles/doubles. Close to the motor park is the *Darma House* on Dusima Rd. For N 170 you can get a basic single with fan and self-contained bath or pay N 230 for air-con; they also have a restaurant. The overpriced *Gabby International Hotel* has not so clean small rooms. Outside town is the *Katsina Motel* where a double with air-con, TV, and fridge costs N 350 plus a deposit of N 400. The restaurant offers dinner for around N 100.

Liyata Palace Hotel (☎ (065) 31165, fax 32690) outside town is the only posh hotel in the area. With tennis courts, pool, and beautifully clean rooms it charges N 1100 plus a deposit of N 700. The restaurant offers Euro/African fare for N 160 to N 200.

For tasty chicken pepper soup and other

Nigerian favourites, try *Katsina City Restaurant* on IBB Way near the Okmos clinic and the hospital. For extremely cheap chop there is the *Horizontal Food Hotel* a bit further on IBB Way.

Getting There & Away

A Peugeot J5 van charges N 50 and a bush taxi costs N 70 for the two-hour ride to Kano; machines are N 5 for short drops.

SOKOTO

In the far north-west corner of Nigeria, Sokoto is known for the **Sultan's palace**, and the **market**, well-known for its handmade leather goods, which is held every day except Sunday (best on Friday).

Sokoto can also be used as a base to visit the spectacular three-day fishing festival held every February in Argungu, 100 km to the south-west. Another good time to be here is at the end of Ramadan. Long processions of musicians and elaborately dressed men on horseback make their way from the prayer ground to the Sultan's palace.

The Sultan of Sokoto is the spiritual leader of the Hausa and of the Muslims in Nigeria. The present Sultan, however, enjoys less respect than the position usually commands. In 1988, after the death of the 17th Sultan, the choice of Ibrahim Dasuki by his patron, President Babangida, who enjoyed little popularity in the north, was marked by riots and arson. If you go to the Sultan's palace on a Thursday between 9 and 11 pm, you can hear **Hausa musicians** outside playing to welcome in the Holy Day (Friday).

When you come to the palace, check out the mosques; there are several on the same

road as well as some dye pits south of the palace.

Places to Stay & Eat

For about N 100 a night you could stay at one of several somewhat grubby bar-restaurant-hotels around Ahmadu Bello Way and Maitatu Rd, just north of the heart of town. The rooms are generally basic but tolerable; some are used by prostitutes. One is the friendly *Good Food Restaurant* at 3 Maitatu Rd; it's fairly clean and has fans. There's also the *Meeting Point Hotel*, with cold beers and OK rooms but awful bathrooms. Another fairly decent one is the *Central Hotel* where you can also eat. On the southern side of town the old government-run *Catering Rest House* (☎ 232 505) near the Post Office is run-down and fairly dirty. The *Mabera Guest Inn* (☎ 233 205) on Kalambaina Rd is better.

The *Shukura Hotel* (☎ 200 019) on Gusau Rd, south of the centre, charges N 750 (N 800 deposit) for an air-con double. The older *Sokoto Hotel* (☎ 237 126) nearby is similarly priced. Both have bars and restaurants.

For less expensive (N 300) but very decent accommodation, try the *Ibro International Hotel* (☎ 232 510) on Abdullahi Fodio Rd north-west of the motor park. The restaurant serves large portions for N 50.

Things to Buy

Sokoto is the home of 'Moroccan leather'. Traditionally, the red goat leather was tanned locally and then taken by camel to be sold in Morocco. There are all sorts of leather goods for sale such as bags, pouffes, belts and purses. Try the traders opposite the Sokoto

---

Hausa Bands

A typical Hausa band consists of three *kakaki*, three *alghaita* and some drums. The kakaki is a remarkably long (about three metres) tin trumpet with an impressive, shattering timbre. It produces barely two notes but its majestic tone augments the orchestral ensemble. The conical alghaita is an African oboe with a metal tube through it that widens out into a bell at the end. What's remarkable about it, apart from its piercing tone, is the way it's played. The musician inhales a large amount of air, puffs his cheeks and remains that way, using the reed in a manner that allows him to play without interruption, for hours on end. ∎

Hotel and those near the Sultan's palace, or the government-run Sokotan factory.

Getting There & Away

Air Nigeria Airways (☎ 232 252) has flights about every other day to Lagos for N 2000.

Bush Taxi & Bus There are lots of bush taxis in Sokoto headed for Kano, Zaria and Kaduna, Lagos and Illela/Birnin-Konni. They leave from the motor park on the northern side of town facing the market. On the Sokoto-Kano route, buses charge N 140, minibuses N 250 and bush taxis N 300; the trip takes eight hours. If you're heading to Niamey (Niger), the route via Gaya is marginally cheaper than via Birnin-Konni but the trip takes slightly longer. Bush taxis do the trip to the border at Kamba (276 km) in three to five hours and charge N 250.

MAIDUGURI

Maiduguri (may-DOO-gou-ree) is the booming capital of Borno State in the far north-eastern corner of Nigeria. From March to May temperatures often reach 48°C in this city of 400,000 inhabitants. It's a reasonably clean city with a relatively clean water

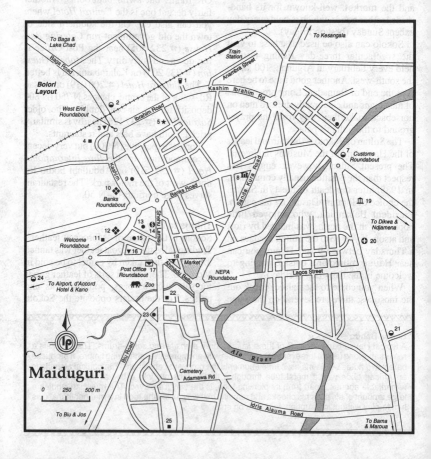

Maiduguri

0   250   500 m

supply and getting around is quite easy and cheap by shared taxi. Very few travellers come here – usually just those on their way to/from northern Cameroun – so it is a good place to buy traditional crafts without too much intense bargaining.

Markets

Gomboru market, or Monday market, is in the heart of town just north of NEPA Roundabout while Kamuri market, or New market, is on the eastern side of town, several blocks east of Kashim Ibrahim Rd and north of Customs Roundabout. Both markets have a little bit of everything including some mysterious local medicines. Artisans in Kamuri market produce things like hoes, knives and bowls from recycled steel.

Museum & Zoo

The city has a small museum and a zoo worth seeing. The museum is on the eastern side of town off Bama Rd and south of Customs Roundabout while the pleasant shady zoo is in the centre on Shehu Lamisu Way.

Places to Stay & Eat

The *Borno State Tourist Centre* charges about N 250 for a ventilated single and N 400 for an air-con double. The water supply is erratic and service at the restaurant is slow but you can get a decent Nigerian meal for about N 90 and a European breakfast for much less. If it's full, try the similar *Royal City Hotel* or *Safari Hotel* by the post office for N 350. The *Ambassador Garden Lodge*

and *Hotel Rainbow* are cheaper at around N 150; both are near the National Oil Depot.

The city's top hotel is the *Deribe Hotel* (☎ 232 662), a block west of West End Roundabout. Rooms (doubles only) cost about N 1000 (plus N 2500 deposit). The *Lake Chad Hotel* (☎ 232 453, telex 82121), just east of Welcome Roundabout, charges N 900 per room (doubles only). It has a pool, good bar and tennis court.

Two other cheap hotels in the same price range on the northern side of town are the *Ali Chaman Guesthouse* (large, pleasant rooms with TV and bucket baths) on Kashim Ibrahim Rd, and, just off that road near the train station, the *Travellers Palace (ventilated rooms and a noisy bar)*.

If you want a good hotel for half the price, there are several north of the Deribe, including the *Safecon Hotel* and the *Merry Joe Guest Inn*.

For Nigerian chop in the heart of town, try the snack bar at the *UTC* store on Kashim Ibrahim Rd, the *Bosco Café* between UTC and the post office, or *Lalle Restaurant* between the post office and the Monday market. *Pujo's Snacks* serves inexpensive food and has air-con; it is by Ares Nightclub. Try some of the excellent tasty suya sold on street corners at dusk. And around the markets be on the lookout for men on bicycles selling yoghurt – it's delicious.

The city's best restaurant, *Chinese Restaurant*, is between the train line and the roundabout; it has reasonable prices and is also a good place to come just for drinks.

Entertainment

For cheap bars and dancing, head for the area north of Kashim Ibrahim Rd and west of the train station. One of the most popular all-night discos in this area is the *Ares Nightclub*, which is often packed on weekends.

Getting There & Away

Air Nigeria Airways has flights almost every day to Lagos and less frequently to Kano. The office is in the centre between Banks Roundabout and Post Office Roundabout.

Bush Taxi & Bus There are four motor parks in town, each serving a different location. Refer to the city map for locations. Bush taxis to/from Kano take from 6½ to eight hours and cost N 250. Yankari Express, one of the bus companies, has connections to Jos.

Train There's one train a week to Lagos and one to Port Harcourt; both involve changes at Kafanchan Junction. According to the schedule the train takes about two days to either city, but it almost always arrives late. Check that the trains are running. They are supposed to arrive on Monday from Lagos and Wednesday from Port Harcourt. The cost to both Lagos and Port Harcourt is N 483/322 in 1st/2nd class.

The train station is on the northern side of town, just north of Kashim Ibrahim Rd.

AROUND MAIDUGURI

Gwoza

Some 115 km south-east of Maiduguri, Gwoza is in the western foothills of the scenic Mandara mountains and is a good place for hiking.

The scenery in this area is some of the most interesting in West Africa but most hikers see it only from the Cameroun side, particularly the area between Roumsiki and Mokolo. If you

sleep in Gwoza (the *Hillside Guest Inn* (N 100) opposite the motor park or the *Government Rest House*), you can then head off in the early morning and return in the late afternoon, thus avoiding the heat of the day. Keep your eyes out for some unusual butterflies and an occasional troop of monkeys.

Although the area is extremely rocky, the people living here have terraced the hills and every available piece of earth is used to grow food. In the last half of the rainy season (August/September) the crops are so high that they reduce your visibility. From Gwoza you can hike four hours east to Ngoshe. The more adventurous can keep heading east towards the Cameroun border not far away, although crossing illegally is not recommended.

If you are in Gwoza on a Saturday take local transport to the village of Karu on the Cameroun border. The village, on the river and frontier, has a huge market full of local colour that attracts folks from both sides of the border.

Baga & Lake Chad

Nigeria is not nearly such a good vantage point for seeing Lake Chad as Chad or Cameroun, because in recent years the lake has been receding northwards across the border. Given this, it is best to go when the water is at its highest, between December and February; Baga, 170 km north-east of Maiduguri, is the place to go. Be sure to get a permit from the International Joint Patrol or you will be stopped by immigration. There is a 13 km canal that goes out to the Nigerian part of Lake Chad and the bird-watching is supposed to be excellent. Check with the Chad Basin Development Authority (CBDA) in Baga for permission to visit. Minibuses and bush taxis leave from the Baga Motor Park in Maiduguri. You can stay at the *Baga State Hotel*. Pay your respects to the police as they are always suspicious.

Senegal

More visitors go to Senegal than to any other country in West Africa. One reason for this must be Dakar, which is many people's favourite West African city, with a relatively cool climate and a fascinating mix of Afro-French characteristics. Another of Senegal's many attractions is the southern Casamance region, where local communities have built a network of cheap African-style rest houses. Using these village *campements* you can travel all over the Casamance region and get a taste of life in rural Africa.

Other visitors may prefer living in luxury: for beach lovers Senegal has two of the three Club Meds south of the Sahara, and several more top quality hotel resorts on the Atlantic shores of Cap Skiring and the Petite Côte.

There's a lot for wildlife enthusiasts too, including Niokolo-Koba National Park, one of West Africa's main game reserves, and the Djoudj and Langue de Barbarie national parks, amongst the most impressive and important bird sanctuaries in the world.

Facts about the Country

HISTORY

Senegal was one of the first parts of West Africa to be inhabited by humans – remains dating from at least 13,000 BC have been found. More recently, it was part of two great empires of West Africa, the Ghana Empire (which flourished between the 8th and 11th centuries) and the Mali Empire (13th to 15th centuries). As the Ghana Empire's grip weakened, Islamic invaders from Morocco reached Senegal, bringing their religion with them. At the same time, long droughts in the Sahara pushed migrations of Wolof, Sérèr, Fulani and Toucouleur people south into the area.

European Arrival

The year 1444 marks medieval Europe's first direct contact with West Africa, when Portu-

REPUBLIC OF SENEGAL

Area: 196,192 sq km
Population: 8.5 million
Population Growth Rate: 3.1%
Capital: Dakar
Head of State: President Abdou Diouf
Official Language: French
Currency: West African CFA franc
Exchange Rate: CFA 500 = US$1
Per Capita GNP: US$650
Inflation: 95%
Time: GMT/UTC

guese traders landed at Cap Vert, near present-day Dakar. They settled on nearby Île de Gorée (Gorée Island), and for the next 150 years Portuguese ships scoured the coast in search of slaves. The Dutch and the English then entered the scene. The islands of Gorée and St-Louis, to the north, changed hands several times before they were finally secured by the French in the late 1600s.

For the next hundred years or so, all along the West African coast, the European nations continued to trade in slaves and other goods such as gold and ivory, assisted by powerful African kings, whose armies raided neighbouring tribes to procure the slaves. In

SENEGAL

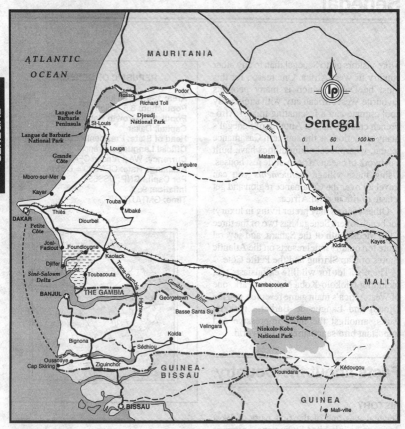

fact, slavery had existed in Africa long before the Europeans arrived, but they 'refined' the trade and made it a coastal operation. Wherever Europeans settled, slaves were always the main export, and the brutality of the trade is evident in the dungeons at Île de Gorée and other forts along the coast.

Through the 18th century, the town of St-Louis grew in size and importance but, when the Council of Vienna banned the slave trade in 1815, the French were forced to look for new sources of wealth. Efforts to introduce commercial crops were a failure until

Louis Faidherbe was appointed governor in 1845. Stationed in St-Louis, he occupied the lands of the local people around the lower Senegal River and forced them to grow groundnuts (peanuts) as a cash crop. From the French point of view, this method was effective: he made the colonial administration self-financing within 10 years.

In the next few decades, French forces systematically moved inland across West Africa, defeating local armies as they went. Senegal became the gateway to the new, and still undefined, territory of *Afrique Occidentale Francaise* (French West Africa).

Suggested Itineraries

There's a lot to see and do in **Dakar**, and you can easily spend three days here, or more if you go to nearby places like **Île de Gorée**. To the north of Dakar, the old capital of **St-Louis** can be reached in a few hours and is also worth a visit for one or two days. From here you can get to two spectacular wildlife reserves (allow one day each), or continue into Mauritania if you're heading north.

If you're going south, from Dakar you can travel to **Ziguinchor**, the capital of the **Casamance** region, via the beaches of the **Petite Côte** (where you can easily spend three days), the interesting town of **Kaolack** (one or two days), and the **Siné-Saloum Delta** (three to five days). This route also passes through The Gambia at Banjul (where you can spend several more days – see The Gambia chapter for details). Alternatively, you can go directly from Dakar to Ziguinchor by road on the Trans-Gambia Highway (allow one long day), or by boat (two days).

You can spend a day or two in Ziguinchor, then tour the rural parts of the Casamance, by foot, bike or local bus, for between three days and three weeks. The tempting beaches at **Cap Skiring** can also add extra days to your time here. From the Casamance you can keep heading south into Guinea-Bissau: regular transport goes from Ziguinchor, and you can reach Bissau in a day if you leave early.

If you're heading east, from Dakar you can take the express train to Bamako (Mali). The trip takes two days. Alternatively, you can join the train in **Tambacounda** (capital of eastern Senegal), which can be reached by road from Dakar (easy) or Ziguinchor (more difficult), or from Banjul by travelling along the length of The Gambia. From Tambacounda you can also get to the **Niokolo-Koba National Park** (for which you'll need about three days for a visit, plus a day at each end to get to/from Tambacounda). ■

The Colonial Period

At the Berlin Conference of 1884-85, following the so-called 'scramble for Africa', the entire continent was divided between powerful European states. While Great Britain (with Germany and Portugal) got most of East and southern Africa, the greater part of West Africa was allocated to France. At the end of the 19th century, French West Africa stretched from the Atlantic to present-day Niger.

Even before this settlement, from 1848, Senegalese delegates had been permitted to sit in the French parliament (although these were White or mixed race). In 1887 Africans living in the four largest towns (Dakar, Gorée, St-Louis and Rufisque) were also granted limited French citizenship. However, most of the 14 million other French West Africans did not become *citoyens* and, compared to the British, the French did little to educate their colonial subjects. Only those needed for the colonial administration received secondary education, delivered by three institutions in Dakar, which by this time had become the capital of French West Africa. (St-Louis remained the capital of Senegal-Mauritania.)

In 1914, Senegal elected its first Black delegate, Blaise Diagne. The same year the first political party in West Africa was established. It soon became fashionable, however, for politically conscious Senegalese to join French parties: from the late '30s, many joined the increasingly powerful Socialists and Communists. In the same period, several Senegalese intellectuals went to France to study. One was Léopold Senghor, who was to become Senegal's most influential politician of the 20th century. After his studies (where Georges Pompidou was a classmate) and graduation, he became the first African secondary-school teacher in France. During this period, he began writing poems; after WW II, he and Alioune Diop founded *Présence Africaine*, a magazine promoting the values of African culture.

Senghor, who couldn't even speak Wolof, the country's predominant native language, was somewhat aloof from the people – a Catholic in an overwhelmingly Muslim country and a Black married to a White French woman. He was politically astute, however, and shrewdly began building a personal power base which resulted in his being elected as Senegal's representative to the French Assembly. When the potential independence of France's African colonies in Africa was raised, he promoted the idea of a strong federal union to prevent France from 'balkanizing' her former colonies – keeping them divided, weak and still dependent on their former ruler. His rival was Côte d'Ivoire's Houphouët-Boigny, who wanted French West Africa split into various small countries, fearing that within a federal union the richer colonies (such as Côte d'Ivoire) would have to subsidise the poorer ones.

Independence

In the late '50s, Senghor gained support from French Soudan (now Mali), Upper Volta (now Burkina Faso) and Dahomey (now Benin) to form a single union, the Mali Federation. Upper Volta and Dahomey, however, withdrew under pressure from both France and Côte d'Ivoire. Senegal gained independence in 1960, and Senghor became the first president. Two months later, the Senegal-Mali union broke up. Houphouët-Boigny had won the day; French West Africa became nine separate republics.

Senegal's early independent years did not always run smoothly. In 1968, in the wake of protests in France and amid mounting economic difficulties at home, students rioted at the University of Dakar. Senghor sent in troops, but the national trade union supported the students and called for a general strike. Even with a show of force supported by French troops stationed in Senegal, Senghor had to make concessions to the union and the students.

The 1970s were less turbulent: Senghor held on to his position and remained a popular figure. In 1980, after 20 years as president, he did what no other African head of state had done before – he voluntarily stepped down. His hand-picked successor, Prime Minister Abdou Diouf, took over.

The 1980s

Soon after gaining the presidency, Diouf was asked to help Dawda Jawara, the president of The Gambia, who had been ousted in a coup. Diouf sent in Senegalese troops and, after considerable bloodshed, Jawara was restored. This co-operation became formalised when the Senegambia confederation was established later the same year.

Meanwhile, Senegalese troops remained on Gambian soil, much to the resentment of most Gambians.

In 1983 eight parties contested the Senegalese elections, which Diouf won with over 83% of the vote. His major opponent, Abdoulaye Wade, received most of the rest. Wade remained a prominent critic of Diouf, and two years later he spearheaded an effort to unite the opposition parties. Diouf was clearly worried and banned the organisation on the grounds that it violated election law.

In the 1988 elections Wade again contested the presidency. During the campaign violence erupted. Diouf's response was to ban all political meetings, station tanks throughout Dakar, and arrest Wade, charging him with intent to subvert the government. Official results showed Diouf with 73% of the vote and Wade with 26%, but rumours of major election fraud were rampant. Wade received a one-year suspended sentence and left for France.

By this time the Senegambia confederation was in trouble (see the chapter on The Gambia for more details), and in 1989 it was dissolved completely. But while Diouf was contending with this break-up and calls for political reform, he had two other major problems to deal with: one was a dispute with Mauritania (see the boxed story on the Mauritanian Crisis), and the other was a campaign against separatists in the southern region of Casamance.

There had been periodic calls for independence in Casamance for many years, but they came to a head in 1989, when rebels from the Movement of Democratic Casamance Forces (MDCF) started attacking government installations. Several people were killed, and the army moved in with tanks and heavy weapons. A cease-fire signed in May 1991 held for several months, but a major clash in September 1992 left another 60 people dead. Quite apart from the effect the fighting had on local people, it also severely hit Senegal's money-spinning tourist industry, as visitors stayed away and tour companies suspended operations throughout the whole country.

Senegal Today

Opposition leader Abdoulaye Wade returned

The Mauritanian Crisis

In 1989, a minor incident on the border between Senegal and Mauritania led to serious riots in both countries in which many people died. It all started in southern Mauritania when two Senegalese peasants were killed by Mauritanian border guards in a clash over grazing rights. In Senegal, people reacted by looting Mauritanian-owned shops in Dakar, and killing several people. Mauritanians retaliated in their country by herding up and deporting thousands of Senegalese; hundreds were killed in the process, and the Senegalese retaliated with more of the same. Large-scale airlifts by humanitarian organisations helped to get the Mauritanians out of Senegal and the Senegalese out of Mauritania but not before horrendous atrocities were committed on both sides.

The problem is complex and stems from centuries of conflicts between the Arabs and Black Africans, dating from the time when Arab armies on horses would raid African villages and take away slaves. In Mauritania the Black slaves developed into a distinct cultural group (the 'Bidan') as they adopted the lifestyle of their Arab masters. Most Senegalese are Muslims and are very pro-Arab, so they certainly do not hate Arabs in general. But their close links with the Arab world, including Mauritania, do not prevent them resenting the centuries of systematic discrimination by Moors in Mauritania against the Blacks, most of whom are Senegalese in origin. It took until 1980 for the Mauritanian government to outlaw slavery; even today there are an estimated 100,000 Black de facto slaves there. What erupted on the Senegalese side was the result of this resentment.

Following the outbreaks of violence, the borders between Senegal and Mauritania were closed, and diplomatic relations were broken off for two years. They were resumed in April 1992, and ambassadors were exchanged a few months later. Today, you can once again travel overland between these two countries. ∎

from political exile in 1990, which brought huge crowds out onto the streets chanting *sopi* ('change' in Wolof). Eight political parties signed a statement calling for Diouf's resignation and free elections. In an attempt at appeasement, in March 1991, the National Assembly approved the restoration of the post of prime minister and the participation of opposition parties in the government. Wade was made Minister of State, but the opposition parties were still not satisfied.

Wade stood against Diouf in the presidential election of February 1993. When the results were released the following month, Diouf had won with an absolute majority of 58% (against Wade's 32%) and was thus elected for a third term. Parliamentary elections were held three months later and while the opposition parties improved their performance over the previous election, Diouf's party still obtained over two-thirds of the seats. This led to violent protests in many parts of the country, particularly in the Casamance where anti-Diouf feeling still ran high. Large numbers of troops were once again sent into the region. After long negoti-

ations between the government and the separatists, a cease-fire was declared in June 1993. In the following months, after further talks and concessions on both sides, full peace returned to Casamance.

However, although the Casamance was quiet again, sporadic outbreaks of anti-government protest continued in other parts of the country. In August 1993, the government introduced a number of austerity measures, including wage-cuts for all civil servants, which led to considerable unrest around the country and a one-day general strike in early September. Unrest continued in the following months and, in February 1994, following more violent demonstrations in Dakar, Abdoulaye Wade was arrested again, along with several of his supporters.

Wade went on trial in March 1994, accused of conspiracy, following the Dakar demonstrations, and on charges related to the murder of a state official. The following May, the charges were dismissed and Wade was released. In July, French officials visited Senegal and attempted to encourage President Diouf to include Wade in the government. If a reconciliation can be

SENEGAL

brokered, Dakar and Senegal are likely to return to normality. If the rift is irreparable, however, there may be more unrest. Travellers should be aware of the current situation before visiting.

GEOGRAPHY

Senegal is the westernmost country on the African continent, with an area of just under 200,000 sq km (slightly smaller than Britain). It consists mainly of flat plains; part of the arid, sandy Sahel. The only hills are in the far south-east along the Guinea border (the northern tip of the Fouta Djalon plateau) and further east along the border with Mali.

The region is transected by three major rivers, which all rise in the Fouta Djalon. In the north is the Senegal River which forms the border with Mauritania. St-Louis, the old capital, is at this river's mouth. The wide flood plains are one of the country's most productive areas: cultivated with groundnuts and millet as the waters retreat. In the middle of the region is the Gambia River, with the small country of The Gambia following its course, completely surrounded by Senegal. In the south is the Casamance River, which gives its name to the surrounding Casamance area, a fertile zone of forest and farmland. Senegal's most beautiful beaches are also here, around Cap Skiring.

Senegal is the most biologically diverse country in the Sahel, with over 550 animal species. It is also important for migrating birds, particularly waterfowl, which return in large numbers each winter from Europe, stopping at one of the world's major bird reserves, Djoudj Park, north of St-Louis.

Desertification throughout the north of the country is an ever-increasing problem. The new Arab-financed Manantalli Dam on the Senegal River is making the northern strip more productive, but the areas outside the waters' reach remain vulnerable to the pressures of overgrazing and the cutting of trees for firewood.

CLIMATE

Dakar is one of the cooler, breezier spots in West Africa, although Senegal's average temperatures lie between 18 and 31°C. In the

north and central parts of Senegal the rainy season is from July to September, while in the Casamance it's longer, from late May to early October. Rainfall ranges from an annual average of 300 mm in the north to almost six times as much in the south, with about 600 to 650 mm annually in Dakar. November to March is the best time to visit, as it's cool and dry, but from December the skies are clouded by the dusty harmattan winds that blow down from the desert.

GOVERNMENT

Senegal is a republic, with the president and 120 members of the unicameral National Assembly elected every seven years and five years, respectively, by universal adult suffrage. Senegal was the first genuinely multiparty democracy in West Africa; Cape Verde and Benin have now joined the ranks. There are several opposition parties, including Wade's party, the Parti Démocratique Sénégalais (PDS), the Ligue Démocratique-Mouvement pour le Parti du Travail and the Parti pour la Libération du Peuple. However, unlike in Cape Verde and Benin, the ruling party, Parti Socialiste Sénégalais (PS), has never been thrown out of power following an election. This is troublesome. The new electoral law has proven cumbersome and the fact that the deputy chief of the Constitutional Commission, which declares official vote counts, was assassinated shortly after the recent parliamentary elections, clearly shows that all is not well with Senegal's democracy. In terms of political stability, however, Senegal has done extremely well since independence. It and Benin are also the least politically repressive of the former French colonies.

ECONOMY

Senegal's economy is based on agriculture (although fishing is a major activity on the coast, supplying both the domestic and export markets) and has been precariously dependent on groundnuts (peanuts) as a cash crop for more than a century. When droughts struck in the 1970s, Senegal was severely affected. Another problem is that less than half the crop is sold to the government as required by law; the rest is sold privately or smuggled into The Gambia. Production levels of subsistence crops such as corn, millet and sorghum are also stagnant or declining and Senegal now imports more than 35% of its food requirements.

Tourism also contributes to Senegal's economy, although this is less than 10% of the total, and activity is restricted mainly to the coastal regions. In the mid-1980s Senegal received about 300,000 visitors per year, mostly package tourists from France, with others from Germany and Scandinavia. Numbers fell in the early 1990s due to fighting in Casamance (see the Senegal Today section, earlier). The first tourists began to return early in 1994. It will probably take a few more years before numbers reach the boom-time levels of the mid-1980s.

The fighting has now ended, and tourists are returning, but Senegal's troubles are far from over. The breakdown of the Senegambia confederation in 1989 was a symptom of a much deeper problem: Senegal's economy has been getting nowhere since the '80s. Real per capita income – about US$650 – has not risen since independence in 1960, when Senegal and Côte d'Ivoire were on a par. Now, per capita income in Côte d'Ivoire is 70% higher. Meanwhile, reserves are low even though Senegal receives more foreign aid per capita than just about any other country in Africa.

In March 1994, the International Monetary Fund (IMF) loaned Senegal about US$60 million to support various economy-boosting schemes such as a reduction in import tariffs, following the devaluation of the CFA franc in January (for details, see the Money section in this chapter). At the same time, various creditor countries (known as the Paris Club) agreed to reduce Senegal's foreign debt by a further $200 million.

POPULATION & PEOPLE

Of the country's estimated 8.5 million people, about 35% are Wolof. Almost all of the remainder are Sérèr (17%), Peul (also called Fulani; 12%), Toucouleur, Diola (JOU-lah), Mandinka and Soninké. You'll find the Wolof everywhere, but particularly in the area north of Dakar and Thiès. The Sérèr are predominantly to the east and south-east of Dakar, the Toucouleur in the north and east along the Senegal River, the Peul in the north, the Diola in the Casamance, the Mandinka more in the central and eastern regions, and the Soninké in the east. Minor groups include the Bassari and Bédik, found in the remote south-east. Until recently, Senegal was also home to about 300,000 Moors, from Mauritania, but most fled the country in 1989 (see the earlier boxed story on the Mauritanian Crisis), although since 1992 some have returned.

Senegal differs from many other West African countries in its high degree of homogeneity among ethnic groups. Most speak or understand the Wolof language and about 85% are Muslim. French efforts to assimilate the Africans into a Gallic way of life also helped to minimise ethnic differences.

CULTURE

Like many African tribes, Senegal's main group, the Wolof, has a highly stratified society, and status is determined by birth. At the top are the traditional noble and warrior

Filigree bead worn by Wolof and Fulani women

SENEGAL

SENEGAL

Toucouleur mask from northern Senegal

families, followed by the farmers, traders and persons of caste – blacksmiths, leather workers, wood workers, weavers and *griots* (GREE-oh). Griots are the lowest of the castes but highly respected as it is they who pass on the oral tradition and are usually the only ones who can recite family or village history. As musicians or songwriters, they used to entertain the royal families. Today, if you're fortunate enough to hear the harp-like *kora* played, the musician will almost certainly be from a griot family.

At the bottom of the social hierarchy were the slaves, taken in wars or bought from traders. Slavery is long gone, but many descendants of former slaves still work as tenant farmers for their former masters. Modernity is eroding this hierarchy. Today, the government official who manifests contempt for the uneducated peasants (even the chief) may actually be a member of a lower caste or slave family who went away to the city and acquired an education.

Music

Senegalese music can be divided very broadly into two types: traditional and modern, although there's considerable overlap. Today's pop stars base their work on traditional sounds and rhythms, and Senegal has produced some of the best-known musicians in Africa, many of them famous all over the world.

The father of modern Senegalese music is Ibra Kassé who founded the Star Band de Dakar to play at his nightclub, The Miami, in the early 1960s. Kassé is now dead but his music is currently enjoying something of a revival. The Miami also still thrives.

Foremost amongst today's stars is Youssou N'dour, who combined traditional *mbalax* music and Western pop, rock and soul into music in which rhythms clatter and shift around a basic pulse behind his wailing voice. He still plays on occasion with his band Le Super Etoile at his Dakar nightclub, The Thiosanne, but since his international breakthrough he is often on tour.

Touré Kunda (meaning Touré Family – the band was founded by four brothers) is another leading exponent of mbalax, as is Thione Seck who started with Orchestra Baobab (a legendary band in Senegal) in traditional Wolof style but moved on to create mbalax rhythms incorporating a Cuban influence with his band, Raam Daam.

Whilst N'dour and Touré Kunda have become more 'international' in their sound and audience, other musicians are regarded as remaining more 'African'. One such is Baaba Maal, a Peul from northern Senegal who sings in his native tongue and plays traditional music as well as electric pop and reggae.

Some of the other names to look out for are: Lamine Konté, a master kora player who mixes traditional kora with rock and folk music; Ismael Lô, sometimes called the Senegalese Bob Dylan, and his band Ilopro; and Idrissa Diop, who sings in Wolof and has performed before huge international audiences with his group, Les Gaiendes (his music features percussion instruments of all kinds). The group Xalam, which developed a unique style combining jazz, rhythm and blues and African music, and was one of the first West African bands to gain recognition in Europe, has not played on stage since the death of their lead singer, but their albums are still popular and widely available. ∎

RELIGION

Over 80% of the population is Muslim, the remainder being primarily Christians and practitioners of traditional religions. The Wolof, Toucouleur and Mandinka are virtually all Muslim while the Fulani (Peul) and Diola are animists by tradition. Many of the Sérèr, who are found mostly around Thiès, along Petite Côte and in the Sine Saloum, are Catholics.

Senegal has its own unique version of Islam that blends magic with a reliance on the priesthood and the veneration of saints. Virtually all adherents are members of one of five brotherhoods, the two principal ones being the Mourides, centred in Touba and Diourbel, and the Tidjanes. At the head of each is a Grand Caliph, the chief *marabout* (mah-rah-bou), or holy man. The Grand Marabout at Touba is held in as much awe by his followers as is the Pope by Catholics. He has secular as well as religious influence and no one, high or low, would make a major decision without consulting him. This is at odds with orthodox Islam, which says that Allah is directly accessible to each believer without intermediary assistance. Senegalese Muslims hold that a disciple, or *talibé*, is linked to Allah through his marabout. Also, the Grand Marabout has only to say the word and his zealots will carry it out.

If you're in Senegal during a Muslim holiday or the Grand Magal, head for Touba. Go to the palace of the Grand Marabout for his benediction, or risk being treated with disdain in the street. You'll see the faithful offering him gifts, while he spits into their hands as a sign of blessing.

LANGUAGE

French is the official language and Wolof the principal African language. The Toucouleur and Peul (Fulani) speak Pulaar (or Fula) while the Sérèr speak Sérèr. Arabic expressions are also widely used and can come in useful. For instance, if you're having problems with taxi drivers in Dakar, as you enter the taxi say 'sah-LAHM ah-lay-KUUM', Arabic for 'peace be with you' (the reply is 'mah-lay-KUUM sah-LAHM'). They'll think you live there and will put on the meter.

If you're being pestered by street vendors,

say in Wolof 'my-mah su-mah gee-AHM' ('leave me in peace') or simply 'jair-ruh-jef' fairly loudly. That usually shuts them up. Other expressions in Wolof include:

Good morning.	*ya-MAHN-gah fah-NIN*
Good evening.	*ya-MAHN-gah YEN-lou*
How are you?	*nang-gah-DEF*
I'm fine.	*mahn-gee fee-REK*
Thank you.	*jair-ruh-JEF*
Goodbye.	*mahn-gah-DEM*

Facts for the Visitor

VISAS & EMBASSIES
Senegal Visas

Visas are not needed by nationals of Denmark, France, Germany, Italy, Ireland, Luxembourg, the Netherlands, the USA and the UK for stays of up to 90 days. All other nationalities need them. (It is particularly hard for citizens of New Zealand to get visas: embassies (in Africa and elsewhere) refer requests to Dakar, and the process can take six months.) Visas are usually good for multiple entries and a stay of three months. They are not available at airports or land borders.

In West Africa, you can get visas for Senegal in Abidjan (Côte d'Ivoire), Bamako (Mali), Banjul (The Gambia), Bissau (Guinea-Bissau), Conakry (Guinea), Freetown (Sierra Leone), Lagos (Nigeria), Niamey (Niger) and Praia (Cape Verde). For details, refer to the Visas & Embassies section of the relevant country chapter.

Outside of West Africa, Senegalese embassies and consulates issue visas without any onerous requirements. The embassy in Washington, for example, issues multi-entry visas valid for stays of up to three months. They cost US$6.50 and require two photos. The Senegalese embassies/consulates in London, Paris and Bonn have similar procedures and requirements.

Senegalese Embassies

Belgium 196 Ave Franklin-Roosevelt, Brussels 1050
(☎ (02) 230-39-11)

France (consulate) 22 rue Hamelin, 75016 Paris (☎ (1) 44-05-38-48)
Germany Argelanderstrabe 3, 5300 Bonn 2 (☎ (0228) 21-80-08/9)
UK 11 Phillimore Gardens, London W8 70G (☎ (0171) 937-0925)
USA 2112 Wyoming Ave, NW, Washington, DC 20008 (☎ (202) 234-0540)

Senegal also has embassies in Addis Ababa, Algiers, Berne, Brasilia, Cairo, Geneva, Libreville, New Delhi, New York, Ottawa, Rabat, Rome, Stockholm, Tokyo, Tunis and Yaoundé, plus consulates in Bordeaux, Lyon, Marseilles, Melbourne, Montreal, Toronto, Vancouver, Vienna and Zürich.

Other African Visas

Cape Verde The embassy is open weekdays from 8.30 am to 12.30 pm and 3 to 6 pm, Saturdays from 8.30 am to 12.30 pm. Visas cost CFA 5000 and take 48 hours, but can be rushed in an emergency.
Côte d'Ivoire The embassy is open weekdays from 8.30 am to 12.30 pm and 3 to 6 pm. Visas cost CFA 5000.
The Gambia The embassy is open Monday to Thursday from 9 am to 3 pm, Friday from 9 am to 1 pm. Visas cost CFA 4000. If you come early, you can get the visa by 2.30 pm, otherwise within 24 hours. Seven-day visas to The Gambia may be available at the border. These cost 50 dalasi (about US$5), which may be payable in CFA, and are renewable.
Guinea The embassy is open weekdays from 9 am to noon. You need CFA 10,000 and a letter of introduction from your embassy. Visas are issued in 24 hours.
Guinea-Bissau The embassy is open weekdays from 8 am to 12.30 pm and 3.30 to 6 pm. Visas cost CFA 5000 and are issued in 24 hours or, occasionally, less. Don't join the queue in front; go round the back to the consul's office.
Mali The embassy is open weekdays from 9 am to 12.30 pm. Visas cost CFA 5000 and take 48 hours.
Mauritania The embassy is open weekday mornings. Visas cost CFA 6000 and are issued on the spot. A letter of introduction from your own embassy is required.
Niger The embassy has closed but may reopen in the future. Visas used to cost CFA 7500 and were valid for one-month stays.
Sierra Leone The consulate issues visas for CFA 3000 (CFA 5000 for Britons), normally in 48 hours, although occasionally on the spot. You may need a letter of introduction from your own embassy.
Zaïre The embassy is open weekdays from 8 am to 1 pm; visas cost a ridiculous CFA 35,000 and take

48 hours. Don't get your Zaïre visa in Senegal unless you're desperate – their embassies elsewhere in Africa generally charge much less.
Other Countries The French embassy issues visas to Togo, Burkina Faso and Chad. Their visa section is open weekdays from 8 to 11.30 am. The fee is CFA 3000 and the process usually takes 24 hours but same-day service is occasionally given. Get a visa for Burkina Faso here rather than in Bamako, where the Burkina Faso embassy charges CFA 9000 for visas.

Foreign Embassies
See the Dakar Information section for a list of foreign embassies found in the capital.

DOCUMENTS
All visitors need a passport and International Vaccination Certificate. If you're driving, you do not need a *carnet de passage*; the customs office issues a free 30-day renewable *passavant de douane*. They'll accept your international insurance and national driving licence as well.

CUSTOMS
CFA 200,000 is the maximum amount of currency foreigners may export (CFA 20,000 for locals). If you carry more, a smile and a plea of ignorance will usually get you through without any major problems.

MONEY
1FF	=	CFA 100
UK£1	=	CFA 775
US$1	=	CFA 500

The unit of currency is the West African CFA franc, which is pegged to the French franc at 100:1. In January 1994 the CFA was devalued overnight from a rate of 50:1, and other hard-currency rates also increased by a similar amount. Prices everywhere increased by between 120 and 200%, and are likely to fluctuate more in the future, but because the exchange rate has doubled, Senegal is now cheaper overall for visitors than it was before.

Banks for changing money include Citibank, CBAO (Compagnie Bancaire de l'Afrique Occidentale), BICIS (Banque Internationale pour le Commerce et l'Industrie Sénégalaise) and BCS (Banque Commerciale du Sénégal). There are banks in all main towns and one at Dakar Airport. If it is closed, you can change at the airport bookshop (where the commission is lower!).

Cashing travellers' cheques is easy in Dakar but difficult elsewhere if they're not in French francs. In Dakar, St-Louis, Ziguinchor and Kaolack, banks will give cash with Visa cards but sometimes only for French cards (eg Carte Bleue) as they are easier to verify. The process can take 24 hours, and there may be a minimum withdrawal.

BUSINESS HOURS & HOLIDAYS
Businesses are open on weekdays from 8 am to noon and 2.30 to 6 pm, and on Saturdays from 8 am to noon. Government offices keep the same hours. Most banks are open on weekdays, typically from 8.30 to 11.30 am and 2.30 to 4.30 pm. On Saturday mornings in Dakar the CBAO is open until 11 am. The bank at the airport is open until midnight.

Public Holidays
1 January, 4 April (Independence), Easter Monday, End of Ramadan, 1 May, Ascension Thursday, Whit Monday, Tabaski, 15 August, Mohammed's Birthday, 1 November, 25 December. The major holidays are Independence Day, the end of Ramadan and Tabaski.

Other festivals include the Grand Magal pilgrimage and celebration, held in Touba 48 days after the Islamic new year, and the Paris-Dakar Rally, which ends in Dakar around the second week of January.

POST & TELECOMMUNICATIONS
Sending letters from Senegal is expensive. The poste restante in Dakar is slow, unreliable, holds letters for only 30 days and charges CFA 250 per letter.

Senegal's internal phone service is reasonable. There are no city codes: the first two figures of a six-figure number indicate the area, but you must dial the whole number. International phone connections to/from Senegal are also good. Dakar has several private *telecentres*, usually open until late evening, for phone calls, telexes and faxes with rates similar

to those at the public SONATEL offices. In addition, phone booths are being installed all over the country, even in small towns, making national and international calls from the rural areas easy. Three-minute calls cost about CFA 5500 to the USA and CFA 4000 to the UK. Reverse-charge (collect) calls can be made to the USA.

PHOTOGRAPHY
Taking photographs in Senegal is not a problem. The government here is the least uptight in West Africa about photos: you can even photograph the presidential palace. However, you should still avoid photographing genuine military installations.

For passport photos (required for visa applications), there are several places in central Dakar. Try the camera shop on the Place de l'Indépendance, or the Kodak shop at the intersection of Blvd de la République and Ave Lamine Gueye.

HEALTH
For emergencies in Dakar, try Hôpital Principal (☎ 23 27 41) on Ave Courbet, or Clinique Hubert (☎ 21 68 48) at 26 Ave Jean Jaures. Two English-speaking general practitioners in Dakar are Dr Hassan Bahsoun (☎ 21 36 14) at 29 Rue du Dr Thèze and Dr J C Bernou at Clinique Internationale (☎ 24 44 21), 33 Blvd Dial Diop. Dakar has many pharmacies. Night pharmacies *(pharmacie de garde)* in Dakar are listed in *Le Soleil* or *Le Dakarois*.

DANGERS & ANNOYANCES
Dakar has the worst reputation of any city in West Africa for thieves. Most of them, however, are unarmed petty criminals and not as life-threatening as those in Abidjan and Lagos, although occasionally knives are used in attacks, particularly at night. Petty theft is also common on the major beaches, and muggings occur there from time to time.

On Dakar's streets, single women are most vulnerable, and should be particularly careful not to wear watches or jewellery (no matter how cheap it may be). The areas around Sandaga market, Ave Pompidou and Place de l'Indépendance (especially – and not surprisingly – outside the banks) have the most pickpockets. Keep your money out of sight, preferably under at least one layer of clothing.

Thieves usually work in groups. One person will touch your back, causing you to stop. A second person then bumps into you and tries to grab your purse or wallet. He then runs while a third person acts as a decoy. Some street traders are also thieves, working in groups like the others. If several traders surround you in Dakar, the chances of being robbed are excellent, so get away from them immediately. Beware too of people offering bracelets as *cadeaux* (gifts): it's just another way to slow you down. Ignore them.

The danger of travelling in the Casamance definitely persists and may have increased. In April 1995 four French tourists were killed, allegedly by rebels.

ACCOMMODATION

Senegal offers a very wide choice of places to stay, from the top class international hotels on the coastal resorts, to dirty dosshouses in Dakar, plus campements (simple hotels) in the rural areas. In the Casamance region, a system of village-run campements raises money for local projects. There are very few organised camp sites in Senegal.

All hotels and campements in Senegal charge a CFA 500 per person tourist tax. Sometimes this is included in the price, and sometimes it isn't. You have to ask.

Some hotels charge by the room so it makes no difference to the price (apart from the tourist tax) if you are alone or with somebody. Even if they do charge for singles and doubles, couples may be allowed to share a single. The price is usually for bed or room only. Breakfast is extra (or not available) unless stated on the hotel's tariff sheet.

FOOD & DRINKS

Senegal is known for having some of the finest cuisine in West Africa. Dakar, among other places, is an excellent place to sample it. Common dishes include: *mafé*, a peanut-based stew, and *poulet yassa*, grilled chicken marinated in a mild chilli sauce. Variations on

the theme, and depending on location, are *poisson yassa* and *viande yassa*. *Tiéboudienne* (chey-bou-jen) is the 'national dish' and consists of rice baked in a thick sauce of fish and a variety of vegetables with pimiento and tomato sauce. *Bassi-salété* ('couscous' on restaurant menus) is millet covered with vegetables and meat; it is frequently served for the evening meal as well as on special occasions and, like many African dishes, can be simple or very complex. Another, equally variable, favourite is *riz yollof* – vegetables or meat cooked in a sauce of oil and tomatoes, served with rice.

A popular snack is *chawarma*: grilled meat in bread, served with salad and sesame sauce, an 'import' originally from Lebanon, now found in towns and cities all over West Africa. Dakar in particular has some excellent chawarma places.

For breakfast, or a cheap snack at any time of day, there are roadside coffee stalls (on many street corners in Dakar, or around the market or *gare routière* (bush taxi park) in most other towns) serving Nescafé, and bread with either butter or mayonnaise. Some also serve tea (made with a Lipton teabag), or even Milo, and the more enterprising *cafémen* might fry up eggs or serve sardines. Sometimes the tea or coffee is made with a weak solution of local herbs called *kinkilaba*, which turns the water brown, and gives the drink a slightly 'woody' taste.

Senegalese beer is good. Gazelle comes in 500 ml bottles and costs between CFA 500 and CFA 875. Flag is a stronger more upmarket brew. A 330 ml bottle costs CFA 500 in a cheap place, up to CFA 1200 or more in posh bars and hotels (where they wouldn't dream of offering Gazelle). Flag is also available in larger bottles and on draught. Soft drinks such as Coke cost CFA 150 from a street vendor, CFA 250 to CFA 300 at a cheap restaurant, CFA 500 to CFA 750 in a posh bar, and CFA 1200 in a nightclub.

Typical Senegalese cold beverages include spicy ginger beer and the very popular, reddish *bissap* (BEE-sap) made from bissap flowers. You'll see lots of bissap being sold on the streets in plastic bags right after the Ramadan fast ends.

Getting There & Away

AIR

To/From the USA

Air Afrique has punctual flights with good service twice a week both ways between Dakar and New York. Most other flights between North America and West Africa are on European airlines, via Europe.

To/From Europe

Airlines from Europe serving Senegal include Air Afrique and Air France (with direct flights 12 times a week via Paris and five times a week via Marseilles), Swissair (via Geneva or Zürich), Sabena (via Brussels), Alitalia (via Rome), Iberia (via Madrid), TAP (via Lisbon) and Aeroflot (via Moscow). Many other European cities are served by the above airlines. For example, you can fly to Dakar from London on Sabena or Alitalia. One-way fares start at US$470, and returns vary from US$600 to US$900, depending on the season and your length of stay.

For a one-way flight back to Europe, Nouvelles Frontières in Dakar (see under Travel Agencies in the Dakar Information section) often have space on charter flights to Paris for around 2000FF (US$350).

To/From West Africa

Dakar is linked to all other capital cities in West Africa, and you have a wide choice of regional airlines. There are four flights a week to/from Bamako (Mali) on Ethiopian Airlines and Air Afrique (the one-way fare is CFA 88,600) and two flights a week to/from Ouagadougou (Burkina Faso), also on Air Afrique. TACV and Air Senegal have three flights per week to/from Praia (Cape Verde); the one-way fare is CFA 85,900 and the round-trip excursion is 50% more.

There is at least one flight a day in both directions between Dakar and Banjul on Gambia Airways, Air Gambia or Air Senegal (the one-way fare is CFA 30,700). Between Dakar and Bissau (Guinea-Bissau) Air Senegal and TAGB Air Bissau have five flights a week (CFA 60,200 one way and CFA 120,400 return); most flights stop in Ziguinchor.

There are flights every day to/from Abidjan on Air Afrique, Nigeria Airways and Air Ivoire (CFA 133,700 one way); almost every day to/from Conakry on Air Afrique, Air Guinée and Ghana Airways; three times a week to/from Accra on Nigeria Airways and Ghana Airways (CFA 92,000); and weekly to/from Niamey on Air Afrique (CFA 164,500). There are also direct connections to/from Casablanca (Morocco) on Royal Air Maroc and Air Afrique, and to/from Rabat (Morocco), Las Palmas (Canary Islands), and São Tomé on TAP and Ghana Airways.

LAND

Bush Taxi & Minibus

To/From Mauritania The main route between Dakar and Nouakchott goes via Rosso (the border). A bush taxi between Dakar and Rosso costs CFA 4500. A *pirogue* (small boat) across the river is CFA 180 or 50 ougiya per person. Between Rosso and Nouakchott costs 750 ougiya (around CFA 3700) by bush taxi. The whole journey (Dakar to Nouakchott) takes about 10 hours. Beware of a possible scam at the border at Rosso. Some travellers have been charged an 'exit tax' of CFA 1550 per person. If this hoax happens to you, refuse to pay. Nicely.

To/From The Gambia Senegal completely surrounds The Gambia, but there is no direct public transport between the two countries: all journeys involve changing vehicles at the border. Only vehicles travelling between north and south Senegal on the Trans-Gambia Highway are allowed to cross the border, although passengers are not allowed to end their journey in The Gambia.

Minibuses and Peugeot 504 bush taxis run regularly between Dakar and the Senegalese border town of Karang beyond Toubacouta. Minibuses take a full day as they stop all along the way. By Peugeot 504 it takes only five hours; the fare is CFA 3100 (CFA 2500 by minibus) plus luggage (notoriously high on this route: you'll need to bargain to get it down to what the locals pay). From Karang you can get a bus (3D), pick-up (9D) or taxi (50D) to the ferry at Barra, via The Gambian border post (one km south of Karang). (You may have to get a taxi or walk between the two border posts before finding transport to Barra.) The ferry starts running at around 8 am. The last ferry from Banjul is around 6 pm, and from Barra at 7 pm; the fare is only 3D. If you are in a hurry and the ferry isn't leaving soon you could take a pirogue across the river. The fare should be no more than the ferry. Going the other way, all prices are the same.

Bush taxis (504s and pick-ups) run regularly between Ziguinchor and the southern border with The Gambia. A 504 from Ziguinchor to the border is CFA 1850, and from there to Serekunda is 20D. Going the other way these sections cost CFA 1750 and 25D because the transport always takes you to the far side of the border. The trip takes three to five hours depending on connections. An early start is better.

It's also possible to travel between Senegal and The Gambia via Tambacounda and Basse Santa Su (see Getting There & Away in The Gambia chapter).

To/From Guinea Transport from Dakar to Labé leaves from the corner of Rue Reims and Rue Des Dardanelles, off Ave Blaise Diagne, a few blocks north of Marché Sandaga. A 20-seater bus leave when full, usually every other day. The cost is CFA 25,000 and you even get a ticket. All the way to Tambacounda the bus stops to pick up and drop off more passengers. At the border, all passengers transfer to 504 bush taxis which go to Labé. The bus driver sorts out payment with the bush taxis. The entire trip takes between 25 and 35 hours. You'll also find trucks trundling between Tambacounda and Labé for about CFA 9000.

To/From Guinea-Bissau Bush taxis and minibuses for Bissau leave from the gare routière in Ziguinchor, going via São Domingos and Ingore. The fare is CFA 2500. You also have to pay 2000 pesos for two ferry crossings on the Guinea-Bissau side.

The road is paved all the way, but the ferries can make the trip between Ziguinchor and Bissau in anything from four to eight hours. It's best to leave by around 8 am. Occasionally vehicles leave as late as 11 am but your chances of making it to Bissau in one day are then greatly reduced.

Train

To/From Mali Between Senegal and Mali, the 'main' road is very bad and traffic virtually nonexistent, so the Dakar to Bamako express train is the cheapest and best way to go. Trains leave twice weekly in either direction on Wednesdays and Saturdays at around 8 am. Each country has its own train: the Senegalese train is newer but now only slightly better than the Malian train, which has coaches dating from the 1950s. Delays are common: between Dakar and Bamako it is scheduled to take 30 hours but 35 hours or longer is more typical.

The trains have three classes: *couchettes* (sleeping berths) which have two-person compartments that are basic and dirty but not shockingly so, although they do get hot during the day as the windows may not open; 1st class with large, comfortable seats; and 2nd class which is more crowded with less comfortable, though adequate, seating. The train has a restaurant car selling beer, soft drinks, sandwiches and good full meals. You can get cheap food at stations along the way.

Tickets go on sale the day before departure. Fares (1st/2nd class) from Dakar are: CFA 14,045/7560 to Kayes, and CFA 29,910/19,735 to Bamako. A couchette from Dakar to Bamako costs CFA 42,390 to CFA 57,870 per person. Student discounts are not available for foreigners, although it might be worth a try. Seats in 1st class can be reserved, but to be sure of a seat in 2nd class, get to the train about two hours before it is due to leave.

At each border post you'll have to take a short hike to the customs office to have your passport stamped. Foreigners sometimes have their passport taken by an immigration inspector on the train, but you still have to collect it yourself by getting off the train and going to the office at the border post. Nobody tells you this so, if your passport is taken, ask where and when you have to go for collection. If you're going into Mali and manage to sleep through the Malian border check and don't get your passport stamped, you can get it done in Bamako. Entering Mali you may also need to get your passport stamped at Kayes, but this seems completely arbitrary.

Theft is a problem on the train: if you leave your seat or couchette, especially at night, ask a fellow passenger to watch your gear.

You can save time and money by doing the section between Dakar and Tambacounda by bush taxi, but then you'll find the train very full in Tambacounda. Some travellers get off at Kayes and take the cheaper 'local' train on to Bamako. The saving is minimal as this requires staying overnight in Kayes, but it breaks the journey and Kayes itself is quite an interesting place to visit (see the Mali chapter for details).

Car

To/From The Gambia & Mauritania Typical driving times from Dakar are five or six hours to Banjul, and seven or eight hours to Nouakchott. In Senegal, the roads get progressively worse the nearer you get to any border.

To/From Mali Driving time from Dakar to Bamako (1423 km) is four days, with overnight stops at Tambacounda, Kayes and Nioro. The Tambacounda to Nioro section is in terrible condition and sometimes impassable in the rainy season; the road via Mauritania is easier but longer (1925 km).

Most drivers heading to/from Mali put their vehicles on the train and sleep in their cars to deter thieves. Taking a car out of Dakar by train can be difficult because heading for Mali it's always full, and you may have to reserve long in advance. Coming out of Bamako is easier. For more information see the Getting There & Away section in the Mali chapter.

SEA

Pirogues go between Senegal's Siné-Saloum Delta and Banjul (The Gambia): see the later section on Djiffer & Palmarin in this chapter

for details. There's also a boat about once a month between Dakar and Praia (Cape Verde); enquire at the port. For a freighter to Europe or along the coast of West Africa, ask at Socopao-Voyages in Dakar (see Travel Agencies in the Dakar Information section). Expect to pay double the air fare.

LEAVING SENEGAL

Departure tax at Yoff Airport (flight information ☎ 23 10 41) is US$15 but most tickets already have it included in the price. Check with your airline when you reconfirm your ticket, so that you're not charged again at the airport.

Getting Around

AIR

For getting around the country by air, Air Senegal has daily flights from Dakar to Ziguinchor (which continue to Cap Skiring four times per week) and weekly flights from Dakar to Tambacounda and Kedougou. For more details see the Dakar Getting There & Away section. There are also flights to Simenti (in the Niokolo-Koba game park); check locally for departure days.

Air Senegal flights are notoriously unreliable. Reservations can be made only in person in an Air Senegal office. If you've reserved a flight from outside Senegal, even though your ticket may read 'OK', your name may not be on the airline's list; try to have your travel agent contact one of the Dakar travel agencies to make the reservation. Wherever you may have booked, when you arrive in Dakar go immediately to the Air Senegal office to confirm once again.

For plane charter, contact Air Afric Service (☎ 20 03 88) in Dakar.

BUS, MINIBUS & BUSH TAXI

Buses (*cars*) carrying 30 to 40 people ply the main long-distance routes between Dakar, Kaolack, Ziguinchor and some other large towns. Minibuses (*petits cars*) carrying 15 to 30 people also run on many routes. These tend to be quite safe, in good condition, leave when full and only stop occasionally. On many routes you also find other minibuses (misleadingly called *cars rapides*): battered, slow, crowded and worth avoiding.

Your other option for long-distance journeys is a bush taxi (*taxi brousse*). On the main routes these are usually Peugeot 504s with three rows of seats: comfortable, safe, and as fast as private vehicles once they're on their way. They seat only three people across, not four or five as in some poorer countries, and you can always buy an extra seat if you want more space. Some sample journeys and fares: Dakar to St-Louis (264 km) takes three hours and costs CFA 3000; Dakar to Ziguinchor (454 km), eight hours, CFA 5600. On rural routes bush taxis are pick-ups (sometimes called *bachés*) seating about 12 people on benches.

Minibuses are typically about a third cheaper than Peugeot 504s, and buses cheaper still. There are no timetables: nearly all minibuses and bush taxis leave when they are full. Fares are fixed by the government. There's generally an extra charge for luggage – this is normally about 10% of the fare, although you may have to negotiate a bit, or check the price with other passengers.

TRAIN

Many visitors take the express train that runs between Dakar and Bamako (Mali), but few travel by train around Senegal itself. Generally, 2nd-class fares are cheaper than road transport, although trains are slower. But if you're not in a hurry, riding the rails through Senegal can be very pleasant and relaxing.

The twice-weekly express between Dakar and Bamako goes via Tambacounda (the last big town in the east of Senegal), and there's another weekly 'local' service which stops at more places. There are also daily trains from Dakar to St-Louis and Kaolack, with new comfortable carriages. For times and fares, see the Dakar Getting There & Away section.

CAR

In Senegal, rental rates are very high, with mainstream operators charging CFA 18,000

a day and CFA 150 per km, plus CFA 2500 a day for car insurance and 20% tax, even for the cheapest cars. If you average 250 km a day, the cost will come to about US$950 a week plus petrol. Some smaller outfits have cheaper deals: from CFA 9000 a day and CFA 90 per km, plus insurance and tax, and you can also find special weekend rates, or *prix promotionals*, which are lower. There are several car rental companies in Dakar, plus a few in St-Louis and Ziguinchor (see these sections for details). You are not obliged to hire a driver in Senegal. Petrol costs CFA 350 per litre.

BOAT

SENTRAM is the Senegal maritime transport organisation. Their new ferry, MV *Joola*, plies the ocean twice weekly both ways between Dakar and Ziguinchor, also stopping at Carabane Island, and is a very pleasant way of travelling. The boat should depart from Dakar on Tuesdays and Fridays and from Ziguinchor on Thursdays and Sundays, but the schedule changes constantly, and departure times depend on the tide, so you should check details at the port in either city (in Dakar ☎ 21 44 35, in Ziguinchor ☎ 91 22 01). The journey takes about 20 hours. The boat has three classes; the cheapest is deck class (CFA 3750) while comfortable reclining seats in 1st class are CFA 7500. The one and two-person cabins with private showers cost from CFA 20,000 to CFA 25,000 per person. Taking a car costs CFA 18,000. The restaurant-bar-TV room serves reasonable meals.

TOURS

Most places of interest in Senegal can be reached by independent travellers using public transport or their own car, but several companies run organised tours (*excursions*) around the country.

Most tours are aimed squarely at groups: they have set departure days and require a minimum of six or eight passengers. This makes things difficult for independent travellers. However, if you can get a group together or want to chance your luck finding another group to join, this can be a good way to see something of the country if time is short or if money is not a concern.

Most tour companies are based in Dakar. Those worth checking include: Africa Travel at 63 Rue Assane Ndoye; Dakar Auto Voyages at 7 Rue Masclary, off Allées Delmas (just north of the Place); and Safari-Evasion (☎ 22 47 38) at 12 Ave Albert Sarraut. Some example prices: around CFA 19,000 to CFA 25,000 per person for a one-day tour to Lac Rose, Joal-Fadiout or the Saloum Delta; CFA 62,000 to CFA 75,000 for a three-day trip to St-Louis; and CFA 150,000 to CFA 165,000 for four or five days to Casamance or Niokolo-Koba.

The friendliest and cheapest of the travel agencies is Inter Tourisme (☎ 22 45 29) at 3 Allées Delmas. They also have a minimum group size of four people on many trips which makes things more viable for independent travellers. Some sample prices: three-day, all-inclusive tours of the Casamance for about CFA 80,000, one-day trips to Joal-Fadiout for CFA 12,500 and to Lac Rose for CFA 6000. They also have information and can make bookings for the various campements in the national parks.

For something a bit more authentic and imaginative, Kinkiliba Tours run excursions in the Casamance region and The Gambia. For more details, and their address, see the Tours section of The Gambia chapter.

Dakar

Dakar gets mixed reviews from visitors. On the positive side, it has a reputation as one of the nicest cities in Africa – temperate climate, a wide variety of restaurants and hotels, and many interesting things to see and do. There are several clubs where popular African groups play, and regular listings magazines are available to tell you what's going on. With tree-lined streets and a relatively small central area, Dakar is not crowded and is easy to walk around despite its population of almost one million.

Despite Dakar's charm, some people hate it. A stroll around town can be ruined by pestering traders who won't take 'no' for an answer. Locals cultivate a nonchalant air in the streets and ignore these traders. This is not likely to work, however, if you've got a rucksack or you're looking around the streets to find your way. Another technique is to look very closely at their goods, then make it quite clear by the expression on your face that you don't like anything. If all else fails, spend more time in sections of the city that tourists, and consequently these hustlers, don't frequent, such as the old Medina or the Île de Gorée. Whatever, don't forget that these aggressive hustlers are not typical. Most Senegalese are genuinely hospitable and wouldn't dream of hassling guests in their country.

Orientation

Dakar is on the Cap Vert peninsula, the westernmost part of the African continent. The peninsula has two points: the southernmost is Cap Manuel, and the city centre begins just north of it. Dakar's focus is the Place de l'Indépendance (often just called the Place) from which all the main streets radiate: Ave Roume heads south in the direction of the Palais Présidentiel; Ave Pompidou (formerly Ave Ponty and still generally called by that name) heads west and is lined with shops, cafés and bars, with the city's largest market, Marché Sandaga, at its western end. Most of the inexpensive hotels and restaurants, and many nightclubs, are in and around this area.

Leading from the eastern side of the Place is Ave Albert Sarraut, at the end of which, one block north, you'll find another market, Marché Kermel, with the main post office one block away.

The wide Blvd de la République extends west from the Palais Présidentiel to the cathedral at the intersection of Place de la République. Around here, and to the south towards Place de Soweto, you'll find the national museum and theatre and many embassies. From Place de Soweto you can head north along Ave Lamine Gueye, past Marché Sandaga, eventually reaching the gare routière and the main autoroute out of the city, which

SENEGAL

SENEGAL

ends at Patte d'Oie. About halfway along the autoroute, another main road leads west, though the residential suburb of Castors.

From Place de la République you can head north-west on Ave Blaise Diagne, passing the area of the Grande Mosquée, the wrestling arena and La Médina. Continuing north-west, Blaise Diagne becomes Route d'Ouakam, passing the university, then suburbs of Point E, Mermoz and Ouakam. Some 10 km from La Médina you'll be in the Pointe des Almadies and Île de N'Gor area, a favourite weekend retreat. The major beaches, some big hotels and good seafood restaurants and the airport are all here. The Route de la Corniche-Ouest runs along the Atlantic Ocean roughly parallel to the Route d'Ouakam; here you'll see joggers and the city's finest homes and embassy residences.

Information

The tourist office has closed, but for details of what's going on around town simply consult one of the free listings magazines, such as Le Dakarois or Panda available in large hotels and travel agencies. For information on national parks you may want to contact the Direction des Parcs Nationaux (☎ 23 07 93 or 21 42 21) in the Point E area.

Money On the western side of the Place are BICIS, CBAO and Citibank, which all change money. CBAO has the quickest service, BICIS is the next best, and Citibank prefer to deal only with their own account holders unless you've got US dollars (cash), but even then rates are low. Each bank has different exchange rates and commissions varying for different currencies, for cash or travellers' cheques, and even for the number of cheques you're changing. If you've got time, do a quick comparison to find the best one for you. For bank hours see Money in the Facts for the Visitor section.

If all the banks are closed, some travel agencies may change French francs cash (and only make a small commission). Or try one of the large hotels. Most will change cash or travellers' cheques, although rates are low or commissions high, or both.

Post & Telecommunications The main post office is on Blvd el Haji Djily Mbaye (formerly Ave Pinet Laprade), two blocks north of Marché Kermel. There's also a smaller office at the eastern end of Ave Pompidou. For phone calls, SONATEL has city centre offices on Rue Wagane Diouf (open 7 am to midnight) and on Blvd de la République (7 am to 11 pm), and at the airport (24 hours). There are also many private telecentres in Dakar offering the same service. The best is on the Place, near the banks.

Foreign Embassies Embassies or consuls in the central area include:

Algeria 5 Rue Mermoz, two blocks south of the IFAN Museum (☎ 22 35 09)
Austria 24 Blvd el Haji Djily Mbaye, formerly Ave Pine*t Laprade (☎ 22 38 86)*
Belgium Route de la Corniche-Est (☎ 21 40 27)
Cameroun 157 Rue Joseph Gomis, near the junction with Ave Nelson Mandela (☎ 22 34 14 or 25 30 89)
Canada 45 Blvd de la République (☎ 23 92 90 or 24 02 30)
Cape Verde 3 Blvd el Haji Djily Mbaye, formerly Ave Pinet Laprade (☎ 21 39 36/18 73)
Côte d'Ivoire 2 Ave Albert Sarraut, one block south of Marché Kermel (☎ 21 01 63, 21 34 73)
Egypt 45 Blvd de la République (☎ 21 24 75)
France 1 Rue Assane Ndoye, near the Novotel (☎ 23 91 81)
The Gambia 11 Rue de Thiong, a block north of Ave Pompidou (☎ 21 44 76)
Germany 20 Ave Pasteur (☎ 22 25 19 or 23 25 19)
Italy On Rue Alpha Hahcamiyou, formerly Rue Seydou Nourou Tall (☎ 22 05 78)
Japan On Blvd el Haji Djily Mbaye (formerly Ave Pinet Laprade), next to the Austrian embassy (☎ 21-0141 or 23 91 41)
Liberia 20 Blvd de la République (☎ 22 53 72)
Mali 46 Blvd de la République (☎ 22 04 73)
The Netherlands 37 Rue Kléber (☎ 22 04 83 or 23 94 83)
Sierra Leone Out at Clinique Bleu at 13 Rue Castor
Spain 45 Blvd de la République (☎ 21 30 81)
Switzerland Rue Alpha Hahcamiyou, formerly Rue Seydou Nourou Tall (☎ 23 58 48)
Tunisia Rue Alpha Hahcamiyou, near the Swiss embassy (☎ 23 47 47)
UK 20 Rue du Dr Guillet, one block south of Hôpital Le Dantec (☎ 23 73 92/99 71, fax 23 27 66, telex 21690)
USA Ave Jean XXIII (☎ 23 34 24/42 96, fax 22 29 91)

The following embassies and consulates are in the Point E and Mermoz areas, four to five km north-west of the central area (take bus No 7 or 12 out along Ave Blaise Diagne and Route d'Ouakam):

Benin In the Sicap area, north of Point E, off Blvd Bourguiba, near Demba Diop stadium (☎ 24 87 08)

Gabon On Ave Cheikh Anta Diop (formerly Rue Leo Frobenius), round the corner from the Zimbabwe embassy (☎ 23 15 29 or 24 09 95)

Guinea On Rue 7, Point E, north of the Nigerian embassy (☎ 24 86 06)

Guinea-Bissau On Rue 6, Point E, north of the Nigerian embassy (☎ 24 59 22)

Mauritania In Mermoz, to the west of Route d'Ouakam, near the intersection with Route de la Corniche-Ouest. Turn off at the junction marked by a large Air Afrique sign, then follow signs to the Nigerian Residence. The embassy is an unmarked private house.

Morocco On Ave Cheikh Anta Diop (formerly Rue Leo Frobenius), round the corner from the Zimbabwe embassy (☎ 24 69 27)

Nigeria On Rue 1, Point E, one block north of Route d'Ouakam (☎ 24 69 22)

Togo Signposted off the Route d'Ouakam, just west of the intersection with Route de la Corniche-Ouest (☎ 25 29 19)

Zaïre On Ave Cheikh Anta Diop (Rue Leo Frobenius), around the corner from the Zimbabwe embassy (☎ 25 19 79)

Zimbabwe At km 5 on the Route d'Ouakam, near the junction of Ave Cheikh Anta Diop (Rue Leo Frobenius) (☎ 23 03 25)

Cultural Centres The American Cultural Centre is on Rue Carnot at the south-western corner of the Place de l'Indépendance. It has copies of the *International Herald Tribune*, *Time* and other magazines and a big library of books in English. It's open weekdays from 8 am to 6 pm; closed for lunch. The French Cultural Centre is five blocks west on the corner of Rue Carnot and Rue Gomis. Both show films. The British-Senegalese Institute, which also has a library, is at 18 Rue 18 Juin, two blocks west of Place de Soweto. They show one film per week, on Wednesday and Friday evenings. Entrance is free.

Travel Agencies Most airlines have offices in central Dakar, and it's best to use them for reconfirming onward or return flights. If you're looking for a ticket home, or elsewhere in Africa, using a travel agency can save you a lot of shopping around, and maybe even some money.

Senegal Tours (☎ 23 31 81, fax 23 26 44) at 5 Place de l'Indépendance, is the agent for American Express. They can make flight reservations and also offer a range of in-country tours. Another first-rate travel agency is Socopao-Voyages (☎ 23 94 16), which is nearby at 51 Ave Albert Sarraut. Socopao is the representative for Diners Club and is open weekdays to 6 pm and Saturdays to noon. Also recommended are M'boup Voyages (☎ 21 18 63) on Place de l'Indépendance near the banks, where the staff speak English, and Travel Booking (☎ 21 39 35 or 22 14 93) just off the Place, near the Hôtel de l'Indépendance. Both have their own reservation terminals. Nouvelles Frontières (☎ 23 34 34), on Ave Pompidou, up a small alley near the Ali Baba snack bar, sometimes has relatively cheap seats available on charter flights back to Europe.

Bookshops Librairie Clairafrique, at the northern end of Place de l'Indépendance, and Librairie aux Quatres Vents on Rue Félix Faure (between Rue Gomis and Rue Blanchot) both have a very wide range of books and magazines (few in English) and also sell maps of Dakar and Senegal (sometimes Guinea-Bissau and Mauritania maps too). The more detailed IGN maps of various areas of the country are only available from the Service Géographique National (☎ 32 11 81), outside the city centre in the Hann area, about one km off the autoroute.

Supermarkets Dakar has three excellent supermarkets in the centre: Le Supermarché just north of the Place, Score on Ave Albert Sarraut, two blocks east of the Place, and Ranch Filfili at 18 Blvd de la République. All are open Monday to Saturday from around 8.30 am until 12.30 pm, and 3 to 7.30 pm. Fruit and vegetable vendors sell their produce outside.

SENEGAL

SENEGAL

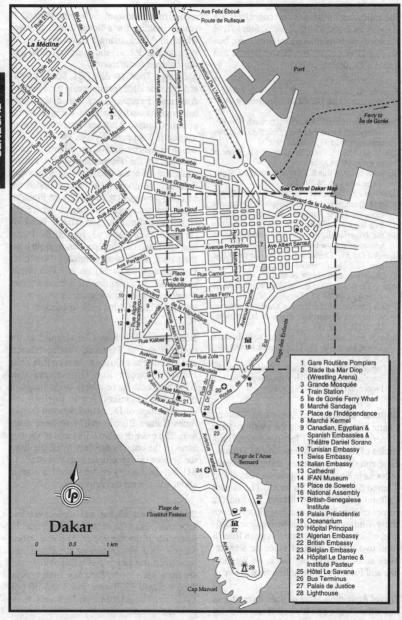

Ave Felix Éboué
Route de Rufisque

La Médina

Port

Ferry to
Île de Gorée

See Central Dakar Map

Boulevard de la Libération

Place de la République

Plage des Enfants

Plage de l'Anse Bernard

Plage de l'Institut Pasteur

Dakar

0   0.5   1 km

Cap Manuel

1 Gare Routière Pompiers
2 Stade Iba Mar Diop
   (Wrestling Arena)
3 Grande Mosquée
4 Train Station
5 Île de Gorée Ferry Wharf
6 Marché Sandaga
7 Place de l'Indépendance
8 Marché Kermel
9 Canadian, Egyptian &
   Spanish Embassies &
   Théâtre Daniel Sorano
10 Tunisian Embassy
11 Swiss Embassy
12 Italian Embassy
13 Cathedral
14 IFAN Museum
15 Place de Soweto
16 National Assembly
17 British-Senegalese
   Institute
18 Palais Présidentiel
19 Oceanarium
20 Hôpital Principal
21 Algerian Embassy
22 British Embassy
23 Belgian Embassy
24 Hôpital Le Dantec &
   Institute Pasteur
25 Hôtel Le Savana
26 Bus Terminus
27 Palais de Justice
28 Lighthouse

IFAN Museum

The Museum of the Institut Fondamental d'Afrique Noir (☎ 21 40 15) on Place de Soweto was renovated in 1994. It's one of the best in West Africa and testimony to former president Senghor's interest in promoting African art and culture. Displays include masks and statues from the whole region (including Mali, Guinea-Bissau, Benin and Nigeria), and provide an excellent overview of styles. You can also see drums, musical instruments, stools and agricultural tools. Open daily from 8 am to 12.30 pm and 2 to 6.30 pm; the entry fee is CFA 200.

Things to See & Do

Dakar's two major markets, **Marché Sandaga** and **Marché Kermel**, are very lively. Marché Sandaga is built in an interesting style; Marché Kermel burnt down in 1993 and only the stalls of merchandise can be seen here (see Things to Buy, later).

The handsome white **Palais Présidentiel**, five short blocks south of the Place along Ave Roume, dates from 1906 and is surrounded by sumptuous gardens. The Buckingham Palace-style guards outside add to its interest. Four blocks west of the Palais Présidentiel is the **cathedral**, open daily, but it is nothing special architecturally. More interesting is the marvellous old **train station**, several blocks north of the Place.

A visit to **Le Village Artisanal** and the nearby fishing village of **Soumbédioune** is good in the late afternoon, when fishing boats return. It can be followed by a stroll along the **corniche** in the direction of the university.

Also out of the city centre is the **Grande Mosquée** (built in 1964) with its landmark minaret that is floodlit at night. The mosque is closed to the public, but it's worth coming here anyway because the area around it, called **La Médina**, while not picturesque, is a lively bustling place contrasting sharply with the sophisticated high-rise city centre.

At the heart of La Médina is **Marché de Tilène**, crowded with the sights and sounds of a traditional African market, and relatively free of tourists (and thieves). The original market hall, built in the colonial days when

La Médina was created as a 'township' for Africans, is interesting but hard to find among the modern sprawl of tin-roofed shops and houses.

Another hassle-free market is in the residential suburb of Castors, on the northern side of the city, about halfway between the centre and the airport. Many of the city buses terminate just west of here.

Beaches

The most popular beach near the city centre is Plage Bel-Air (or Tahiti Plage), two km northeast of the train station. It has a bar and sailboards and catamarans for rent; entry costs CFA 300. Unfortunately the water is not particularly clean. La Plage des Enfants is a more secluded beach down the steep cliff from the Petite Corniche, east of Hôtel Lagon II, but you run a high risk of being robbed here, as you do at the tiny Plage de l'Anse Bernard, just before the Hôtel Le Savana. If you go out along Corniche-Ouest you'll pass two small beaches in Fann, just before the university, and Plage d'Ouakam further out.

One of greater Dakar's biggest attractions is the beach at N'Gor, 13 km from the centre, and the nearby Pointe des Almadies, the westernmost point on the African continent. There is a row of excellent restaurants at Almadies, but the beach is rocky, windy and unsuitable for swimming, so everybody heads to the sheltered beach at N'Gor, just west of the old Meridien hotel. There are more restaurants in this area too, and on weekends half of Dakar seems to be here.

For CFA 500 for the round trip, you can hire one of the many pirogues stationed on the beach to take you over to the beach on nearby Île de N'Gor. The ride takes five minutes and you pay on return. A walk through the narrow streets of the island can be interesting, and snacks and drinks are available, but the beach is just as crowded as the mainland beaches on weekends. During the week, however, it may be possible to rent one of the many rustic weekender huts on the island.

For a more secluded beach, continue eastward for several km, past the turn-off to the airport, to the fishing village of Yoff; long

SENEGAL

stretches of sandy beaches begin there. There's also a cheap campement (see Places to Stay).

Activities

Water Sports All the top-end hotels except the Lagon II have pools. The Savana has a superb, Olympic-size pool and charges CFA 3700 to use it. The pool on top of the Indépendance is not as nice but you can swim there for free if you have a drink plus you get a great view of Dakar from up high.

You can rent a sailboard at Plage Bel-Air or Restaurant Lagon I, 300 metres south of the Place, which also offers water-skiing. You could also splurge and go to the Club Med. You can spend the day there for about CFA 12,500, which includes lunch and use of most of their sports facilities; no reservation is required.

The Kayak Club of Dakar has monthly trips on rivers and the coast around Senegal. Contact Bruno at the Orisha souvenir shop (☎ 22 56 09) on the corner of Rue Assane Ndoye and Rue Mohamed V.

Scuba Diving Along with Sierra Leone, the coast off the Pointe des Almadies offers the

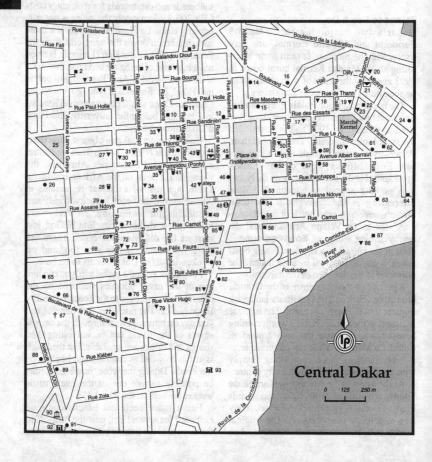

Central Dakar

0   125   250 m

best scuba diving (*plongée sous-marine*) along the West African coast. Around Île de N'Gor, there are protected places where the water is fairly clear with lots of interesting fish. Other popular spots are in the Almadies area and around Île de Gorée, but talk with other divers as there are strong currents and undertows in these areas. The waters are clearer from February to April.

Oceanarium on the Corniche-Est rents equipment (closed Mondays). They also organise diving days graded according to ability. To get there from the Place, go south on Ave Roume to just past the Palais Présidentiel, then left towards the water for a short distance.

Jogging Because Dakar is cool by African standards, you'll see more joggers here than anywhere else in West Africa. The favourite route is along the Corniche-Ouest leading north towards the university.

SENEGAL

PLACES TO STAY	32	Chawarma La Brioche	44	Small Post Office
		& Cinéma Plaza	46	Sabena, M'boup
1 Hôtel Le Grasland	33	Restaurant Keur N'deye		Voyages & CBAO
2 Hôtel Mon Logis	34	Restaurant Chez		Bank
5 Hôtel des Princes		Loutcha	47	Citibank, Aeroflot &
6 Hôtel Al Baraka	35	Ali Baba Snack Bar		Travel Booking
7 Hôtel Continental	37	Sam-Son &	48	BICIS Bank
Annexe		Restaurant '?' 2	52	Socopao-Voyages &
9 Hôtel Continental	40	Café de Paris		Air France
10 Hôtel Farid	42	Restaurant Chez	53	Senegal Tours
13 Hôtel Provençal		Nanette		(Amex Agent)
20 Hôtel du Midi	50	Restaurant La Pergola	54	Air Afrique
22 Hôtel Oceanic	60	Restaurant Le Sarraut	55	Cinéma Le Paris
29 Hôtel Ganalé &		& Le Café Théâtre	57	Air Senegal & Air
Restaurant '?' 1		du Kermel		Bissau
45 Hôtel de	69	Le Hanoi	58	Score Supermarket
l'Indépendance	72	Touba Restaurant	59	Safari-Evasion (Tours)
49 Hôtel Nina	73	Gargotte Diarama	61	Côte d'Ivoire Embassy
51 Hôtel Croix du Sud	79	Le Bambou	63	French Embassy
56 Hôtel Teranga (Sofitel)	81	Restaurant Le	66	Malian & Egyptian
62 Hôtel du Marché		Bilboquet		Embassies
64 Novotel	86	Restaurant-Bar Lagon I	67	Cathedral
65 Hôtel du Plateau			70	Black & White
68 Hôtel St-Louis Sun	**OTHER**			Nightclub & Le
75 Hôtel l'Auberge Rouge				Marseille Nightclub
84 Hôtel Le Miramar	11	Chez Vous Nightclub	71	French Cultural Centre
87 Hôtel Lagon II	12	Librairie Clairafrique	74	Librairie aux Quatres
		(Bookshop)		Vents (Bookshop)
PLACES TO EAT	14	Inter Tourisme (Tours)	76	King's Club
	15	Dakar Autotours	77	Metropolis Club
3 La Pizzalina	16	Austrian & Japanese	78	Ranch Filfili
4 La Pizzeria		Embassies		Supermarket
8 Touba Restaurant	21	Main Post Office	80	Keur Samba Jazz
(formerly Chez		(Poste Restante)		Nightclub
Ousmane)	24	Cape Verde Embassy	82	Nigeria Airways
17 Restaurant Darou	25	Marché Sandaga	83	Ethiopian Airlines
Salam	26	Air Guinée	85	American Cultural
18 Le Tricontin Snacks	28	Le Pacific Nightclub		Centre
19 Restaurant Angkor	36	Orisha & Other Art	88	US Embassy
23 Le Dagorne		Shops	89	The Netherlands
27 New James Restaurant	38	Chez Claudette		Embassy
& Africa Star		Nightclub	90	IFAN Museum
Restaurant	39	The Gambia Embassy	91	Place de Soweto
30 Le Plaza	41	Bar Ponty	92	National Assembly
31 Mateo Pizza	43	Sene Keur Nightclub	93	Palais Présidentiel

Tennis & Squash Most of the major hotels have tennis courts which nonguests can usually pay to use. The best players are at the Cercle de l'Union (☎ 22 24 41), a private club near the Oceanarium, a five-minute walk from Hôtel Teranga. You'll also find squash courts there. You may be able to arrange an out-of-hours lesson with the squash pro for about CFA 1200.

Places to Stay – bottom end

All hotels in Dakar are expensive compared to most other capital cities in Africa. Dakar is also no place to be searching the streets with a rucksack on your back, especially after dark. If you find a room anywhere near your budget, take it for one night, and look for something cheaper the next day.

Cheapest in the city centre is the *Hôtel Mon Logis* (☎ 21 85 25) on Ave Lamine Gueye, between Rue Bourgi and Rue Galandou Diouf, which charges CFA 5000 for grubby rooms with trickling showers and none-too-clean toilets. It's down an alley, upstairs and unmarked. Some of the rooms get very active at night, and the walls are wafer thin. Next in line is the *Hôtel des Princes* (☎ 21 18 55) at 49 Rue Raffenal, three blocks north of Ave Pompidou, another brothel, where rooms are just about OK but the bathrooms are disgusting by any standard and there's never any water. The cost is CFA 6000. Both these hotels are in a part of town which is dark and not the safest at night.

Much better is the *Hôtel Provençal* (☎ 22 10 69), near the Place de l'Indépendance at 19 Rue Malenfant. Very clean singles/doubles with fans cost CFA 8500/9500. The showers and toilets are also cleaned daily. Try and get an upstairs room; they are quiet, airy and have washbasins. Part of the hotel downstairs becomes a brothel at night but it's fairly low-key. The hotel sells cold drinks, and nearby stalls sell snacks and coffee. (Avoid the bread stall opposite the hotel which overcharges tourists.)

Also good is the *Hôtel du Marché* (☎ 21 57 71) at 3 Rue Parent, near Marché Kermel. It charges CFA 6250 for a room (CFA 7500 with private bathroom), plus CFA 500 tax per

person and CFA 625 for a good breakfast. The rooms are not the cleanest and don't have fans but there's a lovely patio at the back and the staff are friendly. Or try the *Hôtel Le Grasland* (☎ 22 55 22) at 34 Rue Raffenal, six blocks north of Ave Pompidou, with clean quiet singles/doubles for CFA 7500/9350. The area is not the safest, but the hotel has good security.

A popular choice is *Hôtel l'Auberge Rouge* (☎ 21 72 56), on the corner of Rue Blanchot and Rue Jules Ferry, with clean rooms for CFA 8700 including breakfast. Another good deal in this range is the *Hôtel du Midi*, opposite the main post office on Blvd el Haji Djily Mbaye, with clean self-contained air-con doubles for CFA 8700.

Outside the centre, near the airport in Yoff village, and only 100 metres from a beach, is the pleasant *Campement le Poulagou* (☎ 20 23 47) which charges CFA 6000 per person in double or triple rooms including breakfast, or CFA 14,000 for full board. If you fly in to Dakar and phone from the airport, the owner will come and pick you up. To get there from the city centre take SOTRAC bus No 7 or 8 and get off in Yoff. The campement is at the end of a small street off the main road. Look for a sign marked 'Menuiserie Metallique Yoff Tonghor'. In the same area, on Route du Cimetière, is the *Campement Adama Diop* (☎ 20 13 67) with simple rooms for CFA 3100 per person.

Even further out of town is the *Campement Touristique de Malika Peul* near the outer suburb of Malika-sur-Mer, about 20 km from Dakar centre. This campement is rated highly by travellers with their own vehicle, and by anyone else who wants to escape the city and spend some time on the huge unspoilt beach. Basic huts cost CFA 3750, and meals are available (around CFA 1250), although there are shops and stalls near the Malika bus terminus (see below) if you want to self-cater. To get here take SOTRAC bus No 21 (marked Malika or Keur Massa) to the terminus. Directly opposite the terminus a sandy street heads towards the ocean (look for the small sign to the campement): it's a 30-minute walk through sand dunes and forest. When groups stay at the campement, local musicians (or even members of the National Ballet) sometimes perform or hold workshops. If you want to learn how to drum or play the kora here, a teacher can be arranged for around CFA 2500 per three-hour session.

If you'll be in Dakar for a week or more, consider getting a room on Île de Gorée, thus avoiding the hassles and high prices of Dakar. Or, if you prefer being near a beach, try renting a small weekender cottage on Île de N'Gor. After some bargaining you should be able to get one for between CFA 3750 and CFA 7500, depending on the facilities.

Places to Stay – middle
All hotels in this range have self-contained rooms and all prices include tax.

The *Hôtel Oceanic* (☎ 22 20 44) is the cheapest in this range, a simple and pleasant old-style hotel at 9 Rue de Thann, a block north of Marché Kermel. It charges CFA 10,400/12,800 for air-con singles/doubles plus CFA 1000 for breakfast, or CFA 1375 if you have croissants. To the north of the Place, at 10 Rue Galandou Diouf, the decent *Hôtel Continental* (☎ 22 38 77) charges CFA 10,000/11,800 for air-con rooms, plus CFA 625 for breakfast. If it's full, try the hotel's annexe (☎ 22 03 71) two blocks west at 57 Rue Blanchot, with rooms at the same rate. Up a notch is the *Hôtel Farid* (☎ 21 61 27), nearby at 51 Rue Vincens, where air-con rooms with reliable hot showers cost CFA 13,000/16,000. In the same area, a few blocks further away from the Place, is the *Hôtel Al Baraka* (☎ 22 55 32, telex 21428) at 35 Rue Bourgi, where rooms with TVs and large bathrooms cost CFA 15,500/18,500. (All the above hotels are in the part of town which is dark and not the safest at night although, to keep things in perspective, you have to be careful everywhere in central Dakar.)

On the other side of town, *Hôtel du Plateau* (☎ 23 15 26/44 20, fax 22 50 24; cards AE, CB) at 62 Rue Jules Ferry, is recommended for its relatively low price, although it's not very clean, with large singles/doubles for CFA 14,250/17,250. Nearby, at 68 Rue Félix Faure is the *Hôtel St-Louis Sun* (☎ 22 25 70) with pleasant rooms at CFA 14,300/17,500 including breakfast. For slightly more you can stay at the modern *Hôtel Le Miramar* (☎ 23 55 98, fax 12 35 05) at 25 Rue Félix Faure, just 100 metres south of the Place, where self-contained air-con rooms with hot showers and TVs with video cost CFA 15,800/20,800 including breakfast. It also has four single rooms (without TVs) for only CFA 11,250, but they're not well publicised. Calmer is the *Hôtel Nina* (☎ 21 22 30, telex 3015; cards AE, D, V, MC) near the Place at 43 Rue du Dr Thèze, where small air-con rooms with TV cost CFA 16,750/18,500, including a good breakfast. In the same area and best value in this price range is the swish new *Hôtel Ganalé* (☎ 21 55 70, fax 22 34 30) at 38 Rue Assane Ndoye with rooms at CFA 16,100/18,500 and breakfast for CFA 1500.

For a place near the beach, try *Club Le Kalao* (☎ 20 05 40) next to the old Meridien at N'Gor, some 10 km west of the city centre. Thatched bungalows cost CFA 17,500. Facilities include a restaurant (CFA 5000 for the menu) and a swimming pool.

Places to Stay – top end
Cheapest is the tall *Hôtel de l'Indépendance*, a poorly managed, overpriced hotel right on the Place de l'Indépendance. The pool on the roof is its only plus and you don't have to stay there to use it, although it costs CFA 1250 for a swim, and almost as much for a beer. A much better deal is the futuristic *Hôtel Lagon II*, 400 metres from the Place perched on stilts at the edge of the ocean. It's well managed and half the price of some other hotels in this range, with excellent rooms and one of the best (but most expensive) restaurants in town. Also in the centre, and another good deal, is the old-style *Hôtel Croix du Sud* at 20 Ave Albert Sarraut, a block east of the Place, also well managed with a pleasant French ambience and an excellent restaurant.

Sofitel's 264-room *Hôtel Teranga* is a favourite with the tour groups. It's also the most centrally located, at one end of the Place de l'Indépendance. The *Novotel*, five blocks east of the Place, is modern and not particularly interesting but just as expensive.

If price is of no concern, go to the new *Hôtel Le Savana*, part of the Pullman chain, which now receives the most accolades. Two km south of the city centre, it's a 100-room low-rise hotel with a beautiful setting on a cliff overlooking the ocean, an Olympic-size pool and many other amenities.

In the N'Gor area you have several more choices. Absolute top of them all is the exceedingly plush *Meridien President* near Pointe des Almadies, which provides every facility (including its own heliport) and charges to match. Close nearby is the action-packed, architecturally striking *Club Med Les Almadies* which is mainly for package tourists but accepts independent visitors for a few nights whenever one of its 300 rooms is available. A few km to the east is the 'old' high-rise *Meridien N'Gor* and the smaller, less expensive *Meridien Diarama*. Both are popular with beach-lovers, have magnificent ocean views and are noted for their sports activities. Meals are OK but expensive.

Hôtel de l'Indépendance (☎ 23 10 19, fax 22 11 17), CFA 28,000/32,500, pool, cards AE, D.

Lagon II (☎ 23 60 31/74 42, fax 23 77 27), rooms CFA 35,000, car hire, sailboards, cards AE, D, V, MC.

Hôtel Croix du Sud (☎ 23 24 10/29 47, fax 23 26 55), rooms CFA 22,500 (CFA 20,000 low season), cards AE, D, V.

Teranga Sofitel (☎ 23 10 44, fax 23 50 51), CFA 43,000 for rooms, long pool, tennis, sauna, car hire, shops, nightclub, cards AE, D, V, MC.

Novotel Dakar (☎ 23 88 49/78 72, fax 23 89 29), rooms CFA 33,700, pool, tennis, car hire, cards AE, D, V, MC.

Hôtel Le Savana (☎ 23 60 23/56 36, fax 23 85 86), CFA 51,000/56,000, pool, tennis, nightclub, sailboards, sauna, gym, cards AE, D, V, MC.

Meridien President (☎ 20 21 22, fax 20 30 30), rooms CFA 62,500, suites CFA 125,000, car hire, conference centre, all facilities, cards D, AE, V, MC.

Meridien N'Gor & Diarama (☎ 23 10 05) CFA 37,500/41,000 at the N'Gor, CFA 31,000/33,700 at the Diarama, pool, tennis, sailboards, sailboats, horse riding, mini-golf, shops, nightclub, casino nearby, car hire, cards AE, D, V, MC.

Club Med Les Almadies (☎ 20 09 21), about CFA 47,500 a person, pool, tennis, sailboards etc, cards AE.

Places to Eat – cheap

For street food, try the stalls near the train station. You can get cheap breakfasts of coffee and bread, or beef brochettes. On many street corners there are stalls selling bread with fillings of butter, chocolate spread, mayonnaise or sardines. Next to some of these, particularly along Rue Assane Ndoye, you'll find women cooking rice and sauce in big pots, and serving hot filling meals for around CFA 300. Most of these places are closed by mid-afternoon though.

Cheap food is also available in Dakar's main supermarkets, but the various imported luxuries can be tempting! Fresh fruit and veg can be bought from traders outside the supermarkets and at Marché Kermel and Marché Sandaga. You can buy soft drinks for CFA 150 from the trolleys that ply the streets, compared to CFA 300 in a basic café.

One of Dakar city centre's cheapest restaurants is the hole-in-the-wall *Gargotte Diarama*, at 56 Rue Félix Faure, with most dishes at CFA 400. *Touba Restaurant*, just around the corner on Rue Gomis, has simple meals like mafé, poisson riz or chicken from CFA 400 to CFA 750. Both places are popular, especially for lunch, reasonably clean and offer large servings. Touba is also open late in the evening. There's another *Touba Restaurant* (formerly *Chez Ousmane*) 4½ blocks north of Ave Pompidou on Rue Wagane Diouf with similar prices, also open evenings, although by then the many lunchtime selections have usually dwindled.

Lebanese chawarma sandwiches make a filling meal and are sold throughout the city for CFA 625. Many travellers' favourite is *Chawarma La Brioche*, on Ave Pompidou, four blocks west of the Place. You can also get filling Lebanese meals here, mostly in the CFA 1250 to CFA 2500 range. At *Ali Baba* snack bar across the street the chawarmas are just as good, but you pay a bit extra for the more classy surroundings. Ali Baba and the nearby *Mic Mac* also serve good hamburgers for CFA 800 to CFA 1000, chips for CFA 400 and several other types of junk food. *Le Tricontin Snacks* on Rue de Thann, a block north-east of Marché Kermel, is similar.

For African food in pleasant surroundings, the best value in this range is *Restaurant '?'* (☎ 22 50 72) on Rue Assane Ndoye, just west of Rue Gomis. The owner has a second restaurant with the same weird name (ask for 'Restaurant Point d'Interrogation') two blocks east on the corner of Rue Assane Ndoye and Rue Mohamed V. These places are clean and friendly, with filling African dishes such as poulet or poisson yassa in the CFA 850 to CFA 1100 range. However, the quality seems to vary according to who's on duty in the kitchen.

Also good value is *Restaurant Darou Salam* on Rue des Essarts, two blocks east of the Place, where filling African meals cost around CFA 750. It's very popular at lunchtime and closed in the evenings.

Places to Eat – more expensive

African Dakar's fanciest African restaurant is *Keur Samba* (☎ 21 60 45), on Rue Jules Ferry, just west of Ave Roume. The quality of the Senegalese food is OK but what's special is the jazz played here.

More reasonably priced, and highly recommended, is *Keur N'Deye* (☎ 21 49 73) at 68 Rue Vincens, two blocks north of Ave Pompidou. Open every day, it offers about six well-prepared Senegalese specialities, including mafé for CFA 1800, grillades for about CFA 2000 and vegetarian dishes. Drinks are expensive (CFA 750 for a small beer), as is the set menu (CFA 4000).

The friendly and popular *Restaurant Chez Loutcha* (☎ 21 03 02) is at 101 Rue Blanchot, one block south of Ave Pompidou. Cape Verdean food is the speciality and 'cuisine Euro-Africaine' is also available. Servings are large, as is the menu, with most dishes around CFA 2500. (Closed Sundays, air-con.) Just down the street is *Chez Maty* offering the same type of food at cheaper prices.

La Pergola (☎ 21 29 14), just off the Place on Rue Le Dantec, specialises in French-Senegalese dishes ranging from CFA 1000 to CFA 2500.

Out of town, at N'Gor beach, try *Baye Mbarrick* (closed Monday), which has a

rustic outdoor setting, strolling kora players and both Senegalese cuisine and seafood.

Italian One of Dakar's most popular moderately priced restaurants, with excellent pizza and other Italian fare, is *La Pizzeria* (☎ 21 09 26) at 47 Rue Bourgi, just west of Rue Raffenal. It's open 24 hours; half/whole pizzas cost CFA 2300/3600. The ambience is better here than at *La Pizzalina* across the street, which has similar prices. You can also get good Italian cuisine in *Le Plaza* (☎ 22 27 68) at 71 Rue Raffenal; its prices, however, are slightly higher (closed Sundays). Another fairly expensive but reputed Italian restaurant is *La Trastevère* (☎ 21 49 20) at 26 Rue Mohamed V on the corner of Rue Carnot (closed Mondays).

French All the top-end hotels serve French dishes in their restaurants, and Dakar also has a wide choice of bars, bistros and cafés doing French food. Two restaurants which offer some of the best value in Dakar are *Le Dagorne* (☎ 22 20 80) at 11 Rue Dagorne, half a block north-east of Marché Kermel, with a bustling, energetic atmosphere, and *Le Bilboquet* at 19 Ave Roume, two blocks south of the Place. A four-course meal at the Bilboquet will cost around CFA 4300 (closed Sundays), while the Dagorne, which is open every day, has a superb menu with many tempting choices, all well-prepared, for CFA 5000 plus 20% tax. Also worth trying is *Restaurant Le Sarraut*, east of the Place on Ave Albert Sarraut, with a CFA 4300 three-course menu.

If money is not a concern, *Le Bambou* (☎ 22 06 45) at 19 Rue Victor Hugo, east of the cathedral, gets top marks for its French and Italian food and good service. It's open for lunch and dinner weekdays and for dinner on weekends.

Out of town, in the N'Gor area, head for *Ramatou* (☎ 20 03 40) on Route de N'Gor. Dishes are around CFA 3750, and there's a choice of menus from CFA 3750 to CFA 5600. (Closed Wednesdays.)

Seafood In central Dakar, three good choices are *Lagon I*, a five-minute walk down from the Teranga, the restaurant at the

SENEGAL

Hôtel Croix du Sud, a block off the Place, and the less expensive *Embarcadero de la Chaloupe*, at the Île de Gorée ferry wharf. The Chaloupe is very popular at lunchtime, with prices from around CFA 2500. At night Lagon I is the more popular because it overlooks the ocean. Best of all is *Le Terrou Bi* (☎ 22 06 99) on the Corniche-Ouest facing Camp Claudel, with a lovely setting.

Most other restaurants known for serving good seafood are at Les Almadies and N'Gor. The cheapest ones are all in a row on the beach near the 'old' Meridien N'Gor. With basic surroundings they have various seafood dishes in the CFA 1250 to CFA 2000 range. Moving up-market, try the nearby *La Madrague* (☎ 20 02 23), open every day, with superb service and a roaring fire in the winter. At Almadies beach, if you want lobster, head for the *La Pointe des Almadies* (☎ 20 01 40). It is the first in the row of restaurants there and offers the best value with dishes (also including steaks and Vietnamese food) in the CFA 2500 to CFA 6200 range (closed Thursdays). On Saturday and Sunday evenings reservations are recommended. For a greater seafood selection and a terrace setting, try the moderately priced *L'Armatan* (☎ 20 05 55) next door (open to midnight; closed Mondays).

Another out-of-town option is *Le Chevalier de Boufflers* (☎ 22 53 64) on Île de Gorée, which has a terrace overlooking the harbour and the most romantic setting, with meals around CFA 2500 and a three-course menu for CFA 4800.

Asian Dakar has a number of moderately priced Asian restaurants. The most colourful is the Chinese *Restaurant Angkor* on Rue Dagorne near Marché Kermel (closed Sundays). Dishes are in the CFA 2000 to CFA 4000 range. For Vietnamese food try *Tonkinoise* (☎ 21 05 82) at 62 Ave Albert Sarraut (closed Tuesdays), *Le Sam-Son* (☎ 21 48 14) at 61 Rue Assane Ndoye, three blocks west of the Place (closed Thursdays) or *Le Hanoi* (☎ 21 32 69) two blocks further west on the corner of Rue Carnot and Rue Gomis, where most dishes are in the CFA 2700 to CFA 3600

range. The Sam-Son has a small but tasty three-course menu for CFA 3600. Another place to try is the *Hong Kong*, near the Île de Gorée ferry wharf, which has Chinese and Vietnamese dishes in the CFA 3000 to CFA 4500 range and takeaways for less.

In the Almadies area, *La Pointe des Almadies* (☎ 20 01 40) has been one of the most popular restaurants for years and is highly recommended but it's more expensive than the others with meals in the CFA 2500 to CFA 6500 range.

Miscellaneous The best Lebanese fare is served at *Hôtel Farid*. Most dishes cost between CFA 2500 and CFA 4000 (closed Wednesdays). You can get a good home-style Portuguese meal at *Restaurant Chez Nanette* on Rue du Dr Thèze, just south of Pompidou. A three-course meal costs CFA 2500.

For a splurge, the all-you-can-eat breakfast buffet at the *Teranga* has been recommended; it costs CFA 4300.

Pastry Shops Dakar has some excellent French-style pastry shops including: *Le Pompidou* on Ave Pompidou, four blocks west of the Place; *La Palmeraie N'Diogonal* nearby at 20 Ave Pompidou; *Gentina* at 22 Ave Albert Sarraut; *La Marquise* on Rue du Dr Thèze near the Hôtel Nina; and *Laeticia* on Blvd de la République opposite the cathedral. All these places are also have ice cream, coffee, crêpes, sandwiches and snacks. Most open for breakfast and close around 7.30 pm. (Le Pompidou closes at 11 pm.)

Entertainment

Bars The best known watering hole in town is the *Bar Ponty* on Ave Pompidou, three blocks west of the Place, which manages to be smart and slightly disreputable at the same time. It's a pick-up joint but the atmosphere is not at all heavy. If you can afford a beer (small Flag for CFA 875), it's worth sampling. (Decent meals here start at CFA 2500.) On the opposite side of the street is the *Café de Paris* which is similar in all respects.

For a taste of lowlife, visit the *Bar Gorée*, almost opposite the Gorée ferry wharf, which has cheap beer (CFA 500 for a small

Flag), snacks and music. This large outdoor place, which often has a band at night, is great for dancing and is popular with seamen, Peace Corps volunteers, and anybody looking for a good time without busting the bank.

Bar Fouquets, on the ground floor of the large pink Immeuble Maginot building opposite the cathedral, has a nice patio garden, and with a beer you get jazz music and snacks thrown in for free. The nearby *Bar Colisée 9*, a few blocks up Ave Lamine Gueye, is popular for after-work drinks but not particularly cheap.

If you want to feel like you're on a cruise ship, the bar at the *Hôtel Lagon II* has professional bartenders and magnificent ocean views, but a piña colada will set you back CFA 3100. There's nothing professional about the *Hôtel de l'Indépendance*, and the drinks are pricey too, but the roof-top bar has a spectacular view of the city at sunset.

Nightclubs Dakar is one of the best cities in West Africa for live music. There are a number of clubs where Senegalese bands perform on weekends. The only one in the heart of town is *Keur Samba* (☎ 21 60 45) at 13 Rue Jules Ferry. A favourite with the Senegalese jet set, it's a small posh jazz club. The most popular place, however, is the flashy *Club Kilimanjaro* (☎ 21 62 55) on the Corniche-Ouest by Le Village Artisanal. Celebrities such as the legendary Youssou N'dour occasionally perform at this hot and crowded place and at the less refined *Club Thiossane* (☎ 24 35 10) on Rue Coulibaly, roughly four km north of Marché Sandaga.

The *Tamango Bar* in the Point E area has good live jazz on Wednesdays, Thursdays and Fridays: it's free to get in but beers are pricey. Check the papers and entertainment guides or call the clubs to see whether a band is playing. If a star is performing, expect to pay about CFA 3100 at the door and about the same for drinks; and don't expect the music to start before midnight.

Reputable discos include the posh *Play Club* at 46 Rue Jules Ferry. Nearby, at 32 Rue Victor Hugo, is the equally fancy *King's Club*. Other possibilities include *The Metropolis Club* nearby on Blvd de la République, *Sene Keur* on Rue du Dr Thèze, two blocks behind Hôtel de l'Indépendance, and the slightly cheaper *La Plantation* a block away on Rue Wagane Diouf. The best, however, is *Le Sahel* out near the Hyperscore supermarket, about three km north-west of Marché Sandaga. For a place of this sort, expect to pay a cover charge of around CFA 4000; this always includes the first drink. No one goes before 11 pm at the earliest.

Most of the big hotels have nightclubs. In the centre these include *Le Mandingo* at the Teranga. In the N'Gor area, the Meridien has a club, or for CFA 12,500 you can go to the nearby *Club Med* from 5 pm to the wee hours of the morning. The price includes dinner, a show and the disco, and no reservation is required. In the same area the *Casino du Cap Vert* (☎ 20 09 74) has a floor show as well as gaming tables, and is open every night.

Theatres There are many cultural events at the Théâtre Daniel Sorano (☎ 21 31 04) on Blvd de la République but they are seldom well publicised. Check the posters outside and at the box office. The Ensemble Instrumental, the Ballet National du Sénégal, the Mudra Dance Group and the Théâtre National du Sénégal perform here on occasion. Also watch for the Semaines Culturelles when there are presentations by other African countries. The Centre Culturel Blaise Senghor at Place de l'ONU has frequent exhibitions and presentations.

Cinemas Dakar has several clean and comfortable cinemas, including Le Vog and Le Plaza, both on Ave Pompidou, and the more expensive Le Paris next to the Hôtel Teranga. New movies arrive in Dakar fairly quickly; consult *Le Soleil* or one of the listings mags for what's showing. Prices are between CFA 750 and CFA 1000 in the afternoon and CFA 250 higher at night. Movies in English are dubbed into French. The British-Senegalese Institute shows films in English.

Wrestling Watching a traditional Senegalese wrestling match *(les luttes)* is a potential highlight of any trip to Dakar. There are usually many matches as they last only a few minutes until one contestant forces the other to the ground (technically one knee touching the ground ends the match). Every section of town has its heroes. The arena *(l'arène)* is in Le Médina at the large Stade Iba Mar Diop on Ave Blaise Diagne. Most matches are announced only on the radio, so it can be a problem finding out when they are held. Saturdays and/or Sundays are the usual days, starting around 4.30 or 5 pm. Matches can be held any time of year, but wrestling activity goes into high gear during the dry season starting around October.

Music Lessons For kora lessons, try the Conservatoire de Musique (☎ 21 25 11) on Ave Faidherbe, or the Campement Touristique de Malika Peul. A good place to learn drumming is on Île de Gorée.

Things to Buy

Market Goods The city's two main markets are Marché Kermel, four blocks east of the Place towards the port, and Marché Sandaga, seven blocks west of the Place on the junction of Aves Pompidou and Lamine Gueye. At Marché Kermel, also known as the European market, all the stalls are out in the surrounding streets, selling mainly clothing, fabrics and souvenirs. There are also several flower and fruit sellers.

At the larger Marché Sandaga there's more in the way of fruit and less in the way of souvenirs, but for visitors the sheer choice of fabric stalls is a real draw. Colourful baggy cotton trousers are 'in' for foreigners, especially women. You may see some ready-made for sale, but the locals prefer to pick their own fabrics and have them made up, usually within 24 hours. Beautiful cloth sold by Lebanese merchants starts at about CFA 1000 per metre; wax cloth is more expensive, especially if it's imported. Tailors are all around the market. As an example of prices, a short-sleeved shirt will cost about CFA 1800, not including the cloth. It's best to leave a model garment with your order.

Unfortunately, both markets are plagued by hustlers, offering to be your 'guide', 'assistant' or simply your 'friend'. Hiring one of these guides, however, will help minimise the hustling from other guides.

The Marché du Port, near the port on Blvd de la Libération, is very much a locals' market with little to interest most tourists. It has food, electrical goods, car spares, second-hand clothes and so on.

Artisan Goods For African art, head for the junction of Rue Assane Ndoye and Rue Mohamed V. You'll find several small shops there including Orisha at 14 Rue Mohamed V and Touba Galerie (☎ 21 32 04) across the street. These shops have lots of high-quality masks and other objects from all over West and Central Africa. Towards Ave Pompidou are several more similar shops – the nearest Dakar gets to a bazaar. Galerie Antenna at 9 Rue Félix Faure, a block west of the Teranga, is good but it's much more expensive.

For souvenir-quality crafts, most tourists head for the government-sponsored Le Village Artisanal on the Corniche-Ouest, a five-minute taxi ride from the centre. A good time to go is the late afternoon when the area next to the Artisanal, Soumbédioune village, comes alive with pirogues returning from their day's fishing. You'll find a tremendous display – wooden carvings, metal work, tablecloths, gold and silver jewellery, ivory, blankets, leather goods and dresses.

The quality at Le Village Artisanal is mediocre at best, prices are high if you don't bargain hard and long, and the vendors are aggressive – all reasons why the locals stay away – but it does give a good idea of what's available. If you don't speak French, don't worry. Chances are the vendor will whip out a pocket calculator. The game begins with the merchant typing in an outrageously high number, then you type in an outrageously low one. Play continues with his lowering and your raising until a price is finally agreed upon. Giving a defiant take-it-or-leave-it expression each time, even sticking the calculator in his face, are acceptable strategies.

However, being friendly but firm is just as effective when hunting for a bargain and a lot more enjoyable as well.

For locally woven fabrics of high quality, head for Caritas Tissage Traditional, a traditional weavers' workshop out on Ave Blaise Diagne/Route d'Ouakam, three km northwest of Marché Sandaga and four blocks beyond the Hyperscore supermarket. Skilfully woven cotton jacquards are made into tablecloths, bedspreads and smaller items, including purses. The fixed prices are high but fair for the quality. If you come here, stop at Hyperscore for a look at the artisanal goods (gold, silver, etc) sold outside.

Gold & Silver For gold and silver, the best place is La Cour des Mours, in a small alley at 69 Ave Blaise Diagne, north of Marché Sandaga. A few of the Mauritanian silversmiths who gave it its name have returned since being expelled a few years ago, and there are numerous Senegalese traders. The silver is priced by weight, typically CFA 625

Ivory

After years of witnessing the wholesale slaughter of the elephant, the world finally came to its senses in 1990. In that year almost 100 countries began honouring an international ban on ivory trade, including Australia (long before the ban), Canada, the USA, Japan and virtually all European countries, among others. The ban has been amazingly effective. Within a year, ivory prices (from US$70 to US$100 a pound before the ban) had tumbled by as much as 80%. In the USA, for example, imports have dropped to near zero and the market has virtually collapsed.

Again taking the USA as an example, under the ban it is illegal to bring ivory into the country (including elephant products gained from sport hunting), but it is not illegal to buy and sell ivory already there. Two exceptions are: antique ivory over 100 years old (significant documentary proof is required), and sport-hunted trophies, provided proper permits are obtained. The first exception makes sense; the latter does not. Violating the law can land you in jail.

The ban came none too late. During the 1980s, the African elephant declined in numbers by at least 50%, or about 80,000 annually. Most were slaughtered by poachers who were financed by intermediaries. Showing incredible loyalty and care to kin, elephants prefer to stay in groups, making them vulnerable to poachers, who pick off entire families at a time. Kenya and Uganda, for example, have lost 89% of their elephants since 1973, from about 160,000 to 17,500. In 1988, the Burundi government in a single catch uncovered 100 metric tons of illegal ivory poached from some 11,000 elephants in neighbouring countries! In some West African countries, poachers have wiped out virtually the entire elephant population. In all of West Africa's game parks and reserves, numbers probably don't exceed 2000, and may be much less. In Central Africa, there are still large herds of forest elephants in some of the most pristine jungle areas. However, the larger elephants found in the plains have been slaughtered unmercifully, particularly in Chad where they are on the verge of extinction, and in Zaïre and the Central African Republic where their numbers are a small fraction of what they were just 15 years ago.

With so many excellent substitutes for ivory, it's a wonder why it has been so difficult to wean people off ivory. Two substitutes are bone and wart-hog tusk; both age very nicely. Unfortunately, the bone is sometimes from an elephant, in which case it's just as bad.

A third substitute is plastic which is almost indistinguishable from ivory, even to experts! The only sure way to tell the difference is to put it under a flame or, better, touch it with a lighted cigarette. Plastic will melt and bone will scorch. Ivory, on the other hand, will not scorch but can be discoloured if the flame is left too long.

Finally, there's malachite jewellery from Zaïre. With the ban and all these alternatives, you shouldn't be tempted to buy ivory, although you definitely will see it still being sold all over West Africa. ■

a gram, but there's still room for minor bargaining, particularly for jewellery. Even if you're not interested in jewellery, a trip to this fascinating old district is highly recommended. You'll also find silversmiths in other parts of Dakar; there's a row of three on Rue Victor Hugo, opposite Restaurant le Bambou. For an ordinary jewellery shop near the Place with good prices, try Galeries at the Hôtel de l'Indépendance, Taj Mahal several blocks down at 18 Ave Pompidou, or Bijouterie at 7 Rue Félix Faure, a block west of the Teranga.

Clothes For ready-made African women's clothes, try Creations ADL, 69 Rue Carnot at the junction with Rue Gomis, and Gorée Boutique several blocks south at 40 Rue Victor Hugo.

Music For cheap cassettes, go to the Marché du Port on Blvd de la Libération. Or try Disco Parade (☎ 21 30 79) at 59 Ave Pompidou, Disquerie at 176 Ave Lamine Gueye and 19 Ave Albert Sarraut, Disco Club (☎ 21 53 71) at 71 Ave Peytavin or Radio Africaine at 15 Ave Jean Jaurès.

Getting There & Away
Air Air Senegal flies daily to Ziguinchor and Cap Skiring (CFA 29,500 and CFA 31,500 one way), twice weekly to Simenti (Parc National de Niokolo-Koba), and once a week to/from Tambacounda (Saturdays) for CFA 32,000. Flights to St-Louis have been discontinued. The airport tax on local flights is CFA 2500.

The following airlines have offices in Dakar:

Aeroflot Place de l'Indépendance (☎ 22 48 15)
Air Afrique Place de l'Indépendance (☎ 22 43 54 or 23 10 45)
Air Algérie Place de l'Indépendance (☎ 23 55 48)
Air Bissau 45-47 Ave Albert Sarraut (☎ 23 49 70)
Air France Ave Albert Sarraut, one block down from Place de l'Indépendance (☎ 23 29 41)
Air Guinée Ave Pompidou, south of Marché Sandaga
Air Senegal 45-47 Ave Albert Sarraut (☎ 23 49 70)
Alitalia 5 Ave Pompidou (☎ 23 3129/38 74)
American Airlines 73 Ave Peytavin (☎ 21 23 78)
Ethiopian Airlines 16 Ave Roume (☎ 21 99 13/32 98)
Iberia Place de l'Indépendance (☎ 23 34 77)
Nigeria Airways 29 Ave Roume (☎ 23 60 68)

Royal Air Maroc Place de l'Indépendance (☎ 21 37 20 or 22 32 67)
Sabena Place de l'Indépendance (☎ 23 49 71)
Swissair Immeuble (building) Faycal, Rue Parchappe (behind Air France), just off Place de l'Indépendance (☎ 23 48 48).
TACV Cape Verde 102 Rue Blanchot (☎ 21 39 68)
TAP Portugal Immeuble (building) Faycal, (☎ 21 01 13/00 65)
Tunis Air 25 Ave Roume (☎ 23 14 35)

Bush Taxi Bush taxis and minibuses for most long-distance destinations leave from Gare Routière Pompiers off Ave Malik Sy, near the end of the autoroute, three km north of the Place. To get there from Marché Sandaga, take SOTRAC city bus No 5, 6 or 18. A taxi from Marché Sandaga or the Place should cost about CFA 625.

Some sample fares for long-distance trips to/from Dakar are listed here. For Ziguinchor, Peugeot 504s charge CFA 5600 and take around eight to 10 hours. Minibuses charge CFA 3900 and take from 10 to 15 hours. There's a short ferry crossing over the Gambia River, about three hours north of Ziguinchor and six hours south of Dakar, where the wait can be anything from a few minutes to more than an hour. The ferry shuts down around 8.30 pm, so you're unlikely to find vehicles leaving for Ziguinchor after noon.

For St-Louis, minibuses/bush taxis charge CFA 2350/3000 (three to five hours), CFA 5250/5580 to Tambacounda (eight to 10 hours), CFA 2800/3250 to the Gambian border at Karang (four to eight hours), and CFA 900 to M'Bour.

If you want to take a 504, ignore the touts who tell you they've all gone and push you onto a minibus (cheaper but slower). There are *always* 504s. For bush taxis to outer suburbs and nearby destinations, go to Gare Routière Kolobane, about two km further away from the centre on the other side of the autoroute. Destinations from here include: Thiès (CFA 800) and Rufisque (CFA 375).

Train Dakar's train station is half a km north of the Place. Dakar to Tambacounda costs CFA 10,165/7455 for 1st/2nd class on the Bamako express. (For details of the train to

Bamako, see the main Getting There & Away section in this chapter.) There's also a weekly *omnibus* service which is CFA 8670/3740.

The train to St-Louis is scheduled to leave Dakar daily at 3 pm and arrive at 8 pm. From St-Louis it leaves at 7 am, arriving Dakar at noon. Fares cost CFA 3150/2100 for 1st/2nd class. The train to Kaolack leaves Dakar daily at 4.50 pm and arrives in Kaolack at 9.30 pm. It leaves Kaolack at 6 am and arrives in Dakar at 11 am. Fares cost CFA 2350/1550 for 1st/2nd class. Both trains are new, but often arrive an hour or two late.

Boat The ferry MV *Joola* sails between Dakar and Ziguinchor, twice per week in each direction, via Carabane Island. For more information see the main Getting Around section in this chapter.

Getting Around

To/From the Airport Dakar's taxis have meters but they are not used for trips to/from the airport. The official rates for taxis to the centre of Dakar are posted in the luggage reception area – CFA 3750 during the day and CFA 4350 from midnight (not before!) to 5 am. The drivers will swear to Allah that the posted rates are old (they aren't), so hard bargaining is required. From the airport you'll be doing well if you can negotiate them down to within CFA 1250 of the posted rate, but going back to the airport you can sometimes get a taxi for less than the official fare. Locals do not tip; many tourists do. If you don't have CFA (it's illegal to bring it in to Senegal from outside the CFA zone, and the airport bank is invariably closed), it's simple enough to pay for a taxi in French francs (cash): between 50 and 100FF for a ride to the city centre.

You can also get to/from the airport by bus. SOTRAC city buses No 7 or 8 go along the main highway, and stop only a few hundred metres from the terminal building. Buses do not run at night between around 9 pm and 6 am.

Facilities at the airport include a bank, car-hire desks and a post office. If you want to avoid night taxis, and are waiting at the airport until the buses start running, there's a small kiosk across the carpark from the arrivals hall, with a pharmacy nearby where some people crash out on the veranda.

Bus The cheapest way to get around Dakar is with the SOTRAC city buses, which cover not just the centre but also the areas north-west out to N'Gor and the airport, north-east to Malika and east to Rufisque. The buses show numbers and destinations clearly and stops are well marked. They cost CFA 120 for short rides, up to CFA 225 for long rides.

Many buses start their northward journeys from the terminus at the Palais de Justice, at the southern end of Ave Pasteur, passing either the Place de l'Indépendance, Marché Sandaga or both. Others start from Place du Maréchal-Leclerc, three blocks north of Marché Kermel, or from Place Lat Dior, at the western end of Ave Peytavin. Some of the major lines are:

No 2 From Place Leclerc, via the Grande Mosquée to Place de l'ONU.

No 3 From Place Leclerc, north and north-east to the suburb of Castors.

No 4 From the train station to Marché Tilène, in the Medina.

No 5 From Place Lat Dior past Marché Sandaga, and the gare routière, then north along the autoroute.

No 6 From Place Lat Dior, past the Place de l'Indépéndence and the station, then north towards the gare routière, past the port and Plage Bel-Air, then north-west along the main road between Grand Yoff and Castors.

No 7 From the Palais de Justice, past the Place, along Ave Pompidou to Marché Sandaga and up Ave Blaise Diagne and Route d'Ouakam past Point E to Almadies, N'Gor, the airport and Yoff.

No 8 From the Palais de Justice, past the Place, along Ave Pompidou, out through the Medina and eventually north up Blvd Bourgiba to Yoff and the airport.

No 9 From the Palais de Justice, past the Grande Mosquée and Place de l'ONU, and then north to the Castors area.

No 10 From the Palais de Justice, along the Corniche-Ouest past the Village Artisanal, Soumbédioune fishing village, Fann and the university, then north through the suburbs to the Castors area.

No 12 From Marché Sandaga, north-west to Point E and beyond.

No 13 From the Palais de Justice, north past the Grande Mosquée, along Ave Mbaké (also called Rue 13) to the Castors area.

No 15 From the Place, east around the bay to Rufisque.

No 18 From Marché Sandaga north to the gare routière and north-east out to the Castors area.

No 21 From the Palais de Justice, north up Ave Lamine Gueye and eventually north-east out of town to Tiaroye-Mer, Malika-sur-Mer and Keur Massar.

Cars Rapides If you don't see a bus going your way, you can always hop on a *car rapide* – a dilapidated blue and yellow minibus stuffed with people. Some are genuinely (frighteningly) rapid; others crawl along. Their prices are about 25% lower than for the SOTRAC buses. They go to most places but their destinations aren't marked, so you'll have to listen carefully to the destinations that the young assistants yell out. The main terminus is near Marché Sandaga.

Taxis Taxis around Dakar are plentiful, but taxi drivers cause tourists more problems than in any other West African city. The taxis have meters, but getting drivers to use them is a never-ending battle. They will try to quote you a flat rate; don't agree as this rate will invariably be higher than the metered tariff would have been.

If you do manage to get the meter running, note that rates double between midnight and 5 am; the normal rate is No 1, the night rate No 2. Drivers may tell you, wrongly, that the night rate begins earlier; moreover, many taxis have old meters that don't show the numbers, making it easy for the driver to put it on the night rate without your knowing. The higher rate ticks over much faster, so the first time you get in a taxi with the numbers marked, note how fast No 1 is ticking; on subsequent taxi rides if the meter ticks more rapidly you'll know you're being gypped.

If you decide to go for the flat rate, a short ride will be around CFA 250 to CFA 375, and from the Place to the main gare routière around CFA 800. Drivers outside top-end hotels will try and charge you much more than this and many will simply refuse to take you if you insist on their using the meter.

For longer hire, taxis should cost CFA 2500 by the hour if you stay within the city centre/N'Gor area; more if you hire it only for an hour or two. The official fare from the centre to Almadies, N'Gor or the airport is CFA 3750. The official all-day (7.30 am to 6 pm) rate is CFA 16,200 plus petrol but only a handful of drivers know this as very few of them have ever negotiated an all-day fare. Trying to include petrol in the price is a mistake as you're asking the driver to speculate. So agree to a daily rate and pay for the petrol you use, but to avoid problems at the end of the day verify first whether his petrol gauge is operating.

Car The major car rental agencies in Dakar are: Hertz (☎ 21 56 23 or 22 20 16, fax 21 17 21) at 64 Rue Félix Faure, with branches at the Novotel and Hôtel Teranga; Avis (☎ 23 33 00/32 30, fax 21 21 83) at 34 Ave Lamine Gueye, near the end of the autoroute; Europcar (☎ 22 06 91, fax 22 34 77) at the junction of Blvd de la Libération and Allées Delmas; and Budget (☎ 22 25 13, fax 22 25 06) at the junction of Aves Lamine Gueye and Faidherbe. They all have similar rates: between CFA 16,000 and CFA 20,000 per day plus CFA 150 to CFA 200 per km for the cheapest models, plus CFA 2500 per day for insurance and 20% tax.

Of the independent outfits, Senecartours (☎ 22 42 86/94 54, fax 21 83 06) at 64 Rue Carnot is long-established and one of the most reliable, with good quality vehicles, and prices lower than the internationals. They also do special weekend rates. The manager is friendly and speaks English. Others include: Seloca (☎ 22 41 05) at 44 Rue Assane Ndoye; Noprola (☎ 21 73 11) at 29 Rue Assane Ndoye (near Hôtel Teranga) and Clinic Auto (☎ 22 24 25) at 58 Rue Vincens. Auto Service Bayeux (☎ 21 42 08) is a repair yard at 106 Rue Gomis, but they sometimes have cheap cars for rent, with no km charge or any other extras.

Nearly all the companies can provide a driver for around CFA 6200 a day, which may be useful if you're unused to West African traffic. Some drivers double as guides. If you take a rented vehicle into The Gambia, be prepared for substantial hassles by Gambian police alleging absurd infractions everywhere you go.

AROUND DAKAR
Île de Gorée

Île de Gorée (Gorée Island) is about three km east of Dakar. Only 28 hectares in area, it is a wonderfully peaceful place, with 1000 inhabitants, no asphalt roads and no cars or bicycles. You'll find colonial-style houses with wrought-iron balconies, the old town hall, the former home of Blaise Diagne, and Le Castel, a rocky plateau at the far end of the island where you can get a good view of the island and of Dakar. The beach next to the ferry ramp is popular on the weekends, when you'll see people having picnics or swimming (although the water here is a bit oily), and pleasure boats from Dakar.

You should also visit the excellent **IFAN Historical Museum** in the Fort d'Estrées at the north end of the island. It has superb pictorial and physical exhibits portraying Senegalese history up to the present. There is also the **Musée Maritime**, between the old town hall and the post office. All three places are open from 10.30 am to 12.30 pm and 2.30 to 6 pm (closed Mondays), and charge a CFA 200 entrance fee. On the rocky **Castel** at the south end of the island are the remains of several fortifications dating from different periods, now inhabited by a group of hippy-ish Baye Fall disciples (see the boxed story on Drumming).

There's a little **tourist market** just behind the row of bars and restaurants facing the

ferry ramp. It's full of souvenir-quality crafts and materials. The bargaining here is far more relaxed than in Dakar so take your time. It's a good place to pick up trinkets for the folks back home.

Places to Stay For a room in a private home, enquire at the row of bars facing the ferry ramp. Finding a room, especially for a number of days, is not difficult. The local

---

La Maison des Esclaves

A visit to Gorée is no light-hearted affair. The island was one of the busiest slave centres in West Africa during the 18th and 19th centuries. La Maison des Esclaves (Slave House), built by the Dutch in 1776 and renovated in 1990 with French assistance, was where slaves were imprisoned before being shipped to the Americas. The guide will explain how people were stuffed into pens measuring six by 10 metres, inspected and priced as though they were animals, how the obstinate ones were chained to the walls and sea water was piped into their rooms to keep them partially submerged, how they fought for food, and how the weaker ones died on the island and were fed to the sharks while the stronger survivors were then branded with the shipping company's insignia and packed tightly into the holds for transportation. ∎

people ask CFA 5000 per night but, with bargaining, you can bring it down: a week should cost about CFA 12,500 for a pleasant room and less for one with just a mattress on the floor. The woman who owns the *Restaurant St-Germain* has been recommended, her rooms cost CFA 3500. She speaks English and also gives discounts in the restaurant.

The only hotel is the mid-range *Chevalier de Boufflers* (☎ 22 53 64), near the ferry ramp, where rooms cost CFA 11,250 to CFA 15,000 each.

Places to Eat As you come off the ferry ramp, you'll see several small bars and restaurants all serving fairly cheap food and drinks for around the same prices: meals are in the CFA 1250 to CFA 1850 range and big Gazelle beers cost CFA 625. Recommended is *Le St-Germain*, where a three-course menu costs CFA 2500. For cheaper fare, try to find *Chez Madame Siga*, a private house between the ferry and the fort, where the locals go to eat. A plate of rice and fish is CFA 650, but may have to be ordered in advance. For more up-market dishes, the *Chevalier de Boufflers* has a well-known seafood restaurant (closed Wednesdays) with dishes from CFA 2500, a three-course menu for CFA 4800.

Getting There & Away A return ticket on the ferry to Île de Gorée costs CFA 1500 for residents and CFA 3000 for foreigners. It leaves from the wharf in Dakar, which is a 10-minute walk north of the Place, and the trip across takes 20 minutes. The schedule (Monday to Saturday/Sunday & Holidays) rarely changes but check it in *Le Soleil*:

departs	*Monday to Saturday*	*Sundays & holidays*
Dakar	12.30*, 6.15, 7.30, 10 & 11 am, 12.30, 2.30, 4, 5, 6.30, 8 & 10.30 pm	12.45, 7, 9 & 10 am, 12, 2, 4, 4.30, 6.30, 7.30, 8.30 & 10.30 pm
Gorée	1*, 7, 8 & 10.30 am, 12, 2, 3, 4.30, 6, 7, 8.30 & 11pm	1.15, 7.30, 9.30 & 10.30 am, 12.30, 2.30, 4.30, 5.30, 7, 8, 9 & 11 pm

* Only on Monday, Friday and the day after a holiday.

Rufisque

Rufisque is a town about 30 km east from central Dakar. It was an important settlement in colonial times, but today it's nothing special though people are friendly and there are beaches nearby. The *Hôtel Koussin* (☎ 36 66 41) in the centre of town, a few blocks south of the main drag, charges CFA 7500 for a room with clean shared bath. (It might be worth staying here if you're arriving late from upcountry and don't want to wander the dark streets of Dakar at night.) On Rufisque's main drag are some cheap restaurants. SOTRAC bus No 15, plus frequent bush taxis and cars rapides, run between Rufisque and Dakar, but the road is notoriously congested and slow, and you might consider taking the train; there are several services each day.

Lac Retba

Lac Retba, more usually called Lac Rose (especially by the tour companies in Dakar) due to its pink colouring, is billed as Senegal's answer to the Dead Sea. Surrounded by dunes, it's 10 times saltier than the ocean but suitable for swimming – on your back, to keep the salt from burning your eyes. The lake is also famous because the annual Paris-Dakar motor rally finishes here.

Drumming

The Baye Fall disciples who live in and around Le Castel are a friendly relaxed bunch of guys, into dreadlocks, ganja and drumming. Robert Kohlhase, who came all the way from California to learn to drum, tells us: 'It's easy to find one of the guys to give you lessons, for about CFA 2000 per hour. The drums are *djembes* and the rhythms come from all parts of Senegal. Some of the guys belong to formal musical groups and do performances and recordings. The drum parts I learned were fairly simple: instruction is casual and the teachers aren't terribly concerned if the students don't know the techniques well. Still, it's a pleasant environment for learning and, once you're into the scene, you'll also find several of them will be happy to sit on the cliffs and drum with you, just for the fun of it.' ■

SENEGAL

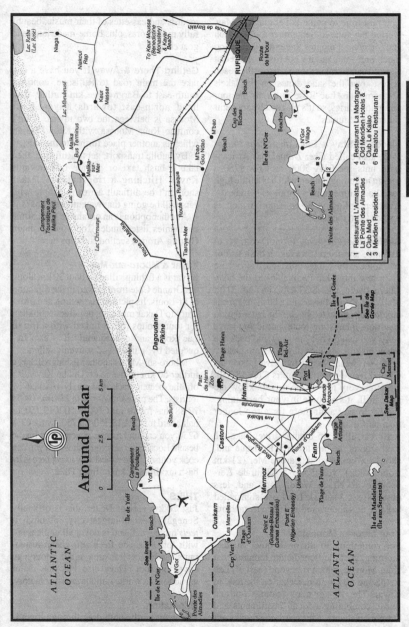

Around Dakar

ATLANTIC OCEAN

ATLANTIC OCEAN

Lac Retba (Lac Rose)
Niaga
Niakoul Rap
Lac Mbeubeusse
Keur Massar
To Keur Moussa (Benedictine Monastery) & Kayar Beach
Route de Bayakh
RUFISQUE
Route de M'bour
Cap des Biches
Beach
M'bao
M'bao Gou Ndao
M'bao Beach
Route de Rufisque
Malika Bus Terminus
Malika-sur-Mer
Lac Youi
Campement Touristique de Malika Paul
Lac Chirouaye
Route de Malika
Tiaroye-Mer
Beach
Cambérène
Plage Hann
Dagoudane Pikine
Stadium
Campement Le Fouljagu
Yoff
Île de Yoff
Beach
Parc de Hann Zoo
Plage Bel-Air
Hann
Port
Île de Gorée
See Île de Gorée Map
Autoroute
Grande Mosquée
Cap Manuel
See Dakar Map
Ave Mbaké
Castors
Blvd Bourguiba
Village Artisanal
Cap Vert
Les Mamelles
Ouakam
Plage d'Ouakam
Point E (Guinea-Bissau & Guinean Embassies)
Point E (Nigerian Embassy)
Mermoz
Université
Route d'Ouakam
Fann
Plage de Fann
Île des Madeleines (Île aux Serpents)
N'Gor
Pointe des Almadies
See Inset
Île de N'Gor

0   2.5   5 km

Inset (upper right):
Île de N'Gor
Beaches
N'Gor Village
Beach
Pointe des Almadies

1 Restaurant L'Armatan & La Pointe des Almadies
2 Club Med
3 Meridien President
4 Restaurant La Madrague
5 Old Meridien Hotels & Club Le Kalao
6 Ramatou Restaurant

The best time to come is February to May. During the June to September rainy season and for several months thereafter there's too much rainwater and it's not rose-coloured at all. You can swim in the ocean too; the beach is just over the sand dunes on the lake's northern side. Lac Rose is on all the tour group itineraries, so it's plagued by souvenir sellers and 'guides'.

Places to Stay & Eat *Campement Niaga-Peul*, also called *Chez Daniel*, has African-style huts for CFA 5000 or CFA 8750 a person including dinner, which is a little high for the campement's modest standards. Another option is *Keur Kanni* which is further from the lake.

Getting There & Away From Dakar, get to Rufisque and from there take a bush taxi or car rapide to the village of Niaga, from where it's a few more km (walkable) to the lake. Alternatively, take SOTRAC bus No 21 to Malika or Keur Massar and a bush taxi or car rapide from there to Niaga. The latter option is a more interesting route, but if you leave early you can go out one way and back the other, making it a nice day trip from Dakar.

If you decide to go by private taxi, the official round-trip taxi fare is CFA 18,750, although very few of the drivers know the rate. Still, it's a guide in your bargaining. Expect to pay a bit more for a trip longer than half a day.

By car, it's a 45-minute drive. Take the road around the bay towards Rufisque and, about six km beyond Tiaroye-Mer (21 km from Dakar), you'll see a 'Centrale Aerosolaire de Niaga Wolof' sign and, less obviously, a 'Visitez le Lac Rose' sign nailed to a tree. It's about another 19 km from there.

Keur Moussa Monastery

For something to do on a quiet Sunday morning, visit the Benedictine monastery at Keur Moussa, which is beyond (east of) Lac Retba and 50 km from Dakar on the road to Kayar. The 10 am mass features unusual music combining African instruments and Gregorian chants. Afterwards the monks sell

records and cassettes of their music, beautifully made koras, plus home-made jams and goat cheese.

Getting There & Away If you have a car, take the main road to Rufisque, continue south-east to Bargny five km further, then head north-east towards Kayar. Keur Moussa is between the two towns. (Don't confuse Keur Moussa with Keur Massar, which is another place further to the west.)

By public transport, get to Rufisque, then take a bush taxi or private taxi towards Kayar. Hitching a ride back to Dakar shouldn't be difficult as many people with cars will be going that way after the mass.

Another option is an organised tour. Some companies listed under Tours in the main Getting Around section run trips here.

Kayar & Mboro-sur-Mer

Kayar is a fishing village, about 30 km along the Grande Côte from Dakar, in the direction of St-Louis. Its picturesque setting and proximity to Dakar make it a popular destination for tour groups (often linked with a trip to Lac Rose) and consequently it is also frequented by 'guides' and souvenir-sellers.

Mboro-sur-Mer is another fishing village, a further 50 km up the coast. Unlike Kayar, it's off the beaten track and rarely reached by tourists. The pleasant *Gîte de la Licorne* (☎ 55 77 88) has rooms for CFA 14,500/ 19,750, or half board for CFA 18,750/ 33,750. Or for CFA 6250 you can rent a basic concrete hut on the beach. Locals will sell you fish which you can cook yourself. The easiest way to get here is by bush taxi from Dakar or from Thiès.

THIÈS

Just 70 km east of Dakar, this is officially Senegal's second-largest city, although it *feels* quite small and is not at all unpleasant, with lots of shade trees and cheap restaurants, and a central area small enough to cover on foot. Thiès also has one major attraction – a world-famous tapestry factory.

Orientation

The main north-south drag through town is

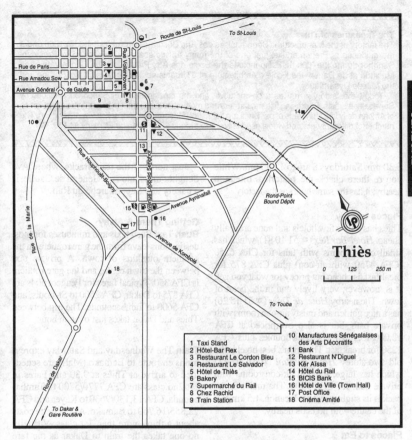

Thiès

0   125   250 m

1 Taxi Stand	10 Manufactures Sénégalaises
2 Hôtel-Bar Rex	des Arts Décoratifs
3 Restaurant Le Cordon Bleu	11 Bank
4 Restaurant Le Salvador	12 Restaurant N'Diguel
5 Hôtel de Thiès	13 Kër Aïssa
6 Bakery	14 Hôtel du Rail
7 Supermarché du Rail	15 BICIS Bank
8 Chez Rachid	16 Hôtel de Ville (Town Hall)
9 Train Station	17 Post Office
	18 Cinéma Amitié

Ave Léopold Senghor. At the southern end is the Hôtel de Ville (town hall) with a large park just in front. As you head north from the park you'll pass several restaurants, petrol stations and banks. Just beyond the first roundabout and train tracks is the junction with Ave Général de Gaulle, a major road which leads west towards the train station and, further on, the well-marked tapestry factory. The core business district is the area just north of the train station including Ave Général de Gaulle. The gare routière is on the southern outskirts of town, about three km from the centre.

Things to See

Don't miss seeing the famous **tapestries** at the Manufactures Sénégalaises des Arts Décoratifs (☎ 51 11 03/31), on Rue de la Marie, about half a km west of the train station. Prices can range into the thousands of US dollars, but the tapestries are worth seeing even if you have no intention of buying. Visitors are allowed only into the factory's exhibition rooms but the most interesting part is touring the factory to see how the tapestries are actually made. If you call a day or two ahead, you may get the full tour. The entrance fee is CFA 500. It's open weekdays from 8 am to 12.30 pm and 3 to

---

The Tapestries of Thiès

The factory of the Manufactures Sénégalaises des Arts Décoratifs was established in 1966 under the guidance of French artists, just one of the many artistic endeavours inspired by President Senghor during the '60s that also include the École des Arts Plastiques, the Conservatoire de Musique et de Danse, the École d'Architecture et d'Urbanisme, the Théâtre Daniel Sorano and the Musée Dynamique.

Today, the factory is run as a co-operative, and the tapestries are all based on paintings by Senegalese artists. Portraying fishers, farmers and mothers with children, they are a visual distillation of African daily life. Hundreds of paintings are submitted for consideration; only a few are chosen. The number of different-coloured wools used is typically around 20, but can be as many as 100. ■

6.30 pm, Saturdays 8 am to 12.30 pm. While you're there check the **historical museum** nearby; it has the same hours as the factory.

Places to Stay

Thiès has only a few hotels and none are really cheap. *Hôtel-Bar Rex* (☎ 51 10 81), which has small clean rooms with fans for CFA 6250 (CFA 8750 with air-con) plus CFA 875 for breakfast, is cheap but pricey for what you get. It is, however, very lively and in the heart of town. The nearby *Hôtel de Thiès* (☎ 51 15 26) has a nice garden and musty air-con rooms with private bath, but is also overpriced at CFA 12,000/13,500 for singles/doubles plus CFA 1250 for breakfast. The town's best hotel is the old two-storey *Hôtel du Rail* (☎ 51 10 13) which has large, tranquil air-con rooms with private bath for CFA 9500. The major drawback is its slightly remote location, 1.5 km east of the centre with no taxis nearby.

Places to Eat

There are many restaurants on Ave Senghor. Recommend for good, cheap food is *Restaurant N'Diguel* (or Chez Adja), seven blocks north of the Hôtel de Ville. Riz poisson costs CFA 450, poulet rôti CFA 875 and mafé CFA 450. Across the street and two blocks south you'll find *Kër Aïssa*, another tiny restaurant with similar prices.

Chez Rachid on Ave Général de Gaulle, two blocks east of the train station, has good chawarmas; *Restaurant Le Salvador*, on Rue de Paris two blocks north of the station, has a wide selection of inexpensive dishes; *Restaurant Le Cordon Bleu* is directly opposite and similar in all respects.

Just north of the train tracks, where Ave Senghor turns into Ave Général de Gaulle, is a bakery and Supermarché du Rail.

Getting There & Away

Bush Taxi Bush taxis and minibuses for most destinations leave from the gare routière on the southern outskirts of town. A private taxi between the town centre and the gare routière is CFA 350. Typical fares for Peugeot 504s are CFA 875 to Dakar, CFA 2500 to St-Louis, and CFA 5600 to Tambacounda. The trip between Thiès and Dakar takes just over an hour.

Train The Wednesday and Saturday express trains en route to Bamako (Mali) are scheduled to arrive at Thiès at 9.30 am. Fares in 1st/2nd class are CFA 7770/5700 to Tambacounda, CFA 13,130/9630 to Kayes and CFA 22,855/16,760 to Bamako. A couchette costs about a third more than 1st class. Virtually no one takes the train to Dakar as the fare (CFA 1380/1010) is not competitive and the train is inevitably delayed.

The Petite Côte

The 150-km stretch of coast running south from Dakar to the Siné-Saloun Delta is called the Petite Côte. This is Senegal's second-best beach area after Cap Skiring. The principal attractions are the beautiful beaches around M'Bour and Sali Portugal and the twin villages of Joal and Fadiout.

M'BOUR, SALI PORTUGAL & NIANING

M'Bour is a small town on the coast, about 80 km south of Dakar. Sali Portugal is a village eight km north of M'Bour, and Nianing is 10 km south. Between Sali (also spelt Saly) and Nianing are at least 10 ocean-front hotels, packed with European tourists during winter and particularly busy over Christmas and Easter. People flock here for the clean white **beaches**, sports and guaranteed sunshine every day. If you want the place to yourself, the time to come is May to October. Accommodation is also much cheaper at this time (although some hotels close completely during the low season).

Places to Stay & Eat – bottom end

Those on a low budget should head for M'Bour, which is the only place with cheap accommodation. M'Bour also has many touts and hustlers who all want to sell you something or be your guide. They even follow you onto the beach and you have to go some way from the town to evade them. However, the touts can be useful if you want to stay with a local family. Expect to pay around CFA 2500 per person for a room. You may be able to arrange breakfast and dinner for an extra CFA 1250.

The cheapest hotel in town is *Fouta Touba*, 10 minutes' walk from the *gare routière*, opposite the school, where clean doubles are CFA 3750. Or try the *Centre d'Accueil et de Séjour au Sénégal* (☎ 57 10 02), better known as Chez Marie, near the market and only 100 metres from the beach. Singles/doubles cost CFA 5500/7500; tax and breakfast are extra. The people are very friendly and there's a wonderful garden.

Another popular place is *Chez Zeyna* (☎ 52 19 09) which has a friendly family atmosphere and three small self-contained rooms for CFA 5000 per person plus CFA 650 for breakfast. It's on the southern side of the town, beyond the Centre Touristique de la Petite Côte, about one km along the sandy street that runs nearest to the ocean.

Another option is the good-value *L'Escale*, on the Dakar side of town near the main junction where the roads to Kaolack

and Joal-Fadiout divide. The rooms are small but clean with mosquito nets and wash-basins, and cost CFA 7900. Even if you don't stay here, it's a good place for a moderately priced French meal, with dishes in the CFA 1800 to CFA 3000 range (closed Mondays).

Other places for eating in M'Bour include *Chez Maurice*, a Senegalese restaurant in between the market and the Centre Touristique, with dishes in the CFA 1700 to CFA 2500 range. Just round the corner is a snack bar with chawarmas at CFA 650 and hamburgers at CFA 850. Near the market and taxi park are several small gargottes.

One of the nicest places to stay in this area is *La Ferme de Saly*, right on the coast, three km north of M'Bour. Here you can enjoy a clean beach and escape the touts. Run by amiable Frenchman Jean-Paul Difolco, it has a nice set of round huts with showers plus a pleasant bar-restaurant. He charges CFA 5000 per person per night, or CFA 62,500 per week for a hut (up to four people). Meals cost CFA 2500. He also has two horses and two camels that can be rented for riding on the beach, and other excursions can be arranged. To get there, heading south from Dakar, five km or so past the turn-off for the big hotels at Sali, you'll see a sign on the ocean side for 'La Ferme'. Follow the dirt road for another three km through grassy sand dunes to reach the farm. If you get lost ask for Chez Jean-Paul.

In Nianing, about 100 metres from the Auberge des Coquillages towards M'Bour, is the small unmarked *Hôtel Le Bintegnier* with simple rooms in a beautiful garden for CFA 5000 per person and excellent French meals for CFA 2500.

Places to Stay & Eat – middle

The best (and only) mid-range hotel in M'Bour is the 70-room *Centre Touristique de la Petite Côte* (☎ 57 10 04, fax 57 10 77). It is very good value with self-contained air-con doubles for CFA 14,750 including tax. Breakfast is CFA 2000 and meals cost around CFA 3000 to CFA 5000. Half board is around CFA 12,000 per person. Nonguests can use the pool for CFA 2000 but if you buy a drink the chances are good you can swim for free. The hotel is set in beautiful gardens and has its own private beach, where touts are not allowed.

At Nianing is the attractive *Auberge des Coquillages* (☎ 57 14 28) where prices start at CFA 8750/12,500 in self-contained bungalows and go up to CFA 21,250 per person for full board. The hotel has a small pool and its own beach. Nearby is an unmarked restaurant serving simple plates of rice and sauce, while the man next door sells coffee, bread and eggs.

Places to Stay – top end

Most of the big hotels are grouped together in a 'resort-complex' at Sali Portugal, which also has restaurants, shops and a casino, and all offer virtually the same activities – fishing, water-skiing, sailing, sailboards, tennis, swimming, pétanque and horse riding. It is unusual to stay at these places for a bed only, so most quote for half or full board. Sometimes the tour companies in Dakar offer special rates at these hotels, especially in the low season.

One of the less expensive is *Hôtel Village Club des Filao* (☎ 57 11 19/80) which charges CFA 20,000 for doubles, half board. They also do a weekend special (Saturday night): CFA 18,750 per person, double occupancy, full board.

Petite Côte & Siné-Saloum Delta

The 92-room *Sali Novotel* (☎ 57 11 67) has more typical prices – CFA 21,250 for doubles, B&B, and CFA 35,000 per person for a full board weekend special. Other hotels with similar prices are: *Hôtel Royam*, the *Palm Beach* (☎ 57 11 37, telex 7755), *Savana Koumba* (☎ 57 11 12), and *Savana Saly* (☎ 57 11 13, fax 57 10 45).

Most expensive of all is *Club du Baobab* (☎ 21 18 86 in Dakar) to the north of Sali, about 70 km from Dakar.

To the south of M'Bour, at Nianing, is the 300-room *Club Aldiana* (☎ 57 10 84, telex 7756). Nearby is the 100-room, French-run *Domaine de Nianing* (☎ 57 10 85, Dakar 22 25 73, telex 7786) which is slightly cheaper.

Getting There & Away
Bush taxis between M'Bour and Dakar charge CFA 1125. To/from Kaolack is CFA 1250, and to/from Karang (Gambian border) is CFA 3250. If you're travelling south down the Petite Côte or into the Siné-Saloun Delta, bush taxis are CFA 460 to/from Joal-Fadiout and CFA 1125 to/from Djiffer or Ndangane.

JOAL-FADIOUT
The twin villages of Joal and Fadiout (sometimes spelt Fadiouth) are 114 km south of Dakar at the end of the tarred road. Joal (the birthplace of former president Senghor) is on the mainland, while Fadiout is on a small island reached by an old wooden bridge. Because this place is picturesque, and an easy day trip from Dakar, all the tour companies run excursions here.

Fadiout is unusual in that the island is made entirely of oyster and clam shells that have accumulated over the centuries. Shells are everywhere, covering the streets and embedded in the walls of houses. Even the topsoil is shells. A walk through Fadiout takes about an hour; afterwards you can hire a pirogue to go to the surrounding islands, including one nearby where you'll see some curious basket-like granaries on stilts.

Unfortunately you cannot tour the town in peace. Immediately you arrive you'll be surrounded by dozens of youths wanting to be your guide. They won't take no for an answer

and they may become quite aggressive and unpleasant, following you and even trying to prevent you from seeing things such as the granaries. It's best either to take a guide or stay away, otherwise they'll ruin your trip.

Places to Stay & Eat
In Joal, the cheapest place to stay is *Campement Les Cocos*, on the road towards Djiffer, which charges CFA 2500 per person for a mattress on the floor of a tatty hut. For cheap eats go to the waterfront where you'll find places selling rice and fish for about CFA 375. The nearby *Relais 114* (☎ 57 61 14), also called Chez Mamadou Balde, has basic clean rooms (for up to three people) with fans for CFA 6250, which includes one breakfast. The restaurant promises 'service rapide' and charges around CFA 1875 for meals, with a three-course menu for CFA 3750. More upmarket but good value is the *Hôtel le Finnio* (☎ 57 61 12), near the bridge over to Fadiout, with comfortable self-contained air-con rooms for CFA 4250 per person. Breakfast (CFA 1000) and other meals (from CFA 3125) are available in the restaurant.

Your other option in this area is the *Mission Catholique de St Joseph* at Ngasobil, about six km north of Joal, where a room in the guesthouse costs CFA 2500 per person. Breakfast is CFA 750 and meals CFA 2500. The mission in Joal does not take guests.

PALMARIN & DJIFFER
These two villages are on the Petite Côte. Both are much more pleasant than Joal-Fadiout (although slightly harder to get to) and handy for exploring the northern part of the Siné-Saloum Delta. Details are included in the Siné-Saloum Delta section below.

The Siné-Saloum Delta

South of the Petite Côte, the 180,000-hectare Siné-Saloum Delta is one of the most beautiful parts of Senegal. Formed where the seasonal Siné and Saloum rivers meet the tidal waters of the Atlantic Ocean, it's a swampy area with mangrove trees, lagoons, open forests, dunes and sand islands. Stretching east towards the city of Kaolack and south to the Gambian border, part of the area is included in the Saloum Delta National Park.

You will not see large mammals here apart from the occasional wart hog and, perhaps, a sea cow (manatee) in the lagoons, but the area abounds with monkeys (including the red colobus) and is particularly good for birding, especially during the migratory season (November to April). And the area is worth a trip for the fascinating scenery alone. A pirogue trip down one of the river branches to see the pelicans, flamingos and other birds, or to visit some of the island fishing villages, is well worth doing, although the spray can be cold, so you should bring some warm and waterproof clothing.

Some people use Kaolack as a base for visiting the Siné-Saloum area. But along the edges of the delta are several hotels and campements, which make much better bases for exploring the area by foot or pirogue.

KAOLACK

Kaolack (pronounced KOH-lack) is a regional capital, with over 200,000 inhabitants, and the centre of Senegal's groundnut industry. Midway between Dakar, Tambacounda and The Gambia, it is often regarded as little more than a junction, but it's a lively city – more active than St-Louis or Ziguinchor – and well worth visiting for a day or two. Things to see include the large Moroccan-style **mosque**, the pride of the Tidjaniya brotherhood, and the second-largest covered **market** in Africa (after Marrakesh) with oriental arches and arcades, a grand entrance and a large central patio. Despite these attractions few tourists come here, so there's very little hassle. It's a great place just to wander around and soak up the atmosphere.

There are several good-value restaurants and bars in the town, and three banks, although if you're caught here on a weekend without local money, you can change cash or travellers' cheques at the Super-Service supermarket on Ave Filiatre.

Places to Stay

The cheapest hotel in town is the *Hôtel Napoléon*, two blocks east and one block north of the market, but it's dirty, smelly and grossly overpriced at CFA 5000 for a double with fan. The food is cheap, however. Nearby is the *Hôtel Adama Cire*, also known as Chez Aida Ba, where the clean self-contained rooms are CFA 7500, although they can sometimes be bargained down to the same price as the Napoléon. The food here is also cheap and filling. Unfortunately this hotel is directly above a bar where the loud music ends at dawn. More tranquil is the *Mission Catholique*, in the south-west part of town, which has spotless self-contained single rooms for CFA 3750 (no sharing allowed) or a dormitory for CFA 2000 per person. Missionaries have priority here, and the rooms are often full.

Moving up-market, but still a very good deal, is the *Caritas Chambres de Passage* (☎ 41 27 30/20 30) a few blocks west of the mission. Caritas is an aid organisation but their hotel-standard rooms are for anybody and cost CFA 6000 per person or CFA 9000 for a couple sharing. You can even phone and reserve a room in advance.

The *Hôtel Le Dior* (☎ 41 16 62) charges CFA 9500/10,000 for air-con singles/doubles plus CFA 500 tax per person and CFA 1000 for breakfast. The best place in town is the French-run *Hôtel Le Paris* (☎ 41 10 19) which charges CFA 13,750 plus tax for an air-con double. The facilities are good and include a small pool. Breakfast is CFA 2500 and good quality meals cost around CFA 5000.

Places to Eat & Drink

All the hotels mentioned above do food. For cheap eats there are several nameless gargottes near the gare routière, and street food can be found around the market. For reasonable snacks and meals try the Lebanese-run *Chez Miriam* and *Chez Marcel*, both in the north-east part of the centre around the intersection of Ave Van Vollenhoven (Senghor) and Ave Noirat, which have chawarmas, burgers and hot sandwiches for CFA 500 to CFA 1000, and meals in the CFA 1875 to

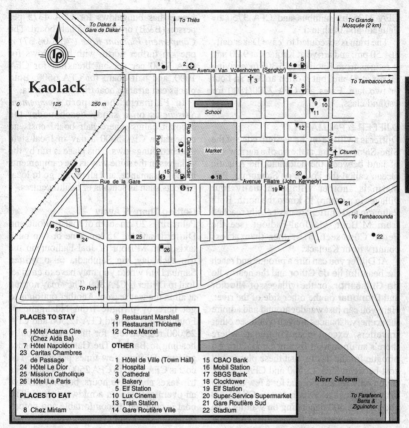

Kaolack

0   125   250 m

To Dakar &
Gare de Dakar

To Thiès

To Grande
Mosquée (2 km)

Avenue Van Vollenhoven (Senghor)

To Tambacounda

School

Rue Galiene

Rue Cardinal Verdier

Market

Rue de la Gare

Avenue Noirot

Church

Avenue Filiatre (John Kennedy)

To Tambacounda

To Port

River Saloum

To Farafenni,
Barra &
Ziguinchor

SENEGAL

PLACES TO STAY		9	Restaurant Marshall
6	Hôtel Adama Cire (Chez Aida Ba)	11	Restaurant Thiolame
7	Hôtel Napoléon	12	Chez Marcel
23	Caritas Chambres de Passage		**OTHER**
24	Hôtel Le Dior	1	Hôtel de Ville (Town Hall)
25	Mission Catholique	2	Hospital
26	Hôtel Le Paris	3	Cathedral
		4	Elf Station
PLACES TO EAT		5	Elf Station
8	Chez Miriam	10	Lux Cinema
		13	Train Station
		14	Gare Routière Ville

15	CBAO Bank
16	Mobil Station
17	SBGS Bank
18	Clocktower
19	Elf Station
20	Super-Service Supermarket
21	Gare Routière Sud
22	Stadium

CFA 2500 range. Nearby is the *Restaurant Thiolame* which has similar prices. Also nearby, and only slightly more expensive, is the recommended *Restaurant Marshall* run by three graduates from the hotel school in Dakar, and serving excellent European and African food in pleasant surroundings.

All the hotels and restaurants sell beer and soft drinks. For less salubrious surroundings visit the *Bar Malibu* between the Restaurant Marshall and the Lux Cinema. Another more lively place, although not for the faint-hearted, is *Chez Alain* below the Hotel Adama Cire.

Getting There & Away

The town has three gare routières: Gare de Dakar, on the north-western side of town (CFA 250 for a taxi or horse-drawn *calesh* from the city centre) for Dakar, Touba and northern destinations; Gare Sud, on the south-east side of the city centre, for Ziguinchor, The Gambia and Tambacounda; and Gare Ville for local bush taxis to the surrounding suburbs and villages. Bush taxis do the 192-km trip to Dakar in about three hours (CFA 1875). Minibuses to the Gambian border towns of Farafenni and Karang charge CFA 875 and CFA 1125, respectively. Kaolack to Tambacounda is

CFA 3125 by minibus and CFA 3750 by Peugeot 504 bush taxi.

The train is scheduled to leave Dakar daily at 4.50 pm, and arrive at Kaolack at 9.20 pm. It returns from Kaolack at 6.30 am, arriving Dakar at 11 am, but it often arrives an hour or two late. Fares are CFA 2700/1800 for 1st/2nd class.

DJIFFER & PALMARIN

Djiffer is a village on the western edge of the Siné-Saloum Delta, at the tip of a narrow spit of land between the delta and the Atlantic Ocean called the Pointe de Sangomar. Palmarin is another village (actually four villages in a group) 15 km to the north. Both Palmarin and Djiffer are most easily reached from M'Bour, via Joal-Fadiout (see the Petite Côte section), rather than across country from Kaolack.

At Djiffer you can hire a pirogue and reach the beautiful Île de Guior and the nearby Île de Guissanor, or the villages of Niodior and Dionouar on the other side of the river. Here you can just wander around and admire the scenery. Chances are you won't see other travellers, except near Dionouar, where there's an up-market fishing camp. Hiring a pirogue for the day to visit these places will cost between CFA 12,500 and CFA 25,000. If you only want a pirogue for a few hours to visit Dionouar it costs between CFA 5000 and CFA 12,500 depending on waiting time and your powers of bargaining. Dionouar used to be linked to Niodior by a footbridge, but this has fallen down and you have to take a short ride for CFA 12 in a dugout canoe. You can also get the public boat which runs between Djiffer and Dionouar for CFA 310 per person, but it only runs once a day in each direction, usually in the afternoon.

Places to Stay & Eat

For a cheap bed in Djiffer you may find a family to put you up; this usually isn't difficult. One place to ask is at Restaurant Lat Dior (which also has excellent food). Expect to pay about CFA 2500 per person. On the north side of the village are two new campements: *Campement Le Pointe de San-*

gomar has bungalows for CFA 4375 per person (B&B) or CFA 6875 half board. The *Campement Flamant Rose* (☎ 35 08 37) is one km further north, with bungalows for CFA 3750 per person, breakfast for CFA 1000, and half board for CFA 6600. Both places can arrange boat trips on the delta.

In Palmarin the superb *Campement Sessene* is on a sandy beach under the coconut palms where half board costs an unbeatable CFA 5000 a day in local-style thatched bungalows. This place is run by the villagers in the same way as the campements in the Casamance, and all profits go to local projects such as schools or health centres.

Getting There & Away

Palmarin is 20 km south of Joal-Fadiout, and Djiffer is another 15 km. One or two bush taxis from M'Bour or Joal-Fadiout do the trip each day, via Sambadia (also written Samba Dia) where you may have to change. Joal to Djiffer is CFA 800. They may not run at all in the wet season. Another option is to get here by pirogue from Ndangane or Foundiougne, around CFA 12,500 and CFA 25,000 respectively for the boat. If you're heading to Banjul (The Gambia), pirogues go from Djiffer a few times per week. The cost is CFA 1250 to CFA 2500 a person. The trip takes about five hours, but may involve an overnight stop on a midway island. The boat is cramped, uncomfortable and notoriously unsafe. You have been warned!

NDANGANE

Ndangane (pronounced n-den-GAN-nee) is the northernmost settlement bordering the delta. On the edge of the village *Le Pelican* (☎ 49 83 20) is a large attractive hotel with a pool and a superb location overlooking the delta. It's also slightly overpriced at CFA 16,250 for a double with air-con. Meals are extra but quite good. A cheaper alternative is the new *Campement Limboko*, a 20-minute pirogue ride (CFA 2500) from the village. Traditional rooms cost CFA 4000 per room, breakfast is CFA 1000 and other meals, CFA 3000. Fishing and bird-watching trips can be arranged. Another option may be staying with one of the pirogue owners in the village. Expect to pay about CFA 5000 per person with meals.

Getting There & Away

By road Ndangane is reached from Ndiosomone (between Tiadiaye and Tataguine) on the M'Bour to Kaolack highway. From here it's 42 km south on a tar road to Ndangane. The hotel is signposted. You can also go from M'Bour by bush taxi via Sambadia (CFA 500) although this is difficult in the wet season. Ndangane is also accessible from Foundiougne (25 km to the east as the crow flies) by pirogue (CFA 12,500 for the boat).

If you're heading next to Banjul (The Gambia), it's possible to take a pirogue from Ndangane. Prices and conditions are the same as the pirogues from Djiffer.

FOUNDIOUGNE

West of Kaolack, the small town of Foundiougne (FOUN-dune) is easy to reach, has a good hotel and an excellent cheap campement, and is another good place to find pirogues for trips around the delta. Some visitors go to the Île des Oisseaux for birdwatching; others go fishing.

Campement Le Baobab, normally called Chez Anne-Marie (☎ 45 11 08), has clean double bungalows with mosquito nets and spotless shared showers and toilets for CFA 5000/5620 including breakfast. The three-course meals are very good and also reasonably priced at CFA 1800. Ishmael, the resident boatman, offers pirogue trips to the Île des Oisseaux and fishing excursions for CFA 12,500 per day for the boat, although these are negotiable according to the petrol and time required.

Nearby is the up-market *Village-Hôtel Les Piroguiers* (☎ 45 11 34) with comfortable air-con bungalows at CFA 13,750/22,500 for singles/doubles and breakfast at CFA 1500, or full board for CFA 18,750 per person. It's in a beautiful spot on the river and has a pool, lovely gardens, a good restaurant and a nightclub. It also offers sailboards, sailing, hunting and fishing.

Getting There & Away

By road Foundiougne is reached from Passi on the highway between Kaolack and the Gambian border at Karang. A bush taxi between Passi and Kaolack is CFA 625; from Passi to Foundiougne is CFA 300. The gare routière is on the southern edge of the town. Continue down the main street to the water's edge then turn left to reach the campement and hotel.

You can also get here from Fatick, 150 km from Dakar on the M'Bour to Kaolack highway, by bush taxi to Dakhonga and ferry across to Foundiougne. The big ferry no longer runs, but pirogues cross regularly for CFA 125 per person. Leaving Foundiougne this way, the first ferry departs at dawn to connect with the first minibus, which goes all the way to Dakar for CFA 1875.

TOUBACOUTA & MISSIRAH

Toubacouta and Missirah are good bases for exploring the southern side of the park, known as the Fathala forest section. It's a dry open woodland with tidal mud flats on the western edge and mangrove swamps beyond. The red colobus monkeys are plentiful but shy; the dry season, when trees have fewer leaves, is best for seeing them. The park headquarters are six km from Missirah and signposted. You actually enter the national park just south of Missirah, where the entrance fee is CFA 2500.

Places to Stay

In Toubacouta you have a choice between two fairly expensive hotels. The *Hôtel Les Palétuviers* (☎ 48 57 14, fax 48 57 06) features a pool, billiards and other games, and colourfully decorated air-con cottages at CFA 9820/12,340 for singles/doubles, plus breakfast at CFA 2000, or 17,420/27,540 for half board. The *Centre de Pêche Keur Saloum* (☎ 48 57 16, Dakar 22 89 70) has air-con bungalows for CFA 13,500/18,000 for B&B, or CFA 15,600/20,300 half board. Both offer hunting and fishing trips, and have pirogues and cars for hire by the hour or day.

Near Missirah, the *Gîte de Bandiala* is

smaller, friendlier and cheaper than the two places at Toubacouta, but harder to reach if you don't have wheels. It's also ideally situated for viewing animals and the mangrove swamps. Hundreds of monkeys, for example, come to eat or drink at the campement's pool. The bungalows have two to four beds each. The price per person is CFA 9750 half board and CFA 14,300 full board. Pirogue trips, fishing excursions and photo safaris are available.

There are three other hotels in this area, all owned by the people who run Les Palétuviers, with the same phone number and the same activities/excursions. One is the newly renovated *Hôtel 'Ile Paradis'* on Paradise Island near Bétanti, west of Toubacouta. The second is the *Plage d'Or* in Djinack on the Gambian border. It's smaller and less expensive with 12 ventilated rooms and is near a beach. The third is the *Village 'Tarzan'* they're constructing in Fadiong which will have three unique cottages built amongst baobab trees.

Another locally owned place is *Hôtel Le Caïman*, at Sokone, on the main road north of Toubacouta, where full board costs CFA 20,000 per day.

The national park headquarters are six km from Missirah. You may be allowed to camp here but be sure to get permission.

Getting There & Away

Toubacouta is just off the main highway between Kaolack and Karang (the Gambian border), about 70 km from Kaolack and 44 km from Karang. A bush taxi from Kaolack is CFA 1125.

To reach the Gîte at Missirah by public transport you have two options: get off at Toubacouta and walk 12 km along a good dirt road, or get off at the village of Santhiou el Haji (about 80 km from Kaolack) and walk six km on a pleasant sandy track through the forest. The Gîte is signposted both ways.

To reach the park headquarters, get to Missirah. The rangers come to the village about once a day and will give you a lift to the park. Ask at the store when they're expected.

The Casamance

The Casamance is the region of Senegal south of The Gambia. It differs geographically and culturally from other parts of the country, being a well-watered fertile area where the majority of people are non-Muslim Diola (Jola). This feeling of difference is so strong that a separatist movement has existed here since the 1950s, leading to war with the 'northern' government (see History in the Facts About the Country section) in the late 1980s.

Until that time the Casamance region had attracted more visitors than any other part of Senegal, but the 'separatist problems' caused tourist numbers to dwindle. Since the ceasefire of July 1993 visitors have started returning, but it will take a few more years before numbers get up to the levels of the 1980s. So now is the time to go: the hotels and campements are rarely full, the beaches are quiet, and prices are being held down to attract custom.

Palm Wine

As you travel along the backroads of Casamance, you'll almost certainly see men collecting 'wine' from the oil palm trees that grow in this region. Each collector climbs his own trees, using a loop of rope (called a *kandab* in Diola) that fits like a large belt around man and tree, holding him close to the trunk. Just below the point where the palm fonds sprout from the tree, the collector punches a hole through the bark into the soft sap. The liquid drips slowly through a funnel (traditionally made from leaves, although these days it's usually a piece of plastic), and is collected in any handy container (once a natural gourd or calabash, today more likely to be a real wine bottle salvaged from a hotel junk heap in Cap Skiring). After a few hours, the collector comes back – the bottle is full and the wine is already fermented and ready to drink! ∎

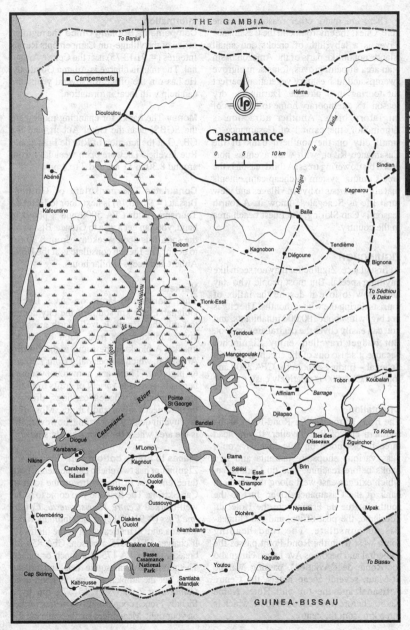

There are many other reasons to come here. One is the environment: the Casamance River is a labyrinth of creeks and small islands not unlike parts of the Amazon basin – an area of palm groves, forests, mangrove swamps and lush estuary vegetation, perfect for touring in a pirogue. During the dry season it's a temporary home to millions of migratory birds. Another attraction is Ziguinchor, the capital of Casamance, a small city on the southern bank of the Casamance River, with wide avenues bordered by flowering trees. A third reason is the area's unique system of cheap campements that allow tourists to live in villages and view rural life as Senegalese know it. A fourth reason is Cap Skiring, the finest beach area in the country.

ZIGUINCHOR

At first glance, Ziguinchor may not seem like anything special. But most people who stay here grow to love it despite the influx of tourists during the winter months. The city is not big, with about 100,000 inhabitants, and you can easily cover the central area on foot. But budget travellers enjoy Ziguinchor because it's also one of the cheapest cities in Senegal – finding a room for CFA 2500 and food for CFA 500 is relatively easy.

Orientation

The heart of town is Le Rond-Point at the southern end of Rue Javelier. If you head three blocks north on Rue Javelier, you'll pass various shops, restaurants and two banks before reaching Rue du Commerce, which extends east-west along the southern bank of the Casamance River. Just to the south, in Rue de France, are the Hôtel du Tourisme, the post office, and the Guinea-Bissau consulate. The road heading south-west from the Rond-Point passes the cathedral and becomes Ave Lycée Guignabo (or Route de l'Aviation), passing Marché St-Maur, several cheap hotels, the Centre Artisanal and the top-end Hôtel Néma Kadior, before reaching the airport, which is three km from the centre.

Information

Campements Booking Office The regional office of the village-run Campements Rurals Integrés (☎ 91 13 75) is at the Centre Artisanal. The man in charge is Adama Goudiaby. He has run the office for several years and can help with local information.

Money The banks for changing money are the SGBS, near the Hôtel Aubert, and the CBAO at the junction of Rue de France and Rue Javelier. They are open weekdays from around 8.30 to 11 am and 3 to 4 pm.

Consulates The consulate of Guinea-Bissau (☎ 91 10 46) is next door to Hôtel du Tourisme. With CFA 5000 and a photo in hand, you can get a visa to Guinea-Bissau on the spot. It is open weekdays from 8.30 am to noon. The French consulate is at the Hôtel Aubert and keeps similar hours.

Markets

The **Marché St-Maur** on Ave Lycée Guignabo, one km south of the city centre towards the airport, is well worth a visit if you're looking for fresh food or knick-knacks. A block to the south is the **Centre Artisanal**, which is open daily from 7.30 am to nightfall. There are numerous vendors here selling a wide variety of crafts from the area, including wooden carvings, dresses, metal objects, silver and fabrics. Most of it is souvenir quality. A warning, however: this is the area where the town's hustlers lurk.

Places to Stay – bottom end

Ziguinchor has two cheap campements, both three km west of the centre on the road to Cap Skiring. The first one you come to is the well-marked *Centre Touristique de Colobane Fass* (☎ 91 15 12) at the landmark radio antenna and 30 metres north of the highway. It charges CFA 1875 a person, CFA 850 for breakfast and CFA 1750 for lunch or dinner. The rooms have mosquito nets and private baths but the ambience is not as good as at *Campement ZAG* (☎ 91 15 57), run by a friendly French couple and 100 metres further on your right. Meal prices are the same but the

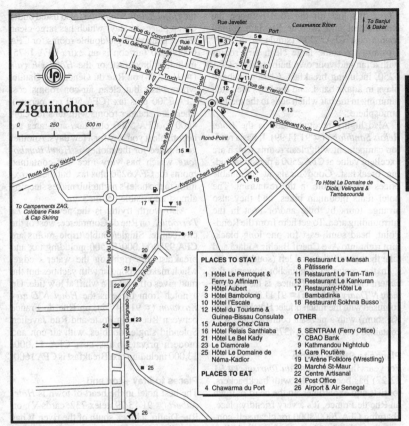

Ziguinchor

0   250   500 m

To Campements ZAG,
Colobane Fass
& Cap Skiring

To Hôtel Le Domaine de
Diola, Velingara &
Tambacounda

PLACES TO STAY	6 Restaurant Le Mansah
1 Hôtel Le Perroquet & Ferry to Affiniam	8 Pâtisserie
2 Hôtel Aubert	11 Restaurant Le Tam-Tam
3 Hôtel Bambolong	13 Restaurant Le Kankuran
10 Hôtel l'Escale	17 Restaurant-Hôtel Le Bambadinka
12 Hôtel du Tourisme & Guinea-Bissau Consulate	18 Restaurant Sokhna Busso
15 Auberge Chez Clara	**OTHER**
16 Hôtel Relais Santhiaba	5 SENTRAM (Ferry Office)
21 Hôtel Le Bel Kady	7 CBAO Bank
23 Le Diamorale	9 Kathmandou Nightclub
25 Hôtel Le Domaine de Néma-Kadior	14 Gare Routière
	19 L'Arène Folklore (Wrestling)
PLACES TO EAT	20 Marché St-Maur
4 Chawarma du Port	22 Centre Artisanal
	24 Post Office
	26 Airport & Air Senegal

local-style rooms cost CFA 2400 a person. There are nets, clean toilets and showers, and a pleasant *paillote* (straw hut). You can also rent bicycles here for CFA 2500 a day.

Also cheap, but not as nice as the campements, is *Le Diamorale*, about two km from the Rond-Point on the road towards the airport. It looks like a tin shack (which it is) with some very basic rooms costing CFA 2500 for one or two people. Slightly nearer the centre, in the area around Marché St-Maur, are some other cheapies. These include the somewhat rustic *Hôtel Le Bel Kady* (☎ 91 11 22) which has been popular

for years with backpackers because of the friendly management, cheap restaurant and general good vibes. The rooms are basic but decent and cost CFA 3000/3750 for singles/doubles without fans. If you're desperate, a few short blocks further north is the *Restaurant-Hôtel Le Bambadinka* which has filthy rooms for CFA 2500 (up to three people). A small place we didn't try, called *Auberge Kadiandou*, and costing CFA 3000 per person, is a five-minute walk from the gare routière – handy if you want to get moving early.

A better deal than all of these, if you don't mind spending a bit extra, is *Auberge Chez*

Clara. It's just off the road between the Rond-Point and Marché St-Maur. Small rooms cost CFA 5000 (single or double). Upstairs are some large clean airy rooms with a fan and your own bathroom for CFA 6250, including breakfast. Clara's husband plays in a jazz band, and the boys are often jamming in the bar which adds to the mellow atmosphere.

Also highly recommended is the *Hôtel Relais Santhiaba* (☎ 91 11 99). It has a rooftop campement with clean rooms which are excellent value at CFA 2500 a person including breakfast. Good meals at reasonable prices are available in the restaurant. The hotel rents mountain bikes, and they also arrange tours by bike and/or boat in the surrounding area. To get here from the Rond-Point, head south-east for one long block, turn right into Ave Cherif Bachir Aidara and take the second dirt road left (south).

In the centre of Ziguinchor, towards the eastern end of Rue de France, is the *Campement N'Daary Kassoum* (☎ 91 11 89; not to be confused with the much pricier Hôtel N'Daary Kassoum) with a pleasant courtyard and self-contained rooms for CFA 4375/5625.

Places to Stay – middle

For years the small *Hôtel du Tourisme* (☎ 91 12 27) has been popular with backpackers, tourists and expatriates. In the heart of town on Rue de France, it's a very friendly place, charging CFA 7000/8000 for clean self-contained singles/doubles with fans, including tax. Some larger double rooms are CFA 9000; the ones upstairs are best. Breakfast is CFA 1000. The bar, which has a shady terrace, is a good meeting place. Meals are good too, with most main courses around CFA 2000. Even if you're not staying, it's worth stopping by for a drink. Veronique, the French woman who runs the hotel with her husband Phillipe, backpacked around the world before settling here and likes to meet travellers (and practice her English!), and can help with local information. The hotel will also store gear for guests touring Casamance or heading for the beach.

Other places in this price category include

the *Hôtel Relais Santhiaba* (also listed under cheap places to stay) which has large clean self-contained single/double rooms for CFA 6000/8500 (air-con is an extra CFA 1875) including breakfast, or the *Hôtel l'Escale* (☎ 91 12 04) on Rue du Général de Gaulle, where basic but clean air-con rooms cost CFA 7500 plus tax (CFA 500 per person). There are cheaper rooms with fans for CFA 4000 to CFA 5000 plus tax, and rates are negotiable if you stay for a few days. Another good place for the money is *Hôtel Bambolong* which has very nice self-contained rooms for CFA 6250 plus tax, but their proximity to the hotel's nightclub makes sleeping almost impossible before 3 am.

Also worth trying is the new *Hôtel Le Perroquet*, on Rue de Commerce, west of the city centre. Single/double/triple rooms are CFA 9250/11,000/16,500 including tax and breakfast. It's right on the water's edge, which makes it popular with yachties but the mud gives off a bit of a whiff at low tide. Up a notch from these is the *Hôtel N'Daary Kassoum* (☎ 91 14 72), on Rue de France between Rue de la Poste and Rue Javelier. Splendid singles/doubles, with air-con and modern private baths cost CFA 11,000/13,000 including tax. Breakfast is CFA 1600.

Places to Stay – top end

The best hotel in the heart of town is *Hôtel Aubert* (☎ 91 13 79, telex 732; cards V), on Rue Diallo, a block south of the river. It has a small pool, car hire and an excellent restaurant. Rooms cost CFA 12,500 to CFA 16,250 for singles and CFA 12,500 to CFA 17,500 for doubles, plus tax (CFA 500 per person). Breakfast is CFA 2000.

Ziguinchor's other top hotel is the *Hôtel Le Domaine de Néma-Kadior* (☎ 91 18 24, telex 7320; cards AE, D, V). It charges around CFA 18,000/25,000 for a single/ double bungalow in the luxuriant garden grounds. The hotel is just over two km from the city centre on the road to the airport. Facilities include a swimming pool (open to nonguests for CFA 1250), tennis, and a somewhat pricey restaurant with a three-course menu for around CFA 6000.

Places to Eat

Cheap A good street for cheap food is Ave Lycée Guignabo, in the area of Marché St-Maur, which has many cafés, bars and gargottes. One of the town's most popular cheapies is *Restaurant Sokhna Busso*, 15 metres down a side alley one block south of the junction with Ave Cherif Bachir Aidara, where you can find meals for only CFA 310 a plate. Or try the *Restaurant-Hôtel Le Bambadinka* across the street, where the meals are similarly priced. The restaurant at *Hôtel Le Bel Kady* is slightly more expensive, but good value with mafé for CFA 500, riz viande for CFA 650, poulet yassa for CFA 1000 and big beers for CFA 500.

For fresh bread and cakes, the *pâtisserie* on the junction of Rue de France and Rue Lemoine is open all day and night. For chawarmas at CFA 650, head for *Chawarma du Port* on Rue du Commerce, near the port. They also do pizzas and sandwiches.

At the gare routière are several coffee stalls and shacks where cheap food is served, including *Sopp Naby* (or Chez Zal) and *Fatou Derme*.

More Expensive Good value in this range is *Restaurant Le Mansah*, a small place on Rue Javelier two blocks up from the river. It has some of the most reasonable prices in town, with poulet grillé, poulet rôti, poisson braisé or tiéboudienne, all with chips, for CFA 1250. In the same price range is *Restaurant Chez Clara*, less than 100 metres south-west of the Rond-Point, across from the cathedral. The service is slow but you can get a three-course menu for about CFA 2000. (It's possible that this place may have closed during 1994, and transferred operations to the Auberge Chez Clara, a few hundred metres away, just off the main road.)

Moving slightly up-market, the tranquil *Restaurant Le Tam-Tam* on Rue de France at the intersection with Ave Lemoine has good European and African dishes, with slow service and prices in the CFA 1500 to CFA 2500 range. Not far away is the large and cavern-like *Restaurant Le Kankuran* where prices are slightly lower.

Other restaurants in this range are joined to hotels. Highly recommended is the *Hôtel Relais Santhiaba* where Gerard the French chef prepares very decent dishes in the CFA 1500 to CFA 2300 range, or the *Hôtel du Tourisme* where prices are slightly higher but the food is also excellent.

Entertainment

Discos Try the flashy nightclub at the *Hôtel Bambolong*, near the centre, half a block south of the river. Beers are about CFA 1200. The *Kathmandou Nightclub* on the east side of the city centre is another popular place where the beer is cheaper.

Cinema Look for what's showing at Le Vox, which is near the centre on the corner of Blvd Foch and Rue de Boucotte.

Wrestling This is one of the main spectator sports in Ziguinchor. Wrestling matches *(les luttes)* take place during the dry season, primarily January to June, on Sundays starting at 4 pm, at Arène Folklore, 50 metres east of Ave Lycée Guignabo and just north of Marché St-Maur. There's no stadium, just a dusty field. Each section of town has its favourites at these festive occasions.

Getting There & Away

Air Air Senegal has an office (☎ 91 10 81) at the airport, and flies everyday between Ziguinchor and Dakar, and three or four times a week to Bissau (Guinea-Bissau) for about CFA 31,500.

Bush Taxi & Minibus The gare routière is one km east of the central area. Bush taxis and minibuses for Dakar (454 km), the Gambian border (120 km), Bissau (139 km), Cap Skiring (71 km) and all destinations in the Casamance leave from here. The fare to Dakar is CFA 5625 by Peugeot 504 bush taxi and CFA 4375 by minibus; the trip normally takes eight to 10 hours by bush taxi and 10 to 15 hours by minibus, depending on delays at the border or the ferry across the Gambia River. Most transport to Dakar leaves between 7 am and noon. You can also travel to Dakar on one of the night buses that leave from Ave Lycée Guignabo near the market between 3 and 8 am, arriving in Dakar about nine to 11 hours later. You can get on the bus any time during the evening or night and sleep there until departure. Or you may be able to arrange to have them pick you up at your hotel. Other fares are: CFA 3125 to Kaolack, CFA 2250 to Kolda and CFA 5000 to Tambacounda via Kolda.

If you are travelling from Ziguinchor to other towns and villages around the Casamance, bush taxis and minibuses to Cap Skiring leave from the gare routière starting around 7 am, with the last one at about 7 pm, although they go most frequently in the morning. The fare is CFA 900 in a minibus, and CFA 1200 in a 504, and the journey takes from one to two hours. By minibus to Oussouye is CFA 775, to Elinkine CFA 750, to Kafountine CFA 1875.

For details on routes to Banjul and Bissau see the main Getting There & Away section.

Hitchhiking Hitching on the main road between Ziguinchor and Cap Skiring is fairly easy, as there's lots of traffic but, just because we say hitching is possible, it doesn't mean we recommend it. On the smaller dirt roads around Casamance your chances of getting a lift are very small as traffic is light.

Boat The most interesting way to travel between Ziguinchor and Dakar is by the ferry MV *Joola* that runs twice weekly in each direction, via Carabane Island. See the main Getting Around section for details.

Getting Around

Taxi Taxis around Ziguinchor city centre and out to the airport (three km) or gare routière (one km) cost CFA 300 to CFA 400. You may have difficulty getting this price coming into town from the airport. For longer trips, a taxi for the day will cost you CFA 12,500 to CFA 15,000 plus petrol if you bargain well. The main taxi rank is at the Rond-Point.

Car For getting around town or around the Casamance region you can rent a car. The only place in Ziguinchor is Casa Auto Location (☎ 91 10 38) whose office is on Rue du Général de Gaulle, one block along from the Hôtel l'Escale. They also have a Cap Skiring depot at the Pirogue Restaurant (☎ 93 51 76). Rates are reasonable and avoid the complex calculations required when you rent from the big outfits in Dakar. The smallest car (a soft-top Citroen, 2WD but fine on all but the sandiest tracks) costs a flat rate of CFA 17,000 per day including insurance, tax and unlimited km. A Fiat saloon with air-con costs CFA 22,000. All you pay is the petrol, and a driver is available if required.

Bicycle For getting around town, or for touring the Casamance in relaxed style, you can't beat a bike. These can be hired from the Hôtel Relais Santhiaba, Campement ZAG, or from outside the Hôtel Aubert. Types vary considerably: there are a few decent mountain bikes (*vélos tous terrains*), but mostly all you can find are old steel roadsters. These are OK if you take your time and don't race around (which you shouldn't do in the Casamance anyway). VTTs cost about CFA 2500 a day; roadsters CFA 1500, although you should be able to negotiate good deals if you want to go for a week or so.

AROUND ZIGUINCHOR

A good place for a short day trip from Ziguinchor is the **Ferme Animalière de Djibelor**, five km outside town on the road towards Cap Skiring, which has an interesting selection of tropical plants and 'wild' animals (the larger ones in cages), where you can walk along pleasant paths through the forest. There is also a farm shop selling good quality fresh fruit. Entrance is CFA 1000.

Another popular day trip organised by many of the hotels and campements is a pirogue ride to the villages of Affiniam and Djilapao, on the north bank of the Casamance River, and the nearby Île des Oisseaux (Bird Island). The main feature at Affiniam is the splendid *impluvium* (see the later section on Enampor for details), while at Djilapao you can visit some two-storey mud houses (*cases étages*) and the house of a local artist which is decorated with relief murals of various designs, some rather risqué. Île des Oiseaux is fascinating, even if you're not greatly into birds. With very little effort you can see pelicans, flamingos, kingfishers, storks, sunbirds, and many more. Prices are around CFA 12,500 per day for the boat.

TOURING THE CASAMANCE

The Casamance is divided into three areas: Basse Casamance (Lower Casamance) is the area west of Ziguinchor and south of the river; Casamance Nord is the area north of the river; and Haute Casamance (Upper Casamance) is the area east of Ziguinchor.

Village Campements

One of the Casamance region's major attractions is its system of village campements (officially called *campements rurals integrés* or CRIs), built by villagers with government loans and run as co-operatives. Profits are reinvested in the villages to build schools, maternity clinics and health centres – an exemplary way to improve village life without introducing many of the poisonous effects generally associated with Western tourism in developing countries. Up until 1989, well over 20,000 tourists stayed in them each year although this number fell in the early 1990s due to the 'separatist problems'. In the next few years, as things pick up, it's likely that these figures will be reached again.

The first village campement was built in 1973 at Enampor. There are now ten in the Casamance: four in the Basse Casamance (Enampor, Diohère, Oussouye and Elinkine)

and six in the Casamance Nord (Koubalan, Affiniam, Tionk-Essil, Baïla, Abéné and Kafountine). The last two are the only ones on the ocean. Prices at all the CRIs are standardised: the price of a bed (with net) is CFA 2300, breakfast is CFA 900, and three-course lunch or dinner CFA 2200. Bucket showers are the norm, and lighting is generally by oil lamp, but bedrooms and bathrooms are always clean and tidy.

The central reservations office for the village campements in Casamance is at the Centre Artisanal in Ziguinchor. At present, reservations are not normally required, as campements are rarely full. Even if things pick up in the next few years, the system only works if you reserve at least a month in advance and do not alter your itinerary, which is OK for organised groups but usually impossible for independent travellers. As things stand, if you turn up on spec you should get a bed. In the unlikely event of the campement being full, there may be another nearby or, failing that, a room will probably be found for you at a private house in the village.

As well as the village campements, there are now many privately owned campements in the Casamance region, which offer similar facilities at similar prices, although the profits go to the owner rather than to the village as a whole.

Suggested Itineraries

The Casamance can be toured by car, public transport, bicycle or foot. The walking is not difficult along the banks of the estuaries although occasionally you will encounter marshy areas. At most tributaries you'll find someone with a pirogue who will be glad to

---

Fromager Trees

Although the fromager tree is found in many parts of West Africa, it has a special significance in the Casamance region, where it also known as the bombax tree or the kapok tree. In other parts of Africa it's called the cotton tree. The tree's most recognisable features are its yellowish bark, large pod-like fruit, and exposed roots, which grow tall and narrow, forming a natural maze around the trunk. The name 'fromager' (meaning cheese in French) comes from the soft, light wood which is especially good for making *pirogues* (dugout canoes).

Many villages are built around an ancient fromager tree because they are believed to have special significance, harbouring spirits who protect the inhabitants from bad luck. The men of the village use the tree as a *palava*, or meeting place; the exposed roots often make comfortable benches or back rests. ∎

take you across for a small fee. If you want to leave the main tracks and follow footpaths through the fields and villages, a local guide is recommended. A daily fee or around CFA 500 to CFA 1000 is appropriate. For cycling, the smaller *pistes* are often too sandy, even for fat-tyred mountain bikes, but there are several good dirt roads in the area which are rideable. Even the main tarred roads are OK on a bike, although you need to keep your eyes and ears open, as what little traffic there is tends to go quite fast, and with little room for error. If you want to avoid the long stretches of tar, or just get tired, you can always load your bike onto a bush taxi.

If you want to combine hiking with public transport, a full circuit of the Basse Casamance can be done in seven to 12 days: go from Ziguinchor by bush taxi to Brin; hike to Enampor, then either hike direct (or bush taxi back via Brin) to Diohèr, Niambalang or Oussouye; hike or bush taxi to Elinkine; take the boat to Carabane Island; return to Elinkine and either retrace through Oussouye or go directly by pirogue to Diakène Ouolof; get a boat or bush taxi to Cap Skiring; head north to Diembéring, then return to Ziguinchor by bush taxi. An extra loop would be from Cap Skiring, south along the beach to Kabrousse, east through the Basse Casamance National Park then north to Oussouye and back to Ziguinchor. Of course, you can lengthen or shorten this circuit, or choose your own, to suit the time you have. There are campements or cheap places to stay in all these villages so a tent isn't necessary. The Basse Casamance National Park is due to reopen in 1994, but the huts at the campement were destroyed during the 'separatist problems' and you may need a tent here until they are rebuilt.

A tour by bike might be: Brin, Enampor, Oussouye, to Elinkine via M'Lomp on the tar road, over to Carabane by boat (leaving the bike at Elinkine), back to Elinkine and then to Oussouye on the old road via Loudia Ouolof, to Cap Skiring and/or Diembéring before returning to Ziguinchor. The sandy track to the Basse Casamance National Park from Oussouye is only just passable by bike but the

track from Kabrousse is too soft for cycling. By bike you can also tour parts of Casamance Nord: from Ziguinchor, you can catch the public ferry across to Affiniam, and ride to Baïla via Tendouk, returning via Bignona to Koubalan, then back to Ziguinchor.

BASSE CASAMANCE
Brin
Brin is a small village on the main road between Ziguinchor and Cap Skiring, where the dirt road to Enampor branches off. For a place to sleep the friendly *Campement Le Filao* set in a lush tropical garden has single/double bungalows for CFA 1500/2500. Breakfast is CFA 600 and a three-course menu is CFA 2000.

Brin is often overlooked, but it's in a nice area. You can walk in the surrounding forest or fields or take pirogue rides on the nearby Casamance River. To get here, take anything heading for Cap Skiring and get off at Brin.

Enampor
Enampor is 23 km directly west of Ziguinchor. The *village campement* is a huge, round mud house, called a *case à impluvium*, which is worth a visit even if you're not staying here. During wartime, the people would shut themselves inside the impluvium for safety. Rain water would be funnelled into a large tank in the centre of the house through a hole in the roof, which also admits a wonderful diffuse light. There are other such houses in the Casamance but this is a particularly good example. The only other genuine impluvium campement is at Affiniam. To sleep and eat here you pay the standard CRI prices. For a visit, the grumpy manager will show you around for CFA 120.

Getting There & Away A daily minibus comes to Enampor from Ziguinchor in the afternoon (CFA 375) and returns in the morning. Or get a bush taxi to Brin and walk the 13 km to Enampor through palm groves, fields and villages, taking the left (southerly) fork at Essil, the halfway point.

Diohèr

Diohèr is a small village on the main road between Brin and Oussouye. The *village campement* was closed in 1994; if it reopens, standard CRI prices will apply.

Niambalang

Niambalang is between Diohèr and Oussouye. The campement here is called *Chez Theodor Balouse* and visitors stay with the friendly Balouse family in very simple surroundings for CFA 1250 per night, with breakfast for CFA 375 and meals CFA 1000 (a full day's notice is required).

Oussouye

Roughly halfway between Ziguinchor and Cap Skiring, Oussouye (OU-sou-yeh) is the main town in the Basse Casamance area. It's a sleepy place, although the market gets lively on some mornings. There's a few good local restaurants and campements. Bikes can be hired from Velo Adiake on the main street, or from Bernard, a Frenchman who also organises cycling tours in the area (ask at the campements for directions).

Places to Stay & Eat The well-run *village campement* is one km north of town on the old (dirt) road leading north-west towards Elinkine. This is a fascinating example of local mud architecture, with two storeys, a central hall and stairway, conical pillars and low doorways. Accommodation and meals are standard CRI prices. The privately owned *Auberge du Routard* is half a km from town on the same road as the village campement and run by its former manager. It has nice bungalows for CFA 1625 a person without food and CFA 4250 for full board. The food is good; many of the vegetables come from the back garden and the chicken you see running around in the morning may be on your platter in the evening. On the outskirts of town, about one km off the road to Ziguinchor, is the smarter *Campement des Bolongs* which has nice bungalows for CFA 3000 per person (CFA 3750 if you want self-contained). Breakfast is CFA 1250, and

meals are around CFA 2000, but reductions are available if you take full board.

For eating in Oussouye, *Restaurant 2000* on the main street has good cheap food, although there's normally only one dish a day. Other places to try are *Chez Rachel* in the market, or *Restaurant Sud* on the main street. For a quiet drink and some people-watching, go to the nearby *Buvette du Rond-Point*.

Getting There & Away All bush taxis between Ziguinchor and Cap Skiring pass through Oussouye, so getting here is easy.

M'Lomp

On the new tar road between Oussouye and Elinkine you'll pass through the village of M'Lomp, which has several two-storey cases étages, and some other single-storey houses with brightly decorated walls and pillars, all unique to this part of Africa. The old lady who lives in the largest case étage near the main road will give you a tour for CFA 100. Tourists on day trips from Cap Skiring also visit M'Lomp, which explains the postcards of Rome and Mont Blanc proudly pinned to the wall, and the local youths outside offering cheap souvenirs.

Pointe St George

Pointe St George lies to the north of M'Lomp and Oussouye on a large bend in the Casamance River. The delightful Hôtel Pointe St George was destroyed during the 'separatist problems', and there are no immediate plans for rebuilding. The people at Hôtel du Tourisme in Ziguinchor will know if it is rebuilt.

Elinkine

Elinkine is a busy fishing village at the end of the new tar road from Oussouye. From here you can get boats to Carabane Island (a port of call for the ferry between Dakar and Ziguinchor), either for the day or to stay at one of the campements on the island.

Places to Stay & Eat The *village campement*, on the edge of Elinkine, signposted on the right as you come in from Oussouye, charges standard CRI prices. It has clean, safe huts (some with showers), cheap beer and is in a perfect setting amongst palm trees (complete with hammocks) on a sandy beach right at the water's edge. Bikes, canoes and sailboards can be hired, and pirogue excursions arranged. The private *Campement Le Fromager* is right next to the road, where all the bush taxis stop. Built in an impluvium-style it charges CFA 2300 a person for clean rooms and spotless shared baths. Breakfast is CFA 900, and meals CFA 2200. This place is busier and noisier than the village campement, as it seems to be a meeting place for local youths. At night, local drummers congregate around a fire in the garden and there's a good atmosphere.

Getting There & Away A minibus runs every afternoon from Ziguinchor to Elinkine; it passes through Oussouye around 4 pm and returns the next day at 7 am. The cost is CFA 875.

Carabane

Carabane (sometimes spelt Karabane) is the name of the island, and the village on it, to the north-west of Elinkine. The village was an important settlement and trading station in early colonial times, but has now been almost totally reclaimed by bush. You can still see the ruined Breton-style church, with dusty pews and crumbling statues, and the remains of a school. Along the beach is an old cemetery with settlers' graves dating from the 1840s, many now half-covered in sand. Carabane is also good for bird-watching and swimming. Dolphins are often seen off the beach.

Places to Stay & Eat The *Campement Cocotier* is a relaxed place with a lively bar popular with local youths and visiting fishers. Rooms cost CFA 1875 a person and meals are CFA 1750.

More tranquil is the *Campement de Malang Badji*, about one km further along the beach, where prices are the same. Malang Badji is a sculptor and painter; he has exhibited in Europe and his works (and those of other local artists)

are on display or for sale here. If you're staying for a few days, and you don't mind paying for materials, you can try your hand at local glass painting or pottery. More up-market is the *Hôtel de Karabane*, on the beach between the two campements. The hotel fell on hard times in the early 1990s, but it was bought by the energetic Augustine Diatta in 1994 and is now undergoing a complete renovation. Augustine is an agronomist by profession and has great plans for turning the hotel grounds into a tropical garden. Rooms range from CFA 2500 to CFA 10,000, depending on their state of repair.

Getting There & Away Carabane village can be reached by motorised pirogue from Elinkine. There is no regular public service, although there's usually a boat across to the island each evening which waits for the daily minibus to arrive from Ziguinchor. It comes back early next morning. Otherwise, you need to hang around on the waterfront until you see a boat leaving. The fare should be CFA 1200, and the ride takes 30 minutes. In reality the local people hang around until they see a group of tourists who have hired a boat (CFA 6500 for the return trip, including waiting time), and then they hitch a ride for nothing.

You can also get to Carabane Island on the MV *Joola* which stops here on its voyage between Dakar and Ziguinchor, twice weekly in each direction. The schedule changes constantly (see the main Getting Around section for details), but if the boat leaves Dakar on a Monday afternoon, it stops at Carabane early on Tuesday morning, arriving in Ziguinchor about 11 am. Going the other way, if the boat leaves Ziguinchor at noon on Thursday, it stops at Carabane a few hours later, then arrives in Dakar on Friday morning. The sailings over Friday to Monday allow some Dakar residents to spend the weekend on Carabane. The fare for deck class between Ziguinchor and Carabane is CFA 875.

Diakène Ouolof

The *Campement Eguaye* lies on an island near the village of Diakène Ouolof, about three km off the main road between Oussouye and Cap Skiring, and is probably the most 'remote' campement in Casamance, but worth getting to if you can. The owner, Abdou N'Diaye, is a friendly guy who speaks English and French. A bed is CFA 1800, breakfast CFA 750 and meals CFA 1500. Fishing and bird-watching trips by pirogue can be arranged. To reach the campement, you first need to get to Diakène Ouolof. Ask to be dropped at the junction three km west of Diakène Diola. The campement is signposted. It's a three-km walk along the sandy track. Keep left at any fork or junction. You need to get there in the morning, in time to find Abdou (ask for his house) and paddle with him out to the campement. Alternatively you can arrange to get there from Elinkine. A motorised pirogue should cost CFA 7500 for the seven-km ride.

CAP SKIRING

The beaches in the Cap Skiring area are some of the finest in all Africa. This is where you find most of Senegal's tourist hotels (although there are some cheap campements as well), and the highest concentration of foreigners in West Africa except for in The Gambia. If you want a few easy days of sun and sand, plus a touch of energetic nightlife, this is the place. But if you're trying to see the 'real' Africa, pass on.

Orientation

Everything revolves around Ziguinchor Junction, which is the intersection of the north-south beach road and the highway to Ziguinchor. Public transport will drop you here if you want. The village of Cap Skiring, with shops, restaurants and the main gare routière, is about one km or so north of that. The hotel strip starts to the north of the village and continues south to Kabrousse, five km away.

Places to Stay & Eat – bottom end

The cheapest places are in Cap Skiring village itself. The lively Bar Kassoumaye has very basic singles/doubles for about CFA 2500/3000 and meals for CFA 1200. There

are several cheap restaurants and gargottes along the main street, all doing cheap dishes in the CFA 350 to CFA 750 range. For cheap beer in local surroundings, try Bar Saraba just off the road towards Diembéring.

For more pleasant accommodation, there's a row of campements about one km from the village, near Ziguinchor Junction, all reached by walking south from the junction for 100 metres, then turning right down a dirt road for 200 metres towards the ocean. First in the line is the simple Campement Keur Samba which has a row of fairly dark rooms costing CFA 2200/4250 for singles/doubles. Meals are CFA 2000. Next is the friendly and popular Auberge de la Paix where well-maintained singles/doubles are CFA 1900/3000 and meals are CFA 2000. There's good music here and at night someone is usually beating the drums. Next is Campement Le Paradis where spotless rooms are CFA 2000 per person, and meals in the nicely decorated bar cost around CFA 2000. This place has the most character and is the best value in terms of facilities. Last in this line is Campement Karabane a small quiet place with rooms at CFA 2000.

Up a bit in price is Campement Mussuwam, wedged between the Paix and the Paradise, but it's no better value with doubles at CFA 4350 with dirty shared baths, or CFA 5200 for self-contained rooms. A larger room (for up to three people) with air-con and hot water is CFA 12,500.

If you want to stay in the village, Auberge La Palmier is recommended, with double rooms at CFA 6250. The bar-restaurant is also popular, with French and Senegalese menus in the CFA 3500 to CFA 4000 range.

The most interesting place to eat, with very reasonable prices, is the Restaurant Toray Kunda, near the beach, just off the dirt road towards the Hôtel Savana. Run by the friendly and very talkative Ali Baba, this place does Senegalese specialities to order for around CFA 2500 per person. You need to go in the morning to see what's available, and to give Ali time to get to the market. Wine, beer and soft drinks can also be ordered.

If you're self-catering, there's an excellent

bakery at Ziguinchor Junction, with a small shop nearby. Cap Skiring village also has local stores and a small fruit market.

Places to Stay & Eat – middle & top end

Best in this range is the good-value *Hôtel Les Cocotiers* (☎ 93 51 51) next to (and managed by) the top-class Hôtel La Paillote. This is a friendly place with a private beach and pleasant self-contained single/double rooms overlooking the ocean for CFA 18,000/21,000. Breakfast is CFA 1500. Half board is CFA 15,500 per person for two people sharing a double. Guests staying here can eat at La Paillote and use their facilities, which include water sports equipment, an excellent French restaurant and a beach bar which also serves cheap snacks. The *Hôtel La Paillote* (☎ 93 14 14) is directly opposite Ziguinchor Junction. It has single/double bungalows for CFA 24,250/31,000. Breakfast is CFA 2500. Half board is CFA 24,250 per person for two people sharing a double. The hotel is renowned for its superb French food and wonderful ambience.

The plush new *Hôtel Savana* (☎ 93 15 52, fax 93 14 92; cards V, D, M, AE) is about two km north of Cap Skiring village, with attractive bungalows for CFA 37,500/46,000 and thatched two-storey houses with individual balconies for CFA 56,000/66,000. Special weekend and low-season rates are often available; ask at reception. Breakfast is CFA 2500; meals CFA 8000. Nearby is the smart bar *Oasis du Cap* with pricey beers, a small menu, and dancing most evenings.

South of Cap Skiring, near Kabrousse, are two large deluxe hotels, which share the same lush grounds and many facilities, catering almost exclusively for package groups, although independent tourists are welcome. These are *Le Kabrousse* and the slightly more expensive *Hôtel Cap Casamance* (☎ 93 51 26, fax 93 51 27; cards V, M, D, AE), where rooms range from 165 to 255FF for singles and 315 to 405FF for doubles depending on the season. Nearby is the smaller *Hotel Houback* (☎ 93 14 36, fax 93 51 12; cards V, M, AE) where pleasant bungalows cost 160FF per person. Most of the

top hotels are closed in August, September and October.

Getting There & Away

Bush taxis and minibuses run regularly all day between Ziguinchor and Cap Skiring, although there's more traffic in the mornings. Leaving Cap Skiring, you can arrange for a bush taxi to pick you up in the morning from your hotel.

You can also go by pirogue between Cap Skiring and Carabane Island. A private hire costs around CFA 20,000 for the whole boat.

Getting Around

Most of the large hotels have bicycles for rent and can also arrange car hire. You can also hire bikes from some of the cheaper campements, or by asking at the repair shop in Cap Skiring village, which also rents mobylettes for the day. All the hotels and campements arrange pirogue trips on the *bolongs* (creeks/backwaters) a few km inland from the coast. A day trip will be around CFA 12,500 for the boat. Alternatively, you can arrange to be dropped at Diakène Ouolof or Elinkine.

Diembéring

To escape the hustle and bustle of Cap Skiring, head for Diembéring (pronounced JEM-bay-ring), nine km to the north and easily reached by bicycle, private taxi (CFA 5000 each way) or the daily minibus from Ziguinchor, which passes through Cap Skiring around 5 pm and returns early next morning. The beach is quiet and hassle-free and there are several places to stay.

At the entrance to the village is the homely *Restaurant Le Diola* with meals around CFA 1850, and one room with two beds for CFA 1500 per person. Opposite is *Campement Asseb* (☎ 93 31 06) where bungalows cost CFA 1850 per person and meals CFA 1750. Slightly nearer the beach, in a great setting on a small hill in the heart of the village, is *Campement Aten-Elou*, where rooms are CFA 2250 per person and meals CFA 1750. At the foot of the hill is the basic impluvium-style *Campement Chez Albert*, where slightly run-down rooms are CFA 1750, and meals CFA 1250.

BASSE CASAMANCE NATIONAL PARK

The Basse Casamance National Park, which measures about seven km by five km, can be reached from Cap Skiring and Oussouye. There are several vegetation zones: tropical forest and dense undergrowth give way to open grassland, tidal mud flats and mangrove swamps. There are quite a few animals, especially red colobus monkey and duiker, as well as bushbuck, porcupine, mongoose, a herd of forest buffalo, crocodile and leopard. The park fee is CFA 1000 per day, plus CFA 5000 for a car. The park has a good network of roads and white sandy trails and there are several hides (called *miradors*) for viewing game.

Places to Stay & Eat

The park was due to reopen in 1994, but the bungalows at the campement were destroyed

during the 'separatist problems'. Your only option is to camp at the park headquarters, or to stay in Oussouye and visit the park for the day by bike or taxi.

Getting There & Away

The park headquarters are 10 km south of Oussouye. From Oussouye go two km west on the main highway towards Cap Skiring, then turn left (south) at the signpost for the park; the park entrance is eight km down the white sandy road towards Santiaba Mandjak. Once you enter the park, keep heading south for half a km, then take your first right to reach the headquarters.

CASAMANCE NORD
Affiniam

Although this village is north of the river in the Casamance Nord area, it is very easy to reach from Ziguinchor by boat, and is a popular day-trip destination. It's worth staying here if you can, however, and spending some time

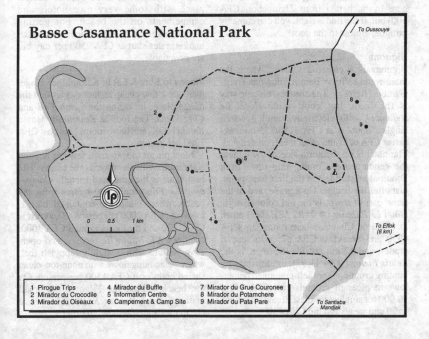

Basse Casamance National Park

To Oussouye

0   0.5   1 km

To Effok
(6 km)

To Santiaba
Mandjak

1 Pirogue Trips
2 Mirador du Crocodile
3 Mirador du Oiseaux
4 Mirador du Buffle
5 Information Centre
6 Campement & Camp Site
7 Mirador du Grue Couronee
8 Mirador du Potamchere
9 Mirador du Pata Pare

in the surrounding area, where the people see few visitors.

The *village campement* is a genuine impluvium, similar in design to the one in Enampor, where you get a bed for CFA 1750 and meals at standard CRI prices. To get there, the public ferry runs between Affiniam and Ziguinchor (the quay is near the Parquet Hotel) every Monday, Wednesday and Friday morning. It stops at 'le port d'Affiniam' (about one km from the campement) for one hour then returns. The fare is CFA 300. If you're coming here by bike or car, you can use the road that turns off the main road south of Bignona and crosses the new barrage to the north-east of Affiniam.

Koubalan

Koubalan is a few km to the east of the main road between Ziguinchor and Bignona. The *village campement*, overlooking a quiet creek, has rooms and meals at standard CRI prices, and good facilities including clean bathrooms with running water. You can get here by bush taxi from Ziguinchor (CFA 500) but, if the tide is right, you can come by pirogue, almost to the door!

Bignona

Bignona is a crossroads town, where the main route to/from Banjul joins the Trans-Gambia Highway. The cheapest place to stay is the basic but good-value *Hôtel Le Kelumack* with electricity, running water, singles/ doubles at CFA 3150/3750, breakfast at CFA 625, and other meals on demand. The hotel is on the north side of town, near the gendarmerie. Coming into town from Diouloulou, turn left at the first rond-point, just after the bridge. Up a grade, and in the same part of town, is the old colonial-style *Hôtel Le Palmier* (☎ 94 12 58), also known as Hôtel de Chasse, where rooms are CFA 4350 and breakfast CFA 875. Up several grades, and 12 km outside the town, is the *Relais Fleuri* (☎ 94 11 93), used mainly by hunting groups, where self-contained bungalows in pleasant grounds cost CFA 7500/ 10,000 for singles/doubles. Breakfast is CFA 1500 and meals around CFA 4300.

Baïla

Just off the main road between Bignona and Diouloulou, the *village campement* at Baïla is a quiet place with clean rooms and good food at standard CRI prices. It's run by a friendly manager who enjoys showing visitors around the village, which is off most tourist itineraries. It's also a very good place to see birds.

Diouloulou

If you get stuck at this village some 20 km south of The Gambian border, where the road to Kafountine branches off, the small *Campement Myriam* has simple singles/ doubles in bungalows for CFA 1850/2500.

Kafountine

Kafountine is a large village, 15 km south of The Gambian border, at the end of the tar road from Diouloulou. In the 1980s it was destined to be Senegal's newest coastal resort, but the 'separatist problems' put a hold on any large-scale development, and today Kafountine remains a small tranquil place with some very nice hotels and campements on the beach. For getting around, bikes can be hired from a shop in the market; rates start at CFA 2500 per day but are negotiable.

Places to Stay & Eat In Kafountine village, there are a few cheap restaurants around the marketplace, including the *Lamp Fall* and *Chez Vieux*. The food at *Restaurant Mama Kendo* is OK, and basic rooms here cost CFA 1200 per person.

Most places to stay are a few km beyond Kafountine village, towards the ocean. The best value is the quiet and friendly *Campement Le Filao*, only 100 metres from the beach, where clean self-contained bungalows cost CFA 2000 per person. Breakfast is CFA 1000 and meals are around CFA 3000. Nearby is *A la Nature Restocases*, a co-operative venture with a slightly hippyish feel, where basic bungalows with none-too-clean shared baths cost CFA 1500 per person. On the beach behind the Filao is the small thatched *Soko Bantan Restaurant* where cheap meals are prepared to order.

In between the village and the beach are several more places, including *Kunja Campement* and *Africa Campement* with rooms at CFA 1850 per person, and meals in the CFA 1000 to CFA 2500 range. Beyond these three places, on the beach, about 700 metres north of the Filao, is the village campement, called *Campement Sitokoto*, with rooms and meals at standard CRI prices. Next door is the more up-market and snappily titled *Robinson Crusoe Fishing Lodge & Mama Karamba Restaurant*, where half board in a bungalow costs from CFA 5000 per person. Even if you're not staying here, the restaurant is well worth a visit, with complete three-course meals between CFA 3500 and CFA 5000. Boat excursions to remote islands in the Casamance delta can be arranged.

On the beach south of the Filao is the new *Hôtel Nandy* where clean self-contained rooms cost CFA 3100 per person. A few km further is the up-market *Hôtel Le Karone* where good quality self-contained bungalows with air-con and hot showers cost CFA 8100 for two people (B&B). Half board is CFA 11,800 per person.

Getting There & Away Kafountine is three hours from Ziguinchor by bush taxi (CFA 1850). Alternatively, get any transport running between Ziguinchor and The Gambian border and change at Diouloulou, from where local bush taxis run on a fill-up-and-go basis to Kafountine for CFA 625.

Abéné

Abéné is six km north of Kafountine, with a selection of places to stay in the village itself, or a few km away on the beach.

In the heart of the village is the tasteful and tidy *Campement La Belle Danielle*, where the Konte brothers charge CFA 1250 per person for a bed, or CFA 5000 for full board, in a room with a net, and shared bath. The nearby *Campement Bantan Woro* charges CFA 2500 per person, but the facilities are not a patch on the Belle Danielle. Both places hire bikes and arrange pirogue trips.

From the village it's two km along a sandy track to the beach and the village-run

Campement Samaba, which charges standard CRI prices for rooms and meals, and seems to be home to several local Rastas. If you stay for more than a few days you can cook for yourself in the kitchen, and with a bit of advance warning you can arrange for a bush taxi to collect you when you want to leave. Nearby is the more up-market French-run *Campement Le Kossy*, usually known as Chez Jeanette, where half board in a self-contained bungalow in the beautiful garden costs CFA 6250 per person.

A few km north of Le Kossy is the more expensive *Village-Hôtel Kalissai* (☎ 93 51 88, fax 93 51 17), which has air-con thatched bungalows set in a shady palm grove very near the beach for CFA 18,700/21,200, or CFA 23,700/35,000 for half board. Sail-boards and 4WDs can be hired.

Getting There & Away You can get to Abéné by any transport heading to Kafountine (see that section), although the village is two km off the main road, and the beach a further two km, which you'll have to walk. The road to Hôtel Kalissai is signposted about three km before the road to the village.

HAUTE CASAMANCE
Sédhiou

Some 100 km east of Ziguinchor, on the north bank of the Casamance River, you may pass through Sédhiou on your way to/from Tambacounda. The town isn't particularly interesting, but the *Hôtel La Palmeraie* (☎ 95 11 02), a hunting and fishing camp, has nice bungalows for CFA 8000 a double in a garden setting by the river and a decent but expensive restaurant. The owner is friendly, rents bicycles, and can be a good source of information about the area. *Le Relais*, owned by his brother, is a similarly priced alternative.

Getting There & Away

Shared taxis from Tanaf on the road from Ziguinchor to Kolda cost CFA 375. You can also get to Sédhiou by ferry from Sandinièri; there are four every day as well as motorised pirogues. Heading north, take a bush taxi to the Bounkilling crossroads; there you'll find vehicles for Dakar.

Kolda

If you're travelling between Ziguinchor and Tambacounda on either the north or south bank of the river, you'll pass through Kolda, and maybe change transport here. The *Campement de la Chasse* has clean self-contained doubles for CFA 11,000.

The Northern Region

TOUBA

Touba is the sacred city of the Mouride Islamic Brotherhood. Each year, about half a million followers of Mouridism come to Touba on a pilgrimage called the Magal, to celebrate the return from exile (in 1907) of the founder of the sect, a marabout called Amadou Bamba. (He had been banished for 20 years by the French authorities, who saw him as a potential threat to their power.) His tomb is inside Touba's beautiful **mosque**, the pilgrims' focus. You can visit it outside prayer hours. Climbing up the minaret for a splendid view of the town should be possible once the repair work is completed. Also, don't miss the **market**.

If you're lucky enough to be in Senegal at the time of the Magal, go if you can. The date is 48 days after the Islamic new year. Be prepared, however: during the three days preceding the holy night, it is almost impossible to find an empty seat in a vehicle headed for Touba, or any place to stay. And, whenever you go to Touba, be very careful of what you do and what you wear. No alcohol or cigarettes are allowed, and men and women should be conservatively dressed with most (or all) of their arms and legs covered. Women are also expected to wear a skirt to well below the knees, or very loose-fitting trousers might suffice.

ST-LOUIS

For a glimpse of what a Senegalese city looked like in the colonial period head for St-Louis,

the first French settlement in Africa, which dates from 1659. Today, the city straddles the mainland, an island and part of the Langue de Barbarie peninsula at the mouth of the Senegal River. You reach the island on the 500-metre-long Pont Faidherbe, and two smaller bridges link the island to the peninsula.

St-Louis was the capital of Senegal-Mauritania until 1958, when the two countries split up. On the island, which was the European quarter, you can see many grand old houses, a few still with gracious wrought-iron and wooden balconies and verandas. The part of St-Louis on the peninsula used to be the African quarter; today it's a thriving fishing community called Guet N'Dar and the liveliest section of town.

Having seen its heyday pass years ago, St-Louis is now quite run-down and some travellers find it fairly dull, while others enjoy its faded elegance. But the Langue de Barbarie peninsula is certainly interesting. From Guet N'Dar this long narrow sandbar extends southwards for about 15 km separating the river from the ocean. On the end of the peninsula is one of Senegal's world-famous bird sanctuaries; a visit here or to the national park at Djoudj, 60 km north of St-Louis, could be the highlight of your trip.

Information

To change money go to the BICIS bank on Rue de France, two blocks north of Place Faidherbe, or the BNDS a block north on the same street. Both are open weekdays approximately from 8 to 11 am and 3 to 5 pm.

Things to See

The only notable sight on the mainland (the Sor district) is the old and architecturally intriguing **train station**. The **Pont Faidherbe** bridge from the mainland across to St-Louis Island is a grand piece of 19th-century engineering, originally built to cross the Danube but transferred here in 1897. The middle section used to rotate to allow ships to steam up the Senegal River. Taxis run across the bridge, but it's worth walking for the view.

Immediately after crossing the bridge you'll see the old **Hôtel de la Poste** on your

SENEGAL

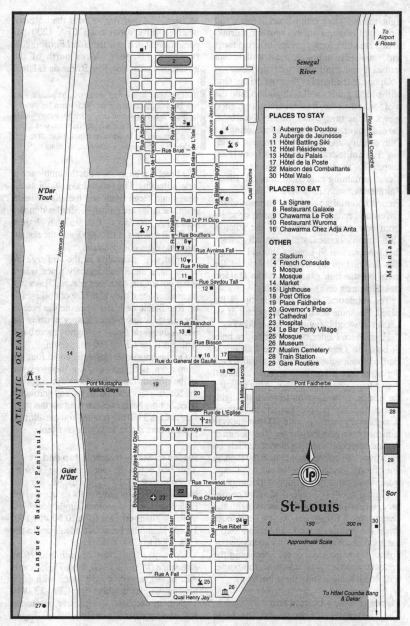

To Airport & Rosso

Senegal River

N'Dar Tout

Rue Adamson

Rue Ababacar Sy

Avenue Jean Mermoz

Rue de France

Rue Brue

Rue Brière de L'Isle

Quai Roume

Rue Blaise Diagne

PLACES TO STAY

1 Auberge de Doudou
3 Auberge de Jeunesse
11 Hôtel Battling Siki
12 Hôtel Résidence
13 Hôtel du Palais
17 Hôtel de la Poste
22 Maison des Combattants
30 Hôtel Walo

PLACES TO EAT

6 La Signare
8 Restaurant Galaxie
9 Chawarma Le Folk
10 Restaurant Wuroma
16 Chawarma Chez Adja Anta

OTHER

2 Stadium
4 French Consulate
5 Mosque
7 Mosque
14 Market
15 Lighthouse
18 Post Office
19 Place Faidherbe
20 Governor's Palace
21 Cathedral
23 Hospital
24 Le Bar Ponty Village
25 Mosque
26 Museum
27 Muslim Cemetery
28 Train Station
29 Gare Routière

Rue Khalifa

Rue Lt P H Diop

Rue Boufflers

Rue Aynima Fall

Rue P Holle

Rue Seydou Tall

Rue Blanchot

Rue Bisson

Rue du General de Gaulle

Rue Millès Lacroix

ATLANTIC OCEAN

Langue de Barbarie Peninsula

Pont Mustapha Malick Gaye

Pont Faidherbe

Mainland

Route de la Corniche

Rue de L'Eglise

Rue A M Javouye

Boulevard Abdoulaye Mar Diop

Guet N'Dar

Rue Thevenot

Rue Chassagnol

Rue Ibrahim Sarr

Rue Blaise Dumont

Rue Neuville

Rue Ribet

Rue A Fall

Quai Henry Jay

St-Louis

0   150   300 m

Approximate Scale

Sor

To Hôtel Coumba Bang & Dakar

right, the most interesting hotel in town, and a pleasant (though pricey) spot for a drink. In this area lurk local 'guides' offering tours and souvenirs, although most will accept refusal if you don't need their services.

Opposite the hotel is the post office. One of the local guides will take you up onto the roof for a small fee, from where you get good views of the bridge and the city. Nearby is the old **governor's palace**, a fort during the 18th century and now a government building. The **cathedral** nearby dates from 1828, despite its modern appearance, and is the oldest remaining church in Senegal. **Place Faidherbe**, with its statue of the famous French colonial governor, is in front of the governor's palace. If you go north or south from here you'll see some of the island's 19th-century houses, still essentially intact, that have earned St-Louis a World Heritage site designation by UNESCO. One of the more outstanding examples is the **Maison des Signares** on Quai Henry Jay.

The **museum**, at the southern tip of the island, has some fascinating old photos of St-Louis and wood carvings including masks.

From Place Faidherbe another bridge links St-Louis to Guet N'Dar on the Langue de Barbarie peninsula. The bridge was called Pont Servatius, but it has been recently renamed Pont Moustapha Malick Gaye. After crossing the bridge, go straight on to reach the lighthouse and the beach. Forget sunbathing though: every morning, some 200 pirogues are launched from here into the sea. They return in the late afternoon – surfing in spectacularly on the waves – to unload their fish on the sand. A line of lorries waits to take the catch to Dakar, from where some fish is shipped to Europe.

Further south is a unique **Muslim cemetery**, where each tomb is covered with the dead person's fishing net. As you head south down the peninsula, you can begin looking for good beach spots. You may be hassled by police if you go looking for beaches in the opposite (northern) direction, as the border with Mauritania is only three km away.

Places to Stay – bottom end

The cheapest place to stay is the basic *Maison des Combattants*, near the hospital, where a dirty room costs CFA 1200 per person. Next in line is the *Hôtel Battling Siki* (☎ 61 18 83), four blocks north of the governor's palace on Rue Brière de L'Isle.

Battling Siki, whose real name was M'Barick Fall, was born in St-Louis and in 1925, when he was 28, he became the first (and only African) heavyweight boxing champion of the world. His reign was short-lived, however, as he was assassinated the same year in the USA. His nephew now runs the hotel.

The hotel is a bit grubby but the ambience is a definite plus. The rooms have washbasins, chairs and clean linen and the shared bathroom facilities are passable. Singles/doubles cost CFA 3700/5000. Couples can share a single. Breakfast is CFA 400, and the restaurant also does cheap meals.

Up a step in quality is the *Auberge de Jeunesse*, a clean and friendly place where B&B costs CFA 4500 per person. Tours can be arranged and they also hire out bikes. It's on Rue Brière de L'Isle opposite the French consulate. A few blocks further north is the new *Auberge de Doudou*, slightly more basic with B&B for CFA 3750 per person.

On the Langue de Barbarie, about four km from town, is *Campement des Vacances*, run by the Hôtel du Palais. It's in a nice setting, near the beach with views out to sea and across the river, but the basic huts are a bit on the steep side at CFA 3750 per person. You are allowed to camp here if you have your own tent.

Places to Stay – middle & top end

Your best bet in the medium range is *Hôtel du Palais* (☎ 61 17 72; cards AE, V) two blocks north of the governor's palace on Rue Brière de L'Isle. Spacious singles/doubles/triples with air-con are CFA 10,500/14,100/17,700 including breakfast. Meals are in the CFA 2500 to CFA 3700 range.

Up a grade is the French-run *Hôtel Résidence* (☎ 61 12 59/60, telex 75119; cards AE, D, V), a very decent place with large air-con singles/doubles for CFA 13,000/16,000, an excellent, if expensive, restaurant and an air-con bar. It's on Rue Blaise Diagne, four blocks north of the governor's palace. The friendly owners know the region well and have 4WDs and bicycles for hire.

The city's most charming hotel, however, is the *Hôtel de la Poste* (☎ 61 11 18/48, fax 61 23 13; cards V, AE), the first place you reach after coming across Pont Faidherbe from the mainland. It has singles/doubles for CFA 14,200/17,200. Breakfast is CFA 1750. Even if you don't stay here, don't miss seeing the hotel's club-like Safari Bar. Beers are expensive, and meals start at around CFA 3000; the French cheese platter is wonderful.

The most modern hotel in the St-Louis area is the attractive 50-room *Hôtel Coumba Bang* (☎ 61 18 50; cards AE, D), but it's recommended only if you have wheels as it's on the mainland, six km from the centre, on the road towards Dakar. There's a tranquil garden with swimming pool and tennis court. You can also windsurf on the lagoon just behind the hotel but the hotel's board is in bad condition. Singles/doubles cost CFA 18,600/21,100 plus tax.

Places to Eat

There are at least three places doing chawarmas for around CFA 600. *Chawarma Arafa*, next door to Hôtel de la Poste, also has other meals, including steak, in the CFA 600 to CFA 1000 range. *Chawarma Chez Adja Anta* is a block to the west on the same street. Best is the slightly more up-market (with tablecloths) *Chawarma Le Folk*, which is two blocks north of Hôtel Battling Siki, where the choices include steak frites for CFA 1000, poisson au riz for CFA 1200 and poulet yassa for CFA 1800.

For good Senegalese food at around CFA 1200 to CFA 1800 a plate, go to *Restaurant Wuroma*, a block north of the Hôtel Battling Siki, and *Restaurant Galaxie* a block further north on the same street. They are all small family restaurants with very decent Senegalese meals (and copious servings) in the CFA 1200 to CFA 1800 range. Another place to try is *Restaurant Aziz*, six blocks south of the governor's palace and east to the wharf.

Entertainment

You can get food at *La Chaumière*, near the lighthouse, but it's really more for drinks. At night there's a cover charge of CFA 1200 per person but the action starts very late. There are several other bars and nightclubs including the *Casino Nightclub* that juts out into the water at the far northern tip of the island at the end of Rue Blaise Diagne. For cheap drinks and lowlife, head for the bar at *Hôtel Battling Siki*. For smarter surroundings and a nice terrace overlooking the river, go to *Le Bar Ponty Village* where the food and drinks are only slightly more expensive, and there's often live music. For dancing, try the nightclub at *Hôtel Walo* on weekends: it's one of the best.

Getting There & Away

Bush Taxi The gare routière is on the mainland (Sor), 100 metres south of Pont Faidherbe. The fare to/from Dakar (268 km) is CFA 3000 by Peugeot 504 and CFA 2300 by minibus. A taxi from here over the bridge to St-Louis Island is CFA 250.

Train The train station is in Sor, immediately north of the gare routière, and only open an hour or so before the train departs. The train to Dakar leaves St-Louis every day at 6.30 am and arrives in Dakar at 11.25 am (although it's often an hour or two late). The fare is CFA 3500/2330 in 1st/2nd class.

Getting Around

For getting around St-Louis and the surrounding area, bikes can be hired at several of the hotels and at the Auberge de Jeunesse, for around CFA 2500 per day. Most of these places can also arrange car hire, and excursions by car and/or boat to the nearby national parks. The Hôtel de la Poste also has kayaks for hire.

AROUND ST-LOUIS

Langue de Barbarie National Park

The Langue de Barbarie National Park is 20 km south of St-Louis covering the southern tip of the Langue de Barbarie peninsula, and a section of the mainland on the other side of the river's mouth. From November to April it is home to numerous **water birds** – pink flamingos, white pelicans, cormorants, herons, egrets and ducks. The park is open daily from 7 am to sunset; entry costs CFA 1200. Camping inside the park is not permitted but camping nearby is OK.

Getting There & Away If you have your own high-clearance vehicle you can approach the park by driving down the peninsula from Guet N'Dar, over the dunes to the tip of the Langue; from there you'll have to hire a pirogue to take you to the main area. It is also possible to get a good way down the peninsula by bike (hired in town), although sand makes the going heavy.

Alternatively, drive or get a bush taxi to Gandiol on the mainland; you can enter the park by pirogue from there as well.

Excursions can be arranged at Hôtel de la Poste, Hôtel Résidence, Hôtel du Palais or the Auberge de Jeunesse. Rates for a one-day excursion vary between the hotels, ranging from CFA 8750 to CFA 13,750, and depend on the size of the group (minimum four persons) and if lunch, drinks or park entry is included. Some guides speak English.

Djoudj National Park

The Parc National des Oisseaux du Djoudj is 60 km north of St-Louis, on a great bend in the Senegal River. It covers an area eight times larger than the Langue de Barbarie park and is one of the three most important **bird sanctuarie**s in the world. If you're in Senegal in winter, don't miss the opportunity of seeing this great spectacle of bird life.

From November to April, some three million birds migrating south from Europe pass through this area. The park is flooded all year, thanks to the dam at Maka-Diama, and is one of the first places with permanent water south of the Sahara. Almost 300 species of bird have been recorded here. Pink flamingos (up to 100,000!), ducks and waders are most plentiful. Others that you might see are white pelicans, spur-winged geese, night and purple herons, egrets, spoonbills, black-tailed godwits, cormorants, great bustards and tree-ducks. November to April, especially January, are the best months and the early morning is the

best time of day to see them. There are few birds in the area between May and October. The park is open all year, however, from 7 am to dusk every day; entry costs CFA 2000.

The *Campement du Djoudj* is at the park entrance with attractive but overpriced bungalows for CFA 15,000. The restaurant serves breakfast for CFA 1700 and other meals for CFA 5000. You can make reservations at several of the travel agencies in Dakar, or ask at any of the large hotels in St-Louis. Camping is allowed at the park entrance, with permission from the warden.

Getting There & Away To get here from St-Louis, take the paved highway towards Rosso for about 25 km. Near Ross-Bethio you'll see a sign pointing to the park, which is about 25 km further down a dirt track. If you don't have your own wheels, the hotels in St-Louis arranging tours to the Langue de Barbarie park can also take you to Djoudj park for approximately the same fare. Alternatively, if you get a small group together, you can save money by hiring a taxi for the day. Typical fares are CFA 10,000 one way and CFA 15,000 for the round trip. Make it crystal clear beforehand what time you plan to return and don't pay the whole fare in advance. You can take a vehicle around the edges of the park, and walking is possible, but since much of the park is inundated with water a pirogue (CFA 2000) is the only way to get to the heart of it.

We've also heard from travellers who paid CFA 11,000 to join a tour from St-Louis. Rather than return with the group, they stayed in the park for four days and then hitched a ride out with some other tourists.

THE SENEGAL RIVER ROUTE
Richard Toll

Some 93 km north-east of St-Louis near Rosso, Richard Toll has little of interest but you might find yourself here if you're following the Senegal River Route. The *Gîte d'Étape* near the gare routière is a nice hotel with air-con doubles for CFA 12,500. Or try *Hôtel Keur Massada* where a room costs

CFA 5000. Taxis to/from St-Louis charge CFA 1625; the trip normally takes 1½ hours.

Podor

At the northernmost point of Senegal on the Senegal River, Podor rarely attracts visitors. The Mission Catholique does not accept guests, which leaves the *campement* (CFA 3750 a room) as the only place to stay. A Peugeot 504 bush taxi from St-Louis costs CFA 2600.

Matam

Matam is 230 km south-east of Podor, and the next settlement of any size along the river. There is no hotel but don't worry: just go to the préfecture and the people there will find you a room for CFA 2500, including breakfast. Minibuses cost CFA 3000 to Podor and CFA 2500 to Bakel.

Bakel

Bakel is the next place you reach, 150 km south-east of Matam, and only 60 km from Kidira on the Senegal-Mali border and the Dakar to Bamako train line, and really in eastern Senegal, although still with the feel of the north. *Hôtel El Islam* is clean and friendly and rents rooms for CFA 3750 (CFA 6800 with air-con). Minibuses charge CFA 875 to Kidira, where you can find another to Tambacounda for CFA 2500.

The Eastern Region

TAMBACOUNDA

In a hot, flat savannah area full of baobab trees, Tambacounda is a major crossroads town, with routes east to Mali, south to the Niokolo-Koba National Park or to Guinea, west to Dakar or The Gambia, and south-west to Ziguinchor. The main avenues are the east-west street running parallel with the train tracks and the road that crosses it which leads south to the park. Most shops, the bank and several restaurants are on these streets.

Places to Stay & Eat

There are three places to stay, all in the southern part of town roughly one km from the centre. The cheapest and furthest out is the unmarked *Chez Dessert*, where the friendly old French owner, Georges, has rooms for CFA 2500 per person. About 200 metres north of Chez Dessert is *Hôtel Niji* (☎ 81 12 50), a mid-range place with good quality self-contained singles/doubles for CFA 7000/8000 (plus CFA 3750 if you want air-con). The new annexe has thatched huts in a shady garden compound – a welcome relief from the hot dusty streets outside.

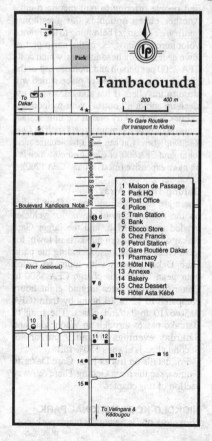

Tambacounda

0   200   400 m

To Gare Routière
(for transport to Kidira)

Avenue Léopold S Senghor

Boulevard Kandioura Noba

To Dakar

River (seasonal)

To Velingara &
Kédougou

1 Maison de Passage
2 Park HQ
3 Post Office
4 Police
5 Train Station
6 Bank
7 Eboco Store
8 Chez Francis
9 Petrol Station
10 Gare Routière Dakar
11 Pharmacy
12 Hôtel Niji
13 Annexe
14 Bakery
15 Chez Dessert
16 Hôtel Asta Kébé

SENEGAL

There is a restaurant and bar (with cheaper drinks in the annexe) and the manager arranges pirogue trips on the Gambia River, or excursions to Niokolo-Koba park.

The city's best hotel is the *Hôtel Asta Kébé* (☎ 81 10 28, fax 81 17 44), 200 metres east of the Niji and up a slight hill, with air-con singles/doubles at CFA 15,000/20,000. It has a restaurant, tennis courts and a pool which nonguests can use for CFA 1800. Breakfast is CFA 1800 and meals CFA 5000. Neither travellers' cheques nor credit cards are accepted. It rents vehicles for self-drive tours of the park, or you can join an excursion.

At the main gare routière you can often find people offering to rent private rooms. Another cheap option is the guesthouse (*maison de passage*) belonging to the French Volontaires du Progrès, in the north part of town near the park headquarters, which costs CFA 2500 per person and includes use of the kitchen. This is the kind of place which will close to travellers if it's abused, so pay up, clean up and don't outstay your welcome.

For cheap food try one of the little restaurants on or near the main streets such as *Chez Khadim*, where you can get a two-course meal for around CFA 600, or *Chez Francis* which is a bit more expensive (meals around CFA 1200).

Getting There & Away

There are two gare routières – Gare Kidira on the eastern side of town, for vehicles headed towards Mali, and the larger Gare Dakar on the southern outskirts of town, for most other destinations, including the park. Gare Dakar swarms with touts, so watch your gear. Bush taxis charge CFA 5800 to Dakar. The trip takes around eight hours compared to 12 or 13 hours by train (CFA 9150/6710 in 1st/2nd class). The train to Bamako passes through on Wednesday and Saturday evenings around 9 pm or so. Second class is always 150% full.

For details on trucks from Gare Dakar to Guinea, see the main Getting There & Away section of this chapter.

NIOKOLO-KOBA NATIONAL PARK

Niokolo-Koba is Senegal's major park, covering about 900,000 hectares, in the south-east corner of the country, some 550 km from Dakar. Although the park has been neglected in recent years it's still very beautiful and worth a visit. It is a relatively flat area, watered by the Gambia River and two major tributaries, with lush and varied vegetation. It is a refuge for eighty-four species of mammal, including the giant derby eland, lion, leopard and the last remaining elephant in Senegal (some estimates say only 20). These are very rarely seen; however, you are likely to see hippo, crocodile, waterbuck, bushbuck, kob, baboon, monkey (green and hussar), wart hog, roan antelope, buffalo and hartebeest. But, as villagers continue to cut down trees to plant crops along the park perimeters, all the animals are seriously threatened. Giraffe and korrigum antelope have disappeared altogether.

Some 350 species of bird have been recorded here, including the red-throated bee-eater, saddlebill stork, spur-winged goose, white-faced tree-duck, kingfisher, Senegalese coucal, crane, ibis, hammerhead, heron, Denham's bustard, the spectacular Abyssinian ground hornbill and violet turaco.

You may be allowed to visit the park at any time, but generally it's open from 1 December to 31 May as this is the dry season. However, the rains are unpredictable and some park tracks are not cleared until a month after the rains have ended, so don't take anything for granted. Even in the dry season all park tracks require 4WD, except between the park gate and the Simenti Hotel which can usually be covered in a saloon car.

The daily entrance fee is CFA 2000 per person and CFA 5000 per vehicle. Trained guides are available for CFA 6000 per day and may be useful if you want to visit the remoter parts of the park and increase your chance of seeing animals. As in all West African parks, the most pleasant time to come is December and January but the best viewing time is the peak of the hot season in April and May, when the tall grass has withered and the animals congregate at the water holes. Simenti's water hole in particular attracts thirsty animals, mostly in the early

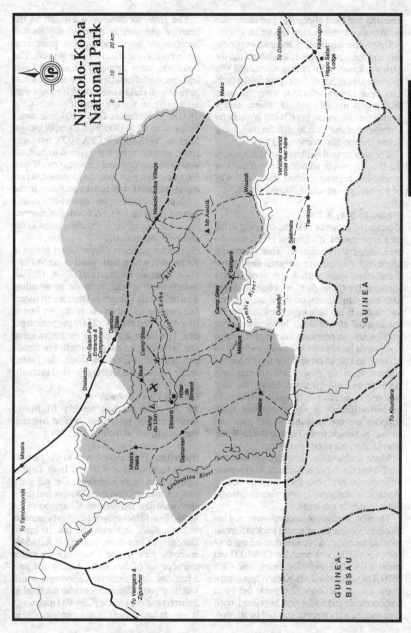

SENEGAL

morning and later afternoon; you can watch them from an observation hut set on stilts.

Up-to-date information about accommodation and track conditions is available from the park headquarters in Tambacounda, and you should call here before setting out for the park. You must have a vehicle to enter the park. Walking is not allowed anywhere, except around the camp sites, but it is still possible for travellers without a car to visit the park, using public transport or an organised tour.

The area around Niokolo-Koba is home to the Bassari people who feature in some tour itineraries, because of their traditional way of life and picturesque villages.

Places to Stay & Eat

Despite the presence of lions, camping in the park is permitted. It's free but you'll need the park rangers' permission. This is usually automatic. There are several designated camp sites, some with a few open rickety shelters. Try *Camp du Lion*, a beautiful spot nine km from Simenti on the Gambia River; swimming is possible here but watch out for the hippos! If you don't have wheels you may be able to persuade the rangers, whose compound is only one km away, to drop you off here and pick you up a few days later. It's a good place for people without transport because animals go there during the day. Wherever you camp in the park, you need to be self-sufficient in equipment and food; supplies are not available in the park and should be bought from Tambacounda. Water is available, but needs purifying.

More problematic than any wildlife are staff from the hotel at Simenti who reportedly search the park for campers, telling them it is dangerous, and almost forcing them to stay at the hotel.

There is a reasonable *campement* at Dar-Salam park entrance, where the track to Simenti turns off the main road. A basic double bungalow costs CFA 6200, with breakfast CFA 1000 and meals CFA 3000. Half-day safaris cost CFA 2500. The hotel in Niokolo-Koba village (on the main route through the park between Tambacounda and Kédougou) has closed, but it may reopen, and camping may still be allowed.

The *Hôtel de Simenti* at Simenti in the heart of the park is more ideally located because the hotel overlooks a permanent water hole where animals come to drink. The hotel was badly managed for several years and became dilapidated, but new owners have recently taken over. Double rooms with air-con (not always working) are CFA 18,000. Breakfast is CFA 1200 and meals cost around CFA 3700. Some simple bungalows are available for CFA 6000, but these rustic constructions are reported to harbour snakes, scorpions and mosquitoes. If you have camping gear, you may manage to persuade the hotel staff to let you camp in the garden. The hotel organises half-day safaris around the park for CFA 6500. For reservations, use one of the companies listed in the earlier Tours section.

Another option is *Hippo Safari Lodge* in Kédougou, where half board in traditional-style bungalows starts at CFA 13,700. Safaris into the park, or in the surrounding area to Bassari villages or Dinndéfélo waterfall (see the end of this chapter), for one to four days, start at CFA 12,000 per person per day. The lodge also has an exclusive camp site, with tents, in the park itself. For details contact Safari-Evasion in Dakar (listed under Tours in the Getting Around section).

Getting There & Away

Air Air Senegal has weekly flights to Tambacounda; some also stop at Simenti. For details, ask at their office.

Bush Taxi The cheapest way to the park by public transport is a bush taxi from Tambacounda heading for Kédougou. Get off at the park entrance at Dar-Salam. Drivers will probably want the full fare to Kédougou (CFA 4250). To save money, you could get a minibus to Diala Koto, and walk the last 10 km to Dar-Salam. Once there, walking is forbidden inside the park, so you'll have to hitch with a tourist or one of the rangers. Failing that, take a half-day safari from the campement which will drop you at Simenti, or radio the hotel in Simenti to send a vehicle (CFA 4000 one way). If private taxi drivers at the gare routière in

Tambacounda say there's no regular transport to Kédougou, don't believe them: there are several bush taxis/minibuses a day. Park fees are not payable if you're transiting the park straight to Kédougou.

Private Taxi You can hire a taxi in Tambacounda for one or two days. The driver pays petrol, plus his own food, lodgings and entrance fees for him and the car, while you pay your own entrance, food and accommodation. Starting prices seem to be around CFA 60,000 for a day, but we've heard from two travellers who paid CFA 30,000 for a two-day trip. Alternatively, hire a taxi to drop you at Simenti or a camp site, and pick you up again after a few days, although this will involve two return journeys. Any taxi driver in Tambacounda will be interested in taking you to the park, but carefully check the condition of his car, and call at the park headquarters to ensure the track to Simenti is passable for 2WD.

Car If you are driving your own vehicle, the entrance to Niokolo-Koba at Dar-Salam is 80 km south-east of Tambacounda, on the road towards Kédougou. (It's an eight-hour drive from Dakar (546 km) on a paved road.) You are not allowed to drive at night in the park. If you don't have your own car, you might be lucky and find a lift by hanging around at the park office or one of the smart hotels in Tambacounda.

Tours Four-day all-inclusive tours from Dakar start at CFA 100,000 a person, with a minimum of four to six people. See under Tours in the Getting Around section for a list of tour companies. In Tambacounda, the Hôtel Niji organises excursions for CFA 87,500 per day, for up to six people, which includes driver, guide, petrol and vehicle park fees, but does not include personal park fees, food and accommodation. The Hôtel Asta Kébé charges CFA 80,000 per day, but this is for the vehicle only; you should add around CFA 25,000 for fuel and CFA 5000 for vehicle entry.

It is much cheaper to arrange half-day or full-day safaris at either Dar-Salam campement, Hôtel de Simenti or Hippo Safari Lodge (see Places to Stay & Eat).

DINNDÉFÉLO
If you have your own vehicle, after touring the park you could head south towards Kédougou and, 30 km away, the village of Dinndéfélo, a two-hour drive from the park. From there it's a 10-minute walk to a spectacular 100-metre **waterfall** with a deep green pool at the bottom, safe and wonderful for cooling off year-round. You can stay at the *Campement de la Cascade* at the edge of the village, which offers simple cement huts, bucket showers, and an attractive thatched paillote where visitors can eat (typically chicken and fonio) and relax.

Sierra Leone

REPUBLIC OF SIERRA LEONE

Area: 72,325 sq km
Population: 4.6 million
Population Growth Rate: 2.6%
Capital: Freetown
Head of State: Captain Valentine Strasser
Official Language: English
Currency: Leone
Exchange Rate: Le 600 = US$1
Per Capita GNP: US$190
Inflation: 20%
Time: GMT/UTC

Until recently Sierra Leone seemed unable to emerge from a long decline since independence; each year the country's economy and the local people's quality of life worsened. This situation did little to attract visitors. Apart from a few thousand package tourists who stayed on the Freetown Peninsula beaches, the country had few visitors, and independent travel upcountry was extremely rare.

But everything changed in 1992. A group of young army officers overthrew the government and, with popular support, began to reform the country. By 1994 they were still in charge and most people seemed happy with their new rulers. Sierra Leone still has a very long way to go before it ceases to be one of the world's poorest countries, but now at least there's food in the shops in Freetown and fuel for the buses to run around the country, while roads and buildings everywhere are being repaired and repainted.

Although package tourists may come to Sierra Leone mainly for the beach and a touch of the 'exotic', adventurous travellers will find the rest of the country interesting for several other reasons. These include several excellent wildlife reserves, most of which can be reached without your own car. And if beaches are your thing, you can still avoid the crowds by escaping to one of the more remote parts of the Freetown Peninsula. Other reasons to visit are the varied landscapes and tropical vegetation, and the eternally friendly people.

Facts about the Country

HISTORY

The region now called Sierra Leone was on the southern edge of the great Mali Empire, which flourished between the 13th and 15th centuries. Even before that time Malinké (Mandingo) traders had entered the region, and integrated with the indigenous people.

Contact with the West began when the first Portuguese navigators landed on the coast in 1462 and called the area Sierra Leone or 'Lion Mountain'. Almost 120 years later, Sir Francis Drake stopped here during his voyage around

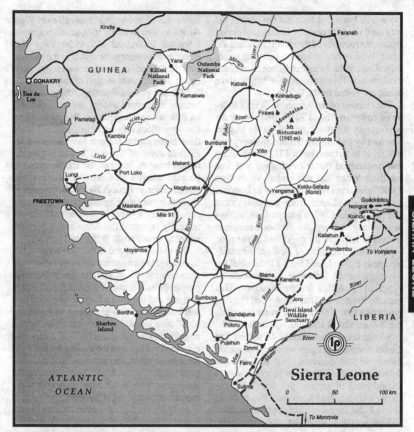

SIERRA LEONE

Suggested Itineraries

Sierra Leone's capital, **Freetown**, is a lively place, with a good atmosphere and some popular beaches nearby. You could easily spend a few days here, or longer if you went down the **Freetown Peninsula** to some of the more remote beaches.

Inland from Freetown, you can head north through **Makeni**, a busy town with a large market (and worth stopping at for one or two days), to **Kabala** which is a much sleepier place, with laid-back people and surrounded by pleasant rolling hills (two to four days). From Kabala you could aim for **Mt Bintumani** (one of the highest peaks in West Africa) or its foothills which are a forest reserve and good wildlife area. You should allow about six days for a trek, plus a few more before and after to get between Kabala and any of the main starting points. From Makeni you could go to **Outamba-Kilimi National Park**, which can be explored by foot or local canoe, and is good for travellers without a vehicle (although reaching it takes a bit of determination). You should allow five days to a week for a visit and travel to/from Makeni.

Your other option from Freetown is eastwards to **Bo** and **Kenema**, both interesting towns which are worth a day or two's visit. Kenema is surrounded by forested hills and there's a number of wildlife reserves in the surrounding area which can easily occupy another week. ■

the world, but the British did not control the area until the 18th century. During this period Britain also dominated the slave trade along the whole West African coast, transporting slaves from Africa to the Americas. Bunce Island, near modern-day Freetown, was a major slave centre controlled by the British.

The turmoil of the American War of Independence in the 1770s provided an opportunity for thousands of slaves to gain freedom by fighting for Britain. (Slavery was still legal in Britain, but a 1772 court ruling had determined that a freed slave was free for life.) When the war ended, more than 15,000 ex-slaves made their way to London, where they suffered from unemployment and poverty. In 1787, a group of philanthropists – inspired by John Wesley's religious revival to improve the condition of the poor – purchased 52 sq km of land on the mainland near Bunce Island from a local chief for the purpose of founding a 'Province of Freedom' in Africa for the ex-slaves. This became Freetown. That same year, the first group of about 400 men and women, including 300 ex-slaves and 100 Whites, arrived.

Within three years, all but 48 settlers had died of disease or in fights with the local inhabitants, or had deserted. But in 1792 the determined British philanthropists sent a second band of settlers, this time 1200 ex-slaves who had fled from the USA to Nova Scotia. Later, they sent 550 more from Jamaica.

The settlers were hardly moralists. According to Richard West in *Back to Africa*, most of the Whites were probably 'debtors, adventurers, men who had failed in other colonies or disgruntled officers from the army or navy'. To the chagrin of the philanthropists, some settlers, both White and Black, joined in the slave trade. In 1808, the British government took over the Freetown settlement and declared it a colony.

The Colonial Period
By the early 1800s, slavery had been abolished in Britain. During the next 60 years, British warships plied the West African coast, trying to intercept slave ships destined for America. Freetown became the depot for

thousands of 'recaptives' from all over West Africa as well as many indigenous migrants from the hinterland. By 1850, over 100 ethnic groups were represented in the colony. Yet they lived in relative harmony, each group in a different section of town.

Like the previous settlers, the recaptives became successful traders and intermarried, so that all non-indigenous Blacks became known collectively as Krios. Cut off from their home and traditions they assumed an English style of life and began regarding themselves as superior to the indigenous peoples. Many were Christian, and received an education at Fourah Bay College outside Freetown, the first English-speaking university in Africa. The British administrators naturally favoured the Krios and appointed many to senior posts in the civil service.

But towards the end of the 19th century, the tide started to turn against the Krios, who were outnumbered 50 to one by the indigenous people. Britain declared the hinterland a protectorate and imposed a hut tax, which led to a war between the two groups, in which many Krios were killed. Lebanese merchants began migrating to the area, and by WW I they had displaced the Krios as the leading traders with the interior tribes. In Freetown, British entrepreneurs favoured the more tractable indigenous people, thereby squeezing Krio merchants further out of business.

In 1924, the British administrators established a legislative council with elected representatives, to the advantage of the more numerous indigenous people. The Krios, who continued to monopolise positions within the civil service, reacted by clinging to the British. While other colonies clamoured for independence, they proclaimed loyalty to the Crown. One group even petitioned against the granting of independence. They were far from enamoured by Wallace Johnson, a liberal Krio journalist, who led the independence movement throughout the 1930s.

Independence
When independence was achieved in 1961, it seemed that Western-style democracy

would work. There were two parties of roughly equal strength but, not unusually in Africa, they became divided along ethnic lines. The Sierra Leone People's Party (SLPP) was the party of the southern Mendes, and represented the tribal structure of the old colony. The All People's Congress (APC), formed by a trade unionist, Siaka Stevens, became identified with the Temnes of the north and voiced the dissatisfaction of the small, modernising elite. The Krio community threw its support behind the SLPP, whose leader, Milton Margai, became the first prime minister.

Following Margai's death in 1964, his brother Albert took over and set about replacing the Krios in the bureaucracy with the Mendes. The Krios took revenge in the 1967 elections by supporting the APC, which won a one-seat majority. A few hours after the results were announced, a Mende military officer led a coup, placing Siaka Stevens under house arrest. Two days later some fellow officers staged a second coup, vowing to end the corruption that was so widespread under the Margai brothers.

Stevens went into exile in Guinea and with a group of Sierra Leoneans began training in guerrilla warfare techniques for an invasion. This became unnecessary when a group of private soldiers mutinied and staged a third coup 13 months later – an African record for the number of coups in such a short period.

Siaka Stevens returned and formed a new government, but his first decade in office was turbulent. He declared a state of emergency, detained many people, banned breakaway parties from the APC and tried a number of SLPP members for treason. Fearing for his life after two assassination attempts in one day in 1971, Stevens took the unusual step of asking President Sekou Touré of Guinea, with whom he made a military pact, for Guinean troops to act as his bodyguards.

Meanwhile, the economy continued to deteriorate. The iron-ore mine closed, revenues from diamonds dropped, the cost of living steadily increased, students rioted, and Stevens again declared a state of emergency. The 1978 election campaign resembled a mini civil war

between the major ethnic groups; the death toll topped 100. Stevens won, and Sierra Leone became a one-party state.

Politically, matters calmed down a bit, but the economy continued to stagnate. Nevertheless, Stevens went ahead with plans to court international publicity by hosting the 1980 Organisation of African Unity (OAU) conference, which involved huge expenditures on deluxe hotels and luxury villas, among other things, for the visiting heads of state. The country sank deeper into debt by about US$150 million.

Despite the one-party system, the 1982 elections were the most violent ever, forcing Stevens to give the Mendes and Temnes equal representation in the cabinet. But economic and social conditions continued to deteriorate: inflation soared, queues for food and fuel became an everyday part of survival, and Freetown was almost totally blacked out every night.

With virtually no support left, Stevens finally stepped down in 1985 at the age of 80, naming as his successor 'the choice of God', Major-General Joseph Momoh, the head of the army.

The economic situation Momoh inherited was far from divine. By 1987 the inflation rate was the highest in Africa (well over 100% annually), budget deficits were astronomical, and smugglers – allegedly with close government connections – were continuing to rob Sierra Leone of up to 90% of its diamond revenue.

Momoh did nothing. While a few well-connected people prospered, the economy remained a mess. Foreign exchange reserves completely dried up, and only with occasional loans from the country's most powerful Lebanese businesspeople was the government able to halt total economic collapse.

Things got worse in late 1989 when civil war broke out in neighbouring Liberia. By early 1990 thousands of Liberian refugees had fled into Sierra Leone. The following year fighting also spilled across the border. The situation was confused, but it seems that Sierra Leonean rebels, opposed to the Momoh régime, formed an allegiance with Liberian rebels and together took control of the strategic town of Koindu, in the far east corner of Sierra Leone. Then the rebels took control of much of the eastern part of the country.

Through 1990 and early 1991 there was growing clamour for reform and multiparty democracy, but the Momoh Government used the civil war in the east as an excuse to postpone elections. Finally, in September 1991, a new constitution was adopted to allow for a multiparty system. As if to emphasise the need for change, in early 1992 the UN published its quality of life index, which placed Sierra Leone at the bottom of the list. But before an election date could be announced, in April 1992, a group of young military officers overthrew Momoh.

Sierra Leone Today
The new leader of Sierra Leone was 27-year-old Captain Valentine Strasser. The National Provisional Ruling Council (NPRC) was set up, and Strasser was sworn in as head of state on 6 May. In December the same year, after another attempted coup, at least 25 suspects were executed by firing squad. Some reports claimed that not all those executed were involved in the coup attempt, and in protest Britain suspended all economic aid to Sierra Leone.

However, by mid-1994 Strasser continued to be a popular leader. Elections, and a return to civilian rule, were promised for 1995. Economic reforms, monitored by the International Monetary Fund (IMF), designed to develop a foreign exchange market and better exploit the country's natural resources, started to have effect. A campaign encouraging people to pay their income tax was successful, and when Freetown's main stadium was reopened for international football the people literally danced in the street.

But, through 1994 the heady optimism that followed the coup started to fade. A major distraction and drain on resources was the continuing fight in the east of the country against the anti-government rebels, now called the Revolutionary United Front (RUF). They were bolstered after the coup by supporters of the previous Momoh régime, and by escaping rebels from Liberia. But it soon became apparent that none of these groups were fighting for a 'cause' or political objective. They were fighting simply to control the territory, and all the diamonds and gold fields it contains. In January 1994 the government army seemed to have the upper hand and the region was gradually coming under control, but by May the same year, the rebels were once again on the offensive and had regained some of their lost territory.

By late 1994 northern and eastern parts of the country were reported to be descending into anarchy with private armies led by local warlords, government soldiers, rebel soldiers and deserters from both sides (from Sierra Leone and Liberia) roaming the area at will, and terrorising local populations. Some have turned to banditry on the main roads. In 1995, the situation for travellers became particularly dangerous after several European volunteers and expatriate workers were abducted and held by RUF rebels.

Because of these bandits and rebels you'll find military checkpoints all over the country. The officials are usually quite friendly and helpful. However, many of these 'checkpoints' are illegal and built by local people, particularly the secret societies. They'll say they're looking for weapons but what they really want is your money. If you pay, you'll move on more quickly, but you may make it very difficult for subsequent travellers to refuse doing the same.

All across Sierra Leone, things remain unclear, and visitors heading upcountry should be aware of the current situation before leaving Freetown.

GEOGRAPHY
Sierra Leone has an area of 72,325 sq km (about the size of Scotland) and can be divided into three main zones: coast, central plateau and mountains.

The coastal zone consists of mangrove swamps and beaches and is flat except for the 40 km-long Freetown Peninsula, which is the only place along the West African coast where mountains rise near the sea. There are also small islands just off the coast such as

Local Attitudes to Wildlife Conservation

Despite its small size, Sierra Leone is endowed with a broad range of vegetation zones, containing a great variety of bird and animal species. The government of Sierra Leone has established several parks and reserves where this wildlife can be protected. However, as the country's human population continues to expand, the pressure on the land for cultivation also increases. Thus, wildlife and people are forced to compete for the same resources.

Rural West Africans regard cultivated or settled land as a legacy from their ancestors. They believe their rights are validated by the fact that their forebears physically cleared the land of wild bush. This link is strong: in some cases, the ancestors were buried on the land itself.

Most people of Sierra Leone, particularly those in the north, view farmland and settlements favourably as places where the bush has been cleared, and where the morals of the ancestors can be upheld. The bush itself is considered a dangerous place of threatening supernatural powers, requiring courage and strength to bring it within the farming cycle. Thus, the Western notion of preserving wilderness areas for their own sake is not always shared by traditional people.

Many local people are struggling to achieve a better standard of living or, in some cases, simply to survive. Most protected nature areas include lands of subsistence farmers, but it's difficult to be a conservationist if your family is hungry.

Although Western attitudes towards the natural environment seem incompatible with local concepts, it is still possible to protect natural ecosystems without local people having to give up their beliefs or ambitions. Rather, conservationists and government officials must create a situation where protecting natural areas and indigenous plant and animal life will offer significant practical advantages for local people.

Parts of this section are extracted from the *Wildlife & Nature Reserves* booklet produced by the Conservation Society of Sierra Leone (CSSL), but they could apply to many other West African countries. The CSSL is supporting a number of schemes where local people are involved in setting up protected areas and benefiting from them in a tangible manner. To support the work of the society, you can buy the above booklet and other leaflets from their offices in Freetown (see the Information section). Even better, visit one of the reserves described in this chapter. ■

Sherbo, Banana and York. Away from the coast, the land rises to become an undulating plateau, which is heavily forested and extensively cultivated. To the north and north-east are the Lola Mountains, with Mt Bintumani (1948 metres), one of the highest points in West Africa, at their centre.

To the south of the Lola Mountains is Koidu-Sefadu, more commonly called Kono, the country's major diamond area. South of Kono towards Kenema, in the region called Tongo Fields, you may see prospectors looking for diamonds along the small streams. These alluvial deposits are rapidly diminishing as the huge forests in this area are being cut down on a massive scale.

CLIMATE

Sierra Leone is one of the wettest countries in West Africa, with an average annual rainfall of over 3150 mm in most of the country. The rainy season stretches from May to early November, the wettest months being July to

September. While the humidity is particularly high in the coastal regions, the sea breeze affords considerable relief. The country's annual average temperature is a fairly moderate 27°C. Temperatures drop in December and January, but the skies are frequently hazy from the harmattan winds that carry dust from the Sahara. This has no effect on travelling but does spoil the views. The absolute best time to visit is late November: after the rains and before the harmattan.

GOVERNMENT

Valentine Strasser remains the head of the NPRC. After the coup parliament was suspended, and party political activity was banned. In early 1993, the NPRC appointed several civilian ministers to the cabinet and in July the same year the Supreme Council of State was created to separate the military from the cabinet. The military government then drafted a new constitution preventing the government from executing political opponents and providing for transition to civilian rule by 1996.

ECONOMY

The future of Sierra Leone's economy is uncertain. At independence, Sierra Leone had the fifth highest per capita income in West Africa but, in the 30 years of mismanagement and corruption that followed, the economy went rapidly and continuously downhill.

Today, the economy is based on subsistence agriculture although the country has large reserves of bauxite, diamonds and gold, which have not been fully exploited due to fighting between the army and rebels in the east. Sierra Leone remains heavily dependent on financial aid from several Western nations.

The coup of 1992 also had a major effect on Sierra Leone's package-tour industry. Quite simply, the tourists (and their vital hard currency) stayed away. In 1994, numbers in the big beach hotels outside Freetown were still down to less than 25% of their 1990 level. While the fighting continues (even though it's far from the beach), tourists are unlikely to return in great numbers.

In March 1994, the IMF approved a resumption of loans of some US$160 million to Sierra Leone. (All IMF funds had been halted in 1988, after the country defaulted on a previous loan.)

In a scheme which sounds crazy to all but global economists, the '94 loan was allowed after the '88 deficit was paid off with money borrowed from several Western countries, including France and the USA.

POPULATION & PEOPLE

With a population estimated at 4.6 million, Sierra Leone is one of the more densely populated countries in West Africa. There are 18 ethnic groups. The two largest are the Temnes and Mendes, about equal in number, together comprising 60% of the population. The Temnes predominate in the north and are mainly Muslim. The Mendes and kindred peoples inhabit mainly the southern and eastern provinces, and are mostly animist. Generally, compared to many other African countries, ethnic strife is minimal.

The Krios number less than 2% of the people – roughly 60,000. Residing mostly in the Freetown area, they have held on to Western traditions and Christianity. Many of the country's intellectuals and professional people are Krios, and many of their leaders are Masons, whom you can see in Freetown going to their weekly meetings in their three-piece suits and fancy cars.

You'll also see a lot of Lebanese and Indian merchants, who began migrating here

---

Temnes & Mendes

Sierra Leone's two main ethnic groups are the Temnes and the Mendes. Although ethnic conflict is minimal (when compared to other West African countries) great differences, and considerable competition, still exist between these groups.

The Temnes inhabit the northern parts of the country, and their cultural traditions have much in common with the savannah-dwelling peoples of Guinea, southern Senegal and southern Mali. They follow Islam, and place considerable importance on the idea of hereditary kingship. Ceremonies that confirm the power of local kings or chiefs are also important, and can be quite elaborate. However, the Temnes are not traditionally warlike, and have generally coexisted peacefully with neighbouring smaller groups, such as the Loko in the west or the Koranko around Mt Bintumani, who all maintain their own language and traditions.

The Mendes inhabit the southern regions of the country. Their culture is linked more to the forest-dwelling peoples of Liberia and Côte d'Ivoire. Traditionally, Mendes are animist, although many have embraced Christianity (which was introduced in colonial times). There are also some Mende Muslims. Mende ceremonies are often connected to the functions of the *Bundus* (secret societies). They traditionally see themselves as superior to neighbouring smaller groups, such as the Gola around Kenema and the Sherbo along the coast, who are gradually abandoning their own traditions, and adopting the Mende language and culture. ■

Music

Sierra Leone's indigenous music, often part of the secret society ceremonies and 'devil' dances described under Culture (below), is played on traditional instruments such as the *khandi* (a thumb piano made from recycled tin cans), the *shake-shake* (a gourd enclosed in a net of buttons or shells), the *balangie* (a wooden xylophone), and various drums.

Modern music in Sierra Leone is not based on traditional sounds as it is in other parts of West Africa, and you don't hear African pop music in the same way as you do in the Francophone countries. Any taxi or disco is more likely to play Western-style dance or Jamaican reggae than anything else.

If you want to sample some home-grown artists, start with the near-legendary Ebenezer Calender, who popularised the *miringa* sound (a unique and lively Krio combination of African and Western rhythms), and S E Rogie, an exponent of 'palm-wine music' (more mellow). Both were active around the time of independence, and Rogie can still be found performing in the USA and Britain.

Today, some of the best Sierra Leonean music comes out of London on the BBC World Service thanks to King Masco, a popular disc jockey whose music is inspired by the disco-calypso rhythms of his compatriots Bunny Mack and Abdul Tee-Jay, who both record in Britain.

If you want to hear local live music, bands to look out for include Sierra Afrique, The God Fathers, Afro National and Afro Combo. Also worth trying is Daddy Loco, a Freetown songwriter who sings about current events, and the somewhat eccentric Dr Oloh who sings through a portable megaphone. ■

SIERRA LEONE

in the 1880s and now number about 10,000. The much smaller European community is involved mainly in commerce, government service, and aid work.

CULTURE

The Mende and Temne peoples both maintain strong traditions. Village chiefs still wield considerable power with primary jurisdiction (rather than the civil judges) over local disputes. The Mendes are known for their culture of 'secret societies', locally called *Bundu* (although this is actually a Krio word). These societies, including the Poro for men and the Sande for women, have considerable influence – their responsibilities include training children (sometimes over many months, or even years) in matters including tribal law and crafts, thus helping with their education and keeping their traditional culture alive. If you see young children with their faces painted white, you'll know that they're in the process of being initiated. Masks are an important feature in Bundu ceremonies, and are highly prized.

At some secret society celebrations, men dressed as 'devils' will dance around the village. They are imposing figures, often dancing themselves into a trance-like frenzy, and are held in considerable respect by the local people. Visitors should show the same

Brass mask (Arabai Aron type) – used when the Temne chiefs are enthroned.

respect. Some devils cannot be seen by outsiders but, for money, some will even agree to pose for a photograph.

RELIGION

About a quarter of the population is Muslim, concentrated in the north. The remainder practise Christianity, particularly along the coast, and traditional religions, which are still strong.

LANGUAGE

English is the official language. There are also about 14 tribal languages, but Krio is most widely spoken. The major ingredient of Krio is English, but it's enriched by various West African languages. Because Krio was imported from different groups of slaves, there are strong differences in the languages, so strong in fact that some people have less problems understanding the Krio from Nigeria than Krio spoken in other parts of Sierra Leone.

Expressions in Krio

Hello.	*KOU-shay*
Hi mate.	*Eh bo*
How are you?	*how-dee boh-dee?*
I'm fine.	*BOH-dee fine*
	no bad (used more often)
Thank God.	*ah tel god tenk-kee*
Thank you.	*TENK-kee*
Please. (with emphasis)	*DOU-yah (ah-beg)*
Goodbye.	*we go see back*
Food.	*chop*
Is there any food?	*CHOP-dah?*
How much?	*Ow mus?*
Sierra Leone	*Salone*

Facts for the Visitor

VISAS & EMBASSIES
Sierra Leone Visas

Visas (or entry permits which, for Sierra Leone, are almost the same) are required by all visitors. They are normally valid for 30 days. You cannot get a visa or entry permit at the border.

In West Africa, you can get visas and entry permits for Sierra Leone in Abidjan (Côte d'Ivoire), Banjul (The Gambia), Conakry (Guinea), Monrovia (Liberia), Lagos (Nigeria), Dakar (Senegal), and possibly Accra (Ghana) as well. For details refer to the Visas & Embassies section in the relevant country chapters. Elsewhere, if you're in a country with no Sierra Leonean embassy, try the British high commission.

In Washington, the Sierra Leonean embassy may insist that you send them a self-addressed envelope in order to get a complete list of visa requirements. Requirements include two photos, US$20, and a letter from your bank or employer, for a three-month single-entry visa. In London, the high commission issues visas for UK£20. The process takes four days, and you need one photo. In Bonn or Berlin, the embassy or consulate charges DM75, requires proof of a round-trip airline ticket and takes three days to process a visa.

Visa Extensions

Available at Immigration (☎ 223023) in Freetown at 44 Siaka Stevens St.

Sierra Leone Embassies

Belgium 410 Ave de Terveuern, Brussels 1150 (☎ (02) 771-00-52)
Germany Rheinallee 20, 5300 Bonn 2 (☎ 0228) 35-20-01/2)
UK 33 Portland Place, London W1N 3AG (☎ (0171) 636-6483)
USA 1701 19th St, NW, Washington, DC 20009 (☎ (202) 939-9261)

Sierra Leone also has embassies in Addis Ababa, Cairo, Lusaka, Madrid and Rome; plus consulates in Amsterdam, Stockholm, Vienna and Zürich.

Other African Visas

Côte d'Ivoire The embassy is open from 9 am to 3 pm, requires US$25 and takes 24 hours to issue visas.
The Gambia The embassy is open from 8 am to 4 pm Monday to Friday, and issues visas in 24 hours. The cost varies: about US$10 for Britons and about US$15 for Americans.
Ghana The embassy is open from 9 am to 3 pm, takes three days to issue visas which cost about US$25.
Guinea The embassy is open from 9 am to 3 pm Monday to Friday. Visas are issued the same day, and cost between US$2 and US$50 depending on nationality. A letter of recommendation may be requested. You can also get a visa to Guinea as a matter of course in Nongoa, which is just across the border from Koindu in the north-eastern corner of Sierra Leone. However, procedures can change, so double-check this with the embassy in Freetown.

Liberia The embassy is closed until the war in Liberia ends.

Mali The embassy is open weekday mornings, and issues visas in 24 hours for US$20.

Nigeria The embassy is open only from 10 am to 1 pm Monday to Thursday. Visas take three or four days to process. As at all Nigerian embassies, the cost varies according to nationality, being very cheap for Americans and very expensive for Britons.

Senegal The Senegalese consul gives same-day service. He's usually there from 9 am to 4.30 pm Monday to Friday and from 9 am to 12.30 pm on Saturdays. Visas cost US$12.

Other Countries The French embassy issues visas to Togo, Burkina Faso, Chad and possibly Mauritania. The visa section is open weekdays from 10 am to noon, and issues visas in 24 hours.

Foreign Embassies
See the Freetown Information section for a list of foreign embassies found in the capital.

DOCUMENTS
All visitors need a passport and an International Vaccination Certificate for yellow fever.

CUSTOMS
Importing or exporting more than the equivalent of US$5 in leones is illegal, and at the airport you cannot convert excess leones back into foreign currency. Currency declaration forms are not used, unless you're taking more than US$5000 in or out of the country. At the airport (not land borders) you have to change US$100/UK£60 (or equivalent) into leones. Rates are the same as banks in town.

Leaving the country, your money will be counted (to make sure it's less than US$5000) and you may be searched, although it's all hassle-free.

You are not allowed to take antiquities out of the country. It's unlikely that you'll find any genuinely old items, but customs officials will definitely challenge you if you try

to take out Bundu masks or *nomolies* (sandstone ancestor figures). If you buy anything that *looks* old, you can get a Certificate of Non-authenticity from the national museum in Freetown. The process is quick and straightforward.

MONEY

1FF	=	Le 100
UK£1	=	Le 850
US$1	=	Le 600

The unit of currency is the leone (Le). Inflation was very high in the early 1990s and is now about 20% annually. However, in real terms, prices are fairly stable so they're quoted in US dollars throughout this chapter. At the top hotels, you have to pay in hard currency.

Banks, and the recently introduced foreign exchange (forex) shops offer free rates; consequently there is no black market. However, rates and commissions vary considerably between banks and forex shops, according to the currency you're changing. Cash gets good rates at the forex shops, especially for large denomination bills. Banks give higher rates for travellers' cheques in US dollars and UK pounds. Anybody offering good rates on the street is probably a con-artist, but you can sometimes get between 5 and 10% more for your money at the stores in Freetown selling imported consumer goods. Wherever you change, be prepared for a rucksack full of small bills.

Banks in Sierra Leone include Barclays and Standard Chartered, with branches in Freetown, Kenema, Bo, Makeni, Kabala and Koidu-Sefadu. In Freetown the banks are on or near Siaka Stevens St, where there's also a row of forex shops; handy for comparisons. At Barclays, you can get cash with your Visa card but it costs about US$7.

SIERRA LEONE

Pounds & Pints

You may hear local people quoting prices in *pounds*, a remnant from the time when the leone was pegged to the British pound at 2:1. A Sierra Leonean pound is two leones, so just double the number.

Another similar term you may hear in markets is *pint*. This is the size of a standard beer bottle (330 ml), used everywhere to measure cooking oil and other fluids. ■

BUSINESS HOURS & HOLIDAYS

Business hours are Monday to Saturday from 8 am to noon and 2 to 5 pm. Government departments are open weekdays from 8 am to noon and 12.30 to 3.45 pm, and alternate Saturday mornings. Banking hours are weekdays from 8 am to 1.30 pm (2 pm on Friday), closed Saturday and Sunday.

Public Holidays

1 January, Easter Friday, Easter Monday, 27 April (Independence Day), 29 April (Day of Revolution), End of Ramadan, Tabaski, Mohammed's Birthday, 25 to 26 December.

If you're in Freetown on Easter Monday, visit the beach for the National Kite-Flying Day celebrations. If you're upcountry around 1 January, the New Year celebration at Kabala is the place to be. Thousands of hip young dudes (and anyone else who can afford the bus fare) come from all over Sierra Leone, and beyond, to meet old friends, strut their stuff, and generally have a good time.

POST & TELECOMMUNICATIONS

The postal service in Sierra Leone is unreliable for both sending and receiving letters. Upcountry, anything in an envelope other than a letter is likely to be removed. Aerograms are available and recommended. Parcel post out of Freetown is reported to be quite reliable.

The telephone network within Freetown, and to some upcountry towns, is fairly good. Phonecards are available for booths around town for calls within the city and upcountry. For international calls use Sierra Leone External Telecommunications (SLET ☎ 222801) on Wallace Johnson St; open daily from 8 am to 7 pm. Reverse-charge calls are possible only to the USA and Canada.

MAPS

The Shell Map of Sierra Leone has the whole country on one side (roads are fairly up to date, but topography is not shown) and a street map of Freetown on the other. It costs US$3 from any Shell petrol station or from street stalls in Freetown.

For detailed government survey maps of the whole country or specific areas, go to the Surveys & Lands Department, at the New England Government Buildings, off Jomo Kenyatta Rd. All maps cost about US$4.

PHOTOGRAPHY

No permit is required but, as always, you should not snap government buildings, military sites, airports, harbours or religious ceremonies.

HEALTH

For emergencies in Freetown try the Netland Hospital in Congo Cross (☎ 231476) or the West End Clinic (☎ 223918). They are generally better than Connaught Hospital (☎ 222101) in the centre on Percival St or the Hill Station Hospital (☎ 222006).

WOMEN TRAVELLERS

Sierra Leonean women have come to expect to be propositioned by men constantly, but these approaches are rarely threatening. Foreign women must be prepared for the same treatment.

DANGERS & ANNOYANCES

Like any city in the world, Freetown has its thieves. You should be on your guard against pickpockets and bag-snatchers, although violent robbery is unlikely during the day. At night you should be OK if you keep to the main streets, but dark alleys and the port area should be avoided. Security is more of a concern around the beach hotels near Lumley Beach and Aberdeen, outside Freetown, particularly after dark. The beaches directly in front of the hotels and restaurants are generally safe during the day, although you should not leave your gear unattended. Further down the beach it's more risky. You'll be asking for trouble if you lounge alone. Even if you jog here, don't tempt someone by wearing a watch or carrying money.

In central Freetown, beware of con-artists who ask for money to help a sick relative. Another regular is the guy who hangs around the travel agencies pretending to be a customs official from the airport. His line goes like this: 'You arrived recently? Don't you remember me helping you through? You're leaving soon? Do you want to avoid trouble? A small tip will settle everything'. It's all crap – ignore him.

Theft is also a problem in upcountry towns, particularly at markets and bus stations, although it's no worse than in most other countries. Keep an eye on your bag, keep your camera out of sight, and don't wear expensive-looking watches or *any* jewellery.

A danger of a different sort, which may affect visitors, is the fighting between the army and rebels in various parts of the country (see the earlier Sierra Leone Today section in this chapter). Banditry and sporadic skirmishes continue, and you should make enquiries about the current situation before leaving Freetown.

ACCOMMODATION

In Freetown you have a wide choice: from dirty doss-pits to smart hotels, with mid-range guesthouses and hostels in between. There's less of a choice when you go upcountry: most large towns have a few cheap hotels and maybe one or two in the lower-middle range. Some missions have guesthouses which are open to travellers. Peace Corps also have some upcountry rest houses where travellers may be allowed to stay for a few dollars a night if there's space, and if other volunteers are present; you have to turn up and ask. However, in the past these places were flooded with travellers, some of whom left without paying, so be prepared for a refusal. (The PC rest house in Freetown is for volunteers only.) Also be prepared for no rest houses at all, as some reports indicate that Peace Corps may pull out of Sierra Leone if the fighting between the army and rebels does not end.

FOOD

Sierra Leonean cuisine is one of the best in West Africa, if not *the* best. You should definitely not pass up the opportunity of trying the cooking here. Every town has at least one *chop bar* (basic eating-house) serving tasty filling food, and in Freetown there are even some 'proper' restaurants specialising in local cooking. Rice is the staple and *plasas* (pounded potato or cassava leaves cooked with palm oil and fish or beef) is the most common sauce. Other typical Sierra Leonean dishes are okra sauce, palm oil stew, groundnut stew, pepper soup and, for special occasions, jollof rice.

Sierra Leone has good street food as well: roasted groundnuts, roasted corn, beef sticks, steamed yams, fried plantain bananas, fried dough balls and fried yams with fish sauce. Keep an eye open for *benchi* (black bench peas with palm oil and fish) usually served with bread at breakfast-time.

DRINKS

The local beer is called Star, and is reasonable. In upcountry towns, most bars are attached to petrol stations (because they have generators for the pumps which also keep the fridge going), although the sight of happy drinkers with cigarettes so close to all those fumes takes some getting use to.

Poyo, the local palm wine, is light and fruity, but getting used to the smell and the wildlife floating in your cup takes a while. The spicy ginger beer sold on the streets is a nonalcoholic alternative, but you can easily get sick from it as the water is rarely boiled.

Getting There & Away

AIR

To/From Europe & the USA

Airlines from Europe serving Sierra Leone include KLM (via Amsterdam), Air France (via Paris), Sabena (via Brussels) and Aeroflot (via Moscow). Return flights start at the equivalent of around US$650, depending on the season and your length of stay. Other services include Air Gambia (from London via Banjul) and Ghana Airways (from London via Accra).

From the USA, you can take Air Afrique from New York, transferring to a regional flight in Dakar or Abidjan. Otherwise you'll have to go via Europe.

To/From West Africa

Freetown is connected to other West African capitals by several regional airlines, including Ghana Airways, ADC, Air Gambia, Gambia Airways (both with return flights to Banjul for US$100), Air Guinée, Guinée Air Service, Nigeria Airways, and Sierra National Airlines (with return flights to Accra for US$380). KLM also flies within West Africa: for example Freetown to Conakry (US$56) or Dakar (US$150). For airline office addresses see the Freetown Getting There & Away section.

LAND

Bush Taxi & Minibus

To/From Guinea There are plenty of minibuses and bush taxis running directly between Freetown and Conakry, via Pamelap (the border). Some vehicles go direct or you may have to change at Pamelap. Either way the trip costs about US$15, and takes 10 to 12 hours but can be done in a day if you leave early. Be prepared for several police checks on this route (in both countries).

It's also possible to cross the border in north-eastern Sierra Leone between Koindu and Nongoa, or at Medina Dula between Makeni and Kindia (see Getting There & Away in the Guinea chapter). Another way to go is via Kabala and Faranah, but you'll have problems finding vehicles close to the border, which is why so few travellers take this route. However, it is feasible by a combination of trucks, bush taxis and, possibly, some walking. In Kabala you can hire a motorbike (and driver) to take you to the border, or all the way to Faranah. See the Kabala section in this chapter for details.

To/From Liberia Travel to Liberia obviously depends on the state of the war in that country; currently it is not possible to enter overland, but if things change, the major route between Freetown and Monrovia will be via Kenema and the Liberian coast, with a change of vehicles (and overnight stop) at Kenema. The whole journey can be done in two days in the dry season. Kenema to Monrovia costs about US$20 by bush taxi.

During the rainy season the road between Kenema and Fairo gets very bad, and can easily take all day to cover, with frequent stops for passengers to get out and push the overcrowded vehicle through the mud.

There are also vehicles every day from Kenema north to Koindu (180 km but an all-day trip even in the dry season), from where you can cross into northern Liberia (again, wars permitting).

Car

To/From Guinea The 330-km drive from Freetown to Conakry via Pamelap takes six to eight hours, and a bit longer in the rainy season; the road is paved except for a 70-km stretch near the border (which opens from 6 am to 6 pm).

You can also drive from Kabala to Faranah, and possibly from Koindu to Macenta via Voinjama (Liberia). See Getting There & Away in the Guinea chapter.

To/From Liberia Once the political situation in Liberia calms down, overland travel between the two countries should resume. The main route goes via Kenema and Fairo, across the Mano River bridge (the border), then along the coast to Monrovia. During the dry season, the drive between Freetown and Monrovia (650 km) can be done in 10 to 12 hours. During the rains, the section between Kenema and Fairo is always a mess but usually passable. Alternatively, drive from Joru to Koindu and enter Liberia from there.

SEA

To/From Guinea A fast luxurious hydrofoil service was operating twice a week between Freetown and Conakry until the end of 1993. The one-way fare was US$40. It may start again, so enquire at Sierra Link Ltd (☎ 222304) at 22 Rawdon St in Freetown, or any travel agency.

LEAVING SIERRA LEONE

Airport departure tax for international flights is US$12.

Getting Around

AIR

Sierra Leone Airlines, affectionately known as Sierra Leone Scare-lines, went bankrupt in the late 1980s. However, in 1993 it was resurrected as Sierra National Airlines with several regional flights to other West African capitals. A domestic service has been promised, probably to Kenema and Bo, so make enquiries locally if you want to get around the country by air.

BUS

The Sierra Leone Road Transport Corporation (SLRTC) run large buses every day between Freetown and the major upcountry towns: Kabala (via Makeni), Kenema, Bo, Koindu and Koidu-Sefadu (Kono). They are reliable, fast, not overcrowded and much safer than bush taxis or minibuses. Fares are cheap: for example, across the country from Freetown to Kabala costs US$6. Naturally, these buses are popular, so getting a ticket requires certain know-how (see the Conakry Getting There & Away section in the Guinea chapter for details).

Private buses cover the same routes. They are about the same price but more crowded and less reliable than the SLRTC buses.

BUSH TAXI & MINIBUS

Because long-distance buses are so popular, bush taxis (usually Peugeot 504s) and minibuses (called *poda-podas*) generally only do relatively short trips (which are reasonably priced) between major towns, for example Bo to Kenema (US$2), or Makeni to Kabala (US$3), although for these journeys they go more frequently than buses.

The major problem with bush taxis and poda-podas is that they're extremely crowded and uncomfortable. It's not unusual for a Peugeot 504 to have 11 passengers inside, plus luggage, children, chickens and occasionally even someone on the roof. Also, some drivers go like mad, occasionally with fatal results.

CAR

Most of the major upcountry towns are connected to Freetown by good tar roads, but they are bendy and the generally poor standard of driving can make them dangerous. Note that many road distances on signposts and maps (including the Michelin) are given in miles. (One km is 0.625 miles.)

Sierra Leone used to suffer from petrol shortages, but since 1992 it has been generally easy to buy (US$1 for two litres).

For details on car rental see Freetown Getting Around.

HITCHING

Sierra Leone is one of the best countries in West Africa for hitching and it's usually the most comfortable way to travel. Drivers are happy to pick up travellers because everyone understands the difficulty of getting around. Most Sierra Leoneans in private vehicles will not expect hitchhikers to pay, although truck drivers will, so you should check before getting in. In general, foreigners here don't expect money from hitchers: they'll presume you're a volunteer.

Freetown

Freetown used to be a shanty town with a capital S. Along with the rest of the country, it had a dirty and decrepit air and very little to recommend a visit. But since the coup of 1992, things have changed: the last few years have seen a sudden surge of activity and optimism. There's running water again, electricity (at least during the day), and the new government has introduced 'National Cleaning Day': on the first Saturday of every month there's a virtual curfew until 10 am while everybody cleans their yard or section of road, and the city is certainly looking better for it. There are waste bins on the main streets – people use them and (even more remarkable) they are regularly emptied. Gangs of local youths have cleared the mud from the drains so that in the rainy season most water flows there instead of in the

SIERRA LEONE

street. Houses are being repainted, roads are repaired and the shops are full of goods.

Things are not perfect though; locals still avoid elevators as they probably haven't been inspected since independence. But apart from the traffic jams at rush hour (which have got worse now petrol is easy to buy), and the problems with thieves (see Dangers and Annoyances) Freetown is not a bad place to visit. As African cities go it's got a good feel and a lot of character.

Orientation

Central Freetown is set out on the usual grid pattern. The major street is Siaka Stevens St which runs north-east to south-west, with the huge Cotton Tree, a major landmark, about halfway along. Within a few blocks of the tree are the national museum, the post office, the markets, a range of hotels, banks, forex shops, restaurants, airlines and embassies.

Overlooking the city is Mt Aureol. As you go out of the central area the streets become more winding as they climb or circle the surrounding hills.

To the east of the centre, the main road out of town is Kissy Rd which passes through many of the older, poorer districts, bordered by Susan's Bay on the north and Mt Aureol on the south. Some taxis and poda-podas heading east from the centre alternatively go along Forah Bay Rd through the dock area.

The main road west of the centre follows Sanders St, Brookfields Rd and Motor Main Rd through the better residential areas towards Aberdeen village and Lumley village(see Greater Freetown map). Some taxis and poda-podas heading west alternatively go via Kroo Town Rd and Congo Town Rd.

The three major beach hotels, including the prestigious Mammy Yoko Sofitel, are all just beyond Aberdeen village at the north-western tip of Freetown Peninsula, roughly 10 km west of the centre. Lumley Beach extends for five km southward from here.

Information

Tourist Office The National Tourist Board has an office at the Bintumani Hotel. The staff try to be helpful, but have no maps or leaflets to give away.

National Parks The Sierra Leone Conservation Society (☎ 229716) at 4 Sanders St, has some good leaflets for sale about the country's protected wildlife areas. Money raised helps fund their various projects. You can also get details (and make reservations for the camp at Outamba-Kilimi) at the Wildlife Conservation Branch (☎ 225352), part of the Forestry Division, in the Government Building at Tower Hill.

Money Barclays is in the heart of town on the corner of Siaka Stevens and Charlotte Sts and is probably the best place to change travellers' cheques in UK pounds or US dollars, although the rates and commissions for other currencies are bad, and the service is slow. The main branch of Standard Chartered is on the corner of Lightfoot Boston and Wilberforce Sts, and Meridien-BIAO is on Lightfoot Boston St, between Charlotte and Gloucester Sts. Freetown also has many foreign exchange (forex) shops, with quick service, giving good rates for cash, especially US dollars or UK pounds, and poor rates for travellers' cheques. Several of these, including First Foreign Exchange and West Africa Forex Bureau, are on Siaka Stevens St near Barclays.

Post & Telecommunications The post office is on Siaka Stevens St, three blocks east of the Cotton Tree. It's open weekdays and Saturday mornings, and the poste restante is free. For sending packages, go to the parcel post office on the waterfront at the foot of Lamina Sankoh St. All Freetown phone numbers are now six-figure. All old five-figure numbers now have a 2 prefix.

Foreign Embassies The following countries have embassies/consulates that issue visas:

Côte d'Ivoire 1 Wesley St, east of Pademba Rd (☎ 223983)
France 13 Lamina Sankoh St, north of Siaka Stevens St (☎ 222477)
The Gambia 6 Wilberforce St, south of Lightfoot Boston St (☎ 225191)

Ghana 16 Percival St, north of Siaka Stevens St (☎ 223461)

Germany Santanno House, 10 Howe St (☎ 222511)

Guinea At the eastern end of Wilkinson Rd, on the left as you're going away from the centre, next to a Fiat-Lada garage

Italy In the offices of Action Aid, 32a Wilkinson Rd, about halfway between Freetown and the Lumley Beach area (☎ 230995/1392)

Ireland 8 Rawdon St, north of Siaka Stevens St (☎ 222017)

Japan 82-88 Kissy Dockyard (☎ 250559)

Mali 40 Wilkinson Rd, 200 metres beyond Aberdeen Junction (☎ 231781)

The Netherlands Above KLM on Lamina Sankoh St (☎ 224444)

Nigeria Nigeria House, Siaka Stevens St near the Cotton Tree (☎ 224202)

Senegal Attached to a shop at 9 Upper East St, a block east of the Leona Hotel

UK Above the Standard Bank, on the corner of Lightfoot Boston and Wilberforce Sts (☎ 223961)

USA 1 Walpole St, near Siaka Stevens St (☎ 226481)

Travel Agencies The two best travel agencies in town are Yazbeck Tours (☎ 222374) and IPC Travel (226860), both in the centre on Siaka Stevens St, between Charlotte and Wilberforce Sts. Yazbeck is the representative for American Express, and IPC also has an office at the Sofitel Mammy Yoko Hotel. Both agencies mainly deal in flights, offering a good and reliable service (credit cards accepted), and also handle excursions and reservations for tour groups. Independent travellers can also make arrangements for upcountry tours, fishing and hunting trips, half and full-day river-boat cruises, and all-day excursions to the Banana Islands where snorkelling and fishing are possible, although most trips require a minimum of eight passengers.

For flights only, try Lion Travel (☎ 223211), 13 Howe St; Freetown Travel Agency (☎ 223109), 28 Walpole St next to the US embassy; or Aureol Travel (☎ 225344) and City Travel Agents (☎ 225493), both on Rawdon St between Lightfoot Boston and Siaka Stevens Sts.

Bookshops & Libraries The best bookshop in Freetown is New Horizons on Howe St, just north of Siaka Stevens St. They have a good selection of general books and paperback novels, all priced in UK pounds and converted at the day's rate. For second-hand books, nearly all in English, browse at the stalls on Garrison St or along Lightfoot Boston St near the basket market.

The Sierra Leone Library is just south of Victoria Park at the junction of Rokel and Gloucester Sts. The British Council nearby has a really nice library with newspapers, magazines, etc. To get there, go south on Gloucester St, and turn left just past the Sierra Leone Library; it's 200 metres up that winding road.

Supermarkets One of the better supermarkets in the centre is A H Mackie on the corner of Siaka Stevens and East Sts; it sells mostly foreign goods as well as 1½-litre bottles of water for US$1. Further west, at the other end of Siaka Stevens St, Choithram's is larger, with a wide range of imported foods. Boys *(bobos)* sell fruit, veg and eggs on the pavement outside. Local expatriates also favour Quik Serve, Atson's and Cold Point, all on Wilkinson Rd to the west of the centre, because 'the parking is better and you don't get hassled by the egg-bobos'.

Things to See
The first order of the day should be a walk along Freetown's major street – Siaka Stevens St. Halfway along here is the 500-year-old **Cotton Tree**, the heart of town and the city's principal landmark. Up the hill from the tree you can see the **State House**. (The drive is closed to the public.) Just to the east of the tree are the **Law Courts**, which were burnt in 1990 (allegedly by arsonists to destroy the court's records) but are undergoing renovation.

On the opposite side of the Cotton Tree is a small old train stop that is now the **National Museum**. It has an entrance fee of US$1, and, among other things, a great collection of Bundu masks used by the Mende and Temne female secret societies. It's open weekdays from 8 am to noon and 1 to 4 pm and is well worth a visit.

On Lightfoot Boston St, on the corner of Gloucester St, is the dilapidated **City Hotel**, where Graham Greene wrote his highly acclaimed novel, *The Heart of the Matter*,

SIERRA LEONE

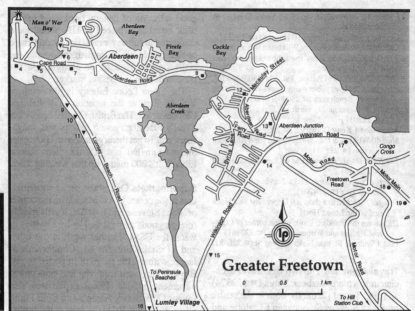

Greater Freetown

while working here for the British Colonial Service during WW II. The hotel was built in the 1920s and looks like it hasn't been maintained since. It's now a brothel; if the bar is open, have a drink for the experience, although it's not particularly friendly and latest reports say they often run out of beer.

On Wallace Johnson St at the foot of Pultney St, right on the waterfront, is **King Jimmy Market**, a small food and clothing market, reached by going down a steep flight of stone steps. Nearby is the Big Market (usually called the Basket Market).

Some of the old wood-framed **Krio houses** scattered throughout Freetown are fascinating. Most date back to the late 19th century, with a few even older.

The new **Parliament** building is on the hill inland from the Paramount Hotel. Tours may be possible: just ask at the gate. On top of Mt Aureol is **Fourah Bay College**, founded in 1827 by the Church Missionary Society, which is the oldest English-language univer-

sity in Africa south of the Sahara. Most people take a taxi, but the college can be reached in about an hour on foot. Head up Parliament Rd from the Paramount Hotel. It eventually turns into Berry St, from which you turn off on Barham Rd to the college.

Activities

The ocean is calm and swimming is generally safe. Several places in front of the beach hotels rent sailboards for about US$10 an hour (and small sailing boats for twice the price), and conditions are good for learning. The three beach hotels and the Brookfields Hotel have pools.

Places to Stay – bottom end

Best value is the *YMCA* (☎ 223608) at 32 Fort St, west of the centre. Both men and women are welcome. Clean single/double rooms with fans, sinks, towels and candles cost US$7/10. The shared bathrooms are also clean. The Y is nearly always full, so your

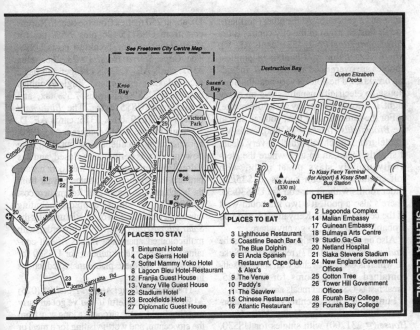

PLACES TO STAY

1 Bintumani Hotel
4 Cape Sierra Hotel
7 Sofitel Mammy Yoko Hotel
8 Lagoon Bleu Hotel-Restaurant
12 Franjia Guest House
13 Vancy Ville Guest House
22 Stadium Hotel
23 Brookfields Hotel
27 Diplomatic Guest House

PLACES TO EAT

3 Lighthouse Restaurant
5 Coastline Beach Bar & The Blue Dolphin
6 El Ancla Spanish Restaurant, Cape Club & Alex's
9 The Venue
10 Paddy's
11 The Seaview
15 Chinese Restaurant
16 Atlantic Restaurant

OTHER

2 Lagoonda Complex
14 Malian Embassy
17 Guinean Embassy
18 Bulmaya Arts Centre
19 Studio Ga-Ga
20 Netland Hospital
21 Siaka Stevens Stadium
24 New England Government Offices
25 Cotton Tree
26 Tower Hill Government Offices
28 Fourah Bay College
29 Fourah Bay College

only chance of a bed may be to wait at the restaurant until someone leaves.

Next best is the *Leona Hotel* (☎ 223587), two blocks south of Siaka Stevens St on the corner of Regent Rd and Back St, where clean self-contained air-con singles/doubles cost $10/12. The restaurant is also good.

For somewhere cheaper, the *City Hotel* on the corner of Lightfoot Boston and Gloucester Sts has historical interest but it's a filthy dump, where rooms are US$3 a night. A better bet is the *Tropic of Cancer Hotel* opposite at 4 Gloucester St, where reasonable rooms cost US$5 per person. Beer and chop (served by the delightful Mrs Williams) is also cheap.

Other possibilities are: the dingy *Lamar Hotel* (☎ 225903) at 21 Howe St, where self-contained singles/doubles are better than the City Hotel but poor value at about US$7/10; the *New Lido Hotel* (☎ 225574) on the corner of Garrison and Charlotte Sts, overlooking Victoria Park Market, with basic grubby rooms for US$8/11 (25% more

with private bathroom) including breakfast; and *Andy's Apartments* at 32 Rawdon St, south of Siaka Stevens St, where large self-contained rooms with a kitchen (but no stove) cost US$10 (monthly rents also available). The *El-Basha Hotel* (☎ 222704) at 23 East St, south of Siaka Stevens St and up a flight of stairs, has dirty self-contained air-con rooms for US$13. (None of the hotels in this bracket have generators, so you should have a torch (flashlight) or candles in case there's a night blackout.)

Sleeping on Lumley Beach or any other beach near Freetown is illegal and if the cops don't get you, muggers probably will.

Places to Stay – middle

Cheapest in this range and very good value is the *Diplomatic Guest House* (☎ 224179) at 152 Circular Rd, near the junction with Fort St. Clean air-con rooms cost US$17/20 with shared baths, or US$20/25 for self-contained rooms. There's also back-up water tanks and a generator. At the other (northern) end of Fort St, right in the city centre, is the *Paramount Hotel* (☎ 224531; cards AE, V), where reasonable self-contained singles/ doubles are overpriced at US$36/67, including breakfast. The hotel is very near the State House so electricity usually stays on every night. If it doesn't, you may get a 30% rebate.

For the same price or less, you can stay at the *Brookfields Hotel* (☎ 241860; cards V), a hotel training school, which is very clean, if slightly faded, in an area where the electricity usually stays on at night, with self-contained air-con rooms at $35/55. Older rooms without air-con are US$30/35. There's also a pool. It's two km south-west of the centre on Jomo Kenyatta Rd, and you probably need a taxi to go anywhere.

Also on the western edge of the centre is the *Stadium Hotel* (☎ 240387), reached from Syke St, which is excellent value with spotless self-contained air-con rooms for US$17/25. Breakfast is US$3, and meals around US$5.

Further west of the centre, very near Aberdeen Junction, is the *Vancy Ville Guest House* (☎ 231200) with singles for US$30, and self-contained doubles with air-con for US$45, including breakfast. The hotel restaurant does a good African buffet on Tuesday lunchtimes. A few km further down the same road is the small and friendly family-run *Franjia Guest House* where clean singles/doubles cost US$17/25 including breakfast. Other meals can be prepared to order. Couples can share a single.

Just across the bridge from here is the good value *Lagon Bleu Hotel & Restaurant* (☎ 272237), with comfortable self-contained air-con bungalows for US$40/45. Breakfast is US$3, meals from around US$6.

Places to Stay – top end

Freetown's three major beach hotels are all about 10 km west of the city centre in the Aberdeen/Lumley Beach area. They have most of the facilities you'd expect at top-class hotels, including pools, tennis courts, water sports etc, and stand-by generators. The best by far is the *Sofitel Mammy Yoko Hotel* (☎ 231176, telex 3416; cards AE, V,

D), about 250 metres from the beach. Rooms cost from US$115/136 plus 7.5% tax for singles/doubles, and breakfast costs US$8. The *Cape Sierra Hotel* (☎ 237266, telex 3367; cards AE, V, D) is cheaper and has a nice relaxing ambience. Singles/doubles cost from US$90/110 plus 7.5% tax, and breakfast is US$5 extra. The *Bintumani Hotel* (☎ 237019, telex 3316; cards AE, D, V), built for the OAU conference in 1980, commands an excellent view but it's going downhill fast, is periodically closed, and has a dreadful atmosphere. The mediocre restaurant and the position, a 15-minute walk from the beach, are also drawbacks. Rooms here cost US$96/134 for singles/doubles, including breakfast. In the shadow of the Bintumani is the *Solar Village Hotel* (☎ 272531; no cards), with multicoloured apartment blocks of self-contained 'studios' with kitchens, for US$80 for two people. All these places make reductions in the low season.

The pleasant *Lungi Airport Hotel* (☎ (025) 345; cards AE) is useful if you've got an early morning flight, as the airport is a long way from the city centre, and worth visiting for a meal or drink (the bar TV has CNN) if you've time to kill before departure. Singles/doubles are US$84/100, or US$25 for day rooms. Breakfast is US$5, and the hotel has a pool.

Places to Eat – cheap

For low priced chop in nice surroundings go to the *Park Café* in Victoria Park, where bowls of rice and sauce are around US$1. With similar food and prices is *Wendy's* on Howe St and *The Cavern* and *Afro-Merik*, on Garrison St. Also, Howe St is good for street food in the evening.

For low prices and cleanliness, it's hard to beat the excellent restaurant at the *YMCA* where you can get breakfast (7.30 to 10 am) and lunch (12.30 to 3 pm) for around US$1, and dinners (6 to 10 pm) such as fish & chips for around US$2.

For low prices and more 'authentic' surroundings head for *Minnie's*, unmarked at 7 Lamina Sankoh St, 60 metres north of Siaka Stevens St. The beloved Minnie, who has been running this chop house since 1960,

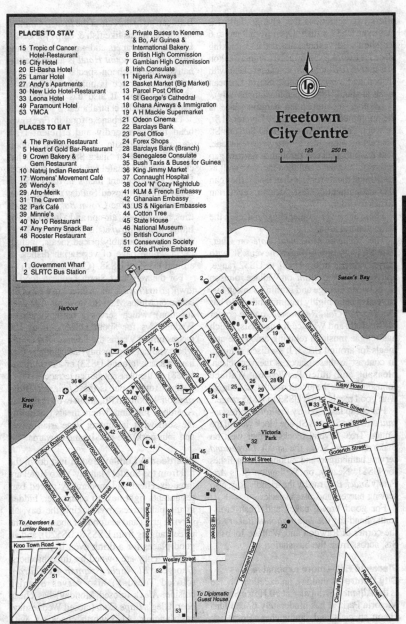

PLACES TO STAY

15 Tropic of Cancer
   Hotel-Restaurant
16 City Hotel
20 El-Basha Hotel
25 Lamar Hotel
27 Andy's Apartments
30 New Lido Hotel-Restaurant
33 Leona Hotel
49 Paramount Hotel
53 YMCA

PLACES TO EAT

4 The Pavilion Restaurant
5 Heart of Gold Bar-Restaurant
9 Crown Bakery &
   Gem Restaurant
10 Natruj Indian Restaurant
17 Womens' Movement Café
26 Wendy's
29 Afro-Merik
31 The Cavern
32 Park Café
39 Minnie's
40 No 10 Restaurant
47 Any Penny Snack Bar
48 Rooster Restaurant

OTHER

1 Government Wharf
2 SLRTC Bus Station

3 Private Buses to Kenema
   & Bo, Air Guinea &
   International Bakery
6 British High Commission
7 Gambian High Commission
8 Irish Consulate
11 Nigeria Airways
12 Basket Market (Big Market)
13 Parcel Post Office
14 St George's Cathedral
18 Ghana Airways & Immigration
19 A H Mackie Supermarket
21 Odeon Cinema
22 Barclays Bank
23 Post Office
24 Forex Shops
28 Barclays Bank (Branch)
34 Senegalese Consulate
35 Bush Taxis & Buses for Guinea
36 King Jimmy Market
37 Connaught Hospital
38 Cool 'N' Cozy Nightclub
41 KLM & French Embassy
42 Ghanaian Embassy
43 US & Nigerian Embassies
44 Cotton Tree
45 State House
46 National Museum
50 British Council
51 Conservation Society
52 Côte d'Ivoire Embassy

**Freetown
City Centre**

0   125   250 m

SIERRA LEONE

offers two selections that change daily for just over US$1 a dish. Open from 9 am to 6 pm, she also serves breakfast, and it's a relaxing place for a drink. Nearby at 10 Lamina Sankoh St is the *No 10 Restaurant*, a smarter place, with air-con and very reasonable Sierra Leonean meals at about US$3 (open lunchtimes only).

Another recommended bargain place is the un-named chop house at 50 Liverpool St, between Pademba Rd and Siaka Stevens St. There's no sign, just a very yellow façade. You have to squeeze through a narrow gap between the house and the fence. As well as traditional meals for less than US$1, they can also do authentic West African vegetarian dishes to order.

There are several other cheap places in the same general area.

The *Women's Movement Café* on Charlotte St, just north of Siaka Stevens St, with African dishes in the US$1 to US$2 range, and *Romie's Restaurant* on Wallace Johnson St, between George and Lamina Sankoh Sts, have also been highly recommended. So has the *Heart of Gold Restaurant*, on the corner of Charlotte and Wallace Johnson Sts, which has reggae music, a relaxing ambience and meals for around US$3. It's a disco at night. In contrast to these places is the very clean, pleasant and quiet *Pavilion* on Wallace Johnson St, near the junction with Charlotte St, with good meals in the US$3 to US$5 range.

For cheap fast food, try the *Rooster Restaurant* on Siaka Stevens St, one block west of the Cotton Tree. Several blocks further west on Siaka Stevens St is the small *Burgerland* serving hamburgers and various African dishes for US$1. Nearby, on Wellington St is *Any Penny Snack Bar*, run by the friendly Ray, also serving burgers and cheap snacks.

For good bread, cakes and fresh croissants, head for the *International Bakery* on the corner of Rawdon and Wallace Johnson Sts, across from the bus station.

Places to Eat – more expensive

City Centre At midday, an excellent choice is the *Alliance Française* at 30 Howe St near Victoria Park; it has moderately priced luncheon specials and sandwiches. Homesick Brits can go to the café at the *British Council*, which has meals like fish & chips for US$4, English newspapers and a great view of the city. The *Paramount Hotel* is another alternative. The luncheon special is reasonably priced, the service is quick, and there's a sandwich menu. It also has the only upmarket bar in the central area.

For the best Lebanese food in Freetown, head for the friendly and efficient *Gem Restaurant* opposite Air France on Wilberforce St, south of Siaka Stevens St. It has chawarma and falafel sandwiches for about US$2 and excellent meals in the US$5 to US$10 range (closed Sunday). Next door, the pâtisserie at the *Crown Bakery* has pastries, hamburgers, air-con and a lot more. For Indian food, *Natruj* at 18 Wilberforce St has excellent, reasonably priced meals, including a whole page of vegetarian dishes, at around US$5 to US$8. (Closed Sunday.)

For the very best Sierra Leonean food in town, go to *Provilac* about three km west of the centre on Motor Main Rd (towards Aberdeen Junction), which serves a buffet lunch on Wednesdays for about US$5. About 100 metres further west is the *Balmaya Art Centre* where you can view (or buy) the paintings, then have a snack (around US$3) or a meal (up to US$8) on the pleasant garden terrace.

Even further out is the *Chinese Restaurant*, on Wilkinson Rd, about two km beyond Aberdeen Junction, where meals (including the somewhat intriguing vegetarian sweet and sour pork) are US$10 and upwards.

Aberdeen & Lumley Beach Just down the hill from the Sofitel Mammy Yoko Hotel are three excellent and moderately priced bar-restaurants right next to each other, hidden in the palm trees overlooking the bay, all serving grills and seafood for about the same price (ranging from US$5 to US$20), and all good places for a drink even if you're not hungry. They are owned by three brothers: George's *El Ancla Spanish Restaurant* (closed Tuesday) also serves Spanish cuisine; *Alex's* (closed Monday) has cheap beer; Oleg's *Cape Club* (closed Wednesday) has dancing. Also worth checking, with meals at similar prices, is the *Lighthouse Restaurant*, on the other side of the bay.

Nearby, on the beach side of the road leading towards the Cape Sierra Hotel are *The Blue Dolphin*, a smart seafood restaurant with meals in the US$10 range, and the *Coastline Beach Bar*, a less pretentious, local-style place, with cheaper food and beer.

A few hundred metres away, right on Lumley Beach, only a few metres from the sea, are some more bar-restaurants which are popular, informal and reasonably priced. They're ordinary-looking at best, but delightfully breezy with roofs to protect you from the sun, and open from mid-morning until the last people go home at night, and ideal for a snack, a meal or just a drink.

At the far southern end of the beach is the long-established *Atlantic Restaurant*, which is fine but not worth the effort unless you've got wheels. Shrimp, lobster and barracuda are its specialities. Open every evening and for Sunday lunch, it has tables that are very near the beach; sometimes there's music later in the evening.

These places are easy to reach during the day: get a shared taxi to Aberdeen Junction, then another to Aberdeen village roundabout (just past the Sofitel Mammy Yoko Hotel) and walk the last few hundred metres. During the day you can return the same way, but at night taxis are hard to find (you cannot phone for one), and walking in this area is not safe. You may be able to find a lift back to town if you ask around in the carpark.

Entertainment

Bars Most of the hotels or restaurants listed above are also bars. For a taste of the past, visit the *Hill Station Club*, above the city with views across the peninsula. This was Freetown's social centre in colonial times (Graham Greene was a member) but the last few years have not been kind and the club is now only a shadow of its former self. You're supposed to be a member, but getting a drink during the day is easy enough. To get here take a taxi up Hill Cot Rd from the Brookfields Hotel (walking is possible but not advised after sunset). For a complete con-

trast, head for Kissy town, where there's a lot of low-life action, although it's best to go here with a streetwise local.

Nightclubs There are many nightclubs, ranging from the real dives to the fairly respectable. Most start warming up at about 10 or 11 pm. A favourite is the *Cool N' Cozy* disco, on Percival St, just south of the Connaught hospital. You can dance there to reggae sounds until the wee hours of the morning. Similar is *Wendy's* on Howe St, very crowded and free to get in, and *Paladios* on Rawdon St (small entrance charge). Or try *Count Down*, a small and smoky reggae club, south-west of the central area on Sanders St, where entrance is US$2. Nearby is *Rico's* and *Peppermint*. More up-market is *Phase 2* on Upper Syke St, which costs US$3 to get in.

In the beach area, tourists and wealthier locals all head for the *Attitude Disco* at the very modern *Lagoonda Entertainment Complex* (near the Cape Sierra Hotel), which also has a restaurant, cinema and casino. Alternatives in this area include *Where Else?* at the Bintumani Hotel, and the inferior *Casino Leone* nearby, between the Mammy Yoko and the Cape Sierra.

Cinemas The best cinema is at the Lagoonda Complex, which shows good quality recent releases. Tickets for evening shows are US$3, or US$1 on Saturday afternoons. In town, your choices include the Odeon Theatre on the corner of Siaka Stevens and Howe Sts, showing mainly kung-fu-quality films, and the Strand Theatre on Waterloo St, which is similar but occasionally has better things. The British Council shows films most Fridays – entrance is free.

Things to Buy

Fabric Sierra Leone is a good place to buy beautiful fabrics including 'country cloth' and *gara*. Country cloth is a coarse material woven from wild cotton into narrow strips that are then joined to make blankets and clothing, then coloured indigo, green or brown using natural dyes. Gara is a thin cotton material, tie-dyed or batik-printed

SIERRA LEONE

SIERRA LEONE

either with synthetic colours or natural dyes. In Freetown, Victoria Park Market probably has the best selection. Material is sold by the *lapa* (about 1.5 metres), and is often pre-cut into 'double-lapa' lengths. For top quality stuff, visit Mrs Kadiatu Kamara who sells gara, batiks and African-style clothing, and has worked with anthropologists studying West African textiles. To reach her workshop go out of the centre on Motor Main Rd, over the stadium bridge, and it's on the right as you go up the hill. Look for the sign.

Artisan Goods First visit Victoria Park Market, then try the shops along Howe St leading down from the market; some of them are run by traders selling things from around West Africa. You could also try the street stalls along Lightfoot Boston St. For carvings, visit the small shop next to No 10 Restaurant on Lamina Sankoh St. For baskets, and just about anything else from saucepans to monkey skulls, head for the Big Market (usually called the Basket Market) at the foot of Lamina Sankoh St, on the port side of Wallace Johnson St.

If the skulls put you off, Charlie's Curio Shop at the Paramount Hotel has an assortment of crafts from around West Africa, and prices are surprisingly reasonable.

For paintings and sculptures by local artists, there are two galleries on Motor Main Rd, west of the centre. Studio Ga-Ga, at the junction with College Rd, acts as an agent for the artists and is generally cheaper. Bulmaya Arts Centre, 300 metres further down the road, is a dealership where the quality of work, and the prices, are generally higher.

Music You can buy cassettes (for about US$2) of various local stars, but the recording quality is terrible. You'll do better buying blank tapes (try New Horizons bookshop) and taking them to places like Pat Paul on Kroo Town Rd, three blocks from the junction with Siaka Stevens St, or Tapes International at 27 Regent St, where you can have an album recorded for about the same price. Both places are open late.

Getting There & Away

Air There are no domestic flights between Freetown and other destinations within Sierra Leone, although Sierra National Airlines may start serving upcountry towns in the future.

Airlines with offices in Freetown include: Ghana Airways (☎ 224781) at 15 Siaka Stevens St near Howe St; Nigerian Airways (☎ 226347) at 11 Siaka Stevens St; Air France (☎ 226075) at 12 Wilberforce St; Sierra National Airlines (☎ 222075) at 25 Pultney St; Air Gambia (☎ 224016) at 5 Gloucester St; Aeroflot (226328) at the junction of Charlotte and Wallace Johnson Sts; Air Guinée (☎ 225534) on Rawdon St between Wallace Johnson and Lightfoot Boston Sts, and KLM (☎ 224444) on the corner of Siaka Stevens and Lamina Sankoh Sts, near the Cotton Tree.

Bus SLRTC buses all leave from the bus station (which was the old train station)on the corner of Rawdon and Wallace Johnson Sts. Buses from Freetown go every day between 7 and 10 am to Kenema (US$6), Bo (US$5), Kambia (US$5) and Koidu-Sefadu, also called Kono (US$8), and every Monday, Wednesday and Friday to Kabala via Makeni (US$6). Add US$1 for large pieces of luggage. The bus typically takes about four hours to Makeni and six hours to Kenema or Kabala. Things change though, so you should go to the bus station the day before you travel to check prices and schedules.

Private buses leave from the street outside the bus station, or from the Kissy Shell station. Fares are about the same, but private buses tend to be unreliable and more crowded.

To get an SLRTC ticket you must follow a routine. First, you need to get to the bus station by the crack of dawn (6 am at the latest) on the day you want to travel. There are several queues around the bus station: join the one for your destination. The ticket staff arrive about 8 am and issue everybody in each queue with a voucher. There's a fair bit of jostling at this stage, so hold on to your place (even if you were fifth in line, people will arrive who 'know' others in front of you, and you'll soon be tenth). Then a man with a megaphone calls out each destination in turn and the whole queue goes to the ticket office, where you surrender your voucher, pay your money, and get your ticket which has your seat number on it. Easy!

Bush Taxi & Minibus Bush taxis and poda-podas (and some private buses) leave from various sites in Freetown (all in the centre or east of the centre), depending on the destination: the corner of Free and Upper East Sts) for Conakry; Dan St for Bo and Kenema; Ashoebi Corner (two km east of the central area on Kissy Rd) for Makeni, Kabala and Koidu-Sefadu (Kono); and, Kissy Shell station (five km east of the central area on Kissy Rd) for various locations including Koidu-Sefadu. But be prepared for changes: because the SLRTC buses are so popular there a fewer bush taxis on the long-distance routes, and there seems to be a move for all private transport to leave from the Kissy Shell station as this avoids the traffic jams. Between the city centre and Kissy Shell a seat in a shared taxi is US$0.50. You may need to walk to the western end of Kissy Rd to find one.

Getting Around
To/From the Airport Freetown's Lungi Airport is about 25 km from central Freetown, on the other side of the bay. There are several ways to reach the city:

Via the Kissy Ferry Getting to/from the airport this way involves a 40-minute ferry ride between the Tagrin (northern) and Kissy (southern) terminals, and a road journey at either end. Many foreigners take the airport bus which drives on to the ferry and drops you off at the Paramount Hotel in the centre of town – handy if you have a lot of baggage: it costs US$20 but doesn't meet every flight. Taxi drivers at the airport demand that much just to Tagrin, only a 15-minute ride away, or about US$50 all the way to Freetown. The private taxi rates to the ferry should be around US$5 to Tagrin ferry terminal and US$35 all the way to Freetown, but you'll have a hard time getting this. To avoid arguments with taxi drivers, do as the locals do: walk 200 metres out of the airport to the main

road and flag down any shared taxi that passes (going towards the left, as you come out of the airport gates). The shared taxi rate is US$0.30. Leaving the airport, your bargaining power is weak: shared taxi drivers may make a small 'tourist baggage' charge (up to US$0.50) but they'll still be much cheaper than the private taxis.

The ferry from Tagrin across to Kissy costs about US$0.50 2nd class, and US$1.50 1st class. The ticketer may try to charge you US$10, but this is for the Express Ferry straight to town (see below). The voyage is very pleasant: get a beer from the bar, lean on the rail, and enjoy the views of Freetown with the mountains behind. Apart from an occasional ferry breakdown, the only problem going this way is timing – the ferry runs once every two to three hours, so you may have a long wait.

From the Kissy ferry terminal private taxis go to Freetown (for about US$5), but most people walk up the hill to the main highway and get a shared taxi from there into the centre for about US$1.

Going from Freetown to the airport via the Kissy ferry, the choices are the same. Call the Paramount Hotel (☎ 224531) to learn the departure hour of the bus – usually three hours before every flight, but it depends on the ferry. Or go by shared taxi to the ferry, and from the other side to the airport. By private taxi, rates are cheaper when you go in this direction.

The most important thing to check are the ferry times, to give yourself plenty of time to reach the airport. All the airline offices have a ferry schedule, but make sure it's up-to-date.

Via the Express Ferry The new Express Ferry is a small fast launch running between the Tagrin terminal and Government Wharf in the city centre. It costs US$10 oneway. The ferry normally ties in with intercontinental flights, but timetables are constantly changing. Once you've got from the airport to Tagrin ferry terminal, if you want to get this ferry it's simply a case of asking when the next departure is. Going from Freetown to Lungi, most airline offices have the schedule.

Via the Hotel Ferry If you're staying at one

of the large beach hotels (10 km west of the centre), you can take the ferry that runs direct between the hotels and Tagrin terminal. Going from the hotels to the airport, ask at you hotel reception or a travel agency in town for details. Going from the airport, ask at Tagrin when the next Hotel Ferry departs. The cost is US$20 oneway.

Helicopter There's a helicopter service between Lungi Airport and the helipad near the large beach hotels. They meet most arrivals from Europe and the cost is US$60 per person, although the service was temporarily suspended in early 1994 following four crashes. Enquire at your hotel or a travel agent in town.

Taxi Taxis around Freetown do not have meters, so for a private hire the price must be negotiated. The official fare, posted in the hotel lobbies, from the centre to the Lumley Beach area is about US$20, but most drivers will accept less if you bargain. For a longer hire, US$10 an hour for city driving would be reasonable, although drivers are reluctant to do this.

Shared taxis run everywhere. To catch one, stand on a street in the direction you want to go and shout your destination. A ride in a shared taxi costs about US$0.30 for a short trip around town. If it's clearly a shared taxi and someone else is inside, then don't discuss the price; just hop in and ask the passengers what the fare is. If you get an empty taxi without discussing the price, you have chartered a private taxi, like it or not.

Car The most reliable car rental agencies are Yazbeck and IPC, although neither are cheap. A car with driver costs US$150 per day for city use, and US$250 if you want to go around the Freetown Peninsula. For upcountry use, 4WDs cost US$350 per day or US$550 for three days.

AROUND FREETOWN
The Beaches
Freetown lies at the northern end of a 40-km-long mountainous peninsula with some of the best beaches in West Africa stretching

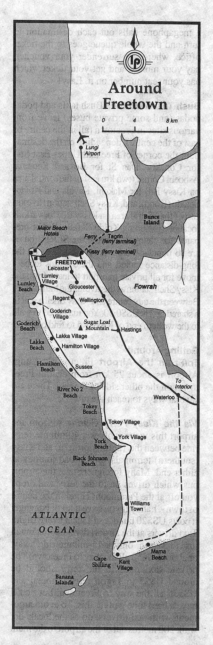

Around Freetown

0   4   8 km

along its western side. **Lumley Beach** is at the northern end, nearest to Freetown, and easily reached by hailing any shared taxi on Siaka Stevens St headed west. Ask for Aberdeen Junction (there's a petrol station at the junction), about five km from the centre, from where shared taxis go to the beach area. Each ride costs about US$0.60.

If you're headed for the other beaches by shared taxi, don't get off at Aberdeen Junction; stay in the taxi to Lumley village, about four km further south, from where bush taxis and poda-podas run down the coast road. Some tracks off the coast road to the beaches are not clear, so you may have to ask for directions.

Going south from Lumley village, four km after passing the junction for Goderich village you reach the turn-off for **Lakka Beach**. Nearby is the YMCA's *Lakka Beach Camping Centre* (ask at the YMCA – listed in Places to Stay – for details). More up-market is the *Cotton Club* where B&B costs US$30 per person. Continuing southwards for another two km you come to Lakka village, and then **Hamilton Beach**.

The choicest beach of all – the one pictured in all the tourist brochures – is **River No 2 Beach**, roughly halfway down the Peninsula. It's quite 'touristy' here, so prices for anything start high. Basic beach huts (where you can sleep) can be hired for US$3 per day. Local people will offer to cook meals for you, or supply some home-brewed firewater if that's your scene. Two characters called Jack and Francis have been recom-

mended: for an all-in fee they can sort you out a hut, food, and wood for the fire to keep the mozzies off. One traveller has written:

'River No 2 is a great place to relax. Sit around the fire at night, and listen to Jack's tales of encounters with devils and spirits, or his views on the French hotel nearby, and the next thing you know your visa's run out...'

You can also get a boat to the **Banana Islands** (see below). Hiring a boat here or from River No 2 is much cheaper than hiring one from Freetown (which costs about US$100 per person), because the travel agencies there use expensive new boats. A local guy called Nicholas arranges day trips costing about US$10 to US$20 each for a group of around seven people, which includes a meal on the island. For a shorter trip, go up River No 2 to the waterfalls and see the crocodiles.

Just south of the mouth of River No 2 is **Tokey Beach**, which is equally nice, and the *Africana Tokey village*, a large expensive Caribbean-inspired resort, with 50 bungalows, a restaurant, pool, and mostly French clients. (A room here costs over US$100 a night, although you can get weekend deals for US$50 per person, half board.)

A few km further south is York village. Even though poda-podas occasionally make it this far south, few tourists do. York Beach and **Black Johnson Beach** just across the bay (but five km by road) are good skin-diving sites. Some 20 km further at the

---

Bunce Island

Bunce (BUN-see) Island is at the mouth of the Sierra Leone River, about 18 km inland from Freetown. The major attraction of this 500-metre-long island is the ruined fortress. First built by the British as a trading base, it was levelled to the ground in 1702 by French men o' war. The ruins you'll see today are of a second fort built shortly thereafter. Within the walls were some warehouses, lodges and, most strikingly, a slave booth.

After the British and French occupations, the fort was held successively by the Dutch, the Portuguese and, again, the British. From 1750 to 1800, this island became notorious as one of the major collection points on the West African coast for slaves destined for Europe and the Americas. (The Gullah people of South Carolina are thought to have come from here.) Concerted efforts are now being made to preserve these long-forgotten ruins.

Hiring a boat to yourself for Bunce is prohibitively expensive, so a tour is the only feasible way to get there for most people. Freetown's major travel agencies have half-day and full-day tours of Bunce. ■

southernmost point of the Peninsula is Kent village, where you can also hire a boat and go over to the Banana Islands.

Diving and snorkelling off the Banana Islands is superb – probably the best along the West African coast. The fishing is said to be good too. In Dublin village, on the northern tip of the main island, there's a Portuguese church and the remains of a slave centre. Tours to the Banana Islands and River No 2 Beach are available from Freetown's major travel agencies.

Regent & Gloucester

These two villages are in the hills overlooking the city, where the cool air is more pleasant for walking around. If you've got wheels, getting here is easy. Otherwise it's a short ride (US$0.50) by bus or poda-poda, via the village of Leicester. Both villages have several interesting old Krio-style houses, some possibly dating from the early-19th century. From Regent you can walk though the Krio villages to **Charlotte Falls** or, if you're feeling fit, climb **Sugar Loaf Mountain**, one of the highest points on the Peninsula. This is a logging area and paths are often indistinct, but you can find guides in Regent. From the top (reached in one to two hours) you get a sweeping panorama of the bay.

The South & East

The southern and eastern parts of Sierra Leone are generally humid and low-lying. This region is also forested, especially in the far east along the border with Liberia. It also contains the country's major diamond-mining areas, notably Tongo Fields between the towns of Kenema and Kono, which along with Koindu are also diamond trading and smuggling centres.

Diamond Mining in Sierra Leone

Sierra Leone has some of the largest and richest diamond deposits in Africa, by far the most valuable of the country's natural resources. The main diamond areas are in the east of the country around Koidu-Sefadu, more commonly called Kono – the country's 'diamond capital'. The headquarters of the National Diamond Mining Company is at Yengema, 15 km to the west of Kono. A particularly rich deposit is Tongo Fields, about 50 km south of Kono.

During colonial times the diamond fields were controlled by the Government Diamond Office. Large scale commercial mining started in the 1930s when an organisation called the Sierra Leone Selection Trust was granted a sole concession to the country's reserves. In many cases, mining the diamonds was a simple task: the deposits were mixed with light alluvial soil only a few metres underground. In some areas where streams cut through the land, the diamonds could literally be picked up from the surface.

Production costs were low, world prices were favourable, and diamonds (along with other minerals such as iron and chromite) were exported from Sierra Leone to many parts of the world, making a vital contribution to the colony's economy.

For the diamond companies, however, this easy access also created a problem. The local people realised how simple it was to collect diamonds and how valuable they were. The diamonds could not be sold legally inside Sierra Leone, so they were smuggled across the border to the neighbouring countries of Liberia and Guinea, or taken further afield by sea.

Many Sierra Leoneans were attracted to the Kono region in search of easy pickings and instant wealth. By the early 1950s the steady flow of new settlers became a 'rush', and by the mid-1950s the export value of these illegally 'mined' diamonds almost equalled the value of the legal trade.

To overcome this problem, in the late 1950s several diamond fields were leased to private concerns and individuals. These people still had to sell their diamonds to the Government Diamond Office, but this scheme was somewhat effective in controlling illegal mining and smuggling, and the colony continued to benefit from the valuable resource.

At independence in 1961, Sierra Leone ranked fifth in a 'wealth league table' of West African nations. This wealth was based largely on the diamond trade, but through the 1960s and 1970s, as Sierra Leone lurched from one political disaster to the next, export revenue from diamonds,

Since 1990, as the war in neighbouring Liberia spilled across the border, many parts of this region have been dangerous and out of bounds to visitors. More recently, the region has been kept closed by the civil war between rebels and the forces of the government which came to power in the '92 coup. In 1994 both wars seemed to be ending, and the towns of Bo and Kenema could be easily reached, but in 1995 things got worse again, so you should make enquiries locally before heading this way.

BO

Bo is some 250 km south-east of Freetown, on the road to Kenema. This is a lively town with a bank, cinema and several places to eat, drink and sleep; a good choice if you're looking for just one upcountry town to visit. Bo is also a good place to buy gara (see Things to Buy in the Freetown section). Ask May-Rose Coker at Coker's Bar to show you her work or to help you find Omar and Mohammed, the two Fulani brothers who make fine cloth. Near the Black & White Hotel there's a man who does good leather work, including small bags with clever hiding places that discourage pickpockets. Called 'Peace Corps bags' by the locals, they are popular and practical.

Places to Stay

In the centre, the *Black & White Hotel & Restaurant* is an old favourite run by the friendly Mr Joe. The only room is a large airy double, almost like an apartment with its own lounge and bathroom, which costs US$17 per night. (African meals start at US$2, or you can have a hamburger for US$3.) Next door is the new *Hotel Sir Milton* (☎ (032) 496), which offers a 'grandfatherly service', with clean self-contained singles/

SIERRA LEONE

and the whole economy which was based upon it, went into terminal decline. In 1972 the world's third-largest diamond (969.8 carats) was discovered in the Kono fields, but this had little effect on the overall situation.

By the mid-1980s, with the country descending into anarchy and foreign exchange reserves completely exhausted, well-organised groups of smugglers – allegedly masterminded by powerful business people with close government connections – were continuing to rob Sierra Leone of up to 90% of its diamond revenue. Every day about US$500,000 worth of diamonds were scraped from the earth and immediately hidden; many of the illegal operators were allegedly police officers and security guards.

After the coup of 1992 when Captain Valentine Strasser came to power, some efforts were made to revitalise legal diamond-mining activities and reduce the smuggling. This had some reasonable success, along with many other economic reforms introduced at the same time. It was hoped that international investors, many of whom had pulled out of Sierra Leone during the 1980s, could be persuaded back to the country's diamond industry. In 1994 there were reports that the giant South African De Beers corporation was to explore for diamonds on the sea-bed off the coast of Sierra Leone. However, the various rebel groups (or their leaders) stand to gain more from continued anarchy in the diamond fields. In early 1995 several expatriate mining engineers were kidnapped by Revolutionary United Front rebels opposed to the Strasser government. The return of more international companies is likely to be stalled until the situation in Sierra Leone is brought under control.

It is also worth noting that although a revitalised diamond mining and export industry would improve Sierra Leone's economic situation in the future, it can never be an instant solution to the country's many deep-set problems. But the income generated by the diamond trade would allow the country to invest in other schemes, such as communications, health and small-scale farming, which would benefit the nation as a whole.

Warning It is illegal to buy, sell, mine (and probably touch) diamonds without a government licence. Police and customs officials would come down very heavily on any tourist caught smuggling and dealing in diamonds. ■

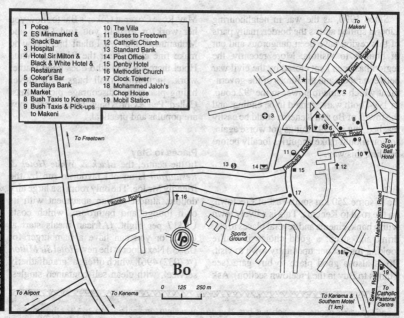

1 Police
2 ES Minimarket & Snack Bar
3 Hospital
4 Hotel Sir Milton & Black & White Hotel & Restaurant
5 Coker's Bar
6 Barclays Bank
7 Market
8 Bush Taxis to Kenema
9 Bush Taxis & Pick-ups to Makeni
10 The Villa
11 Buses to Freetown
12 Catholic Church
13 Standard Bank
14 Post Office
15 Denby Hotel
16 Methodist Church
17 Clock Tower
18 Mohammed Jaloh's Chop House
19 Mobil Station

To Makeni
Kissy Town Road
To Freetown
Fenton Road
To Sugar Ball Hotel
Dambara Road
Tikonko Road
To Airport
To Kenema
0   125   250 m
To Freetown
Bo
Sports Ground
Mahelboima Road
Sewa Road
To Kenema & Southern Motel (1 km)
To Catholic Pastoral Centre

SIERRA LEONE

doubles at US$25/37 for B&B, which is a bit pricey for what you get. The restaurant has a 'wide range of sea and land food' with a three-course *menu du jour* for US$7. The hotel also has an annexe with rooms for US$12.

A cheap and pleasant place is the *Catholic Pastoral Centre* on the south-eastern edge of town, about two km from the centre. Church workers have priority here, but travellers can stay if there's space. Simple rooms with two beds are US$3 per night, better quality ones are US$5. Breakfast is US$2 and meals are US$3. To get here from the centre, take the road towards Kenema and fork left at the Mobil station.

Other cheap options include the *Sugar Ball Hotel* where it costs US$5 for rooms with one bed, and US$7 for two beds. This place is on the east edge of town, about two km from the centre, with a nice village feel. To get there follow Fenton Rd from the roundabout, keeping right at the only major fork. Also out of the centre, on the road towards Kenema, is

the *Southern Motel*, with fairly clean rooms for US$5/8 (US$14 self-contained), and a bar which gets noisy in the evening.

Places to Eat & Drink

A long-time favourite is *Coker's Bar*, in the centre of town, where Pa Coker always has cold beer and his wife, May-Rose, makes good food. A cheap chop house is *Mohammed Jaloh's*, on the road between the clock tower and the Mobil station. Slightly more up-market is *The Villa*, an open-air restaurant and bar on the road between the centre and the Mobil station, where chicken and chips costs US$5. Smartest of all is the *ES Minimarket & Snack Bar* (or Mrs Michael's) serving good Lebanese and European food in the US$4 to US$8 range.

Getting There & Away

The daily SLRTC bus between Bo and Freetown costs US$5. From Bo it leaves the bus stand on Dambara Rd around 8 am. You need to be there at 6.30 am to buy a ticket, although you can supposedly buy them in advance from Mrs Nicholas who has a general store near the clock tower. Bush taxis to Kenema (US$2) go regularly from the bus park on the north side of Fenton Rd; the journey takes one hour along a good tar road. Crowded pick-ups to Makeni (US$3) go from the bus park on the south side of Fenton Rd; the rough cross-country journey takes all day. (If you're driving or hitching, note that the main road between Freetown and Kenema now bypasses Bo, about two km to the south of the town.)

KENEMA

Kenema, some 300 km south-east of Freetown, at the end of the tar road, is a large busy town and Sierra Leone's timber capital. If you're travelling overland to Liberia or eastern Guinea, this is a major junction where you'll have to change vehicles. Don't rush on, though: it's a pleasant place to spend a day or two.

In town, the two large open **markets** to the east of the main drag are worth strolling around. There's also a smaller covered market nearer the centre. If you're looking for something more than dried fish or saucepans, you'll also

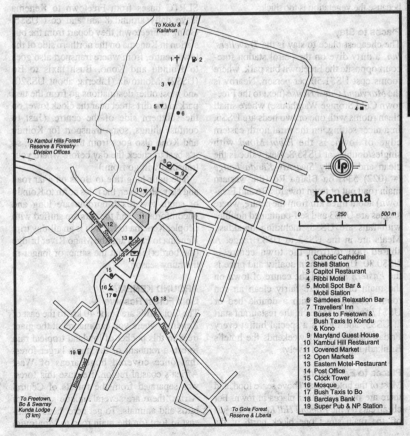

Kenema

0   250   500 m

1 Catholic Cathedral
2 Shell Station
3 Capitol Restaurant
4 Ribbi Motel
5 Mobil Spot Bar &
   Mobil Station
6 Samdees Relaxation Bar
7 Travellers' Inn
8 Buses to Freetown &
   Bush Taxis to Koindu
   & Kono
9 Maryland Guest House
10 Kambui Hill Restaurant
11 Covered Market
12 Open Markets
13 Eastern Motel-Restaurant
14 Post Office
15 Clock Tower
16 Mosque
17 Bush Taxis to Bo
18 Barclays Bank
19 Super Pub & NP Station

To Koidu &
Kailahun

To Kambui Hills Forest
Reserve & Forestry
Division Offices

Maxwell Street

Hangha Road

Dama Road

Blama Road

To Freetown,
Bo & Swarray
Kunda Lodge
(3 km)

To Gola Forest
Reserve & Liberia

SIERRA LEONE

notice that just about every second shop on the main street is a diamond dealer, although you need a licence to buy. While you're strolling around town, check out the murals on the large blue Secretariat Building on the main street, showing Tom Nyuma (a war hero, now a leading member of the government) in an almost Biblical setting, complete with serpent and tiger.

On the edge of Kenema is the **Kambui Hills Forest Reserve**, a surprisingly large and lush area of woodland so close to the town. This is a good place for a day's walk, following wood cutters' paths between the tall trees. You may see monkeys, but you won't get any views because the vegetation is too thick.

Places to Stay

The cheapest place to stay is the *Travellers' Inn*, a dirty dive on the petrol station forecourt opposite the Freetown bus park, where rooms cost US$1.50 per person. Nearby is the *Maryland Guest House* (next to the Freetown Cold Storage Warehouse) where small clean rooms with one or two beds are US$6. In a nicer setting, on the rural north-eastern edge of town, is the *Ribbi Motel* with singles/doubles at US$5/8. Best value is the clean and friendly *Swarray Kunda Lodge* (☎ (022) 534) on Blama Rd (the western main road out of town towards Bo and Freetown) about three km from the centre, where singles are US$3 and self-contained doubles with fans are US$8, including breakfast. Meals are in the US$3 to US$5 range. A shared taxi to/from the town centre is US$0.30. Up a notch in quality and price is the *Eastern Motel* in the centre of town on the main drag, where fairly clean air-con rooms cost US$11 with a double bed or US$17 for two. Meals in the restaurant start at US$3, and there's a special buffet every Friday lunchtime. At weekends the hotel's Braikadi nightclub is lively.

Places to Eat & Drink

Most of the hotels listed above serve food, and there are plenty of other places in town. For cheap eats try the *Kambui Hill Restaurant* just off the main street one block north of the covered market, the *Maryland Spot*, a small wooden hut (which promises 24-hour service) next to the Eastern Motel, or any of the shacks around the bus and taxi parks. Slightly more up-market is the *Capitol Restaurant* (also a cinema) where you can get cold beers and good-value African and Lebanese meals.

For drinking, try the unnamed red shed opposite the Eastern Hotel, the *Mobil Spot Bar* at the Mobil petrol station near the Capitol, *Samdees Relaxation Bar* opposite the Mobil, or *Super Pub* at the NP petrol station on the southern side of the town centre.

Getting There & Away

SLRTC buses from Freetown to Kenema leave daily around 8 am and cost US$6. Going to Freetown, they depart from the bus station in Kenema on the northern side of the town centre, from where transport also goes to Koindu and Kono. Bush taxis to Bo (US$2), Monrovia (Liberia; about US$20) and most other destinations go from the taxi park in the dirt street near the clock tower on the southern side of the centre. (Just to confuse things, some transport for Koindu and Kono also goes from this taxi park, so it's best to check the day before where your transport will go from.)

The hour-long ride to Bo is on a tar road and easy. However, the rides north to Koindu or south towards Monrovia are long and uncomfortable, and the cars are stuffed with people. Kenema to Koindu is an all-day trip. Kenema to Fairo and the Mano River bridge (the border) is about the same, or longer in the rainy season.

AROUND KENEMA
Gola Forest Reserve

The Gola Hills are some 40 km to the east of Kenema, where you can marvel at the giant trees in this pocket of lowland tropical rain forest, a remnant of the much larger forest that once covered huge areas of West Africa's coastal region. Because this forest was separated from the forests of Central Africa, there are several unique species of birds and animals. To get here, head south-east to Joru (on the main road to Monrovia) and then east 10 km to Lalehun, where there's a basic rest house, but no other facilities, and guides are available.

The Sierra Leone Conservation Society (see Freetown Information) has a good booklet containing details on Gola. In Kenema, you can get more information, and check the security situation outside the town, by asking at the Conservation Department in the Forestry Division offices on Maxwell St, west (up hill) from the market.

KOIDU-SEFADU (KONO)

The twin towns of Koidu and Sefadu are usually called Kono, the name of the surrounding area. Some 360 km east of Freetown, Kono is a boom town as it's a major diamond trading centre, and attracts people from all over West Africa, some of whom bring crafts from their native lands for sale. As a result, the **market** is very lively.

Other than the market, however, Kono has little to offer travellers. For a drink, try the colonial-style Sierra Leone Mining Company club, which has a restaurant, bar and videos. If you chat up a member, you may get invited in.

KOINDU

Koindu is in the far eastern corner of the country, at the end of a tongue of territory wedged between Guinea and Liberia, and on the route to both of these neighbouring countries. To get here from Kenema is an all-day journey along bad twisting roads. There's an acceptable little hotel on the eastern outskirts, and chop bars in town. The border with Liberia was frequently closed even before the events of 1990, so even if conditions in Liberia improve the border may not be opened. If that is the case, you can always take a canoe over the river to Nongoa in Guinea. (If you don't have a visa to Guinea, you can easily get one without problem in Nongoa, although you should check in Freetown if this is still the case, as entry requirements can easily change.)

TIWAI ISLAND WILDLIFE SANCTUARY

Tiwai is a fabulous little reserve about 50 km

directly south of Kenema, on a small island (about 13 sq km) in a wide section of the Moa River, which passes just east of Kenema. The forest environment is virtually pristine with one of the highest concentrations of **primates** anywhere on the continent. You can hike on tracks all over the island; with careful stalking, you may see chimpanzee, several types of monkey including the colobus and the most beautiful diana monkey (the symbol of the park), pygmy hippopotamus, crocodile, and more than 120 bird species, including hornbill, kingfisher and the rare white-breasted guinea fowl. Tiwai Island is also home to bats, bush-babies and hundreds of butterflies.

The bad news is it has been impossible to reach Tiwai since 1990 due to the fighting in this area. But there's some good news too. Although the headquarters and camp are destroyed, reports indicate that wildlife on the island is alive and well, and even increasing in number as hunters stay away because they're scared of the rebels.

When the civil war ends, it will hopefully be possible to visit Tiwai again. If you can get here, it could provide your most memorable experience in Africa. You can get up-to-date details from the Sierra Leone Conservation Society in Freetown, or maybe from the Conservation Department in Kenema.

The easiest way to get here is via Potoru, reached from Bo by bush taxi. (If you can't find anything to Potoru, take one going toward Pujehun, get off at the Potoru junction and hitch from there.) From Potoru, head for Kambama village (16 km) along the river's western bank; you may have to walk this bit. At Kambama, hire a canoe to take you over to the island.

If you've got wheels you can go from Kenema. Take the major road east to Joru (30 km), then south towards Fairo (the road to Liberia) for about 50 km to the junction for Baoma village, then go west to Baoma. Mapuma village is two km beyond, on the river's eastern bank, where you can hire a canoe for the island.

The North

The north of Sierra Leone is the homeland of the Temne people, most of whom are Muslim. The landscape here is noticeably higher and drier than the southern and eastern parts of the country. Where they haven't been cultivated, the undulating hills are covered mainly in light bush or savannah woodland, although ribbons of dense forest do run along the major rivers. The hills become mountains in several places, with many peaks rising above 1500 metres. At the heart of the Lola Mountains, in the north-east, is Mt Bintumani (1945 metres) which proudly claims to be the highest point in West Africa, as long as you put Mt Cameroun and several peaks along the Cameroun-Nigeria border, some 2500 km to the east, in Central Africa!

BUMBUNA FALLS

These large waterfalls are about 50 km north-east of Makeni, on the upper reaches of the Rokel River (also known as the Seli) which eventually flows into the Sierra Leone River near Freetown. The falls are a popular weekend spot for expats and one of the few upcountry places that travel agencies in Freetown take tourists to see. But it's also easy to reach by public transport, via Magburaka from where bush taxis run along the brand new 'Bumbuna Highway' that was built to service the HEP station near the falls. In Bumbuna town there are a few bars and eating houses, and if you ask around you may find somewhere to stay. The falls are a short distance outside the town. Swimming is possible, but the turbulent water is not very clean. (Do not confuse Bumbuna Falls with Bumban Falls, near the village of the same name, just to the east of the main road between Makeni and Kabala. This is another spectacular waterfall, but harder to reach without your own vehicle.)

KABALA

Kabala is the largest town in northern Sierra Leone, at the end of the tar road, about 300 km north of Freetown, and the last place of any size you'll pass through on the route to Faranah (Guinea). But even if you're staying in Sierra Leone, Kabala is well worth a visit. It's smaller than Bo and Kenema, and while the big towns buzz with activity, Kabala is quiet and sleepy. It's also a friendly place: spend a few days here and you'll begin to feel like a local.

Places to Stay

Kabala's only hotel is the *Lans Kort*, a nightclub with a few grubby rooms for US$3 per night, bucket showers and occasional electricity. It's on the Freetown road, about half a km from the centre. Much better value and more central is the *Gbawuria Guest House* (pronounced BOW-ree-ah), also known as the Chief's House, next to the chief's office on the west side of town. Very clean rooms with one or two beds cost US$3 a night, and the bathroom is also spotless. Food is not

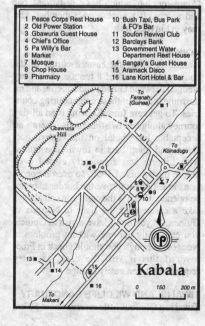

1 Peace Corps Rest House	10 Bush Taxi, Bus Park
2 Old Power Station	& FO's Bar
3 Gbawuria Guest House	11 Soufon Revival Club
4 Chief's Office	12 Barclays Bank
5 Pa Willy's Bar	13 Government Water
6 Market	Department Rest House
7 Mosque	14 Sangay's Guest House
8 Chop House	15 Aramack Disco
9 Pharmacy	16 Lans Kort Hotel & Bar

To Faranah (Guinea)

Gbawuria Hill

To Koinadugu

Kabala

To Makeni

0   150   300 m

available. The lounge seems to be a meeting place for the town's elder dignitaries so you should show respect where necessary. For slightly more salubrious surroundings you can stay in the vaguely colonial *Government Water Department Rest House* on the south-west side of town. It costs US$7 per person to stay here. Officially you're supposed to book in advance at the Water Department offices (Leone House, Siaka Stevens St, Freetown) but if you turn up without a booking the caretaker may be able to help. Nearby is another small guesthouse owned by local businessman Mr Sangay. For details and directions ask at his motor spares shop in the town centre. There's also a *Peace Corps Rest House* on the north side of town, where travellers might be allowed to stay.

Places to Eat & Drink

For coffee, bread, rice and sauce there's a good *chop house* on the main street just north of the bus park. *FO's Bar* at the bus park is a basic place where the beer is always cold. You can get grilled meat and bread from the stalls outside and eat in the bar. More pleasant, with benches on the terrace, is *Pa Willy's Bar*, on the north side of town. Kabala's weekend nightlife revolves around the *Soufon Revival Club*, in the centre on the road towards Freetown, and the *Aramack Disco*, 400 metres along the same road.

Getting There & Away

The bus from Freetown goes to Kabala every Monday, Wednesday and Friday, and returns the next day. The fare is US$6 each way. On the days when there's no bus, a bush taxi goes to Freetown for US$8.

Bush taxis to/from Makeni go regularly throughout the day for US$3, and take about two hours on the good tar road.

If you're heading north to Faranah in Guinea, the road is bad and there are no bush taxis, so you'll have to ask around the bus park and market for a truck. There's one or two per week, usually tying in with Faranah's weekly market (Monday). Alternatively, you can hire a motorbike (and rider) to take you to the border or all the way to Faranah for about US$20.

KAMBIA

Kambia is on the highway to Conakry (Guinea), 13 km from the Guinean border. If you're caught here, you won't find a hotel but travellers could enquire at the *Peace*

SIERRA LEONE

Hiking Around Kabala

If you want to be active in Kabala, head for the surrounding hills. They're high enough to catch the breeze, with cool streams and waterfalls, and perfect for some gentle hiking, with a choice of day-walk destinations. These include the summit of **Gbawuria Hill**, overlooking the town on the eastern side. A path goes up from the old power station. From the broad rocky summit you can head towards the gap between the two prominent pointed peaks directly to the north. Another path approaches Gbawuria summit from the west, branching off the dirt track that leads southwards from the Chief's House, and then south-west out of town. The easternmost of the two pointed peaks can also be approached by following the ridge which starts on the west side of the road towards the Guinea border, about two km beyond the town. The route goes through shady forest for much of the way, but can be difficult to find when the grass is high. On the summit is the remains of an old colonial survey post. There's a maze of paths through the bush on all of these hills: if you haven't got a compass or a good sense of direction, consider taking a local as guide.

For a full scale expedition you might want to strike out for **Mt Bintumani**. From Kabala you can hitch on occasional trucks to Koinadugu and maybe all the way to Firawa. Pay your respects to the chief here and he will help you find a local hunter to be your guide. There's no hotel, but you can eat and lodge with local people, paying what you would in a small hotel. From Firawa it's at least a three-day trek to and from the summit, and you need to be completely self-contained for the entire trip. We heard from some travellers who set out for the mountain from Kabala, but they met such pleasant people and had such a good time in the villages and forest along the way, they decided to give the mountain itself a miss! ∎

Corps Rest House facing the Catholic mission near the market.

MAKENI

Some 190 km from Freetown, Makeni is the capital of the northern province. It's a large and busy town, with a reputation as one of the hottest places in the country during the dry season. The people here are mainly Temnes, and the **mosque** is one of the most beautiful in the country.

Makeni is renowned for two crafts: *shukublais*, distinctive Temne baskets, and *gara* material (see Freetown Things to Buy) which is often cheaper than in Freetown. The vibrant **market** is also a good place to find Bundu masks, but you should also be on the lookout for pickpockets here. And don't forget the carver near the mosque; famous for being famous, he represented Sierra Leone several years ago at the World's Fair in New York!

Places to Stay

Makeni's two hotels are both on the south-western outskirts, where the new Freetown to Kono highway bypasses the town. The

Gbetgbo Hotel (pronounced BET-boh) is by the turn-off to the town centre as you come in from Freetown. Run by the friendly Mr Jamal, prices range from US$3 for small dirty singles to US$8 for large passable doubles with nets and shared bath. The *Thinka Motel* (pronounced TIN-kah) is new and in better condition; rooms with one or two beds cost US$3, or US$4 for self-contained. Both these places have popular bars and can be noisy in the evening.

Quieter and more central is the *Caritas Guesthouse* on Soldier St, about 100 metres north of the central Independence Place. Rooms are run-down but clean and cost US$3 for one or two people. Meals must be ordered in advance; so must electricity, and you have to pay for the fuel for the generator. Otherwise, buy candles. The *Catholic Pastoral Centre* on Teko Rd only takes aid workers, missionaries, or volunteers.

Places to Eat

For cheap eats, there are several chop houses in the bus park: *Tamaraneh Brothers* is one of the nicest, and they also serve coffee and sandwiches. On Mapanda Rd (towards Free-

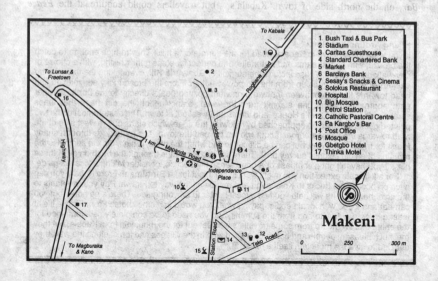

1. Bush Taxi & Bus Park
2. Stadium
3. Caritas Guesthouse
4. Standard Chartered Bank
5. Market
6. Barclays Bank
7. Sesay's Snacks & Cinema
8. Solokus Restaurant
9. Hospital
10. Big Mosque
11. Petrol Station
12. Catholic Pastoral Centre
13. Pa Kargbo's Bar
14. Post Office
15. Mosque
16. Gbetgbo Hotel
17. Thinka Motel

To Kabala

To Lunsar & Freetown

Highway

Rogbana Road

Soldier Street

1 km

Mapanda Road

Independence Place

Station Road

To Magburaka & Kano

Teko Road

Makeni

0   250   300 m

Shukublai Baskets

In the markets of Makeni and other towns in the area you may see *shukublais* for sale. These are large, colourful, almost spherical baskets, traditionally made by Temne women from a long 'rope' of coiled grass which is then wrapped in strips of dyed raffia palm. Small baskets, plates, lids and other decorative items are made in the same way. Shukublais are attractive, unbreakable, light and useful, and many travellers buy them as souvenirs.

It is also possible to buy shukublais at the Mamunta-Mayoso Wildlife Sanctuary. This is a protected area of wetland (see below) where the grass is particularly suitable for basket making. A local women's group makes and sells high-quality baskets and other handmade items. The money earned by the women is one way in which the local communities can benefit from the sanctuary, and is a way of ensuring its continued protection. ∎

town from Independence Place) is the *Solokus Restaurant*, a chop-stop for buses on the Freetown to Kabala/Kono routes. Nearby, next to the cinema, *Sesay's Snacks* sells mainly cakes and other nibbles. There's also a simple restaurant (with illusions of grandeur) in the cinema itself. A Makeni institution is *Pa Kargbo's Bar*, the local volunteers' hang-out, on Teko Rd next to the Catholic Pastoral Centre, where you can get cold beers and delicious meat sticks skilfully marinated and grilled by a guy called Usman. Look for the polished wooden bench inscribed 'Usman's Tastes Awesome' – a gift from some appreciative Peace Corps.

Getting There & Away

The SLRTC buses run between Freetown and Kabala, via Makeni, three times per week in each direction. Bush taxis to/from Kabala go regularly throughout the day for US$3, and take about two hours on the good tar road. You can also get transport to Kamakwie, if you're heading for the Outamba-Kilimi National Park (see below), or on to Kindia in Guinea.

MAMUNTA-MAYOSO WILDLIFE SANCTUARY

This small reserve (only 20 sq km) protects a wetland area about 30 km to the south of Makeni, and provides a vital refuge for many species of bird and small mammal, and the rare short-nosed crocodile. There is a visitors' centre here, but no other facilities. You can camp for free, but donations ensure the reserve continues to exist. You reach the reserve via Magburaka and the main road towards Mile 91. After seven km look for the MMWS signpost. More details, and a leaflet, are available from the Conservation Society (see the Freetown Information section).

MT BINTUMANI

Mt Bintumani (also spelt Bintimani, and sometimes called Loma Mansa) lies at the centre of the Loma Mountains, some 60 km to the south-east of Kabala. At about 1945 metres, this is one of the highest points in West Africa, and just after the rains when the skies are clear the views from the summit are excellent. The area around the mountains is the homeland of the Koranko people, and some sections have been listed as a reserve, protecting the **highland rainforest** that covers the lower slopes. The forest on the west side of the range is more impressive and in better condition. There are several species of monkey, and you're quite likely to see chimpanzees. Above 1500 metres the forest gives way to grassland where you can spot baboon, wart hog, duiker, and porcupine. There are also buffalo up here – not usually a problem unless you surprise them. In the rivers you may see **pygmy hippo** and **dwarf crocodile**, both very rare. Keen bird-watchers get very excited about the endangered **rufus fishing owl** which can be seen in this area.

You can approach the mountain from Kabala via Koinadugu and Firawa (see the boxed story – Hiking Around Kabala), but it's more usual to approach from the village of Yifin, to the east of the dirt road that runs between Kabala and Bumbuna (from where it's at least a four-day walk to and from the summit) or from Kurubonla, north of Kono (three days minimum).

Wherever you start from, take a guide (the forest paths are maze-like or completely overgrown) and possibly porters, as you need to be self-contained with camping gear and food for at least five days. Buy all your food in Makeni, Kabala or Kono.

Pay your respects to the chief in either Firawa, Yifin or Kurubonla (a gift of kola nuts or about US$1 is sufficient), and he will help you find a guide and porters, for which you pay about US$1 per day, and arrange accommodation with local people, for which you should also pay around US$1. Pay a small tip (US$0.50) or give some nuts to the chief of each village where you stay.

On the summit is a cairn and a bottle full of messages. The original bottle, which

---

Koranko Conservation

The Koranko people inhabit the area around the Loma Mountains. Compared to many other ethnic groups in Sierra Leone, they have remained culturally distinct, partly due to their remote location, and partly due to their (not unrelated) proud and independent character.

The Koranko (also spelt Kuranko) entered the Loma Mountain area from the north (present-day Guinea or Mali) some time in the late 1500s. Their language is still closely related to the Malinké spoken in Guinea and Mali (and in many other West African countries) today. For three centuries after their migration, the Koranko were engaged in several clashes with neighbouring peoples. The most destructive battle was in the 1880s when an army from Guinea, led by the legendary war hero Samory Touré, invaded the Loma area. The Koranko were scattered and took refuge in the higher parts of the mountain range, where many of them settled permanently.

The Koranko traditionally farm two types of rice (upland rice and swamp rice) and cassava for their own needs (although surplus crops do occur which are sold or bartered), plus cash crops such as groundnuts, kola nuts and local tobacco. Hunting is also an important activity; mainly of duikers (small antelopes) that inhabit the forest.

The western side of the Loma Mountains Forest Reserve falls within the Koranko chiefdom of Nieni, ruled by the paramount chief, who lives in Yifin. A group of research scientists from Britain recently went to the Loma Mountain region to study the wildlife in the reserve. They also wanted to learn about the Koranko people – to ensure that the conservation aims of the reserve were 'in sympathy with local needs'.

The researchers found that the Koranko were aware of the ecological processes occurring around them, and that they used these processes in several positive and sustainable ways. For example, a traditional system of clearing, burning, planting and harvesting, followed by a period of fallow, is used. But when an area is cleared, not all the trees are felled; some are left to promote quick regeneration during the fallow period. Another example: a type of vegetable with nitrogen-fixing properties is planted along with the rice. This encourages trees to grow, rather than grass, after the rice has been harvested.

However, even though the Koranko people realise the importance of forest conservation, the researchers also found that these people resented the restrictions imposed on them by the reserve. They saw their traditional rights being removed without consultation and (more importantly) regarded the forest guards as representatives of central government, always something to be treated with suspicion. The guards are also reported to be antagonistic and harsh, confiscating crops or imposing fines for breaches (either real or imaginary) of regulations which are often ambiguous anyway.

The researchers concluded: 'The relationship between the indigenous people...and their environment is complex and reciprocal. Any future management plan [for the reserve] must include co-operation and needs of local people, and utilise the great fund of ecological knowledge that they possess...but access to reserve resources is vital if the Koranko are to be able to maintain their traditional way of life'.

The researchers were from the University of East Anglia. Thanks to Phil Atkinson of UEA for providing the material for this section, and for giving us permission to quote from it. ∎

had been on the mountain since the turn of the century, was removed by the president in the 1960s when he reached the top by helicopter. But the messages from the last 30 years still make amazing reading.

Routes

From Yifin The route towards the reserve goes via the villages of Kondembaia and Sinikoro (four hours from Yifin). From there the path goes steeply up hill to reach 'Base Camp', a place for camping between the forest and the grassland, about five to seven hours from Sinikoro. From there to the summit is another four to five hours, but with an early start you can get back to the base camp in a day. It's then another one or two days back to Yifin.

From Kurubonla The route goes through the village of Sokurela (four to five hours from Kurubonla). From there the path goes steeply up to 'Camp Two', where you can pitch a tent, about five to seven hours from Sokurela. From there to the summit is only two hours, which means you can get back to Sokurela or even Kurubonla the same day.

OUTAMBA-KILIMI NATIONAL PARK

The Outamba-Kilimi National Park (sometimes called Kamakwie National Park after the nearby village, or more usually OKNP) is in the remote north-western part of Sierra Leone, near the border with Guinea. OKNP is a beautiful and peaceful place, where you can experience some real West African wilderness, and it's worth visiting if you have time. The park is easy to reach by 4WD car, and you can also get here by public transport during the dry season. There are no roads inside the park, so visitors are encouraged to explore on foot or by canoe (which can be hired). This makes OKNP an ideal park for independent travellers without a vehicle.

The park has two sections. The northern Outamba section consists of rolling hills, grasslands, flood plains and rainforests, dissected by several rivers, including the Little Scarcies. The park headquarters, visitors' centre and camp is in this section, on the banks of the river. Several km upstream is a waterfall and several pools with clear, bilharzia-free water. The Kilimi section to the south-west is much flatter, less ecologically intact and not as interesting.

The park entrance fee is US$8 (cheaper for volunteers and Sierra Leoneans). You can hire a canoe (seats five people) at the park headquarters for about US$2 per day. Skilled guides are also available to accompany you for about the same price.

Large animals in the park include elephant, leopard, buffalo, wart hog, duiker, bushbuck, baboon, chimpanzee and several types of monkey. In or near the rivers you may see otter, hippo and crocodile. The various habitats support many species of bird, including kingfisher, hornbill, heron, hawk, eagle, turaco, weaver, sunbird and the blue plantain eater, one of the most spectacular birds in this region.

Until recently, elephants in the Outamba area were threatened by poaching, which often occurred with the knowledge of local chiefs. Getting caught was not a major concern: the maximum sentence was a fine of less than US$10. But in early 1992 the local chiefs officially requested that this area be made a national park. Villages and farms would remain, but hunting would be stopped. In return, the government and some international conservation bodies agreed to fund several local community development projects. In this way the people could benefit directly from the park. Reports in early 1994 indicated that funding levels were low, and that fees paid by visitors were the park's only source of income. Hopefully this will change.

For information and reservations, enquire at the Wildlife Conservation Branch in Freetown, or at the Conservation Society (also in Freetown).

Places to Stay

At the park camp there are several large double tents with beds and lanterns, where visitors can stay for US$6. There are also some smaller tents for US$3 (which you can hire if you want to explore deeper into the park for a day or two), and it costs US$2 a night to pitch your own tent. There are communal washing and cooking facilities (stoves and pots). Water comes from the river but it needs to be treated. You must bring all the food you need, although if you do run short the rangers may be able to sell you fish or go to nearby villages to buy rice and bananas for you. If you have any spare food when you leave, make a gift of it to the rangers. You should also give the rangers a tip if appropriate; life is pretty tough for them out here and the pay is very low.

Getting There & Away

If you're driving from Makeni, take the main road north towards Kabala. After a few km there's a checkpoint at a junction where a dirt road on the left (west) leads to Kamakwie (about 90 km from Makeni). The park is signposted. Beyond Kamakwie you have to cross the Little Scarcies River on a basic ferry. From there, continue on the road towards Fintonia for seven km to reach the well-marked turn-off to the camp and park headquarters; it's seven km down a dirt track to the east, a total of about 25 km from Kamakwie. In a 4WD, Makeni to the park headquarters takes four hours, along a rough hilly road, which means you can make it from Freetown in a day, if the ferry is working.

If you're on public transport, first get to Makeni from where a bush taxi leaves every morning for Kamakwie (US$3). If you get stuck for the night here, ask around for somewhere to stay (some travellers have reported that the Lebanese garage-owner will let you camp in his yard).

From Kamakwie, pick-ups and lorries go to Fintonia. Seven km after crossing the ferry is the junction where the track leads east to the park. It's a seven-km walk from there. Your other option is to hire a taxi in Kamakwie to take you all the way to the camp for US$15. We've also heard from some intrepid travellers who walked the whole distance: it was a hot haul, but much of the route was in shade, and they did it in a day.

You might be able to hitch into OKNP from Makeni, as the park is popular on weekends. Wait by the checkpoint north of Makeni where the road to Kamakwie turns off.

To get to the Kilimi section of the park, follow the directions above, then stay on the road until you reach Sainya village. The villagers can point out the road leading into the park; the boundary is two or three km along here.

Togo

If there were a popularity contest among countries in West Africa, Togo would probably win. It's only a pencil-thin strip of land but is interesting enough to get rave reviews from travellers. Lomé, the capital city, and the nearby beaches are the main reasons. The ocean is only a block from the heart of town, and you can reach one good beach without even taking a taxi. The market is one of the five best in Black Africa.

Equally famous throughout Africa are the women traders – nicknamed 'Nana Benz' because they all seem to own Mercedes Benz cars. Elsewhere in town, you can buy everything from good pieces of African art and the best sandals in West Africa, to smuggled goods and black-market currency. Taxis are everywhere, more than half of them owned by the Nana Benz, but Lomé is small enough that you can cover the heart of town on foot. In addition, Lomé has an outstanding selection of restaurants and nightclubs. Unfortunately, recent political disturbances have, temporarily, destroyed the city's charm.

There's more to Togo than Lomé and the beaches, however. The people are friendly, and upcountry, you'll pass through some beautiful hills on your way to the game parks where you might spot a few animals; then see the famous fortress-like houses of the Tamberma.

For a totally different environment, travel down the coast to Aného. There you can observe life in a fishing village, watching the men on the beach slowly hauling in their long fishing nets accompanied by the rhythm of guttural singing. Or cross Lake Togo in a canoe and visit Togoville, a centre of the fetish cult in Togo.

Facts about the Country

HISTORY

Togo and Cameroun are the only countries in West and Central Africa with a German past. Afterwards, both of them had French

REPUBLIC OF TOGO

Area: 56,785 sq km
Population: 4 million
Population Growth Rate: 3.6%
Capital: Lomé
Head of State: President Major-General Gnassingbé Eyadéma
Official Language: French
Currency: West African CFA franc
Exchange Rate: CFA 500 = US$1
Per Capita GNP: US$360
Inflation: 1%
Time: GMT/UTC

and British rulers. In Togo, the entire British section eventually became part of Ghana. The resulting boundaries, like a finger pointing into the side of West Africa, are totally artificial. Ever since, Togo and Ghana have acted like a constantly bickering separated couple. Achieving national unity has been a constant theme since independence. What's remarkable is the relatively high degree of unity that now exists.

No one is quite sure what happened in Togo prior to the late 15th century when the Portuguese first arrived. Various tribes moved into the country from all sides – the Ewé (EH-vay) from Nigeria and Benin, and the Mina (MEE-nah) and the Guin from

Ghana. They settled along the coast. When the slave trade began in earnest in the 16th century, the Mina benefited the most. They became ruthless agents for the European slave-traders and would travel north to buy slaves from the Kabyé and other northern tribes. Europeans built forts in neighbouring Ghana (at Elmina) and Benin (at Ouidah), but not in Togo, which had no natural harbours. Some of the slaves who were sent off to Brazil were eventually freed, most of them settling along the coast from Accra (Ghana) to Lagos (Nigeria). They, in turn, became heavily involved in the slave trade. The father of Sylvanus Olympio, Togo's first president, was one of these *Brazilians*.

Colonial Period

When the slave trade started dying out in the mid-19th century, the Europeans turned their attention to trade in commodities – palm and coconut oil, cacao, coffee and cotton. The rivalry between Britain and France was fierce. Germany, which initially showed no interest in colonial expansion, surprised the British and French by sending a ship to the coast of 'Togoland' in 1884. They signed a treaty with a local king, Mlapa, in Togoville agreeing to 'protect' the local inhabitants in return for German sovereignty.

German Togoland, like the neighbouring Gold Coast (Ghana), went through an economic miracle before WW I. Through the introduction and scientific cultivation of cacao, coffee and cotton, Germany developed the colony's agricultural resources, which soon paid for all its colonial expenses. Local tax revenues equalled 5% of GNP, large for the time. They were enough to pay for everything, including a harbour and breakwaters at Lomé, a telegraph system, excellent roads, a brewery, a powerful radio transmitter to Germany, three railroads and the highest level of educational development in Africa – nine out of 10 school-age children were in school in 1914.

The Togolese, however, didn't appreciate the forced labour, direct taxes and 'pacification' campaigns of the Germans, which killed thousands of natives. So large numbers

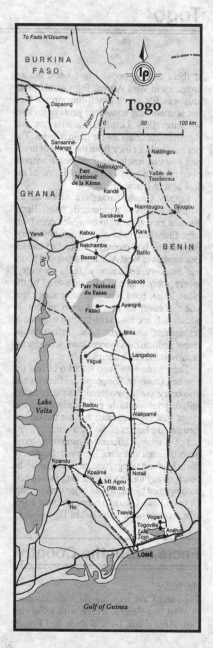

Suggested Itineraries

In years past, **Lomé** was such a gem that some travellers never bothered to venture outside the capital city. These days, several days in Lomé is likely to be plenty because the tension there is obvious. The Friday market in **Vogan** is particularly interesting; you can combine a trip there with one to **Aného**, perhaps spending a few days at **Lake Togo**. Two hours north-east of Lomé is **Palimé**, the country's best hiking area. After several days there, you could head on to **Atakpamé** and the **Akloa waterfalls** outside Badou, then continue on to **Kara**. The area north-east of Kara is the most mountainous in the country and is great for cycling. Several hours further north you'll come to the **Tamberma valley** where you'll find fascinating castle-like structures. Also worth a short visit are Togo's two game parks: **Fazao** in the central region and **Kéran** in the north. ∎

of Togolese started migrating to the Gold Coast. In 1914, with the outbreak of WW I, they welcomed British forces with open arms. Encircled by British and French colonies, the Germans blew up their expensive radio station and surrendered – the Allies' first victory in WW I.

After the war, Togoland was no longer a colony per se. According to the League of Nations mandate, France was to administer the eastern two-thirds of Togoland and Britain the remainder. That was pretty much the end of development in Togoland until the 1950s.

During the colonial period, the Mina, by virtue of their position on the coast and long association with Europeans, came to dominate Togo's economic and political life to the exclusion of northern groups, whom they treated as savages and systematically excluded from any significant participation in the government and economy.

Independence

The dissection of Togoland divided the Ewé. After WW II, political groups on both sides agitated for reunification. Sylvanus Olympio, a Mina from the south, led the cause on the Francophone side. The French were violently opposed. In 1956, hopes of reunification were dashed when British Togoland, in a plebiscite which was irregular and unilateral, voted to be incorporated into Ghana, then on the brink of independence. When independence on the French side came in 1960, the French backed a northern-based party, but Olympio's party won and he became the first president. From the outside, Olympio's régime looked good.

The Mina were bright and knew how to manipulate Westerners. The government, however, was repressive, violent and discriminatory, driving thousands into exile. Northerners were infuriated.

In 1963, Togo became the first country on the continent to experience a military coup following independence, and proved how easy it is to stage a coup. (The continent has averaged over two a year since then, plus many more unsuccessful ones.) It was provoked by Olympio's refusal to hire some 600 Togolese, mainly Cabrais from the north, who had served in the French army and returned to Togo after the Franco-Algerian war. Because they were *petits nordiques*, as Olympio called them, he refused to employ any of them in his small, 250-man army. All it took was a few shots by a band of these men to kill Olympio at the gates of the US embassy as he sought refuge. Thousands of exiles returned. One of them, Nicolas Grunitzky, Olympio's brother-in-law, was put in charge. He lasted four years until being deposed in a bloodless coup headed by Colonel (now General) Étienne Eyadéma (ay-yah-DAY-mah), a northerner.

Eyadéma set out to unify the country, insisting on one trade union confederation and one political party. Every time he made a public appearance, he'd be accompanied by a cheering, dancing crowd of hundreds of women all in identical traditional dress. (Chances are you'll see one of these cheering choruses if you stay long enough.) There's a huge bronze statue of *Le Guide* at the Place de l'Indépendance in Lomé, and you can even buy wristwatches with a picture of Eyadéma that fades and reappears every 15 seconds, plus a comic book where he appears as a Superman character – all in the name of national unity.

The comic book recounts how Eyadéma's private plane crashed in Sarakawa on 24 January 1974. Eyadéma survived but four other passengers were killed. Only two weeks before, he had announced the government's decision to increase Togo's share in the lucrative foreign-owned phosphate mines to 51%. Convinced that 'imperialists' had attempted to assassinate him for this action, nine days later he announced the complete nationalisation of the company. About the same time, following the example of Zaïre's Mobutu, he ordered all Togolese with French first names to replace them with African ones; Étienne Eyadéma became Gnassingbé Eyadéma. It was, however, only a perfunctory strike at colonialism; Togo remained as dependent on the West as ever.

Under Eyadéma's guidance, Togo's economy grew dramatically from 1967 to 1980. Phosphates were the reason. They account for about half of export earnings, making Togo one of the world's largest producers. During that period, Eyadéma's heyday, only Cameroun experienced a higher real growth rate in West Africa. To attract tourists, the government constructed many new hotels, including two five-star hotels, increasing the number of rooms from 200 to over 3000. A new steel plant, a cement works, an oil refinery and sugar operations were other new initiatives.

The 1980s

Eyadéma's attempt to make Togo a sort of 'African Switzerland', attracting a wide range of investors, was all a bit too ambitious, and when the recession of the early 1980s hit and phosphates prices tumbled, the economy was devastated. The cost of servicing the debt reached a staggering 50% of the budget. The International Monetary Fund (IMF) stepped in to help and forced the government to sell numerous unproductive

government enterprises. The star performer was the steel company, leased in 1985 by a flamboyant American entrepreneur. It even expanded with a floating warehouse, selling steel all along the West African coast.

Relations with Ghana continued to be bad, stemming from the division of the Ewé and other ethnic groups at the end of WW I. Every two years or so since Eyadéma came to power, there has been another coup attempt. Each time, Togo has closed the border for months, claiming it was staged by Ghana. Ghana did the same when there were coup attempts there. In 1986, dissidents within Togo – not outside mercenaries – staged a coup that came very close to success. Eyadéma himself fired many of the shots that killed 13 of the attackers. Some of these were backed by the sons of Olympio and other Mina supporters exiled in Paris.

During the last years of the 1980s, relations with Ghana began improving. Relations with the West were even better, especially with the USA. The US embassy in Lomé had tipped Eyadéma off about a rumoured coup attempt in the late 1970s. Since then, American travellers haven't needed visas to come here.

Togo Today

Starting in 1990 with the fall of communism in Eastern Europe and the precedent-setting revolt in neighbouring Benin against one-party rule, France began putting great pressure on Eyadéma to come out in favour of a multiparty system. Eyadéma resisted and through Togo's state-run TV tried to portray African multiparty systems in a negative light by broadcasting scenes of strikes and violence in nearby Côte d'Ivoire and Gabon, two states with ongoing debates on multiparty democracy. The tactic backfired and since then the country has been in a state of near civil war. In early 1991, pro-democracy forces, who were mainly southerners, especially Mina and Ewé, started rioting and calling strikes. Eyadéma responded in his usual way by sending out his troops who proceeded to kill 23 protesters. In April 1991, 28 bodies were dragged out of Lomé-Bé Lagoon.

France and the Togo people, with the backing of a new independent newspaper, were furious, and Eyadéma, who had been fending off coup attempts left and right since he came to power, finally gave in. Just as Kérékou had done a year before in Benin, he agreed with opposition leaders to a national conference in 1991 to decide the country's future, with the identical result – Eyadéma, after 24 years of ruling Togo by slogans and authoritarian dictatorship, was stripped of all powers and made president in name only. Joseph Koffigoh, who created the country's first private human rights league (LTDH), was elected interim prime minister and headed a new civilian government. Four months later, however, on New Year's Eve, the army used heavy artillery and tanks to attack Koffigoh's official residence. At least 17 people were killed but Koffigoh survived and was taken to Eyadéma, who ordered him to form a new transitional team with more of the president's supporters. To save his head, the prime minister agreed. Eyadéma then neutralised the former opposition hero, who began looking like an Eyadéma ally, much to the chagrin of the pro-democracy forces, who branded him a traitor.

Throughout 1992 and 1993 the army kept up its intimidatory tactics, including periodic seizures of the radio station and terror strikes against the independent press. Even more cold-blooded were the assassination attempts on the opposition leaders, including the serious wounding of Gilchrist Olympio, head of the eight-party Union of Forces for Change (UFC) coalition. Although Eyadéma publicly announced regret at the ambush, reports indicated that it was Eyadéma's own son, Ernest, who had headed the commando unit which led the attack. Meanwhile, the promised 'transition' to a democracy came to a complete standstill, with Eyadéma becoming even more intransigent, spurning offers of mediation by European powers and defying aid sanctions by them. The opposition continued calling general strikes, leading to further violence by the army and the exodus of hundreds of thousands of southerners to Ghana and Benin, including many of the oppo-

sition leaders. There were also periodic closings of the border with Ghana whose president, Jerry Rawlings, had a Ewé mother and was a target of Eyadéma's hatred.

Using every intimidating tactic at his disposal and clever political moves that disqualified one opposition party and caused another to refuse to participate, Eyadéma won the 1994 presidential elections unopposed. Since then, the opposition parties have lost much of their steam and Eyadéma's grip on power has become almost as firm as before the crisis began. Most of those who fled the country during this period remain abroad, fearing retribution if they return. The country's appalling human rights record is enough for most Western governments to maintain their distance from the new government without having to decide whether it warrants being called partially democratic.

GEOGRAPHY

Togo measures roughly 540 km by 110 km. In Lomé and along the coast (all flat land) there are lagoons which extend intermittently across the country just behind the sandy coast.

Inland, there are rolling hills covered with forests. The hills around Kpalimé are excellent for growing coffee, while those around Atakpamé afford some pleasant vistas. Central Togo is the location of a major national park, the Forêt de Fazao. North of Kara the hills drop down to savannah plains where you'll find the traditional houses of the Tamberma, and another small park, the Réserve de la Kéran. Sokodé, about halfway between Lomé and the northern border, is the largest city in the interior, with about 40,000 inhabitants, followed by Kara, Kpalimé and Atakpamé.

CLIMATE

Rains fall from May to October. In the south there's a dry spell from approximately mid-July to mid-September. In the drier northern areas, there's no such interlude. The best time to visit is during the dry season. The coast, including Lomé and up to 10 km inland, is a fairly dry area. Mid-February to mid-April is the hottest period.

GOVERNMENT

In mid-1993, President Eyadéma caught the opposition parties off guard by calling the presidential election with little advance notice, cut legal corners and decreed new procedures as he found expedient without regard to the constitution, and reinterpreted election law according to need. With many of their leaders in exile, the opposition parties were unable to group themselves well enough to conduct a campaign. Three candidates opposed Eyadéma. However, the Supreme Court disallowed the candidacy of the leading candidate – Gilchrist Olympio – on trumped up technicalities, and then the other two, Edem Kodjo and Yaovi Abgoyibo, resigned five days prior to the election, citing massive fraud in registration lists and electoral card distribution as well as lack of personal and voter security. Refusing a postponement, Eyadéma won unopposed, with 96% of the vote, but somewhere between 65 and 90% of the registered voters boycotted the elections. Repression immediately returned.

Eyadéma then proceeded with elections to the parliament in early 1994. There was hope that they might be fair because despite a boycott of the elections by supporters of Olympio and the Democratic Opposition Collective (COD-II), there were broadly representative slates in virtually all electoral districts. Leading up to the elections, however, there was widespread shooting almost every night in Lomé, frequent dusk-to-dawn curfews, attacks on military barracks and at least one coup attempt.

On election day, local observers were not permitted in the polling stations. Nevertheless, the main opposition grouping, the Committee for Renewed Action (CAR) headed by Abgoyibo won 34 out of 78 seats, making it the largest party. Kodjo's party, the Union Togolaise Démocratique (UTD) won six seats. Instead of becoming the ruling party, however, the CAR was effectively pushed aside when Eyadéma reached a deal with Kodjo, appointing him prime minister

instead of Abgoyibo. Kodjo, looking more and more like a tool of the president, rewarded Eyadéma by giving some key ministerial posts, including those of defence, foreign affairs and planning, to his supporters and none to the CAR. As a result, Eyadéma is now fully in command as president, with a fully co-operative prime minister and the country's first-ever multiparty parliament, and claims that the country is a democracy, which is far from the truth.

ECONOMY

At the beginning of 1990, the economy was on a modest upturn even though the country's main export crop, cacao, continued to suffer from low world prices. Revenues from tourism were continuing to grow and Togo's Green Revolution programme, started in 1977, was doing well. Even though Togo was ranked by the Population Crisis Committee as 16th (from the bottom) of 130 countries in terms of human suffering (as measured by literacy, clean water, nutrition etc), the country was virtually self-sufficient in food production in non-drought years.

The political crisis changed all this, sending the country into another recession, but far worse than that of the 1980s. As many as 250,000 Togolese have fled the country in the last few years, and the country's once flourishing tourism industry is now all but dead. By 1994, government revenues were down by more than a third and because of the government's severe human rights violations, the USA, Germany and some other countries (but not France) had cut off all foreign aid except humanitarian assistance, damaging the economy still further. And all of this is very visible. Many hotels which were once flourishing have either closed or become dumps. Roads once smoothly tarred are now full of potholes, and most minibuses and bush taxis are now in bad repair.

POPULATION & PEOPLE

With about 40 ethnic groups and a population of four million people, Togo has one of the more heterogeneous populations in Africa. The two largest groups are the Ewé

Life & Death According to the Ewé
One of the more interesting things about the Ewé-related people is their strong attachment to animist beliefs. They believe Mahou, the Supreme Being, created some 600 deities, many representing natural phenomena such as thunder and disease. The Ewé can communicate with these deities by joining a cult and worshipping them, but only these spirits can communicate with God. They believe a person's soul can be reincarnated, and you can influence this by casting a spell. When someone dies, relatives go through a series of funeral rites during the following year to help free the soul of the deceased. Each newborn child is the reincarnation of some deceased person in the area, and a week after birth they determine by divination who that ancestor is. ■

and the Kabyé. The Kabyé, who count President Eyadéma among their number, are concentrated in the north around Kara and central Togo and are known as hard-working people, skilled in terrace farming. Travelling north of Atakpamé, you can tell when you reach the Kabyé area by the design of the houses. The predominantly rectangular huts give way to the round Kabyé houses, that have conical roofs and are joined together by a low wall. The compound is known as a *soukala* (SOU-kah-lah) and is designed for an extended family, where parents with their sons, their sons' wives and their unmarried daughters all live. The granaries are often more interesting than the houses. They are also circular but slightly elevated and about half the size of the regular houses.

The Ewé-related people are concentrated in the south, particularly on the cacao and coffee plantations in the southwest. They include people who call themselves Ewe, such as Anlo, Adja, Peda, Plah, Mina, Guin etc. However, some of these groups, such as the Mina and the Guin, are not ethnic Ewé. The Guin are Ga people from Accra while the Mina are Fanti people from the Ghanaian coast. In Togo, the Mina tend to be somewhat better educated than other groups; many are bureaucrats and merchants.

CULTURE
The Ewé consider the birth of twins a great blessing. By offering kola nuts and water to figurines embodying the spirit of twins, they hope to increase the possibility of having twins. You may see some of these figurines in the market. Not all Togolese consider twins to be a blessing, however. The Bassari consider them to be a misfortune, and used to kill one of the twins, even both of them, whenever this happened a second time to the same mother.

The same contrast in customs is seen with eating habits. In the south, the Ewé eat cat and consider anyone who eats dog to be barbaric, while in the north the Kabyé eat dog but not cat. Another difference is seen in the practice of female circumcision or, more specifically in the case of Togo, infibulation (removal of the labia and closing the vagina by sewing together the vulva). Over 20% of the females in Togo have undergone infibulation, with most cases occurring in the north, especially in the Sokodé region. This spiritual and cultural ritual dates back to ancient Egyptian times, but only in recent years have the health problems associated with this grossly mutilating and primitively performed operation, including the spread of the AIDS virus, gained prominent attention.

RELIGION
Approximately 20% of Togolese are Christians, 10% are Muslims and the remainder are animists. Most of the Christians live in the south, and many of them are Ewé. An equal number of Ewé, however, are animists and believe in reincarnation, a hallmark of their religion.

LANGUAGE
French is the official language. About half the people speak or understand Ewé. The second most widely spoken African language is Kabyé. One word you'll hear everywhere is *yovo*, meaning White person.

TOGO

Expressions in Ewé

Good morning/ evening.	nee-LYE-nee-ah
(response)	MEE-lay
What is your name?	n-koh-WOH-day?
My name is...	nk-nee-N-yay...
How are you?	nee-FOH-ah?
I'm fine.	MEE-foh
Thank you.	mou-DOH, ack-pay-NOW
Goodbye.	mee-AH DOH-goh

Expressions in Mina

Good morning/ evening.	SOH-bay-doh
How are you?	oh-FOIN?
I'm fine.	aihn
Thank you.	ACK-pay
Goodbye.	SOH-day-loh

Facts for the Visitor

VISAS & EMBASSIES
Togo Visas
Nationals of the following countries do not need visas for stays of up to three months: Belgium, Canada, Denmark, France, Germany, Italy, Luxembourg, the Netherlands, Norway, Sweden, the UK and the USA. All other nationals need visas.

French embassies in Africa have authority to issue Togo visas where there is no Togolese embassy.

Visa Extensions
The sûreté in Lomé on Rue du Maréchal Joffre issues visa extensions in 24 hours. They are usually good for 14 days, require four photos and cost CFA 1000.

Togo Embassies
Belgium 264 Ave de Tervueren, Brussels 1150 (☎ (02) 770-17-91)
France 8 rue Alfred-Roll, 75017 Paris (☎ (1) 43-80-12-13)
Germany Beethovenallee 13, 5300 Bonn 2 (☎ (0228) 33-50-91)
USA 2208 Massachusetts Ave, NW, Washington, DC 20008 (☎ (202) 234-4212)

Togo also has embassies in Accra, Kinshasa, Lagos, Libreville and Ottawa. There are consulates in Geneva and Vienna.

Other African Visas
Benin There's no Benin embassy in Lomé but you can get visas at the southern border on the Lomé to Cotonou highway. The border is open 24 hours, but you can't always get visas at night. The visas are good for only two days, cost CFA 2000, and can be extended to one-month at Immigration in Cotonou for CFA 6000 (takes three to five days).

Ghana The embassy (open weekdays from 8 am to 2 pm) requires four photos and takes 48 hours to issue visas. They're good for one-month stays and cost CFA 12,000 (CFA 10,000 for Commonwealth citizens). Three-day transit visas cost CFA 3000. The visa application requires the name and address of a hotel in Accra, so use a well-known place such as the Novotel. In recent years the border between Ghana and Togo has frequently been closed due to political disturbances in Togo. In this case, you may still be able to cross the border with a *laissez passer* from the Ministry of Interior (CFA 500). Or head for Kpalimé; officials at the border nearby usually let travellers cross without laissez passers.

Nigeria The embassy (open weekdays from 8 am to 4 pm) requires one photo and a letter of request from your embassy. It takes from one to three days to issue visas; they cost CFA 1000 to CFA 12,000, depending on your nationality.

Zaïre The embassy (open weekdays from 7.30 am to 3 pm) gives same-day service, requires three photos and a letter of request from your embassy. Single/multiple-entry visas good for stays of one, two and three months, cost CFA 22,000/34,000, CFA 38,000/50,000 and CFA 54,000/62,000.

Other Countries For a visa to Burkina Faso, Central African Republic, Côte d'Ivoire and Mauritania, go to the French consulate. It charges CFA 6000 and CFA 20,000 for visas good for stays of five days and three months, respectively. The consulate is open weekdays from 7.45 to 11.30 am and issues visas in 48 hours. Neither Niger nor Mali has an embassy in Togo. You can get visas to both countries in Ghana, Côte d'Ivoire and Nigeria, as well as Benin (Niger only) and Niger (Mali only).

Foreign Embassies
See the Lomé Information section for details of foreign embassies in the capital.

DOCUMENTS
To enter Togo, everyone needs a passport, except nationals of France and certain

African countries. Everyone needs an International Vaccination Certificate plus an International Driving Permit (IDP) for those who will be driving.

CUSTOMS

There is no restriction on the importation of local currency but declare any large sums you may bring in because the export of foreign currency must not exceed the amount declared on arrival. Theoretically, you're not supposed to export more than CFA 25,000 but in practice customs officials don't seem to care, unless it's a huge amount.

MONEY

1FF	=	CFA 100
UK£1	=	CFA 775
US$1	=	CFA 500

The unit of currency is the West African CFA franc. Lomé has a black market in Ghanaian cedis and Nigerian naira, but since Ghana and Nigeria started floating their currencies the advantages of buying cedis or naira here have greatly diminished and the rates are no better than what you can easily obtain in those countries. The black market dealers will also exchange CFA for hard currencies but their rates, if you're lucky, will only be 1% better than the bank rate. If you change money here, be sure to count your money carefully because Lomé's money dealers are notorious for cheating. If you're near the market and someone is hissing at you, it will almost certainly be one of the dealers. There are also hordes of them at Lomé's Ghanaian border.

Banks for changing money include: Méridian BIAO, UTB (Union Togolaise de Banque), ECO Bank and the BTCI (Banque Togolaise pour le Commerce et l'Industrie).

BUSINESS HOURS & HOLIDAYS

Business hours are weekdays from 8 am to noon and 3 to 6 pm; Saturday from 7.30 am to 12.30 pm. Government offices are open weekdays from 7 am to noon and 2.30 to 5.30 pm. Banking hours are weekdays from 7.30 to 11 am and 2 to 3 pm.

Public Holidays

1 January, 13 January (Liberation Day), 24 January, End of Ramadan, 24 April, 27 April (Independence Day), 1 May, Ascension Day, Whit Monday, Tabaski, 21 June, 15 August, 1 November, 25 December.

POST & TELECOMMUNICATIONS

The poste restante is very reliable and efficient. There is a charge of CFA 150 per letter, and they are held for two months.

The international telephone service is good. There are international telephone and telex facilities at the major hotels, cheaper ones behind the main post office in Lomé.

BOOKS

The Village of Waiting (Vintage Books, 1988) is an interesting observation on life in Togo by George Packer. One of the best books yet on the Peace Corps experience, it's about a volunteer's two years in Lavié and it's quite candid about the country's autocratic politics.

An African in Greenland is by Togo's most famous author, Tété-Michel Kpomassie, who was raised in a traditional Togolese family; his father had eight wives and 27 children. This, Kpomassie's most famous book, is an autobiography containing his fascinating and unique perspective on Arctic life.

MAPS

For detailed maps of Lomé, see the Service Topographique et Cadastre in the centre on the corner of Ave Sarraut and Rue du Colonel de Roux; it's open weekdays.

PHOTOGRAPHY

A photo permit is not required, but be sure not to photograph government buildings and personnel, the airport, the harbour, major industries or, especially, the Presidential Palace. Travellers who have taken photos of the palace have been severely beaten by police.

HEALTH

A yellow fever vaccination is required, as is a cholera shot if you come from an infected area.

The two best places for medical treatment are Clinique de l'Union (☎ 21 77 13), near l'École Française, and the Centre Medical Française on the western side of Blvd du 13

TOGO

Janvier, near the Texaco station. The Hôpital Tokoin (☎ 21 25 01), about three km north of the centre of Lomé on the Route de Kpalimé, is a typical African hospital and should be avoided like the plague, which you might pick up there.

DANGERS & ANNOYANCES

The recent political strife in Lomé has made the city quite dangerous. Even when the situation is 'calm', petty crime is bad. There are lots of pickpockets around the Grand Marché and along Rue du Commerce, and muggings are frequent, some at knife-point. The worst thing you could do is walk along the beach alone at night. Indeed, walking anywhere around the city at night is very dangerous – take a taxi. Even then, avoid the bars in Lomé at the Ghanaian border, which are often full of belligerent drunks. And whenever political strife surfaces, you should probably avoid the city altogether. Outside Lomé, conditions are not nearly so bad except in times of political turmoil, when road blocks may be put up everywhere.

ACCOMMODATION

Accommodation in Togo is among the least expensive in West Africa; finding a room for as little as CFA 3000 per night is not difficult. For just a little more, you'll get a spacious hotel room with private bath and fans. For CFA 6000 to CFA 9000, your room will have air-con. Top-end hotels with pools and amenities can be found in Lomé, Lake Togo and Kara.

FOOD & DRINKS

The food in Togo is some of the best in West Africa, and there are lots of places to try it,

especially in Lomé. In Togo, even a complete dish of various elements is served in a sauce called, quite simply, 'sauce'. Most dishes are invariably accompanied by a starchy substance, such as rice or foufou. One common dish, for example, is rice with peanut sauce, known as *riz sauce arachide*.

Each major Togolese district has its culinary specialities, and in some instances the sauces have more specific names. Along the coast, *lamounou déssi* or simply sauce de poisson (fresh fish sauce) is most popular. Some other sauces include *aglan* (with crab), *gboma* (with spinach), *tomate* (with tomatoes), *aubergine* (with eggplant) and *épinard* (with spinach). One of my favourites is *sauce des légumes avec du crab*; the greens are usually spinach or something like it.

There are a variety of starches used to garnish the sauces, including *pâte* or *akoumé* (a dough-like substance which can be made of millet, corn, plantains, manioc or yams), *ablo* (a slightly sweet pâte made with corn and sugar), *monplé* (a slightly sour pâte made with fermented corn), *gari* (couscous-like grain made with manioc), *djenkoumé* (a red-coloured pâte made with red palm oil, tomatoes and corn) and *foufou* (mashed yams). Other Togolese dishes include *abobo* (snails cooked like a brochette), *egbo pinon* (smoked goat), *koklo mémé* (grilled chicken with chilli sauce), *koliko* (fried yams), which you'll see everywhere on the streets, and *millet couscous*, which is appreciated especially in the north.

Togo also has its fair share of home-made brews. In the north, the preferred drink is *tchakpallo* (CHAK-pah-loh), which is fermented millet with a frothy head and can often be found in the market areas. In the

---

Lamounou Déssi (Sauce de Poisson)

Cut about one kg of saltwater fish (eg sea bass) into small bite-size pieces and three fresh chillies into much smaller pieces, then toss both into a heavy saucepan with a little oil. Add a chopped and seeded green pepper and two large minced onions, and simmer for 10 minutes. Then add a tablespoon of flour and stir, followed by half a kg of peeled and chopped fresh tomatoes (or an equivalent can of tomatoes) and water. Stir in some smoked shrimp and salt and pepper to taste just before serving. Accompanied by rice, this will feed from six to eight people. ∎

south, the most popular brews are *vin du palm* (palm wine) and, to a lesser extent, *sodabe* (SOH-dah-bee), an unusually strong, clear-coloured alcohol which will knock your socks off. All along the southern highway between Lomé and the Benin border you'll see people selling bottles with a white liquid inside; that's palm wine.

Getting There & Away

AIR

From Europe, there are direct flights three times a week from Paris (daily via Abidjan), twice weekly from Amsterdam and once a week from Brussels, Geneva and Frankfurt. The cheapest flights from Lomé to Europe are on Aeroflot, which has flights once a month via Moscow. If you're headed here from Europe or elsewhere, always check comparable fares to Cotonou and Accra as well because if they are considerably less, you could take a flight to one of them and then a three-hour bush taxi ride on to Lomé.

From the USA, you'll have to take Air Afrique or Ghana Airways from New York, transferring in Dakar, Abidjan or Accra, or go via Europe. In June and at Christmas, Friends of Togo sponsors two-week excursions on Air Afrique from New York for about US$1200 (air fare only). See the introductory Getting There & Away chapter.

If you'll be travelling to/from the Sahel, check Air Burkina, which has twice-weekly flights to/from Ouagadougou for about CFA 80,000 one way, which is 20% less than on other airlines.

LAND
Bus

The only large bus ('car') that you might see in Lomé is an X9 bus from Ouagadougou. It used to ply between the two cities once a week, leaving Lomé on Wednesday afternoon. To see if it has resumed service, enquire at the gare routières (bush taxi parks) in Lomé. The fare is about the same as a bush

taxi direct to Ouagadougou, so you wouldn't save any money but it is more comfortable.

Bush Taxi & Minibus
To/From Benin & Ghana Bush taxi Peugeot 504s and minibuses from Lomé to Cotonou (155 km) and Accra (201 km) cost CFA 2000 and CFA 1500 respectively, and take three hours. The Ghanaian border closes at 6 pm sharp whereas the southern Benin border is open 24 hours. There are always lots of vehicles headed in either direction, so the waiting time is minimal.

To/From Burkina Faso Lomé to Ouaga takes about 36 hours, with the night spent at the border, but if you leave Lomé in the late afternoon or early evening, it's sometimes possible to reach Ouaga in as little as 26 hours. If you take a taxi or minibus directly to/from Ouaga, the cost will be CFA 12,500, which is about CFA 4000 more than taking one to Dapaong and the nearby border, and another taxi or minibus from there.

Car
Roads in Togo are in fairly good condition. The one major exception is the stretch between Atakpamé and Kara, which is now full of potholes. Both Accra (Ghana) and Cotonou (Benin) are only three hours by car from Lomé on asphalt road. The more interesting route to Accra is not via the coast but north-west to the mountainous area of Kpalimé. From there, you travel west to Ghana and south-west along Lake Volta, the largest artificial lake in Africa, passing by Akosombo Dam at the southern end. This route is 60% longer but tarred all the way.

Ouagadougou (Burkina Faso) to Lomé is 967 km, an easy two-day drive on asphalt roads. Niamey (Niger) to Lomé takes two long days, whether you go via northern Togo (1192 km) or, better, Benin (1217 km). The roads are paved all the way on both routes, although the roads via Benin are better. Togo's northern border closes around 6 pm but cars can usually get through afterwards by paying a tip.

TOGO

Getting Around

AIR

Within Togo, don't count on flying; almost everybody goes overland. Air Togo, however, charters small planes from Lomé to Kara, Dapaong, Sokodé, Niamtougou and Mango.

TRAIN

For total submersion into African life try the train. Take soft drinks and beer with you, as there's none sold on the train.

There are two lines, Lomé to Kpalimé and Lomé to Blitta. The latter, however, now goes only as far as Wahala, well south of Atakpamé. The former is better because it leaves you in an interesting town to visit, Kpalimé. Both trains leave in the morning from Lomé and return in the evening, taking typically five or six hours to reach either destination.

BUSH TAXI & MINIBUS

For travel upcountry, minibuses are the primary means of transport; most are in fairly good condition. Togo has the most police checkpoints of any country in West Africa except Liberia, so travelling can be agonisingly slow. There is a supplementary charge for luggage and you'll have to bargain furiously because they'll sometimes ask for as much as a third of the price of the seat. To Kpalimé, for example, the fare is CFA 850 and the typical luggage fee is CFA 200; for Dapaong, it's CFA 4250 and CFA 500, respectively.

Lomé

Before the country's political troubles of the 1990s, Lomé was the pearl of West Africa. Travellers motoring their way across West Africa would almost invariably spend a few days camping on the beach outside Lomé. It was not just the on-the-cheap crowd that was attracted to Lomé; the city has two five-star hotels. One of them is 35 storeys high and is the tallest building in Black Africa outside South Africa. French and German tourists flocked here in the winter time. These days, tourists and travellers are fairly scarce in Lomé and many businesses are barely surviving. A few hotels are still doing good business but the majority have a semi-deserted ambience.

Should the country's political disturbances subside, a fast recovery is likely because for a city of roughly 600,000 inhabitants, Lomé has more than its fair share of attractions.

Orientation

Orientating yourself is fairly easy in Lomé because the central area is clearly defined by the straight east-west highway along the beach and the semi-circular Blvd de 13 Janvier (more commonly called Blvd Circulaire) passing around the urban centre.

The heart of town is the intersection of Rue de la Gare and the Rue du Commerce, which beyond the market area becomes the Rue du Lac-Togo, on which the landmark Marox restaurant is located. The market is a few blocks to the east of the intersection and the landmark SGGG (S-troi-ghay) department store is about six blocks north along Rue de la Gare. A block north of the SGGG is Ave du 24 Janvier, which runs east-west. There you'll find the French Cultural Centre and some restaurants. Leading into that avenue are three main north-south arteries: Ave de Calais, better known as the Route de Kpalimé, which leads to the Tokoin district and on to Kpalimé; Ave de la Libération, on which the main post office is located; and Rue Maman N'Danida (formerly Rue d'Amoutive), better known as the Route d'Atakpamé, which leads out to the airport, university and, eventually, Atakpamé and beyond.

Information

Tourist Office The tourist office (☎ 21 43 13), on Rue du Lac-Togo just beyond Chez Marox, usually has maps of Lomé and sometimes, if you ask, great posters of Togo.

Money The major banks, which include BIAO, BTCI, UTB and ECO, are all conveniently together in the centre at or near the corner of Rue de la Gare and Rue du Commerce. Some of these banks have new headquarters to the north, off Blvd Circulaire. ECO Bank's commissions are typical – 2% on travellers' cheques and nothing for cash. Like many banks in West Africa, proof of purchase is required to change travellers' cheques. If you don't have a receipt, try Satrac, a company in the heart of Lomé; it will change money, including travellers' cheques, and its exchange rates without commissions are more favourable.

Foreign Embassies The following countries have diplomatic missions in Lomé:

Belgium Rue Pelletier Caventou (☎ 21 03 23)
Egypt Route d'Aného (☎ 21 24 43)
France Rue du Colonel de Roux (☎ 21 81 83)
Gabon Tokoin (☎ 21 47 76)
Germany Blvd de la Marina, two blocks west of Blvd du 13 Janvier (☎ 21 23 38)
Ghana Tokoin (☎ 21 34 94)
The Netherlands (consulate) Rue du Lac-Togo, facing Marox
Nigeria 311 Blvd du 13 Janvier (☎ 21 34 55/60 25)
Tunisia Rue de Méinas (☎ 21 26 37)
USA Corner of Rue Pelletier Caventou and Rue Vauban (☎ 21 29 91, fax 21 79 52)
Zaïre Blvd du 13 Janvier, at the intersection with Rue du Litimé (☎ 21 51 55)

Honorary consulates include those of Italy, on Rue de l'Ogou, four blocks north of the German embassy, and Norway-Sweden, half a block north of the US embassy.

Travel Agencies There's no lack of travel agencies; many offer excursions to the interior, typically CFA 80,000 for a three-day trip to the north. One of the best is Delmas Voyages (☎ 21 26 11, fax 21 26 12), formerly STCM, in the centre at 2 Rue du Commerce. It has terminals for making airline reservations and is the American Express representative. With your AE card you can obtain US$500 every 30 days and more if you have personal cheques with you. Pronto Voyages (☎ 21 09 14) is a block away on the same street facing Hôtel du Golfe. Also check the travel agency at Hôtel Sarakawa.

Bookshops The two best bookshops are Librairie Bon Pasteur, a block west of the cathedral on Rue du Commerce, and Maladise, about three blocks further east on the same street, south of the market. They have street maps of Lomé (CFA 3000) and occasionally have publications in English such as the *International Herald Tribune* and *Time* magazine. You could also check the American Cultural Centre which faces the US embassy; it has a relaxing air-con library with recent newspapers and lots of books.

Supermarkets The major supermarkets carry foreign goods but not nearly so many as in the years preceding the devaluation of the CFA. Goyi Score on Rue du Kouromé in the centre of town is the largest supermarket, followed by Super Marché Choithram on Ave de la Libération just south of Rue du Commerce. The smaller Marox Supermarché on the eastern end of Rue du Lac-Togo is still another. SGGG is the major department store (also a supermarket); it's in the centre on Rue de la Gare, 100 metres south of Ave du 24 Janvier.

Place de l'Indépendance

The gilded bronze statue of President Eyadéma, carved by North Koreans, and the statue of his mother were taken down in 1991 during the civil disturbances. Across the way is the moribund Hôtel du 2 Février. Going for a drink on the 35th floor could be interesting for the views if the bar there ever reopens. On the Place, you'll also see the Palais des Congrès, previously the headquarters of Eyadéma's party.

National Museum

The entrance to the museum is at the back of the Palais des Congrès. It houses historical artefacts, pottery, costumes, musical instruments, wood carvings, traditional medicinal remedies, including powders for pregnant women, and 'thunder stones' and cowrie shells, both formerly used as legal tender. It's open weekdays from 8 am to noon and 3 to 5.30 pm; entrance costs CFA 200.

Lomé

TOGO

To Gare Routière du Lycée, Airport, University & Kara

To Fetish Market

To Hôtel de la Paix, Hôtel Sarakawa, Ramatou Beach, Lake Togo & Benin

To Gare de Kpalimé, Ghanaian Embassy, Hôtel Agni & Kpalimé

To Ghana Border & Aflad

ATLANTIC OCEAN

Lagoon

Lagoon

MILITARY CAMP

Rond-Point Central

Rue Dhoni
Rue de Nangbéto
Boulevard Houphouët-Boigny
Rue de France
Route d'Atakpamé (Rue d'Atakpamé)
Rue Kalitzan
Boulevard Lagunaire
Avenue de la Libération
Boulevard du 13 Janvier (Bvd Circulaire)
Rue Maman N'Danida
Rue d'Aného
Boulevard Notre Dame
Rue d'Aného
Rue Pelletier
Cavenou
Rue Vauban
Rue du Lac-Togo
Rue Maman N'Danida
Avenue du 24 Janvier
Rue du Chemin de Fer
Rue Alsace
Lorraine
Ave de la Libération
Rue Foch
Rue de la Gare
Rue du Kouroni
Boulevard de la Marina
Avenue du Nouveau Marché
Avenue Pompidou
Avenue du Golfe
Rue Koketi
Rue Koketi
Avenue Sarakawa
Ave de Calais (Route de Kpalimé)
Ave Nicolas-Grunitsky
Rue Mitterrand
Avenue de Gaulle
Avenue de la Présidence
Avenue Duisberg
Boulevard de la République (Bvd de la Marina)
Boulevard du 13 Janvier (Bvd Circulaire)
Avenue Joseph Strauss
Ave de la Kozah
Rue de Togo
Rue Houndagbe
Rue d'Armoudre
Rue du Commerce
Boulevard de la Marina
Rue de la Gare
Rue du Grand Marché
Rue Galliéni
Rue Joffre
See Inset

To Restaurant Pili-Pili
Rue du Litmé
Rue de l'Entente

0 250 500 m

PLACES TO STAY

9 Hôtel du Boulevard
11 Hôtel Mawuli
23 Hôtel du 2 Février
40 Hôtel Avenida
41 Hôtel Ahoefa
43 Hôtel Copacabana
49 Hôtel Tindano
57 Secourina Hôtel
60 Hôtel Ahodikpé
   Éboma
67 Hôtel Le Galion
   Annexe & Italian
   Consulate
68 Hôtel Le Galion
   (Chez Mamy)
69 Hôtel California
71 Hôtel Lily
72 Salam Motel
74 Hôtel Le Maxime
75 Hôtel L'Abri
76 Hôtel de la Plage &
   Bric à Brac
81 Hôtel Le Bénin
91 Hôtel Palm Beach &
   Ethiopian Ailines
95 Hôtel du Golfe

PLACES TO EAT

1 Tanty Hanu
   Restaurant
3 China Town
   Restaurant & Hôtel
   Lymakos
4 Restaurant
   Le Shanghai
10 Restaurant
   Fouta-Djalon
14 Restaurant Au Relais
   de la Poste
27 Restaurant au Relais
   des Iles
28 Restaurant
   Mini-Brasserie &
   Abrevoir Nightclub
29 Domino Snack Bar
31 Restaurant Au Feu de
   Bois & Papillon
32 Mic-Mac
33 Restaurant Le
   Phénicien
36 Ristorante Claudio
39 Restaurant Keur
   Rama
42 Ristorante da Silvia &
   Swiss Consulate
44 Restaurant Le Berry
47 La Pirogue

55 Chez Marox
58 Golden Crown
   Restaurant
61 Restaurant
   l'Oriental
64 Café du Centre
65 Le Belvedère
70 Restaurant Layalina
83 Restaurant de l'Amitié
84 Restaurant Le Lautrec
86 No-Name
   Restaurant
98 Boulangerie
   Bopato, Snack
   Vendome & BTCI
103 Restaurant
   Sénégalais de la
   Paix
108 Good Street Food &
   Artisan Vendors

OTHER

2 Maquina Loca
   Nightclub
5 BOAD Bank HQ
6 CDEA HQ
7 BTCI Bank HQ
8 Marché Amoutive
12 Mosque
13 Post Office
15 Café des Arts
16 French Cultural
   Centre
17 Café Santa Fé
18 Hertz
19 Train Station
20 Le Tabou Nightclub
21 Museum & Palais de
   Congrès
22 Place de
   l'Indépendance
24 Stadium
25 Sûreté
26 SGGG Department
   Store
30 Boston Pub
34 Le Pacha Nightclub
35 Avis
37 Le Byblos Nightclub
38 Nigerian Embassy
45 Stadium
46 Zaïre Embassy
48 Oro Nightclub
50 American Cultural
   Center &
   Norway-Swedish
   Honorary Consulate
51 US Embassy
52 Maladise Bookshop

53 Gare de Cotonou
   (Aného & Cotonou)
54 Lufthansa, the
   Netherlands
   Consulate, Renault
   & Yamaha Dealers
56 Tourist Office
59 Bar Fifty-Fifty
62 Peace Corps Office
63 WHO Office
66 FAO Office
73 German Embassy
77 Tennis Club
78 United Nations
79 French Consulate
80 Presidential Palace
82 Service
   Topographique et
   Cadastre
85 Music Store
87 Grand Marché
88 Goyi Score
   Supermarket
89 BCCI Bank, Sabena,
   KLM, Immeuble
   Tabac & Cinéma
   Elysses
90 Air Gabon, Air Zaïre &
   Ghana Airways
92 Samaze Arts Primitifs
   & Arts d'Afrique
   Noire
93 Church
94 Bookshop
96 Nigeria Airways &
   Batik Sellers
97 Balkan Air, Atlas
   Voyage & Peace Air
   Togo
99 Delmas Voyages
100 Pronto Voyages
101 Le Squire Taverne
102 Satrac
104 UTB Bank,
   Air Afrique & Air
   France
105 King Cash
   Supermarket
106 BIAO Bank
107 Choitram
109 Telephone/
   Fax Place
110 Librairie Bon Pasteur
111 ECO Bank
112 Cathedral
113 Moneychangers

TOGO

Marché des Féticheurs

The fetish market is in the Akodessewa area, four km north-east of the centre. It has a remarkable supply of traditional medicines used by sorcerers, including skulls of monkeys and birds, porcupine skin, wart hog teeth and all sizes of bones and skulls. It's also a great place to buy gris-gris, which are worn around the neck and ward off various evils. They only work, however, if they've been blessed by a fetish priest.

Take a shared taxi along Blvd Notre Dame from the Grand Marché; the cost is CFA 175 (about CFA 500 for a taxi to yourself). This photogenic place has become quite touristy, so be prepared for lots of young boys descending on you, offering to show you where all the fetishes are sold.

Amoutive

Amoutive (ah-mou-TEEVE) is another interesting section of town, starting around the intersection of Blvd du 13 Janvier and Rue Maman N'Danida. This is a very animated area and one of the best places for late night street food.

Activities

The surf in Lomé is very dangerous because of a strong undertow; drownings are not uncommon, so be cautious. Many of the **beaches** are also used by locals as toilets. The best by default is in front of the ever-active Hôtel Le Bénin. Or better, take a cab (CFA 1000; CFA 125 shared) and head for the more secluded and protected Robinson's Plage, nine km east from the centre.

As for pools, the Sarakawa's is Olympic size and the best in West Africa, but it costs CFA 2000 for nonguests. Hôtel Le Bénin and the Foyer des Marins charge nonguests CFA 1000 and CFA 600, respectively, to use their pools, which are clean but sometimes crowded on weekends.

Places to Stay – bottom end

If a low price is your only concern, head for the *Hôtel Atlantique* on the western outskirts of town, half a block from the customs office at the Ghanaian border. A room with no ventilation but passably clean shared toilets costs CFA 1500, and prostitutes and potential muggers abound.

The best by far near the central area is the quiet *Hôtel Mawuli* (☎ 21 55 05). Secure doubles with fan and clean shared bath cost from CFA 2500 to CFA 3000. It's on a dirt road (21 Rue Maoussas), one km north of the centre in the very African Zongo district, a block or two south of Blvd du 13 Janvier. Just ask for the mosque; it's a block east thereof.

The new *Salam Motel* on Blvd de la Marina has a breezy breakfast area with views of the ocean, and clean cramped rooms with twin beds, fans and spotless shared baths for CFA 3000. Several blocks beyond on the same road is *Hôtel Lily* which has small ventilated rooms with private baths for CFA 3300. There are cheap eateries nearby.

Better value is the *Hôtel California* (☎ 21 18 75), which is a poorly signposted four-storey establishment two blocks from the Abri and just a block off the water. Singles/doubles with fans, balconies and private hot-water showers cost CFA 3500/4200. There's a good restaurant and a paillote bar outside.

If you don't mind paying a bit more, check the more active *Hôtel Le Galion* or Chez Mamy (☎ 22 00 30), around the corner at 12 Rue Houndjagoh and two blocks north of the beach road. There's a lounge upstairs with relaxing armchairs and shelves full of books, and a popular bar downstairs where you can meet all kinds of locals and travellers. Bright attractive doubles with fans and clean private baths cost CFA 5500 (CFA 7500 with air-con), and Americans receive a 20% discount.

The six-storey *Hôtel Ahodikpé Éboma* (☎ 21 47 80), also on the western side of town at 45 Blvd du 13 Janvier, has rooms with fans and super comfortable double beds for CFA 3500 (CFA 6000 with air-con).

Two possibilities on the eastern side of town are the *Hôtel du Boulevard* (☎ 21 15 90) at 204 Blvd du 13 Janvier, half a block west of the intersection with Route d'Atakpamé, and the *Hôtel Ahoefa* (☎ 21 42 48) further east, a block behind the Hôtel Avenida. They charge CFA 3500 and CFA 4000, respectively, for a tidy room with fan and private bath, and CFA 2000 more with air-con. The Boulevard has been spruced up a bit and is in a good location that's lively at night, while the Ahoefa is on a quiet side street and has a more African feel, a small shady area outside for drinks plus polite service – the hotel's hallmark.

Camping *Le Ramatou* (☎ 21 43 53) has big plain bungalows with up to four single beds, mosquito nets and shared baths for CFA 2000 and rooms with fans and private baths for CFA 5000 (CFA 8000 with air-con). Camping here costs CFA 800 a person.

Robinson's Plage next door has a slightly more formal atmosphere and superb restaurant (expensive). Camping costs CFA 500 a person. The spacious thatched-roof bungalows have twin beds and mosquito nets and cost CFA 3000 (CFA 5000 with interior bath); rooms have air-con and private baths and cost CFA 6000 (CFA 8000 with two beds). Both hotels have clean bathrooms and showers. Walking on the beach at night is very dangerous (people have been robbed on the beach even in broad daylight) and you must keep an eye on your luggage.

Le Ramatou and Robinson's Plage are nine km from the centre. The well-marked turn-off is one km east of the large roundabout at the port. A taxi from the Grand Marché should cost no more than CFA 400 but the drivers will ask for much more. A shared taxi from the main road into town costs CFA 125. On weekends, catching a ride is easier.

Chez Alice (☎ /fax 27 91 72) is in a tiny village four km further east of Robinson's Plage. It costs CFA 750 for camping, CFA 2500 for primitive bungalows with petrol lamps and shared baths, and CFA 3500 for rooms with fans and clean shared baths (CFA 6000 with private baths and closer proximity to the ocean). Chez Alice is further out than the others but conveniently located just off the highway to Aného. To get to Lomé, simply flag a bush taxi (CFA 125).

Places to Stay – middle
A great place for the price is the *Foyer des Marins* (☎ 27 53 51, fax 27 77 62) on the Route d'Aného just before the Rond-Point du Port. It has singles/doubles with fans and shared baths for CFA 4500/6000 (CFA 7000/9000 for apartments with kitchens). Other features include a pool, snack bar and a bar. The only problem for travellers is that the owner must give first priority to sailors, so call before coming here because it's five km east of the central area, half a km beyond Hôtel Sarakawa. Regardless, you can come here for a swim for CFA 600, and every Saturday there's fresh home-made bread for which this place is famous.

For a place closer to the centre, try *Hôtel Le Maxime* (☎ 21 74 48), 1.5 km west of the centre on the beach road, facing the ocean. This long-standing French-run place has air-con rooms with private baths for CFA 7300, a pleasant patio and an excellent restaurant.

Another good place for the money and closer to the centre is the *Secourina Hôtel* (☎ 21 60 20, fax 21 01 96) on the opposite side of town on Rue du Lac-Togo, two blocks east of Marox. It has air-con singles with showers and telephones for CFA 6300 to CFA 8300, and doubles for CFA 7600 to CFA 9600, a decent restaurant and a nice shady drinking area in front.

Hôtel Agni (☎ 21 47 34, telex 5047), three km north of the centre across the lagoon in Tokoin and next door to the Chinese embassy, charges CFA 8500/10,000 for small but decent singles/doubles. This place has gone downhill, however, and is far inferior to the well-maintained *Hôtel Avenida* (☎ 21 46 72, fax 21 34 76), which is closer to the centre, half a block off Blvd du 13 Janvier near the eastern end. It has a decent restaurant and singles/doubles for CFA 8000/9600. Both places readily offer discounts.

Places to Stay – top end
The best buy among the top-end hotels is unquestionably the long-standing *Hôtel Le Bénin* (☎ 21 24 85, telex 5264; all cards) on Blvd de la Marina, half a km west of the town centre. At this well-maintained independence-era hotel, renovated singles/doubles cost CFA 21,000/25,000. The pool, poolside restaurant and piano bar are all very

TOGO

popular, and a beach is just across the street. The restaurant has reasonably priced dishes for CFA 2000 to CFA 2500.

A popular new high rise in the centre of town, *Hôtel Palm Beach* (☎ 21 85 11, fax 21 87 11, telex 5184; all cards), has singles/doubles for CFA 45,000/51,000. Features include a pool, weight room and cable TV.

The best beach-front property is the PLM *Hôtel Sarakawa* (☎ 21 65 90, fax 21 71 80, telex 5354; all cards), three km east of the town centre. Expect to pay CFA 35,000 a room (CFA 40,000 with ocean view). Features include sailboards, a wonderful pool, horse riding, tennis, a hairdresser and shops.

The only other ocean-view property is the fast declining *Hôtel de la Paix* (☎ 21 52 97, fax 21 23 02, telex 5252; cards AE, D, V, CB), which has a beach across the street, a pool and tennis court. Rooms cost from CFA 21,000 to CFA 30,000.

Places to Eat

Bar Fifty-Fifty on the western side of Blvd du 13 Janvier, just north of the Hôtel Ahodikpé, is very popular and lively. Food is served only in the evenings.

A block to the east on Rue de la Gare, across from the BIAO, are two adjacent places popular with travellers: *Snack Vendome*, good for sandwiches, and *Boulangerie Bopato*, a bread and pastry shop. The city's best pastry shop, however, is *Au Choid Croissant* on Rue du Kouromé, 100 metres north of the Hôtel Palm Beach on the opposite side of the street. It also serves excellent brewed coffee.

Another area with inexpensive food is around the SGGG department store on Rue de la Gare. Facing SGGG is *Café du Centre*, with draught beer for CFA 400. The nearby *Restaurant Mini-Brasserie* has a convivial atmosphere and is such a long-standing favourite as to be a landmark. It's open every day from 6 am to 1 am. The food is good but main dishes are mainly in the CFA 2000 to CFA 4000 range. Even if you don't eat here, it's one of the best places to meet other travellers and have an ice-cold *pression* (draught beer) for CFA 400.

Another popular place is *Chez Marox*, an open-air German beer parlour/delicatessen. However, the food is not cheap and the service is slow. Sandwich prices range from CFA 650 to CFA 1400. Open until 10 pm, it's near the eastern end of Rue du Lac Togo near the ocean. Next door is a small *delicatessen* where you can buy German sausages, cheese etc.

If you're on Ave du 24 Janvier, head for *Mic-Mac*. It's a fancy bar at the eastern end of that avenue but outside they grill huge hot dogs for CFA 500 as well as fish. You can also get cheap food at the *Boston Pub* facing the French Cultural Centre.

For a splurge, try the yummiest ice cream in town at the air-con *Papillon*, which is between these two establishments. They have elaborate ice-cream concoctions for CFA 700 to CFA 1800 and wonderful fresh fruit juices for CFA 175 to CFA 1500.

African Lomé has one of the best selections of African restaurants of any West African city. The cheapest is *Tanty Hanu* on Ave du Nouveau Marché, five blocks north of Blvd du 13 Janvier. It closes around 9 pm.

One of the best areas for African street food, day and night, is along the Route d'Atakpamé for several blocks just north of Blvd du 13 Janvier. A great place on Blvd du 13 Janvier is *Restaurant Fouta Djalon*. Open nightly until 10 pm, this 'Senegalese' restaurant offers several authentic African dishes such as riz sauce arachide (CFA 400).

In the heart of town, a terrific, cheap, unmarked place is half a block directly behind (north of) the UTB bank on a north-south side street. It has four sauces to choose from; the sauce aubergine is great, as is the sauce de poisson; CFA 250 worth is filling and you can eat at tables out the back.

Another popular place three blocks away is the *Restaurant de l'Amitié* at 17 Rue du Grand Marché, west of Rue de la Gare. Its dishes, which are mostly Senegalese, are all in the CFA 500 to CFA 1000 range. *Restaurant Sénégalais de la Paix* is at the intersection of Rue du Commerce and Rue de la Gare. Most of the dishes are in the CFA 800 to CFA 1300 range. Both places are open until around 8 pm. If you're in Tokoin, look for the popular *Bar Nopegali* facing the hospital; it's a good place for African sauces.

For a more up-market African restaurant, head for *Pili-Pili*, on the eastern side of town on Rue de l'Entente behind Hôtel de la Paix. The menu is varied with Togolese dishes for CFA 2000. It has good recorded music and sometimes a live band on Friday and Saturday evenings (closed Tuesday).

Another place on the eastern side of town is *Keur Rama*. It's also slightly up-market with air-con and similar prices. The cuisine is Senegalese and Togolese and most dishes cost from CFA 1750 to CFA 1850. The restaurant (closed Monday) is well marked on Blvd du 13 Janvier, opposite the Nigerian embassy.

Restaurant La Pirogue, several blocks south on the same street, has similar prices, and offers about six African selections as well as French dishes. It's open every day and has a relaxed outdoor ambience. On the same street, several blocks east of Ave du Nouveau Marché near Café des Arts, is *Le Kilimanjaro*, the city's only Ethiopian restaurant. For a huge plate of vegetarian sauces and injera (Ethiopian fermented wheat bread), which is plenty for two people, they charge CFA 2000, slightly more with meat.

Lebanese The three best restaurants, all moderately priced, are *Le Phénicien*, near the centre on Rue Maman N'Danida; *Restaurant Layalina* (☎ 21 21 83), at the western end of Blvd du 13 Janvier, next to Hôtel de la Plage; and *Restaurant Oriental*, half a km north on the same street. Very popular with the Lebanese community, the Restaurant Oriental has lots of Lebanese selections, mostly in the CFA 1500 to CFA 2000 range. Le Phénicien is recommended for the mezzas as the portions of the other dishes tend to be small and the service is rushed. It's closed on Monday.

Italian *Restaurant Le Belvedère* on the western side of town on Ave Duisberg, three blocks west of Blvd du 13 Janvier, has wonderful pizzas for CFA 1800. If you go eastward around Blvd du 13 Janvier to *Ristorante Da-Claudio* (☎ 22 26 65) you'll find pizzas for CFA 1800 to CFA 3600, pasta dishes for CFA 1800 to CFA 3000 and, best of all, a choice between air-con dining inside and a wonderful relaxing terrace outside. It's open every day. The best Italian restaurant in town is *Ristorante da Silvia*, further east on the same street and about 250 metres before the ocean road. It's expensive, with most main courses starting at CFA 5000, but their three-course menu du jour costs CFA 4900. Pizza costs from CFA 3500.

Chinese The best Chinese restaurants are all on Blvd du 13 Janvier. Starting at the eastern end at the intersection with the ocean road, there's the long-standing *Golden Crown* (moderate prices; good quality). Halfway around Blvd du 13 Janvier near the commissariat is the Chinese-run *Le Shanghai* (☎ 21 00 52). Closed Wednesdays, it's the best and most popular and has an extensive menu. Dishes are pricey at CFA 3000 to CFA 3800. Further west you'll come to *China Town Restaurant*, which is better value. Dishes cost from CFA 1900 to CFA 2000.

French *Au Relais de la Poste* has a friendly atmosphere, and wandering minstrels sometimes play during the meal. An omelette and a large portion of chips costs CFA 800. Open every day, it is on Ave de la Libération next to the post office.

For a French meal in the CFA 2300 to CFA 3000 range, try *Hôtel Le Galion*. It may be the only place in town to get Vietnamese food as well. A block away towards the beach is the similarly priced *Le Maxime*. And in the centre at *Restaurant Le Lautrec* on Rue de la Gare, you can get a decent three-course plat du jour for CFA 2300.

For years, *Restaurant Le Berry* has been Lomé's most exclusive restaurant. It is a formal place with excellent food and outstanding service. It's on the eastern side of town, just north of Rue de l'Entente and two blocks east of Blvd du 13 Janvier. (Open daily except Sunday.)

Seafood The *L'Auberge Provençale*, on the coastal road near the Ghanaian border, is

TOGO

fairly expensive and has become a culinary institution – its seafood is very good. The cuisine is southern French, and you can dine inside or outside daily except on Tuesday.

Also good is the attractively decorated *Alt München*, on the ocean road just east of the Sarakawa. The seafood is particularly good here and the service is excellent. It's closed on Tuesday.

Less expensive, but nine km east of town, is *Robinson's Plage*, which is open every day with daily menus for CFA 3000 to CFA 5000. Expect a long wait.

Entertainment

Bars Lomé is a great place for bars because the brew in Togo is the cheapest in West Africa. Two of the most popular slightly up-market places are *Chez Marox*, near the town centre at the eastern end of Rue du Lac-Togo, and the air-con *Mini-Brasserie*, in the centre on Rue de la Gare, one block south of the SGGG department store. Both cater primarily to foreigners. Large draught beers at these places cost CFA 400. There's also the air-con *Le Squire Taverne* in the heart between the Hôtel du Golfe and the ocean road – Lomé's attempt at an English pub.

The *Café des Arts* is maybe the liveliest terrace bar of its kind on the West African coast. It's popular with Africans and foreigners, has draught beers (CFA 150), good music, and a friendly manager. Open late, this gem is on Blvd du 13 Janvier at the intersection with the Route d'Atakpamé.

In the town centre are several places with cheap beers for CFA 100 or less. One of the more popular is *Panjar Bar* (or Jungle Bar), two blocks to the west on the eastern side of Goyi Score. A second is *Bar Mawuena*, on the south-east corner of the Grand Marché. If you're at Gare Routière de Kpalimé, ask around for *Sweet Mother*; it's four streets north of the lagoon on the Route de Kpalimé, then three or four streets west. This not-so-hidden treasure has pressions for CFA 75, with two bars no less, a jukebox, pinball machine and a football table.

Nightclubs Among the nightclubs (*boîtes de*

nuit) with an African feel, *African Queen* in Tokoin is cheap, safe, always crowded, open every night and great for dancing. Large beers cost CFA 250; admission is also CFA 250 (weekends only). Take Ave de la Libération north, one km beyond the Blvd du 13 Janvier and across the lagoon; it is on your left.

The European-oriented, disco-like nightclubs are much more expensive and have entrance fees, typically CFA 2000, which usually include a drink. The hottest and best known is *L'Abreuvoir*, in the centre on Rue de la Gare, half a block south of SGGG. It's open every night. Small beers are CFA 1500, and there's a snack bar on the roof. *Le Pacha*, on the eastern side of town on Blvd Notre Dame, is open from Thursday to Saturday nights, and afternoons on Sunday. It's one of the biggest and one of the few that sponsors occasional live performances; look for announcements. The entrance charge is CFA 2000. Not far away on Rue du Litimé, a block east of Blvd du 13 Janvier, you'll find the *Oro*, one of the city's flashiest nightclubs. Moving westward along Blvd du 13 Janvier you'll come to *Le Byblos*, which is open only on weekends and frequented by rich young Togolese. Still further west at 8 Ave de Nicolas Grunitsky, just north of Hôtel de 2 Février, is the long-standing and popular *Maquina Loca*. Occasionally it has live bands.

Live Music For live entertainment, head for *Chez Alice* on the coastal highway to Aného, about 12 km from the heart of Lomé. Every Wednesday night, the Togolese dance group Sakra performs here. It's great fun and always packed till the early morning hours. The cost to nonresidents is about CFA 300.

Cinemas The best cinema is at the 2 Février hotel, with shows at 6.30 and 9 pm.

Things to Buy

Fabrics The 2nd and 3rd floors of the Grand Marché are the domain of the Nana Benz and are loaded with colourful cotton material, most of it wax cloth from Holland and cheaper African material. It's sold by the *pagna* (PAHN-yah), almost two metres, the complete package being three pagnas. Don't be surprised if they sometimes refuse to sell less than the entire three pagnas – it's not always easy to sell the remainder because most African women want three pagnas, the amount needed for a complete outfit. Don't expect to bargain much either. If you can get the price down 10%, you're probably doing well. Nonetheless, prices here are lower than anywhere else in West Africa. With handmade African material, such as the multicoloured *kente* cloth from Ghana, it's a different ball game – you can bargain all day. The market is open every day except Sunday, and closes at 4 pm sharp.

Artisan Goods For wooden carvings and brass work, take a walk on the Rue des Artisans, a short alley in the centre along the eastern side of the Hôtel du Golfe, where there are many Senegalese and Malian traders. Their opening prices are usually ridiculously high, so expect lots of hard bargaining. Most pieces are of low quality.

For high-quality art, your best bet by far is Bric à Brac (☎ 21 02 45), next door to the well-known Hôtel de la Plage on Blvd de la République. Messie Catherine, the friendly owner, has a showroom of top-quality pieces from around West Africa and her fixed prices are very reasonable. Also, unlike in many West African countries, exporting such pieces requires no clearance from a museum. In short, this is one of the best shops in West Africa for buying good quality African art and small discounts may be offered if you purchase in quantity.

Other shops with high-quality African art, mostly wooden carvings, include Samaze (☎ 21 26 49), Arts d'Afrique Noire and, most expensive, Galerie Yassine (☎ 21 45 37), which are all a stone's throw from the northern end of Rue des Artisans. However, their opening prices are usually off the scales and unless you're a near expert on African art, the chances are good you'll be ripped off.

For ready-made African dresses and batik material, look for street vendors along Rue du Grand Marché from Goyi Score east to Rue de la Gare.

The Village Artisanal on Ave du Nouveau Marché, between Ave du 24 Janvier and Blvd du 13 Janvier, is an easy-going place to shop. You'll see Togolese artisans weaving cloth, carving statues, making baskets and lamp shades of rattan, sewing leather shoes, and constructing cane chairs and tables – all for sale at reasonable fixed prices. You can also pick up jewellery, tablecloths, napkins and ceramic pottery.

Lomé is famous for its leather sandals. They were originally all made at the Village Artisanal but now you can also buy them around the market for about CFA 2500.

Another place for Togolese handicrafts, mostly cloth items with tie-dye designs, is the Centre Prohandicap, an outlet for a workshop in Niamtougou for the mentally and physically challenged. It's on the eastern end of Blvd du 13 Janvier, one block inland from the ocean road.

Music For cassettes, try the unmarked music shop in the centre on Rue du Grand Marché, just east of the intersection with Rue de la Gare. Its African selection is fairly good. Around the Grand Marché you may find others. Leading Togolese musicians include the group As du Golfe, Ouye Tassane, Dama Damaozan, and the female vocalists Akofa Akoussah and Fifi Rafiatou, who have beautiful voices, and Angelique Kidjo, one of the brightest new stars with international fame.

Getting There & Away

Air Most of the major airlines are in the heart of Lomé and include: Ghana Airways (☎ 21 56 91), Ethiopian Airlines, Sabena, Air Gabon and Air Zaïre, at or next door to Hôtel Palm Beach; Air Afrique (☎ 21 20 42/10 58) and Air France (☎ 21 69 10) on Rue du Grand Marché, behind the UTB bank; and Balkan Airlines/Atlas Voyages (☎ 21 79 60) and Nigeria Airways (☎ 58 26 32) on Rue Foch. Aeroflot (☎ 21 04 80), which has the cheapest flights to Europe, is on Ave 24 Janvier, while Swissair (☎ 21 31 57) and Lufthansa are on the eastern side of town on Rue du Lac-Togo near Marox. Air Burkina (☎ 26 78 21) also has an office in Lomé.

TOGO

Most of the airlines accept credit cards but not all of them. Air Afrique, for example, accepts only Visa and MasterCard.

Train The train station is in the centre at the intersection of Ave du Nouveau Marché and Ave du 24 Janvier. The train to Kpalimé costs CFA 550 and is scheduled to leave every day at 6 am from Lomé and at 1.20 pm from Kpalimé. The trip typically takes six hours even though the schedule says five; occasional breakdowns can make it much longer.

The train to Wahala leaves Lomé around 7 am. It is ridiculously slow, taking up to five hours to Wahala. Both trains have only one class and no bar or restaurant. Take water; food can be bought at stations along the way.

Bush Taxi & Bus Taxis and minibuses travelling east to Aného and Cotonou leave from the new Gare d'Akodessewa (five km east of the centre and one km beyond Bé market, or one km north of the port) and, more conveniently, from the smaller gare routière on Rue du Commerce (or Gare de Cotonou) just south of the market. Buses for Accra leave from just across the Ghanaian border in Aflao; those for Kpalimé leave from Gare de Kpalimé, three km from the centre out on the Route de Kpalimé; and most of the rest, including those for Kara, Atakpamé, Dapaong and Ouagadougou leave from Gare Routière du Lycée, which is several km north of the centre towards the airport. The Nouvelle Gare Routière (or Gare de Kara), which is about 10 km north of the centre in the Agbalepedo area, off the road to Atakpamé, is a big flop and not used very much.

A shared taxi from Akodessewa to the Ghanaian border should cost no more than CFA 150, but getting that price is difficult. Most minibuses are in excellent condition and cost CFA 850 to Kpalimé (two hours), CFA 1200 to Atakpamé (three hours), CFA 1500 to CFA 2000 to Cotonou (three hours), CFA 2400 to Sokodé (six to seven hours), CFA 2800 to Kara (seven to nine hours) and CFA 4225 to Dapaong (12 to 15 hours). There's an extra charge for baggage. Taxis to Ouagadougou cost CFA 12,500 direct and

CFA 8225 if you go to Dapaong and get another from there. For information on whether the large X9 buses from Ouagadougou have resumed the weekly service to Lomé, enquire at Gare du Lycée and Gare du Kara.

Getting Around
To/From the Airport A taxi into Lomé (six km) costs at least CFA 2000, but only CFA 1000 from town to the airport.

Taxi The city has no public buses, so your only choice is a taxi. They are abundant, even at night, and have no meters. Fares are CFA 175 for a shared taxi (CFA 200 after 6 pm), more to the outlying areas, and CFA 500 for a *course* (short trip in a taxi to yourself). At the hotels, you'll pay more, and rates double at midnight. A taxi by the hour should cost CFA 1500 if you bargain well. By the day, you can get a taxi for CFA 10,000 to CFA 12,000 plus petrol.

Car Hertz (☎ 21 44 79, telex 5208), Europcar-National (☎ 21 13 24, telex 5275) and Avis (☎ 21 05 82, telex 5214) all have booths at the airport. In town, Europcar is on the western end of Blvd du 13 Janvier while Avis is at 252 Blvd du 13 Janvier, next door to Café Santa Fé and across the street from Hertz. A Toyota Starlet with air-con costs roughly CFA 25,000 per day plus petrol if you travel 150 km. Other agencies to enquire about are Transcar (☎ 21 45 40) and Loc-Auto (☎ 21 42 50) on Blvd du 13 Janvier.

AROUND LOMÉ
Davié
If you're driving north from Lomé, stop off on the way in Davié (dah-vee-AY) for a look at the unusual cemetery, with gravestones depicting the occupation of the deceased (for example, a chauffeur's grave will have a steering wheel).

Lake Togo
This bilharzia-free lake is 30 km east of Lomé and is part of the inland lagoon which stretches all the way from Lomé to Aného. The lake is good for sailing, sailboarding and

water-skiing. You can lunch or stay overnight here as well as hire a pirogue for a ride across the lake to Togoville.

Places to Stay & Eat There are three hotels on the southern side of Lake Togo. From Lomé, the first one you'll come to is *L'Auberge du Lac*, which is about halfway to Aného and is signposted well on the Lomé to Cotonou highway. It's one km north thereof, just outside the village of Kpéssi (pay-SEE). The Auberge is beautifully situated among palm trees on an elevated knoll overlooking the lake. It has a friendly manager, a restaurant, and spacious comfortable bungalows with two beds and private baths for CFA 7000. Discounts, however, are usually offered as business is slow. Most dishes are in the CFA 1100 to CFA 2000 range.

Several km further on the Lomé to Cotonou highway you'll find the cosy, well-marked *Hôtel Suisse-Castel* (☎ 35 00 07) in Agbodrafo village, 30 metres from the water's edge. Popular with Germans, it has modestly priced rooms for CFA 4000 with fans and shared baths, CFA 5000 with private bath, and CFA 7000 with air-con. Most dishes on the menu are in the CFA 1000 to CFA 3000 range. Public canoes for Togoville leave periodically throughout the day from here and cost CFA 600 return.

The 'top' hotel on the lake is the French-run *Hôtel du Lac* (☎ 35 00 05), a bit further east and well off the main highway. Facilities include a good restaurant, a saltwater pool (CFA 700 for nonguests), sailboards (CFA 3000 per hour), speed boats with water-skis (CFA 3000 per trip) and sailboats for hire. Air-con singles/doubles cost CFA 14,000/ 19,000; they also offer weekends specials (eg CFA 26,000 for two people with full board) on occasion. The menu du jour is CFA 5000, but you can get snacks at the bar.

Getting There & Away The cheapest way to get to the lake from Lomé is to hop on a minibus to Aného and get off at the entrance point for whichever hotel you choose. Your driver should know where to drop you; if not, look for the hotels' signs.

Togoville

On the northern banks of Lake Togo, Togoville is mainly interesting for its history. It was from here that voodoo practitioners were taken as slaves to Haiti, now a major centre for voodoo. And it was here in 1884 that chief Mlapa III signed a peace treaty with the German explorer Nachtigal and gave the Germans rights over all of Togo. Today, the only attractions are the chief's house, the church and the Artisanal. The **Artisanal** is between the village's main pier and the nearby church. The art co-operative consists of several buildings with artisans working in each; most of the men are wood carvers and their carvings are not cheap or of high quality, so chances are you'll be disappointed. Regardless, you're sure to be pestered by young boys insisting on being your guide. The nearby **church** has some beautiful stained-glass windows and pictures of the gruesome deaths of some famous African martyrs.

About 100 metres west of the church is the chief's house, called the **Maison Royal**. It's an uninteresting modern structure with a gold Mercedes in front. The only reason to come here is to meet the chief, Mlapa V Moyennant, who will gladly show you a room ('museum') with some interesting old photos of his grandfather as well as his throne. A gift may be expected. The best time to visit is on early Saturday morning when he holds court (*fait la justice*) on the patio of his compound. Check out the small market, which is a 100 metres north of the church. Market day is Wednesday but there are always a few people there.

For something unusual, from Togoville (or from Agbodrafo across the lagoon) you could offer one of the local fisher people a small *cadeau* (gift) to take you with them on their daily fishing excursion, departing around 5.30 am and returning around noon.

Places to Stay & Eat The cheapest accommodation is at the dumpy *Auberge l'Arbre à Palabre* (or Chez Polica), two blocks east of the market. It has about six cell-like rooms without electricity which rent for CFA 5000 a month, so you should be able to get one for CFA 1000 or so. It has a spacious area for eating, but for food you'll have to look around the quarter for an African woman to fix you a meal.

The best place to stay by far is the surprisingly nice *Hôtel Nachtigal* (☎ 21 64 82), a new two-storey hotel 100 metres west of the market. Spotlessly clean small rooms with fans and private baths cost CFA 5300 (CFA 7500 to CFA 8500 with air-con). There is also a large attractive paillote where you can get sandwiches for CFA 1000 to CFA 2000 or a decent three-course meal for CFA 4500. You can play ping-pong here and then go have a drink at the nearby *Bar Happy Day* or the *Jerusalem Bar-Dancing* next door.

Getting There & Away Getting here from Lomé is a bit of a hassle. You must either go eastward all the way to Aného and around the lagoon and then back (westward) for 10 km or so to Togoville or, much quicker, go about halfway to Aného and stop off at Hôtel Suisse-Castel in Agebodrafo. From the hotel you can take a collective canoe across the lagoon for CFA 600 return; the trip takes about 20 minutes and canoes leave periodically during the day. You can also get to Togoville by bush taxi from Aného, about 12 km away. If you hire a canoe to yourself, with hard bargaining expect to pay about CFA 1500 for the trip over and back.

Vogan & Agoégan

The famous Friday **market** at Vogan is one of the largest and most colourful in Togo and should not be missed. It's not a good place for artisan goods other than pots but for more practical items it's great. There's also a well-stocked voodoo section. The activity starts fairly early in the morning and lasts until mid-afternoon. If you stay for the night, try *Hôtel Medius* (☎ 33 10 10) not far from the market. It has clean rooms with fans for around CFA 3500 and a bar-restaurant.

On Monday, there's also a **market** in Agoégan, which is on the intercoastal canal dividing Togo and Benin and is less than half an hour's taxi ride from Aného. It's one of

the most picturesque in Togo, relatively untouched by foreign influences.

Getting There & Away The road from Lomé is paved all the way and the trip takes one hour and costs about CFA 400. Go to Aného and take a left (north) to Vogan, circling around the lagoon. On Friday morning, finding a minibus in Lomé at Station d'Akodessewa direct to Vogan should be no problem; otherwise, change in Aného. From Togoville, you can find bush taxis headed here only on Friday morning. Instead of returning by bush taxi directly to Lomé, you could take a taxi south to Togoville, cross the lake in a pirogue and hail a bush taxi from there.

The South

ANÉHO

A 45-minute ride east of Lomé brings you to Aného (ah-NAY-hoh), the colonial capital of Togo until 1920. The Benin border is two km beyond. Aného looks like it's going with the wind but it can be interesting to walk around and look at the **old buildings** that are still standing. Particularly interesting are the daily activities of the **fishers**, including their deft navigation of the boats and the hauling in of the nets in the late afternoon. The major attraction is the **beach**. The best place to swim is off a strip of sand that separates the lagoon and the ocean, which can easily be seen from the bridge over the lagoon. Be careful because the undertow is quite swift.

At night, Aného comes alive with a surprising amount of activity for such a tiny town. Along the streets you'll hear music playing and find vendors selling a variety of food, including agouti (bush rat). The street is as good a place as any to eat, have a few beers and watch people.

The town is cut in two by the lagoon's outlet to the ocean; the more modern section is on the western side of the bridge. There you'll find the market, taxi stand, SGGG department store, bank, petrol station and the post office.

Guin Festival

If you're in Togo in the second week in September, don't miss the Guin Festival in Glidji, four km north of Aného. The festival lasts four days, starting on the first or second Thursday of the month and ending on a Sunday. Opening day is attended with great pomp and ceremony; it's when the locals determine the colour of the sacred stone that will be used in the various celebrations. If it's white, the year will be good; if black, the opposite. Blue denotes a rainy year and red indicates the year will be dangerous. A seat in the arena costs only CFA 100. You'll see parades of women in traditional dress, adorned with coral necklaces and silver ornaments in their hair. On Friday the people pay tribute to the elders, while the last two days are for celebrating, with much dancing and drinking. Since voodoo is the traditional religion, people going into trances are a common, but bizarre, sight. ■

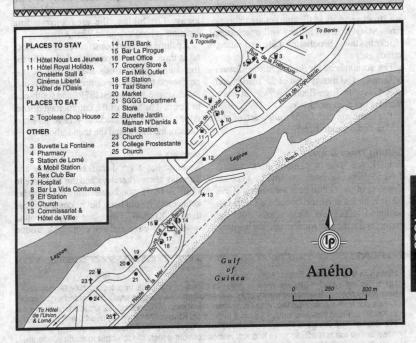

PLACES TO STAY

1   Hôtel Nous Les Jeunes
11 Hôtel Royal Holiday,
    Omelette Stall &
    Cinéma Liberté
12 Hôtel de l'Oasis

PLACES TO EAT

2   Togolese Chop House

OTHER

3   Buvette La Fontaine
4   Pharmacy
5   Station de Lomé
    & Mobil Station
6   Rex Club Bar
7   Hospital
8   Bar La Vida Contunua
9   Elf Station
10 Church
13 Commissariat &
    Hôtel de Ville

14 UTB Bank
15 Bar La Pirogue
16 Post Office
17 Grocery Store &
    Fan Milk Outlet
18 Elf Station
19 Taxi Stand
20 Market
21 SGGG Department
    Store
22 Buvette Jardin
    Maman N'Danida &
    Shell Station
23 Church
24 College Prostestante
25 Church

To Vogan & Togoville

To Benin

Rue de la Préfecture

Route de Togo-Benin

Rue de l'Hôpital

Lagoon

Beach

Lagoon

Route de Togo-Benin

Route de la Mer

Gulf of Guinea

Aného

0   250   500 m

To Hôtel de l'Union & Lomé

TOGO

Places to Stay

The best place to stay is *Hôtel de l'Oasis* (☎ 31 01 25). Rooms with fans and interior baths cost CFA 4300, or CFA 6300 with air-con, but they're usually all taken on the weekends. It's on the water's edge 40 metres east of the bridge, and has beautiful views.

The dumpy looking *Hôtel Royal Holiday* (☎ 31 00 27), two blocks away on a noisy street, asks a ridiculously high CFA 6300 for a large, clean, room with private bath (often

no water) and fan (CFA 7300 with air-con), but you can bargain the price down by 25% or more. If not, *Nous Les Jeunes*, a private home (blue and white) east of the gare routière, has small rooms (CFA 2500) with saggy beds and bucket showers.

The *Hôtel de l'Union* (☎ 31 00 69, fax 31 10 47), at the western entrance to town on the main highway and well away from the water, is overpriced at CFA 13,500 with air-con and bath.

Places to Eat & Drink

On the eastern side of the bridge, there's a good pâte and sauce lady hidden behind the Hôtel Royal Holiday. You have to go to the end of the alley beside SCOA to find her. Several blocks further east, there's a woman who serves food in a no-name hut facing the Buvette Fontaine. She's 200 metres due east of the gare routière and just east of the intersection with the road north to Vogan.

On the western side of the bridge, there are street vendors in the market area across from SGGG. At night they sell omelettes, chicken, stews, brochettes, pâte and sauce, salads etc.

For a drink, head for *Buvette Jardin Maman N'Danida*, 150 metres west of the market and SGGG on the Togo-Benin highway. It has a relaxing open-air ambience.

For dancing, try *Le Maquis* east of the bridge down a side street.

Getting There & Away

From Lomé, take a minibus from Station d'Akodessewa or from the smaller Gare de Cotonou in the centre near the market (CFA 300). Vehicles in Aného bound for Lomé can be found at the taxi stand across from the market and at the gare routière near the hospital.

KPALIMÉ

A two-hour ride (120 km) north-west of Lomé brings you to Kpalimé (pah-lee-may), a mountainous cacao and coffee region, considered by many to be the prettiest area in Togo. With an altitude of 250 metres, Kpalimé is noted for its mild climate, market, artisans' co-operative, the refreshing Campement de Klouto nestled high up in the cool outlying hills, fantastic butterfly areas nearby, and Mt Agou (986 metres), Togo's highest peak, 20 km away. For hiking, the area surrounding Kpalimé is hard to beat in West Africa.

Kpalimé is spread out so covering it on foot takes time. The city's pattern is defined by the four major paved roads leading out of it – north-west towards the campement, north-east to Atakpamé, south-west to Ho, and south-east to Lomé. The heart of the commercial district is the triangular area marked by the Rond-Point Texaco, the mairie and the train station.

Markets

Kpalimé has a good market. Saturday and Tuesday are market days and the best time to visit. A fairly good selection of Ghanaian kente cloth is sold here, but prices are higher than in Kumasi. There are people around town who weave and sell cloth; ask around

Hiking in the Kpalimé Area

Hiking in the woody Kpalimé area is great because of the thick vegetation, hilly terrain and noticeably cooler climate. But what's unique are the butterflies. Some areas are loaded with them. Take a taxi from Kpalimé up the hill to Campement de Klouto (670 metres), 12 km to the north-west of Kpalimé. From the campement you can hike up **Mt Klouto** (741 metres) nearby and look over into Ghana. The village of Klouto, some 600 metres from the campement, is the starting point for hikes to see the butterflies. You'll find any number of young men all too eager to guide you to the butterfly areas. Taking a guide often destroys the peacefulness of the hike but you'll need one if you want to go to the best sites for seeing butterflies. Potential guides will demand a fortune but with bargaining you can get the rate down to CFA 200 per person in a group. Afterwards, you could then hike alone and take some back routes down to Kpalimé. Getting lost shouldn't be a problem if you know the general direction.

One km or so before the campement you'll pass the paved turn-off for **Château Viale**. It's an astonishing medieval-style fortress of stone built by a visionary Frenchman in 1944 as a retreat for his wife. She spent three days there, then split for France. On a clear day, there are views of Lake Volta (Ghana), but since the government purchased the château it has been off limits to the public. It's now a frequent weekend retreat for Eyadéma.

Alternatively, you could climb the **Pic d'Agou** (986 metres), 20 km south-east of Kpalimé. On a clear day you can see Lake Volta but during the harmattan season the views are disappointing. To get there, take a taxi to the base of the mountain at Agou Nyogbo where the Hôpital Évangélique is located. Finding for their shops. More famous than the market is the long-standing Centre Artisanal, about 1.5 km north from the centre on the road to Campement de Klouto. You'll find a vast array of wooden carvings, including chiefs' chairs and tables carved out of solid blocks of wood, as well as pottery, macramé and batiks. It's open Monday to Saturday from 7 am to noon and 2.30 to 5.30 pm, Sunday and holidays from 8.30 am to 1 pm.

Places to Stay – bottom end

The cheap, dumpy, mud-constructed *Chez Solo* has cell-like dirty rooms with filthy shared toilets for CFA 1200 (CFA 1500 with fan). However, Solo sometimes offers discounts. It's on the south-eastern side of town on the Route du Zongo, one km from the centre.

The friendly *Auberge Amoto Zomanyi* (☎ 41 01 94), on the south-western outskirts of town on the road to Ho, is a 20-minute walk to the centre. It has clean, spacious singles/doubles with fans and shared baths for CFA 2000/3000 (CFA 4000 with a large bed and interior bath), and they're likely to offer you a discount immediately. You can get food here as well.

In the centre, you can't beat the long-standing ever-popular *Hôtel Domino* (☎ 41 01 87), which faces the Texaco Rond-Point.

Its small rooms with fans and clean shared baths cost CFA 2500 (CFA 3000 with private bath and CFA 6000 with air-con).

In the village of Klouto there's the friendly *Auberge des Papillons*. It's fairly primitive but clean. A double costs CFA 1500, and cheap meals are available.

Places to Stay – middle

For solitude or a cooler climate, stay at the 16-room *Campement de Klouto*, which was a German hospital before WW I. It's on top of a mountain, 12 km north-west of Kpalimé on the road to Ghana. The woody tropical environment up there is simply fabulous. It is quiet, shady, moist and cool, with a constant breeze. Fairly large singles/doubles cost CFA 4000/5500. You can also camp here for about CFA 1000 a person.

All of the mid-range hotels are north of town. The best for the money is *Auberge Don Berger* (☎ 41 02 18), one km north of the centre on Rue Missahoe towards the campement. The spacious but somewhat bare rooms with fans and hot-water baths cost CFA 3300 (CFA 5000 with air-con).

Another possibility is *Hôtel La Détente* (☎ 41 01 43), 100 metres off the Route d'Atakpamé, about 1.5 km from the town

a shared cab (CFA 200) headed to Agou can be difficult except on Friday, which is market day there, so you may have to charter one. In Agou hire a boy to guide you for the first hour of hiking. After that just ask people along the way. The walk to the top takes three hours. The top itself is disappointing because of the antenna, fences and guards, but the walk up is peaceful and beautiful. Bring your passport because there's a sensitive TV station antenna on top and police guards there may ask to see your documents. Alternatively, you could take a taxi all the way to the top of the mountain (about CFA 3000). From there you could hike back down to the main Kpalimé to Lomé highway.

Another alternative would be to go to **Les Cascades de Kpimé** (Kpimé Falls) north of town. You can get there by taking a taxi or a minibus headed for Atakpamé. These very high falls are fairly spectacular during the rainy season and almost bone dry the rest of the year. From the base you could hike to the top of the cascades, where there's a lake and a panoramic view, and then hike back to Kpalimé, perhaps taking a remote back route. Going north from Kpalimé on the Atakpamé road, after nine km you'll come to Kpimé-Séva, a village with a large sign announcing the falls. You can see them clearly in the distance. There's no need for a guide; just walk westward down the main track for 30 minutes until you reach a closed gate, then walk through a gap in it. The base of the falls is 100 metres or so away.

Yet another possibility would be to climb in the **Plateau de Danyi** area. To get there, continue north another nine km beyond Kpimé-Séva to Adéta and take a left there on a tarred road for the plateau. You'll find the seven-room *Motel Concordia* in N'Digbé, which is on the plateau, and a few km further both the *Benedictine Convent* and the *Benedictine Monastery*. These peaceful places have accommodation and serve meals. ■

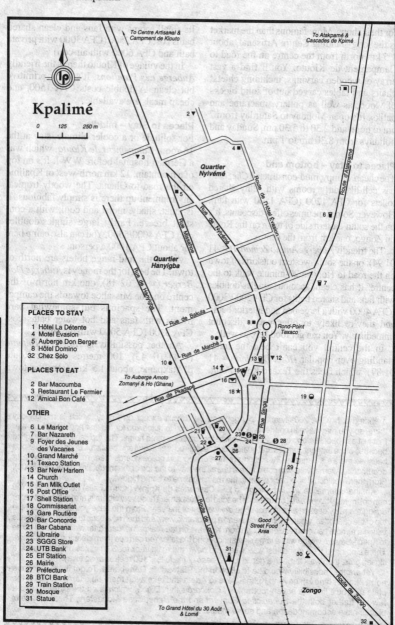

Kpalimé

0   125   250 m

To Centre Artisanal &
Campment de Klouto

To Atakpamé &
Cascades de Kpimé

Quartier
Nylvémé

Quartier
Hanyigba

Rond-Point
Texaco

Rue de Misahoe

Rue de Hanyigba

Rue de Bakula

Rue de Marché

Rue de Pkadape

Rue de Lome

Rue Singa

Route de Zongo

Route de l'Hôtel Evasion

Rue de Nyatanu

Route d'Atakpamé

To Auberge Amoto
Zomanyi & Ho (Ghana)

Good
Street Food
Area

Zongo

To Grand Hôtel du 30 Août
& Lomé

PLACES TO STAY
1   Hôtel La Détente
3   Motel Évasion
5   Auberge Don Berger
8   Hôtel Domino
32 Chez Solo

PLACES TO EAT
2   Bar Macoumba
3   Restaurant Le Fermier
12 Amical Bon Café

OTHER
6   Le Marigot
7   Bar Nazareth
9   Foyer des Jeunes
    des Vacanes
10 Grand Marché
11 Texaco Station
13 Bar New Harlem
14 Church
15 Fan Milk Outlet
16 Post Office
17 Shell Station
18 Commissariat
19 Gare Routière
20 Bar Concorde
21 Bar Cabana
22 Librairie
23 SGGG Store
24 UTB Bank
25 Elf Station
26 Mairie
27 Préfecture
28 BTCI Bank
29 Train Station
30 Mosque
31 Statue

centre and marked with a small sign on the highway. Its rooms with fans and shared baths cost CFA 3500 (CFA 6000 with air-con and private bath). This is a quiet, pleasant place and food is available. The mosquitoes can sometimes be bad here, so bring a mosquito net or bug repellent. It's similar in many respects to the tranquil but inconveniently located *Motel Évasion* (☎ 41 01 85), one km due north of town on a dirt road, between Rue Missahoe and the Route Atakpamé. Singles/doubles with fans cost CFA 3550/4900 (CFA 6900 with air-con), but discounts are offered. The bungalows are attractive and you can get food as well.

Places to Stay – top end

The tranquil three-storey *Grand Hôtel du 30 Août* (☎ 41 00 95; cards AE, D, V), two km south of town, has large air-con singles/doubles for CFA 6500/8500. The nicest hotel in the area, *L'Auberge de Bethania* (☎ Lomé 21 35 51), has bungalows, a pool and tennis courts, but it's 30 km south of Kpalimé on the road to Lomé.

Places to Eat

Several women on Route du Zongo, 100 metres south-east of the mairie, serve cheap Togolese food – CFA 200 for sauce de poisson. If you're staying at *Chez Solo*, you can eat there. A typical meal costs CFA 350. There are also women selling similar fare, including delicious yam chips, in the heart of town a block south of the Rond-Point. That's where you'll also find *Amical Bon Café* where meals range from CFA 300 to CFA 1300. If you're looking for a good guide, the owner can introduce you to Ali Samo Souliman, a pleasant young man who frequents this place and the Domino.

For an up-market restaurant serving Togolese fare, try the attractive open-air *Bar Macoumba* on the northern outskirts of town. The tempting menu includes poulet Togolais for CFA 1600 and gbomadess for CFA 3000 as well as Continental selections.

For European food, two of the best places for the price are *Auberge Don Berger* and *Restaurant Le Fermier*. The latter, open for lunch and dinner every day except Monday,

has excellent food and the best ice cream in town, CFA 100 per tiny scoop. It's 250 metres north of the Auberge, then 50 metres left down a dirt road. Tourists usually eat at the *Grand Hôtel du 30 Août*, which has a big thatched-roof eating area and dance floor.

Entertainment

The best place for dancing is *Le Marigot*, a new open-air 'boîte' on the road to Kpalimé. Very African in ambience, it has a large dancing area with good African sounds and is the most lively on weekends. *Bar Macoumba* is another but it's better for drinks than dancing. For a disco, try the *Akpéssé* at the 30 Août; it's liveliest on weekends too. The lively *Bar Concorde* is good for drinks any night and has dancing on weekends. It's near the centre, just west of the mairie. Also near the centre and a bit nicer, is the *Bar Nazareth* on the Atakpamé road, not far from the Rond-Point.

Getting There & Away

The cheapest and most interesting way to travel from Lomé to Kpalimé is by train. The trip takes about six hours and costs CFA 550. Trains leave from Lomé every day at 6.30 am and from Kpalimé around 1.20 pm. The station in Kpalimé is two blocks east of the post office. Most people, however, take a minibus. To get one in Lomé, go to Station de Kpalimé on Route de Kpalimé; they charge CFA 850 and take about 2½ hours to do the 120-km trip, with about four police checks along the way. In Kpalimé the station is in the heart of town, two blocks east of the Shell station. Minibuses for Lomé start leaving around 4.30 am, with the last departure around 6.30 pm.

If you're headed to Atakpamé (CFA 700), you'll find a minibus at the station more easily in the morning than in the afternoon. The trip takes two hours. You can also get minibuses here direct to Kara (CFA 2500) and to the Ghana border (CFA 300), which closes at 6 pm sharp, as well as direct to Ho (Ghana). There are only one or two minibuses every morning direct to Ho and they can easily take up to three hours or more to fill up. The fare is CFA 900

TOGO

and the border crossing is usually hassle free but time consuming.

Getting Around

To get from Kpalimé to the Klouto area, most people charter a taxi. The price should be no more than CFA 1500 but the drivers will ask for up to CFA 3000. At the campement, there's a telephone for calling taxis to pick visitors up. Taking a shared taxi is much cheaper, usually CFA 125 from town to the police checkpoint. From there it's an easy walk to either the campement or Klouto village. To get a taxi back to Kpalimé, go to the checkpoint and wait for shared taxis to pass by. They are usually full, so waits of up to an hour are common.

ATAKPAMÉ

A 2½ to three-hour ride north of Lomé brings you to Atakpamé (ah-TAC-pah-may). The favourite residence of the German administrators, it is at 500 metres altitude in the heart of a mountainous area. It's also the centre of Togo's cotton-growing belt and has a textile mill. You may see tourist posters in Lomé of dancers on stilts, sometimes five metres high; they come from here. There's a good public pool near the gare routière at the SOTOCO complex; the cost is CFA 500 but it's frequently not functioning.

The southern entrance to town is marked by a T-junction, the east leg of which bypasses the city and continues on to Kara. The north leg goes into town towards the market, which is the heart of the city, passing six hotels and the gare routière.

Les Cascades d'Ayomé, about 17 km south-west of town on the asphalt road to Kpalimé, are picturesque in the rainy season.

Places to Stay – bottom end

The Peace Corps' *La Maison de Passage* is still open to travellers, so treat the volunteers well as fewer and fewer of these rest houses accept travellers. The cost is CFA 1500 a person, which includes a mattress with sheets and mosquito nets. It's a yellow and blue house centrally located two blocks south and up a hill from Station de Kpalimé; everybody in that quarter knows where it is.

On the southern outskirts of town on the road to Kara is the Total station and a no-name adjoining *hotel*. Its 10 rooms with shared baths are small, dark and cell-like but the cost is only CFA 1500 (CFA 2000 with fan), plus there's a bar at the petrol station and cheap restaurants nearby. For a slightly larger room, try the *Auberge Le Retour*, which is across the highway from the main gare routière. Rooms with bucket showers cost CFA 2000, but there are no fans or running water. Nearby, 150 metres north of the gare routière and 75 metres to the east, you'll find the poorly marked *Centre Communautaire des Affaires Sociales*. This dormitory-like place has no restaurant but its bare clean rooms with shared baths, fans and one or two beds are a good deal at CFA 2000 (CFA 3000 with air-con and private bath).

A much better place with a pleasant, relaxing ambience is the homy *Hôtel Miva*. Entering town from the south, you'll see the sign on the left 100 metres north of the T-junction where the international route takes its sharp turn right (east) for Kara. It has three, small, spotless singles/doubles with fans and clean shared baths for CFA 3000/3500.

Places to Stay – top end

The best is the *Hôtel Roc* (☎ 40 02 37), just up the hill from Station de Lomé. It's on a plateau with a panoramic view of the city and surrounding hills. Air-con singles/doubles cost about CFA 7300/9600 including tax.

Hôtel Le Kapokier (☎ 40 02 13), which is much inferior, has the advantage of being closer to the centre, on the main drag 200 metres east of the market. It has decent spacious air-con rooms with private baths for CFA 5000 and a terrace bar-restaurant.

Relais des Plateaux (☎ 40 02 32), on the main drag between Hôtel Le Kapokier and the gare routière, is more expensive and no better. Its bar-restaurant has similar prices. Rooms with fans and interior showers and basins for one/two people cost CFA 4500/5900 (CFA 5900/6400 with air-con) and

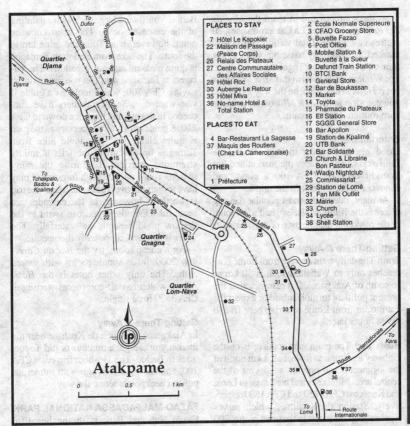

PLACES TO STAY

7 Hôtel Le Kapokier
22 Maison de Passage
   (Peace Corps)
26 Relais des Plateaux
27 Centre Communautaire
   des Affaires Sociales
28 Hôtel Roc
30 Auberge Le Retour
35 Hôtel Miva
36 No-name Hotel &
   Total Station

PLACES TO EAT

4 Bar-Restaurant La Sagesse
37 Maquis des Routiers
   (Chez La Camerounaise)

OTHER

1 Préfecture

2 École Normale Superieure
3 CFAO Grocery Store
5 Buvette Fazao
6 Post Office
8 Mobile Station &
   Buvette à la Sueur
9 Defunct Train Station
10 BTCI Bank
11 General Store
12 Bar de Boukassan
13 Market
14 Toyota
15 Pharmacie du Plateaux
16 Elf Station
17 SGGG General Store
18 Bar Apollon
19 Station de Kpalimé
20 UTB Bank
21 Bar Solidarité
23 Church & Librairie
   Bon Pasteur
24 Wadjo Nightclub
25 Commissariat
29 Station de Lomé
31 Fan Milk Outlet
32 Mairie
33 Church
34 Lycée
38 Shell Station

Atakpamé

0   0.5   1 km

seem overpriced as they are a bit cramped and are not particularly neat.

Places to Eat

A great place for African food is *Buvette à la Sueur*, just behind the Mobil station near Hôtel Kapokier. During the day you'll find several women here with four or five sauces for sale, and if you order a drink you can eat inside at the buvette. For Western-style food, you'll have to pay more. One of the best places for the price is *Bar-Restaurant La Sagesse* on Rue Djama, 100 metres north of the market. This rustic place, which is open from 11 am to 2 pm

and from 6 pm to midnight, serves surprisingly good food. There are lots of choices, mostly around CFA 1500, and the service is efficient. *Bar Apollon*, which is just west of the market and down the hill, is mainly for drinks and serves no food but they'll run and get you some foufou if you ask.

These places are better for food than the *Bar Solidarité*, which is 200 metres south of the market. This rustic bar is a better place for a large cold beer (CFA 245) than for a meal, which is typically limited to riz sauce for CFA 300 (CFA 800 with steak) and café au lait and bread for CFA 300.

At the southern end of town the *Maquis des Routiers* (or Chez La Camerounaise), 20 metres east of the Total station and poorly marked, is extremely basic but you can get four or five delicious Togolese dishes here. For Western-style food in this area, your best bet is *Hôtel Miva*. Also, on the way into town you can stop at the *Fan Milk* outlet near the gare routière for ice cream.

Entertainment

Good places for beer include the *Bar de Boukassan*, which faces the market and has draught beer for CFA 100 a glass, and *Buvette Fazao*, a block to the north.

At night, one of the most popular dancing places is the *Wadjo Nightclub*, half a km south of the market in the direction of the mairie.

Getting There & Away

Train The daily train service from Lomé now reaches only to Wahala, which is 50 km or so south of Atakpamé. If it resumes after the present political turmoil subsides, expect the 7 am train from Lomé to arrive here five to seven hours later.

Bush Taxi The main gare routière is on the highway leading into town, half a km north of the T-junction and one km south-east of the central area. Minibuses and bush taxis to Lomé and Kara cost CFA 1150 and CFA 1800 respectively. Station de Kpalimé, which serves Kpalimé and Badou, is in the town centre, 200 metres south of the market. Minibuses charge CFA 700 to either town and leave fairly frequently throughout the day to Kpalimé and less frequently to Badou. In Lomé you'll find minibuses for Atakpamé at Gare Routière du Lycée, not Gare de Kara. The trip from Lomé takes about three hours. Roads are tarred and in good condition to Lomé, Kpalimé and Badou but the stretch between Atakpamé and Kara is now full of potholes.

BADOU

Badou, in the heart of the cacao area, is 88 km west of Atakpamé by paved road. The major attraction is **Les Cascades d'Akloa**, south-east of town. Just before entering Badou, you'll see a large rock with a painting of the cascades on it. The main entrance point, however, is at Tomagbé, nine km to the south. The hike from Badou to Tomagbé is quite pleasant and not strenuous. The villagers at Tomagbé won't let you pass without paying CFA 500, which includes a guide if you want one. Some travellers have succeeded in negotiating the price down to CFA 250. A guide isn't really necessary as the path is quite clear. The 40-minute hike from Tomagbé up the hill to the falls is mildly strenuous, particularly during the rainy season. You'll pass through forests and may have to clamber over rocks and trees. The trip is worth it, however, as the cascades are beautiful. Once there you can swim in the shallow pond beneath the waterfalls. The water is safe and supposedly therapeutic.

For a cheap room, try the *Bar au Carrefour 2000*. It has simple rooms with shared baths. The only other hotel is the *Hôtel Abuta*, which has air-con rooms starting at CFA 3800 for a single.

Getting There & Away

In Atakpamé at Station de Kpalimé near the market you can get a minibus or old Toyota truck to Badou. The 1½-hour trip costs CFA 700, and the road is rough with numerous police checkpoints along the way.

FAZAO-MALFACASSA NATIONAL PARK

Fazao National Park is in the beautiful Malfacassa mountains of central Togo, an area of thickly wooded savannah with a variety of waterfalls, cliffs and rocky hills. Most people come for the wildlife. Park fees are paid at the lodge. The park itself is closed from September to the end of November, but there's nobody there to collect an entrance fee or tell you not to enter.

The park has not been well managed, so the chances of seeing much wildlife other than birds and monkeys are not good. Some of the other animals that you might see are waterbuck, duiker, hippo, oribi, buffalo, bush pig, wart hog, hyena, vervets, baboon and, if you're very lucky, elephant and lion.

Adjoining Fazao is the Malfacassa Zone

de Chasse. It's excellent for hiking as parts of it are amazingly beautiful. From the mountain tops, you can see the countryside roll away for many km. You might also see elephants; in the Malfacassa section they gather along the Sokodé to Bassar road during the dry season.

If you want to hike, ask the warden for permission; he may insist you take a guard. Hikers should fill up with water at the river in Malfacassa as other streams in the park aren't always reliable sources.

There are two major problems with hiking, however. The first is lions – hiking may be officially prohibited because of their presence. The second is that Malfacassa is a hunting zone and hiking during the dry season (when tourists are most likely to hunt) could be very risky. There are many good animal trails to follow in Malfacassa; the best run along the mountain tops and head south into the park. Orientation is easy even when you're hiking off trails because of the wide views from the mountain tops. In the rainy season, walking up the slopes through the tall grass takes considerable effort. Along the streams, the forest grows thick and gets difficult to penetrate.

Places to Stay & Eat

Perched on a hill and shaped like an African village, the *Hôtel du Fazao* has air-con rooms and an interesting restaurant. Occasionally in the evening, the locals perform dances of hunting scenes. Doubles cost CFA 13,000 and the mediocre meals are overpriced at CFA 4500. Call Hôtel Sarakawa in Lomé for reservations. You can also camp here for a small fee. It's open from December to May. There are no hotels in Malfacassa but there are many good places to camp along the mountain tops.

Getting There & Away

The marked turn-off for the Fazao section of the park is the village of Ayengré , on the international highway 50 km south of Sokodé. You may have to wait a while for a ride to the lodge at Fazao, although you could also walk the 23 km. If you're driving from Lomé, the trip should take about 4½ hours. To get to the

Malfacassa section, catch a minibus from Sokodé towards Bassar and get off at the semi-abandoned village of Malfacassa, which is at the pass over the highest point of these small mountains. From there, hike south of the highway into the park.

The North

SOKODÉ

There's nothing to see per se in Sokodé (SOAK-oh-day) other than the central market, which is particularly active on Mondays. Nevertheless, Togo's second-largest city, with some 45,000 inhabitants, mostly Muslims, is quite pleasant. The town is spread out with shade trees everywhere, especially colourful flamboyants and mango trees. So walking around you shouldn't get too hot. The heart of town is the T-junction just south of the market; the post office and a branch of the UTB bank are there as well.

Places to Stay – bottom end

Le Campement charges CFA 2000/2500 for spacious, neat, singles/doubles with clean sheets, fans and private baths. You can also get a set three-course meal here for CFA 1750. It's in a tranquil setting – up the hill from the douane on the southern end of town, a good walk from the centre.

Le Centre Communautaire des Affairs Sociales has even cheaper accommodation. It's on the far western side of town and has beds in dormitory rooms for CFA 1500, plus there's good street food outside. It's better than *Hôtel Tchaoudjo*, which is more conveniently located than either of these. It's next to the market and has grubby rooms, sagging mattresses and filthy outside bathrooms for CFA 1500 – the mosquitoes are free. *Hôtel Konodji*, which is a block south, offers equally bad rooms for the same price.

Hôtel Les Trois Fontaines, about 200 metres south of the city's main junction, represents much better value and is centrally located. It charges CFA 2300 for a large room with fan, fresh sheets and clean shared baths.

TOGO

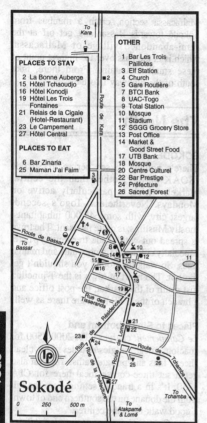

PLACES TO STAY

2 La Bonne Auberge
15 Hôtel Tchaoudjo
16 Hôtel Konodji
19 Hôtel Les Trois
    Fontaines
21 Relais de la Cigale
    (Hotel-Restaurant)
23 Le Campement
27 Hôtel Central

PLACES TO EAT

6 Bar Zinaria
25 Maman J'ai Faim

OTHER

1 Bar Les Trois
   Paillotes
3 Elf Station
4 Church
5 Gare Routière
7 BTCI Bank
8 UAC-Togo
9 Total Station
10 Mosque
11 Stadium
12 SGGG Grocery Store
13 Post Office
14 Market &
    Good Street Food
17 UTB Bank
18 Mosque
20 Centre Culturel
22 Bar Prestige
24 Préfecture
26 Sacred Forest

Sokodé

0   250   500 m

The ambience here is quite active but not noisy and you can get drinks at the bar as well as all kinds of food. Further south on the main highway the *Relais de la Cigale* has neat spartan rooms with fans and clean shared baths for CFA 2500.

If you're desperate, try *Hôtel Alhamdou*, one km east of the town centre near the stadium or, better, *La Bonne Auberge*, two km north of the centre. The former has simple rooms with fans for CFA 2000 (CFA 3000 with air-con), while the latter has small clean rooms with private bath and air-con for CFA 5300.

Places to Stay – top end

The city's top address is *Hôtel Central* (☎ 50 00 03), a large quiet hotel on shady grounds at the southern entrance to town on the main north-south drag. It has clean, spacious rooms and tiled baths with hot water for CFA 6000 (CFA 9000 for bungalows). There is also a thatched-roof bar and a decent restaurant.

Places to Eat & Drink

Hotels serve the best European food in town. The most attractive and relaxing hotel restaurant in town is the one at *Relais de la Cigale*. Most selections on the long menu are in the CFA 1500 to 2500 range. For the best genuine Togolese food, head for *Maman J'ai Faim*, on the southern side of town, about 200 metres east of Hôtel Central as the crow flies. Well known by taxi drivers, prices are low, eg CFA 300 for a filling meal of pâte or foufou with gboma sauce. For street food, try the area around the central market.

A good place for beer is *Bar Prestige*, on the main drag south of the central area. It's a lively open-air place with loud African music and small draught beers for CFA 100. If you're on the far northern side of town, check the *Bar Les Trois Paillotes*, which is well-marked on the main drag, over two km north of the central area. The *Bar Sans Souci*, on the same side of town, has good brochettes and cheap brew. If you're hot to go dancing, head for *Bar Zinaria* on Route de Bassar, on the western side of town near the gare routière. In addition to loud music it has food, typically a plat du jour for CFA 600.

Getting There & Away

The gare routière is several blocks west of the central market. Minibuses cost CFA 600 to Kara and CFA 2400 to Lomé. You may also find minivans in the centre around the market.

BASSAR

Renowned for its traditional hunters, Bassar is 57 km on asphalt road to the west of Sokodé. It is also the site of the annual yam *(igname)* festival in September, involving lots of native dancing, including fire dances, and traditional clothing.

The cheapest place to stay is *Le Campement*. If it's full, try the *Mission Catholique*. The best place is the state-run *Hôtel de Bassar*, but its bungalows are relatively expensive.

KARA

Formerly called Lama-Kara, Kara is in Kabyé country. Because President Eyadéma comes from Pya, a Kabyé village not far to the north-east, he has pumped a lot of money into Kara, including a second brewery, a modern radio station and, most impressively, the party headquarters. As a result, the town has grown quickly to about 40,000 people.

Laid out by the Germans on a spacious scale, it's a pleasant town. Much more interesting than Kara is the area to the north, where many tourists are headed.

The Mobil station intersection on the Route Internationale is where the paved roads east to Benin and west to Ghana begin. The gare routière, Station de Tomdé, is just to the right and the core central area is over half a km to the west. That's where you'll find the market; the big day is Tuesday.

Places to Stay – bottom end

The cheapest place to stay is the *Centre Communautaire des Affaires Sociales* (☎ 60 61 18), 100 metres east of the gare routière on the highway to Benin. This large, well-run centre with a bar-restaurant and TV charges CFA 1000 per person for a dorm bed in rooms with three bunk beds, clean sheets and fans. The shared bathrooms are clean. A private room with fan costs CFA 2000 (CFA 4000 with air-con and bath). A notch up price-wise is the popular, well-maintained *Auberge de la CNTT* (☎ 60 62 32), on the south side of town on the main road, about one km south of the gare. It charges CFA 2500/3500 for singles/doubles with fans (CFA 5000/6000 with air-con). There are also several dorm rooms with very clean private baths; CFA 1500 per person.

West of the market in the direction of Hôtel Kara are several cheap hotels which are all fairly central. *Hôtel Dacoma* charges CFA 1000 for a room with reasonably clean sheets and baths but no fans. There's a bar and TV here. It's a block from *Hôtel Sapaw*, which

charges CFA 1500/2000 for plain, ventilated singles/doubles and clean shared baths with forceful cold showers (CFA 2500 with private bath and CFA 4500 with air-con). You can get food here as well. A block away is *Hôtel Idéal*; CFA 2300 for a large ventilated room. The sheets and bathrooms, however, are not so clean and the ambience here is a bit dreary.

Further west and about 100 metres south of Hôtel Kara down a dirt road is the small *Hôtel Le Coin*, which has a sign in front. This friendly, homy establishment charges CFA 1500 for a reasonably clean room with a fan and shared bath (CFA 3500 with air-con). You can't get food here but there is a TV room and drinks are available. Several hundred metres to the west, behind the SAFGRAD office, is the better known but more isolated *Hôtel Parisien*. Rooms here are a bit overpriced at CFA 3500 with fan (CFA 5500 with air-con), however, the restaurant and bar here are both popular.

Rooms at *Hôtel-Restaurant Mini-Rizzerie* (☎ 60 61 54) cost CFA 3500 with fan and CFA 5300 with air-con, and they are no better. However, it's much closer to the centre, several blocks north of the market, and there's a popular bar and restaurant. Another possibility is the Peace Corps' *Maison de Passage*. In the past the volunteers have charged CFA 1500 a person, but it's not clear whether they accept travellers any longer. To enquire, from the market head south on the paved road across the river and continue several hundred metres; the Maison de Passage is on your left and unmarked.

Places to Stay – top end

The *Hôtel Kara* (☎ 60 60 21/3, telex 7204) has a pool, tennis court, shops, nightclub and three classes of rooms, from CFA 18,500 to CFA 25,000 (singles) and CFA 21,500 to CFA 28,500 (doubles). It's on the road to the Ghanaian border, past the market and the BID bank. *Hôtel-Restaurant Le Jardin* is west from the market towards Hôtel Kara, just off the road on the left. This attractive, popular place with a garden ambience has four small pleasant rooms with air-con (CFA 5300), and Kara's top restaurant.

The tranquil *Hôtel Le Relais* (☎ 60 62 98) is much cheaper but not nearly so nice. The rooms, which are a bit dark, cost CFA 2800 with fan and CFA 4300 with air-con. They have fresh sheets, fans and private tiled baths. You can also eat here; the fixed three-course menu costs about CFA 2400. It's half a km down a dirt road leading north from the gare routière; follow the signs.

Places to Eat

African Kara has a number of dirt cheap places serving superb Togolese food. One of the most popular is the open-air *Bar Colombia*. The women pound away all morning on the corn and millet; by lunchtime it's hard to find a seat. Their specialities are pâte and foufou. It's one block west of the market; you can't miss it. *Zongo Bar*, two blocks west of the market and south of the Colombia, is run by the same family and just as good, with a variety of Togolese sauces to choose from. Both places are open until around 10.30 pm (closed Sunday). In the same area, 50 metres in front of the Colombia in the direction of the market, is a Ewé lady who makes reputedly the best pâte in town.

European For reasonable prices and good quality, you can't beat *Le Château* (☎ 60 60

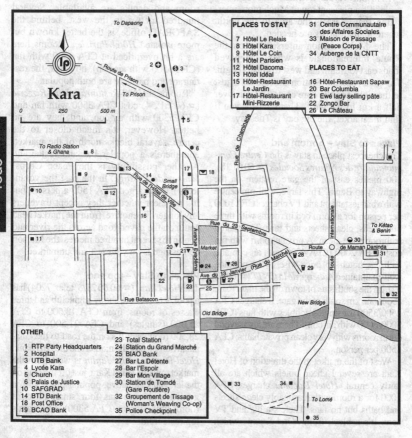

Kara

0   250   500 m

To Dapaong
To Prison
Route de Prison
To Radio Station & Ghana
Rue de l'Hôtel de Ville
Small Bridge
Rue de Chaminade
Avenue Eyadema
Market
Rue du 23 Septembre
Ave du 13 Janvier (Rue du Marché)
Rue Batascon
Old Bridge
New Bridge
Route Internationale
Route de Maman Daninda
To Kétao & Benin
To Lomé

PLACES TO STAY
7   Hôtel Le Relais
8   Hôtel Kara
9   Hôtel Le Coin
11 Hôtel Parisien
12 Hôtel Dacoma
13 Hôtel Idéal
15 Hôtel-Restaurant Le Jardin
17 Hôtel-Restaurant Mini-Rizzerie
31 Centre Communautaire des Affaires Sociales
33 Maison de Passage (Peace Corps)
34 Auberge de la CNTT

PLACES TO EAT
16 Hôtel-Restaurant Sapaw
20 Bar Columbia
21 Ewé lady selling pâte
22 Zongo Bar
26 Le Château

OTHER
1   RTP Party Headquarters
2   Hospital
3   UTB Bank
4   Lycée Kara
5   Church
6   Palais de Justice
10 SAFGRAD
14 BTD Bank
18 Post Office
19 BCAO Bank
23 Total Station
24 Station du Grand Marché
25 BIAO Bank
27 Bar La Détente
28 Bar l'Espoir
29 Bar Mon Village
30 Station de Tomdé (Gare Routière)
32 Groupement de Tissage (Woman's Weaving Co-op)
35 Police Checkpoint

TOGO

40), an attractive pub-restaurant 50 metres east of the market on Rue d'SGGG. It has ice-cold pressions for CFA 200, sandwiches for CFA 900 to CFA 1600, and an extensive menu with both African and Continental dishes. It also serves expensive desserts such as crêpes suzettes and ice-cream sundaes for CFA 850. The popular balcony is the best place in town for people-watching.

Another winner is the long-standing *Mini-Rizzerie* on Ave Eyadéma, about 250 metres north of the market and opposite the post office. Except for breakfast, which costs CFA 850, the restaurant is reasonably priced with most dishes in the CFA 1000 to CFA 1600 range as well as sandwiches for CFA 600 to CFA 1200. It also serves three-course French meals for CFA 2500 and will prepare Togolese food if you order in advance.

The city's best restaurant is at *Hôtel-Restaurant Le Jardin*. The crêpe chocolat there is particularly good and well worth the price. For cheaper non-African fare, try the nearby *Hôtel-Restaurant Sapaw*.

For something special, try *La Paillote du Village*, a restaurant run by the French-run orphanage group SOS in Lassa, six km east of Kara on the road to Kétao and Benin. Open every day except Monday, it serves delicious French meals and wine in a tranquil setting and the proceeds go to the orphanage.

Entertainment

The hottest African nightclub in town is the *Bar l'Espoir*, half a km east of the market in the direction of the main gare routière. *Bar Mon Village*, a block away, is not nearly so lively these days. Both places are open every night. The disco at the *Hôtel Kara*, which is open only on weekends, has a cover charge of about CFA 500.

Things to Buy

For African fabrics and tablecloths check the Groupement de Tissage des Femmes de Kara on the eastern side of town. This women's co-operative was set up with the assistance of Peace Corps volunteers, and has assisted greatly in giving the women weavers an alternative source of income. It sells high-quality

pagnas for CFA 2500 to CFA 4000 and tablecloths for CFA 12,000 to CFA 15,000. From the Mobil station intersection, take the paved road east for 200 metres and just beyond Affaires Sociales turn right, heading south on a dirt road, and follow the signs.

Getting There & Away

The main gare routière is Station de Tomdé at the Mobil station intersection on the international highway. Minibuses cost CFA 2800 to Lomé and CFA 1560 to Dapaong. To Parakou in Benin, the 193-km trip can be easily done in one day, with taxi changes at the border and Djougou. The chances of making it in one day to Tamale (256 km) in Ghana are not as good. Both routes are paved only in Togo. Station du Grand Marché, in the centre next to the market, is better at night for catching vehicles as the other station is relatively dead at that time.

To rent a vehicle for the day, enquire at your hotel. One traveller reported that the cook at Hôtel Sapaw found her a Peugeot 504 and after some serious bargaining paid CFA 10,000 for the day, including the driver and petrol to Tamberma country and back.

AROUND KARA
Sarakawa

Sarakawa, 23 km to the north-west of Kara, is not worth a special visit, but if you pass through check out the huge monument commemorating the site where Eyadéma's plane crashed in 1974. The statue has Eyadéma pointing to the ground and saying, 'They almost killed me here'. To get there, take the international route north for about 10 km, then the paved highway westward for 13 km.

Mont Kabyé Area

Mont Kabyé is roughly 15 km north-east of Kara (as the crow flies) in a hilly region. Try not to miss travelling in this area as it is one of the most scenic in Togo. Typically, the first stop is **Landa**, a village 15 km north-east of Kara and several km off the paved highway towards Benin. The women there make artisan goods that some people find interesting. Four km further east is **Kétao**, which is

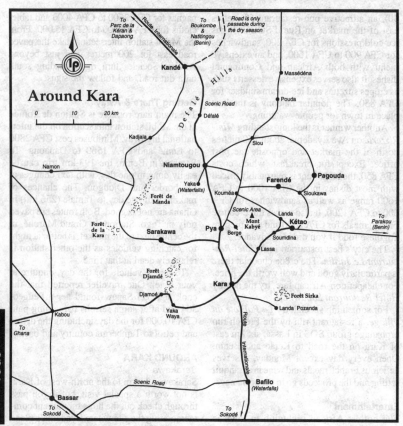

Around Kara

To Parc de la
Kéran & Dapaong

Route Internationale

To Boukombe
&
Natitingou
(Benin)

Road is only passable during the dry season

Kandé

Défalé Hills

Masséddéna

Pouda

Scenic Road

Défalé

Kadjala

Siou

Namon

Niamtougou

Farendé

Pagouda

Yaka
(Waterfalls)

Kouméa

Sloukawa

Forêt de
Manda

Scenic Area

Landa

Kétao

To
Parakou
(Benin)

Forêt
de la
Kara

Sarakawa

Pya

Mont
Kabyé

Berge

Soumdina

Lassa

Forêt
Djamdé

Kara

Djamdé

Forêt Sirka

Kabou

Yaka
Waya

Landa Pozanda

To
Ghana

Route Internationale

Scenic Road

Bassar

Bafilo
(Waterfalls)

To
Sokodé

To
Sokodé

0   10   20 km

TOGO

---

on the main highway. The huge Wednesday market there is fascinating and the second-largest in Togo. From there you could head north on a dirt road for about 20 km or so to **Pagouda** where you can hear traditional music if you ask the chief and if the musicians are in town. The main attractions there, however, are the scenic mountains, including Mont Kabyé, and the stunningly located tourist hotel. From there you can proceed westward towards **Farendé**, renowned for its metal workers, and on to **Pya** (PEE-ah), Eyadéma's village on the north-south international route, then south for about 14 km back to Kara.

The *Tourist Hôtel* in Pagouda has a bar-restaurant and charges CFA 5600 for one of its spacious air-con chalets.

NIAMTOUGOU
Niamtougou is 34 km north of Kara on the north-south international route and because of its tourist hotel is frequently used as a base camp for side trips to Tamberma country. The traditional Sunday **market** there is one of Togo's most vibrant and fascinating, particularly for those interested in baskets and ceramic bowls. In addition, there's a great **Centre Artisanal** on the southern side of

town; it has well-made cloth, dresses (CFA 5000) and tablecloths.

The *Tourist Hôtel* is similar to the one in Pagouda and has rooms for about CFA 5500.

VALLEY OF THE TAMBERMA

Kandé is on the international route 28 km north of Niamtougou; the stretch between these two towns is the most scenic on the entire highway. The valley of the Tamberma people is accessible from Kandé. If you ask around, you should be able to find one of the dirt tracks leading east for about 27 km to one of the Tamberma villages near the Benin border; their fortress-like houses are the major attraction.

In Kandé you can find boys, or they'll find you, who will offer you huts for CFA 500 a person.

Getting There & Away

Most travellers without vehicles end up walking the 27 km from Kandé to the Tamberma villages. Not only is walking more interesting, but the people are much more likely to give you a warm welcome. You'll have to bring your own food and water. From Kandé, walk east for 20 km to Warengo, then another seven km to Nadoba, the most important village. Alternatively, you might try your luck looking in Kandé for

a shared taxi; this is much easier on Tuesday, which is market day.

KÉRAN NATIONAL PARK

The other major attraction during the dry season is Kéran National Park. As you're driving north from Kandé towards Dapaong, look for a sign pointing to the park's entrance. The officials there will insist you take a guide. You are forbidden to stop the vehicle, speed (ie over 50 km/h for cars and over 40 km/h for trucks) or take photographs on the international highway cutting through the park.

In the past, the park rangers were known for giving stiff fines frequently and arbitrarily. For example, a fine of CFA 20,000 would be typical for speeding, or hitting a guinea fowl. Taking less than 92 minutes (115 minutes for trucks) could be used as evidence that you were speeding; taking more than 92 minutes could be taken as proof that you stopped along the way. Fortunately they're not so strict now, but clearly if you exceed the speed limits (50 km/h during the day and 40 km/h at night), you may run into problems. Consider synchronising your watch with the soldiers at the park entrance when they give you a form. Going north, at the 30-minute mark (37 minutes for trucks), you should be in Naboulgou, the site of another well-marked hotel, Hôtel Naboulgou.

Tamberma Country

A typical Tamberma compound, called a *tata*, consists of a series of towers connected by a thick wall with only one doorway to the outside. In days past, the castle-like nature of these extraordinary structures helped ward off invasions by neighbouring tribes and, in the late 19th century, the Germans. Inside, there's a huge elevated terrace of clay-covered logs where the inhabitants cook, dry their millet and corn, and spend most of their leisure time. Skilled masons, the Tamberma use no tools other than their hands, and the only materials they employ are clay, wood and straw. The walls are banco – a mixture of unfired clay and straw, which is used as a binder. The resulting environment is fairly cool all day long, unlike a more modern cement dwelling which gets hotter as the day progresses. They use the towers, capped by picturesque conical roofs, for storing corn and millet and other rooms for sleeping, bathing and, during the rainy season, cooking. Downstairs, they keep the animals, protecting them from the rain.

Many Tamberma, who are usually scantily clothed, get irritated by tourists staring at them, but you may be lucky and get to see inside one of their compounds. You'll find the interior very dark but light enough to decipher things including, possibly, fetish animal skulls on the walls and ceilings and a tiny altar for sacrificing small animals such as chickens. If you're really lucky, you might even see a man and his son going off to hunt with bows and arrows. When the son gets old enough to start his own family, he shoots off an arrow and where it lands is where he'll construct his tata. ∎

You can forget about this mad trip schedule if you're staying overnight there.

Unless you're very lucky, you won't see many animals. Every so often fires get out of hand; if you pass by then, all you're likely to see is an antelope or two and maybe a couple of monkeys. Potentially, however, you might see elephant, giraffe, buffalo, antelope, wart hog, hippo, monkey and various birds including stork, crane and marabou. Lions are extremely scarce if not nonexistent, so walking here is reasonably safe but it may be officially prohibited. There are a number of good tracks throughout the park which are clearly marked on the map at the lodge. The main track heading south from the lodge is the one the locals use to get to the villages beyond the southern boundary, and it's the best track during the rainy season because unlike other paths it remains dry for the most part.

Places to Stay & Eat

Kandé At the southern end of the park, Kandé has a run-down *Campement* with rooms for CFA 2300 (CFA 3800 with air-con); it's on the main drag.

Naboulgou Naboulgou is inside the park on the international highway, 32 km north of Kandé and 50 km south of Mango. A sign-post at the guard post of Naboulgou marks the road to the *Motel de Naboulgou* two km away. It has round bungalows designed like African soukalas; they are comfortable and cost CFA 7000 with air-con (CFA 9000 with private bath). The set menu costs CFA 2500 and beers are three times the normal price. The staff are friendly, and there is a safari vehicle for hire, but it's not always in working condition. You can also camp here, or sleep on the terrace of the bar. The charge of CFA 1000 includes use of the showers and bathrooms in the lodge.

Sansanné-Mango Mango is a small village at the northern edge of the park. Stop here if you're interested in seeing hippos; they can be found in the Oti River nearby. The *Hôtel-Bar l'Oti* on the main drag to the north of the village centre has rooms for CFA 1500 to CFA 2500. It's very clean and the friendly owner will arrange private lifts going south. At the restaurant you can get cheap drinks and a meal for CFA 550. The *Hôtel Au Bon Coin des Savanes*, very near the market, has rooms in the CFA 2000 range; the restaurant serves decent African food. For a drink, try one of the several bars in town.

DAPAONG

Located in the far north only 30 km from Burkina Faso, Dapaong (population 20,000) is a pretty little town with a mild climate. It is on a group of small hills overlooking the countryside, providing a slight break in the otherwise flat landscape. The Route Internationale passes around the city on the eastward side, so it's possible to pass this place and see virtually nothing of it. The people here like to joke that their market town is at the end of the earth, but in reality it's almost modern compared to some more remote villages. There are air-con hotels, bars with draught beer and restaurants with seafood and ice cream. Dapaong is noted for its **market**; Saturday is the big day. In the corner of the market you'll find tchakpallo, which is made from millet and the only indigenous beer with a good head.

Places to Stay – bottom end

The cheapest place is the *Centre Communautaire des Affaires Sociales* on the northern side of town and south of the international highway. A bare, slightly grubby room with a bed, dirty sheets, shared baths and running water costs CFA 1600 (CFA 2000 with

Cotton war belt (Mango)

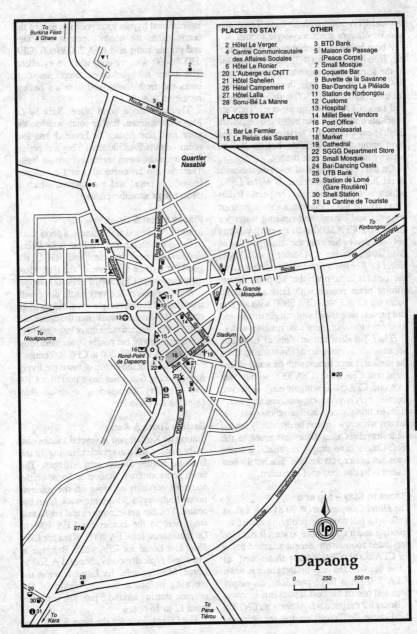

PLACES TO STAY	OTHER
2 Hôtel Le Verger	3 BTD Bank
4 Centre Communicautaire	5 Maison de Passage
des Affaires Sociales	(Peace Corps)
6 Hôtel Le Ronier	7 Small Mosque
20 L'Auberge du CNTT	8 Coquette Bar
21 Hôtel Sahelien	9 Buvette de la Savanne
26 Hôtel Campement	10 Bar-Dancing La Pléiade
27 Hôtel Lafia	11 Station de Korbongou
28 Sonu-Bé La Manne	12 Customs
	13 Hospital
PLACES TO EAT	14 Millet Beer Vendors
1 Bar Le Fermier	16 Post Office
15 Le Relais des Savanes	17 Commissariat
	18 Market
	19 Cathedral
	22 SGGG Department Store
	23 Small Mosque
	24 Bar-Dancing Oasis
	25 UTB Bank
	29 Station de Lomé
	(Gare Routière)
	30 Shell Station
	31 La Cantine de Touriste

To Burkina Faso
& Ghana

Route Internationale

Quartier
Nasablé

To
Korbongou

Route de Nasablé

Route de Korbongou

Grande
Mosquée

To
Nioukpourma

Rue du Stade

Stadium

Rond-Point
de Dapaong

To
Kara

Rue du Marché

Rue de SGGG

To
Pana
Tiérou

Dapaong

0   250   500 m

TOGO

fan and CFA 3000 with air-con). There may also be cheaper dormitory-style rooms.

About half a km further north is the state-run *Hôtel Le Verger* (☎ 70 81 39). Because of the somewhat remote location, it attracts few customers. However, the rooms are good for the price of CFA 2300 with private baths and fans (CFA 4800 with air-con). They are spacious and have clean baths and beds with fresh sheets. They also serve cold drinks and food under a large paillote, but the lack of activity makes the place dreary.

On the opposite side of town on the main street leading to the centre is *Hôtel Lafia*, which is similar in many respects. It has clean rooms with fans, clean sheets, interior showers and basins, and running water for CFA 2300 (CFA 3800 with air-con); you can get cold drinks here but the atmosphere is as dead as the Verger's. Another possibility is *Hôtel Le Ronier*, a few blocks north-west of the central area near the hospital. It has similar plain rooms with fans and shared baths for CFA 2300 (CFA 3800 with air-con and private baths) and you can get drinks and food here too, but there's no running water.

Hôtel Sahelien attracts lots of travellers because it's in the heart of town across from the market. Large rooms with fans and shared baths cost CFA 2600 (CFA 3300 with private bath and CFA 5200 with air-con). However, there is rarely any running water and they won't offer to bring you a bucket unless you ask. Rooms without a fan can be dreadfully hot, so some travellers drag their mattresses to the roof. Others have simply negotiated a lesser price just to sleep on the roof. The hotel's best feature is its thatched-roof restaurant.

Places to Stay – top end

The *Hôtel Campement* (☎ 70 81 59), a short walk up a hill from the centre, is attractive, relaxing and a good place to stay. It has nice ventilated rooms with decent attached baths for CFA 6000 (CFA 8000 with air-con), an active bar with the only draught beer in town (CFA 350 for a large pression), an empty pool and one of the best restaurants in town.

Better for the price is *L'Auberge du CNTT* at the Bourse de Travail on the semi-circular international bypass route, one km east of the centre. Units for one/two people with fans and private baths cost CFA 2300/3600 (CFA 4300/ 5600 with air-con) and are excellent. The rooms have balconies, telephones, tiled baths and fresh sheets, and there's a paillote restaurant.

There is also a good place, *Sonu-Bé La Manne Restaurant*, further south-west on the same road near Station de Lomé. It has four rooms (about CFA 3500 each). They are spotless and have fans, clean sheets and private baths. There is also an enclosed area for camping (negotiable price) and a restaurant, which is under a large attractive paillote.

Places to Eat & Drink

In addition to food at the hotels, a good place to eat, drink and meet travellers is *Le Relais des Savanes* near the centre and SGGG. It's good for a drink any time of the day. Most dishes are in the CFA 300 to CFA 1000 range.

Bar Le Fermier is a very rustic place with sand floors. It's best at night when there's more activity. A 30-minute walk from the centre, it's on the north-western outskirts of town, north of the main highway, but poorly signposted. Most dishes are in the CFA 200 to CFA 800 range.

For a drink in the centre of town the lively *Bar-Dancing Oasis* has large beers for CFA 250. Also try the spacious open-air *Bar-Dancing La Pléiade*.

Getting There & Away

Station de Korbongou is several blocks east of the market and has vehicles leaving for the Burkina border and nearby villages. The main gare routière is Station de Lomé on the southern outskirts of town on the international highway, a 30-minute walk from the centre. You can get minibuses and bush taxis from here to the border for CFA 400, to Ouagadougou for CFA 4000, Kara for CFA 1560 and Lomé for CFA 4225. Baggage is extra and typically costs about CFA 500 to Lomé. Most vehicles for Lomé leave in the morning before 8 am and again in the evening starting around 5 pm. The trip takes from 12 to 16 hours.

For Ouaga, look for the large STCB bus;

there is usually one leaving every day around 8 am (CFA 4000). Alternatively, you could take a truck to Koupéla in Burkina Faso (CFA 2500) and from there make connections to Ouaga or Niamey. Travel between the border and Ouaga is extremely slow because of the dozen police stops along the way. If you can find a Peugeot 504 in Dapaong or at the border, take it because the baggage searches with the minibuses take much longer.

LA FOSSE AUX LIONS

If you'd like to take a hike through some typical savannah woodland, the Fosse aux Lions might be of interest even though it's a

tiny and fairly insignificant reserve. It's 12 km south of Dapaong; the main international highway runs right through it, making access easy. A sign marks the entrance and there's no entrance fee.

The Fosse lies in a flat area of woodland savannah at the base of a steep ridge; hike up the cliffs for an excellent view of the surrounding countryside. Several seasonal streams flow through the savannah but stock up on food and water in Dapaong as the water is not safe and you're not likely to find much food in the smaller villages around the reserve unless you happen to hit one when a market is going on.

Glossary

abusua – clan or organisation of the Akan

adinkra – hand-made printed cloth from Ghana worn primarily by the Ashanti on solemn occasions

Afro-beat – a fusion of African music, jazz and soul originated and popularised by Fela Anikulapo Kuti of Nigeria; along with *juju* it's the most popular music in Nigeria

alghaita – an African oboe with a metal tube through it that widens out into a bell at the end

alizé – trade wind blowing from the ocean

alkalo – chief

aloco – fried bananas with onions and chille

ancien combattant – WW II veteran

animism – the base of virtually all traditional religions in Africa; the belief that there is a spirit in all natural things and the worship of those spirits, particularly human spirits (those of ancestors) which are thought to continue after death and have the power to bestow protection

Ashanti – the largest tribe in Ghana, concentrated around Kumasi, and one of the few matrilineal societies in West Africa

aso adire – a broad term for dyed cloth, a common handicraft found in many markets in Nigeria

attiéké – grated manioc; a side-dish (Côte d'Ivoire)

auberge – traditionally a simple guesthouse, but some auberges in West Africa are quite smart hotels

autogare – another name for *gare routière*

baché – type of bush taxi; covered pick-up

balafon – xylophone

Bambara – the major ethnic group of Mali concentrated in the centre and south and famous for their art, especially wooden carvings

benchi – black bench peas with palm oil and fish

bidon – large bottle

bolongs – creeks; backwaters

brochettes – beef kebabs

bundus – secret initiation societies in Liberia, and in certain parts of Sierra Leone and Côte d'Ivoire

buvette – small bar

cadeau – gift; also a hand-out

campement – simple hotel or guesthouse, usually a group of bungalows or huts

car rapide – minibus, often slow and dilapidated

carrefour – literally crossroads, but also used to mean meeting place (carrefour des jeunes: youth centre)

cases étages – two-storey mud houses

CFA – the principal currency of the region, used in Benin, Burkina Faso, Côte d'Ivoire, Mali, Niger, Senegal and Togo. There are actually two CFAs – the West African CFA (Communauté Financière Africaine) and the Central African CFA (Cooperation Financière en Afrique Centrale). The latter is used in Cameroun, Congo, the Central African Republic, Chad, Equatorial Guinea and Gabon. Although both are linked to the French franc, they are not the same currency.

chakalow – millet beer

chambres de passage – low-grade accommodation, a bare-minimum guesthouse

chawarma – a popular snack of grilled meat in bread, served with salad and sesame sauce, an 'import' originally from Lebanon, now found in towns and cities all over West Africa.

chèche – light cotton cloth, in white or indigo blue, that Tuareg men wear to cover their head and face

chiwara – a headpiece carved in the form of an antelope used in ritualistic dances by the *Bambara*

chop house – cheap restaurant (English-speaking countries)

commissariat – police station

couchette – sleeping berth on a train

croix d'Agadez – Tuareg talisman that protects its wearer from the 'evil eye'

dash – bribe, tip (see also *cadeau*)

déplacement – a taxi or boat that you 'charter' for yourself

djembe – type of drum

Dogon – people found in Mali, east of Mopti; famous for their cliff dwellings and art (carved doors and locks). Dogon masks are some of the most sought after in West Africa.

Eid-ul-Fitr – feast to celebrate the end of Ramadan

fanals – large lanterns, also the processions during which the lanterns are carried through the streets (Senegal and The Gambia)

fanicos – washerpeople (Côte d'Ivoire)

foutou – sticky yam or plantain paste similar to fufu; a staple in Côte d'Ivoire

fromager tree – found throughout West Africa and also known as the bombax, kapok or cotton tree, it is recognisable by its yellowish bark, large pod-like fruit and exposed roots

fufu – a staple along the southern coast of West Africa (made with fermented cassava, yams, plantain or manioc) which is cooked and puréed

fula-fula – converted truck or pick-up; rural public transport (Niger)

Fulani – nomadic cattle raisers by tradition, they live throughout West Africa; also known in French-speaking areas as Peul or Foulbé

gara – thin cotton material

garage – bush taxi/bus park (The Gambia, Guinea-Bissau)

gare routière – bush taxi/bus park

gare voiture – term for *gare routière* (Guinea)

gargotte – simple basic eating house or stall in Senegal, parts of Mali and The Gambia

gasoil – diesel fuel

gendarmerie – police station/post

girba – water bag

Gold Coast – pre-independence name for modern state of Ghana

grand boubou – the common name for an elaborate robe-like outfit. For men this is an embroidered garment reaching the ground with pants and shirt underneath; the woman's boubou is similarly regal, long and embroidered.

grisgri – charm worn around the neck to ward off evil

griot – a member of a cast responsible for maintaining an oral record of tribal history in the form of music, poetry and storytelling

groundnuts – peanuts

harmattan – the light winds from the north which carry tiny particles of sand from the desert, causing skies to become hazy throughout West Africa from December to March

Hausa – centred mainly in northern Nigeria and southern Niger, they are mostly farmers, traders and merchants

highlife – a style of music, now passé, which originated in Ghana and was the first to combine West African and Westernised influences

hôtel de ville – town hall

IMF – International Monetary Fund

impluvium – large round traditional house, with roof constructed to collect rain water in central tank or bowl

juju music – the music style characterised by tight vocal harmonies and sophisticated guitar work, backed by traditional drums and percussion; it is very popular in southern Nigeria, most notably with the Yoruba

kakaki – a remarkably long (about three metres) tin trumpet with an impressive, shattering timbre

kanaga – bird-like mask

kandab – a large belt used to climb trees to collect palm wine (Senegal)

kandonga – pick-up (Guinea-Bissau)

kedjenou – a mild stewed-chicken dish with vegetables (Côte d'Ivoire)

kente cloth – probably the most expensive material in West Africa, made with finely woven cotton, and sometimes silk, by Ghana's Ashanti people

kojo – millet beer

kola nuts – extremely bitter nuts sold everywhere on the streets and known for their mildly hallucinogenic and caffeine-like effects; they are offered as gifts at weddings and other ceremonies

kora – harp-like musical instrument with over 20 strings

koutoukou – a clear 100-proof alcohol home-made in Côte d'Ivoire

kwotenai kanye – earrings

lumo – weekly market (Senegal, The Gambia)

luttes – wrestling matches

lycée – secondary school

mairie – town hall; mayor's office

Makossa music – the distinct music of Cameroun which is a fusion of Camerounian *highlife* and soul; strongly influenced by Congo music

malafa – crinkly voile (Mauritania)

Malinké – Guinea's major ethnic group, and also found in southern Mali, north-western Côte d'Ivoire and eastern Senegal; closely related to the *Bambara* and famous for having one of the great empires of West Africa

maquis – rustic open-air restaurant originating in Côte d'Ivoire, serving primarily braised fish and braised chicken with *attiéké*, and traditionally open only at night

marabout – Muslim holy man

mestizos – people of mixed Caucasian and African decent (Guinea-Bissau)

mobylette – French-made moped

Moors – also called Maurs, the predominant nomadic people of Mauritania; now also well known as merchants and found scattered over French-speaking West Africa

Mossi – the people who occupy the central area of Burkina Faso and comprise about half the population of Burkina Faso as well as the bulk of Côte d'Ivoire's migrant labour force

nomalies – sandstone ancestor figures

OAU – Organisation of African Unity

pagne – a length of colourful cloth worn around the waist as a skirt

paillote – thatched sun shelter; straw hut

palava – meeting place

palm wine – a milky-white low-strength brew which is home-made and a staple in villages along the coast

peintures rupestres – rock paintings in the desert

petits cars – minibuses

pétrole – kerosene

pinasse – medium-sized motorised riverboat for hauling people and cargo

pirogue – small dugout canoe

plasas – pounded potato or cassava leaves cooked with palm oil and fish or beer

poda-poda – minibus (Sierra Leone)

préfecture – police headquarters

pression – draught beer

riz sauce – very common basic meal (rice with meat sauce)

rôtisserie – food stall selling roast meat

Sahel – dry savannah area; most of Senegal, The Gambia, Mali, Burkina Faso and Niger

sambuia – ferry

sept-places – Peugeot 504 seven-seaters (usually carrying up to 12 people)

sharia – Muslim law

shukublai – distinctive baskets, traditionally made by Temne women

sodabe – similar to *koutoukou*; made in Togo

soukala – a castle-like housing compound of the Lobi tribe found in the Bouna area of southern Burkina Faso

Songhaï – ethnic group located primarily in north-eastern Mali and western Niger along the Niger River

sûreté – security police

Tabaski – Eid-al-Kabir; also known as the Great Feast, this is the most important celebration throughout West Africa

taguelmoust – shawl or scarf worn as headgear by Tuareg men

tama – hand-held drum

tata somba – a castle-like house of the Betamaribe tribe in north-western Benin
taxi brousse – bush taxi
togu-nas – traditional Dogon shelters where men sit and socialise
tro-tro – small wooden bus (Ghana)
Tuareg – nomadic descendants of the North African Berbers; found all over the Sahara, especially in Mali, Niger and southern Algeria

voodoo – the worship of spirits with supernatural powers widely practised in southern Benin and Togo

Yoruba – a major ethnic group concentrated in south-western Nigeria; their well-known art is found in museums around the world
yovo – White person (Togo)

WHO – World Health Organisation
Wolof – Senegal's major ethnic group; they're famous also found in The Gambia

zemi-johns – motorcycle-taxis (Benin)
zrig – a Moorish drink of dried milk, sugar and water

Index

ABBREVIATIONS

MAPS

912

TEXT

Map references are in **bold** type.

Thanks

Annie Angle (Aus), Frank Audenaerd (Nl), Sam Barnett (UK), Stefanie Beck (C), Nancy Bell (USA), Miriam Benac (F), Penelope Bender (USA), J M Benduiet, Jan Berbee (Nl), Lars Bernd (G), Tasha Bertoire (USA), Jim Beuduiet (BF), Charles Biorley (USA), Martin Bohnstedt (A), Robert Bonem (USA), Martin Bottenberg (Nl), Tina Bursoe (D), Guy Catherine, Sharon Caulder (USA), Cavan Champion (UK), Deborah Chapman (USA), Alfousseyni Cissokho (Sen), Rick Cline (USA), Steven Clues (Aus), James Coonan (Aus), Judith Coppock Gex (USA), Christina Cordoza (USA), Craig Cowbrough (UK), A Cox-Farr (USA), Brian Cram (USA), Blaithin Crombie (UK), Maria Csendesne Takacs (H), Barbara Cyrus (G), P Davey (UK), Phil Detweiler (USA), François Dophemont (Nl), Ronald & Gloria Duber (USA), Chris Duvall (Gh), Andrew Eather (UK), Thomas Eberle (B), Joseph & Phyllis Edelman (USA), Geri Eikaas (USA), Steve & Elly (Aus), Nick Elzinga (Nl), J D Evans (Ire), Marijke Fackelday (Nl), Ferdinand Fellinger (A), Gazda Ferenc (H), Christiane Fischer (D), Chan Floyd, Alana Fowler (NZ), Mark Fraser (Aus), Sarah Fry (USA), Ingelise Gerrand (Nl), Issa Guindo Gerant, Florence Gisserot (F), Patrick Gonzalez (USA), Klaus & Edith Gosmann (G), Bart Govaeart (B), Alison Grant, Leslie Gray (USA), Michael Groll (K), Bob Hammond (UK), Mette Hansen (D), Nina Hansen (D), Frank Hempel (G), Claus Herting (G), Bob Hesterman (Nl), Andy Hibbert (UK), Andy Higgs (UK), Greg Hillen (USA), Mark Hillon, Lone Winge Hoier (G), David Hooper (C), Foar Hovoa (N), Claire Hughes (C), Sonja Imhoff (A), Jürgen Jacobsen (Sw), Patrick Janjaud (F), Martin Jensen (Nl), Helen Johns (UK), Dan Judge (USA), Mark Kaib (USA), Bamidele & Daniel Kammen (USA), G & K Kelly (UK), Michael Kevane (USA), Franya Kilodziejczyk (USA), David Klassen (Ng), Abdoulaye Kone, Teppo Koskinen (Fin), David Kucera (CR), Shamma Laiquddin (G), Bill Lamb (USA), Peter Lamb (C), Sallie Lang (USA), R E Laurin (C), Bruce Lilley (USA), Phillip Livingston (USA), Dawn Lock (UK), Peter Lowe (USA), Robert Lowe (USA), Jonas Ludvigsson (Sw), Gabriella Malnati (Swz), A L McArthur (Aus), Paul McGrory (UK), Blair McLaren (NZ), Darren McLean (Aus), Barbara McMillan (USA), Neil McTaggart (UK), Gert Vander Meijiden (Nl), Tonia Melville (C), Matthew Mendelsohn (C), Thomas Micholitsch (A), Miriam Miedema (Nl), Jenny Milne (UK), Karla Milne (UK), Duff Mullin (USA), Peter Munday (UK), Kelly Murad (Isr), Andrea Nussbaum (USA), Bill O'Donnell (USA), Anne-Marie O'Farrell (UK), David Olsen (C), Dr T Peter Omari, Kenneth Orosz (USA), A K Padi, Steve Payne (C), Barry Pell (USA), Christine Pieters (B), Christine & Jean Pieters (B), Greg Pilley (UK), Elise Pinners (Nl), Ignace Pollet (B), Yves Potier (F), Ellen Psychas (USA), Matthew Rappaport (USA), Mike Raship (USA), François de la Roche (USA), Johannah Rodgers (USA), Jörg Romeis (G), Julia Roloff (G), Edward Rother (USA), Jenny Roxman (Sw), Jose J L Sadaba (Sp)Tasha & Sal (USA), Momo & Toru Sasaki (Jap), Eleanor Saunders (UK), Clifford Sayre (USA), Erix Schokker (Nl), Claire Scott (C), Sally Scott (USA), Donald Shaffer (USA), P L Shinnie (C), Ritva Siikala (Fin), Ezra Simon (USA), Brenda Sloan (USA), April Smith, Steve Specht (USA), Rae Spector (USA), Jackie Stanley (UK), Maud Steeman (Nl), T Stuart (UK), Rodney Stutzman (USA), Richard Supple (USA), Marijke Swart (Nl), Greg Taylor (UK), Diana Temple (UK), Enric Torres (Sp), Lona Ulrich (Sw), Lona Ulrich (USA), Roger van der Maelen (B), Serge Van Donkelaar (Nl), Martijn van Walwijk (Nl), Marco Veul (Nl), M Wakefield (UK), Stephen Wanne (Aus), Nell Westerlaken (H), Richard Wheelhouse (UK), Jay Yasgur (USA), Robert Yates-Earl, Isabel Zimmer (Swz), Robert Zimmerman (USA) and Ethan Zuckerman (USA).

A – Austria, Aus – Australia, B – Belgium, BF – Burkina Faso, C – Canada, CR – Czech Republic, D – Denmark, F – France, G – Germany, Gh – Ghana, H – Hungary, Ire – Ireland, Isr – Israel, J – Japan, N – Norway, Ng – Nigeria, Nl – The Netherlands, NZ – New Zealand, Sen – Senegal, Sp – Spain, Sw – Sweden, Swz – Switzerland, UK – United Kingdom, USA – United States of America.

Update – February 1997

BENIN

Visas are now required by all except nationals of ECOWAS countries.

In downtown Cotonou, the Financial Bank is the only bank offering cash advances on Visa credit cards.

An outbreak of yellow fever has been reported by the World Health Organization in north-east Benin. There is little danger for travellers in contracting the disease outside this region. Proof of vaccination is required to enter the country.

CÔTE D'IVOIRE

Visas are required by all, except US citizens, for stays of less than 90 days.

SGBCI is the only bank that offers cash advances on Visa cards, and which will exchange Thomas Cook and American Express travellers' cheques. BIAO will change only Thomas Cook.

Road travel by night is not recommended due to frequent accidents and sporadic incidents of ambushing and banditry.

GHANA

Most prices in Ghana have at least doubled since 1995 due to inflation.

GUINEA-BISSAU

Australians now need a visa and a three-month one costs £20 from the UK Embassy.

Be prepared for petty corruption by officials. Have plenty of small-denomination notes handy. Vehicle owners should be scrupulous about having all their papers in order and having the required equipment, such as a warning triangle and a fire extinguisher.

Visas for Guinea now cost US$40; visas for Côte d'Ivoire (available at the French embassy) cost FF 60 for five days, FF 200 for a month.

Changing money in Bissau was easy at the BIGB on Au Amilcar Central. The exchange counter is on the far right.

Sailing times are not posted at the Rodofluvial office; lots of questioning and cross referencing is required to ascertain just what's going on. To Bubaque

was P90,000; returning on a different boat cost P70,000. Both boats left right on time.

S McCarthy

LIBERIA

A peace accord was signed by all warring factions in late 1995, but this failed in a dramatic manner in early 1996, when rival factions went on an orgy of killing and looting in Monrovia. Since then, the ECOMOG peacekeepers have stopped the fighting. The situation remains very tense and the infrastructure is practically nonexistent. Hopes for peace are again alive since the induction of the country's first woman head of state, Ms Ruth Perry.

MALI

Travellers report queuing for three days to buy tickets for the Bamako/Senegal train. The delay was caused by ticket touts who blocked the queue and sold their tickets at 100% commission. There are also touts at the Senegal end but they don't cause as many problems and don't take such a cut on their tickets.

Tuareg attacks in the north continue sporadically, so make sure you know the current situation before entering the region.

It seems that you are more frequently charged for changing French francs to CFA in Mali than in Niger, where I wasn't charged at all. Better to change in Niger if you are there before Mali.

Barbie Campbell Cole

MAURITANIA

Visas can cost as much as US$20 or more. You might have to specify your date of departure, and the visa will be valid until then. When entering from Senegal you will need to have UM 100 for the entry tax, but you don't need (nor are allowed to have) any more, despite what the Senegalese money-changers will tell you. When leaving, keep enough UM for the departure tax. One traveller entering Mauritania at Rosso was told to leave his CFA at the border post – it was still there when he returned!

A traveller reports that it is possible to join a convoy 'through the minefields' between Dakhla (Morocco) and Nou Ydhibou. However, the embassy in Rabat requires you to have an air ticket into Mauritania before they will issue a visa. You can buy an air ticket in Rabat to get your visa then get a refund on the ticket. Many agents will help you with this, taking 10 or 20% of the refund as a fee. This is technically illegal. The Mauritanian embassy in Senegal might ask you for a letter from your embassy, but travellers have managed to talk their way out of this.

NIGER

In early 1996 the government was overthrown in a military coup lead by Ibrahim Bare Mainassara. The coup leaders announced that they did not plan to end multi-party democracy, although their coup displaced the country's first democratically elected president. Neighbouring Mali has denounced the coup, so crossing between the two countries might not be easy for a while.

NIGERIA

Following the execution of environmental campaigner Ken Saro-Wiwa in late 1995, the Nigerian government has been increasingly shunned in Africa and around the world. It was suspended from the Commonwealth

membership. The European Union in January 1997 extended its sanctions against Nigeria for another six months. Nigeria has reacted belligerently, and travellers with British and Canadian passports might have some trouble and/or expense in getting a Nigerian visa.

It seems likely that officials will be paying close attention to foreigners in south-eastern Nigeria, the Ongoni area that Saro-Wiwa was fighting to protect from environmental devastation caused by exploitation of the oilfields by the Shell company.

Crime and corruption are on the rise in Nigeria, and unauthorised roadblocks are becoming a dangerous feature of road travel.

It might not be possible to get Nigerian visas in Togo or Benin. The Burkina Faso embassy in Lagos has moved to 170 Moshood Olhbani Rd. It charges N 1040 for a 15-day visa, twice as much for 30 days.

The best place to exchange travellers' cheques are the bureaux de change as banks are useless. Thomas Cook travellers' cheques attract the official exchange rate of US$1 to N 80 but American Express travellers' cheques apparently only get the lower rate of N 70.

The prices have also apparently doubled since the publication of this guide.

SIERRA LEONE

Captain Valentine Strasser, the head of state since 1992, was deposed in a bloodless coup by his deputy, Julius Amaada Bio, in early 1996. Bio subsequently won an election which was marked by chaos, corruption and bloodshed. Rural areas did not participate because they remain beyond the control of the government. The situation is very dangerous.

There's a US$25 departure tax.

TOGO

Visas are required for all except nationals of ECOWAS countries.

There are frequent reports of hassling at the checkpoints set up at night on Blvd de la Marina and elsewhere in Lomé. A foreigner was killed at one in 1996.

LONELY PLANET PRODUCTS

Lonely Planet is known worldwide for publishing practical, reliable and no-nonsense travel information in our guides and on our web site. The Lonely Planet list covers just about every accessible part of the world. Currently there are eight series: *travel guides, shoestring guides, walking guides, city guides, phrasebooks, audio packs, travel atlases* and *Journeys* – a unique collection of travel writing.

EUROPE

Amsterdam • Austria • Baltic States phrasebook • Britain • Central Europe on a shoestring • Central Europe phrasebook • Czech & Slovak Republics • Denmark • Dublin • Eastern Europe on a shoestring • Eastern Europe phrasebook • Estonia, Latvia & Lithuania • Finland • France • French phrasebook • German phrasebook • Greece • Greek phrasebook • Hungary • Iceland, Greenland & the Faroe Islands • Ireland • Italian phrasebook • Italy • Mediterranean Europe on a shoestring • Mediterranean Europe phrasebook • Paris • Poland • Portugal • Portugal travel atlas • Prague • Russia, Ukraine & Belarus • Russian phrasebook • Scandinavian & Baltic Europe on a shoestring • Scandinavian Europe phrasebook • Slovenia • Spain • Spanish phrasebook • St Petersburg • Switzerland • Trekking in Greece • Trekking in Spain • Ukrainian phrasebook • Vienna • Walking in Britain • Walking in Switzerland • Western Europe on a shoestring • Western Europe phrasebook

Travel Literature: The Olive Grove: Travels in Greece

NORTH AMERICA

Alaska • Backpacking in Alaska • Baja California • California & Nevada • Canada • Florida • Hawaii • Honolulu • Los Angeles • Mexico • Miami • New England • New Orleans • New York City • New York, New Jersey & Pennsylvania • Pacific Northwest USA • Rocky Mountain States • San Francisco • Southwest USA • USA phrasebook • Washington, DC & the Capital Region

CENTRAL AMERICA & THE CARIBBEAN

Bermuda • Central America on a shoestring • Costa Rica • Cuba • Eastern Caribbean • Guatemala, Belize & Yucatán: La Ruta Maya • Jamaica

SOUTH AMERICA

Argentina, Uruguay & Paraguay • Bolivia • Brazil • Brazilian phrasebook • Buenos Aires • Chile & Easter Island • Chile & Easter Island travel atlas • Colombia • Ecuador & the Galápagos Islands • Latin American Spanish phrasebook • Peru • Quechua phrasebook • Rio de Janeiro • South America on a shoestring • Trekking in the Patagonian Andes • Venezuela

Travel Literature: Full Circle: A South American Journey

ANTARCTICA

Antarctica

ISLANDS OF THE INDIAN OCEAN

Madagascar & Comoros • Maldives• Mauritius, Réunion & Seychelles

AFRICA

Africa - the South • Africa on a shoestring • Arabic (Moroccan) phrasebook • Cape Town • Central Africa • East Africa • Egypt • Egypt travel atlas• Ethiopian (Amharic) phrasebook • Kenya • Kenya travel atlas • Malawi, Mozambique & Zambia • Morocco • North Africa • South Africa, Lesotho & Swaziland • South Africa, Lesotho & Swaziland travel atlas • Swahili phrasebook • Trekking in East Africa • West Africa • Zimbabwe, Botswana & Namibia • Zimbabwe, Botswana & Namibia travel atlas

Travel Literature: The Rainbird: A Central African Journey • Songs to an African Sunset: A Zimbabwean Story

MAIL ORDER

Lonely Planet products are distributed worldwide. They are also available by mail order from Lonely Planet, so if you have difficulty finding a title please write to us. North American and South American residents should write to Embarcadero West, 155 Filbert St, Suite 251, Oakland CA 94607, USA; European and African residents should write to 10 Barley Mow Passage, Chiswick, London W4 4PH; and residents of other countries to PO Box 617, Hawthorn, Victoria 3122, Australia.

NORTH-EAST ASIA

Beijing • Cantonese phrasebook • China • Hong Kong • Hong Kong, Macau & Guangzhou • Japan • Japanese phrasebook • Japanese audio pack • Korea • Korean phrasebook • Mandarin phrasebook • Mongolia • Mongolian phrasebook • North-East Asia on a shoestring • Seoul • Taiwan • Tibet • Tibet phrasebook • Tokyo

Travel Literature: Lost Japan

MIDDLE EAST & CENTRAL ASIA

Arab Gulf States • Arabic (Egyptian) phrasebook • Central Asia • Iran • Israel & the Palestinian Territories • Israel & the Palestinian Territories travel atlas • Istanbul • Jerusalem • Jordan & Syria • Jordan, Syria & Lebanon travel atlas • Middle East • Turkey • Turkish phrasebook • Turkey travel atlas • Yemen

Travel Literature: The Gates of Damascus • Kingdom of the Film Stars: Journey into Jordan

ALSO AVAILABLE:

Travel with Children • Traveller's Tales

INDIAN SUBCONTINENT

Bangladesh • Bengali phrasebook • Delhi • Hindi/Urdu phrasebook • India • India & Bangladesh travel atlas • Indian Himalaya • Karakoram Highway • Nepal • Nepali phrasebook • Pakistan • Rajasthan • Sri Lanka • Sri Lanka phrasebook • Trekking in the Indian Himalaya • Trekking in the Karakoram & Hindukush • Trekking in the Nepal Himalaya

Travel Literature: In Rajasthan • Shopping for Buddhas

SOUTH-EAST ASIA

Bali & Lombok • Bangkok • Burmese phrasebook • Cambodia • Ho Chi Minh City • Indonesia • Indonesian phrasebook • Indonesian audio pack • Jakarta • Java • Laos • Lao phrasebook • Laos travel atlas • Malay phrasebook • Malaysia, Singapore & Brunei • Myanmar (Burma) • Philippines • Pilipino phrasebook • Singapore • South-East Asia on a shoestring • South-East Asia phrasebook • Thailand • Thailand travel atlas • Thai phrasebook • Thai audio pack • Thai Hill Tribes phrasebook • Vietnam • Vietnamese phrasebook • Vietnam travel atlas

AUSTRALIA & THE PACIFIC

Australia • Australian phrasebook • Bushwalking in Australia • Bushwalking in Papua New Guinea • Fiji • Fijian phrasebook • Islands of Australia's Great Barrier Reef • Melbourne • Micronesia • New Caledonia • New South Wales & the ACT • New Zealand • Northern Territory • Outback Australia • Papua New Guinea • Papua New Guinea phrasebook • Queensland • Rarotonga & the Cook Islands • Samoa • Solomon Islands • South Australia • Sydney • Tahiti & French Polynesia • Tasmania • Tonga • Tramping in New Zealand • Vanuatu • Victoria • Western Australia

Travel Literature: Islands in the Clouds • Sean & David's Long Drive

THE LONELY PLANET STORY

Lonely Planet published its first book in 1973 in response to the numerous 'How did you do it?' questions Maureen and Tony Wheeler were asked after driving, bussing, hitching, sailing and railing their way from England to Australia.

Written at a kitchen table and hand collated, trimmed and stapled, *Across Asia on the Cheap* became an instant local bestseller, inspiring thoughts of another book.

Eighteen months in South-East Asia resulted in their second guide, *South-East Asia on a shoestring*, which they put together in a backstreet Chinese hotel in Singapore in 1975. The 'yellow bible', as it quickly became known to backpackers around the world, soon became *the* guide to the region. It has sold well over half a million copies and is now in its 9th edition, still retaining its familiar yellow cover.

Today there are over 240 titles, including travel guides, walking guides, language kits & phrasebooks, travel atlases and travel literature. The company is the largest independent travel publisher in the world. Although Lonely Planet initially specialised in guides to Asia, today there are few corners of the globe that have not been covered.

The emphasis continues to be on travel for independent travellers. Tony and Maureen still travel for several months of each year and play an active part in the writing, updating and quality control of Lonely Planet's guides.

They have been joined by over 70 authors and 170 staff at our offices in Melbourne (Australia), Oakland (USA), London (UK) and Paris (France). Travellers themselves also make a valuable contribution to the guides through the feedback we receive in thousands of letters each year and on our web site.

The people at Lonely Planet strongly believe that travellers can make a positive contribution to the countries they visit, both through their appreciation of the countries' culture, wildlife and natural features, and through the money they spend. In addition, the company makes a direct contribution to the countries and regions it covers. Since 1986 a percentage of the income from each book has been donated to ventures such as famine relief in Africa; aid projects in India; agricultural projects in Central America; Greenpeace's efforts to halt French nuclear testing in the Pacific; and Amnesty International.

'I hope we send people out with the right attitude about travel. You realise when you travel that there are so many different perspectives about the world, so we hope these books will make people more interested in what they see. Guidebooks can't really guide people. All you can do is point them in the right direction.'

– Tony Wheeler

LONELY PLANET PUBLICATIONS

Australia
PO Box 617, Hawthorn 3122, Victoria
tel: (03) 9819 1877 fax: (03) 9819 6459
e-mail: talk2us@lonelyplanet.com.au

USA
Embarcadero West, 155 Filbert St, Suite 251,
Oakland, CA 94607
tel: (510) 893 8555 TOLL FREE: 800 275-8555
fax: (510) 893 8563
e-mail: info@lonelyplanet.com

UK
10 Barley Mow Passage, Chiswick,
London W4 4PH
tel: (0181) 742 3161 fax: (0181) 742 2772
e-mail: lonelyplanetuk@compuserve.com

France:
71 bis rue du Cardinal Lemoine, 75005 Paris
tel: 1 44 32 06 20 fax: 1 46 34 72 55
e-mail: 100560.415@compuserve.com

World Wide Web: http://www.lonelyplanet.com
or AOL keyword: lp